Lecture Notes in Networks and Systems

Volume 220

The series "Lecture Notes in Networks and Systems" publishes the latest developments in Networks and Systems—quickly, informally and with high quality. Original research reported in proceedings and post-proceedings represents the core of LNNS.

Volumes published in LNNS embrace all aspects and subfields of, as well as new challenges in, Networks and Systems.

The series contains proceedings and edited volumes in systems and networks, spanning the areas of Cyber-Physical Systems, Autonomous Systems, Sensor Networks, Control Systems, Energy Systems, Automotive Systems, Biological Systems, Vehicular Networking and Connected Vehicles, Aerospace Systems, Automation, Manufacturing, Smart Grids, Nonlinear Systems, Power Systems, Robotics, Social Systems, Economic Systems and other. Of particular value to both the contributors and the readership are the short publication timeframe and the world-wide distribution and exposure which enable both a wide and rapid dissemination of research output.

The series covers the theory, applications, and perspectives on the state of the art and future developments relevant to systems and networks, decision making, control, complex processes and related areas, as embedded in the fields of interdisciplinary and applied sciences, engineering, computer science, physics, economics, social, and life sciences, as well as the paradigms and methodologies behind them.

Indexed by SCOPUS, INSPEC, WTI Frankfurt eG, zbMATH, SCImago.

All books published in the series are submitted for consideration in Web of Science.

More information about this series at http://www.springer.com/series/15179

Nancy L. Black · W. Patrick Neumann ·
Ian Noy
Editors

Proceedings of the 21st Congress of the International Ergonomics Association (IEA 2021)

Volume II: Inclusive Design

 Springer

Editors
Nancy L. Black
Département de génie mécanique
Université de Moncton
Moncton, NB, Canada

W. Patrick Neumann
Department of Mechanical and Industrial
Engineering
Ryerson University
Toronto, ON, Canada

Ian Noy
Toronto, ON, Canada

ISSN 2367-3370   ISSN 2367-3389 (electronic)
Lecture Notes in Networks and Systems
ISBN 978-3-030-74604-9   ISBN 978-3-030-74605-6 (eBook)
https://doi.org/10.1007/978-3-030-74605-6

This Springer imprint is published by the registered company Springer Nature Switzerland AG
The registered company address is: Gewerbestrasse 11, 6330 Cham, Switzerland

Preface

The International Ergonomics Association (IEA) is the organization that unites Human Factors and Ergonomics (HF/E) associations around the world. The mission of the IEA is "to elaborate and advance ergonomics science and practice, and to expand its scope of application and contribution to society to improve the quality of life, working closely with its constituent societies and related international organizations" (IEA, 2021). The IEA hosts a world congress every three years creating the single most important opportunity to exchange knowledge and ideas in the discipline with practitioners and researchers from across the planet. Like other IEA congresses, IEA2021 included an exciting range of research and professional practice cases in the broadest range of Human Factors and Ergonomics (HF/E) applications imaginable. While the conference was not able to host an in-person meeting in Vancouver, Canada, as planned by the host Association of Canadian Ergonomists/*Association canadienne d'ergonomie*, it still featured over 875 presentations and special events with the latest research and most innovative thinkers. For this congress, authors could prepare a chapter for publication, and 60% chose to do so. The breadth and quality of the work available at IEA2021 are second to none—and the research of all authors who prepared their publication for this congress is made available through the five volumes of these proceedings.

The International Ergonomics Association defines Human Factors and Ergonomics (HF/E) synonymously as being:

> the scientific discipline concerned with the understanding of interactions among humans and other elements of a system, and the profession that applies theory, principles, data and methods to design in order to optimize human well-being and overall system performance.

> Practitioners of ergonomics and ergonomists contribute to the design and evaluation of tasks, jobs, products, environments and systems in order to make them compatible with the needs, abilities and limitations of people.

> Ergonomics helps harmonize things that interact with people in terms of people's needs, abilities and limitations. (https://iea.cc/definition-and-domains-of-ergonomics/)

The breadth of issues and disciplines suggested by this definition gives one pause for thought: what aspect in our lives is not in some way affected by the design and application of HF/E? For designers and managers around the world, a similar realization is growing: every decision made in the design and application of technology has implications for the humans that will interact with that system across its lifecycle. While this can be daunting, the researchers and professionals who participated in IEA2021 understand that, by working together across our disciplines and roles, we can achieve these lofty ambitions. This is especially relevant as we continue our collective journey into an increasingly "interconnected world"—the theme for the 21st IEA Congress. With the rise of a myriad of technologies as promulgated by Industry 4.0 proponents, we need now, more than ever, the skills and knowledge of HF/E researchers and practitioners to ensure that these tools are applied in a human-centric way towards resilient and sustainable systems that provide an enduring and sustainable road to prosperity—as advocated in the new Industry 5.0 Paradigm (Breque et al. 2021). Where the trend of Industry 4.0 aims primarily at encouraging technology purchasing and application, Industry 5.0 includes goals of resiliency and sustainability for both humans and our planet. These proceedings provide examples of research and development projects that illustrate how this brighter, human-centred future can be pursued through "*Ergonomie 4.0*", as stated in the French theme of the Congress.

While the theme of the Congress concerns human interactions within a rapidly evolving cyber-physical world, the devastating impact of the COVID-19 pandemic has given an added dimension to the Congress theme and its delivery model. As the pandemic began to engulf the world, the traditional in-person Congress became increasingly less viable and gave way to the creation of a hybrid model as a means to enhance international participation. In early 2021, it became clear that holding an in-person event would not be possible; hence, the Congress was converted to a fully virtual event. The uncertainty, mounting challenges and turbulent progression actually created new possibilities to engage the global HF/E community in ways that were never previously explored by the IEA. Indeed, one of the scientific tracks of the congress focuses explicitly on HF/E contributions to cope with COVID-19, and readers will find some submissions to other tracks similarly focus on what HF/E practitioners and researchers bring to the world during this pandemic period. This journey epitomizes broader transformative patterns now underway in society at large and accentuates the urgency for resilience, sustainability, and healthy workplaces. No doubt, the notion of globalization will be redefined in the wake of the pandemic and will have far-reaching implications for the connected world and for future society, and with new paradigms emerge a host of new human factors challenges. The breadth of topics and issues addressed in the proceedings suggests that the HF/E community is already mobilizing and rising to these emerging challenges in this, our connected world.

IEA2021 proceedings includes papers from 31 scientific tracks and includes participants from 74 countries across 5 continents. The proceedings of the 21st triennial congress of the IEA—IEA2021—exemplify the diversity of HF/E, and of the association, in terms of geography, disciplines represented, application domains, and aspects of human life cycle and capability being considered. Our diversity mirrors the diversity of humans generally and is a strength as we learn to weave our knowledge, methods, and ideas together to create a more resilient and stronger approach to design than is achievable individually. This is the strength of the IEA congresses, in the past, in the current pandemic-affected 21st occasion, and in the future. There is no other meeting like it.

A substantial number of works were submitted for publication across the Scientific Tracks at IEA2021. This gave us the happy opportunity to group contents by common threads. Each volume presents contents in sections with papers within the track's section presented in alphabetical order by the first author's last name. These proceedings are divided into five volumes as follows:

VOLUME 1: SYSTEMS AND MACROERGONOMICS (ISBN 978-3-030-74601-8)

Activity Theories for Work Analysis and Design (ATWAD)
Systems HF/E
Ergonomic Work Analysis and Training (EWAT)
HF/E Education and Professional Certification Development
Organisation Design and Management (ODAM)

VOLUME 2: INCLUSIVE AND SUSTAINABLE DESIGN (ISBN 978-3-030-74604-9)

Ageing and Work
Ergonomics for children and Educational Environments
Ergonomics in Design for All
Gender and Work
Human Factors and Sustainable Development
Slips Trips and Falls
Visual Ergonomics

VOLUME 3: SECTOR BASED ERGONOMICS (ISBN 978-3-030-74607-0)

Practitioner Case Studies
Aerospace Ergonomics
Agricultural Ergonomics
Building and Construction Ergonomics
Ergonomics in Manufacturing
HF/E in Supply Chain Design and Management
Transport Ergonomics and Human Factors

VOLUME 4: HEALTHCARE AND HEALTHY WORK (ISBN 978-3-030-74610-0)

Health and Safety
Healthcare Ergonomics

HF/E Contribution to Cope with Covid-19
Musculoskeletal Disorders

VOLUME 5: METHODS & APPROACHES (ISBN 978-3-030-74613-1)

Advanced Imaging
Affective Design
Anthropometry
Biomechanics
Human Factors in Robotics
Human Modelling and Simulation
Neuroergonomics
Working with Computer Systems

These volumes are the result of many hours of work, for authors, Scientific Track Managers and their reviewer teams, student volunteers, and editors. We are grateful to Springer for making it available to you in book form and are confident you will find these works informative and useful in your own efforts to create a better, more human-centred future.

References

Breque, M., De Nul, L., Petridis, A., 2021. Industry 5.0: Towards More Sustainable, Resilient and Human-Centric Industry, in: Innovation, E.D.-G.f.R.a. (Ed.), Policy Brief. European Commission, Luxembourg, p. 48. https://ec. europa.eu/info/news/industry-50-towards-more-sustainable-resilient-and-human-centric-industry-2021-jan-07_en

International Ergonomics Association (2021) Definitions and Domains of Ergonomics. https://iea.cc/definition-and-domains-of-ergonomics/; accessed March, 2021

Nancy L. Black
W. Patrick Neumann
IEA2021 Scientific Co-chairs

Ian Noy
IEA2021 Conference Chair

IEA2021 Acknowledgements

The IEA Congress organizing committee acknowledges many individuals whose contributions to the event have been invaluable to its success.

First and foremost, we acknowledge with deep appreciation the tremendous work of Steve Marlin, CEO of Prestige Accommodations, International Inc. His firm, hired to assist with organizing and executing the Congress, delivered unparalleled service throughout the planning process. Tragically, Steve passed away in early 2021. He provided outstanding support and wise counsel, always with a smile. He is sorely missed. We remain indebted to the Prestige staff, whose expertise and outstanding professionalism guided us through the planning process. In particular, we are grateful to Laurie Ybarra, Sr. Meetings Manager, who oversaw the many diverse aspects of our ever-changing plans and Christine Reinhard, Director of Operations, who skilfully managed the budget, website and registration system. Laurie and Christine's friendly approach, and their unique combination of technical and interpersonal skills, made it a pleasure to work with them. Marie-Hélène Bisaillon, Executive Director of the Association of Canadian Ergonomists/ *Association canadienne d'ergonomie*, supported their work.

The Organizing Committee is also indebted to those contributors who were instrumental in developing and promoting IEA2021. Joanne Bangs, our freelance Communications Specialist, provided engaging news blogs and other promotional collateral to help get the word out about the Congress. Sadeem Qureshi (Ryerson University), Elizabeth Georgiou, Elaine Fung, and Michelle Lam (Simon Fraser University) helped to create widespread awareness of the Congress as well as the HF/E field and profession through creative use of digital and social media. We are also grateful to those who worked diligently to ensure that the Congress provided meaningful opportunities for students and early career researchers, including Daniel P. Armstrong and Christopher A.B. Moore (University of Waterloo), Owen McCulloch (Simon Fraser University), Dora Hsiao (Galvion, Inc.), Chelsea DeGuzman and Joelle Girgis (University of Toronto), and Larissa Fedorowich (Associate Ergonomist, self-employed). The ePoster presentation option, new to IEA triennial congresses in 2021, was defined with care by Anne-Kristina Arnold (Simon Fraser University). Colleen Dewis (Dalhousie University) was key to interpreting our technical submission software and adapting its capacities to our needs. Hemanshu Bhargav (Ryerson University), Rachel Faust (Université de Québec à Montréal), Myriam Bérubé (Université de Montréal), Charlotte Bate, Vanessa DeVries, Caleb Leary, and Marcelo Zaharur (Fanshawe College), Tobi Durowoju (EWI Works), Issa Kaba Diakite, Mariam Keita, Mouhamadou Pléa Ndour, Shelby Nowlan, Faouzi Mahamane Ouedraogo, Jenna Smith, and Israël Muaka Wembi (Université de Moncton), and the aforementioned Larissa Fedorowich assisted with technical submission database verification and clean-up. We are particularly grateful that so many came to us through the Association of Canadian Ergonomists/Association canadienne d'ergonomie, witnessing to the active and motivated ergonomics and human factors community in IEA2021's host country.

The organizers are especially grateful to our sponsors, whose generous contributions made the Congress possible and readily accessible to the global HF/E community. Their recognition of the Congress as a valuable opportunity to advance the field of HF/E, as well as their steadfast support throughout a very trying planning period, was critical to the success of the Congress. The IEA 2021 sponsors include:

Benefactor Level:
>   Amazon.com, Inc.

Platinum Level:
>   Anonymous

Diamond Level:
>   Healthcare Insurance Reciprocal of Canada

Gold Level:
>   Huawei Technologies Canada
>   Institute for Work and Health (Ontario)
>   WorkSafe BC

Silver Level:
>   Fanshawe College
>   Simon Fraser University
>   Aptima, Inc.

Organization

IEA2021 Organizing Committee

IEA2021 Congress Chair

Ian Noy — HFE Consultant and Forensic Expert, Toronto, Ontario

Technical Program Committee Co-chairs

Nancy L. Black — Department of Mechanical Engineering, Faculté d'ingénierie, Université de Moncton

W. Patrick Neumann — Human Factors Engineering Lab, Department of Mechanical and Industrial Engineering, Ryerson University

Media Outreach

Hayley Crosby — Options Incorporated

Developing Countries

Manobhiram (Manu) Nellutla — Actsafe Safety Association

ePosters Coordinator

Anne-Kristina Arnold — Ergonomics, Simon Fraser University

Exhibits Coordinator

Abigail Overduin — Workplace Health Services, The University of British Columbia

Early Career Researcher Program Coordinator

Sadeem Qureshi   Human Factors Engineering Lab, Department
                                        of Mechanical and Industrial Engineering,
                                        Ryerson University

Media Relations

Heather Kahle   Human Factors Specialist/Ergonomist,
                                        WorkSafeBC
Jenny Colman   Human Factor Specialist, Risk Analysis Unit,
                                        WorkSafeBC

Events/Social

Gina Vahlas   Human Factors Specialist/Ergonomist,
                                        Risk Analysis Unit, WorkSafeBC
Era Poddar   Specialist Safety Advisor-Ergonomics,
                                        Manufacturing Safety Alliance of BC, Canada
Alison Heller-Ono   CEO, Worksite International

French Language Coordinator

François Taillefer   Faculté des sciences, Université de Québec à
                                        Montréal

Communications Coordinator

Joanne Bangs   Free-lance consultant

EasyChair Platform Technical Liaison

Colleen Dewis   Department of Industrial Engineering,
                                        Dalhousie University

Scientific Committee of IEA2021

Nancy L. Black (Co-chair)   Université de Moncton, Canada
W. Patrick Neumann   Ryerson University, Canada
  (Co-chair)
Wayne Albert   University of New Brunswick, Canada
Sara Albolino   Coordinator of the system reliability area
                                        for the Center for Patient Safety—Tuscany
                                        Region, Italy
Thomas Alexander   Federal Institute for Occupational Safety
                                        and Health (BAUA), Germany
Anne-Kristina Arnold   Simon Fraser University, Canada

Rafael E. Gonzalez	Bolivarian University, Petróleos de Venezuela, S.A. (PDVSA), Venezuela
Ewa Górska	University of Ecology and Management in Warsaw, Poland
Maggie Graf	International Ergonomics Association - Professional Standards and Education, Certification Sub-committee, Switzerland
Alma Maria Jennifer Gutierrez	De La Salle University—Manila, Philippines
Jukka Häkkinen	University of Helsinki, Finland
Gregor Harih	University of Maribor, Slovenia
Veerle Hermans	Vrije Universiteit Brussel, Belgium
Dora Hsiao	Revision Military, Canada
Laerte Idal Sznelwar	Universidade de São Paulo, Brazil
Rauf Iqbal	National Institute of Industrial Engineering (NITIE), India
Nicole Jochems	University of Luebeck, Germany
Marie Laberge	Université de Montréal, Centre de recherche du CHU Ste-Justine, Canada
Fion C. H. Lee	UOW College Hong Kong, Hong Kong
Yue (Sophia) Li	KITE, Toronto Rehabilitation Institute— University Health Network, Canada
Peter Lundqvist	SLU - Swedish University of Agricultural Sciences, Sweden
Neil Mansfield	Nottingham Trent University, UK
Márcio Alves Marçal	Universidade Federal dos Vales do Jequitinhonha e do Mucuri, Brazil
Blake McGowan	VelocityEHS, USA
Ranjana Mehta	Texas A&M University, USA
Marijke Melles	Delft University of Technology, Netherlands
Marino Menozzi	Swiss Federal Institute of Technology, ETH Zurich, Switzerland
Francisco Octavio Lopez Millan	TECNM/Instituto Tecnológico de Hermosillo, Mexico
Karen Lange Morales	Universidad Nacional de Colombia, Colombia
Ruud N. Pikaar	ErgoS Human Factors Engineering, Netherlands
Dimitris Nathanael	National Technical University of Athens, Greece
Yee Guan Ng	Universiti Putra Malaysia, Malaysia
Jodi Oakman	La Trobe University, Australia
Udoka Arinze Chris Okafor	University of Lagos, Nigeria
Paulo Antonio Barros Oliveira	Federal University of Rio Grande do Sul, Brazil
Vassilis Papakostopoulos	University of the Aegean, Greece
Maria Pascale	Uruguayan Association of Ergonomics (AUDErgo), Uruguay

Gunther Paul	James Cook University, Australia
Chui Yoon Ping	Singapore University of Social Sciences, Singapore
Jim Potvin	McMaster University, Canada
Valérie Pueyo	Université Lumière Lyon 2, France
Sadeem Qureshi	Ryerson University, Canada
Sudhakar Rajulu	NASA - Johnson Space Center, USA
Gemma Read	University of the Sunshine Coast, Australia
David Rempel	University of California Berkeley; University of California San Francisco, USA
Raziel Riemer	Ben-Gurion University of the Negev, Israel
Michelle M. Robertson	Office Ergonomics Research Committee, Northeastern University, University of Connecticut, University of California, Berkeley, USA
Martin Antonio Rodriguez	Universidad Tecnológica Nacional Buenos Aires FRBA, Argentina
Gustavo Rosal	UNE (Spanish Association for Standardisation), Spain
Patricia H. Rosen	Federal Institute for Occupational Safety and Health (BAUA), Germany
Ken Sagawa	AIST, Japan
Paul M. Salmon	University of the Sunshine Coast, Australia
Marta Santos	Universidade do Porto, Portugal
Sofia Scataglini	University of Antwerp, Belgium
Lawrence J. H. Schulze	University of Houston, USA
Rosemary Ruiz Seva	De La Salle University, Philippines
Fabio Sgarbossa	Norwegian University of Science and Technology, Norway
Jonas Shultz	Health Quality Council of Alberta, University of Calgary, Canada
Anabela Simões	University Lusófona, Portugal
Sarbjit Singh	National Institute of Technology Jalandhar, India
John Smallwood	Nelson Mandela University, South Africa
Lukáš Šoltys	Czech Ergonomics Association, Czech Republic
Isabella Tiziana Steffan	STUDIO STEFFAN—Progettazione & Ricerca (Design & Research), Italy
Daryl Stephenson	Occupational Health Clinics for Ontario Workers, Canada
Gyula Szabó	Hungarian Ergonomics Society, Hungary
Shamsul Bahri Mohd Tamrin	Universiti Putra Malaysia, Malaysia
Andrew Thatcher	University of the Witwatersrand, South Africa
Giulio Toccafondi	Center for Clinical Risk Management and Patient Safety GRC, WHO Collaborating Center, Florence, Italy

Andrew Todd   Rhodes University, South Africa
Judy Village   University of British Columbia, Canada
Christian Voirol   University of Applied Sciences Western
                                 Switzerland, University of Montreal,
                                 Switzerland
Michael Wichtl   AUVA-Hauptstelle, Austrian Ergonomics
                                 Society, Austria
Amanda Widdowson   Chartered Institute of Ergonomics and Human
                                 Factors (CIEHF), Thales, UK
Sascha Wischniewski   Federal Institute for Occupational Safety
                                 & Health (BAuA), Germany

Contents

Part I: Ageing and Work (Edited by Jodi Oakman)

Ageing Factors and Forecasting Tool for Companies

Bernard Michez[✉]

Ergotec Company, 213 Av de Muret, 31300 Toulouse, France
bernard.michez@ergotec.fr

Abstract. Improving age management in companies and administrations and increasing the employment rate of seniors is a major challenge. The methods for analyzing and acting on this topic need to be applied on a large scale, despite the fact that there is a huge amount of publications on this subject. We found poor return of practical experience about the application of tools, the possible actions, the assets, the impediments, etc. This paper summarizes a prospective analysis of aging at work. It highlights the stakes about the economic level, the health of employees, the share of knowledge in the company, as possible actions to be taken. The main aspects of the methods are exposed, as some results, and the actions steered afterwards in the company

Keywords: Ageing in companies · Forecasting methods · Costs estimation · Action plan

1 Context and Objectives

The company is of a worldwide dimension. The perimeter of the study covered 10 sites. We focused this presentation on 6 production sites. The kind of production changes considering each site, but the organization of the workshops, the tools, the management, are very similar. The social and cultural factors introduce differences among the working population.

The request was about a prospective analysis of aging at work, its impact on the company and possible actions to be taken. The results were used to develop the action plan and prioritize the actions to be implemented.

The study followed this sequence:

- Data analysis about the population on each site: ages range, years of experience, absenteeism, pathologies
- Construction of hypothesis about the absenteeism and pathologies factors, using human factors models
- Interviews with production managers and human resources managers belonging to the different sites, in order to share the interpretations, and to collect information about the age management strategy

N. L. Black et al. (Eds.): IEA 2021, LNNS 220, pp. 3–9, 2021.
https://doi.org/10.1007/978-3-030-74605-6_1

- Integration of all the results in a steering group, including top managers, occupational medicine, human resources department, prevention department
- Creation of a mind map about the over ageing factors and the ageing management
- Creation of a set of actions, assigned to different project managers (Fig. 1)

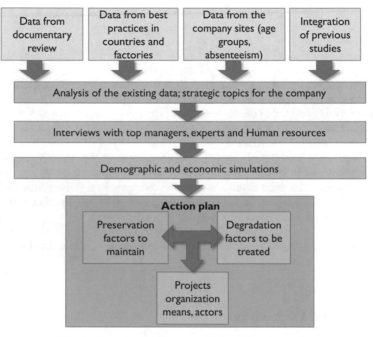

Fig. 1. Overview of the steps followed by the study

All along the study, the staff management was involved, including for the adaptation of the operational organization in the different teams.

2   Findings

The amount of findings is important; we show here some of them which appear to be relevant and useful for the actions (Fig. 2).

2.1   Differences Among the Population's Sites

The sites numbered 4, 5, 6 have a younger population than the other sites while the site numbered 2 shows a large workforce in the older age groups, with 45.6% of employees aged 50 and over.

Some sites show a more or less pronounced peak in the 45 to 59 age groups. This peak will lead to a large proportion of older employees in the years to come (sites 1, 2, 3).

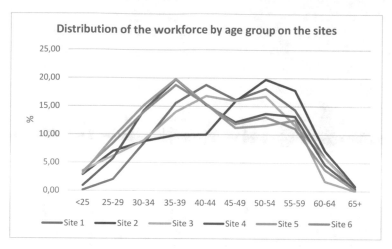

Fig. 2. Ages in the employee population

Connected to qualitative analysis, health data and absenteeism, this statistic led to those conclusions:

- The site number 2 needed a quick action, in order to cope with the rise of absenteeism, and to prevent as much as possible the premature wear of employees in previous age groups. More specifically, the workstations analysis showed a high exposure to Musculoskeletal Disorders. Those workstations have been redesigned, using anthropometric and physiologic human factors models.
- The expertise possessed by the elderly population had to be transmitted to the younger employees. Several crucial aspects of this expertise were identified, and companionship room were settled. The training sessions were designed using human factors models on expertise and cooperation.

2.2   Age and Absenteeism

The cross analysis of the data provided these conclusions (Fig. 3):

- The absenteeism rate is linked to different reasons depending on the age. For the younger groups, the factors a more related to family requirements. For the older groups, the factors a more related to health issues.
- The absenteeism is more homogeneous in the younger population, and more concentrated in the older population.
- The Fig. 4 below shows the proportion of absenteeism among young and old population. The stakes are underlined: elders present the greatest cost for the company, due to their health issues. But the younger groups will soon or later develop the same pathologies.

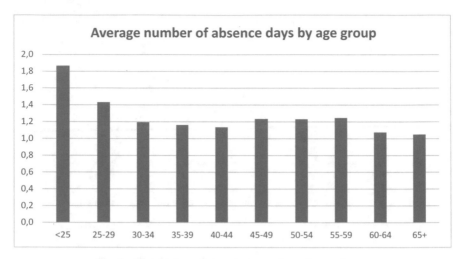

Fig. 3. Distribution of absenteeism among the employees

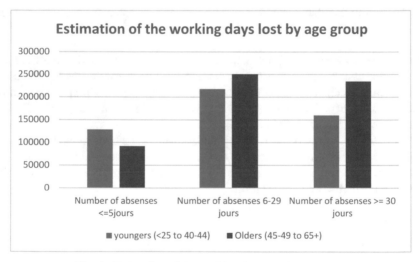

Fig. 4. Estimation of the working days lost by age group

Figure 4 divides the population into two groups. The median is between the 40–44 and 45–49 age groups.

The cross analysis of the data provided these conclusions:

- 45% of the lost working days are due to 31% of the working population
- This part of the population was particularly exposed to difficult working conditions.
- The research for solutions showed that for most of the population presenting health issues, the only possible way is to place them in a position suitable for disability. The action therefore inventoried these positions within the workshops and created an assignment process.

- This solution was not satisfactory, because it did not prevent the premature wear for other age groups. It was therefore decided to make changes to the workstations

The next question was how to finance the improvement of the working conditions. We created a solution through a simulation, presented below.

3   A Simple Tool for Forecasting

At this step, we had a lot of data about the population, and processed this data in order to give us a cost estimation.

- We use data on the working population and break if down by age groups
- We associate the absenteeism rates identified in the existing situation with the age groups, at T0
- Then, we carry out the projection of the evolution of the number of people by age groups 5 years later, and we evaluate the volume of associated days of absence

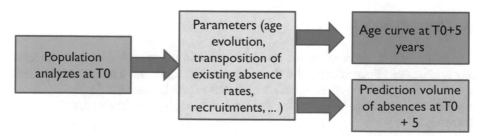

Fig. 5. Forecasting tool for absenteeism cost estimation

The parameters were settled with the human resources department. They took into account the recruitment policy (Fig. 5).

The results shown on the Fig. 6 led to those conclusions:

- An increase of the absenteeism for around 3% in the 5 years to come
- The calculations carried out with the human resources department established the costs of this absenteeism.
- This estimation established the budget for the improvement of working conditions. The approach was completed by a hierarchizing of the workstations to be processed, considering their discrepancy with the human requirements.

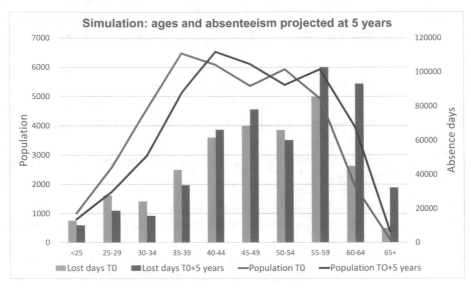

Fig. 6. Results of the projection 5 years later

4 Discussion

The major impact obtained was on the highlighting of the relationships between ages, absenteeism and financial costs for the company. The tools that we created were used by the steering group to make a prediction of those costs for the next 5 years.

The demonstration used human factors knowledge on 3 levels, applied to the company:

- Normal ageing, with the loss of strength, senses, cognitive capabilities, …
- Natural compensatory processes, with the density of social networks, the expertise, knowledge of the company's history, the values, …
- Accelerated aging, due to discrepancies between human capacities/limitations, and the tools provided, work organization, stress management, …

As other studies, this one shows that limiting the impacts of aging requires action before the arrival of operators in the 50-year age group. This implies that there is currently a skyrocketing effect, for the 50-year-old generation and beyond. Actions to limit these effects, require a coordination of several dimensions in the company.

An impediment for the actions was on the lack of data of health in the statistics. It appears that the health of an operator at some point in his professional life depends on the different jobs and workstations held. This aspect was not covered in the data, and was one important point for improvement.

5 Conclusion

A good way to deal with the ageing topic is to bring up the issue of costs. Actions to improve working conditions may seem too expansive at a first glance, but by placing the economic stakes in front of the investment, the arguments are favorable to the investment.

We have used many human functioning models to interpret the data collected. These models are not familiar to the management in charge of the production sites. We had to bring them to light, step by step, throughout the study. The pedagogic aspect of consultancy is a good mean to change the representation of the stakeholders.

References

1. Bureau de Normalisation du Québec- BNQ 9700–811/2018- Guide de bonnes pratiques pour favoriser l'embauche, le maintien et le retour en emploi des travailleurs expérimentés
2. Marquié, L.C., Paumès, D., Volkof, S.: La travail au fil de l'âge. Ed Octarès, Toulouse (1995)
3. Lemaire, P., Bherer, L.: Psychologie du vieillissement, une perspective cognitive. De Boeck, Paris (2005)
4. Travail, santé, vieillissement: Relations et évolutions – Collection Colloques. Octarès, Toulouse (2001)
5. A guide to managing and aging workforce-Alberta Labour workplace and Career Planning - HR Series for employers - alis.gov.ab.ca/publications
6. Working and ageing: Guidance and counselling for mature learners » CEDEFOP. Publications Office of the European Union, Luxembourg. www.cedefop.europa.eu (2011)
7. ED 6097: Bien vieillir au travail- juin. INRS (2011)
8. Chi, M.T.H., Glaser, R., Farr, M.J.: The nature of expertise. Lawrence Erlbaum Associates, Hillsdale (1998)
9. Reed, S.K.: Cognition-Théories et applications. De Boeck, Paris (1999)
10. Delay, B., Huyez-Levrat, G.: Le transfert d'expérience est-il possible dans les rapports intergénérationnels? Sociol Pratiq. **12**, 37–50 (2005)
11. Towards age-friendly work in Europe: a life-course perspective on work and ageing from EU Agencies –Report, Cedefop, Eurofound, EIGE, EU-OSHA (2017)
12. ED 6097: Bien vieillir au travail- juin. INRS (2011)
13. Forette, F.: Santé, travail et vieillissement. International Longevity Center France (ILC-France) 20 mars (2014)
14. Sustainable development in the European Union: Monitoring report on progress towards the SDGS in an EU context- Eurostat (2017)
15. Quennec, Y., Teiger, C., De Terssac, G.: Repères pour négocier le travail posté. Octarès, Toulouse (2008)

Are My Employees Able to and Do They Want to Work? The Baseline Investigation in a Follow up Study Regarding Managers' Attitudes and Measures to Increase Employees' Employability in an Extended Working Life

Kerstin Nilsson[1,2]([⊠]) and Emma Nilsson[1]

[1] Division of Occupational and Environmental Medicine, Lund University, Lund, Sweden
kerstin.nilsson@med.lu.se
[2] Department of Public Health, Kristianstad University, Kristianstad, Sweden

Abstract. Background: The demographic change affects the retirement age, which has been postponed in many countries. Therefore, the number of senior employees is increasing in the world. However, managers' attitudes towards their employees' employability affect the employees' possibilities regarding whether they can and want to work.

Objective: The aim of this study was to evaluate managers' attitudes towards their employees' employability and what factors and measures that affect whether employees can and want to work in an extended working life.

Method: The study population in this study consists of 249 municipality managers in Sweden, from a baseline investigation in a follow up study following the swAge-questionnaire. The data was analysed through the method of logistic regression.

Results: 79% of the managers stated that their employees 'can' work and 58% that their employees 'want to' work until 65 years or older. Managers believed their employees' health, physical work environment, skills and competence were associated to if they *would be able to* work until 65 years or older. Lack of support in the social work environment and lack of possibilities to arrange relocations if needed were associated to whether managers believed their employees *want to work*.

Conclusions: The results indicate that the postponement the retirement age must be followed by measures in the employees' work situation in order to decrease demands, increase rotation or change work tasks if needed, as well as increased possibilities to recuperate through reduced workload, reduced work pace and reduced working hours. The results will hopefully contribute to the understanding of needed organisational measures in the process of extending working life.

Keywords: Demography · Work environment · Employability · SwAge-model · Age management

N. L. Black et al. (Eds.): IEA 2021, LNNS 220, pp. 10–16, 2021.
https://doi.org/10.1007/978-3-030-74605-6_2

1 Introduction

Retirement is a possible and socially acceptable way for employees to withdraw from working life if the employee experiences their physical and mental work environment as well as the social situation in the workplace to be insufficient, or because they lack the experience of stimulation and motivation in their work tasks and do not have the opportunity of utilizing their skills and competence when executing work tasks [1–4]. However, the working population of the world is ageing, therefore a larger amount of senior employees need to participate in working life for a longer time, due to the demographic change in many countries [5–7]. Consequently, the retirement age has been postponed in many countries and seniors are forced to keep working and participating in the labour force for as long as possible. This demographic situation stresses the importance of factors motivating senior employees to experience that they both can and want to work until an older age.

Managers hold a key role in the organisation of work and on how to motivate and make measures in the work situation to enable employees to extend their working lives. The managers' attitudes towards their employees affect the employees' work situation and possibility of extending their working life [8–12].

Previous research has identified nine determinant areas connected to whether individuals can and want to work or not [1–4, 13–15]. Those nine areas are described in the theoretical swAge-model (sustainable working life for all ages) and are: (1) self-rated health, diagnoses, functional diversity; (2) physical work environment; (3) mental work environment; (4) work schedule, work pace, time for recuperation; (5) personal finances; (6) personal social environment; (7) work social environment; (8) work tasks, stimulation, motivation, self-crediting; (9) knowledge, skills, competence.

To facilitate a sustainable extended working life it is of particular interest to examine managers' beliefs regarding whether their employees 'can' and 'want to' work until an older age, associated with the nine determinant areas. Furthermore, in order to better understand how managers can motivate employees and make working life more sustainable until an older age, more information is needed regarding managers' beliefs of determinant factors for their employees' labour force participation.

1.1 Objective

The aim of this study was to evaluate managers' attitudes towards their employee's employability and factors that affect whether employees can and want to work in an extended working life. Furthermore, the aim of this study was to investigate what measures the managers thought could increase their employees' participation in an extended working life.

2 Methodology

2.1 Material

The dataset used in this study comes from a baseline survey of a longitudinal study with municipality managers. The respondents consisted of 456 managers employed in one of the largest municipalities in Sweden. After two reminders, 249 managers (29% male and 71% female) responded to the web questionnaire. This corresponded to a response rate of 54.6%, with an age distribution of 25–67 years of age (median age 50.4 years). The managers' sectoral work areas were: 38.6% Educational work (child, adolescent and adult education); 14.5% Care, health care, rehabilitation work, housing, home services; 11.6% Social and curative work; 9.2% Technology, IT, city environment, water maintenance, electric operation maintenance, kitchen and food distribution; 4.4% Library, archive, culture, tourism, municipality leisure activities; 21.7% Administration, support functions (HR, finance, law, administrative support functions, management, communication, digitalization).

2.2 The Questionnaire

The questions in the survey have been tested and used previously in other studies. The questions in the survey were subdivided into the nine theoretical themes of determinant areas in the swAge-model [1–4], i.e.: (1) health; (2) physical work environment; (3) mental work environment; (4) work schedule, work pace, time for recuperation; (5) personal finances; (6) personal social environment; (7) work social environment; (8) stimulation and motivation of work tasks; (9) knowledge, skills, competence.

2.3 Statistical Analysis

The two outcome variables in the analysis were for how long the managers believed their employees would be able to and for how long the managers believed their employees would want to work, where the breaking point was set to 65 years, i.e. whether the managers believed that their employees 'would want to work until 65 years of age or beyond' and/or 'would be able to work until 65 years of age or beyond'. The response options for the statements, based on the questions divided into nine determinant areas, were dichotomised from four to two variables, i.e. from both highly agree and partly agree to just 'agree', and from both partly disagree and highly disagree to just 'disagree'. The statistical method of logistic regression analysis was used to investigate the association between different factors in the work situation, measured by statements, and generating odds ratios (OR), as well as 95% confidence intervals (CI) for the statement's association with the two outcomes.

3 Results

The proportion of managers who stated that most of their employees 'want to work until 65 years or beyond' was 58%. At the same time, the proportion of managers who stated that most of their employees 'can work until 65 years of age or beyond' was 77%.

3.1 Statements Associated with Whether the Managers Believed That Their Employees Could Not or Would Not Want to Work Until 65 Years of Age or Beyond

The 40 statement from the nine determinant areas in the survey were analysed in association with whether the managers believed that their employees would be able to and would want to work until 65 years of age or beyond, respectively.

The strongest observed statistically significant association in the multivariate model, regarding whether the managers believed their employees could not work until 65 years of age or beyond was the statement "I do not experience that my employees have a reasonable physical work load" (OR 4.8, CI 1.5–15.4), followed by the statements "My employees in general have many tasks involving a physically demanding work load and heavy lifting" (OR 4.7, CI 1.8–12.2), "I do not experience it being important to keep elderly employees in the organization based on their competence" (OR 3.6, CI 1.6–8), "I do not experience that my employees have access to sufficient technical support" (OR 2.8, CI 1.1–7.2), and "My employees in general have some kind of diagnosis or chronic disease" (OR 2.7, 1.1–6.8 CI).

The strongest observed statistically significant association in the multivariate model regarding whether the managers believed their employees would not want to work until 65 years of age or beyond was the statement "My employees in general do not receive sufficient support from me to be able to work until ordinary retirement age" (OR 5.0, CI 1.3–19.6), followed by the statement "In my experience it is hard to find work tasks to relocate employees who experience their work environment as too physically demanding" (OR 2.8, CI 1.6–4.8).

3.2 Measure Activities Associated with Whether the Managers Believed That Their Employees Could Not or Would Not Want to Work Until 65 Years of Age or Beyond

The 28 possible measure activities stated in the survey were also analysed in association with whether the managers believed that their employees would be able to and would want to work until 65 years of age or beyond, respectively.

The highest statistically significant corresponding measure activity associated with whether managers believed that their employees "could work" until 65 years of age or beyond was the measure "Decrease of physical work demands" (OR 2.9, CI 1.6–5.3), followed by the measures "Other work tasks in the workplace" (OR 2.2, CI 1.2–4.3), "Rotation between different work tasks to decrease physical work load and strain" (OR 2.1, CI 1.1–4.0), "Rotation between different work tasks to decrease mental work load and strain" (OR 1.9, CI1.0–3.4), and "Decrease of mental work demands" (OR 1.8, CI 1.0–3.3).

Furthermore, the 28 possible measure activities were analysed in association with whether the managers believed that their employees "would want to work" until 65 years of age or beyond. The highest statistically significant corresponding association was the measure activity "Decreased work pace" (OR 2.1, CI 1.2–3.9) followed by "Increased time for recuperation between work shifts" (OR 1.7, CI 1.0–2.9).

4 Discussion

In this study factors associated to whether managers believed their employees could work in an extended working life or not were investigated. Previous research and the theories of the swAge-model state that the health effects of the work environment are related to employability [1–4, 10–16]. The results from this study state that the highest statistically significant association regarding whether managers believed that their *employees could not work until 65 years of age or beyond* was if their employees had a reasonable physical workload, followed by whether the employees had many tasks involving a physically demanding workload and heavy lifting. These results relate to earlier research which states that a poor physical work environment and work conditions increase the risk of work accidents, leave people worn out and push them to leave working life early [1–4, 10–20]. Sound self-rated health, diagnoses and functional diversity are stated to be of importance to whether individuals can participate in working life at all [1–4, 10–16]. Furthermore, the results of this study state the employees' health status to be of importance regarding whether the managers believed their employees could work until an older age. Additionally, according to the results of this study, the managers belief that their senior employees could not continue working in an extended working life proved to be statistically significant and associated with whether their employees did not have proper access to sufficient technical support. Earlier research state the possibility to continue working in an extended working life to be associated with the possibility to execute the work tasks properly [1–4, 13–15, 21]. However, in spite of age, anyone would surely experience problems to keep working if there is no proper support or measures for that need to be facilitated. Furthermore, the results of this study state that the managers do not experience it being important to keep elderly employees in the organization based on their competence. Previous research states that managers' attitudes towards their employees, and whether employees are treated as important to the organisation, affect their possibility to continue working in an extended working life [8–12].

In this study, the strongest observed association regarding whether the managers believed their employees would not *want to work until 65 years of age or beyond* was analysed. Previous research and the swAge-model state employees' employability to be associated with social support as well as proper skills and the possibility to execute work tasks [1–4, 13–15, 21, 22]. The results of this study state that whether managers believed their employees would not want to work until 65 years of age or beyond was highly statistically significantly associated with whether they received sufficient support from the managers, as well as whether work tasks could be found to relocate employees who experience their work environment as too physically demanding.

Measures in working life are needed in order to increase the possibility for more senior employees to participate in the labour force until an older age when the retirement age in many countries is postponed [5–7]. The results of this study state that the managers believed that offering employees other work tasks in the workplace if needed was a measure that could affect whether their employees would be able to and would want to participate in an extended working life. Further possible measures mentioned were the opportunity to decrease demands, the opportunity to increase rotation between different work tasks to reduce workload and wear in order to enable the employees to continue working in an extended working life, as well as reduced work pace and a reduction of working hours (i.e. increased leisure time between work shifts).

5   Conclusions

This study states that different determinant areas of work life participation were associated with whether managers' believed their employees *would not be able to work* or *would not want to work* until 65 years or beyond. The areas of particular importance to whether managers believed that their employees could not work until 65 years of age or beyond were the employees' health, the physical work environment, as well as skills and competence. The areas most important to whether the managers believed that their employees did not want to work until age 65 or beyond were the social work environment, whether the employees received enough support from the managers, and the possibility of arranging relocation within the organisation if the employees needed to. The results strengthen the theoretical framework of the swAge-model regarding factors of importance for employability and determinant areas for a healthy and sustainable working life for all ages [1–4].

The analysis of the managers' attitudes indicate that postponing the retirement age must be followed by measures in the employees' work situation with possibilities to decrease demands, increase rotation or change work tasks if needed, as well as increased possibilities to recuperate through reduced workload, reduced work pace and reduced working hours. The managers' perspectives on why their employees *can* and *want to* work will hopefully contribute to the understanding of organisational measures in the process of extending working life.

Organisational measures and activities are needed throughout the entire working life in order to increase the possibility to extend the working life and to create a healthier and sustainable working life for all ages. Hopefully, the results of this study will make a contribution to the understanding of the process of extending working life, and be used in the critical debate of employability, as a background to workplace interventions and toward future research for a sustainable working life.

References

1. Nilsson, K.: A sustainable working life for all ages – the swAge-model. Appl Ergon. **86**, 103082 (2020). https://doi.org/10.1016/j.apergo.2020.103082
2. Nilsson, K.: Conceptualization of ageing in relation to factors of importance for extending working life – a review. Scand. J. Publ. Health **44**, 490–505 (2016)
3. Nilsson, K.: Should I stay or should I go? The SwAge model = Sustainable Working life for All Ages. Report 5, pp. 1–67, S2018: 10. The Swedish governments' official investigations, Delegation for Senior Workforce, Stockholm (2019) (in Swedish)
4. swAge-models Homepage. https://swage.org/. Accessed 2 Aug 2021
5. OECD: Pensions at a glance 2019: OECD and G20 indicators. OECD Publishing, Paris (2019). https://doi.org/10.1787/b6d3dcfc-en
6. World Economic Forum. Global Agenda Council on Ageing (2016). https://www.weforum.org/communities/global-agenda-council-on-ageing/

7. Hess, M.: Rising preferred retirement age in Europe: are Europe's future pensioners adapting to pension system reforms? J. Aging Soc. Policy **29**(3), 245–261 (2017). https://doi.org/10.1080/08959420.2016.1255082

8. McGoldrick, A.E., Arrowsmith, J.: Discrimination by age: the organizational response. In: Glover, I., Branine, M. (eds.) Ageism in Work and Employment, pp. 75–96. Ashgate Publishing Ltd., Stirling (2001)

9. Stypinska, J., Konrad Turek, K.: Hard and soft age discrimination: the dual nature of workplace discrimination. Eur. J. Ageing **14**(1), 49–61 (2017). https://doi.org/10.1007/s10433-016-0407-y

10. Nilsson, K.: Managers' attitudes to their older employees - a cross-sectional study. Work **59**(1), 49–58 (2018)

11. Nilsson, K.: Managers' attitudes towards their older employees. Report 15, pp. 1–47, S2018: 10. The Swedish governments official investigations, Delegation for Senior Workforce, Stockholm (2019) (in Swedish)

12. Nilsson, K.: Attitudes of managers and older employees to each other and the effects on the decision to extended working life. In: Ennals, R., Salomon, R.H. (eds.) Older Workers in a Sustainable Society. Labor, Education & Society. Peter Lang Verlag, Frankfurt, pp. 147–156 (2011)

13. Nilsson, K.: Why work beyond 65? Discourse on the decision to continue working or retire early. Nordic J. Work. Life Stud. **2**(3), 7–28 (2012). https://www.nordicwl.com/nilsson-2012-why-work-beyond-65-discourse-on-the-decision-to-continue-working-or-retire-early/

14. Nilsson, K., Rignell-Hydbom, A., Rylander, L.: Factors influencing the decision to extend working life or to retire. Scand. J. Work Environ. Health **37**(6), 473–480 (2011). https://bmc publichealth.biomedcentral.com/articles/10.1186/s12889-016-3438-6

15. Nilsson, K.: The influence of work environmental and motivation factors on seniors' attitudes to an extended working life or to retire. A cross sectional study with employees 55–74 years of age. Open J. Soc. Sci. **5**, 30–41 (2017). https://file.scirp.org/pdf/JSS_2017071013594273.pdf

16. Nilsson, K., Rignell-Hydbom, A., Rylander, L.: How is self-rated health and diagnosed disease associate with early or deferred retirement: a cross sectional study with employees aged 55–64. BMC Public Health 886 (2016). https://doi.org/10.1186/s12889-016-3438-6

17. Ilmarinen, J.: Toward a Longer Working Life: Aging and Quality of Working Life in the European Union. Helsinki, Finnish Institute of Occupational Health (2006)

18. Oakman, J., Wells, Y.: Retirement intentions: what is the role of push factors in predicting retirement intentions? Ageing Soc. **33**, 988–1008 (2013)

19. von Bonsdorff, M.E., Rantanen, T., Törmäkangas, T., Kulmala, J., Hinrichs, T., Seitsamo, J., von Bonsdorff, M.B.: Midlife work ability and mobility limitation in old age among non-disability and disability retirees: a prospective study. BMC Public Health **16**(1), 154–161 (2016). https://doi.org/10.1186/s12889-016-2846-y

20. Torgén, M.: Physiological ageing – physical capacity and occupational performance. In: Vingård E (ed) Healthy workplaces for women and men of all ages, vol. 8, pp. 75–85. Swedish Work Environment Authority, Stockholm (2016)

21. Hovbrandt, C., Håkansson, C., Karlsson, G., Albin, M., Nilsson, K.: Prerequisites and driving forces behind an extended working life among older workers. Scand. J. Occup. Ther. **28**, 1–13 (2017). https://doi.org/10.1080/11038128.2017.1409800

22. Gyllensten, K., Wentz, K., Håkansson, C., Nilsson, K.: Older assistant nurses' motivation for a full or extended working life. Ageing Soc. **39**(12), 2699–2713 (2019)

Management, Measures and Maintenance: Success and Setbacks in Interventions Promoting a Healthy and Sustainable Employability and Working Life for All Ages

Kerstin Nilsson[1,2(✉)] and Emma Nilsson[1]

[1] Division of Occupational and Environmental Medicine, Lund University, Lund, Sweden
kerstin.nilsson@med.lu.se
[2] Department of Public Health, Kristianstad University, Kristianstad, Sweden

Abstract. Background: The labour force is ageing due to the demographic change and the postponement of old-age retirement in many countries.

Objective: In order to increase the possibility for employees to maintain their employability and to keep working in an extended working life this intervention project tested a distance education as a technique to integrate a theoretical model for a sustainable working life for all ages (the swAge-model) as a practical management tool in fourteen municipality managers' ordinary work situation.

Results: Most of the participating managers had difficulty completing the entire training program in this intervention project due to external circumstances, such as the COVID-19 pandemic and re-organisations, and because no extra time during working hours had been allocated to the managers to participate in the intervention project. Despite this, all participating managers appreciated being given the opportunity to participate and take part in the content of the intervention. Everyone considered the theoretical model, the wage model, on which the intervention project was based, to be very useful and to have given them new insights into their managerial duties.

Conclusions: If society and organisations want a larger amount of employees to participate in working life until an older age, they also need to allocate working hours for managers to acquire new knowledge on how to create healthy and sustainable workplaces for all ages, as well as to implement these tools, measures and working methods permanently in the daily organisational work.

Keywords: Demography · Work environment · Employability · swAge-model · Age management

1 Introduction

In most countries the old age dependency ratio is increasing right now [1, 2]. The increasing average life expectancy is a positive sign of a healthy community. However, the rapidly ageing population is also one of the most powerful transformative forces to affect society and the national economy. Because of this, the retirement age has

© The Author(s), under exclusive license to Springer Nature Switzerland AG 2021
N. L. Black et al. (Eds.): IEA 2021, LNNS 220, pp. 17–24, 2021.
https://doi.org/10.1007/978-3-030-74605-6_3

been postponed, the working population is ageing and correspondingly increasing in many countries [1, 2]. Increasing age causes vision, hearing, sensation and reactivity to deteriorate, and increases the risk of chronic diseases, aches and pains, furthermore, the risk of sick leave, occupational injuries and early retirement increases with older age [3, 4]. Therefore, if the pension system postpones the retirement age without planning measures, activities and awareness of the ageing workforce, it can strike back with an increased risk of suffering and increased costs due to a larger amount of work injuries, accidents and illness [5, 6]. Age needs to be considered in working life if a larger amount of people should be able to work until an older age [4, 7]. Though, a recent review states that although the risk of occupational injuries increases with older age and seniors suffers from more occupational injuries, there is a lack of evaluated intervention studies and knowledge on practical activities and measures to enable a sustainable and healthier working life for senior employees [8]. Therefore, additional intervention studies on how to promote a healthy and sustainable working life for all ages are of vital importance [1, 2]. There is a great need for intervention studies with the intention of reducing the risks of ill health and increasing healthiness in working life for senior employees.

Managers have a significant role to play in the work environment and the possibility for senior employees to be able and want to maintain their ability to work [9–11]. Because of this managers need knowledge and tools on how to manage their employees' work situation and employability in order to make workplaces and working life more sustainable in relation to the employee's age.

1.1 Objective

The aim of this intervention study was to try out and evaluate a distance education initiative of the swAge model's measures and action proposals for managers to adapt in their own supervisory functions and to utilize as lasting tools for a sustainable and age-conscious leadership.

2 Methodology

2.1 Material

The implementation of the intervention project was designed from a bottom-up perspective and was carried out in collaboration with managers and the human resource (HR) department in a larger Swedish municipality. The project was well established in the management of the municipality, furthermore, a political decision had been made for this kind of initiative and measures to increase the opportunity for older employees to continue working until an older age as well as to increase the possibilities for a sustainable extended working life.

The intervention project consists of an online education program regarding theories and practical tools for age conscious leadership and how to create a healthy and sustainable working life.

The participants in the intervention project were recruited through the HR department's distribution of information through e-mail to 103 managers in the municipality regarding the program and the managers' possibility to participate. 17 of the informed managers announced their interest to participate in this intervention project. However, of the 17 participating managers, 3 managers dropped out before the online education had begun. One of those managers stated that her reason to drop out was because she was a head manager, and she assumed the course was more directed towards first line managers. The other two stated that they had to enter an additional mandatory course in the municipality, and thought it too much to attend two courses at the same time. Finally, 14 managers, 3 men and 11 women, from six different administrations in the municipality, participated in the online education program of this intervention project (Table 1).

Twelve of the participating managers accepted to be individually interviewed one month after the education program had ended, in order to investigate success factors and setbacks of the educational program in the intervention project. Two managers stated that they did not have time to participate in the interview and that they had not followed through with the educational program.

Table 1. The participating managers (men and women) in the intervention projects educational program, working in different administrations.

Administration	Total	Men	Women
City management administration	2	1	1
Social administration	2	1	1
Labour market administration	1		1
Cultural administration	1		1
Care and welfare administration	4		4
School and leisure recreation administration	6	1	5

2.2 The Design of the Education Program in the Intervention

The interventions' action in this project was an educational program designed for managers with practical tools to address the objective of increasing the senior employees' possibility to participate in a healthy and sustainable extended working life. The course was given on the educational online platform Canvas. The online design of the educational program gave the participating managers the possibility to take part of the education whenever they could and want to during a period of five months (November 2019–April 2020).

The education consists of 28 recorded lectures, reflection assignments related to each lecture, as well as a final examination on how the managers should utilize what they have learnt during the education through developing an action plan for measures in the work place based on a workplace analysis and a workplace matrix.

2.3   The Content of the Education Program in the Intervention

The content of the lectures, assignments and examination was based on and followed a theoretical model for intervention tools, the swAge model (the acronym swAge stands for "Sustainable working life for all ages"). The swAge model encompasses four determinant spheres of employability, i.e. i) health effects of the work environment; ii) financial incentives; iii) relationships, social support, participation in a community; iv) execution of tasks [4, 7, 12] and has been developed by our research group through grounded theory method. The swAge model addresses factors that are important to participate in working life, consisting of the four determinant spheres of employability, which are divided into nine different determinant areas: (1) self-rated health, diagnoses and functional diversity, (2) physical work environment, (3) mental work environment, (4) working hours, work pace and time for recuperation, (5) personal finances, (6) personal social environment with family and leisure situation, (7) work social environment with support, group dynamics, attitudes of managers, ageism, discrimination, (8) job satisfaction, motivation and self-crediting tasks and activities, (9) skills, knowledge, competence development [13–15]. The swAge-model also includes theories of gerontology regarding ageing, i.e. biological, chronological, social and cognitive age, and links these with the possibilities and demands of the work situation and the work environment, i.e. the four determinant spheres of employability. Theories, developed strategies and tools for a sustainable working life and age-conscious leadership are included in the overall model. These age-appropriate leadership tools can be utilized by all managers with regard to the needs and opportunities that exist in the workplace [16, 17].

3   Results

3.1   The Design of the Education Program in the Intervention Project

Of the interviewed managers only two had completed the entire educational program, sent in the document and matrix of the final examination which they had carried out in their workplaces. One manager stated that she had finished the entire educational program and the final examination in their workplace, but had not sent in the examination documents. Nine managers had watched all or some of the 28 recorded lectures online, done the reflection assignments related to the lectures and also looked at the matrix and how to perform the final examination, though had not completed the examination.

Most of the participants stated that the design of the educational program as an online course, i.e. on an educational course platform where they could take part of the recorded lectures and assignments whenever they wanted to, gave them a better opportunity to adapt their participation to their daily work tasks. However, some of the participants stated that they were not familiar with educational platforms, that it was a very long time ago they had participated in any education and stated this as a hindrance to complete the education program.

The managers stated that a great problem within the educational program was that no time had been allocated by their employer to participate in the educational program during working hours. Therefore, several managers stated that they had to take part of the lectures during their leisure time in order to complete the educational program, competing with other things they would do in their spare time. All the managers who do not completed the education program, but also the three managers who completed it, i.e. utilized what they learnt during the education through a final examination of creating a workplace analysis and action plan, stated that the hindrance to fully complete all parts of the educational initiatives were the managers' ordinary work tasks and the prioritization of acute unforeseen circumstances. For example one manager described it in the following way: *"There is so much else that us managers have to do that I have not had time for. It's really sad and I'm ashamed that I did not have time to complete the examination task, but there are urgent things that need to be taken care of. Now, there is also a pandemic and there is no time left at all to do this. It's a shame because I really see the benefits I would have had from this"*. Examples of unforeseen circumstances that affected the possibility to complete the educational program were re-organisations in the municipality that took longer time than expected, as well as the COVID-19 pandemic which unfortunately occurred shortly after the intervention project began and burdened the manager's daily work in a way they had not anticipated.

3.2 The Content of the Education Program in the Intervention Project

The content of the educational initiative seemed to be very satisfactory based on the managers' statements. The managers stated that it had been an eureka moment to take part of the swAge-model and the lectures. They described they had started to reflect on the fact that there were several different ways of defining age. Furthermore, they described that they had not fully understood their own significance in relation to the retirement pension being postponed in society before. For example, one manager stated: *"I feel that the knowledge I gained through the intervention project has given me a completely new perspective that I did not have before. Today I reflect more on the importance of age in working life. It was something I have not done before at all"*. Another manager stated: *"I now see and better understand my own importance as a manager to support my employees to work until an older age. I had not reflected on that before"*.

The managers participating in this intervention project who had the opportunity to prioritize the educational initiative in their regular work tasks were the most satisfied and had developed their own strategies for using the swAge-model in their leadership and work environment management, in order to promote a healthy and sustainable workplace for all ages. For example, one manager described it like this: *"The model (i.e. the swAge model) and the matrix that we used for the workplace analysis in the examination assignment are very useful in the daily work as a manager. /.../ The model contains all the perspectives in a single picture. That's really good for me. /.../ We will also use the model in our collaboration group (i.e. the collaboration group for employers, employees, union representatives and safety representatives) in the work environment set up"*.

An intent of the intervention project was for the managers to achieve a reflection based understanding of the swAge model in relation to the needs of their own employees in their organisation. The results showed that all managers who completed the entire or most of the educational program stated that they had gained a better understanding, not only of the swAge-model, but also of how they could use the swAge-model in their work and make it more individual-oriented for their employees of any age.

4 Discussion

The labour force is ageing in most countries and age-dependent deterioration increases the risk of occupational injuries and accidents [1, 2]. However, we know that in a healthy work environment and work situation where people experience well-being, more employees are able to and want to continue working until an older age [3–5, 12–17]. Measures to maintain and increase employability are needed throughout working life, especially when you have become a senior employee. If the employee does not have, for example, the skills, capacity or physical conditions needed, they are not as employable and also risk causing declines in productivity. It is the manager's task to draw attention to risks of reduction in employability and to implement the necessary measures together with the employee and others based on the matter and the problem.

A great problem with this intervention project was that only two participating managers completed the entire educational program. However, it was completely voluntary to participate and the organization or the researchers could not force the participants to complete. All of the managers had stated the topic of the intervention project to be important and took the time to sign up. Furthermore, the municipality's top management, politicians and HR director had stated the topic to be of such importance that the institution allowed the researchers to execute this intervention project in their organisation. It is well known that managers have a key role to senior employees' possibility to continue working until an older age [9–11]. However, in spite of this the managers did not receive any allocated time to participate and had to perform the educational competence development program as an additional task in their already burdened working hours. The managers described their lack of time, having too many different tasks and assignments during a working day and that they were relieved of none of their ordinary tasks despite their participation in an education during their working hours. Therefore, even if they themselves registered their interest and experienced the program as very useful for them to participate in, they experienced difficulties completing their participation in this educational initiative. Furthermore, most managers stated that they always had to prioritize urgent actions over investing time and energy in long-term strategies, such as strategies to create a healthy and sustainable workplace and working life for all ages. Despite the intention to complete the educational program and implementation, unforeseen circumstances seemed to change the focus of the daily work of the managers participating in this intervention project. Especially since the intervention project took place during the COVID-19 pandemic. This work situation is probably similar for most managers, i.e. even managers who did not participate in this particular project. Therefore, organisations need to realize that managers need to be relieved of some other tasks and allocate working hours if they are to have a reasonable opportunity to complete an intervention project and implement their new skills in the workplace to benefit the organisation in a long term perspective.

Despite the problem for all managers to complete all the tasks of the educational program, all the managers stated that they had absorbed new knowledge and had started to consider a new age management perspective. All the managers stated that they perceived the benefits of using the swAge model in their managerial assignments. Additionally, they were all satisfied with having participated in this intervention project. The managers' new knowledge, the swAge-model and their reflections based on the lectures might hopefully influence the managers to develop an implementation of measures in their daily leadership and work situation in the future.

5 Conclusions

If organizations and enterprises want to achieve a more sustainable working life for all ages, they need to be supportive and offer managers time and latitude to work with this issue during their ordinary working hours, through relieving of or removing other tasks. Otherwise, new measures to promote a more sustainable working life for all ages are very difficult to develop and implement in the managers' daily managerial tasks.

Most of the participating managers in this intervention project experienced difficulties in finishing their final examination due to external circumstances such as the COVID-19 pandemic. That is a great bias of this project and the result could not be generalized. However, intervention projects are usually implemented in smaller groups of participants and are therefore difficult to generalize.

Though, all managers who participated in the educational program (in total or in some part) stated that they perceived the swAge-model as highly relevant to their age-consistent supervision, due to the knowledge and tools it contains to increase the employability for different age groups. Owing to those statements, as well as previous research, the swAge-model gives the impression to be considered as a genuine tool in the work to establish healthier workplaces and a sustainable working life for all ages.

References

1. OECD: Pensions at a Glance 2019: OECD and G20 Indicators. OECD Publishing, Paris (2019). https://doi.org/10.1787/b6d3dcfc-en
2. World Economic Forum: Global agenda council on ageing (2016). https://www.weforum.org/communities/global-agenda-council-on-ageing/
3. Torgén, M.: Physologichal agein – physical capacity and occupational performance. In: Vingård, E. (ed.) Healthy Workplaces for Women and Men of All Ages, vol. 8, pp. 75–85. Swedish Work Environment Authority, Stockholm (2016)
4. Nilsson, K.: Conceptualization of ageing in relation to factors of importance for extending working life – a review. Scand. J. Publ. Health. **44**, 490–505 (2016)
5. Fridriksson, J.F., Tómasson, K., Midtsundstad, T., Mehlum, I.S., Hilsen, A.I., Nilsson, K., Albin, M., Poulsen, O.M.: Working environment and work retention. TemaNord, vol. 559, pp. 1–121. Nordic Council of Ministers, Copenhagen (2017)
6. Nilsson, K., Östergren, P.-O., Kadefors, R., Albin, M.: Has the participation of older employees in the workforce increased? Study of the total Swedish population regarding exit working life. Scan. J. Pub. Health. **44**, 506–516 (2016)
7. Nilsson, K.: A sustainable working life for all ages – the swAge-model. Appl. Ergon. JERG_103082 (2020). https://doi.org/10.1016/j.apergo.2020.103082
8. Nilsson, K.: Interventions to reduce injuries among older workers in agriculture: a review of evaluated intervention projects. Work. J. Prev. Assess. Rehabil. **55**(2), 471–480 (2017). https://content.iospress.com/articles/work/wor2407
9. Nilsson, K.: Active and healthy ageing at work – a qualitative study with employees 55–63 years and their managers. Open J. Soc. Sci. **5**, 13–29 (2017)

10. Blomé, M., Borell, J., Håkansson, C., Nilsson, K.: Attitudes toward elderly workers and perceptions of integrated age management practices. Int. J. Occup. Saf. Ergon. **26**(1), 112–120 (2020)
11. Jensen, P.H., Juul Møberg, R.: Age management in Danish companies: what, how and how much? Nordic J. Working. Life. Stud. **2**(3), 49–65 (2012)
12. swAge-models Homepage (2021). https://swage.org/. Accessed 08 Feb 2021
13. Nilsson, K.: Why work beyond 65? Discourse on the decision to continue working or retire early. Nord. J. Work. Life Stud. **2**(3), 7–28 (2012). https://www.nordicwl.com/nilsson-2012-why-work-beyond-65-discourse-on-the-decision-to-continue-working-or-retire-early/
14. Nilsson, K., Rignell-Hydbom, A., Rylander, L.: Factors influencing the decision to extend working life or to retire. Scand. J. Work Environ. Health. **37**(6), 473–480 (2011). https://doi.org/10.1186/s12889-016-3438-6. https://bmcpublichealth.biomedcentral.com/articles/
15. Nilsson, K.: The influence of work environmental and motivation factors on seniors' attitudes to an extended working life or to retire. A cross sectional study with employees 55–74 years of age. Open J. Soc. Sci. **5**, 30–41 (2017). https://file.scirp.org/pdf/JSS_2017071013594273.pdf
16. Nilsson, K.: Managers' attitudes towards their older employees. Report 15, S2018:10. The Swedish governments official investigations, pp. 1–47. Delegation for Senior Workforce, Stockholm (2019). (in Swedish)
17. Nilsson, K.: Should i stay or should i go? The SwAge model = sustainable working life for all ages. Report 5, S2018:10. The Swedish governments official investigations, pp. 1–67. Delegation for Senior Workforce, Stockholm (2019). (in Swedish)

The Retention of Airline's Customer Service Agents Within the Framework of the Digitalization of the Service Relationship

Lucie Reboul[1]([⊠]), Catherine Delgoulet[2], and Corinne Gaudart[3]

[1] PACTE, Grenoble-Alpes University, Grenoble, France
[2] CRTD/CNAM, Paris, France
[3] LISE/CNAM, Paris, France

Abstract. This paper presents the results of research aimed at understanding the increase in health problems among airline customer service agents in a context of multiple transformations: an overall aging population, downsizing, and the digitalization of the service relationship. This action-research combines a synchronic and diachronic approach to health/work relations in order to understand the occurrence of a health problem in a present situation while situating it in the evolution of working conditions and employees' career paths. The results analyze the tensions between work and worker transformations. These tensions arise from the way in which decision-makers manage change, considering digitalization only from the point of view of progress and ageing only from the point of view of decline. Consequently, these tensions produce an intensification of work depriving experienced employees of their strategies, built up over the course of their career, and which aim at the quality of the service relationship, preservation of health and safety. This prolonged exposure to constraints ultimately leads to the departure of former employees from their jobs. These results insist on integrating a participatory approach when introducing a new technology, which takes into account the real work and the skills - often tacit - that agents develop to deal with hazards, manage quality and preserve their health.

Keywords: Ageing · Work trajectory · Digitalization of the service relationship · Health and performance · Airline

1 Introduction

The production systems of industrialized countries are caught up in a twofold evolution linked to the aging of the active population [1], and the spread of technologies, particularly in the tertiary sector [2–4]. This is the case of a major French airline company that is experiencing a gradual digitalization of tasks relating to the service relationship. The digitalization consists mainly in the implementation of automatons to supplement the

© The Author(s), under exclusive license to Springer Nature Switzerland AG 2021
N. L. Black et al. (Eds.): IEA 2021, LNNS 220, pp. 25–32, 2021.
https://doi.org/10.1007/978-3-030-74605-6_4

various operations that were previously performed by customer service agents[1]. Their population is also ageing and recruitment has been halted in a context of a significant reduction in the workforce (10% between 2009 and 2013). More and more of them are also presenting medical restrictions[2], starting at 30, which raises concerns about their job retention for occupational health and human resources service providers. This was the starting point for an action-research project built within the framework of an agreement between the airline company and the GIS-CREAPT research team[3]. Generally speaking, the measures recommended to keep "aging" employees in employment are struggling to materialize. One of the obstacles identified comes from persistent stereotypes regarding the learning or adaptation capacities of seniors, particularly when it comes to new technologies. These stereotypes tend to retain only aspects of the aging process that are in decline (cognitive and physical functions, etc.), at the expense of acquired [5]. As a result, the modes of change management and workforce management tend rather to exclude these employees [6, 7]. This action-research aims at understanding the links between the digitalization of the service relationship - and the organizational and prescription transformations it entails - and the health and skills paths of agents. The objective is also to initiate transformations aimed at "sustainable" work [8, 9], i.e. work that is favorable to the construction of health and the development of skills throughout the career path.

2 Theoretical Framework

The service relationship can be defined as a process of "coaction" and "co-production" in order to achieve a common goal between agents and clients [10, 11]. This definition emphasizes the cooperation required between clients and agents to produce a service. However, this cooperation takes place within the framework of an asymmetrical relationship, since agents possess multidimensional and specific skills acquired in the trade [12]. The efficiency of service production depends, among other things, on the information and signs available, the time and organization of queues, the workspace, the physical environment, etc. [11, 12]. Quality is multi-criteria, covering the company's definitions, customer expectations and agents' self-prescriptions that emerge from their own experience of the service relationship [13, 3].

As for digitalization, it leads in part to the transfer to the customer of certain tasks previously assigned to agents. This is more broadly in line with the trend towards "putting clients to work" [14], which modifies the modalities of cooperation between agents and clients, making them more complex and/or encouraging the deployment of new collective skills [11]. Digitalization can also help to reduce waiting time for agents and customers

---

[1] The tasks are: 1) removal of boarding pass and baggage tag at the Self-Service Kiosks (BLS); 2) drop off baggage at the Automatic Baggage Drop-off (DBA); 3) access to boarding the plane via automatic "Self-Boarding" gates; 4) customer reception and dispatching in the terminal at the Reception-Dispatch station (AD).

[2] Issued by the occupational health authorities to protect employees with certain constraints by setting up workstations.

[3] Conducted between 2015 and 2019, before the COVID-19 epidemic, Convention ANR Project ANR 14 - CE 30 - 0006. GIS-CREAPT - Scientific Interest Group, Research Center on Experience, Age and Working Populations.

and increase responsiveness and flexibility, but sometimes at the cost of accelerating work rates [4]. This acceleration of work rates potentially accentuates an intensification of work that is already well established in all industrialized countries [15, 16] and which continues to strengthen for the commercial agent categories [17]. Work intensification is induced by a) an accumulation of industrial and market constraints [1], b) a regime of permanent change [18, 19] and c) an acceleration of the latter [20]. These configurations are a source of haste and rush, generate shortcuts in decision-making and consequently increase the risks of errors and omissions [21]. This temporal pressure accentuates the painful feelings induced by physical constraints [22, 23] that often precede the onset of a musculoskeletal disorder [2–24]. The intensification of work weakens, above all, the career paths at both ends of the age pyramid [25]: on the one hand, employees at the beginning of their working lives more frequently accumulate several temporary contracts and do not have sufficient time to learn a trade and the specificities of the professional environment in which they are inserted [26]. On the other hand, high time constraints and frequent changes destabilize the strategies of older employees and deprive them of their experience, potentially leading to early departures or dismissal for unfitness. This action-research aims to elucidate the effects of the digitalization of the service relationship on the activity of ground personnel in an air company.

3 Methodology

The objective was to situate medical restrictions in the dual evolution of the work system (digitalization of the service relationship) and socio-demographic characteristics (evolution of generations at work: workforce, age, health, skills). To do this, we combined qualitative and quantitative analyses, in a diachronic and synchronic perspective [27]. The first consists in characterizing the technical-organizational and socio-demographic transformations. The second aims to analyze the articulations or tensions between these different transformations based on work activity. In this perspective, quantitative analyses were carried out using the company's databases to trace socio-demographic evolutions (workforce fluctuations, states of health, overall ageing). The qualitative analyses included fifteen semi-directive interviews with decision-makers (HR manager, production manager, manager, occupational physicians, etc.) in order to gather their point of view on these transformations and to understand their management methods. Five biographical interviews were conducted with the agents in order to reconstruct their work history (date of joining the company, the various positions held, projections, state of health, etc.). From a synchronic perspective, we mobilized the ergonomic analysis of the activity [28], proceeding by systematic observations of five agent shifts (F34, F39, F42, M50, F52) in two types of situations: the tasks of the digitized customer itinerary (reception-dispatch (AD): reception and dispatching of customers in the check-in area, (BLS, DBA and self-boarding gate) and the tasks of the "manual" customer itinerary (operations carried out at the check-in counter or at the boarding gate). The indicators systematically recorded were: the different postures adopted; communications (with colleagues and customers); and load carrying. These observations were supplemented by post-activity interviews with the agents observed. The analysis of their frequency according to these two types of situation allowed to understand the transformation of the activity in terms of the arduousness associated with the postures, the possibilities of cooperating with colleagues and with clients. These results are cross-referenced with the analysis of the agents' career paths and the evolution of the generations (changes in age, workforce, health).

4 Results

The results show that the problems of health and therefore of the retention of agents are less due to a given age than to the way in which human resources and digitalization are considered. Indeed, while digitalization is essentially perceived as progress, age is considered only in terms of decline (Sect. 4.1). Digitalization is therefore accompanied by work intensification and deskilling, potentially leading to accelerated attrition and early departure from the profession (Sect. 4.2).

4.1 An Aging Incompatible with the Digitalization of Tasks?

For department heads and managers, digitization above all makes it possible to reduce waiting time for customers and agents, the main criterion used to assess customer satisfaction: *"We mainly measure waiting time. The customer only wants to go fast."* [Customer Manager]. This automation would also be an opportunity to improve agents' working conditions by reducing a workload estimated based on the number of customers to be processed: *"There is no longer the pressure to say, 'I'm at a counter and I have 150 customers to register'; that's over! It's over!"* [Quality Manager]. This would justify the sharp reduction in staff numbers and thus support cost reduction. On the other hand, health difficulties are mainly associated with aging and declines in cognitive and physical function. *"Aging causes restrictions in standing posture. What do we do with these agents when we have to accompany the client in a standing position?"* [Client Manager]. As for the skills developed in the service relationship and which are aimed at multiple objectives, these are discredited or even perceived as a brake in these phases of change to which it is mainly a question of adapting. Finally, weakened agents are encouraged to retrain in order to escape the hardship of their work in a context where organizational solutions are increasingly rare (outsourcing of so-called "soft" jobs): *"I know that they are encouraged to move in other directions. Because in operations, you're working off-beat, you're running in all directions. You have the customers in front of you, you need stamina, you need physical strength and you need psychological strength"* [Customer Service Manager].

These difficulties in maintaining the employment of weakened personnel are partly the result of the actors' representations, anchored on an aging process essentially based on decline and therefore incompatible with the physical demands of digitalization.

4.2 An Intensification of Work

In order to assess the effects of digitalization on the transformation of the intensity of agents' work, let us look at the postures adopted by agents throughout their shift, the modalities of the service relationship and the actual interactions with other professionals.

Digitized Tasks: An Increase in "Stand-up" Work

All of the digitized tasks are carried out standing up, and in general, the five agents spend nearly half of their time (excluding breaks) performing "standing" tasks and a little less than half "sitting". For the majority of the agents, the tasks performed "standing" and "sitting" are alternated, but for some, the maintenance of the "standing" posture continues throughout the tasks. This is the case for F39, who performs two tasks standing for 2 h, then two other tasks while still standing for 2 h and 10 min, and ends her shift with a task during which she remains standing for 60 min and 50 min sitting at a workstation. In total, this agent spends 38.1% of her time in a "static standing" posture (i.e. 3 h 30 min over 9 h of presence)[4] and 24.3% of her time in a "dynamic standing" posture (2 h 07 min). Moreover, the digitized tasks are those that offer the least leeway to change posture: the "AD" task, for example, is essentially performed in a "static standing" manner. This constraining posture leads agents to look for micro-regulations by trampling or looking for support (on one leg, holding their back, on an automaton) to relieve them. In these conditions, agents express discomfort and pain (in the knees and feet) related to postures induced mainly by the new tasks associated with the digitized client path (AD, BLS, DBA): *"we really trample on what (...) we all have a little back pain, our feet are full of bunions on our toes..."* [F39]. These difficulties lead the agents to question their ability to remain in the trade until retirement age: *"we say to ourselves, can we do this until 60, is it possible..."* [F39]. Maintaining the "standing" posture can also awaken or accentuate specific health problems: this is the case of F42 whose low back pain has been reactivated by these new constraints. These pains lead to a medical restriction, and in the near future, they will lead to a departure from the profession: *"I am considering changing my restriction because unfortunately I cannot resume recording"* [F42]. Moreover, there are fewer and fewer varied schedules that allow for alternating "sitting" and "standing" tasks. This is due to the increase in the number of people with medical restrictions, who have schedules mainly composed of "sitting" tasks, and the decrease in these "sitting" tasks with digitalization.

Digitized Tasks, More Frequent and Briefer Interactions with Customers

The new configurations of the stations appearing with the digitization modify the inter-actions between agents and customers, in number and duration. In fact, we can see that F52 devotes an average of 37 s per customer to the "AD" task (161 customers managed in 1 h of work), whereas it gives them an average of 6 min during the "check-in counter" task (26 customers managed in 2 h 25 min). F52 must therefore manage a greater number of clients simultaneously and therefore respond more quickly, in the context of direct contact, since there is no longer a clearly defined workstation. The main objective of this AD task is to direct customers on their journey through the airport. However, analyses show that the agents do much more than checking the eligibility of customers to go to the next step, since this eligibility concerns only 53% of customers. In 47% of cases, agents take care of other problems: inviting customers in advance to come back later (16% of cases), handling a complex case requiring special handling (15%), or redirecting the customer who has not completed all the operations (no label, no boarding pass) to the BLS (11%). Finally, they also inform customers in 5% of cases. Thus, this requires

---

[4] The duration of a session is normally 8 h, the session of this agent lasted 9 h due to a contingecy.

the agents to be extremely vigilant in identifying the various cases and to decide in a very constrained timeframe on the response to be given to the customer. In addition, responses that impede the client's progress along the way (27% of them) can lead to tense exchanges. The agents who performed the "AD" task expressed weariness due to the repetitive nature of the task and dissatisfaction with the quality of the customer relationship and the service provided: *"We always repeat the same thing 'your boarding passes, your identity papers'. It has to go very fast, you get up and put your head down for an hour, it's exhausting. [...] It's also a very bad service that doesn't please the customers and it's not fluid"* [F52]. Finally, for the agents, these changes are accompanied by the feeling that they are no longer doing their job. An employee who has been working for 27 years underlines the gap between the job for which she was recruited and the missions she is currently carrying out: *"We all passed tests to be recruited on certain criteria at the outset. We like the welcome and the commercial side, but that's impossible.... We're doing machine assistance now"* [F52].

5 Discussion

Concerns about the retention of customer service agents suggested that aging agents and digitalization were not compatible. This short-term vision does not take into account the role of prolonged exposure to physical and temporal constraints on the fragility of all employees, nor the role of the skills developed in the service relationship in coping with customer variability and preserving their health. Digitalization is accompanied by an intensification of work resulting in a) an increase in awkward postures; b) a greater number of customers to manage within shorter deadlines; c) a decrease in exchanges with colleagues. This intensification undermines the strategies of the agents built up over the course of their careers and which are aimed at quality of the service relationship, safety and the preservation of their health. These results qualify the optimistic representations of digitalization: they can indeed facilitate the customer journey by saving time, but only for a part of the customers (who are used to these technologies and to travelling, who are not late and do not encounter any hazards along the way). Indeed, the "putting to work" [14] of customers does not lighten the physical and mental load of agents in any way, since the results show an increase in cognitive, physical and temporal demands. Finally, these technologies are most often imposed without taking into account the way in which they transform the collective organization of work and sweep away agents' experience. These results then insist on the importance of participatory approaches when introducing new technologies that take into account real work [29]. They also underline the need to develop reflections on a long-term scale on the design of work paths that combine health and employee skills [30, 31].

References

1. Volkoff, S.: Dérives et inerties dans la démographie de la population salariée. In: Molinié, A.-F., Gaudart, C., Pueyo, V. (eds.) La vie professionnelle: âge, expérience et santé à l'épreuve des conditions de travail, pp. 21–30. Octarès Éditions, Toulouse (2012)

2. Prunier-Poulmaire, S.: Flexibilité assistée par ordinateur: Les caissières d'hypermarché. Actes de la recherche en sciences sociales **134**, 29–36 (2000)
3. Caroly-Flageul, S.: Différences de gestion collective des situations critiques dans les activités de service selon deux types d'organisation du travail. PISTES **4**(1), 34 (2002). https://doi.org/10.4000/pistes.517
4. Bobillier-Chaumon, M.-E.: Évolutions techniques et mutations du travail: émergence de nouveaux modèles d'activité. Le Travail Humain **66**(2), 161–192 (2003)
5. Cau-Bareille, D., Gaudart, C., Delgoulet, C.: Training, age and technological change: difficulties associated with age, the design of tools, and the organization of work. Work **41**, 127–141 (2012)
6. Sewdas, R., de Wind, A., van der Zwaan, L.G.L., van der Borg, W.E., Steenbeek, R., van der Beek, A.J., Boot, C.R.L.: Why older workers work beyond the retirement age: a qualitative study. BMC Public Health **17**(672), 2–9 (2017)
7. Behaghel, L., Caroli, E., Roger, M.: Age-biased technical and organizational change, training and employment prospects of older workers. Economica **81**(322), 368–389 (2014)
8. Shani, A.-B., Docherty, P., Forslin, J.: Creating Sustainable Work Systems – Emerging Perspectives and Practices. Routledge, London (2002)
9. Volkoff, S., Gaudart, C.: Working conditions and «sustainability»: converting knowledge into action. Rapport de recherche, 92, Centre d'études de l'emploi, Noisy-le-Grand (2015)
10. Gadrey, J.: Les relations de service et l'analyse du travail des agents. Sociologie du travail **36**(3), 381–389 (1994)
11. Cerf, M., Valléry, G., Boucheix, J.M.: Les activités de services: enjeux et développements. In: Falzon, P. (ed.) Ergonomie, pp. 565–581. PUF, Paris (2004)
12. Falzon, P., Lapeyrière, S.: L'usager et l'opérateur: ergonomie et relations de service. Le travail humain **61**(1), 69–90 (1998)
13. Ughetto, P.: La relation de service, source inévitable de contrainte pour les travailleurs? Relations industrielles **61**(3), 490–512 (2006)
14. Dujarier, M.A.: Le travail du consommateur – De Mac Do à eBay, comment nous coproduisons ce que nous achetons. La Découverte, Collection «Poches/essais» (2014)
15. Gollac, M., Volkoff, S.: Ciltius, altius, fortius (l'intensification du travail). Actes de la recherche en sciences sociales **114**, 54–67 (1996)
16. Parent-Thirion, A., Biletta, I., Cabrita, J., Vargas Llave, O., Vermeylen, G., Wilczyńska, A.: Sixth European Working Conditions Survey – Overview report? European Foundation, Dublin (2016)
17. Bèque, M., Mauroux, A.: Quelles sont les évolutions récentes des conditions de travail et des risques psychosociaux? Dares Analyses **082**, 10 (2017)
18. Demers, C.: De la gestion du changement à la capacité de changer. L'évolution de la recherche sur le changement organisationnel de 1945 à aujourd'hui. Gestion **24**(3), 131–139 (1999)
19. Bradley, G.: The information and communication society: how people will live and work in the new millennium. Ergon. **43**(7), 844–857 (2000)
20. Algava E., Davie E., Loquet J., Vinck, L.: Conditions de travail – Reprise de l'intensification du travail chez les salariés. Dares Analyses **49**. https://travail-emploi.gouv.fr/2014-049-conditions-de-travail,17845.html (2014)
21. Weill-Fassina, A.: Le développement des compétencesprofessionnelles au fil du temps, à l'épreuve des situations de travail. In: Molinié, A.-F., Gaudart, C., Pueyo, V. (eds.) La vie professionnelle: âge, expérience et santé à l'épreuve des conditions de travail, pp. 117–144. Octarès Éditions, Toulouse (2012)
22. Volkoff, S., Buisset, C., Mardon, C.: Does intense time pressure at work make older employees more vulnerable? A statistical analysis based on a French survey «SVP50». Appl. Ergon. **41**(5), 754–762 (2010)

23. Volkoff, S., Delgoulet, C.: L'intensification du travail, l'intensification des changements dans le travail: Quels enjeux pour les travailleurs expérimentés? Psychologie du travail et des organisations **25**(1), 28–39 (2019). https://doi.org/10.1016/j.pto.2018.09.002
24. Arnaudo, B., Hamon-Cholet, S., Waltisperger, D.: Les contraintes posturales et articulaires au travail. Dares Premières Synthèses **11**(2), 6 (2006)
25. Gaudart, C.: Intensification du travail: le temps soustrait. In: Thébault-Mony, A., et al. (éd.) Dans Les risques du travail, pp. 196–206. La Découverte, Paris (2015)
26. Cloutier, E., Ledoux, E., Fournier, P.-S.: Knowledge transmission in light of recent transformations in the workplace. Ind. Relat. **67**(2), 304–324 (2012)
27. Molinié, A.-F., Gaudart, C., Pueyo, V.: La vie professionnelle: âge, expérience et santé à l'épreuve des conditions. De travail. Octarès Éditions, Toulouse (2012)
28. Guérin, F., Laville, A., Daniellou, F., Duraffourg, J., Kerguelen A.: Understanding and Transforming Work. The Practice of Ergonomics. ANACT, Lyon-Montrouge (2007)
29. Rocha, R., Mollo, V., Daniellou, F.: Le débat sur le travail fondé sur la subsidiarité: un outil pour développer un environnement capacitant. @ctivités **14**(2) (2017). https://doi.org/10.4000/activites.2999
30. Gaudart, C., Ledoux, E.: Courses of work and development. In: Falzon, P. (ed.) Constructive Ergonomics, pp. 117–132. CRS Press Taylor, Francis Group, Boca Raton (2014)
31. Buchmann, W., Mardon, C., Volkoff, S.: Peut-on élaborer une approche ergonomique du «temps long»? Une étude des douleurs articulaires liées au travail, dans une grande entreprise. PISTES **20**(1) (2018). https://doi.org/10.4000/pistes.5565.

Analyzing the Influence of Work Demands and Work Organization on Workability Based on Age

Camila A. Ribeiro[1]([⊠]), Teresa P. Cotrim[1,2] [ID], Vítor Reis[3], Maria João Guerreiro[3], Susana Candeias[3], Ana Sofia Janicas[3], and Margarida Costa[3]

[1] Ergonomics Laboratory, FMH, Universidade de Lisboa, Lisbon, Portugal
tcotrim@fmh.lisboa.pt
[2] CIAUD, Faculdade de Arquitetura, Universidade de Lisboa, Lisbon, Portugal
[3] Health and Safety Department, Municipality of Sintra, Sintra, Portugal

Abstract. The reduction in work ability over the years is due to the imbalance between the work demands and individual resources and is strongly affected by a set of factors. This study aims at analyzing the influence of work demands and work organization on work ability based on age. The results were extracted from a prospective study that accomplishes three time periods. Was used a self-administered questionnaire composed of sociodemographic questions, the Portuguese version of the Work Ability Index (WAI) and the scales related to work demands and work organization from the Portuguese medium version of Copenhagen Psychosocial Questionnaire (COPSOQ II). In 2015 the sample included 885 participants, in 2017, 1167 participants, and in 2019, 1331 participants. The results pointed out that the ability to work decreased over the years. Also, workers over 50 years old, from the operational assistant category, with a degree in basic education presented lower WAI, representing a more vulnerable group. Regarding the COPSOQ II, the scales of "quantitative demands", "work pace" and "cognitive demands" showed better results as age increases. Better values in the scales "meaning of work", "workplace commitment" and "cognitive demands" determined better results in WAI, playing a protective role on the work ability. To conclude, psychosocial factors affect differently workers from different age groups and professional categories and has an important role on work ability. This must be taken into consideration to propose intervention measures.

Keywords: Work ability · Work demands · Cognitive demands · Work organization · Workplace commitment

1 Introduction

To better understand the concept of work ability, we first reflect on the concept of disability established by the International Classification of Functionality, Disability and Health: a person's functionality and disability are conceived as a dynamic interaction between health conditions and contextual factors; disability is not an attribute of the

N. L. Black et al. (Eds.): IEA 2021, LNNS 220, pp. 33–40, 2021.
https://doi.org/10.1007/978-3-030-74605-6_5

person, but a complex set of conditions that results from the interaction between person and environment (OMS 2004).

Disability is the generic term for disabilities, activity limitations and participation restrictions. It corresponds to the negative aspects of the interaction between an individual (with a health condition) and its contextual factors (environmental and personal) (OMS 2004). The work ability can be defined, therefore, by a sustainable balance between factors of work and human resources (physical and mental) (Ilmarinen 2012).

Maintaining the work ability of workers has been the focus of many studies, since professional life has been prolonged over the past decades and there is a concern to reduce occupational risks and promote quality of life and health among the aging workforce (Ilmarinen 2012; Oakman et al. 2016). In the European Union, it is estimated that by 2030, workers aged between 55 and 64 will make up the majority of the workforce in many countries (EU-OSHA 2016; Ilmarinen 2012).

The current changes in working life, increase the challenges for everybody, especially aging workers, since these changes are not accompanied by the pace of biological aging (Ilmarinen 2019).

Several studies have sought to understand how the emergent risk factors of psychosocial origin affects workers life and how they interfere on mental health for older workers (Collins and O'Sullivan 2015; Leijten et al. 2015). Among the results obtained, it was possible to identify that high physical, emotional demands and less autonomy at work were associated with reduced health among older workers. On the other hand, the promotion of commitment at work was a favorable factor and could be beneficial to health, especially the mental health of the older group (Leijten et al. 2015). The work demands also influence the risk of musculoskeletal injuries what can reduce the ability to work over the years (Collins and O'Sullivan 2015; Oakman et al. 2016).

Therefore, it is justified to develop a study that contemplates the analysis of the ability to work over the years and the characterization of the factors that influence this variation, regarding sociodemographic characteristics, work demands and work organization, aiming to contribute to the promotion of the permanence of workers in their workplace and improve health.

2 Methodology

2.1 Study Design

The study is cross-sectional but has a longitudinal design in which it seeks to analyze the aspects related to time and the changes that occur in individuals, integrating three time periods.

2.2 Methods

The analysis was done using a self-administered questionnaire composed by questions related to the sociodemographic variables, the Portuguese version of the Work Ability Index (WAI) (Silva et al. 2011) and the scales related to work demands and work organization from the Portuguese medium version of Copenhagen Psychosocial Questionnaire (COPSOQ II) (Silva et al. 2012).

The Work Ability Index is a self-administered instrument developed in Finland, which evaluates the worker's perception on how well they can perform work in function of work demands, health, physical and mental resources. Seven dimensions compose the WAI, with a final score ranging from 7 to 49 (better score). The results are classified as poor, moderate, good or excellent (Silva et al. 2011).

The COPSOQ is an instrument developed by the National Occupational Institute of Denmark, and tested in several studies, in order to standardize and monitor different psychosocial aspects in the workplaces (Silva et al. 2012). The scales from the Work demands, Work organization of the Portuguese medium version of COPSOQ II, regarding Quantitative demands, Work pace, Emotional demands, Cognitive demands, meaning of work, Commitment to the workplace, were used in this study. The scales are scored with a 5-point Likert scale and classified as critical, intermediate and favourable, based on two cut-off points.

2.3 Population and Sample

The population of this study included 1,667 workers of a Portuguese municipality. In 2015 the response rate was of 54%, with a total of 888 participants. In 2017, the sample comprised 1167 participants, corresponding to a response rate of 70%. In 2019, the global sample of workers in the Municipality was higher than in previous years, comprising 1997 workers. From this sample, we obtained 1325 valid questionnaires, making an overall response rate of 66.3%.

2.4 Procedures

The questionnaire was self-administered during the years 2015, 2017 and 2019. The inclusion criteria were to have a valid WAI and be a municipality worker for at least one year. 20 questionnaires were excluded from the analysis in 2015, 14 questionnaires in 2017 and 6 questionnaires in 2019. Missing values were excluded. The confidence level assumed for the statistical analysis was 95%.

At the end of the study, focus groups will be held to evaluate measures that can be implemented in the workplace.

3 Results

3.1 Sociodemographic Characterization

The sample showed an average age of 46.9 years (sd = 8.3) in 2015, 48.4 years (sd = 8.7) in 2017, and 49.5 years (sd = 9.2) in 2019. The mean age had an increase in both follow ups and the differences were statistically significant (F(2): 22,217; p $\leq$ 0,001). Looking at the age groups, it's clear that in 2019, the group aged 50 years and more had a high percentage (Table 1).

The largest part of our sample has an undergraduate level and belong to a lower hierarchical level (Table 1). In the first two moments, workers in the technical assistant category had a higher percentage, and in 2019 we obtained a higher participation of workers in the operational assistant category (Table 1).

Table 1. Sociodemographic characterization

		2015		2017		2019	
		N	%	N	%	N	%
Age groups	<50	521	61,2%	593	52,8%	589	46,7%
	≥50	330	38,8%	530	47,2%	671	53,3%
Qualifications	Basic level	242	28,2%	314	27,9%	397	31,4%
	Secondary level	324	37,8%	411	36,5%	474	37,5%
	Graduated/post graduated	291	34,0%	402	35,7%	392	31,0%
Professional category	Operational assistant	287	33,7%	370	32,7%	468	37,6%
	Technical assistant	336	39,4%	431	38,1%	445	35,7%
	White collars	229	26,9%	330	29,2%	333	26,7%

Looking at the occupational category and age, workers in the Operational Assistant category are mostly aged 50 and over, and, comparing with the other occupational categories, the differences were statically significant [2015: F(2): 25,808; p ≤ 0,001; 2017: F(2): 25,538; p ≤ 0,001; 2019: F(2): 21,327 p ≤ 0,001].

The qualifications also correlate with age [2015: F(2): 50.090; p ≤ 0,001; 2017: F(2): 81,924; p ≤ 0,001; 2019: F(2): 73,876; p ≤ 0,001]. Workers with a Basic level of education are mostly aged 50 and over.

3.2 COPSOQ II Dimensions

The scales belonging to the Work demands of COPSOQ II, correspond to those in which the highest value is the most critical result: "Cognitive demands", "Emotional demands", and "Work Pace". These scales had the worst results. Comparing the three years of research the Work demands scales that had significant differences were the "Work pace" (F(2) = 6,199; p = 0,002) and "Emotional demands" (F(2) = 4,663; p = 0,009). The results were worse in 2015 comparing with the subsequent moments (Table 2).

Concerning the scales from the Work Organization and Content dimensions, from those whose lower value corresponds to the most critical result: "Commitment to the workplace" and "Meaning of work"; the scale "Commitment to the workplace" had the lowest values. Comparing the years of research, we found that the "Meaning of work" (F(2) = 4,760; p = 0,014) had statistically significant differences, presenting worse results in 2015 (Table 2).

Regarding the analysis comparing the COPSOQ II Scales between professional categories, declining scores in the scales "meaning of work" [F(2): 16,002; p ≤ 0,001] and "workplace commitment" [F(2): 11,723; p ≤ 0,001] were found in 2019 among the technical assistants.

Table 2. COPSOQ II dimensions characterization

Year		2015		2017		2019	
N		888		1167		1313	
		Mean	S.D.	Mean	S.D.	Mean	S.D.
Work demands	Quantitative demands	2,3	0,9	2,3	0,8	2,2	0,9
	Work pace*	3,0	1,0	2,9	1,0	2,9	1,1
	Cognitive demands	3,5	0,8	3,6	0,7	3,5	0,8
	Emotional demands*	3,3	1,2	3,1	1,2	3,1	1,2
Work organization and content	Meaning of work*	3,9	0,8	4,0	0,7	4,0	0,7
	Commitment to the workplace	3,2	0,9	3,3	0,9	3,3	0,9

* $p \leq 0,050$;

The White collar workers presented worst results on a greater number of scales: "quantitative demands" [2015: F(2): 37,780; $p \leq 0,001$; 2017: F(2): 45,775; $p \leq 0,001$; 2019: F(2): 57,678; $p \leq 0,001$], "work pace" [2015: F(2): 22,553; $p \leq 0,001$; 2017: F(2): 38,846; $p \leq 0,001$; 2019: F(2): 31,550; $p \leq 0,001$] "cognitive demands" [2017: F(2): 40,020; $p \leq 0,001$; 2019: F(2): 26,207; $p \leq 0,001$], "emotional demands" [2017: F(2): 8,438; $p \leq 0,001$; 2019: F(2): 4,628; $p = 0,010$].

Analysing the COPSOQ II scales and age, the scales of "quantitative demands" (2015: $r = -0,17$; $p \leq 0,001$; 2017: $r = -0,12$; $p \leq 0,001$; 2019: $r = -0,18$; $p \leq 0,001$), "work pace" (2015: $r = -0,09$; $p \leq 0,001$; 2017: $r = -0,09$; $p \leq 0,001$; 2019: $r = -0,13$; $p \leq 0,001$) and "cognitive demands" (2015: $r = -0,18$; $p \leq 0,001$; 2019: $r = -0,12$; $p \leq 0,001$) correlated with age, showing better results as age increases.

3.3 Work Ability Index

The WAI of the municipal workers showed, in 2015, an average of 40.7 points (s.d = 5,1), in 2017, 40.2 points (s.d = 5,1) and in 2019, 39.9 points (s.d = 5,5). In the three time periods, the average value obtained corresponds to a classification of "good" work ability. The differences in the mean WAI values between 2015, 2017 and 2019 were statistically significant (F (2) = 6,366; $p = 0,002$), indicating a decrease in the ability to work in recent years (Table 3).

Age was negatively correlated with WAI (2015: $r = -0.15$; $p \leq 0.001$; 2017: $r = -0.18$; $p \leq 0.001$; 2019: $r = -0.15$; $p \leq 0.001$), that means when age increases, the ability to work decreases.

Workers over 50 years old (2015: $t = 4,266$; $p \leq 0,001$; 2017: t:5,541: $p \leq 0,001$; 2019: t: 4,775: $p \leq 0,001$), from the operational assistant category [2015: F(2) = 5,519; $p \leq 0,001$; 2017: F(2) = 18,301; $p \leq 0,001$; 2019: F(2) = 9,576; $p \leq 0,001$], with a

Table 3. WAI scores

Year	N	Mean	Min.	Max.	S.D.
2015	885	40,7	14	49	5,1
2017	1167	40,2	7	49	5,1
2019	1331	39,9	12	49	5,5

degree in basic education [2015: $F_{(2)}$: 11,494; $p \leq 0,001$; 2017: $F_{(2)}$: 26,005; $p \leq 0,001$; 2019: $F_{(2)}$: 9,972; $p \leq 0,001$] presented lower WAI (Table 4).

Table 4. WAI and sociodemographic characterization

WAI		2015			2017			2019		
		N	Mean	S.D.	N	Mean	S.D.	N	Mean	S.D.
Age groups	<50	521	41,3	4,7	593	41,0	4,5	589	40,7	5,4
	≥50	330	39,8	5,6	530	39,3	5,6	671	39,2	5,6
Qualifications	Basic level	242	39,6	5,6	314	38,6	5,7	397	39,2	5,8
	Secondary level	324	40,8	5,2	411	40,2	4,8	474	39,7	5,7
	Graduated/post graduated	291	41,7	4,3	402	41,3	4,6	392	40,9	5,0
Professional category	Operational assistant	287	40,3	5,6	370	38,9	5,6	468	39,5	6,0
	Technical assistant	336	40,6	5,1	431	40,4	4,9	445	39,6	5,2
	White collars	229	41,7	4,1	330	41,2	4,6	333	41,1	4,8

WAI also correlates with the scales of COPSOQ II. Better values in the scales "meaning of work" (2015: $r = 0,27$; $p \leq 0,001$; 2017: $r = 0,25$; $p \leq 0,001$; 2019: $r = 0,27$; $p \leq 0,001$), "workplace commitment" (2015: $r = 0,13$; $p \leq 0,001$; 2017: $r = 0,16$; $p \leq 0,001$; 2019: $r = 0,16$; $p \leq 0,001$) determined better results in WAI.

4 Discussion

The average age of the samples was higher in the follow up, what corresponds to the ageing process of the working population.

The samples presented a majority of workers in the Technical assistant category in 2015 and 2017. In 2019 the number of workers in the Operational assistant category increased and these workers were mostly aged 50 and over, with a degree in basic education, belonging operational assistant category, in all moments of the research, representing a more vulnerable group. The hierarchical level and the nature of work activities is correlated, the lower the hierarchical level, the greater the physical demands of the activity, which may affect workers' health (Rugulies et al. 2010).

The COPSOQ II scales, in this study, presented worse results in 2015, what can be explained by the changes made in public administration on the last years. The psychosocial risks also affected professional categories in a different way, similar to other studies (Metzler and Bellingrath 2017), making it important to assess specific groups to better understand how psychosocial risks are present and affect the health of these groups. While lower hierarchical levels have more physical demands, higher levels have higher cognitive demands (Rugulies et al. 2010). Furthermore, high qualification at work is related to reduced risk of work exit generally and health-related exit specifically (Fleischmann et al. 2017).

The scales of "quantitative demands", "work pace" and "cognitive demands" correlated with age, showing better results as age increases. There is a longitudinal association between changes in exposure to psychosocial work factors and health, what needs to be considered deploying measures to improve the psychosocial work environment of aging workers (Havermans et al. 2018). With advancing age, although workers are less physically fit, they can be mentally capable, therefore, their work should be less physically demanding and more demanding in terms of mental abilities, which were developed throughout their professional career (Tuomi et al. 2001).

Regarding the WAI, results confirmed that work ability has a complex structure that includes the interactions between skills, individual and work characteristics. In line with other studies, there was a negative correlation between age and work ability (Ilmarinen et al. 1997). Aging is associated with a decrease in physical aptitudes and an increase in musculoskeletal injuries what can reduce the individual's ability to work at the same rhythm and requirements for productivity (Oakman et al. 2016). On the other hand, higher results at scales meaning of work and workplace commitment were correlated with better results on work ability, similar to other studies where, regarding psychosocial factors, the development of opportunities and the meaning of work are characteristics that contribute to the maintenance of work ability (Ilmarinen 2012).

5   Conclusion

To conclude, psychosocial factors that play a protective role on work ability must be taken into consideration in order to be included in intervention measures, especially knowing that cognitive demands tend to decrease over the years.

In this way, companies should promote the possibility of training and acquiring new skills over the years, developing strategies that improve the workplace commitment, the meaning of work and optimize other organizational aspects, considering that it seems to be a good way to maintain work ability.

In the future, studies with focused groups will be conducted to identify the specific group requirements in order to propose interventions that seek to promote healthier workplaces for all workers.

References

Collins, J.D., O'Sullivan, L.W.: Musculoskeletal disorder prevalence and psychosocial risk exposures by age and gender in a cohort of office based employees in two academic institutions. Int. J. Ind. Ergon. **46**, 85–97 (2015). https://doi.org/10.1016/j.ergon.2014.12.013

EU-OSHA: Healthy Workplaces for All Ages Promoting a sustainable working life (2016). https://www.healthy-workplaces.eu/

Fleischmann, M., Carr, E., Stansfeld, S.A., Xue, B., Head, J.: Can favourable psychosocial working conditions in midlife moderate the risk of work exit for chronically ill workers? A 20-year follow-up of the Whitehall II study. Occup. Environ. Med. (2017). https://doi.org/10.1136/oemed-2017-104452

Havermans, B.M., Boot, C.R.L., Hoekstra, T., Houtman, I.L.D., Brouwers, E.P.M., Anema, J.R., van der Beek, A.J.: The association between exposure to psychosocial work factors and mental health in older employees, a 3-year follow-up study. Int. Arch. Occup. Environ. Health **91**(1), 57–66 (2018). https://doi.org/10.1007/s00420-017-1261-8

Ilmarinen, J., Tuomi, K., Klockars, M.: Changes in the work ability of active employees over an 11-year period. Scand. J. Work Environ. Health **23**, 49–57 (1997)

Ilmarinen, J.: Promover o envelhecimento ativo no local de trabalho. Agencia Europeia de Saúde e Segurança No Trabalho. Bruxelas: OSHA, 1–9 (2012)

Ilmarinen, J.: From work ability research to implementation. Int. J. Environ. Res. Public Health **16**(16) (2019). https://doi.org/10.3390/ijerph16162882

Leijten, F.R.M., van den Heuvel, S.G., van der Beek, A.J., Ybema, J.F., Robroek, S.J.W., Burdorf, A.: Associations of work-related factors and work engagement with mental and physical health: a 1-year follow-up study among older workers. J. Occup. Rehabil. **25**(1), 86–95 (2015). https://doi.org/10.1007/s10926-014-9525-6

Metzler, Y.A., Bellingrath, S.: Psychosocial hazard analysis in a heterogeneous workforce: determinants of work stress in blue- and white-collar workers of the European steel industry. Front. Public Health **5** (2017). https://doi.org/10.3389/fpubh.2017.00210

Oakman, J., Neupane, S., Nygård, C.H.: Does age matter in predicting musculoskeletal disorder risk? An analysis of workplace predictors over 4 years. Int. Arch. Occup. Environ. Health **89**(7), 1127–1136 (2016). https://doi.org/10.1007/s00420-016-1149-z

OMS, O.M. de S.: CIF: Classificação Internacional de Funcionalidade. Calssificação Internacional de Funcionalidade, Incapacidade e Saude, 238 (2004). https://doi.org/10.1590/S1415-790X2005000200011

Rugulies, R., Aust, B., Pejtersen, J.H.: Do psychosocial work environment factors measured with scales from the Copenhagen psychosocial questionnaire predict register-based sickness absence of 3 weeks or more in Denmark? Scand. J. Public Health **38**(3 Suppl), 42–50 (2010). https://doi.org/10.1177/1403494809346873

Silva, C., Rodrigues, V., Pereira, A., Cotrim, T., Silvério, J., Rodrigues, P., Sousa, C.: Índice de Capacidade para o Trabalho-Portugal e Países Africanos de Língua Oficial Portuguesa. FCT - Fundação Para a Ciência e Tecnologia, pp. 1–6 (2011)

Silva, C., Amaral, V., Pereira, A., Bem-Haja, P., Pereira, A., Rodrigues, V., Nossa, P.: Copenhagen Psychosocial Questionnaire - COPSOQ - Portugal e países africanos de língua oficial portuguesa, pp. 1–46 (2012)

Tuomi, K., Huuhtanen, P., Nykyri, E., Ilmarinen, J.: Promotion of work ability, the quality of work and retirement. Occup. Med. **51**(5), 318–324 (2001)

A Hybrid Approach to the Evaluation and Design of Workstations for Manufacturing Industries: A Tuscan Case Study

Francesca Tosi, Mattia Pistolesi[✉], and Claudia Becchimanzi

Laboratory of Ergonomics and Design (LED), Department of Architecture, University of Florence, 93 Sandro Pertini Street, 50041 Calenzano, Florence, Italy
{francesca.tosi,mattia.pistolesi,claudia.becchimanzi}@unifi.it

Abstract. The aim of the study was the experimentation with a hybrid approach for the evaluation of some workstations of 5 Tuscany manufacturing companies, with the aim of defining standard operating guidelines for the improvement of safety and usability of the industrial machinery and workstations, and to improve the working conditions of the operators of all ages. 3 mechanical companies and 2 fashion-leather companies took part in this study. 37 users with variable age, gender and experience were involved. The study, financed by INAIL Toscana, bases its scientific reliability on the integration of skill and methodologies of two different fields of ergonomics, such as occupational ergonomics (curated by INAIL) and Human-Centred Design (curated by LED). The heuristic approach involved the application of a series of methodologies and the direct participation of operators to assess, identify and explore possible problems and discrepancies from the point of view of human-workstation interaction and workers' perceptions. The following methodologies have been used: User Observation, Thinking Aloud, Interview, Questionnaire, Workstation Observation and Work Environment Observation. The data emerged were compared and evaluated also in consideration of the results of the evaluation carried out by INAIL experts within the framework of Occupational Ergonomics. The use of this hybrid approach allowed the researchers to collect qualitative and quantitative data, such as opinions, thoughts, expectations and critical points experienced by operators, sometimes silent and hidden due to the low participation of the operators in the company decisions. This article shows the methodology used and the findings.

Keywords: Ergonomics in design · Hybrid evaluation approach · Workstations · Older workers

1 Introduction

For many years now, the manufacturing industry has been a highly productive sector for the Italian economy and Tuscany as well. Today this sector offers employment to many categories of workers, including operator over 50.

Demographic trends in active population in the EU countries indicate that the age range between 55 and 64 will increase by around 16,2% (9.9 million) between 2010

© The Author(s), under exclusive license to Springer Nature Switzerland AG 2021
N. L. Black et al. (Eds.): IEA 2021, LNNS 220, pp. 41–49, 2021.
https://doi.org/10.1007/978-3-030-74605-6_6

and 2030, while all other age groups will decrease from 5,4% (40–54 years) to 14,9% (25–39 years) [1]. As regards Italy, forecasts indicate that between 2010 and 2050, the age group of 20 to 65 years is predicted to decrease while the age group of 65+ is predicted to increase [2]. This is also reflected in the employment rate that among the Italian population between 55 and 64 years has constantly increased since 2002 and was at 43% in 2013 [2].

Some scientific evidence shows [2–5] how the ageing of the employed population poses challenges related both to the protection of health and safety conditions in the workplace (incongruous postures, prolonged fatigue, repetitive work, working time, etc.) and to the increase in safety levels and usability-simplicity of use of high and medium complexity machinery.

For these reasons, the aim of the study, financed by INAIL Toscana, was the ergonomic evaluation of standard operating guidelines for the improvement of safety and usability conditions of industrial machinery and workstations, together with the enhancement of working conditions of the operators of all ages. The study bases its scientific reliability on the integration of skills and methodologies of two different fields of ergonomics, such as occupational ergonomics (curated by INAIL) and Human-Centred Design (HCD) (curated by LED).

3 mechanical companies and 2 fashion-leather companies were involved in the study.

This paper shows the approach used during the study.

2   Method

The research was aimed to the ergonomic evaluation of workstations in 3 companies in the metalworking sector (2 large private companies with more than 250 employees, and 1 medium private company with less than 250 employees) and 2 companies in the fashion-leather sector (1 large private company and 1 medium private) (see Table 1).

A heuristic approach was followed, experimenting with a hybrid survey methodology, which involved the combined application of a series of methodologies and the direct participation of operators to assess, identify and explore possible problems and discrepancies from the point of view of human-workstation interaction, and workers' perceptions. The methodological approach is based on the application of methods for evaluating the usability and safety use of product-system [6].

After a careful review of the scientific literature of the sector [6–10], the following methodologies have been used, involving the direct participation of the user, as follows: (i) User Observation, (ii) Thinking Aloud, (iii) Interview, (iv) Questionnaire, (v) Workstation Observation and (vi) Work Environment Observation.

37 users with variable age, gender and experience were involved, recruited from the safety managers of each company.

After a preliminary discussion with the safety managers, we selected the workstations focusing on the most sensitive and critical from the operator's point of view and from the layout point of view. We also assumed that the selected workstations are the most common in Italian manufacturing companies.

Table 1. Characterization of companies, workstations and subjects

Sector	Company	Company category		Workstation	Operator	Age	Gender
		<250	>250				
Mechanical engineering	A	•		Grinder	01	51	Male
				Welding torch	02	49	
				Grill and bending	03	52	
				Assembly	04	49	
					05	34	
					06	22	
	B		•	Assembly components	01	43	Male
					02	32	
				Packing	03	29	
					04	50	
					05	21	
				Armour plating	06	49	
	C		•	Assembly components	01	57	Male
					02	35	
					03	26	
					04	37	
					05	52	
					06	32	
Fashion and leather goods	D	•		R&D	01	44	Female
					02	46	Male
				Prototyping dept	03	49	Female
					04	47	Female
					05	56	Male
					06	31	Male

(*continued*)

Table 1. (*continued*)

Sector	Company	Company category		Workstation	Operator	Age	Gender
		<250	>250				
	E		•	Assembly components	01	28	Male
					02	30	Male
				Finishing	03	51	Female
				Assembly components	04	64	Female
					05	50	Male
				Product verification	06	31	Male
					07	43	Female
					08	42	Female
					09	42	Female
				Packaging verification	10	25	Male
					11	24	Male
				Packing	12	25	Male
					13	50	Male
Total	5	2	3	–	37	–	–

2.1 User Observation

The User Observation, an empirical qualitative usability methodology, was conducted in the work environment. During the observation phase audio and video recordings were performed for each workers at every work stage. This method allowed researchers to observe how operators were working, as they were interacting with the workstation without interfering with the usual working operations.

For repetitive tasks, User Observation sessions lasted 2 h while for variable tasks, User Observation sessions lasted 4–6 h.

2.2 Thinking Aloud

During Thinking Aloud, each operator was asked to continue his work though telling aloud what he was doing, how he was doing it and what critical issues and difficulties he was finding, at first spontaneously and then guided by specific questions.

The Thinking Aloud is an empirical qualitative usability methodology, which leads the operators to express aloud their thoughts during their job activities [7].

Each Thinking Aloud session lasted 1–2 h and was aimed at identifying what follows: (i) User Experience (UX), focusing on both the actual "quality of interaction" (ease of use, comprehensibility, possibility of error) and the "perceived experience" (emotional impact, pleasantness, and enjoyment of the experience), (ii) operative difficulties, postural and visual discomforts.

2.3 Interview

The purpose of the semi-structured interviews was to stimulate and initiate a dialogue among the participants in order to achieve an open discussion within the framework of the study on object and to generate a wide range of interesting insights (critical issues, opinions and considerations). The success of an interview depends on the experience and the empathy of the interviewer [8] towards the interviewee. In order to make the interviewees [7, 8] feel comfortable and receive honest and useful information for the research, the interview was conducted in the real work context. This allowed the increase of the researcher-interviewee's level of confidence [11]. Each session lasted 1 h.

2.4 Questionnaire

Each user submitted a thematic questionnaire which included information related to biographical data, work activity, workstation and work environment questions. Questionnaire is an indirect approach which supports the quantitative survey from a methodological point of view. It is useful because it allows the interviewee to express opinions freely [7]. Thanks to the evaluation questionnaire, researchers could check if what emerged from the questionnaire was different, similar or equal to what they observed [11].

2.5 Workstation and Work Environment Observation

The workstations and the work environment were observed in this phase.

For each workstation, the researchers collected general data such as morphology, materials, possibility of adjusting and/or customizing the components, any possible presence of visual or sound signifiers and action feedback, button mapping and finally the human-machine interface, both physical and digital.

As regard the working environment, the context of use of the workstations was observed and analysed, including lighting, both natural and artificial, temperature and the level of noise exposure to which operators may be subjected.

Each session lasted 1 h.

3 Results

The hybrid approach used for the analysis phase produced a considerable amount of relevant data, which were compared in order to define an overall mapping of problems. The results of the analysis are summarised in Table 2.

The data emerged were compared and evaluated also taking into account the results of the evaluation carried out by INAIL experts within the framework of Occupational Ergonomics. This allowed to define the common indications of intervention.

3.1 Personal Protective Equipements (PPEs)

Some workers do not wear PPEs (e.g. gloves, helmets, burns, prevention sleeves, etc.) or use them only occasionally / not continuously. This may be due to the lack of suitability of PPEs for certain tasks.

Table 2. Correlations between the companies involved in the study and the critical issues identified in the analysis phase

Criticità	Company				
	01	02	03	04	05
PPEs	•	–	–	•	•
Working area	•	•	•	•	•
Tools and aids	•	•	•	•	•
Operator position	•	•	•	•	•
Lighting	•	•	•	–	–
Temperature	•	–	•	–	
Acoustics	–	–	–	•	•

4   Working Area

The main critical points emerged are the following:

- the presence of elements on the ground (as cables, pallets, etc.) which can increase the risk of accidental fall or stumbling block;
- when working at heights (>1.00 ml), the operators do not take the necessary precautions or measures to limit the risk of falls and/or stumbling block;
- some workstations are poorly organised, forcing operators to move frequently in order to obtain the necessary tools. This factor causes stress and worsens the work performance of each individual operator;
- other workstations are not correctly dimensioned or adjustable in height, forcing operators to use improvised support surfaces and/or assume incorrect positions.

4.1   Tools and Aids

The critical points highlighted concern work tools that emit vibrations and hot temperatures and that can cause a feeling of discomfort in the hands, wrists and arms.

The interview and the questionnaire showed that some workers complain of discomfort because of this equipment. In addition, the observation shed light upon the fact that some operators do not use work tools to perform tasks that require a lot of force.

4.2   Positions Assumed by the Operators

The main critical points highlighted are the following:

- some workstations are unsuitable or lack support surfaces, forcing some operators to adopt incorrect positions, as well as performing work operations on improvised and random surfaces;

– some workstations are too high or non-adjustable, leading the operator to work in standing position or to assume incorrect postures for the neck, back, elbow and wrist. The interview and the questionnaire showed up that some operators suggest the adoption of a height-adjustable workstation or part of it. Scientific studies show that the healthiest activities for humans are "mixed activities", that is to say activities that allow the alternation of sitting and standing positions [10–12];
– the design and organisation of some workstations force some workers to frequently twist their upper bodies during working hours.

4.3 Temperature, Lighting and Acuostics

As regards the temperature of the working environment, only the operators working for 2 metalworking companies complained of difficulties in working during the hot period of the year (June–July) due to the high temperature caused by the machines in operation.

Whilst, as regards lighting, only few operators stated that they would prefer global lighting with adjustable intensity in order to limit shaded areas and glare.

Finally, in consideration to the level of acoustics, some operators state that the noise in the workplace, although acceptable, is annoying because it is constant and continuous.

5 Discussion

This article shows the methodology used and the results that emerged from the case study that involved some essential companies in the Tuscany manufacturing sector.

The use of this hybrid approach allowed the researchers to collect qualitative and quantitative data, such as opinions, thoughts, expectations and critical points experienced by operators, sometimes silent and hidden due to the low participation of the operators in the company decisions.

However, a limitation for this study is the number of companies involved. The Italian manufacturing fabric is made up of about 400.000 companies (small-medium-large), located in 20 Italian regions. In the present study only 5 significant Tuscan companies were involved and, consequently, they cannot be considered fully representative neither at a regional nor at a national level.

Such a study should require a lot more resources, time and staff compared to the purpose of this research.

6 Conclusion

In summary, the results of the evaluation phase were useful for the definition of the common indications of intervention, which are not presented in this article as the companies involved have just received the results of the study and they will have full freedom to decide which workstations to improve. For this reason, subsequent studies will be carried out to assess whether the improvements introduced bring benefits in terms of operator performance, safety, well-being and ultimately operator satisfaction.

Overall, the main problems emerged in the following areas: the position assumed by the operators during the various work phases, the work area, work tools and aids, personal protective equipment (PPEs) and the working environment.

The results of this study showed that current workstations and their working environments need immediate adaptation to achieve a significant improvement in operator performance, safety, well-being and satisfaction.

This study emphasises that companies, whether small, medium or large, must take a more pragmatic and decisive view regarding the operator, whether young or old, with his own skills and needs, who can offer to the company useful indications on how to improve the workplace.

Acknowledgements. The authors would like to thank the INAIL experts Mario Papani, Fernando Renzetti, Sabina Piccione. Many thank also to all workers directly involved in the research.

Funding. This work was financed by INAIL Toscana.

Article Contributions. Francesca Tosi is the scientific director of the research program. Francesca Tosi and Mattia Pistolesi contributed to the research planning. Francesca Tosi, Mattia Pistolesi and Claudia Becchimanzi have contributed equally to the analysis and interpretation of the results as well as to the drafting of this paper.

References

1. Ilmarinen, J.: Promoting active ageing in the workplace. European Agency for Safety and Health at Work (EU-OSHA), Bilbao, pp. 1–6 (2012)
2. European Agency for Safety and health at Work (EU-OSHA): Safer and healthier work at any age – country inventory. European Agency for Safety and Health at Work, Italy (2016)
3. International Labour Office (ILO): World employment and social outlook, Trends 2015. International Labour Office, Geneva (2015)
4. Nilsson, K., Hydbom, A.R., Rylander, L.: Factors influencing the decision to extend working life or retire. Scand. J. Work Environ. Health **37**(6), 473–480 (2011). https://doi.org/10.5271/sjweh.3181
5. Blomé, M.W., Borell, J., Håkansson, C., Nilsson, K.: Attitudes toward elderly workers and perceptions of integrated age management practices. Int. J. Occup. Saf. Ergon. **26**(1), 112–120 (2020). https://doi.org/10.1080/10803548.2018.1514135
6. Rubin, J., Chisnell, D.: Handbook of Usability Testing: How to Plan, Design, and Conduct Effective Test, 2nd edn. Wiley, Hoboken (2011)
7. UNI 11377-2:2010: Usabilità dei prodotti industriali, parte 2: metodi e strumenti di intervento. Ente Italiano di Normazione, Milan (2010)
8. Stanton, N.A., Young, M.S., Harvey, C.: Guide to Methodology in Ergonomics, Designing for Human Use, 2nd edn. CRC Press, Taylor and Francis Group, Boca Raton (2014)
9. Wilson, J.R.: A framework and a contest for ergonomics methodology. In: Wilson, J.R., Corlett, E.N. (eds.) Evaluation of Human Work. Taylor & Francis, Londra-Philadelphia (1995)
10. Chengular, S.N., Rodgers, S.H., Bernard, T.E.: Kodak's Ergonomic Design for People at Work, 2nd edn. The Eastman Kodak Company, Wiley, Hoboken (2004)

11. Tosi, F., Pistolesi, M.: Ergonomics evaluation of workstations for mechanical engineering companies with particular attention to older workers. In: Bagnara, S., Tartaglia, R., Albolino, S., Alexander, T., Fujita, Y. (eds.) Proceedings of the 20th Congress of the International Ergonomics Association (IEA 2018). Advances in Intelligent Systems and Computing, vol. 824, pp. 410–420. Springer, Cham (2019). https://doi.org/10.1007/978-3-319-96071-5_44
12. Pheasant, S., Haslegrave, C.M.: Bodyspace: Anthropometry Ergonomics and the Design of Work. CRC Press, Boca Raton (2006)

Aging Workers in Industry and Retail Sector – A Holistic Approach for an Age-Related Evaluation and Design of Work

Matthias Wolf[1]([⊠]) and Sandra Maria Siedl[2]

[1] Institute for Innovation and Industrial Management, Graz University of Technology, Graz, Austria
Matthias.wolf@tugraz.at
[2] LIT Robopsychology Lab, Johannes Kepler University Linz, Linz, Austria
sandra.siedl@jku.at

Abstract. The demographic change leads to an on average older workforce. Aging is associated with a decrease of physical abilities and an increase in physical disorders. However, guidance for the evaluation of age-critical work tasks and workplaces is needed. Using a mixed method approach, we collected data from 37 interviews with employees and management representatives and descriptively analyzed archival data sources of two large Austrian companies. Empirical findings suggest that data on different levels should be considered in analysis to derive measures that are tailored to the specific needs of industrial application.

Keywords: Demographic change · Ageing workforce · Work design · Mixed methods

1 Introduction

Demographic changes in OECD countries follows not only an average increase in the age of workers, but also lead to raised retirement ages and prolonged periods of working lives [1]. As we know from previous studies, the age of workers is negatively related to work absenteeism and productivity mainly caused by musculoskeletal disorders [2, 3]. One reason might be that the physical workload at the workplace remains constant while physical performance prerequisites decrease with increased age [4, 5].

Moreover, many industrial workers are still exposed to material handling (32% of the EU working population), repetitive movements (60%) and awkward body postures (43%) [6] which pose the health of workers at risk and promote the development of musculoskeletal disorders (MSD). In order to reduce work-related injuries or illnesses and allow for an age-appropriate task execution, a fit between the worker and the job is needed [7]. Therefore, the group of older employees in physically demanding occupations is of particular relevance in this [8].

In industry so called safety health and environmental (SHE) management systems are in place for promoting workers' health and wellbeing. As part of such management

© The Author(s), under exclusive license to Springer Nature Switzerland AG 2021
N. L. Black et al. (Eds.): IEA 2021, LNNS 220, pp. 50–60, 2021.
https://doi.org/10.1007/978-3-030-74605-6_7

systems age-management combines all measures of health promotion, personnel management, work organization and work design to maintain the work and employability of all employees throughout their working lives [4].

Therefore, a resource-oriented understanding of the workability is used to analyse and optimize the interaction between human resources and the work demands [9]. Serval tools supporting age-management in industry are available in literature. On managerial level concepts like the "House of Work Ability" [10], or KPI based management model [11] can be used to explain relations and identify risk areas.

On work system level the evaluation of physical demands is at the focus of considerations and different tools to evaluate the remaining capacities and compare them with work demands have been introduced (cf. [12]). Available approaches range from stress based worker reallocation planning [13, 14], to age-based ergonomic stress assessments and workplace modifications [15, 16].

In regard to the worker itself several assessment tools for identifying human related issues e.g. the holistic and resource centred "Work Ability Index" [17] or specific assessments of remaining physical capacities with functional capacity evaluation (FCE) (e.g. [18]) are used in industry.

However, as the methods and tools summarized here are either tailored to specific industries or very generic it remains a challenge for industrial practitioners to conduct meaningful analysis and to derive concrete measures on workplace level [12]. Further an integrated management perspective and a holistic evaluation framework for businesses is still lacking [19]. This is where this paper aims to extend existing literature and management practice. The aim of this study was to identify existing challenges, critical factors at workplace level and important fields of work design in relation to an ageing workforce in the specific environment of an Austrian food retail company and fire truck producer, occupations that have been widely neglected in this research field so far. Based on a field study, a holistic picture of industry-relevant issues and requirements for work design are to be derived to assist age-appropriate work settings.

2   Case Setting and Methodology

The case study was conducted in two Austrian companies as part of a larger-scale research project from September, 2017 to June, 2020. Case company A is an international operating retail company. The divisions participating in the research project employ about 30.000 people in over 1200 stores. Case company B is an international operating producer of firefighting trucks and equipment. At 16 international production facilities about 3.600 workers are employed. To ensure comparability of these different cases the units of analysis within the companies were carefully selected.

The case study applies a mixed method approach, combining qualitative and quantitative methods. Within each company, qualitative data was collected from semi-structured interviews with representatives from management, health and safety experts, and worker. To check for convergence in the findings, qualitative data collection was accompanied by a quantitative descriptive data analysis based on archival data such as previous evaluations on physical stress and workplace ergonomics, age-structure and sick leave statistics and documented exit interviews.

Qualitative Data and Analysis Procedure

In total, 37 interviews were conducted, recorded, partly transcribed, screened and coded. We led seven interviews with management representatives including the CTO, the general HR manager and further executive staff members. Ten interviews addressed the field of industrial health and safety, more precisely involving the participation of two occupational medicines, an occupational psychologist, two work council members and five health and safety officers. Additionally, 20 blue-collar workers working agreed to be interviewed on work demands, physical limitations, health impairments in relation to work and potential improvements. Interviews took between 40 and 90 min. For data analysis, we used a code-based form of content analysis that allows to identify individual challenges and opportunities for work design.

To better understand age-specific work stress, available ergonomic workplace assessments results were aligned with the strain perceptions of participants in different age groups.

Quantitative Data and Analysis Procedure

The quantitative date gathered for this research contained statistics of sick days of 44,592 employees, sick leave data for two departments with 6,218 and 3,655 employees respectively in 2018. The data was analyzed according to the available age-structure and age-related differences. Furthermore, detailed sick leave statistics were provided by one company. This data was analyzed in a group comparison for different age groups and different reasons for sick leave, as well as a cross-department comparison normalized to age groups. In addition, 3,117 interviews in case of leaving the company were provided from the year 2017. These exit interviews results were post processed in a descriptive analysis and reasons for leave were aggregated to meaningful groups and analyzed according to a Pareto analysis to identify most relevant reasons in relation to different age groups.

3   Findings

This section provides an overview of relevant findings of the field study and the analysis of quantitative data. First the qualitative findings from the interview study are reported. Second, insights gained by comparing ergonomic assessment results in comparison with worker perception are reported. Last, results in the quantitative data analysis are provided.

3.1   Qualitative Findings for Age-Management Practice in Industry

Information Base for Age-Management

Statements made by representatives of the management and executive staff indicate limited knowledge regarding the situational awareness of age-specific issues and associated problems on the shop floor. This is illustrated by references made to the lack of related KPIs (e.g. sick leave statistics, ability limitation statics fluctuation analysis, etc.) and availability of aggregated data as a basis of decision-making. Based on a missing holistic assessment decision making is not supported by current work place assessment and improvement procedure. Since economical disadvantages or benefits of ergonomic work design and improvements are not evaluated, the topic of maintaining worker's health and workability is only taken into consideration to the point of legal compliance. Interviewees also addressed insufficient continuous attention to age-management as opposed to daily business issues and highlighted missing resource allocation in this context.

Perception of Age Critical Work Factors
The experience gained during work life was perceived as an asset especially in terms of more complicated work tasks. Individual experience was described to be useful to lower work stress by knowing suitable techniques for work execution. Nevertheless, caused by the increasing number of physical problems of older workers most interviewees considered the elderly to be less productive. Most managers, experts and workers surveyed identified a problem for older employees in relation to physical resilience, followed by problems in specific tasks as heavy lifting, and working in strenuous postures as well as a high overall physical exertion in body movements (walking, climbing ladders, etc.). Further, environmental conditions as heat, cold, or draught were named as a stress factor, particularly by the higher age workers. Based on ergonomic assessments these factors were available at most workplaces under consideration.

Origin and Severity of Health Complaints
Interestingly, some participants linked the increasing number of physical complaints more to private reasons (sports, accidents, etc.) than to working conditions. Others reported to suffer from job-related physical complaints themselves or referred to colleagues concerned with health problems due to work tasks. Some of these persons stated that they regularly leave work with pain in different body parts originating from physical stress at their workplace. Most health issues were reported in relation to low back, knee and shoulder issues, and limitations in heavy lifting. According to the current physical state in relation to work requirements, several workers expressed the belief that they will not be able to conduct their job until reaching official retirement age.

Worker-Workplace Fit and Associated Measures
The adaption of workplaces to worker needs was perceived as an important measure to increase the possibility to reintegrate workers. In this context, improvement suggestions for age-related workplace adaptions addressing the occurrence of awkward body postures, the use of mechanical assisting devices and organizational redesign of task modifiers (layout, pieces per load carrier, lifting aids) were given as examples. Moreover, participants mentioned the extension of target times that enable individual breaks, a reduction of overall physical workload, teams as a combination of younger and older workers and individual technical support if needed can enhance a better fit between worker and workplace in relation to ageing. Workers added that means of individual support such as bandages, shoe insoles, orthoses can additionally have a positive impact on this perceived fit. Further, organizational measures (team work, division of work based on individual strengths and limitations, part time work, partial retirement etc.) were reported as suitable measures. However, as available ergonomic workplace assessment tools are not tailored to workplace requirements, nor worker age several limitations

(e.g. multi-tasking, different ability profiles, age-related or individual interpretation of results) exist for evaluating the as is situation and derive suitable measures.

Shortcomings of Current Practice

However, interviewees addressed the need for a more systematic and proactive approach for work design in relation to demographic developments taking into account changing abilities of older workers in workplace assessment and worker allocation. Incident-driven responses to a worker's physical limitations that prevent him or her from further task execution appear too narrow and reactive. This includes for example the medical evaluation of a worker's remaining physical capacities after a long-term sick leave associated with the occasion-related search for an alternative workplace. Since the number of cases where such individual solutions are needed is increasing, suitable "light duty" workplaces become harder to find.

3.2 Quantitative Date Provided by Industry Partners

Statistics of Sick Leave Days and Age-Structure Analysis

Sick leave data on aggregated level showed that 77.2% of the workforce was younger than 50 years and only 22.8% were older. However, 36% of lost days due to incapacity to work were attributed to the latter age group. For workers younger than 50 years the average value of incapacity to work days is 8.4 days per year, while it is approximately twice as long (16.3 days) for a worker aged 50 or older (overall average 10.2). It can be concluded that about a quarter of the workforce employed causes over a third of all sick days and the average amount of sick days for the older group is double the amount of the younger group. This strongly implies a need for consideration of elderly workers as a special target group.

Statistics and Reasons for Sick Leave

The subsequent analysis of the age structure for two departments with 6,218 and 3,655 employees, respectively, provides the basis for future planning. The existing age structure was quite balanced in age groups except that after the age of 50 years there are disproportionally little workers in employment (see Table 1). The forecast for the next five years indicates that the group of workers older than 50 years should slightly more than double. However, according to current numbers of employment in this age group most of these experiences workers might retire or leave the company. In relation to the sick leave statistics described in the previous section, this increases the importance of the topic of age-related work design even more for the department.

An age sensitive analysis for the data sets reported in Table 1 showed that the amount of cases per worker slightly decreases with age but the duration per case drastically increases by the threefold from the youngest (6.8 days) to the oldest age group (21.1 days). As the increase in duration outweigh the decrease in cases, the overall sick leave per 100 workers more than triples from the youngest (<24 years) to the oldest (>55 years) age group. Clearly the number of sick days per case show a high correlation with age in both departments and this tendency is in line with data reported in literature.

Table 1. Sick leave data of two departments (data provided by company)

Dep./Age	Workers		Total cases		Total sick leave days		Sick leave per 100 worker		Sick days per case	
	A	B	A	B	A	B	A	B	A	B
Till 24	1,693	1,136	1,741	774	12,251	5,286	724	465	6.8	7.0
25–34	1,451	797	1,439	645	13,419	6,451	925	809	10.0	9.3
35–44	1,335	673	1,075	594	14,556	7,251	1,090	1,077	12.2	13.5
45–54	1,401	768	1,153	750	18,169	11,569	1,297	1,506	15.4	15.8
>55 y.	538	281	469	262	10,359	5,538	1,925	1,971	21.1	22.1
Total	6,418	3,655	5,877	3,025	68,754	36,095			11.9	11.7

The data shows that there is a need for action in preventing cases of elderly workers, since they are on average more severe resulting in a longer time for recovery. A cross-department comparison shows that while the trend in sick days per case is the same in both departments (linear increase to the 3-fold, see Fig. 1 left), the amount of cases per 100 workers and age group is different. For the cases itself, the numbers show different trends for the two departments which might indicate different approaches towards the work design. As the number of sick leave cases for categories of physical complaints like musculoskeletal disorders (MSD) is related to physical overload, this variance might indicate a different approach in relation to work environment, the physical work stress, or the handling of the ageing worker.

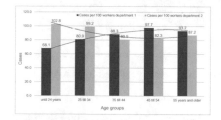 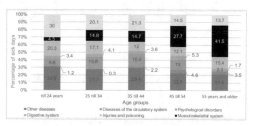

Fig. 1. Comparison of sick leave days (left) and ICF classification of cases (right) per age group (data provided by company)

Further information about sick leaves can be retained when analyzing in detail the reasons for the cases. While for the young age group, the categories of respiratory diseases and other diseases are the predominant reasons for sick leave, musculoskeletal disorders (MSD) outweigh all other reasons in higher age. For MSD the percentage of sick days steadily increases from 8.6% in the youngest to almost 40% in the oldest age group while all other types of disease show a declining, or almost constant trend. Also the amount of cases increases from 4.7% to 32.1% for MSD (see Fig. 1 right). This implies a high relevance of physical work design in relation to an ageing workforce.

Statistics and Analysis of Company Leaves
The Pareto analysis of the exit interview data showed that out of 25 reasons covered in the survey for leaving the company the top three categories included: working hours (13%), personal reasons (11%), health and physical reasons (10%) (see Fig. 2) Thus, this data showed that the health status and physical reasons, as well as the experienced workload (5%) are main reasons to leave the job. The comparison of different age groups revealed that while the type of work is the main reason for younger employees the main reasons for older employees (>50 years) are in relation to health and physical workload. This shift in reasons for leaving the job is the same in in service job with a lower physical workload (n = 1,975) and in logistic work with a high physical workload (n = 119) as illustrated in Fig. 2.

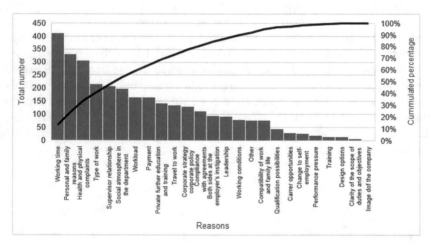

Fig. 2. Pareto analysis of reasons for leaving the company (data provided by company)

For jobs with a lower overall physical stress level, the type of work, and personal reasons are important motives for younger worker to leave their job. However, these reasons show a decline in importance with increasing age. In contrary, the workload, physical health and physical complaints are of low importance for younger workers, but increase in importance with age. As a third category, the working time is particularly relevant for the middle aged workers. In jobs with a high physical load in contrast the payment is an important reason why younger worker leave the job. With age, however, physical complaints and the climatic working conditions become highly important reason to leave. Thus for logistics jobs, health and physical complaints and the working conditions can be considered as especially relevant for elderly workers (see Fig. 3).

In conclusion the exit interviews showed that especially health and physical complaints in combination with the workload or working conditions cause elderly workers to leave their jobs. Overall the increase in health and physical complaints as a reason to

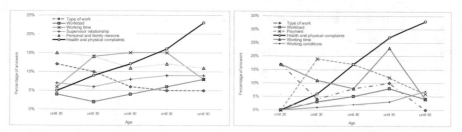

Fig. 3. Top 6 reasons for leaving the job in a department with low physical workload (left) and high physical work load (right)

leave the job stands out in comparison to all other reasons. The change in motives for leaving can be used to derive suitable incentives for workers of all age groups.

4 Conclusion

In this work a strong focus was put on incorporating outlined findings to tailor the proposed framework for work evaluation and design to industrial requirements. It can be concluded that a holistic approach of age sensitive work evaluation and design should focus on suitable KPI's to build awareness and derive management goals for the elderly workforce. Further, it should include the adaption of the workplace to the worker to minimize ability-requirement mismatches. Lastly it should focus on a participatory design process for workplace improvements. Table 2 summarizes required data, data analysis procedures and potential findings of such a holistic approach.

The conducted analysis suggests that sick leave days and reasons for sick leave in combination with an age structure analysis can help to identify age-related problems in physical work. Broken down on different departments, or in comparison with an industry benchmark fields of action can be identified. Specifically, a root cause analysis of sick leave statistics per department can support the understanding of these differences. In addition, the qualitative investigation into the workforce perception can provide information about existing issues, challenges and improvement suggestions. This data can further be supported by quantitative finding as the analysis of exit interviews. However, measuring impact of changes by relating it back to the defined goal is key to achieve long term improvements.

The mixed methods approach applied in this research enables to draw a holistic picture of challenges, and opportunities for an ageing workforce in industry and retail. These findings that extend existing literature by industry specific age-critical work requirements and possible counteractions in the field of heavy machinery production and retail, an industry field that had been largely neglected in literature so far. The framework assists in building awareness and provides a starting point to support industrial practitioners in implementing age appropriate work settings.

Table 2. Data for age-based work evaluation basis for work design

Domain	Data to consider	Data analysis procedures	Potential findings
KPI's for goal setting	Employee list including age, seniority, work schedule and workplace	Age structure analysis Cross department comparison	• Identification of old/imbalanced areas • Need for action related to age
	Aggregated or individual sick leave statistics on employee base and department level	Group comparison for different age groups Comparison of reasons for sick leave/job attendance Cross-department comparison normalized to age groups Benchmark with similar industries	• Building awareness on the as-is situation • Need for action according to health issues • Identification of problem areas for older workers based on sick leave
	Worker fluctuation data and exit interviews	Descriptive statistics Pareto analysis Age group comparison	• Reasons for leaving the job including potential fields for action
Worker workplace mismatches	Worker surveys to detect physical (dis)abilities and high work stress (physical and mental)	Department and age-group comparison for: Work ability (e.g. WAI) Ability limitations (e.g. FCE) Subjective complaints (e.g. Nordic questionnaire) Perceived strain from work (e.g. grading scales)	• Reduced work capacity (work years/financially) • Physical complaints in relation to work • Perception of work in relation to workability
	Ergonomic evaluation of workplaces	Ergonomic assessment with suitable tools(e.g. KIM, EAWS) in workplace observation interviews	• Identification of workplaces with high risk ratings
	Interview study on expert and worker level	Structured content analysis	• Worker needs • Possible improvements
Measures	Other sources (Certificates, health promotion information, etc.)	Structured content analysis	• Overview of solutions offered for older worker in the company
	Participatory process for work improvement	Creativity techniques	• Idea generation for individual measures that are accepted by workers

All in all, the intention was to propose a first version of a framework that considers age aspects in work analysis and design by linking the experiences from the industrial case study to relevant research. Further research should be conducted based on mixed method case study approaches to obtain deeper insights in the connections of age, health and workability in relation to physical work stress during the working life.

Acknowledgments. We'd like to acknowledge the case study companies and the Austrian Research Promotion Agency for its financial project support.

References

1. UNDP: World population prospects 2019: median age by region, subregion and country, 1950–2100, United Nations, Population Division (2019)
2. EUOSH: Work-Related Musculoskeletal Disorders: Back to Work Report, European Week for Safety and Health at Work, vol. 3. Office for Official Publications of the European Communities, Luxembourg (2007)
3. Institute of Medicine: Musculoskeletal Disorders and the Workplace: Low Back and Upper Extremities. National Academy Press, Washington (DC) (2001)
4. Ilmarinen, J.: Aging workers. Occup. Environ. Med. **58**, 546 (2001)
5. Kenny, G., et al.: Physical work capacity in older adults. Implications for the aging worker. Am. J. Ind. Med. **51**(8), 610–625 (2008)
6. Eurofound and International Labour Organization: Working Conditions in a Global Perspective. Publication Office of the European Union, Luxembourg (2019)
7. Snook, S.: Approaches to preplacement testing and selection of workers. Ergonomics **30**(2), 241–247 (1987)
8. Seeberg, K., et al.: Effectiveness of workplace interventions in rehabilitating musculoskeletal disorders and preventing its consequences among workers with physical and sedentary employment. Syst. Rev. **8**(1), 1–7 (2019)
9. Frerichs, F.: Alternsmanagement im Betrieb – Herausforderungen und Handlungsansätze. In: Bäcker, G., Heinze, R. (eds.) Soziale Gerontologie in gesellschaftlicher Verantwortung, pp. 185–195. Springer VS, Wiesbaden (2013). https://doi.org/10.1007/978-3-658-01572-5_13
10. Ilmarinen, J., Tempel, J., Giesert, M. (eds.): Arbeitsfähigkeit 2010: Was können wir tun, damit Sie gesund bleiben? VSA-Verlag, Hamburg (2002)
11. Kugler, M., Sinn-Behrendt, A., Bruder, R., Baumann, G., Hodek, L., Niehaus, M.: Empowering corporate ageing management by interconnecting existing data: a case study from the German automotive industry. In: Deml, B., Stock, P., Bruder, R., Schlick, C. M. (eds.) Advances in Ergonomic Design of Systems, Products and Processes, pp. 431–449. Springer, Heidelberg (2016). https://doi.org/10.1007/978-3-662-48661-0_28
12. Landau, K., et al.: Musculoskeletal disorders in assembly jobs in the automotive industry with special reference to age management aspects. Int. J. Ind. Ergon. **38**(7–8), 561–576 (2008)
13. Boenzi, F., et al.: Modelling workforce aging in job rotation problems. IFAC-PapersOnLine **48**(3), 604–609 (2015)
14. Egbers, J.F.: Identifikation und Adaption von Arbeitsplätzen für leistungsgewandelte MitarbeiterInnen. Dissertation, TUM (2013)
15. Keil, M., Spanner-Ulmer, B.: Conception and evaluation of an age-differentiated task analysis and screening method. In: ElMaraghy, H. (ed.) Enabling Manufacturing Competitiveness and Economic Sustainability, pp. 178–183. Springer, Berlin (2012). https://doi.org/10.1007/978-3-642-23860-4_29

16. Wittemann, P.: Konzeption eines Verfahrens zur Ableitung ergonomischer Gestaltungslösungen für fähigkeitsgerechte Arbeitsplätze. Dissertation, Technische Universität Darmstadt, Darmstadt (2017)
17. Ilmarinen, J.: The work ability index. Occup. Med. **57**(2), 160 (2006)
18. Rademacher, H., et al.: Capability related stress analysis to support design of work systems. In: Schlick, C., Frieling, E., Wegge, J. (eds.) Age-Differentiated Work Systems. Springer, Berlin (2013). https://doi.org/10.1007/978-3-642-35057-3_10
19. Varianou-Mikellidou, C., et al.: Occupational health and safety management in the context of an ageing workforce. Saf. Sci. **116**, 231–244 (2019)

Part II: Ergonomics for Children and Educational Environments (Edited by Lawrence J. H. Schulze)

Establishment and Discussion of the Design Criteria for Training Chopsticks for Children

Yu-Hui Chen and Jo-Han Chang[✉]

Department of Industrial Design, National Taipei University of Technology, Taipei, Taiwan
t108588023@ntut.org.tw, johan@ntut.edu.tw

Abstract. For children living in East Asia, chopsticks are important eating utensils. Providing children with appropriate training chopsticks to help them learn how to hold chopsticks properly facilitates not only better hand muscle development, but also fine motor skills. However, commercially available children's training chopsticks come in a variety of designs and styles that have different effects on the way children hold them. Because of the lack of scientific research exploring chopstick design criteria, there are no data for designers to refer to when designing chopsticks. To help resolve this issue, we collected and compiled chopstick design studies and analyzed the designs of commercially available chopsticks to develop 10 systematic design criteria for the design of training chopsticks. Subsequently, we used the analytic hierarchy process (AHP) and conducted interviews with three experts who were familiar with children's chopstick usage behavior and/or who had experience in designing children's tableware to derive the weights of the criteria. The results showed that operating part design (the design of the upper-chopstick), bridge size, and chopstick material were the primary design criteria that designers should consider when designing children's training chopsticks.

Keywords: Training chopsticks for children · Ergonomic product design · Design criteria

1 Introduction

As of 2020, any search of online shopping platforms such as Amazon, eBay, Alibaba, and PChome will reveal that these platforms offer many children's training chopsticks. These chopsticks come in a variety of forms and styles, affecting the way children hold them. The design of training chopsticks has a direct effect on how children hold them. Studies have shown that learning how to hold chopsticks correctly offers children numerous advantages, including facilitating their cognitive development (attention) [4], enhancing their inner and outer palm muscle strength, allowing them to develop fine motor skills [15], and increasing their flexibility, adaptability, stability, and efficiency [2, 8]. Therefore, scientific research that explores the design of children's training chopsticks should be performed so that designers are provided with the referential data they need. Several domestic and foreign studies have investigated the effects of chopstick design and users' chopstick-holding posture on users' efficiency in picking up food [1, 3, 5–7, 9, 12–14]. For this study, we first collected and compiled chopstick design studies and analyzed

N. L. Black et al. (Eds.): IEA 2021, LNNS 220, pp. 63–70, 2021.
https://doi.org/10.1007/978-3-030-74605-6_8

the design of commercially available chopsticks before developing design criteria for children's training chopsticks. Subsequently, we adopted the analytic hierarchy process (AHP), conducted expert interviews, and consulted three experts who were familiar with children's chopstick usage behavior and/or who had experience in designing children's tableware. We used this data to assign weights to the various design criteria.

The objective of this study is to provide designers with the referential data they need to design children's training chopsticks. Such referential data consists of (1) criteria for assessing children's training chopstick designs; (2) the weights of the various criteria; and (3) matters to pay attention to when designing children's training chopsticks.

2 Literature Review

2.1 Analysis of Chopstick Design Studies

Many domestic and foreign studies have investigated the effects of the design of various aspects of chopsticks on users' chopstick-operating efficiency and stability. For example, Mukai, Y. and Hashimoto, K. [11] maintained that the ideal chopstick length is 1.1–1.2 times the length of the user's hand. They obtained this data by dividing chopstick length by hand length for users of all ages. This finding revealed that when designing chopsticks, one must consider chopstick length. Subsequent studies have explored the effects of chopstick length on accuracy in picking up food, stability in moving food, efficiency in picking up food, and level of comfort; results showed that adult chopsticks with a length of 24 cm demonstrated favorable efficiency in both picking up food and degree of comfort [6, 14], and that children's training chopsticks with a length of 18 cm and with the presence of a bridge allowed increased accuracy in picking up food and stability in moving food [7]. Regarding chopstick cross-sectional design, a diameter of 6 mm [13] with a square handle provided optimal efficiency in picking up peanuts; whereas a diameter of 6 mm with a rounded square handle provided optimal efficiency in picking up butter beans [12]. Concerning chopstick tip design, a diameter of 4 mm, an angle of 2° [13], and the presence of grooves in the chopstick tip provided optimal efficiency in picking up food [3, 5, 9]. With respect to chopstick materials, chopsticks made of bamboo or wood offered optimal efficiency in picking up food [5, 9]. Bridges with a width of 1.5 cm placed 1/3 of the way up from the bottom of the chopsticks offered optimal operability [7]. In this study, we used the above results to determine chopstick lengths, cross-sectional design, tip design, materials, and bridge size (see Table 1). Next, commercially available chopsticks were analyzed to identify the remaining design criteria.

2.2 Analysis of Chopstick Design Studies

We purchased children's training chopsticks from PChome, Taiwan's largest e-commerce platform, between 2017 and 2020, and studied several variables among the designs, namely operating part design (the upper-chopstick on which the thumb, index finger, and middle finger are placed), stabilizing part design (the chopstick held in place against the ring finger), and bridge design (the device connecting the chopsticks). Analysis revealed

Table 1. Factors affecting efficiency and stability in picking up food and their effects (com-piled by this study)

Design criterion	Independent variable (cause)	Dependent variable (effect)	Related studies
Chopstick length	Length of adult chopsticks/length of children's training chopsticks	Efficiency in picking up food	[6]
	Length of children's training chopsticks/chopsticks with (or without) a bridge	Accuracy in picking up food/stability in moving food	[7]
	Length of adult chopsticks	Efficiency in picking up food/level of comfort	[14]
Chopstick cross-sectional design/tip design	Diameter of handle/ tip angle	Efficiency in picking up food	[13]
	Shape of handle/shape of tip/chopsticks with (or without) grooves	Efficiency in picking up food/stability in picking up food	[3]
	Diameter of handle	Efficiency in picking up food	[1]
	Shape of handle	Efficiency in picking up food	[12]
Chopstick materials	Materials/chopsticks with (or without) grooves	Efficiency in picking up food	[9] [5]
Bridge size	Bridge width/position	Efficiency in picking up food/ stability in picking up food	[7]

six operator assistive designs (ring restraints, thumb alignment, flat grooves, semi-ring supports, protrusion supports, and purlicue supports); and two stabilizer assistive designs (ring restraints and protrusion supports). Accordingly, we formulated design criteria for both operating part design and stabilizing part design. With respect to developing assistive designs for children's training chopsticks, Chen, Y.J. and Wu, F.K. [4] offered five recommendations: (1) the thumb should be placed at the 1/4 mark away from the bottom of the chopstick as a fulcrum; (2) the base of the thumb should act as the fulcrum; (3) the distal interphalangeal of the ring finger should act as a second fulcrum; (4) the chopstick to be moved should be the one held by the distal interphalangeal of the index and middle fingers; and (5) to prevent the chopsticks from crossing each other, designers should think about the locations of the fulcra, the chopstick maximum angles, and the positioning of the assistive design elements. Accordingly, this study derived two additional design criteria (i.e., main fulcrum position and maximum angle). Finally, because studies have shown that the weight of chopsticks influences how children hold them [10], and that commercially available chopsticks fail to account for this factor, this study also added weight as a design criterion.

From the literature review, we developed the following 10 design criteria for children's training chopsticks: length, cross-sectional design, tip design, fulcrum position, operating part design, stabilizing part design, bridge size, maximum angle, weight, and materials, as shown in Fig. 1. The design criteria were then assessed using the analytic hierarchy process (AHP) to obtain their relative weights.

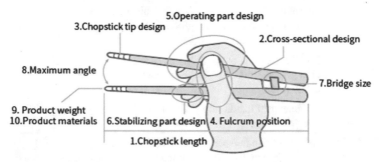

Fig. 1. Design criteria for children's training chopsticks (illustration provided by this study)

3   Methods

Between Jun. 24 and Jul. 6, 2020, we met with three experts who were familiar with children's chopstick usage behavior, who had experience in designing children's tableware, and who had over four years of related experience: a Montessori educator, a children's tableware designer, and a children's functional therapist. Table 2 shows details about these experts. Next, an AHP and semi-structured interview were performed. The AHP entailed the experts assessing the relative weights of the 10 design criteria (from which the final weights, rankings, and importance of the criteria were obtained), and the expert interview involved the experts offering their design recommendations.

Table 2. Expert information (compiled by this study)

Expert no.	Job title	Years of experience	Specializes in
Expert A	Montessori preschool educator	4 years	Montessori education preschool development research
Expert B	Children's tableware designer	5 years	Tableware design for infants and children
Expert C	Functional therapist for children	15 years	Children's visual perception and fine motor training

4 Conclusions

4.1 Weights and Rankings of the Design Criteria for children's Training Chopsticks

Table 3. Weights and rankings of the design criteria for children's training chopsticks (compiled by this study)

Design criterion	Weight assigned by the experts							
	Expert A		Expert B		Expert C		Total weight	
	Weight	Ranking	Weight	Ranking	Weight	Ranking	Average value	Standard deviation
(1) Chopstick length	4.06%	9	5.57%	6	2.31%	10	4.00%	2.00%
(2) Cross-sectional design	6.12%	8	1.12%	10	6.79%	6	4.67%	3.21%
(3) Tip design	0.53%	10	1.73%	9	2.53%	9	2.00%	1.00%
(4) Main fulcrum position	15.39%	1	3.26%	8	3.24%	8	7.00%	6.93%
(5) Operating part design	12.31%	6	13.94%	2	28.64%	1	18.33%	9.29%
(6) Stabilizing part design	12.38%	5	7.78%	4	5.92%	7	8.67%	3.06%
(7) Bridge size	12.91%	3	4.87%	7	11.08%	3	9.67%	4.16%
(8) Maximum angle	8.70%	7	11.49%	3	7.39%	5	9.00%	2.00%
(9) Product weight	12.62%	4	5.93%	5	21.59%	2	13.67%	8.02%
(10) Product materials	14.99%	2	44.32%	1	10.52%	4	23.33%	18.01%

The weights of the design criteria are presented as percentages. As shown in Table 3, the top three design criteria with the highest average weights were materials (23.33%), operator design (18.33%), and weight (13.67%). However, the standard deviations for these criteria were 18.01%, 9.29%, and 8.02%, respectively, which were relatively high. We surmised that the reason for the large standard deviations was because the three experts work in different fields, causing them to have different focuses. Thus, we asked the three experts to explain why they chose the respective design criteria as the top three design criteria.

Expert A maintained that the top three design criteria, listed in descending order, were main fulcrum position (15.39%), materials (14.99%), and bridge size (12.91%), where main fulcrum position had a substantial effect on operational stability and sense of direction. Expert B contended that the top three design criteria, listed in descending order, were materials (44.32%), operator design (13.94%), and maximum angle (11.49%), where materials were the most important criterion when designing children's products. Expert C asserted that the top three design criteria, listed in descending order, were operator design (28.64%), weight (21.59%), and bridge size (11.08%), where operator design was key to developing correct chopstick-holding posture; weight helped children train their hand muscles; and bridge size should be approximately the linear distance between the metacarpophalangeal joints of the thumb and index finger in children. Because at least two experts agreed that operating part design, bridge size, and product materials were the most important, they were determined to be the three most important design criteria to be considered when designing children's training chopsticks.

4.2   Suggestions for the Design Criteria for children's Training Chopsticks

Because the literature and experts' suggestions for the design criteria for children's training chopsticks feature both similarities and differences, they are summarized in Table 4 to serve as a reference for product designers.

Table 4. Suggestions for the design criteria for children's training chopsticks (compiled by the authors)

Design criterion	Recommendations from the literature and experts	Learned from
(1) Chopstick length	(a) Should suit user's hand length (b) Must also consider chopstick weight	Literature and Experts A and B Expert C
(2) Cross-sectional design	(a) Should use circular and rounded square (general chopsticks) handles (b) Should guide placement of fingers (c) Should rest against user's purlicue	Literature Expert A Expert B
(3) Tip design	(a) Should have grooves (b) Must be made from appropriate materials (to allow the user to feel the food effectively)	Literature and Experts A and B Expert C
(4) Main fulcrum position	(a) Should be at the 1/3 and 1/4 mark up from the bottom of the chopstick (b) Should be where the bridge is (c) Should be near the center of the chopsticks	Literature Literature and Experts A, B, and C Experts A and C
(5) Operating part design	(a) Groove and protrusion should be clearly marked (b) Should be adjustable	
(6) Stabilizing part design	(c) Should be near the center of the chopsticks (d) Design should not be excessively assistive	Experts A, B, and C
(7) Bridge size	(a) Should be approximately the linear distance between the metacarpophalangeal joints of the thumb and index finger in children	Literature and Experts A, B, and C
(8) Maximum angle	(a) Should be within 5 cm	Expert C
(9) Product weight	(a) Must allow the user to feel the weight	Experts A, B, and C
(10) Product materials	(a) Should be non-slip, heat resistant, and easy to clean	Experts A, B, and C

Table 4 shows that the literature and the experts differed on main fulcrum position. In the literature, it was argued that it should be at the 1/3 or 1/4 mark up from the bottom of the chopsticks, whereas the experts contended that it should be near the center of the chopsticks. Concerning operator and stabilizer design, the experts provided concrete design suggestions. However, their suggestions were not scientifically verified. Therefore, these three design criteria will need to be confirmed in subsequent scientific experiments.

5 Conclusions

(1) The three experts invited to participate in this study had different specialties and thus different focuses. Expert A paid more attention to hand-eye coordination and chopstick materials. Expert B prioritized chopstick materials and environmental protection. Expert C believed that guiding the correct use of chopsticks was the most important factor. These differences of focus resulted in considerable deviation in their weighting of the criteria.

(2) Despite operating part design and stabilizing part design both being related to chopstick-holding position, the average weight of the former was more than twice that of the latter, according to the three experts. Therefore, this study posits that among children with favorable finger-control abilities, designers need not focus too much on stabilizing part design.

(3) Both literature and the experts agreed that the main fulcrum position (where the thumb should be placed) should be parallel to the location of the bridge, and that chopstick length should suit the hand length of the child. Additionally, Expert C suggested that bridge size should be approximately the linear distance between the metacarpophalangeal joints of the thumb and index finger in children. Careful attention should be paid to these matters when designing children's training chopsticks.

(4) Because literature and the experts have yet to reach a consensus on main fulcrum position, operating part design, and stabilizing part design, further research should be carried out in these areas. Cross-sectional design is affected by operating part design, and stabilizing part design.

References

1. Chan, T.: A study for determining the optimum diameter of chopsticks. Int. J. Ind. Ergon. **23**(1), 101–105 (1999)
2. Chen, S.W., Liang, J.I., Lai, K.Y., Ting, Y.T., Peng, Y., Hsu, H.Y., Lai, K.H., Su, F.: Kinematics analysis of chopsticks manipulation. In: World Congress on Medical Physics and Biomedical Engineering, vol. 25, pp. 410–413. IFMBE Proceedings, Germany (2009)
3. Chen, Y.L.: Effects of shape and operation of chopsticks on food-serving performance. J. Appl. Ergon. **29**, 233–238 (1998)
4. Chen, Y.J., Wu, F.K.: Assessing the design criteria for assistive devices added to toddler's training chopsticks. Ind. Des. **127**, 113–118 (2012)

5. Ho, C.P., Wu, S.P.: Mode of grasp, materials, and grooved chopstick tip on gripping performance and evaluation. Percept. Mot. Skills **102**(1), 93–103 (2006)
6. Hsu, S.H., Wu, S.P.: An investigation for determining the optimum length of chopsticks. Appl. Ergon. **22**(6), 395–400 (1991)
7. Lee, Y.C., Chen, Y.L.: An auxiliary device for chopstick operation to improve the food serving performance. Appl. Ergon. **39**(6), 737–742 (2008)
8. Lin, L., Dong, Q., Sun, Y.Q.: Comparison of chopstick-using skills between 3–7 year old children and adults. Acta Psychologyica Sinica **33**(03), 40–46 (2001)
9. Lin, T.F.: The study of the effects of pinching operation, material of chopsticks, and carved groove on food-serving performance (2002)
10. Li, T., Chang, J.H., Fan, C.K.: The effect of spoon weight on spoon usage behavior. In: Lung, H.W. (ed.) Ergonomic Design, Situational Technology, and Smart Manufacturing. Ergonomics Society of Taiwan Annual Meeting and Conference, Sun Moon Lake Youth Activity Center (2019)
11. Mukai, Y., Hashimoto, K.: A study on the length of chopsticks. J. Home Econ. Jpn. **28**(3), 230–235 (1977)
12. Wu, S.P., Tsai, W.H.: Handle cross section and chopsticks grasping mode effects on foodserving performance. J. Work Leisure 1–10 (2012)
13. Wu, S.P.: Effects of the handle diameter and tip angle of chopsticks on the food-serving performance of male subjects. Appl. Ergon. **26**(6), 379–385 (1995)
14. Yang, T., Zhong, Y.Z., Liu, M.H., Tang, R.X.: Ergonomic analysis and joints movement model during chopstick using. Chin. J Appl. Psychol. **2**, 127 (2016)
15. KingNet   (2019).   https://www.kingnet.com.tw/knNew/news/single-article.html?newId= 43587. Accessed 31 May 2019

Study on the Optimal Time for Intervention to Guide the Development of the Static Tripod Grip in Toddlers

Chiao-Yun Cheng and Jo-Han Chang[✉]

National Taipei University of Technology, Taipei, Taiwan
t107588012@ntut.org.tw, johan@mail.ntut.edu.tw

Abstract. Utensil manipulation can help toddlers develop control of their hands. However, as toddlers go through the stages of muscular development, they should be given the appropriate tools for different stages of development to encourage autonomous learning. In this study, the authors investigated and summarized the development of fine motor skills and spoon grasp patterns in toddlers through a review of the literature, and concluded that progressing from a radial grasp to the static tripod grip is critical to the later adoption of the dynamic tripod grip, which allows toddlers to freely manipulate a spoon and other tools. Through our review of past studies, we also concluded that toddlers aged 18–24 months who have developed forearm supination and finger differentiation skills may be provided with a training spoon designed to guide the development of the static tripod grip. In order to verify the conclusions of this study and establish important items for future evaluation, the authors developed a semi structured questionnaire focused on the static tripod grip on spoons as well as the assessment of forearm supination and finger differentiation skills. The questionnaire was used in an interview conducted with three occupational therapists. The therapists' opinions regarding the optimal time for intervention to guide the development of the static tripod grip on a spoon were compiled and five conclusions were derived from the data.

Keywords: Toddler · Static tripod grip · Learning to use a spoon · Fine motor skill

1 Introduction

Currently, most parents opt to spoon-feed their children, resulting in a lack of independent practice opportunities for toddlers (Kuo et al. 2014). However, utensil manipulation can help toddlers develop control of their hands (Nagao, 2004; van Roon et al. 2003). As they go through the various stages of muscular development, toddlers between the ages of 12 and 18 months begin to use the radial grasp with forearm pronation to manipulate a spoon (Connolly and Dalgleish 1989); they fully develop the forearm supination and finger differentiation skills needed to manipulate a spoon with the tripod grip after two years of age (Chang 2019). The tripod grip can be differentiated into the static and dynamic tripod grips; the former involves the use of wrist movement to support the

© The Author(s), under exclusive license to Springer Nature Switzerland AG 2021
N. L. Black et al. (Eds.): IEA 2021, LNNS 220, pp. 71–79, 2021.
https://doi.org/10.1007/978-3-030-74605-6_9

grip, while the latter enables the three fingers to move freely (Ho 2015). The optimal time for a toddler to progress from a radial grasp to the static tripod grip needs to be carefully considered to prevent muscle compensation. Assessment should be made using a variety of assessment methods to determine whether or not the toddler has developed the skills needed to learn how to hold a spoon using the static tripod grip. In this study, we conducted interviews with professional occupational therapists to determine the optimal time for toddlers to progress to the static tripod grip as well as suitable motor skill development assessment methods. To sum up, the four objectives are as follows:

1. Summarize the development of fine motor skills and spoon grasp patterns in toddlers;
2. Develop assessment methods for motor skills;
3. Interview experts to determine the optimal time for toddlers to progress to the static tripod grip for spoon manipulation (in terms of age and motor skills);
4. Interview experts to determine how to assess the motor skills required for toddlers to progress to the static tripod grip.

2   Literature Review

2.1   The Development of Fine Motor Skills in Toddlers

At six months of age, toddlers develop forearm pronation skills (see Fig. 1). By nine months old, toddlers begin to develop slight forearm supination (see Fig. 2) (Sacrey et al. 2012). Once wrist control is developed, toddlers begin to learn how to use the intrinsic muscle groups and extrinsic muscle groups in their hands separately (Wu 2012). The intrinsic muscles are responsible for finger movement while the extrinsic muscles contribute to wrist stability (Wu 2013). At age 12–18 months, toddlers are developing forearm supination skills, allowing them to use spoons, pencils, and other tools (Case-Smith 2006; Augustyn et al. 2009). At 18 months old, toddlers can effectively use the radial grasp (Claxton et al. 2009).

Fig. 1. Forearm pronation

Fig. 2. Forearm supination

2.2   The Development of Spoon Grasp Patterns

Toddlers adopt different grip patterns depending on the progress of their musculoskeletal development (Connolly and Dalgleish 1989). At one year old, toddlers begin to develop the ability to use a spoon with a pronated grasp. Between 13 and 15 months of age, toddlers gradually develop a more stable spoon grasp pattern and can hold a spoon with the radial grasp or ulnar grasp (Yun 2017). Between 12 and 18 months of age, most toddlers use the transverse palmar grip to hold a spoon (Connolly and Dalgleish 1989). After two years old, they fully develop the forearm supination skills required to manipulate a spoon using the tripod grip (Chang 2019) and ultimately adopt the dynamic tripod grip commonly (Connolly and Dalgleish 1989). The tripod grip is most commonly used with tools requiring complex movements. It separates the hand into two operating parts; this is known as the dissociation of the two sides of the hand. The thumb, index, and middle fingers are on the skill side and the ring and small fingers are on the stabilizing side. The static tripod grip involves using wrist movement to support the three fingers holding the spoon, while the dynamic tripod grip enables the three fingers to move freely (Ho 2015). The table below shows the different spoon grasp patterns (see Table 1).

Table 1. Spoon grasp patterns (re-illustrated for this study)

Illustration					
Age (months)	12-18	18-24	13-15	-	24
Grasp pattern	Transverse palmar grip	Transverse digital grip	Ulnar grasp	Static tripod grip	Dynamic tripod grip
	Radial grasp				

2.3   Toddler Motor Skill Assessment Methods

From the above, it can be inferred that when it comes to fine motor development in the hands, Toddlers develop forearm supination skills before they develop finger differentiation skills. The development of these manual motor skills are important indicators of the adoption of different grasp patterns in toddlers. In this study, we developed assessment methods based on previous studies.

Forearm Supination Assessment Methods
In this study, we used the forearm supination manual muscle testing method (Relive Occupational Therapy, 2017) and a forearm supination stability development activity (Gillette Children's web) to develop two assessment methods for forearm supination skills (see Table 2).

Table 2. Forearm supination assessment methods developed in this study

Method	Steps	Illustration	References
I	1. The toddler keep their upper arm close to the body and supinate their forearm by 90 degrees. 2. The toddler rotates their wrist outwards. 3. The angle is between 80 and 90 degrees, passes the assessment.		(Relive Occupationa l Therapy, 2017)
II	1. Place a Slinky spring toy in front of the toddler. 2. The toddler keep their upper arm close to the body. 3. The toddler holds the Slinky and supinate their forearm. 4. The angle is between 80 and 90 degrees, passes the assessment.		(Gillette Children's web)

Finger Differentiation Assessment Methods
In this study, we referenced the second edition of *Peabody Developmental Motor Scales* (PDMS-2) and used its cube grasp test to assess toddlers' fine motor skills (M. Rhonda Folio et al. 2000). We then used the finger differentiation activity introduced in the book Fine Motor ABC (Stacie Erfle 2016) to develop the three-stage assessment method for finger differentiation skills (see Table 3).

Table 3. The preliminary finger differentiation skills assessment methods drawn up in this study

Stage	Steps	Illustration	References
I	Instruct the toddler to grasp a cube with thumb opposed to the index and middle finger pads with space visible between cube and palm.		(M. Rhonda Folio &Rebecca R.Fewell,2000)
II	Instruct the toddler to grasp two cubes with one hand and hold them for three seconds.		
III	Instruct the toddler to hold a ring with their ring and little fingers, then grasp a cube with their thumb and index and middle fingers.		(Stacie Erfle,2016)

2.4   Conclusions

Based on the literature, the authors of this study concluded that progressing from a radial grasp to the static tripod grip is critical to allow toddlers to freely manipulate a spoon and other tools. Toddlers develop forearm supination skills before finger differentiation skills. The authors therefore concluded that the optimal time to guide the development of the static tripod grip in toddlers is between 18 and 24 months of age, after the development of the forearm supination and finger differentiation skills.

3   Methods

Through interviews with professional experts, we determined the optimal time for toddlers to progress to the static tripod grip and recommended appropriate methods to assess toddlers' motor skills. In March 2020, we also conducted individual semi structured interviews with three professional occupational therapists who specialize in child development. A questionnaire was provided beforehand.

3.1   Interview Subjects

We interviewed three occupational therapists (referred to as A, B, and C in this study) with over five years of clinical experience in the motor development of children. Before each interview, we asked the interviewees to fill out their personal information, including their name, employer, occupation, and years of experience (see Table 4).

Table 4. Interviewee information

Interviewee	Occupation	Years of experience	Place of work
A	Occupational therapist	5	New Taipei City, Taiwan
B	Occupational therapist	7	Taipei City, Taiwan
C	Occupational therapist	15	Taipei City, Taiwan

3.2 Semistructured Questionnaire

The experts' answers in the interview were based on their own professional experience. The questionnaire consists of two sections focusing on different topics that the authors wished to investigate (see Table 5). The first section revolves around the fine motor skills indicators required for the adoption of the static tripod grip in toddlers; the second section concerns the clinical assessment methods for forearm supination and finger differentiation skills developed from the literature review. The interviewees provided the authors with suggestions and important notes on the preliminary assessment methods drawn up in this study (see Tables 2 and 3).

Table 5. Contents of the semi-structured questionnaire

Topic		Interview questions
Optimal time for toddlers' adoption of the static tripod grip to hold a spoon		1. At how many months of age is it appropriate for toddlers to adopt the grip? 2. What fine motor skills are required of toddlers before adopting the grip?
Assessment of toddlers' motor skills	Forearm supination	1. At how many months of age should toddlers develop this skill? 2. Please provide suggestions and important notes on the the the preliminary assessment methods drawn up in this study
	Finger differentiation	1. At how many months of age should toddlers develop this skill? 2. Please provide suggestions and important notes on the the the preliminary assessment methods drawn up in this study

4 Results

4.1 The Optimal Time to Guide Toddlers to Adopt the Static Tripod Grip to Hold a Spoon

Recommended Age for Toddlers to Adopt the Static Tripod Grip to Hold a Spoon
The three experts held different opinions on the optimal learning age: Expert A suggested that toddlers begin learning at three years of age, the recommended age for learning to hold a pencil; Expert B suggested that toddlers begin learning at two years of age, after the development of fine motor skills; Expert C took toddlers' fine motor skills and cognitive development into account and suggested that toddlers begin learning at 2.5 years of age. All three experts believed that this study's proposed age of 18–24 months was too early for toddlers to adopt the static tripod grip. (See Table 6).

Recommendations Regarding the Motor Skills Needed by Toddlers to Adopt the Static Tripod Grip to Hold a Spoon
In response to the question concerning the motor skills needed to adopt the static tripod grip when using a spoon to eat, the three experts agreed that toddlers should develop fine motor skills in their hands before attempting to adopt the static tripod grip. In addition to the finger differentiation and forearm supination skills concluded in this study, Experts B and C also specified that the development of hand arch, wrist stability, thumb opposition, and the related cognitive abilities were necessary precursors to the adoption of the static tripod grip. (See Table 6).

Table 6. Comparison of study conclusions and expert recommendations on the optimal time for the adoption of the static tripod grip to hold a spoon

	Optimal learning time	Study conclusions	Expert recommendations
Agreeing	Based on skill indicators	Finger differentiation, forearm supination	Finger differentiation (A, B, and C), forearm pronation and supination (B and C)
Opposing		–	Thumb opposition (C), hand arch (B and C), wrist stability (B, C), cognitive abilities (C)
	Based on age	18–24 months	24 months (B), 30 months (C), 36 months(A)

4.2 Recommendations for Motor Skill Assessment Methods for Toddlers

Recommendations for the Forearm Supination Assessment Methods Developed in This Study

The three experts agreed that the development of forearm supination is not limited to a specific age range. The experts offered the following recommendations for the assessment methods developed in this study: the concept of manipulating a spring toy is not understood by children aged two years or younger (A); muscle compensation in the upper arm should be avoided during assessment (B); the supination angle of the forearm required for eating is small, and the pronation angle is roughly between 0 and 45 degrees when using the static tripod grip to hold a spoon (C) (see Table 7).

Table 7. Expert recommendations for the preliminary forearm supination assessment methods developed in this study

Met hod	Illustrations of the assessment methods in this study	Expert recommendations
I		• The supination angle of the forearm required for eating is small, and the pronation angle is roughly between 0 and 45 degrees when using the static tripod grip to hold a spoon (C). • Muscle compensation in the upper arm should be avoided (B).
II		• The ability to understand the concept required for toddlers to perform this action is generally developed after age two (A). • Muscle compensation in the upper arm should be avoided (B).

Suggestions for the Finger Differentiation Assessment Methods Developed in This Study

The three experts agreed that the development of finger differentiation is not limited to a specific age range. The experts offered the following recommendations: the movements in stage I can be achieved by toddlers aged around one year old and do not require hand arch development (B, C); the achievement of the movement in stage II requires hand arch development (B); the movement in stage III is more difficult and requires the development of comprehension skills and the dissociation of the two sides of the hand (A, C) (see Table 8).

Motor Skill Assessment Criteria

The three experts agreed that toddlers should only be required to complete the movement specified in each stage once to be deemed capable of that skill. Expert C generally gives each toddler three chances to complete each task and continues to observe the toddlers' following two attempts whether or not they successfully complete the task on their first try.

Table 8. Expert recommendations for the preliminary finger differentiation assessment methods developed in this study

Stage	Illustrations of the assessment methods in this study	Expert recommendations for the assessment methods	Observation
I		• Achievable by simply opening and closing the hands without using the hand arch (B) • Achievable at one year of age (C)	Thumb opposition
II		• Requires the use of the hand arch to achieve (B)	Hand arch development
III		• Difficult for toddlers aged 18 to 24 months (A) • Requires comprehension of instructions to achieve (C)	Finger differentiation

4.3 Interview Conclusions

Based on the content of the aforementioned expert interviews, the following five conclusions were reached:

1. In addition to finger differentiation and forearm supination, toddlers require hand arch development, wrist stability, thumb opposition, and the related cognitive skills when using the static tripod grip to hold a spoon.
2. The supination angle of the forearm required for eating is small and does not need to reach 80–90°. Wrist stability in toddlers should be assessed to prevent muscle compensation in the upper arm.
3. Toddlers aged 24–36 months old should begin learning to use the static tripod grip to hold a spoon.
4. A three-stage assessment of fine motor skills should include the assessment of thumb opposition, hand arch development, and finger differentiation.
5. When assessing a skill, toddlers should be given at least three chances to complete the task and should only be required to complete it once to be deemed capable of the skill.

5 Discussion and Recommendations

For this study on grasp development in toddlers, the authors examined fine motor development in toddlers' hands and hypothesized that after the required forearm supination and finger differentiation skills are developed, toddlers may be guided to adopt the static tripod grip to hold a spoon at between 18 and 24 months of age. After interviewing experts with clinical experience, the authors added the development of the related cognitive abilities and stability in tool manipulation as prerequisites to learning the static tripod grip. The experts agreed that toddlers should begin learning after 24 months of age. When conducting an applied interdisciplinary study, in addition to conducting a literature review, practical experience should also be obtained through expert interviews.

References

Augustyn, M., Frank, D.A., Zuckerman, B.S.: Chapter 3 - Infancy and toddler years. In: Developmental-Behavioral Pediatrics, 4th edn., pp. 24–38 (2009)

Case-Smith, J.: Chapter 7 - Hand skill development in the context of infants' play: birth to 2 years. In: Hand Function in the Child: Foundations for Remediation, pp. 117–141 (2006)

Chang, Y.C.: When will you learn to feed yourself, my child?—development of self-feeding skills. Mennonite Christian Hospital (2019). https://ftt.tw/uXVwR

Claxton, L.J., McCarty, M.E., Keen, R.: Self-directed action affects planning in tool-use tasks with toddlers. Infant Behav. Dev. **32**(2), 230–233 (2009)

Connolly, K., Dalgleish, M.: The emergence of a tool-using skill in infancy. Dev. Psychol. **25**(6), 894–912 (1989)

Ho, E.S.: Measuring hand function in the young child. J. Hand Ther. **23**(3), 323–328 (2010)

Ho, J.: Child development series: use of the first three fingers [Video] (2015). https://ftt.tw/X7PRE

Kuo, Y.S., Lin, H.C., Huang, T.Y., Chang, Y.A.: Investigation of eating behaviors in preschool children—case study of a kindergarten in Shengang District, Taichung City. J. Health Care Sci. **2**(1), 106–119 (2014)

Sacrey, L.A.R., Karl, J.M., Whishaw, I.Q.: Development of rotational movements, hand shaping, and accuracy in advance and withdrawal for the reach-to-eat movement in human infants aged 6–12 months. Infant Behav. Dev. **35**(3), 543–560 (2012)

Nagao, T.: Joint motion analysis of the for eating upper extremity required activities. Bull. Health Sci. Kobe **19**, 13–31 (2004)

Ross, E.: Chapter 9 - Eating development in young children: understanding the complex interplay of developmental domains. In: Saavedra Jose, M., Dattilo, A.M. (eds.) Early Nutrition and Long-Term Health, pp. 229–262. Woodhead Publishing (2017)

van Roon, D., Kamp, J., Steenbergen, B.: Constraints in children's learning to use spoons. J. Learn. Disabil. 75–93 (2003)

van Roon, D., Steenbergen, B.: The use of ergonomic spoons by people with cerebral palsy: effects on food spilling and movement kinematics. Dev. Med. Child Neurol. **48**(11), 888–891 (2006)

Wu, Y.Y.: Fine motor skills – how nimble hand movements develop in children. UDN Blog (2013). https://ftt.tw/dtALX

Wu, Y.Y.: Fine motor skills – thumb movements part 1. UDN Blog (2012). https://ftt.tw/dtALX

Yun, T.: Fine motor development guide for toddlers aged 0–2 years: move your hands, grow your brain! Mom and Baby (2017). https://ftt.tw/1blwd

The FRAM Error Model Within a System Theoretical Work System to Support Conceptually the Development of a Technical Learning System for Learning from Errors

Marvin Goppold[1]([✉]) [iD], Sven Tackenberg[2] [iD], Martin Frenz[1] [iD], and Verena Nitsch[1] [iD]

[1] Institute of Industrial Engineering and Ergonomics,
RWTH Aachen University, Aachen, Germany
{m.goppold,m.frenz,v.nitsch}@iaw.rwth-aachen.de
[2] Laboratory of Industrial Engineering, University of Applied Sciences
and Arts Ostwestfalen-Lippe, Lemgo, Germany
sven.tackenberg@th-owl.de

Abstract. New learning media approaches in technical vocational education offer multiple opportunities to revolutionize learning processes in apprenticeship. One approach tries to facilitate learning from errors in real work processes with the help of augmented reality (AR). Therefore, FRAM as a systemic error model can support the product development process of such AR learning media. The article shows how to combine FRAM with an extended work system model. Engineering design methods complement both system theoretical models in order to simulate erroneous and perfect solutions in work processes. In majority, the results present a good fit of FRAM's functional dimensions that allows fostering synergies. The extended work system helps in combination with engineering design methods to convert difficult and ill-defined dimensions into a compatible shape for discrete event simulations. The investigation is limited on the assumptions of the underlying models and illustrates just one possible modelling solution. Moreover, resilient work design can profit from the outcomes on the integration of FRAM into an early staged product and work process design.

Keywords: Workplace learning · Augmented reality · Human action · Product development · System theory · Simulation

1 Motivation

In technical vocational education and training (TVET), there is a high demand for supporting learning media using new digital opportunities. One innovative approach that might offer highly beneficial learning opportunities for apprenticeships of dual or company education systems [1, 2] in TVET focuses on errors [3]. Today supervisors and apprenticeship trainers try to avoid dangerous or expensive incidents and accidents to provide safe workplaces, sustainable environments, and cost-efficient training processes. Therefore, this behavior sadly prevents to learn effectively from errors.

N. L. Black et al. (Eds.): IEA 2021, LNNS 220, pp. 80–87, 2021.
https://doi.org/10.1007/978-3-030-74605-6_10

Augmented Reality (AR) technology offers solutions to use neglected negative error consequences virtually for learning without a real negative impact. Figure 1 illustrates an example of a setup that is necessary to track vocational actions in work processes at the workplace. Digital twins build on empirically collected data. Later on, these digital twins digitally map the structure and behaviour of the real learning environment.

Based on standardized machine data interfaces and secondary devices, such as smart tools, precise detection of a person's actions can be achieved. Furthermore, cameras and artificial intelligence solutions support to identify actions as well. The virtual testbed as the core of the system merges all information [4] and builds a digital twin of the real work process state in order to simulate consequences [5]. Thereupon, head-mounted displays visualize consequences of errors to learners while working a learning task in our AR-system. All processed data is stored in a database. After completing the vocational learning task, a cloud solution for didactical use in a reflection phase stores a compressed and pre-evaluated replay dataset.

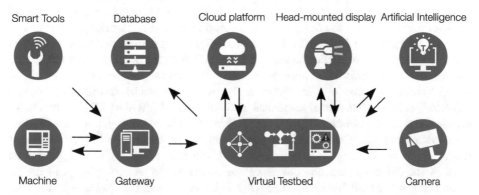

Fig. 1. Technical system setup for action tracking and data processing in work processes

Consequently, there is a need for a methodology to analyze and design entire work processes, identify action errors based on detected system states, and simulate human actions' consequences. The developed system can be integrated into different approaches for individual work-based competence fostering [6, 7]. Therefore, the need arises to integrate preliminaries of didactic concepts into the technical development process of learning media.

2 Theory

Learning from errors in the context of a TVET should take place in real work systems. Therefore, one has to find a solution on how to design technical learning media for technical occupations in professional workplaces using augmented errors [8]. In addition to the work system's description, this also requires a detailed analysis of work processes.

In contrast to Anglo-American approaches [9, 10], methods of work humanization [11] match the perspective of German TVET best to develop a learning system that includes error based learning. A detailed overview of the required data collection and the corresponding empirical data can be found in (Goppold et al. 2020).

There are two dimensions to the development of such a learning system. In addition to the development and design of the didactic learning concept, it is mainly about the technical system's design and implementation. While didactics uses work analysis results to build a learning concept, whereas the disciplines involved in technical developments reformulate them as requirements to clear technical obstacles. The interfaces between the disciplines involved in the development consist of requirements [12]. Didactics describes additional requirements on the learning media from a learning perspective while technology development brings in suggestions on technical solutions as well as rejections due to technical feasibility.

Both disciplines are able to align with a socio-technical system view and integrate typical design principles [13]. A suitable representation of elements and relations within socio-technical systems are a part of work systems. A work system describes the work processes and the influencing factors in a technically formal way and thus creates the basis for an algorithm-based representation [14, 15]. For a systematic development of the learning system, we use design methods compatible with the work system [16, 17].

Various error models describe the occurrences, characteristics, and effects of errors [18]. A systemic error model needs to be embedded in the work system due to the socio-technical system choice, aims of German TVET and arguments on organizational perspectives in error models [19]. Systems-Theoretic Accident Modeling and Processes (STAMP) [20] and Functional resonance analysis method (FRAM) [21] are two well-elaborated systemic error models and methods to consider. In general, both complement the work system well. On the contrary, identifying interdependencies between different design levels in macroergonomics [22] as STAMP's main advantage does neither meet most of the didactical learning outcomes nor contribute to technologies main design level. For this and additional reasons, FRAM is the error model to integrate in the work system.

This article investigates whether the FRAM model can provide the basis for developing an error-based learning system based on the extended work system. Furthermore, the main objective illustrates which adaptions have to apply on FRAM and the extended work system.

3 Methodology

An extended work system [15, 23] is based on empirical work studies and summarizes information of a work process in a structural system theoretical representation. The structural information feed into a discrete state description of the observed work process (illustration of one state in Fig. 2). Using a formal language to describe a system [24], the extended work system model is capable of being transferred to a digital twin simulation development method [5]. When designing a learning system, formal language allows using model-based design methods from engineering [17].

Therefore, the FRAM error model must be adapted to a formal language description to integrate into the extended work system. Because FRAM and the extended work systems are function-oriented approaches, both are suitable for comparison to reflect strengths and weaknesses of both of them. FRAM describes functions that represent actions in work processes within six dimensions in order to identify potential interdependencies of their variability (compare Fig. 3).

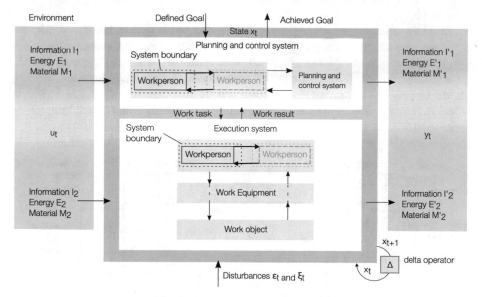

Fig. 2. Extended work system [15]

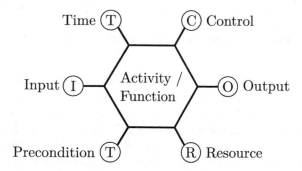

Fig. 3. Function dimensions of FRAM [21]

4 Results

The control and time dimensions fit best to model assumptions of the extended work system. The former dimension arranges well because of the distinction between execution subsystem and planning and control subsystem. The latter dimension builds on the temporal system boundaries [14]. This consideration is relevant since they show different system states and possible functions (actions) in detail. One should emphasize that work system's functions and the structure are time-dependently.

From a function-oriented perspective, an intended output is always closely related to the function's objective and is the end state of a transformation of inputs [15, 17]. The transformation process can face optimizations by considering further constraints to achieve best feasible end states. However, the FRAM model does not fully represent this point of view.

In addition, inputs in FRAM and the extended work system belong to different types, for instance material, energy or information. Input characteristics can vary over time that enforces to complement them with a set of states. Therefore, operands describe the transformation of system states [17] in order to simulate actions of humans. Actually, FRAM already has a precondition dimension delivering required state descriptions to process a function. Simulations need preconditions necessarily defined as different states to describe actions usefully, see Fig. 4.

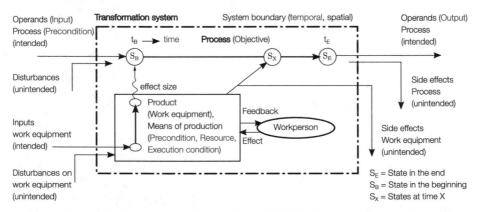

Fig. 4. Transformation process with red-coloured FRAM dimensions [adapted from 17]

The resource dimension looks at the work equipment when it mediately transforms an input state into an intended output state. Therefore, one should neglect to interpret such resources as inputs of the transformation process. These resources place within the system boundaries of a transformation process and hold a separate set of necessary inputs and outputs to connect to the environment shown in Fig. 4. Since resources can also change over time, a set of conditions (preconditions) describes resource states, too. Moreover, execution conditions must fulfil during the whole transformation process. Within a discrete simulation of work systems, this provokes a conflict due to the distinction of preconditions and execution conditions. The extended work system will treat the execution conditions in the same way as the preconditions to solve this conflict.

Consequently, there is a first test whether the precondition and the execution conditions are present. If the test is true, the transformation process will start and triggers a state change in the work system. Secondly, a check on fulfilment of execution conditions takes place during the transformation process.

5   Discussion

First, FRAM's view on action variability improves the extended work system to evaluate the system elements and their relations concerning errors. The other way round, due to its deep roots in system theory, the extended work system clarifies the ambiguous descriptions of dimensions in the FRAM model.

Furthermore, the extended work system should handle its planning and control subsystem in a function-oriented way. While both models can sufficiently represent the dimension time, it is difficult to describe functions running in parallel [25]. If there are no relations between these functions, they are independent of each other. In this case, a deterministic sequence of the states of the work system is not given. Additional methods such as TAFEI [26] can heal this disadvantage.

Minor adjustments of the input and output dimensions in both models with embedded preconditions enable using engineering design methods and discrete event simulation models. The discussion of preconditions hints that there is a need for a combined description of elements and their associated states.

Last, execution conditions have to exist for operands and work equipment until the intended output leaves the transformation process. On this behalf, preconditions and execution conditions behave the same in discrete simulations, neglecting the need for a technical distinction.

Nevertheless, FRAM is a well-founded combination of a systemic error model and supplies a suited methodical framework for error identification. The results bridge the gap between human action perspective versus system state perspective [25]. Furthermore, the results support previous statements in literature that FRAM fits existing socio-technical systems better than for developing ones [27].

As a limitation, the results of the depicted considerations focus on applying the extended work system with all its historical assumptions and references. In addition, they show one solution that depends on many assumptions and interpretations in system modelling but offers transferability to other socio-technical studies.

6   Conclusion

Overall, the article illustrates the synergies of the extended work system that describes work processes and FRAM that identifies relations in the work process as well as their unintended outcomes. The integration of both models leads to a simulation-ready description of possibly error-prone actions. Not only do both models support understanding and analyzing work processes, but also the interdisciplinary communication of didactics, engineering and informatics. Indeed, the integration of FRAM as a systemic error model encourages the technical development process e.g. of an error-based AR learning media in TVET. Using the strength of FRAM, one can see that most preliminary assumptions fit perfectly to industrial engineering approaches of the extended work system. Additionally, the extended work system combined with the engineering design method of Heidemann [17] compensate some inadequately defined dimensions of the FRAM model.

The results offer many chances for transferring insights to similar socio-technical system models to design resilient work systems. The next development activities need to evaluate the model by way of example on a technical prototype before applying it on two use cases in CNC drilling and injection moulding.

Acknowledgement. The contribution of this article is part of the project "FeDiNAR—Didactical Use of Errors with the Help of Augmented Reality". It is funded by the Federal Ministry of Education and Research (BMBF) as part of the "Digital Media in Vocational Education and Training" programme and is supported by the German Aerospace Center (DLR) under the funding code 01PV18005A.

References

1. Cedefop: Vocational education and training in Germany. short description. Publications Office of the European Union, Luxembourg (2020)
2. Lensjø, M.: Stories of learning: a case study of norwegian plumbers and apprentices in TVET at the construction site and in a training agency. IJRVET **7**, 148–166 (2020)
3. Atanasyan, A., Kobelt, D., Goppold, M., Cichon, T., Schluse, M.: The FeDiNAR project: using augmented reality to turn mistakes into learning opportunities. In: Geroimenko, V. (ed.) Augmented Reality in Education. A New Technology for Teaching and Learning, pp. 71–86. Springer, Heidelberg (2020)
4. Reitz, J., Rosmann, J.: Automatic integration of simulated systems into OPC UA networks. In: 2020 IEEE 16th International Conference on Automation Science and Engineering (CASE), pp. 697–702. IEEE (2020)
5. Schluse, M., Priggemeyer, M., Atorf, L., Rossmann, J.: Experimentable digital twins—streamlining simulation-based systems engineering for industry 4.0. IEEE Trans. Ind. Inf. **14**, 1722–1731 (2018)
6. Billett, S.: Learning through work: workplace affordances and individual engagement. J. Workplace Learn. **13**, 209–214 (2001)
7. Engeström, Y.: Learning by Expanding: An Activity-Theoretical Approach to Developmental Research. Cambridge University Press, New York (2015)
8. Gerds, P.: Shaping and evaluating vocational training offers. In: Rauner, F., Maclean, R. (eds.) Handbook of Technical and Vocational Education and Training Research, pp. 523–530. Springer, Dordrecht (2008)
9. Brannick, M.T., Levine, E.L., Morgeson, F.P.: Job and Work Analysis: Methods, Research, and Applications for Human Resource Management. SAGE Publications, Los Angeles (2019)
10. Fleishman, E.A.: The Fleishman-Job Analysis Survey (F-JAS). Consulting Psychologist Press, Palo Alto (1992)
11. Luczak, H.: Task analysis. In: Salvendy, G. (ed.) Handbook of Human Factors and Ergonomics, pp. 340–416. Wiley, New York (1997)
12. Mattmann, I., Gramlich, S., Kloberdanz, H.: Mapping requirements to product properties: the mapping model. In: Marjanović, D., Štorga, M., Pavković, N., Bojčetić, N., Škec, S. (eds.) Proceedings of the DESIGN 2016 - 14th International Design Conference, pp. 33–44. Cavtat-Dubrovnik, Croatia (2016)
13. Clegg, C.W.: Sociotechnical principles for system design. Appl. Ergonomics **31**, 463–477 (2000)
14. Hubka, V., Eder, W.E.: Theory of Technical Systems. Springer, Heidelberg (1988)
15. Schlick, C., Bruder, R., Luczak, H.: Arbeitswissenschaft. Springer, Berlin (2018)

16. Pahl, G., Beitz, W., Feldhusen, J., Grote, K.-H.: Engineering Design: A Systematic Approach. Springer, London (2007)
17. Heidemann, B.: Trennende Verknüpfung. Ein Prozessmodell als Quelle für Produktideen. VDI-Verl., Düsseldorf (2001)
18. Dekker, S.: The Field Guide to Understanding 'Human Error.' CRC Press, Boca Raton (2014)
19. Hollnagel, E.: Safety-I and Safety-II: The Past and Future of Safety Management. Ashgate, Surrey (2014)
20. Leveson, N.: Engineering a Safer World: SYSTEMS thinking Applied to Safety. MIT Press, Cambridge (2011)
21. Hollnagel, E.: FRAM, the Functional Resonance Analysis Method: Modelling Complex Socio-Technical Systems. Ashgate, Surrey (2012)
22. Hendrick, H.W.: An overview of macroergonomics. In: Kleiner BM, Hendrick HW (eds) Macroergonomics. Theory, Methods, and Applications Lawrence Erlbaum, Mahwah, pp. 1–24 (2002)
23. International Organization for Standardization: Ergonomics principles in the design of work systems 13.180 (2016)
24. Ropohl, G.: Philosophy of socio-technical systems. Soc. Philos. Technol. Q Electron. J. **4**, 186–194 (1999)
25. Nouvel, D., Travadel, S., Hollnagel, E.: Introduction of the concept of functional resonance in the analysis of a near-accident in aviation, p. 9 (2007)
26. Baber, C., Stanton, N.A.: Task analysis for error identification: a methodology for designing error-tolerant consumer products. Ergonomics **37**, 1923–1941 (1994)
27. Moškon, M., Tkalec, M., Zimic, N., Mraz, M.: Towards the declaration of inter-functional protocol for FRAM. In: Annual reliability and maintainability symposium (RAMS), pp. 1–6 (2019)

Applying a Systems Approach to Developing Interventions to Increase Physical Activity Among Primary School Children While Distance Learning During the COVID-19 pandemic- the Stand up Kids Study

Judith I. Okoro[1,4]([⊠]), Brittany Ballen[1,2,4], Melissa Afterman[2,4], Carisa Harris Adamson[1,2,4], and Michelle M. Robertson[3,4]

[1] University of California, Berkeley, CA 94720, USA
judithokoro@berkeley.edu
[2] University of California, San Francisco, San Francisco, CA 94143, USA
[3] Office Ergonomics Research Committee, Yarmouth Port, USA
[4] Center for Occupational Environmental and Health, University of California, Berkeley, USA

Abstract. Sedentary behaviour among school children has been associated with musculoskeletal pain, adverse cardiometabolic disorders and reduced cognitive performance, all of which may be negatively impacted by distance learning during the COVID-19 pandemic. We present the methodology used to design and develop interventions to increase physical activity in 4th graders using a participatory, systems process during distance learning. Formative evaluation of training is being conducted with key stakeholders to facilitate this iterative process.

Keywords: Participatory ergonomics · Instructional systems design · Primary grade students · COVID-19

1 Introduction

Research indicates that, for primary school children, sitting for greater than 2 h is associated with many undesirable health consequences, including: increased risk of childhood obesity, lower cardio-respiratory fitness, lower physical fitness, reduced cognitive performance, lower academic achievement, unfavourable pro-social behaviour and lower self-esteem [1–6]. The impact of COVID-19-based distance learning on sedentary time and associated health outcomes among 4th graders is unknown.

Our primary study aim is to compare the impact of three primary school-based interventions, including health education, ergonomic training, and curricular integration of physical activity using a systems participatory approach involving key stakeholders to design an integrated well-being curriculum for 4th graders delivered through distance learning technology. Here, we describe the process of designing the interventions used to develop these curricular interventions aimed at increasing movement through physical activity, posture changes, and healthy learning habits while distance learning.

N. L. Black et al. (Eds.): IEA 2021, LNNS 220, pp. 88–94, 2021.
https://doi.org/10.1007/978-3-030-74605-6_11

2 Methodology

This is a quasi-experimental randomized control trial with three elementary schools (8 classes) in Northern California. Interventions were allocated by school. Three interventions were designed and developed, including: 1) eight 20-min interactive educational classes on healthy habits; 2) two 30-min classes on ergonomics with a focus on changing postures to reduce prolonged sitting; and 3) the integration of pedometer-based step counts into curricular lessons designed to support physical activity during school and leisure time. Key stakeholders including teachers, parents, principals, and students were involved in designing the integrated curriculum using the formative evaluation process as training materials were developed and implemented. The instructional systems design approach was used to develop the educational training programs for this pilot study [7–9].

2.1 Designing the Interventions

We used the Instructional Systems Design (ISD) model (Table 1) to structure the design of the three intervention trainings. The ISD model has a five step instructional process: 1) Analysis, 2) Design, 3) Development, 4) Implementation, and 5) Evaluation [7].

Analysis. The design team curated a literature review to address the problem of physical inactivity and its impact on risk of musculoskeletal pain, cardiometabolic disorders and reduced cognitive performance. The team identified multiple contributing factors to this health concern: 1) lack of knowledge about healthy habits, 2) increased sitting time, and 3) lack of physical activity.

We hypothesize that students may not be knowledgeable about healthy best practices related to nutrition, hydration, sleep, and physical activity. Without intentional education on these issues, students unknowingly carry on behaviours that could be detrimental to their health. This may be exacerbated by distance learning during the COVID-19 pandemic since kids have less opportunity for guided physical activity in physical education (PE) or recess. We also hypothesized that students could reduce sitting time if they were knowledgeable about how to use tablets and other learning devices in other postures like standing. Further, we assumed that many students would not have a dedicated desk or workspace that fits their smaller stature while schooling from home. Therefore, providing parents, teachers, and kids additional support on how to apply basic ergonomic principles and posture changing strategies to reduce sitting throughout the day could be beneficial. Thirdly, we hypothesized that increasing physical activity among school children would require a systems approach involving the child, their parents and their teachers. Thus, providing a pedometer to each child and using tracked step counts in the student's curriculum with strategies to increase physical activity before, during and after school may facilitate an increase in physical activity.

Design. The design team consists of Subject Matter Experts (SMEs) in the Occupational Health and Ergonomics areas, and included student researchers, ergonomic consultants, an engineer, a physician, and an instructional web designer. This pilot study was designed for 3 key stakeholders: parents, teachers, and 4th grade primary students. The

Table 1. Intervention design using the instructional systems design model

Interventions	Analysis	Design	Development	Implementation	Evaluation
Training 1: healthy habits education	Lack of knowledge	Increase knowledge of core health habits	Online education of healthful habits	Design team delivers Zoom sessions online during class time on Fridays	Increase in pre- and post-learning assessed by Kahoot learning game --short term Improved self-reported healthful habits --long term
Training 2+: ergonomic training	Increased sitting time	Reduce sitting time during school and leisure time	Online education of healthful habits and ergonomic training with integrated problem-solving strategies	Design team delivers two Zoom sessions online during class time on two Fridays	Increase in duration time spent in variable postures --long term Students' ability to share ergonomic solutions with teachers and parents --short term
Training 3++: curricular integration of pedometers	Lack of physical activity & changing postures	Increase physical activity during school and leisure time Changes in computing learning postures	Curricular integration of physical activity, postural movement; optimal learning environment set-ups	Design team holds bi-weekly meetings with teachers and parents to revise subsequent curricula as present in Training 2+	Increase in weekly reported pedometer step count --short term Improved cognition --long term Improved cardiometabolic biomarkers --long term

design team identified three instructional objectives to increase knowledge of core health habits, reduce sitting time during school and leisure time, increase physical activity during school and leisure time. The specific goals of Training 1 include new knowledge of healthy habit goals such as, limiting added sugar consumption, decreasing non-educational screen time, getting adequate sleep, and increasing physical activity. Training 2+ goals include increasing knowledge of ergonomics with a focus on home workstations that utilize different postures and frequent postural changes. Training 3++ goals include providing strategies in and out of school to increase physical activity and using a pedometer to provide feedback on the step count goals. For training 3++, key stakeholders were actively involved in providing feedback to the training materials to promote commitment and ownership of the training materials for their student learners as well as to encourage parents to apply the training materials and relevant handouts to assist their child in setting up a comfortable learning environment that encourages postural movement and physical activity.

Development. The design team set a major goal of decreasing sitting time, postural movements, and increasing physical activity in children by educating them on healthy habits, ergonomics, and physical activity which were integrated into the school curricula.

The Healthy Habits educational series focuses on nutrition, sleep, reducing sitting time and physical activity. Eight 30-min live zoom sessions include a 3-min movement break, pre-post assessment of knowledge and 20 min of content. The primary educational messages include getting:

- at least 60 min of physical activity per day
- at least 6 cups of water per day
- at least 8 h of sleep per day (with no screen time 1–2 h before bed)
- less than 25 g of added sugar per day
- reducing non-educational screen time to less than 2 h per day

The Ergonomic educational series, "StandUp Kids: An Ergonomics Lesson for Students at Home and School," is an interactive online training that teaches basic content on using school devices in different postures and how varying their postures throughout their school day may help prepare their brain and body for learning. The training provides ideas for at home low-cost environmental design alternatives to enable postural flexibility/variability. Teachers will take the same training as the kids and are provided handout with tips for facilitating and modeling posture changes while learning.

Increasing physical activity can be challenging for kids, particularly during the pandemic when recess and breaks do not offer opportunities to play with other children. With each day spent at home, it can be challenging for kids to know just how much physical activity they engage in. To address this, a pedometer (step counter) was provided to each student in one of the schools. Step counts are being tracked using a log that incorporates operational math activities such as adding, averaging and graphing. Teachers discuss step count goals and incorporate "challenges" using provided curricula. For example, students will climb Mt Everest by comparing their step count with the number required to climb the mountain. During their climb, they learn about geography, customs and the physical impact of climbing a mountain with a backpack at elevation. To support kids in their climb, house-based, class-based and family-based activities that increase step counts are suggested. This intervention utilizes the people closest to the student to support increases in their physical activity.

Implementation. All interventions are occurring on Zoom Communications, Inc. The materials are being delivered through this platform and integrated into their school curriculum. The design team delivers the Healthy Habits (Schools 1–3) and Ergonomic sessions (Schools 2–3) every week during class. Teachers incorporate the step count activities as part of their regular curriculum throughout the week (School 3).

Evaluation. Short term goals include the assessment of pre- and post-learning knowledge of the Healthy Habits and Ergonomic training through Kahoot! learning game. For Training 3++, weekly step count logs compare weekly change in step counts by class. This information is reported back to the parents and teachers for feedback on revising subsequent curricula and to encourage their learners to increase their physical activity and postural changes. Formative evaluation of the training materials occurs as the teacher uses the materials in their curriculum and observes the reactions of the learners to the training materials and their effectiveness in teaching the instructional objectives.

Long term goals will be assessed in a smaller cohort of participants and will include the assessment of self-reported habits by survey. Questions on knowledge and implementation of healthy habits and ergonomic lessons will be assessed. End of school year physical activity and time spent in different postures will be compared to baseline measurements using the ActivPAL inertial measuring unit (PAL Technologies Ltd., Glasgow, UK) Cognitive skills such as attention, memory, and executive functions will be assessed using the Attention Network Test [10], Wisconsin Card Sorting Test [11], and the Working Memory Span Test. Changes in body mass index (height and weight) and waist: hip circumference measurements will be recorded.

Feedback on perceived benefits and challenges of all three training curriculum while distance learning is received from parents and teachers during bi-weekly scheduled meetings. Through this formative evaluation process, parents have requested for the inclusion of new content addressing anxiety and depression during the pandemic which may be impacting their individual students. This has allowed the design team to revise the upcoming educational plans. Parents have also reported on how parental involvement or lack of involvement could impact a child's step count.

3   Results

Formative evaluation of the training materials is being conducted with the targeted learner audience. A brief survey was completed by the trainees' to measure the initial reaction to the training materials and the appropriateness of the learning materials for the identified students [12]. Teachers, principals and parents provided feedback on the training materials as well and was adapted for the teacher and parent's needs, specifically learning about ergonomic principles and the importance of setting up one's computer environment and taking healthy computer breaks along with incorporating movement into their virtual teaching day. An overview of the formative evaluation including outcomes and impact on the design of the interventions will be presented.

4   Discussion

Given the high prevalence of obesity and sedentary behaviour among primary school children before the pandemic, and the unknown impact of distance learning on sedentary behaviour and associated health consequences, this 8-month field study will investigate the effects of three interventions on children's health and well-being during the ongoing COVID-19 pandemic. This presentation will provide an overview of the participatory approach and formative evaluation process used to design educational, environmental and curricular interventions that may impact sedentary behaviour, physical activity and associated physical and cognitive outcomes.

4.1 Limitations

As stated before, this study is being conducted during the COVID-19 pandemic, therefore, all participants are distance learning. Overall, obstacles include active participation in learning from home, varied attendance, difficulty in assisting students and facilitating the online surveys, difficulty in implementing cognition testing, and successfully receiving ActivPAL devices back from students once they have been distributed.

5 Conclusion

This virtual poster session will provide an overview of the three training interventions, the design of each intervention, and the formative evaluation of the training materials. It will review how a systems approach can be used to promote the active involvement of stakeholders for the betterment of our children's health.

Acknowledgements. The authors would like to thank the StandUp Kids Foundation for their financial support, Jessica Gorsuch for the development of the ergonomics webinar, and the teachers and students at the participating San Pablo elementary schools.

References

1. Arundell, L., Hinkley, T., Veitch, J., Salmon, J.: Contribution of the after-school period to children's daily participation in physical activity and sedentary behaviours. PLoS One. **10**(10), e0140132 (2015)
2. Bacardí-Gascon, M., Pérez-Morales, M.E., Jiménez-Cruz, A.: A six month randomized school intervention and an 18-month follow-up intervention to prevent childhood obesity in Mexican elementary schools. Nutr. Hosp. **27**(3), 755–762 (2012)
3. Benden, M.E., Blake, J.J., Wendel, M.L., Huber, J.C.: The impact of stand-biased desks in classrooms on calorie expenditure in children. Am. J. Public Health. **101**(8), 1433–6 (2011)
4. Mazzoli, E., Teo, Wei-Peng., Salmon, J., Pesce, C., He, J., Ben-Soussan, T., Barnett, L.: Associations of class-time sitting, stepping and sit-to-stand transitions with cognitive functions and brain activity in children. Int. J. Environ. Res. Public Health **16**(9), 1482 (2019)
5. Strugnell, C., Turner, K., Malakellis, M., Hayward, J., Foster, C., Millar, L., Allender, S.: Composition of objectively measured physical activity and sedentary behaviour participation across the school-day, influence of gender and weight status: cross-sectional analyses among disadvantaged Victorian school children. BMJ Open **6**(9), e011478 (2016)
6. Minges, K.E., Chao, A.M., Irwin, M.L., Owen, N., Park, C., Whittemore, R., et al.: Classroom standing desks and sedentary behavior: a systematic review. Pediatrics **137**(2) (2016). https://pediatrics.aappublications.org/content/137/2/e20153087

7. Robertson, M.M., Amick, B.C., Hupert, N., Pellerin-Dionne, M., Cha, E., Katz, J.N.: Using participatory ergonomics to develop a workshop on computer ergonomics for young knowledge workers. In: Systems, Social, and Internationalization Design Aspects of Human-Computer Interaction. CRC Press (2001)

8. Robertson, M.M., Amick, B.C., Hupert, N., Pellerin-Dionne, M., Cha, E., Katz, J.N.: Effects of a participatory ergonomics intervention computer workshop for university students: a pilot intervention to prevent disability in tomorrow's workers. Work **18**(3), 305–314 (2002)

9. Robertson, M.M.: Macroergonomics: theory, methods, and applications. In: Macroergonomics of Training Development Systems (2001). https://www.routledge.com/Macroergonomics-Theory-Methods-and-Applications/Hendrick-Kleiner/p/book/9780805831917

10. Fan, J., McCandliss, B.D., Sommer, T., Raz, A., Posner, M.I.: Testing the efficiency and independence of attentional networks. J. Cogn. Neurosci. **14**(3), 340–347 (2002)

11. Grant, D.A., Berg, E.A.: A behavioral analysis of degree of reinforcement and ease of shifting to new responses in a Weigl-type card-sorting problem. J. Exp. Psychol. **38**(4), 404–411 (1948)

12. Kirkpatrick, D.: Techniques for evaluating training programs. Train Dev. J. (1979). Accessed 15 Oct 2020, https://agris.fao.org/agris-search/search.do?recordID=US201302107125

Investigation on Ergonomic Well-Being for Academician's Work from Home Arrangements by Using Association Rules Technique

Charles Ramendran SPR[1]([✉]), Anbuselvan Sangodiah[1], Lilis Surienty Abd Talib[2], Norazira A. Jalil[1], Au Yong Hui Nee[1], and Suthashini Subramaniam[1]

[1] Universiti Tunku Abdul Rahman, 31900 Kampar, Perak, Malaysia
`{charlesr,anbuselvan,noraziraj,auyonghn,suthashini}@utar.edu.my`
[2] Universiti Sains Malaysia, 11800 Gelugor, Penang, Malaysia
`lilis@usm.my`

Abstract. Corona virus or most popularly known as the Covid-19 has paralyzed the people movement as well as various sectors that includes the education sector. Henceforth, it gave a breakthrough for academia to venture themselves into work from home with the aid of information technology. It is known as online teaching and learning (OTL). Frequent and continuous usage of OTL to conduct lessons for learners from home may take a toll on the health aspect of academicians. Demographic factors associating with the factors related to ergonomic settings among academicians will be the focus of this study. Data was collected from private universities in Malaysia by using online platform. Association rules technique based on unsupervised approach had been used to find interesting patterns between demographics and ergonomic settings. With association rules, finding co-occurrences of demographics factors leading to the factors of ergonomic settings is the main strength of the technique. Despite many researchers in the past has done ergonomics studies in various areas/fields, only simple and descriptive statistical techniques were used. At present, there is no research work reported using the association rules technique in the educational field in the context of ergonomics. Association rules algorithms FP-Growth and Apriori were used and the evaluation metrics used in this study were support, confidence and lift. The results from this study indicated that the academic group with demographic factors *(Married, Male)* particularly vulnerable to the risk of mental health while the academic group *(Married, Female, Years of experience is less than 10 years)* did not have adequate ergonomics facilities at home and lacked a better sense of interpretation of the information provided to them by the management in the process of executing OTL. The results could facilitate further improvements to establish good working conditions for academicians to use OTL from home. The management could undertake the necessary initiatives targeting specific academic groups to address the issues facing them.

Keywords: Online teaching · Ergonomic · Association rules technique · Academician · Covid-19

N. L. Black et al. (Eds.): IEA 2021, LNNS 220, pp. 95–104, 2021.
https://doi.org/10.1007/978-3-030-74605-6_12

1 Introduction

The deadliest Corona virus or better known as Covid-19 has taken big waves and drown many lives of various nation's citizen. Many have lost their employment, businesses, career dreams and most importantly next of kin. While many industries were struggling to sustain in the market, one industry were stand still and begun to transform the way of performing the task which is education industry. The academia world has its space to cope with the assistance of technology by inspiring professional academics to adapt and adopt to the instant revolution of digital teaching. The comfort of teaching in physical mode has taken to online teaching for the first time in Malaysia in the history of education. The workload of academicians increased as they have taken a lot of time and effort to cultivate students as well as prepare teaching method that matched with the student's learning style [1]. When Covid-19 landed in Malaysia, a very early precaution was quickly taken by the Malaysian government in order to curb the spreading of the virus to entire country. Various industries were asked to move on to online and those who unable to process such transmission had to let down the employees as well as the business. But academics switched their original routine to the new norm of delivering their lectures and it just took a certain software to be installed and of course equipment such as a laptop, a personal room convert to office room and a proper WIFI connection. However, many lecturers were satisfied with sufficient facilities but ignored on the ergonomic part of working from home. Due to the new normal in the world of educational institutions, both academicians and students experienced psychological anxiety and heightened mental in response to remote teaching and online learning [2]. It has becoming intolerable in long run if the most important aspect were unseen but affecting the human body due to inefficiency and discomfort relating to designed in the working environment. Academics were trained to conduct and handle classes via online, the setting up of their personal room follow the ergonomic way were given to respective lecturers to follow their comfort. Unfortunately, improper set up has excruciating pain not only mentally but psychically.

In contrast, Iwai [3], has indicated that academicians having a resistance of utilizing technological tools and inconvenience to deliver lectures and tutorials. For the new or unfamiliar applicator, implement online teaching can become a complex process for them [4]. These processes collectively affect the lecturer's psychological well-being [5]. For academicians, working from home should have basic office facilities and silence and comfortable office space [6]. According to Institution of Occupational Safety and Health [7], people who work from home will bring health and safety hazards to the employees such as risk assessment issues, including work environment, work equipment and well-being. The working conditions of employees including space, light and equipment may become difficult due to the lighting in the workplace, unfavorable posture during work, duration of the work shift and equipment [8]. Apart from that, excellent ergonomic design can make employee's mental healthier, reduce long-term health problems and psychological problems and increase productivity. According to Lee et al. [9], the bad working condition will influence the person's psychological well-being, due to ergonomic risk factor like musculoskeletal illness, the effect of job stresses and job satisfaction from the previous studies. The long-term discomfort caused by poor ergonomic design may lead to related physical injuries such as musculoskeletal diseases. In the earlier study identified that physical illnesses such as back, neck, and eye diseases can aggravate employees' stress and affect their mental health and stress has come from workload affected a person's motivation in work. Therefore, inappropriate workstation design may happen physiological or psychological consequences like influence job satisfaction, increase the level of stress, fatigue and high blood pressure [10].

2 Problem Statement

Undeniably, United Nations's played huge role in promoting sustainable development goals (SDGs) throughout the world focusing on all occupations, industries and jobs and goal number three on good health and well-being at the same time goal number eight on decent work are significantly related with academic field but since the transformation to online teaching and learning, does the goals represents for the academicians' well-being in terms of ergonomics? According to Robertson and Mosier [11], the area of the workplace which suitable for most activity and equipment requirement is at least 2 m x 2 m; if an academic has used a computer for work, the work surface should have 66 cm high and at least 60 cm deep or include an ergonomic chair. If academics doesn't follow this guideline to design their workplace and place their equipment, it will increase the chance to face stress and musculoskeletal problems, because these ergonomic factors are used to improve a workplace design and can address the psychological health of employee [11]. Consistently, due to soaring workload, academician staring at gadgets the whole day with seamless connectivity may causes complications to body psychically and mentally [5]. Problems with ergonomics in the workplace can cause other diseases and affect the mental health of workers. Nearly 50% of respondents did not work with a desk or office chair, while 53% of respondents faced shoulder pain. 46% of the respondents involved neck pain, and some respondents faced back pain [12]. The study has shown that sitting in front of the desk to working 5.41 h and 7 h sleeping at night had a great impact on the physical and mental health due to increase in workload while 55% of worker's working hours or 7.7 h per day is in sedentary postures that increase intradiscal pressure [13]. With prolonged sitting in poor posture, the ergonomic risk factors increased that involved neck problems, lower back, slip disc, painful joints and Carpel tunnel syndrome [13]. In other words, poor ergonomics workplace will increase the physical stress on a academic's body and lead to work-related musculoskeletal disorders. Academicians who work from home due to the Covid-19 pandemic will use a computer/laptop for a long time due to workload increases, the number of times they use mouse and keyboard will increase, and the fatigue of their hand will also increase. Besides, people must have a proper posture of hand to using the keyboard and mouse to prevent injury of hand muscle. According to Kumar Shrawan [14], due to the imbalance demands on different muscles, the different muscles operating a joint may lead to different amounts of fatigue and also different in the rate they feel fatigue in short term.

As in the current era of digitalization, by incorporating all the scientific disciplines in the research, the experimental design and the implementation of the statistical methods are the crucial factors to evaluate the research findings [15]. However, in relation to the ergonomics studies, most analysis had done only simple and descriptive statistical techniques which unable to find out desired interesting knowledge and information such as finding trends, patterns and association in the data collected [16, 17]. Therefore, the application of data mining could overcome such problems. Data mining include the analysis and prediction of data to search for the previous unknown data, pattern and relationships [18]. Data mining techniques are classified into 7 categories including classification, clustering, regression, outer, sequential patterns, prediction and association rules [19, 20].

This study attempted to fill the gap by investigating ergonomics well-being of those academician who working from home. It is crucial to understand the physical setup while having online teaching and learning that affect Malaysian private universities academician due to work from home. Therefore, the impact of this situation also become a warrant for us to investigate physical impacts on the psychological well-being of academician private universities in Malaysia.

3   Data Sets

In this study, a total of 60 responses have been obtained from academic staff from several private universities in Malaysia which intends to find relationships between attributes of the background of academic staff and ergonomic characteristics in respect of cognitive, physical, work, and mental overload. This study goes beyond the common research or studies of the past by focusing on ergonomic characteristics at workplace and associating them with physical injuries. In addition to looking into attributes or factors related to workplace settings and the resultant factors of physical injuries, factors related to demographic of academic staff, their cognitive and mental overload assessments have also been taken into account to ensure the completeness of investigation on ergonomic well-being for academician's work. The aforementioned responses were collected via a survey consisting of questions covering five aspects or categories which are demographic, work, physical, cognitive and mental overload. A brief description of each of the five categories is shown in the Table 1.

Table 1. Description of survey categories

Category	Description
Demographic	To identify gender, age, income, marital status, academic qualification, academic position, years of experience
Work	To identify the ergonomic workplace characteristics while working at home
Physical	To identify the physical activities faced by the academicians throughout handling works from home
Cognitive	To investigate the level of stress faced by the academicians
Mental overload	To assess the dependence of the amount of information required throughout the execution of works from home along with the level of mental readiness of academic

In the survey, there were 27 questions arranged in 5 sections which are open closed-ended questions type - yes no except for the demographic category where some of the questions are multiple-choice type.

4 Data Pre-processing

As there were a lot of attributes in the survey and in order to make it easier to make a reference to each question, labels were used and tagged to questions. For an instance, the first question in the work category was labeled as W1, similarly, for the cognitive category, the third question was labeled as C3. Apart from that, the values Yes/No were converted to 0s and 1s respectively in order to use association rules algorithms. Attributes from all the categories were used except for some attributes in the demographics category which are age, qualification, position and income were removed as the number of responses is quite low where this may not create much variation among the responses based on the attributes that were removed.

In the next section, the concepts and examples of patterns derived using association rules methods will be presented.

5 Association Rules Algorithms

According to Kaur and Kang [21], market basket analysis (MBA) is a data mining technique to discover association rules in large data sets. It is very popular in the retail industry where it can be used to determine the products which are bought together by customers. In the context of MBA, association rules are used to find interesting association rules or patterns among a large set of data items. In this study, let $I = \{i_1, i_2, ..., i_m\}$ be a set of items (e.g. a set of demographic factors and other ergonomic factors for a particular ergonomic record of academic staff) and $C = \{c_1, c_2, ..., c_n\}$ be a set of database ergonomic information (transaction) where each ergonomic record c_i contains a subset of items chosen from I. Each interesting association rules between items is called an itemset. The itemset with k items is called k-itemset. For instance, 3-itemset is $\{Gender\_Male, W2, C2\}$ while 8-itemset can be $\{Gender\_Married, Gender\_Female, C2, M4, W6, P1, M1, W3\}$.

An association rule of itemset can be expressed as $A \rightarrow B$, where A and B are disjoint itemsets. The antecedent is A and the consequent is B. Frequent association rules or known as frequent itemsets can be derived using support and confidence as threshold levels [22].

Generally, *Confidence* measures the reliability of the inference of a generated rule. A higher confidence for A $\rightarrow$ B signifies that the presence of B is highly visible in the transactions having A. While *Lift* of the rule makes an association with the frequency of co-occurrence of the antecedent and the consequent to the expected frequency of co-occurrence. A lift value greater than 1 indicates positive interdependence between the antecedent and the consequent, while a value smaller than 1 indicates negative interdependence, a value of one designates independence [23]. *Confidence* measure can be misleading if the consequent is frequent in the transactions despite having weak relationship between antecedent (A) and consequent (B). *Lift* measure was introduced to overcome the weakness [24, 25]. In order to have a better interpretation of the strength of the relationship between A → B, *Lift* measure had been used in this study.

In this study, the minimum support is capped at 30% while minimum confidence at 70%, respectively. The main reason to set such minimum support is to avoid generating trivial frequent itemsets when the minimum support is lower than 30% or missing the interesting patterns and associations between factors of demographics, work, physical, cognitive and mental overload when minimum support is higher than 30%.

There are several association rules algorithms such as FP Growth, Apriori, Eclat, RElim, and others that can be used to carry out market basket analysis (MBA). However, in this study, FP Growth and Apriori had been used. PyCharm IDE tools with Python and mlxtend API were used in this study as they are popular in academic research [26, 27].

6   Results and Discussion

As there are a lot of association rules were generated using FP growth and Apriori which are more than 100,000, the search space for finding interesting patterns was narrowed down. Association rules with antecedent consisting of demographic factors/items and with consequent containing other factors (work, physical, cognitive and mental overload) were sought. In the next section, association rules that have the highest *Lift* by gender that were generated by each algorithm type were selected and would be presented.

Table 2. Frequent itemset using FPGrowth for male gender

FPGrowth (Gender – Male)					
No	Frequent itemset	Support	Confidence	Lift	Length
1	Marital_Status_Married, Gender_Male → W2, P2, C2, M1, W5, M4, M2, W3, W6, M5	67%	80%	1.2	12
2	Marital_Status_Married, Gender_Male → W2, P2, W1, C2, M1, W5, M4, M2, W3, W6	67%	80%	1.2	12

The patterns of the association rules obtained from *FPGrowth* and *Apriori* based on gender type of male resemble each other in both Table 2 and Table 3. Not only that, the results of *support*, *confidence* and *lift* measures between the two association rules (Rule 1 and Rule 2 in both tables) algorithms appear to be the same. In Rule 1 and Rule 2, the academic staff who are married, male, and regardless of years of experience appears to be the frequent antecedent in the frequent itemsets. This frequent antecedent has associated co-occurrence factors and outcomes that are present in the consequent. In the consequent part, it appears that the factors/outcomes from work and

Table 3. Frequent itemset using Apriori for Male Gender

Apriori (Gender – Male)					
No	Frequent itemset	Support	Confidence	Lift	Length
1	Marital_Status_Married, Gender_Male → M4, C2, W5, W3, P2, M5, W6, W1, W2	67%	80%	1.2	11
2	Marital_Status_Married, Gender_Male → M4, M1, C2, W3, W5, P2, M2, W1, W2	67%	80%	1.2	11

mental overload occur more frequently than the factors/outcomes from cognitive and physical categories. Based on the confidence level, it indicates that 80% of the academic staff group as mentioned above, demands minimal physical involvement in OTL (no occurrence of factors – *P1, P3, P4, P5, P6*) but instead requires more knowledge and the ability to manage classes (*P2*). This group of academic staff experiences information overload in respect of instructions, SOP from management during the period of the Covid-19 pandemic despite there is adequate information system support to deliver the excessive non-academic information (occurrence of factors – *M1, M2, M4, M5*). This situation may result in pressure for this group of academic staff as evidenced by the co-occurrence of the *C2* outcome that indicates the involvement of academic staff in working extra time/overtime. The co-occurrence of multiple factors *(W1, W2, W5)* from the *work* category alongside other factors from other categories implies that the academic staff has good facilities at home in respect of ergonomic support to deliver OTL. This could be explained by better awareness of the risk involved in using computers and having financial stability among the married and male academic staff did not hinder them to invest in tools or equipment in establishing better settings of ergonomics at home. The *Lift* value which is slightly above 1 indicates there is a positive relationship between the factors in the antecedent and consequent respectively. On the whole, it can be concluded that the pressing issues facing the group of academic staff are receiving on an unprecedented large scale of non-academic information and putting them in practice in the process of delivering OTL which may affect significantly the mental state of academic staff.

As with the patterns of the association rules shown in Table 2 and Table 3, the patterns of the association rules shown in Table 4 and Table 5 based on gender type of female resemble each other including the association rules measures. In Rule 1, the academic staff who are married, female, and years of experience is less than 10 years appears to be the frequent antecedent in the frequent itemsets. In contrast to Rule 1 and Rule 2 in Table 2 and Table 3, in the consequent part, it appears that the factors/outcomes from work and mental overload categories occur less frequently in particular. Based on the confidence level, it indicates that 72% of the academic staff group as mentioned above, demands minimal physical involvement in OTL and knowledge and skills to manage

Table 4. Frequent itemset using FPGrowth for Female Gender

FPGrowth (Gender – Female)

No	Frequent itemset	Support	Confidence	Lift	Length
1	Marital_Status_Married, Gender_Female, Years < 10_Years → M2, P6, W6, C2	33%	72%	1.3	7
2	Gender_Female → M4, P2, W6, P4, M2, M1, W1, W2, W5	33%	100%	3	10

Table 5. Frequent itemset using Apriori for Female Gender

Apriori (Gender – Female)

No	Frequent itemset	Support	Confidence	Lift	Length
1	Marital_Status_Married, Gender_Female, Years < 10_Years → C2, P6, M2, W6	33%	72%	1.3	7
2	Gender_Female → M4, P2, W6, P4, M2, M1, W1, W2, W5	33%	100%	3	10

classes (no occurrence of factors – *P1, P3, P4, P5, P2*). Besides, despite this group of academic staff experiences information overload in respect of instructions, SOP from management during the period of the Covid-19 pandemic, the absence of co-occurrence factors (*M1, M4, and M5*) led to the interpretation that there is a lack of support system to deliver unambiguous and clear information. This probably had resulted in limited choices in respect of teaching methods or techniques for this group of academic staff in conducting classes and to some extent, they may not aware that the information they receive from the management is not related to the execution of academic tasks.

The absence of several co-occurrence factors *(W1, W2, W3, W5)* from the *work* category implies that the academic staff did not have good facilities at home in respect of ergonomic support to deliver OTL. This could be due to the lack of awareness about the physical risks associated with OTL among the academic staff.

The *Lift* value which is slightly above 1 indicates there is a positive relationship between the factors in the antecedent and consequent respectively. On the whole, this group of academic staff may be facing issues such as receiving information that is lacking in clarity and ambiguous, and a lack of adequate ergonomic settings at home to deliver OTL.

Rule 2 in Table 4 and Table 5 closely resembles *Rule 1* and *Rule 2* in Table 2 and Table 3 respectively. However, the *Lift* value of the former which is 3 indicates a strong positive relationship between factors in antecedent and consequent.

7 Conclusion and Future Work

This paper proposed and evaluated the ergonomics well-being of the academician who working from home based on association rules data mining. The results showed that the academic group with demographic factors (Married, Male) is more vulnerable to the risk of mental health. Meanwhile, the academic group (Married, Female, Years of experience is less than 10 years) did not have the proper ergonomic facilities at home and lacked a better sense of interpretation of the information provided to them by the management in the process of executing OTL. For these academic groups, the management at the respective university can undertake several initiatives such as conducting specific workshops to create awareness of health risks from OTL and may hold talks with the respective government agencies to provide incentives to facilitate academics to establish better ergonomics settings at home. Through the results of the current study, a promising ergonomic evaluation using the association rule has been implemented. For future work, the number of respondents would be increased to gain more insights by evaluating the relationship between data and the implementation of other data mining methods such as clustering and prediction to further analyze the interesting information related to the ergonomic well-being of the academician.

References

1. Islam, N., Beer, M., Slack, F.: E-learning challenges faced by academics in higher education. J. Educ. Train. Stud. 3(5), 102–112 (2015)
2. Kaur, N.: The face of education and the faceless teacher post COVID-19. Horizon 2, 39–48 (2020)
3. Iwai, Y.: Online learning during the COVID-19 pandemic. Sci. Am. (2020)
4. Malik, S.A., Holt, B.: The impact of new working methods – a psychosocial risk perspective. In: IIRSM Technical Paper (2014)
5. Thestar.   https://www.thestar.com.my/opinion/letters/2021/01/18/look-into-mental-health-needs-of-lecturers, Accessed 26 Jan 2021
6. Shareena, P., Shahid, M.: Work from home during COVID-19: employees perception and experiences. Glob. J. Res. Anal. (2020)
7. Institution of Occupational Safety and Health: Home Office, Mobile Office: Managing Remote Working (2014)
8. Bakotic, D., Babic, T.: Relationship between working conditions and job satisfaction: the case of Croatian shipbuilding company. Int. J. Bus. Soc. Sci. 4(2), 1–8 (2013)
9. Lee, B.J., Park, S.G., Min, K.B., Min, J.Y., Hwang, S.H., Leem, J.H., Kim, C.K., Jeon, S.H., Heo, Y.S., Moon, S.H.: The relationship between working condition factors and well-being. Ann. Occup. Environ. Med. 26(1), 34 (2014)
10. Christy, D., Duraisamy, D.S.: Ergonomics and employee psychological well being. Int. J. Manag. 11(3), 435–438 (2020)
11. Robertson, M.M., Mosier, K.: Work from home: human factors/ergonomics considerations for teleworking (2020)

12. International Labour Organization Managing Work-Related Psychosocial Risks During The COVID-19 Pandemic (2020)
13. Dubey, N., Dubey, G., Tripathi, H.: Ergonomics for desk job workers-an overview. Int. J. Health Sci. Res. **9**(7), 257–266 (2019)
14. Kumar, S.: Theories of musculoskeletal injury causation. Ergonomics **44**(1), 17–47 (2001)
15. Fox, B., Mines, D., Cort, J., Jones, M., Lu, M.-L., Potvin, J., Rempel, D.: The design of experiments in occupational ergonomics research: issues and challenges. Proc. Hum. Factors. Ergonomics Soc. Annu. Meet. **63**(1), 1005–1007 (2019)
16. Asif, R., Merceron, A., Ali, S.A., Haider, N.G.: Analyzing undergraduate students' performance using educational data mining. Comput. Educ. **113**, 177–194 (2017)
17. Dutt, A., Ismail, M., Herawan, T.: A systematic review on educational data mining. IEEE Access **5**, 15991–16005 (2017)
18. Harahap, M., Husein, A.M., Aisyah, .S, Lubis, F.R., Wijaya, B.A.: Mining association rule based on the disease's population for recommendation of medicine need. In: Journal of Physics: Conference Series, vol. 1007, no. 1 (2018)
19. Taranu, I.: Data mining in healthcare decision making and precision. Database Syst. J. **6**(4), 33–40 (2016)
20. Agrawal, S., Agrawal, J.: Survey on anomaly detection using data mining techniques. Procedia Comput. Sci. **60**(1), 708–713 (2015)
21. Kaur, M., Kang, S.: Market basket analysis: identify the changing trends of market data using association rule mining. Procedia Comput. Sci. **85**, 78–85 (2016)
22. Das, S., Dutta, A., Avelar, R., Dixon, K., Sun, X., Jalayer, M.: Supervised association rules mining on pedestrian crashes in urban areas: identifying patterns for appropriate countermeasures. Int. J. Urban Sci. **23**(1), 30–48 (2019)
23. Adamov, A.Z.: Mining term association rules from unstructured text in Azerbaijani language. In: IEEE 12th International Conference on Application of Information and Communication Technologies, AICT 2018 - Proceedings, Kazakhstan (2018)
24. Berzal, F., Blanco, I., Sanchez, D., Vila, M.A.: Measuring the accuracy and interest of association rules: a new framework. Intell. Data Anal. **6**(3), 221–235 (2002)
25. Wright, A., Chen, E.S., Maloney, F.L.: An automated technique for identifying associations between medications, laboratory results and problems. J. Biomed. Inf. **43**(6), 891–901 (2010)
26. Raschka, S.: MLxtend: providing machine learning and data science utilities and extensions to python's scientific computing stack. J. Open Source Softw. **3**(24), 638 (2018). https://doi.org/10.21105/joss.00638
27. Shetty, A.R., Ahmed, F.B., Naik, V.M.: CKD prediction using data mining technique as SVM and KNN With pycharm. Int. Res. J. Eng. Technol. **06**(05), 4399–4405 (2019)

Workload Level Assessment of Online Classes of College Students in Technological Institute if the Philippines Manila Using NASA Task Load Index (NASA TLX)

Janina Elyse A. Reyes[✉], Karl Bryant P. Buan, Roi Vincent B. Limin, and John Roy D. Marucot

Technological Institute of the Philippines, Arlegui, Manila, Philippines
{jereyes.ie,mkbpbuan,mrvblimin,mjrdtmarucot}@tip.edu.ph

Abstract. Online classes or the online learning is the new found system that was implemented and absorbed by the education system. Even though the system looks new, this thing was already practiced by other institution before. But today's educational system was purely online related and technology dependent with the thought that everyone could be at par with the changes in the system. This new system is far different from the traditional education practice since instead of physically going to school to learn, the students can use gadgets to study and learn while at home or anywhere. But this system was forcedly implemented that is why many problem arises, saying that this new system makes it more difficult to cope up compared to traditional system. This issue affected many students, most especially their mental health. The main purpose of this study is to assess the current level of workload given to students and decrease online fatigue experienced by college students with the use of NASA Task Load index.

Keywords: Online classes · Educational system · Mental health · College students · NASA Task Load Index

1 The Problem and Its Background

1.1 Introduction

In this world that everything is changing so fast, there some things that are seemingly remaining constant, or maybe having occurrence of little changes, but it is still the same. Just like the Education system. Looking back to the past, the said system are still being implied in the way where it started. Some said that there could be an underlying reason why it is not changing, some said that it is not changing because no one is trying to change it. But in the recent years, it can be noticed that there are occurrence of changes in the system where the technology is being used in the system, which is a sign of changes in the system. It seems good and convenient as per those who tried doing this improved system. But by the time that this new system called "Online Classes" were

N. L. Black et al. (Eds.): IEA 2021, LNNS 220, pp. 105–112, 2021.
https://doi.org/10.1007/978-3-030-74605-6_13

implemented, those underlying reasons why no one is changing the traditional systems started to show up. This system that looks convenient in every situation since it can be done anytime and anywhere. However, in reality is causing more struggles due to lack of resources and it consumes more time to students and teachers that causes stress and fatigue.

1.2   Statement of the Problem

This study aims to assess the workload level of college students during online classes. Specifically, this study aims to identify the source that contributes more work load in terms of;

- Mental Demand,
- Physical Demand,
- Temporal Demand,
- Performance,
- Effort, and
- Frustration Level.

1.3   Objectives of the Study

This study aims to achieve the following objectives:

- To assess if the current workload level of students is at par with the acceptability level
- To find ways that can decrease online fatigue based on the research findings.

1.4   Scope and Limitations

This study will be limited to the students of Technological Institute of the Philippines Manila Campus. They will be the respondents who will answer the questionnaires to attain the result of the study. This study was conducted for 6 weeks using the NASA Task Load Index. With the findings of this study, the researchers will try to assess the workload level to decrease the online fatigue experienced by college students due to online class workloads.

2   Review of Related Literature and Study

According to Ghimire (2020) [1], children have no option but to attend online classes because of the COVID19 pandemic. Although being on screen can cause harm for the toddlers, the students still have no choice but to pursue online learnings. This lessen the time of the children to enjoy what they normally enjoy at their age. Ghimire also stated that the Indian State of Karnataka banned all online classes for students up to the fifth grade. This decision came up after the National Institute of Mental Health Neurosciences in India pointed out that kids again six years old and below should not on screen for more 1 h as it can cause psychological effects. While the parents are struggling for the tuition fee of their kids, the students are suffering from the psychological impacts that online classes can cause.

According to Sherdan (2020) [2], Most instructors are already familiar with many advantages and disadvantages of online learning, but it is worth going over a few of them here. Online courses are self-paced; Students can speed up or slow down if needed. They can skip the material that they already know and focus on topics they most want or need to learn. Geographical barriers are eliminated. They also appreciated the flexibility of the online format since many of them had day jobs and family commitments. Despite the obvious advantages of online education, several disadvantages stand out stand out. Often, both students and instructor must master the technological learning curve. Some students may be at the very beginning stages of understanding how to use the internet and the requirements of operating the online course may frustrate or overwhelm them. With online training, students have little or no direct contact with the instructor or support personnel. This makes it more difficult for a student with questions or one who does not understand part of the training to seek and obtain help.

According to Singhal (2020) [3], the pandemic brought by COVID19 made people work in their homes. With many teachers that are also having problems in facing the reality of online learning, she listed 10 ways to reduce stress when teaching online. Be patient and be kind, this mind set is very helpful to reduce stress, because while people are adjusting to new normal, it is best for the teachers to be patient and understanding. This is both helpful to the teacher and the student. Set boundaries in communication, let the students know how to contact the instructors. This will make them more comfortable and can also make the teacher reach the students easier. Outline the learning objectives, this will ensure that the students will easily understand the lessons and could make them more focused in learning outcomes. Provide a time-on-task estimate for each lesson assessment, this gives students the ability to set aside the time needed to succeed in the course. Make assignments lower or no stakes if the teacher using a new platform, do not give the students hard time in online classes. Avoid giving them high stakes exam or assessment, because this will stress them out and eventually the teacher will suffer from stress too. Utilize supplemental material to improve learning outcomes and competencies, always maximize the use of multimedia and apps online. This will reduce the pressure that the teacher will experience. If you are making videos, keep them short. Viewers tune for only about 3–4 min, having long videos will only make the students bored and ignore all the learnings from the video. Assign assessments with instant detailed feedback, this will give you more time for other tasks and for yourself. Do not get consumed with best practice. For now, do what you can and what you have to do. Focus on the most important assignments such as those that will cover the course material, but also prepare students for the follow-up course. And finally, remember, you will not recreate your classroom; you will reinvent your classroom. Make some breaks, but do not ignore the call of the students. Teachers must still be accessible for the students.

3 Research Methodology

This chapter contains the methods used in this research and sources of data in this study. It includes how the researchers able to get the ideas contained by previous chapter and enhancing the study, gathering data, collection of the related information and the designs used in this study.

3.1 Method of Research Used

In order to gather the data for this study, the researchers used survey. Survey is a qualitative and/or quantitative strategy poses set of questions that can reach mass of respondents and is often rated in numerical. The researchers used survey to identify the respondent's in-depth information and reasoning.

3.2 Respondents of the Study

The respondents of this study has a total of 200 college students at Technological Institute of the Philippines S.Y. 2020–2021. Their age ranges from 18–24 yrs old, consists of 90 male (45%) and 110 female (55%).

3.3 Sampling Technique

The Slovin's formula was used to determine the number of the student-respondents involved in this study. Enrolled students of Technological Institute of the Philippines would serve as respondents in this study. The samples to be taken are expected to possess characteristics that is identical to those of the population. The data gathered from the respondents have been tabulated and interpreted. The researchers used a marginal error of 7% as the basis and used the Slovin's formula.

$$n = N/(1 + Ne2) \tag{1}$$

where:
n = number of samples
N = total population
e = margin of error

The researchers applied the Slovin's formula that gives the data needed in finding the sample with 7% margin of error. A sample size of 192 college students out of the total population of 7660 is needed. But the gathered response was 200, so the 7 extra respondents were still considered as 'counted' since the number of excess is not that much.

3.4 Data Gathering Procedure

The researchers gathered data and information through NASA-TLX tool on the students. NASA-TLX is an assessment tool used to rate workloads in order to assess the given tasks. In the survey questionnaire, the respondents were asked about their insights on Online Classes and were asked to rate the sources that contributes to their workloads. These data were thoroughly analyzed and interpreted to be able to find out factors that can decrease online fatigue experienced by college students.

3.5 Research Paradigm

Figure 1 shows the Research Paradigm of the study. The Input Process Output model was used to show how the researchers will attain the result of the conducted study using the demographic profile of the respondents as input, and the NASA TLX tool to gather and interpret the data.

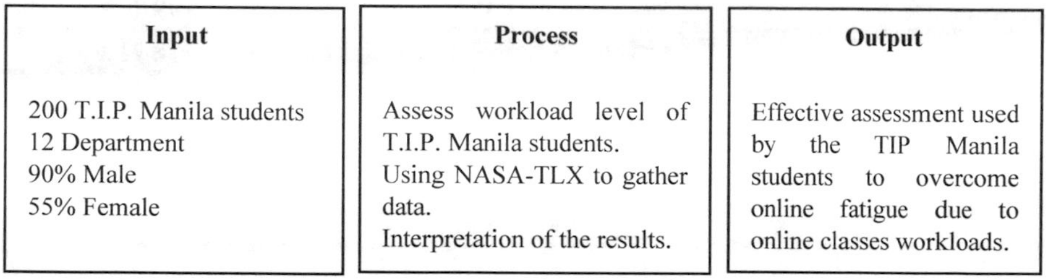

Input	Process	Output
200 T.I.P. Manila students 12 Department 90% Male 55% Female	Assess workload level of T.I.P. Manila students. Using NASA-TLX to gather data. Interpretation of the results.	Effective assessment used by the TIP Manila students to overcome online fatigue due to online classes workloads.

Fig. 1. Research paradigm

4 Presentation, Analysis, and Interpretation of Data

Table 1. Example worksheet in analyzing gathered data (per respondent)

Sources	Weight	Raw rating	Adjusted rating
Mental demand	4	85	340
Physical demand	0	75	0
Temporal demand	4	100	400
Performance	1	75	75
Effort	4	100	400
Frustrations	2	90	180
Weighted rating: 93		**Average raw rating: 1395**	

Table 1 shows the analysis and computation of gathered data per respondents. The weight was acquired from the Comparison of Sources of Workload (pairs = 15) and the raw rating was acquired from Sources Rating Scale of 1–20 increment of 5. And by multiplying the weight and the raw rating, the adjusted rating will be acquired. Then the sum of adjusted rating will be divided to 15 to get the weighted rating.

Table 2. Average of adjusted ratings and total weighted rating

Source	Average of adjusted ratings	Percentage
Mental demand	266.63	23.08%
Physical demand	121.80	10.54%
Temporal demand	174.40	15.10%
Performance	163.35	14.14%
Effort	210.40	18.21%
Frustration	218.53	18.92%
Total weighted rating: 77.01	**Total sum of adjusted ratings: 1155.10**	**Total: 100%**

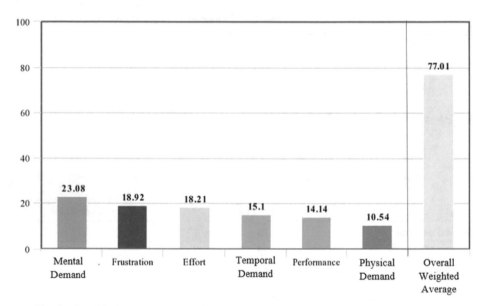

Fig. 2. Graphical representation of average of adjusted rating and total weighted rating

Table 2 shows the tabular value of the mean of all the gathered data from the survey questionnaire answered by the respondents. The Fig. 2 shows the graphical representation of the computed value of all the sources according to their contribution to the workload of the students. The data shown above were analyzed and weighted so this will explain the findings of this study about contribution of sources to the workload. From the graph, it can be seen that the Mental Demand got the highest weighted rating of 23.08% out of 100%. This concludes that the given task, which is taking online class, is mentally demanding. The next is Frustration with weighted rating of 18.92% out of 100%. This means that online classes are frustrating for the students. It was followed by effort with weighted rating of 18.21% out of 100%. It can be interpreted that the students still try to give their best effort in online class even though it was mentally demanding and frustrating. The next is Temporal Demand with weighted rating of 15.10% out of 100% which means that even though they are not that rushed in doing their tasks, they still feel exhausted because of the number of workloads. And with weighted rating of 14.14% out of 100%, the result in terms of Performance means they are not able to perform well during online classes, due to other factors such as slow internet connection. And lastly, the Physical demand that got the lowest weighted rating of 10.54%. This means that online class is not physically demanding, which is an obvious or expected result since online classes does not really require too much physical effort. And the Total Weighted rating is 77.01% which is noticeably high, means the given task, or the online class has a high level of chance in causing fatigue to the students. According to Eitrheim, M. H. R., and Fernandes, A, (2016) [4] workload below 50 is perceived as acceptable. And higher workload scores were associated with low acceptability among the participants. This means that the workload level of online classes, which has a rating of 77.01%, is also associated in low acceptability since it is very far from the acceptability level.

5 Findings, Recommendations, and Conclusions

5.1 Summary of Findings

The survey conducted shows that majority of the respondents prefer having traditional face-to-face class rather than online class. The majority stated that traditional face-to-face classes are more convenient. They also emphasize that online class can drain more energy rather than having face-to-face classes. The level of difficulty that the respondents are experiencing in online class is way higher than the traditional face-to-face classes. And the findings of the study satisfied the objectives of the researchers.

To Assess if the Current Workload Level of Students is at Par with the Acceptability Level. Based on the findings of the study, the researchers found out that the current workload level of the students for the online class is far above the acceptability level. The level of acceptability is 50 and below, anything above 50 is associated in low acceptability level. Even the results are weighted according to their demographic profile, the results are still the same. This can be perceived as the current system of online class is unhealthy and does not fit for the students.

To Find Ways that Can Decrease Online Fatigue Based on the Research Findings. The researchers are able to find ways to decrease online fatigue experienced by the students based on the research findings. The survey questionnaire helped in finding answers that are full of concerns and suggestions of the students why are currently taking online class. This helped the researchers in formulating their recommendations.

5.2 Conclusion

It was shown on the interpretation of data that the total findings of this study says that the student have great chances of experiencing online fatigue because of the current set up of the education system now which is called online class due to the current level of their workload. And having too much workload greatly affects the students, not only on their performance, but also on their chances of having conducive learning during the current situation.

5.3 Recommendation

Based on the results shown in the data, the majority of the students' difficulty in having online class is having poor internet connection and energy draining activities conducted through online. The researchers recommend to the students to upgrade their internet connection to avoid lags, delays, and internet loss while having online class and each student must have an organized and comfortable study area. The researchers also recommend that the school should make adjustments to the workloads of the students that is at par with the level of workload acceptability. It was shown on the findings that the current workload is very high and far from the level of acceptability. It was shown on the findings that the current workload is very high and far from the level of acceptability. Also, the school should always try to address the occurrence of problems on the platform used by the students for online classes because those problem contributes more to the frustrations of the students. They should also cater the complaints of the students. Many students are complaining about the piled up number of requirements, so the school should assign specific numbers of activities given per day and give extensions for the deadlines. Also, the time and attempts given in taking quizzes and exams should be more considerate, make it longer and give more than one attempts so the students have chances in case they encountered problems given that many are having struggles, mostly on internet connection. More consideration from the school are needed by the students. And lastly, the researchers recommend that the school should have a proper scheduling for synchronous and asynchronous classes.

References

1. Katmandu Website. https://kathmandupost.com/national, Accessed 28 Sept 2020
2. eLearning Industry. https://elearningindustry.com, Accessed 03 Oct 2020
3. Inside Higher Ed. https://www.insidehighered.com/news, Accessed 03 Oct 2020
4. Eitrheim, M.H.R., Fernandes, A.: The NASA Task Load Index for rating workload acceptability. Research Gate (2016)

Investigation on Mental Health Well-Being for Students Learning from Home Arrangements Using Clustering Technique

Anbuselvan Sangodiah[(✉)], Charles Ramendran SPR, Norazira A. Jalil,
Au Yong Hui Nee, and Suthashini Subramaniam

Universiti Tunku Abdul Rahman, 31900 Kampar, Perak, Malaysia
{anbuselvan,charlesr,noraziraj,auyonghn,suthashini}@utar.edu.my

Abstract. The excitement of travelling from hometown to a university, well dressed along with carrying notes and laptop, attending classes physically with friends has become a myth in year 2020 and perhaps until the end of the year 2021. COVID-19 has robbed the lifestyle of being a university student and transformed the learning system into online. However, from the perspective of digitalization, it's an achievement but a sudden change has stirred many conflicts on the mental health of students in terms of accepting drastic movement taken by the university due to the COVID-19 pandemic. Academic performance of students is in limbo as they tend to avoiding registered for subjects due to lack of absorbance of changes in the mode of learning with limited facilities to support them along the way. In response, it gives monumental pressure to grasp the subjects via online where it can affect the academic performance of students. This study investigated the state of mind of students who are undergoing classes via online. As such, mental state, physical and ergonomic factors associating with academic background among students will be the focus of this study. Data had been collected from a private university in Malaysia by using online platform. We used non-parametric clustering technique K-medoids based on unsupervised approach and Davies-Bouldin Index to measure cluster quality. Though in the past a few researchers have investigated similar studies, there is no research work reported using the clustering technique to study the aforementioned factors. A total of 8 distinct clusters were obtained. The patterns in the clusters indicated that high mental stress, poor ergonomic settings, alongside high potential risk of injuries were present in students in the clusters regardless of academic background. In particular, the two groups of clusters namely C4, C5, C6, C7 and C1, C2 need immediate attention in respect of mental, health and pedagogy support. As of result, the management of university, family members and university stakeholders should play their part by providing students with psychological support, comfortable study workspace, appropriate pedagogy support.

Keywords: Online teaching and learning · Mental health · Clustering technique · Students · COVID-19

1 Introduction

In recent years, the term 'mental health' has come to the limelight in many countries. Mental health is defined by the status of our emotional, psychological, social well-being, and quality of life. It encompasses how we think, feel, behave, the way we handle stress and how we make choices [1]. Generally, it affects the way we respond to something and it affects everyone, ranging from kids to adulthood. In Malaysia, based on the recent National Health and Morbidity Survey on adolescent mental health [2], three out of 10 adults aged 16 years and above suffer from some form of mental health issues. Mental health issues are triggered by many factors such as economics, social, environmental and cultural factors [1]. The recent global factor for mental health issues is the COVID-19 pandemic. This pandemic changed everything in the world; the way things are done, people's lifestyle, perspectives, daily routine, education and many more [3]. COVID-19 has forced everyone worldwide to stay at home, work, and study online.

In Malaysia, the government has set the "stay at home" order to control the pandemic. With the enforcement of such an order, people are at home working online and all levels of education are conducted online, including tertiary education. Students started to learn from home. Past studies indicate that university students were already having mental health crisis before the pandemic [4, 5]. These study results show that university students are more prevalent to experience depression and anxiety compared to the general population. Now with the pandemic, the stress level of the students has increased [6]. They have to stay at home all the time, cannot see their friends and some of them are staying alone near the university campus far from their home. Furthermore, the lectures are held online without the normal physical touch. All these contribute to their mental health well-being, causing anxiety, depression, and unwanted feelings. Researchers have found that students' education does get affected by poor mental health [7].

2 Literature Review

The instability situation of COVID-19 has created uncertainty for many industries, some businesses were stagnant and some were struggling however few were sustaining and education is listed as an on-going process. Higher education has decided to adopt online teaching and learning platform to safeguard students, administrative staff and lecturers from exposing towards the deadly virus and lower the risk of further transmission of the virus. This movement brought a very positive response from various parties in the absence of focusing at the core of the matter. At the beginning of the implementation, it was effective however as semester goes by the online learning became susceptible to psychological issues for students. According to Patricia Aguilera-Hermida [8], university students complained that stress level is at the peak due to online learning and completing their assignments. Some of the challenges shared by the students were exhausted looking at the screen, lack of peer tutoring and library resources and virtual communication with professors not as effective as physical. Bower [9] added that limitation on social connection and cognitive engagement among students due to online learning has an effect on mental health.

According to Horita et al. [10], the finding shows students are going through distress in terms of mental health since they need to get ready to accept e-learning which is completely new norm for the students. Students' preparation for facing a drastic transition in a short period of time on mode of learning could cause shock to the state of mind. It is further supported that students find it difficult to absorb the online continuous assessment because shifting to online mode happens at a quick manner [11]. In a study conducted by Hamza et al. [12], students without previous mental health issues experienced tremendous challenges on mental health such as sadness, depressive and anxiety symptoms as well as burdensomeness due to online learning transition. Khattar et al. [13] added prolonged closure of universities and remote learning due to pandemic has adversely affected mental health of students. It is because remote learning isolated the students from engaging with others compare with physical classes, viewing the screen long could cause eye problem, frustration due to lack of access to resources and lack of personal one to one contact with students and lecturers has detrimental effects on mental development of students.

Several statistical studies were conducted for the past one year to evaluate the mental health status of university students during the pandemic COVID-19. Akhtarul Islam et al. [14] applied Binary logistic regression to identify variables that influencing depression and anxiety among students, while Son et al. [15] analyzed the collected data through descriptive statistics and thematic analysis to analyze the students' demographics and level of stress respectively. Other similar studies that used statistical approach include [16–18].

3 Data Sets

In this study, a total of 215 responses have been obtained from students from a private university in Malaysia which intends to find relationships between attributes of the academic background of student and their mental health being characteristics in terms of mental overload, ergonomic settings, and physical risks of injuries. This study is unique in that it used the non-parameter clustering technique to group students based on the aforementioned attributes to find its relationships. In addition to looking into attributes or factors related to mental health and demographics of student, factors related to ergonomic setting and physical injuries have also been taken into account to ensure the completeness of investigation on mental health well-being for students. The aforementioned responses were collected via a survey consisting of questions related to the aforementioned attributes and they were grouped into demographic, mental overload, ergonomic settings and physical risk of injuries categories. A brief description of each of the four categories is shown in Table 1 below.

In the survey, there were 40 questions arranged in 4 sections which are open closed-ended questions type - yes no except for the demographic category where some of the questions are multiple-choice type.

Table 1. Description of survey categories

Category	Description
Demographics	To identify gender, age, academic performance, years of study
Physical risk of injuries	To identify the physical activities and effects faced by the students throughout handling classes from home
Mental overload	To investigate the level of stress faced by the students
Ergonomic settings	To identify the ergonomic workplace characteristics while studying at home

4   Data Pre-processing

As there were a lot of attributes in the survey and in order to make it easier to make a reference to each question particularly questions from ergonomic settings, physical risk of injuries mental overload categories, labels were used and tagged to questions. For an instance, the first question in the ergonomic settings category was labelled as E1, similarly, for the physical risk category, the third question was labelled as P3. All the responses that were collected were in the form of non-numeric and no conversion of data was made. Some attributes that were highly correlated in their respective category were removed to reduce the computational complexity.

In the next section, the concepts and examples of patterns derived using association rules methods will be presented.

5   Clustering Algorithms

The clustering technique is an unsupervised approach for analyzing data in statistics, machine learning, pattern recognition, and data mining. This technique allows similar objects or items to be collected together to form a group or cluster [19]. Each cluster contains objects that are similar to each other but dissimilar to the objects of other groups. When a dataset is composed of a set of attributes $A = \{gender, current\_study, e1, p2,...,\}$, attribute or feature clustering consists on partitioning them into a set of K disjoint clusters $C = \{C_1,..., C_K\}$ such that $\bigcup_{k=1}^{K} C_k = A$. The technique has been widely in various fields as reported in [20, 21].

Generally, clustering techniques have broadly been classified into two types, hierarchical and partitional. In this study, partitional clustering was used. Common algorithms in use for partitional clustering are *K-means*, *K-medoids*, *K-modes* and others. Despite *K-means* is commonly used in applications [22], it is only well known for clustering on numerical data. Since this study deals with categorical data, *K-medoids* was used instead. This algorithm is more robust than *K-means* and has the ability to deal with numerical and non-numerical data [23]. As for similarity measure to group or cluster attributes of non-numerical data, *simple matching coefficient (SMC)* was used [24]. Though there have been various variants and types of clustering algorithms and similar measures, we only used the basic *K-medoids* and *SMC*.

In this study, in order to measure the quality of clustering such as well separateness between clusters and objects within clusters, the index named *Davies–Bouldin (DBI)* [25] was used. A low value in the index signifies high intra-cluster similarity and low inter-cluster similarity. The main aim of any clustering algorithm is to produce a low index value of *Davies–Bouldin*. As partitional clustering requires determining k number of clusters before running *K-medoids*, we experimented with several *k-values* and chose the k-value which provides the lowest value of *DBI*. PyCharm IDE tools with Python and RapidMiner were used in this study as they are popular in academic research [26, 27].

6 Results and Discussion

A total of 8 distinct clusters or groups were formed from the dataset used in this study. The selection of the appropriate number of clusters (k-value) was determined using Davies–Bouldin index (DBI). The author experimented with several k-values ranging from 3 to 15 and found that the k-value of 8 produced the lowest value of DBI. In the next section, tables depicting cluster size and a description of clusters would be presented.

Table 2. Cluster size

Cluster No	Demographic description of clusters	Items
Cluster 1 (C1)	Male, 1st year, 3.00–3.49	39
Cluster 2 (C2)	Male, 3rd year, 2.00–2.99	31
Cluster 3 (C3)	Male, 2nd year, 2.00–2.99	30
Cluster 4 (C4)	Male, 3rd year, 3.50–4.00	10
Cluster 5 (C5)	Male, 1st year, 2.00–2.99	13
Cluster 6 (C6)	Female, 3rd year, 3.00–3.49	7
Cluster 7 (C7)	Male, 3rd year, 2.00–2.99	26
Cluster 8 (C8)	Male, 1st year, 3.50–4.00	59

Table 2 above shows that, cluster 8 *(C8)* appears to be the largest cluster while *C6* is the smallest. Generally, the proportion of female students is very much lower than the proportion of male students in the dataset. And this will be self-explanatory for the cluster size *C6*. Clusters *C1, C2, C3* and *C7* are quite uniform in size. The total 8 clusters have good coverage of values for the current *year of study* of student and *CGPA* demographic attributes. This will facilitate comparing demographic category with mental stress, ergonomic and physical risk categories between clusters which are presented in Table 3.

Table 3 shows that all the clusters except for C8, have high potential for physical risks of injuries regardless of *gender, year of student* and *CGPA*. Students from these groups of clusters experienced and suffered physical strains on their body parts such as the spinal cord, muscles, joints and eyes. These clusters which exhibit lack of good ergonomic

Table 3. Description of clusters

Cluster label	Demographics	Mental stress level	Ergonomic settings	Physical risks of injuries
C1	Male, 1st year, 3–3.4	No signs of depression and high stress level, but lack of interest and interactions during OTL is evident	Conducive environment for OTL but lack of ergonomic support for sitting posture (spinal/back)	High physical risks
C2	Male, 3rd year, 2–2.9	No signs of depression and high stress level but lack of interest during OTL is evident	Conducive environment for OTL and good ergonomic support	Moderate to High physical risks
C3	Male, 2nd year, 2–2.9	Mental overload is evident despite no signs of depression, lack of interest and interactions during OTL	Modest environment for OTL but lack of ergonomic support for sitting posture (spinal/back)	High physical risks
C4	Male, 3rd year, 3.5–4	Indication of depression and lack of interactions are present despite no signs of mental overload and lack of interest and interactions during OTL	Poor ergonomic settings	High physical risks
C5	Male, 1st year, 2–2.9	Signs of depression, lack of interest and interactions during OTL are present	Conducive environment for OTL but lack of ergonomic support for sitting posture (spinal/back)	High physical risks

(*continued*)

Table 3. (*continued*)

Cluster label	Demographics	Mental stress level	Ergonomic settings	Physical risks of injuries
C6	Female, 3rd year, 3–3.4	Signs of depression, lack of interest and interactions during OTL are present	Poor in ergonomic settings and OTL environment	High physical risks
C7	Male, 3rd year, 2–2.9	Signs of depression, lack of interest and interactions during OTL are present	Conducive environment for OTL and modest ergonomic support	High physical risks
C8	Male, 1st year, 3.5–4	Overall better mental resilience, no signs of depression and lack of interest and interactions during OTL are evident	Conducive environment for OTL and good ergonomic support	Low physical risks

support could be the strong reason for students vulnerable to having high physical risk of injuries. With the exception of *C8* cluster, where students from this cluster were found to be having low in physical risks of injuries. A conducive environment and good ergonomic support are the main reasons preventing them from experiencing physical strains during OTL. When this cluster *(C8)* is compared with other clusters *(C1, C5)* where the former and the latter have commonalities in the *year of study* and *gender* but varies in *cgpa*, certainly the perception between these two groups of students varies in terms of ergonomic settings at home. Students from *C8* cluster may have the perception that the OTL may continue for a longer period of time due to COVID-19 pandemic and driven by their desire to maintain *cgpa* hence they are willing to invest in establishing good ergonomic settings at home. However, the students from *C1* and *C5* clusters may think otherwise.

Generally, students in the *third* year of study cluster particularly clusters *(C4, C6, C7)* regardless of *cgpa* and *gender* were found to be giving less importance to ergonomic settings at home. This group of students is nearing the completion of studies and they may have the perception that investing in equipment or tools that have good ergonomic support may not be worthwhile. The irony is that the same group of students was experiencing mental depressions and boredom during OTL. This could be due to the fact that the students were not prepared for OTL in terms of lesson delivery and assessment. They have been accustomed to face-face physical teaching and learning and abrupt change in teaching and learning methods may have led them to mental depressions.

In short, delivering lessons via OTL in the face of the COVID-19 pandemic has an adverse impact on students regardless of their academic performance, gender and year of study. In the long term, high mental stress, poor ergonomic settings, alongside high potential risk of injuries facing them can be detrimental to their health and academic performance. Certainly, the management of a university can step in to mitigate the aforementioned impacts on students. For instance, the management can set up a special committee to extend emotional support and to conduct special workshops to create awareness on health risks for clusters particularly *C4, C5, C6, C7* that are acute in terms of mental stress and physical risks of injuries. As for clusters *C1, C2* where students demonstrated lack of interest in OTL, the management with the assistance of academics should look into the current teaching and learning strategies in OTL to improve the delivery of lessons that are interesting and effective. Apart from that, the cluster size shown in Table 2 can be useful for the management in prioritizing formulating of solutions and their executions on clusters. In the event of immediate execution of the solutions with limited resources at hand, the management could target larger clusters over smaller clusters. On the whole, the clustering technique used in this study allows the management to identify the shortcomings facing different clusters and subsequently formulate different strategies and solutions based on the characteristics of clusters presented in Table 3.

7   Conclusion

This study investigates the patterns of academic background, mental state, physical risk and ergonomic settings among students at the private university in Malaysia in using OTL during the pandemic COVID-19. The patterns indicated that high mental stress, poor ergonomic settings, alongside high potential risk of injuries were present in students in the clusters regardless of academic background. In particular, the two groups of clusters namely *C4, C5, C6, C7* and *C1, C2* need immediate attention in respect of mental, health and pedagogy support. The adverse effects affecting students are more apparent during the pandemic. In view of this, the management of university, family members and university stakeholders should play their roles by providing students with psychological support, comfortable study workspace, appropriate pedagogy support. Future work will compare k-medoids algorithm with other algorithms in the clustering technique to observe for any variation of patterns.

References

1. Barry, M.M., Clarke, A.M., Petersen, I., Jenkins, R. (eds.): Implementing Mental Health Promotion. Springer, Heidelberg (2019)
2. National Health and Morbidity Survey: Adolescent Mental Health, Ministry of Health, Malaysia (2017)
3. Pfefferbaum, B., North, C.S.: Mental health and the Covid-19 pandemic. New Engl. J. Med. **383**(6), 510–512 (2020)
4. Pedrelli, P., Nyer, M., Yeung, A., Zulauf, C., Wilens, T.: College students: mental health problems and treatment considerations. Acad. Psychiatry **39**(5), 503–511 (2014)

5. Evans, T.M., Bira, L., Gastelum, J.B., Weiss, L.T., Vanderford, N.L.: Evidence for a mental health crisis in graduate education. Nat. Biotechnol. **36**(3), 282–284 (2018)
6. Elsalem, L., Al-Azzam, N., Jum'ah, A.A., Obeidat, N., Sindiani, A.M., Kheirallah, K.A.: Stress and behavioral changes with remote E-exams during the Covid-19 pandemic: a cross-sectional study among undergraduates of medical sciences. Ann. Med. Surg. **60**, 271–279 (2020)
7. Cornaglia, F., Crivellaro, E., McNally, S.: Mental health and education decisions. Lab. Econ. **33**, 1–12 (2015)
8. Aguilera-Hermida, A.P.: College students' use and acceptance of emergency online learning due to COVID-19. Int. J. Educ. Res. Open **1**, 100011 (2020)
9. Bower, M.: Technology-mediated learning theory. Brit. J. Educ. Technol. **50**, 1035–1048 (2019)
10. Horita, R., Nishio, A., Yamamoto, M.: The effect of remote learning on the mental health of first year university students in Japan. Psychiatry Res. **295**, 113561 (2021)
11. Sahu, P.: Closure of universities due to coronavirus disease 2019 (COVID-19): impact on education and mental health of students and academic staff. Cureus **12**(4), e7541 (2020)
12. Hamza, C.A., Ewing, L., Heath, N.L., Goldstein, A.L.: When social isolation is nothing new: a longitudinal study psychological distress during COVID-19 among university students with and without pre-existing mental health concerns. Can Psychol/Psychologie Canadienne (2020)
13. Khattar, A., Jain, P.R., Quadri, S.M.K.: Effects of the disastrous pandemic COVID 19 on learning styles, activities and mental health of young Indian students-a machine learning approach. In: 2020 4th International Conference on Intelligent Computing and Control Systems (ICICCS), pp. 1190–1195 (2020)
14. Akhtarul Islam, M., Barna, S.D., Raihan, H., Nafiul Alam Khan, M., Tanvir Hossain, M.: Depression and anxiety among university students during the COVID-19 pandemic in Bangladesh: A web-based cross-sectional survey. In: PLoS ONE, 15(8 August), pp. 1–12 (2020)
15. Son, C., Hegde, S., Smith, A., Wang, X., Sasangohar, F.: Effects of COVID-19 on college students' mental health in the United States: interview survey study. J. Med. Internet Res. **22**(9), 1–14 (2020)
16. Aiyer, A., Surani, S., Gill, Y., Iyer, R., Surani, Z.: Mental health impact of COVID-19 on students in the USA: a cross-sectional web-based survey. J. Depression Anxiety **9**(5), 375 (2020)
17. Wathelet, M., Duhem, S., Vaiva, G., Baubet, T., Habran, E., Veerapa, E., Debien, C., Molenda, S., Horn, M., Grandgenèvre, P., Notredame, C.E., D'Hondt, F.: Factors associated with mental health disorders among university students in France confined during the COVID-19 pandemic. JAMA Netw. Open **3**(10), e2025591 (2020)
18. Abisha Meji, M., Dennison, M.S.: Survey on general awareness, mental state and academic difficulties among students due to COVID-19 outbreak in the western regions of Uganda. Heliyon **6**(11), e05454 (2020)
19. Dutt, A., Ismail, M.A.: A Systematic review on educational data mining. Int. J. Comput. Commun. Netw. **9**(3), 39–42 (2020)
20. Althari, S., Najmi, L.A., Bennett, A.J., Aukrust, I., Rundle, J.K., Colclough, K., Molnes, J., Kaci, A., Nawaz, S., van der Lugt, T., Hassanali, N., Mahajan, A., Molven, A., Ellard, S., McCarthy, M.I., Bjørkhaug, L., Njølstad, P.R., Gloyn, A.L.: Unsupervised clustering of missense variants in HNF1A using multidimensional functional data aids clinical interpretation. Am. J. Hum. Genet. **107**(4), 670–682 (2020)
21. Shalchyan, V., Farina, D.: A non-parametric Bayesian approach for clustering and tracking non-stationarities of neural spikes. J. Neurosci. Methods **223**, 85–91 (2014)

22. Elmer, J., Jones, B.L.: Nagin DS (2020) Comparison of parametric and nonparametric methods for outcome prediction using longitudinal data after cardiac arrest. Resuscitation **148**, 152–160 (2019)
23. Nirmal, S.: Comparative study between K-means and K-medoids clustering algorithms. Int. Res. J. Eng. Technol. **6**(3), 839–844 (2019)
24. Xavier, J.C., Canuto, A.M.P., Almeida, N.D., Goncalves, L.M.G.: A comparative analysis of dissimilarity measures for clustering categorical data. In: Proceedings of the International Joint Conference on Neural Networks, pp. 1–8 (2013)
25. Sitompul, B.J.D., Sitompul, O.S., Sihombing, P.: Enhancement clustering evaluation result of davies-bouldin index with determining initial centroid of k-means algorithm. J. Phys. Conf. Ser. **1235**(1), 1–6 (2019)
26. Naik, A., Samant, L.: correlation review of classification algorithm using data mining tool: WEKA, Rapidminer, Tanagra, Orange and Knime. Procedia Comput. Sci. **85**(Cms), 662–668 (2016)
27. Shetty, A.R., Ahmed, F.B., Naik, V.M.: CKD prediction using data mining technique as SVM and KNN With pycharm. Int. Res. J. Eng. Technol. **06**(05), 4399–4405 (2019)

Ergonomics Checkpoints for Educational Environments

Lawrence J. H. Schulze[✉]

IEA Committee for Ergonomics for Children in Educational Environments, Department of Industrial Engineering, University of Houston, Houston, TX 77204-4008, USA
ljhs@uh.edu

Abstract. The IEA's Committee on Ergonomics for Children in Educational Environments originally focused on ergonomic initiatives in educational environments and studies that have used children as the participants in their research effort(s). However, as the committee has grown in size and diversity of its membership, it was soon realized that there are a number of aspects of children and ergonomics that are inseparable. As technology has been integrated into nearly every student's life from Pre-K though college the effort has been expanded to include all educational environments. Due to the emergence of SARS-COV-2 (COVID-19), additional emphasis is now being focused on the learning from home environment. The approach taken here is to provide examples, not an exhaustive nor complete summary of the efforts that are either on-going or should be started that are focused on ergonomics in educational environments. Ergonomics Checkpoints have been developed to date, provide guidelines for educational environments that teach a generation or generations of young people who will bridge the gap between children to whom no ergonomic thought has been given regarding their exposures to adult-like conditions and a generation or generations who will have everything ergonomic. More research will need to be conducted, better definitions and guidelines will need to be developed, and education and training of all people involved with children, from students, parents, and teachers to furniture manufacturers and school purchasing agents will have to be provided. Specific examples of Ergonomic Checkpoints, from furniture through functional environment are be presented.

Keywords: Ergonomics · Children · Educational environments

1 Introduction and Background

Ergonomic studies involving children is increasingly being accorded the importance it rightly deserves. For instance, the Institute of Ergonomics & Human Factors [1] in the United Kingdom has supported the development of a website known as "Ergonomic 4 Schools". The initiative presents a practical and interactive approach towards the promotion and adoption of ergonomics principles related to children and their specific needs within a school environment. The website aims to promote learning about ergonomics among high school students.

© The Author(s), under exclusive license to Springer Nature Switzerland AG 2021
N. L. Black et al. (Eds.): IEA 2021, LNNS 220, pp. 123–129, 2021.
https://doi.org/10.1007/978-3-030-74605-6_15

The International Ergonomics Association (IEA) has a technical committee called the "Ergonomics for Children in Education Environments" (ECEE) formed in 2000 by Cheryl Bennet [2]. This committee has focused on bringing together research (related to issues associated with children) from around the world within an educational framework. ECEE looks at a range of emerging issues, ranging from the use of computers in the education environment to load-bearing activities such as the carrying of backpacks by children and now the home-schooling environment. In addition, the ECEE is now in the ISO TC59/SC16 Working Group Accessibility an Usability of the Built Environment focussing on Children with Disabilities.

The checkpoints are developed for both existing and emerging educational environments in which an anthropometric variety of students use the same or similar educational environment(s) and in which technology is being continuously integrated in hopes of enhancing the educational experience.

2 Method

The checkpoints focused on educational environments follow the format of the Ergonomics Checkpoints previously published by the IEA [3]. The checkpoints are based on reviewing published research. The sources are not limited to 'ergonomics' related research but include educational science, psychology, medicine, physical therapy, etc. to ensure that the recommendations that are made are as widely applicable as possible.

The checkpoints are designed to be applicable worldwide and across a wide range of individual characteristics and include both formal teaching environments and home-school environments. The checkpoints were developed to address the following topics of interest: (1) Accommodation (physical and cognitive); (2) environment (heating, air conditioning, ventilation, temperature, etc.); (3) furniture (classroom and home); (4) Health (diet, exercise, general health, posture, hygiene, backpack use, etc.); (5) teaching methods; (6) technology (the use and integration of technology in teaching environments); and (7) transportation (to, from and in-and-around educational environments including way-finding). Other topic areas are welcome and encouraged.

This effort is not exclusive only to the IEA ECEE, any individual with an interest in ensuring that children are provided the best environment in which to learn and thrive are encouraged to participate. As Schulze [4] and Schulze and Ginsberg [5] indicated, ergonomics for children will be impacted by current and future technology development and implementation.

3 Results

Example Ergonomic Checkpoints are presented below following the format of Ergonomic checkpoints created by the International Ergonomics Association [3]. The example checkpoints presented here are a timely focus on the home-school environment that has become an increasing focus due to the SARS-COV-19 pandemic.

3.1 Ergonomic Checkpoint 1

Ensure multiple breaks throughout the day for outdoor activity.

Why?: As children spend more time in front of the screen, they increase their chances of vision problems such as myopia. A study in the Investigative Ophthalmology and Visual Science journal was able to show that elementary aged students who spent greater than 10 h a week outside or doing outdoor sports decreased their chances of developing myopia in their middle school ages [6].

Risks/Symptoms

- Myopia
- Blurry Vision
- Eye strain

How

1) Schedule times during children's home school day to allow for outdoor breaks.
2) Allow students to partake in after school outdoor sports if accessible.

More Hints
Encourage students to spend time outdoors.

Points to Remember
Increase student's outdoor time.

3.2 Ergonomic Checkpoint 2

Adjust room lighting for optimal viewing of computer screen.

Why?: Oftentimes, students are in environments that are not conducive to proper viewing of computer screens. The computer may be in an environment that is too bright and can cause a glare on the screen. Screen glaring can potentially lead to Computer Vision Syndrome (CVS).

Risks/Symptoms

- Computer eye syndrome

How

1) Reduce lighting in the room that computers and laptops are in to ensure there is not a glare on screen.
2) In order to prevent glare, do not place the computer or laptop screen directly in front of a window. Computers should try to be out of direct sunlight or should be perpendicular to windows. Example can be seen in Fig. 1 below.

Fig. 1. Graphic depicting a person sitting at a desk near a window. Left side shows improper placement of the screen near the window. Right side shows proper placement of the screen near a window (graphics by Mary Scurlock).

More Hints
If you cannot adjust the lighting in the room or placement of the computer, The American Optometric Association recommends obtaining a glare filter for your computer screen [7]. Most flat panel and laptop displays are glare-reducing except for displays and laptops design for gaming or for enhancement of video presentation.

Points to Remember
Adjust lighting in the room or the computer's position near a window when using the computer to prevent glare.

3.3   Ergonomic Checkpoint 3

Incorporate use of desktop computers instead of laptop computers when students need to use computers.

Why?: According to a study done by Straker et al., utilizing laptop computers increases neck strain in users, causing neck pain and poor posture (1997). In this study, the average neck angle for a laptop computer was 57.3° and the average neck angle for a desktop computer was 50.8°. It suggested that laptop use equated to poorer posture. It also suggested a trend of increased neck pain due to poorer neck postures when using laptops [8].

Risks/Symptoms

- Poor posture
- Neck Pain

How

1) Utilize desktop computers over laptop computers when possible.

Points to Remember
Desktop computers put less strain on a student's neck.

3.4 Ergonomic Checkpoint 4

Educate parents to help promote healthy behavior for children.

Why?: Many parents believe that schools should be primarily responsible for educating their child on healthy eating habits [9]. Most of these parents have a lack of knowledge on dietary and exercise habits that should be met for their children.

Risks/Symptoms

- Type II diabetes
- Weight gain\Obesity
- Cardiovascular disease

How

1) Parents should learn about dietary guidelines.
2) Parents should start teaching their kids about the importance of eating healthy and exercising.
3) Parents and teachers should have good communication to identify any health issues with students.

More Hints
If parent does not participate or get involved, his/her student's health problems due to bad eating habits and lack of exercise will be higher.

Points to Remember
Parents are an important part in the growth of the student. Improving parental health habits and awareness can lead to a healthy student (Fig. 2).

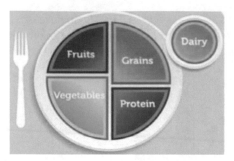

Fig. 2. Choose my plate proportions [10].

4 Discussion and Recommendations

As can bee seen from these few examples, Ergonomic Checkpoints for Educational Environments has the potential to positively effect the present and future of those who are our future. What more needs to be done to remedy the situation and create a healthier and safer environment for the children? The following are recommendations, not all inclusive, for what should be done to promote the proper use of ergonomics for children. If there are additional recommendations that are deemed important, they should be sent to the corresponding author for inclusion in these important efforts.

A. Collect anthropometric data for all grade levels for use in furniture specification and design
B. Develop ergonomic guidelines for the use of technology in schools;
C. Develop ergonomic guidelines for use of technology in homes
D. Educate furniture designers/manufacturers regarding furniture adjustability
E. Train teachers, students, parents, and purchasing agents of school districts in the principles and application of ergonomics
F. Conduct more evaluations of classroom conditions
G. Conduct epidemiological studies to identify the impact of technology, including computer games, on the health of children
H. Conduct studies comparing workstation configuration and child anthropometry in homes
I. Conduct studies comparing workstation configuration and child anthropometry in publicly accessible places such as libraries
J. Develop additional on-line ergonomics assistance for home and school computer use and include assistance for the use of laptop computers
K. Conduct research on the long-term effects of poor ergonomics on children
L. Develop assistance for parents in understanding the relationship between their children's health, activity levels, exposure to technology and the development of cumulative trauma disorders later in life.

References

1. Legg, S.: Ergonomics in schools (editorial). Ergonomics **50**(10), 1523–2529 (2007)
2. IEHF. Ergonomics4Schools.com (2010). www.ergonomics4schools.com
3. International Labour Office. Ergonomics Checkpoints: Practical and easy-to-Implement Solutions for Improving Safety, health and Working Conditions, Geneva (1996)
4. Schulze, L.J.H.: ErgoKids: how will future generations deal with current exposures. International Ergonomics Association. Seoul, Korea (2003)
5. Schulze, L.J.H., Ginsburg, R.A.: ErgoKids 2: protecting today's children from tomorrow's pain. In: Schulze, L.J.H. (ed.) Building Bridges to Healthy Workplaces (2004)
6. Jones, L.A., Sinnott, L.T., Mutti, D.O., Mitchell, G.L., Moeschberger, M.L., Zadnik, K.: Parental history of myopia, sports and outdoor activities, and future myopia. Invest. Ophthalmol. Visual Sci. **48**(8), 3524 (2007) https://doi.org/10.1167/iovs.06-1118
7. Computer Vision Syndrome (Digital eye strain) (n.d.). https://www.aoa.org/healthy-eyes/eye-and-vision-conditions/computer-vision-syndrome?sso=y
8. Straker, L., Jones, K.J., Miller, J.: A comparison of the postures assumed when using laptop computers and desktop computers. Appl. Ergonomics **28**(4), 263–268 (1997)
9. Hart, K.H., Herriot, A., Bisop, J.A., Truby, H.: Promoting healthy diet and exercise patterns amongst primary school children: a qualitative investigation of parental perspectives. J. Human Nutr. Diet **16**(2), 89–96 (2003)
10. United States Department of Agriculture. Choose my plate. https://www.myplate.gov/sites/default/files/styles/large/public/2020-11/myplate-brand--labelled.png?itok=m2Kvz_MN

Distance Ergonomics Laboratory Using Flipped Classroom and Smartphone Application as Learning Tools – A Case Study

Liyun Yang[1,2]([✉]) [iD], Malin Håkansson[2] [iD], Malin Engquist[3] [iD], Carl Mikael Lind[1] [iD], and Linda Barman[3] [iD]

[1] Institute of Environmental Medicine, Karolinska Institutet, Stockholm, Sweden
Liyun.yang@ki.se
[2] Division of Ergonomics, School of Engineering Sciences in Chemistry, Biotechnology and Health, KTH Royal Institute of Technology, Stockholm, Sweden
[3] Department of Learning in Engineering Sciences, School of Industrial Engineering and Management, KTH Royal Institute of Technology, Stockholm, Sweden

Abstract. Distance laboratory training in ergonomics with a flipped-classroom approach and smartphone applications as a tool was designed, implemented, and evaluated at two Swedish universities. Most students (10/13) were satisfied with the laboratory training. In this small-scale study, sufficient preparation time, tailored instructions and timely support during the pre-lab work were identified as factors that may improve students' learning. This case study points to that distance laboratory training can be a feasible method in future ergonomics education. The findings also contribute to better understanding on the design of distance laboratory training in the future.

Keywords: Ergonomics education · Digital learning · Distance education · Laboratory · Flipped classroom

1 Introduction

The U.S. National Center for Education Statistics reported over 6.6 million students who took at least one distance education course in postsecondary institutions in 2018, which equals to a proportion of 33% of the total students enrolled [1]. In the European Union in 2019, 8% of people aged 16 to 74 reported that they took an online course in the last 3 months, and in the top two countries Finland and Sweden the percentages were 21 and 18% [2]. The growth in distance education is anticipated, but it has also been escalated during the COVID-19 pandemic when schools and universities were required to transform to distance learning [3]. Such transformation has created new challenges, such as to conduct laboratory work at a distance. Examples of various forms of laboratory training outside of a traditional laboratory space include: online laboratory, where the learners access simulated experiments or instruments through internet; remote

N. L. Black et al. (Eds.): IEA 2021, LNNS 220, pp. 130–134, 2021.
https://doi.org/10.1007/978-3-030-74605-6_16

laboratory, where the learner access real experiment or instrument virtually through internet; and distance laboratory, where the learner perform hands-on experiment at home through e.g. take-home lab kits [4]. Laboratory training is essential for students to gain a deeper understanding of ergonomics and to apply current methods in practice. Traditionally, students gain pre- and post-laboratory thinking by reading and attending lectures/seminars, but perform the ergonomics assessments using various tools/methods in the classroom setting. When laboratory training needs to be performed off-campus, it can be a challenge for the educators to provide a beneficial lab environment.

Facing the COVID-19 pandemic, the laboratory trainings in two master courses in ergonomics at two Swedish universities were rapidly changed from campus to distance education. Currently, the research is scarce on how educators can provide high quality ergonomics laboratory trainings at a distance [5] and how students perceive these distance laboratory trainings in ergonomics. In addition, with an expected increase in distance laboratory training, such knowledge is needed for guidance and improvement of distance ergonomics laboratory in the future.

This study aims to evaluate how students perceive distance laboratory training in ergonomics and to identify what factors the students' perceived as facilitating and hindering their learning.

2   Methods

The distance laboratory training was held at two universities, with five students in a technical university (TechUniv) and 15 students in a medical university (MedUniv). The participating students from the TechUniv were in their first year of a two-year full-time master program in Technology, Work and Health, which used to have on-campus education. The participants from the MedUniv were in their second semester of a two-year half-time master programme in Work and Health, which, before the pandemic, used to have a combination of distance education for lectures and group work, and on-campus laboratory trainings and supervisions. For the distance laboratory training, the intended learning outcome was that students will learn about how to evaluate work postures using technical measurement methods, analyze the data and present risk assessment results. The focus of the lab exercise was the risk assessment of the upper arm postures and movements, using a freely available and validated smartphone application – ErgoArmMeter [6]. The laboratory training was performed using a flipped-classroom approach.

Before the online seminar, the students were provided with instructions regarding the topic and what they were expected to prepare. The students at the MedUniv received the instructions two days before the online seminar, whilst the students from the TechUniv had one week to read and perform exercises. Students at the TechUniv also received a sport armband to put the smartphone on their arms, whilst students at the MedUniv were instructed to use their own sport armband or find alternative ways to put the smartphone on the arm, such as a rubber band, due to limited resources. The lab instructions included reading of one book chapter on "Work in awkward postures", a three-page lab instruction including the user manual for the app, and a five-minute video lecture. They were instructed to perform an ergonomics assessment of themselves or another person available at home for a cleaning or another self-chosen task involving arm movements for about five minutes, using the ErgoArmMeter. The students were instructed to either video record their performance, or to write down timeframes of each subtask for later analysis. After the assessment, they were expected to analyse the summative result from the app, plot the measurement data in a time sequence using Microsoft Excel, and prepare a 5-min presentation for the seminar regarding their findings. The students were also provided with questions aiming to trigger their reflections about how to interpret the risk assessment result and identify strenuous subtasks, how to improve the work task, as well as advantages and disadvantages of the applied assessment method.

During the online seminar, which lasted about one hour, students presented their results and discussed about the difficulties and reflections on the assessment task together with the teacher. The seminar with the TechUniv students were conducted in the whole group setting since only 5 students were present whilst the MedUniv students conducted their presentations in smaller groups and the teacher visited each Zoom break-out room to listen and to comment. The students at the MedUniv had a tighter schedule with several other online sessions held on the same day of this online seminar.

Seven weeks after the seminar, the students received an online questionnaire. Four students from the TechUniv and 9 from the MedUniv replied. The questionnaire included the students' educational background, previous experiences of distance education, satisfaction and preparation time for the lab. It also included open questions on students' experiences of the difficult/challenging and positive aspects regarding the lab, and the support needed. The questionnaire results were analysed with Microsoft Excel (Microsoft Corp., Redmond, WA, USA) using descriptive statistics for quantitative data and thematic analysis for qualitative data.

3   Results

All students participating in this study from the TechUniv and two thirds of students at MedUniv were satisfied with the distance lab. Previous experiences of distance learning were not positively associated with the students' learning experience of the distance laboratory training. However, individually reported preparation time was found to be moderately associated with students' satisfaction of the lab ($r = 0.36$).

The four students participating in this study from the Tech-university, stated that they received sufficient support. The students expressed that they could perform the task by themselves beforehand and that the seminar focused on analysing results. They were also satisfied with the time to perform the task before the seminar, the clear instructions, and that the teachers were available during the whole course.

At Med-university, 6/9 of the students reported having difficulty analysing data using Microsoft Excel and wished for clearer instructions about how to use Excel for this purpose. One reason for this difficulty, that became clear during the online seminar, was the different terms used for the decimal settings in the software as instructed in the video (in English, using period '.') versus the settings in the students' computers (in Swedish, using comma ','). Five of the students also reported having too little time to prepare for the lab and they would need more time for reading instructions and perform the tasks. A few students ($n = 3$) stated more breaks were needed during the day when this online seminar took place, as they had to attend several other online sessions from the same course on the day as well. Two students reported that they had preferred to perform laboratory-work on site instead of at a distance. Still, three students appreciated conducting the task by themselves and two students stated the laboratory went well.

4 Discussion

This case study evaluated how students perceive the distance laboratory training in ergonomics and what factors the students perceived as facilitating and hindering their learning. Most (10/13) students in both universities were satisfied with the distance laboratory training. However, distinctive differences in how the two student groups perceived the distance laboratory were reported. One factor was the time that students had to perform the lab task (risk assessment) before the online seminar. The timeframe between instructions and sessions, is one important pillar in the flipped classroom approach. In this case, the laboratory exercise was performed individually by the students, but only the TechUniv students had sufficient time to do the lab work, due to the rapid shift during the pandemic.

Another factor was students' previous knowledge of relevant software, as students at MedUniv expressed the need for clearer guidelines of software use. The different settings of the software in the teacher's versus students' computer also led to the difficulty for students at MedUniv to perform one of the data analysis task during the pre-lab work. Extra support, in forms of e.g. live online instruction before the seminar may help to solve the potential software problem timely and improve students' learning. This was also in accordance with previous findings about the barrier to asking timely questions in non-traditional labs [4].

A limited number of students were involved in this evaluation study. However, the reply-rates were quite high, and since there are very few studies about distance laboratory training in ergonomics, these findings are of relevance to educators. The size of the groups also differed between the two universities, as students at MedUniv were divided into break-out rooms when presenting their pre-lab work. However, the effect of group sizes was not examined in the study.

Still, this case study showed that it is feasible to perform ergonomic laboratory training at a distance with most of the students being satisfied. The satisfaction rate was comparably much higher than those reported by students from a chemical engineering program, where only about 45% of students agreed the designed online lab work was useful [3]. Future studies can involve larger student groups and look at different lab designs and how they affect students' learning.

5 Conclusions

To conclude, the design of the distance ergonomics laboratory using the flipped-classroom format and valid smartphone applications points to a potential for future distance laboratory training, or online workshops with the aim to educate usage of ergonomics tools and methods. Enough preparation time, tailored instruction based on the need of student groups and timely support during the pre-lab work were identified as factors that may improve students' learning.

References

1. Snyder, T.D., de Brey, C., Dillow, S.A.: Digest of education statistics 2018, 54th Ed. NCES 2020–009 (2018). https://nces.ed.gov/programs/digest/d18/
2. Eurostat. People expanding their knowledge by learning online. Accessed 25 Jan 2020, https://ec.europa.eu/eurostat/web/products-eurostat-news/-/EDN-20200517-1
3. Dietrich, N., Kentheswaran, K., Ahmadi, A., Teychené, J., Bessière, Y., Alfenore, S., Laborie, S., Bastoul, D., Loubière, K., Guigui, C., Sperandio, M., Barna, L., Paul, E., Cabassud, C., Liné, A., Hébrard, G.: Attempts, successes, and failures of distance learning in the time of covid-19. J. Chem. Educ. **97**(9), 2448–2457 (2020)
4. Faulconer, E.K., Gruss, A.B.: A review to weigh the pros and cons of online, remote, and distance science laboratory experiences. Int. Rev. Res. Open Dist. Learn. **19**(2), 155–168 (2018)
5. Duarte, W.A.H., Bernal, L.G.G.: Teaching-learning ergonomics in virtual and distance education: bibliometric review. In: Advances in Intelligent Systems and Computing, vol. 1211 AISC, pp. 112–117 (2020)
6. Yang, L., Grooten, W.J.A., Forsman, M.: An iPhone application for upper arm posture and movement measurements. Appl. Ergonomics **65**, 492–500 (2017)

Part III: Ergonomics in Design for All (Edited by Isabella Tiziana Steffan and Ken Sagawa)

Seniors' Perception of Smart Speakers: Challenges and Opportunities Elicited in the Silver&Home Living Lab

Leonardo Angelini[1]([⊠]) [iD], Maurizio Caon[2] [iD], Emmanuel Michielan[3],
Omar Abou Khaled[1] [iD], and Elena Mugellini[1] [iD]

[1] HumanTech Institute, HES-SO, 1705 Fribourg, Switzerland
{leonardo.angelini,omar.aboukhaled,elena.mugellini}@hes-so.ch
[2] School of Management, HES-SO, 1705 Fribourg, Switzerland
maurizio.caon@hes-so.ch
[3] Pro Senectute Fribourg, 1705 Fribourg, Switzerland
emmanuel.michielan@fr.pro-senectute.ch

Abstract. As the European population is getting older, there is an increasing need in maintaining older adults living independently at home. Vocal assistants may offer various services that can be beneficial for senior citizens. In the context of the Silver&Home living lab, we tested the Google Home Smart speaker connected to smart lighting installation with 7 people to understand the strengths, weaknesses and possible usage for improving the quality of life of older adults. The test and the questions asked to participants were framed according to the Unified Theory on Acceptance and Use of Technology (UTAUT2). Participants generally appreciated the interaction with the smart speaker, although they also identified some barriers, such as the "OK Google" wakeword or the assistant speaking too fast for some answers. Finally, they considered it particularly adapted to people living alone.

1 Introduction

As the European population is getting older, there is an increasing need in maintaining older adults living independently at home. Vocal assistants integrated in smart speakers may offer various services that can be beneficial for senior citizens. Although smart speakers are nowadays particularly affordable and voice interaction is particularly robust, these devices were not built with seniors in mind as target users [1]. This might lead to services that are not appealing for older adults and to a mismatch between the mental model needed to interact with the device and the mental model that seniors actually adopt. On one side, as vocal interaction is a natural communication manner for seniors, they may adopt a mental model typical of human-human conversation, which brings to higher expectations compared to the conversation that vocal assistants can actually manage. On the other hand, when considering vocal assistants as a computer, seniors might borrow a mental model from the more familiar Graphical User Interfaces, which provide a more consistent and seamless experience (one icon corresponding to one outcome), compared to vocal assistants, which, conversely, may still suffer from speech misrecognition [2].

N. L. Black et al. (Eds.): IEA 2021, LNNS 220, pp. 137–144, 2021.
https://doi.org/10.1007/978-3-030-74605-6_17

In the context of the Silver&Home Living Lab in Switzerland, we conducted 4 test sessions to understand the appropriateness of this solution for older adults. During each test, each participant had the possibility to explore several features of the Google Home Smart speaker, including the possibility to control a smart lighting system. Our paper sheds additional light on opportunities and pitfalls of such devices.

To position our work, we report in Sect. 2 previous studies with commercial smart speakers. Then, we detail the testing methodology, in particular explaining the test environment of the Silver&Home living lab and the testing framework based on the UTAUT2 model [3]. Finally, in Sect. 4 we report the results of the tests, which are discussed in Sect. 5.

2 Related Work

2.1 Smart Speakers

First commercial release of Smart speakers dates to 2015, when Amazon release the Echo. Shortly after, in 2016, Google launched the Google Home (renamed as Google Nest in 2019) and, in 2018, Apple announced the HomePod. All these smart speakers rely on the respective proprietary conversational agent technology, which is also available in the smartphones. Worldwide adoption of smart speakers did not happen until 2018, when proper language models were trained for each country. As Switzerland has three national languages and its market is quite fragmented, Amazon Echo is still not officially available in this country. Smart speakers are actually mostly unknown by the older Swiss population. Since commercial smart speakers are targeting the very large public, their design may have forgotten the special needs of older adults. To better address older adults' needs, El Kamali et al. [4] co-designed a smart speaker and the underlying conversational agent together with older adults from four European countries. This device is still currently under test. In the next subsection, we discuss the insights collected by previous research on commercial smart speakers.

2.2 Previous Tests of Smart Speakers with Older Adults

Conversational agents for assisting older adults have been developed and tested since several years by the research community. However, smart speakers are nowadays proposing a mature technology to the mass at an affordable price and they open new interaction scenarios also for older adults. In order to assess the usability and usefulness perceived by older adults, recently, several researchers tested the Amazon Echo or Google Home with older adults.

Trajkova and Martin-Hammond [5] interviewed 36 seniors that were enrolled for testing the Amazon Echo in USA for over 1 year. Most of the users used seldom the device and only 18% used it daily. The authors reported that most common uses of the Echo were listening to music/radio, setting alarms/timers/reminders, asking for the weather and latest news. In general, non-adopters complained with the lack of useful functions, considering the device "a toy" rather than a device that can be beneficial for their life and well-being. Indeed, they wished that it could promote prevention plans and that could better integrate with health data (at the same time they were also scared by privacy issues). They also considered the Echo particularly useful for people with disabilities.

After testing the Amazon Echo Dot with 7 older adults with low technology proficiency, Pradhan et al. [6] analyzed the users' perception of the Alexa assistant in terms of social companionship. They found that Alexa was never clearly *personified* or *objectified*, but rather a mix between the two. Although users referred to it as "she" and as someone to talk to, they also considered Alexa often as a machine rather than as a person. Nevertheless, they often used politeness forms, for example for thanking Alexa. In a later article, [2] the authors reported that the most interesting features for the users were the possibility to look for health-related information and to set reminders for supporting memory (although this latter was seldom used in the end). Although participants had difficulties in identifying the right keywords for interacting and the experience was not faultless, they were still willing to continue using the device after the testing period.

Kowalski et al. [7] tested the Google Home speaker with seven older adults with good ICT skills in a living lab in Poland. The smart speaker was connected to a smart home setup composed by a lighting system, a TV and a fan connected to a Wi-Fi relay. Participants were particularly enthusiastic of the interaction possibilities enabled by the smart speaker and found that it increased the accessibility of smart home technology compared to screen-based interfaces.

The results of previous studies are often discordant and may depend on the users' ICT literacy level as well as on the way participants were interviewed or prompted in focus-group discussions, where ideas may converge towards stereotyped considerations for "other older adult end-users", rather than for themselves [8]. In the next sections we present our methodology, and we discuss how our results relate to previous studies.

3 Methods

3.1 Living Lab and Installation

Silver&Home is a living lab in Fribourg, Switzerland, aiming at sensitizing senior citizens and healthcare professionals to the opportunities that gerontechnologies can offer for increasing the seniors' quality of life. A 3.5-room apartment was furnished to recreate a senior's home environment and about 40 devices that can be used for improving the quality of older life were installed in this apartment. We invited senior citizens to visit this showroom with the purpose to discover such technology and to test some of the devices installed in the apartment. In particular, for this study, a Google Home Smart speaker was connected to the Homey home automation controller, to a Spotify account and to a Samsung smart TV. The Homey box controlled the ceiling lights through the Qubino wireless relays and a floor lamp through a smart plug. The lighting system could be controlled also with a wireless button (double click to switch on all lights and long press to switch off all lights) as well as with a smart frame able to recognize swipe gestures. Lights were associated to the different rooms in the apartment (bathroom, living room, kitchen, etc.) and configured in the Google Home app prior to the test. Finally, a *routine* was configured in the Google Assistant: when prompted with "Good Morning", Google Home switched on the lights, spoke about the weather, reminded about the next appointments in the calendar and, as final action, played music from a local radio. In order to avoid confusion and unwanted answers during the discussion with the participant, the smart speaker was configured as to not listen for new commands after the vocal assistant reply.

3.2 Testing Framework

After introducing the device with a commercial video by Google, we asked visitors to interact with the smart speaker and we interviewed them to understand the factors that might influence the adoption of such device in their daily routines. The questions were inspired by the UTAUT2 framework for technology acceptance and use [3]. This framework is used for all the tests in the Silver&Home living lab, in order to understand which are the factors that can affeect technology acceptance and use. Tests and questions are adapted for each product but reflect a similar structure in order to explore all the factors of the UTAUT2 model, namely: Performance Expectancy, Effort Expectancy, Social Influence, Facilitating Conditions, Hedonic Motivation, Price Value, Habit, Behavioral Intention [3].

After a visit of the Silver&Home showroom, participants filled in a consent form and a questionnaire about personal information and previous knowledge of technology (Habit factor). Participants were introduced to the device with an official advertisement video of the product. Then, users had the opportunity to test different features of the smart speaker, namely: T1) asking for generic questions such as a recipe, weather and transport information; T2) asking for music, such as a preferred song or artist; T3) turning on lights in the apartment; T4) triggering Google Home Routines. 21 questions framed according to the UTAUT2 model were asked to the participants. The detailed steps and questions of the test are reported in the following list (in parenthesis are reported the corresponding factors of the UTAUT2 model):

- *V1. Product presentation video*
- Q1. Does this product seem useful to you? (Performance Expectancy)
- *T1. Please, ask a question about a recipe, the weather or transport information for nearby city*
- Q2. Was it easy to speak with the Google Home assistant? (Effort Expectancy)
- Q3. Do you think that the "OK Google" wakeword is natural/convenient? (Effort Expectancy)
- Q4. Do you think that the assistant voice was clear? Do you prefer a male or female voice? (Hedonic Motivation)
- Q5. Are you satisfied by the assistant answer? Was it coherent with your question? (Performance Expectancy)
- *T2. Please, ask to play a song or a music genre that you like, then try to increase or decrease the volume*
- Q6. Do you think that playing a song and adjusting the volume was easy? (Effort Expectancy)
- Q7. Are you satisfied by the assistant answer? Was it coherent with your question? (Performance Expectancy)
- Q8. How do you consider the music/audio quality? (Hedonic Motivation)

- *T3. Please, ask to switch on/off the lights of the apartment or of a specific room*
- Q9. Was it easy to switch on/off the lights? (Effort Expectancy)
- Q10. Are you satisfied by the assistant answer/action? Was it coherent with your question? (Performance Expectancy)
- *T4. Please, say "Good Morning" to test the preregistered routine*
- Q11. Do you think that this routine could be useful for you? (Performance Expectancy)
- Q12. Which information would you like to get at the beginning of the day? (Performance Expectancy)
- Q13. Do you like the physical design of the Google Home? (Hedonic Motivation)
- Q14. The price of the Google Home is about 150CHF. Do you think that this price is reasonable for the features that it offers? (Price Value)
- Q15. In order to benefit of all the music selection, you will need an additional abonnement to Spotify of 12.95 CHF per month. Do you think that the price of this service is appropriated? (Price Value)
- Q16. In order to equip an apartment like this with voice-controlled lights you need additional equipment for around 600 CHF. Do you think that the price is adequate for the functions offered? (Price Value)
- Q17. Do you think that the speaker sound is loud enough? (Effort Expectancy)
- Q18. In order to set up the system, a couple of apps and accounts should be configured. Do you think that somebody could help you with this task? (Facilitating Conditions / Social Influence)
- Q19. How often would you use this product? (Behavioral Intention)
- Q20. Would you recommend this product to your acquaintances? (Behavioral Intention)
- Q21. Do you have any suggestions or improvements for this product?

3.3 Participants

7 participants (4 female) volunteered for the test. 6 participants were 50+ (2 of them were 80), while 1 participant was a caregiver working with older adults affected by memory problems. All participants lived in couple, or in a house with more than 3 people. 6 participants had a smartphone or tablet, the other person had a computer. All participants used these devices at least once per day. 4 participants use from time to time the vocal assistant integrated in the smartphone. Even if all participants are acquainted with technology, about 1/3 of participants were rather skeptical about technological innovation, whereas the others were rather interested in the new technologies. All participants were native French speakers and interacted with the Google Home Smart speaker in this language.

4   Results

4 participants considered the Google Home very useful after watching the advertisement video, only 2 not so useful (Q1). The skeptical participants perceived the Google Home rather as a technological gadget. One person suggested that the device could be useful for people with mobility impairments whereas another thought that the device would be helpful for people living alone.

During the first test, 2 people had trouble interacting with the vocal assistant, having to repeat the questions before getting the correct answer. They judged the easiness of the interaction as average, saying that it would require some time in order to get used to the device, while most of the other people considered the interaction easy or very easy (Q2). All participants considered the speed of the voice during the first interaction (a recipe) too fast (Q4), but appreciated the possibility to receive the link to the recipe in the smartphone. 3 people regretted that the assistant did not reply to thanking with a "you're welcome". 3 people considered difficult the "OK Google" wakeword. All participants considered the voice very natural (Q3). Female participants said that they would have preferred a male voice, considering it more reassuring, while males appreciated the current female voice (Q3). While some answers to the first questions did not satisfy completely all the users (Q5), reply to the music questions (T2) were very satisfying, most of them being surprised of the capability of the assistant to find their songs, being them not so popular (Q7). 6 people found the quality of the sound excellent, while 1 person, an audiophile, found it just about good (Q8). All people found intuitive giving commands for the musique and adjusting the volume (Q6). However, one participant noted that one should know in advance the exact name of the song, which could be difficult in case of memory troubles.

Participants found very intuitive also the interaction with lights (T3), although more than one person remarked the need of preparing the right question in advance, as the speaker interpret the question as soon as the user stop speaking (Q9). The fact that the exact name of the room should be spelled out in order to switch on the lights of this room was considered as a limiting factor as synonyms of the room names were not recognized (Q10). One user also suggested that the device should understand the user location and habits in order to facilitate this task. Considering the test about the Google Routine (T4), only one person found this feature not so useful (Q11). Nevertheless, two participants highlighted the difficulty to use this feature when living in couple, as each person would have different routines, concluding that this feature would be particularly useful for people living alone. In general, participants would include in the routine the weather information (5 people), reminders about calendar appointments (5), news (4), other reminders (2), automatic lighting (2) and nearby events, festivals, or new films at the cinema (1) (Q12). The physical design of the Google Home was also appreciated, being discreet and modern (Q13) and the sound volume was considered satisfactory by all participants (Q17). They thought that it could blend well in the living room or kitchen, whereas they generally would not install it in the bedroom. The price of the Google Home was considered adequate by all participants, because of all the features offered without any additional monthly fees (Q14). A participant complained about the fact that it is generally not possible to test these kinds of products in the shops and that they are available only in specialized consumer electronics shops. Conversely, most participants found inadequate the monthly fees for services like Spotify (Q15). Besides the price for a feature that might not be interesting for them, they were particularly worried about the additional burden of managing all the subscriptions. One participant suggested that it would be much easier for the seniors if all these services were included in a unique offer from a trustable provider (for example, their Internet provider). The additional price for the lighting system was considered as reasonable by all participants (Q16). However, while one participant said that it would be good especially in future perspectives of reduced mobility, another said that most peoples in their 70s were not used to spend money on non-essential goods. Participants also shared their concerns about the risk of sedentariness that the lighting system could introduce, considering it really useful only for people with reduced mobility. Concerning the difficulty for configuring the Google Home, all participants said that they could easily find help from their family or friends (Q18). After the test session, 5 participants said that they would use the device daily, about once per month the others (Q19). Most participants considered that they would particularly appreciate such kind of interactions if they were living alone, since it could decrease the sense of loneliness. All the participants would also recommend the product to their acquaintances, although some people noted that they might still not need it at this stage (Q20). Among the suggestions for improvements (Q21), participants highlighted the importance of personalizing the wakeword and of having a detailed user manual with the possible questions and keywords. One also suggested to use the speaker to send daily reminders to people with cognitive problems.

5   Discussion and Conclusion

Although smart speakers are still considered by some older adults as tech gadgets, they offer services that might be useful for older adults. The participants to our test considered that Google Home would be particularly useful for people living alone, since the vocal interaction could partly relieve the sense of loneliness. Although interacting with Google Home was generally intuitive for most participants, many improvements are still required for increasing the device accessibility. The "OK Google" wakeword is often difficult, especially for non-English speakers, and, in the case of the recipe, the speech was too fast to be remembered by the users. For some participants, it was difficult to figure out how to properly formulate a question. They eventually had a pause in the middle of the question to think about the next part of the phrase, and Google Home interpreted just the first part, without giving time to the participant to finish the phrase. A participant advocated the need of a more advanced artificial intelligence, able to better understand their wishes and context of use, such as the user location and habits. The ambiguous feeling of the assistant being neither "human" or "object" highlighted by Pradhan et al. [6] was probably present also in our participants, although never explicitly expressed (in French there is no neutral pronoun). However, participants highlighted the importance of adding politeness forms, to give it an additional "touch of humanity". In the end, although most of them said that they would use the device daily, they also highlighted possible conflicts in usage in couples. Therefore, although the answer to our question on Behavioral Intention to use the device was generally positive, we think that an important gap between intention to use and actual adoption still exist.

Acknowledgments. The authors thank Paul Vergères for the tests conducted in the Silver&Home living lab. The Silver&Home project has been supported by HES-SO, SwissUniversities and all the project sponsors, which we also thank.

References

1. Sayago, S., Neves, B.B., Cowan, B.R.: Voice assistants and older people: some open issues. In: Proceedings of the 1st International Conference on Conversational User Interfaces, pp. 1–3 (2019)
2. Pradhan, A., Lazar, A., Findlater, L.: Use of intelligent voice assistants by older adults with low technology use. ACM Trans. Comput.-Hum. Interact. (TOCHI) **27**, 1–27 (2020)
3. Venkatesh, V., Thong, J.Y., Xu, X.: Consumer acceptance and use of information technology: extending the unified theory of acceptance and use of technology. MIS Q. **36**, 157–178 (2012)
4. El Kamali, M., Angelini, L., Caon, M., Khaled, O.A., Mugellini, E., Dulack, N., Chamberlin, P., Craig, C., Andreoni, G.: NESTORE: mobile chatbot and tangible vocal assistant to support older adults' wellbeing. In: Proceedings of the 2nd Conference on Conversational User Interfaces, pp. 1–3 (2020)
5. Trajkova, M., Martin-Hammond, A.: "Alexa is a Toy": exploring older adults' reasons for using, limiting, and abandoning echo. In: Proceedings of the 2020 CHI Conference on Human Factors in Computing Systems, pp. 1–13 (2020)
6. Pradhan, A., Findlater, L., Lazar, A.: "Phantom Friend" or "Just a Box with Information" personification and ontological categorization of smart speaker-based voice assistants by older adults. In: Proceedings of the ACM on Human-Computer Interaction, vol. 3, pp. 1–21 (2019)
7. Kowalski, J., Jaskulska, A., Skorupska, K., Abramczuk, K., Biele, C., Kopeć, W., Marasek, K.: Older adults and voice interaction: a pilot study with google home. In: Extended abstracts of the 2019 CHI Conference on Human Factors in Computing Systems, pp. 1–6 (2019)
8. Pradhan, A., Jelen, B., Siek, K.A., Chan, J., Lazar, A.: Understanding older adults' participation in design workshops. In: Proceedings of the 2020 CHI Conference on Human Factors in Computing Systems, pp. 1–15 (2020)

Social Presence Despite Isolation - Insights into the Relation Between Psychological Distance and Sensory Synchronization in Computer-Mediated Communication

Stina Becker[1]([✉]), Tim Schrills[2], and Thomas Franke[2]

[1] Julius Maximilians University of Würzburg, Würzburg, Germany
stina-becker@web.de
[2] Institute for Multimedia and Interactive Systems, University of Lübeck, Lübeck, Germany
{schrills,franke}@imis.uni-luebeck.de

Abstract. Whilst social distancing (e.g., during a pandemic), electronic communication allows users to keep in touch with social contacts, thereby fulfilling needs for human interaction. Accordingly, it is important to examine social closeness in the context of computer-mediated communication in more detail and to take a closer look at the relation between the feeling of presence to achieve the maximum potential for such communication. In this paper we introduce the concept of sensory synchronization as a predictor for perceived social presence. To this end, social activities conducted virtually during the Covid-19 pandemic were surveyed and analyzed to understand the connection between a feeling of presence and possible sensory synchronization of communication partners. Context of activities were collected in preliminary interviews and examined more closely in an online survey ($N = 234$). Most frequently reported activities included video calls, playing virtual games and virtual meals. The results showed that there is a significant positive correlation between sensory synchronization and social presence in all activity categories. The activity categories significantly explain different variances of the evaluated social presence and sensory synchronization. The results of this work motivate further research on the topic of sensory synchronization and social presence. New predictors in social presence research were identified and a questionnaire for the assessment of sensory synchronization and social presence was developed.

Keywords: Social distancing · Social presence · Construal-Level Theory · Computer- mediated communication · Sensory synchronization

1 Introduction

On 31st December 2019, first cases of Covid-19 caused by SARS-CoV-2 in Wuhan City, China, were reported for the first time by the World Health Organization, followed by a variety of restrictions worldwide. With *social distancing* (i.e., maintaining physical distance and minimizing close contact to others [1]) being one of the most important

N. L. Black et al. (Eds.): IEA 2021, LNNS 220, pp. 145–153, 2021.
https://doi.org/10.1007/978-3-030-74605-6_18

measures to combat the virus, many people found themselves in prolonged isolated situations such as home office or separated from family members and friends. Beginning in mid-March 2020 social contact and participation in social activities in the context of physical meetings decreased significantly [2]. In this time, usage of internet-based applications as a remedy to isolation increased [3], with users reporting that social distance became more bearable through electronic communication [4]. This unique situation regarding social proximity in the context of electronic communication motivated further research, not only to prepare for similar situation in the future, but also as a basis for understanding human needs in electronic communication, such as *social presence*.

In 1976, social presence was described by Short et al. as the salience of interaction partners and their interpersonal relationship in a transmitted communication medium [5]. It is not always clear which factors influence social presence and which possibilities electronic communication or the context of an activity must increase social presence. Therefore, new approaches to understanding social presence and to identify influencing factors are necessary.

One possible approach, which we seek to introduce to the context of electronic communications and describe in the context of social presence is *sensory synchronization*. Sensory synchronization can be defined as the parallel processing of sensory information by two or more communication partners. Ramseyer et al. showed in studies of non-verbal synchronization in psychotherapy positive effects in therapy outcome as well as a link to relationship quality and attachment styles through non-verbal synchronization [6].

In typical video calls, however, non-verbal or expanded sensory synchronization as described above is only possible to a limited extent. Even within this limited scope, a range of research questions remains, including 1) the specific role of sensory synchronization in improving social presence in virtual calls, 2) how additional stimuli (e.g., shared music while gaming) can increase synchronicity, or 3) if feelings of psychological distance are affected by sharing rituals (e.g., communal breakfast over webcams).

The objective of this paper was to explore users' feelings of social presence in relation to their sensory synchronization. To this end, we first conducted a preliminary expert interview study to determine typical electronic communication situations during social distancing. In a follow-up exploratory online survey, users rated their experiences regarding social presence and sensory synchronization during these situations.

2 Background

Construal-Level-Theory. Liberman & Trope (2003) deal with the dimensions of the construct of psychological distance within the framework of the Construal-Level Theory [7]. This theory serves as the basis for the operationalization of social presence in the context of the present work. They discuss whether proximity and distance should be understood as two opposite poles, which implies a mutual dependence of proximity and distance [8]. In other words: the smaller the distance between two people in a space, the closer they are to each other. Conversely, this assumption makes it possible to measure distances in order to obtain information about proximity. As such, the observation of absolute proximity is the direct experience in the here and now of the perceiving person and is considered purely subjective. [7] further assume that distance is created by varying the distance of probabilities, as well as temporal, spatial, and social distances.

1) *Distance of probabilities* deals with estimating the probabilities of a situation occurring in the future and can be neglected in the context of this research, as it is not transferable to electronic communication [9].
2) *Temporal distance* is the subjective feeling of difference between the here and now and the future or the past. For example, remembering the pros and cons of summer vacation from five years ago to better plan this year's summer vacation. It has been confirmed that mental representation takes place at a higher level when comparing events that are distant in time to events that are closer in time [10].
3) *Spatial distance* describes the localization of an object and what information is available through a change in position. The closer an object is, the more detailed it is perceived. More information is available to process the situation and an abstraction of possible information is not necessary [11].
4) *Social distance* describes the feeling of belonging to a group, the familiarity between people, the perception of status differences or the influence on people's behavior [11]. Interpersonal similarity is a form of social distance. Social distance is lower when social contacts are similar [12].

In this research, a new aspect of synchronization will be investigated: The sensory synchronization of spatially separated communication partners. Sensory synchronization is defined in this paper as the synchronization of the perception of the sensory modalities (visual, auditory, tactile-haptic, gustatory, olfactory) of two or more communication partners. Auditory synchronization can be the joint listening to a song or gustatory-olfactory and visual sensory synchronization can be the simultaneous consumption of identical breakfast during a joint video call. The gustatory-olfactory synchronization takes place by tasting and smelling one's own coffee and the visual synchronization is that the communication partners both have a breakfast table in front of them. In the context of online gaming, for example, the sensory synchronization would be the visual and auditory synchronization, since all players see the same playing field and hear the same game sound.

3 Method

3.1 Participants

The survey was distributed to the student body of the University of Lübeck via an email distribution list. In addition, social networks (Facebook, Instagram, nebenan.de, online forums of the homepage pcgames.de and WhatsApp status) were used to acquire participants. There was no prerequisite for participation in the online survey. The survey had a retrospective question structure in which respondents were asked to recall their electronic communications in April 2020. The survey was accessible from 09.06. to 29.06.2020. A total of 279 participants took part. Of these 279 participants, 45 were excluded (resulting in $N = 234$). This was due to incomplete responses or recognizable response patterns throughout the questionnaire (i.e., consistently selecting the answer response in the same spatial position).

3.2 Procedure

In the main study, participants gave answers in self-report measure, which was repeated across the three categories, defined in a pre-study: Video Call (VC), Virtual Game Playing (VGP), and Virtual Meal (VM).

The self-report items (see Table 1) were based on the questionnaires "Multimodal Presence Scale for Virtual Reality Environments" (MPSVRE) by [13] and "Presence Questionnaire" (TPQ) by [14] and were supplemented by items on sensory synchronization and on the psychological distance dimensions [13, 14]. The MPSVRE was chosen as an important reference point for the questionnaire construction, as it also addresses social aspects of proximity, not included in TPQ [14, 15]. Furthermore, it is based on the work and conception of the Theory of Presence by [16], which considers three aspects of presence in the virtual world: physical presence, social presence and self-presence [13] and has overlapping aspects to construal level theory [11].

The 16 items of social presence were classified as reliable and internally consistent in the respective conditions video call ($\alpha = .791$), playing virtual games ($\alpha = .884$) and virtual meal ($\alpha = .918$). Due to technical problems, the item number SYN5 "…tasted the same as my communication partner" could not be included in the statistical evaluation. The other five items of sensory synchronization can be classified as reliable as well as internally consistent only in the video call ($\alpha = .704$) and virtual meal ($\alpha = .829$) conditions. In the virtual game playing activity category with a Cronbach's alpha of $\alpha = .506$, reliability and internal consistency cannot be assumed [17, 18].

Items were answered on a 6-point Likert scale: 1 = "Don't agree at all", 2 = "Don't agree to a large extent", 3 = "Rather don't agree", 4 = "Rather agree", 5 = "Agree to a large extent", 6 = "Agree completely". Participants also had the option of not giving an answer.

In order to control for influencing factors, demographic data (age, gender, occupation) and the affinity for technology through the Affinity for Technology Interaction Scale questionnaire [21] were recorded for each condition. In addition, the software used was queried to exclude a possible influence on the relationship between social presence and sensory synchronization.

Table 1. Self-report items translated in English

Temporal distance	Social distance
TD1: During __, my interactions with my communication partner were like those in a real conversation	**SOD1:** During __ I felt as if I were in the presence of my communication partner
TD2: During __, the flow of conversation with my communication partner, was like that in a real conversation	**SOD2:** During __ I interacted with my communication partner in the same way as if I were in a real __ in real surroundings
TD3: During __, I felt that I was close in time to my communication partner	**SOD3:** During __ I was consciously aware of my communication partner's emotions

(continued)

Table 1. (*continued*)

Temporal distance	Social distance
TD4: During __ I lost track of time	**SOD4:** During __ I talked about the same topics with my communication partner as during a real __ in real surroundings
TD5: During __, my communication partner's movements seemed natural	**SOD5:** During __ I behaved exactly as I would in a real __
	SOD6: During __ I felt socially distanced from my communication partner
Spatial distance	Sensory synchronization
SPD1: During __ I had a feeling as if I were in the same place with my communication partner	**SYN1:** I saw the same things as my communication partner
SPD2: During __ the environment of my communication partner seemed real to me	**SYN2:** I heard the same things as my communication partner
SPD3: During __ I felt spatially distanced from my communication partner	**SYN3:** I smelled the same things as my communication partner
SPD4: During __ I had the feeling of seeing only an image of my communication partner	**SYN4:** I felt the same things as my communication partner
SPD5: During __ I had the feeling that I was present in a virtual room	**SYN5:** I tasted the same things as my communication partner
SPD6: During __ I had the feeling that the virtual and real worlds were blurring into each other	**SYN6:** I felt distant while talking to my communication partner

Notes: temporal distance (TD), spatial distance (SPD), social distance (SOD), sensory synchronization (SYN)

4 Results

4.1 Correlation of Synchronization and Social Presence

Mean values, variances and standard deviations were calculated for the different variables (see Table 2). Pearson correlations were calculated to analyze a possible correlation between perceived social presence and sensory synchronization in more detail. Significant results were found in all conditions. Social presence correlated with sensory synchronization in a video call ($r = .34, p < .001$), virtual game play ($r = .45, p < .001$) and virtual meal ($r = .76, p < .001$) category.

Table 2. Descriptive data for sensory synchronization and social presence in each condition

	Video call		Virtual game play		Virtual meal	
	Sync.	Presence	Sync.	Presence	Sync.	Presence
N	219	219	88	88	57	57
M	3.29	3.85	3.63	3.94	3.45	4.04
MD	3.40	3.82	3.60	4.06	3.40	4.06
SD	0.766	0.718	0.841	0.833	1.19	0.913
Min	0.400	1.88	1.60	1.24	1.00	2.35
Max	5.20	5.65	5.80	5.71	6.00	6.00

Notes: sensory synchronization (Sync.), social presence (Presence)

4.2 Predictors of Experienced Presence and Synchronization

Regression analyses was used to investigate whether the activity categories can be understood as a predictor for the relationship between experienced social presence and sensory synchronization. From the regression analyses of the conditions, it can be concluded that the activity context explains significantly different variances in the assessed social presence. In the video call category, the regression suggests that sensory synchronization can be considered a predictor of subjectively experienced social presence ($\beta = .32, t\ (216) = 5.50, p < .001$). Sensory synchronization and Affinity for Technology Interaction thus explain a significant proportion of the variance in social presence in the video call ($R^2 = .14, f^2 = 0.157, F\ (2,216) = 16.95, p < .001$).

Significantly more variance was explained in the virtual game playing and virtual meal category. In the virtual game playing category, sensory synchronization was also hypothesized to be a predictor ($\beta = .44, t\ (85) = 4.51, p < .001$), as it was in the virtual meal category ($\beta = .59, t\ (54) = 8.68, p < .001$). The variables sensory synchronization and Affinity for Technology Interaction explained a significant amount of the variance in the virtual game playing category ($R^2 = .21, f^2 = 0.263, F\ (2,85) = 11.23, p < .001$), as well as in the virtual meal category ($R^2 = .58, f^2 = 1.398, F\ (2,54) = 37.7, p < .001$). The fit as well as the transfer of the regression models was confirmed in all three activity categories video call ($RMSE = 0.666$), virtual game playing ($RMSE = 0.737$) as well as virtual meal ($RMSE = 0.584$). Due to the strong differences in variance resolution in the conditions and the difference in effect sizes, it can be confirmed that the relationship between rated sensory synchronization and social presence is dependent on the activity context.

4.3 Quality of Electronic Communication Software

To identify possible differences of quality between electronic communication software, we queried the tool used for the respective condition. Due to the small number of users in the activity category playing virtual games and virtual meal, only the tools of the video call ($N = 219$) were considered. In this way, meaningful and generalizable results were achieved. For the video call, WhatsApp was chosen in 33.8% of cases. This was followed by Skype (23.3%), Facetime (12.3%), Zoom (10.5%), WebEx (8.7%), Discord (6.4%), Other (4.1%) and Microsoft Teams (0.9%). Due to the high user rate of WhatsApp (N = 74) in this study, as well as having two billion users worldwide [19], WhatsApp was considered as the reference level of software in the regression and not Skype. The latter had a sample of 51 participants and an estimated 1.67 billion users worldwide [20] and thus fewer users than WhatsApp.

Adding the software used as a factor in the regression model didoes allow for more variance to be explained ($R^2 = .20$, $f^2 = 0.256$, $F(9,209) = 6.32$, $p < .001$) than compared to the regression model without adding the software used ($R^2 = .136$, $f^2 = 0.157$, $F(2,216) = 16.9$, $p < .001$), but only the software Zoom weakened the effect of the association between rated social presence and sensory synchronization ($\beta = -.46$, $t(209) = -2.90$, $p = .004$). Thus, it can be assumed that only occasionally the communication tool used has an influence on the correlation between social presence and sensory synchronization.

5 Discussion

5.1 Summary of Results

The aim of this study was to further investigate a possible connection between sensory synchronization and subjectively experienced social presence in electronic communication. During the period of social distancing due to the pandemic 2020, all respondents were found to have increased their use of video calling to stay in touch with friends and family members. In addition, it was found that a variety of new social activities supported by electronic communication tools were used. Especially virtual meals and virtual games were pursued by respondents to maintain social contacts despite physical distance.

Considering the statistical analysis of the online questionnaire, a connection between sensory synchronization and social presence can be assumed. It was confirmed that sensory synchronization in different activity contexts has a moderate to strong effect on the experienced social presence and can thus be used as a predictor.

However, the effect of differently selected tools on the experienced sensory synchronization as well as on the social presence could not be generally confirmed.

5.2 Implications

Looking at the numerous mentions of new online-based activities, as was the case in this work, shows that new economic branches have emerged in the Covid-19 pandemic. Services can create solutions to unprecedented situations in a noticeably short time and emerge stronger from such a pandemic. Besides the therapeutic setting, where for example sensory synchronization could positively influence the patient-therapist relationship, sensory synchronization could be an approach to increase interpersonal closeness in many virtual settings. As mentioned earlier, the number of people living alone is increasing [21].

In the context of the Covid-19 pandemic, the at-risk group of elderly people in nursing homes were subjected to strict prophylactic isolation measures and in some cases an absolute ban on visits applied. In Germany, about one in three Covid-19 deaths lived in a nursing home where there was consequently a lack of human proximity [22]. Regardless of the Covid-19 virus, patients receiving chemotherapy and who are to receive a stem cell transplant are particularly at risk of infection and are also isolated in hospital for a few weeks to be protected from external influences [23]. These groups lack social proximity and to compensate for social proximity, the integration of sensory synchronization through video call could provide greater psychological support. For example, in nursing homes and hospitals, joint family meals could be organized by means of electronic communication, in which the sensory synchronization of taste, smell and even haptic information promote social closeness. Similarly, the synchronization of screens could enable movie nights with the family in the hospital and at home at the same time, to make the period of therapy more pleasant as well as more social.

The potential of video games has been shown in other works, e.g. [13, 24] confirmed positive social effects in the field of online gaming in their study. We found similar effects that can be possibly related to synchronously performed activities. Further research may aim to compare online games with high visual and auditory synchronization and online games with low visual and auditory synchronization could be analyzed.

In summary, the integration of sensory synchronization in private, in home office, as well as in clinical contexts can offer numerous positive effects, with many possible avenues available for further research.

6 Conclusion

This work offers new possible predictors in the study of social presence and presents a reliable, internally consistent questionnaire developed to assess sensory synchronization and social presence. While the significant relationship between sensory synchronization and subjective social presence requires further empirical investigation, this study gives integral insights for this topic of research. The potential for future sensory synchronization shows promise in therapeutic, private, and economic contexts.

References

1. Lockerd Maragis, L.: Coronavirus, Social and Physical Distancing and Self-Quarantine (2020)
2. Juhl, S., Lehrer, R., Blom, A.G., Wenz, A., Rettig, T., Reifenscheid, M., Naumann, E., Möhring, K., Krieger, U., Friedel, S., Fikel, M., Cornesse, C.: Die Mannheimer Corona-Studie: Gesellschaftliche Akzeptanz politischer Maßnahmen und befürchtete Konsequenzen für die Wirtschaft, pp. 1–14 (2020)
3. Krex, A.: Die Stunde der Avatare (2020)
4. von Gehlen, D.: Durch Corona wird das Internet zur Selbstverständlichkeit (2020)
5. Short, J., Williams, E., Christie, B.: The Social Psychology of Telecommunications. John Wiley & Sons, New York (1976)
6. Ramseyer, F.: Nonverbale Synchronisation in der Psychotherapie. Systeme **24**, 5–30 (2010)
7. Liberman, N., Trope, Y.: Construal level theory of intertemporal judgment and decision. In: Loewenstein, G., Read, D., Baumeister, R. (eds.) Time and Decision: Economic and Psychological Perspectives on Intertemporal Choice, pp. 245–276 (2003)

8. Thiersch, H.: Nähe und Distanz in der Sozialen Arbeit. In: Dörr, M. (ed.) Nähe und Distanz: Ein Spannungsfeld pädagogischer Professionalität. pp. 42–51. Beltz Juventa in der Verlagsgruppe Beltz, Weinheim Basel (2019). https://doi.org/10.1024/2297-6965/a000214

9. Trope, Y., Liberman, N.: Construal-level theory of psychological distance. Psychol. Rev. **117**, 440–463 (2010). https://doi.org/10.1037/a0018963

10. Nussbaum, S., Trope, Y., Liberman, N.: Creeping dispositionism: the temporal dynamics of behavior prediction. J. Pers. Soc. Psychol. **84**, 485–497 (2003). https://doi.org/10.1037/0022-3514.84.3.485

11. Liberman, N., Trope, Y., Stephan, E.: Psychological distance. In: Kruglanski, A.W., Higgins, E.T. (eds.) Social Psychology: Handbook of Basic Principles, pp. 353–381. The Guilford Press, New York (2007)

12. Heider, F.: The Psychology of Interpersonal Relations. Wiley, Oxford (1958)

13. Makransky, G., Lilleholt, L., Aaby, A.: Development and validation of the multimodal presence scale for virtual reality environments: a confirmatory factor analysis and item response theory approach. Comput. Hum. Behav. **72**, 276–285 (2017). https://doi.org/10.1016/j.chb.2017.02.066

14. Witmer, B., Jerome, C., Singer, M.: The factor structure of the presence questionnaire. Presence Teleoper. Virtual Environ. **14**(3), 298–312 (2005). https://doi.org/10.1162/105474605323384654

15. Lessiter, J., Freeman, J., Keogh, E., Davidoff, J.: A cross-media presence questionnaire: the ITC-sense of presence inventory. Presence Teleoper. Virtual Environ. **10**(3), 282–297 (2001). https://doi.org/10.1162/105474601300343612

16. Lee, K.M.: Presence, explicated. Commun. Theory. **14**, 27–50 (2004). https://doi.org/10.1093/ct/14.1.27

17. Cripps, B.: Psychometric Testing: Critical Perspectives. Wiley, Hoboken (2017)

18. Gliem, J.A., Gliem, R.R.: Calculating, interpreting, and reporting Cronbach's alpha reliability coefficient for Likert-type scales. In: Midwest Research-to-Practice Conference in Adult, Continuing, and Community Education (2003)

19. WhatsApp: Two Billion Users -- Connecting the World Privately. https://blog.whatsapp.com/two-billion-users-connecting-the-world-privately, Accessed 17 July 2020

20. Poleshova, A.: Prognose zur Anzahl der registrierten Nutzer von Skype in den Jahren 2009 bis 2024. https://de.statista.com/statistik/daten/studie/185958/umfrage/registrierte-und-zahlende-skype-nutzer-seit-2007/, Accessed 17 July 2020

21. Chen, Y., While, A.E.: Older people living alone in Shanghai: a questionnaire survey of their life experience. Health Soc. Care Commun. **27**, 260–269 (2019). https://doi.org/10.1111/hsc.12648

22. Kampf, L., Riedel, K., Pittelkow, S.: Pandemie in Deutschland Corona-Zone Altenheim (2020). https://www.tagesschau.de/investigativ/ndr-wdr/coronavirus-pflegekraefte-101.html, Accessed 17 July 2020

23. Beckmann, I.A.: Leukämie bei Erwachsenen. Stiftung Deutsche Krebshilfe (2016)

24. Trepte, S., Reinecke, L., Juechems, K.: The social side of gaming: how playing online computer games creates online and offline social support. Comput. Hum. Behav. **28**, 832–839 (2012). https://doi.org/10.1016/j.chb.2011.12.003

Luminance Contrast Standards, the Boy Who Could, and Visionary Pathfinders

Penny Galbraith[1][✉] and Richard Bowman[2]

[1] Centre for Universal Design Australia, Sydney, Australia
penny@box50.com.au
[2] Intertile Research, Brighton East, Australia
slipbusters@gmail.com

Abstract. Visual contrast is crucial to how users experience their environment. While this has been recognized in standards, which utilise the light reflectance value, there is no universally acknowledged method of measuring and calculating luminance contrast, particularly on site. Past standards' developments have only partially addressed some issues. This paper highlights how the standards have evolved and the work of pathfinders seeking to achieve better outcomes in our environment and society. Issues such as bulky measuring equipment and poor translation of lab measured LRVs to on-site measurements, have hindered provision and maintenance of compliant facilities. Practitioner frustration led to recent research to develop a portable measuring tool as well as to develop a validated image analysis algorithm to allow ready measurement of LRV on site. Issues remain that LRV alone is inadequate to reflect user experience. Further research is suggested to assist improve some parameters, but particularly luminance contract calculation methods.

Keywords: Luminance contrast · Standards · Image analysis · Measurement tool · Visual contrast · Bowman-Sapolinski

1 Introduction

Vision is our dominant sense and is the process of deriving meaning from what is seen. About 80% percent of our perception, learning, cognition, and activities are mediated through vision [1]. Visual contrast sensitivity is a vital part of human vision (different to acuity) allowing detection of objects and discriminating objects or details from their background. Visual contrast is crucial to human experience of environments [2]. Poor visual contrast thus has a significant impact on people with vision impairment. Worldwide, luminance contrast is recognised in Standards and Codes for new buildings, transport, and information, as the most relevant measure of how a person visually perceives their environment. Luminance contrast is required for signs, stair nosings, doorways, glazing contrast marking, handrails, tactile surface ground indicators (TGSIs)[1] and other situations to facilitate improved universal design [3].

---

[1] TGSIs are also known as guiding blocks, detectable walking surfaces, tactile warning surfaces.

© The Author(s), under exclusive license to Springer Nature Switzerland AG 2021
N. L. Black et al. (Eds.): IEA 2021, LNNS 220, pp. 154–162, 2021.
https://doi.org/10.1007/978-3-030-74605-6_19

Luminance contrast is recognised as crucial for safety and is vital to remove environmental barriers for people with a vision impairment. However, luminance contrast is only a tiny fraction of total building compliance. Further, lack of affordable and portable measuring equipment leads to lack of luminance measurements on site. As such, new facilities often fail to achieve acceptable luminance contrast outcomes. Another issue is that standards' methodologies emphasize measuring pure colour of surfaces with a controlled light source (colorimeter), rather than reflected light, and thus do not replicate how users experience their environment. While photometers can be used on site, they are bulky and sensitive to changes in lighting conditions. Existing standards provide partial technological solutions but need further development.

For existing buildings, public spaces, and transport, as surfaces become worn and soiled, the on-going luminance contrast requirements are challenged. Achieving better luminance contrast outcomes for all users of the built environment firstly requires luminance to be measured, expressed as a light reflectance value (LRV). Secondly, luminance contrast should be calculated.

While professionally researched luminance contrast standards should provide everyone with safe and easy to access and use of the built environment, the recent history of standards development has created more problems in use than they have solved. While Standards' committees might hope for one solution that fits all, a rational approach must be taken to fulfil a range of stakeholder needs.

This paper provides some luminance contrast history to illustrate past and present problems with standards development and their application. It proposes a new image analysis technique to measure luminance that reflects user experience of the built environment, rather than a theoretical colour construct. It will hopefully encourage a new research-based approach to both measuring and calculating luminance contrast that better reflects the user experience of the built environment.

2 Developing Australian Standards and Codes

When Bowman was asked in 1995 to confirm that some porcelain TGSIs complied with the AS 1428.4 (1992) standard [4], there was a hiccup with the 30% luminance contrast requirement. Bowman asked the standards committee what test method was to be used for measuring luminance and how the calculation should be performed. The reply invited Bowman to create a test method and stipulate the calculation.

Bowman recommended the use of a tristimulus colorimeter or spectrophotometer for laboratory-based measurements, where it might also be used on site. Bowman [5] considered the available equations and recommended an equation used in AS 2422: 1981, *Glossary of micrographic terms*. This better enabled his derivation of an algorithm for multicoloured surfaces. For solidly coloured units, the percentage luminance contrast, C, could be calculated from Eq. (1) (Table 1), where L2 was the larger (lighter) of two light reflectance (or CIE Y tristimulus) values. Bowman stressed the need to visually verify his interim solutions using appropriate cohorts.

Bowman also recommended that wet luminance measurements should be made on porous materials, such as concrete, due to the extent of their darkening on wetting, and made this a significant component of the testing procedure. He provided worked examples of the limiting effects of porous materials becoming darker [5].

Recognising one size does not fit all, Bowman subsequently proposed speculative 45% and 60% contrast requirements for the evolving uniform discrete and composite discrete indicators, again stressing the need for practical verification. These requirements were incorporated in AS 1428.4 (2002) [6] without independent confirmation.

2.1   The Boy that Could

In 2008, Sapolinski, a high school student, contacted Bowman about his luminance contrast research project. Sapolinski [7] produced 48 full-sized ETDRS eye charts using greyscale and colour combinations: a mixture of high, medium, and low luminance contrast between the font and background colours. He designed a logarithmic scale visual acuity scoring system and tested 80 subjects positioned 6m from the eye charts at 500 lx illumination. Sapolinski took a morning paper round for 6 months to fund his research, including the verification that Bowman had been seeking.

Sapolinski found the AS 1428.4:2002 Eq. (1) provided better correlation than both the Weber Eq. (2), as used in the Americans with Disabilities Act Accessibility Guidelines (Section A4.30), and Cook's simple difference Eq. (3), which had been adopted in the British Building Regulations 2001 - Approved document AD(M).

Sapolinski [7] recognised that humans better differentiate between darker colours than lighter colours, and corrected the AS 1428.4 Eq. (1) to declare a new evidence-based Bowman-Sapolinski Eq. (4). Sapolinski also stated that while the 30% requirement was quite satisfactory, a 40% requirement would be preferable based on the data. This could have been achieved by changing the coefficient from 250 to 187.5, while still retaining a declared (but essentially meaningless) 30% requirement. In fact, further optimization of Bowman-Sapolinski Eq. (5) could be achieved by carefully adjusting the coefficient based on further evidence, such as that of Lukman et al. [8].

Table 1.   A summary of luminance contrast algorithms, and (where determined) the root mean square values for the correlation between visual acuity scores and the luminance contrast values for the visually impaired (VI) and normal vision (NV) cohorts.

Equation			R^2 VI	R^2 NV
1	AS 1428.4:2002	$C = 200 (L2 - L1)/(L1 + L2)$	0.8270	0.8227
2	Weber	$C = 100 (L2 - L1)/L2)$	0.7672	0.7659
3	Simple difference	$C = Y2 - Y1$	0.8167	0.7755
4	B-Sapolinski derived	$C = 250 (L2 - L1)/(L1 + L2 + 25)$	0.9254	0.9122
5	B-Sapolinski optimized	$C = 187 (L2 - L1)/(L1 + L2 + 25)$	0.9254	0.9122
6	Michelson	$C = 100 (L2 - L1)/(L1 + L2)$	–	–
7	B-Sapolinski altered	$C = 125 (L2 - L1)/(L1 + L2 + 25)$	0.9254	0.9122

Sapolinski could have derived an evidence-based modified form of the Weber Eq. (2), but chose to only improve the existing requirement. Sapolinski confidently wrote [7] "the Bowman-Sapolinski equation has been adopted as the new equation for luminance contrast in AS 1428.1:2009". However, this did not occur, seemingly due to discussions pertaining to the inaugural ISO luminance contrast standards, which adopted an altered Sapolinski Eq. (7), where the coefficient in Eq. (4) was halved without subsequent explanation. ISO 23599:2019 [9] notes the Sapolinski formula is a modification of the Michelson Eq. (6), but Sapolinski never considered Eq. (6) in [7].

Since the Michelson and Weber formulae are known to be problematic when achieving appropriate contrast with dark colours, standards such as ISO 21542:2011 [10], require a minimum LRV value of 50 or 60 points for the lightest surface, depending on circumstances, where visual contrasts are specified in terms of Eq. (2) with the amount of required difference varying between 15 points (door hardware) and 60 points (top of stairs). Floor patterns should have a visual contrast of less than 20 points difference, where this presumably applies in both wet and dry conditions.

On the other hand, ISO 23599:2019 [9] requires use of the Michelson Eq. (6) to calculate luminance contrast values. To compensate for problems with dark surfaces, the lighter surface must have a LRV value of at least 40, much less than required by ISO 21542:2011 [10].

While the ISO standards contain lengthy bibliographies and some useful informative visual contrast content, their different unexplained approaches are not helpful. The adoption of flawed algorithms has necessitated the use of further arbitrary controls. They failed to exploit the potential benefits of Sapolinski's work.

In AS 1428.1:2009 [11] and AS 1428.4.1:2009 [12], a new Bowman-Sapolinski Eq. (7) was published, though it differed from the same named original Eq. (4) (in [7]). Lukman et al. [8] noted the discrepancy of outcomes between the new [11, 12] and former [6] Australian standards (Eqs. (1) and (7)).

2.2 Luminance Contrast Compliance Benchmarks

Observing that the creation of definitive accessibility guidelines is complicated when there is no universally acknowledged method of measurement or calculation, Lukman et al. [8] set out to determine whether the minimum 30% level of contrast required in the Australian standards was sufficiently visible for 12 people with visual impairment in dry conditions. It should be noted their specimens included many coloured discrete tactile indicators and stainless steel/composite tactile indicators, with 45 and 60% requirements, respectively. Lukman et al. found the number of participants who rated a combination as being subjectively good in terms of visibility did not necessarily reflect the measured luminance contrast rank order. Bentzen et al. [13] similarly found safety yellow detectable warnings with as little as 40% contrast with an adjoining surface were more detectable to persons with low vision than detectable warnings of other colours having up to 86% contrast. The calculated luminance contrast values did not reflect user experience for people with a vision impairment.

Nevertheless, Lukman et al. [8] found a 30% contrast requirement enabled most of the participants to detect the TGSIs from relatively safe distances. Given the more demanding nature of Eq. (7), are the much higher 45 and 60% requirements for discrete and composite TGSIs still appropriate, particularly where the dominant paving material has a significant change in LRV on wetting? Where ISO 23599 [9] has a 30% minimum contrast value for the Michelson formula generally, the required minimum for discrete units is 40% and for hazards only 50%.

2.3   Evidence Base

While there are various ISO and national standards that contain various luminance contrast algorithms, one should consider the negative consequences of the adoption of the lower coefficient in the mandated Bowman-Sapolinski Eq. (7) rather than the derived Eq. (4) or the optimized Eq. (5).

To determine if the luminance contrast between TGSIs and an adjacent surface is acceptable, Bowman's test requires surfaces to be soaked in water, since concrete and other porous surfaces become darker when wet! AS 1428.4 requires that there be an acceptable contrast between the TGSI with both the wet and the dry background. This significantly increases the unacceptable range of luminance values, compared to other standards. In fact, there have reportedly been situations when it has no longer been possible to install discrete TGSIs due to the low coefficient of the transmuted algorithm, Eq. (7). There are similar wet and dry requirements in the ISO standards, but there are no worked examples, and it is not spelled out whether the minimum LRV requirements for lighter surfaces must be met in both wet and dry conditions.

The "boy that could" may have put us on the right path, but he did not reckon on the fallibility of standardization procedures. His evidence-based algorithm was inexplicably altered making it difficult to obtain the required luminance contrast, with the choice often restricted to either white or black non-porous TGSIs. While safety yellow TGSIs may be more readily detected than compliant TGSIs, that is a separate problem to be addressed elsewhere. Where Australian standards are referenced documents in the National Construction Code (NCC), they are hard to change, particularly when they are integral to the Disability Discrimination Premises Standards legislation.

Standards committees sometimes lack the necessary expertise to ensure that stakeholders' needs can best be met. When external experts identify problems and derive potential solutions, their advice should be heeded throughout all stages until the standard is finalized. Standards committees need to ensure that all elements are fit for purpose, not just when installed but also at the end of an economically reasonable life cycle. Ensuring the safety and slip resistance of TGSIs is another element of the right path approach, where we must ask ourselves what we might do today to leave a legacy for the future. Privacy, confidentiality, and cost considerations can frustrate the contribution of capable experts, although many might also be locked out of the standardization process by the lack of publicly accessible documentation. Where does that leave practitioners?

3   Applying Standards in Practice

As an accessibility and compliance practitioner, Galbraith routinely observed that LRV was not measured on new construction, nor as part of ongoing maintenance of existing assets. A barrier to measurement was thought likely to be the expensive and/or bulky equipment prescribed in the Australian Standards' methodology, namely colorimeters and photometers. This equipment is well established and has been since the standards were developed decades ago; indeed, well before the digital technological advancements we take for granted today.

Galbraith (2017) carried out a survey of access practitioners (n = 84) that revealed 66% relied on 'by eye' judgement to determine luminance contrast compliance with the NCC. For specified finishes, some designers/consultants obtained laboratory LRV test certificates, based on controlled lighting test conditions to develop compliant designs. However, when tested using photometers, lab based LRVs were not replicated in as-installed situations, indicating that the sole reliance on lab LRV values would not guarantee as-built compliance.

Colorimeters, when used on site to determine LRV, typically have a controlled light source and measure the 'pure' colour of a surface (specular component inclusive). Such measurements do not reflect ambient lighting nor how users experience an environment. To illustrate this, consider the effect of either too much light or too little light on a colour. In low light, pure white can appear grey. In excess light, black can appear grey. User experience of an environment is contingent on the available light and the colour and finish of the surfaces from which light is reflected to the eye [14].

The objective of Galbraith's privately funded research was to better understand how practitioners achieved compliant design and construction, and if appropriate develop a readily available portable tool that could measure LRVs representative of user experience. Representative LRVs could then be used to calculate the luminance contrast experienced by users in a particular setting.

3.1 Image Analysis Algorithm

The research hypothesis was based on the premise that cameras capture the scene, 'as seen'. Camera images are specular component exclusive, allowing for prevailing light conditions and the amount of light reflected from a surface to the eye (or camera).

Extensive research was carried out bringing together print, web and photographic technology to examine and test a range of image analysis algorithms. AS 1428.4.1 clause E3.3(e) states "A more accurate calculation [of LRV] might be based on the relative proportions of each colour (where these proportions might be determined by image analysis techniques)" [12] in relation to Bowman's colorimeter method. However, it is equally valid for Galbraith's proposed approach.

With known lux and luminance values, the LRV results from the preferred image analysis algorithm were validated against the LRV obtained with the ISO 21542 formula, Eq. (8) where L = luminance cd/m^2; E = lux; and X_{lrv} = LRV [10]:

$$L = (E \times X_{lrv})/\pi \qquad (8)$$

The resultant image analysis algorithm was incorporated into a smart phone application to provide a portable and affordable tool. The App, *Get Luminance* [15], is free, and practitioners typically have use of a mobile smart phone! A key benefit of the App is that shadowing, glare, gloss, and uneven surfaces can have their LRV measured and that the LRV reflects user experience at that given time under the prevailing circumstances.

3.2   Limitations of Calculation Methods

Having validated an image analysis algorithm to determine the LRV, the next step was to measure LRV for two adjoining surfaces and calculate the luminance contrast. The App includes four common calculation methods for luminance contrast where L1 is the lighter colour LRV and L2 the darker colour LRV:

1. Simple difference $[C = L1 - L2)]$ Eq. (3)
2. Bowman-Sapolinski (transmuted) $[C = 125 (L1 - L2)/ (25 + L1 + L2)]$ Eq. (7)
3. Weber Proportional difference $[C = (L1 - L2)/L1]$ Eq. (2)
4. Michelson $[C = (L1 - L2)/ (L1 + L2)]$ Eq. (6)

What many may not initially appreciate, is just how widely different the luminance contrast calculation results can be. Figure 1 shows some results for the luminance contrast calculation methods using two LRVs, deliberately set at 30 points apart, since a luminance contrast difference of 30% is a common compliance benchmark. Each calculation method provides quite different answers, but none necessarily provides a true indication of sufficient contrast. This is an ongoing consideration (concern) for assessing luminance contrast, where there is much debate about the calculation methods. There is no consensus worldwide. The choice of calculation method provides the single biggest factor affecting luminance contrast outcomes.

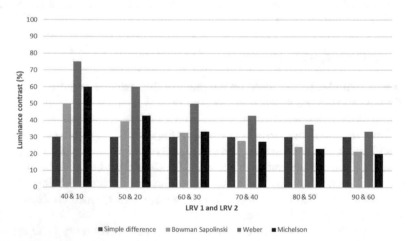

Fig. 1. Luminance contrast results for Eqs. 3, 7, 2 and 6 compared for LRVs 30 points apart.

3.3   Further Research

An extension of this work was to seek a better understanding of why there is such a discrepancy between lab and site measurements. Not only for compliance purposes but to achieve accessible design outcomes.

A key difference between lab and site measurements is the use of a controlled light source in the lab (specular component inclusive) and ambient light conditions on site (specular component exclusive). This is important for designers who rely on lab-based LRV data to develop their design without appreciating that lab-based LRVs are only indicative of performance and do not factor in the gloss of surfaces.

As we have shown, Sapolinski [7] addressed the problem of dark colours in good viewing conditions. However, as both low light and excess lighting conditions reduce the luminance contrast in practice, the user experience of contrast cannot be solely addressed through LRVs [3]. Contrast formulae must be based on the parameters influencing contrast perception. Furthermore, contrast ratios will only be valid within a limited range and may not apply to extremely high or low luminance conditions [3].

The human eye is highly adaptable to a range of light conditions [16]. But what is the maximum and minimum difference in luminance (cd/m^2) that the human eye can discern, particularly for smaller objects or narrow architraves or nosing strips? Is this different for people with a vision impairment? Research into the effect of low and excess light may assist the refinement of the luminance contrast algorithms. Such research may also indicate that LRVs should be used within a range of reference lighting conditions [3]. A good example of the link between LRV and illuminance is fine work such as sewing a dark fabric with dark thread. Excess light will assist the task even though the contrast of the materials is minimal.

4 Conclusions

While we all have a vested interest in optimizing universal access, unexplained Standards' decisions that occur behind closed doors can be counterproductive. If poor decisions are made, experts should be able to access the relevant documentary evidence to propose alternative solutions. Where is the published evidence that should be driving the evolution of such standards, while also informing interested parties such as manufacturers and other code and standards writers?

Despite many years of standards' development, there is still no universally acknowledged method of determining luminance contrast. However, we contend that LRV alone, despite numerous algorithms and attempts to improve them, does not provide solutions that always translate from lab to site. Practitioners need evidence-based standards and methodologies to deliver safe and accessible environments that account for user experience. Practitioner-led research has demonstrated how image analytical techniques can be used and incorporated into a smart phone Application to provide a portable, affordable on-site luminance contrast measurement tool that reflects user experience. It would benefit from further research that yields a consistent luminance contrast calculation reflecting human visual experience. Both innovations are required to achieve safe and accessible outcomes in the built environment.

References

1. Romih, T.: Humans Are Visual Creatures (2016). https://www.seyens.com/humans-are-vis ual-creatures/, Accessed 21 Mar 2021

2. Feigusch, G., Steffan, T.S.: Accessibility and visual contrast: a proposal for a better evaluation of this physical quantity. In: Proceedings of the 20th Congress of the International Ergonomics Association (IEA 2018), pp. 1642–1648. Springer, Cham (2018)
3. CSTC. Tableur Contrastes Connaissances de base (2017). https://www.cstc.be/index.cfm?dtype=tools&doc=Contrastes_Conaissances_de_base_tableur_v1.0.pdf&lang=fr, Accessed 26 Feb 2021
4. Standards Australia. AS 1428.4, Design for access and mobility - Tactile ground surface indicators for the orientation of people with vision impairment (1992)
5. Bowman, R.: Inadequate colour contrasts and other illuminating considerations. Tile Today 48 (1999). https://www.researchgate.net/publication/344393224_Inadequate_colour_contrasts_and_other_illuminating_considerations
6. Standards Australia. AS/NZS 1428.4, Design for access and mobility - Tactile ground surface indicators (2002)
7. Sapolinski, J., Garth, S.M., Garth, I.M.: An improved metric for luminance contrast using colour modified clinical eye charts. Redeemer Baptist School, North Parramatta, Australia. https://redeemer-baptist-school.squarespace.com/s/Sapolinski-Color_Contrast_Scientific_Report.pdf, Accessed 26 Feb 2021
8. Lukman, A.L., Bridge, C., Dain, S.J., Boon, M.Y.: Luminance contrast of accessible tactile indicators for people with visual impairment. Ergonomics Des. 28(2), 4–15 (2020)
9. International Organisation for Standardisation. ISO 23599:2019. Building Construction – Accessibility and Usability of the Built Environment. ISO, Geneva (2019)
10. International Organisation for Standardisation. ISO 21542:2011. Assistive products for blind and vision-impaired persons – Tactile walking surface indicators. ISO, Geneva (2011)
11. Standards Australia. AS 1428.1, Design for access and mobility – New building work (2009)
12. Standards Australia. AS 1428.4.1, Design for access and mobility - Means to assist the orientation of people with vision impairment - Tactile ground surface indicators (2009)
13. Bentzen, B.L., Nolin, T.L., Easton, R.D.: Detectable warning surfaces: Color, contrast and reflectance. Cambridge, MA: U.S. Department of Transportation, Federal Transit Administration, Volpe National Transportation Systems Center. Report No. VNTSC-DTRS-57-93-P-80546 (1994)
14. Konica Minolta, Precise Color Communication. Konica Minolta, Japan (2007)
15. Box 50 Pty Ltd., Get Luminance (2019). www.box50.com.au, Accessed 21 Mar 2021
16. Oyster, C.W.: The human eye: structure and function. Sinauer Associates, Sunderland (1999)

Research Through Co-design for Connecting Design for All and Policy Ergonomics

Daniele Busciantella-Ricci[1](✉) ⓘ and Sofia Scataglini[2] ⓘ

[1] Design Research Lab, Department of Humanities, University of Trento, Trento, Italy
d.busciantellaricci@unitn.it
[2] Department of Product Development, Faculty of Design Sciences, University of Antwerp,
Antwerp, Belgium
sofia.scataglini@uantwerpen.be

Abstract. This paper frames theoretical reflections to connect the Design for All (DfA) approach with Policy Ergonomics (PE) through the Research Through Co-design (RTC) theory. We used the RTC theory for connecting variables of the RTC model with DfA by assuming the context of policy-making. We also used a polynomial to express the diversity in the RTC model. As a result, we obtained the Polynomial of Diversity (PoD) to make the diversity as a tangible value in the RTC model. The PoD describes the diversity in terms of different weights of the co-designers in the RTC model. In practical terms, the PoD helps practitioners, designers, designers-researchers, policy-makers to reflect on those variables that can influence the application of the DfA approach in the context of policy-making. At the same time the application of the RTC theory through the PoD has the potential of co-creating useful knowledge for identifying innovative, sustainable and inclusive policies in different policy-making contexts. Finally, this paper provides a theoretical connection among DfA, RTC and the policy-making context highlighting the need to define the field of study in PE.

Keywords: Research through co-design · Control system theory · Policy ergonomics · Design for all

1 Background

1.1 Problem Statement

Design for All (DfA) is historically and culturally linked with policies and the public sector (see [1]). At the same time, the interest in embedding design thinking in the public sector and policy-making contexts is growing from several perspectives [2]. Moreover, the Research Through Design (RTD) is affirming its value as a type of design research that recognises its source in design [3] and as a cybernetic mode of inquiry [4]. In addition, the Research Through Co-design (RTC), that is based on RTD and the control system theory [5], has been recently discussed as a model that can contribute to the policy-making context [6]. Theoretical and robust connections are still not established among the three fields of studies as described above.

N. L. Black et al. (Eds.): IEA 2021, LNNS 220, pp. 163–171, 2021.
https://doi.org/10.1007/978-3-030-74605-6_20

1.2 Research Question and Objective

This paper frames theoretical reflections to connect the DfA approach with Policy Ergonomics (PE) through the RTC theory. Is the RTC model a method of inquiry that enhances the ergonomics of the policy-making through participative design procedures? Is the RTC model representative of ergonomics methods for enhancing inclusive, democratic, emancipatory design-driven innovations for the society?

With these questions, this paper investigates possibilities for connecting PE as an inclusive field of study through the RTC model by integrating the DfA philosophy in the form of variables of the RTC model.

2 Methodological Approach

2.1 RTC as a Model_for

We used the RTC as a "model_for" [3] connecting the variables of the RTC model with the DfA philosophy by assuming the context of the policy-making. As discussed by Junginger [7, 8], we started considering the process of policy-making as designing. In contemporary era, designing by its nature "is shifting to the concept of 'co': to collaboration, co- creation and co- design as a central feature, emphasizing the explicit involvement of users, partners, suppliers and other stakeholders in the design process" [2]. Also, if we consider design "as a projective process, human-centered process, innovation process, emancipatory process, political/social process" [9] in a second-order cybernetic system we can understand its role as a knowledge generator. It is the case of the Research Through Design (RTD) that is a type of research that "recognises its source in design, and which uses the insights and understandings of design in its pursuit" [3]. When we mention RTD, we mean that category of design research [10] as an "embodied/situated/intentional observer inside a design/inquiring system, generating knowledge and change through active participation in the design/inquiring process" [9]. Therefore, what we know about RTD can take advantage of the contemporary nature of design that is substantially shifting on models and processes of doing design in a collaborative way. Accordingly, the RTD is naturally going in the direction of research methods of inquiry driven by co-design processes; and this is the case of the RTC theory [11, 12].

Consequently, if we consider the process of policy-making as designing we can also consider its role in producing knowledge by a co-design process. Or better, as we framed in previous works [6] we can consider policy-making as a process that can take advantages from the RTC model where the policy-maker can act as a designer-researcher [13, 14]. This is also supported by the idea that "the generation of new, innovative and transformative policies depends on the ability of policymakers to inquire into situations before they turn into problems" [8]. If we consider the problem or question to be addressed in policy-making as a research question, and the policy-making process as the co-design process, we can consider the RTC as a model for giving answers to the need of inclusive and innovative policies through participative and democratic mechanisms.

2.2   The RTC Model as a Neural Network for the Context of Policy-Making

The RTC is a mathematical model of cognitive control that can be useful for understanding how co-creating knowledge through a co-design process in a wider research process. This model allows to frame how to reach a research answer C(s) through a co-design process G(s) where at least two persons collaborate (Co $\geq$ 2) to find the design answer(s) C1 with the aim to understand its capacity to respond at the research question R(S) according to its relevance with the error E(s) after the testing H(s). Figure 1 reports the transfer function of the model and graphically describes the RTC model.

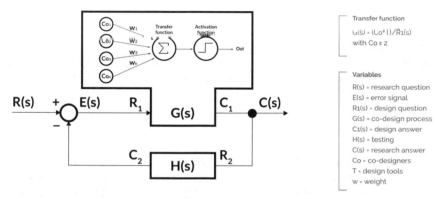

Fig. 1.   Graphical representation, variables, and transfer function of the RTC model.

We can represent G(s) as a neural network where each co-designer can be represented as a node that communicates with one or more co-designers. This neural network mechanism of co-designing is such a computing neural model that serves as algorithms to train and simulate the elaboration of a research answer through a co-design process minimizing the error between the obtained research answer C(s) and pre-fixed research question R(s). Accordingly, the nodes are like neurons of biological mechanisms [15] augmenting consciousness, through learning and consequently creating knowledge. Human intelligence is the capability to accomplish complex goals requiring judgment, creativity, empathy, interaction, and multi-domain expertise. This can be distinguished by the consciousness that it also depends on subjective experience. In RTC, each co-designer presents his own consciousness that serves as algorithms for the estimations of the best sets of interconnection weights based on their experience and domain.

Co-design joins different expertise, fields of knowledge, background and experiences in design; it puts together people that collaborate in terms of working together towards a common interest, project and goal [16]. In G(s) the co-designers are nodes, as neurons of a brain, with different backgrounds, knowledge, competencies and relational intelligence respect to designing. If we consider them as nodes of a neural network, they have different weights (the variable w in Fig. 1). From a DfA perspective, this diversity is a value for the whole design process. From these reflections emerged how to consider diversity as a representative value of the DfA philosophy in the RTC process. Every node is a person, and every person is different in real life. This means every person participating in the design process has a different weight (w) which cannot be under-estimated. Following a real inclusive philosophy in establishing a participative design process means that nobody can decide who is including or excluding whom in a design process. Potentially everybody should be included in the design process - especially in complex and democratic-driven circumstances such as it is expected in the case of policy-making contexts. But this is not always possible or achievable.

Therefore, how can we understand the weights (w) of the different co-designers in the design process? What are the best weights needed to be really representative of diversity as a value?

We used the RTC process as a cybernetic model to guide our reflection and identify a structure for describing the different weights of the nodes that is the diversity of the co-designers as a value. This diversity of the nodes (co-designers in G(s)) is described with a mathematical expression consisting of variables - a polynomial [17]. In the form of variables of the RTC model in G(s), the polynomial links factors that can determine the inclusions/exclusions when we design and elements that can influence the DfA philosophy through the nodes (Co).

2.3   The DfA in the RTC Model

The European network EIDD-Design for All Europe [18] defines DfA as the design "for human diversity, social inclusion and equality" and as a holistic and an innovative approach that "constitutes a creative and ethical challenge for all planners, designers, entrepreneurs, administrators and political leaders. Design for All aims to enable all people to have equal opportunities to participate in every aspect of society [...] and requires the involvement of end users at every stage in the design process". We can also read this definition highlighting that DfA fights exclusion through design by (i) spreading participation and equality, (ii) reinforcing the interaction with the context, (iii) exploring diversity as a creative resource. Also, fighting exclusion through design means addressing the aspects in the society can create the exclusion. Therefore, we used five exclusion factors [19, 20] with the aim to understand how to relate the concept of exclusion with representative elements of the DfA variables in the RTC model according to the context of policy-making. Finally, we used the RTC model as a 'model_for' understanding the variables for designing inclusive policies.

3   Results

3.1   Design for All Variables

As the main result, we identified the "Design for All variables" in the RTC model that generates a significant influence in the output of the RTC system. Therefore, as this connection is established in the policy-making context, we identified the touchpoints where the DfA approach in the RTC model generates an influence in this context.

In practice, we designed a polynomial that can be useful in the RTC as a process for designing inclusive policies through the DfA approach. We defined it as the Poly-nomial of Diversity (PoD) because it considers five exclusion factors (a, b, c, d, e) as values to be multiplied by the elements (x, y, z) that guarantee the diversity as the main representative value of the DfA approach in the RTC system. Therefore, these elements are the participation (x) of the different people/actors in the RTC process; the context (y) in terms of a significant interaction of the design beneficiaries with the context; the personalization (z) as an intrinsic attitude of the self/auto-regulation feature of the RTC system in favour of the different people/actor's needs.

The Elements of the PoD. The three identified elements that determine the basic representation of the DfA approach through variables in the neural network (G(s) in Fig. 1) are detailed explained in the following paragraphs.

The Participation (x). This is the variable that multiplied with the five exclusions factors allows to guarantee the effective presence of the diversity as a creative value in the design process (G(s)). For 'participation' we mean the presence in the RTC system of the different systems' actors as co-designers in the design process (G(s)). They are nodes of the neural network; and every node is different from each other. More the diversity is represented in the G(s), greater is the possibility to reach an inclusive design answer (C1).

The Context (y). This is the variable that multiplied with the five exclusions factors allows to consider the interactions with the different contexts. We assume that the utopian term 'for all' in DfA can be translated to specificities of the context, especially in the area of policy design. Therefore, as we consider the act of policy-making as designing, we assume that every inclusive policy can be based on universal principles such as democracy and human rights, but the application is context-related. Accordingly, every design of inclusive policy depends on the actor's relations with the contexts and we can consider the knowledge of the context as a variable to be expressed in the RTC process. The context elements cause an imbalance in the system and can push the RTC system in an opposite direction, or they can affect G(s). They can be considered design conditions that allow the respect of the nature of the context. For instance, the environmental sustainability, compliance with environmental standards, ergonomics standards or anthropological conditions can be interpreted as design constraints given by the context which must be considered as a variable that affects G(s).

The Personalization (z). This is the variable that multiplied with the five exclusions factors allows to consider the different needs of the people in front of a design solution - for instance a new policy. By definition, the RTC process is a self/auto-regulation process. It finds an equilibrium through the close-loop circle and by the co-design process G(s). This system mechanism also favours the formulation of customizable design solutions that have greater possibility to respect the different needs of the system actors. The greater is the personalization of the design solutions, the greater is the possibility to match the system actor's needs. And this is more valuable in the context of policy-making.

The Exclusion Factors of the PoD. We used five factors that can determine exclusions (i.e. physical and cognitive, cultural, social, political, economical). They can also be described as design domains to be considered in a holistic manner [19] for facilitating the findings of inclusive design answers. These aspects are translated into variables of the PoD for understanding the weights of the co-designers in the context of policy-making.

The first factor concerns physical and cognitive aspects of the individuals and considers aspects such as how people physically and cognitively interact with physical objects and spaces, physical and digital systems inherent to the policies considering aspects such as vision, hearing, thinking, dexterity, and locomotion. In this case, this domain mainly focuses on inclusive approaches for designing physical and digital products and spaces related to the design answer that is a policy solution.

The second factor concerns cultural aspects of the individuals and considers how these influence the policy and how the diversity, different ways of living, and different values are treated by the policy. This factor mainly focuses on inclusive approaches for designing solutions with a strong impact on the knowledge, the training and the education of all the stakeholders that affect the policy.

The third factor concerns social aspects of the individuals and considers how they affect the possibility to create relationships, social support, and solidarity through the policy. This factor mainly focuses on inclusive approaches for designing solutions that enhance the support, the mutual help, the solidarity and the collaboration among the stakeholders and the society.

The fourth factor concerns political aspects and considers how legislation, policies and practices affect the level of the democracy and the opportunity of participating in public life through the new policy. This factor mainly focuses on inclusive approaches for designing solutions related to the policies and how these aspects can be integrated or can influence governments and policy makers.

The fifth factor concerns economical aspects and considers how the economic status of the people, the costs, the labour condition and the economical sustainability is considered in the policy. This factor mainly focuses on inclusive approaches for designing solutions related to the management and the distribution of the resources, and aspects such as the labour conditions and the redistributions of the roles.

Each factor considers how the single aspect can describe every node; therefore, how the single aspect can describe the capacity of the inclusion/exclusion of a policy for a single person in the neural network G(s).

3.2 The Polynomial of Diversity

The multiplication of the elements - i.e. the participation (x), the context (y), and the personalization (z) - with the five exclusions factors - i.e. physical and cognitive (a), cultural (b), social (c), political (d), economical (e) defines the PoD as a P or polynomial in the RTC process. It is described by the Eq. (1).

$$P = (a + b + c + d + e)(x + y + z) \tag{1}$$

The polynomial describes the weight that is called "learning of the perceptron" [21] that categorizes the diversity of each co-designer in the co-design process G(s). The sum of the products of the weight and the input in each node are computed at perceptron function G(s) that need to pass a threshold that fires (Fig. 1). The firing represents the capability or not of the success to determine the research answer through a co-design process G(s). We discussed possible DfA variables in the RTC model which could influence the constitution of a threshold in the model. These variables are related to the diversity of individuals as a resource with respect to the DfA approach. Therefore, the G(s) in the RTC model is basically a neuronal network, therefore a network where all the diversities collaborate. Potentially, the threshold to exit G(s) is crossed or not if this diversity is respected, if the design answer (C1) through the co-design process is truly representative of the different weights. At the same time, the threshold should also be able to measure the fact that one exits from G(s) only with innovative solutions. Therefore, the threshold considers some values that allow us to say that under a certain threshold there is no innovative solution - or better there is not an inclusive innovation solution. In the threshold there will also be an equation that will take into account both the variables of the diversity and that of the context as elements that also determine the level of innovation. Furthermore, we defined a threshold that takes into account DfA variables as key elements of innovation for all, but also general elements of novelty. These elements may be given by previous investigations that can be made either before G(s) or within G(s); for instance, to carry out operations such as a simple survey of the state of the art. In G(s) we must therefore insert a variable that influences an initial state and allows us to evaluate a final state of the design solution. This is an operation that should be within G(s) because H(s) is a testing to understand if the identified design solutions allow to respond to research question R(s) and are able to generate innovations for all.

4   Discussion

From a design perspective, the PoD helps practitioners, designers, designers-researchers, policy-makers to reflect on those variables that can influence the application of the DfA approach. This is even more effective in the case of the application of the RTC model in the context of policy-making that requires democratic, participative and innovative interventions. At the same time, the variables we identified in the PoD have the potential to enrich both the RTC model and the DfA approach. Also, the positioning of the variables and the possibility to calculate and simulate the model with these new variables reinforce the role of the DfA philosophy as a driver in research processes. Finally, the same variables facilitate the identification of ergonomic procedures for making policies for all. It means giving inclusive and democratic answers from the RTC model applied in the policy-making contexts by describing a research process.

The RTC works as a research process for identifying innovative answers for inclusive policies, and it is strongly oriented to understand the interactions among humans and the other elements of the systems exploiting the potential of co-design as an innovation process for the well-being of the society. Potentially, as applied in the policy-making context with the DfA approach, the RTC system allows to find research answers as new forms of knowledge for the well-being of the citizens. The RTC model can favour the designing of policies and the identification of new forms of civic knowledge in order to improve the interaction among citizens and other elements of the system. Therefore, we can recognise this process as an ergonomic set of procedures for studying - in this case - how to achieve an ergonomic output, so an ergonomic policy. The set of studies that deal with the understanding of the interactions between the society and the build of policies can be named as PE. Therefore, the main strength of this study is the connection between the DfA approach and the PE through the variables that can be represented and applied through the RTC model.

5 Conclusion

We argue the connections presented in this paper can positively influence multiple contexts and research domains such as ergonomics, design research, and policy studies also through inclusive approaches in design such as DfA. We studied how to link the DfA philosophy, the RTC theory and the policy-making contexts. They are three determinants domains for the development of innovative, sustainable and inclusive futures for the global society. However, this perspective requires a systematic investigation through design in order to (i) empower the interactions among citizens and the other systems, and (ii) reduce wicked gaps such as those among real people's needs and policy-makers; or those among governments and environmental sustainability - just to name a few. We defined the field that should be the catalyser of these inquiries as the PE field of study. It is a field of study that deals with the ergonomics in policy-making for enhancing participative, democratic, and emancipatory models to spread design-driven innovation for the society. In these terms, PE has the potential to match democratic, inclusive and design-driven research processes with the extensive scientific knowledge of the ergonomics disciplines.

Finally, the main limitation of this work is represented by the lack of applied cases and the difficulty in finding tangible examples of how the connections among the three fields can find a more tangible application. For this reason, about the next steps of this study we consider the collection of cases and data for simulating the model in the policy-making context.

References

1. Bendixen, K., Benktzon, M.: Design for All in Scandinavia - A strong concept. Appl. Ergonomics **46**, 248–257 (2015)
2. Bason, C.: Design for Policy. Routledge, Abingdon (2016)
3. Glanville, R.: A (cybernetic) musing: certain propositions concerning prepositions. Cybern. Human Knowing **12**(3), 87–95 (2005)
4. Jonas, W.: A cybernetic model of design research: towards a trans-domain of knowing. In: Rodgers, P.A., Yee, J. (eds.) The routledge companion to design research, pp. 23–37. Routledge, Abingdon (2014)
5. Levine, W.S.: The Control Handbook: Control System Fundamentals, 2nd edn. CRC Press, Boca Raton (2011)
6. Busciantella-Ricci, D., Scataglini, S.: Discussing research through co-design in policy-making. In Rebelo, F., Soares, M. (eds.) Advances in Ergonomics in Design. AHFE 2020. Advances in Intelligent Systems and Computing, vol. 1203, pp. 3–9. Springer, Cham (2020)
7. Junginger, S.: Design and innovation in the public sector: matters of design in policy-making and policy implementation. Ann. Rev. Policy Des. **1**(1), 1–11 (2013)
8. Junginger, S.: Towards policy-making as designing: policy-making beyond problem-solving & decision-making. In: Bason, C. (eds.) Design for Policy, pp. 104–121. Routledge, Abingdon (2016)

9. Jonas, W.: Research through design is more than just a new form of disseminating design outcomes. Constructivist Found. **11**(1), 32–36 (2015)
10. Frayling, C.: Research in art and design. Roy. Coll. Art Res. Papers **1**(1), 1–5 (1993)
11. Busciantella Ricci, D., Scataglini, S.: A co-model for research through co-design. In Di Nicolantonio, M., Rossi, E., Alexander, T. (eds.) Advances in Additive Manufacturing, Modeling Systems and 3D Prototyping. AHFE 2019. Advances in Intelligent Systems and Computing, vol. 975, pp. 595–602. Springer, Heidelberg (2020)
12. Busciantella-Ricci, D., Scataglini, S.: Making design knowledge democracy happen. Disegno Industriale – Ind. Des. (DIID) **71**, 80–87 (2020
13. Cross, N.: Design research: a disciplined conversation. Des. Issues **15**(2), 5–10 (1999)
14. Cross, N.: Designerly Ways of Knowing. Springer, London (2006)
15. Barrett, D.G., Morcos, A.S., Macke, J.H.: Analyzing biological and artificial neural networks: challenges with opportunities for synergy? Curr. Opin. Neurobiol. **55**, 55–64 (2019)
16. Zamenopoulos, T., Alexiou, K.: collective design anticipation. Futures **120**, 1–13 (2020)
17. Barbeau, E.J.: Polynomials. Springer, New York (2003)
18. EIDD Design for All Europe. What is DfA. https://dfaeurope.eu/what-is-dfa/, Accessed 09 Feb 2021
19. Busciantella Ricci, D., Rinaldi, A., Tosi, F.: Supporting inclusive approaches in service design with netnography. In: Di Bucchianico, G. (eds.) Advances in Design for Inclusion. AHFE 2018. Advances in Intelligent Systems and Computing, vol. 776, pp. 290–301. Springer, Heidelberg (2019)
20. Busciantella Ricci, D., Dong, H., Rinaldi, A., Tosi, F.: Discussing about "Inclusion in Sharing-Based Services". A design workshop using an analytic tool. Des. J. **20**(sup1), S4671–S4677 (2017)
21. Rosenblatt, F.: The perceptron: a probabilistic model for information storage and organization in the brain. Psychol. Rev. **65**(6), 386–408 (1958)

A Highly Legible Font for All

Marco Canali[1]([⊠]), Christina Bachmann[2], and Federico Alfonsetti[1]

[1] EasyReading Multimedia srl, Turin, Italy
canali@easyreading.it
[2] Centro Risorse, Clinica Formazione e Intervento in Psicologia, Prato, Italy

Abstract. Reading is a frequent activity in everyday life for most people all over the world. A highly legible font represents an effective and inexpensive device to help reading in an accurate and less fatiguing fashion. The EasyReading® font was originally conceived to alleviate the hindrance experienced by dyslexic readers, but its design has soon evolved to encompass the broader public. To this end the Design for All methodology has represented a constant guiding reference.

Examples of the solutions adopted in the design of roughly one thousand glyphs are presented to illustrate the simplicity of the main concept at the foundation of EasyReading®.

The results and the conclusions of three independent scientific investigations are reported and briefly discussed. In two cases the main question concerns the effectiveness of EasyReading® vs. Times New Roman as an aiding tool for dyslexic pupils compared to normal readers of the same educational level. The third case offers a challenging point of view about the effectiveness of a font as an aiding device.

Finally, a brief overview is offered about possible practical applications and future developments of the font.

Keywords: High legibility · Font · Dyslexia · Ergonomics · Design for All

1 Introduction: A Highly Legible Font

The absolute relevance of reading as a daily activity needs no assessment. The act of reading is so frequent and - after a reasonable training period - automatic, that one can safely state that we read almost with the same frequency as we breathe, and possibly almost with the same urgency. As with breathing, the more natural and effortless reading is, so much the better. Hence the importance of choosing a font that, all other conditions being equal, makes reading smoother, faster and less prone to errors.

1.1 Main Features of a Highly Legible Font

It widely accepted that a text, at least one written in a language and/or composed using letters of Greek or Latin origin, is so much more legible as it features:

– a sans serif font

N. L. Black et al. (Eds.): IEA 2021, LNNS 220, pp. 172–179, 2021.
https://doi.org/10.1007/978-3-030-74605-6_21

– adequate horizontal (between characters/words) and vertical (interline) spacing
– adequate character size

The absence of embellishments in the glyphs of a sans-serif font makes reading easier, because the eye is not distracted in deciphering non-meaningful information. Widening the horizontal spacing reduces the possible misreading of certain groups of characters, when some common fonts are used (Times New Roman among them!); augmenting the interline further counters the perceptive confusion known as the crowding effect; and enlarging the size of the signs up to a practical limit makes the written message more readable, albeit more space consuming.

It is worth noting that normally the spacing and size of the characters can be adjusted and adapted as an alteration to an original work, whereas the serif/sans-serif attribute is inherent to the font of choice.

1.2 Some Clarity About Dyslexia

Dyslexic readers report several difficulties when confronted with a written message, often described in terms of revolving and/or levitating characters, place-swapping words, mixing up lines, and similar. These misperceptions seem to be fundamentally related to the incapability of recognizing with sufficient precision, confidence and speed the single signs and groups of signs contained in the text. It is as if the eyes literally bounced left to right, up and down, struggling to grasp some point to hold on and lock in.

The above observations have led in the past to conceive and design *specific* fonts *dedicated* to dyslexics, e.g., Dislexie. In order to tackle the most common difficulties, their glyphs were expressly designed to feature thick, bold and heavy strokes, so that they would not fly, rotate, nor revolve. Gravity does the trick here!

While the effectiveness of such solutions has been widely challenged, two questions are worth considering:

– is the use of a *specific* font for dyslexics perhaps too much connoting (and maybe discriminating)?
– is a *dedicated* font for dyslexics useful, or just neutral, or even detrimental to normal readers?

1.3 EasyReading®: A Highly Legible Font for All

When in 2008 Federico Alfonsetti started designing a new font, he had a clear goal in mind: To provide dyslexic young students with an effective tool to alleviate their learning disorder. Early into the project, though, he envisioned his creation as being both attractive and useful for any readers, not just dyslexics.

Refraining from the needless features found in the existing, single-purpose fonts, while at the same time forging a universally valid instrument was the defying task. The goal throughout years of refinements, testing and enhancements has been to effectively make EasyReading® a truly inclusive, highly legible typeface for any reader, not just dyslexics.

To Serif or Not to Serif. The first myth to debunk is that pure sans-serif font ought to be the natural choice. As matter of fact, the careful crafting of a *hybrid* font, in which serif and sans-serif characters coexist, goes a long way in reducing visual misperceptions (see Fig. 1).

Fig. 1. Examples of selected, non-symmetrical glyphs of EasyReading®

Essentially, adding *ad hoc* stems to and slightly altering the strokes of selected letters and numbers breaks the symmetry usually found in the same glyphs of most fonts, thus mitigating the confusion induced by the rotating/revolving letters effect.

Countering the Crowding Effect. We have mentioned that wider horizontal and vertical spacings enhance the visual deciphering of a text; and that spacing is a formatting choice normally available even to the casual typist. The glyphs of EasyReading® are so designed as to be intrinsically more spaced in both dimensions. The beneficial consequence is a considerable reduction of the crowding effect (see Fig. 2).

Fig. 2. Built-in spacing in the glyphs of EasyReading® and Calibri.

A Truly Inclusive Solution. None of the aesthetic attributes of EasyReading® identifies the font as specifically designed for dyslexics. The bold strokes, 'heavy' characters and other mundane expedients introduced in almost every "dyslexia-friendly" font are notably absent. EasyReading® aims to be by any count a highly legible font for all *and* helpful for dyslexics, a distinctive hallmark of a truly Design for All solution.

2   EasyReading® Put to the Test

The claims that EasyReading® is both a highly legible, good for all font and a valid compensating tool for dyslexic readers have been subjected to close inspections in the last eight years. The font has been the topic of a number of scientific studies, published articles and doctoral theses.

Positive evidence from the first, fundamental investigation, and from of one of the most recent works is briefly presented and it appears strongly encouraging. A more challenging result is also reported and discussed.

2.1 Bachmann et al., 2013–2018

In a study published in 2013 [1] and subsequently revised in 2018 [2], Bachmann illustrated the findings of a research conducted in two phases on a population of 89 and then 533 pupils, including both normal readers and children with various diagnosed learning disorders, including dyslexia. The stated objective of the investigation was to assess whether a font can be considered a compensating tool for readers with dyslexia. A sketched description of the methodology follows.

Phase One. The subjective preferences for EasyReading® vs. the widely used Times New Roman font were gathered in the first phase. Texts printed with both fonts were administered and questionnaires were proposed, where the subjects indicated their level of agreements – according to a Likert scale – about several characteristics of the two fonts. A statistically significant score in favor of EasyReading® ensued.

Phase Two. The natural question arose: Are readers' preferences suggesting or implying any degree of effectiveness for dyslexics or even for normal readers? Moving from possibly subjective biases to actual performance measurements was in order to dispel this legitimate doubt. Fluency and accuracy were then scrutinized in hundreds of fourth grade pupils, divided into four groups according to the relative reading prowess. Several different tests were fielded, and the specific results are detailed in the bibliographic references.

The Conclusions. In 2018 the seminal work was revised, expanded and translated in English. Excerpts from the new publication are quoted (emphasis added):

*"Results show a **statistically relevant** difference between performances undertaken with EasyReading™ font as opposed to Times New Roman. The EasyReading™ font proved to have positive impact on reading fluency across all reading tests (excerpts, words and non-words).*

Dyslexic children scored significantly better in reading accuracy with EasyReading™. Consequently, the EasyReading™ format was not only preferred by most of the students (phase 1 of the present research), but also helped to improve their reading performances (phase 2)."

*"The improvement in reading fluency (syllables per second) when using the EasyReading™ font, is **statistically and clinically significant -** an improvement of 0.16 [syllables per second] in reading fluency in non-words and of 0.52 [ditto] in excerpts, surpassing the natural, annual improvement [of 0.14 and 0.30 syllables per second respectively [3]]"*

*"Based on the evidence collected and the consistent results, it can be concluded that the EasyReading™ font **facilitates reading** for both normal and dyslexic readers and can rightfully be considered **a very effective compensating tool for dyslexia and a facilitating font for all readers**".*

We strongly encourage the reader to consult the complete published papers for a deeper analysis and further conclusions.

2.2 Mengoni, Castagna, 2020

More recently Mengoni and Castagna [4] obtained similar results and drew comparable conclusions examining a small, yet statistically relevant group of 7 to 11-years old pupils. Like in Bachmann's work, several texts written in EasyReading® and Times New Roman were presented – excerpts, lists of words, lists on non-words - and reading speed and accuracy were measured.

The final scores show a statistically significant ($p < 0.005$) improvement of the performances across speed and accuracy in both the excerpt and word-list tests, whereas the improvement in the test with lists of non-words does not appear to be statistically sound. The Authors note, though, that the incidence of non-words has little practical relevance in normal life.

Selected remarks in the Authors' final conclusions seem noteworthy (freely, not verbatim quoted):

a. The use of an effective font, easily deployed in learning environments in written texts and on multimedia device, can help reducing the sense of diversity experienced by pupils affected by Specific Learrnig Disorders.
    Again, this is the goal of the Design for All methodology!
b. Further tests should include a control group of normal readers alongside with SLD, dyslexic or otherwise impaired individuals.
    So true, in fact, that Bachmann's Phase 2 study involved four groups of pupils, one of them composed of normal readers.
c. Further investigations are in order as to whether the performance improvements in speed and accuracy be correlated with the text content comprehension capability.

This is particularly stimulating and, together with questioning the incidence of the readers' age and educational level, is certainly worth deeper research.

2.3 Galiussi et al., 2020

In a paper published in 2020 [5] Galiussi et al. seriously challenged the claim that inherent morphological features of a dyslexia-friendly font be anyhow beneficial for a speedier and more accurate reading experience. Namely, EasyReading®, with its dedicated serif, longer ascenders and descenders, and wider built-in inter-letter spacing has been put under scrutiny.

The research specifically disputes that the sheer *spacing*, be it inter-letter, inter-word or interline, coupled with any choice of serif/sans serif glyphs, can effectively mitigate the crowding effect and enhance the recognition of characters. It rather attributes the largest share of positive effects, if any, to the *size* of the signs used in the written text. In addition, it correctly points out that studies ought to be carried out on groups of more adult (i.e., more trained and educated) readers. It goes overall at great length to dissect and illustrate several aspects of the employed methodology and statistical evidence.

Although a well argued, sharp, and critical attitude certainly represents a welcome stimulus – and a sort of appreciation – a few observations contained in the article seem frankly off-mark. To wit:

Spacing is mostly irrelevant and after all it can be adjusted: EasyReading® has an optimal horizontal and vertical spacing built-in, a definite advantage over other fonts. And quite a few studies demonstrate that spacing is relevant indeed. See Fig. 3.

Wider-spaced fonts/texts make for shorter sentences, and these are inherently more easily readable: true, but Bachmann's works [1, 2] are not plagued with this bias.

Statistical evidence attributes no advantage to any font: while this remains yet to be decided, the sheer subjective preference for EasyReading® expressed by the majority of pupils in Bachmann, Phase 1 [1, 2] might suggest that a more enjoyable, endurable reading experience awaits those readers, who can use their font of choice.

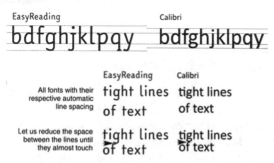

Fig. 3. Interline spacing in EasyReading® compared with Calibri. Longer ascenders and descenders reduce vertical crowding.

3 State of the Art and Future Developments

We believe that EasyReading ® represents an efficient, cost-effective, easily portable and deployed solution, allowing anyone to enjoy reading in faster, less fatiguing fashion, all else being equal. Our opinion is supported by a growing number of investigations, together with positive feedbacks from the general public.

3.1 Where We Stand

As of this writing, February 2021, EasyReading®:

- is the only dyslexia-friendly font, that underwent and passed many scientific examinations - most of them with flying colors
- is a proven highly legible font
- offers over 1,000 glyphs in six different styles, covering the Latin, Greek and Cyrillic alphabets
- is a standard TTF font, readily installed on any platform or device that allows font customization
- is widely adopted by public and private organizations: publishers, associations, foundations, enterprises
- is freely available for non-commercial use [6].

But we are not done yet. Both supporting and skeptical studies encourage the team at EasyReading Multimedia to pursue further developments.

3.2 What Lies Ahead?

A brief overview of promising scopes follows:

Research. While dyslexia, particularly in early stages of life, rightly deserves attention, we feel that the more general realm of high legibility should be explored. To this end we would gladly welcome and foster investigations encompassing broader population groups in terms of age, educational level, and reading impairments.

Different Cultures. The diffusion of dyslexia among the alphabetized populations has been measured in areas of the world, where the prevailing written languages are based on the Greek alphabet and its most widespread derivatives, Latin and Cyrillic alphabets. The current design of EasyReading® adapts and modifies the characteristics of the signs contained in those alphabets. We wonder whether and how our solution could be applied to vastly different ways of writing; and how high legibility would be attained.

Practical Applications. Written messages are ubiquitous in everyday life. Just think of books, magazines, newspapers, mail; and of course computer screens and printed documents. Now include user instruction manuals, road signs, posters, billboards, timetables; TV programs subtitles and of course the evermore commonplace tablets and smartphones. Add warning signs, drug description leaflets, …: Dyslexia and learning disorders are not the only issues here, legibility for all is.

EasyReading® can very well be put to good use in any of these places and contexts, wherever and whenever the need arises to convey a written message with clarity, accuracy, and urgency. Or, in other words, where and when a *highly legible font for all* stands as an *inclusive, universal ergonomic tool.*

3.3 An Enticing Agenda

Putting everything together, a couple of practical, intriguing questions come to mind and suggest a possible to-do list:

- Should Hebrew be immediately considered as a natural extension of the EasyReading® glyph set?
- How common is dyslexia in those areas, where the written languages are stroke- rather than character-based, such as Chinese, Arab, Korean and others? Would readers in those languages benefit from a specially, dyslexia friendly font? And how would high legibility be practically implemented into, say, Japanese kanji?

No, we are not done yet!

References

1. Bachmann, C.: Può un font essere uno strumento compensativo per i lettori con dislessia? Dislessia. Giornale italiano di ricerca clinica e applicativa **10**(2) (2013)
2. Bachmann, C., Menghero, L.: Dyslexia and fonts: is a specific font useful? Brain Sci. **8**(5) (2018). https://www.mdpi.com/2076-3425/8/5/89/htm

3. Tressoldi, P.E., Stella, G., Faggella, M.: The development of reading speed in Italians with dyslexia: a longitudinal study. J. Learn. Disabil. **34**(5), 414–7 (2001)
4. Mengoni, V., Castagna, L.M.: Confronto delle prestazioni di lettura di testi in Times New Roman e in EasyReading in soggetti con DSA e DA. DIS. Giornale italiano di ricerca clinica e applicative **1**(2) (2020)
5. Galliussi, J., et al.: Inter-letter spacing, inter-word spacing, and font with dyslexia-friendly features: testing text readability in people with and without dyslexia. Ann. Dyslexia **70**, 141–152 (2020). https://doi.org/10.1007/s11881-020-00194-x
6. https://www.easyreading.it/en/users-license/

An Inclusive Design Approach for Designing an Adaptive Climbing Wall for Children with CP

Maria Rita Canina(✉), Chiara Parise, and Carmen Bruno

IDEActivity Center, Design Department, Politecnico di Milano, Via Durando 38/A, 20158 Milan, Italy
{marita.canina,chiara.parise,carmen.bruno}@polimi.it

Abstract. The increasing awareness of social diversity has attracted the interest and attention of designers who more than ever before have started to design solutions aimed at enabling everyone to obtain increased independence for performing everyday tasks. The inclusive design approach has been largely applied in adaptive sports, to improve levels of functioning in daily living activities, increase physical capability, physiological capacity, levels of employment, social status and sense of belonging. Designing for inclusiveness is a complex and challenging activity that requires the adoption of a specific inclusive design process to create human-centred solutions based on user desire and needs. The paper shows the inclusive design process adopted to support a design team to identify the inclusive requirements for designing a climbing wall for rehabilitation that considers children's diversity. This process is presented through a project whose aim is to use the climbing sport as a tool for recreational rehabilitation for children with Cerebral Palsy (CP). The inclusive design approach enables to involve in the design process the CP children and all the relevant actors that deals with their rehabilitation and the climbing sport: the children family, physiotherapists, climbing instructors, professional climbers, and the project researchers. This allowed to identify the design requirement by broadly and deeply considering their needs, desires, knowledge, experience and expertise.

Keywords: Adaptive sports · Inclusive design process · Co-design approach

1 Introduction

In recent years, Europe has been moving towards a concept of inclusivity as highlighted by the sixteenth goal of the 2030 Sustainable Development Goals Agenda that promotes peaceful and inclusive societies [1–3].

The increasing awareness of social diversity has attracted the interest and attention of designers who more than ever before have started to design solutions aimed at enabling everyone to obtain increased independence - in terms of help and social support - for performing everyday tasks [4].

Indeed, designing for inclusivity not only opens the use of products and services to a wider and more heterogeneous audience, but it also reflects how people are. Understanding diversity is one of the main goals of inclusive design and design should catch

© The Author(s), under exclusive license to Springer Nature Switzerland AG 2021
N. L. Black et al. (Eds.): IEA 2021, LNNS 220, pp. 180–188, 2021.
https://doi.org/10.1007/978-3-030-74605-6_22

these important human diverse characteristics to design products that reflect it. Inclusive design, therefore, aims to lower the level of ability required to use a specific product/service in order to improve the user experience for a broad range of customers in a variety of situation [5].

The inclusive design approach has been largely applied in sports, in particular in adaptive sports, to improve levels of functioning and independence in daily living activities, increase physical capability, physiological capacity, levels of employment, social status and sense of belonging. All of these components influence an individual's quality of life. Adaptive sports can become a way to promote involvement as an active part in the rehabilitation exercise to stimulate neuromotor recovery, in particular in children with disabilities. Rehabilitation tools that involve the child in a natural way, that exploit the propensity to play, to sport, to compete, to stimulate the execution of specific exercises, can transform this effort into a game and multiply the effectiveness of the rehabilitation process [6].

Designing for children rehabilitation is a complex and challenging activity that requires the adoption of an inclusive design approach in order to create human-centred solutions based on user desire and needs. Also, the adoption of such inclusive approach allows to converge in a solution that could be accessible and used by as many people as reasonably possible [5].

This paper describes the inclusive design process adopted by the authors to identify the inclusive requirements needed to design a climbing wall for rehabilitation that considers children's diversity. This process has been applied within the ACCEPT project, in which the authors are involved as Polimi design team, whose aim is to use the climbing sport as a tool for recreational rehabilitation for children with Cerebral Palsy (CP). The inclusive design approach allowed to involve in the design process the CP children and all the relevant actors that deals with their rehabilitation and the climbing sport: the children family, physiotherapists, climbing instructors, and the project researchers. This allowed to identify the design requirement by broadly and deeply considering their needs, desires, knowledge, experience and expertise.

2 ACCEPT - Adaptive Climbing for CErebral Palsy Training

ACCEPT project aims to design and build a reconfigurable and interactive climbing wall optimised for the rehabilitation of CP children aged 6–13 by harnessing the expertise of research groups from the different university department.

Children with CP can in many cases recover some of their motor skills with intense rehabilitation work, especially if this begins during the early years of life, and climbing has been considered as a suitable mean of rehabilitation to stimulate reaching, grasping, supination, which are movements typically affected by the lesion of the neuro-motor system [7].

Indeed, ACCEPT introduces CP children to climbing making it accessible and inclusive, with the aim of helping children with different degrees of disability to build trust and awareness of their potentialities, and a sense of accomplishment while training problem-solving and decision-making skills [8].

From a motor point of view, the adaptive wall helps children to exercise balance, to become aware of the different parts of the body, to increase muscle strength, while the sensorised, reconfigurable and interactive surface wall provides doctors with precious data to guide therapy allowing to modulate the exercises based on the progress observed. Indeed, the sensors implemented in the wall enable different activities to be tested during motor rehabilitation sessions, providing the medical staff with a valid tool for qualitative and quantitative analysis of progress in a context that is stimulating and functional for the child.

The design of a climbing wall for CP children requires special attention for inclusiveness and the involvement of several professionals and actors in order to bring together climbing, the special needs of CP children and rehabilitation. Therefore, to define these requirements it has been necessary to identify a methodology that could lead to a coherent and effective solution, using a Human-Centred Design (HCD) approach based on the principles of inclusive design. Starting from the solutions on the market as the Everlast Adaptive Climbing Wall, the multidisciplinary research team studied the needs and desires of the users through co-design sessions organised with the qualified staff of the FightTheStroke association (Association of families of children with CP) and the other stakeholders involved. The complexity of the project required different skills to be brought into play, ranging from the design of the sensors and the climbing structure (mechanical, electronic, IT, design and ergonomics), to the medical and social knowledge necessary to involve children and to follow and guide them in the rehabilitation treatment.

The inclusive design methodology allowed to collect and understand from all the actors involved in the process the relevant information to improve the climbing experience and the wall itself, prioritizing the needs of children with CP. During the co-design sessions, the experience of FightTheStroke and the professionals involved enabled the definition of both the design, anthropometric and ergonomic requirements in terms of grips modularity, protrusions and proprioceptive inputs (colours, textures, sounds and lights) that help to improve sensory integration and to identify effective methods of analysing the interaction between children and ACCEPT.

To achieve the project goal, the climbing facility must be seen by the child as a playground and an adventure that is easily understood and used by children with different characteristics and that allows them to enjoy an experience. At the same time, it should provide the medical staff responsible for rehabilitation with the tools to stimulate the child to perform the specific exercises, but also to quantitatively measure the child's progress in performing these exercises. The project therefore uses the principles of inclusive design for adopting a holistic view that not only identifies the product requirements but also builds the user interaction experience.

3   Methodology

This paragraph defines the inclusive design process that supported the design team to identify the design requirements to create a climbing wall for rehabilitation of CP children. A HCD approach have been adopted aiming at clarifying the needs of CP children by deeply exploring their various abilities and by integrating the experience of physiotherapists, instructors and parents on the concepts of inclusion, rehabilitation, play, sport and safety. To this end, the IDEActivity method, developed by the authors, were adopted. The method is composed by a process - based on the Double Diamond divergent and convergent thinking model - and a set of tools - centred on the synergy between creativity techniques and design tools - to enable collaborative actions aimed at identifying and solving design problems through the direct involvement of users [9].

IDEActivity's process converges on two main consequent stages, Explore and Generate, and a total of four explicit process steps, each one with specific objectives and characterized by specific activities. Within the Explore stage an understanding of needs, hopes, and aspirations is crucial, and an analytical process of information interpretation is fundamental to identify opportunities. Explore is divided in two main steps: Clarify goal and Define Opportunities. The second stage, Generate, aims at the generation of suitable concepts in line with the given context and the prototyping of innovative ideas. It is divided in two main steps: Ideate and Prototype.

The newly developed inclusive design process is based on the comparison integration of the IDEActivity process and the "Inclusive Double Diamond" [10, 11]. The four phases of the "inclusive Double Diamond", also based on the British council model, have been adopted as a starting point to analyse the inclusive specific aspects to transfer to the new "IDEActivity inclusive process" (Fig. 1).

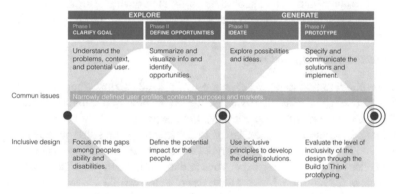

Fig. 1. IDEActivity inclusive design process created by comparing and integrating the IDEActivity process and the Inclusive Double Diamond (Sooshin Choi)

The Explore stage of the process started with a series of qualitative interviews with stakeholders (Fighthestroke, physiatrist and Italian Climbing Federation instructor) to better understand the challenges and weaknesses related to rehabilitation through sport climbing. A play session in the gym organised by Fighthestroke with 10 children with CP allowed direct observation of these children's abilities to approach climbing. These preliminary activities were fundamental to gather the information to define the objective of the co-design sessions, moving to the Generate stage of the process. POLIMI researchers then worked on the identified scenarios, comparing the literature and the results produced in the co-design session to create the guidelines, specific requirements and project challenges to be addressed. The process steps here summarized are described in detail in the next sub-sections.

3.1 Phase 1: Clarify Goal

The first phase allowed to investigate and understand the problems abilities of CP children through the direct experience of the people.

The Accept project sees the involvement of a multidisciplinary research team in which the presence of the FightTheStroke co-founder, mother of a CP child, has been fundamental to catch the everyday life difficulties of a CP children. The possibility of interviewing physiotherapists, climbing instructors and climbers, as experts in their fields, gave an all-round insight into the situation. The diversity of people backgrounds has been a great source of enrichment for defining the physiotherapeutic aspects and understanding the characteristics of climbing. At the same time, it has also been difficult to combine worlds with very different languages. The presence of staff qualified in climbing and rehabilitation allowed the design team to gather information and identify gaps and needs related to this hitherto unknown new rehabilitative practice for children with CP performed through climbing.

The results that emerged in this first phase, enhanced by desk research and validation of the data collected, made it possible to identify some interconnections between climbing and the rehabilitation of children with CP. Specifically, some typical movements of upper limb rehabilitation that should be stimulated during climbing were identified: hand opening, hand prone-supination, elbow extension, and thumb opposition.

3.2 Phase 2: Define Opportunity

The second phase aimed to converge, not only by synthesizing what has been gathered in the first research phase but also by reflecting on the potential impact that requirements identified could have on the people involved in the project.

The insight gathered from the Clarify goal phase has been subsequently defined and translated into precise tools in order to organize a co-design workshop with all the experts to generate ideas on the climbing experience and the wall itself, prioritizing the needs and requirements of CP children. Making the data collected visible and easy to communicate was fundamental to be able to convey the information also to less experienced people, or those with different backgrounds that participate in the co-design activities. This phase saw the use of IDEActivity tools such as scenario definition, persona creation, and graphic visualizations to define the context and the target that ACCEPT wants to address. The inclusive design asks to consider the whole range of human diversity and the average user (if it exists) cannot be considered as a good reference point for design because it implies an ideal design solution for a restricted group. Considering the whole range of diversity by including also the less common characteristics, undoubtedly allows reaching a wider audience. We therefore decided to use the personas tool not to identify similarities but to highlight differences. In order to give an overview of the behaviours and difficulties that a child with CP may experience, three personas were defined, each one affected by CP with a different degree of disability according to the MACS scale (Manual Ability Classification System for Children with Cerebral Palsy 4–18) [12] (Fig. 2).

Activity templates were created to guide the experts during the co-design session thus allowing the construction of a shared vision that leads to an inclusive climbing experience. The IDEActivity method foresees that each template is accompanied by an

Fig. 2. Co-design personas templates (Canina, Parise, Bruno)

explanation card with How and Why, which is given to each participant so that he/she always has this information at hand (Fig. 3).

Fig. 3. Co-design activities templates (Canina, Parise, Bruno)

3.3 Phase 3: Ideate

The Generate stage is focused on exploring possibilities and inclusive ideas. The co-design workshop objective was to co-generate ideas for stimulating the specific movements of the hands and for engaging children with CP during the climbing experience [13]. To this end, to co-design the climbing experience, some of the requirements highlighted in the research were shared and validated, also analysing the pre- and post-activity, delimiting specific objectives to be investigated, such as: definition of the tactile experience and cognitive engagement; identification of preparatory routes for climbing including observation of peers in the pre-activity; design of the route both as placement of holds and type of holds during the activity; and finally in the post-activity incentive to perform the rehabilitation activity continuously (rewards for children, goals to be achieved, etc.). The decision to focus the workshop activities on the climbing experience and not on finding technical solutions is in line with the philosophy of inclusive design, which aims to make the user experience satisfactory for all, responding appropriately to everyone's differences. Including diversity when designing experiences allows for better solutions for all.

To reach these goals experts from the ACCEPT team, climbing instructor, engineers, designers, and CP specialists, have been involved. The workshop consisted of two main activities: in the first one, the participants were invited to think of different interactions with surfaces, materials, objects, shapes to stimulate a given movement; in the second one, they tried to contextualize the emerged ideas in the climbing experience. Participant were guided by the tools and templates designed in the previous which highlighted their skills and experiences and made them accessible to everyone during the session. They facilitated the communication among people bringing out their strengths and helped in concretizing everyone's experience into tangible ideas. The ideas emerged aimed at the rehabilitation of the upper limbs and focused on engaging the children and make them feel like protagonists in the climbing game; others, instead, were concentrated on stimulating tactile and cognitive learning, proposing activities to involve children also in observing and visualizing movement from the other children.

3.4   Phase 4: Prototype

The last phase "involves testing out different solutions at small-scale, rejecting those that will not work and improving the ones that will" [14].

Following the workshop, the data and suggestions that emerged were collected and concretized in specific activities tested during one week of summer camp where children and a staff of professionals qualified in adapted motor sciences therapy and physiotherapy, participate in an intensive period of introduction to sport and rehabilitation. The introduction of an ordinary climbing wall allowed the experimentation of the activities built with the Build to Think technique, giving the opportunity to observe and validate the insights that emerged from research activities done on the previous phases. As the goal of the workshop was to understand how to readjust climbing for children with CP, solutions mostly related to the compressive experience of the child emerged, finding solutions in materials, activities, and goals to be achieved rather than defined products. For this reason, it was decided to transfer this information using the Build to Think technique, not testing a physical product, but an experience or behaviour. In this way, the principles of rehabilitation collected during the research phase have been adapted to a climbing experience. The activities included integrated exercises to be carried out in the warm-up pre-climbing activity and to stimulate and involve the child during the climbing phase.

In order to take note of children's behaviours and stimulated movements, an observation grid based on the identified requirements was provided to be used during the summer camp. It provided a series of general information about the holds and the interest shown by the children and specific questions for the observation of specific movements stimulated during the reference exercise. The results that emerged from this first phase of testing are subsequently guiding the design of the climbing wall and holds, in order to reach the project goal. Following the observation of the children during camp, a number of evaluations emerged which saw a preference for certain types of holds over others. In particular, jug and pocket holds were well used, as they encouraged the children to put their hand in the cavity and encouraged thumb opposition and prone - supination of the hand.

4 Results and Discussion

The methodology described in this paper shows how the inclusive design process can help in the definition of design requirements to create a climbing wall for CP children rehabilitation that combine play with physical exercise making the experience more fun and effective. In order to design a solution that can include a broad spectrum of diversity, we followed some of the simple steps that characterise this process, starting from the principle that inclusive design is participatory, and inclusivity is co-created with people at risk of exclusion. Involving people directly throughout the process is therefore fundamental and is the basis of our HCD approach, which has been enriched by inclusive design methods. The first step in inclusive design is to learn to recognise exclusions. This meant analysing the design objective by checking at each step of the way whether any of the mapped diversity could be excluded from the user experience. The second step is to learn from diversity by recognising bias. Everyone can bring his or her own biases into the project and this happens because we tend to use our own skill levels. The tools designed allowed new and different perspectives to emerge from the workshop, which are the key to true insight by avoiding bias. The design of different ways of experiencing climbing that are equivalent to each other was valued, thus fulfilling the third step for inclusive design. The opportunity to test some of the ideas that emerged during the co-design session at a summer camp with children with CP provided significant feedback for the design of the climbing wall.

The need to have specially designed holds that combine therapeutic exercises with the climbing movements, strongly emerged, as well as the idea to create paths for the association of perception. Indeed, holds installed on the wall with different textures could suggest to the child the correct movement and stimulate a tactile sensitivity of the injured side. For CP children is important to prioritize symmetrical shape in order to stimulate the child to approach them in a two-handed grip and to have tubular shapes and recesses that encourage children to use the hold correctly. Another important requirement is to engage children and give a sense of familiarity with the new experience they are approaching but at the same time create a flexible environment in order to adapt the climbing experience according to the special needs of each child.

The use of an inclusive methodology of double diamonds allowed the ACCEPT wall to be designed in a way to be a scalable product, able to be exported to a wider social system, and to adopt an inclusive approach so as to involve a wide range of users and not only users with disabilities.

References

1. United Nations Department of Global Communications: Transforming our world: the 2030 Agenda for Sustainable Development (2015). https://doi.org/10.1163/157180910X12665776 638740
2. Hunt, V., Prince, S., Dixon-Fyle, S., Yee, L.: Delivering through Diversity, p. 42. Mckinsey Co. (2018)
3. Dixon-Fyle, S., Dolan, K., Hunt, V., Prince, S.: Diversity wins! How inclusion matters, pp. 1–12. McKinsey Co. (2020)

4. Persson, H., Åhman, H., Yngling, A.A., Gulliksen, J.: Universal design, inclusive design, accessible design, design for all: different concepts—one goal? On the concept of accessibility—historical, methodological and philosophical aspects. Univers. Access Inf. Soc. **14**, 505–526 (2015). https://doi.org/10.1007/s10209-014-0358-z
5. Waller, S., Bradley, M., Hosking, I., Clarkson, P.J.: Making the case for inclusive design. Appl. Ergon. **46**, 297–303 (2015). https://doi.org/10.1016/j.apergo.2013.03.012
6. Reljin, V.: Effects of adaptive sports on quality of life in individuals with disability. Williams Honors College, Honors Research Project 822 (2019)
7. Vitrikas, K., Dalton, H., Breish, D.: Cerebral palsy: an overview. Am. Fam. Physician. **101**, 213–220 (2020)
8. Christensen, M.S., Jensen, T., Voigt, C.B., Nielsen, J.B., Lorentzen, J.: To be active through indoor-climbing: An exploratory feasibility study in a group of children with cerebral palsy and typically developing children. BMC Neurol. **17**, 1–20 (2017). https://doi.org/10.1186/s12 883-017-0889-z
9. Dong, H., McGinley, C., Nickpour, F., Cifter, A.S.: Designing for designers: insights into the knowledge users of inclusive design. Appl. Ergon. **46**, 284–291 (2015). https://doi.org/10. 1016/j.apergo.2013.03.003
10. Clarkson, P.J., Waller, S., Cardoso, C.: Approaches to estimating user exclusion. Appl. Ergon. **46**, 304–310 (2015). https://doi.org/10.1016/j.apergo.2013.03.001
11. Clarkson, P.J., Coleman, R., Hosking, I., Waller, S.D.: Inclusive DesignToolkit (2011)
12. Malak, R., Gajewska, E., Sobieska, M., Samborski, W.: Manual ability classification system for children with cerebral palsy. Fizjoterapia Pol. **10**, 69–77 (2010)
13. Cassim, J., Dong, H.: Interdisciplinary engagement with inclusive design - the challenge workshops model. Appl. Ergon. **46**, 292–296 (2015). https://doi.org/10.1016/j.apergo.2013. 03.005
14. DesignCouncil: What is the framework for innovation? https://www.designcouncil.org.uk/ news-opinion/what-framework-innovation-design-councils-evolved-double-diamond

Ergonomics Aspects in Workstation Development During the Covid-19 Pandemic

Cristiane Nonemacher Cantele[(✉)], Fabrício Santin, Jairo Beninca, Tiago Cezne, Maurício Veigel, Samuel Matté Madalozzo, and Jeferson A. Gevinski

Cavaletti Professional Seating S.A, Erechim, RS 99706-540, Brazil
{ergonomia,fabricio.s,jairo,tiago.c,mauricio.v,samuel.m,
jeferson}@cavaletti.com.br

Abstract. One of the main concepts of Ergonomics is to understand the adaptation of Jobs and the needs of its users, the Covid-19 pandemic presented new situations and new needs, with global impacts. Among the impacts are the repercussions of the international and financial scenario Market that has been assuming great proportions, directly affecting world markets, raising in investors the concern about the impacts on the global economy, such as the survival of companies after the pandemic. In addition to the financial impact, the virus affected the way of working with the prioritization of the Home Office and, gradually, the return to the work areas and the perspective of what the work environments will be like. How to adapt the work environments in order to preserve the health and safety of workers? What would be the best solution? To find a solution, a Brazilian company located in the south of the country developed a study whose main theme included the application of macro ergonomic concepts with the objective of designing a workstation that would meet the functional needs of its users and in a new perspective of work therefore, this work aims to demonstrate the application of the concepts of macroergonomics in the design and production of chairs through the involvement of workers and users and as specific objectives, the demonstration of the commercial needs and respective users with the multidisciplinary team involved, as well as highlighting the results end of the product and its perspective of relevance in the national and international market in times of global pandemic. Methodically semi-qualitative questionnaires based on the concepts of macro ergonomics were applied at all stages of the process, involving teams of development, process and manufacturing, marketing and users. It was concluded that the concepts of macro ergonomics applied proved to be effective in the design and definition of the ergonomic and functional characteristics of the product. In addition to being essential to list the functional needs of products and users.

Keywords: Ergonomics · Macro ergonomics · Ergonomic product

1 Introduction

The design when aligned with ergonomic concepts can generate an improvement in the quality and functionality of various products. In the design Project all the desired

N. L. Black et al. (Eds.): IEA 2021, LNNS 220, pp. 189–196, 2021.
https://doi.org/10.1007/978-3-030-74605-6_23

qualities are planned, combined with the procedural methodology. The Covid-19 pandemic generated large impacts in the world economy changing the work relationships and the way of achievement, to this end companies sought a readjustment/adaptation. Using analysis tools makes it easier to design projects that involve ergonomics-based priorities.

2   Theoretical Framework

2.1   Design Concept

According to Bcheche et al. (2013), Brandão (2011) the design seeks to cater the individual by promoting their well-being. For him, the design has expanded from various sciences, like architecture, engineering and advertising.

2.2   Ergonomics Design

Pequini (2005) ergonomics is related to various aspects such as: posture, body movements, environmental factors, perception factors, controls, as well as task analysis.

2.3   Macro Ergonomics

According to IDA (2005), the Macro ergonomicsappear as a development in man interaction – machine environment/organization occurring on a macro level. Macro ergonomicsalso called participatory ergonomics is a discipline of ergonomics that approaches how different professional approaches are involved in the design process. With that in mind, the concepts are integrated since the beginning of the processes, considering the organizational, technological, physic and organizational aspects, within considering the opinion of the interested people, promoting the professional's participation of various segments, as well as its mutual interaction. In that way the employee involvement in the design and operationalization of tasks significantly increases the chances of success in implementing the respective suggestions.

For Vink (2005) macro ergonomics can be described as the environment adaptation and the human being's needswith the involvement of its own participants of the process and users.

According Guimarães (2006), the AMT - Ergonomic Macro Analysis of Work is an analysis method that can be used by the researcher and ergonomist, as well as those responsible for the implementation of ergonomic actions, also emphasizes its focus of acting involving several stages of implementation, as well as its participatory character. Still, Guimarães (2006) reassures that the participation of the employeesin the restructuring of the work environment, added to the expert evaluation, it is extremely important to incorporate the necessary changes and to improve the conditions within the systems.

3 Methodology

The Project was based on the principles of macro ergonomics, in a way to relate the reality of the national and international context of Covid-19.

According to Guimarães (2006) the macro ergonomics is based in a participatory method, in which the public involved in the work process contributes to greater assertiveness of the interventions aiming at reducing the margin of error and increasing acceptance. In general its way of evaluation it is a unique approach of the four subsystems that include technological, environmental and interpersonal variables that interfere with productivity (Medeiros 2005; Kleiner 1998). Based on this applicability, the following steps were established:

Step 01 Selection of participants and survey guidelines· Through qualitative and quantitative research through an open and semi-structured questionnaire. Being the participants: National and international participant, commercial representatives related to market trends, internal workers involved in the process of designing, manufacturing and shipping the products.

Within this context the project's review focused on the ergonomic needs of the users, which were passed on to the design and engineering teams, as well as pertinent information to the commercial and marketing demands, data from competitors, and items that will compose the work environment. With emphasis on safety and health aspects. *Step 02 Product development:* After receiving the questionnaires the data was compiled and presented to the multidisciplinary team involved in the process: ergonomist, engineers, designers, architects, representatives of the commercial sector. Besides the representatives of the manufacturing process of the sectors: stapling, upholstery, carpentry, shipping, sewing and foam. Step 03 Product design development:According to the information collected, the product project was developed and the team involved was presented. Step 04 Project approval: After the approval the manufacturing steps were verified and together with the workers the improvements and optimization of the production process were defined. Step05 Prototype/mockup development: The mockups/product prototypes were presented to the team, associating the survey of improvements. Step06: Finalization of the product and its inclusion in the product portfolio. Step 07: Documentation, all steps were documented and statistically evaluated.

About sample the initial survey was carried out internally at the manufacturer of the product with representatives of the sectors, totaling 12 workers, externally through online questionnaires distributed to users by retailers and representatives, 865 responses were collected.

4 Results and Discussion

4.1 Results Regarding the Questionnaire Macro Ergonomic Concepts Applied to Representatives, Internal and External Commercial Team

4.1.1 Semi Quantitative Analysis

Regarding the current market needs, it was verified that 37% of the interviewees related the creation of collective spaces with security, 59% already reported the adaptation of collective spaces with security, 3% emphasized the resumption of the economy and 1% the retention of talents in companies.

Participants were also asked about the list of products offered by the main competitors in the market, company X was mentioned by 42% of participants, company Y was mentioned by 36% of participants and finally company W was mentioned by 22% of participants.

Still on the products manufactured by the competitors, they were asked which products were more representative in the market in relation to the current moment, 56% of the participants mentioned product X and 44% mentioned product Y.

Participants were also asked about the characteristics that a product should present to meet the current moment 59% related to isolation, 23% to safety and 18% to accessible value.

4.2   Results with Regard to the Questionnaire Related to the Macro Ergonomic Concepts Applied to the Users of the Company Products

Relationship product expectations for the current moment, which characteristicsshould be observed, the characteristics mentioned were described in Table 1.

Table 1. Product's expectations

Product's expectations		
Safe product	Customized product	Colorful product
Flexibility for the posture	Authentic product	Facility for sanitization
Notebook adaptation	Isolation	Privacy

4.3   Results Regarding the Project, Mockup and Final Product

4.3.1   Product's Features

Based on the information collected and data from the market, it was thought of a product with the following goals: Adaptation with privacy for collective environments,increase of the user's productive capacity, acoustic comfort, various forms of use, ease of use, possibility of customization.

4.4   Project Development

Based on the research data, the project consisted of meeting the main demands of the market (Fig. 1).

4.4.1   Mockup Development

Product test mockups were performed as shown in Fig. 2a, b and c.

Fig. 1. Product project, Source Authors

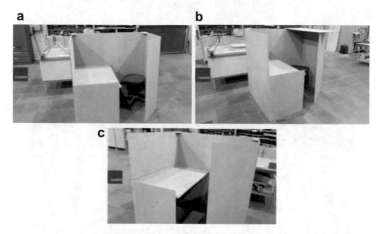

Fig. 2. Mockup product, Source Authors

4.4.2 Final Product and Respective Versions

After the resistance and durability tests, the final versions of the product were carried out (Fig. 3a and b).

4.4.3 Adjustments and Components

After approval of the final product, the coating components were inserted (Fig. 4).

4.4.4 Final Product

The final version of the product included the characteristics scored in the survey (Fig. 5).

a   b

Fig. 3. First version, Source Authors

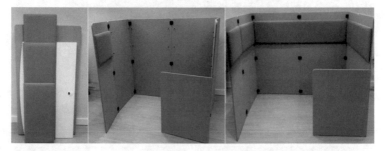

Fig. 4. Assembly components, fixing the hinges, placement of the acoustic boards, Source Authors

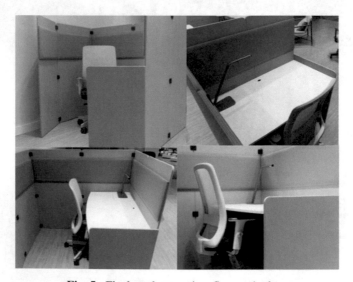

Fig. 5. Final product version, Source Authors

The Covid-19 context had a great impact on the world economy, in the context of corporate environments there were profound changes in the sense of readjusting spaces to resume the economy, as well as there was a great demand in the adaptation of home environments for home office/work.

For the companies in the furniture segment, there was an awakening to the Market opportunities, in this sense we sought a product that would serve the current needs maintaining the quality pattern in the process and in the product, always considering the ergonomics aspects in product design and manufacture.

Considering that the users spend most of their time seated it is important to maintain the ergonomics and comfort parameters in products, for that reason the company Cavaletti S/A has a commitment with the ergonomic of their products and processes.

It is known that ergonomics cause an impact in the quality of processes such as in the ergonomics criteria of products, it is understood that in the product's Project, must be taken into account the features, capacities, skills, aptitudes e the person's limitation.

Thus, the concepts are integrated from the beginning of the processes, considering the organizational, technological, physical and organizational aspects, besides considering the interested opinions, promoting the professionals participation of several segments, as well as its mutual interaction.In this way, the involvement of workers in the design and operationalization of tasks significantly increases the chances of success in the implementation ofrespective suggestions.

Based on these concepts we try to optimize this methodology continuously in a way to achieve our users and professionals involved in the design and manufacture of products.

5 Final Considerartions

This study aimed to demonstrate the enforcement of macro ergonomics in the design and production of a workstation adapted to the urgency of the new parameters of work environments dictated by the Covid-19.

It was found that when applying the principles of macro ergonomics in the creative process favored the knowledge of the users' needs, as well as the participation of internal teams and commercial agents.Favored the development of the product as well as the acceptance in the corporate market.

All the development process lasted for about 2 months, a record time for the company since it usually takes at least a year to design a new product, but the market and our users demanded a position that would serve that peculiar moment.

However even in a short period and in urgency condition the company prioritized the macro ergonomics concept associated to its product and process,being the product finalized and successfully accepted by the Market the methodology once again became efficient in order to add knowledge and experiencemainly because it considers the opinion of users and the entire team involved.

According to previous experiences, ergonomics is part of the process, the application of macro ergonomic concepts are part of the company's ergonomics routines and corporate routine.

References

Abrantes, A.F.: Ergonomics in the office environment. Technical Article (2001). https://www.inf
  ohab.org.br/entac2014/2006/artigos/ENTAC2006_1030_1039.pdf. Accessed 10 Feb 2018
Câmara, J.J.D., Vaz, C.S.: Design versus ergonomics: considerations about the practice of
  ergonomics by professionals from design schools. Ergon. Action 1(2), 72 (1999). Ergonomics.
  III Ergonomics Seminar in Bahia. Salvador: ABERGO
Diniz, R., Barbosa, Rengel, Raposo (orgs.) et al.: Ergonomics design usability interaction.
  ERGODESIGN/UFJF, Juiz de Fora (2013). 183 p.
Ettinger, K.: Management and Productivity. Direction, Organization and Administration of
  Companies. Teaching Manual 1. São Paulo, IBRASA (1964)
Graf, M., et al.: An assessment of seated activity and postures at five workplaces. Int. J. Ind. Ergon.
  15, 81–90 (1995)
La Ville, G., et al.: Understand the work to transform it. Translation: Giliane M. J. Ingratta, Marco
  Maffei. Edgar Blucher, São Paulo (2001). 200 p. Original title: Comprendreletravailpourletrans-
  formerla pratique de l'ergonomie
Guimarães, B.M.L. (org).: Macroergonomics: putting concepts into practice. In: Ergonomic
  Monographic Series c.1. FEENG/UFRGS, Porto Alegre (2010a)
Guimarães, B.M.L.: Historic. Environment. In: Process Ergonomics, vol. 1, 5th edn.
  FEENG/UFRGS, Porto Alegre (2010b)
Guimarães, L.B.M., Fogliato, F.S.: Macroergonomic design. I Africa Meeting
Haines, H., et al.: Validating a framework for participatory ergonomic. Ergonomics 45(4), 309–327
  (2002)
Ida, I.: Ergonomics- Design and Production, 2nd edn. Edgard Blücher, São Paulo (2005)
Ios, N., Imada, A.S.: A macroergonomic approach to produce design (1998)
Karwowski, W.: Plysical tasks: analysis, design and operation. In: Savendy, G. (ed.) Handbook of
  Industrial Engineering, 3rd edn. Wiley, New York (2001)
Kmita, S., Pastre, T., Guimaraes, L.: Ecodesign, design for assembly (DFA) and Vink, P. Com-
  fort. Inaugural Address, Faculty of Design, Construction and Production, Delft University of
  Technology, June 2002
Kroemer, K.H.E., Grandjean, E.: Manual of ergonomics: adapting work to man. Translation by
  Lia Buarque de Macedo Guimarães. 5th edn. Bookman, Porto Alegre (2005)
Noro, K.: Participatory ergonomics. In: Karwowski, W., Marras, W.S. (eds.) The Occupational
  Ergonomic Handbook. CRC Press, Boca Raton (1999)
Vink, P.: Comfort and Design- Principles and Good Practice. CRC Press Taylor & Francis, Boca
  Raton (2005)

Leef Chair: Application of the Equid Methodology and the Principles of Macro Ergonomics in Product Design

Cristiane Nonemacher Cantele[1](✉), Marc Sapetti[2], Jairo Benincá[1], and Giovanna Nonemacher[3]

[1] Cavaletti Professional Seating S.A, Erechim, RS 99706-54, Brazil
ergonomia@cavaletti.com.br
[2] Sapetti GmbH, Hinterbergstrasse 36, 6330 Cham, Switzerland
marc@sapetti.com
[3] ErgoIdea Ergonomic Solutions, San Diego, USA

Abstract. The concepts of Ergonomics are based on cognitive, emotional and physical interfaces. When designing products, the analysis of these interfaces is paramount. A Brazilian company located in the south of the country has developed a chair based on ergonomics with the objective of meeting the functional needs of users, as well as favoring market acceptance through efficient interaction in corporate environments. Thus, this work aims to demonstrate the application of macro ergonomic concepts and the Equid/2008 tool in the design and production of the Cavaletti Leef product, as specific objectives, the demonstration of commercial needs, analysis of the interdisciplinarity involved in the study, impacts of the product in relation to production process compared to the previous product. As well as the verification of the final results of the product and the respective relevance in the national and international market. Methodologically, semi-qualitative questionnaires were applied based on the precepts of the Equid/2008 tool and macroergonomics concepts were applied in all stages of the process, involving the development, process and manufacturing team, marketing and users. It was concluded that the Equid tool and the concepts of macro ergonomics have proven to be effective in the design and definition of the product's ergonomic and functional characteristics, this being the third product that the company designs and launches on the market based on these tools that once again demonstrated efficiency. In addition, they are essential to list the functional needs of the product and the team of workers involved in its manufacture.

Keywords: Ergonomics · Macro ergonomics · Product ergonomics

1 Introduction

The design, when aligned with the concepts of ergonomics, can generate an improvement in the quality and functionality of several products. In the design project, all the desired qualities are planned, combined with the procedural methodology.

© The Author(s), under exclusive license to Springer Nature Switzerland AG 2021
N. L. Black et al. (Eds.): IEA 2021, LNNS 220, pp. 197–204, 2021.
https://doi.org/10.1007/978-3-030-74605-6_24

2 Referential

2.1 Design Concept

According to Bcheche et al. (2013) Brandão (2011) design seeks to meet the individual through the promotion of their well-being. For him, the design has been expanded from various sciences, such as architecture, engineering and advertising, and makes it necessary to consider the design so that the product design considers aspects of ergonomics and usability.

2.2 Ergonomics Conception

Pequini (2005) ergonomics is related to several aspects such as: posture, body movements, environmental factors, perception factors, controls, as well as task analysis. According to Guimarães (2002), the growing concern with people's quality of life has increased the commitment of companies to product and process conception.

2.3 Macro Ergonomics

According to Ida (2005), Macro ergonomics emerges as a development in the man - machine environment/organization interaction occurring at a macro level. Macro ergonomics also called participatory ergonomics is a discipline of ergonomics that studies how different approaches professionals are involved in the design process.

2.4 Ergonomic Design Quality (Equid)

According to the publication of the International Ergonomic Association IEA (2008) the Equid method was developed to provide guidance on the term "ergonomically designed product". In order to properly use this description, the product must have been developed using a process that incorporates principles of ergonomics during the design process. In this way, it is mentioned in the document as: "Equid Design Process", and the main users of this document include ergonomists and designers of products and services, together with the managers responsible for development, it is worth noting that the methodology does not have the pretension to enter conflict or replace other standards. According to IEA (2008) the application of the requirements of the Design Process Equid has the following benefits to the organization, both in the design of the product or service.

3 Methodology

According to Guimarães (2006) the macro ergonomics is based on a participatory method, in which the public involved in the work process contributes to the assertiveness of the interventions in order to reduce the margin of error and increase the acceptance. According to studies by Noro (1999), Haines et al. (2002) and Vink et al. (2002), with the aim of the participatory ergonomic process, some steps were established for this study in order to allow the needs of the workers to be considered. In this way the following steps were established:

Step 01- Preparation: In order to carry out a comparative study, the definition of the last model with similar characteristics was carried out, Cavaletti Essence model 20501 was chosen. Through the informed consent form, the participants were informed of the research and respective objectives.

Step 02- Analysis of tasks: The tasks and work performed were studied through interviews, questionnaires and observation. The questionnaires were delivered to the workers involved in the process with the following questions:

In the current production process, which ones do you find difficult to carry out the task of sewing? In the current production process, which ones do you have difficulty in performing the cheating task? In the current production process, which ones do you have difficulty in performing the task of stapling? If so, what are the main difficulties? What are your suggestions for improving the process and the product?

Data from the production process were also accounted for, responses were counted and statistical analysis was subsequently performed to measure the results. This way you can identify which topics are related to process and product improvements.

Step 03- Pilot study with the improvements: Testing a new design to perform the tasks.

Step 04- Implementation: Improvements in the manufacturing process are implemented, as well as the workers were guided in relation to the new improvements.

In the field of product design, the Equid-Iea protocol for the product design and manufacturing steps, followed by the steps suggested as shown in the annex.

3.1 Sampling

The research was carried out in the productive area of the company, commercial representatives, buyers and users of the previous products. To answer the questionnaire related to the process, 22 workers participated in the survey; regarding the application of the product questionnaire about 1200 people including users and buyers answered the survey. Data were compiled and analyzed, resulting in specific charts.

4   Results and Discussion

4.1   Results Related to the Macro Ergonomic Concepts Questionnaire Applied to Workers Involved in the Production Process

The production process of both products can be described as a cellular process based on the concepts of macro ergonomics, with all workers performing all stages of the process and all sectors involved reported difficulties in carrying out the current process. Through this study it was verified that the processes that need intervention are the glue and sewing process, so it was understood that these would be modified through the new project, the improvements in the production process were prioritized.

There were major improvements in the production process resulting in less fabric, number of pieces and number of staples. In addition, process steps, production time weight reduction of the final product were reduced, thus facilitating the delivery and usability of the product (Table 1).

Table 1. Process improvements

Sector/Activity	Essence model	Leef model
Sewing/parts sewing/day	8–10 parts	18–20 parts
Sewing/process time	23 min	17 min
Sewing/material used	7,33 m^2	3 m^2
Cut/number of pieces	49	8
Stapling/staple quantity	300	100
Weight	53 lb	44 lb

4.2 Results Regarding the Application of the Equid Methodology in the Design of the Product

4.2.1 Understanding Users

In the current context it appears that most people spend a large part of their time sitting in office chairs, even in the managerial/executive areas Among the users interviewed, 8% were between 18 and 25 years old, 13% were between 25 and 35 years old, 27% were between 35 and 45 years old and 52% were over 45 years old, Among the users interviewed, 70% were male and 30% female.

About the function 25% of the interviewees were executive directors, 34% were managers and 41% were directors from other areas.

4.2.2 Product Expectation

Regarding the characteristics that the chairs must have, 25% of the users infer that the chair must have adjustments, 17% of the users infer that the chairs must have adjustments that are easy to operate, 11% of users would like the chairs to have a younger appearance, 20% of users say that the product must have support for the spine, 18% users would like chairs with more elegant colors and 9% of users would like more cheerful colors in the product.

4.2.3 Analysis of the Current Product

The essence chair (Figs. 1a and b) was used as a comparison parameter for the development of the new product.

In order to understand the need for improvements to the developed product, questions were asked regarding the current product specific to end users. Users were asked which points of the product interfere with the comfort of the product, 47% of users said it was difficult to adjust, 32% of users said the chair was too big, 13% of users said the chair did not fit properly on the table and 08% of users reported that the seams need maintenance.

Users were asked what the points of improvement in the current chair would be 37% of users infer that the shape of the seat should be changed, 23% infer that the shape of the backrest should be modified, 12% say that the colors should be warmer, 18% infer that the chair should be less square and 10% infer that the chair should be more rounded.

Fig. 1. Essence current product;

All the considerations about the mentioned items were relevant in the conception of the new product.

4.3 Design Based on the Opinion of the End Users

All the tests and analyzes of the interpretations of the data related to the results found resulted in a new project. The objective was focused on the segment of the following aspects: angle of the back and hip, seat height to the floor, seat depth, armrest (height, width, length, shelter, edges), distance from the popliteal region and buttocks, safety distance in the popliteal region, shapes to the contours of spine (horizontal, vertical and support for the lower back adjustments), rounding of the front edges, with seat and backrest sizing design related to youthfulness, different colors of coating and customization of seams.

4.3.1 Results: Testing with Seat Prototypes

The prototypes were tested by users and the laboratory for the purpose of verifying the resistance of the product, all improvements to the prototypes were passed on to the team with approval from the company's management. The results of the research carried out were considered from the initial stages of the project.

4.3.2 Design Interventions

The modifications of the product object of this study in relation to the previous product were in relation of the lumbar support to the angle of the backrest, the angle of the armrest, adjustment of the approximation of the armrest, adjustment of the depth of the seat, high and low backrests (Figs. 2a, b, c, d and e).

4.4 Sustainability

In this way was used recyclable material in its components through the production of recyclable engineering polymer completely chromium-free product and silver-paint inks colorless of heavy metals. One of the main topics is that the product eliminates the use of wood in both the backrest and the seat. Initially, the Essence product had wood on both sides of its back and the new design included the elimination of wood and the use of recyclable polymers.

Fig. 2. Desing interventions, source the authors;

4.5   Outstanding Result

The final product that was the object of this research was launched nationally and internationally, with the qualification of the sales teams, thus achieving the expected results and the return on financial investment (Figs. 3a, b and c).

Fig. 3. Final product, source Cavaletti S/A

The final product obtained excellent acceptance in the market, adapting itself to different work environments (Figs. 4a and b).

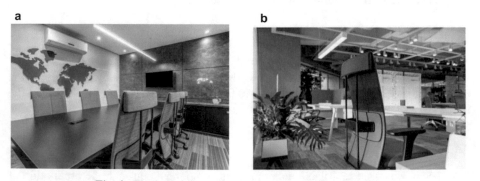

Fig. 4. Final product application case, source Cavaletti S/A

5 Final Considerations

Since 2003, the company has been developing participatory ergonomics programs in its process. Over time, ergonomics has become an essential pillar for both products and processes.

Based on this perspective for the third time, the application of the concepts of macro ergonomics and the Equid/2008 tool was used in the design and production of the Leef product. It was found that when applying the principles of macro ergonomics in the production process, it favored the participation of the team, as well as the modifications made had a significant impact on product improvement, as well as on the process.

Both tools were indispensable in understanding the needs and expectations of our users, directly reflecting in the conduct of the product development process, especially when related to the user interface.

The study and applicability of ergonomics can be a challenge mainly in the design of a product, but with adequate tools, pre-defined process steps, participation and engagement of the team involved are essential factors in the success of the project.

The application of the Equid tool, mainly in the intervention with the end users, it can be noticed that usually the dynamic chairs are not used in an appropriate way, in this way, strategically specific training of the commercial teams involved and the end users were carried out. It is noteworthy that considering the opinion of users and associating with research was fundamental for the success of the project, so that the company already developing another product for launch in 2023 and we are already applying the respective tools again.

We understand that the dissemination of both tools should be encouraged in order to expand applicability and results, as they can be fundamental to professionals in the area, in order to obtain all the benefits both in process and in products.

It is concluded in this way that the success and longevity of use of the products in our segment definitely depend directly on the design ergonomics being considered from the design, manufacturing process until the final use by the end user.

References

Bcheche, I.C., Costa, H.F.A., Azevedo, A.C.: Ergonomics of design: a marketing strategy for the valorization of products. Interdiscip. J. Contemp. Stud. 33–41 (2013). Nova Serrana, September/December

Bins Ely, V.H., Turlienicz, B.: Attribute grid method: evaluating the relationship between user and environment. Built Environ. 5(2) (2005)

Brandão, E.: Laboratory of ergonomics and usability of interfaces in a human-technology system. https://wwwusers.rdc.puc-rio.br/leui/eduardobrandao/eduardo-brandao_capitulo-02.pdf. Accessed 15 Nov 2017

Brazil of Ergonomics V. Latin American Congress of Ergonomics. IX Brazilian Congress on Ergonomics. III Ergonomics Seminar in Bahia. ABERGO, Salvador (1999)

Design Process Guidelines Equid. International Association of Ergonomics Equid (Ergonomic-Quality In Design) Technical Committee All rights reserved. Copyright 2008 by the IEA

Garcia-Acosta, G., Lange-Morales, K., Puentes-Lagos, D.E., Ruiz Ortiz, M.R.: Addressing human factors and ergonomics in design process, product life cycle, and innovation: trends in consumer product design. In: Karwowski, W., Soares, M., Stanton, N. (eds.) Handbook of Human Factors and Ergonomics in Consumer Product Design: Methods and Techniques (Chap. 9), pp. 133–154. CRC Press Taylor & Francis, Boca Raton (2011)

Guimarães, B.M.L. (org).: Macroergonomics: putting concepts into practice. In ergonomic monographic series c.1 Porto. FEENG/UFRGS, Alegre (2010a)

Guimarães, B.M.L.: Historic. Environment. In: Process Ergonomics, vol. 1, 5th edn. FEENG/UFRGS, Porto Alegre (2010b)

Guimarães, B.M.L.: Process Ergonomics I, 5th edn. FEENG/UFRGS/EE/PPGEP (2006). 436 p.

Ida, I.: Ergonomics-Design and Production, 2nd edn. Edgard Blücher, São Paulo (2005)

Intenational Standart Book Number 978-0-9976041-0-8. IEA - EQUID 1/10 Project Process Requirements

Ios, N., Imada, A.S.: A macroergonomic approach to produce design (1998)

Lange-Morales, K., Garcia-Acosta, G., Bruder, R.: The EQUID approach: improving ergonomics quality in product design and development. In: Ahram, T., Karwowski, W., Marek, T. (eds.) Proceedings of the 5th International Conference on Applied Human Factors and Ergonomics AHFE 2014, Kraków, Poland, 19–23 July 2014 (2014)

Moraes, A.: Ergonomics and product design, information, human-computer interaction interfaces and architectural spaces: teaching and research. ENEGEP (2003)

Requirements for the managment of ergonomic quality in the product and service design process Version 2.0 EQUID Technical Committee (Ergonomic Quality In Design). International Ergonomics Association. All rights reserved. Copyright 2008 by the IEA. Published by IEA Press

Vink, P.: Comfort and Design-Principles and Good Practice. CRC Press Taylor & Francis, Boca Raton (2005)

Opportunities and Challenges of Digital Technologies for Inclusion

Maurizio Caon[1] , Isabella Tiziana Steffan[2] , and Alessandra Rinaldi[3(✉)]

[1] University of Applied Sciences and Arts Western Switzerland (HES-SO),
Fribourg, Switzerland
maurizio.caon@hes-so.ch
[2] Studio Steffan – Design and Research, Milan, Italy
info@studiosteffan.it
[3] Department of Architecture, University of Florence, Florence, Italy
alessandra.rinaldi@unifi.it

Abstract. Digital technologies are profoundly changing our daily life and our society more in general. This transformation brings new opportunities and challenges also in terms of inclusion. Indeed, some technologies can present barriers in terms of adoption and accessibility; for this reason, it is important to elaborate new methodologies that can guide the design process in order to be more inclusive. At the same time, digital services and products can empower citizens to fight social exclusion, or assist people with disabilities for enabling them to perform activities that they have not been able to do before, or to increase participation of disadvantaged people in social and economic activities. This paper shows the current trends in terms of design applied to digital technologies and highlights the importance and urgency of this topic calling all researchers from academia and industry for action to leverage "design for all" methods in order to increase inclusion in our connected world.

Keywords: Digital technologies · Inclusive design · Design for all/universal design · Human-computer interaction

1 Introduction

Inclusive design is a complex matter presenting multiple facets and this session aims at sharing experiences and debating on how digital technology can be leveraged to provide universal access to people, empowering diversity and overcoming cognitive and physical barriers, such as cultural and societal differences in this connected world. Identifying new opportunities and challenges in leveraging digital technology to foster inclusion requires bringing together researchers from academia and industry and practitioners to create a multidisciplinary community interested in facilitating knowledge transfer and synergy, the connection, the gaps between the different research domains, paving the way for common purposes.

N. L. Black et al. (Eds.): IEA 2021, LNNS 220, pp. 205–208, 2021.
https://doi.org/10.1007/978-3-030-74605-6_25

A symposium is the perfect platform to showcase good practices and discuss future directions for the development of digital solutions for inclusive design, where interactive exchange of ideas and opinions will be encouraged and valued.

The impact of digital technologies is affecting the world of research and industry, in the field of products, public and private services and the fruition of cultural heritage, investing also in the Human Factors and Ergonomics domains. It is no coincidence that the IEA has dedicated the 2021 conference to the general theme of "HFE (Human Factors and Ergonomics) in a connected World and on Ergonomics 4.0".

It is therefore very important to address the issue of digital technologies for inclusive design, so topical, in a multidisciplinary way in order to have a vision from different perspectives and open a discussion on the topic.

2 Digital Technology Impact on Design for Inclusion

Digital technologies have transformed the contents and tools of design and manufacturing, but they also create different ways for end users to use spaces, architectures, objects and services, facilitating interaction, security and creating innovative transmedia communication modality.

Inclusive Design is neither a new genre of design nor a separate specialism, but it is a general and transversal design approach that can be applied in various design sectors, from communication systems to built environment, from services to product-service system, so that each environment/product/service can be used by as broad a range of population as possible [1, 2].

Terms such as "inclusive design", "design for all", "universal design", "accessible design", "barrier-free design", and "transgenerational design" are often used interchangeably with the same meaning. They share a similar inclusive design philosophy, that is designing, developing, and marketing products, environments, programmes and services to be accessible and usable by as broad a range of users as possible, without the need for adaptation or specialized design. ID does not exclude assistive devices for particular groups of persons with disabilities where this is needed. ID is explicitly cited in British Standard, UD is considered as the necessary approach to grant accessibility in UNCRPD art.2, DfA is applied in EU standards [3]. The adoption of these approaches brings forth on two concepts which should be based on design targeting the widest possible range of user capabilities: accessibility and usability [4–11]. Accessibility refers both to the process of design, in that it is a goal, and to the product of the design process, in that it provides a basis for measuring the extent to which the product can be used. It is a concept that relates to the interaction between the user and product or service, expressed in terms of the achievement of task goals. The concept of usability is associated with the interaction between the user and the product and not with the product in itself. Increasing the quality of interaction is considered fundamental for the goal of increasing the levels of accessibility achieved in software products. The concepts of accessibility and usability overlap and are interdependent, as well as a product that cannot be used to achieve task goals is never going to be effective, and therefore is neither usable nor accessible. It is important to understand in relation to these two concepts the context of use and the context of design.

Aging and the various social changes of today challenge designers to design products, services and environments that take into account the largest range of users possible [12]. This means addressing the diversity of the population, in the design process and design goals, that derives from differences in age, gender, ability, ethnicity, profession, culture, language, nationality, situation, etc. In this context, digital technologies have a fundamental role in terms of interaction with our surrounding world. The development of digital technologies and their diffusion in the fabric of everyday life, through the application to everyday products such as: household appliances, furniture for indoor and outdoor environments, communication devices, services, just to name a few, are changing the modalities and the Design of interaction, towards a better quality of life, both individually and collectively. There are many researches and studies on the use of digital technologies, in various academic sectors, that address human diversity in design of product, services and built environments, with the view to Design for Inclusion. For example: smart urban furniture aimed at facilitating cultural diversity interaction [13, 14]; smart habitat for the eldery [15, 16], addressing the challenge of migrant integration through ICT-enabled solutions [17], increasing interaction between people through technology [18, 19].

We find ourselves taking advantage of the many possibilities offered by the digital transformation that has affected all areas of our life. The ubiquitous computing that is pervasive in the urban environment; Internet of Things and artificial intelligence, which make home living environments and not only interactive and adaptive; wearable devices, smart fabrics, smart garments, often used for health and stress monitoring; real-time communication technologies, which make us continuously connected to the virtual environment and find all the necessary answers in real time. Those are some of the technological opportunities that a designer faces when exploring possible new scenarios to increase the quality of life and well-being of people and their habitat. Targeted at inclusion, these technologies can help to address the various challenges that society is facing today. On the one hand, for example, the aging of the population, with a growing demand for new solutions aimed at the most fragile groups of users, such as the elderly, with temporary or permanent physical and cognitive disabilities, to extend their autonomy and health for longer possible, or to assist them in daily tasks. On the other hand, the migratory flows of people from different countries and the globalized society, with the consequent demographic, cultural, political, and economic transformation of urban areas. This phenomenon brings out new barriers linked to the diversity of culture and of cultural levels, to social and gender barriers.

Last but not least, another challenge is the overcoming of the transgenerational digital divide, an issue that, if not addressed in an inclusive manner, could lead to the exclusion of the less young and less digitized users from many digital services.

References

1. Clarkson, P.J., Coleman, R.: History of inclusive design in the UK. Appl Ergon **46**, 235–247 (2015)
2. Clarkson, P.J., Coleman, R., Hosking, I., Waller, S.: Inclusive design toolkit. Engineering Design Centre, University of Cambridge, Cambridge (2007)
3. EN 17210:2021 Accessibility and usability of the built environment (2021)

4. ISO 9241-171:2008 Ergonomics of human-system interaction — Part 171: Guidance on software accessibility. Annex F (2008)
5. ISO 9241-210:2019 Ergonomics of human-system interaction — Part 210: Human-centred design for interactive systems (2019)
6. ISO/DIS 21542:2020, Building construction — Accessibility and usability of the built Environment (2020)
7. ISO 9241-112: 2017 Ergonomics of human-system interaction. 3.15 (2017)
8. EN 301549:2019 Accessibility requirements for ICT products and services (2019)
9. EN 17161:2019 Design for All - Accessibility following a Design for All approach in products, goods and services - Extending the range of users (2019)
10. CEN/CLC Guide 6 Guide for addressing accessibility in standards (2014)
11. ISO GUIDE 71 Guide for addressing accessibility in standards (2014)
12. Van der Linden, V., Dong, H., Heylighen, A.: From accessibility to experience: opportunities for inclusive design in architectural practice. Nordic J. Archit. Res. **28**(2), 33–58 (2016)
13. Rinaldi, A., Caon, M., Abou Khaled, O., Mugellini, E.: Designing urban smart furniture for facilitating migrants' integration: the co-design workshop as approach for supporting inclusive design. In: Congress of the International Ergonomics Association, pp. 461–470. Springer, Cham (2018)
14. Rinaldi, A., Angelini, L., Abou Khaled, O., Mugellini, E., Caon, M.: Codesign of public spaces for intercultural communication, diversity and inclusion. In: International Conference on Applied Human Factors and Ergonomics, pp. 186–195. Springer, Cham (2019)
15. Kaner, J., Maestre, R., Lameski, P., Isaacson, M., Taveter, K., Tomesone, S., Melero, F.: SHELDON Smart habitat for the elderly. Cetem Technology (2019)
16. Palumbo, F., Crivello, A., Furfari, F., Girolami, M., Mastropietro, A., Manferdelli, G., Rizzo, G.: "Hi this is NESTORE, your personal assistant": design of an integrated IoT system for a personalized coach for healthy aging. Front. Digit. Health **2**, 20 (2020)
17. European Commission, Horizon (2020). https://ec.europa.eu/programmes/horizon2020/en/h2020-section/europe-changing-world-inclusive-innovative-and-reflective-societies. Accessed 21 Jan 2021
18. Caon, M., Carrino, S., Ruffieux, S., Abou Khaled, O., Mugellini, E.: Augmenting interaction possibilities between people with mobility impairments and their surrounding environment. In: International Conference on Advanced Machine Learning Technologies and Applications, pp. 172–18. Springer, Heidelberg (2012)
19. Caon, M., Mugellini, E., Abou Khaled, O.: A pervasive game to promote social offline interaction. In: Proceedings of the 2013 ACM conference on Pervasive and Ubiquitous Computing Adjunct Publication, pp. 1381–1384. ACM, New York (2013)

6Ws in the Ergonomics Review of Macro and Micro Workplace Design

Justine M. Y. Chim[1,2(✉)] and Tienli Chen[3]

[1] Student of Doctoral Program in Design, College of Design, National Taipei University of Technology, Taipei, Taiwan
jchim@my-ergonomics.com
[2] Principal Consultant, Chim's Ergonomics and Safety Limited, 17/F, No. 80 Gloucester Road, Wan Chai, Hong Kong, Hong Kong
[3] Professor of Department of Industrial Design, College of Design, National Taipei University of Technology, 1, Sec. 3, Zhongxiao E. Rd., Taipei 10608, Taiwan

Abstract. The application of ergonomics in the occupational setting concerns the understanding the fitting of workers and the components of a work system which include work task, workstation setting, workspace and work environment. Ergonomics considerations in the workplace design bring the benefits to minimize the risk of musculoskeletal injuries, promote health and safety, create a worker-friendly workplace and enrich the employees' wellbeing. The paper aims to summarize the systematic process to conduct an ergonomics review of workplace design proposals. Ergonomist applies theory, principles, data and methods to evaluate and review in the ergonomics review process. The ergonomics review discussed in this paper has been used in newly designed control room, call center and offices. This paper will answer the following questions: (1) What are the objectives of ergonomics review of workplace design? (2) Why is ergonomics review of workplace design important? (3) Who should be involved in the ergonomics review of workplace design? (4) When should an ergonomics review of workplace design be conducted? (5) Where should be included in the ergonomics review of workplace design? (6) How should the ergonomics review of workplace design be conducted? Upon completion of the ergonomics review, the consolidated result and recommendations for improvement as well as the final decision of the design proposal should be well-documented for project reference in the next stage of the design process.

Keywords: Workplace ergonomics · Workplace design implementation · Employee wellness · Healthy workplace · Occupants' comfort

1 Introduction

Ergonomics is a human-centered approach to understand the interactions among humans and other components of a system. (ISO6385: 2016) In the application of ergonomics in occupational function, it is concerned to understand the fitting of the components of a system between workers and other elements of task requirements and design, workstation

© The Author(s), under exclusive license to Springer Nature Switzerland AG 2021
N. L. Black et al. (Eds.): IEA 2021, LNNS 220, pp. 209–216, 2021.
https://doi.org/10.1007/978-3-030-74605-6_26

setting, workspace and work environment. There is interdependence between a working person and the task requirements, workplace settings and components, environment, and body movements and postures. A workplace with a suitable workplace design will minimize the risk of musculoskeletal injuries, promote workplace health and safety, greater productivity and work efficiency, higher comfort level, create worker-friendly environment and enhance employees' wellbeing. (Chim 2009, 2019; Ibrahim 2020; Saha 2016).

Ergonomics review of workplace design is a process of verification and validation of ergonomic design elements during the design proposal stage. The purpose of this systematic review aims to confirm the meeting of ergonomics consideration and legal compliance in the workplace design proposal in accordance with the target occupants, task and operations, workstation and furniture, workspace, floor plan and layout, architectural features and workplace environment. Ergonomist together with the design project management team aims to generate recommendations and solutions for improvement before making final confirmation on the design proposal. The pre-occupancy and post-occupancy check should have further study on ergonomics and occupational safety and health aspects.

Universal design strategy was conceptualized by the American Architect, Ronald L. Mace in the middle of the 1980s which universal design was defined as "the design of products and environments to be usable by all people, to the greatest extent possible, without the need for adaptation or specialized design". The universal design applying in the environment which has the purpose of inclusive different users no matter the age, size or ability and without the need for adoption in the architectural design (Nygaard 2017).

Coleman 2002, p. 756 stated that "Good design can inspire and support productivity, creativity, social interaction, and a sense of community, as well as physical and psychological well-being. Individual subjective taste obviously plays a role, but good design is more universal…". The workplace design concerns both the work and non-work areas. An ideal workplace environment creates a feeling of joyful, comfortable, relaxed, positive, motivation and satisfaction and a human-centered workplace should be well-considered ergonomics, work health and safety and employees' wellness. The World Health Organization proposed that "The wealth of business depends on the health of workers" and the well-being of the workers are significantly important to business success (WHO 2010).

The physical work environment and the psychosocial work environment are two elements for creating a healthy workplace. The physical work environment such as air quality, workplace layout and structure, furniture and production processes in the workplace, can affect workers' physical safety and health, mental health and well-being. The psychosocial work environment, such as organizational culture, values and daily practices of the organization which also correlated to the mental and physical well-being of employees (WHO 2010).

Explained the conceptual relationship between the physical work environment and healthy workplaces. The benefits of creating a healthy workplace include increased employee satisfaction, better health condition, attract potential employees and create positive corporate image and lower health medical costs. Furthermore, employees are also expected to have a better quality of life and employees' well-being (Jensen and van der Voordt 2019).

In the Interior design handbook of professional practice, Heerwagen suggested that more clients are demanding justification for design proposals and clients would like to ask for evidence to prove the design if the designer claims that the interior design idea can increase productivity. In addition, when the designers present the design concept to the clients, they will need to demonstrate that the interior design can meet the goals and strategic interest of the organization on top of the user's comfort and aesthetic perspectives (Coleman 2002). The ergonomics consideration in the workplace becomes the necessary important nutrition to develop a healthy workplace environment (Chim 2019).

2 Aims and Methodology

The paper aims to summarize the systematic considerations and processes to conduct ergonomics review of workplace design proposals. This paper will answer the 6Ws in ergonomics review of macro and micro workplace design. The methodology of the ergonomics review discussed in this paper has been used in newly designed control room, call center and offices.

3 Discussion

In the workplace design, ideally, an ergonomics professional is invited to participate and contribute in the preliminary stage of the design process. The early involvement and collaboration with the project team which can give appropriate influence in the workplace users comfort, safety and productivity aspects (Bligard and Berlin 2019). However, if the ergonomics professional is not able to involve in the early design process, the ergonomics review becomes necessary to ensure the ergonomics considerations are fully taken and identify the ergonomics issues before the confirmation of the design proposal.

3.1 What Are the Objectives of Ergonomics Review of Workplace Design?

The objectives of ergonomics review of workplace design are to offer professional advice on ergonomics in the design proposal. The ergonomics review also allows preliminary verification and validation of the workplace design in regard to ergonomics design principles, international standards, local legislation and relevant guidelines. The ergonomics review exercise can provide preliminary guidelines information on the workstation and furniture design and selection after conducting the ergonomics operational analysis and task analysis. The considerations of ergonomics are taken into account for creating a suitable workplace environment accordingly.

3.2 Why is Ergonomics Review of Workplace Design Important?

During the ergonomics review, the industry guidelines and international standard are used for allowing the discussion for the meeting of occupant satisfaction and comfort. By going through the ergonomics review of workplace design, it can optimize the occupants' comfort, optimize human reliability and operational efficiency as well as ensure legal compliance with occupational safety and health regulations. The occupant's satisfaction and comfort level in the workplace environment will be enhanced.

Vischer (2008) proposed three levels of environmental comfort levels to workplace users and more recently, Kwon and Remøy (2019) proposed the similar explanation. The environmental comfort levels are:

(a) The fundamental level is physical comfort which includes temperature, thermal comfort, ventilation comfort and lighting comfort. The application of building codes and standards belongs to physical level.The fundamental level is physical comfort which includes temperature, thermal comfort, ventilation comfort and lighting comfort. The application of building codes and standards belongs to physical level.

(b) The next level is functional comfort which is defined as environmental support for users for performing the work-related tasks and activities and productivity enhancement.

(c) The top level of occupant satisfaction and well-being is psychological comfort so the workplace design can create the occupant's feelings of belonging, ownership and control over the workspace. It shows the importance of considering the employees' comfort level in the workplace design process.

Rothe et al. (2012) proposed the employees' satisfaction is based on Herzberg's two-factor theory: (i) motivating factors increase employee satisfaction and (ii) poor hygiene factors decrease employee satisfaction. The work environment needs represent the hygiene factors which means dissatisfaction increases if the needs are not met in the workplace setting whereas preference represents the motivating factors so when the work environment preferences are met, the satisfaction is increased.

During the ergonomics review of the design proposal, it allows the ergonomist and project team to ensure the suitable workplace settings are well considered. Figure 1 displays the relationship between needs, preferences, and requirements and implementation on workplace settings and occupants' satisfaction.

3.3 Who Should Be Involved in the Ergonomics Review of Workplace Design?

The ergonomics review should be completed by a team led by an ergonomist together with the team members such as designers' team, architect and construction consultant, project team, operational team, administrative and facilities officers, and focus group with employees' representatives.

Bligard and Berlin (2019) describes the tasks for ergonomists for the participation or leading for the workplace design process. For instance, in operation design level, ergonomist performs:

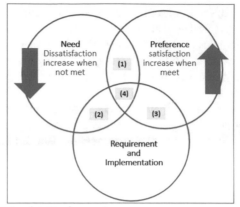

(1) Compromise (Need + Preference):
    Is needed and preferred if not implemented, cause dissatisfaction
(2) Necessity (Need + Requirement and implementation):
    Is needed and implemented, does not increase satisfaction
(3) Bliss (Preference + Requirement and Implementation):
    Is preferred and implemented, increases satisfaction
(4) Must have (Need + Preference + Requirement and Implementation):
    Is needed, preferred and implemented, increase satisfaction

Fig. 1. Relationship between needs, preferences, and requirements and implementation on occupants' satisfaction (Rothe et al. (2012); Kwon and Remøy (2019)

(a) the analysis of work system goals and functions in the given workplace;
(b) the investigation and specification the intended use and user requirements; and.
(c) the evaluation of the intended activities with workforce participation in the design process.

In architecture design level, ergonomist performs:

(d) the analysis of the work process by understanding the workspace requirements and task sequential process in the available space;
(e) the investigation the workplace's physical constraint with considering the architectural layout in the intended operational process; and
(f) the workforce participation exercise during the layout-planning stage.

A clear definition of the roles and responsibilities of ergonomists in the ergonomics review as well as a good collaboration and effective communication within the project team can make a significant contribution in the ergonomics review exercise.

3.4 When Should an Ergonomics Review of Workplace Design Be Conducted?

The ergonomics review should be conducted once the preliminary design is prepared so that the findings and recommendations can be provided to the design and project teams for preparation of the final design. The ergonomics review plan should be presented and confirmed by the project team in the earliest stage of the workplace design so the timeline for ergonomics review is included in the project plan. The ergonomist can provide ergonomics information to the design team as references which help to provide guidance notes for the development of the workplace design objectives, direction and strategies.

Early and consistent participation by ergonomists in the workplace design can bring sufficient contribution throughout the workplace design process. Ergonomics professionals are well-trained to apply theory, principles, data and methods to design who can make contributions in the workplace design project with collaboration with other professionals in the design management project team. (ISO6385: 2016; Bligard and Berlin 2019).

3.5   Where Should Be Included in the Ergonomics Review of Workplace Design?

The ergonomics review should include both work and non-work areas and both in macro and micro perspectives:

(a) From the macro-perspectives, the design parameters compose of the workplace overall layout, room layout, equipment layout, colour scheme, architectural finishes and materials and furniture, storage arrangement, breakout room, restroom, canteen as well as the environment aspects, such as ventilation, acoustic, indoor air quality, artificial and natural lighting, passages, sound insulation and windows.

(b) From the micro-perspectives, the design parameters cover the areas of workstation and work bench design, workstation specifications, seating, reach distance and; control and display (Chim 2019; Vischer 2008).

The design parameters consider the dimensions, shape and product specifications according to the physical, functional and psychological comfort in the workplace setting.

3.6   How Should the Ergonomics Review of Workplace Design Be Conducted?

The following steps are proposed to conduct the ergonomics review of workplace design:

(Step 1) The scopes of workplace design ergonomics review should be identified which include to define the number of staff concerned, main staff position concerned, types of workstation in the workplace and the concerned workplace locations in the ergonomics review.

(Step 2) Ergonomist retrieves the international standard, legislation, industry guidelines and references relevant to the country, operation and task in that particular workplace.

(Step 3) Ergonomist understands the overall operations, jobs and tasks involved in this newly designed workplace.

(Step 4) Ergonomist selects user population and the relevant anthropometric data for the use in the review. The application of the anthropometric data is for considering the workspace, furniture selection and workstation fitting evaluation.

(Step 5) After all the preparation in the previous step, in this step, the ergonomist should have fully understood the design objectives, layout plan, location and specification of

the functional room and equipment room and the design parameters in the macro perspectives. A checklist on relevant legislative requirements, international standard and guidelines on ergonomics aspects can be developed for the ergonomics review on each parameter. Focus group shall be formulated to collect the users' feedback on the current workplace setting as well as to understand their needs for the future workplace. Regular meeting with the focus group is useful to obtain the feedback from time to time throughout the ergonomics review process.

(Step 6) In the ergonomics review of workstation design, the similar techniques used in the macro perspectives in step 5 can be used in this step. The result of task analysis and anthropometric data can be used for the workstation-user-fitting evaluation with the participation of a focus group. Participatory ergonomics approach is very helpful to obtain occupants' feedback as well as confirm the user fitting to the workstation design. *(Final Step)* The consolidated result including the findings of the ergonomics review and recommendations for modification of the workplace design should be well-discussed within the project team and a full report should be prepared as the documentation of the project.

4 Conclusion

The paper aims to introduce the technique and experience to conduct ergonomics review of workplace design. Ergonomics consideration included in the workplace design that brings positive value on occupants' comfort, workplace health and safety and productivity. Ergonomics principles should be well-considered in the design of a workplace. The ergonomics review exercise allows a systematic process of verification and validation of ergonomics design elements with well reference to the international standard, legislation and industry references in the relevant domains. The outcomes of the ergonomics review can provide useful information, recommendations for workplace design improvement and expect to maximize the occupants' comfort and satisfaction with throughout considerations in the design stage. A successful ergonomics review can bring ultimate benefits to the final design proposal and construction of a future workplace.

Acknowledgement. This work was supported by Chim's Ergonomics and Safety Limited. The paper was prepared by considering the real case experience from working with clients in ergonomics review on workplace design.

References

Bligård, L.O., Berlin, C.: ACD 3 as a framework for design of ergonomic workplaces. Work **62**(1), 5–12 (2019)

Chim, J.M.Y., Ng, P., Tai, S.: Winning telebet centre, design: apply participatory ergonomics to promote work health & safety, employee wellness and operational efficiency. In 17th World Congress on Ergonomics, International Ergonomics Association, Beijing, China (2009)

Chim, J.M.Y.: 6Ws in ergonomics workplace design. In: Bagnara, S., Tartaglia, R., Albolino, S., Alexander, T., Fujita, Y. (eds.) Proceedings of the 20th Congress of the International Ergonomics Association (IEA 2018). IEA 2018. Advances in Intelligent Systems and Computing, vol. 824. Springer, Cham (2019)

Coleman, C.: Interior design handbook of professional practice. McGraw-Hill, New York (2002). https://www.academia.edu/36218043/Interior_Design_Handbook_of_Professio nal_Practice. Accessed 20 Mar 2020

ISO 6385: 2016: Ergonomic Principles in the Design of Work Systems, International Organization for Standardization (2016)

Jensen, P.A., van der Voordt, T.: Healthy workplaces: what we know and what else we need to know. J. Corporate Real Estate **22**, 95–112 (2019)

Kwon, M., Remøy, H.: Office employee satisfaction: the influence of design factors on psychological user satisfaction. Facilities **38**, 1–19 (2019)

Nygaard, K.M.: What is Universal Design-Theories, terms and trends (2017)

Ibrahim, P.A.: Ergonomic Workplace Design for Micro, Small and Medium Enterprises: A Conceptual Model. IUP Journal of Management Research, 19(2) (2020)

Rothe, P., Lindholm, A.L., Hyvönen, A., Nenonen, S.: Work environment preferences–does age make a difference? Facilities **30**, 78–95 (2012)

Saha, S.: A study on impact of workplace design on employee's productivity in selected it companies in Pune region. Int. J. Bus. Gen. Manag. **5**(1), 2319–2267 (2016)

Vischer, J.C.: Towards an environmental psychology of workspace: how people are affected by environments for work. Archit. Sci. Rev. **51**(2), 97–108 (2008)

WHO: Healthy Workplaces: a model for action- for employers, workers, policy-makers and practitioners. World Health Organization (2010)

The Effect of Cognitive Styles on the Effectiveness of Visual Search Tasks with Different Familiarity

Yu Ju Chiu$^{(\boxtimes)}$, Zi Xuan Chen, and Yung Ching Liu

Department of Industrial Engineering and Management, National Yunlin University of Science and Technology, Yunlin, Taiwan
m10821023@gemail.yuntech.edu.tw

Abstract. The study explored the differences in visual search tasks for people with different cognitive styles of field independence and field dependence when browsing the different sequence of application layout on computer desktops. This experiment is a 2 (Cognitive styles: field independence vs. field dependence) * 2 (Familiarity: familiar vs. un-familiar) * 2 (Sequence of application layout: name vs type) design of mixed factors. The response time and fixation times of searching computer application were the dependent variables. The experiment meth-od is: All participants took the test with the Group Embedded Figures Test (GEFT), the top 25% and bottom 25% of the test scores are divided into styles of field-independent and field-dependent. They per-formed visual search tasks in different sequence of application layout on computer desktops with eye tracking devices. Each participant per-formed a total of 4 search tasks.

It was found that there was a significant difference in the response time of the participants searching for familiar and unfamiliar applications. When the participants searched for familiar applications, their reaction time and number of fixations were significant differences. The difference between this research and previous research on people with different cognitive styles is that the previous research for field independent people can quickly find the target in an unfamiliar environment, but in this research, field independents did not find this feature in the search task for computer applications.

Keywords: Cognitive style · Visual search · Familiarity

1 Introduction

With the advancement of Internet of Things (IoT) technology and the popularization of artificial intelligence, people's lives or business increasingly do not require media or devices to transmit information. From the traditional desktop computer, it is necessary to use the mouse and keyboard to control the computer interface, now people can use the hand or voice to control the interface. The Ericsson Mobile Trends report shows that the number of smartphone users worldwide has increased by 620 million in 2019, and it is estimated that by 2025, it will reach 1 billion users [1]. In people's lives, there are

© The Author(s), under exclusive license to Springer Nature Switzerland AG 2021
N. L. Black et al. (Eds.): IEA 2021, LNNS 220, pp. 217–222, 2021.
https://doi.org/10.1007/978-3-030-74605-6_27

also more and more smart home appliances appearing, such as: sweeping robots, smart switches, smart cameras, etc. All only need people's simple hand movements or sounds to make these devices automatically help us service. Now even the eyes can be used to help people control the interface [2], and these eye tracking devices are becoming more and more accurate, which will open up the infinite possibilities of human-computer interaction.

The age of digitization, people pay more attention to the protection of personal privacy. The most commonly used methods to verify identity are the input of passwords, the recognition of graphics or fingerprints. After identity verification, whether it is a mobile phone or a computer, if it is continuously unlocked, it is may increasing the risk of personal information leakage, and causing major property losses. In order to increase the protection of personal privacy, nowadays, in addition to facial recognition, it may also be possible to make judgments and achieve the purpose of identity verification based on the eye movement path of users who usually use computers or mobile phones.

Eye trackers have become ideal measurement tools for various researches. For example, using PowerPoint (PPT) lectures as the theme, investigating students' attention on slides, and using eye movement data to evaluate their learning performance, it turns out that students' attention to the text area next to the slide is more frequent than that on the slide. There are many pictures, but in the image area, the students spend more gaze duration than the text area [3]. Eye tracking technology can also be used to evaluate the interface. Compared with the better interface, a poor interface will cause the eyeball to have more duration and similar gaze points in a certain position of the interface. From these eye movement data, it can increase the user's understanding of the interface, and then improve the accuracy of the interface evaluation [4].

The eye tracker data also enables us to better understand people's viewing behaviors based on similar professional knowledge [5, 6], as well as understanding the user's attention when viewing natural environments and urban scenes. Concentration and dispersion. Some studies have pointed out that when people are watching natural environment scenes, the number of eye fixations is smaller than that of urban scenes [7]. Dynamic biometric recognition is currently one of the most popular eye movement research fields and has been applied to many information systems. These information systems are embedded with high-precision identification modules to protect users who have been identified in the information system and prevent other users from stealing the data inside. There are many types of biometric recognition in information systems, such as fingerprints or palm prints [8], iris [9], electrocardiogram (ECG) analysis [10], face recognition [11, 12] and body part recognition [13]. The eye movement data can provide some characteristics of humans when viewing rich information. Although it is not easy to observe, it may provide unique biometric data as one of the safe biometric features.

Our study will explore whether the eye movement path of the user when viewing the computer desktop after the computer is turned on will cause different eye movement paths due to the influence of the viewing screen or the behavioral habits of the participant. In the selection of the desktop background picture of the computer, a natural picture with a smaller number of eyes and a smaller moving distance is selected as the desktop background [7] to avoid the influence of the desktop background on the participant. In terms of user behavior, this study classifies the participants using the theory of field dependence and field independence [15–17]. For the test participant who is easily affected by the test environment or picture, it is called field dependence; for the test participant who relies more on their own experience without being affected by the environment or picture, it is called field independence. The test method is to use Embedded Figures Test (EFT), which is designed to guide the participant to find simple pat-terns hidden in complex patterns. During the test, it will go through cognitive stages such as attention concentration, attention control, and goal matching. Since EFT is suitable for individual testing, in order to consider group testing, this study uses its modified version of the Group Embedded Figures Test (GEFT) as a measurement tool. Those with higher scores tend to be field-independent; those with fewer scores, It tends to be field-dependent.

2 Method

2.1 Design

The experiment is a 2 (Cognitive styles: field independence vs. field dependence) * 2 (Familiarity: familiar vs. unfamiliar) * 2 (Sequence of application layout: name vs type) design of mixed factors. The dependent variable is the reaction time for the participants to find the specified application and the number of fixation times for viewing the specified application. The reaction time is the first fixation point of the participants' eye track moving to the specified application, and the number of fixation times is the number of times the participant repeatedly watches the specified application.

2.2 Participants

Thirty-six volunteer participants were recruited for participation. The average age of all participants was 25 years and their education level were above university level. All participants took the test with the Group Embedded Figures Test (GEFT), the top 25% and bottom 25% of the test scores are divided into styles of field-independent and field-dependent. Among them, the experimental data can be used as the analyzed field-independent and field-dependent cognitive types of 9 participants each, a total of 18 participants.

2.3 Apparatus

In this study, an eye-tracking instrument was used to perform visual search tasks in the order of arrangement of different applications on the computer desktop. Before the experiment, collect computer applications frequently used by students and make computer desktops with different sequence of application layout. And save the desktop screenshot of the arranged application as a file, input it into Mangold Vision related software, and combine the Mangold Vision portable eye tracker with the Dell E6364 laptop, and then place the eye tracker and the laptop on the desktop. The distance between the instrument and the participants is 60 cm.

2.4 Procedures

When the participant enters the lab, the researchers explain the purpose of the experiment and ask him to sign a consent form, and ask them to fill out a questionnaire with basic personal information and application familiarity to understand their familiarity with the computer application in the experiment. Participants took a Group Embedded Figures Test (GEFT) test to understand their cognitive style. After filling in all the information and the test, the participant would be seated in the designated position for eyeball correction.

At the beginning of the formal experiment, the participants would first see a video that simulates the computer power-on screen, and at the end of the movie, they would see a computer desktop in the order in which an application is arranged for 11 s. After watching the computer desktop, a black screen will appear. At this time, the participant would hear the search application assigned to him by the researcher. Then, the computer desktop with the same application arrangement sequence as before would start to search. When participant finding the specific application, using the guidance tool on hand to point to the application on computer desktops, and the researcher immediately press the left button of mouse to stop the search task. Each participant performed a total of 4 search tasks, and the experiment ended.

3 Result

3.1 Reaction Time

The results of the experiment found that in terms of the reaction time of the participants searching for the specified application, there was no significant difference in the reaction time of the participants of different cognitive types to the search task; while there is also no significant difference in different layout. However, there is a significant difference in the reaction time between the participants searching for familiar and unfamiliar applications [F $(1,16) = 11.363, p = 0.004$]. When the participant is searching for applications, he searches for the familiar reaction time (1629.139 ms) is shorter than the response time of searching for unfamiliar applications (5342.611 ms).

3.2 Number of Fixation Times

There was no significant difference in the number of fixation times between different cognitive types; while there is also no significant difference in different layout. However, there is a significant difference in the number of fixation times between the participants searching for familiar and unfamiliar applications [F$(1,16) = 19.337, p < 0.001$]. When the participants were searching for apps, they watched familiar apps (33.694) less than they watched unfamiliar apps (82.5228). And the number of fixations of familiarity and the number of fixations of cognitive style have a significant interaction [F$(1,16) = 6.383, p = 0.022$] (see Fig. 1).

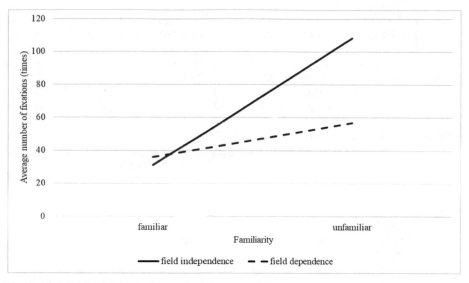

Fig. 1. The figure shows the interaction between different cognitive styles and familiarity of different computer applications. The field independent participants had lower average fixation times than the field dependent participants when watching familiar computer applications, but higher average fixation times than the field dependent participants when watching unfamiliar computer applications.

4 Conclusion

In the study, field independent and field dependent cognitive types of participants were analyzed. There was no significant difference in reaction time and number of fixations between the two cognitive types of participants in the task of searching computer desktop. However, there were significant differences between all participants in searching familiar and unfamiliar desktop applications. When searching familiar applications, the reaction time and number of fixations were shorter. The biggest difference between this study and previous studies on people with different cognitive styles is that previous studies [16] found that field independents can quickly search for targets in unfamiliar environments. In the study, field independents did not find this feature in the search task of computer applications.

References

1. Jonsson, P., Davis, S., Linder, P., Gomroki, A., Zaidi, A., Carlsson, P.A., Opsenica, M., Sorlie, I., Elmgren, S., Blennerud, G., Baur, H., Svenningsson, R.: Ericsson Mobility Report (2020). https://www.ericsson.com/4adc87/assets/local/mobility-report/documents/2020/november-2020-ericsson-mobility-report.pdf
2. Wobbrock, J.O., Rubinstein, J., Sawyer, M.W., Duchowski, A.T.: Longitudinal evaluation of discrete consecutive gaze gestures for text entry. In: Proceedings of the 2008 Symposium on Eye Tracking Research & Applications, pp. 11–18. ACM, March 2008

3. Yang, F.Y., Chang, C.Y., Chien, W.R., Chien, Y.T., Tseng, Y.H.: Tracking learners' visual attention during a multimedia presentation in a real classroom. Comput. Educ. **62**, 208–220 (2013)
4. Goldberg, J.H., Kotval, X.P.: Computer interface evaluation using eye movements: methods and constructs. Int. J. Ind. Ergon. **24**(6), 631–645 (1999)
5. Tatler, B.W., Macdonald, R.G., Hamling, T., Richardson, C.: Looking at domestic textiles: an eye-tracking experiment analysing influences on viewing behaviour at Owlpen Manor. Text. Hist. **47**(1), 94–118 (2016)
6. King, A.J., Bol, N., Cummins, R.G., John, K.K.: Improving visual behavior research in communication science: an overview, review, and reporting recommendations for using eye-tracking methods. Commun. Methods Measures **13**, 149–177 (2019)
7. Franěk, M., Šefara, D., Petružálek, J., Cabal, J., Myška, K.: Differences in eye movements while viewing images with various levels of restorativeness. J. Environ. Psychol. **57**, 10–16 (2018)
8. Cappelli, R., Ferrara, M., Maltoni, D.: Minutia cylinder-code: a new representation and matching technique for fingerprint recognition. IEEE Trans. Pattern Anal. Mach. Intell. **32**(12), 2128–2141 (2010)
9. Hollingsworth, K.P., Bowyer, K.W., Flynn, P.J.: Improved iris recognition through fusion of hamming distance and fragile bit distance. IEEE Trans. Pattern Anal. Mach. Intell. **33**(12), 2465–2476 (2011)
10. Biel, L., Pettersson, O., Philipson, L., Wide, P.: ECG analysis: a new approach in human identification. IEEE Trans. Instrum. Meas. **50**(3), 808–812 (2001)
11. Parkhi, O.M., Vedaldi, A., Zisserman, A.: On-the-fly specific person retrieval. In: 2012 13th International Workshop on Image Analysis for Multimedia Interactive Services, pp. 1–4. IEEE, May 2012
12. Huang, Y., Xu, D., Cham, T.J.: Face and human gait recognition using image-to-class distance. IEEE Trans. Circuits Syst. Video Technol. **20**(3), 431–438 (2009)
13. Ramanan, D., Forsyth, D.A., Zisserman, A.: Tracking people by learning their appearance. IEEE Trans. Pattern Anal. Mach. Intell. **29**(1), 65–81 (2006)
14. Zhang, Y., Juhola, M.: On biometrics with eye movements. IEEE J. Biomed. Health Inform. **21**(5), 1360–1366 (2016)
15. Witkin, H.A., Lewis, H.B., Hertzman, M., Machover, K., Meissner, P.B., Wapner, S.: Personality through perception: An experimental and clinical study (1954)
16. Witkin, H.A., Goodenough, D.R.: Field dependence and interpersonal behavior. Psychol. Bull. **84**(4), 661 (1977)
17. Witkin, H.A., Moore, C.A., Oltman, P.K., Goodenough, D.R., Friedman, F., Owen, D.R., Raskin, E.: Role of the field-dependent and field-independent cognitive styles in academic evolution: a longitudinal study. J. Educ. Psychol. **69**(3), 197 (1977)

Designing the University of Manitoba Technology for Assisted Living Project (TALP): A Collaborative Approach to Supporting Aging in Place

Mohamed-Amine Choukou[1,2(✉)], Jacquie Ripat[1,2], Shauna Mallory-Hill[2,3], and Reg Urbanowski[1]

[1] College of Rehabilitation Sciences, University of Manitoba, Winnipeg, MB, Canada
Amine.choukou@umanitoba.ca
[2] Centre on Aging, University of Manitoba, Winnipeg, MB, Canada
[3] Faculty of Architecture, University of Manitoba, Winnipeg, MB, Canada

Abstract. Emerging technologies are critical to support older adults to live independently and safely at home. This manuscript describes the collaborative approach used to build the "University of Manitoba Technology for Assisted Living Project" (TALP), a research and assessment facility dedicated to independent and safe living for older adults.

Keywords: Ambient assistive living · Telemonitoring · Telepresence · Patient-oriented · Accessibility · Usability

1 Problem Statement

Quality of life and the cost of healthcare are paramount considerations for older adults living in the community [1, 2]. Older adults prefer to remain in their homes as long as possible [3, 4], which reduces the strain on healthcare institutions [5]. This concept is known as "aging-in-place," which can be defined as "remaining living in the community, with some level of independence, rather than in residential care" [6]. The field of gerontological environmental design links the importance of addressing the needs of older adults through physical changes to the home, such as removing barriers or adding assistive devices in order to enhance independence and well-being [7, 8]. More recently, emerging ambient assistive living (AAL) approaches seek to enable older adults to remain independently and safely in their homes and communities by making connections to health and social supports and services. AAL technologies are defined in this paper as wireless, minimally invasive technological solutions embedded within the home that passively, autonomously, and continuously monitor and react to individuals in their home environment [9–13].

Smart home technology was first proposed as a solution for energy management and automation in the home environment. However, because of its promising features, the use

© The Author(s), under exclusive license to Springer Nature Switzerland AG 2021
N. L. Black et al. (Eds.): IEA 2021, LNNS 220, pp. 223–228, 2021.
https://doi.org/10.1007/978-3-030-74605-6_28

of remote monitoring and responsive automation technology has extended to health care and security applications. In particular, the use of smart home technology for applications such as telehealth is rapidly increasing worldwide. Different sensing technologies placed around the home can monitor the activities of the inhabitants and provide personalized services and supports, customized to their individual activities and behaviours. AAL has included sensing technologies such as wearable, ambient, and multimedia sensors to monitor activities and to allow the users to communicate with others. This paper focuses on how these technologies can be used to support telemonitoring and telepresence.

2   Objectives

To describe the collaborative design process used to develop the Technology for Assisted Living Project (TALP) and to outline the approaches followed to initiate collaborative research and services to support older adults living with chronic medical conditions to age-in-place.

3   Process

The TALP development involved two phases, a collaborative, interdisciplinary design phase to create a research facility to prototype and test solutions and a research and innovation phase to build capacity in AAL technology to support aging in place.

- The collaborative design process aimed at repurposing a space in the Winnipeg Health Science Centre, a tertiary care facility, to develop a fully sensorized apartment (FSA) to be used to initiate research on emerging ambient assistive technologies. This phase included a series of meetings involving researchers, healthcare professionals, architects, designers, engineers, private companies, foundations, and facility managers. The research team led the meetings, coordinated the decisions and outcomes, and monitored the design and construction progress. In parallel with building the FSA, the research team continued to develop and/or deploy a series of technologies for residents' evaluation and training purposes.
- Research and innovation activities included building research capacity in this novel area and the conceptualization of interdisciplinary research projects. TALP includes state of the art human activity monitoring sensors (1) installed in the FSA, and (2) available as a set of portable equipment for use in the community (e.g., health institution, individual homes). A custom cloud-based information system was developed to manage the data collection and interpretation both in the FSA and in the community (Fig. 1).

3.1   Research Facility

The FSA is a 700 ft^2, one bedroom apartment with accessible design features and furnishings throughout (Fig. 2). The space integrates the needs and uses for resident assessment, research, and education.

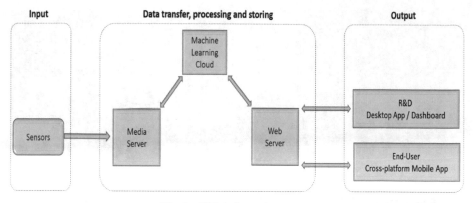

Fig. 1. FSA information system

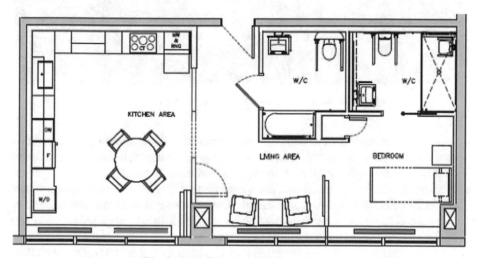

Fig. 2. FSA floorplan (MMP architects)

The FSA includes:

- An adjustable kitchen comprising of five task zones, each outfitted with unique data gathering technology to capture and model kitchen tasks in 3D to assess and customize the ideal ergonomic fit between older adults and surface heights. This innovative space provides the infrastructure to initiate the first research project aimed at observing how differences in physical and functional characteristics of older female adults relate to the usability of work surface areas in each kitchen task zone. The kitchen was developed as part of an industry-academia partnership with a kitchen cabinet design company interested in improving the ergonomic fit between consumers and their products to allow for aging in place. Figure 3 shows a virtual model of the kitchen developed as part of the TALP.

Fig. 3. Accessible, adjustable and sensor-embedded kitchen

- A bedroom including the latest lift and environmental control technologies (e.g., lights, electronics, call system) using new and emerging technologies for environmental control, and the capacity for monitoring a person while in bed,
- A standard bathroom, modelled after current home design, but with flexibility and adjustability in the adaptive aids installed, allowing students and clinicians to evaluate older adults for safety when returning home (e.g., establishing appropriate toilet seat height or bath equipment to facilitate safe transfers),
- A smart bathroom featuring an overhead track system for resident transfers, with fully sensorized toilet, faucets, heat and light, and a wheel-in shower, and
- A capacitance sensorized flooring (smart floor) to wirelessly study pedestrian behaviour, level of activity, and space usage.

3.2 Building Research Capacity

- Telemonitoring: Our research team has developed an information system that manages the data collection in the FSA (Fig. 1). The information system consists of a media server (Kurento), a machine learning cloud (Azure Machine learning) and a webserver (Azure Webserver). The established media server allows data collection from several sensors including, but not limited to, depth cameras, motion sensors, and the smart floor. An artificial intelligence solution (deep learning convolutional neural networks) is applied to quantify activity and identify behaviours that require attention depending on the clinical needs/application (e.g., fall) as compared to standardized profiles (anomaly detection). The programs are run on a webserver capable of sending emails and/or text messages. For example, in the context of monitoring individuals with dementia, real-time alerts about hazardous behaviours are sent to the caregiver through an application downloaded on a tablet/smartphone.

- Wireless Activity Monitoring: Our research team has developed a computer vision based real-time remote activity monitoring platform designed for community-based projects (Fig. 4). The platform uses depth cameras (or any other cameras such as web-cameras or surveillance cameras) installed in the assessment areas and data is processed as explained in Fig. 1, without any breach of the occupant(s)' identity. This platform includes customized detection algorithms based on an open source library: OpenPose, a real-time multi-person keypoint detection library for body, face, hands, and foot estimation. Our applications include the wireless detection of occupant(s) presence, sedentary behavior, and the assessment of gait parameters.

Fig. 4. Computer vision based real-time remote activity monitor

- Telepresence: Communication between care providers, patients and informal care-givers is key in addressing the patient's needs, especially for older adults. Through the TALP, telepresence robots are deployed for use with individuals living in the community with mild to moderate dementia, with the intent of combating loneliness and social isolation.
- Virtual reality: The research team has developed a multi-user virtual apartment (a clone of the FSA) allowing for evaluation and training, and for conducting research on cognitive rehabilitation (e.g., attention, spatial recognition and memory) (Fig. 3).

4   Conclusion

The TALP is a collaborative initiative between a multidisciplinary university research team, a health institution, and industry partners. Through the TALP, our aim is to identify the best ways to support healthy aging in the community through research, education, and outreach. The collaborative design approach of the TALP took into consideration the needs of users, clinicians and the team worked with an international network to develop a unique array of services, educational, and research initiatives. The TALP is designed as an innovation hub rooted in its ecosystem and enables growing research capacities including inclusive design, ergonomics, telehealth and virtual reality-based rehabilitation with the aim of improving quality of life and enabling social participation for persons with disabilities and older adults.

References

1. Statistics Canada: Population projections: Canada, provinces and territories, 2018 to 2068 2019 (2019). https://www150.statcan.gc.ca/n1/daily-quotidien/190917/dq190917b-eng.htm? CMP=mstatcan
2. Muscedere, J., Andrew, M.K., Bagshaw, S.M., Estabrooks, C., Hogan, D., Holroyd-Leduc, J., et al.: Screening for frailty in Canada's health care system: a time for action. Can. J. Aging/La Revue canadienne du vieillissement. **35**(3), 281–297 (2016)
3. Binette, J., Vasold, K.: 2018 Home and Community Preferences: A National Survey of Adults Ages 18-Plus. AARP Research, Washington, DC (2018)
4. Turcotte, P.-L., Carrier, A., Roy, V., Levasseur, M.: Occupational therapists' contributions to fostering older adults' social participation: a scoping review. Br. J. Occup. Therapy **81**(8), 427–449 (2018)
5. Karlsen, C., Ludvigsen, M.S., Moe, C.E., Haraldstad, K., Thygesen, E.: Experiences of community-dwelling older adults with the use of telecare in home care services: a qualitative systematic review. JBI Database Syst. Rev. Implement. Rep. **15**(12), 2913–2980 (2017)
6. Wiles, J.L., Leibing, A., Guberman, N., Reeve, J., Allen, R.E.S.: The meaning of "aging in place" to older people. Gerontologist **52**(3), 357–366 (2011)
7. Saray, G.P.H., Silva, E.C.: The gerontological design: a practice to improve life quality of the elderly. Nurs. Care Open Access J. **5**(4), 205–209 (2018)
8. Lawton, M.P., Windley, P.G., Byerts, T.: Competence, environmental press, and the adaptation of older people. In: Aging and the environment: Theoretical Approaches. Springer, New York (1982)
9. Aloulou, H., Mokhtari, M., Tiberghien, T., Biswas, J., Phua, C., Kenneth Lin, J.H., et al.: Deployment of assistive living technology in a nursing home environment: methods and lessons learned. BMC Med. Inform. Decis. Making **13**, 42 (2013)
10. Blasco, R., Marco, A., Casas, R., Cirujano, D., Picking, R.: A smart kitchen for ambient assisted living. Sensors (Basel) **14**(1), 1629–1653 (2014)
11. Cavallo, F., Aquilano, M., Arvati, M.: An ambient assisted living approach in designing domiciliary services combined with innovative technologies for patients with Alzheimer's disease: a case study. Am. J. Alzheimer Dis. Other Dementias **30**(1), 69–77 (2015)
12. Marschollek, M., Becker, M., Bauer, J.M., Bente, P., Dasenbrock, L., Elbers, K., et al.: Multimodal activity monitoring for home rehabilitation of geriatric fracture patients–feasibility and acceptance of sensor systems in the GAL-NATARS study. Inform. Health Soc. Care **39**(3–4), 262–271 (2014)
13. Mitseva, A., Peterson, C.B., Karamberi, C., Oikonomou, L., Ballis, A.V., Giannakakos, C., et al.: Gerontechnology: providing a helping hand when caring for cognitively impaired older adults-intermediate results from a controlled study on the satisfaction and acceptance of informal caregivers. Curr. Gerontol. Geriatr. Res. **2012**, 401705 (2012)

Developing a Standard One-Fits-All Boarding Assistance System as a Universal Accessibility Solution

Martin Dorynek(✉) ⓘ, Anne Guthardt, and Klaus Bengler ⓘ

Chair of Ergonomics, Technical University of Munich, Boltzmannstraße 15, 85747 Garching, Germany
martin.dorynek@tum.de

Abstract. To make mobility and thus participation in social life accessible for as many people as possible, the present work, therefore, deals with developing a concept for a boarding aid for different means of transport. Many public places and vehicles have not yet been adapted to this goal. In addition, there are differences in height and gap widths, which cannot be technically overcome in any other way. In the long term, many of these public transit vehicles will remain in operation due to their holding time. Besides, new, alternative forms of mobility use virtual stops without the corresponding infrastructure. This is where this work comes in and examines how this challenge could be solved as simply, safely, and cost-efficient as possible without compromising the ergonomic requirements. Particular focus is placed on the later users, who often face these problems in their everyday lives. The central question here was: What expectations and requirements do users have of entry-level systems?

Keywords: Accessibility · Mobility Impaired · Boarding · Assistance · MaaS · On-Demand-Mobility

1 Introduction

The German Basic Law (Article 3 (3) GG) states that no one must be "disadvantaged because of their disability." According to a provision of the Passenger Transportation Act (§8 Paragraph 3 Sentence 3 PBefG), means of public transportation must therefore be barrier-free from 2022.

Accessibility is defined in the Act on Equal Opportunities for Persons with Disabilities (§4 BGG) as follows: "Structural and other facilities, means of transport, technical commodities, information processing systems, acoustic and visual sources of information and communication facilities as well as other designed areas of life are barrier-free if they can be found, accessed and used by persons with disabilities in the generally customary manner, without particular difficulty and, in principle, without outside assistance. In this context, the use of disability-related aids is permissible."

However, many public places and vehicles have not yet been structurally adapted to this goal [1]. Also, there are height differences and gap widths between platforms and

© The Author(s), under exclusive license to Springer Nature Switzerland AG 2021
N. L. Black et al. (Eds.): IEA 2021, LNNS 220, pp. 229–238, 2021.
https://doi.org/10.1007/978-3-030-74605-6_29

means of transport that cannot be implemented in any other technical way. Furthermore, there is the option of future Mobility-as-a-Service concepts, where different means of transport can be used in combination [2]. These results are multimodal, virtual stops whose infrastructure will not necessarily be designed to be barrier-free. The lack of accessibility is a major problem for people with (mobility) disabilities.

For an entrance to be considered barrier-free under DIN 18040–3 [3] the height of the steps and the width of the gap between the edge of the train or bus platform and the vehicle must not exceed 5 cm. If greater differences exist, these must be compensated by suitable measures, at least one access point. If the value of the step height and/or the gap width is between 5 cm and 10 cm, the access, especially for wheelchair users, is only possible with the help of third parties or with difficulties [4]. If the gap width is too large, there is also a risk that a wheel of a wheelchair can become jammed between the train/bus platform and the vehicle [5]. Figure 1 shows the permissible dimensions for step height and gap width graphically.

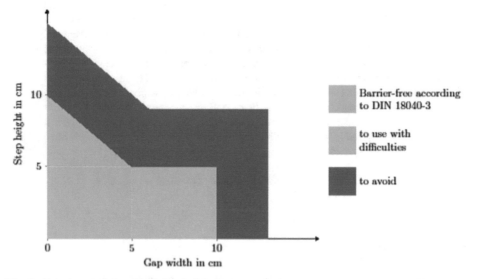

Fig. 1. Recommended residual step height and gap width - own representation according to [6].

In order to be able to guarantee the goal of barrier-free access despite the restrictions as mentioned above, entry aids such as lifts or ramps are a good idea, as they are already widely used.

2   Methods

In the following investigation, an extensive literature review and a more detailed interview study were conducted. Therefore, different user groups, which for various reasons are considered to be mobility-impaired, were defined and interviewed at the beginning. A distinction must be made between the mobility-impaired in the narrower and the broader sense. The former group includes: Walking, arm and hand impaired, wheelchair users, visually impaired and blind, the hard of hearing and deaf, and the learning and mentally handicapped. In a broader sense, mobility-impaired persons include travelers with luggage, bicycles or baby carriages, passengers with dogs, expectant mothers, people who are overweight or who do not know their way around or speak their language, as well as small children and elderly persons. These are shown in Fig. 2.

Fig. 2. Mobility impairments have different characteristics and cannot be lumped all together - own illustration designed with humaans and Freepik.

In semi-structured interviews, 11 people were asked about their experiences regarding getting on and off different means of transportation. Six subjects were male, and five were female. The average age was 58.36 years, with a standard deviation of 17.59 years. Three subjects reported mobility limitations due to carrying a stroller. Three subjects had physical limitations with which they were able to walk, but which significantly limited the musculoskeletal system; one of these participants was also short in stature. The other half of the subjects were dependent on a wheelchair due to various physical disabilities. The structure of the interview questions was based on the study by [7]. Due to different physical limitations and different residence places in Germany, the subjects' living situations cannot be compared. This could be a reason for the partly different opinions and answers of the subjects.

3   Results

3.1   Specify Requirements of Mobility Impaired People

The subjects evaluated the entry and exit options of the means of transport they use frequently and occasionally. The assessment of the boarding and alighting facilities of subway and exit options of subway and commuter trains. The test persons rated the suburban train boarding as "mostly handicapped friendly" or "no problem". The only critical comment made about the subway was that there was no time in the timetables to install a ramp, which meant that the timetables could not be adhered to in such a case.

For buses and passenger cars, there are major differences in the subjects' assessments. Newer models are often accessible at ground level. There are often ramp systems, and the buses are lowering to the side, the so-called "kneeling". So the remaining height differences are reduced. In the case of older buses, passenger cars, and especially long-distance buses designed as high-floor buses, the entrance was critically evaluated. It was noted that the height differences were far too great, making it very difficult to overcome them.

According to the respondents, there are not yet many barrier-free long-distance buses. Since 2016, it has been a legal requirement that newly registered long-distance buses be usable for people with limited mobility, and since January 1, 2020, this requirement has also applied to older buses, which since then have had to be retrofitted accordingly (Sect. 62 (3) PBefG). Basically, it is possible to board a long-distance bus with a lift. However, drivers were often not sufficiently trained and did not know how to operate the lift.

In addition to height differences, gaps between the vehicle and the curb are also a major problem. Bus drivers would often not stop directly at the curb because they were instructed to protect the vehicle's tires. The transport companies contradict this claim. However, for wheelchair or stroller boarding, this is suboptimal. If the gaps are too wide, the wheels can tilt in the gaps and make it impossible to get in without assistance from the driver or other passengers (see Fig. 1). Also, bus and streetcar lines often have very tight schedules.

The subjects reported that some drivers did not want to fold out ramps and sometimes left wheelchair users standing at bus stops, or lift them onto the bus or tilt their wheelchairs to board the bus. For the persons concerned, however, this is very unpleasant. They do not feel comfortable and would like to be able to board vehicles independently, just as it is possible for people without mobility impairments. People with baby carriages would also be very reluctant to wait. It was stated that boarding with a ramp was much easier, but a bus driver would never fold it out for a stroller because it would be too much effort. In a regulation of the [8] it is pointed out that the use of ramps for passengers with strollers is not appropriate for operational reasons, which mainly include time delays.

Only the subjects in wheelchairs rated riding the train. Those with other mobility impairments did not report riding the train. The statements of the test persons are therefore very similar. In the case of trains with large height differences and gap widths, boarding with a wheelchair is very difficult. Another problem is that the trains are not adapted to the platform heights and it may be necessary to board a train upwards as well as downwards. Deutsche Bahn offers a "mobility service" for people with limited mobility, which is described on their website [9]. The test persons basically assessed this as a good facility. However, it was also noted that using the mobility service would require a great deal of organizational effort. People had to be at the station much earlier, were tied to a train, and had to plan their trip well in advance. Spontaneous excursions are therefore not possible. In addition, there are nor lifts neither staff at every station. As a result, there are always situations in which people with wheelchairs missed their connecting trains, were diverted or had to wait until a lift and staff were organized, which led to considerable delays in the trains.

The main user-needs can be described after the interviews as follow:
Requirements for boarding aids:

– Time aspect:

  o It should be possible to operate the boarding aid as quickly as possible.
  o The entry itself should be possible as quickly as possible.

- Height differences should be as small as possible.
- Gap widths should be avoided.
- The system should be usable and available everywhere (in as many different means of transport as possible).
- The system should be able to be used spontaneously and should not require any planning in advance.
- Ramps are a preferd solution, as long as they do not exceed 6% slope.
- Lifting devices should only be used if the height differences due to the resulting slope are too steep for the use of ramps.
- There are also groups of people who can get in better by using stairs than by using a ramp.
- An electrical control panel is advantageous to be able to use systems independently.
- In the event of technical faults, manual operation should also be possible.
- Since the driving personnel is not always trained, the operation should be intuitive and straightforward.

3.2 Create Design Solutions and Develop an Assistive Boarding Aid

The literature work provided an overview of the theoretical background, regulations and currently available systems. The normative specifications were compared with test subjects' recommendations and statements and are summarized into a list of requirements, which is presented in Table 1.

Table 1. List of requirements after [10–13] - technical requirements for a boarding aid.

Requirement	Description	Value/Range
Wide	Recommended width of the boarding aid	900 mm
Length	Minimum length of the boarding aid	1200 mm
Load capacity	Recommended maximum permissible weight with which the boarding aid may be loaded	350 kg
Weight	Maximum total weight of the boarding aid	not defined
Control	Entry aid should be electrically controllable and operated at the push of a button be operable	–
Operability	Entry aid should be manually operable in case of emergency	–
Speed	Maximum extension speed of the boarding aid	0.6 m/s
Time required	Maximum duration until the entry aid is fully extended	not defined
Entry width	Recommended width of the vehicle door in the entrance area	800 mm
Entry height	Maximum height difference between a stop and the vehicle interior	not defined

(*continued*)

Table 1. (*continued*)

Requirement	Description	Value/Range
Step height	Maximum height difference between the individual steps of a staircase	250 mm
Gradient	Maximum gradient of a ramp	6%
Roll-off protection	Lateral roll-off protection for ramps and lifts	50 mm
	Frontal roll-off protection for lifts	100 mm
	Width of a side colored marking on ramps	450–550 mm
Surface	Anti-slip finish	–
Edge	Maximum vertical height difference of the edge between floor and ramp	4 mm
Edge rounding	Radius for rounding outer edges	2.5 mm
Corner rounding	Radius for rounding outer corners	5 mm

Surprisingly, there is still no unified standardization for barrier-free entrances in the mobility sector, neither in the European area, nor worldwide. In residential and house construction, this is already more advanced. All accessibility systems are based on individual solutions or offers from smaller modification companies.

According to the general model of product development, there are several prerequisites for developing an overall solution for the objective: a clear task, a detailed list of requirements, and a spectrum of subfunctions and associated partial solutions [14].

Sub-function	Partial solution 1	Partial solution 2	Partial solution 3
System	Ramp	Lift	Steps
Drive	manual	electric	
Control	manual	electronic (push button)	electronic (app)
Implementation	vehicle-linked	self-sufficient	built in infrastructure
Storage	foldable/extendable	one piece	
Dimensions	fixed	variabel	

Fig. 3. Representation of the implementation of partial functions concerning the concept of this work in a morphological box.

For a clear representation, these sub-functions were entered in a morphological box and connected to an overall solution. The implementation in relation to the concept of this work can be seen in Fig. 3. Here, no connections between individual partial solutions have been drawn to create an overview of all possible solutions of the partial functions first.

4 Discussion

Since the system sought should be universally applicable and functional in as many different situations as possible, it is advisable to implement it in a vehicle-bound manner. This means that users are not dependent on a boarding aid's presence at the respective stop when boarding. This option offers many advantages, especially with regard to future mobility-as-a-service concepts in which no fixed stops are defined. However, some aspects speak in favor of a self-sufficient or stop-bound implementation of the boarding aid. In the case of fixed stops, there is the possibility that the self-sufficient realization of the concept can save costs by requiring fewer boarding aids than vehicles. When implementing the boarding aid in the stop, it should be noted that it would be necessary to instruct the vehicles to the millimeter to enable safe boarding. This could be realized using sensors or magnets, for example.

When implementing the boarding aid in a vehicle, it is also important to consider whether the system should be installed at the vehicle's side or rear. Safety when exiting the vehicle should be considered. This may be limited by passing cyclists or stops in the middle of a street - as is sometimes the case with streetcars. The dimensions of the boarding aid and bus/train platform described in Sect. 3 must be observed in any case. The space required for side boarding is illustrated in Fig. 4 and the space required for boarding at the rear of the vehicle in Fig. 5.

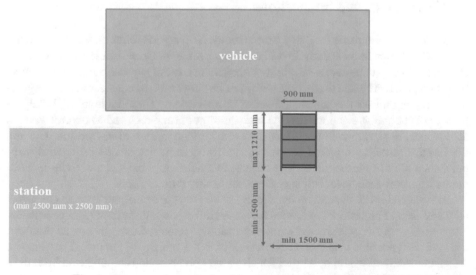

Fig. 4. Space requirements for side entry and exit - own illustration.

When entering the vehicle from the side, it should be noted that the vehicle's movement area should be wide enough to allow wheelchair users to turn in the direction of travel.

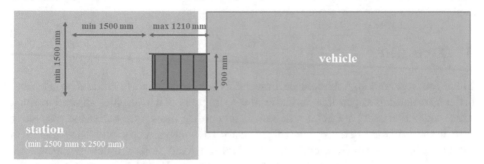

Fig. 5. Space required for entry and exit at the rear of the vehicle - own illustration

According to [15], the requirements should be discussed, critiqued, and prioritized for subsequent action following the generation of several ideas. This step serves to filter out the idea from all the proposed solutions that can best be applied to the task and the existing problem [15]. It should form the basis for the subsequent design and creation of prototypes, which in turn are tested with users [16]. This will be done in upcoming papers.

On the basis of these systems, a possibility was sought to combine the advantages of the different systems and, at the same time, reduce the problems. The system was built as a prototype and subjected to a detailed expert evaluation.

5   Conclusions and Suggestions

Mobility is commonplace for many people today, as everyone relies on the use of transportation systems in their daily lives. However, people who are unable to use existing transportation systems due to a mobility impairment can only appreciate its importance. In summary, it can be said that people with mobility impairments consider various aspects of getting on and off the bus as in need of improvement. These include the large differences in height and gap widths, the high amount of time required to operate various access aids, the organizational effort involved in planning a barrier-free journey, and the fact that mobility-impaired persons cannot travel as independently as persons without such a mobility-impairment. The different vehicles used in local and long-distance public transport each have their specific accessibility requirements.

Travel disabilities depend on the situation and purpose of the journey and can affect all passengers. Framework conditions for an overall ergonomic system must be created, allowing access for as many different and mobility-impaired user groups as possible. This makes it possible to guarantee accessibility to the vehicle for almost all passengers. A general standard would be a relief for all parties involved and should be strived for in a timely manner.

In the foreseeable future, not all passenger transport vehicles will be barrier-free, which is why such systems are still needed. However, the goal should be to design vehicles for commercial passenger transportation considering ergonomic requirements as described. This would avoid retrofitting. A vehicle concept is needed that provides optimal access for commuters, seniors, families, students, and users with limited mobility. It would be desirable to apply this on a large scale because such a design would benefit all groups.

References

1. Schwedes, O.: Verkehrspolitik. Springer Fachmedien Wiesbaden, Wiesbaden (2018)
2. Hahn, A., Pakusch, C., Stevens, G.: Die Zukunft der Bushaltestelle vor dem Hintergrund von Mobility-as-a-Service – Eine qualitative Betrachtung des öffentlichen Personennahverkehrs in Deutschland. HMD **57**, 348–365 (2020). https://doi.org/10.1365/s40702-020-00589-9
3. DIN 18040–3: Barrierefreies Bauen – Planungsgrundlagen – Teil 3: Öffentlicher Verkehrs- und Freiraum (2014)
4. Allgemeiner Deutscher Automobil-Club e.V.: Mobilitätssicherung im ländlichen Raum, München (2015)
5. Reinhardt, W.: Öffentlicher Personennahverkehr: Technik - rechtliche und betriebswirtschaftliche Grundlagen, 1st edn. Praxis. Vieweg+Teubner Verlag / Springer Fachmedien Wiesbaden GmbH Wiesbaden, Wiesbaden (2012)
6. Rebstock, M., Gerbig C.„, Köster, K.: Leitfaden zur Veranschaulichung der Checkliste Mindeststandards für barrierefreie Verknüpfungspunkte SPNV/StPNV. Institut Verkehr und Raum der Fachhochschule Erfurt (2014)
7. Wretstrand, A., Ståhl, A., Petzäll, J.: Wheelchair users and public transit: eliciting ascriptions of comfort and safety. Technol. Disability **20**, 37–48 (2008). https://doi.org/10.3233/TAD-2008-20104
8. Verband Deutscher Verkehrsunternehmen e. V.: Mitnahme von Mobilitätshilfen in Bussen (2014). https://knowhow.vdv.de/documents/mitnahme-von-mobilitatshilfen-in-bussen/. Accessed 22 Jul 2020
9. Deutsche Bahn AG, Unternehmensbereich Personenverkehr, Marketing eCommerce (2020) Barrierefreies Reisen. https://www.bahn.de/p/view/service/barrierefrei/uebersicht.shtml. Accessed 05 Oct 2020
10. Nationaler Umsetzungsplan (2017) Nationaler Umsetzungsplan der Bundesrepublik Deutschland: zu den Technischen Spezifikationen für die Interoperabilität bezüglich der Zugänglichkeit des Eisenbahnsystems der Union für Menschen mit Behinderungen und Menschen mit eingeschränkter Mobilität (TSI PRM, VO (EU) 1300/2014): gemäß Artikel 8 in Verbindung mit Anlage C der VO (EU) 1300/2014. https://ec.europa.eu/transport/sites/transport/files/rail-nip/nip-prm-tsi-germany.pdf. Accessed 11 Dec 2020
11. DIN 18040–3 (2014) Barrierefreies Bauen - Planungsgrundlagen - Teil 3: Öffentlicher Verkehrs- und Freiraum
12. Europäische Kommission: Verordnung (EU) Nr. 1300/2014 der Kommission vom 18. November 2014 über die technischen Spezifikationen für die Interoperabilität bezüglich der Zugänglichkeit des Eisenbahnsystems der Union für Menschen mit Behinderungen und Menschen mit eingeschränkter Mobilität: TSI PRM (2014). https://eur-lex.europa.eu/legal-content/DE/TXT/PDF/?uri=CELEX:32014R1300&from=DE

13. UN/ECE R 107: Regelung Nr. 107 der Wirtschaftskommission für Europa der Vereinten Nationen (UNECE) - Einheitliche Bestimmungen für die Genehmigung von Fahrzeugen der Klassen M2 oder M3 hinsichtlich ihrer allgemeinen Konstruktionsmerkmale (2018). https://eur-lex.europa.eu/legal-content/DE/TXT/PDF/?uri=CELEX:42018X0237&from=RO Accessed 06 Oct 2020
14. Kirchner, E.: Werkzeuge und Methoden der Produktentwicklung. Springer, Heidelberg (2020)
15. Wilson, C.: Brainstorming and Beyond: A User-Centered Design Method. Elsevier Science, Burlington (2013)
16. Gerling, A., Gerling, G.: Der Design-Thinking-Werkzeugkasten: Eine Methodensammlung für kreative Macher, 1. Auflage. dpunkt.verlag, Heidelberg (2018)

Inclusion Design and Functionalities of a Personalized Virtual Coach for Wellbeing to Facilitate a Universal Access for Older Adults

Mira El Kamali[1]([⊠]), Leonardo Angelini[1], Maurizio Caon[1,2], Francesco Carrino[1], Carlo Emilio Standoli[3], Paolo Perego[3], Giuseppe Andreoni[3], Filippo Palumbo[4], Alfonso Mastropietro[5], Omar Abou Khaled[1], and Elena Mugellini[1]

[1] HumanTech Institute, HES-SO, Fribourg, Switzerland
{mira.elkamali,leonardo.angelini,maurizio.caon,
francesco.carrino,omar.aboukhaled,elena.mugellini}@hes-so.ch
[2] School of Management, HES-SO, Fribourg, Switzerland
[3] Politecnico di Milano, Milan, Italy
{carloemilio.standoli,paolo.perego,giuseppe.andreoni}@polimi.it
[4] Institute of Information Science and Technologies "A.Faedo" National Research Council,
Pisa, Italy
filippo.palumbo@isti.cnr.it
[5] Institute of Biomedical Technologies, CNR, Segrate, Italy
alfonso.mastropietro@itb.cnr.it

Abstract. The current research proposes a technological system "NESTORE" designed for and with older adults in four different countries in order to improve and sustain their wellbeing. The system personalized activities and architecture, co-designed interfaces, and its multilingual aspect aim to establish an 'inclusion' criterion based on the user's sociocultural profile and health condition.

Keywords: Virtual Coach · Conversational Agent · Inclusive Design · Wellbeing · Older adults

1 Introduction

1.1 Problem Statement

In Europe, the population of older adults is increasing. ICT can help older adults to improve their lifestyle and therefore their health.

NESTORE is a virtual coach, co-designed with older adults in four different countries (Italy, Spain, The Netherlands and UK). The coach aims to help older adults in five domains of wellbeing: physical, nutritional, social, cognitive and emotional. The whole intervention is based on a behavioral change model called HAPA [2]. It is also supported by a decision support system [1] to make the system personalized according to user's preference, needs and short- and long-term habits. The virtual coach comes in different types of interfaces: a mobile application, a chatbot and the tangible coach[5], a physically embodied vocal assistant co-designed and built in the frame of the NESTORE project. The NESTORE coach is also connected to different sensors, environmental sensors, beacons and bracelets to get different type of information about the user during his or her day lifestyle.

Older adults are a heterogeneous group with different preferences, needs and lifestyles. This prompted us to adopt an inclusive design based on the users' socio-cultural profile and health conditions. However, recognizing the resource and timeframe of the project, it was determined that NESTORE might have to be developed in a staged approach providing varying formats and functionalities to be able to target diverse social groups. In addition, NESTORE would not target users with severe chronic health conditions, where users should seek expert medical help, although it could provide additional healthy lifestyle support. Thus, NESTORE e-coach is designed to be universal through its personalized wellbeing activities, co-design process and its multilingual capacity.

The goal of this paper is to present a virtual coach that is suitable for all older adults with different needs, preferences, user profile and capacities.

1.2   Co-design Process for an Inclusive Design

Co-design is an approach to design, which actively involves all stakeholders in the design process to help ensure the result meets their needs and is usable. According to [4], stakeholders cannot only serve as a need-forecasting group but also show us actively new and upcoming possibilities. The traces they leave help us to detect general patterns and could determine which artefacts should be – or should not be – designed as universal design products. In particular, co-design process has seen used in several previous work to older adults [6–8]. Several works have also shown that co-designing products or services for older adults are successful [9]. Moreover, older adults' inputs are very important to create ideas during the co-design process and older adults shows enthusiasm during co-design [10]. Hence, co-designing can help at the end to create an inclusion design to facilitate a universal access to users.

NESTORE therefore adopts co-design tools and methods that will seek to engage and elicit information related to perception, acceptance and usability of technology to support healthcare. It is co-designed in four different countries whereas each country has its own language and culture, with users with different opinions, gender and ethnicity. Thus, this will lead to have an inclusive design that works with different communities of different culture and language. First of all, we created a multi-lingual survey and sent it to four different countries to understand coaching activities preferences, pathways interest and the number of hours of interaction interest with a virtual coach. Second, we conducted five workshops in the four countries mentioned above, where we codesigned with users the virtual coach interfaces. Finally, we created an interface to translate all the messages that are fed to the conversational agents according to each countries culture of language and famous expressions. The tangible coach and the chatbot are based on Natural Language Understanding technology, powered by the RASA framework, and were manually trained with expressions from each country to detect the different intents, i.e., questions that the coach is able to answer. Section 2 presents the methodology steps used to create a universal coach; Sect. 3 presents the results of some of the experiments mentioned in the methodology section.

2 Methodology

This section describes three main activities that were carried out to take into account the sociocultural differences of the NESTORE users: 1) to provide coaching activities that are valid and appreciated by the target users, we conducted a survey about their usual activities and the activities that they would do in NESTORE; 2) to provide usable coach interfaces, we conducted several co-design workshops; 3) to tailor the coaching content, we developed a translation interface where project partners could manually adapt the system to the local language and their typical expressions.

2.1 E-coaching Activities Survey

The complete coaching plan, activities, path and recommendations are backed by a decision support system personalized to each user according to her/his needs, preferences, and conditions [3]. In fact, the virtual coach follows each user's journey by collecting data from sensors, beacons and environmental sensors and through also its main conversational agents' interfaces: the "chatbot", which is a text messaging application, and a "tangible coach", which is a vocal assistant in a physical device [4]. To understand user preferences in the different activities of wellbeing, we conducted a survey in four different countries (11 participants from Spain, 7 from UK, 6 from the Netherlands and 2 from Italy). The survey aimed at prioritizing the development of the preferred coaching activities and goals based on user's feedback. Figure 1 shows a part of the survey sent to the user. A shortened version of the survey is also included in the system in order to tailor the recommended activities according to the user preferences.

Fig. 1. E-coaching activities survey

2.2 User Interface Co-design Workshops

We held five workshops in four countries (Italy, Spain, UK, Netherlands) where we codesigned with users the virtual coach interfaces. The aim of the first workshop was to build understanding of design features of current digital interfaces that participants find helpful/unhelpful. Each participant was invited to place counters with either a tick or a cross by particular technology interfaces they found particularly helpful or unhelpful and record with the camera. Figure 2 shows the participants giving opinions about the different digital interfaces.

The aim of the second workshop was to find out the persona users would like to have in the coach. We showed video clips to users that brings life to existing personas and to support the technologists in understanding the audience for whom NESTORE would reach. Figure 4 shows the different personas that the virtual coach can have.

The aim of the third workshop was to map out the potential pathways NESTORE could provide to guide how a user might navigate the system. Participants were presented with a series of cards as examples of scenarios of use based on users' profile, their needs/requirements and activities. For instance, the e-coach would need to understand who the user is, male or female, and maybe whether the system is being used by an individual or couple. The e-coach needs to understand the intent of the user as to whether they wish or choose to improve their health and engage in familiar activities, or whether there is recognition that a behavior change is needed, and they will need a motivational and suggestive prompt. The workshop presented opportunity to visualize a systematic approach to mapping out and creating different pathways and scenarios for NESTORE from a user perspective. Figure 3 shows the creation of pathways through real-life scenario.

The aim of the fourth workshop is to set the tangible coach in context. Participants were encouraged to present an imaginary day based on activities that might in reality happen over a longer period of time. These were mapped on a template created by the design team.

The aim of the fifth workshop is to co-design the tangible coach physical appearance and features with older adults.

Fig. 2. Analysis of digital probes WSP4

Fig. 3. Pathway creation

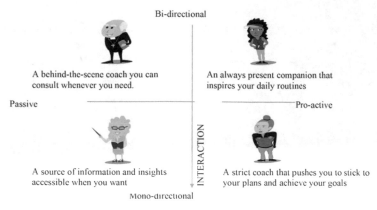

Fig. 4. E-coach personas

2.3 Translation Interface

We designed an interface to translate all the conversations in the mobile application, chatbot and the tangible coach and the intents and entities words to have natural conversations with our two conversational agent interfaces (chatbot and the tangible coach). This will lead to make our system as much flexible as possible with user's native language. This has also helped us also to write conversations depending on user's culture. The system allows also to adapt the content to the user's gender. Figure 5 and 6 shows respectively the web application interface for conversations and intents.

Fig. 5. NESTORE Translation Page (Conversations)

Fig. 6. NESTORE Translation Page (Intents)

3   Results and Discussion

3.1   Results of the E-coaching Activities Survey

We collected and then analyzed the data from our survey. Results were preliminary. However, we established some differences and similarities between each individual and each country. According to our survey, it seems that each country has preferred activities that is very culturally understandable. In fact, 6 out of 6 of older adults from Netherlands already cycle and walk however, they do not dance nor run whereas in Spain, 9 out of 11 of older adults like to dance and walk and do not cycle at all. In fact, it is widely known the importance of cycling in the Netherlands and the culture of dancing in Spain. In terms of pathways, older adults from Spain rated "Improve or maintain body flexibility" as their first choice to tackle whereas the other countries rated "Improve or maintain aerobic fitness" as their first choice. In the cognitive domain, "Improve or maintain memory" were the most wanted in UK and Italy whereas "Improve or maintain broader thinking skills" were mostly wanted by Spain and the Netherlands. One can conclude that users have different goals. Moreover, participants were also interested to try new things: In Spain, 6 participants out of 11 said they already write, however "engaging in commercial brain training app" was something Spanish people were interested in. In the social part, Spanish older adults (8/11) volunteers with others and would like to maintain doing this activity. After analyzing the whole results of the survey, we implemented these preferred activities in the system to propose them to users. In addition, we created a different pathway design where each user will have the ability to choose what pathway he or she would like to tackle in each domain of wellbeing [2].

3.2   Outcomes of the User Interface Co-design Workshops

Multiple themes emerged through the first workshop in relation to the design facets of existing technologies, user requirements, and virtual coach design interfaces. Participants understood the necessity to input personal data to the system but were cautious and considerate about the amount of data that were willing to share. Positive characteristics of existing technological interfaces included easy access of information, voice activated, convenience of portability and gestural control. There were mixed responses from the group with respect to multi-function products. Some people liked to have many functions in one device whereas others preferred a customized one. However, one common thing was the importance to have a full consultation with end-users before creating a product.

During the second workshop, feedback suggested that the personas should provide a better gender and ethnic balance. Plus, the e-coach is helping to improve the health of older adults; however, it is not a doctor but simply a coach.

Next, the cards used in the third workshop have provided an important co-design tool and tangible interface that ensured that the NESTORE partners have adopted a collective and coherent understanding of the complex variables presented in the system.

The outcomes of the fourth workshop were related to issues concerning the appearance, interaction, coaching style and data. Participants commented that they would prefer an e-coach that can "blend into the environment", "beautiful", "a piece of art", and is also controlled by the user, telling it what to do. Participants also suggested that the tangible coach should be "a knowledgeable peer" and its attitude might be different in different activities. Finally, participants felt that the data provided by the tangible coach needs to be meaningful and relevant to the user. Figure 7 shows the final prototype of the tangible coach design, co-designed with users by the using the double diamond-process for creating inclusive designs [11] in the fifth workshop.

Fig. 7. Tangible Coach Design

4 Conclusion

NESTORE is a virtual coach designed for older adults' wellbeing. Our study proposes a universal model by co-designing the virtual coach with older users. In our process, we carried out surveys to discover user's preferences wellbeing activities in order to create a personalized coaching system. Moreover, we conducted five workshops in order to create the different pathway intervention, e-coach interfaces and capacities and e-coach persona and design. Finally, our virtual coach can adapt to each user's culture and language thanks to a translation interface. Hence, this made the e-coach an inclusive design accessible universally. The system has been tested since October 2020 on a 3-month pilot study in Italy, Spain and the Netherlands. Results of the pilot will be reported in a further publication.

References

1. Orte, S., Subías, P., Maldonado, L. F., Mastropietro, A., Porcelli, S., Rizzo, G., Boqué, N., Guye, S., Röcke, C., Andreoni, G., Crivello, A., Palumbo, F.: Dynamic decision support system for personalised coaching to support active ageing. In: AI* AAL@ AI* IA, pp. 16–36 (2018)
2. Angelini, L., Mugellini, E., Khaled, O. A., Röcke, C., Guye, S., Porcelli, S., Mastropietro, A., Rizzo, G., Boqué, N., del Bas, J.M., Subias, P., Orte, S., Andreoni, G.: The NESTORE e-coach: accompanying older adults through a personalized pathway to wellbeing. In Proceedings of the 12th ACM International Conference on PErvasive Technologies Related to Assistive Environments, pp. 620–628, June 2019
3. El Kamali, M., Angelini, L., Caon, M., Lalanne, D., Abou Khaled, O., Mugellini, E.: An embodied and ubiquitous E-coach for accompanying older adults towards a Better lifestyle. In: International Conference on Human-Computer Interaction, pp. 23–35. Springer, Cham, July 2020
4. De Couvreur, L., Goossens, R.: Design for (every) one: Co-creation as a bridge between universal design and rehabilitation engineering. CoDesign 7(2), 107–121 (2011)
5. El Kamali, M., Angelini, L., Caon, M., Khaled, O.A., Mugellini, E., Dulack, N., Chamberlin, P., Craig, C., Andreoni, G.: NESTORE: mobile chatbot and tangible vocal assistant to support older adults' wellbeing. In. Proceedings of the 2nd Conference on Conversational User Interfaces, pp. 1–3, July 2020
6. Lehto, P., Rantanen, T.: Robotics in homecare: the development process through a case study. In: Proceedings of the International Technology, Education and Development Conference. Valencia, Spain, pp. 3444–3452 (2017). https://doi.org/10.21125/inted.2017.0864
7. How, T.-V., Hwang, A.S., Green, R.E.A., Mihailidis, A.: Envisioning future cognitive telerehabilitation technologies: a co-design process with clinicians. Disability Rehabilitation Assistive Technol. 12, 244–261 (2017). https://doi.org/10.3109/17483107.2015.1129457
8. McGee-Lennon, M., Smeaton, A., Brewster, S.: Designing home care reminder systems: lessons learned through co-design with older users. In Proceedings of the 6th international conference on pervasive computing technologies for healthcare. IEEE, San Diego, USA (2012).https://doi.org/10.4108/icst.pervasivehealth.2012.248684
9. Merkel, S., Kucharski, A.: Participatory design in gerontechnology: a systematic literature review. Gerontologist 59, e16–e25 (2019). https://doi.org/10.1093/geront/gny034
10. Davidson, J.L., Jensen, C.: Participatory design with older adults: an analysis of creativity in the design of mobile healthcare applications. In: Proceedings of the 9th ACM Conference on Creativity and Cognition—C&C'13. ACM Press, Sydney, Australia, p. 114 (2013). https://doi.org/10.1145/2466627.2466652
11. West, J., Meldaikyte, G., Raby, E.: Developing the Double Diamond Process for Implementation-insights from a decade of Inclusive Design projects. DESIGN4HEALTH, 310 (2017)

Flat Cushion vs Shaped Cushion: Comparison in Terms of Pressure Distribution and Postural Perceived Discomfort

Iolanda Fiorillo[1]([⊠]), Yu Song[2], Maxim Smulders[2], Peter Vink[2], and Alessandro Naddeo[1]

[1] Department of Industrial Engineering, University of Salerno, 84084 Fisciano, SA, Italy
ifiorillo@unisa.it
[2] Faculty of Industrial Design Engineering,
Delft University of Technology, 2628 CE Delft, Netherlands

Abstract. A proper seat is crucial not only for preventing health issues but also for the (dis)comfort perception. In the design of a seat, the seat pan's geometric shape, either in or under the cushion, plays a vital role as it constrains the deformation of the foam it supports. The contact area and pressure distributions between the foam and the human body, closely associated with (dis)comfort, are influenced by those constrained deformations. In this paper, using a comparative study, the aim is to determine if opportunely shaped seat pans are better than a standard flat pan regarding postural comfort and pressure distribution. Two cushions with the same type of foam but two different seat pans were used in the comparison. The first seat pan is the standard one used in current aircraft seats and the second is a shaped seat pan, which was designed following the mean buttock-thigh shape of an international population (including P5 females and P95 males). Twenty-two international participants (11 males and 11 females, with BMI between 16 and 30) took part in the blind experiment. Results indicated that the cushion with shaped seat pan performed better as it led to less postural comfort, a larger contact area and more uniform pressure distribution. Also, 64% of participants favored the cushion with the shaped seat pan as they felt it was more comfortable and suitable for the buttock shape.

Keywords: Seat-pan · Comfort · Human-center-design · Pressure map

1 Introduction

Designing a comfortable seat often needs to study factors of the human body, such as anthropometry [1, 2], 3D body shape [3, 4], body sensitivity [5, 6], postures [7, 8], perceived (dis)comfort [9, 10]. During seating, the interactions between the human body and the seat are often affected by the body shape, the postures [11, 12], the seat's design and the seating duration. Remaining seated for extended periods increases the risk of

The original version of this chapter was revised: [Fiorillo, I., Song, Y., Vink, P. & Naddeo, A. 2021, Designing a shaped seat-pan cushion to improve postural (dis)comfort reducing pressure distribution and increasing contact area at the interface. In: Proceedings of the Design Society, pp. 1113. doi:10.1017/pds.2021.111. The correction to this chapter is available at https://doi.org/10.1007/978-3-030-74605-6_101

N. L. Black et al. (Eds.): IEA 2021, LNNS 220, pp. 247–254, 2021.
https://doi.org/10.1007/978-3-030-74605-6_31

pressure ulcers development over the buttocks, as the soft tissue in this area is squashed between two surfaces: the top of the seat cushion and the bones of the pelvis [13, 14]. Also, the blood flow in these regions is significantly decreased when sitting 3 h without moving the body [15, 16]. Therefore, both (dis)comfort perception and health issues should be considered in the seat's design.

Literature study indicates that a seat with ideal pressure distribution [9, 17, 18] could lead to more comfort than a seat with self-chosen adjustments on a more than 2 h' drive [19]; however, the contributions of different components of the seat, e.g. the types of foam, the seat pan, to the pressure distribution were not fully explored. For instance, the seat pan's geometric shapes could influence both the contact area's size and the pressure distribution by constraining the deformation of the foam in different manners.

This work aims to fill literature gaps by investigating the effects of different types of seat pans on the perceived (dis)comfort and the pressure distribution on aircraft seats. In general, a lower average pressure and a more uniform pressure distribution are often accompanied by less discomfort [20]. A larger contact area might in lower mean pressure correlated to a higher comfort level [21–23]. One way to achieve this is to design a "shaped seat pan" for aircraft seat that follows the buttock-thigh shape of the international population (including P5 females and P95 males) based on the hypothesis: the shaped set pan could have more benefits than the standard flat pan regarding comfort. To validate this hypothesis, a research question was initiated as: having two cushions with seat pans in different shapes, which seat pan is preferred regarding both postural comfort and pressure distribution?

2 Materials and Methods

A blind experiment was designed to answer the proposed research question. The experiment protocol was approved by the Human Research Ethical Committee at Delft University of Technology (HREC, TU Delft), in the Netherlands. Participants were explained about the protocol and asked to fill the Informed Consent before experiments.

2.1 Materials for Experiments

Seat cushions with different seat pans. Two aircraft seats with different cushions were used in the experiment. The seats' inclination angle was fixed at 4 degrees regarding the floor, representing the aircraft's real condition. The two types of cushions used in the experiment were: 1) "Foam on flat seat pan" as commonly used in standard aircraft seats; 2) "Foam on shaped seat pan" which was built using the same type of foam but with a shaped seat pan. The 3D shape of the seat pan was designed to follow the buttock-thigh contour based on the mean pressure profile of an international population [24]. Both cushions were covered with the same textiles to avoid any potential influences on the participants' perceptions and expectations [25].

Pressure mat. A Xsensor LX210:48.48.02 pressure mat was used to record the pressure distribution of the participants during the experiment. The total sensing area and the mat's thicknesses were 24×24 in. (~61×61 cm) and 0.03 in. (~0.08 cm), respectively. With this mat, contact pressures of a wide range of population could be recorded without influencing perceived (dis)comfort.

Questionnaires. Three different types of questionnaires were prepared using Google Forms. The first one was the "short-term questionnaire" composed by a Body Part Discomfort (BPD) questionnaire [26] where each body part was associate with a 5-point scale ranging from 1 = "no discomfort" to 5 = "extreme discomfort". This questionnaire was designed to investigate the discomfort levels after each posture per cushion for detecting the discomfort levels over time [27].

The second was the "long-term questionnaire" composed by three questions: 1) Overall perceived discomfort (1 = No discomfort, 2 = Low Discomfort, 5 = Discomfort, 7 = High Discomfort, 9 = Extreme Discomfort); 2) Overall perceived comfort (1 = No Comfort, 2 = Low Comfort, 5 = Comfort, 7 = High Comfort, 9 = Extreme Comfort); and 3) Personal feelings about cushions (Soft/Hard, Cozy/Uncomfortable, Firm/Loose, Adequate/Inadequate, Shaped/Flat). This questionnaire was used to detect participants' overall perceived discomfort, comfort and sensations after experiencing a cushion for 42 min (7 min × 6 postures).

At the end of the experiment where the subject experienced both cushions, the third questionnaire was asked with a closed question regarding the cushion's preference (the first or the second cushion since experiments were blind-tests) and an open question for explaining the reasons of choice.

2.2 Participants

Prior to the experiments, a statistical power calculation was conducted to determine the minimal sample size N of the experiment using the GPower software [28]. Results showed that at a confidence interval of 80%, a sample number N = 21 was needed to identify the difference regarding (dis)comfort using a one-tail Wilcoxon signed-rank test. Base on this result, 22 (11 males and 11 females) international participants (Chinese, Egyptian, Italian, Colombian, Mexican, Indonesian, Dutch) were recruited through social channels of TU Delft and emails to obtain a large sample of the international population with high variability on age, height, weight, and ethnic groups. The anthropometric data of the subjects are presented in Table 1.

Table 1. Anthropometric data of participants (n = 22)

	Average	Median	SD	Max	Min
Age	28.73	27.50	5.55	48.00	24.00
Weight (kg)	64.64	62.50	13.00	95.00	48.00
Height (cm)	169.32	167.00	9.42	193.00	155.00
BMI (Kg/m2)	22.40	22.06	3.05	29.40	16.60

2.3 Experiment Protocol

The cushion and posture orders have been planned for each participant adopting the Latin Square Method to randomize the order while keeping the experiments' repeatability [29–31]. Five sitting postures, which were often observed in the airplane, were selected based on literature [32]. They are:

1) *Upright*: The participant had to assume the upright posture, angle back-legs around 90° and legs raised at 90° at the knee.
2) *Elbow on legs*: The participant should bend forward placing the elbows on the legs, and both thighs were on the seat.
3) *Legs crossed*: The participant had to lay against the backrest and to have leg crossed, with the right leg on the left leg.
4) *Arm on armrest*: The participant should bend to the right side placing the arm on the armrest.
5) *Legs crossed + arm on armrest*: Crossing the legs (the left leg on the right leg), the participant should bend to the right side placing the arm on the armrest

During the experiment, the backrest angle was fixed; therefore, the slouched/relaxed posture was hard to achieve and was not included in this study. Besides these 5 postures, participants could choose a desired posture as the last posture, reproducing the situation in which participants could assume their comfortable posture freely during a flight.

3 Results and Discussions

The postural discomfort data collected from the "short-term" questionnaires were categorized and analyzed regarding different postures, two types of cushions and the time. Figure 1 shows perceived discomfort over time regarding the flat cushion and shaped cushion per posture, starting with the first assumed posture and ending with the last performed posture, i.e., the grouped postures refer to the order, without any distinction of postures' types. The line LBD (Lower Body Discomfort) represents the mean global perceived discomfort of lower limbs for a better comparison of two cushions' discomfort trends. Results show that the perceived discomfort for the flat cushion (LBD range: 1.76–2.00) is higher than the shaped cushion (LBD range: 1.56–1.78). Wilcoxon Sign Rank tests were performed to check inter- and intra-cushions significant differences. Results indicated that there were significant inter-differences ($\rho \leq 0.05$) for Posture 3 ($Z = -2.076$, $\rho = 0.038$), Posture 4 ($Z = -1.957$, $\rho = 0.050$) and Posture 6 ($Z = 2.210$, $\rho = 0.027$). Instead, there is only one significant intra-difference for the shaped cushion between Posture 3 and Posture 4 ($Z = -2.298$, $\rho = 0.022$), and no intra-differences for the flat cushion. The absence of significant intra-differences could mean that the 7-min per posture were not long enough for participants to be aware of the differences in perceived discomfort between postures. However, the presence of significant inter-differences could mean that participants were aware of different perceived discomfort regarding different cushions, where the shaped cushion is associated with significantly lower perceived discomfort.

Figure 1 shows also perceived discomfort scores of the BPD questionnaires regarding different posture. The flat cushion scored higher discomfort scores than the shaped cushion. The Wilcoxon Sign Rank test results indicate that for the cushion with the shaped seat pan, there is only one significant difference between postures "Arm on Armrest" and "Leg Crossed" ($Z = -2.300$, $\rho = 0.021$). However, there are no significant differences of discomfort scores among different postures regarding the cushion with the flat seat pan. Similarly, significant inter-differences have been identified ($\rho \sim 0.040$) between the same posture (for example, LBD of Upright posture calculated for Flat cushion with LBD of Upright posture calculated for the shaped cushion).

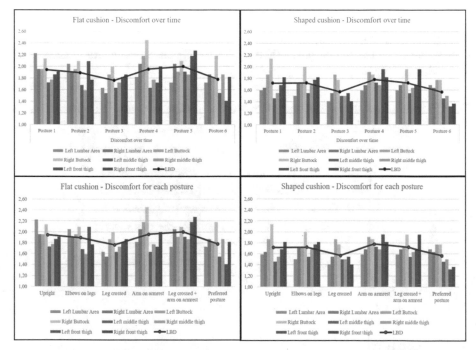

Fig. 1. Result from LPD (with 5-point Likert scale) of "short-term" questionnaires - perceived discomfort overtime and for each posture while sitting on the flat and shaped cushions. The line LBD stands for Lower Body Discomfort, the mean score of perceived discomfort indexes for each posture.

The "long-term" questionnaire was rated after sitting on one cushion for 42 min. The shaped cushion scored lower perceived discomfort (3.7) and higher perceived comfort (6.5) than the flat cushion (disc. 4.5; comf. 5.5). Wilcoxon Sign Rank Test results also showed significant intra- and inter-differences ($\rho \leq 0.05$) of the perceived discomfort and perceived comfort regarding these two cushions. As far as the descriptive adjectives, the flat cushion appeared firmer than the shaped cushion.

After experiencing both cushions, participants were asked to choose their preferred cushion without knowing the difference between them (as it was a blind experiment), and explained their reasons. Results showed that 64% of participants chose the shaped cushion. Answers of the open question were analyzed, and the keywords were categorized to advantages and disadvantages for each cushion. Participants felt the shaped cushion softer, more comfortable and more adequate for their body shape. Indeed, they declared that the shape fitted their lower body better. The disadvantages were more pressure on the front thigh and less firmness. Instead, the flat cushion gave more support, but they felt more pressure on the lower body areas.

Objective data have been gained from the pressure mat. The first analysis allowed comparing cushions in terms of pressure distributions and contact areas. Indeed, data from cushions have been subtracted: negative values of average pressure indicated the pressure distribution on the shaped cushion is lower than the flat cushion; positive values of contact area indicated that the shaped cushion shows a wider contact surface than the flat one. Thus, results showed that the shaped cushion presented less pressure and higher contact area than the flat cushion (Table 2). Thus, objective results are in accordance with subjective data.

Table 2. Result from the pressure mat: differences of average pressures and contact areas per each posture.

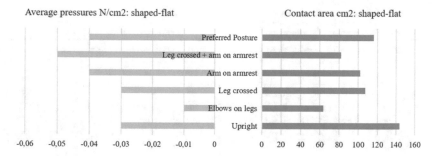

4 Conclusions

Sitting is an everyday activity that for a prolonged amount of time could lead to discomfort and in the worst case, even health problems. For these reasons, it is essential to design a comfortable seat preventively. Less pressure distribution variations in the contact interface between the seat pan and buttock-thigh area could lead to higher perceived comfort or a discomfort reduction. The experiments performed at TU Delft with 22 participants demonstrated that a cushion with a shaped seat pan (designed as the buttock-thigh shape) was more comfortable than the standard cushion with a flat seat pan regarding both subjective (dis)comfort perceptions and objective data of pressure distributions. However, the two cushions have different fabrication process that could have influenced results. Another limitation of the study is that only one type of foam for the shaped cushion was used in the experiment. In the future study, more types of foams will be included, the same fabrication process will be considered, and the backrest influence will be investigated.

References

1. Casadei, K., Kiel, J.: Anthropometric Measurement. Treasure Island (FL) (2020)
2. Molenbroek, J.F.M., Albin, T.J., Vink, P.: Thirty years of anthropometric changes relevant to the width and depth of transportation seating spaces, present and future. Appl. Ergon. **65**, 130–138 (2017). https://doi.org/10.1016/j.apergo.2017.06.003
3. Smulders, M., Berghman, K., Koenraads, M., et al.: Comfort and pressure distribution in a human contour shaped aircraft seat (developed with 3D scans of the human body). Work **54**, 1–16 (2016)
4. Hiemstra-van Mastrigt, S., Smulders, M., Bouwens, J.M.A., Vink, P.: Chapter 61 - Designing aircraft seats to fit the human body contour. In: Scataglini, S., Paul, G. (eds.) DHM and Posturography. Academic Press, pp. 781–789 (2019)
5. Vink, P., Lips, D.: Sensitivity of the human back and buttocks: The missing link in comfort seat design. Appl. Ergon. **58**, 287–292 (2017). https://doi.org/10.1016/j.apergo.2016.07.004
6. Rosaria, C., Alessandro, N., Chiara, C.: Comfort seat design: thermal sensitivity of human back and buttock. Int. J. Ind. Ergon. **78**, 102961 (2020). https://doi.org/10.1016/j.ergon.2020.102961
7. Apostolico, A., Cappetti, N., D'Oria, C., et al.: Postural comfort evaluation: experimental identification of range of rest posture for human articular joints. Int. J. Interact. Des. Manuf. **8**, 109–120 (2014). https://doi.org/10.1007/s12008-013-0186-z
8. Smulders, M., Naddeo, A., Cappetti, N., et al.: Neck posture and muscle activity in a reclined business class aircraft seat watching IFE with and without head support. Appl. Ergon. **79**, 25–37 (2019). https://doi.org/10.1016/j.apergo.2018.12.014
9. Zenk, R., Mergl, C., Hartung, J., et al.: Objectifying the comfort of car seats. In: SAE 2006 World Congress & Exhibition. SAE International (2006)
10. Anjani, S., Kühne, M., Naddeo, A., et al.: PCQ: preferred comfort questionnaires for product design. Work **68**, S19–S28 (2021). https://doi.org/10.3233/WOR-208002
11. Naddeo, A., Califano, R., Vink, P.: The effect of posture, pressure and load distribution on (dis)comfort perceived by students seated on school chairs. Int. J. Interact. Des. Manuf. (2018). https://doi.org/10.1007/s12008-018-0479-3
12. Smulders, M., Vink, P.: Human behaviour should be recorded in (dis)comfort research. Work **68**, S289–S294 (2021). https://doi.org/10.3233/WOR-208027
13. Stephens, M., Bartley, C.: Understanding the association between pressure ulcers and sitting in adults what does it mean for me and my carers? seating guidelines for people, carers and health & social care professionals. J. Tissue Viability **27** (2017). https://doi.org/10.1016/j.jtv.2017.09.004
14. Schubert, V., Perbeck, L., Schubert, P.-Å.: Skin microcirculatory and thermal changes in elderly subjects with early stage of pressure sores. Clin. Physiol. **14**, 1–13 (1994). https://doi.org/10.1111/j.1475-097X.1994.tb00484.x
15. McManus, A.M., Ainslie, P.N., Green, D.J., et al.: Impact of prolonged sitting on vascular function in young girls. Exp. Physiol. **100**, 1379–1387 (2015). https://doi.org/10.1113/EP085355
16. Thosar, S., Bielko, S., Mather, K., et al.: Effect of prolonged sitting and breaks in sitting time on endothelial function. Med. Sci. Sports Exerc. **47** (2014). https://doi.org/10.1249/MSS.0000000000000479
17. Mergl, C., Klendauer, M., Mangen, C., Bubb, H.: Predicting Long Term Riding Comfort in Cars by Contact Forces Between Human and Seat (2005). https://doi.org/10.4271/2005-01-2690
18. Kilincsoy, U., Wagner, A., Vink, P., Bubb, H.: Application of ideal pressure distribution in development process of automobile seats. Work **54**, 895–904 (2016). https://doi.org/10.3233/WOR-162350

19. Hiemstra-van Mastrigt, S.: Comfortable passenger seats: Recommendations for design and research (2015)
20. Noro, K., Fujimaki, G., Kishi, S.: A theory on pressure distribution and seat discomfort, 33–39 (2004). https://doi.org/10.1201/9781420038132.ch3
21. Fan, F., Shen, L., Chen, Y., Yuding, Z.: A method for measuring the weight of body segment based on human model and body pressure distribution, pp. 735–741 (2016)
22. Zemp, R., Taylor, W.R., Lorenzetti, S.: Seat pan and backrest pressure distribution while sitting in office chairs. Appl. Ergon. **53**, 1–9 (2016). https://doi.org/10.1016/j.apergo.2015.08.004
23. Dangal, S., Smulders, M., Vink, P.: Implementing spring-foam technology to design a lightweight and comfortable aircraft seat-pan. Appl. Ergon. **91**, 103174 (2021). https://doi.org/10.1016/j.apergo.2020.103174
24. Fiorillo, I., Song, Y., Vink, P., Naddeo, A.: Designing a shaped seat-pan cushion to improve postural (dis)comfort reducing pressure distribution and increasing contact area at the interface. Proc. Des. Soc. **1**, 1113–1122 (2021). https://doi.org/10.1017/pds.2021.111
25. Naddeo, A., Cappetti, N., Califano, R., Vallone, M.: The role of expectation in comfort perception: the mattresses' evaluation experience. Procedia Manuf. **3**, 4784–4791 (2015). https://doi.org/10.1016/J.PROMFG.2015.07.582
26. Grinten, M.P.: Development of a pratical method for measuring body part discomfort. In: S.K. (ed.) Advances in Industrial Ergonomics and Safety IV, pp. 331–318. Taylor and Francis, London (1992)
27. Helander, M., Zhang, L.: Field studies of comfort and discomfort in sitting. Ergonomics **40**, 895–915 (1997)
28. Faul, F., Erdfelder, E., Lang, A.-G., Buchner, A.: G*Power 3: a flexible statistical power analysis program for the social, behavioral, and biomedical sciences. Behav. Res. Methods **39**, 175–191 (2007). https://doi.org/10.3758/BF03193146
29. Fisher, R.A.: Statistical methods for research workers. In: Kotz, S., Johnson, N.L. (eds.) Breakthroughs in Statistics: Methodology and Distribution, pp. 66–70. Springer, New York (1992)
30. Fiorillo, I., Piro, S., Anjani, S., et al.: Future vehicles: the effect of seat configuration on posture and quality of conversation. Ergonomics **62** (2019). https://doi.org/10.1080/00140139.2019.1651904
31. Piro, S., Fiorillo, I., Anjani, S., et al.: Towards comfortable communication in future vehicles. Appl. Ergon. **78** (2019). https://doi.org/10.1016/j.apergo.2019.03.008
32. Liu, J., Yu, S., Chu, J.: The passengers' comfort improvement by sitting activity and posture analysis in civil aircraft cabin. Math. Probl. Eng. **2019**, 3278215 (2019). https://doi.org/10.1155/2019/3278215

Accessibility Performance for a Safe, Fair, and Healthy Use of the Elevator

Elena Giacomello[1]([⊠]), Mickeal Milocco Borlini[2], Daniele Pavan[3], Christina Conti[2], and Dario Trabucco[1]

[1] IUAV University of Venice, Terese, Dorsoduro, 2206, 30123 Venice, Italy
{elenag,trabucco}@iuav.it
[2] Dipartimento Politecnico di Ingegneria e Architettura, Università degli studi di Udine, via Delle Scienze, 206, 33100 Udine, Italy
{mickeal.milocco,christina.conti}@uniud.it
[3] TK Elevator Italia, via Alessandro Volta, 16, 20093 Cologno Monzese (MI), Italy
daniele.pavan@tkelevator.com

Abstract. The elevator is a machine, a transport system, a space. It is the solution *par excellence* addressed to everyone. Its installation and use should be simple, and open to all users. The accessibility (for all), safety, and hygiene aspects of the elevator are constantly evolving: on these topics, this research takes its first steps and deepens each subject connected to 'the vertical travel'. The paper introduces the European Standards on elevator's accessibility, defines the declination of DfA/HCD methodology applied to product design processes, and shows some innovative product solutions inspired by the health emergencies, which are suitable for inclusion and safety above the current circumstances. Finally, the interaction of the studies represents the base for future research collaboration about the safe and fair use of elevators and vertical journeys.

Keywords: Elevators · Accessibility · Safety · Fair use · Equity · Standards · Design for all · Human-centered design · Product innovation

1 Introduction

The context of research is within the European accessibility standards, which defines general requirements "to be solved" at a national level, improving existing and future solutions aimed at the creation of suitable architectural, ergonomic, and product standards for all. The authors represent 3 distinct research groups who, in close fields, have collaborated and are involved in designing accessibility and product innovation.

The group based at the IUAV University of Venice explores the subject of the design, and integration of elevators including their accessibility in buildings [1, 2] In synergy with the important Italian elevator industry, the group has published books and articles on accessibility [3] and carried out regular teaching activities and academic dissemination on these topics (Conferences "Beyond the square and the X" ed. 2013, 2015, 2017, 2020).

N. L. Black et al. (Eds.): IEA 2021, LNNS 220, pp. 255–262, 2021.
https://doi.org/10.1007/978-3-030-74605-6_32

The group based at the University of Udine (dalt – Environmental accessibility and universal design Lab.) has been dealing with research on Inclusive Living [4] for almost a decade, focusing on the reduction of architectural barriers; the group declines also the HCD methods and deals with the active participation of the users in the analytical design process; the group also investigates the sensory-perceptive aspects of the "vertical travel" [5].

TK Elevator, a multinational leader in the production of elevators, represents the third group. The research groups of the universities of Venice and Udine are part of the AA-Environmental Accessibility Cluster of The Italian Society of Architectural Technology (SiTdA). The paper discusses the accessibility of elevators through the analyses of the EU standards, the DfA/HCD method, and product innovation. Finally, future lines of research are defined considering the improvement, usability, and fair use of vertical devices.

2   Elevator Accessibility in EU Standards

2.1   The European Current Standards on Elevator Accessibility

In Europe performance of elevators are regulated by several standards (EN standards) developed by CEN; CEN member Countries are obliged to comply. For what concerns accessibility the regulation frame is composed by the following standards:

1. **Directive 2014/33/EU** [6]: the Lift Directive is the main reference text for the development of the standards. Among a number of requirements, it states that "its accessibility [of the elevators] is a RES-Essential Safety Requirement of the Lift Directive 2014 [pp. 96; 271].
2. **EN 81–20** [7]: it complies to the RES requirements of the Lift Directive, including the accessibility. This standard is a fundamental wide reference text for every aspect of safety requirements and protective measures of elevators.
3. **EN 81–70** [8]: it is dedicated to safety rules for the independent accessibility of elevators for a wider range of persons, including passengers with disabilities. This standard – applicable according to the EN 81:20 [7] – raises the elevator requirements to facilitate the use by all. The 5 Appendixes of the text are important and interesting, deepening: general considerations on disabilities, what disabilities have been considered in the standard, a risk analyses, hypoallergenic materials, and guidelines for visually impaired.
4. **CEN/TS 81–76** [9]: it deals with technical specific rules for the evacuation of people with impair abilities and how to train persons to evacuate people with impair abilities using elevators;
5. **EN 81–80** [10]: it is defined as a good practice standard, not harmonized – it does not comply to the RES requirements of the Lift Directive [6] – but it implements the

Recommendations 95/216 EC [15] giving a methodology for improving the safety of existing elevators with the aim of reaching an equivalent level of safety of new installed elevator (elimination of cabin barriers, leveling the cabin to floors, phone call system, …).

6. **EN 81–82** [11]: consequent to the 95/216/EC [12], it is dedicated to improve the accessibility of existing lifts by persons with impair abilities. It corresponds to the EN 81:70 [8], but the application is to existing lifts.

2.2 The Elevator Accessibility in the Holistic Approach of the EN 17210

The EN 17210 [13] is a new European Standard dedicated to minimum functional requirements and recommendations for the accessibility of the built environment. The objective of the standard is to decrease discrimination, while addressing the largest number possible of users, according to the principles of DfA, and Universal Design (UD). It was developed: (1) to facilitate public processes of built environments following the principles of DfA, (2) to provide a mechanism by which public contractors have access to an online toolkit for harmonized requirements in the building process [18, p. 2]. Concerning the issues of accessibility of lifts, the EN mentions EN 81–70 [8] and EN 81–20 [7], however, it introduces some new functional elements including (a) the tip-up seat inside the lift cabins installed in particular buildings (i.e. health facilities); (b) the *braille* language on the command panels; (b) the high contrast of the controls. This standard appears to be considerably advanced because the issue of accessibility is treated holistically, with fundamental recommendations including the continuity of spaces/surfaces and the DfA. Its potential impact, when used as a building process regulation tool, can be huge in terms of accessible upgrading.

3 Design for All/Human-Centered Design Approaches for Improving Elevator Accessibility, Usability, and Perception

A DfA/HCD approach applied to the vertical transport should "create a continuous relationship between everyone, accepting physical, sensory, cognitive and behavioral diversity as a distinctive trait of each one" [14].

The definition of the project requirements must consider the proxemic-spatial perception through the senses and the different intellectual faculties of users, including those with disabilities.

The ongoing research aim is to obtain qualitative and quantitative data (taxonomies) of vertical transport devices, to find solutions "reasonably accommodated" [15, art. 2] between the needs of users and the presence/absence of services and functions, referring to the "user journey" throughout a building. To achieve so, the next step is to carry out participatory experiments in confined environments, such as lifts, to integrate the data already collected in other users tests in urban and building contexts; thus, participation is an extremely important method; collecting data through subjective mapping to the largest pool of users possible, allows us to determine the critical elements in the "elevator environment" that need to be solved in the design processes [16, 17].

As the urban environment, the elevator is also a subjective space [18] and can be interpreted and being interacted with by each user. Therefore, the cognitive strategies implemented by users are an integral part of the analysis for an inclusive vertical transport design, to improve its communication, and – specifically – its dimensional, multisensory, perceptual, and orientation aspects. The DfA and HCD methodologies have improved product innovation, which can inspire new environmental safety standards for the elevators, and the building's distribution spaces connected to the vertical devices. The elevator naturally belongs to a family of devices that overcome architectural barriers; its cabin is also space, a room, connected to other distribution areas of the building system. We consider the spaces connected to the lift and their distribution, function, and design, as an integral part of the vertical travel's design; the elevator is "an environment", a "place of living", and it is part of growing attention [15] to the requirements that ensure an accessible and safe use for all. Therefore, the analysis, study, and control of interactions between the users and the built environment is the key to ruling out obstacles and barriers that cause discomfort or inaccessibility [15].

The interaction between users, distribution spaces, and machines involves several cognitive strategies aimed at redefining the places according to elements of reference, coordination, orientation, and recognition and giving audio support for help (voiceover) and destination commands by typing the buttons of the panel inside and outside the cabin, finally, entering/exiting the cabin, choosing the right direction.

Elements that indicate, suggest, orient are indispensable distribution aids to allow the user to have a complete experience from the point of view of wayfinding, usability, and safety. These elements include visual devices, tactile devices, and auditory aids that facilitate the interaction between the human being and the space that surrounds him; those actions can be touch-less (ICT).

The mentioned methodology can improve and implement future product innovations and research.

4   Most Recent Innovations for Accessibility from TK Elevator Product Research Division

Elevators are enclosed, restricted spaces that often lack ventilation, making them a potential hazard during situations as the current global pandemic. The aerosols in the air, viruses, and bacteria in the cabin interior may endanger the safety of passengers, even on subsequent elevator rides. Thus, it is important to continuously purify and sanitize the cabin air to prevent exposure to risk infection.

Two innovative integrated systems, produced by the leading elevator industry TK Elevator, are hereby introduced (Fig. 1).

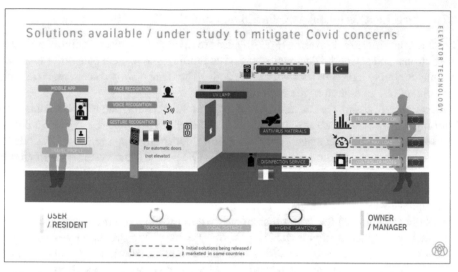

Fig. 1. Diagram of TK elevator solutions to mitigate Covid-19 risks. Source: TK elevator

4.1 Sanitization Systems and Air Purification of the Cabin

4.1.1 Elevator Cabin Air Purification with Ozone

It is a system that purifies the air in lift cabins using ozone, creating a clean and hygienic environment, free from harmful microorganisms. It also removes other noxious chemical compounds, including those that cause unpleasant odors.

Ozone successfully combats airborne biological contaminants (bacteria, viruses, molds, pollen, and mites) and sterilizes the cabin air. Ozone also neutralizes spores and dust and eliminates gases and smoke.

4.1.2 Elevator Cabin Sanitization with UV Light

Studies have shown UV-C wavelengths to be effective against bacteria and viruses by penetrating their cells and damaging the DNA or RNA containing their genetic code. The sanitization device uses a small UV lamp to provoke photo-catalyst oxidation. Thereby the cabin air is purified. The device can be retrofitted into existing systems to reduce exposure to the risk of contagion and ensure the safer use and maintenance of elevators. The UV lamps are combined with a mechanical ventilation device with 3 small integrated fans and equipped with a coated filter – a molecular material of slowly released chlorine dioxide, which is a powerful and non-poisonous disinfectant. Air is withdrawn from the elevator and is cleansed of viruses and bacteria before being released back into the elevator. The air sanitizer eliminates almost all microorganisms from the cabin air (99%). The device is automatically activated if the presence sensor detects a person entering the elevator. The delayed shutdown function will continue disinfection for 30 min, once the person leaves the elevator.

4.2 Touch-Less Technology for Facilitated and Safe Use of the Elevator

The TK contactless call system allows the user to operate the elevator without touching the buttons, and select the destination from the landing; passengers can either use their mobile or simply a printed pass with a QR code. There are 4 simple scenarios available for contact-less operation of the elevator.

Scenario 1–Using the TK Elevator app: it is suitable for owners or tenants of a building who use the elevator regularly. Once the user has installed the app, the solution can work offline: (a) user selects the destination floor (b) the app creates a QR code on the phone (c) in the landing, the user scans the QR code (d) the system automatically generates the call to the destination both on the landing and in the COP-Car operating panel; *Scenario 2–Mobile scenario without TK Elevator app*: it is intended for visitors or guests who do not use the app. Via the app or a dedicated web platform, a resident or concierge can generate QR codes that are needed to travel within the building and send it to their smartphones (this is dedicated to the hotels). Then the journey is similar to Scenario 1; *Scenario 3–Solution without mobile device:* the solution also works without a mobile device. It is suitable especially for elderly passengers or occasional visitors; it is possible to print QR codes on cards and use them just like a boarding pass at an airport gate to get to the destination floor; *Scenario 4–Mobile scenario QR code*: using a smartphone, the passenger scans the QR code located near the elevator door or inside the cabin. A virtual image of the elevator's landing and cabin operation panel is brought up on the screen, which can then be used to call the elevator or select the destination floor (Fig. 2).

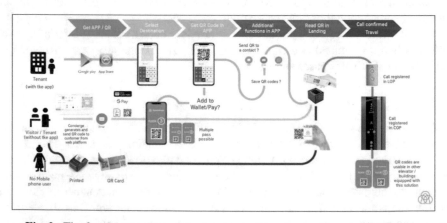

Fig. 2. The first 3 contactless control systems of the elevator. Source: TK Elevator.

5 Discussion and Open Problems

As briefly introduced, the European standards dedicated to elevator accessibility defines mature progress in the matters discussed. Moreover, since January 2021 Europe has adopted the EN 17210 standard, which represents a promising instrument to regulate the accessibility design of the built environment. This standard impacts also the elevators. Meanwhile, the elevator industry, motivated by the Covid-19 pandemic, has generated product innovations for a healthier and safer use of the cabin and the commands. These innovations (sanitization devices and touch-less systems to drive the elevator) represent a significant upgrade for the accessibility above the current health emergency. Therefore they surpass the standard.

DfA and HCD suggest a more inclusive approach to accessibility design [19], providing comfort and safe use to all users. Furthermore, the applied method to develop more inclusive elevators should analyze, with an inductive approach, all the abilities of users to define specific requirements and performance. It is reasonably foreseeable that flexible functions, customization, multisensory, site-specific, and traffic analyses will be the driving design and research approach. The active participation of users with and without disabilities is the core of the future elevator design process. That is the way to extend usability and autonomy to the population living in the built environment, where elevators play a leading role in its fruition.

In conclusion, a relevant research topic raised by the research group is how/where to apply the innovations in the field of elevator usability. The goal is to develop an operative approach to evaluate and choose the best devices in their real contests (customization), to guarantee both the best answers in terms of fair access and economic/environmental sustainability while respecting the minimum standards, and the users.

6 Conclusion

The innovation of this research derives from the intercultural approach between researchers in DfA/HCD and industries who, working together, identify the gaps in the current state of the art about elevators' accessibility and hypothesize new performance that may affect a larger number of stakeholders with and without disabilities.

The broad vision of accessibility for all, applied to "the machine" and the neighboring spaces would not otherwise be possible.

Functional flexibility in commands usability, deepening all abilities and disabilities, the analysis of flows, and destinations of use represent the winning approach for the maximum possible social inclusion. Proving this research in the field of accessibility of elevators means working in a more integrated way with all the stakeholders in this multidisciplinary, integrated, and jointed research process. Finally, the intent is to expand the research group by creating innovation synergies between researchers, industries, and users to improve the process of promoting a fair use and design of elevators – integrated into different building systems – and the best suitable application of the design innovation.

References

1. Trabucco, D., Giacomello, E., Alberti, F.: L'ascensore in architettura. Progettazione, dimensionamento, normativa e casi studio. Franco Angeli, Milano (2018)
2. Giacomello, E., Alberti, F., Trabucco, D.: Architectural barriers vs Universal Design/Barriere architettoniche vs Universal Design. In: (multiple authors) "The accessible world/Il mondo accessibile", Volpe Editore (2018)

3. Trabucco, D., Giacomello, E., Belmonte, M.: Mobilità verticale per l'accessibilità – Oltre il Quadrato e la X, Vertical Mobility for Accessibility. Anteferma, Conegliano (2020)
4. Baratta, A.F.L., Conti, C., Tatano, V. (eds.) Abitare Inclusivo/Inclusive Living. Anteferma (2019)
5. Conti, C., Milocco Borlini, M., Tubaro, G.: Vertical travel. the multi-sensory accessibility of vertical transition environments in museum itineraries. In: Trabucco, D., Giacomello, E., Belmonte, M. (eds.): Mobilità verticale per l'accessibilità – Oltre il Quadrato e la X, Vertical Mobility for Accessibility. Anteferma, Conegliano (2020)
6. Directive 2014/33/EU of The European Parliament and of the Council of 26 February 2014 on the harmonization of the laws of the Member States relating to lifts and safety components for lifts; Annex Essential Health and Safety Requirements §1.2, §1.6.1, p. 96/271
7. UNI EN 81–20: Safety rules for the construction and installation of lifts - Lifts for the transport of persons and goods – Part 20: Passenger and goods passenger lifts
8. EN 81–70: Safety rules for the construction and installation of lifts – Particular applications for passenger and goods passenger lift – Part 70: Accessibility to lifts for persons including persons with disability
9. CEN/TS 81–76: Safety rules for the construction and installation of lifts – Particular applications for passengers and goods passenger lifts – Part 76: Evacuation of disabled persons using lifts
10. EN 81–80: Safety rules for the construction and installation of lifts – Existing lifts – Part 80: Rules for the improvement of safety of existing passenger and goods passenger lifts
11. EN 81–82: Safety rules for the construction and installation of lifts – Existing lifts – Part 82: Rules for the improvement of the accessibility of existing lifts for persons including persons with disability
12. 95/216/EC: Commission Recommendation concerning the improvement of the safety of existing lifts
13. EN 17210: 2021 Accessibility and usability of the built environment – Functional requirements
14. Laurìa, A.: Progettazione ambientale & accessibilità: note sul rapporto persona-ambiente e sulle strategie di design. Techne 13, 55 (2017)
15. UN: Convention on the Rights of Persons with Disabilities
16. Bucknell, A.: Touch It, Smell It, Feel It: Architecture for the Senses (2018). https://www.archdaily.com/903925/touch-it-smell-it-feel-it-architecture-for-the-senses. Retrieved Oct 2019
17. Pratt, A., Nunes, J.: Interactive Design: An Introduction to the Theory and Application of User-centered Design. Rockport Publishers (2012)
18. Malagugini, M.: Spazio e percezione Appunti di progetto, Alinea Editrice (2008)
19. Cellucci, C., Di Sivo, M.: F.A.AD. CITY Città fiendly, active, adaptive, Pisa. University Press (2018)

Improving Accessibility and Inclusiveness of Digital Mobility Solutions: A European Approach

Sabina Giorgi[1(✉)], Rebecca Hueting[1], Andrea Capaccioli[1], Floridea di Ciommo[2], Gianni Rondinella[2], Andrés Kilstein[2], Imre Keseru[3], Samyajit Basu[3], Hannes Delaere[3], Wim Vanobberghen[4], Miklós Bánfi[5], and Yoram Shiftan[6]

[1] Deep Blue Srl, 00198 Rome, Italy
{sabina.giorgi,rebecca.hueting,andrea.capaccioli}@dblue.it
[2] CambiaMO|Changing Mobility, 28012 Madrid, Spain
{floridea.diciommo,gianni.rondinella,
andres.kilstein}@cambiamo.net
[3] Vrije Universiteit Brussel, Brussels, Belgium
{Imre.Keseru,Samyajit.Basu,Hannes.Delaere}@vub.be
[4] Imec-SMIT-VUB, 1050 Brussels, Belgium
wim.vanobberghen@imec.be
[5] Mozgássérültek Budapesti Egyesülete, Budapest 1136, Hungary
banfi.miklos@kjk.bme.hu
[6] Technion, Israel Institute of Technology, 32000 Haifa, Israel
shiftan@technion.ac.il

Abstract. This paper presents the main results of the co-creation activities carried out in the first phase of INDIMO (INclusive DIgital MObility solutions), a three-year EU-funded Horizon 2020 project that aims to extend the benefits of digital mobility and delivery solutions to vulnerable people that currently face barriers in using such solutions due to physical, cognitive and socio-economic limitations. On the one hand, results concern needs, capabilities and requirements of vulnerable-to-exclusion users and non-users of digital mobility and delivery services that have been collected in the five pilot sites of the project. On the other hand, findings highlight drivers and barriers for the development and deployment of inclusive and accessible digital mobility services from the viewpoint of developers, operators and policy makers. These results are the basis for the development of the main outcome of the project, i.e. the Inclusive Digital Mobility Toolbox.

Keywords: Digital mobility and delivery solutions · Accessibility · Inclusiveness · User and non-user needs · Requirements · Universal design

1 Introduction

The proliferation of smartphones and digital technologies have produced a quickly expanding array of digital services in mobility and logistics. While significant achievements have been made mainly in terms of improving physical accessibility of transport,

© The Author(s), under exclusive license to Springer Nature Switzerland AG 2021
N. L. Black et al. (Eds.): IEA 2021, LNNS 220, pp. 263–270, 2021.
https://doi.org/10.1007/978-3-030-74605-6_33

digital accessibility and inclusion have marginally been addressed. There is a risk that these new digital mobility and logistics services will not be available and accessible to all members of society. 22% of all European households still do not have access to broadband internet especially in rural areas. Mobile broadband penetration also shows a high variation within Europe with 70 subscriptions per 100 persons in Hungary as a lowest value. In some EU Member States, over 25% of the population still does not regularly go online. Almost 10% of EU citizens have never used the internet, with a high number of non-users among those with low education levels, aged over 55, retired or inactive [1]. This data shows that internet-enabled mobility is not an obvious choice for millions of Europeans although internet access is just one of the reasons why they may be excluded.

Access to digital services may be limited due to physical or cognitive barriers, but digital accessibility has so far only been addressed at the level of websites and applications. In addition, from the inclusiveness perspective, various socio-economic, demographic, financial and functional barriers may prevent people from using digital mobility and logistics services (e.g. educational level, gender, language, immigration status, poor access to transport or digital networks, affordability, etc.) [2].

Digital mobility solutions are mainly developed for general use according to the assessment of the needs of average users. This practice may, however, lead to the exclusion of several groups. Implementing universal design principles and accessibility standards could lead to more inclusive applications: past experience proved that including special features for broadening customer palette increased the overall usability.

Inclusivity features cover two main topics: service related and interface related issues. Improving service inclusivity usually results in the increase of inclusivity of the related application as well. However, improvement may require high investment on service development, especially on informatics and technologies. Development should focus on providing additional information, functions, and options for possible vulnerable users. Increasing interface accessibility refers to adapting universal design [4] in the development process of graphical user interfaces, which may lead to iterative processes and can affect previous steps (e.g., database modelling). The process also requires an extended testing phase to verify inclusiveness.

This paper addresses the lack of accessibility and inclusivity of mobility services and proposes the application of the universal design principles and a co-creation approach to overcome these barriers. It discusses needs, capabilities and requirements of vulnerable-to-exclusion users and non-users of digital mobility and delivery services, and findings highlight drivers and barriers for the development and deployment of inclusive and accessible digital mobility services from the viewpoint of developers, operators and policy makers.

2   The INDIMO Project: An Overview

The INDIMO project aims both at filling the knowledge gap about accessible-by-design digital mobility services and improving the inclusiveness and equity of the interconnected transport systems. Pursuing this mission, INDIMO explores needs, capabilities, barriers and requirements of vulnerable-to-exclusion users on the one hand, and the challenges that developers, operators and policy makers face, on the other hand.

To this aim, the main outcome of the project will be the Inclusive Digital Mobility Toolbox, which includes a universal design manual for digital mobility services, guidelines for improving the design of interfaces, guidelines for cybersecurity and personal data protection and a policy evaluation tool for policy makers.

Overall, the INDIMO methodology consists of a user-centric approach. The INDIMO Inclusive Digital Mobility Toolbox will be co-designed with local communities of practices in five pilot sites (i.e. Italy, Belgium, Galilee, Spain, Germany) and with an international co-creation community including policy makers, user representatives, industry, academia, and developers, during the three years of the project.

The INDIMO co-creation process is designed as a five-stage process. *Stage 1* is devoted both to the identification of user and non-user needs, capabilities and requirements, and the investigation of needs and concerns of developers, policy makers and operators when introducing digital mobility and delivery solutions (DMS/DDS). *Stage 2* concerns the co-designs of the INDIMO Inclusive Digital Mobility Toolbox to bridge the digital mobility gap, on the basis of needs, capabilities, requirements and barriers identified in the stage 1. *Stage 3* regards the co-implementation of the tools included in the INDIMO toolbox. Their impact and usability will be tested in the five pilot sites through the redesign of the pilots' digital mobility and delivery solutions and their implementation made according to the INDIMO toolbox guiding principles. *Stage 4* focuses on the co-evaluation, feedback and redesign. Pilots engagement will provide feedback in order to improve the INDIMO toolbox. An evaluation will be carried out, both in terms of inclusion and accessibility assessment of the pilots' digital mobility and delivery services, and of process evaluation of the INDIMO Toolbox. Finally, *stage 5* concerns the transferability assessment and the deployment of the toolbox as an online toolkit.

This paper presents and discusses the results emerged from the research carried out in the first stage of the co-creation process, whose methodology is described more in detail in the next section.

3 Identification of Needs, Capabilities, Requirements and Barriers: The Methodology

In the first phase of the project, needs, capabilities and requirements of vulnerable-to-exclusion users and non-users of digital mobility and delivery services have been collected in the five pilots. The process started with the definition of users' characteristics and the general analysis framework of qualitative data collection. Each pilot site addressed specific user profiles and characteristics and focused on certain digital mobility or delivery services that will be tested and re-designed during the project to be improved from the accessibility and inclusiveness points of view (see Table 1).

In total, 58 semi structured interviews (SSIs) with digital mobility services' users and non-users and 25 interviews with stakeholders representing users have been carried out. SSI structure was set-up according to several dimensions identified in the general analysis framework (e.g. goals/value of using the service; accessibility and inclusion: reasons for not using the service; needs; etc.). SSIs and short interviews were firstly documented in debrief documents by including the more relevant excerpts of the interviews and, secondly, analysed trough a coding process. This was performed through

Table 1. Pilots' names and user profiles

Pilot name and country	User profiles (and characteristics)
• Introducing digital technology to enable e-commerce in rural areas (Emilia Romagna-Italy)	Older people and migrants/ foreign people who receive/send parcels (lack of digital knowledge; residing in peri-urban locations; lack of digital services; lack of dedicated network infrastructures; language barriers; low income, ...)
• Inclusive traffic lights (Antwerp–Belgium)	Vulnerable pedestrian (i.e. older people; people with reduced mobility; people with reduced vision)
• Informal ride-sharing in ethnic towns (Galilee) • Cycle logistics platform for delivery (Madrid-Spain)	Informal ride-sharing users (ethnic minority man/women; residing in the periphery; language barrier; lack of digital skills) Healthy food delivery users (people with reduced mobility; people with reduced vision; socially isolated-unwanted loneliness; not-connected people; low income; COVID-19 isolated)
• On-demand ride-sharing integrated into multimodal route planning (Berlin-Germany)	On demand ride-sharing users (caregivers of children/ impaired/ elders; women; lack of services; lack of digital skills, residing in peri-urban locations)

the Quirkos CAQDAS (Computer Assisted Qualitative Data AnalysiS) software. Relevant verbatims from interviews were labelled with appropriate codes to analyse data in terms of similarities, differences, and relationships. The final step consisted of the thematic analysis to organize the identified codes in meaningful crosscutting themes [3]. The main results emerged from these research activities are relevant themes concerning needs, capabilities and requirements of digital mobility services' users and non-users (see Sects. 4.1 and 4.2).

In order to support changes that can extend the benefits of digital mobility services and applications equally to the vulnerable-to-exclusion groups, it is necessary to understand what the drivers and barriers are for the development and deployment of inclusive and accessible digital mobility services from the viewpoint of developers, operators and policy makers. For this purpose, 10 deployment case studies were performed to investigate how new digital mobility services have been introduced in European cities and regions. The case studies included desktop data collection, 20 semi-structured interviews with developers, service operators and policy makers, and a thematic analysis to determine the key barriers and drivers. The main results concerning this part of the study is described in Sect. 4.3.

4 Main Results

4.1 Identification of Users and Non-users' Needs

The insight from the pilots, with different user profiles, locations and mobility solutions, allowed us to identify needs of the users and potential users. Also, stakeholders on behalf of specific groups of population, provided their inputs to build a narrative that moves across geographies and profiles. Needs vary across groups, but there are threads as "space", "time" and "trust" that are points of contact and common areas.

The first thread is the "space". In the case of environments characterized by scattered rural villages, such as in the pilots of Emilia Romagna and Galilee, digital mobility solutions (e.g. Apps) may compensate the lack of infrastructure, the transport poverty and the difficulties for personal mobility. In the case of Emilia Romagna, there are logistic problems to reach remote areas. The digital locker for deliveries could overcome distances and enhance accessibility, especially for older people for whom picking up parcels demanded a great amount of effort. In the case of Galilee there is a need of mobility alternatives given the lack of public transport and good connectivity in the Arab rural villages. This need is even greater for Arab women, since cultural barriers and a hostile atmosphere prevent many of them to drive and ride the public transit. But there are additional needs related to the spatial configuration of this place. Most of the mobility apps have severe difficulties to match the digital mapping with the real geography. There are rural streets with no names nor numbers; this implies a difficulty for the user to order a ride.

In the Antwerp pilot, people with reduced mobility or reduced vision find a number of obstacles in the physical environment that prevent their everyday activity. The needs have to do with the adaptation of traffic lights but also the adaptation of the surroundings to overcome these limitations: the short time provided by the traffic lights, the uncertainty about when it is going to change, the uneven pedestrian spaces, the height of the button to ask for a traffic light change and so on are the main needs to be addressed.

The second thread articulating needs is "time". Time is a valuable resource and the importance of making a good use of it appears in the different pilots. It presents a very sensitive treatment in the Berlin pilot, covering a ride-sharing app for caregivers (focusing on women). Time needs to be flexible: the driver and the remaining passengers should be tolerant to the fact that a mother may be delayed (because the child is more unpredictable, he/she doesn't want to go out, the mother spends time picking items needed by the child etc.), and also the caregiver needs the driver to be punctual (because of the difficulty of waiting in the public space with a child or the time constraints typical of the role).

In the case of Madrid, the existence of a food delivery app may save time, and the convenience of it is often remarked. The point here is that an app of delivery allows to give a different quality to time: time to relax instead of time to cook; a gained time instead of a time devoted to a domestic chore. Nevertheless, in Madrid certain vulnerable to exclusion groups perceived the app as an assistance they do not need; as a help that undermines their own autonomy.

Finally, the last thread that may organize the needs across the pilots is "trust" and having human contact behind the digital interface. Human contact is a requirement to overcome all the fears contained in the digital domain; it is the ultimate safety net for vulnerable to exclusion population that venture into the unknown digital world. In Emilia Romagna, an assistant at the locker spot will be helpful to overcome digital-skills-related problems; in Antwerp, target population are very much depending on the help of passers-by to overcome physical obstacles, this assistance narrowed for fears raised by the COVID pandemics; in Galilee, having direct contact with the driver is a requirement to trust them, to overcome fears related with physical insecurity; in Madrid, the possibility of ordering food through WhatsApp or arranging details of delivery through a call to the rider were very frequents claims to the service; and finally, in Berlin there was a request of humanity directed to the driver: women need drivers to care about the needs of a mother and to help her onboard and offboard. Human contact is a key value to provide all needs in inclusive digital services.

4.2 User Requirements Towards the Digital Interconnected Transport System

The stakeholders' interviews in each pilot underline the potential of the INDIMO mobility services to meet certain goals that increase opportunities for the target groups in each pilot site. However, the stakeholder interviews show similar basic concerns across the five pilots to meet those goals. Providing an inclusive service by solely working on an easy to use and accessible digital interface (icons, fonts, read-aloud features, etc.), although important, will not be sufficient to engage the different vulnerable end user categories.

Five key activities will be important by the pilots to meet user requirements. Building a trust relationship is the first one. It is only because a certain trusted public or private organization or a trusted individual (relative, friend) recommends using the digital system, that users will know the service and try it out. Pilots will have to develop a good "social" marketing strategy to get their service to the target audience as well as involve such organizations closely in the whole service deployment. Building trust also involves the service agent appearance, tone of voice and behaviour, important for the driver in ride-sharing services (Berlin, Galilee) and the delivery person in delivery services (Madrid). Providing dedicated assistance and support mechanisms are a second key activity. Dedicated training opportunities that go beyond an introduction will be especially needed in the case of older people to tackle digital skills (Emilia Romagna) or blind people for integrating a smart traffic light in their road usage (Antwerp). The third important key activity is being reliable. Since the pilot services are targeting people with specific needs, they also count on these services and their provision in the structuration of their lives. In the case of vulnerable pedestrians, a non-working traffic lights either keeps the person at home (reduce mobility) or forces him to take another route (mobility hindrance). In case the service is not functioning sending out a warning message is important as well as communicating when the service is working again. The fourth activity will be to provide a service that in its strategic choices builds in "flexibility", meaning that it can't be too rigidly organized but should be able to incorporate unanticipated events at the end user side (for example cancelling a ride close to the agreed time or changing a pick-up location). The final key activity is increasing awareness about privacy and data sharing in order to prevent misuse, especially in use cases working with elderly (Emilia Romagna and Madrid) and cognitively impaired persons (Madrid).

4.3   Understanding the Process of the Deployment of Digital Mobility Services

In the first stage of the INDIMO project, drivers and barriers related to the development and deployment of accessible and inclusive digital mobility services were also explored from the viewpoint of developers, operators and policy makers.

The results of our case studies and the stakeholder workshop have pointed out several key barriers to the deployment of inclusive and accessible digital mobility services. The regulatory framework is often non-existing or outdated. There may be a lack of co-operation or trust between private and public organisations. The users are often not involved in the development of services. There is a lack of knowledge among developers about potential vulnerable-to-exclusion users. Unstable market pushes development towards 'typical' users with no or limited inclusive features. Finally, there is limited willingness to share (mobility) related data and information with public authorities and other operators.

A number of drivers can help to make existing or new services more inclusive and accessible: stable market conditions supported by a comprehensive regulatory framework; the integration of digital services into the public transport service network where minimum accessibility and inclusivity guidelines have been set; consultation with users and their representatives to have more knowledge of potential users can all be beneficial. Using inclusive design as a cornerstone of the service development, bottom-up co-creation events; open communication with other stakeholders, which includes sharing of information about best/worst practices and local support schemes (subsidies or incentives) can further help to introduce accessibility and inclusiveness features.

The differences between the services studied showed that there is no single method to develop more inclusive services. The issues most of the services are struggling with are similar (co-creation, communication, data-sharing etc.), but they might need different approaches depending on the type of service, region and people. The results of the analysis will help to create a framework and guidelines for developing inclusive and accessible digital mobility services, which are more aligned with the needs and expectations of vulnerable-to-exclusion groups.

5   Discussion and Conclusions

The INDIMO project's main contribution concerns the co-creation of the Inclusive Digital Mobility Toolbox. It will cover relevant aspects for fostering the Universal Design approach throughout the planning and design process of digital mobility applications and services, by integrating the perspective of vulnerable-to-exclusion groups since the beginning. Such approach represents a shift of paradigm from the design-as-usual where experts "know what users need", thus increasing the users' acceptance of digital mobility and delivery solutions.

We contribute at filling the knowledge gap about accessible-by-design digital mobility services and improving the inclusiveness and equity of the interconnected transport systems by exploring needs, capabilities, barriers, and requirements of vulnerable-to-exclusion users on the one hand, and the challenges that developers, operators, and policy makers face, on the other hand. This was achieved through various semi structured interviews and co-creation workshop from five case studies in different European sites.

Concerning findings coming up from this first phase of the project, they show that providing an inclusive service by solely working on an easy to use and accessible digital interface (icons, fonts, read-aloud features, etc.), although important, will not be sufficient to engage the different vulnerable end user categories. It is crucial to build trust among users, to provide dedicated assistance and support mechanism for the service to be reliable and provide flexibility, and finally, ensure privacy and prevent misuse in data sharing. Further, the differences between the analysed digital mobility services showed that there is no singular method to develop more inclusive services. The issues most of the services are struggling with are similar (co-creation, communication, data-sharing, lack of frameworks, etc.) but might need different approaches depending on the type of service, region, and people. There is need for co-creation with potential users resulting in a bottom-up approach and improve communication between stakeholders and exchange of knowledge about potential users, especially those vulnerable to exclusion.

Overall, the results offer a qualitative take allowing for a deep grasping of various dimensions of exclusion and inclusion ranging from interface to socio-economic and cultural factors.

References

1. European Commission: Digital Economy and Society Index (DESI) (2020)
2. Lucas, K., Martens, K., Di Ciommo, F., Dupont-Kieffer, A.: Measuring transport equity. 1st edn. Elsevier (2019)
3. Rosala, M.: How to Analyze Qualitative Data from UX Research: Thematic Analysis (2019). Nielsen Norman Group webpage. https://www.nngroup.com/articles/thematic-ana lysis/. Accessed 07 Feb 2021
4. Story, M.F., Mueller, J.L., Mace, R.L.: The Universal Design File: Designing for People of All Ages and Abilities. Revised Edition. Center for Universal Design, NC State University (1998)

A Study on the Acceptance Towards Blockchain-Based Access to Biobanks' Services Using UTAUT2 with ITM and Perceived Risk

Fouad Hannoun[1(✉)], Francesco Carrino[1], Omar Abou Khaled[1], Elena Mugellini[1], and Maurizio Caon[2]

[1] HumanTech Institute, HES-SO Fribourg, Fribourg, Switzerland
{Fouad.Hannoun,Francesco.Carrino,Omar.AbouKhaled,
Elena.Mugellini}@hes-so.ch
[2] School of Management Fribourg, HES-SO, Fribourg, Switzerland
Maurizio.Caon@hes-so.ch

Abstract. The blockchain technology offers reliability, decentralization, security and credibility. Blockchain solutions can be based on smart contracts and on the use of utility tokens which may represent a utility of a company like limited fashion items, cars, car parts or even human biological samples stored in biobanks. However, decentralization comes with responsibilities: people must take care of storing those tokens in a safe place (commonly denominated as "wallets") knowing that losing a wallet or wallet key means losing the owned tokens. This concept is still new to people and might sound scary. The success of such services relies on the extent of customers intending to adopt them and very few studies target this intention.

The current research proposes a model combining of the unified theory of acceptance and usage of technology (UTAUT2) with the initial trust model (ITM) and the perceived risk construct in order to evaluate the factors affecting the behaviour and use intention of people towards a blockchain technology that enables access to biobank services. An online questionnaire was built and sent to swiss university students. The 72 results showed that simplifying the access to blockchain-based technologies will facilitate inclusion, enabling people with lower digital literacy to access these technologies.

Keywords: Blockchain · Biobanks · UTAUT2 · ITM

1 Introduction

A biobank is a stock of biological samples, i.e., stem cells or blood, and associated information, i.e., height or weight; the samples are stored for research, diagnostic and therapeutic purposes. Every biobank has its own goal; therefore, the types of the collected specimens and the offered services vary accordingly.

The blockchain technology's transaction ledger is public, decentralized, encrypted and constantly audited; therefore, all the network's participants (miners) can make sure the data is correct. Miners have a stored copy of the blockchain's past data so any modification or inconsistency is immediately detectable, adding data traceability and immutability. The technology also allows the deployment of smart contracts, adding autonomy and accuracy, making biobanks' services safer, more transparent and more accessible. We believe that increasing the acceptance of blockchain-based technologies is a first step to increase their accessibility and, consequently, the inclusiveness of the services provided via this technology.

The goal of this study is to propose a model that evaluates the factors affecting the intention toward the adoption of blockchain-based technologies facilitating access to biobank services and to get a first understanding about its acceptance. Many hypotheses were suggested for every construct of the model, regarding its impact on the behavioural intention and use behaviour. Each hypothesis was represented by questions and then validated or rejected based on the answers.

2 Theoretical Background

2.1 UTAUT and UTAUT2

The unified theory of acceptance and use of technology (UTAUT) was forumlated by [1], with the goal of combining the schemes provided by a wide range of models like TAM (Technology acceptance model), TPB (Theory of planned behaviour), TRA (Theory of reason action), IDT (Innovation diffusion technology). Its goal is to interpret the factors affecting users' acceptance and use of a new technology.

The UTAUT's four key constructs are [1]:

Performance expectancy (PE) representing the extent to which the use of the technology lets the user achieve gains and improvements in some tasks.

Effort expectancy (EE) expressing the intuitiveness associated by the consumer to the technology's use. Given the blockchain's complexity, effort expectancy could be important in establishing the intention to use.

Social influence (SI) is to what degree the consumer suppose that friends and close relatives will think that he/she should use the technology.

Facilitating conditions (FC) represents the consumer's beliefs in the availability of needed resources and help to support the use of the technology.

The objective of UTAUT2 [2] is to broaden UTAUT's scope by taking into consideration the consumer use context due to the variance of the answer between the customers and organization context.

UTAUT2 appends three constructs to UTAUT:

Hedonic motivation (HM) is illustrated by the feeling of fun derived from the technology usage.

Price Value (PV) is the "consumer's cognitive trade-off between the perceived benefits of the application and the monetary cost of using it". The price value is positive when the benefits of using the technology are perceived to be greater than the associated monetary cost and such price value has a positive impact on intention. This construct was excluded from the questionnaire because the participants didn't know about the cost of the technology.

Habit (HB) represents the learning curve and the extent to which learning automates tasks to be done with the technology [3]. It is also equated to automaticity by [4]. Blockchain technologies currently require some technical background so it is expected that habit affects intention to use and adopt positively.

The defined constructs are expected to be moderated by the variables: age, gender and experience; with experience being the occasion to use a technology that varies since the system was used for the first time [1, 4].

2.2 Initial Trust Model

The functional goals of our application allow it to be brought closer to a mobile banking or e-banking design. Given the fact that blockchain technologies are still relatively new to the market, consumers tend to be cautious and that the offered service might seem risky. To consider this aspect, we propose to extend UTAUT2 with ITM (Initial trust model) and add perceived risk as an additional key construct. **Initial trust (IT)** does not rely on experience or knowledge, it reflects the willingness of a person to take risks to accomplish a certain task [5]. Trust has an important role in determining customers' intention to adopt mobile banking technologies [6–8].

ITM's three main constructs are:

Structural assurance (SA) in the form of documents helping building trust in the service.

Personal propensity to trust (PPT) represented by the tendency of the person to rely on others in various situations [9].

Firm's reputation is also an important construct of the model; however, we chose to discard it given that, in our study, the participants did not know the company offering the service.

2.3 Perceived Risk

Perceived risk (PR) is represented by the perceived potential loss due to using the offered solution [10]. It is commonly used as extension of the UTAUT model [11]. This construct will also be moderated by experience.

3 Hypotheses and Methodology

The proposed model is a combination of the UTAUT2 model with the ITM model and the perceived risk construct. Our model is shown in Fig. 1.

3.1 Hypotheses

In our model, a hypothesis represents the influence of a latent variable on another.

H1, H2, H3, H4a, H5, H6a, H10: PE, EE, SI, FC, HM, HB and IT will have a positive effect on behavioural intention.

H7: PR will have a negative influence on behavioural intention.

H8, H9: SA and PPT will have a positive influence on initial trust.

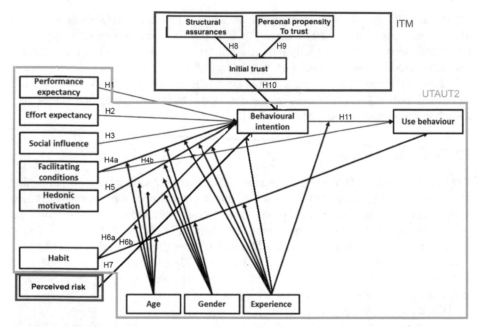

Fig. 1. Our research model showing the UTAUT2 (without the price value variable), ITM (without the firm's reputation variable) and the perceived risk construct

H4b, H6b, H11: FC, HB and behvaioural intention will have positive effects on use behaviour.

The questionnaire was distributed to university members in Switzerland (students, employees and professors). Qualtrics [12] was the chosen platform on which the questionnaire was created and hosted. The broadcast was done via email. Some questions were eliminated (either due to unrelatedness to our technology or due to lack of knowledge available on the participants' side).

4　Results

We had a total of 82 participants, 10 questionnaires had been disregarded due to missing answers. The majority was masculine (between 18 and 40 years) and most of the participants held a bachelor degree or a master. The fact that most of the contributors had higher education does not directly correlate to their digital literacy or their understanding of blockchain-based technologies. In this concern, participants were asked about their experience with crypto-currencies and e-banking. 19 participants had less than a year of online banking experience. Only 2 participants considered themselves very familiar with crypto-currencies and interaction with the blockchain, 11 participants had previously bought crypto-currencies while the rest had no prior interaction with such a technology.

Table 1. Validity and reliability of the latent variables

	Item	Factor loading	Indicator reliability	Fiability composite	AVE	Rho_A
BI	BI1	0.935	0.877	0.938	0.883	0.871
	BI2	0.944	0.891			
EE	EE1	0.570	0.324	0.786	0.557	0.693
	EE2	0.873	0.761			
	EE3	0.765	0.585			
EXP	EXP1	0.971	0.943	0.971	0.943	0.940
	EXP2	0.971	0.942			
FC	FC1	0.820	0.671	0.871	0.628	0.803
	FC2	0.799	0.638			
	FC3	0.780	0.608			
	FC4	0.770	0.592			
HB	HB1	0.752	0.565	0.836	0.721	0.797
	HB2	0.933	0.875			
HM	HM1	1	1	1	1	1
IT	IT1	0.931	0.866	0.928	0.763	0.907
	IT2	0.948	0.899			
	IT3	0.848	0.719			
	IT4	0.754	0.568			
PE	PE1	1	1	1	1	1
PPT	PPT1	0.903	0.815	0.665	0.415	0.779
	PPT2	0.759	0.576			
	PPT3	0.516	0.265			
	PPT4	−0.023	0.0005			
PR	PR1	0.865	0.748	0.944	0.849	0.976
	PR2	0.946	0.894			
	PR3	0.951	0.905			
SA	SA1	0.528	0.278	0.732	0.597	0.719
	SA2	0.956	0.914			
SI	SI1	0.947	0.896	0.929	0.867	0.880
	SI2	0.916	0.838			
USE	USE1	0.833	0.694	0.832	0.625	0.778
	USE2	0.845	0.714			
	USE3	0.684	0.467			

5 Discussion

The results showed that simplifying the access to blockchain-based technologies will facilitate inclusion, enabling people with lower digital literacy to access these technologies. We have noticed that a significant part of the answers was neutral (neither agree nor disagree). This is probably due to the complexity and novelty of the presented technology:

The blockchain concept is still unclear. Most of the participants were quite confident that they could understand and use our solution and they found that this technology facilitates the access to biobank services. About 25% intends to use the technology.

The questionnaires were collected and analyzed using the partial least squared method (PLS) based on variance-based structural equation modeling by using the Smart-PLS software [13]. A representation of the model was made on SmartPLS in order to analyze the factors that influence the willingness to use and adopt the technology.

In order to ensure the reliability and validity of the latent variables, their external loads, their composite reliability, the extracted mean variance and its square root are studied (these data are calculated and exported via SmartPLS). The conditions that these indicators must meet are as follows:

- Indicator reliability is acceptable if it's above 0.7, it is considered acceptable if it's an exploration context and its value is above 0.4.
- Internal consistency reliability is acceptable if it's above 0.7 or above 0.6 in case of exploratory research.
- Convergent validity is acceptable for values equal to 0.5 or higher

There are 4 elements below the acceptable limit level (0.4) for indicator reliability (EE1, PPT3, PPT4 and SA1). The personal propensity to trust has a mean variance greater than 0.4 which is acceptable if the reliability component passes the threshold of 0.6 [14]. All items pass the threshold for the reliability component and the rho_A (Table 1).

Discriminant validity is established by checking that the square root of the average variance extracted (AVE) (in bold on the diagonal in Table 2) is greater than other correlation values between latent variables. We include experience in the chart because a strong moderating effect was noticed.

The results of the measurement model indicate good consistency reliability, indicator reliability, convergent validity and discriminant validity, ensuring distinction and usefulness of the latent variables for testing the structural model.

The model explains 86% of the variation in behavioural intent and 51.4% of the utilization behaviour. It also indicates that social influence (0.258), habit (0.351) and experience (0.526) are strong predictors of behavioural intention while the rest do not really affect it. The same is true for facilitated conditions (0.245), habit (0.161) and experience (0.430) for use behaviour.

According to the results analysis, the suggested model reached acceptable levels in terms of fitness, reliability and validity. The effect of added constructs like perceived risk or initial trust is not very significant on behavioural intention. The fact that only a small party doesn't trust the technology (less than 15% had negative answers when it comes to trust or propensity to trust) and that experience and habit influence behavioural intention the most shows how important it is that people get familiar with using the technology. Therefore, designers should focus on simplifying the use of blockchain-based technologies to facilitate inclusion.

Table 2. Discriminant validity. This picture shows the correlation between variables and the square root of the AVE (in bold)

	USE	BI	EE	EXP	FC	HB	HM	IT	PR	PE	PPT	SI	SA
USE	**0.791**												
BI	0.543	**0.939**											
EE	0.603	0.673	**0.747**										
EXP	0.608	0.807	0.688	**0.971**									
FC	0.54	0.612	0.754	0.606	**0.792**								
HB	0.495	0.799	0.653	0.613	0.658	**0.85**							
HM	0.402	0.342	0.474	0.414	0.586	0.456	**1**						
IT	0.556	0.592	0.632	0.588	0.688	0.606	0.54	**0.874**					
PR	− 0.295	− 0.234	− 0.335	− 0.289	− 0.422	− 0.236	− 0.297	− 0.516	**0.922**				
PE	− 0.112	− 0.174	0.06	− 0.118	− 0.068	− 0.165	− 0.046	− 0.136	0.047	**1**			
PPT	− 0.235	− 0.244	− 0.424	− 0.288	− 0.318	− 0.299	− 0.441	− 0.408	0.363	− 0.11	**0.644**		
SI	0.569	0.688	0.758	0.528	0.761	0.754	0.494	0.723	− 0.307	− 0.164	− 0.429	**0.931**	
SA	0.416	0.403	0.358	0.375	0.399	0.453	0.21	0.631	− 0.395	0.156	− 0.261	0.395	**0.772**

5.1 Limitations and Future Research

This study presents some limitations that should be tackled in future research. In particular, the participants have not tested the solution but a video of a prototype was presented with an explanation about the solution and blockchain technology. In addition, the fact that the blockchain technology is very new and was never used before by many participants was a barrier for some of them who perceived this technology as very complex and the goal of the proposed service unclear; this resulted in some incomplete surveys. Finally, the survey was only sent to people with an academic background. A more diversified audience (i) might give more importance to other constructs (ii) and allows generalizing the results to general population.

Finally, it is also important to keep in mind that people will get more and more familiar with the blockchain technology in general and that habit and experience will grow up more and more in this field.

6 Conclusion

The adoption of biobanks services using blockchain technology was studied in this research by suggesting a new model joining UTAUT2, ITM and the perceived risk construct. The additions to the UTAUT2 model turned out to be with negligible influence on the behavioural intention and use behaviour. We found out that the inclusion of such a technology relies on how easy it seems for users. Further studies should maybe let users use the technology for a certain period of time before handing in the questionnaires.

References

1. Venkatesh, V., et al.: User acceptance of information technology: toward a unified view. MIS Q. **27**, 425–478 (2003)
2. Venkatesh, V., Thong, J.Y.L., Xu, X.: Consumer acceptance and use of information technology: extending the unified theory of acceptance and use of technology. MIS Q. **36**, 157–178 (2012)
3. Limayem, M., Hirt, S.G., Cheung, C.M.K.: How habit limits the predictive power of intention: the case of information systems continuance. MIS Q. **31**, 705–737 (2007)
4. Kim, S., Malhotra, N., Narasimhan, S.: Research note—two competing perspectives on automatic use: a theoretical and empirical comparison. Inf. Syst. Res. **16**(4), 418–432 (2005)
5. Kim, K.K., Prabhakar, B.: Initial trust and the adoption of B2C e-commerce: the case of internet banking. ACM SIGMIS Database: DATABASE Adv. Inf. Syst. **35**(2), 50–64 (2004)
6. Alalwan, A.A., et al.: Consumer adoption of internet banking in Jordan: examining the role of hedonic motivation, habit, self-efficacy and trust. J. Financ. Serv. Mark. **20**(2), 145–157 (2015)
7. Luo, X., et al.: Examining multi-dimensional trust and multi-faceted risk in initial acceptance of emerging technologies: an empirical study of mobile banking services. Decis. Support Syst. **49**(2), 222–234 (2010)
8. Zhou, T.: An empirical examination of initial trust in mobile banking. Internet Res. **21**(5), 527–540 (2011)
9. McKnight, D.H., Cummings, L.L., Chervany, N.L.: Initial trust formation in new organizational relationships. Acad. Manag. Rev. **23**(3), 473–490 (1998)

10. Featherman, M., Pavlou, P.: Predicting e-services adoption: a perceived risk facets perspective. Int. J. Hum. Comput. Stud. **59**(4), 451–474 (2003)
11. Williams, M., Rana, N., Dwivedi, Y.: The unified theory of acceptance and use of technology (UTAUT): a literature review. J. Enterp. Inf. Manag. **28**(3), 443–488 (2015)
12. Qualtrics Homepage. https://www.qualtrics.com/. Accessed 29 Jan 2021
13. SmartPLS Homepage. https://www.smartpls.com/. Accessed 29 Jan 2021
14. Fornell, C., Larcker, D.: Evaluating structural equation models with unobservable variables and measurement error. J. Mark. Res. **18**(1), 39–50 (1981)

How to Increase Users of Products, Services and Environments - Concept and Methods of Accessible Design

Nana Itoh[1]([✉]), Kenji Kurakata[2], and Ken Sagawa[1]

[1] National Institute for Advanced Industrial Science and Technology (AIST), Tsukuba, Japan
{nana-itoh,sagawa-k}@aist.go.jp
[2] Waseda University, Tokyo, Japan
kurakata.kenji@waseda.jp

Abstract. One of the most important concepts of accessible design is to increase users of products, services and environments to cover the widest range of human characteristics and capabilities. There are two possible methods on how to do it; one is to provide multiple means of information presentation or operation, and the other is to set design parameters of products etc., so that they accommodate diverse human characteristics and capabilities as much as possible. Both methods are addressed as basic strategies of accessible design to make products more accessible (i.e., used by more people). Conducting and repeating this step, products can reach an ideal goal of being universal. In this paper, the concept and methods of accessible design regarding the increase of users are discussed with some examples.

Keywords: Accessible design · Older persons · Disabilities · Increase of users · Multiple means · Accommodation to diverse human abilities

1 Introduction

Several design concepts for taking care of older persons and persons with disabilities have been proposed since 1960s starting from Normalization in Northern European countries followed by Barrier Free Design, Universal Design, Design for All, Inclusive Design, Transgenerational Design, and Accessible Design. They all have a similar goal for making products, services and environments easy and comfortable to use for persons who have special needs due to their physical limitations.

Among those design concepts, accessible design, which is a focus of this paper, has developed its own design concepts and methods for approaching to the common goal, and differs from other design concepts mentioned above. One of the concepts of accessible design, which is introduced and discussed here, is to increase users of products, services and environments to cover the widest range of human characteristics and capabilities. The increase of users is intended to include older persons and persons with disabilities who need special care as addressed in other design concepts. To implement this design concept, accessible design has several methods which are described as design strategies in ISO/IEC Guide 71:2014 [1]. In this paper, two major design methods are introduced and discussed.

© The Author(s), under exclusive license to Springer Nature Switzerland AG 2021
N. L. Black et al. (Eds.): IEA 2021, LNNS 220, pp. 280–285, 2021.
https://doi.org/10.1007/978-3-030-74605-6_35

2   Increasing Users: A Basic Concept of Accessible Design

Accessible design, as well as other design concepts, is considered in a simple meaning that the design is for solutions of problems or inconveniences that older persons and persons with disabilities have in their using products, services, and environments. There are so many things around us that people cannot readily use due to some physical limitations caused by aging or disabilities. For example, a jar with a tightly sealed lid that is difficult to open for older women with weak muscle strength. Designers try to solve those problems in their designing so that those people can use them. This is accessible design. This design means from another perspective that the products come to be used by those people with special needs by applying accessible design. Therefore, increasing users has comparable intention and meaning with making things accessible.

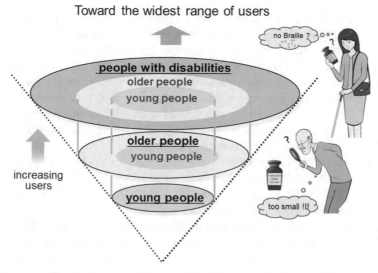

Fig. 1. A concept of accessible design to increase users [2]

Figure 1 illustrates this concept more clearly by taking a packaging label as an example [2]. There are many packages that have a label with small printed letters hard to read for older people who have low visual acuity due to aging. Therefore, the packages or products are not usable for those older people, and only young people can use this. To solve the problem, designers try to design the label with a larger font size so that older people could read it. Then this product can include older people among its users. This is one step of increasing users. Furthermore, if the designers additionally put Braille on the label, people with visual disabilities could read it and use the product. This is also another step of increasing users: visually impaired people in this case. Another additional design may be possible for solving other users' problems or inconveniences. Like these steps, the product can increase its users more and more toward the final goal that includes all types of people, which will be regarded an ideal design for all.

It should also be mentioned that increasing users does not cause dropping out already existing users. There might be some cases in which a new design consequently excludes a part of former users due to some change of the product. This should not be the case of accessible design. As Fig. 1 clearly illustrates, the original user group (in this case young people) always remains in the center of the user groups, but is never excluded. This is also an important aspect of increasing users in the concept of accessible design.

3 Design Methods for Increasing Users

3.1 Method 1: Multiple Means of Information Presentation and Operation

Among several methods that are addressed in ISO/IEC Guide 71:2014 as design strategies [1], there are two basic methods for increasing users. One is to use multiple means of information presentation and operation. This is already illustrated in Fig. 1 at the 2nd to the 3rd level from the bottom where Braille is additionally introduced for use by persons with visual disabilities. If the package label is originally equipped with Braille, persons with visual disabilities would be able to use and be counted as users of the product from the first. However, it used to be considered redundant to have the same meaning in another format once the printed information is provided. But now, being based on the concept of accessible design, this redundancy is very necessary and crucially important to increase users. Moreover, using graphic or pictorial symbols in addition to letters may also be useful especially for persons with cognitive disabilities who have difficulties in reading letters. Those different formats such as printed letters, graphics and Braille, are regarded as multiple means of information presentation.

Another good example is floor guidance of an elevator as shown in Fig. 2a, which uses printed information (numbers), speech announcements, and Braille (or raised tactile letters). With these three means of information presentation, the floor guidance can convey its information to people as many as possible.

Multiple means do not necessarily apply for human different senses. It also applies to different mode of presentation within one sense. A good example is a combination of color and text or color and shape. Color is frequently used to differentiate things like a pie-chart as shown in Fig. 2b. The pie-chart usually have colors to identify each part of the chart and the legend shows which color means which part. However, some persons with defective color vision cannot discriminate some colors and they often have confusion on which part means which. If there is a description within the chart like Fig. 2b, it can be clearly understood by persons with defective color vision or older persons, or even persons with normal color vision but in a dim lighting condition.

Operation of products should also have multiple means to increase users. Computer devices have now a large variety of means for input and output of information, for example. However, as is often seen, one computer has only one input-output system, namely a keyboard and a display and it would be very inconvenient to use, or sometime unable for some people who have difficulties in typing a keyboard. If there is a voice input system or output system like a screen reader, more users could be included who use those additional devices. The method of multiple means of operation is also very effective to increase users, and to increase accessibility consequently.

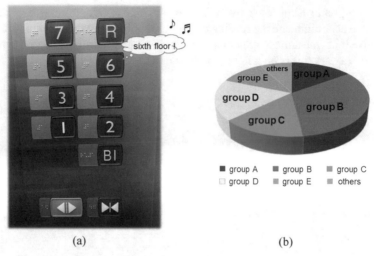

| (a) | (b) |

Fig. 2. An example of multiple means of information presentation: (a) floor guidance of visual, hearing and tactile information, and (b) a pie-chart using color and text [2].

3.2 Method 2: Accommodation to Diverse Human Characteristics and Capabilities

The other method for increasing users is to accommodate products to diverse human characteristics and capabilities. Undoubtedly human characteristics and capabilities have a large variety due to aging and various types of disabilities. Designing products should take account of these different human abilities, though it is not an easy task. Setting appropriate parameters of products is one of the important aspects of design in order to increase users. There are so many everyday products around us that are not easy to use for older people due to their age-related changes in human abilities, such as too small letters to see, too soft sounds to hear, too complex operations to understand, and so on. Products are used to be designed to fit young adults as a major group of users, but this design strategy is changing to cover more people including older persons and persons with disabilities by accommodating their design parameters to fit those people too.

The exact method of design to accommodate diverse human abilities is shown in Fig. 1 with an example of using a larger font size to meet the needs of older people. Enlarging font size makes letters legible to older people and then the product can be used by a new user group of older people. This is another method to increase users.

There is also another example concerning with font size, which is how to increase users of people with low vision for printed information or visual signs. Low vision means extremely low visual acuity due to various type of visual impairments. They usually need a much larger font size to see text and pictures. Figure 3 shows one example of data on minimum legible font size of characters for Japanese 59 persons with low vision who were tested legibility of different types of characters and font styles at a usual viewing distance (0.5 m) [3]. They showed that nearly 100 pt of font size was required at least to read a single character slightly depending on different characters and font styles. For a comparable viewing condition, young and older people show their minimum legible font size of 5 pt and 12 pt respectively. This means that about 10 times larger font size is required to accommodate the reading ability of people with low vision. It is also clear that negative font (meaning a lighter text on a darker background) has an advantage over positive one (a darker text on a lighter background).

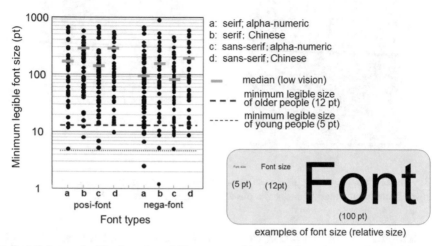

Fig. 3. Minimum legible font size of 59 persons with low vision when reading a character of alpha-numeric and Chinese characters in positive and negative font type at 0.5 m viewing distance. Each dot in the graph means individual data of participants and green bar the median of the 59 participants. Red dashed line and a blue dotted line mean minimum legible font size at the same viewing condition for older and young persons respectively. An inset figure in the lower-right corner is an illustration of different font sizes (relative scale) to show an image of minimum legible font sizes for three different groups (young, older, and low vision persons respectively from the left).

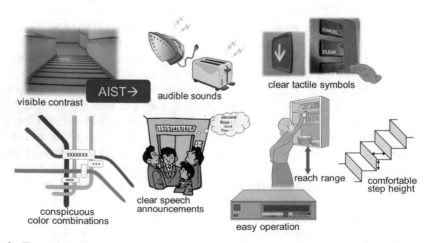

Fig. 4. Examples of human data and design items regarding human sensory, physical and cognitive functions.

It is obvious that ergonomics data on human ability are required for the Method 2. There are so many human body functions and we need data for those functions to accommodate users of older persons and persons with disabilities who have degraded human abilities. Figure 4 shows typical examples of human functions in use of home appliances. Of course, those data should be provided to be readily applicable in designing products, including sensory, physical, and cognitive functions. Among those functions, it is noted that cognitive data are quite lacking in the literature.

Though not exhaustive, some useful database for human abilities are becoming available now. Recently, ISO (International Organization for Standardization) has published a technical report on human data on sensory, physical and cognitive characteristics and capabilities [4]. This is one of the useful data sources for accessible design.

4 Summary

Increasing users is one of the important design concepts of accessible design. It aims to expand user groups step by step toward the ultimate goal of all people. Any step, tiny or big, is worth trying and be acceptable. To proceed this we need useful ergonomics data, which are not sufficiently supplied yet. However, once excellent data sources are provided, accessible design will be more and more common in our daily lives.

References

1. ISO/IEC Guide 71:2014, Guide for addressing accessibility in standards (2015)
2. Sagawa, K., Kurakata, K., Itoh, N.: Accessible design–Human oriented design taking account of sensory and cognitive characteristics and capabilities of older persons and persons with disabilities, NTS Co. Ltd, Tokyo (2019) (in Japanese)
3. Itoh, N., Sagawa, K.: Spatial resolution of people with low vision. In: Proceedings of Light and Lighting Conference with Special Emphasis on LEDs and Solid State Lighting (CD-ROM)
4. ISO/TR22411 2nd edition:2021, Ergonomics data for use in the application of ISO/IEC Guide 71:2014

Ergonomic Design, Evaluation and Application of a 3-Dimensional Simulation of a Clinical Setting for People with Lower Limb Disabilities

Stephen Ong[1,4], James D. McGlothlin[1,4](✉), Bradley S. Duerstock[2,4],
Philip S. Dunston[3,4], and James F. Schweitzer[1,4]

[1] School of Health Sciences, Purdue University, West Lafayette, USA
jdm3@purdue.edu
[2] School of Industrial Engineering, Purdue University, West Lafayette, USA
[3] School of Civil Engineering, Purdue University, West Lafayette, USA
[4] Envision Center, Purdue University, West Lafayette, USA

Abstract. The goal of this project was to use ergonomic design principles to evaluate a 3-dimensional computer simulation of a manikin in a clinical laboratory setting for individuals with lower limb disabilities. The first step was to use the University of Michigan 3D Static Strength Prediction Program (3D SSPP) to determine biomechanical challenges from three simulated work postures commonly performed among clinical workers. Findings were then imported into the Purdue Envision Center's 3D simulation of the Accessible Biomedical Immersion Laboratory (ABIL) located at Purdue's Discovery and Learning Research Center (DLRC). Positions assumed in the 3D ABIL simulation for each task were predicted, using the 3D SSPP software, to be achievable by at least 90% of the population. Collection of data from four subjects performing standardized clinical tasks while in wheelchairs allowed for real-world validation of the 3D simulation model. Additional ergonomic analysis was conducted using the Rapid Upper Limb Assessment (RULA) tool along with subject questionnaires to determine upper limb work risk factors associated with clinical tasks and workstations. RULA and questionnaire data showed the presence of potential upper limb risk factors that may need to be incorporated into the 3D simulation model, especially during pipetting tasks when performed by female subjects. This pilot study showed promise as a clinical facility design tool. Further research is needed to fine tune the 3D ABIL simulation as a useful tool to create clinical facilities for those with lower-limb disabilities.

Keywords: Ergonomic design · 3D simulation · Clinical setting · Lower limb disabilities

1 Introduction

Less than one in five (19.3%) of persons with a disability were employed according to the U.S. Bureau of Labor Statistics [1]. In contrast, the employment-population ratio

© The Author(s), under exclusive license to Springer Nature Switzerland AG 2021
N. L. Black et al. (Eds.): IEA 2021, LNNS 220, pp. 286–293, 2021.
https://doi.org/10.1007/978-3-030-74605-6_36

for persons without a disability was 66.3%. The unemployment rates for both persons with disability were more than twice that of workers without a disability, 7.3% versus 3.5%, respectively [1]. Musculoskeletal disorders (MSDs) have been an ongoing issue in the workplace; they are the leading cause of pain, discomfort, loss of productivity, and disability in the United States [2]. These disorders include a wide range of inflammatory and degenerative conditions that are caused by several workplace factors such as repetition, awkward postures, force, insufficient recovery time, static loading, temperature, and vibrations. The correlation between these work factors and MSDs were further confirmed in a study performed by Punnett and Wegmann [3]. The Occupational Safety and Health Administration (OSHA) observed a seven-fold increase of MSD cases demonstrating the increasing magnitude of MSDs [2]. OSHA has also estimated that MSDs cost employers approximately $15–18 billion a year in workers' compensation claims, greatly affect quality of life, and account for a large portion of occupational injuries worldwide [2].

In the clinical setting, several tasks require repetitive movements, sustained static postures, and high levels of concentration. These factors have led to reports of discomfort in the head, neck, back, and upper extremities by clinical workers [4]. Laboratory tasks that utilize microscopes, pipettes, and other equipment accentuate the risk when performed over extended periods of time. Ramadan and Ferreira performed a study in 2006 that demonstrated the association between work risk factors and MSDs in a clinical pathology laboratory: of 120 subjects, 86.7% reported symptoms in the past work year [5].

To help reduce the occurrence of MSDs in the workplace, ergonomic programs have been established as simple and effective solutions, resulting in substantial savings in workers' compensation costs, increased productivity, and decreased turnover [6]. Another method used to reduce the number of MSD cases is the redesign of the workplace to accommodate the work force. In a 2011 study that researched the design of a laboratory for special needs workers, a Purdue laboratory facility was redesigned according to standards provided by the Americans with Disabilities Act (ADA) and enhanced with ergonomic principles [7]. The modified workspace provided the proper accommodations for those with lower-limb disabilities, allowing for leg clearance under sinks and ventilation hoods, reasonable reaching of switches and knobs, and better visibility of sink contents. While these changes were made specifically for wheelchair accessibility, such accommodations could also be used by able-bodied workers while sitting.

While most of the population is composed of able-bodied workers, it is estimated that 56.7 million people out of 303.9 million non-institutionalized populations had a disability [8]. However, there are an increasing number of veterans with disabilities where 21.6 million veterans in the civilian non-institutional population ages 18 and over [9]. With 3.0 million veterans reported having a service-connected disability.

It is important to note that there is a correlation between the severity of one's disability and economic status. Those with severe disabilities are more likely to be in poverty compared to those with non-severe or no disability. These negative trends will continue to worsen as veterans return home and attempt to reenter the workforce. For example, during the end of Operation Iraqi Freedom and Operation New Dawn the total number of amputations by December 2012 was over 1,700 including major and minor limbs

[10]. In addition to the many capable individuals who are restricted to wheelchairs, including many disabled veterans, there is need for well-designed clinical facilities that are accessible to this cadre of workers.

2 Methods

Manikins were used in the 3D SSPP software program to provide initial postures and determine potential risks associated with the static postures engaged during each task. The 3D SSPP tool is a program built from accumulated research by the University of Michigan to analyze the forces various body parts experience during a given task. Manikins were positioned in seated positions to mimic the three common clinical tasks for this study: microscopy, micro-pipetting tasks, and slide preparation for the 5th, 50th, and 95th percentiles for both males and females. This resulted in a range of evaluation from the 5th percentile female to the 95th percentile male. Once these figures were set to their desired positions, screen shots were submitted to Purdue's Envision Center, where the figures were converted to 3D models and placed in a virtual replica of the ABIL located in Purdue's Discovery and Learning Research Center (DLRC).

To supplement the simulation from the 3D models, four human subjects participated in the study: two females and two males. The two females were able-bodied partic-ipants while both males possessed lower-limb disabilities. Participants performed the same clinical tasks for up to two hours each in a wheelchair provided to them (female subjects), or while utilizing their own wheelchair or a Tracer LX hospital wheelchair (male subjects).

Following the methods from redesign of the ABIL facility, web cameras were set up at each workstation for the four human subjects. One webcam was placed to capture the side profile of each subject performing each task. Another was placed directly over the workstations to capture a birds-eye-view of each task performed. All subjects were given simulated common clinical procedures for microscopy, pipetting, and slide smearing tasks.

The Rapid Upper Limb Assessment (RULA) tool was utilized, following the published protocol by McAtamney & Corlett to make direct observations of the tasks performed by each subject [11]. Videos were recorded to document the work risk factors for the three simulated clinical procedures. Anthropometric measurements were collected to provide additional information on how subjects fit in the workstations. A questionnaire developed and used during the redesign of the ABIL facility was distributed among the volunteers to gather information regarding demographics, occupational history, medical history, and workplace variables. The Nordic Musculoskeletal Questionnaire (NMQ) was included to analyze the specific areas of the subjects' bodies that were affected by MSDs. These observations and responses were then compared and contrasted with the computer-generated outcomes. No statistical analysis was performed because of small sample size.

3 Results

The 3D SSPP tool indicated that none of the sustained postures that would be assumed during each task fell below 90% of each population group. Thus, predicting that 90%

of each size percentile population would be able to achieve the postures during the task. The 3D SSPP manikins and corresponding data were submitted to the Purdue's Envision Center, where the 3D simulation prototype was created. This 3D prototype recreated the manikin postures and placed them into a virtual laboratory environment modeled after the specifications of the ABIL facility. Each manikin was able to fit within the design parameters, providing support that the ABIL specifications can accommodate workers who fall within the 5th percentile female to 95th percentile male range. An example of this range is shown in Figs. 1a and 1b, where the manikins are pipetting in the redesigned fume hood station.

(a)   (b)

Figs. 1. a and 1b (left figure: 5% female 3D SSPP manikin, right human performing pipetting tasks; right figure: 95% male 3D SSPP manikin, right human performing pipetting tasks.

The four human subjects observed for this study, two males and two females per-formed the simulated clinical tasks in wheelchairs. As mentioned, the two males had lower-limb disabilities that required the use of a wheelchair for everyday use, while neither female had such disabilities. The heights of the subjects ranged from 5'0'' to 6'4'' (Table 1), providing a simplified population spectrum from the 5th percentile female to the 95th percentile male.

Table 1. Height, weight, and categorization of volunteer subjects.

Subject	1	2	3	4
Gender	Male	Male	Female	Female
Age	26	23	21	24
Height (cm)	6'4" (193)	5'11"(180.3)	5'4"(162.6)	5'0"(152.4)
% Group	95%	50%	50%	5%
Weight lbs. (Kgs)	230 (104.33)	130 (58.97)	125 (56.7)	91 (41.28)

Using RULA, it was shown that all subjects obtained scores indicating some change was needed for each task. The scores, while assuming adequate leg support, showed that the task most in need of change was slide preparation. It was also observed that the females may need some changes to improve the pipetting tasks as their dominant hands achieved scores of 5 or 6. The females generally had an increase in their pipetting score of one point per hand. These increased scores indicated that more immediate changes may be needed to avoid future risks of MSDs.

The distributed questionnaires provided insight on what the subjects experienced. The 95th percentile male reported that there were no difficulties performing the tasks or using the workstations. The 50th percentile male reported difficulty in handling test tubes during the pipetting task, discomfort in using the microscope and slight (3 on a scale of 1 to 10) fatigue and discomfort in his hands and wrists and a little discomfort and fatigue (1 on a scale of 1 to 10) in his eyes. The 50th percentile female reported difficulty in accessing the fume hood, performing the pipetting tasks within the fume hoods, and fatigue and discomfort in her arms. The 5th percentile female noted difficulty and slight discomfort (3 on a scale of 1 to 10) during test tube handling, difficulty accessing the fume hoods, and fatigue in her arms and back.

The NMQ portion of the questionnaire provided additional background information on the MSDs experienced by the subjects from past work. The 95th percentile male reported MSDs in his neck and both shoulders in the past year but no recent problems in the previous week. He also noted that his MSDs did not prevent him from working. The 50th percentile male reported MSDs in both shoulders in the past year that did prevent him from working. The 50th percentile female reported MSDs in her neck during the past year, while the 5th percentile female reported no MSDs.

To assess the consistency of the ergonomic analyses in this study, the 3D SSPP outputs, prototype, RULA outcomes, and questionnaire responses were compared with one another. The 3D SSPP program predicted that there would be no risks from the assumed postures required for the tasks (Table 2). These predictions and postures were successfully recreated in the virtual ABIL facility. Once the tasks were performed and RULA scores and questionnaire responses were gathered, potential risk factors were revealed for each task. The 50th percentile male indicated discomfort and difficulties for each task, while the 5th and 50th percentile females reported issues with the pipetting tasks.

Table 2. Comparison of university of Michigan 3D SSPP; Envision center's prototype; RULA outcomes; and NMQ questionnaire responses.

Subjects observed	3D SSPP	Prototype	RULA	NMQ questionnaire
Male	Problems?	Problems?	Change needed?	Discomfort/ Difficulty
50th – Microscopy	No	No	Change may be needed	Yes
95th – Microscopy	No	No	Change may be needed	No
50th – Pipetting	No	No	Change may be needed	Yes
95th – Pipetting	No	No	Change may be needed	No
50th - Slide prep	No	No	Change soon	Yes

(*continued*)

Table 2. (*continued*)

Subjects observed	3D SSPP	Prototype	RULA	NMQ questionnaire
95th - Slide prep	No	No	Change soon	No
Female				
5th – Microscopy	No	No	Change may be nceded	No
50th – Microscopy	No	No	Change may be needed	No
5th – Pipetting	No	No	Change soon	Yes
50th – Pipetting	No	No	Change soon	Yes
5th - Slide prep	No	No	Change may be needed	No
50th - Slide prep	No	No	Change soon	No

The redesigned workstations were also evaluated to determine if the new specifications are usable by those who fall in the 5th percentile female to 95th percentile male range (Table 3). Each station had its own individual task with pipetting performed at the fume hood, slide preparations done at the sink, and microscopy done at the adjustable work surface. All subjects were able to perform and complete the assigned tasks at each station, showing that the adjusted specifications can be used by approximately 90% of the population.

Table 3. Workstation dimensions and subjects ability to perform associated tasks.

	Fume hood specs	Sink specs	Adjustable surface
Height surface (cm)	**34 in. (86.4)**	**34 in. (86.4)**	**30–50 in. (76.2–127)**
Width (cm)	**48 in. (121.9)**	**40.5 in. (102.9)**	**60 in. (152.4)**
Depth (cm)	**17 in. (43.2)**	**18 in. (45.7)**	**30 in. (76.2)**
Height clearance (cm)	**31 in. (78.7)**	**28.5 in. (72.4)**	**29–49 in. (73.7–124.5)**
Tasks achievable?	**Yes**	**Yes**	**Yes**

4 Discussion

The ABIL facility was designed in a previous study to allow for improved accessibility [7]. The redesign allowed for better workstation accessibility by workers with lower-limb disability but the percentage of the population that could use the new specifications was not determined. The creation of a simplified spectrum would demonstrate that the facility designed according to the American with Disabilities Act (ADA) standards can accommodate 90% of the population, especially those with lower-limb disabilities. The 3D simulation prototype created a virtual range, showing that the current ABIL specifications should accommodate those who fall within the 5th percentile female to the 95th

percentile male range. The number of subjects observed did not limit the ability to create a real-world spectrum as the two ends, a 5'0" female and a 6'4" male, were analyzed along with a male and female from the 50th percentile to help confirm that the facilities can accommodate this 90% range. Each subject was able to complete all of the designated tasks providing qualitative support that the ABIL specifications are sufficient for a range of workers with lower-limb disabilities. In comparing the computerized outcomes and those collected from subject analyses, it was consistently seen that the two tools differed in outcomes, despite 3D SSPP and RULA being proven to be reliable and useful in the field of ergonomics. The computer-based programs generated outcomes based on averages of the population data. This led to 3D manikins with proportioned anthropometric lengths; however, not every worker is proportioned in such a manner. Because of these individual variances, assessment tools such as RULA and questionnaires were needed to gather more specific data. Analysis of the tasks by RULA, while subject to observer bias, revealed that there were still potential biomechanical and postural load risks, despite the subjects being able to assume the necessary postures. The questionnaire responses revealed specific discomforts and difficulties each subject experienced while performing each task.

The RULA scores provided further information on risk factors associated with each posture assumed during the task; there was indication that all the tasks needed potential change. While each subject scored a 3 or higher for each task, several factors affected how each task was performed, directly affecting the RULA score. These factors include but are not limited to size of the subject, type of wheelchair used, extent of the disability, and prior lab experience. It was also noted during the redesign of ABIL that the RULA tool may potentially underestimate the risk factors of the task as the tool is primarily used on able-bodied workers.

5   Conclusions

This study determined that a 3D simulation is an adequate representation of an accessible clinical laboratory. The positions assumed in the 3D ABIL Simulation Prototype for each task were predicted to be achievable by at least 90% of the population, according to the 3D SSPP tool. The 3D prototype provided virtual "proof of concept" that the ABIL facilities can accommodate 90% of the population. The additional collection of data from four subjects allowed for the creation of a real-world range, providing additional support. Further ergonomic analysis was conducted through RULA and individuals' questionnaires to determine work risk factors associated with the assigned tasks and their corresponding workstation. The presence of potential risk factors coupled with subjective observation of the tasks performed revealed worker characteristics that will need to be further incorporated into the 3D simulation. The current 3D prototype provides a realistic image of how various lab workers can be accommodated at each workstation. Subject analysis also demonstrated that the observed tasks can be performed and completed at each workstation. The final 3D ABIL simulation could ultimately evolve to provide a very comprehensive tool for others to use to create similar accessible facilities, further expanding the clinical job market to those with lower-limb disabilities.

References

1. U.S. Bureau of Labor Statistics. Persons with a Disability: Labor Force Characteristics Summary. USDL-20–0339. https://www.bls.gov/news.release/disabl.nr0.htm Accessed 26 Feb 2020
2. U. S. Department of Labor. (Feb. 12th, 2020). Prevention of work-related musculoskeletal disorders. https://www.cdc.gov/workplacehealthpromotion/health-strategies/musculoskeletal-disorders/index.html Accessed 12 Feb 2020
3. Punnett, L., Wegman, D.: Work-related musculoskeletal disorders: the epidemiologic evidence and the debate. J. Electromyogr. Kinesiol. **14**(1), 13–23 (2004)
4. Thompson, S., Mason, E., Dukes, S.: Ergonomics and cytotechnologists: reported musculoskeletal discomfort. Diagn. Cytopathol. **29**(6), 364–367 (2003)
5. Ramadan, P.A., Mario, F. Jr.: Risk factors associated with the reporting of musculoskeletal symptoms in workers at a laboratory or clinical pathology. Ann. Occup. Hygiene **50**(3), 297–303 (2006)
6. U. S. Department of Labor. Prevention of work-related musculoskeletal disorders. https://www.cdc.gov/workplacehealthpromotion/health-strategies/musculoskeletal-disorders/index.html Accessed 12 Feb 2011
7. Chen, W.-C.: Ergonomic design and evaluation of a clinical laboratory for people with disabilities of the lower limbs (2012)
8. Brault, M.: Americans with Disabilities: Current Population Reports. US Census Bureau vol. 2012 no. 3 (2010)
9. U. S. Department of Labor. Disabled Veterans and the Labor Force. Washington, DC, Retrieved from https://www.bls.gov/opub/ted/2012/ted_20121109.htm 2012
10. Fischer, H.: U.S. Military casualty statistics: Operation New Dawn, Operation Iraqi Freedom, and Operation Enduring Freedom (2012). https://www.fas.org/sgp/crs/natsec/RS22452.pdf
11. McAtamney, L., Corlett, E.N.: RULA: a survey method for the investigation of work-related upper limb disorders. Appl. Ergon. **24**(2), 91–99 (1993)

Information Design and Plain Language: An Inclusive Approach for Government Health Campaigns

Claudia Mont'Alvão(✉) ⓘ, Livia Clemente ⓘ, and Tiago Ribeiro ⓘ

Graduate Program in Design, Laboratory of Ergodesign and Usability of Interfaces, Pontifical Catholic University of Rio de Janeiro, Rua Marquês de S. Vicente, 225, Gávea, RJ, Brazil
cmontalvao@puc-rio.br

Abstract. This paper presents an ongoing study aiming to evaluate Brazilian health campaigns' graphical aspects considering Plain Language as an inclusive approach. One of the barriers to this informative material for health promotion is language. Texts must be easy to read and comprehend to allow all populations to access health information and make decisions as needed. This scenario reveals the need for government health communication, proposing a research question: the messages presented in government health campaigns are clear and accessible for citizens? This paper presents part of broader research that aims to analyze the federal government's comprehensibility in health information and education, considering Plain Language aspects. Data analysis is still ongoing at the time of writing, but results highlight a lack of information in health campaigns.

Keywords: Information design · Inclusive design · Plain language · Health promotion · Human Factors/Ergonomics

1 Problem Statement and Context

The Ottawa Charter for Health Promotion [1], signed by the Brazilian government, highlights all elements' equity to create favorable environments, changing health in global responsibility.

According to Buss [2], based on the health promotion concept proposed by Sutherland & Fulton (1992), educational tools are fundamental to promote behaviour changes. Informative materials are essential for an individual to live and control his/her diseases and treatment options.

Reberte et al. [3] propose that printed information in primary healthcare is usual once this material can help patients clarify their doubts. The study and design of manuals, leaflets, and posters are a contribution to health promotion.

One of the barriers to this informative material for health promotion is language. Texts must be easy to read and comprehend to allow all populations to access health information and make decisions as needed. One of the primary responsibilities of democratic governments is to inform their citizens about their rights, duties, transactions, among other services.

© The Author(s), under exclusive license to Springer Nature Switzerland AG 2021
N. L. Black et al. (Eds.): IEA 2021, LNNS 220, pp. 294–298, 2021.
https://doi.org/10.1007/978-3-030-74605-6_37

This context is found in Brazil, an upper-middle-income country [4], as in many other countries worldwide, where the population's low levels of literacy and reading skills. As Inaf Brasil report [5]: 20% of Brazilians are unable to read and write or express information literally (illiterate or rudimentary level); 34% can select one or more units of information, performing small inferences (elementary level); 25% can find 'literally' expressed information in either journalistic or scientific texts, performing small inferences (intermediate level) and 12% can understand documents of greater complexity based on elements of a given context and can provide an opinion on the positioning or style of the author (proficiency level).

This scenario reveals the need and urgency for government communication following Plain Language guidelines.

In Brazil, in 2020 was published the first official guidelines about Plain Language [6]. These guidelines that follow the ones established by the Plain language movement in many countries must be considered in the information design of all kinds of communication.

The Human Factors/Ergonomics approach allows a better investigation of citizens' characteristics, abilities, and capacities, aiming for better instructional and educative information projects.

2   Objective and Method of This Study

It aims to analyze the federal government's comprehensibility that aims health information and education, considering Plain Language aspects, proposing a research question: messages presented in government health campaigns are clear and accessible for citizens?

This research supposes that health promotion materials must bring elements - as images and text – that can support the message and reach the citizens. Here, health promotion and information design are associated.

This research's first step was a literature review and statistical data about health and deaths in this country. It was considered informative materials from the Brazilian Ministry of Health (BMH), considering both digital and printed pieces in the last five years as a second and side activity. This period was selected once they rely on different governors and different approaches for health information.

The third step was to define how to analyze and compare all data collected. This need led the research team to develop a method for analyzing archives of images, considering authors that explored this topic [7–11]. These authors point out the need to fulfil some concepts for a graphical analysis: consistency, gama, framework, positioning, proxemics, naturalism; typography used for both title and text body; alignment; type of images included (photos, images, illustration) to convey a graphic message.

Additionally, it was observed if Plain Language guidelines set in Brazil [6] were followed. This document, entitled 'Matrix of a text analysis' suggest that words must be replaced if they: have orthographical errors; are long; are difficult; are in another language; is an abbreviation or acronyms; are jargons or technical words; are sexists, pejorative or discriminatory; are action verbs in infinitive; are nouns indicating actions; or abstract nouns. The document also mentions that long sentences make it challenging to understand the text content and readers' concentration and be divided into more than one sentence.

3 Preliminary Results

This research, commenced in August 2020, highlighted that since 2013, BMH broadcasted 159 campaigns on several topics such as Cancer, Malaria, Flu, Sexually Transmitted Infections (STI), Smoking/Tobacco, Tuberculosis, among others.

It also included seasonal campaigns (e.g., for Carnival), the ones that follow international initiatives (e.g., World Health Day, World AIDS Day), or incentives for voluntary donations (e.g., Blood, Organs, Breast milk).

Table 1 shows an example of how the same topic was advertised, or if following international campaigns, involving the idea of warning, voluntary action, or vaccination.

Table 1. Example of health campaigns.

Campaign topic	Years analyzed	Type of campaigns
AIDS	2014 to 2019	During Carnival
AIDS	2014 to 2018	World AIDS Day
Breast milk donation	2014 to 2020	Local, annual
Blood donation	2014 to 2020	Local, annual
Flu	2014 to 2020	Annual vaccination
HPV and Meningitis	2014 to 2018	Annual vaccination

Some statistical data collected points out that the country expended around US$1 billion in vaccines and vaccination initiatives in 2018 [12] and around US$ 32,5 million in public health advertisements per year [13]. For a middle-income country, it is an expressive investment in public health.

4 Discussion and Future Steps

After analyzing all the material collected, blood donation Flu, and STI campaigns, were selected from 2013 until 2020. The criteria represent both the involuntary and voluntary participation of citizens.

Once the data collection and analysis are ongoing, it was possible to identify how different media was used to reach the citizens. Both printed and digital material was used by BHM, primary posters in A3 format, pamphlets, videos, Instagram, and Facebook.

Once considering the Plain Language approach, it is possible to say that technical terms are the main words used, representing a challenge for citizens. Another point to be highlighted is the adequacy of images and their compatibility with text that can make difficult the information presented.

It is expected that after the analysis of all selected campaigns, an experiment can be conducted to compare the comprehensibility of this information design in a health campaign using or not a Plain language approach.

Acknowledgements. The authors would like to thank the Brazilian National Council for Scientific and Technological Development (CNPq), Coordenação de Aperfeiçoamento de Pessoal de Nível Superior - Brasil (CAPES - Finance Code 001) and Pontifical Catholic University of Rio de Janeiro (PUC-Rio) for the financial support of this study.

References

1. World Health Organization (1986). The Ottawa Charter for Health Promotion, 1986. https://www.who.int/healthpromotion/conferences/previous/ottawa/en/. Accessed 29 Jan 2021.
2. Buss, P.M.: Promoção da saúde e qualidade de vida. Ciência & Saúde Coletiva **5**(1), 163–177 (2000)
3. Reberte, L.M., et al.: Process of construction of an educational booklet for health promotion of pregnant women. Rev. Latino-Am. Enfermagem. Ribeirão Preto. **20**(1), 101–108 (2012). https://doi.org/10.1590/S0104-11692012000100014
4. World Bank Data & Research by county (2020). https://data.worldbank.org/country/brazil.
5. Inaf Brasil Resultados preliminares. Estudo especial sobre alfabetismo e mundo do trabalho. São Paulo (2018). https://acaoeducativa.org.br/wp-content/uploads/2018/08/Inaf2018_Relat%C3%B3rio-Resultados-Preliminares_v08Ago2018.pdf Accessed 29 Jan 2021
6. Brasil. Governo do Brasil, Matriz para análise de um texto – Linguagem Simples. 2 p. (2020). https://www.gov.br/pt-br/guia-de-edicao-de-servicos-do-gov.br/publicacoes-e-cursos/matriz-para-analise-de-um-texto.pdf/. Accessed 29 Jan 2021
7. Ashwin, C.: The ingredients of style in contemporary illustration: a case study. Inf. Des. J. **1**, 51–67 (1979)
8. Bento, A.A., Fonseca, L.P.: Graphic analysis of Bonde Circular magazine. In: Proceedings of the 8 th CIDI and 8 th CONGIC Guilherme Santa Rosa; Cristina Portugal (orgs.) Sociedade Brasileira de Design da Informação – SBDI, atal, Brazil, (2017) ISBN 978-85-212-1305-5
9. Moreira, L.A., Fonseca, L.P.: A proposal for a data gathering form for the analysis of archives of images.Proceedings of the 8th CIDI and 8th CONGIC Guilherme Santa Rosa; Cristina Portugal (orgs.) Sociedade Brasileira de Design da Informação – SBDI Natal, Brazil (2017) ISBN 978-85-212-1305-5
10. Borba, M.R., Waechter, H.N., Borba, V.R.: Contributions of graphic design for effective communication in the health campaigns. In: Spinillo, C.G. et al. (orgs) Proceedings of the 7th Information Design International Conference, CIDI 2015, [Blucher Design Proceedings, no. 2, vol. 2, São Paulo, Blucher (2015). https://doi.org/10.5151/designpro-CIDI2015-cidi_86
11. Lócio, L.M., Waechter, H.N.: Reconstruindo e adaptando fichas: proposta de instrumento de análise gráfica. Fadel, L., Spinillo, C., Horta, A., Portugal, C. (orgs) Proceedings of the 9th CIDI and 9th CONGIC Sociedade Brasileira de Design da Informação – SBDI Belo Horizonte, Brazil (2019) https://doi.org/10.5151/9cidi-congic-5.0365

12. BRASIL. Ministério da Saúde. 3° Relatório Quadrimestral de Prestação de Contas. Brasília, DF (2020). https://bvsms.saude.gov.br/bvs/publicacoes/3_relatorio_quadrimestral_prestacao_contas_2019.pdf . Accessed 29 Jan 2021
13. Portal Transparencia Publicidade de Utilidade Pública (2020). https://transparencia.gov.br/programas-e-acoes/acao/4641-publicidade-de-utilidade-publica. Accessed 29 Jan 2021

"Progetto di Vita" and Design for All: An Integrated Approach in Supporting Collaborative Housing Projects for Persons with Disabilities

Cristiana Perego(✉) , Angela Silvia Pavesi , and Ilaria Oberti

ABC Department, Politecnico di Milano, 20133 Milan, MI, Italy
{cristiana.perego,angela.pavesi,ilaria.oberti}@polimi.it

Abstract. "Progetto di Vita" (PdV Life Project) represents the guarantee element for respect of rights and Quality of Life of people with disabilities. It is based on the principle of resilient community that welcomes vulnerability conditions by interpreting "disability" in the semantic meaning of "different abilities" and of resource, triggering a process implementable when institutions, research and welfare services operate according to a holistic approach.

In Italy, Law 112/16 identifies in PdV the principle of paths aimed at fully implementing right to social inclusion expressed by UN Convention. The law provides measures allowing parents to face the future of their children with disabilities in the so-called "Dopo di Noi" (after us). PdV represents a key principle for that holistic approach necessary to address the multidimensional character of disability that can impact on design and management of built environment. Actions in this direction cannot but be supported by a wider infrastructure, through the transdisciplinary approach essential for pathways of social inclusion related to accompanying disabled people to autonomy (where possible).

This paper reports the results of the first stages of a research path aimed at the development of procedural guidelines at meta-project level for the design of new residential models for people with disabilities built around PdV holistic approach foreseen by Law 112/16.

Keywords: Disability · "Progetto di Vita" (PdV) · Inclusion · Design for All (DfA) · Process · Collaborative housing

1 Introduction

In Italy, Law 328/00 introduced the concept of "Progetto individuale" (Individual Project), more commonly called "Progetto di Vita" (PdV), aimed at the global taking charge of the person with different abilities [1].

The standard provides that for each person having a "physical, mental or sensory, stabilised or progressive" disability [2] a PdV is prepared which includes, in addition to the diagnostic-functional assessment, care and rehabilitation services, services to the person, with particular reference to recovery and social integration, as well as the economic measures necessary to overcome social exclusion conditions [3].

PdV allows the creation of personalised pathways coordinating interventions in a targeted manner to maximize benefits and responding overall to needs and aspirations of the beneficiary. The innovative approach considers PdV as an act of planning articulated over time on the basis of which institutions, welfare services and the entire territorial community can create conditions for interventions to materialise in positive actions, accompanying families and listening to needs and interests of the person in order to nurture and promote its potential [4]. In the same way the "Two-year action programme for the promotion of the rights and integration of people with disabilities", adopted for the first time by Italian Government in 2013 [5, 6], provides for the full implementation of PdV as an enforceable right related to the same path of certification and ascertainment of different abilities [4].

Subsequently, Law 112/16 containing "Provisions on assistance for people with severe disabilities without family support" [7], identifies in PdV the principle for activating paths aimed at fully implementing right to social inclusion expressed by UN Convention on the Rights of Persons with Disabilities [8]. The law, better known as "Dopo di Noi" (after us), provides for measures enabling parents and caregivers to face the issue of the future of their sons with disabilities when they will no longer be with them in the so-called "Dopo di Noi". In this sense PdV represents the "heart" of a law that among its founding principles focuses precisely on the deinstitutionalisation of people with disabilities and the greater freedom in identifying eligible models to accompany them to a "new life" in which a greater degree of autonomy is achieved through a process of greater social inclusion. In the construction of PdV lies the guarantee of respect of rights and the Quality of Life of people with disabilities to the extent that it is able to invest life of the person in its entirety, in aspects related to health, living, accompaniment to autonomous adult life, through school inclusion, formation, work integration and the creation of a "generative network of networks", with a view to generative and community welfare.

PdV represents a key principle for the adoption of that holistic approach deemed necessary to address the multidimensional character of the "different abilities", as it is configured as a system in which all components related to person's life should be treated in close synergy with each other starting from the issue of "living". As a matter of fact, house represents a fundamental spatial environment, being configured as a pivotal place for the design of the "Dopo di Noi" in function of "durante noi" (during us), both in terms of implementation of open, inclusive and widespread collaborative housing projects on the territory, and for the human and social experience of "inhabiting a place" as a lever able to experience collective belonging for the creation of an inclusive welfare [9].

Fostering the process of housing autonomy means making sure that the community around the person with disabilities is able (capable) of absorbing that part of "different ability" and transforming it into a resource, a virtuous circle observable from experiences that leads the person with his or her different abilities to put in place in turn resources that are useful to the community.

This is the background of the research project launched by Comitato Officina Dopo Di Noi (CODDN) with the aim of setting up a digital Observatory to monitor the implementation of Law 112/16 and to disseminate best practices emerged from the concrete implementation of this measure on the national territory[1].

To support this project, CODDN has activated a doctorate whose objectives include the elaboration of procedural guidelines at meta-project level for the activation of housing autonomy paths for people with disabilities and the design of new residential models built around PdV holistic approach foreseen by Law 112/16. With respect to this objective, this paper aims to report the results obtained so far.

2 Research Objective and Methodology

The multidimensional character of disability can deeply impact on spaces design and processes organisation within the built environment. Starting from this assumption, the doctorate initiated with the aim of investigating the issue of disability inclusion in the housing sphere in order to elaborate meta-project and procedural guidelines for the design of innovative models of inclusive collaborative housing. The research is articulated into eight phases:

- definition of principles underlying the evolution of the legislative framework with regard to PdV approach through the analysis of data collected within the aforementioned Observatory;
- framework and description of PdV that is configured as an innovation element to address the multidimensional character of disability through a holistic approach and analysis of its interactions on the built environment. This phase is realised through the review of the scientific literature on the topic, corroborated by the dialogue with a multiplicity of stakeholders involved in various ways on the subject;
- mapping of current practices for construction of housing autonomy paths for people with disabilities and projects for new residential models built around the PdV approach. To this end, a benchmark analysis is conducted with the aim of identifying case studies with respect to the issue of inclusive living both through desktop research, using specific keywords, and through special interviews and cases identified in a research-action path;
- mapping of possible user clusters in relation to the different types of disabilities to define specific needs framework at meta-project level through a research phase that crosses data relating to the International Classification of Functioning, Disability and

---

[1] CODDN is the promoter and responsible of Officina NET project financed by Cariplo and Compagnia di San Paolo foundations and realised in partnership with ABC Dept. of Politecnico di Milano, Istituto per la Ricerca Sociale (IRS), Fondazione FITS! per l'Innovazione del Terzo Settore and BES Cooperativa Sociale, which deals with formation and work integration of people with disabilities. To support Officina NET project, a PhD has been activated, through the support of the abovementioned foundations, in co-financing with the ABC Dept. of Politecnico di Milano.

Health (ICF) [10] with elements emerged from the analysis of best practices. The objective is to outline the needs framework that represents the basis for the definition of the guidelines;
– critical analysis of case studies identified from the benchmark analysis to extract a set of indicators characterising the PdV approach and to analyse the fallout that latter can outline with respect to Design for All (DfA) approach and vice versa, also in function of the needs framework identified in the previous phase;
– preliminary elaboration of meta-project and procedural guidelines according to the performance requirements approach to support the spaces design and processes organisation for the disability inclusion in the housing sphere that integrate the PdV approach with the DfA one;
– theoretical validation conducted through the sharing of the preliminary document containing the guidelines (in the form of need–requirement–performance) with a selection of stakeholders involved in the topic. The validation phase involves the completion of questionnaires and the realisation of targeted interviews;
– final elaboration of the guidelines in the light of the theoretical validation phase conducted with the identified network of stakeholders.

3   Results

Results achieved so far relate to the first three phases and are reported below.

3.1   PdV: A Legislative Framework

The first phase of the research focused on the construction of the regulatory framework at national and international level with respect to the concept of PdV and then focusing on Law 112/16 that identifies precisely in the definition of this "Project" the principle for the activation of social inclusion pathways for people with disabilities through an interdisciplinary approach. In this regard, an in-depth analysis of data collected within the Observatory was conducted. Individual regional implementation programs of the law issued on the national territory were analysed, collecting in a monitoring grid qualitative and quantitative data related to different dimensions including regulatory references, regional governance systems, characteristics of beneficiaries, of multidimensional need assessment and of individual project, as well as the distribution of national financial resources of "Dopo di Noi" Fund foreseen by the legislation. The recent debate suggests how the implementation of monitoring systems to detect the state of implementation of norms such as "Dopo di Noi" Law and the analysis of projects already in place in the different territorial realities is proving to be an increasingly essential action for the implementation of welfare policies.

This first phase of the research allowed to outline the principles underlying the evolution of the legislative framework in the field of PdV.

3.2 PdV: A Holistic Approach

The second phase of the research path had the objective of framing PdV with the aim of defining its characteristics and the main phases through which to formulate it so that it can be configured as a guarantee element for the Quality of Life of people with disabilities. The theme has been deepened through a review of the scientific literature on the topic aimed at the creation of an annotated bibliography with respect to specific keywords and a programmatic document that outlines distinctive features of PdV identified by the analysis. This phase of the path was corroborated by the dialogue with a multiplicity of subjects within the "generative network" promoted by CODDN, intended as a bond among institutions, Third Sector, volunteering, families and active citizenship.

This second phase allowed to identify the key principles that configure PdV as an innovation element able to address the multidimensional character of disability through a holistic approach, specifically investigating its interactions on the built environment. In the light of this in-depth study, it was possible to define a series of guiding criteria used for the case studies analysis that is the object of the subsequent research phase.

3.3 PdV and Collaborative Housing: A Benchmark Analysis

The third phase took the form of a benchmark analysis conducted in order to identify a series of case studies deemed demonstrative and characteristic with respect to the design of new residential models built around the PdV interdisciplinary approach foreseen by Law 112/16. To this end, about twenty projects related to the construction of housing autonomy paths for people with disabilities have been mapped in summary sheets with the aim of identifying models and best practices at national level.

Housing experiences have been analysed whose projects have been triggered through a bottom-up approach and through the activation of co-design pathways that have involved primarily beneficiaries and their families. Particular attention has given to all projects that provided forms of accompaniment to living aimed at social inclusion, able to bring people from an individualistic conception to a collective and participatory approach to community life, developing that sense of belonging and "taking charge" of the other ("my neighbour as a resource"), which allows people to feel part of a group and therefore of a community. Data collection for the filing of case studies has been conducted through an in-depth analysis carried out with respect to specific keywords and through the implementation of specific interviews with various stakeholders involved in the experiences that are the object of the analysis. All the information was catalogued and included in a specific survey form (see Fig. 1) in which each project was examined with respect to a set of common indicators summarised in six sections: 1. main information of the intervention; 2. project objectives; 3. stakeholders involved; 4. financial resources deployed; 5. project characteristics; 6. services for accompaniment to living.

The outcome of this phase led to the creation of an atlas of best practices that, together with the previously obtained results, constitutes the basis for the development of subsequent phases envisaged by the research path.

|  | Keywords:
Inclusive living, Possible autonomies, PdV

User target:
People with physical or mental disabilities, including severe ones

Total surface of intervention: 250 sqm.
No. of accommodations: 1
No. of beds: 6 | |

PROJECT TITLE	Localisation	Year of completion
CASA MIA. Una casa accogliente per persone con disabilità	Correggio, Reggio Emilia	2020 - in progress

OBJECTIVE

"Casa Mia" is a project promoted by "Dopo di Noi" Foundation of Correggio and implemented by "Andria" Cooperative of Inhabitants that foresees the realisation of a collaborative housing project in which young people with disabilities will go to live for their free and conscious choice. The project perfectly interprets Law 112/16, better known as "Dopo di Noi", triggering a **bottom-up** approach that involved from the beginning future inhabitants and a network of different actors including institutions, Cooperatives of Inhabitants and Third Sector, assuming a strategic importance because it presents scalability features in its design, construction, in method and evaluation of the produced social impact.

STAKEHOLDERS INVOLVED

☒ Public	Amministrazione comunale di Correggio, Amministrazione regionale Emilia-Romagna, Unione Comuni Pianura Reggiana, Università di Parma
☒ Private	Donations from private and banks
☒ Private social/Third Sector organisations	"Andria" Cooperative of Inhabitants, Fondazione «Dopo di Noi – Verso Casa» Onlus, CORESS Social Cooperative, Auser Correggio

FINANCIAL RESOURCES

☒ Resources from "Dopo di Noi" Fund [Law 112/16]	€ 120.000 approx. (DGR no. 637 of 29/04/2019 - Annex B)
☒ Other financial resources	"Casa Mia" will be realised with an investment of about € 450.000, one third of which provided by the Emilia-Romagna region and another € 130,000 collected thanks to donations from private, banks or associations that have launched a solidarity race, the rest comes from capital of "Dopo di Noi" Foundation and a substantial contribution from Manodori Foundation of Reggio Emilia. The Municipality has made the area available free of charge in surface right for 33 years (after which, except for extensions, the house will become municipal asset, therefore of the community) and individual families have also contributed, each for their own part. "Casa Mia" and the community centre "Laboratorio Caleidoscopio" are owned by "Dopo di Noi" Foundation.

PROJECT CHARACTERISTICS

"Casa Mia" intends to respond concretely to the fragility: children, people with disabilities, in the belief that a neighbourhood that knows how to listen and welcome the weakest is a neighbourhood that expresses greater quality for all. The project foresees the realisation of **a home for "Dopo di Noi"** of about 250 sqm. composed of 6 bedrooms (of which one is reserved for care staff and 5 for guests), two bathrooms, a kitchen and a large living room, as well as a community centre. "Casa Mia" is developed on one floor, with accessible green areas and an adjacent parking space. The home fits within a consolidated urban and social context and connected to the main services. Adjacent there is an area intended for the construction of a second housing block that will be designed with the same criteria. The intervention is part of "Caleidoscopio" project, a new neighbourhood in an area of **urban redevelopment** of buildings disused by Correggio Municipality, in philosophical and urban-environmental continuity with the neighbourhood of Coriandoline "Le case amiche dei bambini e delle bambine" [awarded numerous prizes, including international ones, and visited by many people every year]. In addition to "Casa Mia", the project includes the urban restructuring of an area that currently houses an old rural building, later converted into a kindergarten, in which it is planned the construction of housing "Caleidoscopio" consisting of 23 homes of different types arranged around a large central park.

SERVICES FOR ACCOMPANIMENT TO LIVING

"Casa Mia" project sees the involvement of **care staff** for whom a room is provided for the overnight stay of an operator. To avoid the isolation of structures from the rest of the neighbourhood, the intention is to provide "Casa Mia" with a structure called "Laboratorio Caleidoscopio - creative armonie condivise", which will offer moments of meeting and sharing among inhabitants, the neighbourhood and the community, promoting virtuous relationships with a view to a real social inclusion. The project foresees a **community room** of about 50 sqm. connected to "Casa Mia" but accessible directly from outside, which will be managed by inhabitants and open to the whole community for the organization of events that promote the social integration with the community. "Laboratorio Caleidoscopio" will host multiple activities including theatre in homes, the market vegetables-bio km 0, cultural aperitifs, reading groups, parties and neighbourhood meetings and creative workshops.

Sources

Vita: Casa Mia. Il Dopo di Noi ha trovato casa nel laboratorio dell'abitare condiviso. Vita – La casa possibile, p. 52 (2020).

Legacoop: CASA MIA. Un ponte verso il Dopo di Noi. Legacoop informazioni, p. 15 (2019), https://www.legacoopabitanti.it, last accessed 2020/06/23.

Pavesi, A.S, Zaccaria, R., Borghi, L., Cia, G., Perego, C.: "CASA MIA": A cooperative living experience for "durante e dopo di noi", in Adolfo F. L. Baratta, C. Conti, V. Tatano, INCLUSIVE LIVING. Design for an autonomous and independent living, Anteferma Edizioni (2019).

Regione Emilia-Romagna: Scheda di sintesi del Progetto, https://www.territorio.regione.emilia-romagna.it, last accessed 2020/06/25.

Images source: "Andria" Cooperativa di Abitanti (2019).

Fig. 1. Example of benchmark analysis survey form

4 Discussion/Conclusions

Law 112/16 promotes a cultural paradigm shift for the construction of a community welfare, stimulating to redesign the relationship between institutions and citizens for the construction of a welfare "bottom-up" that knows how to structure the "personalisation" of PdV in initiating paths aimed to disincentivise institutionalisation. The recent debate reveals the need to lay the foundations for the construction of innovative co-design contexts that can generate and regenerate new trust bonds among families, services and institutions, beyond the provision of a service. These contexts can only be built starting from the observation of projects already implemented in the different territorial realities. Analysing these experiences allows to transform the innovation niches into transformation vectors of the system, building an organ of transmission between the existing right and that still to be realised and nurtured through the value of the "acted experience" [11].

From the projects analysed within the current research, which incorporate the PdV approach in the realization of new residential models, some typical aspects of new forms of collaborative housing emerge, where design approach for the construction of housing offer changes significantly. There is a shift from top-down design to shared bottom-up design, which in the specific case of the construction of housing autonomy paths for people with disabilities, means moving from the orientation of a "welfarist" type of housing offer to a capacitive approach in which housing, services to person and service-spaces connected to housing function are strongly interrelated and able to design both a single functional space and the relations of the community. According to this approach, idea of "home forever" is also modified in favour of a design "in progress", subject to continuous changes from spatial and morphological point of view so as to adapt to needs of different users over time or of users who progressively change the possibility of interacting with space. Moreover, the attention to flexibility aspects, which in the specific case of disability is a condition to be configured ex ante in the project ("embedded system"), requires the foreshadowing of new "technical modalities" both in the implementation phase and in the subsequent operation and management phases.

The framework outlined through the analysis of the activated experiences brings to attention another fundamental element: the need for closer interconnections and a more stringent and timely dialogue among various areas of intervention related to the realization of PdV, aimed at building a network capable of supporting processes for the promotion of active social inclusion [11].

Even the United Nations emphasizes that addressing the multidimensional nature of disability requires a cross-sectoral response by triggering dialogue and collaboration among a multiplicity of actors [12]. The need for a cross-sector approach is also reflected in the increasingly urgent need to set up "interdisciplinary working teams" capable of progressively intercepting roles and skills that are transversal with respect to the areas of the PdV for the implementation of multidisciplinary strategies that can change according to the type of disability and the housing context. The systemization of joint actions has to be implemented starting from involvement of families and, where possible, of the person with disabilities, starting with the identification of needs, interests, expectations and desires of the person, allowing to identify formal and informal supports able to ensure the respect of rights, the Quality of Life and the social inclusion, according to a logic of full implementation of citizenship policies. Today experience can provide with interesting hints: where Regions set up an application path concerted with local authorities and Third Sector, the structure has been built; where, on the other hand, application has been tackled without close inter-institutional concertation and without the involvement of Third Sector, everything has been more difficult.

The outlined scenario and the results emerged from first stages of the research return the need to develop a set of recommendations (procedural guidelines) for the scalability of collaborative housing models designed and built around disability. In fact, the overall picture shows a lack of homogeneity among projects and among processes for their implementation. In this process the DfA approach can become a tool for guiding and validating a design type that can incorporate innovative characters of PdV interdisciplinary approach emerged from the research carried out so far.

References

1. Rasconi, M.: Ci vuole un Progetto di Vita. Osservatorio nazionale sulle politiche sociali (2018). https://welforum.it. Accessed 21 Jan 2021
2. Law no. 104/92, Official Gazette of Italian Republic no. 39 of 17th February 1992
3. Law no. 328/00, Official Gazette of Italian Republic no. 265 of 13th Nov. 2000
4. Anffas – Associazione Nazionale Famiglie di Persone con Disabilità Intellettiva e/o Relazionale, Progetto di vita. https://www.anffas.net. Accessed 25 Jan 2021
5. Decree of President of Italian Republic of 4th October 2013, Official Gazette of Italian Republic no. 303 of 28th Dec 2013
6. Decree of President of Italian Republic 12th October 2017, Official Gazette of Italian Republic no. 289 of 12th Dec 2017
7. Law no. 112/16, Official Gazette of Italian Republic no. 146 of 24th June 2016
8. United Nations: Convention on the Rights of Persons with Disabilities (2009). https://www.un.org. Accessed 02 Feb 20212
9. Pavesi, A.S., Oberti, I., Morena, M., Cia, G.: The impact of social demand on the project: the inclusive living of vulnerable people. In: Mussinelli, E., Lauria, M., Tucci, F. (eds.) Producing Project, Maggioli, Santarcangelo di Romagna (2018)
10. World Health Organization (WHO): International Classification of Functioning, Disability and Health (ICF). https://www.who.int. Accessed 02 Feb 2021
11. Bollani, M.: Innovazione e cambiamento del sistema nella legge 112/16. Osservatorio nazionale sulle politiche sociali (2018). https://welforum.it. Accessed 26 Jan 2021
12. United Nations: Policy Brief: A Disability-Inclusive Response to COVID-19, p. 17 (2020). https://www.un.org. Accessed 27 Jan 2021

Humane Design for Inclusion

Audrey Reinert[(✉)] and David S. Ebert

Data Institute for Societal Challenges, The University of Oklahoma, Norman, OK, USA
{areinert,ebert}@ou.edu

Abstract. The positive and negative consequences of engineering and technical decisions are unequally distributed across the population. Members of marginalized groups are uniquely vulnerable to the negative consequences while having little structural power to alter policy. As a discipline, Human Factors Engineering occupies a unique position within the engineering and decision-making sciences when it comes to assessing and addressing the ramifications of intentionally and unintentionally exclusionary designs. This paper focuses on how person-centered design philosophies and human factors engineering practices can be used to design humane services that minimize negative consequences.

Keywords: Design · Discrimination · Diversity and inclusion · Inclusion by design · Humane design

1 Introduction

A designed system, product, or service reflects the values of the socio-cultural environment in which the designer resides [1, 2]. Despite our best efforts and intentions, the tools, products, services, and systems we design are imprinted with unconscious and conscious biases. Sometimes these biases are blatantly obvious, while others are more subtle, insidious, and pernicious. So, while we may not intend to hang a sign saying *Marginalized Peoples Not Welcome* on our design, the sign will still be hung [3].

Many people bristle at the insinuation that a system they are involved in or product they have designed systemically reinforces inequalities. This does not mean the system designer, stakeholders, or users actively ascribe to problematic beliefs. It simply means the system produces unequal outcomes even when decision makers hold no animus towards a marginalized group. It should be noted that we are not discussing inequities resulting from perceptual or ability deficiencies, but rather issues of race, gender, and sexuality.

As designers and engineers, it is important to identify and respond to design decisions that reinforce problematic and unequal outcomes. This chapter focuses on how person-centered design philosophies and human factors engineering practices can be used to develop humane services that minimize negative consequences.

N. L. Black et al. (Eds.): IEA 2021, LNNS 220, pp. 307–316, 2021.
https://doi.org/10.1007/978-3-030-74605-6_39

1.1 Problem Context and Definitions

On a surface level, drawing conclusions about the beliefs of a designer based on where they put a gender-neutral or all-gender restroom appears unfair. We know that designers must account for physical, economic, and process constraints. After all, floor space is limited, and installing new plumbing is expensive. However, we have all had a firsthand experience where it would have been more convenient to use an all-gender restroom. We may have been traveling with a grandparent, taking care of an infant, or enjoying the day with a gender non-conforming friend.

Is this to say that a designer holds special malice towards populations who would benefit from an all-gender restroom when one is not easily accessible? No. Rather, while the designer may not have intended to send an exclusionary message, their design communicates a degree of disinterest towards those individuals' experiences.

While we may set out with a determination to create positive change, we carry our own unique perspectives, preferences, prejudices, and beliefs with us throughout the design process. Sometimes these preferences can be trivial -i.e., preferring a specific shade of blue over another- while other times, the preference can be more profound- i.e., an absence of gender-neutral restrooms. Intentionally or not, our designs and the design processes we use to encode a particular set of cultural, social, and technical values into the finished product.

Before continuing, it is important to establish the definitions of commonly used terms. A *marginalized group* is any group that has suffered from social exclusion, the process in which individuals are blocked from -or denied full access to- various rights, opportunities, and resources that are normally available to members of a different group and which are fundamental to social integration and observance of human rights within that particular group [4]. Historical examples include, but are not limited to, indigenous groups, LGBT persons, disabled individuals, women, and religious and ethnic minorities.

Any conversation centered on how privilege influences how individuals experience a designed system rests on a solid definition of the term *privilege*. The dictionary definition is a special right, advantage, or immunity granted or available only to a person or group [5]. The term also refers to certain social advantages, benefits, or degrees of prestige and respect that an individual has by virtue of belonging to a certain social identity group. The term privilege is often used in conjunction with a modifier like white privilege, male privilege, or middle-class privilege.

A useful paradigm for conceptualizing privilege and oppression is the Matrix of Oppression [6]. Individual characteristics such as race, age, sex, gender identity and class, affect an individual in significantly different ways, in such simple cases as varying geography, socioeconomic status, or simply throughout time. This is a useful framework for understanding how one can interact with different groups, the groups one finds themselves in, and the type of social networks one forms. One of the main utilities of the matrix of oppression is the observation that one may be afforded privilege due to one aspect of their identity. Yet, they can be oppressed in a different aspect of their identity. For a more detailed discussion about privilege, we recommend the listed sources [7–14].

Finally, exclusionary design is a set of design choices that exclude or intimidate a group of individuals away from a space. Unintentionally exclusionary designs occur when a designer does not consider the *foreseeable* broader ramifications of their design choices and how design constraints can disproportionally impact users e.g., designing remote learning content dependent on a high-speed internet connection for correct functionality.

What is Humane Design: There are multiple operational definitions of Humane Design. The term is often used in the context of architectural studies [15, 16], ecological aesthetics [17], communication design [18], and According to S. Toofan [19], humane design is concerned with the livability of all constituents of the global ecosystem. similar work by Ruth Stevens et al. [20] considers humane design as one that fosters human flourishing and development. While both definitions are aspirational, they do not address issues of engrained prejudice. In this context, humane design is defined as: *A design process that recognizes and accounts for the intersecting needs and collective historical experiences of marginalized communities.*

2 Privileged Design

We have all had an interaction with a system or product which left us feeling that the system itself was not designed for our use.[1] For example, most commercially produced products -including household items, computer input devices, and pencils- are designed for right-handed individuals. With 90% of the population being right-handed, designing products for the largest customer base makes sense in economic terms [21]. However, left-handed individuals are either forced to use a system or product which could cause physical harm [22] or discomfort when used or purchase a more expensive version of the same product designed for left-handed use [23].

Admittedly, this example does seem trivial and easy to dismiss or justify. Afterall, why wouldn't you want to make a product that served most of the user population? It is because of how trivial and seemingly invisible right-handedness is that this example serves as a useful introduction to the concept privileged design. *Privileged design* can be defined as a design which systematically benefits one group of users at the expense of another group. While there are instances where left-handed individuals do have some relative advantage, most of the world is designed for right-handed individuals. Being a right-handed individual using a left-handed object is an inconvenience. Being a left-handed individual in a right-handed world is a reminder of your otherness.

2.1 Examples of Privilege in Designed Systems

The following section details two examples of privilege in designed systems: the hiring process and location tracking applications. These examples were chosen because they highlight how privilege can unconsciously be bred into a system by individual designs. Further, these examples are relevant to human factors discipline for reasons discussed in subsequent sections.

The Hiring Process: An example of how privilege functions in practice comes from a study of labor markets and hiring decisions [24]. In this study, researchers sent out

---

[1] This does not apply to instances where an individual is interacting with mobility or accessibility aids.

resumes of fictitious individuals with a randomly assigned African American- or White-sounding name in response to help-wanted ads in two major cities. The authors found that resumes with white-sounding names received %50 more callbacks than resumes with African American sounding names. A subsequent study, conducted over ten years later, demonstrated that last names may -under certain circumstances- be a weak indicator of racial identity [25].

Similar research into the prevalence of hiring discrimination suggests that non-white applicants "Whiten" their resume by concealing or downplaying racial cues to avoid hiring discrimination [26]. Different minority groups will use different techniques- such as Black applicants dropping the word Black from professional societies or Asian applicants using a nick-name- to whiten the resume. Similar research has demonstrated a similar effect among LGBT identified individuals [27, 28].

Appearing white, straight, and cisgender confers a small, subconscious benefit upon an applicant during the hiring process in the form of being offered the benefit of the doubt when their resume is reviewed. An employment gap will be viewed more positively, or a lack of relevant qualifications will be excused. This does not mean such an applicant is guaranteed to get the job. Rather, they have a greater chance on average of getting the job.

Similar issues arise in the context of internships. On a surface level, internship programs are a win-win for a company and students as internships provide students with industry connections they can leverage in the future while companies can cultivate talent pools. However, the dynamics behind internships work against first-generation college students, especially those from low-income families. It should be noted that most first-generation college students identify as Black or Hispanic [9, 10]. First-generation college students are often in financial situations that make taking an unpaid or low-paying internship untenable. It is difficult to justify taking a low paying internship, even one in your preferred field when you do not have the financial resources to support that choice. This loss of opportunity, along with a lack of professional support, can make it difficult for first-generation college students to get their foot in the door for various professions. This lack of opportunity leads to self-reinforcing or self-fulfilling cycles of unintentional exclusion.

Location Tracking and Data Privacy: Between Google Maps, Apple Maps, Facebook, and other social media services, an individual's cellular phone provides near constant information about where they have been. This location data can provide a wide range of beneficial services to users, especially those in the LGBT community. This location data can help find community-specific support networks such as transgender support groups or legal support networks when properly secured and sanitized. However, location data can out someone as a member of the community LGBT or revealing gathering spaces for LBGT individuals without their consent or knowledge. Depending on local laws and norms, this poses a non-trivial risk to individual health, safety, and employment. An example of this concern in practice was a COVID-19 tracking application deployed in South Korea, which used cell-phone data to track where the user had been so public health officials could engage in contract tracing [29]. This practice sounds neutral and even beneficial until you realize that the data produced by this app could be used to link individuals to LGBT friendly spaces.

2.2   Why Does This Happen?

To explain why privileged design occurs, we need to understand how privilege affects an individual's lived experiences. This explanation will focus on two types of privilege, socio-economic privilege and cis-gender privilege, and discuss ways each privilege manifests. Socio-economic privilege centers on one's ability to access resources such as money or capital. This type of privilege manifest as an ability to routinely afford healthy foods and regular health checkups, have access to a reliable car (or other reliable means of transportation), and the ability to afford to participate in extracurricular activities. Cis-gender privilege centers on one's gender identity and manifests as being able to use restrooms without fear of harassment and the ability to interact with the world without being targeted.

When taken as a whole, each of these privileges interact to confer a systematic advantage upon some applicants. Those students who could afford extracurricular activities are granted a slight benefit when applying for college relative to those who cannot afford to participate. This does not mean a student who does not have an extracurricular activity on the application will not get into college. Rather, since the admission system gives more weight to extracurricular activities, it means that on average the student has a lower chance of being admitted.

The simplest explanation for why privileged design occurs is that individuals are often blind to their own privileges and advantages.There are a variety of reasons why this occurs, including the just world fallacy [30] or ego-protection [31–33], which are beyond the scope of this paper.

Consequences for Human Factors: There are two main consequences of privileged design which are immediately relevant to the human factors' profession. The first consequence can be neatly summarized as a loss of user confidence in the design process. Note, this is not a discussion of an individual's ability to trust the veracity of a recommendation, the accuracy of an outcome, or the functionality of the system. Rather, it is the belief that the designers did not account for the lived experiences of a diverse user base.

Disparities hiring and employee evaluation processes [34–36] provide insight into why individuals lose confidence in a process. The hiring process *appears* fair as resumes are graded by their content by an automated system and not on human judgement. However, there have been cases where a seemingly neutral process has shown the systematic bias of the designers. A recent example of this was Amazon's recruiting system appearing to not like women because it was trained on resumes, which overwhelming skewed males [37]. This is especially troubling as companies are increasingly using AI during the hiring process.

The second consequence is a loss of engagement with the system and with the design process. This consequence has two more profound impacts. First, it creates the necessary preconditions and justification for continued exclusionary design. Individuals with an identity label feel the system works against them which leads them to stop using the system. This removes external incentives to fix the issue. Since the issue is unaddressed, more people stop coming. Further, when people don't feel their experiences or concerns are being taken seriously during the design process, they don't feel welcome. This causes them to leave the room, taking their talent and perspective with them.

3 What Can We Do?

There is no patch-fix for hundreds of years of systematic oppressions and deeply ingrained behavioral patterns. Changing these deeply engrained patterns will require constant time and effort. As a discipline, Human Factors Engineering occupies a unique position within the engineering and decision-making sciences when it comes to identifying, assessing, and addressing the ramifications of intentionally and unintentionally exclusionary designs which propagate systematic oppression. The following sections discuss the near- and long-term actions which the human factors discipline can take to minimize negative consequences.

3.1 Near Term Actions

Questions to Ask Yourself: A concrete action we as human factors engineers can take to ensure the needs and experiences of diverse and marginalized communities are represented in the near term is to use a checklist. Completing this checklist will remind a designer to elicit feedback from diverse populations.

1. Do most of my stakeholders or team members look like me or have a similar background?

   a. If so, who is not in the room, and how can we bring them into the room?

2. What barriers are preventing other group's opinions from being heard or considered?

   a. Have we put effort into deconstructing or mitigating the effects of these barriers?

3. Has the design team articulated how their personal perspective and previous experiences may blind them to alternative experiences?

Learn about the issues facing marginalized communities: All the examples used in this paper are well-documented in both academic literature and individual lived experiences. Thanks to the internet, finding first-hand accounts of people being discriminated against for a variety of reasons is now relatively simple. Learning to identify the common issues and why these issues emerge can help to avoid repeating them. Further, these experiences can help create more diverse and nuanced user personas for testing the system. This leads to the next point.

Foster diverse perspectives in the design process: There is an extensive body of literature detailing the benefits of having diverse teams [38–41]. A specific benefit of note is that diverse teams in hypercompetitive environments [42] produce a greater variety of actionable results. There are several actions human factors engineers can employ to foster diverse perspectives in the design process. The first is to acknowledge your privilege and explore how said privilege will influence your design. The second is to listen to the voices and experiences of diverse members of your design and testing team. When they mention that something about the design feels suspect, listen to them, and take their feedback seriously. Individuals from marginalized backgrounds will have a variety of different experiences based on other elements of their personal identity. As such, the experiences of one individual may differ from the experiences of others.

Learn to recognize your privilege: Talking about privilege can be a difficult exercise as it requires us to ask potentially uncomfortable questions. Acknowledging one's privilege does not mean you actively ascribe to problematic beliefs. It is a simple acknowledgment that aspects of your identity afford you certain advantages.

3.2 Long-Term Actions

Questions to Ask Yourself: As with the near-term actions discuss above; we can use a checklist to ensure the needs and experiences of diverse and marginalized communities are represented.

1. What are the hidden costs or barriers to entry which keep us from growing a more diverse talent pool and academic pipeline?

    a. What are our plans to eliminate those barriers to access or minimize their effect?

2. What is our plan to build sustainable, trust-based relationships with marginalized communities?
3. Have we built in space for the design to evolve as our understanding of the needs of our user's changes?

Rethink Recruitment and Retention: The aim of rethinking recruitment and retention is to find an answer to the question *Why do individuals with a specific identity not feel welcomed in the human factor's profession?* Answering this requires examining how we train the next generation of human factors professionals and the environment we train them in. Evidence suggests that minority students do not leave a major because they are unqualified, but because they worry about discrimination [43, 44]. As a discipline, it behooves us to develop a talent pipeline reflective of the diversity of the users we work with. Such diversity benefits the discipline by increasing the multitude of unique perspectives and experiences. This wealth of knowledge will help address issues of privilege.

Eliminate Barriers to Access: Returning to the previously mentioned example of internships, a part of rethinking the talent recruitment and retention process involves a systematic examination of potential barriers to access. Unpaid or low-paying internships represent a barrier to access, which functionally keeps low-income college students out of certain professions. A way to address this issue is to make the conscious choice to expand the recruitment and retention pool by developing connections with underserved communities and institutions. This could entail providing seed funding for HFES chapters at these schools or providing financial aid for low-income students.

Design for Inclusion: Despite our best efforts, as designers or engineers, we must accept that our designs will have unintended, potentially exclusionary consequences. One way to address this is to design systems with an expansive view of diversity. Build-in processes which allow future designers and system stakeholders to modify the system to meet current needs.

3.3 Humane Design: The Next Step

Humane Design represents the logical next step to ensure equitable human-centered design. Human-centered design aims to make systems usable and useful by focusing on the users, their needs, and requirements, and by applying human factors/ergonomics, and usability knowledge and techniques. While human-centered design does consider the context in practice, it does not offer tailored approaches which account for historical and cultural context. As such, human-centered design only considers the user solely in individual terms and not as a member of the community.

However, individual and community experiences are shaped by a variety of social and cultural forces. These social and cultural forces such as oppression, bigotry, and sexism leave a legacy which results in some groups having relative privilege over others. Privileged aspects of one's identity shape one's perceptions and definitions of concepts such as fairness. Failing to account for historical experiences of oppression shape perceptions or how current political and social events influence decision-making risks creating systems which entrap some users. Humane design builds on the successes by considering how an individual's privilege affects their ability to access and utilize the system. Such a design philosophy would consider the user's experience through a matrix of oppression. This lens would enable designers to account for subtle but specific differences in how individuals may view the system.

References

1. Forlizzi, J.: The product ecology: understanding social product use and supporting design culture. Int. J. Des. **2**(1), 11–20 (2008)
2. Lin, R., Sun, M.-X., Chang, Y.-P., Chan, Y.-C., Hsieh, Y.-C., Huang, Y.-C.: Designing 'culture' into modern product: a case study of cultural product design. In: International Conference on Usability and Internationalization, pp. 146–153. Springer, Heidelberg (2007)
3. Reinert, A.: All are welcome but terms and conditions apply. In: Advancing Diversity, Inclusion, and Social Justice Through Human Systems Engineering, p. 109. CRC Press (2019)
4. Adams, M., Blumenfeld, W.J., Castaneda, R., Hackman, H.W., Peters, M.L., Zuniga, X.: Readings for Diversity and Social Justice. Psychology Press, London (2000)
5. Definition of PRIVILEGE. https://www.merriam-webster.com/dictionary/privilege. Accessed 07 Feb 2021
6. Collins, P.H.: Black Feminist Thought: Knowledge, Consciousness, and the Politics of Empowerment. Routledge, London (2002)
7. Gewirtz, S., Ball, S.J., Bowe, R.: Parents, privilege and the education market-place. Res. Pap. Educ. **9**(1), 3–29 (1994)
8. Pattillo, M.: Black Picket Fences: Privilege and Peril among the Black Middle Class. University of Chicago Press, Chicago (2013)
9. Rose, J., Paisley, K.: White privilege in experiential education: a critical reflection. Leisure Sci. **34**(2), 136–154 (2012)
10. McIntosh, P.: White privilege and male privilege: a personal account of coming to see correspondences through work. In: Privilege and Prejudice: Twenty Years with the Invisible Knapsack, p. 7 (2020)
11. Romano, M.J.: White privilege in a white coat: how racism shaped my medical education. Ann. Fam. Med. **16**(3), 261–263 (2018)

12. Tatum, B.D.: Why Are All the Black Kids Sitting Together in the Cafeteria?. And Other Conversations About Race **64**(2) (2009)

13. Benjamin, R.: Race after technology: Abolitionist tools for the new jim code. Social Forces (2019)

14. Nixon, S.A.: The coin model of privilege and critical allyship: implications for health. BMC Public Health **19**(1), 1–13 (2019)

15. Naderi, J.R., Shin, W.-H.: Humane design for hospital landscapes: a case study in landscape architecture of a healing garden for nurses. HERD: Health Environ. Res. Des. J. **2**(1), 82–119 (2008)

16. Trocka-Leszczynska, E., Jablonska, J.: Interior architecture and humane design. In: International Conference on Universal Access in Human-Computer Interaction, pp. 390–400 (2015)

17. Verbeck, B.J., Scott Lakey, J.: Ecological aesthetics, humane design. In: Engineering Approaches to Ecosystem Restoration, pp. 398–403 (1998)

18. McNely, B.: Big data, situated people: humane approaches to communication design. Commun. Des. Q. Rev. **1**(1), 27–30 (2012)

19. Toofan, S.: Importance of humane design for sustainable landscape. Int. J. Eng. Technol. **6**(6), 508 (2014)

20. Stevens, R., Petermans, A., Vanrie, J.: Design for human flourishing: a novel design approach for a more 'Humane' architecture. Des. J. **22**(4), 391–412 (2019)

21. Papadatou-Pastou, M., et al.: Human handedness: a meta-analysis. Psychol. Bull. **146**, 481–524 (2020)

22. Coren, S.: Left-handedness and accident-related injury risk. Am. J. Public Health **79**(8), 1040–1041 (1989)

23. Dossey, L.: Left-handedness: in support of the ten-percenters. Altern. Ther. Health Med. **9**(5), 10 (2003)

24. Bertrand, M., Mullainathan, S.: Are Emily and Greg more employable than Lakisha and Jamal? a field experiment on labor market discrimination. Am. Econ. Rev. **94**(4), 991–1013 (2004)

25. Darolia, R., Koedel, C., Martorell, P., Wilson, K., Perez-Arce, F.: Race and gender effects on employer interest in job applicants: new evidence from a resume field experiment. Appl. Econ. Lett. **23**(12), 853–856 (2016)

26. Kang, S.K., DeCelles, K.A., Tilcsik, A., Jun, S.: Whitened résumés: race and self-presentation in the labor market. Adm. Sci. Q. **61**(3), 469–502 (2016)

27. Mishel, E.: Discrimination against queer women in the US workforce: a résumé audit study. Socius **2**, 2378023115621316 (2016)

28. Flage, A.: Discrimination against gays and lesbians in hiring decisions: a meta-analysis. Int. J. Manpow. **46**, 671–691 (2019)

29. Strother, J.: South Korea's coronavirus contact tracing singles out LGBTQ community. The Week (2020)

30. Crandall, C.S., Eshleman, A.: A justification-suppression model of the expression and experience of prejudice. Psychol. Bull. **129**(3), 414 (2003)

31. Lawrence, C.R.: The id, the ego, and equal protection: reckoning with unconscious racism. Stanf. Law Rev. **39**, 317–388 (1987)

32. Delgado, R.: Two ways to think about race: reflections on the id, the ego, and other reformist theories of equal protection. Geo. LJ **89**, 2279 (2000)

33. Lawrence, C., III.: Unconscious racism revisited: reflections on the impact and origins of the id, the ego, and equal protection. Conn. L. Rev. **40**, 931 (2007)

34. Morton, S.: Understanding gendered negotiations in the academic dual-career hiring process. Sociol. Perspect. **61**(5), 748–765 (2018)

35. Seymour, E.: The loss of women from science, mathematics, and engineering undergraduate majors: an explanatory account. Sci. Educ. **79**(4), 437–473 (1995)
36. Marra, R.M., Rodgers, K.A., Shen, D., Bogue, B.: Women engineering students and self-efficacy: a multi-year, multi-institution study of women engineering student self-efficacy. J. Eng. Educ. **98**(1), 27–38 (2009)
37. Turner-Lee, N., Resnick, P., Barton, G.: Algorithmic bias detection and mitigation: Best practices and policies to reduce consumer harms. Brookings. Brookings, October, vol. 25 (2019)
38. Minbaeva, D.B.: Building credible human capital analytics for organizational competitive advantage. Hum. Resour. Manag. **57**(3), 701–713 (2018)
39. Smith-Doerr, L., Alegria, S.N., Sacco, T.: How diversity matters in the US science and engineering workforce: a critical review considering integration in teams, fields, and organizational contexts. Engag. Sci. Technol. Soc. **3**, 139–153 (2017)
40. Tasheva, S., Hillman, A.J.: Integrating diversity at different levels: multilevel human capital, social capital, and demographic diversity and their implications for team effectiveness. Acad. Manag. Rev. **44**(4), 746–765 (2019)
41. Glover, J., Kim, E.: Optimal team composition: Diversity to foster implicit team incentives. Management Science (2021)
42. Hoisl, K., Gruber, M., Conti, A.: R&D team diversity and performance in hypercompetitive environments. Strate. Manag. J. **38**(7), 1455–1477 (2017)
43. Funk, C., Parker, K.: Diversity in the STEM workforce varies widely across jobs. Pew Research Center, Washington DC, January, vol. 9, p. 2018, (2018)
44. Astorne-Figari, C., Speer, J.D.: Drop out, switch majors, or persist? the contrasting gender gaps. Econ. Lett. **164**, 82–85 (2018). https://doi.org/10.1016/j.econlet.2018.01.010

Bridging the Gap: An Ergonomically Designed Motorized Tricycle Accessible by Persons with Disability Using Anthropometry and Rapid Entire Body Assessment (REBA)

Janina Elyse A. Reyes[✉], Carlo John M. Barbosa, Mon Eleazar B. Nonato, Tommy N. Olayres, and Emmerson R. Tamba

Technological Institute of the Philippines, Arlegui, Manila, Philippines
{jereyes.ie,mcjmbarbosa,mmebnonato,mtnolayres, mertamba}@tip.edu.ph

Abstract. Mass transportation offers accessibility and access to jobs for individuals, city support, health services, treatment, and places for leisure. This supports those who would like to travel. Along with others who have no other choice: over three-quarters of users of public services do not buy a vehicle and do not have a vehicle. They have to rely on public services. Mass transit provides these residents with a simple transportation service. Persons with Disabilities have difficulties in using this public transportation. Most especially those who tend to use some mobility aid for their accessibility. They also need city support in terms of acquiring needed health services. The researchers come up with an idea of resolving those difficulties they faced in accessing some public transportation in creating a schematic designed for a motorized tricycle. The researchers used some statistical tools, anthropometric measurements from the literature, and Rapid Entire Body Assessment. REBA is an ergonomic tool used to evaluate the risk of musculoskeletal disorder in a specific task and to know if there's some risk and the current design needs to improve. The researchers also used the Slovin's Formula to identify the number of respondents needed in this study. The findings of this study suggest that the current design needs to enhance and re-engineered to accommodate all commuters that use this kind of transportation.

Keywords: Motorized tricycle · Public transportation · Persons with Disabilities · Musculoskeletal disorders · Rapid Entire Body Assessment

1 Introduction

The world suffers another pandemic. An infectious disease rapidly spread across the world. According to the World Health Organization, the Severe Acute Respiratory Syndrome Coronavirus 2 (SARS-CoV-2) also known as Covid-19, an infectious disease

© The Author(s), under exclusive license to Springer Nature Switzerland AG 2021
N. L. Black et al. (Eds.): IEA 2021, LNNS 220, pp. 317–324, 2021.
https://doi.org/10.1007/978-3-030-74605-6_40

caused by a newly discovered coronavirus infected many people that might experience mild to moderate respiratory illness, and some are not required to have a special aid to recover. Millions of people died because of this virus. The infection spreads through the droplets of saliva, coughs, and sneeze of the infected person. The government strictly implemented the health protocols to stabilized the numbers of the infected.

Our health sector faces many struggles in controlling the numbers of infected, where they built a facility and testing centers. Health care facilities are funded by numerous organizations across the world to support our healthcare system. Though not only this Covid-19 needs to be cured, there also have illnesses and diseases that need to address.

People need to consult with their doctors but the problem is where they can afford to ride. Individuals who need daily check-ups. Consultations and needs to be cured. To practice social distancing, the government only allows the Public Utility Buses (PUB) to support the commuters in their daily access to go to their respective works. Some of the Public Utility Jeep (PUJ) have their routes to support the daily crisis faces by the commuters but how about those Persons with Disability (PWDs). Supposed our Public transport has a great problem in supporting all the commuters.

The tri-wheel vehicle or a tricycle is the most practical and convenient means of transportation where you can go anywhere at any time. Though it is the simplest mean of transportation, physically disabled person has difficulties in riding the tricycle especially those who use a wheelchair. The researchers think of a way where Persons with Disability (PWDs) ease their access to this most convenient means of transportation. Although there are already existing designs in some places, the researchers seize an improvement on those existing PWD-friendly tricycles to ensure the safety of the passengers.

1.1 Statement of the Problem

This research is conducted to identify the certain struggles faced by Persons with Disability in riding a tricycle. Mobility of any commuter is guaranteed to make an exceptional design for the safety of anyone especially Persons with Disability who is in need to have an accessible means of transportation where they can go and do daily check-ups in the hospital.

Moreover, this study specifically endeavors to answer the following:

1. Demographic profile of the respondents in terms of Age, Sex, mobility aid, and medical condition.
2. Common struggles faced by Persons with Disability in using the motorized tricycle.
3. How the Physically Disabled Person can ride on to the platform of the motorized tricycle?
4. Does the proposed design satisfy the ordinary commuter, Physically Disabled Person, and the tricycle driver?

1.2 Objectives of the Study

General Objectives
This study aims to provide a design of a motorized tricycle that is accessible by Persons with Disability especially those who use a wheelchair as a mobility aid and to guarantee the safety of all commuters.

Specific Objectives

- To determine the common struggles faced by the commuters riding a motorized tricycle.
- Create a schematic diagram of a designed motorized tricycle for all commuters.

2 Related Literature

Accessibility is one of the most important outcomes of the transportation system. Public transport accessibility has gained vital importance in designing and evaluating the transit system in terms of mobility and sustainability. Apart from the transport system itself, public transport accessibility has a considerable impact on life satisfaction in the form of perceived accessibility.

Public transport (PT) in urban areas has gained greater attention in recent years for improving sustainability and the quality of urban life. The economic and environmental performance of cities can be enhanced by connecting resources to destinations effectively and facilitating mass mobility [2]. Public transport can be more attractive by providing "Door to door mobility" and the development of transportation services is an important factor of social quality [3]. Sustainability of transportation, environmental conditions of an area, public health, and economic condition of residents can be raised by shifting from private transport to public transportation, walking, and cycling [4]. This shifting will happen in the condition that public transportation is widely available and accessible to the public.

Noted that negative public acceptance is the outcome of stigmatization and discrimination of the society towards individuals with disabilities, which caused reduced self-esteem and feelings of isolation among PWD. To identify the predictors of the intention (acceptance) of the public towards the involvement of PWD in physical activity, this the study explores the influence of exposure and public attitude towards disabled people [5]. Cities and their spatial management remain unadapt to all groups of users, despite the efforts of city authorities, and this leads to the exclusion of individual social groups. Failure to adapt to their needs can be observed in the architecture of buildings (limited access to the interior and limited movement inside them), public spaces (uneven pavements, absence of ramps, lifts), and the public transport system [6].

Desire to be accepted by other people is one of the basic human needs. Social acceptance by normal people towards physical activity participation for the disabled play a vital role in motivating them to get more involved in physical activity. Past researches often approach these issues from two perspectives which focus on the external and internal factors. The external factors are related to exposure which concerns with previous experience, knowledge, and contacts [7].

3   Methodology

The quantitative approach was used to evaluate the data gathered in the conducted survey and analyze the anthropometric measurements gathered from the references to create a schematic design of a motorized tricycle. Analyzing the ergonomic assessment tools such as REBA (Rapid Entire Body Assessment) would be a basis in creating a design to prevent having awkward postures that may result in musculoskeletal disorder. This design help the researchers determine how a physically Disabled Person can safely ride and simply enters the platform of the motorized tricycle. The techniques used were further discussed in this chapter (Fig. 1).

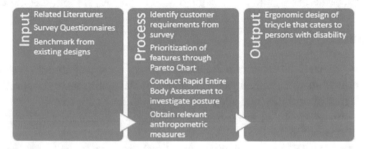

Fig. 1. Research framework

Research Locale. Region IV was split into two separate regions, Region IV-A (Calabarzon) and Region IV-B (Mimaropa). Region IV-A is formally known as Southern Tagalog Mainland. The region comprises five provinces; Cavite, Laguna, Batangas, Rizal, and Quezon. While provinces, comprising Region IV-B include Oriental Mindoro, Occidental Mindoro, Marinduque, Romblon, and Palawan. The researchers gather the number of PWDs work in the government service in Region IV. 616 PWDs worked in the government.

Data Analysis Technique. The researchers used Rapid Entire Body Assessment (REBA) as a tool for data analysis of the study. Rapid Entire Body Assessment (REBA) is a tool used to evaluate the risk of musculoskeletal disorders (MSDs) associated with specific tasks within a job. This is to identify the awkward postures of the neck, trunk, and legs that could trigger the postures of the arms and wrist. This study uses REBA to prevent having awkward postures and to serve as a basis in creating a schematic design. With the use of the REBA worksheet, the data gathered can be simply analyzed.

4   Results

The researchers conducted a survey to PWDs and tricycle drivers to identify the features that needed to be included for the proposed design of the tricycle that caters to PWDs and ordinary commutes. The features to be considered are prioritized using Pareto principle.

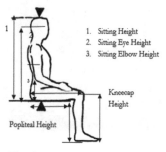

Fig. 2. Relevant anthropometric measurements for the tricycle for PWDs

Table 1. Anthropometric measurement for sitting [8].

	Measurement (cm)
Sitting height	92.00
Sitting eye height	80.00
Sitting elbow height	27.00
Popliteal height	47.00
Knee height	55.90
Buttock knee length	61.90
Buttock popliteal length	52.00

The first feature considered in improving the design of any public transportation is the spaces in the seats and inside the vehicle. Choosing the right material on the platform is also suggested. The platform must be an anti-slip perforated sheet to prevent accidents. A safety strap is attached to the wheelchair of the PWD to ensure safety while the vehicle is moving.

4.1 Selection of Dimensions

Anthropometric Measurement is a vital part of this study to know the ideal measurements in making a design. The researchers gather the required body dimensions of a person to the literature (Fig. 2). This literature has body dimensions that are needed to acquire the appropriate measurements of the schematic design of a motorized tricycle (Table 1).

Design for Proposed Motorized Vehicle

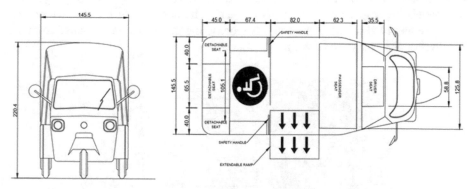

Fig. 3. Front view and top view

The figures above are the orthographic projection of the proposed design of a motorized tricycle. The dimension of the proposed design is based on the anthropometric

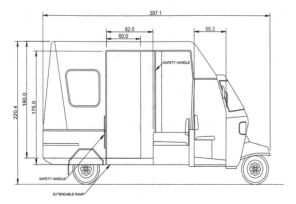

Fig. 4. Side view

measurements of both males and females. The height of the doorway is measured on the vertical measurement of a person. There are two doorways to serve as an entrance to the user; the doorway on the right side has a ramp where a wheelchair can aboard onto the platform of the motorized tricycle, while the left side serves as the entrance for the ordinary commuter. The width of the doorway for wheelchair users is measured based on the measurement of a standard wheelchair. The passenger seats where a commuter sits is measured on the sitting anthropometric measurement of both male and female (Figs. 3 and 4).

This design is a PWD-friendly vehicle where all commuters can access. This design is created to overcome the difficulties faced by PWDs especially the wheelchair user because of the narrow space of the old design tricycle.

4.2 Analysis Using Rapid Entire Body Assessment (REBA)

The posture of PWDs on the existing tricycle model versus the proposed design were evaluated using Rapid Entire Body Assessment. The positions of the neck, trunk and legs were observed to obtain the Score A score while the Score B is obtained from the positions of arm and wrist (Fig. 5).

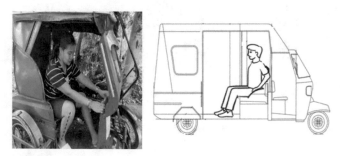

Fig. 5. Postures observed using Rapid Entire Body Assessment

Table 2. Analysis using Rapid Entire Body Assessment Worksheet

Alternatives	Existing model	Proposed model
Neck score	2	1
Trunk score	2	1
Leg score	1	1
Posture A score	3	1
Force load score	0	0
Score A	3	1
Upper arm score	3	2
Lower arm score	1	1
Wrist score	1	1
Posture score B	3	1
Coupling score	0	0
Score B	3	1
Table C score	3	1
Activity score	1	1
Final REBA score	**4**	**2**

In Table 2, Score A consists of the neck, trunk, and leg Analysis. This analysis got 3 points. Meanwhile, Score B consist of arm and wrist analysis got 3 points. The results of the sum for these two scores are 4 points based on table c scoresheet. The activity score is 1 point because the PWD had rapid changes in postures when the vehicle starts to move. Therefore, the REBA score is 4 which means the said activity is "Medium Risk. Further, Investigate and need to Change Soon."

Score A consists of the neck, trunk, and leg analysis got a score of 1. While Score B consist of arm and wrist analysis got a score of 1. The result of the sum of the two scores is 1 based on table C scoresheet. The activity score is 1 point because the PWD had rapid changes in postures when the vehicle starts to move. Therefore, the REBA score is 2 which means the said activity is "Low risk, change may be needed."

5 Conclusion and Recommendations

This chapter includes a summary of findings, conclusions, and recommendations based on the data analyzed in the previous chapter. The proposed design of the motorized tricycle using an ergonomic assessment tool was analyzed to attain the objectives of the study.

Summary of Findings. This study is conducted to identify the common struggles faced by PWDs in riding a tricycle. The data results from the ergonomic assessment tools used by the researchers prove that there are dimensions of the current tricycle design that may trigger awkward postures. By analyzing the gathered anthropometric measurements from the literature and through observation, the researchers create a schematic design of a motorized tricycle.

Conclusion. Based on the findings of the study, the current design of the motorized tricycle is not accessible for PWDs. The design can occur awkward postures that may result in musculoskeletal disorder. In proposing a design, used of ergonomic assessment tool such as REBA and anthropometric measurements of both male and female must consider. And lastly, the proposed design of a motorized tricycle is accessible for all commuters who need to have city support and continue their daily lives.

Recommendation. The researchers recommended future researchers to identify the risk of having this kind of design on roads and highways and widen their knowledge on how to enhance the proposed design. To Local Government Units (LGUs), impose this design and come up with some improvements to provide accessibility for all commuters especially PWDs. And lastly to Tricycle drivers, make use of this design of motorized tricycle to cater to all commuters and to continue to gain more profit.

References

1. LNCS Homepage. https://www.springer.com/lncs. Accessed 21 Nov 2016
2. Bok, J., Kwon, Y.: Comparable measures of accessibility to public transport using the general transit feed specification. Sustainability. **8**(3), 224–236 (2016). https://doi.org/10.3390/su8030224
3. (Jackiva) Yatskiv, I., (Budiloviča) Budilovich, E., Gromule, V.: Accessibility to Riga public transport services for transit passengers. Procedia Eng. **187**, 82–88 (2017). https://doi.org/10.1016/j.proeng.2017.04.353
4. Elias, W., Shiftan, Y.: The influence of individual's risk perception and attitudes on travel behavior. Trans. Res. Part A Policy Pract. **46**(8), 1241–1251 (2012). https://doi.org/10.1016/j.tra.2012.05.013
5. Cummins, Lau: Journal of Applied Research in Intellectual Disabilities, 23, 132–142 (2003)
6. Misiewicz, M.: Miasto przyjazne niepełnosprawnym, Niepełnosprawność – Zagadnienia, Problemy, Rozwiązania, tom II/2014, nr 11, 80−94 (2014)
7. Ferrara, K., Burns, J., Mills, H.: Public attitudes towards people with intellectual disabilities after viewing Olympic or Paralympic performance. Adapt. Phys. Act. Q. **32**(1), 19–33 (2015)
8. Del Prado-Lu, J.: Anthropometric measurement of Filipino manufacturing workers, 499–500 (2007). https://web.njit.edu/~sengupta/IE665/anthropometry%20of%20philipine%20workers.pdf

Digital Technologies as Opportunity for Facilitating Social Inclusion and Multicultural Dialogue

Alessandra Rinaldi[(⊠)] and Kiana Kianfar

Innovation in Design and Engineering Lab, Department of Architecture, University of Florence, Via della Mattonaia 8, 50121 Florence, Italy
{alessandra.rinaldi,kiana.kianfar}@unifi.it

Abstract. Cities worldwide increasingly reflect the cultural diversity of a globalized society as the result of the immigration of people with different backgrounds. The social and cultural barriers evocate an inequality access and, mostly, use of urban spaces in contemporary cities. On the other hand, at the same rhythm of these socio-cultural changes, the cities are undergoing the radical changing by information and communication technologies to improve the various aspects of the cities such as: the quality of life for their citizens, the local economy, environment, and interaction with government, in an increasingly smart perspective. These technological and socio-cultural changes can find a common and fertile ground in urban spaces with the approach of inclusive design. The development of product-service systems, that derives from the progressive growth of digital technologies, applied in the urban environment, have the potential for further studies, research and projects in terms of design for inclusion of cultural diversity. In our knowledge, there is still a lack of design solutions aimed to multicultural inclusion in urban areas through the use of digital technologies. Based on Research through Design methodological approach, the tools of human-centered design and service design thinking were used for the development of a pilot case, M-eating, an EU-funded research project. M-eating is conceived with the goal of designing digital technologies-embedded urban furniture system aimed at facilitating social inclusion, multicultural dialogue and conviviality. The present paper concludes with a holistic and new approach for design for inclusion of cultural diversity in urban space.

Keywords: Design for inclusion · Product-service system design · Social innovation · Urban design

1 Introduction

According to the Nail's recent account [1], large-scale movements of immigrants continue to transform urban areas around the world demographically, culturally, politically, and economically [2]. As Sandercock argued the need to look closely at what happens when "strangers become neighbors" [3], now after twenty years, we are faced with a

N. L. Black et al. (Eds.): IEA 2021, LNNS 220, pp. 325–333, 2021.
https://doi.org/10.1007/978-3-030-74605-6_41

growing multiculturalism in cities across the world. Public space constitutes a physical place for crystallization of certain behaviors and forms of usage that, if not carefully managed, can generate situations of tension first and then social segregation and therefore social exclusion [4]. Social exclusion refers to the inability of people to participate fully in the society in which they live [5]. It is characterized by multiple dimensions: social, economic, political and cultural [6]. The ethnic, racial, language, religion, political beliefs, values, and national history are related to the cultural identity and with reference to the cultural dimension of social exclusion, peoples' cultural identity influence their point of view regarding urban space and how they engage with it [7]. We are witness to ethnically based territorialization of the public spaces, also a changing sound landscape as a result of the voices, sounds produced by immigrants [4].

There is growing attention to the challenges and potentials of conviviality with migration diversity in urban public spaces in terms of perceptions of otherness and belonging, in different academic fields [8], that put forth the importance of social inclusion. Based on intercultural citizenship approach to diversity in society, which emphasizes the importance of face-to-face contacts between people, the public spaces have the potential to become hubs to promote this approach and they lead to diversity-awareness and diversity recognition by all citizens living in society, and to predisposition to share a common public space and thereby social inclusion [9].

In the design field, several design approaches aspire to take into account the largest range of users possible during design, such as: universal design, inclusive design and design for all [10]. All these approaches share a similar purpose, which is to include as many people as possible. "Any interaction with a product or service typically requires an iterative cycle where the user perceives, thinks, acts, where for the most part, perception requires sensory capacity, thinking requires cognitive and acting requires motor capacities" [11]. Exclusion occurs when the sensory, cognitive and motor demands for a task performance exceed the corresponding capabilities of the user [12]. So, in the context of inclusive design, the different abilities of people are mostly defined in motor, cognitive and sensory capacities and they are addressed in the design solutions in terms of accessibility and usability. It has emerged that inclusive design can be understood in multiple ways and in this article, it has been interpreted for addressing the cultural diversity in the urban spaces.

On the other hand, at the same rhythm of these socio-cultural changes, the cities are undergoing radical changes by digital technologies to improve the various aspects of the city, in an increasingly smart perspective [13]. Digital technologies have given a boost to service innovation and the way services can be delivered, as well as it is said that "the service revolution and the information revolution are two sides of the same coin [14]". Based on the recent approach to services, as processes of value co-creation [15], technology-enabled product service systems can create the opportunity to support the engagement of citizens as potential service users and to promote communication among citizens for exchanging mutually meaningful social experiences online and also in a shared physical space [13].

In this perspective the role of design, strictly related to value creation processes, confirms the recurrent definition of it as "[devising] courses of action aimed at changing existing situations into preferred ones" [16]. Urban spaces require design enabled innovative solutions, taking advantage of digital technologies, to promote social inclusion.

As we already mentioned the cultural diversity in the cities has changed the user experience and sensorial qualities of the cities, it must be perceived also in urban furnishing. In the urban studies, there are some research studies that show the use of digital technologies to create a different use of public space such as public art intervention, public display, city gamification and innovative urban services for convivial food consumption [17]. In the field of inclusion, some research has already been conducted on the use of technology, in forms of application and websites for the integration of immigrants in new countries [18]. But in our knowledge, there are no examples of urban design solutions dedicated to multicultural inclusion. From the literature review, it was highlighted that in order to promote the social inclusion of cultural diversity in urban spaces, it requires strong engagement, inclusionary and active participation by sharing user experience at 360°, to obtain social awareness and consequently a social acceptance of diversity. In this context, the research project focuses on two main questions:

- Can design and digital technologies push towards a different way of living public space and promote a shared sense of citizenship to foster the social inclusion of people with cultural diversity?

- Is it possible to support intercultural communication and to facilitate social inclusion through the design of innovative smart urban furnishings?

The general objective was to use Research Through Design [19] methodological approach for the development of a pilot case, M-eating, an EU-funded research project [20], by using the methods and tools of human-centered design and service design thinking [21], in order to contribute a holistic and new approach for design for inclusion of multicultural diversity in urban space.

M-eating is an innovative product-service that exploits the potential of digital technologies embedded in urban furniture to foster inclusion and intercultural dialogue. This pilot project aims to address the following objectives:

- providing a greater cultural diversity-awareness and diversity-recognition by enhancing them;
- fostering socialization and communication by offering shared multisensory experience and storytelling;
- increasing the motivation by inclusive engagement and active participate and collaboration;
- co-creation of values and sense of belonging to an inclusive society.

2 Methodological Approach

Based on the main research objectives to be achieved and with reference to Research Through Design methodological approach [19], the pilot project was organized in 4 phases as described in Fig. 1.

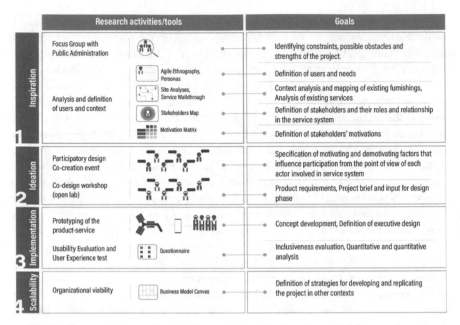

Fig. 1. Research phases showing the applied methods and correlated research goals.

The research activity for investigating the design opportunities of smart solutions aimed to an inclusive and intercultural society in urban spaces, was started by international activities of context understanding (2 focus groups and 2 world cafè) [17]. Subsequently through two co-design workshops, with the involvement of immigrants and cultural mediators, aimed to exploration ideas for the design of innovative urban furniture and services, integrating smart technologies, four Scenarios Design Orienting (DOS) have emerged [22]. M-eating developed and implemented one of the emerged DOS, which exploited the concept of culinary culture, as a catalyst for socialization and cultural exchange through the design of smart urban furnishings connected to an application. The service involves various stakeholders and users. As the public space was the application area of design, it requires the involvement of public administration as an important stakeholder. So, it has been organized a focus group with the three municipalities involved in the project, aimed at identifying constraints, possible obstacles and strengths of the project. The second stage of inspiration phase was dedicated to investigate the following aspects: i) definition of users and their needs and expectations through agile ethnography and personas; ii) context analysis through site analysis and mapping of existing furnishings; iii) analysis of existing services, close to M-eating idea, through service walkthrough tool to have a more complete vision of the context, motivations and interactions, in which these operate; iv) definition of stakeholders and their roles, motivations, and relations through the tool of stakeholder map and motivation matrix. In the ideation phase, two participatory events were conducted. The first one was a co-creation event with the involvement of end users and various stakeholders identified in the previous phase. The event aimed to investigate the motivating and demotivating factors that influence the participation according to the interests of each individual actor involved in the project (Fig. 2). During a second co-design workshop the project requirements have been identified with the collaboration of users and stakeholders, taking part in the design process (Fig. 2). Subsequently, the research team developed the concept identified in the previous phases, by the definition of executive design for the prototyping an application and an interactive urban furniture. In the last stage of implementation phase, there were conducted product-service's usability evaluation and the user experience test, using different design tools. The qualitative and quantitative analysis was carried out by two different questionnaires. Moreover, it was used the tool "Sharinc" [23], which is aimed to analysis of sharing-based services and at the assessment of the inclusiveness of services. It has allowed us an in-depth assessment of M-eating's inclusion skills (cultural and social). For the scalability phase, it was used the business model canvas tool to identify the strategies for developing and replicating the project in other contexts and for making it adaptable to existing furnishings.

Fig. 2. Two co-creation and co-design events conducted in the implementation phase.

3   Results and Discussion

Initially the project was conceived as an APP connected to urban furniture equipped with accessories for cooking. Through the APP, the event planner publishes his/her culinary event to make his/her traditional dishes known, in which other community members can participate by booking it. The event planner prepares traditional food on the location to share, in a convivial way, his/her culinary culture with the other people. During the inspiration phase some fundamental challenges have been highlighted related to this initial idea: i) how to motivate the event planner to organize an event; ii) how to face the issues concerning safety and hygiene of the cooked food in the public spaces; iii) how to involve and motivate users from different cultures to participate in the various events; iv) how to engage the supplier-type stakeholders to have an active participation in the service.

To solve the first challenge, it was introduced a reward system, i.e., the event planner obtains scores and when he/she reaches a certain score, he/she is invited to organize other events with concessions, through the rating and feedback system insertion (Fig. 3). In order to tackle the safety and hygiene issues, it was developed the idea to involve actors operating in catering sector to be part of M-eating community.

To address the third challenge, another stakeholder as a supplier type for the entertainment, named entertainment supplier has been included. The event planner will not only present the traditional dishes of a country, but will also be able to raise awareness of the cultural heritage of that place through socio-cultural activities, which are supported by the entertainment provider, such as traditional dances, arts and crafts, literature, poetry, etc.

Finally, to increase the engagements of the stakeholders, both event planner and suppliers, the service offers an innovative approach in relation to supply and demand. The event planner does not choose the offers already set up by suppliers but rather, specify the characteristic dish of his culinary culture and/or entertainment activity representative of his culture as it shows in (Fig. 3) and in this way the suppliers try to provide the best offer to be selected by the event planner.

M-eating, as the result of this action research, is a pilot prototype of a product-service system, which consists of an APP connected to specific interactive furnishings located in the urban parks. The project aimed at fostering conviviality, dialogue and communication between citizens from different cultures, by sharing both the culture of food and other socio-cultural activities. These activities allow people to know the traditions of different cultures (for example music, dance, art, crafts, poetry). Through the APP it is possible to: i) organize an event where event-planners can share the culinary traditions of their countries; ii) book the interactive urban furnishings connected to the service; iii) share topics regarding social and cultural aspects related to the same country; iv) participate in an event organized by others. M-eating furniture consists of tables and benches designed for conviviality, with embedded digital components connected to the APP. The furniture is equipped with a series of accessories (barbecue or the different accessories to store and cook food etc.) and smart locks. The furnishings are recognizable due to the presence of signage in their proximity that indicates the state of the furniture, if free or booked. (Fig. 3).

Fig. 3. M-eating application and the interactive urban furniture

The evaluation of the inclusiveness of the service, through the use of "Sharinc" tool, revealed new potential stakeholders that could be involved in the project and new development perspectives concerned: i) role of service provider, which can also be carried out by social cooperatives and multiservice; ii) matching system, which can provide by the collaboration with nonprofit associations, and which must include elderly people with digital divide.

All these observations were used to define the business model canvas and strategies for replicating the project in other contexts. A possible solution that emerged is to adapt existing furniture already installed in parks and connect those to the M-eating APP, thanks to an Internet of Things kit to be installed on this furniture. With this solution, it is possible to adapt the existing furniture to M-eating service, just buying some accessories and the IoT kit, that is: service signs to communicate the state of the furniture (reserved or not); barbecue or the different accessories to store and cook food, equipped with smart locks; junction elements to join more furniture and optimize the conviviality.

4 Conclusions

The adoption of digital technologies in the urban environment to foster inclusion and intercultural dialogue is a little tested field that introduces new paradigms in the sector of inclusive design in urban spaces. Thanks to the Research Through Design methodological approach, M-eating has been experienced with the use of human-centered design and service design thinking tools. This research project starts from a reflection on social and cultural factors that can compromise the use and access to urban spaces and services by all citizens causing exclusion and intends to make its contribution to the knowledge of inclusive design linked to the inclusion of multiculture in the urban environment. The project encourages conviviality, dialogue and communication between cultures, through sharing the culture of food and other accessory socio-cultural activities, which provide a greater cultural diversity-awareness. Through the involvement of the various stakeholders: citizens, social and cultural associations, catering operators, public administrations, urban park managers, entertainment suppliers, trade associations and third sector entities, a greater motivation for active and collaborative participation was possible. The project aims to enhance cultural diversity, by making it known in a multisensorial and rich experience, not only linked to food but also to the cultural heritage of a country, tangible and intangible, such as music, poetry, dance, art and craft. The sharing experience offered to multicultural users is created through design for storytelling, a very important tool for engaging participants.

It was highlighted the need for a systemic design approach to enhance engagement, active participation and motivation of people with cultural diversity and different stakeholders by offering a rich multisensory experience, in order to obtain the co-created values and sense of belonging to an inclusive and sustainable society.

Note: the article is the result of the joint work of the authors; the texts were written specifically by Alessandra Rinaldi par 1, 4; Kiana Kianfar par 2, 3.

Acknowledgements. We would like to thank the following for their collaboration in research: Leonardo Angelini and Mickael Reynaud, of Human Tech Institute, HES-SO; Maurizio Caon, Digital Business Center, HES-SO; Municipality of Signa, Municipality of Sesto; Municipality of Calenzano; Progetto Parco Renai; Metalco Group; Serena Barilaro, Daniele Busciantella Ricci, Gabriele Di Salvo, Mark Abou Khaled, Jingyi Wang, Shuang Liang.We thank also all the participants of the co-design workshops, who contributed in a significant manner to the development of the concepts presented in this paper.

References

1. Nail, T.: The Figure of the Migrant. Stanford University Press, California (2015)
2. Price, M., Chacko, E.: Migrants' inclusion in cities: Innovative urban policies and practices. In: Conference: UN-Habitat Conference (2012)
3. Sandercock, L.: When strangers become neighbours: managing cities of difference. Plann. Theory Pract. **1**(1), 13–30 (2000)
4. Lauria, A., Vessella, L., Romagnoli, M.: Public space and life in the city. Six challenges for a society in transformation. Journal Valori e valutazioni (24), 131–149 (2020).
5. van Bergen, A.P., van Loon, A., de Wit, M.A., Hoff, S.J., Wolf, J.R., van Hemert, A.M.: Evaluating the cross-cultural validity of the Dutch version of the Social Exclusion Index for Health Surveys (SEI-HS): a mixed methods study. PLOS ONE **14**(11), 1–15 (2019)
6. Mathieson, J., Popay, J., Enoch, E., Escorel, S., Hernandez, M., Johnston, H., Rispel, L.: Social Exclusion Meaning, measurement and experience and links to health inequalities. A review of literature. WHO Social Exclusion Knowledge Network Background Paper 1 (2008)
7. Egerer, M., Ordóñez, C., Lin, B.B., Kendal, D.: Multicultural gardeners and park users benefit from and attach diverse values to urban nature spaces. Urban Forestry Urban Greening **46**, 126445 (2019)
8. Ganji, F., Rishbeth, C.: Conviviality by design: the socio-spatial qualities of spaces of intercultural urban encounters. URBAN DESIGN Int. **25**, 215–234 (2020)
9. Zapata-Barrero, R.: Republicanism, diversity and public space in contemporary political theory: the normative basis of intercultural citizenship. Citizenship Stud. **24**(8), 1066–1083 (2020)
10. Heylighen, A., Van der Linden, V., Van Steenwinkel, I.: Ten questions concerning inclusive design of the built environment. Build. Environ. **114**, 507–517 (2017)
11. Clarkson, P.J., Coleman, R., Hosking, I., Waller, S.: Inclusive Design Toolkit. Engineering Design Centre. University of Cambridge, Cambridge (2007)
12. Clarkson, P.J., Coleman, R.: History of inclusive design in the UK. Appl. Ergonomics **46**, 235–247 (2015)
13. Ismagilova, E., Hughes, L., Dwivedi, Y.K., Raman, K.R.: Smart cities: advances in research— an information systems perspective. Int. J. Inf. Manage. **47**, 88–100 (2019)
14. Ardolino, M., Saccani, N., Gaiardelli, P., Rapaccini, M.: Exploring the key enabling role of digital technologies for PSS offerings. Procedia CIRP **47**, 561–566 (2016)
15. Morelli, N., De Götzen, A., Simeone, L.: Service Design Capabilities. Springer Nature, Cham (2021)
16. Tosoni, I.: Innovation Capacity and the City: The Enabling Role of Design. Springer Nature, Cham (2019)
17. Rinaldi, A., Caon, M., Abou Khaled, O., Mugellini, E.: Designing urban smart furniture for facilitating migrants' integration: the co-design workshop as approach for supporting inclusive design. In: Congress of the International Ergonomics Association, pp. 461–470. Springer, Cham (2018)
18. Ntioudis, D., Kamateri, E., Meditskos, G., Karakostas, A., Huber, F., Bratska, R., Kompatsiaris, I.: Immerse: a personalized system addressing the challenges of migrant integration. In: 2020 IEEE International Conference on Multimedia & Expo Workshops (ICMEW), pp. 1–6. IEEE Computer Society, London (2020)
19. Zimmerman, J., Forlizzi, J.: Research Through Design in HCI. In: Olson J., Kellogg W. (eds) Ways of Knowing in HCI. Springer, New York (2014)
20. DESIGNSCAPES, Design-enabled Innovation in Urban Environment. https://designscapes.eu/funded-initiatives/. Accessed 15 Nov 2020

21. Stickdorn, M., Hormess, M.E., Lawrence, A., Schneider, J.: This is service design doing: applying service design thinking in the real world. O'Reilly Media, Inc., Canada (2018)
22. Rinaldi, A., Angelini, L., Abou Khaled, O., Mugellini, E., Caon, M.: Codesign of public spaces for intercultural communication, diversity and inclusion. In: International Conference on Applied Human Factors and Ergonomics, pp. 186–195. Springer, Cham (2019)
23. Busciantella Ricci, D., Dong, H., Rinaldi, A., Tosi, F.: Inclusion in Sharing-Based Services (I-SBS): An Analytical Tool. In: International Conference on Applied Human Factors and Ergonomics, pp. 207–219. Springer, Cham (2017)

Type to Be Seen and Type to Be Read

Elisabete Rolo[✉]

CIAUD, Lisbon School of Architecture, Universidade de Lisboa, Rua Sá Nogueira, Pólo Universitário do Alto da Ajuda, 1349-063 Lisbon, Portugal
erolo@fa.ulisboa.pt

Abstract. This research is based on bibliographic research and critical literature, and intends to address, in a didactic way, the graphic problem of choosing typography – an essential element for the reproduction of text and thought. To make this choice, one must take into account the purpose of the graphic object and the text it conveys, that is, one must pay attention to whether the text is intended to be "read" or to be "seen". Here, we essentially address the problem of texts to be read and, consequently, the concepts of legibility and readability. There are multiple factors to consider in order to compose a readable text. On one hand, typographic extrinsic factors (macro- and micro-typography), on the other hand, typographic intrinsic factors, such as upper-case or lower-case, proportions (x-height and its relation to ascenders and descenders), serif or sans serif, and also thickness and contrast. In this context it is also important to focus the fonts with optical sizes, which consist in the digital recovery of a resource from the manual typesetting era, when metal typefaces were crafted by punchcutters, with slight drawing variations intended to achieve the ideal perception, balance and expressivity of type.

Keywords: Graphic design · Typography · Reading · Readability · Optical sizes

1 Introduction: Display Type and Text Type

"No one would use the same shoes to go dancing, run a mile, climb the north face of the Eiger, and walk to the office (...). This also applies to type. Sometimes the letters have to work hard to get across straight facts or numbers, or they may need to dress up the words a little to make them seem more pleasant, more comfortable, or simply prettier." (Spiekermann, E., Ginger, E.M., 1993, p. 41)

The first aspect to consider when choosing a typeface is that "typography is the visible face of language" (Lupton 2006) and that "typography exists to honour content" (Bringhurst 2004 [1992], p. 17). Besides, it is also necessary to take into account the purpose of the graphic object and the text it conveys, that is, it should be taken into consideration whether the text is intended to be "read" or to be "seen" (Unger 2018).

Regarding this, we must distinguish between the display "situations" or text "situations". A **"display situation"** refers to one in which the text is short comprising one word, expression or isolated sentence. For example, texts on magazine covers, posters, information signs, logotypes, headings and subheadings in publications, among so many

N. L. Black et al. (Eds.): IEA 2021, LNNS 220, pp. 334–341, 2021.
https://doi.org/10.1007/978-3-030-74605-6_42

others. A **"text situation"** is one in which the text appears sequentially and extensively: words within sentences, within paragraphs. For example, a book flowing text (excluding headings) or the text of a newspaper or magazine article.

A **"display typeface"** is one whose design is not specifically intended to work in continuous reading situations but manages to be legible in small amounts of text (display situations). In text situations it is barely or not at all legible. A **"text typeface"** is one whose design is optimized to be readable in continuous conditions. Therefore, it is readable in text situations and also in display situations (Moreira, n.d., pp. 9–11). Texts to be "seen" are usually composed in larger sizes and smaller quantities, so the readability issue takes on secondary importance. Texts to be "read" are usually composed in smaller sizes and greater quantity and should aim to "induce a state of energetic repose, which is the ideal condition for reading", and also invite the reader to read, reveal the tenor and meaning of the text, and clarify its structure and order. (Bringhurst 2004 [1992], p. 24).

2 How Do We Read?

2.1 Word Recognition

In the context of choosing typefaces, it is important to clarify how we recognize words, a subject which, here, we can only approach very superficially.

According to Larson (2018) – a Microsoft's recognized researcher – there are three word recognition models: the "word shape" model, the "Serial Letter Recognition" model, and the "Parallel Letter Recognition" model.

In the "word shape" model, we bear in mind the "word superiority effect" phenomenon, which claims that we better recognize letters within words than isolated letters or letters presented in groups that do not form words. According to this model, lower-case text is more readable than upper-case text, since lower-case text produces patterns of ascending, descending and neutral characters. On the contrary, in the upper-case text, all characters have the same size, which makes them more difficult to read.

Nowadays, the most widely accepted model for explaining the reading process is the "Parallel Letter Recognition" model, which states that the letters in a word are recognized simultaneously and that information about these letters is used to recognize words.

In front of the visual stimulus of a word, the first processing step is to recognize the main components of the individual letters, such as horizontal lines, diagonals, and curves. These components are then sent to the letter detection level, where each one of the stimulus-word letters is recognized simultaneously. The letter detection level then activates the word detection level, and each of the recognized letters activates a set of possible words, according to its respective position. For example, considering the English word "WORK", the letter "W" will activate all words with "W" in the first position (WORD and WORK), the "O" will activate all words with "O" in the second position (FORK, WORD and WORK) and so on. While FORK and WORD activate three of the four letters, WORK activates more, because it has all four letters activated and is, therefore, the recognized word.

Larson considers that this model's evidence is attested by the most recent literature on eye movements, which has been developed partly due to the great technological evolution that provides fast eye trackers and increasingly powerful computers (Fig. 1).

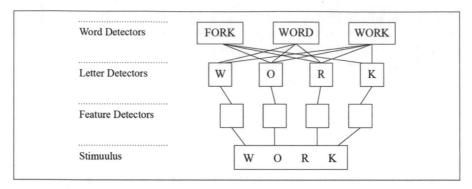

Fig. 1. Parallel letter recognition.(Larson 2018).

2.2 The Reading Process

As Larson states, it has long been known that when we read, our eyes do not move smoothly across the page, but rather through discrete jumps from word to word. We focus on one word for a brief period of time, approximately 200–250 ms, and then make a ballistic movement to another word. These movements are called saccadic movements and usually take 20–35 ms. Most saccadic movements are forward directed (and comprise about 7 to 9 letters), but 10–15% of these are regressive movements. The average length of saccadic movements and fixation times vary by language (Larson 2018). With average text size, such as that used for books, a saccadic movement holds about 5–10 letters, or about 1–2 words in English.

Information is absorbed only during the fixation period, and from up to 10 letters, only 3–4 are sharply focused during the fixation period: the rest is perceived by the eye indistinctly and through context. If the meaning of the text is not clear, the eye jumps back in saccadic regression movements to check again what has already been "read" (Hochuli 2009, p. 8).

Most readers are completely unaware of the frequency of regressive movements during reading. The location of fixation is not random, it never occurs between words and usually occurs in the first half of a word. Not all words are fixated; short words and especially functional words are often ignored. Figure 2 shows a diagram of the fixation points of a typical reader.

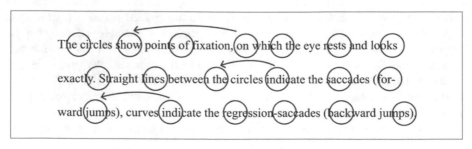

Fig. 2. Saccadic eye movements. (Hochuli 2009, p. 9).

The more experienced the reader is, the shorter the fixation periods and the larger the saccadic movements. If these become too long and the fixation periods too short – that is, when one reads too fast – the text is "guessed". In this case, at least with simple content, the redundancy of language makes comprehension easier, since word pictures that have already been stored in the reader's visual memory are read more quickly than unfamiliar ones (Hochuli 2009, p. 8).

2.3 Legibility and Readability

In this process of effective apprehension of words and textual meaning, it is important to clarify the concepts of legibility and readability.

As David Jury states, "Legibility is the degree to which individual letters can be distinguished from each other" (Jury 2004, p. 58), and readability is related to the ability of reading. "Good typography encourages the desire to read and reduces the effort required to comprehend. Comprehension is the reason for all reading" (Jury 2004, p. 64). Walter Tracy adds that "The term [readability] describes the quality of visual comfort – an important requirement in the comprehension of long stretches of text (…)" (Tracy 1986, p. 31). For all this, legibility is more related to the recognition of characters, individually or in small groups, and readability is related to the process of continuous reading.

As Gerard Unger (2007, p. 149) declares, legibility and readability do not depend only on the shapes of typography. They depend to a large extent on the spaces between letters and words, the spaces within letters, the spaces between lines and the space around the text as a whole. In other words, readability is dependent on the principle of continuity, which refers that to correctly perceive a written message composed by several signs in sequence (words, sentences, paragraphs) their information units (letters, syllables, words, lines of text) must share the same characteristics (type, colour, size, spacing, etc.), without breaks in the text texture.

This idea comes in line with the idea that readability depends on the structure of the graphic object, which should aim for a kind of transparency, as said by Beatrice Warde in the essay "The Cristal Goblet" (Warde 1995 [1955]) and by Robert Bringhurst (2004, p. 17) when he affirms that "typography with anything to say (...) aspires to a kind of statuesque transparency".

Over the more than 500 years of its existence, the typesetting process has developed and refined rules and conventions that determine the legibility and readability of printed communication.

3 Intrinsic Typographic Factors that Determine Readability

3.1 Upper and Lower-Case

One of the aspects that first determine the readability of a text is whether it is set in upper or lower-case, as previously mentioned concerning the word recognition and reading processes. Texts composed in upper and lower-case favour the "word superiority effect", as they provide more detail to each character, making it easier and faster to distinguish them. On the other hand, upper-case letters have all the same height, which makes it more difficult to differentiate them.

3.2 X-Height

X-height (Fig. 3) is the distance between the baseline and the height of the lower-case letters, corresponding to the height of the lower-case "x" of each font. It is a highly variable measurement, even in fonts with the same body size, and has a great influence on legibility and readability. The height of a given body size is always the same, regardless of the typeface, but the x-height is always different, and the larger it is, the smaller the ascenders and descenders (and vice-versa).

Fig. 3. Comparison between two typefaces whose x-heights are very different: Centaur (with small x-height) and Swift (with large x-height). (Author, 2021)

A large x-height typeface looks larger than a small x-height typeface and, therefore, a large x-height allows smaller body and leading spacing, saving space and giving the feeling that the font size is large. (This is why the majority of publications with narrow columns – newspapers and magazines, for example – tend to use large x-height type) (Moreira s.d., Jury 2004, p. 58). However, this solution is not always the best. When x-height is large, the letter ascenders and descenders may become too small and even unreadable, especially on small bodies (Haley 2020). If a type has a small x-height, it means that the ascenders and descenders are large. And because they are large, the degree to which a letter, word, or sequence of words can be decoded is faster, as ascenders and descenders help to better differentiate characters. As reading in situations of large column width (books, for example) tends to be tiring, the existence of large ascenders and descenders favours readability (Moreira, n.d.).

It should also be noted that when combining different fonts, choosing those with similar x-heights, generally creates a feeling of greater typographic harmony.

3.3 Serifs

Readability and legibility in serif and sans serif typefaces is an old debate and there is no definitive answer to which of the two categories is more readable. It depends on many factors, such as the font design, the configuration of the text, the amount of text, among others.

When dealing with short texts, if we consider isolated words, studies show that serif type slows down reading a little more than sans-serif type because it has more detail, and the shapes take longer to be perceived. In other words, sans serif type is more legible because it is simpler.

In the case of continuous reading text, it is generally agreed that serifs improve readability because they provide more detail for word recognition and also because serifs allow words and lines to better flow. The structure of sans serif text is looser and seems to favour vertical movements through the text, which interferes with the horizontal line structure (Unger 2007, p. 166; Jury 2004, p. 74). The serifs, being mostly horizontal, counterbalance the vertical lines and guide the reader through the lines of text. As Gerard Unger states, "Serifs seem to act as a kind of attention safety net" (Unger 2007, p. 166).

3.4 Thickness and Contrast

Another aspect that has a lot of influence on the legibility and readability of a typeface is its thickness. Originally, typefaces had only two design variants – regular and italic – but in the 20th century bold versions were added, and after the second half of the 20th century, a wide range of thicknesses, such as ultralight, light, thin, medium, semi-bold, heavy and extrabold[1]. Concerning readability, studies in typography indicate that the normal (or regular) version is the most suitable. However, all the other variants are useful because they enable to differentiate and establish hierarchies between different text categories, which is extremely useful in complex editorial objects, such as newspapers.

Closely related to thickness is contrast – a decisive feature in typeface design, which concerns the relationship between the thinner and thicker parts of a typeface. The greater the difference between thin and thick stems, the greater the contrast. The smaller the difference, the lower the contrast.

Very contrasted types favour neither legibility nor readability, as the very thin strokes tend to disappear and cause the text area to produce a kind of vibration that inhibits comfortable reading. Types with little or no contrast produce a very homogeneous and uniform text block that causes a certain monotony, which is also not inviting to reading. Types with medium contrast produce more balanced text blocks that combine a certain rhythm with some homogeneity, which makes them the most suitable for readability.

3.5 Optical Sizes

In the metal and wood type era, typefaces were designed specifically for the size at which they were going to be used, and each body size was adapted, by the punchcutter, with slight variations in weight, contrast and proportions, in order to maintain its legibility and character. Generally, fonts designed for small sizes had lower contrast, greater width and x-height, and wider spacing, to confer legibility. Versions designed for larger sizes had finer details, greater stroke contrast and less white space inside and outside the characters. All this to achieve the most pleasing alternation of black and white (Unger 2007, p. 96).

With the advent of phototypesetting and, later, the computer (with Postscript fonts), typefaces could be scaled freely and the process of individually casting typefaces was abandoned. This originated a loss in typographic quality, with display type looking too fragile or too ornate at small sizes and text type looking clunky and uninteresting when presented at larger sizes. (Peters 2014; Optical sizes, n.d.; Condensed 2017).

To address this problem, type design has recently gone back to the solution of the past and returned to the practice of optical size mastering, with some type families now

---

[1] And alongside these, there were also width variations, with fonts ultra-condensed, condensed, extended, etc.

offering specific versions for each type of use according to the body sizes in which they are to be used (Peters 2014). These are called Opticals or optically sized fonts. Generally, these fonts include text, display, intermediate and caption versions. And, although the nomenclature varies, in summary we can say that there are six main categories: **Caption:** for legibility at between 6 and 8 points; **Small text:** for text at small sizes of 8 to 11 points; **Body text:** for the ideal reading sizes of 11 to 14 points; **Subhead:** for setting short phrases between 14 to 24 points; **Display:** for setting large headings above 24 points; **Poster:** for the text in posters above 36 point. (Optical Sizes, s.d.).

4 Conclusion

With this study we have compiled information about typography and readability, and present it in a clear and simple manner, with a useful didactic perspective.

First of all, we have distinguished display and text situations and types, which determine the needs to be taken into account when choosing a typeface. Next, we tried to address the processes of word recognition and reading, which are the functional basis for legibility and readability. Finally, we focused on the intrinsic factors of typography that restrain or favour readability. Aspects such as case, x-height, serifs, thickness and contrast are the main topics that we can observe in a typeface and that determine reading efficiency. In this context, it is important to mention typefaces with optical sizes that allow suitable type for each body size, in order to achieve clarity, balance and also hierarchy in the communication object, and which should therefore be preferred by graphic designers.

References

Ahrens, T., Mugikura, A.: Size-specific adjustments to type designs. https://justanotherfoundry. com/size-specific-adjustments-to-type-designs

Bringhurst, R.: The Elements of Typographic Style. Hartley & Marks Publishers, Point Roberts (2004)

Condensed, B.: Inside the fonts: optical sizes (2017). https://www.typenetwork.com/news/article/ inside-the-fonts-optical-sizes

Haley, A.: Fontology: X-Height (2020). https://www.fonts.com/content/learning/fontology/level-1/type-anatomy/x-height

Hochuli, J.: Detail in Typography. Hyphen Press, London (2009)

Jury, D.: About Face: Reviving the Rules of Typography. Rotovision, London (2004)

Larson, K.: The science of word recognition (2018). https://docs.microsoft.com/en-us/typography/ develop/word-recognition

Lupton, E.: Pensar com Tipos. Cosac Naify, São Paulo (2006)

Moreira, L.: Tipografia, a face visível da linguagem. Instituto Politécnico de Tomar, Tomar (s.d.)

Nix, C.: What is optical sizing and how can it help your brand? (2019). https://www.monotype. com/resources/articles/what-is-optical-sizing-and-how-can-it-help-your-brand

Spiekermann, E., Ginger, E.M.: Stop Stealing Sheep & find out how type works. Adobre Press, Mountain View California (1993)

Rolo, E.: White space in editorial design. In: Rebelo, F., Soares, M. (eds.) Advances in Ergonomics in Design. AHFE 2017. Advances in Intelligent Systems and Computing, vol. 588. Springer, Cham (2017)

Strizver, I.: TypeTalk: Optical and Size-specific Fonts (2016). https://creativepro.com/typetalk-optical-and-size-specific-fonts

Strizver, I.: Serif vs. Sans for Text in Print. https://www.fonts.com/content/learning/fontology/level-1/type-anatomy/serif-vs-sans-for-text-in-print (s.d.)

Tracy, W.: Letters of Credit: A View of Type Design. David R. Godine Publisher, Boston (1986)

Unger, G.: While you are Reading. Mark Batty Publisher, New York (2007)

Unger, G.: Theory of Type Design. NAI Publishers, Rotterdam (2018)

Warde, B.: The crystal gobelet or printing shoul be invisible. In Typographers on Type, pp. 73–77. W.W. Norton & Company, New York and London (1995)

Usability Evaluations Focused on Children with Down Syndrome: A Systematic Literature Review

Lizie Sancho Nascimento[1,2](✉) 🆔, Laura Bezerra Martins[1] 🆔, Nelson Zagalo[2] 🆔, and Ana Margarida Pisco Almeida[2] 🆔

[1] Federal University of Pernambuco, Recife, PE 50670-901, Brazil
`laura.martins@ufpe.br`
[2] University of Aveiro, 3810-193 Aveiro, Portugal
`{nzagalo,marga}@ua.pt`

Abstract. A previous literature review indicated the lack of studies about how to develop accessible games for children with Down syndrome and evaluate their interfaces. With that in mind, the research team decided to do a new one focusing only on finding usability methods that can be applied with this specific audience regarding their safety and their conditions. Therefore, this analysis used the Cochrane methodology organized into: research question, location and selection of the study, critical evaluation of the studies, data analysis, and content analysis. In total, 22 articles were selected from Scopus and Web of Science, in which the observational analysis method was the most used one, maybe because it does not require the user to communicate verbally a lot nor to remember his entire journey. Other methods found were heuristic evaluation, interview, focus group, and questionnaires. Some initiatives must be mentioned such as the research of Lazar et al. which used the assistance of an illustrator to help the volunteers in expressing their ideas during a workshop, and finally, the review permitted to create a list of precautions and recommendations before and during a test with children with Trisomy 21.

Keywords: Down syndrome · Usability evaluation · Literature review · Intellectual disability · User research

1 Introduction

Although the user research field and its methods are widespread in the literature, there are some challenges and precautions that should be taken care of when dealing with children, like how to motivate parents and kids to participate of the experience, how to communicate with them, how to avoid stress and develop engaging activities.

Joyce [1], Barendregt and Bekker [2], and Hanna, Risden and Alexander [3] researches present some guidelines of how to conduct a usability test with children, but since the last literature review pointed the lack of studies that considered the Trisomy 21 children difficulties and frameworks of how to develop accessible games [4],

© The Author(s), under exclusive license to Springer Nature Switzerland AG 2021
N. L. Black et al. (Eds.): IEA 2021, LNNS 220, pp. 342–349, 2021.
https://doi.org/10.1007/978-3-030-74605-6_43

this new review intends to be more specific and find game user research methods that can be applied with them and can grant their safety. In other words, the question from the review of 2020 wanted to find usability and accessibility guidelines, game development frameworks and game balance. This new one wants to search only the first part of the project, which permits to shorten the number of keywords and also an in-depth study.

2 Methodology

The systematic literature review is a method to search what has been done in the research field, which difficulties were found and questions that couldn't be answered, to find references that can contribute to future studies, for example. To sum up, it intends to update the state of the art of the object.

In this way, this review will follow the Cochrane Method [5] organized into a research question, location and selection of the study, critical evaluation of the studies, data analysis, and content analysis.

The first step, as said, is to establish the question that should be addressed. For that matter, Cochrane [5] advises to consider the ethical aspects and the feasibility of the research, define a clear aim and scope and certify with previous studies or with the target audience that it is the right question to ask. Then, the research team should extract the main keywords and the combinations from the question established, decide which scientific databases use and the criteria to select or dismiss an article, which data will be collected and evaluated, after that, a qualitative or quantitative analysis is carried out considering the research problem.

3 Results

3.1 Research Question

The research question established was: what are the usability evaluations that can be applied with children with Down syndrome?

3.2 Location and Selection of the Study

After defining the research question, the keywords used in the review were extracted from it and combined among themselves. Moreover, the terms selected were "Down syndrome", its synonyms, and "usability". Hence, the search sentence established was: "Down syndrome" or "Trisomy 21" or "intellectual disability" or "cognitive disability" or "mental disability" and "usability".

Since to search on the Google Scholar platform seemed harder than the other scientific databases due to the small keyword field, for this new one, Scopus and Web of Science were chosen, also because of their interdisciplinary aspect and broad content [6, 7].

3.3 Inclusion and Exclusion Criteria

The second step was to define the criteria to select or exclude a publication from the results. Since, in Scopus, you have to scan the sentence first and then, filter the results, it was decided not to apply any filter at first, because it had only 109 outcomes. As for the second database, Web of Science, besides the keywords selected, a period time (2009–2019) was also defined.

With the first results, an inclusion criterion was established to select the ones that could answer the research question. Hence, the researchers started reading the titles, abstracts, keywords, conclusions, to check the availability to download the articles, analyze their relationship with digital technologies and language (only written in Portuguese, English, or Spanish).

Therefore, the 1st filter considered the following aspects:

- Title, abstract, keywords, and conclusions: must be related to the search question.
- Access to the research: only the ones with full access and free of charge.
- Should be related to digital technologies (RV, AR, websites, mobile devices, computer).
- Should be a scientific paper, not only an abstract.
- Languages: only Portuguese, English, and Spanish.

After the 1st screening, 43 articles from Scopus and 22 from Web of science were selected to the 2nd filter, in which only the ones that the research was submitted to people with Trisomy 21 and had the methodology described in detail were chosen. Moreover, the duplicated ones were excluded, resulting in 22 articles from Scopus and Web of Science (view Fig. 1). Works that were duplicated or were an extension of a previous study without any new contribution were excluded.

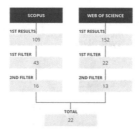

Fig. 1. Number of publications found per database

3.4 Data Collection and Analysis

To analyze the data gathered from the 22 articles selected, a spreadsheet was created with the following columns: title, brief description, keywords, publisher, country of origin, institution, year, user profile, age, number of volunteers, methods used, time per session, the purpose of the research.

The keywords were traced to help future literature reviews, in this way, the most used ones were: Down syndrome (12), usability (10), interaction (8), game (5), disabilities (5), and accessibility (5). The publisher column was used to identify academic events or journals that were interested in the theme. Universal Access in the Information Society, International Conference on Universal Access in Human-Computer Interaction, and International Conference on Human Computer Interaction were the publishers with the largest number of publications.

As for the country of origin, Spain, Mexico, Brazil, and Malaysia were responsible for 56% of the 22 articles, and it is possible to notice on Fig. 2 that the interest for this subject is growing year by year.

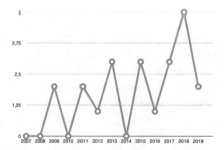

Fig. 2. Number of publications per year from 2007 to 2019

About the other data collected, like the time per session, they will be presented on the Discussion topic.

4   Discussion

About the methods found, the most applied one was observational analysis, which consists of collecting data through the observation of user's behaviors and attitudes, as stated by Sangin [8]. The reason why researchers may have chosen this type of assessment resides on its advantage of not depending on the participant's interpretation, communication, and memory. As some works described, people with Trisomy 21 can have memory deficits, difficulty in verbal communication, and the understanding of abstract concepts [9, 10]. Fact explained in the article by Rico-Olarte et al. [11] in which, they explain the difficulty of children in answering questions that involve subjective factors, such as the feelings experienced. Among the limitations of the observational method, it is important to note that it may be influenced by the researcher's perspective due to his responsibility in interpreting the data collected.

The techniques found in these 16 articles, which used the aforementioned method, ranged from behavioral studies through physiological analysis (eye-tracking and facial expression, for example) to performance during use. For example, the article by Santos et al. [12] used the AffeDex SDK to map facial expressions indicating user involvement, while the Macedo et al. article [13] created a list of behavioral indicators to assess the fun and engagement of children with Down syndrome.

Regarding the choice of how to conduct the tests, Alfredo et al. [14] and Brown et al. [15] opted for co-discovery and peer-tutoring, the former refers to an assessment carried out in pairs, where the participants must initially explore the system and then seek to fulfill the established objectives. While peer-tutoring is a technique in which a user, after becoming experienced in performing the tasks should assist a novice.

For the authors, those techniques aim both to avoid negative thoughts to those submitted to the tests, since they are not alone, as well as to analyze the communication established between peers, through a less embarrassing version of the think-aloud. Although they highlight these advantages, it was not reported in the articles the difficulties of dealing with children, considering that, Joyce [1] explains that age influences the engagement in a team activity, for example, the person who is watching instead of interacting with the interface can get bored.

Usability assessments can have predefined tasks to be performed by volunteers or not. The informal walkthrough is a usability test that does not establish an activity or an objective to be achieved, it aims to understand how the user navigates through the system and how intuitive its interface is [16, 17]. Ramli and Zaman [18] advise that the researcher should draw up a list of all the features before starting. Cortés et al. [19], one of the 4 articles to apply this technique, justify its use considering that people with Trisomy 21, generally, have a reduced short-term memory, and therefore, they can forget what they should do during the activity.

In addition to observational studies, eye-tracking is a hardware that analyzes the user's gaze, so it allows identifying the size of the pupil, where the gaze is directed, which are their points of interest, and the study of this information serves as indicative of the "difficulty of the task, attention, fatigue, mental activity, and intense emotions" [18, p. 31]. Jennett et al. [21] used this system to measure the player's immersion and concluded that, when the player is immersed, the dispersion of his gaze is less.

Considering the results, only the work of Alonso-Virgós et al. [22] used this device, but the researchers opted to use a notebook, due to the possibility of manipulating the screen to adjust to the user's eyes and taking into account the difficulty of that they can have in maintaining the same position throughout the assessment. The body position influences the calibration of the system, therefore, the importance of hardware capable of adapting to adverse conditions.

In this sense, the Tobii brand created an eye-tracker in the form of glasses that allows mobility during the tests, but for those who wear glasses, they need to buy an additional lens to plug, since the device cannot be used on top of it, resulting in additional cost. When dealing with children with Down syndrome, this factor is essential considering that 60 to 70% of them already wear glasses before the age of 7 [23]. Moreover, biometric assessments such as eye-tracking itself are expensive because of the low demand.

Regarding the evaluations that measure the participant's performance (task performance), the tasks are established by the researcher before they are applied, as well as the metrics, which will serve as a basis for the collection and quantitative analysis of the results. The time of completion of the activity, the number of errors and successes, percentage of users who completed the task optimally are some of the metrics. This type of technique can identify usability problems that can be improved, but it does not investigate subjective aspects such as the feeling about the experience during the interaction or motivations. Among the outcomes, 7 publications used that technique.

About the interviews and questionnaires, the approach of Alonso-Virgós [22] seemed interesting due to the participation of health professionals in the creation and approval of the questionnaire to be submitted to people with Down syndrome. In this way, their recommendations are relevant to have greater participation and collection of feedback. In short, one should avoid long sentences and abstract concepts, reduce the number of responses and illustrate what you want to communicate.

Finally, most articles demonstrated the concern of getting advice or assistance from educators, health professionals, or parents of people with cognitive disabilities during the app or game development. About this, the work from Lazar et al. [24] should be highlighted since they used an illustrator to help the volunteers in expressing their ideas throughout a workshop focused on creating an app to teach good eating habits. They explained that this action improved the group motivation.

In summary, the results of the literature review appointed the following aspects:

- Finding volunteers can be difficult, so it is interesting to establish a relationship with associations from the beginning.
- Try to limit the tests to a maximum of 30 min to avoid tiredness.
- In some cases, the audience may have difficulty in communication, such as answering interviews or questionnaires alone. Therefore, the research team should avoid long sentences or use abstract terms. Use images to represent their responses or to illustrate any moment in the interaction, and if possible, have the assistance of a health professional or educator during the development and application of tests.
- Eye-tracking assessments can be difficult to perform because the person must be in the same position the whole time. To deal with this problem, the research team of Alonso-Virgós et al. [22] chose to use a notebook due to the flexibility of the screen.
- Co-discovery and peer-tutoring can help to avoid negative thoughts, but it is important to observe the age of the participants, as this factor can influence the engagement of the participants and the researcher's control during the activity.
- When creating a focus group, allow extra time for volunteers to feel comfortable.
- Informal walkthrough can favor the interest of participants and does not require them to be reminded of an objective to be achieved.
- An illustrator can be useful to identify motivations and facilitate the visualization of the ideas and results discussed, considering that people with Trisomy 21 understand better through images.
- Avoid doing the think-aloud analysis alone to prevent biasing the research.
- Tests with AFFDEX were not accurate in recognizing facial expressions of people with Down syndrome.
- Oculus Rift may cause dizziness in the investigated public.

5 Conclusion

This article intended to find if there was in the literature a set of usability evaluation methods that could be used with children with Down syndrome. In this way, this team chose to follow the Cochrane literature review method [5], which permitted to find 22 works in Scopus and Web of Science, scientific databases.

The results pointed out that the observational methods were the most used associated with task performance technique, face expressions analysis or informal walkthrough. The probable reason why lays out in the fact that observational studies can give more feedback than self-related tests. Even though, they also can suffer from the researcher's biases. Also, the assistance of health professionals or educators seemed very helpful when creating and interpreting the data collected from the tests.

Aside from the traditional evaluations, the DEVAN method presented parameters to apply a video analysis that proved to be useful to evaluate the fun and engagement of the children with Trisomy 21 [13]. Also, the co-discovery technique seemed to be very helpful in avoiding negative attitudes and to motivate them to participate.

Therefore, considering the user's profile, the difficulty of getting volunteers and interpreting the data collected, it's also important to look for the support of health professionals, educators, and associations.

The next step of this research is to evaluate which ones can be used to test the mobile games and if there is any need of adapting them. Moreover, another literature review should take place to find engagement evaluations.

Acknowledgment. This study was financed in part by the Coordenação de Aperfeiçoamento de Pessoal de Nível Superior - Brasil (CAPES).

References

1. Joyce, A.: Usability Testing with Minors: 16 Tips. Nielsen Norman Group (2019). https://www.nngroup.com/articles/usability-testing-minors/. Accessed 27 Jul 2020
2. Barendregt, W., Bekker, M.M.: Guidelines for user testing with children, Eindhoven, Netherlands, Technical report, pp. 1–4 (2003).
3. Hanna, L., Risden, K., Alexander, K.: Guidelines for usability testing with children. Interactions 4(5), 9–14 (1997)
4. Nascimento, L.S., Martins, L.B., Zagalo, N., Almeida, A.M.: Mobile game development focused on children with down syndrome: a systematic literature review. In: XX Congresso Brasileiro de Ergonomia (2020)
5. Cochrane Training, Cochrane Handbook for Systematic Reviews of Interventions, 6.0. Cochrane (2019)
6. Clarivate Analytics, "Web of Science." https://apps.webofknowledge.com/WOS_GeneralSearch_input.do?product=WOS&search_mode=GeneralSearch&SID=F6ktpa3nI5CUPRU VpOA&preferencesSaved=. Accessed 10 Feb 2020
7. Scopus, "What is Scopus Preview?" https://service.elsevier.com/app/answers/detail/a_id/15534/supporthub/scopus/#tips. Accessed 10 Jan 2021
8. Sangin, M.: Observing the player experience. In: Drachen A., Mirza-Babaei, P., Nacke, L.E (eds.) Games User Research. Oxford University Press, Oxford (2018)
9. Jarrold, C., Baddeley, A.D.: Short-term memory in Down syndrome: Applying the working memory model. Down Syndr. Res. Pract. 7(1), 17–23 (2001)
10. Nascimento, L.S.: Diretrizes Projetuais e Instrumentos de Avaliação do Mobile Game Parque das Galáxias Criado para Desenvolvimento Psicomotor das Crianças com Síndrome de Down," Universidade Federal de Pernambuco (2017)

11. Rico-Olarte, C., López, D.M., Narváez, S., Farinango, C.D., Pharow, P.S.: Haphop-physio: a computer game to support cognitive therapies in children. Psychol. Res. Behav. Manag. **10**, 209–217 (2017)
12. Santos, D.A.A., Szturm, D.R., Castro, L.X., Hannum, J.S.S., Barbosa, T.A.: Wearable Device for Literacy Activities with People with Down Syndrome. In: 2017 IEEE MIT Undergraduate Research Technology Conference (2017)
13. Macedo, I., Trevisan, D.G., Vasconcelos, C.N., Clua, E.: Observed interaction in games for down syndrome children. In: Proceedings of the Annual Hawaii International Conference on System Sciences, 2015, vol. 2015-March, pp. 662–671 (2015)
14. Alfredo, M.G., Alvarez, F.J.R., Jaime M.A., Rusu, C., Francisco, A.E., Ricardo, M.G.: A cooperative process for a learnability study with Down Syndrome children. In: XVII International Conference on Human Computer (2016)
15. Brown, D.J., McHugh, D., Standen, P., Evett, L., Shopland, N., Battersby, S.: Designing location-based learning experiences for people with intellectual disabilities and additional sensory impairments. Comput. Educ. **56**, 11–20 (2011)
16. Yussof, R.L., Zaman, H.B.: Usability evaluation of multimedia courseware. Kuala Lumpur: Springer, pp. 337–343 (2011)
17. Yussof, R.L., Paris, T.N.S.T., Abas, H., Zaman, H.B.: Mixed usability evaluation during the development cycle of 'MEL-SindD.' Procedia - Soc. Behav. Sci. **105**, 162–170 (2013)
18. Ramli, R., Zaman, H.B.: Designing usability evaluation methodology framework of augmented reality basic reading courseware (AR BACA SindD) for down syndrome learner. In: 2011 International Conference on Electrical Engineering and Informatics (2011)
19. Cortés, M.Y., Guerrero, A., Zapata, J.V., Villegas, M.L., Ruiz, A.: Study of the usability in applications used by children with down syndrome. In: Computing Colombian Conference (2013)
20. Lalmas, M., O'Brien, H., Yom-Tov, E.: Measuring User Engagement. Synth. Lect. Inf. Concepts Retrieval Serv. **6**(4), 1–132 (2014)
21. Jennett, C., et al.: Measuring and Defining the experience of Immersion in Games. Int. J. Hum. Comput. Stud. **66**(9), 641–661 (2008)
22. Alonso-Virgós, L., Baena, L.R., Espada, J.P., Crespo, R.G.: Web page design recommendations for people with down syndrome based on users' experiences. Sensors **18** (2018)
23. da Silveira, A.C.F.: Síndrome de Down: Educação Diferenciada. Escola Superior de Educação Almeida Garrett (2012)
24. Lazar, J., et al.: Co-design process of a smart phone app to help people with down syndrome manage their nutritional habits. J. Usability Stud. **13**(2), 73–93 (2018)

Revising Recommendations for Evacuating Individuals with Functional Limitations from the Built Environment

Yashoda Sharma[1], Waqas Sajid[1], Cesar Marquez-Chin[1,2], Brad W. R. Roberts[3], Abdulrahman Al Bochi[1,4], Steven Pong[1], Mark Weiler[5], Albert H. Vette[3,6(✉)], and Tilak Dutta[1,2(✉)]

[1] KITE–Toronto Rehabilitation Institute, University Health Network, Toronto, ON, Canada
tilak.dutta@uhn.ca
[2] Institute of Biomedical Engineering, University of Toronto, Toronto, ON, Canada
[3] Department of Mechanical Engineering, University of Alberta, Edmonton, AB, Canada
[4] Department of Chemistry and Biology, Ryerson University, Toronto, ON, Canada
[5] Wilfrid Laurier University, Waterloo, ON, Canada
[6] Glenrose Rehabilitation Hospital, Alberta Health Services, Edmonton, AB, Canada

Abstract. Background: The rate of disability is rising in Canada as many individuals are now experiencing functional limitations due to aging, joining those with injuries and permanent or temporary impairments. In emergency situations, these individuals as well as first responders are at an increased risk of injury due to evacuation guidelines in Canada being out of date and not based on best available evidence. The Canadian evacuation guidelines were published in 2002, highlighting the immediate need to revise egressibility standards for individuals with functional limitations.

Objective: The objective of this project is to summarize the best available evidence on solutions for evacuating individuals with functional limitations from the built environment.

Methods: We will perform a scoping review to identify current solutions used to evacuate this population. The literature search will be structured around three concepts: functional limitation, evacuation, and built environment.

Results: Two-dimensional matrices will be created – the first to list solutions appropriate for existing buildings and the second to list solutions appropriate for new buildings. Each matrix will list building types across one axis and individual functional limitations along the other axis, with each cell containing a list of possible evacuation solutions for a given building type and individual with a specific limitation.

Conclusions: Results will inform the public on current evacuation protocols for individuals with functional limitations and highlight areas for improvement regarding safe egressibility. The outputs of this project will also provide a comprehensive toolkit useful for improving protocols for evacuating this population from the built environment.

Keywords: Built environment · Egressibility · Evacuation · Emergencies · Disability · Functional limitations

N. L. Black et al. (Eds.): IEA 2021, LNNS 220, pp. 350–356, 2021.
https://doi.org/10.1007/978-3-030-74605-6_44

1 Introduction

1.1 Evacuation Guidelines for Individuals with Functional Limitations

While our built environment has become increasingly accessible, in most circumstances, little work has been done to ensure individuals with disabilities can be evacuated from these spaces in the event of an emergency. Egressibility can be defined as the potential for building occupants to evacuate to a safe location, in emergency situations [1]. Evacuation from the built environment is different than accessibility, because it considers the well-being of building occupants during an emergency as opposed to routine building use [2]. Moreover, previous research has shown that the likelihood of death or injury is eight times higher when individuals with disabilities are present in a building in the event of a fire [3].

In Canada, one in five individuals aged 15 and older experience a disability [4], with the majority of individuals experiencing either a short-term or life-long form of impairment during their lifetime [5]. The rate of disability and impairment increases with age [4] and will continue to rise with the rapidly growing aging population in Canada. There are many forms of impairment, including those that affect our physical, cognitive, or sensory systems [6]. These impairments can affect an individuals' involvement in everyday activities and can be termed functional limitations [7].

Canada has a goal to advance the accessibility of public spaces for all individuals by the year 2030 [2]. However, the most recent evacuation guidelines in Canada were issued by the National Research Council in 2002 [8]. Since the publication of these guidelines almost two decades ago, much has changed within the population and with technological advancements in Canada, demonstrating the immediate need for their revision.

Today, Canadians have a longer life expectancy, with activity and functional limitations being more prevalent in the later stages of life [9]. Among those who experience these limitations, more than 80% require assistive devices (e.g., wheelchairs) [10]. In fact, we are seeing a greater use of higher-level power assistive devices among older adults with physical limitations such as powered wheelchairs and scooters [11] which are typically larger than unpowered versions. However, it has also been shown that the built environment may be putting power assistive device users at a disadvantage [11]. Constricted hallways or shopping aisles and inaccessible bathroom stalls are examples of ways the built environment fails to recognize the needs of individuals using larger assistive devices [11]. Next, over the last two decades, there have been technological advancements in evacuation strategies. For example, virtual reality training has been introduced to simulate fires for building residents and first responders to perform appropriate egress preparation [12]. This technology can help first responders estimate the time to exit a building [12], providing these teams with more confidence and a stronger knowledge base on the effectiveness of certain evacuation strategies.

The objective of this project is to provide the foundation for future revisions of egressibility standards by summarizing the best available evidence and theories on evacuation strategies for individuals with functional limitations, with the goal of supporting organizations' development of improved evacuation plans. This project has two aims: (1) to perform a scoping review to identify best practices recommended in the scientific literature used for evacuating individuals with functional limitations from the built environment; and (2) to present the results of the review in a pair of egress matrices for existing and new buildings. Each matrix will categorize type of functional limitation (e.g., physical, sensory etc.) along one axis and building type (e.g., high rise, low rise etc.) along the other axis to create a comprehensive list of all potential egressibility solutions in the built environment.

2   Methods

2.1   Search Strategy

The scoping review search strategy will be conducted in accordance with the Arksey and O'Malley six-stage framework [13] and the Joanna Briggs Institute Methodology for JBI Scoping Reviews [14]. Relevant studies will be identified through the following databases: CINAHL (via EBSCO); Ei Compendex and Inspec (via Engineering Village); Embase and MEDLINE (via Ovid); Korean Journal Database (KCI), Russian Science Citation Index (RSCI), Scientific Electronic Library (SciELO) Citation Index, and the Web of Science Core Collection (via Web of Science); and Scopus (via Elsevier). The search strategy consists of controlled vocabularies (e.g. Medical Subject Headings (MeSH)) and keywords. These terms are joined by Boolean operators. Boolean NOT operators have also been included with certain keywords to ensure irrelevant studies linked to our search concepts were excluded. A unique set of Boolean NOT operators were used in each database to better accommodate the different ways databases describe each main concept.

Studies that do not report evacuation solutions for individuals with functional limitations, or report solutions for areas unrelated to the built environment (i.e., outdoor venues or transportation) will be excluded from the review. Only studies published after 2002 will be included in this review.

2.2   Matrix Development

The development of two egress matrices is ongoing. A multi-disciplinary research team composed of engineers, designers and rehabilitation specialists is providing its perspectives on the viability of evacuation solutions available for individuals with functional limitations, based on their own knowledge and experiences. Identification of viable solutions includes results of a rapid review of evacuation solutions for individuals with functional limitations, preliminary results of the scoping review, and team discussion. The following description represents the information included for the egress matrix created for existing buildings.

A list of functional limitations was created in accordance with the International Classification of Functioning, Disability and Health (ICF) [15]. Each group of functional limitations was broken down into more specific limitations, e.g., visual and hearing impairments within the sensory impairment family. Types of buildings were collected based on commonly found buildings within Canada and through team discussion. Building categories were combined based on their similar evacuation solutions (e.g., combining multistorey educational and industrial buildings).

Evacuation solutions were divided into three categories: (1) notification, (2) wayfinding, and (3) egress. Solutions were weighted and ranked based on four criteria: (1) cost, (2) safety, (3) complexity, and (4) usability. These criteria were chosen by team consensus, their impact on the feasibility of implementation and importance to various stakeholders (e.g., cost being of importance to building developers). Each cell within both matrices provides a ranking of each solution. Rankings are based on how a given solution compares to other solutions within a category. Types of solutions and weighting scales will be finalized via an iterative process by working in conjunction with the following stakeholders: individuals with functional limitations, their caregivers, first responders, and other experts in the field. We will also consult the literature on basic costs and complexities of these technologies.

The next step in matrix development includes creating an egress matrix for new buildings. Both matrices will also include appropriate solutions for different types of emergencies (i.e., fire, flood, power outage, etc.).

3   Results

3.1   Preliminary Scoping Review Search Results

There are three main concepts used for the search strategy of the scoping review: functional limitation, evacuation, and built environment. Within each main concept are sub-concepts. For example, "built environment" is comprised of sub-concepts such as "houses", "stadiums", or "high-rises". These sub-concepts were the basis for constructing the search strings. Preliminary findings show that, as of February 2021 a total of 14,547,581 articles were found for "functional limitation", 771,799 articles for "evacuation", and 15,305,293 articles for "built environment". The number of articles found per concept was calculated prior to deduplication. A total of 2954 articles were found when all three main concepts were combined into a single search (i.e., functional limitation AND evacuation AND build environment) after deduplication and 9 articles were hand searched.

4   Preliminary Egress Matrix for Existing Buildings

Figure 1 and Fig. 2 represent a preliminary egress matrix for existing buildings (high-rise and single storey respectively), that has been displayed as two for presentation purposes only. The left-most column of the matrix lists the general functional limitations of individuals. The "specific limitation" column represents sub-categories within each respective "function" family.

The "Evacuation Solutions Per Activity" column represents the three categories of solutions formed for each type of functional limitation: (1) notification, (2) wayfinding, and (3) egress. Notification solutions are meant to inform and alert the individuals in a building that there is an emergency taking place. Examples of notification solutions are audible alarms, broadcast messages, and strobe lights. Wayfinding solutions direct individuals to the nearest emergency exit, or to a safe refuge to wait for help during an emergency. Examples of wayfinding solutions include appropriate evacuation and exit signage or posted floor plans. Finally, egress solutions are ones that provide individuals with a way to safely evacuate from a building or safely wait for help during an emergency. Egress solutions include using stairwells, fire elevators and evacuation sleds or waiting at a safe refuge. Innovative evacuation solutions found in the literature or created by the research team for consideration in future designs and development will be included in this matrix. The matrix also captures various types of buildings found within our environment. Building types not displayed in these examples, but that will be included, are mid-rise buildings (i.e., between five to eleven stories [16]). Final evacuation solution rankings are delineated with shaded circles. Fully shaded circles represent solutions that are most favorable within a specific category, whereas unshaded circles represent solutions that are least favorable. Partially shaded circles describe solutions that are neutral, meaning they are not considered more favorable or less favorable compared to other solutions within a single category (e.g., wayfinding category).

Function	Specific Limitation	Evacuation Solutions Per Activity			High Rise (11+ Storeys)			
		Notification	Wayfinding	Egress	Cost (Lower Cost)	Safety (Safer)	Complexity (Less Complex)	Usability (Better)
Mobility	All Mobility Impairments	Audible Alarm						
		Broadcast Message						
			Evacuation Signs					
			Floorplans					
	Nonambulatory Impairment (Wheelchairs and Scooters) & Pregnancies			Evacuation Sled				
				FireFighter's Carry				
				Fire Elevator				
				Safe Refuge				
				Firetruck Ladder				
	Ambulatory Impairment (Walker, Cane, Crutch, Slow Gait)			Use Stairs				
				Fire Elevator				
				Firetruck Ladder				
				Safe Refuge				
Sensory	Blind/Partial Vision Impairment	Audible Alarm						
		Broadcast Message						
	Deaf/Hard of Hearing	Strobe Lights						
	Deafblind	Vibrating Alarm						
	Blind/Partial Vision Impairment		Alarm/PA System					
	Deaf/Hard of Hearing		Evacuation Signs					
			Floorplans					
	Deafblind		Tactile Maps					
	All Sensory Impairments			Use Stairs				
Cognitive	Memory, Attention, Comprehension	Other People						
		Lockbox						
			Other People					
			Evacuation Signs					
			Floorplans					
				Use Stairs				

Fig. 1. Example egress matrix categorizing type of evacuation solution available for high-rise buildings and functional limitations.

A second egress matrix will be developed for new buildings following the same format as the matrices shown in Fig. 1 and Fig. 2. This second matrix will also include innovative evacuation solutions found and created in a similar way as described above. The information presented in the second matrix will help advise the design of new buildings and other industrial structures.

5   Discussion and Conclusion

There is a need to revise current evacuation guidelines for individuals with functional limitations in Canada. The number of individuals with functional limitations is rapidly

Function	Specific Limitation	Evacuation Solutions Per Activity			Single Storey			
		Notification	Wayfinding	Egress	Cost (Lower Cost →)	Safety (Safer →)	Complexity (Less Complex →)	Usability (Better →)
Mobility	All Mobility Impairments	Audible Alarm				●	●	◐
		Broadcast Message			◐	●	●	◐
			Evacuation Signs		◐	●	●	●
			Floorplans		◐	●	◐	●
	Nonambulatory Impairment (Wheelchairs and Scooters) & Pregnancies			Evacuation Sled	◐	◐	◐	◐
				FireFighter's Carry	●	○	◐	◐
				Fire Elevator	●	-	-	-
				Safe Refuge	○	◐	●	●
				Firetruck ladder	-	-	-	-
	Ambulatory Impairment (Walker, Cane, Crutch, Slow Gait)			Use Stairs	-	-	-	
				Fire Elevator	-	-	-	
				Firetruck ladder	-	-	-	
				Safe Refuge	○	◐	●	●
Sensory	Blind/Partial Vision Impairment	Audible Alarm			◐	●	●	◐
		Broadcast Message			◐	●	●	◐
	Deaf/Hard of Hearing	Strobe Lights			○	●	◐	○
	Deafblind	Vibrating Alarm			◐	◐	○	○
	Blind/Partial Vision Impairment		Alarm/PA System		○	●	●	◐
	Deaf/Hard of Hearing		Evacuation Signs		◐	●	●	●
			Floorplans		◐	●	◐	◐
	DeafBlind		Tactile Maps		◐	●	○	◐
				Use Stairs	-	-	-	
Cognitive	Memory, Attention, Comprehension	Other People			●	◐	●	●
		Lockbox			◐	●	○	◐
			Other People		●	◐	●	●
			Evacuation Signs		◐	●	●	●
			Floorplans		◐	●	◐	◐
				Use Stairs	-	-	-	

Fig. 2. Example egress matrix categorizing type of evacuation solution available for single storey buildings and functional limitations.

rising, with this population living longer. Previous guidelines were developed in 2002, prior to important changes in available technologies and population demographics.

Results of the scoping review will provide information on evacuation solutions available to individuals with functional limitations. This information will help to inform future recommendations for revising evacuation guidelines for this population in Canada as well as provide a reference for other jurisdictions around the world. This review will also help to advise the development of our egress matrices. Finally, the search strategy and protocol developed for this review are encouraged to be adapted and repeated in the near future. Repeating this search on a scheduled basis (e.g., every 5 years) will help identify more effective and viable solutions for individuals with functional limitations to ensure their safety when evacuating the built environment.

Key contributions of this study include informing current egressibility standards in Canada and increasing awareness of the wide range of functional limitations that exist among Canadians. This work will also inform the public on current evacuation protocols and highlight areas for improvement regarding safe egressibility. Our research team will work to promote knowledge translation to various stakeholders such as building developers, contractors, and owners of existing buildings to present a list of recommendations for safely and effectively evacuating individuals with functional limitations from the built environment.

The strengths of this project include the involvement of a multidisciplinary team of researchers and scientists in developing the scoping review and egress matrices. Members of the research team each bring a unique perspective to the potential solutions. The egress matrices will be discussed with stakeholders of various backgrounds including individuals with functional limitations, caregivers, first responders, contractors, and owners of existing buildings. Connecting with stakeholders adds to the strength and credibility of our results, as solutions were discussed and affirmed by individuals of emergency preparedness teams and end users.

Limitations of the present study include the solutions derived by the research team not taking into account building codes and city laws. Therefore, some of the solutions presented in the matrices may not be feasible to implement into a built environment due to factors such as cost, maintenance, and/or technical requirements. Future research should also focus on validating the articles identified in the scoping review to accurately improve evacuation guidelines in Canada.

The outputs of this project will provide a comprehensive toolkit that will be useful for developing evacuation protocols for individuals with functional limitations from the built environment while also highlighting areas where future research is needed. The development of the matrices will be ongoing until September 2021. We are currently searching for individuals that would like to provide feedback on the development of the matrices. If you are interested in sharing your insights, please get in touch with the corresponding author via email.

References

1. Proulx, G.: Evacuation Time and Movement in Apartment Buildings. Fire Saf. J. **24**, 229–246 (1995)
2. Draft CCBFC Policy Position Paper - Accessibility in Buildings. Canadian Commission on Building and Fire Codes, 1–34 (2018).
3. Lin, Y.S.: Life risk analysis in residential building fires. J. Fire Sci. **22**(6), 491–504 (2004)
4. Morris, S., Fawcett, G., Brisebois, L., Hughes, J.: Canadians Survey on Disabilities: A demographic, employment and income profile, 2017. Statistics Canada, 1–3 (2018)
5. Chapter 1: Understanding disability. World report on disability, pp. 1–17 (2011)
6. Government of Canada, "Accessible Canada Act - Loi canadienne sur l'accessibilité." Ministry of Justice, 1–82 (2019).
7. Verbrugge, L.M., Jette, A.M.: The disablement process. Soc. Sci. Med. **38**(1), 1–14 (1994)
8. Proulx, G.: Evacuation planning for occupants with disability. National Research Council Canada, IRC-IR-843, pp. 1–26 (2002)
9. Decady, Y., Greenberg, L.: Ninety years of change in life expectancy. Statistics Canada, Health Glance. **82**, 1–10 (2014)
10. Disability in Canada: initial findings from the Canadian Survey on Disability. Statistics Canada (2013)
11. Korotchenko, A., Hurd Clarke, L.: Power mobility and the built environment: the experiences of older Canadians. Disabil. Soc. **29**(3), 431–443 (2014)
12. Aizhu, R., Chi, C., Yuan, L.: Simulation of emergency evacuation in virtual reality. Tsinghua Sci. Technol. **13**(5), 674–680 (2008)
13. Arksey, H., O'Malley, L.: Scoping studies: Towards a methodological framework. Int. J. Soc. Res. Methodol. Theory Pract. **8**(1), 19–32 (2005)
14. The Joanna Briggs Institute: The Joanna Briggs Institute Reviewers' Manual 2015 edition / Supplement. The Joanne Briggs Institute., pp. 1–24 (2015)
15. How to use the ICF: A practical manual for using the International Classification of Functioning, Disability and Health (ICF). World Health Organization, Exposure draft for comment (2013)
16. Tall Buildings Guidelines. City of Toronto. (2013)

From Accessibility to Inclusion in People Centered Design

Erminia Attaianese[1], Francesca Tosi[2], and Isabella Tiziana Steffan[3(✉)]

[1] University of Naples Federico II, Naples, Italy
erminia.attaianese@unina.i
[2] University of Florence, Florence, Italy
francesca.tosi@unifi.it
[3] STUDIO STEFFAN – Progettazione and Ricerca (Design and Research), Milan, Italy
info@studiosteffan.it

Abstract. The paper discusses synergies and difference in several people centered design approaches, in order to clarify processes and methods focusing on human diversity. Thanks to a design methodologies review, common grounds and focus are identified by analyzing theoretical basis and applications to different design context, for improving and widening their comprehension and practice. The contribution of Human-Centered Design methods to their application is also discussed.

Keywords: Accessible built environment · Products and service · Human variability · Usability · Universal Design · Design for All

1 Introduction

Although the accessibility concept is not new, there are probably two focal reasons today for considering the relevance of a people-centered approach in design. The first pertains to demographic changes that show globally a constant increase of the elderly population so that, by 2050, one in six people in the world will be aged 65 years or over [1]. The second pertains to the need for leaving 'no one behind' at the global level, which calls for inclusive development. This means equitably including the most vulnerable people and marginalized groups in the development process within countries and internationally, including migrants, refugees, the disabled, indigenous people, and future generations in social life participation [2]. Thus, the need for developing products, environments, and services not only accessible and usable for older adults and people with reduced levels of autonomy but inclusive for all increasingly results in both a necessity, solicited by the social policies and an opportunity for the companies and the market.

Nevertheless, there is no consensus on formulating the concepts of accessibility or inclusion neither on the different approaches of design based on these concepts, and all this probably hinder the adoption of inclusive principles on a wider scale, thus possibly limiting the potential benefits [3].

© The Author(s), under exclusive license to Springer Nature Switzerland AG 2021
N. L. Black et al. (Eds.): IEA 2021, LNNS 220, pp. 357–366, 2021.
https://doi.org/10.1007/978-3-030-74605-6_45

There are several people-centered design approaches, developed in different geographic areas from the 50s, in different contexts of application. They show similarities in that they all are processes aiming at improving quality in use for achieving accessible contexts, including the built environment, products, and services.

However, they present also differences in focus and methodology, which may lead to confusion and be the reason for the current limitations in design applications. Striving synergies in these different design approaches are challenging but can be relevant because they can foster the right application of design principles people-centered and thus facilitate the way products and environments are made more compliant to users' variability through design practices.

2 Design Approaches Centered on Humans

2.1 From Accessibility to Inclusion in Design Approaches

The initial term used around the world was barrier-free design, and it related to efforts that began in the late 1950s in the United State for removing barriers for "disabled people" from the built environment. This concept was later replaced in many countries with the term accessibility, which focused on issues of mobility, such as wheelchair access. Universal Design was first used and promoted in the United States too, by Mace in 1985 for communicating a design approach that could be utilized by a wider range of users. Universal Design remains the dominant terminology in Japan, although increasingly in the United States it is used interchangeably with Inclusive Design. The movements that drove the spread of Universal Design (America, 1985), Inclusive Design (the UK, the 60s), Design for All (Scandinavian countries, 60s), have different roots and motivations. Nevertheless, they seem to share the same content and goals, inspiring similar movements, such as, the International Association for Universal Design (IAUD) born in Japan in 2003, based on the reality of an aging population, and the Design for All Institute of India founded in 2005, focused on social disability and diversity. The European Union supports accessibility with a Design for All approach: in the political framework of the European Disability Strategy 2010–2020 (EC- Employment, Social Affairs and Inclusion 2010) and the Convention on the Rights of Persons with Disabilities [4] there are a set of regulatory actions for accessibility and inclusion.

2.2 Accessibility/Disability-Related Approaches

This group includes design approaches based on accessibility by focusing on disability, i.e. on what people are able/not able to do. Starting from the barrier-free design, developed in the building and urban design area, designing for the access goals has been gradually included in ICT and interactive systems areas, for answering to the right of individuals of full participation to society irrespectively of physical disability. From a semantic comparison of their descriptions , some recurrent terms emerge, such as special (needs), specific (technology), non-standard (people), impairment, adaptations, aids. Thus, one of their most evident common features is the assistive role of design, by proposing mainly specialized solutions for the special demands of specific targets (Table1).

Table 1. Accessibility/Disability-related approaches

Design approach		Main areas	Ref
Barrier free design Accessible design Design for disability Design for special needs	Based on principles of extending standard design to persons with some type of performance limitation to maximize the number of potential customers who can readily use a product, building or service People with disability engaged as experts of their situations, invited to collaborate closely with the designers	Building and home equipment; product and services; learning environment, education	[5] [6] [20]
Assistive Technology Rehabilitation Engineering User-sensitive Inclusive design	Fitting "non-standard users" to standard technology by means of an assistive components. Focused on a "special" category of technologies specific to people with specific needs	ICT/interactive systems, aid	[7] [8] [9]
Design for user empowerment	Including people with disabilities as the designers and engineers creating accessible technologies	Product, equipment, disability aid	[10]

2.3   Value-Related Design Approaches

This group includes methodologies that base their approach on moral values by including social factors in the design process. Developed in the area of ICT and interactive systems, they are aimed at creating accessible technologies for people with disabilities. From a semantic comparison of their descriptions, recurring terms are mostly ability (over disability), user empowerment and self-determination, whose indicating the common focus on the active involvement of final users in all design steps. The most evident feature of this group of methodologies is the ethical role of design, expressing in proposing technical solutions aware of and responsive to users' abilities, and of which users are conscious (Table 2).

Table 2. Value-related approaches

Design approach		Main areas	Ref
Value-sensitive design Design for social accessibility	Considering the moral values not only of the users but all others impacted by the technologies, including social factors in the design process Tripartite methodology: conceptual, empirical and technical investigations Users develop the project, design the requirements and features, develop the prototypes, test the prototypes, and analyze the results of testing to refine the design	ICT/Interactive systems	[11] [12]
Ability-based design	Emphasizing ability over disability, and advocate systems aware of and responsive to users' abilities Ability, Accountability, Adaptation, Transparency, Performance, Context, Commodity	Interactive systems	[13]
Design for user empowerment	Including people with disabilities as the designers and engineers creating accessible technologies Based on self-determination and technical expertise of disabled users, that have the power to solve their own accessibility problems	Product, equipment, disability aid	[14]

2.4   Inclusion-Relates Design Approaches

This group includes design approaches based on the inclusion/inclusivity concepts. They focus on people diversity, to the greatest extent possible and in a wide variety of situations, without the need for adaptations or specialized solutions. Starting from the product design, inclusive goals have been gradually included in all areas, comprising not only ICT and built environment, but also education and services in order to improve accessibility by providing solutions to the before-excluded categories of the population. From the semantic point of view, their comparison highlights that terms like equality, context/contextual, mainstream over special are recurring. The inclusive role of design is their most evident common features, by proposing solutions that, even though firstly conceived for intended users, are then designed for broadening their beneficial impact for

Table 3. Inclusion-related approaches

Design approach		Main areas	Ref
Universal design Design for all Inclusive design	Focused on all people, to the greatest extent possible, without the need for product adaptation or specialized design. Assistive devices for particular groups of persons with disabilities where this is needed not excluded Designing, developing, and marketing artifacts to be accessible and usable by as broad a range of users as possible. UD is explicitly cited as the necessary approach to grant accessibility in UNCRPD art.2, DfA is applied in EU standard; ID in British Standard Using 7 UD Principles (Equitable Use, Flexibility in Use, Simple and Intuitive Use, Perceptible Information, Tolerance for Error, Low Physical Effort, Size and Space for Approach and Use) plus: Respectful, Safe, Healthy, Functional, Comprehensible, Sustainable, Affordable, Appealing - Inclusive, Responsive, Flexible, Convenient, Welcoming, Realistic	Built environment, products, and services, ICT	[15] [3] [16] [17] [26–29] [30] [32] [33]
Transgenerational design	Focused on different ages, with active involvement of the user in the design process, trying to obtain a clear understanding of the exact task requirements, involving an iterative design and evaluation process, and utilizing a multi-disciplinary approach	Built environment, products, and services, ICT	[21] [22]
User centered design	Focused on the active involvement of the user in the design process, trying to obtain a clear understanding of the exact task requirements, involving an iterative design and evaluation process, and utilizing a multi-disciplinary approach. Active involvement of users and clear understanding of user and task requirements; Appropriate allocation of function between user and system; Iteration of design solutions; Multi-disciplinary design teams	Built environment, products, and services, ICT	[18] [19]

all, recognizing that exclusion can happen to anyone interact with an artifact, depending on the particular circumstances (Table3).

3   Human-Centered Design Methods to Design for Inclusion

Nowadays the term accessibility has widened its meaning towards inclusion, considering not only people with disabilities but any person, with their diversity and specificity - physical-perceptual, cognitive or cultural - in the interaction with an artefact. For this reason, the concept of accessibility is increasingly associated with that of usability, as an essential condition to guarantee inclusion and participation, in autonomy and safety, as many people as possible, according to the so-called "Design for All" approach, promoted by European Union. The Inclusive Design approach is located in a very similar direction, today considered fully part of the Human-Centered Design theoretical and methodological approach. As E. Elton and C. Nicolle wrote (2015, pp. 300–301), *"the inclusive design approach, which aims to deliver 'mainstream products and/or services that are accessible to, and usable by, people with the widest range of abilities within the widest range of situations without the need for special adaptation or design'* (BS 7000-6 2005). *Accessibility and usability are the key criteria of this approach. Accessibility refers to allowing users access to the features of products and/or services through their sensory, physical and cognitive capabilities. In essence, inclusive design can be categorized as a specific type of human-centered approach to design. The inclusive design approach specifically focuses on understanding the needs, capabilities and attitudes of people who have some form of impairment and then applying this knowledge to mainstream design. Thus, ergonomics/human factors play a significant role in the inclusive design approach"*.

As Inclusive Design, design for inclusion, Design for All and Universal Design have the same aim and approach, we could say that this is extendable in general to all similar terms.

Human-Centered Design HCD and Design Thinking methods are now widely applied in many areas of Design, from product and interior design, to the design of services up to the entire transversal area of Digital design with particular attention to the field of communication. Methods increasingly centered on the evaluation of User Experience and based on the involvement of people in the design process. The development of this area of research and experimentation, which finds wide confirmation also in the standards, is located in particular in the field of Design, which today is increasingly characterized by a marked capacity for transversal intervention in the various areas of the project, and by the synthesis between the multiple and different disciplinary and professional fields involved in the Design process [25].

As we know, there are a very large number of evaluation and design methods used today in HCD, including Task Analysis, Questionnaires, Focus Groups, etc., all of which widely applicable in all area of the project [24]. The Table 4 below shows some of the main HCD evaluation and design methods fully applicable in all application sectors of product and architecture design and, in particular, in the context of design for inclusion.

The interest in the results, and the ability to involve the user/person in the design process today takes on a strategic importance that offers important development opportunities in all areas of the project, and in particular in the field of architecture in an

Table 4. Some examples of HCD and Design for Inclusion (DfI) methods*

Methods/Tools	Description
Interviews	Interviews are the most commonly methods, which allows the researcher to interview a user by analyzing each aspect of their criticism. This test's positive outcome depends heavily on the experience and empathy of the evaluator The interview may be carried out in a lab, in a pre-established scenario or in a real context. The test may be rendered ineffective in the first two cases, due to the embarrassment experienced by the user in an artificial situation. The third case offers easier conditions for the user and allows us to collect data about their actual experience, as well as their "spontaneous" observations
Observation	Observation is useful for evaluating physical tasks and usability, as users are not always able to explain how to use the product in detail (whether they normally use it or it is the very first time) and they may have a distorted view of how they behave in various real usage situations There are currently various types of observation techniques, including direct observation, indirect observation and participant observation Generally, two people are required for any type of observation: one or more researchers and the participant
Thinking aloud	This method allows the researcher to gather and obtain information that would be otherwise unobtainable, relating to the strategies employed by the user when performing the tasks, the difficulties encountered during the test, his thoughts and his expectations. Recording audio and video is advised, so everything that happened during the test session can be reviewed at a later date
Scenario	It realistically describes the sequence of actions that a person carries out when using a product/system or service in one or more specific usage contexts, typically via images. Scenarios allow the designer or the design team to explore how a product must work in detail (it allows us to consider the desired characteristics of potential users, their tasks and their environment and allows us to simulate possibility usability issues), in order to ensure a good User Experience and satisfy the pre-established objectives
Co-Design	It is a creative process between designers and people who are not experts in Design, who work together to generate ideas and for the concept of a new product and / or service. The users involved have the role of "top experts of their own experience" and the designers synthesize the design solutions by offering tools for the design and development of the project

* cfr. Tosi F., Brischetto A., Pistolesi M., "Human-Centred Design—User Experience: Tools and Intervention Methods". In Tosi, F.: Design for Ergonomics. Springer (2020)

inclusive design vision. In particular, the ability to involve the user in every phase of the design makes it possible to orient the project in a perspective of strong versatility of the product and its customization according to the different needs of users, an approach that has excellent opportunities of application also in architecture. The same design strategies used today for the customization of products and services are also appropriate in the field of designing physical environments and their components. The way forward is the design of products that guarantee the maximum level of usability to the maximum number of people possible, and that provide for the possibility of inserting aids, accessories, and/or adjustment systems that allow the product to be adapted during the time to change the physical, perceptive and/or cognitive abilities of the person, or to adapt it, case by case, to the needs of different users or to the different conditions of use. The problem is therefore the exact identification of which are the real or possible recipients of the project, and what is the range of needs to which the project will be able to respond. In this context, co-design methods are essential, aimed at gathering the needs, expectations and opinions of users, methods in which users are the greatest experts of their experience and designers play the role of facilitators. offering design synthesis skills and tools for the design and development of the project [23]. Some examples of customizable solutions are bathroom furniture systems characterized by a basic configuration that can be personalised, or implemented with accessories and aids (for example, to facilitate the mobility of people on wheelchair) that can be inserted according to your needs. Similar examples are kitchen furnishing systems that provide different configurations, from solutions of maximum accessibility (e.g. clear knee space under the work surfaces) that can also be used from the sitting position, to solutions for the best use of the available space, with the insertion of e.g. height-adjustable kitchen cabinets.

4 Discussion and Conclusion

According to the comparative study, summarized above, it seems that many official definitions and approaches are available at academic publications. Actually, it seems that there is still some confusion between "Design for Disability" - focused on one/more disability- and "Design for Inclusion" -focused on the widest range of abilities within the widest range of situations - and between terms such as e.g. "Universal Access/ Accessibility" - i.e. a right of the citizens - and "Universal Design/Design for All/Inclusive Design" - i.e. the approach to guarantee it.

As said above, nowadays the term Accessibility has widened its meaning towards inclusion, considering not only people with disabilities but any person, with their diversity and specificity - physical-perceptual, cognitive or cultural - in the interaction with an artefact, which is related to the concept of usability as defined in ISO 9241–11:2018 "extent to which a product, a service and the built environment can be used by specified users to achieve specified goals with effectiveness, efficiency and satisfaction in a specified context of use". Accessibility and usability for everyone "is achieved by considering the diversity of human abilities and their associated functional requirements as a basis of design. In this way, systems and solutions can be developed that suit the needs of diverse users, so all people regardless of their age, size or ability have access to the broadest range of systems and environments" [26]. Accessibility is often used as synonymous of usability in standards such as in ISO 21542:2021 [31, 34], EN 17161:2018 and EN 17210:2021, according to ISO 9241–11:2018, which is an important reference for Ergonomics. Standards constitute a global common basis for conceiving, creating and verifying inclusive artifacts, services, and built environment.

Some sectors of intervention are particularly mature and currently applying ergonomic tools and methods (e.g. in ICT, product, services) to achieve these design objectives for inclusion, but it is clear that could be applied also to the built environment [27], very successfully, by using a global approach.

References

1. UN: World Population Ageing 2019 (2019)
2. Gupta, J., Baud, I., et al.: Sustainable Development Goals and Inclusive Development. POST2015/UNU-IAS Policy Brief #5. Tokyo: United Nations University Institute for the Advanced Study of Sustainability (2014)
3. Persson, H., Ahman, H., Yngling, A.A., Gulliksen, J.: Universal design, inclusive design accessible design, design for all: different concepts—one goal? On the concept of accessibility— historical, methodological and philosophical aspects. Universal Access in the Information Society (UAIS), vol. 4(14) (2014)
4. UN: Convention on the Rights of Persons with Disabilities (2006)
5. Chew, S.: An approach to design with people who have special needs. In: Stephanidis, C. (ed.) HCI International 2013 - Posters' Extended Abstracts. HCI 2013. Communications in Computer and Information Science, vol. 373. Springer, Heidelberg (2013). https://doi.org/10. 1007/978-3-642-39473-7_45
6. Zabunova, P.G., Tsvetanova, Y.: Introduction of issues regarding people with special needs to design education. In Proceedings if International Conference on Engineering and Product Design Education, University of Twente, The Netherlands (2014)
7. Borg, J., Larsson, S., Östergren, P.-O.: The right to assistive technology: for whom, for what, and by whom? Disabil. Soc. 26(2), 151–167 (2011)
8. Scherer, J.: Living in the State of Stuck: How Technologies Affect the Lives of People with Disabilities. Brookline Books, Cambridge (1993)
9. Newell, A., Gregor, P., Morgan, M.M., Pullin, G., Macauly, C.: User-sensitive inclusive design. Univers. Access Inf. Soc. 10(3), 235–243 (2011)
10. Ladner, R.E.: Design for user empowerment. Interactions 22(2), 24–29 (2015)
11. Friedman, B., Kahn, P.H., Borning, A.: Value Sensitive Design: Theory and Methods. UW CSE Technical Report 02-12-01 (2002)
12. Shinohara, K., Wobbrock, J.O., Pratt, W.: Incorporating social factors in accessible design. In: Proceedings of the 20th International ACM SIGACCESS Conference on Computers and Accessibility, pp. 149–160 (2018)
13. Wobbrock, J.O., Kane, S.K., Harada, S., Froehlich, S.: Ability-based design: concept, principles, and examples. ACM Trans. Access. Comput. (TACCESS) 3(3), 1–27 (2011)
14. Ladner, R.E.: Design for user empowerment. Interactions 22, 2, 24–29 (2015)
15. Ostroff, E.: Universal design: an evolving paradigm. In: Preiser, W., Ostroff, E. (eds.) Universal Design Handbook, first edition. McGraw-Hill, New York (2001)
16. Steffan, I.T. (ed.) Design for All. The project for everyone. Methods, tools, applications. First part. Maggioli, Santarcangelo di Romagna, Rimini, Italy (2014)
17. Elton, E., Nicolle, C.: Inclusive Design and Design for special population. In: Wilson J.R., Sharples S. (eds) Evaluation of Human Work, (4° ed.). CRC Taylor & Francis group, Boca Raton, Florida (2015)

18. Norman, D.A., Draper, S.W.: User-Centered System Design: New Perspectives on Human-Computer Interaction. CRC Press, Boca Raton (1986)
19. Astbrink, G., Beekhuyzen, J.: The Synergies Between Universal Design and User-Centred Design, Brisbane, Australia: Griffith University School of Computing and Information Technology (2003)
20. DePoy, E., Gilson, S.: Disability by design. Rev. Disabil. Stud. Int. J. **6**(3) (2010). https://dsq-sds.org/article/view/1247/1274
21. Pirkl, J.J.: Transgenerational design: a heart transplant for housing. In: Kohlbacher F., Herstatt C. (eds.) The Silver Market Phenomenon. Springer, Heidelberg (2011). https://doi.org/10.1007/978-3-540-75331-5_10
22. Pirkl, J.J.: Transgenerational Design: Products for an Aging Population. Van Nostrand, New York (1994)
23. Tosi, F., Brischetto, A., Pistolesi, M.. In: Human-centred design—user experience: tools and intervention methods. In: Tosi, F (ed.) Design for Ergonomics. Springer (2020). https://doi.org/10.1007/978-3-030-33562-5_6
24. Tosi, F.: Ergonomics and design for all: design for inclusion. In Tosi, F (ed.) Design for Ergonomics. Springer (2020). https://doi.org/10.1007/978-3-030-33562-5_9
25. Attaianese, E.: Increasing sustainability by improving full use of public space: Human Centered Design for easy-to-walk built environment. In: Rebelo, F., Soares, M. (eds.) Ergonomics in Design: Proceedings of the Ahfe 2016 International Conference on Ergonomics in Design, 27–31 July 2016, Walt Disney World, Florida, USA. Springer (2016). https://doi.org/10.1007/978-3-319-41983-1_43
26. EN 17210:2021 Accessibility and usability of the built environment (2021)
27. EN 301549:2019 Accessibility requirements for ICT products and services (2019)
28. EN 17161:2019 Design for All - Accessibility following a Design for All approach in products, goods and services - Extending the range of users (2019)
29. FprCEN/TR 17621:2021 Accessibility and usability of the built environment - Technical performance criteria and specifications (2021)
30. ISO 9241–210:2019 Ergonomics of human-system interaction—Part 210: Human-centred design for interactive systems (2019)
31. ISO 21542:2021 Building construction—Accessibility and usability of the built Environment (2020)
32. ISO 9241-112: 2017 Ergonomics of human-system interaction. 3.15 (2017)
33. ISO 9241-171:2008 Ergonomics of human-system interaction—Part 171: Guidance on software accessibility. Annex F (2008)
34. ISO/IEC Guide 71:2014 Guide for addressing accessibility in standards (2014)

Good Lighting and Visual Contrast to Improve Accessibility in the Built Environment-A Literature Study

Gregorio Feigusch[1], Isabella Tiziana Steffan[2]([✉]), and Doris Ossberger[3]

[1] European Ergonomist, Via G. Severano 35, 00161 Rome, Italy
feigusch@mclink.it
[2] STUDIO STEFFAN – Progettazione and Ricerca (Design and Research), Milan, Italy
info@studiosteffan.it
[3] Court Certified Expert for Accessibility/Universal Design, Vienna, Austria

Abstract. In the general context of accessibility, the theme of considering the needs of people with visual impairments and of older people, by means of adequate lighting and visual contrast of building elements, is growing in importance and in interest by stakeholders. The authors describe the parameters mostly used to assess visual contrast. The discussion focuses on the alternative between the use of the LRV (Light Reflectance Value) and the CIE Y tristimulus value, but also on the algorithms which best quantify the visual contrast between two adjacent surfaces, according with human perception. Attention is also devoted to the distinction between the assessment of the reflectance properties of building elements in the laboratory, and the check of the luminance contrast in the field. The paper compares some international and national accessibility standards, examining the quantities considered for the expression of visual contrast (e.g. luminance, LRV, CIE Y tristimulus value) and the algorithms used to quantify visual contrast. The comparison highlights a growing tendency to abandon the LRV difference formula, focusing on formulas using a ratio, which are more suited to simulate human perception.

For the future, the authors suggest that the TGs working at "vertical" international and national standards, containing references to accessibility for people with visual impairments, take into account this new approach, which is to be considered as an important step forward for the evaluation of visual contrast.

Keywords: Accessible built environment · Visual contrast · Impaired vision · LRV · CIE Y

1 Visual Accessibility in the Built Environment

In the general context of accessibility in the built environment, the theme of taking into account the needs of people with visual impairments (including older people) is growing in importance and in interest by stakeholders (public administrations, standardization bodies, disability movements and associations, designers, manufacturers, etc.).

Consequently, the more recent evolution of international standards and guidelines about accessibility pays great attention to the definition of design considerations for a

N. L. Black et al. (Eds.): IEA 2021, LNNS 220, pp. 367–375, 2021.
https://doi.org/10.1007/978-3-030-74605-6_46

visual environment aimed at facilitating the perception of information, orientation and safety of movements.

Although requirements concerning lighting are generally expressed in terms of illuminance, the only parameter that determines human vision is luminance, that is the photometric quantity which quantifies the sensation of brightness.

By the fact, the possibility to distinguish and recognize two adjacent surfaces, as for instance a door in a wall, or the symbol on a signal, depends on two factors:

1. A sufficient difference in lightness of the two surfaces generally referred to as "visual contrast", or "luminance contrast" (the term lightness is used here to express the extent to which an object reflects the incident light, not as a parameter of a colour space system);
2. An adequate lighting for them.

These factors are both essential: without a sufficient lighting, even two surfaces with an adequate difference in lightness could be hard to discriminate; on the other hand, even a good lighting could be not sufficient to grant the perception of two adjacent surfaces too similar in lightness.

In fact, while people with normal vision and ability to discriminate colors can rely on both luminance contrast and color differences, many people with visual impairments and older people may have difficulties in color recognition, being able to distinguish adjacent surfaces essentially by their luminance contrast. This is the reason for which accessibility standards usually make reference only to luminance contrast for the assessment of visual contrast.

Among the two factors listed above, the requirement for adequate lighting is generally covered specifying a minimum medium maintained illuminance on the reference plane (a typical value is 100 lx), or else referring to lighting standards. On the contrary, the requirement for visual (or luminance) contrast is much more controversial.

This paper originates by an in-depth examination of technical literature about this matter, which the authors performed also to contribute to work in progress for the definition or update of International and European standards. Nevertheless, this paper reflects only the personal opinions of the authors, without any direct implication on the activities of the various TCs now working at the implementation or revision of the standards.

2 Luminance Contrast

When dealing with lighting, vision, and photometry, one cannot do without referring to CIE. CIE is the French acronym for "Commission Internationale De l'Eclairage", which is the international technical, scientific and cultural non-profit organization more deeply involved in the Matter of vision and lighting.

Both CEN and ISO have established agreements with CIE aimed at a reciprocal cooperation in the elaboration of standards [4]. Also for this reason, when dealing with light and vision, as it is the case with visual and luminance contrast, one should as much as possible refer to CIE publications, CIE definitions of photometric quantities and related measurement methodologies.

CIE definition for luminance is a very complex one, but for the purpose of this paper it will be enough to remember that luminance is the photometric quantity related to the human sensation of brightness and it is expressed in candela per square meter (cd/m^2).

It is important here to define the luminance contrast: we will refer to CIE vocabulary definition (17-22-091):

Luminance Contrast:*quantity relating to the difference in luminance between two surfaces.*

Note 1 to entry: Widely accepted definitions include:

$C = (L_1 - L_2)/L_1$ *with* $L_1 > L_2$ *(positive contrast),*

$C = (L_1 - L_2)/L_1$ *with* $L_1 < L_2$ *(negative contrast),*

$C = (L_1 - L_2)/(L_1 + L_2)$ *with* $L_1 > L_2$,

where C is the luminance contrast and L_1 *and* L_2 *are the luminance values of the two surfaces.*

As one can see, all the "accepted definitions" are based on ratio formulas. As explained above, an adequate luminance contrast between an object and its background is essential to perceive objects and recognize building elements, signals and so on, provided that lighting is sufficient. But the more correct way to quantify and evaluate the reflecting properties of surfaces is just one of most debated and controversial topics in both international and national accessibility standards, and in guidelines. Furthermore, current accessibility standards sometimes fail to stress the difference between laboratory type tests and on-site acceptance tests.

Laboratory type tests should be performed on samples of building elements (such as control panels and buttons for lifts, symbols and background on signage, etc.), so that manufacturers can publish in their technical data sheets the reflectance properties of their products, to be used by architects and designers at the design stage. Instruments with high accuracies (typically spectrophotometers or colorimeters), compliant with standardized measuring conditions (illumination and observation geometry, standardized light source), should be used for this type of tests.

On-site tests should be performed under real lighting conditions and should be aimed essentially at evaluating if the luminance contrast value planned at the design stage has been achieved and if the lighting of the scenario (e.g. a door in a wall, the control plate in a lift, a signage for wayfinding, etc.) can be deemed as adequate in connection with the luminance contrast. Even if the instruments needed (typically a luminance meter or a luminance meter camera, mounted on a tripod) are fairly expensive and ask for skilled operators, measurements should be regarded as "industrial grade measurements", due to the difficulty to reproduce the geometric conditions required by the different standards and to assess the lighting conditions.

Similar measurement arrangements might be used, as well as in the field, also in laboratory, for instance in order to enable a lift manufacturer to check the compliance of the setup for a car at the design stage, before series production.

3 Methodologies Currently Used to Assess the Luminous Reflectance Properties of Surfaces and Building Elements

Until now, we have not yet highlighted an essential aspect of the problem: the inputs into the luminance contrast formulas in the CIE definition (17-22-091) are (obviously enough) the luminance values of the two adjacent surfaces under test; that is, they are relative to a specific installation and lighting scenario, or else to a specific simulation in laboratory.

But, what about the methodologies currently used by the most relevant accessibility standards and guidelines to assess and measure the intrinsic reflectance properties of a surface and the achievable degree of visual contrast between two adjacent surfaces? The authors had the opportunity to compare several accessibility standards (both international and national) and guidelines, with specific reference to these methodologies. This work is the natural prosecution of studies began some years ago [12].

Until now most of the standards and guidelines evaluate the lightness of a surface, referring to a quantity named LRV (Light Reflectance Value).

Then, for the assessment of the visual contrast between two adjacent surfaces, several standards use simple difference formulas, of the type:

$$LRV_1 - LRV_2 \tag{1}$$

where LRV_1 and LRV_2 are the Light Reflectance Values of the lighter and of the darker surface.

This approach is in contradiction with the great majority of researches on vision, which show that human perception of brightness changes approximately with the ratio between luminance values, rather than with the difference. For this reason, formulas using ratios should be preferred to simple difference formulas, in order to assess the visual contrast between two surfaces; the CIE definition itself (17-22-091) is an enforcement of this assumption.

Going back to the use of LRV (Light Reflectance Value), it would be preferable to quantify the intrinsic reflectance properties of a surface, referring to the Y tristimulus value, as defined by CIE.

The debate of using CIE Y tristimulus value rather than LRV is mostly a vocabulary matter; in fact, we can say that all the standards and guidelines using Light Reflectance Values clearly state that "LRV is the same as CIE Y".

So, why should we prefer a definite reference to CIE Y rather than a systematic reference to LRV, even if followed by the note "LRV is the same as CIE Y"?

The main reason is that LRV is not defined properly. A typical definition is that in ISO 21542:2011 [16], (3.41):

light reflectance value (LRV).

proportion of visible light reflected by a surface at all wavelengths and directions when illuminated by a light source.

NOTE 1 LRV is also known as the luminance reflectance factor or CIE Y value (see International Commission on Illumination, CIE, Publication 15:2004, 3rd Edition, Colorimetry).

NOTE 2 The LRV is expressed on a scale of 0 to 100, with a value of 0 points for pure black and a value of 100 points for pure white.

This definition seems to describe LRV as a ratio between the reflected light and the incident light on the sample, rather than as a ratio between the two luminance values of the sample under test and of a white perfect reflecting diffuser, identically irradiated and viewed. Moreover, the definition fails to specify that the energy reflected at each wavelength is to be weighted by the spectral sensitivity of the standard photometric observer CIE 1931 V (λ). Finally, the definition fails to specify that the measurement of LRV has to be performed according to a standardized geometry for the incident and the reflected rays and with reference to a standard light source.

An obstacle to a complete replacement of LRV by CIE Y is the fact that LRV is diffusely used in commercial environment: for instance, many paint companies post the LRV value of a color right on the fan deck of colors, so it is easy for architects and designers to choose colors to use for building elements.

A good trade-off, between this commercial widespread use of LRV and the need for maximum scientific accuracy could be obtained reversing the current approach: the authors are favorable to a systematic reference to CIE Y in the scientific publications and standards, with the specification that in commercial applications the most used term is LRV, which has in principle the same meaning and definition.

The second aspect which needs to be revised refers to the assessment of the visual contrast between two adjacent surfaces.

As explained above, formulas using ratios should be preferred to simple difference formulas. One of the most used ratio formulas is the Michelson contrast formula:

$$(Y_1 - Y_2)/(Y_1 + Y_2) \tag{2}$$

for use when the reflectance properties of a building element have been published by the manufacturer or have been measured in laboratory, or

$$(L_1 - L_2)/(L_1 + L_2) \tag{3}$$

for use if the luminance of the two adjacent surfaces has been measured in the field (the replacement of CIE Y values with luminance values can be made without significant errors only in case of diffusing, non-shiny, surfaces.).

Other formulas using ratios are those by Weber and by Bowman - Sapolinsky:

$$(L_1 - L_2)/L_2 \text{(Weber contrast formula)} \tag{4}$$

$$125 \times (Y_1 - Y_2)/(Y_1 + Y_2 + 25)\text{(Bowman - Sapolinski contrast formula)} \tag{5}$$

In the above formulas, L_1 stands for the luminance of the brighter area and L_2 stands for the luminance of the adjacent darker area, whether Y_1 and Y_2 are the corresponding CIE tristimulus values.

4 Existing Standards and Recommendations – A Literature Study

The authors examined several accessibility standards, recommendations and guidelines with a focus on the assessment of visual contrast [1–11, 13–23]. In this paper are summarized the requirements of just a few publications, chosen not only for their relevance, but also in order to highlight the different approaches (Table 1).

Table 1. A comparison between visual contrast requirements in some standards

Document	Lighting	Visual contrast determination method	Visual contrast for large surfaces	Visual contrast for small surfaces, potential hazards	Visual contrast for small surfaces, text information
ISO 21542:2011 [16]	Minimum light level in different areas is specified[1]	LRV difference in points[2]	LRV difference ≥ 30 p	LRV difference ≥ 60 p	LRV difference ≥ 60 p
ISO/DIS 21542:2020 [15]	Minimum maintained illuminances in different areas are specified[3]	Michelson formula for building elements Weber formula for small elements	$C_M \geq 30$ or $C_W \geq 45$ min plus LRV of lighter surface ≥ 40	$C_M \geq 60$ or $C_W \geq 75$ plus LRV of lighter surface ≥ 50	$C_M \geq 60$ or $C_W \geq 75$ plus LRV of lighter surface ≥ 70
ÖNORM B 1600:2017[4] [21]	LRV values apply for illuminance $\geq$ 100 lx[5]	LRV difference without unit indication	Level II K ≥ 30	Level I K ≥ 50	Level I K ≥ 50
BS 8300–2:2018 [3]	Average and minimum maintained illuminances are specified	LRV difference in points	LRV ≥ 30 p LRV ≥ 20 p. acceptable, if illuminance ≥ 200 lx		LRV ≥ 70 p
AS 1428.1:2009 [1]		Bowman – Sapolinsky Formula	$C \geq 30$	$C \geq 30$	

Note 1: (e.g.: 100 lx for horizontal surfaces indoors)
Note 2: for lighting conditions lower than specified, the difference in LRVs should be higher;Michelson, Weber, Sapolinsky formulas are also mentioned
Note 3: (e.g.: 100 lx for horizontal surfaces indoors)
Note 4: section on visual contrast is currently under revision
Note 5: for minimum lighting requirements, the standard makes reference to EN 12464-1 and EN 12464-2, "Light and lighting - Lighting of work places" (additional lighting required for workplaces of partially sighted persons)

Without any doubt, the most relevant standard dealing with accessibility of buildings is ISO 21542:2011, "Accessibility and usability of the built environment".

In this standard, the method for determination and specification of visual contrast was based on the difference in LRV of the two adjacent surfaces, or of an element and its background (LRV$_1$–LRV$_2$). In its revised version (to be published in 2021), ISO/DIS 21542:2020 [15] incorporates a different approach, which represents a substantial improvement in the assessment of visual contrast.

Although confirming the use of LRV for the description of the reflectance properties of building elements, the new standard will introduce the following important improvements:

- a better definition for LRV (proportion of visible light reflected by a surface, weighted for the spectral sensitivity to light of the human eye);
- a clear statement of the equivalence between LRV and CIE Y, together with the specification that the latter "is evaluated with reference to the standard illuminant CIE D65 and to the geometry dif/8°";
- the adoption of Michelson formula or Weber formula for the determination of luminance contrast instead of the simple difference formula LRV$_1$-LRV$_2$;
- a very detailed and correct treatment of visual contrast;
- an exhaustive treatment of recommended measurement methodologies, with a clear distinction between tests more suitable in the laboratory and those more suitable in the field.

While the former LRV difference formula was based on a study by Cook and Bright [2] - which, by the way, was also the main source for contrast requirements in British Standard 8300:2018 [3] -, the recommendation in a guideline published by the "Centre Suisse pour la construction adaptée aux handicapés" in 2017 [22] might have had an impact on the decision to switch to Michelson and Weber formula in the revision of ISO 21542:2011.

Considering, that e.g. the Austrian national standard ÖNORM B 1600:2017, "Barrierefreies Bauen - Planungsgrundlagen" [21] will probably undergo a similar modification by changing from LRV difference to Michelson formula in the current revision, one might assume there is a general tendency to focus on formulas using a ratio.

Another interesting approach is suggested with introduction of the Sapolinsky formula in the national Australian standard "Design for Access and Mobility" [2], which makes a clear distinction between tests in the laboratory and tests in the field.

5   Authors' Proposal

The authors are definitely satisfied with the new approach to visual contrast assessment introduced in the revision of ISO 21542 now at the stage of ISO/FDIS.

The adoption of the ratio formulas by Michelson and Weber instead of the difference formula recommended by ISO 21542:2011 is an important result.

The new text, with its comprehensive description of visual contrast, will promote a more extended application of the standard, both at the design stage, and in the tests in the field.

For the future, the authors suggest that the TGs working at "vertical" international and national standards containing references to accessibility for people with visual impairments, take into account the new approach in ISO 21542, reaping the rewards of the work done.

In this way, the confusions that today still originate by the diversity between the different existing standards will be gradually eliminated, with great benefits for the stakeholders and the users of buildings.

Certainly, there is a need for the prosecution of researches aimed at a deeper comprehension of the perception of visual contrast by people with visual impairments in order to define algorithms capable to offer the best achievable correlation between the visual contrast values produced by the formula and the visual perception by the human eye.

In this context, it would be useful to study the possibility of taking into account, besides the visual contrast, also an additional contribution by colour contrast, which persons who are capable of colour discrimination at least to a certain degree would benefit from. A very precious guide, for this goal, is ensured by the EN ISO 24502:2010 [18].

6 Conclusion

The use of Michelson and Weber formulas, according to the recommendations in the ISO/DIS 21542:2020, is a great step forward in order to evaluate visual contrast.

Nevertheless, further research work, in cooperation between scientists of different fields, could bring to algorithms capable to offer the best achievable correlation between the visual contrast values produced by the formula and the visual perception by the human eye, contributing to improve accessibility of built environment.

References

1. AS 1428.1:2009 Design for access and mobility, Part 1: General requirements for access - New building work
2. Bright, K. et al.: Colour, Contrast & Perception - Design Guidance for Internal Built Environments. Revised edition. The University of Reading, UK (2004)
3. BS 8300–2:2018 Design of an accessible and inclusive built environment, Part 2: Buildings. Code of practice
4. CIE liaison: https://cie.co.at/about-cie/liaisons. Accessed 4 Feb 2021
5. Code on Accessibility in the Built Environment 2019, Singapore: Building and Construction Authority
6. CSA B651:2018 Accessible design for the built environment, Standard Council of Canada
7. DIN 18040–1:2010 Barrierefreies Bauen - Planungsgrundlagen - Teil 1: Öffentlich zugängliche Gebäude
8. DIN 32975:2009 Gestaltung visueller Informationen im öffentlichen Raum zur barrierefreien Nutzung
9. EN 16584–1:2017 Railway applications - Design for PRM use - General requirements - Part 1: Contrast
10. EN 16584–2:2017 Railway applications - Design for PRM use - General requirements - Part 2: Information

11. EN 81–70:2020 Safety rules for the construction and installation of lifts—Particular applications for passenger and goods passenger lift—Part 70: Accessibility to lifts for persons including persons with disability
12. Feigusch, G., Steffan, I.T.: Accessibility and Visual Contrast: A proposal for a better evaluation of this physical quantity. In: Bagnara, S., Tartaglia, R., Albolino, S., Alexander, T., Fujita, Y. (eds.) Proceedings of the 20th Congress of International Ergonomics Association - IEA 2018: Advances in Intelligent Systems and Computing, vol. 824, 1642–1648, Springer, Cham, Switzerland (2019). https://doi.org/10.1007/978-3-319-96071-5_168
13. FprCEN/TR 17621:2021 Accessibility and usability of the built environment - Technical performance criteria and specifications
14. Hauck, N.: Barrierefreie Beleuchtungslösungen für sehbehinderte Menschen in Innenräumen sowie Entwicklung einer Kontrastbestimmungsmethode. Wien: Dissertation TU Wien (2018)
15. ISO/DIS 21542:2020 Building construction—Accessibility and usability of the built Environment
16. ISO 21542:2011 Building construction—Accessibility and usability of the built Environment
17. ISO 24502:2010 Ergonomics-Accessible design-Specification of age-related luminance contrast for coloured light
18. ISO 9241 -303:2008 Ergonomics of human-system interaction- Part 303 Requirements for electronic visual Displays
19. ISO 3864–1:2002 Graphical symbols—Safety colours and safety signs- Part 1: Design principles for safety signs in workplaces and public areas
20. Mühlthaler, E., et al.: Barrierefreies Bauen - Kontrastreiche Gestaltung öffentlich zugänglicher Gebäude. Deutscher Blinden- und Sehbehindertenverband e. V. - DBSV, Berlin (2016)
21. ÖNORM B 1600:2017 Barrierefreies Bauen – Planungsgrundlagen
22. Schmidt, E., Buser, F.: Contrastes visuels - Directives "Conception et determination de contrastes visuels", Ed. Centre Suisse pour la construction adaptée aux handicapés, Zurich (CH), (2017)
23. SIA 500:2009 Hindernisfreie Bauten

Towards Innovative Bathroom Solutions for All - A Needs Analysis

AnnaKlara Stenberg Gleisner$^{(\boxtimes)}$ ⓘ, Andrea Eriksson ⓘ, Mikael Forsman ⓘ,
and Linda M. Rose ⓘ

KTH Royal Institute of Technology, Stockholm, Sweden
ansg@kth.se

Abstract. To be able to age in place, the home environment often needs to accommodate users' needs throughout their life span. Bathrooms are an especially demanding space for the user, but also for those supporting the user, for example nursing assistants, in their daily life. This study investigated factors of importance for creating well-functioning bathrooms – for both nursing assistants and users, identifying needs concerning access to assistive devices for these groups. Semi-structured interviews were carried out. In total 13 nursing assistants, occupational therapists and users participated in the interviews. The overall results emphasize the importance of space, assistive devices and to be able to customize the bathroom to accommodate the user's needs throughout their life span. These factors are of importance in order to enable independency and safety for the user in the bathroom, and at the same time, enable a safe work environment for those supporting the user. The results help us to understand the complexity of this problem and the results can be used in the work of reducing injury risks and create sustainable work environments.

Keywords: Work environment · Autonomy · Nursing assistants · Accessibility · Assistive devices · Ageing

1 Introduction

Our societies are facing a significant structural change due to an increasing ageing population [1]. People will need to live at home longer and many types of treatments and care will be provided at home. A safe home environment is important for its residents to be able to age in place, and many homes are also work environments for health and home care staff, such as nursing assistants [2]. In particular, residential bathrooms can constitute a challenging environment [3], since they often lack sufficient space for accommodating both the care recipient (hereafter called "user"), their assistive devices and in addition, one or two health or home care staff (hereafter called "nursing assistants").

Nursing assistants often have a high workload. A common reason for sick-leave for this group is work-related musculoskeletal disorders, MSDs, which manifests, for example, as back pain after adverse exposures, such as lifting and moving users during unfavorable conditions [4]. Often opposed to residential bathrooms, the bathrooms in

N. L. Black et al. (Eds.): IEA 2021, LNNS 220, pp. 376–383, 2021.
https://doi.org/10.1007/978-3-030-74605-6_47

nursing homes are in most cases large, which makes it easier for the nursing assistants to move around and support the user. However, large bathrooms have longer distances between support points such as grab bars, which the user can hold on to, and larger distances between the toilet, the sink and the shower/bath tub. This may increase the risk of falling for the user [5].

Assistive devices, such as walking aids, toilet seat raisers, transferring devices and grab bars, can be used to increase independence and safety in the bathroom, both for the user and the nursing assistants [6]. The World Health Organization (WHO) defines assistive devices as equipment that is used to help the individual, due to health condition, to complete an activity [7]. In Sweden, most assistive devices are prescribed and provided by occupational therapists.

This study is a part of the first step in a project, which focuses on, to both improve the work environment for the nursing assistants who support users in their bathroom activities, and to improve user autonomy and safety in the bathroom. The specific aim of this study was to investigate factors of importance to create well-functioning bathrooms as well as factors that are challenging in these spaces – for both nursing assistants and users. This included identifying needs concerning access to assistive devices for nursing assistants, and for the users.

2   Method

In order to address the aim of the study, semi-structured interviews [8] with open-ended questions were carried out. In total, 13 nursing assistants, occupational therapists and users participated in the interviews. Table 1 provides information about occupation, gender and the number of participants in each category. The nursing assistants and the occupational therapists were recruited through inquiries to various municipalities in Sweden. Inclusion criteria were that they, in their daily profession, work with elderly people in the users own homes, or in residential care. The participating users were recruited via the research team's contacts. Criteria for inclusion for the users were; seventy years of age or more and living at home.

Table 1. Occupation, gender and number of participants.

	Number of participants		
Occupation/Role	Female	Male	In total
Nursing assistant	3	1	4
Occupational therapist	3	-	3
User	5	1	6
In total	**11**	**2**	**13**

Two interview guides were developed, one for the professionals – the occupational therapists and the nursing assistants, and one for the users. The guides contained questions about for example; how bathrooms are perceived as a work environment and if the bathrooms fit the user's needs. Other questions were; what factors are perceived as problems in bathrooms, what is needed to make the user independent in bathrooms and questions on the existence of assistive devices and the usage of such devices.

The participants gave oral consent before the interview started. Each interview lasted between 30–60 min and the interviews were conducted and recorded via telephone and then transcribed verbatim. The interview material was sorted at topic level and analyzed using qualitative content analysis [9]. The material was then categorized into the themes "Work Environment", "Autonomy and Independency", "Assistive Devices", "Other aspects" and the result is presented within these themes.

3   Results

3.1   Work Environment

The results point to a number of factors that are challenging for nursing assistants when helping a user in their bathroom. Bathrooms in the own home are generally not built for accommodating the user, assistive devices as well as nursing assistants. Often these bathrooms are small with limited space to move around. For nursing assistants, helping a user with activities in daily living (ADL) in the bathroom often includes standing or kneeling in adverse working postures. Stated by all interviewed professionals, a common problem is lack of space on the sides of the toilet. If there is almost no space on the sides, the nursing assistants need to stand in front of the user resulting in an awkward working posture.

The bathroom floor can become wet and slippery during showering and is perceived as a risk factor both for users and for the nursing assistants. Beside the risk of slipping on a wet floor, helping a user with showering can also result in a moist indoor climate in the bathroom. Oftentimes the bathroom lacks sufficient ventilation, which aggravates the problem, resulting in a demanding work environment for the nursing assistants.

The need for education about how to use different assistive devices was also identified. In addition, three out of four nursing assistants confirmed that courses in lifting and moving techniques are provided, but that the courses do not focus on lifting and moving techniques in cramped spaces, such as small bathrooms.

Nursing assistants have limited or no influence on changing the bathroom layout to make it better to work in, e.g. for example; removing the bathtub in order to install a shower. This includes removing bathroom cupboards that are in the way or removing or putting carpets on the floor. This refers to that the user often is unwilling to change the interior of the bathroom, and does not consider his or her bathroom as a work environment.

3.2   Autonomy and Independency

The layout of the bathroom, as well as the size of the room is of importance. Small bathrooms are difficult to move around in when having one or more assistive devices, for example a shower seat and a walker.

All six interviewed users stated that they had a need for customizing the bathroom in order to better accommodate their needs. A toilet that is mounted to standard height is in most cases too low for a person with difficulties sitting down and standing up. The bathroom door width and the height of the threshold are design features that are crucial for whether or not a user with an assistive device (such as a walker or wheelchair), depends on help. Although shower chairs per se may be stable, an uneven floor makes the chair unstable. This is often the case in bathrooms designed with a drop to make it easier for the water to flow away towards the drain. The move from a wheelchair or a walker to an unstable shower chair is risky and may result in the user becoming dependent on help to take a shower.

3.3 Assistive Devices

Poorly equipped bathrooms were a common problem among the nursing assistants, the occupational therapists and the users interviewed. The need for well-functioning assistive devices, such as manual lifts, toilet raisers, mobility devices, transferring aids and grab bars was identified as a key factor for achieving both improved work environments and increased user autonomy, e.g. better working postures and increased safety for both parties. Other needs identified good lighting, contrast-colored toilet seats, and supports for users with impaired vision, or cognitive impairments.

Grab bars provide an important extra support for the user when moving around in the bathroom. Five out of six interviewed users expressed a need for mounting grab bars, especially in the shower. Some of the users interviewed have had contact with an occupational therapist, but none of them had, for example, grab bars mounted in "the right" places in the bathroom. Three of the users interviewed stated that instead of grab bars, they used the objects closest to them when sitting down, rising up and moving around in the bathroom - objects such as the sink, the shower mixer, the shower, the bathroom cabinet and the door case.

There was also a perception among most interviewees (11 out of 13, both professionals and users), that assistive devices such as walkers and wheelchairs often do not fit in the bathroom due to lack of space. One user did not have home care service, but did have the need to make their bathroom more accessible. The user was unaware of that the occupational therapist working in the municipality could prescribe and provide assistive devices.

3.4 Other Aspects

The results also pointed towards the need for a clarification of the role "occupational therapist", for example when recommending and providing the users with assistive devices. In Sweden, the occupational therapist is often contacted by the home care service or health care when they discover that a person is in need for assistance, or more assistance, in their daily life. For elderly people, the use of home care often starts with cleaning service or help with grocery shopping. Two out of three interviewed occupational therapists believed that if they worked more preventive and were involved from the beginning when the elderly person starts to use home care service, they could help the user to stay independent for a longer time. They believe that the use of assistive devices in the own home from an early stage would prevent the need for more assistance from home care service further on.

4 Discussion

4.1 Discussion of Results

The results point to a number of factors that are important to form a well-functioning bathroom. Often the layout and the size of the bathrooms in private housing differ from the bathrooms in health care and residential care. Yet, the private bathroom becomes a work environment when a disability occurs and the user needs help from home care service. It is difficult to overlook the fact that sufficient space is required, for example, if one or two assistants are going to be able to work in good working postures. How can a small bathroom constitute a good work environment in such cases? More research is needed on how the size and the layout in small bathrooms affects the functionality, accessibility and safety as well as how different assistive devices function in such spaces.

In our study, poorly equipped bathrooms were a common problem among the participants. Stevens et al. [11] approve that installing assistive devices (called "safety equipment" in the article), such as grab bars around the toilet and both inside and outside of the shower or bathtub, will improve safety in the bathroom. The absence of these features leads to dependency, loss of function and autonomy for the user. The results are in line with the results from a study [12] on measuring "Universal Design" features in bathrooms. Mullick [12] reported that accessible fixtures and features, such as a wider door opening, grab bars and a higher toilet with fold down grab bars, result in higher level of performance and independency for people living with disabilities.

It is crucial that the assistive devices can be used both when entering and when being in the bathroom. Our study showed that it was common that the assistive devices, such as walkers and wheelchairs, did not fit in the bathroom. Previous research by De-Rosende-Celeiro and colleagues has found that having access to, and be able to use assistive devices in the bathroom, increase independence and safety [6]. Based on the results in that study, De-Rosende-Celeiro et al. suggested that people who use more categories of assistive devices in the bathroom were less likely to receive personal help.

The results from the interviews also implicate that courses in lifting and moving techniques are often held in large hospital or in nursing home bathrooms and not in "small" bathrooms with restricted space. This is challenging for the nursing assistants working in a user's home as they are often exposed to several adverse postures when helping a user in a small bathroom. Implications from this study are thus that the education for lifting and moving techniques, held for those who work in home care, should be focusing on lifting and moving techniques in small and cramped spaces such as small bathrooms.

This study contributes to the knowledge on what is needed to make a bathroom well-functioning, both for the nursing assistants and for the users. As stated in the introduction we can expect that people will have to live at home longer and treatments and care will be given in the own home to a larger extent. It is also expected that the proportion of older people in the oldest age groups will increase [10]. In Sweden, the policy is that people should primarily age in place. That means that a person has to have an extensive need for care that cannot be given in their own home, in order to be qualified to move to residential care. There are other housing options on the market for people in need for an accessible housing, such as "senior housing", but by making the own home more accessible, moving to a new housing, can be avoided. Thus, bathrooms which enable tailored adaptions to user needs over time, would enable ageing in place throughout a longer period of people's life span.

Mullick [12] states that the accessible bathroom features (assistive devices such as grab bars, toilet raiser) support people with disabilities and can at the same time benefit other users. But unlike the accessible bathroom, a "universal design bathroom" supports all users equally and improves the functional independence. This can be achieved, according to Mullick [12], for example by having the functional benefits of accessible bathrooms as a baseline and having a high flexibility in design so users can customize their bathrooms. This approach invites not only people with disabilities to be able to use the bathroom, but all people, for example children, young adults, short as well as tall people and overweight people. More research is needed in this area how this approach affects the bathroom usage for all people. As stated in the results section, this study identified a need for making the bathroom more accessible for both users and nursing assistants. The study also pointed to a need for customizing the bathroom to fit the specific users' personal needs. Having for example height adjustable sinks and toilets would have solved many of those problems along with grab bars mounted to adequate places. The results of this study implicate that in order to fit users' needs throughout their life span and to be able to age in place, the bathroom needs to be flexible in its design, with for example height adjustable bathroom furniture, as well as having sufficient space and access to assistive devices.

4.2 Discussion of Methods

The design of the semi-structured interview allows the interviewer to have a structured guide with questions and at the same time be able to ask follow-up questions to the participants [8]. In this study, the methods used have made it possible to obtain knowledge on the same topic from both users and professionals – nursing assistants and occupational therapists. The questions in the interview guide allowed us to identify which problems occur when using the bathroom and draw conclusion of what could have been a better solution. Due to the current global Covid-19 pandemic, the interviews were conducted via telephone instead of in person. The consequences of that choice of method were among others that we were not able to photo document the users' bathrooms and make an analysis of the size and the layout of the bathrooms. This is perceived by the research team as important information and is included in the next steps of the project. There is also a possibility that the interview material would have been of larger content if the interviews had been conducted in person. It is likely that the human encounters had contributed to even richer and deeper answers from the interviewees [13]. Although this study is based on a small sample size of thirteen interviews, it likely presents a snapshot of what the reality looks like.

4.3 Future Work

The results in this study identified a number of needs in the bathroom, which can be used for improving safety and enabling independency. Such improvements would benefit users as well as the nursing assistants. Beside the three interviewed groups in this study there are other stakeholders who can contribute with their perspectives, for example representatives from the Swedish trade union and the Swedish work environment authority. They have a broad knowledge on the work environment for nursing assistants and the consequences of such environments. As mentioned above, the project is ongoing and the work will continue with a larger study, and further interviews with other types of stakeholders will take place as well as product evaluation and testing.

5   Conclusions

This study has identified a number of factors of importance for well-functioning bathrooms and needs concerning assistive devices in the bathroom. The results emphasize the importance of the following factors; space, accessibility, access to assistive devices and to be able to customize the bathroom to accommodate the user's needs throughout the life span. These factors are important in order to enable independency and safety for the user in the bathroom, and at the same time, enable a safe work environment for those supporting the user.

Acknowledgements. The authors thank the participants of this study.

References

1. United Nations: World population prospects 2019 (2019). https://population.un.org/wpp/Publications/Files/WPP2019_10KeyFindings.pdf. Accessed 02 Mar 2020
2. Sveriges Kommuner och Landsting: Framtidens vårdbyggnader (2017). (in Swedish). https://webbutik.skr.se/sv/artiklar/framtidens-vardbyggnader.html. Accessed 04 Sep 2019
3. King, E.C., Holliday, P.J., Andrews, G.J.: Care Challenges in the bathroom: the views of professional care providers working in clients' homes. J. Appl. Gerontol. **37**(4), 493–515 (2016)
4. Andersen, L., Clausen, T., Mortensen, O., Burr, H., Holtermann, A.: A prospective cohort study on musculoskeletal risk factors for long-term sickness absence among healthcare workers in eldercare. Int. Arch. Occup. Environ. Health **85**(6), 615–622 (2011)
5. Daram, L., Lilliehorn, P.: Badrumssyndromet. En förstudie om förutsättningar för bra badrum för äldre och god arbetsmiljö för vård- och omsorgspersonal. Rapport 1. Arkus och Hjälpmedelsinstitutet, Stockholm (2014). (in Swedish)
6. De-Rosende-Celeiro, I., Torres, G., Seoane-Bouzas, M., Ávila, A.: Exploring the use of assistive products to promote functional independence in self-care activities in the bathroom. PloS One **14**(4), E0215002 (2019)
7. World Health Organization: Measuring Health and Disability Manual for WHO Disability Assessment Schedule International Classification of Functioning, Disability and Health (2010). https://www.who.int/standards/classifications/international-classification-of-functioning-disability-and-health/who-disability-assessment-schedule. Accessed 22 Jan 2021
8. Patton, M.Q.: Qualitative Research & Evaluation Methods: Integrating Theory and Practice, 4th edn. SAGE Publications Inc, Thousand Oaks (2015)
9. Graneheim, U.H., Lundman, B.: Qualitative content analysis in nursing research: concepts, procedures and measures to achieve trustworthiness. Nurse Educ. Today **24**(2), 105–112 (2004)

10. Socialdepartementet: Framtidens äldreomsorg – en nationell kvalitetsplan (2018). (in Swedish). https://www.regeringen.se/49ee56/contentassets/faebe5c0bff14b9fb7cd9df7 625d2e10/framtidens-aldreomsorg--en-nationell-kvalitetsplan-2017_18_280.pdf. Accessed 04 Sep 2019
11. Stevens, J.A., Mahoney, J.E., Ehrenreich, H.: Circumstances and outcomes of falls among high risk community-dwelling older adults. Injury Epidemiol. **1**(1), 1–9 (2014)
12. Mullick, A.: Measuring universal design: case of the bathroom. In: Proceedings of the Human Factors and Ergonomics Society Annual Meeting, pp. 557–562, Human Factors and Ergonomics Society, Los Angeles, CA (1999)
13. Novick, G.: Is there a bias against telephone interviews in qualitative research? Res. Nurs. Health **31**(4), 391–398 (2008)

Designing Smart Ring for the Health of the Elderly: The CloudIA Project

Francesca Tosi[1], Filippo Cavallo[2,3,4], Mattia Pistolesi[1(✉)], Laura Fiorini[2], Erika Rovini[3,4], and Claudia Becchimanzi[1]

[1] Laboratory of Ergonomics and Design (LED), Department of Architecture, University of Florence, 93 Sandro Pertini street, 50041 Calenzano, Florence, Italy
{francesca.tosi,mattia.pistolesi,claudia.becchimanzi}@unifi.it
[2] Department of Industrial Engineering, University of Florence, via Santa Marta 3, 50139 Florence, Italy
{filippo.cavallo,laura.fiorini}@unifi.it
[3] The BioRobotics Institute, Scuola Superiore Sant'Anna, Viale Rinaldo Piaggio, 34, 56025 Pontedera, Italy
erika.rovini@santannapisa.it
[4] Department of Excellence in Robotics and AI, Scuola Superiore Sant'Anna, Pontedera, Pisa, Italy

Abstract. This paper describes the design and development of a wearable device, able to monitor physiological data, movement and falls, for fragile older person who require health care. Some approaches of Universal Design and Human-Centred Design were used, which allowed to evaluate and design the interaction between the person and the system. From a design point of view, studies on wearability and the most appropriate landmarks of the human body were carried out, suitable for monitoring heartbeat, movement and falls. From an engineering point of view, the main challenge was the miniaturization of the electronic components for the development of a wearable device to be placed on a small surface of the body, able to allow the performance of daily activities without altering the natural movements of the user, also considering the physical limitations of older and fragile people. Our results indicate how digital technologies, specifically wearable, can be a resource to support the independence and psycho-physical well-being of old people. The next step of the research program concerns the experimentation with a significant sample of typical users (elderly and socio-health professionals), both in nursing home and at home.

Keywords: Wearable · Smart ring · Elderly · Human-Centred Design · Universal design · Multidisciplinary approach

1 Introduction

The process of population aging is occurring throughout the world and the number of older people is expected to grow steadily over the coming decades, both at European and global level [1, 2]. According to ARS Toscana [3], the Regional Health Agency that deals

N. L. Black et al. (Eds.): IEA 2021, LNNS 220, pp. 384–392, 2021.
https://doi.org/10.1007/978-3-030-74605-6_48

with consulting and research for elderly in Tuscany, by 2060 almost a third of Europeans will be over 65 and demographic trends in Tuscany are even more pronounced. A study conducted by ARS in 2014 demonstrated that elderly in Tuscany were 916.640 and will increase up to 36% of the population in 2050.

Old people are more subject to illness and disability, in fact around 51% of the elderly in Tuscany declare to suffer from a chronic or long-term illness [3]. However, despite health problems, most of them hope to be able to live in their own home as long as possible. Although such desire can be interpreted as an improvement in the quality of life, it is strongly related to the risk of domestic accidents, such as falls, and social isolation, such as depression and loneliness. This condition often requires that the older persons should move from their home to the nursing home, radically changing their everyday life.

The demand for products and services dedicated to the care and support of the elderly at home is becoming increasingly high, especially for what concerns diagnostic, health monitoring and care devices.

Nowadays digital technologies represent a resource to support ageing at home since they can effectively monitor physiological data and support the elderly's performance of daily domestic activities promoting their own safety [4]. This condition offers new exciting challenges for designers, ergonomists and engineers, both from a technical/functional perspective as well as from an aesthetical and socio-emotional point of view.

The paper describes the methodology used and the results achieved by the *CloudIA* research program, a project co-funded by the *POR FESR Toscana 2014–2020* program, which involved a partnership of 5 social cooperatives and 2 university of Tuscany Region.

1.1 Digital Technologies for the Elderly

New digital products, objects connected to the network and to each other (IoT) and wearable technologies (wearable computers) are playing and may play a key role in the near future.

Compact and miniaturised health devices can be effective for monitoring physiological data and maintaining health status, but also for promoting the safety of the elderly at home and supporting the performance of daily and household activities.

Such devices have vast potential and can be applied in different areas, depending on the user's needs [5, 6]. Integrated into watches, shoes, socks, bracelets, necklaces etc., increasingly powerful wearable device that enhance human abilities are becoming an integral part of everyday life, blending into more traditional interactions with objects or generating new modes of action.

The challenges of wearable health devices to overcome demographic changes can be summarised as [4]:

– continuous sensor-based monitoring can bring new sources of information and insights to help care providers understand each individual's situation and needs and help researchers better understand diseases and their cures;
– monitoring and caring for elderly or frail users requiring long-term care, either at home or in nursing homes or hospitals;
– reduction of healthcare costs as on-site clinical monitoring.

2   Needs Study

2.1   Evaluation Phase

Thanks to Human-Centred Design (HCD) [7] methods, such as interviews [8–10], brainstorming sessions [10, 11] with facility managers and coordinators and social and health professional (social and health workers, caregivers, nurses and rehabilitation therapists), user observation [9, 10], Task Analysis [9, 10] and scenario-based design [8–12], it was possible to investigate the needs, expectations of each single operator, current or potential criticalities and problems during the implementation of the activities [13].

The interview and brainstorming sessions made it possible to discuss together with the facility managers (directors and social workers) each daily activity carried out in the nursing home and at home. A total of 10 operators participated in this phase. Questions have been raised over the tools commonly used for work management and over the improvements needed to make health care more efficient.

The observation of the users was useful to evaluate how the operators work and how the users behave in the real context of use.

The Task Analysis (TA) involved the breakdown of the actions necessary to achieve goals for each character involved in the pathway (elderly person) and in the care process (formal and/or informal caregiver, and health or social worker).

Following the evaluation phase, it was possible to identify the main criticalities felt by the people involved, the areas of intervention and the relative design solutions.

It is important to point out that the co-operatives involved expressed the need for a wearable device compatible with the users' lifestyles, i.e. simplified devices addressed to elderly with compromised abilities. Specifically, the need of a wearable device emerged, i.e. a ring which monitors physiological data, movement and possible falls of the elderly person.

Finally through the scenario-based design, it was possible to define the following functions of wearable devices suitable for the users and the contexts of use at issue:

- monitoring the patient's health status, in terms of heart rate and its variations, movements and falls;
- monitoring of the patient's sleep;
- and support to the health worker in control activities.

3   Smart Ring Description

To ensure that the wearable technology encounter the user's needs, the Universal Design (UD) approach was followed. The UD includes and recognizes the variety of abilities and circumstances of various users allowing to become aware of them and how to deal with them. The UD principles [14, 15] are strongly linked to usability, as good usability allows users to employ technology consistently and easily [15, 16].

Considering the UD principles, the HCD approach has been applied for the design of the new wearable device, based on the needs of the target users. This means that it has been designed considering two categories of users: health professional and elderly people.

The UD challenge, which also bases its effectiveness on the HCD approach, consists in the design and development of the product system, based on the real needs, expectations and aspirations of the users involved during the evaluation phase.

As a result, the new wearable has the function of supporting health professional in providing care services to the elderly, whilst, as far as the elderly are concerned, its purpose is monitoring their physiological parameters and movements, as well as eventual falls. The collected data will be sent to a cloud platform able to analyse them in real time. In case of detection of any abnormal event, a web interface will be able to communicate it to the social health professionals. The user interface on the Cloud platform is designed to facilitate and optimize the social health professionals workflow.

The wearable ring-shaped device has been defined starting from the development of a flexible electronic board, modeled on studies based on wearability [17] and on the most suitable landmarks of the human body, suitable to monitor heart rate, movements and falls. It has to be placed in contact with the first phalanx of the index finger to detect the signal of movement, HR, HRV and SpO2.

From the design point of view, the main challenge was to ensure a product with high usability standards but not invasive from a morphological perspective and stigmatized from a perceptual viewpoint (see Fig. 1).

The ring is made of 2 covers, both printed in 3D in commercial material produced by Formlabs. One cover is made of Flexible resin material (flexible and compressible elastomer) inside which is inserted the flexible electronic board (see Fig. 2), whilst the other cover performs the function of closure and protection, and it is made of Tough Resign (elastomer with high resistance to stress) (see Fig. 3).

3.1 Flexible Electronic Board

The flexible printed circuit board (PCB) layout of the electronic board has been developed according to the requirements identified (mainly wearability, comfortability, ease of use). This type of circuit is very practical and suitable for applications where flexibility, space savings are required, as in the case of finger device. At the same time, they are also very expensive, easily damaged and requires a more difficult assembly process. A PCB consists of two basic parts: a substrate (the board) and printed wires (the copper traces). The substrate provides a structure that physically holds the circuit components and printed wires in place and provides electrical insulation between conductive parts. The PCB layout integrates all the main components of the ring-shaped device, i.e., microcontroller, Bluetooth module and Inertial Measurement Unit and physiological sensors.

The ring-shaped wearable device for psychophysical monitoring proposed in CLOUDIA has been developed based on an STM32-F103 controller (STMicroelectronics, Italy) that integrates ARM®Cortex™-M3 32-bit MCU technology and represents a good trade-off between power consumption and size. The system is equipped with the LSM9DS1 9-axis sensor, which is the latest generation of inertial MEMS (STMicroelectronics, Italy). The inertial sensor includes a 3D digital linear acceleration sensor (selectable full scale: $\pm$ 2/$\pm$ 4/$\pm$ 8/$\pm$ 16 g), a 3D digital angular rate sensor (selectable full scale: $\pm$ 245/$\pm$ 500/$\pm$ 2000 dps), and a 3D digital magnetic sensor (selectable full scale: $\pm$ 4/$\pm$ 8/$\pm$ 12/$\pm$ 16 gauss). The system is also equipped with a Rigado BMD-350

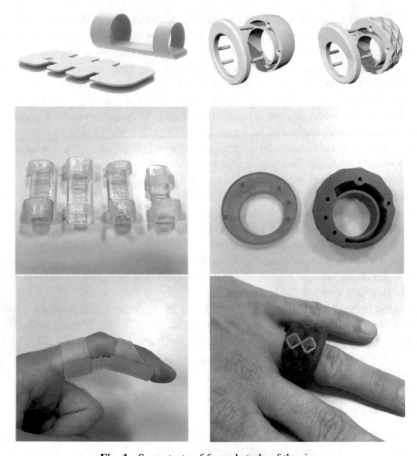

Fig. 1. Some tests of formal study of the ring.

Fig. 2. Detail of the flexible electronic board inserted in the ring cover.

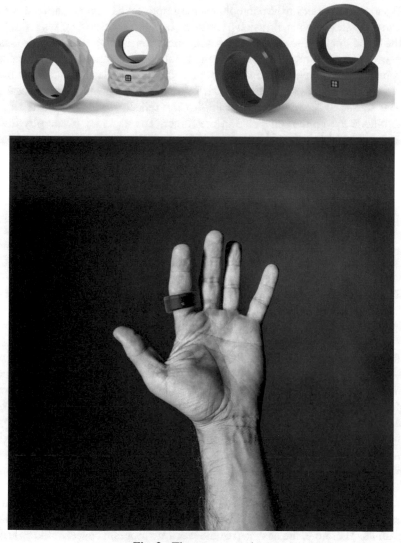

Fig. 3. The new smart ring.

Bluetooth serial device for wireless communication towards a generic control station and it is supplied by a rechargeable LiPo battery. The sampling rate for data acquisition is set at 50 Hz.

The system has been already preliminary validated comparing the accuracy of its measurements with those obtained from an optoelectronic system (i.e., Vicon system) as reported in [18].

Furthermore, the smart ring includes the MAX30102 (Maxim Integrated™, San Jose, CA, USA), a sensor for the measurement of physiological parameters. Indeed, it allows measuring heart rate (HR), heart rate variations (HRV) and blood oxygen saturation

(SpO2) parameters based on the photoplethysmography (PPG) signal. The analysis of the PPG signal, by studying the diffusion of infrared rays in the tissues, makes it possible to study the blood supply. The very low energy consumption, miniaturisation and robustness with respect to motion artefacts with a high signal-to-noise ratio (SNR), were decisive aspects for the selection of this sensor. The placement of the device on the first phalanx of the index finger allows detecting HR, HRV and SpO2 signals via peripheral blood flow. The sensor, indeed, works according to the reflective mode, i.e., the LED and the photodiode are on the same side of the finger. The accuracy of the physiological measurements has been already tested in lab environment involving healthy and young subjects as reported in [19].

4   Conclusion

The results presented in this article have relevance in the design and healthcare sectors. This research is particularly aimed at providing at designing and developing a novel ring solution that monitor the total movements and the physiological parameters of older adults over the day. This device has also an impact on the work of social and health professionals, for whom it is essential to improve health conditions – for the elderly – and working conditions – for health professionals.

Digital technologies represent a resource to support the independence and mental and physical well-being of old people and pose many challenges to design. The research presented in this article also highlights how UD and HCD approaches, in synergy with engineering expertise in the field of Ambient Assisted Living, can offer an important contribution to the identification and analysis of unspoken needs and expectations, in order to create truly useful and acceptable products. Design, when user-centred, can have disruptive results as well as incremental innovation [20], providing a concrete contribution in terms of product innovation and business competitiveness. On this basis, the purpose of design is the design of technologies based on usability, effective and intuitive interaction, absence of stigma, reliability and security to ensure a positive user experience both hedonic and functional.

The technical bench test performed on the flexible electronic board suggest a good accuracy in the measurements. However, the tests were conducted with healthy and young adults. Therefore, the next step of the research program concerns the experimentation with a significant sample of typical users (elderly and health professionals), both in nursing home and domiciliary environments.

Acknowledgements. The author would like to thank the guests and the social-health workers of the social cooperatives of Tuscany for their participation. Special thanks to Jacopo Francesco Montalto for his fundamental contribution for the development and design of the new ring.

Funding.   Research was pursued within the CloudIA project (Regione Toscana, POR CREO FESR 2014–2020, CUP 165.24052017.112000015).

References

1. World Health Organization: World health statistics: monitoring health for the SDGs, sustainable development goals. World Health Organization, Geneva (2018). https://www.who.int/docs/default-source/gho-documents/world-health-statistic-reports/6-june-18108-world-health-statistics-2018.pdf
2. Eurostat: Population structure and ageing, Statistic Explained (2019). https://ec.europa.eu/curostat/statisticsexplained/index.php/Population_structure_and_ageing
3. Agenzia Regionale di Sanità ARS Toscana: Il profilo di salute degli anziani in cifre (2014). https://www.ars.toscana.it/aree-dintervento/la-salute-di/anziani.html
4. Cook, D.J., Schmitter-Edgecombe, M., Jonsson, L., Morant, A.V.: Technology-enabled assessment of functional health. IEEE Rev. Biomed. Eng. **12**, 319–322 (2018). https://doi.org/10.1109/RBME.2018.2851500
5. Piwek, L., Ellis, D.A., Andrews, S., Joinson, A.: The rise of consumer health wearables: promises and barriers. PLoS Med. **13**(2), 1–9 (2016). https://doi.org/10.1371/journal.pmed.1001953
6. Møller, T., Kettley, S.: Wearable health technology design: a humanist accessory approach. Int. J. Des. **11**(3), 35–49 (2017)
7. Meguire, M.: Method to support human-centred design. Int. J. Hum.-Comput. Stud. **55**, 587–634 (2001). https://doi.org/10.1006/ijhc.2001.0503
8. Rubin, J., Chisnell, D.: Handbook of Usability Testing: How to Plan, Design, and Conduct Effective Test, 2nd edn. John Wiley and sons, NJ (2011)
9. Stanton, N.A., Young, M.S., Harvey, C.: Guide to Methodology in Ergonomics, Designing for Human Use, 2nd edn. CRC Press, Taylor and Francis Group, Boca Raton, FL (2014)
10. Fisk, A.D., Rogers, W.A., Charness, N., Czaja, S.J., Sharit, J.: Designing for older adults. Principle and creative human factors approaches. 2nd edn., CRC Press, Taylor and Francis Group, Boca Raton (2009)
11. Gyi, D., Shalloe, S., Wilson, J.R.: Participatory ergonomics. In: Wilson, J.R., Sharples, S. (eds.) The Evaluation of Human Work, 4th edn., pp. 883–906. CRC Press, Taylor and Francis Group, Boca Raton (2015)
12. Rosson, M.B., Carroll, J.M.: Narrowing the gap between specification and implementation in object-oriented development. Scenario-based design. In Carroll, J.M. (ed), Envisioning Work and Technology in System Development, pp. 247–278. John Wiley & Sons, NY (1995)
13. Pistolesi, M., Becchimanzi, C.: Metodologie dell'ergonomia per il design di dispositivi indossabili e robot in cloud per anziani: Introduzione al progetto di ricerca applicata CloudIA. Rivista Italiana di Ergonomia **19**, 20–43 (2019)
14. Erlandson, R.F: Universal and Accessible Design for Products, Services and Processes. CRC Press, Taylor and Francis Group, Boca Raton (2008)
15. Story, M.F.: Maximizing usability: the principles of universal design. In: Assistive Technology, vol. 10(1), pp. 4–12 (1998). https://doi.org/10.1080/10400435.1998.10131955
16. Wentzel, J., Velleman, E., Van der Geest, T: Wearable for all: development of guidelines to stimulate accessible wearable technology design. In. Gay, G., Guerriero, T. (eds.) W4A 2016: Proceedings of the 13th Web for All Conference, vol. 34, pp. 1–4. Association for Computing Machinery, NY (2016). https://doi.org/10.1145/2899475.2899496
17. Tomberg, V., Schulz, T., Kelle, S.: Appliying universal design principles to themes for wearables. In: Antona, M., Stephanidis, C. (eds.): UAHCI 2015, Part II, LNCS 9176, pp. 550–560, Los Angeles, CA (2015). https://doi.org/10.1007/978-3-319-20681-3_52

18. Rovini, E., Galperti, G., Fiorini, L., Mancioppi, G., Manera, V., Cavallo, F.: SensRing, a novel wearable ring-shaped device for objective analysis of reach-to-grasp movements. In: Proceedings 42nd Annual International Conference of the IEEE Engineering in Medicine & Biology Society (EMBC) 2020, pp. 4020–4023, Montreal, QC, Canada (2020). https://doi.org/10.1109/EMBC44109.2020.9176116
19. Fiorini, L., Cavallo, F., Martinelli, M., Rovini, E.: Characterization of a PPG wearable sensor to be embedded into an innovative ring-shaped device for healthcare monitoring. In: Proceedings 10th Forum Italiano Ambient Assisted Living (ForItAAL), Ancona, Italy (2019)
20. Giacomin, J.: What is human centred design? Des. J. **17**(4), 606–623 (2014)

Passenger Activities, Postures, Dis(Comfort) Perception, and Needs During Train Travel

Sumalee Udomboonyanupap[1,2(✉)], Stella Boess[1], and Peter Vink[1]

[1] Faculty of Industrial Design Engineering, Delft University of Technology, Landbergstraat 15, 2628CE Delft, The Netherlands
S.udomboonyanupap@tudelft.nl
[2] Occupational Health and Safety Department, Institute of Public Health, Suranaree University of Technology, 111 University Avenue, Nakhonratchasima, Thailand

Abstract. This study aims to collect data on the activities, postures, dis(comfort), and needs of train passengers. Observations in the trains and questionnaires completed by train passengers were used. The online questionnaire was completed using the smartphone of the passengers during the train trip. The most often observed activity of the passengers was using a smartphone while travelling. They used a smartphone to listen to music, chat or type, look at a video or picture, and to read. Most passengers reported that they hold a smartphone with both hands and used a smartphone with the right hand also. The thigh support and the armrests of the seat showed the lowest comfort and certainly have room for improvement. Future research could be considered to design the seat to increase passenger comfort while using a smartphone.

Keywords: Train · Smartphone · Discomfort · Activities · Posture

1 Introduction

From 2016 to 2020 the number of smartphone users worldwide continuously increased from 2.5 to 3.5 billion. The Global Digital Report (2019) showed that internet usage via a mobile device has jumped from 26% in 2014 to 48% in 2019. Smartphones can be used in many locations, for example in bed, on the airplane, and on the train. Observations by Kilincsoy and Vink (2018) in the train in the Netherlands showed that smartphone use increased from 12.1% in 2014 to 48.3% in 2018 and the activities that are done using the smartphone differed in duration. Honan (2015) described that smartphone use influences the neck flexion, eye strain, and pain in the arm, wrist, and fingers. More pain and fatigue were reported when the smartphone was used for a long period (Kim and Koo 2016). This might lead to Musculoskeletal disorders (MSDs) or Smartphone Syndrome.

The smartphone is also used on trains and facilitating smartphone use by reducing neck flexion might be a way to attract more passengers on the train, besides creating more comfort. Postures and activities on the train have been studied previously (Branton and Grayson 1967; Bronkhorst and Krause 2004; Groenesteijn et al. 2014; Kilincsoy and Vink (2018). However, the interaction with information and the communication

© The Author(s), under exclusive license to Springer Nature Switzerland AG 2021
N. L. Black et al. (Eds.): IEA 2021, LNNS 220, pp. 393–400, 2021.
https://doi.org/10.1007/978-3-030-74605-6_49

technology possibilities have been changing drastically. For example, previous studies by Kilincsoy and Vink (2018) and Kamp et al. (2011) observed passenger activities on the train. But both studies collected several activities: sleeping, reading, talking or discussing, and others. However, the activities of the passenger in the 2018 study on the train changed drastically. Thus, new knowledge on postures and activities is needed to optimize train interiors to facilitate that the traveller can both work and relax optimally. More background knowledge is needed to define which part of the interior should be optimized. The 3 main research questions for this study are: 1) How much smartphone use can be observed in train passengers in Thailand? 2) What activities are performed on the smartphone? 3) How is it linked to posture change and dis(comfort) perception?

2 Methods

To answer above mentioned questions train passengers were observed, and asked to complete questionnaires. This study is based on the methods used by Groenesteijn et al. (2014). The observation focused mainly on the percentage of passengers using a smartphone, while the questionnaires were used to collect the performed activities and tasks while using a smartphone. The researchers collected the data in a sprinter train starting at Nakhonratchasima train station in Thailand in 2020. A pilot test was conducted with 40 paper questionnaires and 18 online questionnaires using a mobile phone. 19 copies were returned of the paper version and 11 were completed. All 18 persons who joined the online questionnaire returned their questionnaire completed. For this reason, the online questionnaire was selected. Based on the pilot nine postures were defined and a tenth 'other' was added (Fig. 1). Five researchers were trained to conduct the research. The researchers started each session by explaining the project objective and benefit to the participant. Then they recorded an observation using an observation form. The main characteristics of the ride were noted (three inputs): train, class, and railway carriage number. Then the total number of passengers, and passengers who use a smartphone were noted by the observers. Then the train passenger was asked to fill in their performed activities, posture, dis(comfort) experience, and their needs in the online questionnaire. They sat on the seat and conducted their normal activities while completing the comfort questionnaire on their smartphone. The global and local discomfort scores were collected using a CR-10 scale (Borg 1982). For each body part, they could rate discomfort on a scale of 1–10 (1 = No discomfort at all, 10 = Extreme discomfort) using a local discomfort map by Corlett and Bishop (1976). The first part of the questionnaire provided the consent form, in which the participants could make their decision to participate or not. After that, they completed the questionnaire and uploaded it by clicking a submit button.

Fig. 1. The corresponding posture related to smartphone use.

3   Results

3.1   Observation Results of the Main Activities Performed by the Train Passengers

The observation could answer the research question on which percentage of train passengers use a smartphone. The researchers collected the overall number of train passengers, then the number of people who use a smartphone were recorded on the observation form. The results showed that out of 606 train passengers, 57.43% were using a smartphone during the trip. This is a 9.13% increase in smartphone use from the last publication by Kilincsoy and Vink (2018) as shown in Fig. 2.

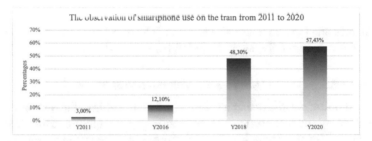

Fig. 2.   Smartphone use in the train in several studies from 2011 to 2020.

3.2   The Questionnaire on Activities, Postures, Dis(Comfort), and Needs of the Train Passengers

The questionnaire was completed by 119 passengers who used a smartphone on the train. Mainly female passengers were in the study population (61.2% female, 37.3% male, and 1.5% considered themselves as others). Their reported average height was 164 cm, which varied from 150 cm to 183 cm. The weight varied from 40 kg to 100 kg, with an average of 64 kg. The ages of the participants varied from 18 to 67 years (average 31 years). Their jobs were a low-intensity 64.3%, followed by the moderate-intensity 27.0%, and 8.7% high-intensity. 47.97% of passengers travelled by train to visit their family, while, 20.27% and 18.24% stated that their trip was for holiday and commuting purposes respectively.

3.2.1   Main Activity of the Train Passengers

The passengers used a smartphone for 88.9% of the time and did other activities for the remainder. The last activities they did before answering the questions on the smartphone were listening to music (36.6% of the time), chatting or typing (22.2%), looking at a video or reading (17.9%, 16.1% respectively). For the questions what the passengers did on the smartphone for the whole trip, it was listening to music for 24.4% of the time, 18.9% chatting or typing on the screen. Looking at a video or picture for this groups was 16.9% of the time, and reading 13.39% as presented in Fig. 3.

Fig. 3. The last activities performed on a smartphone before answering the questionnaire and activities estimated by the passengers over the whole trip.

The average duration for the main activity was approximately 98 minutes. However, they performed the tasks on a smartphone for 30 to 120 minutes. The minimum time was 10 minutes and the maximum 420 minutes. The travel time for the whole trip was on average 6.48 hours and the duration varied from 2 to 12 hours.

3.2.2 The Postures While Using a Smartphone on the Train

The observed postures while using a smartphone on the train are shown in Fig. 4. This picture include by the last posture before completing the questionnaire, and the posture as estimated for the whole trip. The two most common postures were holding the smartphone in the right hand, and using the armrests for 30.5%, and 23.3%, 26.3%, and 36.4% were using both hands to hold their devices, then using the arm support. Lower percentages were observed for the other postures.

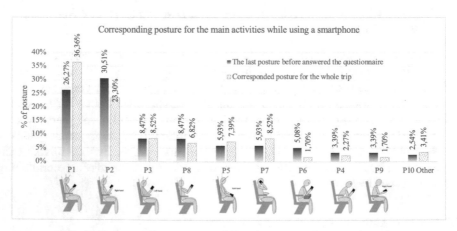

Fig. 4. Corresponding postures while using a smartphone on the train.

The passengers preferred to hold a smartphone with the right hand, and 20% used the armrests when listening to music. 10% held the devices with both hands, and put their elbows on the arm supports for chatting or typing, and assumed the same posture for 5.83%, and 5.00%, for listening to music, and reading, respectively. The corresponding posture and the performed activities of train passengers are shown in Table 1.

Table 1. The postures and the performed activities of train passengers (%).

	P1	P2	P3	P4	P5	P6	P7	P8	P9	P10
Main activities	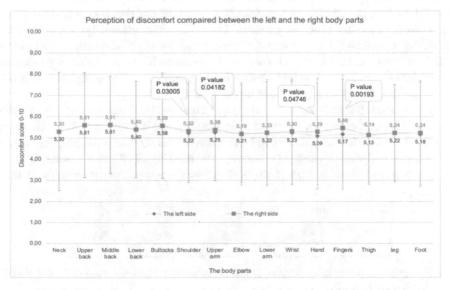									
Listen to music	5,8	20,00	1,67	1,67	1,67	0,00	1,67	2,50	1,67	2,50
Chating or Typing	10,00	1,67	2,50	1,67	1,6	1,67	0,00	2,50	0,83	0,00
Looking at a video	2,50	4,17	2,50	0,00	2,50	0,83	0,0	2,50	0,00	0,83
Reading	5,00	2,50	1,67	0,00	2,50	0,0	0,0	0,00	0,00	0,83
Playing games	0,00	0,83	0,00	0,00	0,00	0,	0,00	0,00	0,00	0,00
Other	1,67	0,83	0,00	0,00	0,00	0,00	0,00	0,83	0,00	0,00
Shopping	1,67	0,00	0,83	0,00	0,0	0,00	0,00	0,00	0,00	0,00
Making a phone call	0,00	0,00	0,00	0,00	0,00	0,00	3,33	0,00	0,00	0,00

3.2.3 Dis(Comfort) Perception

Overall comfort and discomfort experience while using a mobile device on the train was
5.6 and 5.7 on a scale from 1 to 10 respectively. The seat pan was rated with the highest
comfort score: 6.0. The upper backrest, lower backrest followed by a score of 5.8 and 5.6
respectively. For thigh support comfort score was lowest: 4.4. The comfort perception
of legroom, armrests, and headrest were 4.99, 5.00, and 5.15.

Fig. 5. Discomfort per body part for left and the right side of the human body.

Discomfort perception per body part showed that the upper back and middle back had the highest scores (5.6), followed by the buttocks, the right fingers, the lower back, and the right upper arm (5.6, 5.56, 5.4, and 5.4). Figure 5 illustrates the comparison of discomfort between the left and the right body parts. The Wilcoxon signed-rank test showed a significant difference for the shoulder, upper arm, hand, and fingers (P < .05). The right side showed a higher level of discomfort than the left side.

3.2.4   The Train Passengers' Needs Related to Comfort During Smartphone Use

On the general question "Which improvements are needed for comfortable smartphone use?" The Wi-Fi and charger score highest. 21% of the passengers preferred to have Wi-Fi and a charger. 18% mentioned that they needed a better seat pan, for example by increasing the softness and the width of the seat or by changing the cover material to reduce slipping while seated. 17% mentioned the cleanliness inside the train and physical problems like maintaining the same posture over time. Also, passengers mentioned improvement of the armrests such as by installing armrests between the two seats and improving the width and softness of the armrests. Additionally, the high level and the size of arm supports was mentioned by 15% of passengers. 12% of them preferred to have a headrest, and 12% needed more legroom.

4   Discussion

Kamp et al. (2011) found three main activities while people travelled by train: reading, talking/discussing, and relaxing. Seven years later Kilincsoy and Vink (2018) observed three tasks, smartphone use, staring/sleeping, and reading from paper. Groenesteijn et al. (2014) found 3 main activities: staring/sleeping, relaxing, and watching. The corresponding postures of the last study are presented in Fig. 6. Although smartphone use was not one of the main activities, the passengers held the smartphone with both hands or in the right hand, while using an armrest. This result is comparable with a previous publication by Gold et al. (2012), who found that 46.1% of the subjects use a smartphone with both hands, and 36.2% use a mobile phone on the right hand.

In this study, the main activity was using a smartphone. This may have been influenced by the rapid change of information and technology leading up to 2020. However, the other activities not related a smartphone use were the same as previous publications, for example, sleeping, watching or observing, and relaxing. But there was some decrease in percentages for some of these, such as sleeping, shopping, and eating on the train.

Fig. 6. Significant postures for sleeping (a and b), relaxing (a) and watching (c/d/e): studied by (Groenesteijn et al. 2014)

During smartphone use, upper back and middle back have the highest discomfort score. Udomboonyanupap et al. (2020) showed that passengers using a smartphone on the airplane mentioned highest discomfort in the neck. An explanation could be that the heights of the participants were completely different. The average height of this study was 164 cm, while in the airplane study it was 175 cm. Moreover, the main activities in this train study were mainly listening to music (36.6%) and then neck flexion is not needed most of the time.

The results of this study indicate that comfort can also be linked to the armrests. For the two main postures observed, passengers used armrests while holding the devices. (Gustafsson et al. 2017) have reported ergonomic recommendations for texting on a smartphone. A forearm support was preferred while typing, to avoid the neck bending forward and during fast typing when using a small device. Van Veen et al. (2014) reported that discomfort decreases significantly for the neck with forearm support, but arms and hands were not significantly different. It was also because participants were able to adjust the height level of arm support to fit the participant's anthropometry and bring the screen closer to eye height.

Thigh support of the train seat in this study was also an issue. It was too high and the seat pan was too long. When passengers were sitting on the seat and they tried to put their feet on the floor it created more pressure on the thighs. This result is in alignment with Zenk et al. (2012), who reported that when there is too much load at the front of the seat, discomfort increases. Moreover Vink and Lips (2017) found that out of all body parts in the buttock, the area contacting the front area of the seat pan had the highest sensitivity levels, significantly higher than other areas in the buttock.

5 Conclusion

The main activity observed among 606 train travelers is using the smartphone. The smartphone is used for listening to music, chatting, looking at videos, pictures, and reading. Passengers report two main body postures during a train trip in which they use a smartphone. They preferred to use a smartphone with both hands, and resting their arms on the arm support. Also, passengers used frequently the right hand to hold a smartphone. In the seat, the thigh support and the armrests showed the lowest comfort score. These results might be useful for redesigns for train seats to increase passenger comfort, now that the activities they do have changed.

A limitation of this study was that some passengers preferred to sleep or were unwilling to answer the questionnaire. In future research it would be ideal to observe the duration of all of the other activities as well.

Acknowledgements. State railway of Thailand.
The Ministry of Higher Education, Science, Research and Innovation, Thailand.

References

Borg, G.A.: Psychophysical bases of perceived exertion. Med. Sci. Sports Exerc. **14**(5), 377–381 (1982)
Branton, P., Grayson, G.: An evaluation of train seats by observation of sitting behaviour. Ergonomics **10**(1), 35–51 (1967)

Bronkhorst, R.E., Krause, F.: Designing Comfortable Passenger Seats, 1st edn. CRC Press, Boca Raton (2004)

Corlett, E.N., Bishop, R.P.: A technique for measuring postural discomfort. Ergonomics **9**, 175–182 (1976)

Gold, J.E., Driban, J.B., Thomas, N., Chakravarty, T., Channell, V., Komaroff, E.: Postures, typing strategies, and gender differences in mobile device usage: an observational study. Appl. Ergon. **43**, 408–412 (2012)

Groenesteijn, L., Hiemstra-van Mastrigt, S., Gallais, C., Blok, M., Kuijt-Evers, L., Vink, P.: Activities, postures and comfort perception of train passengers as input for train seat design. Ergonomics **57**, 1154–1165 (2014)

Gustafsson, E., Sara Thomee, S., Grimby-Ekman, A., Hagberg, M.: Texting on mobile phones and musculoskeletal disorders in young adults: a five-year cohort study. Appl. Ergon. **58**, 208–214 (2017)

Honan, M.: Mobile work: Ergonomics in a rapidly changing work environment. Work **52**, 289–301 (2015)

Kamp, I., Kilincsoy, Ü., Vink, P.: Chosen postures during specific sitting activities. Ergonomics **54**(11), 1029–1042 (2011)

Kilincsoy, U., Vink, P.: Increase of smartphone use in transport. Tijdschrift voor Hum. Factors **43**(4), 16–18 (2018)

Kim, S., Koo, S.: Effect of duration of smartphone use on muscle fatigue and pain caused by forward head posture in adults. J. Phys. Ther. Sci. **28**, 1669–167 (2016)

Udomboonyanupap, S., Boess, S., Ruiter, I.A., Vink, P.: Discomfort perception per body part while using a smartphone in an aircraft seat. In: ACED-SEANES 2020 Proceedings (2020)

Van Veen, S.A.T., Hiemstra-van Mastrigt, S., Kamp, I., Vink, P.: Improving car passengers' comfort and experience by supporting the use of handheld devices. Work **49**, 215–223 (2014)

Vink, P., Lips, D.: Sensitivity of the human back and buttocks: the missing link in comfort seat design. Appl. Ergon. **58**, 287–292 (2017)

Vink, P., Bazley, C., Kamp, I., Blok, M.: Possibilities to improve the aircraft interior comfort experience. Appl. Ergon. **43**, 354–359 (2012)

WEARESOCIAL Homepage. https://wearesocial.com/blog/2019/01/digital-2019-global-int ernet-use-accelerates. Accessed 2 Sept 2020

Zenk, R., Franz, M., Bubb, H., Vink, P.: Technical note: spine loading in automotive seating. Appl. Ergon. **43**(2), 290–295 (2012)

Part IV: Gender and Work (Edited by Marie Laberge)

Working Conditions in Educational Establishments: Research on Ergonomics and Gender Among Teachers in Pandemic Context

Pamela Astudillo[(⊠)] and Carlos Ibarra

Occupational Ergonomics Program, Kinesiology Department, Faculty of Health Sciences, Atacama University, 1533722 Copiapó, Chile
pamela.astudillo@uda.cl

Abstract. In Chile, there are few studies that documented indicators of teacher occupational health, but do not show evidence regarding the ergonomic working conditions, as well as possible solutions to improve their working conditions. **Objectives:** Describe the working conditions in schools in Chile during the pandemic context, providing a diagnosis from the ergonomic and gender analysis. **Material and Methods**: Case study, observational descriptive cross-sectional design with mixed approach. A total of 101 teachers answered the survey (n = 72 women/ n = 29 man) from 4 educational establishments, that includes the Goldberg General Health Questionnaire (GHQ-12), the Nordic musculoskeletal questionnaire and a questionnaire on working conditions in educational establishments with a specific section in teleworking. **Results:** We found a high prevalence of conditions considered ergonomically unsuitable for teleworking at home, to a greater extent for female, 91,7% of women and 82,8% of men have discomfort at the end of the telework shift, like muscle aches (neck, shoulders, elbows, back, etc.) for a 48,3% of men and 77,8% of women; head-ache (men 24,1%; women 50,0%) and irritation or sore throat (men 41,4%, woman 22,2%). An 44,6% of workers they are at the level of psychopathology with the GHQ-12, and a higher average time spent on housework on work days for women than men. **Conclusions.** This work can provide important evidence from ergonomics and integrating gender, for making public policy decisions that help to improve working conditions, which would benefit working men and women in this sector.

Keywords: Ergonomics · Gender · Teachers · Teleworking · COVID-19

1 Introduction

The education sector in Chile is in full transformation due to the pandemic situation and there is a lack of evidence on ergonomic working conditions and gender. Considering the COVID-19 pandemic facing the global community, this has generated a change in the labor reality in schools, which faces teachers, technicians and professionals supporting a new modality of remote work, impacting their health. In Chile there are no studies that

N. L. Black et al. (Eds.): IEA 2021, LNNS 220, pp. 403–412, 2021.
https://doi.org/10.1007/978-3-030-74605-6_50

describe ergonomic working conditions by gender in schools previously. The aims of this research are describing the working conditions in schools in Chile during the pandemic context, providing a diagnosis from the ergonomic and gender analysis, to know the occupational exposures of workers has with the teleworking identifying the effects on general health, musculoskeletal disorders, psychological health and the interferences in the balance of work-family that these workers experience during this process of work transformation.

2 Methodology

Study Design: It's a mixed descriptive cross-sectional study with the research-action approach. The study is based on the model of the work situation centered on the person in activity [1] through the approach of ergonomic analysis of the work activity [2, 3], integrating gender [4]. The research considers a stage of interviews and observations in the workplace.

Participants and Educational Establishments: The study has a total of 220 participants, of which 101 are teachers (n = 72 women/n = 29 man) from 4 educational establishments included in the study. Women are an average age of 43 years (+−10 years) and men are an average age of 45 (+−12 years). The 4 educational establishments correspond to 2 schools with secondary level; 1 school with primary and secondary levels; and 1 elementary school for students with disabilities. Three of the schools were in the city of Copiapó and one in the city of Santiago, both in Chile.

Survey: An online survey was conducted between August and December 2020. The survey included the Goldberg General Health Questionnaire (GHQ-12), the Nordic musculoskeletal questionnaire and a questionnaire on working conditions in educational establishments with a specific section in teleworking, with a total of 157 questions. The survey and informed consent were sent by email to each worker of the four educational establishments, reaching a total of 220 respondents, of which 101 were teachers, who responded anonymously to the survey on the SurveyMonkey platform.

Data Analysis: The statistical analysis was using the statistical program SPSS version 21. We carried out stratifying the results of each question by sex. The analyzes qualitative of the ordinal variables were performed using the non-parametric tests for independent samples (Sex) such as the Mann-Whitney U and for nominal variables, the Chi-square test and Fisher's exact test were used if necessary. Quantitative variables were analyzed with Student's T-test for independent samples. Always considering confidence intervals of 95 and 99%.

Observations and Verbalizations: It is considered the verbalizations carried out with the workers during the stage of preventive intervention workshops in ergonomic issues.

Ethical Aspects: Each participant was informed about the purpose of the study, the procedures that would be carried out, the benefits of the research-intervention, the confidentiality of personal data, as well as the scope of the study of the job. Their voluntary participation was requested with oral and written consent, respecting the criteria of the Declaration of Helsinki, regarding the privacy and confidentiality of the data collected throughout the process. The study was approved by the ethics committee of the University of Atacama.

3   Results

Ergonomic working conditions show statistically significant differences for the condition Place without privacy, with annoyances and interruptions with a 37,9% for men and 64,4% for women.

However, in most conditions considered ergonomically unsuitable for teleworking at home, the trend is that the prevalence of this type of conditions is unfavorable to a greater extent for female worker, highlighting: Chair not adjustable in height (women 72,2%; men 69,0%); Chair without height adjustable armrests (women 86,1%; men 79,3%); Does not have a notebook boost (women 90,3%; men 86,2%); Without wireless mouse (women 80,6%; men 79,3%); Screen position does not allow keeping the neck straight (women 61,1%; men 55,2%) and No microphone with headphones for classes (women 58,3%; men 55,2%), among others.

On the other hand, 91,7% of women and 82,8% of men stated Discomfort at the end of the telework shift. Significant differences were observed according to sex for Muscle aches (neck, shoulders, elbows, back, etc.) with a 48,3% for men and 77,8% for women; Headache (men 24,1%; women 50,0%) and Irritation or sore throat (men 41,4%, woman 22,2%). More detail in Table 1.

Table 1. Ergonomic conditions and effects of teleworking at home

Ergonomic conditions and effects of teleworking at home	Men (n = 29)		Women (n = 72)		Total (n = 101)		P-value
	N	%	N	%	N	%	
Place without privacy, with annoyances and interruptions	11	37,9%	54	75,0%	65	64,4%	**0,00****
Insufficient work surface to position all work items	7	24,1%	25	34,7%	32	31,7%	0,30
The desk or table does not allow to support the forearms	11	37,9%	30	41,7%	41	40,6%	0,73

(*continued*)

Table 1. (*continued*)

Ergonomic conditions and effects of teleworking at home	Men (n = 29)		Women (n = 72)		Total (n = 101)		P-value
	N	%	N	%	N	%	
Insufficient space under the table or desk	3	10,3%	17	23,6%	20	19,8%	0,17
Chair not adjustable in height	20	69,0%	52	72,2%	72	71,3%	0,74
Chair without height adjustable armrests	23	79,3%	62	86,1%	85	84,2%	0,39
Chair without lumbar support or poor	12	41,4%	34	47,2%	46	45,5%	0,59
Does not have a notebook boost	25	86,2%	65	90,3%	90	89,1%	0,73
Screen not separated	29	100%	72	100%	101	100%	------
Without wireless mouse	23	79,3%	58	80,6%	81	80,2%	0,89
Without wireless keyboard	29	100,0%	69	95,8%	98	97,0%	0,56
Screen cannot adjust to eye level	13	44,8%	38	52,8%	51	50,5%	0,47
Screen position produces glare	7	24,1%	20	27,8%	27	26,7%	0,71
Screen position does not allow keeping the neck straight	16	55,2%	44	61,1%	60	59,4%	0,58
Distance to the Screen is less than an extended arm	8	27,6%	27	37,5%	35	34,7%	0,34
Feet cannot rest on the ground	9	31,0%	17	23,6%	26	25,7%	0,44

(*continued*)

Table 1. (*continued*)

Ergonomic conditions and effects of teleworking at home	Men (n = 29)		Women (n = 72)		Total (n = 101)		P-value
	N	%	N	%	N	%	
No microphone with headphones for classes	16	55,2%	42	58,3%	58	57,4%	0,77
Insufficient lighting to easily read documents	3	10,3%	17	23,6%	20	19,8%	0,17
Discomfort at the end of the telework shift	24	82,8%	66	91,7%	90	89,1%	0,29
Muscle aches (neck, shoulders, elbows, back, etc.)	14	48,3%	56	77,8%	70	69,3%	**0,00****
Eye discomfort, such as burning, fatigue, etc	20	69,0%	46	63,9%	66	65,3%	0,63
Irritation or sore throat	12	41,4%	16	22,2%	28	27,7%	**0,05***
Dysphonia	3	10,3%	6	8,3%	9	64,4%	0,71
Headache	7	24,1%	36	50,0%	43	31,7%	**0,02***

Furthermore, the results of the Nordic musculoskeletal questionnaire in Table 2 they show a high prevalence of symptoms for both sexes being always greater for women in all areas of pain localization. There are statistically significant differences for pain in the upper extremities, with the Shoulders (woman 73,6%; man 51,7%); Elbows/Arm (woman 76,4%; man 44,8%); Hands/Wrists (woman 68,1%; man 44,8%) and for the Dorsal column (woman 58,3%; man 34,5%). In addition, 78,2% of the workers reported having discomfort in the last 7 days, the difference between women and men being significant (woman 88,9%; man 51,7%) and a 72,3% of workers has 4 or more symptoms, this is more prevalent in women with 80,6% compared to men with 51,7%, the difference being significant.

Table 2. Results of the Nordic musculoskeletal questionnaire

Pain zone	Men (n = 29)		Women (n = 72)		Total (n = 101)		P-value
	N	%	N	%	N	%	
Neck	20	69,0%	58	80,6%	78	77,2%	0,21
Shoulders	15	51,7%	53	73,6%	68	67,3%	**0,03***
Elbows / Arm	13	44,8%	55	76,4%	68	67,3%	**0,00****
Hands / Wrists	13	44,8%	49	68,1%	62	61,4%	**0,03***
Dorsal column	10	34,5%	42	58,3%	52	51,5%	**0,03***
Lumbar spine	20	69,0%	57	79,2%	77	76,2%	0,28
Hips / legs	10	34,5%	38	52,8%	48	47,5%	0,10
Knees	14	48,3%	40	55,6%	54	53,5%	0,51
Ankles / feet	10	34,5%	23	31,9%	33	32,7%	0,81
Discomfort in the last 7 days	15	51,7%	64	88,9%	79	78,2%	**0,00****
No Symptoms	4	13,80%	3	4,20%	7	6,90%	0,81
1 Symptom	1	3,40%	3	4,20%	4	4,00%	0,51
2 Symptoms	2	6,90%	4	5,60%	6	5,90%	0,63
3 Symptoms	7	24,10%	4	5,60%	11	10,90%	**0,001****
4 or more symptoms	15	51,70%	58	80,60%	73	72,30%	**0,001****

Likewise, the results of the Goldberg General Health Questionnaire (GHQ-12), in Table 3 they show for both sexes a score of 6,26 (+−2,6), being significantly higher for women with 6,64 (+−2,7) points compared to men with 5,31 (+−2,1)points, placing them in the Suspicion Threshold (5–6).

Nevertheless, for an 44,6% of workers they are at the level of psychopathology for Chilean standards, being significantly higher for women with 52,8% compared to men with 24,1%. The main problems referred to are: Inability to deal with their own problems 68,3% (woman 68,1%; man 69,0%); Inability to enjoy daily life 79,2% (woman 80,6%; man 75,9%); Loss of sleep 75,2% (woman 81,9%; man 58,6%); Constantly under tension 73,3% (woman 83,3%; man 48,3%); among others.

Table 3. Results of the Goldberg General Health Questionnaire (GHQ-12)

Question GHQ-12	Men (n = 29)		Women (n = 72)		Total (n = 101)		P-value
	N	%	N	%	N	%	
A. Lack of concentration	11	37,9%	13	18,1%	24	23,8%	**0,04***
B. Loss of sleep	17	58,6%	59	81,9%	76	75,2%	**0,01****
C. Useless to others	13	44,8%	38	52,8%	51	50,5%	0,47
D. Inability to make decisions	16	55,2%	47	65,3%	63	62,4%	0,35
E. Constantly under tension	14	48,3%	60	83,3%	74	73,3%	**0,00****
F. Inability to solve their own problems	8	27,6%	26	36,1%	34	33,7%	0,41
G. Inability to enjoy daily life	22	75,9%	58	80,6%	80	79,2%	0,60
H. Inability to deal with their own problems	20	69,0%	49	68,1%	69	68,3%	0,93
I. Sad or depressed	8	27,6%	45	62,5%	53	52,5%	**0,00****
J. Loss of self-confidence	4	13,8%	22	30,6%	26	25,7%	0,08
K. Feel worthless	1	3,4%	10	13,9%	11	10,9%	0,13
L. Unhappiness	20	69,0%	51	70,8%	71	70,3%	0,85
SCORE mean	Men (n = 29)		Women (n = 72)		Total (n = 101)		P-value
	5,31 (+-2,1)		6,64 (+-2,7)		6,26 (+-2,6)		**0,02***
Psychopathology cut point	Men (n = 29)		Women (n = 72)		Total (n = 101)		P-value
	N	%	N	%	N	%	
Absent (0–4)	10	34,5%	16	22,2%	26	25,7%	**0,01****
Suspicion Threshold (5–6)	12	41,4%	18	25,0%	30	29,7%	**0,01****
Present (7 or more)	7	24,1%	38	52,8%	45	44,6%	**0,01****

In addition to the above, Fig. 1 shows that there are statistically significant differences in the average time spent on housework on work days (not weekends) between woman and men. Male teachers dedicate less than 1 h a day to domestic work activities with a 62,0%, while women dedicate more than 2 h a week in 38% and between 1 h and 2 h a week with 44.4%.

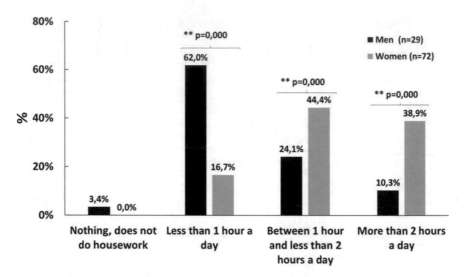

Fig. 1. Average time spent on housework on work days (not weekends)

4   Discussion

In relation to the determinants of teachers' work activity, which have been analyzed according to the Person-Centered Work Activity Model [1, 2]. In the category of determinants "Means offered by the workplace", we find that the main effects on the Health of teachers that can be associated with work activity are linked to the organization of telework, carrying out teaching work with classes in synchronous or asynchronous mode, which is defined by the organization as a result of the exceptional condition caused by the pandemic.

This determinant generates an unusual context for carrying out the work and shows various difficulties for effective performance, among them the imposition of unusual class schedules in the different types of schools studied. As well as the schedule arranged to organize meetings with the parents of the students or the "teachers' councils" where it is mandatory to attend, because in these instances work guidelines, requirements, information on deadlines or class verification records are delivered, etc.

Also, at the level of the technical device determinant, teachers have less access to tools provided by their employer to carry out teleworking at home, which generates discomfort, fatigue, pain, being this inadequate to develop the teaching function and exposing risks of WDMS and Mental Health problems. In general, the workers were not prepared to carry out telework and tele-education, they had to adapt to this new context quickly without having the appropriate conditions due to the pandemic, presenting a series of problems of discomfort, fatigue, pain, stress that limit the development of their work, especially since they do not have appropriate devices such as adapted chairs and tables, notebooks, mouse, microphone, hearing aid, etc. Which is affecting men and women, but is being more demanding for women teachers as it was observed in our results.

In this order, it is important to consider the nature of the teaching work activity, in which it is possible to visualize that the activity requires centrally oral communication, this implies having communication skills with the different actors: students, teacher colleagues, parents, heads, etc., adding to this overload in the use of the voice, a phenomenon already described as a common problem in teachers [5, 6]. and that in current conditions it is maintained and other factors are added such as exposure to computer display screens for a long time, use of the keyboard and mouse, static work sitting, among others, generating ostéomusculaires symptoms Both elements determine the different critical situations that demand greater emotional and cognitive efforts to respond to the different demands, representing a greater effort in the circumstances where they must exercise their role as educators, in the face of the irascible behavior that some students or Faced with the misunderstanding of parents and managers.

Regarding the determinant "Tasks and Requirements", the teachers in person mode began their work at 08:00 am in the classrooms. However, with the outbreak of the pandemic, it was found that the day, especially in high schools with the highest vulnerability index, the day with students currently begins at 11:00 am. This occurs because public schools in Chile must achieve levels of student attendance to classes close to 100%, so as not to lose the economic subsidy that the State transfers through the Ministry of Education and with which salaries are paid. It is for this reason that teachers have the requirement to move the start of classes, to grant access to the majority of students. This may partly explain the high level of interference from work in the domestic sphere, which does not allow responding to the demands of raising their own children at home, who are also in tele-education. which reduces their room for maneuver to respond to the production objectives of the education service and at the same time achieve their personal objectives [1, 2, 4]. This dimension is affecting women more and makes visible the double workload they have in our context due to the lack of parental co-responsibility of men in general in reproductive work and is invisible to decision makers who do not take into account the gender in the management of production and occupational risks [7, 8].

Regarding the determinants related to the "Social environment", we can say that in some cases teachers feel isolated in the performance of their pedagogical activity. The instances of meetings have been reduced, in many cases for fear of the managers to promote instances of collective complaints related to the poor working conditions, for which they do not have the means to improve them either. Paradoxically, these instances of deliberation and collective meetings serve to maintain cohesion among teachers and benefit communication, which could reduce psychological distress. Given the circumstances of pandemic and quarantine, teachers and others professionals and technicians have increased qualitatively different demands from those used to be, as well as interference between domestic work and paid work, which has affected more to the female workers, with poor ergonomic working conditions at home and without support from the establishments in the implementation of telework for both genders, reflected in a poor perception of general health, increased stress at work and MSDs, among other problems. This has shown that the education sector is a forgotten sector for OSH policies, making the risks of work invisible, particularly for women workers, a phenomenon described in Chile [9] and in other parts of the world [5, 6].

5   Conclusion

Despite the demanding conditions of work activity in schools, they are not a priority for OSHA management. This new work context transforms work activity and ex-poses to uncertainties that increase work stress and affect a large number of women and men who work in this sector of activity. Although the ergonomic conditions for teleworking are equally poor for men and women, without distinction between sex, the lack of freedom and frequent interruptions is mostly high for women.

This work can provide important evidence from ergonomics and integrating gender, for making public policy decisions that help to improve working conditions, which would benefit working men and women in this sector, but at the same time the entire society, which benefits from the important work carried out by teachers in all societies.

NOTE: The present study was financed with funds from the DIUDA-Initiation project ATA N ° 22376 of the University of Atacama, Chile.

References

1. Vézina, N. : La pratique de l'ergonomie face aux TMS : ouverture à l'interdisciplinarité. In : Comptes-rendus du 36ème congrès de la Société d'ergonomie de langue française (SELF) et du 32ème congrès de l'Association canadienne d'ergonomie (ACE), pp. 44–60. SELF and ACE, Montréal (2001)
2. St-Vincent, M., Vézina, N., Bellemare, M., Denis, D., Ledoux, É., Imbeau, D.: Ergonomic Intervention. Institut de recherche robert-sauvé en santé et en sécurité du travail (IRSST), Montréal, QC, Canada (2014)
3. Guérin, F., Laville, T., Daniellou, F., Durrafourg, J., Kerguelen, A.: Comprendre le travail pour le transformer: La pratique de l'ergonomie. ANACT, Lyon (2006)
4. Messing, K., Lefrançois, M., Saint-Charles, J.: Observing inequality: can ergonomic observations help interventions transform the role of gender in work activity? Comput. Support. Cooperative Work (CSCW), 1–35 (2018)
5. Seifert, A.M., Messing, K., Riel, J., Chatigny, C.: Precarious employment conditions affect work content in education and social work: results of work analyses. Int. J. law Psychiatry 30(4–5), 299–310 (2007)
6. Riel, J., Major, M.E.: The challenges of mobilizing workers on gender issues: lessons from two studies on the occupational health of teachers in Québec: Les défis de mobiliser les travailleur. ses sur la question du genre: Constats issus de deux recherches portant sur la santé au travail d'enseignant. es du Québec. New Solutions J. Environ. Occup. Health Policy 27(3), 284–303 (2017)
7. Messing, K.: One-Eyed Science: Occupational Health and Women Workers. Temple University Press, Philadelphia (1998)
8. Astudillo, P., Ibarra, C.: La perspectiva de género, Desafíos para la Ergonomía en Chile: Una revisión Sistemática de Literatura. Ciencia trabajo 16(49), 28–37 (2014). https://doi.org/10.4067/S0718-24492014000100006
9. Molinero, E., Cortés, I.: Identificación de factores de riesgo del entorno de trabajo en un instituto de enseñanza secundaria. Arch. Prev. riesgos Labor.(Ed. impr.), 38–45 (2005)

Agile Development of Prevention Tools in Occupational Health and Safety: A Gender Consideration

Myriam Bérubé[1,2,3](✉) ⓘ, Marie Laberge[1,2,3] ⓘ, Céline Chatigny[3,4] ⓘ,
and Denys Denis[5] ⓘ

[1] Rehabilitation School, University of Montreal, Montreal, QC H3C 3J7, Canada
`myriam.berube@umontreal.ca`
[2] Sainte-Justine UHC Research Center, Montreal, QC, Canada
[3] CINBIOSE Research Group, Université du Québec à Montréal (UQAM), Montreal, QC, Canada
[4] Department of Special Education and Training, UQAM, Montreal, QC, Canada
[5] Department of Physical Activity Sciences, UQAM, Montreal, QC, Canada

Abstract. The Work-Oriented Training Path (WOTP) is a Quebec school program offering people aged 15 to 21 to develop their employability by alternating between school and internships. Among other tasks, teachers in this program must ensure that students are healthy and safe in their work environment. Our team wishes to develop new technological tools to address this role. The work activity of the WOTP teachers is complex and modulated by several determinants. It could be assisted by technological tools, which will change this activity in a way that can be anticipated through the Future Activity Approach. The tools must also consider the influences of sex and gender in occupational health and safety prevention. The design team has proposed an Agile approach for the technology's development. A methodological questioning is necessary to assess the capacity of these three approaches to be mobilized in an integrated way. To do so, a content analysis of articles describing the methods has been carried out (Future Activity Approach, Gender-Based Analysis+, Agile methods). They all promote an iterative approach with flexible steps. In theory, the stages of these approaches can be superimposed. Their combination address some of their respective criticisms and could have an added value. Since they come from different fields of expertise, combining them could be challenging; it requires a multidisciplinary approach that is not always available. The combination represents an advantage in the face of a complex work situation influenced by sex and gender, for which a technology development is being considered.

Keywords: Design process · Methodologies · Work activity analysis · Future Activity Approach · Agile software development · Sex and gender

1 Introduction

The Work-Oriented Training Path (WOTP) is a Quebec school program offering young people aged 15 to 21 the opportunity to develop their employability by alternating

N. L. Black et al. (Eds.): IEA 2021, LNNS 220, pp. 413–420, 2021.
https://doi.org/10.1007/978-3-030-74605-6_51

between school and internships. The program targets students who are at least two years behind academically. Some of the teaching staff at the WOTP are involved in the placement, monitoring and evaluation of students in internships. This mandate requires ensuring the health and safety of students through occupational health and safety (OHS) learning and workplace supervision. Prevention measures are important since this population is vulnerable in terms of OHS: young people with learning disabilities are at greater risk of suffering a workplace injury [1].

Despite the importance of their OHS prevention mandate, WOTP teachers rarely have any training in that field. This is why a group of teachers is working in partnership with a research team to develop an OHS management model adapted to their situation and supported by technologies. Few adequate tools exist for them and none are digital. However, the use of digital technology would be an asset given the complexity of the decisions to be made in their work, and the diversity of the population. They need to consider several factors including the type of difficulty of the student, the type of internship, their geographic location and the data collected during the last visit. The tools could help prioritize students for supervision or promote real-time communication with the placement environment.

Before determining the design process for the technological tools, the team reflected on the design issues in this project. The following contextual elements were considered.

- The work activity of internship supervision (e.g. placement, supervising strategies, communication with workplaces) is influenced by several determinants that are important to consider before developing OHS solutions. The analysis of the work activity developed in ergonomics would allow the variability of situations to be documented and understood.
- In ergonomics, the Future Activity Approach is an iterative process aimed at improving working conditions and taking into account human activity in the context of an investment project [2]. It allows to project oneself in the future activity.
- The work environment is still highly segregated by sex and gender in the program. The risks for girls and boys differ whether they are in a traditional job according to their sex or not [3]. This fact calls for an approach that is sensitive to the gendered division of work. The team decided to adopt a Gender-Based Analysis+ (GBA +) in its willingness to be fairest and to consider sex and gender issues in the dynamics of work integration and occupational health [4, 5].
- The design partner group proposes to develop technologies with Agile design methods. In design and software engineering, Agile methods propose iterative design loops aimed at rapidly developing functional parts of a product [6, 7]. They allow for frequent feedback and efficient adjustments to changes in user requirements [7, 8].

In short, the Future Activity Approach, Agile Methods and GBA+ are all adequate for this project. It is not clear, however, whether these three approaches are usable at the same time, and if so, how they can interact together.

This communication will offer a review of three design approaches with the aim of evaluating their capacity to be mobilized in an integrated way for the same project. Special attention will be given to the steps and challenges of the methods. In a world where ergonomists are called upon to be increasingly involved in technological design processes, this type of questioning is critical to their inclusion in the multidisciplinary team. In addition, considering sex and gender makes it possible to optimize certain ergonomic interventions.

2 Methods

A content analysis of three design processes was conducted using NVivo software: 1) Future Activity Approach, 2) Agile Methods and 3) GBA+. To select the relevant literature, the opinions of experts (partners and research team members) were sought. In addition, a literature search was conducted using various sources of information from white and grey literature. To do so, the names of the processes were used as keywords, in English and French, in the Google search base and the Google Scholar, Web of Science and IEEE Xplore databases. The 30 most cited articles from each of the databases, for each of the three design processes, were sorted by title and abstract. Then, a snowball search technique was performed for all relevant literature. Finally, a complete reading of the articles was carried out.

In order to be selected, the works had to explicitly mention the design process and provide a complete description of the steps involved, in either French or English. Publications dealing with the design process in an innovative or atypical context were rejected. It was expected to have 2 to 3 works per process meeting these criteria so as to saturate the definitions and explanations of each approach. At the end, three writings have been selected for each approach and are presented in Table 1.

Table 1. Selected writings for the content analysis

Title	Document type	Number of citation
Les apports de l'ergonomie participative dans le cadre de projets industriels ou architecturaux [2]	Article	9
La prévention des troubles musculo-squelettiques en conception: quelles marges de manœuvre pour le déploiement de l'activité? [9]	Doctoral Thesis	95
L'ergonomie dans la conduite de projets de conception de systèmes de travail [10]	Article	177
Agile Software Development Methods: Review and Analysis [6] First in 2002	Technical report	2050
Agile Modeling, Agile Software Develpment, and Extreme Programming: The State of Research [8]	Litterature review	399
Empirical studies of agile software development: A systematic review [7]	Litterature review	2650

(continued)

Table 1. (*continued*)

Title	Document type	Number of citation
Se montrer à la hauteur du défi: l'analyse des influences du genre et du sexe en planification, en élaboration de politiques et en recherche dans le domaine de la santé au Canada [4]	Book	83 (en.) 2 (fr.)
Better science with sex and gender: Facilitating the use of a sex and gender-based analysis in health research [5]	Article	237
L'analyse comparative entre les sexes plus (ACS +) [11]	Web Site	s.o

3 Results

3.1 Constituent Elements

In total, eight constituent elements emerged from the content analysis of the literature. We define a constituent element as an essential item in the description of a design method. This presentation will focus on the steps and temporality and the challenges of each method (Table 2). They were selected because they are the two elements allowing a critical analysis of the theoretical applicability at this point.

Table 2. Constituent elements

Constituent element	Definition
Steps and temporality	Steps of the method and temporal markers of the process
Challenges	Considerations, criticisms or problems, actual or potential, concerning the method, whether at the social, individual, organizational or other level

Steps and Temporality All three methods are defined as iterative, but only the GBA+ has no real beginning or end [6–8]. Its reflexive process can begin with the birth of any research project and continues as long as the project evolves, without defined steps [6–8]. The Future Activity Approach and Agile methods have opening and closing stages [2, 6]. Their iterative loops are carried out with the central steps [2, 6].

The Future Activity Approach has five well-defined steps: 1) Analysis of baseline situations, 2) Development of characteristic action situations (CAS), 3) Drafting of design benchmarks, 4) Reconstruction of the future activity, 5) Prognosis of the future activity [2]. The fourth step is where the iterations mostly occur. Agile methods also have defined steps, but they vary slightly from one method to another [6]. The majority have an opening, iteration loops, and a closing [6–8]. GBA+ is a reflective posture to ensure that all influences of sex and gender are considered at every decision-making stage [4, 5, 11]. Aspects proposed by Clow and al. (2009) are: the issue, population, data, implications, and recommendations [4]. Definitions of these steps and aspects are presented in Table 3.

Table 3. Definitions of the steps of the design approaches

Future activity approach	Agile methods	GBA+
The methodology has five phases [2]: 1. Analysis of baseline situations: it may be a baseline situation or a situation similar to the future situation [2, 9, 10] 2. Developing Characteristic Action Situations (CASs): Identifying the elements that make up the current activity (current CASs) with the aim of moving those that are relevant into the future (likely future CASs) [9, 10] 3. Writing Benchmarks for Design: Descriptive (current knowledge), prescriptive (to be found in the design) and procedural (steps, meetings) benchmarks [2, 10]. Allows the ergonomist to share observations and forward them for the drafting of the specifications [10] 4. Reconstruction of the future activity: Verbalizations or simulations by the workers, via the future probable CASs [2, 9, 10]. Social and collective design to confirm or modify design choices [9, 10] 5. Prognosis of future activity: Prognosis of health and production in the new system [2, 10]. Adjustments can be made and resubmitted to a simulation [10]. Then solutions are implemented, followed by start-up, evaluation and readjustments [9]	Each Agile method has its specific steps, although they all have an iterative process [6–8] Example of steps for SCRUM [6]: 1. Pre-Game, including two sub-steps: *Planning* – write the requirements, prioritize them and estimate their development time, and *Architecture* - prepare the design according to known requirements 2. Development - agile and iterative part in the form of development sprints, from one week to one month, during which a constant re-evaluation of needs and resources is carried out 3. Post-game - the stakeholders have all judged the product ready and it is beginning to be prepared for delivery, there are no more possible changes At the beginning of each loop, the team meets to discuss the objectives. At the beginning of each day, a brief update meeting takes place (15 min). At the end of each loop, a results presentation meeting is held	Problem: Who thinks there is a problem, why, according to which interpretations. What is their place in the hierarchy? Effects of the interventions, on whom [4] Population: An inventory of the target population is essential, including gaps in knowledge about it and what has already been learned [4, 11]. Focus on the systemic barriers they experience, their needs and perceptions [11] Data: What source, what quality, what limitations [4, 5]. Must be of a reciprocal nature and sources [4, 5, 11] Implications: Identify the differences that are present and those that would be desirable [4, 11] Recommendations: Consider the socio-political context, obstacles and risks, and the strengths of the recommendations depending on the context. Know the audience, and its ability to assimilate the concepts or apply the recommendations [4] Most processes begin by analyzing data according to the sex (disaggregated by sex), but must extend to gender roles, identities and relationships [4, 5, 11]. Other groups of factors and their interactions with each other need to be addressed [5, 11]

The Future Activity Approach and GBA+ are more effective if they are undertaken earlier, but they can be implemented at any time during the project [2, 5, 10]. Their total duration depends on the project for which they are applied [2, 5, 10]. As for Agile methods, they are normally undertaken for small or medium sized projects that last from one to four years [7, 8].

At this point, it is possible to imagine these methods working together on the same project. The GBA+ would be present at all stages, ensuring no sub-population is forgotten I the decision-making process. The Agile method would start a little later than the Future Activity Approach in order to be able to use the specifications developed by this method. The iterative stages of prototype production (step 2 of Agile) and simulation (step 4 of the Future Activity Approach) would take place at the same time.

Challenges. All three processes face challenges that need to be addressed to be effective. In particular, the horizontal, or even bottom-up hierarchical structure of the Future Activity Approach is sometimes poorly received by managers [2, 10]. Some people in the design group may feel that their expertise is being challenged as other groups need to validate their solutions [9, 10]. Agile methods are criticized for a lack of empirical evidence of their benefits [6–8]. Choosing the best Agile method for the circumstances can be difficult and, in fact, they are almost always modified by teams that use them [6, 7]. They are demanding methods for developers and customer [6, 7]. When applying GBA+, one must be attentive to all voices involved in the project, not just those of the usual interlocutors who are usually in a position of power [4, 5, 11]. Identifying relevant actors and t the gendered power dynamics surrounding them is central to this analysis [4].

Combining the three processes could address some of the criticisms they face. In particular, the Future Activity Approach reduces the risk of forgetting important actors for GBA+. On the other hand, GBA+ could facilitate the analysis of social interactions necessary to the Future Activity Approach by considering power dynamics in a more thorough way. However, this combination could require even more time from participants, which was already an issue for individual approaches.

4   Discussion and Conclusion

Despite their apparent differences, these approaches have some core resemblances. They all promote an iterative approach with flexible steps. This type of approach could be interesting for other research teams aiming at developing technologies for a complex work activity. However, a combination of the three would imply an increase in the number of people working on the project. Gathering the expertise to successfully carry out the three approaches could represent a challenge for some research teams. Moreover, once brought together, it is essential to work cohesively, which could become an obstacle for those who are not accustomed to interdisciplinary work in OHS [12]. The multidisciplinary issue arising from the alliance of ergonomics and design methods was also mentioned by Guerlesquin (2012) [13]. A solution could be to assign specific roles to the ergonomists working on the project: activity analyst, agile team member and sex and gender specialist, as long as they receive an appropriate training.

The hypothesis that considering sex and gender in design enriches the results is not new and some teams have already exploited the richness of overlapping approaches [14,

15]. A number of authors have also addressed the influences of sex and gender in technology [16, 17]. Mejias and Soares (2014) put forward a conceptual model that proposes to reconcile Macroergonomics, Design and Cultural Ergonomics, also arguing that this will optimize the results [18]. The superposition of several approaches is therefore not new and has already given encouraging results. The analysis presented here is only a first step in formalizing the association of three specific methods of design.

Although temporalities seem to be consistent in theory, we foresee that the proposed methodology will undoubtedly require several adaptations depending on the context. The duration of the Agile loops could be shorter than the duration of the Future Activity Approach, which would allow only one out of two prototypes to be tested in simulation. However, adaptability is central to all three methods. Far from distorting, this adaptation represents the strength of this combination of solutions and the interest of partnership research.

Acknowledgement. This study was funded by the Institut de recherche Robert-Sauvé en santé et sécurité du travail (IRSST), Québec, Canada / (#2018–0001).

The first author received financial support from Équipe GESTE - for knowledge sharing on modeling the integration of sex and gender in occupational and environmental health knowledge translation interventions (CIHR Grant # 153464), the Canada Graduate Scholarships – Master's program of CIHR (2020–2021), the Master's Scholarship of the IRSST (2019–2021) and the Master's Training for Applicants with a Professional Degree of the Fonds de recherche du Québec - Santé (FRQS) (2020–2022).

References

1. Breslin, F.C., Pole, J.D.: Work injury risk among young people with learning disabilities and attention-deficit/hyperactivity disorder in Canada. Am. J. Public Health **99**(8), 1423–1430 (2009)
2. Bellemare, M., Garrigou, A., Ledoux, É., Richard, J.-G.: Les apports de l'ergonomie participative dans le cadre de projets industriels ou architecturaux. Relat. Industrielles/Ind. Relat. **50**(4), 768–788 (1995)
3. Messing, K., Punnett, L., Bond, M., Alexanderson, K., Pyle, J., Zahm, S., Wegman, D., Stock, S.R., de Grosbois, S.: Be the fairest of them all: challenges and recommendations for the treatment of gender in occupational health research. Am. J. Ind. Med. **43**(6), 618–629 (2003)
4. Clow, B., Pederson, A., Haworth-Brockman, M., Bernier, J.: Se montrer à la hauteur du défi: l'analyse des influences du genre et du sexe en planification, en élaboration de politiques et en recherche dans le domaine de la santé au Canada. Centre d'excellence de l'Atlantique pour la santé des femmes, Halifax, Nouvelle-Écosse (2009)
5. Johnson, J.L., Greaves, L., Repta, R.: Better science with sex and gender: facilitating the use of a sex and gender-based analysis in health research. Int. J. Equity Health **8**(1), 1–11 (2009)
6. Abrahamsson, P., Salo, O., Ronkainen, J., Warsta, J.: Agile software development methods: Review and analysis. arXiv preprint arXiv:1709.08439 (2017)
7. Dybå, T., Dingsøyr, T.: Empirical studies of agile software development: a systematic review. Inf. Soft. Technol. **50**(9–10), 833–859 (2008)
8. Erickson, J., Lyytinen, K., Siau, K.: Agile modeling, agile software development, and extreme programming: the state of research. J. Database Manage. (JDM) **16**(4), 88–100 (2005)

9. Coutarel, F.: La prévention des troubles musculo-squelettiques en conception: quelles marges de manœuvre pour le déploiement de l'activité? , Université Victor Segalen-Bordeaux II (2004)

10. Daniellou, F.: 21. L'ergonomie dans la conduite de projets de conception de systèmes de travail. In: Ergonomie. pp. 359–373. Presses Universitaires de France, Paris cedex 14 (2004)

11. Gouvernement du Canada: Guide pour la recherche en ACS+. https://cfc-swc.gc.ca/gba-acs/guide-fr.html le (2017). Accessed 18 Jun 2020

12. Lortie, M., Denis, D., Lapointe, C., Lapierre, J., Mayer, F., Patry, L., Vézeau, S.: Transfert des connaissances en SST dans un contexte d'interdisciplinarité: Définition d'un cadre de référence et pour le développement d'une programmation thématique. In. Institut de recherche Robert-Sauvé en santé et en sécurité du travail du Québec, Citeseer, (2006)

13. Guerlesquin, G.: Articulation Ergonomie-Design-Conception Mécanique: approche méthodologique de la convergence multidisciplinaire. Université de Technologie de Belfort-Montbeliard (2012)

14. Källhammer, E., Wikberg-Nilsson, Å.: Innovation: change initiated by a design and gender approach. In: ISPIM Innovation Symposium (2011)

15. Schiebinger, L.: Gendered innovations: harnessing the creative power of sex and gender analysis to discover new ideas and develop new technologies. Triple Helix 1(1), 1–17 (2014)

16. Venkatesh, V., Morris, M.G.: Why don't men ever stop to ask for directions? Gender, social influence, and their role in technology acceptance and usage behavior. MIS quarterly, 115–139 (2000).

17. Weber, K., Custer, R.L.: Gender-based preferences toward technology education content, activities, and instructional methods. J. Technol. Educ. 16(2), 55–71 (2005) (spring 2005)

18. Mejias, S., Soares, M.: The evaluation of work systems and products: considerations from the cultural ergonomics. Adv. Ergon. Des. Usability Spec. Popul. Part I 16, 329 (2014)

Methods for Considering Sex and Gender During Intervention-Research Studies: What Do Researchers Say?

Vanessa Blanchette-Luong[1,2](✉) ⓘ, Marie Laberge[1,2,3] ⓘ,
Véronique Poupart-Monette[1,2] ⓘ, and Karen Messing[2] ⓘ

[1] Sainte-Justine UHC Research Center, Montreal, QC H1T 1C9, Canada
[2] CINBIOSE Research Group, Université du Québec à Montréal, Montreal,
QC H3C 3P8, Canada
`blanchette-luong.vanessa@courrier.uqam.ca`
[3] Rehabilitation School, University of Montreal, Montreal, QC H3C 3J7, Canada

Abstract. The purpose of this study is to review the methods used to integrate sex and gender (s/g) in intervention research (RI) projects. The findings are based on a retrospective analysis of twelve IR projects. A thematic content analysis of the twelve in-depth interviews conducted with the researchers involved in the IRs was carried out. The results show a wide variety of methods used to integrate s/g throughout all the phases of the project. All the IRs used mixed research designs (multiple data sources, qualitative and quantitative data), yielding g a wide variety of data (physical, psychosocial, social and organizational information). Various strategies were used for gender-based analyses: data comparing men and women, statistics stratified by gender and detailed analyses related to the mechanisms potentially explaining observed differences. Also, the analysis led researchers to reflect on such issues as the way to address s/g with partners and workers involved in the project (directly or gradually) and the limits of methodological tools (e.g.: the range of methods that facilitate the integration of s/g). We conclude that the methods used, and their effectiveness seem to be influenced by the context in which the IR takes place and that further analyses is needed to inform researchers on the contextual elements that influence the choice and effectiveness of methods used to integrate s/g.

Keywords: Sex-gender based analysis · Work activity analysis ·
Intervention-research studies · Occupational · Health and safety

1 Introduction

Integrating sex and gender (s/g) in OHS intervention studies is necessary to achieve occupational justice, but it has its pitfalls. Workplaces are still highly segregated between sexes, both horizontally and vertically [1, 2], which explains why the effects of work do not appear in the same way for young women and men [3]. Integrating s/g in ergonomic interventions can be difficult, due to the many difficulties that can arise, such as the risk of perpetuating stereotypes or encouraging increased discrimination in employment.

Our team at CINBIOSE have long been interested in s/g integrated analysis in occupational health studies to improve women's working conditions and counter systemic discrimination against women [4–8]. In that vein, CINBIOSE responded to a call from the Canadian Institutes of Health Research by creating the "GESTE-for knowledge translation" team with the objective of describing diverse knowledge transfer initiatives in occupational and environmental health that have integrated s/g.

The team's studies showed the importance of not only describing the differences between women and men, but also the mechanisms that underly these differences [9]. For example, it is not sufficient to demonstrate a tighter link between heavy load handling and musculoskeletal symptoms in women. In order to act to eliminate risk factors, it is also necessary to show the differentiated demands of gender-typical load handling (handling people vs. boxes) and work contexts (job control, decision latitude, social support).

The purpose of the present study is to contribute to the development of methods to consider s/g in research that could help orient the development of preventive interventions in OHS. There are three objectives: 1) to review the range of methods used in the twelve intervention studies, 2) to understand how these methods facilitate gender integration in the analysis and 3) to explore the levers for and barriers to the use of these methods.

2   Methodology

A multiple case study was conducted based on a retrospective analysis of 12 intervention-research (IR) projects conducted by occupational health researchers of the GESTE team. The team was created to describe ways of taking s/g into account in knowledge translation interventions in occupational health. The findings presented in this paper are based on in-depth qualitative interviews with researchers who contributed to these IRs. All the IRs were occupational health interventions, usually ergonomic interventions (9/12). The topics covered included the origin and conduct of the IR, the relationship with partners, the methods used, the difficulties encountered, the levers to successful integration of s/g, and the impacts of taking s/g into account.

The research ethics committee at the Université du Québec à Montréal (UQAM) approved the study proposal. A project committee was established to validate each step of the research protocol. The findings presented in this article stem from the first phase of the project for which the committee met six times over a year and a half period.

2.1   Population and Data Collection

A call to the 17 researchers of the GESTE team elicited an initial list of 27 IR projects integrating s/g. Using the maximum variety method [10], 12 IRs were selected with a view to in: researchers involved, period of the project (years in which the project was conducted), nature of the intervention context (workplace, community), point of integration of s/g (at the beginning or during the course of the study), workers involved (men and women, only women in traditional women's jobs, only women in traditional men's jobs or unspecified jobs) and whether or not the IR was conducted in the context of a specific 19-year multidisciplinary partnership with the three largest union confederations in Québec). Twelve semi-directed interviews were conducted with the researchers involved in the selected IRs (5 individual interviews and 7 collective interviews). The interviews were divided into three themes: origin and development of the study, partnership (relationship with and involvement of the partners) and s/g integration (methods, difficulties, facilitators, strategies, impacts, etc.). The interviews lasted 1–2 h. All interviews were transcribed verbatim to facilitate further analysis.

2.2 Data Analysis

The first step of the analysis was the creation of fact sheets describing the IRs. Second, a gender-focused thematic content analysis was carried out using NVivo 10 software. This first phase of the thematic analysis was carried out in a broad manner; an inductive approach led to the emergence of three coding themes: context, methods, and impacts. The results of an initial analysis concerning the impacts of integrating s/g have been, and a more detailed description of the methods that lead to the categorization can be found in that article [11].

Table 1. Categories and definition of the methods analysis

Category	Definition
Investigation of the initial request	Methods used to investigate the initial request for the project, as expressed by the partners
Participant recruitment	Methods used to recruit participants to the project
Data collection	Methods used to collect data during the project
Data analysis	Methods used to analyse data during the project
Participative structures	Methods used to manage the participative and decision-making structures (e.g.: committees, meetings, etc.)
Knowledge translation	Methods used to divulge the results of the project, including any knowledge transfer initiated between the beginning and the end of the project
Transformations	Methods used to manage transformations of the workplace as suggested by the IR

A second thematic content analysis was conducted, specifically on the methods used during the studies. The categories that emerged and their definition can be found in Table 1. This list of categories represents the different phases of the IR process where the various methods were used (investigation of the initial demand, recruitment, data collection, data analysis, participative structures, knowledge translation and transformations). The second step of the analysis consisted of the creation of project sheets in which all the verbatim extracts for each category were summarized. The themes and sub-themes that emerged from those twelve project sheets are presented in Table 2. These themes and subthemes were then used to create a synthesis of the range of methods used. The final step of the analysis was to create a second synthesis table presenting the researchers' reflection on the integration of s/g in their methods, from which we could extract difficulties experienced and strategies used by the researchers in terms in s/g integration.

Table 2. Themes and subthemes of the Methods analysis

	Theme	Subtheme	Definition
Data analysis	Work analysis	General	Analysis that gives a general idea of the work activity (from preliminary observations for example)
		Detailed	Analysis that allows the access to details of fine operations of the work activity (from in-depth observation data for example)
	Data analysis	Reflexive	Analysis based on the reflection of different stakeholders on the date collected/results presented (research team meeting, meeting with partners, individual questioning, etc.)
		Triangulation	Converge data from multiple sources into common outcomes
		Statistics	Quantitative analysis of collected data
	S/g analysis	Composition	Establishing the number of women and men in the environment studied
		Comparative	Comparison between women's and men's situations
		Differentiated/ mechanisms	Understanding the mechanisms underlying the differences between women's and men's situation
Data collection	Indicators	Physical	Data collection on physical aspects (pain, health conditions, job demands, etc.)
		Psychological	Data collection on psychosocial aspects (motivations, values, etc.)
		Social/ organizational	Data collection on social aspects (relationships, support, hierarchy, etc.)

(*continued*)

Table 2. (*continued*)

	Theme	Subtheme	Definition
Participative structures	Committees	Decision-making	Committee primarily formed to make decisions about the project
		Reflexive	Committee essentially formed to reflect/construct the project
General	Methodological design	Cross-sectional	Study taking place at a specific time
		Longitudinal	Study with several time points
	Cases	One case	Single case study (a community, an organization, etc.)
		Multiple cases	Multiple case study (several organizations, several legal cases, etc.)

3   Results

3.1   Range of Methods Used

The choice of methods depends on the research question and the context in which the project is conducted. For the twelve IRs analyzed, an important part of the context depends on the configurations of the partnership. Most of the time, the research question comes from a request from a company or an institutional partner (e.g. a trade union), leading to the integration of s/g in multiple ways. For some projects, s/g considerations were part of the initial request (e.g., evaluate women's work in the context of pay equity law) and for others, s/g integration depended on the researcher's sensitivity to gender issues and a feminist perspective. Between those two ways of integrating s/g, the projects came from diverse contexts: an initial demand targeting gender-sensitive issues, emergence of s/g issues during preliminary investigations, detailed analyses highlighting differences between men and women, or management of transformation projects raising s/g issues (e.g., choice of the size of future workstations).

One constant among the 12 IRs is the use of mixed research designs with a wide variety of configurations including multiple data sources and both qualitative and quantitative data (all IRs had at least two data sources). As well, the research projects looked at data from multiple categories of participants (11 studies), with the main category being the workers involved (11 studies). The three main sources of data analyzed in the studies were observations of work in situ (9 studies), verbalisations (mainly through qualitative interviews) (9 studies), and questionnaires (7 studies). The richness of the data collected in each RI was also noted; most of the studies combined data on physical workload, psychosocial components, and social and organizational dynamics within the study environments. For the gender-based analyses specifically, several strategies were implemented, such as data comparing men and women (8 studies), statistics stratified by gender (7 studies), as well as detailed analyses related to the mechanisms explaining the observed differences (5 studies).

All the projects analyzed had a project committee. Four committees were intended to make project-related decisions while eight were supposed to reflect on the issues at stake. Half of the "reflexive committees" came from IWCP project the burden of women's work (described in the methodology section).

3.2 Difficulties and Strategies in Data Collection and Analysis

Addressing Gender Issues Head-On? An important reflection raised by the researchers concerns the way to address gender issues with partners and workers. The main issue in the approach to gender issues is to either name and explore them directly and explicitly vs. name and explore them indirectly and implicitly. One of the important aspects influencing the way gender issues are approached is the context in which the project is taking place: is s/g part of the initial demand? Does the partner seem sensitive to gender issues? One of the sources of reluctance to address gender issues in a direct way is linked to the workers' initial reaction. When workers are asked about gender issues or differences, the answer is always the same: there is no difference, there are no problems between men and women. This observation made by the researchers gives rise to several concerns.

Firstly, addressing s/g issues head-on seems to be linked to a firm attitude on the part of the partners or workers involved in the project. In this situation, workers may not feel free to be open about their experiences and attitudes, a situation that paradoxically blocks researchers' access to their lived experience of gender issues in the workplace. Thus, researchers' objective of learning about s/g in the workplace is blocked by the project *a prioris*. Secondly, this problem, mentioned by the researchers, poses concerns about their data collection tools: do the tools allow them to gather information about gender issues? This question was primarily raised by ergonomics researchers, who identified some difficulty in keeping gender in mind when analysing work. Their methodological tools (interviews, observations) are oriented towards the analysis of the work activity *in situ*, which provides little direct, observable information on social dynamics and gender issues. In fact, ergonomics researchers are becoming more and more conscious of the necessity to analyze collective aspects of work, an effort that requires new tools [12, 13]. To counter this difficulty, three types of strategies were mentioned by the participants: 1) adapt methodological tools so they can capture gender issues; 2) capture gender issues in the analysis part of the research process; 3) capture gender issues during the validation/feedback stage of an ergonomic RI. For the first type of strategy, keeping a logbook of gender reflections was an example of tool suggested by researchers to make sure that s/g is integrated throughout the whole study. Another example of adaptation aimed the length of interviews: extending the length of qualitative interviews seemed to build a bond of trust between the interviewee and the interviewer that allowed the latter to access sensitive s/g issues experienced by the interviewees. Another point brought up by the researchers was that their access to gender-sensitive data collection tools was limited, and that further research was needed to expand the range of tools available. For the second type of strategy, several researchers who had decided to keep s/g implicit, used their analysis methods to capture gender issues. For instance, in one IR, participants were teachers, and they were asked if they use different approaches with their boy or girl students. Their automatic response was no. Facing this absence of findings about differentiated approaches, researchers rather proposed to analyze ways that teachers spoke about specific students when they give examples or anecdotes. To do so, researchers compile separately part of verbatim talking about a girl student vs a boy student, to analyze the differentiated discourse. This strategy allowed the researcher to have access to information about gender differences. For the third type of strategy, ergonomics researchers gained access to information about gender issues during the final or validation steps of an intervention, when their conclusions and suggestions for solutions were presented to representative groups of those whose work had been observed. Although the researchers could not always be confident that the workers felt free to speak about gender in this setting, many frank comments could be heard.

Several researchers also discussed their resistance or difficulties in implementing methods that openly targeted gender differences or underlined the difficulty of women's work in environments that were traditionally male dominated. Highlighting gender issues may reveal other social conflicts between research partners (employers vs. unions) or between distinct groups of workers, such as different parts of the production process. These issues need further research.

The participants that used reflexive committees as part of the project's participative structure found them helpful for the integration of s/g. According to them, reflecting with the partners on the results whilst they emerged allowed the researchers to gradually give the partners access to s/g issues, which limited their resistance.

4   Discussion

The context in which the RI takes place is an important element of the selection of the methods to be used and can determine their effectiveness for integrating s/g in the project. Laberge et al. (2020) have described four categories of characteristics regarding the origin, design, interest, and projected output of the IR (see Table 3 of Laberge et al. (2020) for details [11]). The research presented here adds to this list of characteristics, contextual factors such as those linked to the stakeholders' background, inclusion of s/g questions in the initial request for the IR and its social, political and economic context.

As mentioned in the methodology section above, the results presented in this article come from the first phase of the GESTE team research program. A second phase consisted of interview of the partners of the IRs. Some of the results emanating from the retrospective analysis of the IR by the partners have been presented in Génier et al. (2019) [14] and will be presented at this IEA conference by Poupart-Monette et al. (2021) [15]. An analysis of the context and methods of each IR will be carried out in order to identify those factors that influence their efficacy for integrating s/g.

5   Conclusion

The results illustrate the quantity and originality required of methods used to analyze work with a "gender lens". Among these methods are the detailed observation of work in situ, the choice of situations (including both men and women, chronology, tasks performed…), techniques for explaining work and sensitivity to gendered tensions in work collectives. The research also provided recommendations to avoid negative effects of such integration such as gender-based discrimination.

Aknowledgement. This study was funded by the Canadian Institutes of Health Research (CIHR)/Institute of gender and Health (# IGK 153464 / GESTE Team).

This work was carried out with the financial support of the SAGE Interdisciplinary Research Team on work "Health, Gender, Equality" (FRQ-SC grant).

References

1. Laberge, M., Vézina, N., Saint-Charles, J.: Safe and healthy integration into semiskilled jobs: does gender matter? Work **41**(1), 4642–4649 (2012)
2. Laperrière, E., Messing, K., Bourbonnais, R.: Work activity in food service: the significance of customer relations, tipping practices and gender for preventing musculoskeletal disorders. Appl. Ergon. **58**, 89–101 (2017)
3. Messing, K., Punnett, L., Bond, M., Alexanderson, K., Pyle, J., Zahm, S., Wegman, D., Stock, S.R., de Grosbois, S.: Be the fairest of them all: challenges and recommendations for the treatment of gender in occupational health research. Am. J. Ind. Med. **43**, 618–629 (2003)
4. Vézina, N., Courville, J.: Integration of women into traditionally masculine jobs. Women Health **18**(3), 97–118 (1992)
5. Dumais, L., Messing, K., Seifert, A.M., Courville, J., Vézina, N.: Make me a cake as fast as you can: Determinants of inertia and change in the sexual division of labour of an industrial bakery. Work Employ. Soc. **7**(3), 363–382 (1993)
6. Lippel, K.: Compensation for musculoskeletal disorders in Quebec: systemic discrimination against women workers? Int. J. Health Serv. **33**(2), 253–281 (2003)
7. Messing, K.: Physical exposures in work commonly done by women. Can. J. Appl. Physiol. **29**(5), 139–156 (2004)
8. Chatigny, C., Riel, J., Nadon, L.: Health and safety of students in vocational training in Quebec: a gender issue? Work **41**(1), 4653–4660 (2012)
9. Messing, K., Mager Stellman, J.: Sex, gender and women's occupational health: the importance of considering mechanism. Environ. Res. **101**(2), 149–162 (2006)
10. Patton, M.Q.: Qualitative Evaluation and Research Methods, 4th edn. Sage Publications, Newbury Park (2015)
11. Laberge, M., Blanchette-Luong, V., Blanchard, A., Sultan-Taïeb, H., Riel, J., Lederer, V., Saint-Charles, J., Chatigny, C., Lefrançois, M., Webb, J., Major, M.-È., Vaillancourt, C., Messing, K.: Impacts of considering sex and gender during intervention studies in occupational health: Researchers' perspectives. Appl. Ergon. **82**, 102960 (2020)
12. Lefrançois, M., Saint-Charles, J., Riel, J.: Work/Family balancing and 24/7 work schedules: network analysis of strategies in a transport company cleaning service. New Solutions **3**, 319–341 (2017)
13. Caroly, S., Clot, Y.: Du travail collectif au collectif de travail : développer des stratégies d'expérience. Formation Emploi **88**(1), 43–55 (2004)
14. Génier, M-L., Riel, J., Lederer, V.: Analyse rétrospective de recherches-intervention en santé au travail intégrant le sexe et le genre: le point de vue des partenaires. Annual congress of ACFAS, Association francophone pour le savoir, Gatineau (2019)
15. Poupart-Monette, V., Laberge, M.: Facilitators and obstacles to sex/gender-conscious partnership research on occupational health: investigators and partners point of view. Accepted at the 21st Triennial Congress of the International Ergonomics Association. Vancouver (2021)

"This Is a Job for Women, Isn't It?": The Evolution of a Traditional Gendered Occupational Segmentation in a Portuguese Industrial Cluster

Liliana Cunha[1,2(✉)] ⓘ, Daniel Silva[2] ⓘ, and Mariana Macedo[1]

[1] Faculty of Psychology and Educational Sciences of the University of Porto, Porto, Portugal
{lcunha,up201405206}@fpce.up.pt
[2] Centre for Psychology at University of Porto (CPUP), Porto, Portugal
danielsilva@fpce.up.pt

Abstract. Cork industry is most expressive in Portugal. However, within the sector, the activity is very differentiated, either when it is looked at from a gender perspective or from the point of view of its automation-driven evolution. The cork stoppers are manufactured by men, whereas their selection is performed by women. Our study presents findings based on fieldwork carried out in two Portuguese cork processing companies. While the limitations of automation in avoiding the waste of cork have perpetuated up to now the use of manual drills by men, the working methods in the selection activity performed exclusively by women are being reconfigured due to automation. The recent introduction of new automated machines is built upon the female workers' experience, requiring from them new "uses of oneself". With these changes, some risks remain barely visible, and their impacts on health are still unrecognized, despite the importance of these work practices in the "revaluation" of a unique industrial territory.

Keywords: Cork Industry · Gender · Automation

1 Introduction

1.1 Cork Industry in Portugal: A Unique Sector

Cork sector is the only one where Portugal is a world leader, in terms of production and transformation as well as exports [1]. Notwithstanding, a look that intersects, simultaneously, a macro and a micro level of analysis sheds light on other singularities of this sector, beyond the economic dimension. A few examples thereto are (i) its "territorial agglomeration" [2], in what is acknowledged as the largest pole of cork transformation, in Northern Portugal (Municipality of Santa Maria da Feira), which gave a contribution for its recognition as an "industrial district" [3]; (ii) the predominance of the cork stoppers production subsector (72% of the sector's production) – composed essentially by micro and small-sized companies whose activity is to some extent regulated by a large company; and (iii) a strong gendered segmentation of the work activities [4].

N. L. Black et al. (Eds.): IEA 2021, LNNS 220, pp. 429–437, 2021.
https://doi.org/10.1007/978-3-030-74605-6_53

In the cork industrial path, some activities, more than others, are being transformed by automation. Is this transformation affecting men and women differently? How can the automation of certain tasks be analyzed from a gender perspective?

1.2   Automation from a Gender Lens: An Invisible Issue in Cork Companies?

Though the processes to produce cork stoppers integrate a significant component of manual labor, a certain dynamic of technological innovation is being introduced in the sector over the last few years, aiming at responding to the demands that challenge the sustainability of these micro and small companies. On the one hand, productivity demands, with deadlines that grow continuously shorter and, on the other hand, quality demands regarding the natural cork stoppers to face the growing competitiveness of synthetic stoppers in the market [5].

From a gender point of view, the characterization of this "industrial district" highlights that men and women living in the territory perform an activity in the sector. However, an analysis that takes into consideration the work territories reveals instead well delimited frontiers between the activities performed by men and by women. This work division, though visible in the contexts where it takes place, tends to be normalized [6] and diminished its pertinence when compared to other changes the sector is going through. Given this context, what does the assumption of a gender perspective reveal [7–10]. How does a gender-related analysis contribute to the knowledge about the automation processes in industrial context and to the discussion of their impacts?

The analyses that sustain our reflection have still an exploratory nature and report to two activities that are undergoing technological transformation processes: punching, reserved to men, and cork stoppers selection ("choosing"), performed exclusively by women. The punching stage is related to the manufacture of the natural cork stoppers, when the operators, using a manual drill, perforate the cork plank giving rise to the cork stopper. In turn, the activity of selecting involves the identification of defective stoppers and/or separation of stoppers according to their quality classes.

The introduction of automatic and semi-automatic drills was considered a huge technological breakthrough in the history of the sector [5]. For the cork stoppers selection, which was entirely manual, the 80s and 90s brought automatic selection machines [4], that categorize the cork stoppers in pre-defined quality classes, according to the microscopic look of their surface [5].

Although the introduction of these automatic machines is not entirely recent, the pertinence of this analysis is twofold: on the one hand, due to the debate about the automation limits, enabled by the point of view of the work activity, in a moment when the speeches about automation, digitalization and robotics have gained recrudescence; and, on the other hand, due to the fact that the activities segmentation in the cork sector encompasses differentiated risks for men and women, risks that tend to be less visible with the automation of certain tasks.

1.3   Objectives

In this frame, our objective is to analyze the progressive tasks automation in the cork industry and its differentiated impacts, from a gender perspective [11]. Which questions do the men, and the women activities raise concerning the automation processes and their limits? Which commitments are built by women and men in the face of new determinations of the "use of oneself" [12]?

2   Method

2.1   Participants

Twelve male and female workers from two small companies specialized in the production of cork stoppers participated in the study: 8 choosing operators, aged 51 years old on average, and 31 years of seniority in the sector; and 4 punching operators, aged 54 years old on average, and 36 years of seniority in the sector (see Table 1).

Table 1.   Characterization of participants workers.

Code	Activity	Company	Sex	Age	Seniority in the company	Seniority in the sector
Ch1	Chooser (Ch)	1	Female	52	10 years	18 years
Ch2		1	Female	58	37 years	43 years
Ch3		1	Female	55	30 years	41 years
Ch4		1	Female	51	4 years	30 years
Ch5		2	Female	58	12 years	45 years
Ch6		2	Female	55	2 months	34 years
Ch7		2	Female	54	2 months	37 years
Ch8		2	Female	26	3 years	3 years
PO1	Punching operator (PO)	2	Male	47	11 years	34 years
PO2		2	Male	67	2 months	53 years
PO3		2	Male	59	1 month	26 years
PO4		2	Male	45	4 years	31 years

2.2   Data Collection and Analysis

We carried out work activity analyses in real context [13], using as resources (i) interviews with the companies' top managers (to explore the landmarks in each company in terms of technological innovation; and to collect the workers' sociodemographic indicators); (ii) observations including verbalizations and video recordings, and individual on-the-job interviews; and (iii) collective sessions with the workers (see Table 2).

Table 2. Data collection in each company.

	Interviews	On-the-job observations and interviews	Collective sessions
Company 1	4 interviews with managerial staff, quality manager and foreman (in a total of 5 h)	20 h (video and verbalizations recording)	Two collective sessions to return and validate results (lasting 1 h each one)
Company 2	2 interviews with managerial staff and foreman (in a total of 3 h)	13 h (video and verbalizations recording)	One collective session (1 h)

During the on-the-job observation moments, we have tried to get to know the work content, its demands (e.g., physical, time-related, cognitive), the risks evolution due to the introduction of automatic machines, and the perceived impacts work has on health. Additionally, diachronic data about the workers' professional paths were also collected, exploring how the job is learned and which are the pivotal-points that trigger change in their professional histories [14]. These results were returned and validated in collective sessions.

The data analysis focused on the description of the work activities performed by choosers and punching operators; on mapping the introduction of automatic machines and the changes caused in the work content; and on the identification of significant landmarks in their professional paths that translate the construction of experience, and the consolidation of the knowhow, in both activities.

3   Results and Discussion

3.1   Changes in the Work Content Due to Automated Machines

As far as the punching activity is concerned, performed exclusively by men, the activity is defined by handling a drill to manufacture the stoppers by a foot pedal. It is an activity that requires the repetition of the foot movement to operate the drill and the arms to slide the strips synchronized with the rhythm of the foot and the movement of the drills. Currently, this activity can be performed through automatic equipment. However, that does not happen in these companies, and they choose so to avoid the cork waste. The automatic drill is known by the punching workers as a "blind drill", i.e., it manufactures stoppers in every points of the cork strips, even in the points where the strips show quality flaws. During observations, a worker emphasized this issue, while showing a cork strip and pinpointing where he would manually perforate it: *"No automatic drill can do this, these are blind drills, they perforate everything, and it is a waste of cork. Can you imagine what it would be like to waste this strip? This is worth a lot of money!"* (PO2).

To do so, the operators use the touch to determine the exact point where the manual drill will perforate the cork strip, as explained by the workers while performing the activity: *"Our fingers are sensors. They read the highs* [in the belly of the cork strip], *and we know that we have to remove a "cavaquinho"* [Portuguese word used by the workers to name a little prominence in the cork strip]. *I don't look at the belly anymore, the fingers have eyes* [...] *If it has a low, we let the lever go up a little bit and the drill perforates slightly to the middle* [of the strip]*"* (PO1). This manual know-how allows to minimize the production of defective stoppers (see Fig. 1a), as well as a greater use of cork.

a   b

Fig. 1 a. Defective stopper. b. Manual selection of stoppers.

Unlike what happened in the punching operators' activity, the choosing activity, performed by women, involves the use of automated machines. However, the manual stoppers selection has not been eliminated from the work processes. Currently, all the natural cork stoppers are firstly selected by the automatic machines and then subject to manual selection (see Fig. 1b). This process is now faster, although the machines do not identify all types of defects in natural cork, as explained by the workers during the on-the-job observations and interviews: *"This one* [points at the flaw] *is the same color of the cork, it cannot go through, it's a defect. The machine does not notice it because it has the same color the cork stopper has and so it lets it go"* (Ch5); *"The machine does not know yet that the "bug" is a defect and it confuses it with the cork pores, not all of them, but it happens, the selection machine lets this defect pass. We can see it is a defect because the hole is rounder* [spherical]*"* (Ch7).

In this context, new demands are posed to these female workers, to judge upon the quality of each stopper. Turning the "choosing" automatic imposed new tasks to these workers, related to supply, supervise and clear jams in the machines: *"Sometimes, the automated machine might well be stopped. This machine causes a lot of trouble with smaller caliber stoppers, the stopper does not fit the channel properly, either it stands aside or actually falls and jams the machine* [...] *We go there and set it free, the machine is restarted, but between one jam and the other we barely have the time to reach the manual choosing conveyor belt* [and the automated machine is placed right behind the manual conveyor belt]*"* (Ch2).

On the other hand, the selection machines are programmed using the same criteria the workers use, for each class of stoppers. Thereto, during the automatic selection the machines do, in a process known as "make the sample", the choosers choose manually a sample of 250 stoppers per quality class and compare it to the selection the machine is doing. In the event of significant differences (e.g., stoppers from an upper class "chosen" as belonging to a lower class), the machine is stopped to be reprogrammed according to the standards the choosers followed in the manual selection.

The most recent technological change with an impact on the work content took place in 2020, with the smell selection machines, also known as "sniffing" machines. These machines were introduced with the purpose of assuring the quality of the cork stoppers, given the risk of contamination of the stoppers by an odor (TCA - Tricloroanisole) that may contaminate the wine. As such, now the choosers, in addition to the visual selection, have to do a "sniffing" selection, which consists in smelling the cork stoppers after they are previously heated by the "sniffing" machine.

3.2 The Automation Limitations from the Point of View of the Work Activity

The introduction of automated machines is one of the main sector strategies to face the challenges ahead; nevertheless, given the limitations in their performance, in some cases it is not the best solution ever. As mentioned before, to prove this point we mentioned the deliberate option from one of the companies not to make such an investment for the punching operators' activity. The company considers the maintenance of the pedal drill together with the punching operators experience make it possible to surpass one of the sectors' main obstacles today – the loss of quality of the "cork in the woods" (i.e., planks of raw cork, before the transformation process that will result in cork stoppers). Nowadays, the incidence of defects in the cork planks is higher, due to the forest exploitation, but also because the stabilization period of the cork planks is shorter, before and after boiling (see Fig. 2, defects 1 e 2, respectively). When the punching operators notice these defects, they guide the drill so to perforate the cork strip precisely where it is flawless.

Fig. 2. Cork plank with some defects: 1 designated as *verdura* ("greenness", which is a defect visible by the superficial accumulation of water in cork plank); and 2 as *prego* ("woody", which is characterized by the presence of sharp nodes in the belly of cork planks).

The technological innovation in cork stoppers production is particularly obvious in the choosers' activity. The automated machines provide an answer to the emergent demands in the sector, such as, guarantee high productivity levels through the automated selection machines; or assure maximum quality in the final product, with the "sniffing". However, though these machines significantly increase sustainability and reinforce these companies' place in the sector, the work activity shows these automatisms have limitations – when the automatic operation of the selection machines, to meet such demands, is only achievable by calling for the know-how the choosers have previously developed throughout years of experience in this activity. The moments of "making the sample" to reprogram the machine, when the visual selection criteria prevail, as referred, are an example of such limitations, and the identification of defects that the machines optical reading cannot detect is another.

3.3 "I Am a Woman…, I Knew I'd Choose Stoppers"

Historically, assigning the women the selection was based on certain stereotypes that depict the work in selecting cork stoppers as "lighter", when compared for example to the punching operators. Additionally, the job requires greater visual acuity, and higher perceptual eye-hand detailed ability, enhancing the perception that women, rather than men, could select the defective cork stoppers with greater precision and speed.

Furthermore, initiating and learning an activity in this sector is conditioned from the start by these gender stereotypes: then the women join this sector, they begin by learning the selection activity whereas men are taught other activities, such as punching. Moreover, these female workers, given their work experience in manual selection, developed know-how that only the thickness of time can give, setting them apart from other workers from the same sector.

Apart from the work division in the sector, female and male activities were built in separate employment segments: until 2008 the punching operators were part of a better paid group of activities (Collective Bargaining Labor Agreement) [15]), while the choosers were part of a group whose wage level was two steps below.

The introduction of automated machines could possibly redesign the meaning of the activities considered exclusively female or male. Despite not being the case in this industrial district, one of the choosers that participated in this study had previously been a punching operator (with automatic drill) in another company. Still, that is not the case for the choosing activity. The know-how of the female choosers is called so to compensate the operation limitations of the selection automated machines. This is what seems to justify to this day the activity is gender defined. In fact, the perpetuation of the word "escolhedora" (Portuguese word which means "woman chooser") to designate the person working in the selection section is an evidence.

4 Conclusions

The development of automation interacts with gender segmentation. The activity analyses we developed enable this issue to be discussed from different perspectives. The punching operator activity, traditionally performed by men, was once performed by one of the women that participated in this study, when she worked at the sector's major company, with automatic drills. Automatization, in this case, seems to have diluted the borders that define this as a male activity. But is this (automation) the unmistakable direction for the sectors' development? The introduction of automatic drills in smaller companies, such as the ones in this study, is being delayed due to the fact they lead to more waste of cork, with undeniable costs for the sustainability of these type of companies, compared to the manual activity associated with the experience and know-how of these workers.

Although it is acknowledged that women are more at risk of seeing some of their tasks become automated given their repeatability [16], as far as choosing is concerned automatization was not the answer to decrease the demands of the women's activity; quite the opposite, both the work complexity (e.g., supervise the quality of the machine selection), and the invisibility of certain risks (e.g., sniffing selection) seem to have increased. Yet, it was also not the key to turn the women's activity territories permeable to men. The choosers assess the quality of the automated selection, scrutinizing this quality given a reference sample they define based on their experience consolidated over several years of manual choosing. And this story, of the professional path from men and women in this sector, is not neutral in the face of automatization.

However, if the effects of automation do not determine the permeability of borders between the male work and the female work in this sector, is this an opportunity to grant higher visibility to the recognition of these workers know-how in the preservation of this industrial district and in its anchor to the territory?

Acknowledgments. This work is supported by the Fundação Calouste Gulbenkian ("CORK-In" project); and by the Centre for Psychology at University of Porto (FCT UIDB/00050/2020). The authors thank the funders for their support.

References

1. Associação Portuguesa da Cortiça: Anuário de cortiça 18/19. APCOR, Santa Maria de Lamas (2018)
2. Parejo, F., Rangel, J-F., Branco, A.: Aglomeración industrial y desarrollo regional. Los sistemas productivos locales en Portugal. Revista latinoamericana de estudios urbano regionales **134**, 147–168 (2019)
3. Becattini, G.: Italian industrial districts: problems and perspectives. Int. Stud. Manage. Organ **21**, 83–90 (1991)
4. Mendes, A.: A economia do sector da cortiça em Portugal. Evolução das actividades de produção e de transformação ao longo dos séculos XIX e XX. Universidade Católica Portuguesa, Porto (2002)
5. Pereira, H.: Production of cork stoppers and discs. In: Pereira, H. (ed.) Cork: Biology Production and Uses, pp. 263–288. Elsevier Science, Lisbon (2007)
6. Brito, J.: Trabalho e saúde coletiva: O ponto de vista da atividade e das relações de gênero. Ciência e saúde coletiva **10**(4), 879–890 (2005)
7. Messing, K.: Integrating Gender in Ergonomic Analysis. European Trade Union Institute, Brussels (1999)
8. Cunha, L., Santos, M., Barros-Duarte, C.: Quand tenir compte du genre transforme l'analyse mais aussi le projet d'intervention. In: Proceedings of the 45th Annual Conference of the Association of Canadian Ergonomists (ACE 2014). Association of Canadian Ergonomists, Montreal (2014)

9. Messing, K., Lefrançois, M., Saint-Charles, J.: Why do we often forget gender during ergonomic interventions? In: Bagnara, S., Tartaglia, R., Albolino, S., Alexander, T., Fujita, Y. (eds.) Proceedings of the 20th Congress of the IEA 2018. AISC, vol. 826, pp. 245–250. Springer, Cham (2019)
10. Lacomblez, M.: How the gender perspective alters workplace health research? In: Communication presented on the Conference "The Future of Health and Safety in Europe: 30 Years After the Framework Directive on Health and Safety in Europe, What's the Way Forward?". European Trade Union Institute, Brussels (2019)
11. Laberge, M., Caroly, S., Riel, J., Messing, K.: Considering sex and gender in ergonomics: Exploring the hows and whys. Appl. Ergon. 85, 103039 (2020)
12. Schwartz, Y.: Le paradigme ergologique ou un métier de philosophe. Octarès, Toulouse (2000)
13. Lacomblez, M., Bellemare, M., Chatigny, C., Delgoulet, C., Re, A., Trudel, L., Vasconcelos, R.: Ergonomic analysis of work activity and training: basic paradigm, evolutions and challenges. In: Pikaar, R., Koningsveld, E., Settels, P. (eds.) Meeting Diversity in Ergonomics, pp. 129–142. Elsevier, Boston (2007)
14. Cunha, L., Pereira, C., Santos, M., Lacomblez, M.: Self-management process after a work accident: a gender analysis. In: Bagnara, S., Tartaglia, R., Albolino, S., Alexander, T., Fujita, Y. (eds.) Proceedings of the 20th Congress of the IEA 2018. AISC, vol. 826, pp. 287–293. Springer, Cham (2019)
15. Boletim do Trabalho e Emprego número 41, 8/11/2008: Contrato Coletivo de Trabalho entre a APCOR e a FETICEQ. Ministério do Trabalho e da Solidariedade Social (2008)
16. Piasna, A., Drahokoupil, J.: Gender inequalities in the new world of work. Transfer Eur. Rev. Labour Res. 23(3), 313–332 (2017)

The Rules, the Strategies and Gender Regarding Safety

Fabienne Goutille(✉) ⓘ and Alain Garrigou ⓘ

Population Health Research Center - Inserm - EpiCEnE team – University of Bordeaux, Cedex 33076 Bordeaux, France

Abstract. The constraints faced by women and men at work deserve to be apprehended for the development of more effective prevention solutions regarding chemical exposure and occupational cancer. So far, the constraints, as so as the resources mobilize by the people at work to preserve productive and safety activity, are not included to the design of the prevention of chemical exposures. As part of a research-intervention on occupational chemical risk prevention, we mobilized ergotoxicology. This approach, which aims to involve workers in the analysis of chemical risk work situations, from a chemical metrology integrated into the work activity, has made it possible to document essential element to build the prevention at different scale. The intervention demonstrated that the documentation of the strategies developed by workers according gender (in order to save their bodies, reduce the discomfort of the presence of chemical substances, put into words the impact of work on health or to preserve and protect others workers) could help to better prevent chemical exposures, particularly indirect chemical exposures. The results also show that the methodology for analyzing risk situations which makes it possible to build prevention at different levels (operation, company, state) deserves to be enriched in order to document the gendered strategies from which to think about the design of safety situations (at work and in its continuity).

Keywords: Chemical risks · Ergotoxicology · Gender · Safety · Workers strategies

1 Problem Statement

Safety rules regarding chemical risks are most of the time constructed from standards based on laboratory research and established for an average man. The classical security model is in this way mainly based on risk management and administration, prevention rules are not design and implemented according to real work and gender-differentiated safety strategies. The focus is to prevent risk and not to design safety situations at work regarding health.

2 Objective

We show how the ergotoxicological approach, which links toxicology and ergonomics, makes it possible and acute to consider the distinct working strategies to build safety at work in toxic environment. We focus this paper of the strategies stated by workers, in particular those concerning gender, to build adapted safety rules and situations of work according to the particularities of the workers and according to their different risk of exposure to chemical substances [4].

3 Methodology

Ergotoxicology equates situations of occupational exposure to chemicals as puzzles that can be accessed through the ergonomics analysis of work activity. Each of the actors (operators, managers, scientists, rulers, etc.) has fragments of this enigma. The confrontation and the articulation of distinct actors, with collective discussion (focus group) based on real work, allow it to be understood and formulated [1]. From this perspective, Ergotoxicology assumes that the worker facing chemical work situation is an expert in his exposure, an expert of exposure conditions whose can contribute, as practitioner, to construct safety situations of work. The worker's points of view, that could be formalized by the ergonomist, are debated with the expertise of prevention specialists to arrive at a shared diagnosis of the exposure situation. Based on a social construction with the internal and external company's stakeholders, the methodology revolves around the analysis of real exposure situations with the objective of collectively developing constructed security resources. The analysis of the activity in situation is guided by the toxicological knowledge of the dynamics of chemical substances in the environment and their modes of penetration and action in the organism which could differ according to the gender and to the way to accomplish activity at work (productive and safety activities).

The use of intermediary objects (workers testimonies, targeted measurements – as chemical concentration and heart and ventilatory rates - synchronized with video of the activity) show a face of work that may be frequently absent from the rules and procedures of prevention [2]. This picture of real work confronts actor's risks representations and perceptions and invite to consider real workers practices to reinforce chemical risk prevention. Compromises and avoidance behaviors developed by operators confront prescriptions of prevention specialists and ultimately questions the entire systemic functioning of the organization, in particular the prevention policy [3]. Also, the open nature of these confrontations enable Ergotoxicology practitioners to establish bridges between life and safety at work and outside of work (by showing the transfer of chemical risk in the family environment - contaminated vehicle and work clothes, exhalation of solvents, etc.). These links, mobilizing the private and intimate sphere of workers, are used as a resource to build prevention at several levels (operation level, company level and beyond).

Gender is not a usual analysis criterion in ergotoxicology. Investing several months work situations (made up of men and women subjected to toxic environments), allowed us to understand how much endangerment and risk avoidance strategies could be gendered, due, in particular, to the possibility, as a man or woman in a determined social group, to say his exposure, or quite simply to say himself, or to sound the alert regarding indirect chemical danger. Thus, our study did not set up a specific methodology to study gender. In the analysis of the interviews conducted (30 individuals interviews and 7 collective interviews) we considered the capacities of people at work to be able to protect themselves and others (workers and members of the family) in terms of their gender, a gender nested in a specific social context (at the scale of the company and of the French society).

4 Results

The intervention was carried out in a factory using carcinogenic resins in the manufacture of wooden furniture. The analysis of risky work situations, by an ergotoxicological app-roach (participatory observation, work analysis synchronized to metrology, discussion of work and risky situation by using video of activity, confrontation of representations about risky situations at work) [2], enabled us to identify protection and preservation strategies (individual, collective, organizational, personal). These strategies and differ-ent possibilities of being able to mobilize these strategies at work (and outside of work) or during exposure situations have been enlighten as factors of exposure and safety to be considered to a built prevention. In the facts, protecting oneself from physical and chem-ical risks was conditioned by gender of workers and social acceptance of the changes brought about by workers in their work activity at several levels.

Example 1: While the younger men increased their chemical exposure by forcing physically during the activities, the few women in the factory, as well as a man involve in a union, gave themselves the possibility of using the pallet trucks. This allowed them to protect their backs but also to be in less contact with chemicals and therefore to reduce their exposure (as physical efforts can enhance the absorption of toxics). One of the women from the work team that we have integrated (during participatory observation) had a singular floor mat at her workstation which allowed her to work with more comfort. This workstation arrangement was initiated by her to reduce the efforts to accomplish the repetitive operations carried out in binomial. This type of strategy improves working conditions, in the physically and chemically aspects (reduction of the effects linked to trampling, reduction of the efforts linked to lifting the arms in an activity where the height difference between two team members is significant $-1m55$ vs $> 1m75$, respiratory tract further away from the source of pollution). The same woman that we have observed during several days also had the possibility of stopping professional activities when they became too dangerous. Indeed, "as a woman" in a predominantly male job, she has the possibility of using her sensitivity (perception of chemical risk) and to mobilize physiological sensations (itching of the eyes and nose, mucous membranes or skin irritation, etc.) to sound the alarm. She refers on her nose and her olfactory perceptions to detect odors of resins too strong. In this way, a metrological evaluation of the formaldehyde could be launched which in certain cases led to the evacuation of this toxic environment by the entire workers. Male team members were less likely to express their perceptions of chemical and physical hazards. On the contrary, they put themselves in danger "to keep their job", get a "more advantageous employment contract" or "to show that they are strong men" (strengthening virility facing risk).

Example 2: In this factory which uses dangerous chemicals, it is the employer who is responsible for cleaning work clothes. The transfer of work clothes to the private sphere could contaminate the workers' relatives. The interviews with the workers made it possible to understand how a migration of occupational chemical risk could take place in the domestic sphere despite the established safety rules (odors on underwear, on the hair, on the skin which emerge at night). Beyond the set safety rules, workers put in place strategies to protect their family members outside the company. Our results show that men and women do not have the same capacity to speak out and preserve themselves in productive activity and protection activity. However, the strategies that men and women develop, depending on the social acceptance of these strategies, can help companies to increase safety regarding chemical risks, especially in situations where the risk is often not very perceptible without the workers contribution to the risk assessment.

5 Conclusion

Understanding the sources of tension between perceived risk (economic, employment, physical health, chronic disease) and the objective to be achieved (production, employment, self-preservation, environment consideration) is essential for understanding exposure situations and supporting their transformation into safety situations. Therefore the ergotoxicological approach aims to promote the workers' power to act in the transformation of work situations.

Producing an analysis of the strategies of workers (involved in chemical risk situations), within the scope of the genre, has enabled us to better document the conditions of exposure and the ways to prevent them. However, this documentation of strategies needs to integrate the fact that the expression of risk and the strategies of risk taking, and risk avoidance are socially constructed. Thus, considering the private sphere of workers, and their risk management strategies require for future the development of specific methods that integrate gender in the analysis and transformation of work situations with chemical risk.

References

1. Galey, L., Goutille, F., Mohammed-Brahim, M., Ergotoxicologie, G.A.: In: Brangier, E., Valléry, G. (eds.) Dictionnaire encyclopédique de l'ergonomie : 150 notions-clés, chapter Ergotoxicologie. Dunod, Paris (In press).
2. Galey, L., Judon, N., Goutille, F., Jolly, C., Albert, M., Morelot, S., Lhospital, O., Martin, P., Noel-Suberville, C., Pasquereau, P., Mohammed-Brahim, B., Aublet-Cuvelier, A., Garrigou, A.: Proposition méthodologique en ergotoxicologie pour révéler les expositions à des produits chimiques. Activités **16**(1), 1–27 (2019)
3. Goutille, F., Galey, L., Rambaud, C., Pasquereau, P., Jackson Filho, J.M., Garrigou, A.: Prescrição e utilização de equipamentos de proteção individual (EPI) em atividades com exposição a produtos químicos cancerígenos, mutagênicos e reprotóxicos (CMR): Pesquisa-ação pluridisciplinar em uma fábrica francesa de decoração para móveis. Laboreal **12**(1), 23–38 (2016)
4. Mohammed-Brahim, B., Garrigou, A.: Une approche critique du modèle dominant de prévention du risque chimique. L'apport de l'ergotoxicologie. Activités **06**(1), 49–68 (2009)

Gender in the Literature of Healthcare Workers Operating in War Settings

Rima R. Habib[1](✉) (iD), Dana A. Halwani[1], Diana Mikati[2], and Layal Hneiny[3]

[1] Department of Environmental Health, Faculty of Health Sciences,
American University of Beirut, Beirut 1107 2020, Lebanon
`rima.habib@aub.edu.lb`
[2] Faculty of Medicine, American University of Beirut, Beirut 1107 2020, Lebanon
[3] Saab Medical Library, American University of Beirut, Beirut 1107 2020, Lebanon

Abstract. The occupational health literature has established that gender plays an important role in all dimensions of the workplace. This review aims to identify the most recent approaches in the integration of gender in the literature on healthcare workers in conflict settings. We updated the search of a previous review by including the period between 2019 and 2020. Five articles were included in the final review. The findings of this update have identified a dearth of articles with adequate consideration of gender in their study design and a shortage of articles aiming to explore gender differences in their research. It also highlighted the limited use of gender sensitive approaches hindering the researchers' ability to reveal gender-related differences in the exposures and outcomes of male and female participants. The results of the original review and its update have found similar gaps in the literature on healthcare workers in conflict settings, which identified inadequate consideration of gender throughout the different phases of the research process in the reviewed literature. Minimal progress in the integration of gender have been made in recent studies following our published review. This implies that the most recent literature on this topic has not given adequate attention to this important research angle. Our results highlight the need to strengthen the efforts to encourage gender integration in occupational health research. There is a need for more comprehensive tools and strategies to improve the integration and evaluation of gender in research and support better evidence-based policies and practices.

Keywords: Gender · Gender integration · Healthcare workers · Scoping review ·
Occupational health and safety · Conflict setting

1 Introduction

The occupational health literature has established that gender plays an important role in all dimensions of the workplace [1, 2]. Men and women often hold different positions in the labor market, which subjects them to varied occupational exposures and consequently different health outcomes [3]. Furthermore, even within the same job position, male and female workers can have differentiated work tasks and job assignments, which can lead to different exposures and experiences [4]. For example, a study found that female health care aides were more involved in physically demanding tasks, compared to their male colleagues in the same position working at the same hospital [4]. The gender-based segregation of work and job tasks are influenced by various factors including socially constructed roles, expectations, and stereotypes [1]. This division of labor has led to differences in working conditions and uneven distribution of occupational exposures between male and female workers [5]. In addition, due to biological and socially constructed differences, male and female workers can experience the same occupational exposure and health outcome in different ways [3, 5].

Similarly, gender can influence the experiences, exposures, and health outcomes of healthcare workers. For example, studies have found that work-related musculoskeletal pain and workplace bullying is more common among female healthcare workers compared to their male colleagues [6, 7]. Additionally, healthcare workers practicing in war and conflict settings are prone to face hazardous and precarious conditions, however these experiences and exposures often differ between male and female workers [8].

Despite the importance of gender at the workplace, research in occupational health have been criticized for the dearth of gender-sensitive approaches [2, 3]. Various studies assessing the health and safety of workers have not dedicated enough attention to gender considerations in the various phases of the research, from conceptualization to the analysis and interpretation of results [3, 5]. Moreover, many studies continue to recruit single sex populations and assume that the results are generalizable to both male and female workers [5]. In addition, an underestimation of hazards in women's work is encountered in published occupational health research [2]. Accordingly, researchers have not dealt appropriately with gender in studies with populations that include both male and female workers, possibly overlooking gender differences in work experiences, risks, and outcomes [2, 3].

Therefore, scholars have emphasized the need for new and more comprehensive methods that allow for adequate gender integration in occupational health research [2, 5, 9]. With the present labor market becoming more diverse than ever, this is essential to guide sound evidence-based policies which can help improve the health and wellbeing of all workers [5, 10].

A recent scoping review was published to assess how sex and gender are considered in the occupational health literature on healthcare workers in conflict settings [8]. The study reviewed 47 relevant articles published between 1999 and 2019 and found a shortage of articles addressing this topic with adequate consideration of sex and/or gender in their study design [8].

To this end, this paper presents a review that aims to identify the most recent approaches in the integration of gender in the literature on healthcare workers in conflict settings. We updated the search of the previous review [8] by including the period between 2019 and 2020 to assess the latest developments and trends in gender integration in the latest research published on this topic.

2   Materials and Methods

2.1   Study Design and Protocol

We followed the PRISMA extension for Scoping Reviews (PRISMA-ScR) in this study [11]. The methods and protocol used in this scoping review were published elsewhere [8].

2.2   Eligibility Criteria

The eligibility criteria used in the selection process were as follows:

- Study Design: primary studies including quantitative (e.g., surveys, cross-sectional, cohort, case control) and qualitative (e.g., interviews, focus groups). We excluded editorials, commentaries, reviews, and studies published only in abstract form.
- Population of interest: Healthcare workers.
- Setting of interest: Conflict setting.
- Language: Articles published in English language.

2.3   Literature Search

A comprehensive search strategy was developed with the assistance of a medical librarian, using an inclusive set of Medical Subject Headings, keywords, and Boolean terms. The following four concepts were used in the search strategy: (1) healthcare workers, (2) armed conflict or war setting, (3) sex/gender, and (4) occupational health. Details of the full search strategies are found in the published report [8]. The search used nine electronic databases: Medline, Web of Science, Scopus, EMBASE, Cochrane, PubMed, CINHAL, Global Index Medicus, and Global Health. The search was limited to records published between 2019 and 2020 (capturing records published up to October 2020: the date of the search).

2.4   Selection Process

The records retrieved from the search were managed and screened using the reference management software EndNote X8 (Clarivate Analytics, Philadelphia, USA). Duplicates were removed using the Endnote feature and manually by one of the reviewers. Guided by the pre-established eligibility criteria, two stages for the screening and selection of articles were carried out independently and in duplicates by two reviewers. The fulltexts of the records that were deemed eligible for inclusion by the two reviewers during the title and abstract screening phase were retrieved and screened at the full-text stage. Disagreements between reviewers about inclusion in the full text screening were resolved through discussion until consensus was reached between the two reviewers.

2.5   Data Abstraction

A data abstraction form was used to extract relevant information from the included articles. Information relating to the study characteristics and the results were extracted from each included study.

2.6 Data Synthesis

The analysis protocol adopted in this scoping review was published elsewhere [8].

3 Results

The new search of the literature databases identified 592 records. After the removal of duplicates, 389 records were screened during the title and abstract phase. Thirty-one records were deemed eligible and were screened during the full-text phase, out of which 5 articles were included in the final review.

Four of the reviewed studies were cross-sectional, half of which employed qualitative research designs [12, 13], while the other half used quantitative designs [14, 15]. In addition, one study employed a mixed method approach [16]. The reviewed articled studied healthcare workers in various regions including, Middle East and North Africa (n = 1) [14], Sub-Saharan Africa (n = 1) [12], Latin American and Caribbean (n = 1) [13], East Asia and Pacific (n = 1) [16], and Europe and Central Asia (n = 1) [15].Two of the reviewed studies had a sample size between 50 and 99 participants [12, 16], while one study had a sample size of less than 50 participants [13]. The remaining reviewed articles had a sample size between 100 and 499 (n = 1) [15], and a sample size of more than 1000 participants (n = 1) [14]. Three studies assessed mental and social health outcomes [14–16], one study assessed working conditions [12], and one study assessed several outcomes including mental and social health, physical health, workplace violence, and working conditions of healthcare workers practicing in conflict settings [13].

Four of the reviewed articles recruited both male and female participants, of which, 1 had higher proportions of males [14], and 3 had higher proportions of females [12, 15, 16]. All studies that recruited unequal ratios did not justify the sample recruitment strategy. In addition, one study did not specify the gender of their participants [13]. Most articles (n = 4) did not have well-defined objectives related to exploring gender-related findings [12, 13, 15, 16]. Only one study had objectives related to exploring sex/gender differences/similarities, reported on sex/gender related findings, and interpreted gender specific outcomes to identify underlying causes [14]. Most reviewed articles (n = 4) did not consider sex/gender in their qualitative and/or quantitative analysis [12, 13, 15, 16]. While only one used sex/gender as an exploratory variable in univariate models [14].

4 Discussion

Despite the established importance of gender in the occupational health literature, there is a lack of gender integration in the reviewed research that may result in knowledge gaps that undermine evidence-based policies and practices recommended to protect healthcare workers practicing in conflict settings.

The results identified unequal ratios of male and female participants across the reviewed articles, without justifications for the recruitment strategies. Moreover, although most of the reviewed articles recruited both male and female study partici-pants, only one had objectives related to exploring gender similarities or differences. In addition, most of the reviewed articles did not consider gender in their analyses, limiting the researchers' ability to identify possibly overlooked gender-related differences in the exposures and outcomes of male and female participants. This is evidenced by the fact that most reviewed studies did not report gender-related findings.

The current update reveals that minimal progress in the integration of gender have been made in the latest occupational health studies on healthcare workers in conflict settings following our published review [8]. This implies that the most recent literature on this topic has not given adequate attention to this important research angle. The findings of this update have reinforced and increased the certainty of our results and conclusions in the published review.

The results of this update mirrored the findings of the previous review, which identified inadequate consideration for sex/gender throughout the different phases of the research process in most of the reviewed literature. These findings have been reiterated in other studies evaluating both sex and gender integration in health research [2, 5, 17, 18]. Scholars have argued that perhaps researchers' limited expertise and experience in sex and gender issues have hindered their ability to address these factors in their studies [19]. Similarly, the European Commission identified that the lack of familiarity and practice with sex and gender integration tools among researchers may have hindered their ability to integrate these factors in their work [20].

A recent study discussed four challenges that researchers encounter in the integration of sex and gender in health research [21]. The first challenge relates to the use of inconsistent terminologies, whereby sex and gender are often used interchangeably without proper acknowledgment of the definitions and dimensions of these terms[1] [21]. This challenge is particularly amplified in occupational health studies, where distinguishing between sex and gender is difficult when considering job and task assignments [10]. Moreover, researchers may encounter difficulties in acknowledging and understanding the impact of sex and gender on the outcomes they are assessing and in applying those factors in their studies [21]. Capturing sex and gender factors, such as differences in jobs and tasks and their relationships to biological variations and to societal roles and expectations, often mandate researchers to think about these factors during the conceptualization and research formation phase; this leads to changes in research questions, use of different study designs, assessment of different phenomena, and shapes the orientation of the analysis, interpretation and reporting of the results [23, 24].

Moreover, the emergence of the concept of intersectionality has further challenged the application of gender and sex factors in research, which has prompted more sophisticated analyses to account for the ways in which sex and gender interact with additional factors such as race, ethnicity, age, etc.… [10, 21, 25]. In addition, obtaining relevant and sufficient data to allow adequate exploration of sex and gender factors is another challenge for researchers [21]. Researchers who rely on large data sets for data collection often encounter challenges, where data on gender factors may be limited [26]. Also, data collection tools may not allow researchers to capture these factors as needed [21]. In the

---

[1] According to the Canadian Institutes of Health Research (CIHR), sex is defined as "the biological and physiological characteristics that distinguish males from females" and gender is "the socially constructed roles, expectations, relationships, behaviors, relative power, and other traits that societies ascribe to women, men and people of diverse gender identities" [22].

occupational health field specifically, some quantitative tools refer mainly to exposures faced by male workers as a frame of reference, and thus occupational health researchers may face challenges in finding instruments to capture the unique components of women's working environments [10].

In order to overcome these challenges, researchers need proper guidance for a more comprehensive integration of sex and gender in their studies [21]. Efforts have been made toward developing resources and guidelines to support researchers in this integration, such as case studies showing the advantages of integrating sex and gender in health research [9, 27], a criteria for sex and gender integration in Cochrane systematic reviews [28], the Sex and Gender Equity in Research (SAGER) guidelines [29], and recommendations for exploring sex and gender differences in health [30]. In addition, steps have been taken to encourage researchers to integrate sex and gender in their research studies, where various international funding agencies, including the World Health Organization (WHO), the European commission Directorate-General for Research and Innovation, the CIHR, and the United States National Institutes of Health (NIH), have established policies that mandate the integration of sex and gender in research proposals [21]. Also, a number of peer-reviewed journals have established policies for sex and gender reporting [31]. The Canadian Institutes of Health Research (CIHR) has also proposed a series of criteria to evaluate the integration of sex and gender in the various phases of research that include human participants [32].

Yet despite the widespread dissemination of these resources and initiatives, it is possible that researchers are still struggling with the implementation of the proper methods to incorporate sex and gender in their research as evidenced in the limited and incomplete integration of these factors in the reviewed studies [33]. While acknowledging the importance of these resources, a 2019 editorial suggests that sex and gender considerations have not yet been consistently adopted by researchers as a standard practice in health research since institutional ethics committees do not mandate the inclusion of sex and gender considerations in research [17]. Moreover, journals and grant review groups implement varying degrees of sex and gender integration standards [17]. Therefore, as the authors noted "a clear misalignment" is present in the scientific workforce's readiness to plan and implement sex and gender integration in health research [17]. In addition, there is a lack of standardized educational programs that enable researchers to recognize and understand the relevance of sex and gender in their research fields [17].

5   Conclusion

Similar to other health research, most occupational health studies on healthcare workers in conflict settings have marginalized gender in important ways. The findings of this review highlight the need to strengthen the efforts to encourage gender integration in occupational health research. While various resources and guidelines have been proposed and developed, there is a need for more comprehensive tools and strategies to improve the integration and evaluation of gender in research and support better evidence-based policies and practices.

Funding agencies could mandate the inclusion of adequate gender considerations in their call for proposals in order to incentivize researchers to rigorously integrate gender in their studies and address the current literature gap. Educational programs and professional training initiatives that enhance understanding and provide tools for integrating gender in all phases of the research process are essential to enable researchers to successfully integrate gender in their studies. These educational and training programs need to be developed by scientific researchers and educational experts in order to establish international evidence-based standards with universal applications.

Gender integration in research paves the way for designing workplace health and safety interventions that may require distinct control measures for males and females. Therefore, gender-sensitive approaches can help implement effective interventions to address the various hazards facing male and female healthcare workers in conflict settings.

References

1. International Labor Organization (ILO): Working paper 10 Keys for Gender Sensitive OSH Practice – Guidelines for Gender Mainstreaming in Occupational Safety and Health. ILO, Geneva (2013)
2. Messing, K., Punnett, L., Bond, M., Alexanderson, K., Pyle, J., Zahm, S., et al.: Be the fairest of them all: challenges and recommendations for the treatment of gender in occupational health research. Am. J. Ind. Med. **43**(6), 618–29 (2003)
3. Artazcoz, L., Cortès, I., Escribà-Agüir, V.: Gender, work and health: a step forward in women's occupational health. In: Gideon, J. (ed.) Handbook on Gender and Health, pp. 165–188. Edward Elgar Publishing, Cheltenham (2016)
4. Messing, K., Stock, S., Côté, J., Tissot, F.: Is sitting worse than static standing? How a gender analysis can move us toward understanding determinants and effects of occupational standing and walking. J. Occup. Environ. Hyg. **12**(3), D11–D7 (2015)
5. Quinn, M.M., Smith, P.M.: Gender, work, and health. Ann. Work Exposure Health **62**(4), 389–92 (2018)
6. Barbosa, R.E.C., Assunção, A.Á., de Araújo, T.M.: Musculoskeletal pain among healthcare workers: an exploratory study on gender differences. Am. J. Ind. Med. **56**(10), 1201–12 (2013)
7. Ariza-Montes, A., Muniz, N.M., Montero-Simó, M.J., Araque-Padilla, R.A.: Workplace bullying among healthcare workers. Int. J. Environ. Res. Public Health **10**(8), 3121–39 (2013)
8. Habib, R.R., Halwani, D.A., Mikati, D., Hneiny, L.: Sex and gender in research on healthcare workers in conflict settings: a scoping review. Int. J. Environ. Res. Public Health **17**(12), 4331 (2020)
9. Johnson, J.L., Greaves, L., Repta, R.: Better science with sex and gender: facilitating the use of a sex and gender-based analysis in health research. Int. J. Equity Health **8**(1), 1–11 (2009)
10. Armstrong, P., Messing, K.: Taking gender into account in occupational health research: continuing tensions. Policy Pract. Health Saf. **12**(1), 3–16 (2014)
11. Tricco, A.C., Lillie, E., Zarin, W., O'Brien, K.K., Colquhoun, H., Levac, D., et al.: PRISMA extension for scoping reviews (PRISMA-ScR): checklist and explanation. Ann. Intern. Med. **169**(7), 467–73 (2018)
12. Baba, A., Theobald, S., Martineau, T., Sabuni, P., Nobabo, M.M., Alitimango, A., et al.: "Being a midwife is being prepared to help women in very difficult conditions": 'midwives' experiences of working in the rural and fragile settings of Ituri province, democratic republic of congo. Rural Remote Health **20**(2), 5677 (2020)

13. Santos, R.S.D., Mourão, L.C., Almeida, A.C.V.D., Santos, K.M.D., Brazolino, L.D., Leite, I.C.D.M.: The armed conflict and the impacts on the health of workers acting in the Family Health Strategy in the city of Rio de Janeiro, RJ, Brazil. Saúde e Sociedade **29**, e180850 (2020)
14. Alhaffar, B.A., Abbas, G., Alhaffar, A.A.: The prevalence of burnout syndrome among resident physicians in Syria. J. Occup. Med. Toxicol. **14**(1), 1–8 (2019)
15. Güngör, A., Uçman, A.G.: Depression and hopelessness in Turkish healthcare workers: the moderating and mediating roles of meaning in life. Glob. Public Health **15**(2), 236–46 (2020)
16. Posselt, M., Baker, A., Deans, C., Procter, N.: Fostering mental health and well-being among workers who support refugees and asylum seekers in the Australian context. Health Soc. Care Commun. **28**(5), 1658–70 (2020)
17. Regensteiner, J.G., Libby, A.M., Huxley, R., Clayton, J.A.: Integrating sex and gender considerations in research: educating the scientific workforce. Lancet Diab. Endocrinol. **7**(4), 248–50 (2019)
18. Habib, R.R., Hojeij, S., Elzein, K.: Gender in occupational health research of farmworkers: a systematic review. Am. J. Ind. Med. **57**(12), 1344–67 (2014)
19. Science for all. Nature **495**(7439) (2013)
20. European Commission: Final report of the study on the integration of science and society issues in the 6th Framework Programme (EUR 22976). EC, Brussels (2007)
21. Day, S., Mason, R., Lagosky, S., Rochon, P.A.: Integrating and evaluating sex and gender in health research. Health Res. Policy Syst. **14**(1), 75 (2016)
22. Canadian Institutes of Health Research (CIHR), What is gender? What is sex? https://cihr-irsc.gc.ca/e/documents/igh_s17_infographic_gender_sex-en.pdf. Accessed 06 Feb 2021
23. Nieuwenhoven, L., Klinge, I.: Scientific excellence in applying sex-and gender-sensitive methods in biomedical and health research. J. Women's Health **19**(2), 313–21 (2010)
24. Day, S., Mason, R., Tannenbaum, C., Rochon, P.A.: Essential metrics for assessing sex & gender integration in health research proposals involving human participants. PloS One **12**(8), e0182812 (2017)
25. Habib, R.R., Elzein, K., Younes, N.: Intersectionality: The value for occupational health research. In: Gideon, J. (eds) Handbook on Gender and Health, pp. 189–202. Edward Elgar Publishing, Cheltenham, UK (2016)
26. Nowatzki, N., Grant, K.R.: Sex is not enough: the need for gender-based analysis in health research. Health Care Women Int. **32**(4), 263–77 (2011)
27. Schiebinger, L., Klinge, I.: Gendered innovation in health and medicine. GENDER–Zeitschrift für Geschlecht, Kultur und Gesellschaft **7**(2), 9–10 (2015)
28. Doull, M., Welch, V., Puil, L., Runnels, V., Coen, S.E., Shea, B., et al.: Development and evaluation of 'briefing notes' as a novel knowledge translation tool to aid the implementation of sex/gender analysis in systematic reviews: a pilot study. PloS One **9**(11), e110786 (2014)
29. Heidari, S., Babor, T.F., De Castro, P., Tort, S., Curno, M.: sex and gender equity in research: rationale for the SAGER guidelines and recommended use. Res. Integrity Peer Rev. **1**(1), 2 (2016)
30. Springer, K.W., Mager Stellman, J., Jordan-Young, R.M.: Beyond a catalogue of differences: A theoretical frame and good practice guidelines for researching sex/gender in human health. Soc. Sci. Med. **74**(11), 1817–24 (2012)
31. European Association of Scientific Editors, Gender Policy Committee. https://www.ease.org.uk/about-us/gender-policy-committee/. Accessed 06 Feb 2021
32. Canadian Institutes of Health Research (CIHR), Criteria for Evaluating the integration of sex & Gender [Research with Human Participants]. https://cihr-irsc.gc.ca/e/documents/clinical_research_guidelines-en.pdf. Accessed 06 Feb 2021
33. Mason, R.: Doing better: eleven ways to improve the integration of sex and gender in health research proposals. Res. Integrity Peer Rev. **5**(1), 15 (2020)

Training M.Sc. Students in Ergonomics to Integrate a Sex/Gender-Sensitive Approach

Marion Inigo[1,2,3](✉) [iD], Marie Laberge[1,2,3] [iD], Martin Chadoin[3,4] [iD],
and Karen Messing[3] [iD]

[1] Rehabilitation School, University of Montreal, Montreal, QC H3C 3J7, Canada
[2] Sainte-Justine UHC Research Center, Montreal, QC H1T 1C9, Canada
[3] CINBIOSE Research Group, UQAM, Montreal, QC H3C 3P8, Canada
[4] School of Management (ESG UQAM), UQAM, Montreal, QC H3C 3P8, Canada

Abstract. We trained M.Sc. students learning a work activity-centered approach to ergonomics to use a sex- and gender-sensitive lens. Such a lens is useful for ergonomic analysis because gender can affect exposure to some workplace health determinants. Sex and gender training was given in two sessions during students' final year, as part of an intervention internship. We present here three categories for potential sex and gender inclusion in an ergonomics intervention. These categories are: (1) investigating and modeling work activity by integrating sex and gender; (2) implementing solutions with consideration of sex and gender; (3) exchanging with stakeholders on sex/gender issues. We propose that these categories could be useful for examining work activity-centered ergonomic interventions. Student questionnaires revealed that they were satisfied with this training, thought it useful for their practice, and felt that they were well-trained. They rated the training as important and ethically relevant for all ergonomists. However, students did not feel they integrated sex and gender enough in their interventions and they perceived some obstacles to integration. Our results nevertheless support the idea that improving knowledge around sex and gender could be a lever for more inclusive and health-centered ergonomics interventions.

Keywords: Sex and gender consideration · Training future ergonomists · Ergonomic intervention

1 Theoretical Introduction

1.1 Problem Statement

Work activity ergonomics is a scientific discipline that aims to understand work in order to improve it. Ergonomic interventions can be performed at different levels, such as workplace and tool design, training and knowledge translation, and well-being at work [1]. Each of these levels stems from work activity analysis, whose purview includes individual and social aspects such as sex and gender. In this presentation we refer to sex as an individual biological characteristic, and to gender as a relational, social determinant; both can affect health and thus affect ergonomic interventions [2].

© The Author(s), under exclusive license to Springer Nature Switzerland AG 2021
N. L. Black et al. (Eds.): IEA 2021, LNNS 220, pp. 450–456, 2021.
https://doi.org/10.1007/978-3-030-74605-6_56

Gender segregation of the labour market affects working conditions and health effects for men and women. Ergonomists normally act on the working environment, rather than on individual characteristics. Some ergonomists therefore tend to exclude gender considerations from their analysis [3]. However, "gender" also refers to norms and constructs shared by a work team, so it can be considered as a determinant of the work environment [2], of work demands, and of the operational leeway available to workers [4]. This perspective can therefore enlarge the scope of an ergonomics intervention.

Integrating sex and gender in ergonomic interventions requires some delicacy, since making women more visible as women can encourage reifying sex differences and undervaluing women's abilities and contributions. On the other hand, taking sex and gender into account during ergonomics interventions can also help to provide a more inclusive environment by correcting injustices and adapting work practices. It can be hoped that attention to sex and gender integration in ergonomics interventions, under controlled circumstances could lead to more equity at work.

The GESTE research team has developed training content to raise awareness of sex and gender considerations in ergonomic interventions and to point out ways that such considerations can be integrated. The content was constructed based on Canadian Institutes of Health Research, the scientific literature [2], and interventional approaches developed by our collaborators [5]. This training was first provided to students enrolled in two master's level university programs in Québec, Canada.

1.2 Objective

The communication presents the content of this training program on integration of sex and gender consideration in ergonomics interventions and describes the level of satisfaction and the intention to use this content among the students receiving the training.

This communication is part of the GESTE research team's activities aimed at modeling the consideration of gender in knowledge transfer interventions in occupational and environmental health. It is complementary to other presentations at this symposium.

2 Methods

We describe the training context and content, then the constructs employed in this study: categories used for the content of training, for student evaluation of the training and for their intention to make use of the training.

2.1 The Content of Training

The training was given to ergonomics students in two Quebec universities during the final year of their master's degree program, during their intervention internship. The university program presents a work activity-centered approach [1], which proposes various steps in the conduct of ergonomics intervention. For each step, the training offers ways of considering and integrating sex and gender considerations, depending on the intervention context.

This training consists of interactive presentations at two key points during interventions: (A) before the beginning of field work investigations, and (B) just prior to presentation of preliminary results to the workplace participants, before any recommendations are made. These training sessions covered basic notions of sex and gender, their relevance to ergonomic interventions, and practical steps to include sex and gender considerations.

To extract and classify themes covered by the training, we recorded these two interactive presentations, and conducted a short content analysis of this material. After iterative listening, we performed an emerging themes analysis. Watching videos of the training sessions, yielded ideas and suggestions for better consideration of sex and gender in ergonomic interventions. We next conceived a grid to compile ideas and suggestions with reference to some categories of activities usually done by ergonomists, including investigating and modeling work activity by integrating sex and gender (1), implementing solutions with consideration of sex and gender (2), and exchanging with stakeholders on sex and gender issues (3).

2.2 Satisfaction and Intention to Use

Thirteen ergonomic students (8 women and 5 men) participated in A and B training sessions (offered at both universities) and responded to an adapted version of the CDP Questionnaire [6]. The CDP consists of a short questionnaire including 13 items, intended to evaluate the students' intention to adopt new behaviors after receiving continuing professional development training. Each item includes a 7-point response scale (1 – strongly disagree to 7 – strongly agree; or 1 – extremely difficult to 7 – extremely easy; 1 – useless to 7 – useful; 1 – harmful to 7 – beneficial), except for one item which had 5 response choices (0–20%; 20–40%; 40–60%; 60–80%; 80–100%). We calculated the mean (μ) and standard deviation (SD) for 7-point scale items and the frequency for the other one. Descriptive analyses were done using SPSS©.

This questionnaire was completed at the end of students' internships, a few months after the second training session.

3   Results

3.1   The Content of Training

Three main categories and fifteen subcategories were extracted from videos and are detailed in the following Table 1. These categories comprise different ways of taking sex and gender into account in the usual actions during an ergonomic intervention. "Investigating and modeling work activity by integrating sex and gender" includes analysis and understanding of work situations through a sex and gender lens. "Implementing solutions with consideration of sex and gender" includes all actions related to creating solutions whether in work committees (e.g., with workers' representatives) to recommendations. "Exchanging with stakeholders on sex and gender issues" is also an important aspect, because debates can occur, and having a sex and gender lens can stimulate reflection among collaborators and clients.

We also considered these categories to be potentially useful for integrating sex and gender in ergonomic interventions.

Table 1. The content of training.

Categories	Subcategories
Investigating and modeling work activity by integrating sex and gender	Study multiple work situations including men and women Choose valid et relevant methods to do such studies Sample men and women, especially if the job is gender-mixed, even if it is mainly held by one gender When documenting elements of the context, take gender into account Be careful to focus on sex and gender issues and not on people
Implementing solutions with consideration of sex and gender	Suggest tools to biological differences among workers Ensure workers' representativity in terms of gender in project committees Identify stereotypes perpetuated during project management Consider the influence of work culture on sex and gender when proposing transformations Search levers and methods for integrating sex and gender in the specific work environment Propose ways to create environments conducive to knowledge sharing and not based on an expert approach
Exchanging with stakeholders on sex and gender issues	Provide factual data related to sex and gender in the specific workplace Promote access for all even in highly segregated male or female jobs Suggest including gender equity as a valid mandate among the other ergonomic considerations Take care not to perpetuate prejudices when presenting gendered data (e.g., women's work is easier)

3.2   Satisfaction and Intention to Use Sex and Gender in Ergonomic Intervention

Regarding satisfaction and intention to use, we found students were sensitive to this training. Descriptive analysis showed (Table 2) that the students wanted, felt confident and had the ability to integrate sex and gender in their future practice. They also thought that learning how to integrate sex and gender was beneficial for them.

They thought they had learned something new and complementary to the rest of their academic training. For students, this training had an ethical importance, they found it useful and relevant for training in ergonomics. They thought that all ergonomists should know how to integrate sex and gender in their work.

However, students thought that they did not integrate enough sex and gender in their ergonomics interventions, and perceived that few of their colleagues had succeeded in doing so (5 students thought that between 0 and 20% of their colleagues had integrated sex and gender, 7 thought that 21% to 40% had succeeded, and one thought that 61% to 80% had succeeded). They also perceived a certain amount of difficulty in integrating sex and gender.

Table 2. Means and standard deviations of items with 7-point scales ($N = 13$).

Items	M	SD
As part of my internship, I took specific steps to ensure that I applied certain principles of differentiated analysis according to sex and gender	3.23	1.54
For me, applying the principles of differentiated analysis by sex and gender is: [degree of difficulty]	4.23	0.93
In my future practice, I intend to apply the principles of differentiated analysis by sex and gender	4.54	1.51
With the training received, I am confident that I can apply the principles of sex and gender differentiated analysis in my future professional practice if I want to	4.85	.090
I can apply the principles of differentiated analysis according to sex and gender in an ergonomic intervention	4.92	0.76
We should ensure that all ergonomists are adequately trained to apply the principles of differentiated analysis by sex and gender	5.62	1.04
I learned things that I hadn't seen in other classes	5.77	0.93
In general, I think that applying the principles of differentiated analysis according to sex and gender in an ergonomic intervention is: [degree of utility]	5.85	1.07
Overall, I think applying the principles of sex / gender analysis in an ergonomic intervention would be for me: [degree of benefit]	5.92	1.04
The two sessions (on sex and gender) complement the training received in the rest of the master's degree program	5.92	0.86
These two sessions are relevant to my training as an ergonomist	6.00	0.71
I consider it ethical to apply the principles of differentiated analysis according to sex and gender in an ergonomic intervention	6.54	0.66

4 Discussion

This paper presents some ideas and suggestions for developing a sex- and gender-sensitive approach in ergonomic interventions. We present here various ways of offering this training and of meshing the content with the various steps of an ergonomic intervention. We will also discuss some ideas about how to implement the approach.

4.1 Sex and Gender During Ergonomic Intervention

According to St-Vincent et al. (2014) an ergonomic intervention with a work activity-centered approach follows six steps: (1) the request for an analysis; (2) preliminary investigations and pre-diagnosis; (3) choice of work situations to analyze; (4) diagnosis; (5) consensus on the issues to prioritize – recommendations; (6) in-depth work activity analysis while designing and implementing, in a participative way, the situation changes. In this paper, we suggest three main categories of ideas which are suggestions for better consideration of sex and gender in ergonomic interventions. These categories can be relevant in all different steps of an ergonomics intervention because they are all usual activities of an ergonomist. Having a "sex and gender lens" is worthwhile to assess the negative effects of work activity on workers' health with fairness.

These elements should be considered as a non-exhaustive list of possible suggestions to better consider sex and gender in ergonomic interventions.

4.2 Sex and Gender Approach Are Evaluated as Useful

A sex and gender-sensitive approach is considered useful and relevant by ergonomics students for their intervention, but also more globally, for all ergonomists. This training was satisfying, and students think they have learned something. They also feel the implementation is not so easy, and few of them think they succeed enough in their own interventions. Although the students generally gave a positive evaluation of their training, we have not determined whether they in fact used the training during their interventions. Analysis of this question is ongoing.

We should emphasize that the sex and gender training was introduced as a supplement to students' training rather than being integrated with it. Also, the trainer was not the same professor who taught the rest of the course, which may mean that the terms and concepts used did not fully mesh with the rest of the training. Conversely, we do not know whether the professor in charge of the course integrated the sex and gender concepts during the rest of the course. This situation could have imposed an additional cognitive load on students. We suggest it may be better to integrate the sex and gender lens into all ergonomics training. In addition, it would be relevant to provide opportunities for students to think about gender equality and about how to take account of sex differences in the context of ergonomics interventions.

More broadly, ergonomists should be encouraged to critically examine of their own positions and practices regarding the integration of sex and gender in their interventions.

5 Conclusions

This training about integrating sex and gender into ergonomic interventions was appreciated by students. It seems to be a promising and important topic for ergonomics, such as expressed by two reviewers. This paper aimed to increase knowledge around sex and gender to improve equity and health among ergonomists. These reflections are not exhaustive and allow an interesting debate for the scientific track "gender and work" in the "knowledge Transfer, Gender and Ergonomics" symposia series.

Acknowledgements. This study was funded by the Canadian Institutes of Health Research (CIHR)/Institute of gender and Health (# IGK 153464 / GESTE Team).

References

1. St-Vincent, M., Vézina, N., Bellemare, M., Denis, D., Ledoux, É., Imbeau, D.: Ergonomic Intervention. IRSST, Montréal (2014)
2. Laberge, M., Blanchette-Luong, V., Blanchard, A., Sultan-Taïeb, H., Riel, J., Lederer, V., Major, M.-È.: Impacts of considering sex and gender during intervention studies in occupational health: Researchers' perspectives. Appl. Ergon. **102960**(82), 1–9 (2020)
3. Vézina, N., Chatigny, C., Calvet, B.: L'intervention ergonomique : Que fait-on des caractéristiques personnelles comme le sexe et le genre ? Perspectives interdisciplinaires sur le travail et la santé **18**(2), 1–19 (2016)
4. Coutarel, F., Caroly, S., Vézina, N., Daniellou, F.: Marge de manoeuvre situationnelle et pouvoir d'agir : Des concepts à l'intervention ergonomique. Le Travail Humain **78**(1), 29 (2015)
5. Riel, J., Bernstein, S., Cox, R., Laberge, M., Lederer, V., Messing, K., Saint-Charles, J.: Perspectives interdisciplinaires sur les inégalités sociales et de genre en santé au travail : constats et défis pour l'action. In: 86e congrès de l'ACFAS, Chicoutimi (2018)
6. Légaré, F., Borduas, F., Freitas, A., Jacques, A., Godin, G., Luconi, F., Grimshaw, J.: Development of a simple 12-item theory-based instrument to assess the impact of continuing professional development on clinical behavioral intentions. PLoS One **9**(3), 1–10 (2014)

Considering Sex/Gender in the Design of a Technology-Supported Work Injury Prevention Model Among Adolescents with Learning Difficulties

Marie Laberge[1,2,3](✉) ⓘ, Myriam Bérubé[1,2,3] ⓘ, Aurélie Tondoux[2],
Céline Chatigny[3,4] ⓘ, and Denys Denis[5] ⓘ

[1] Rehabilitation School, University of Montreal, Montreal, QC H3C 3J7, Canada
marie.laberge@umontreal.ca
[2] Sainte-Justine UHC Research Center, Montreal, QC, Canada
[3] CINBIOSE Research Group, Université du Québec à Montréal (UQAM), Montreal, QC, Canada
[4] Department of Special Education and Training, UQAM, Montreal, QC, Canada
[5] Department of Physical Activity Sciences, UQAM, Montreal, QC, Canada

Abstract. Adolescents with a low education level and learning difficulties are particularly vulnerable to work injuries. In Québec (Canada), these adolescents can take part in the Work-Oriented Training Path (WOTP) program, where they have the opportunity to develop general employability skills, by spending half of their school time doing a pre-work traineeship. This communication aims to describe, through a sex/gender lens, Occupational Health & Safety (OHS) prevention activities among key stakeholders involved in the WOTP, and to document their needs for new technological OHS resources. We used multiple data sources to collect school principals, teachers, and students opinions. School principals mentioned they are quite far from the students' day-to-day OHS considerations, despite acknowledging that they have some responsibilities in this matter. They did not perceive any issues related to sex/gender and OHS. Teachers expressed feeling personally concerned by OHS, but they focused mainly on students' attitudes and behaviors. They mention that they treat men and women students similarly, but they recognize that some workplaces have specific issues in terms of OHS (e.g. garage, hairdressing salon); however, it is uncertain whether they see any gendered trends in this observation. Male teachers seem more proactive in involving companies in prevention with their students. Finally, students can identify several hazards in their traineeship workplace. Male students tend to name a larger number of potential dangers, but only women name stress and anxiety as specific hazards. Men usually report receiving more OHS training than women, throughout their traineeship.

Keywords: Sex and gender · Adolescents · Vocational training · Injury prevention · Stakeholders perspectives

1   Introduction

Adolescents with a low education level and who experience learning difficulties are particularly vulnerable to work injuries [1, 2]. In the Province of Québec (Canada), these adolescents can take part in the Work-Oriented Training Path (WOTP) program where they have the opportunity to develop general employability skills. The WOTP is intended to improve chances for students who have an uncertain academic future to succeed in accessing the job market. The WOTP is recognized as an innovative program for reducing social inequalities in education and work. This program offers students the opportunity to do a traineeship (300 h/year) that leads to certification for a semiskilled trade chosen according to their interest and capacity. Trades can be found in all activity sectors and are recognized by the Ministry of Education; a list can be consulted here: https://www1.mels. gouv.qc.ca/sections/metiers/index_en.asp. Most of these trades are gender-segregated [3]. According to the Act respecting industrial accidents and occupational diseases, these students are considered to be employed by the educational institution because they are undergoing a traineeship without remuneration. School principals and teachers play a key role in work-related injury prevention, since they organize traineeships and are in contact with companies who have accepted to train the students [4]. As explained by Laberge et al. [5], schools have a duty to ensure that companies are equipped and managed in a safe manner for their trainees and they therefore participate in the identification, control, and elimination of risks.

2   Objective

To help WOPT stakeholders in playing their key role in Occupational Health and Safety (OHS) prevention among WOPT students, we are currently launching a broad study aimed at developing a prevention model adapted to the WOPT population, and supported by technology. WOPT apprentices are predominantly male, whereas their supervising teachers are predominantly female. In addition, apprentices predominantly enroll in practicums that correspond to stereotypes for their gender. This sexual division of jobs implies different OHS risks for male and female apprentices. Based on the larger study, this communication aims to describe OHS prevention activities among key stakeholders involved in the WOPT program, including apprentices, and to document their needs for new resources and tools. This study will use a sex/gender-based analysis (GBA+).

3   Methods

The data were collected in two school boards among diverse categories of participants: 1) semi-directed interviews with four school principals (2 men | 2 women); 2) short-answer questionnaires from 45 trainees/students (35 men | 12 women); and 3) in-depth interviews with twelve teachers supervising traineeships (4 men | 8 women). Ratios of M/W in the samples are proportional to the population in each subpopulation. OHS practices, OHS risk perceptions, and needs for new technological tools, were extracted from each source. As mentioned above, we applied GBA+ with all data.

4 Findings

4.1 School Principals' Perspectives

All four school administrations knew very little about OHS prevention activities for the students nor did they know whether their teaching staff was properly trained in that regard. The OHS issues potentially encountered by male or female students were not considered by any of the school administrators. Agreement signed with internship companies carried certain OHS clauses. The OHS requests coming from teachers concerned solely the purchase of personal protective equipment (PPE) for some students who needed it, mostly male. All school principals feel concerned about OHS issues, but they feel far from the reality on the ground. They trust their teachers to address this topic, and they assume the teachers would contact them if required (severe cases).

4.2 Teachers' Perspectives

Among the OHS activities mentioned, nearly all teachers declared making sure students had the proper PPE. Many teachers reported feeling uncomfortable speaking about OHS with employers, although male teachers showed more confidence in addressing these topics. When OHS matters are discussed with employers, such discussion typically concerns methods and rules that the apprentice should learn (attitudes, behaviors). However, one of the male teachers stood out by reason of his vision of OHS prevention. He mentioned having many years of experience as a worker and supervisor in a plant. He talked about a large array of prevention approaches, such as risk identification, motor learning, environment modification, expressing the right to refuse unsafe work, and, in case of great danger, the removal of a student from a traineeship location. He showed confidence regarding OHS, granting him credibility with companies. When asked about their OHS needs, the supervisor teachers expressed wanting more computerized management tools to help monitor risks and students' activities. Such tools would be devised to help students efficiently recognize inherent risks in their traineeship environment or they could be videos able to raise awareness. Teachers willingly admitted being open to adapting their teaching approach to the specific needs, desires and interests of their students and in relation to the various employment markets they seek. However, they did not envision adapting their teaching approach according to the sex or gender of their students.

4.3 Students' Perspectives

The surveyed students were between ages 15 and 19; they chose a total of 17 different trades that were usually stereotypically gender-based: women mainly chose the food, animal and/or people service sectors, whereas men mostly favoured the food, retail, mechanics, recycling, transformation and/or fabrication sectors. Most students were aware of one or two hazards present in their workplace. Such risks concerned both men and women and included burns, cuts and hazards related to handling heavy loads. The number and variety of identified risks were relatively more significant for men. While women were the only ones to identify stress-related risks, men, were keen at detecting risks linked to machinery and equipment, collisions, explosions/electrocutions, or respiratory risks. In most cases, men stated having received more OHS training than women throughout their internship.

5 Discussion

The preliminary findings of this action-research study provide insight about the challenges encountered in the development of an OHS prevention model adapted to the reality of the WOTP. Future technological resources should help principals get better insight into the students' day-to-day reality, and become aware of the needs, means and resources required by teachers and workplace stakeholders in their OHS mandates. Such tools should also help teachers take a more proactive role among workplace stakeholders. Presently, they are rather reluctant to raise OHS issues with companies, because they are afraid of having their students refused for traineeship places. In addition, technological resources should offer assistance in identifying gendered OHS risks and prevention approaches by taking into account the sex and gender of the students. This would avoid the underestimation of certain invisible risks and ensure that women have adequate training.

The purpose of this research project was to enable WOTP stakeholders to become key players in OHS prevention strategies, notably by providing them with new technological resources to support their supervising role with WOTP students. Our preliminary results and analysis offer some working hypotheses that consider sex and gender as part of a comprehensive prevention model. The next step will be to record the perspective of workplace stakeholders on these same issues.

6 Conclusion

The originality of this research lies in the multiple cross-gender perspectives of apprentices, supervising teachers, and stakeholders in traineeship companies, as suggested by Laberge et al. [5]. This view includes the dual preoccupations of making sure that sex/gender-differentiated risks are considered in the prevention model, while fostering awareness of certain unconscious gender biases about how students should be supported in their job training.

Acknowledgement. This study was funded by the *Institut de recherche Robert-Sauvé en santé et sécurité du travail (IRSST)*, Québec, Canada / (#2018–0001). Special thanks to Jena Webb for reviewing and advices.

References

1. Lay, A.M., Saunders, R., Lifshen, M., Breslin, F.C., LaMontagne, A., Tompa, E., Smith, P.: Individual, occupational, and workplace correlates of occupational health and safety vulnerability in a sample of Canadian workers. Am. J. Ind. Med. **59**(2), 119–128 (2016)
2. Breslin, F.C., Lay, A.M., Jetha, A., Smith, P.: Examining occupational health and safety vulnerability among Canadian workers with disabilities. Disabil. Rehabil. **40**(18), 2138–2143 (2018)

3. Laberge, M., Vézina, N., Calvet, B., Ledoux, E.: Parcours de formation axée sur l'emploi au secondaire: Quelles sont les implications pour la santé et la sécurité du travail? Travail et santé **26**(2), S7-13 (2010)
4. Laberge, M., Tondoux, A., Camiré Tremblay, F. : Élaboration des critères de conception d'un outil d'aide à l'évaluation des risques pour la SST par les enseignants superviseurs de stage du Parcours de formation axée sur l'emploi. IRSST (R-968), Montréal (2017a)
5. Laberge, M., Tondoux, A., Camiré Tremblay, F., MacEachen, E.: Supervising the Occupational Health and Safety of apprentices enrolled in a semiskilled vocational training program: How gender identity impacts teachers' strategies and power relationships with placement sites? New Solutions J. **27**(3), 382–402 (2017b)

Work-Related Musculoskeletal Disorders Interventions in a Seasonal Work Context: A Scoping Review of Sex and Gender Considerations

Marie-Eve Major[1,2]([✉]) [ID], Hélène Clabault[1,2] [ID], and Audrey Goupil[1] [ID]

[1] Faculté des sciences de l'activité physique, Université de Sherbrooke,
2500 Boul. de l'Université, Sherbrooke, QC J1K 2R1, Canada
`marie-eve.major@usherbrooke.ca`

[2] CINBIOSE Research Centre, Université du Québec à Montréal, Succ. Centre-Ville,
C.P.8888, Montreal, QC H3C 3P8, Canada

Abstract. Many industry sectors that involve a large proportion of seasonal workers are characterized by working conditions that are demanding from a musculoskeletal perspective and by a gendered and sex-based division of labor. This paper aims to address the important issue of musculoskeletal disorders (MSDs) among seasonal workers by examining recommendations and interventions undertaken to prevent MSDs within a context of seasonal work and by assessing how sex and gender are considered. A scoping review was conducted in seven scientific databases and into ergonomics and occupational health and safety websites using descriptors and keywords (English and French). A total of 16 documents were included. Findings show six main categories of transformation targets, with the most reported category being the one on technical devices/physical environment. Only a few studies incorporated a sex/gender analysis and considered the influence of the seasonal context in the intervention-research study design. Indeed, the few studies that did investigate sex/gender mainly approached the idea in terms of inter-individual differences between the workers when designing an intervention to meet physiological needs. Only a few studies also looked at how sex/gender exposed workers differently in terms of working activity or other related dimensions in these types of atypical working contexts. Our study illustrates the need to address occupational health inequalities in a seasonal work context to better design interventions for this underserved and understudied population.

Keywords: Seasonal work · Musculoskeletal disorders · Sex and gender · Review · Interventions · Ergonomics

1 Introduction

Seasonal work exists within various industries characterized by demanding musculoskeletal conditions (e.g., agriculture, forestry, food processing, fishing). These industries are marked by a division of labor along sex and/or gender (sex/gender) lines, as well as by their seasonal nature, a situation that imposes substantial organizational, time-based, and physical constraints that are generally accepted because they last only a season. However, studies on seasonal workers have evidenced significant musculoskeletal disorders as well as a higher prevalence of MSDs among seasonal workers performing the same or similar jobs as permanent workers [1]. Furthermore, female seasonal workers appear to be especially at risk of developing chronic disorders [2]. All of this highlights the need for developing preventive measures that are both context appropriate and sensitive to sex/gender inequalities. The aim of this paper is to examine the published interventions and recommendations meant to prevent MSDs in seasonal work and to assess how both seasonality and sex/gender are considered.

2   Methodology

The project entailed performing a scoping review on the topic according to the framework proposed by Arksey, O'Malley [3] and the guidance for conducting systematic scoping reviews [4]. Peer-reviewed scientific articles, scientific reports, and theses published in English and French between 2000–2017 were searched in seven electronic databases: Medline & Medline In-Process, Academic Search Complete, EconLIT, PsycINFO, ABI/INFORM Collection, Scopus, and Google Scholar. A manual search into ergonomics and occupational health and safety websites was also conducted. Combinations of keywords related to two main themes (seasonal work and musculoskeletal disorders) as well as synonyms were considered. The search strategies were validated by a librarian specialized with this literature review approach and with bibliographic search in ergonomics and occupational health.

Independently, three reviewers selected and screened the documents. This paper focuses on studies involving a prevention-oriented intervention or integrating research recommendations on conducting MSD interventions in a seasonal work context. An intervention was considered as such if it led to, or intended to lead to transformations (technical, organizational, physical, social, individual, political, etc.), or to recommendations for improving worker health, working conditions, productivity at work [5], or equity between women and men at work [6]. Documents without a methodology or those that did not include qualitative and/or quantitative data were excluded. All documents were screened by the three reviewers independently, first on the title, then on the abstract and full text.

The selected documents were then read in-depth and analyzed from a qualitative perspective (descriptive, categorical, and content analyses). The information extracted by one team member was confirmed by a second member and co-analyzed. Based on the preliminary readings, two grids were constructed for systematically extracting and compiling data. The first grid served to document fairly linearly the data concerning the study aims, the methodology (approach, design, population, sex/gender considerations, methods of data collection and analysis, sex/gender-sensitive analysis), findings (considerations to sex/gender and seasonal work context), elements of discussion, study limits and avenues for future research. The second grid was to extract data on the industry sector, the time period and length of the study, the MSDs of the seasonal workers, the risks of MSDs, the working conditions, the actions or measures recommended to prevent MSDs, the transformation projects established or targeted within the interventions put into place, as well as the difficulties encountered with respect to the seasonal work context (methodological difficulties, timing, entities involved in the intervention, etc.) as well as sex/gender considerations, if these elements were mentioned. Thirdly, using a qualitative content analysis, we constructed a portrait of the interventions and recommendations identified in the literature that targeted MSD prevention in a seasonal working context.

3   Results and Discussion

After eligibility and screening, a total of 16 documents were included. This first result already illustrates that seasonal workers represent an understudied and underserved population. According to the literature examined, the issue of MSDs in seasonal workers has been identified in Canada [7–13], in the United States [14–19], in France [20], as well as in New Zealand [14, 21, 22]. The agricultural sector was represented in the greatest number of studies (n = 7, 44%), followed closely by the food processing sector (n = 6, 38%), and finally, by the sectors of forestry (n = 2, 13%) and fishing (n = 1, 6%).

3.1   Seasonal Workers and Musculoskeletal Disorders

According to the studies selected, our synthesis enabled us to demonstrate that seasonal workers report MSDs for various areas of the body (e.g., back, hands, wrists, shoulders, hips, feet, etc.) and this is irrespective of their working sector, as shown in Fig. 1a. Our analyses also attempted to underscore the differences in reporting with respect to areas of the body and sex/gender, in the related sectors. Notably, in agriculture, the pains most commonly reported by seasonal workers were localized in the hands, the wrists, the shoulders, the neck, the back, the knees, and the hips [12, 15, 18–21]. Certain data mentioned in the studies lead us to suppose that these results were most likely obtained from male workers (e.g., a mention of the over-representation of men in the sector, etc.) [10, 20]. In the seafood processing sector, considerable and chronic pains have been reported in a significant way for the upper extremities (in particular, the shoulders) by female seasonal workers. The few studies published about the forestry sector have highlighted pains in the back and lower extremities and seem to have been gathered from male participants [10, 11]. Finally, in the fishing sector, the regions of the body most often reported were the lower back, followed by a similar fashion by the hands, the wrists, and the shoulders in both men and women [17]. Beyond Lipscomb *et al.* (2004) who studied MSDs in a differentiated way in terms of sex/gender and the study by Major and Vézina (2011; 2015; 2016) who were specifically studying MSDs in female seasonal workers, most studies on seasonal workers did not specify MSDs in terms of the sex/gender of the individuals or simply did not mention the sex/gender of the participants (Fig. 1b). And yet, a great number of these industry sectors are recognized as being very demanding from a musculoskeletal perspective as well as involving a gendered division of labor [17, 23, 24] which can expose women and men differently to the risk of MSDs.

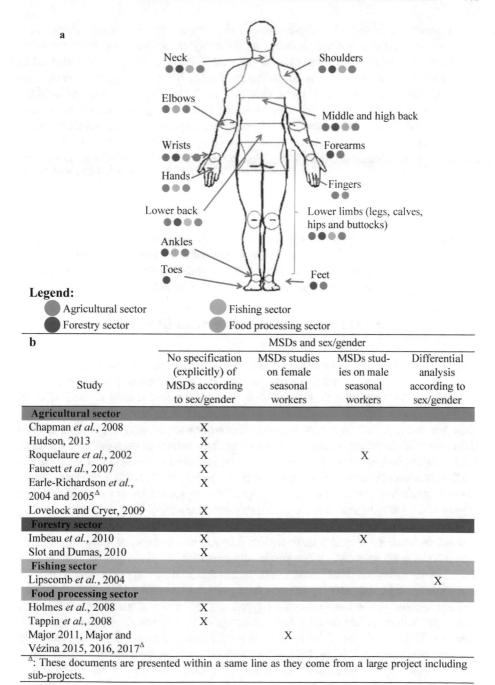

Legend:

| ● Agricultural sector | ● Fishing sector |
| ● Forestry sector | ● Food processing sector |

Study	No specification (explicitly) of MSDs according to sex/gender	MSDs studies on female seasonal workers	MSDs studies on male seasonal workers	Differential analysis according to sex/gender
Agricultural sector				
Chapman *et al.*, 2008	X			
Hudson, 2013	X			
Roquelaure *et al.*, 2002	X		X	
Faucett *et al.*, 2007	X			
Earle-Richardson *et al.*, 2004 and 2005$^\Delta$	X			
Lovelock and Cryer, 2009	X			
Forestry sector				
Imbeau *et al.*, 2010	X		X	
Slot and Dumas, 2010	X			
Fishing sector				
Lipscomb *et al.*, 2004				X
Food processing sector				
Holmes *et al.*, 2008	X			
Tappin *et al.*, 2008	X			
Major 2011, Major and Vézina 2015, 2016, 2017$^\Delta$		X		

(b) MSDs and sex/gender

$^\Delta$: These documents are presented within a same line as they come from a large project including sub-projects.

Fig. 1. a. Localization of MSDs reported among seasonal workers in the sectors of agriculture, forestry, fishing and food processing. Figure adapted from [2]. b. Integration of sex/gender regarding MSDs and sectors in the included studies.

Furthermore, in several of these sectors and particular in the seasonal context, the work is such that it is normal to accept its difficulty as an integral part of the work, and even more so because it lasts for only a season [9, 25]. The pain is perceived as inevitable [17] and endured through various means [8]. These perceptions appear to be shared by the employers [22, 25] who then rely on the resilience and capacities of the seasonal workers for the duration of the season. Moreover, a great number of seasonal industries involve a lot of competition between the companies, further enhanced by the seasonal nature of the work. The companies are competing for a single resource whose availability and lifetime are temporally limited and dependent on climate and weather conditions [26]. This context contributes to an intense focus on production which can then put the brakes on MSD prevention if strong links between production and health are not demonstrated [2]. In this sense, the data missing from the literature in terms of MSDs and a differentiated portrait according to sex/gender in a seasonal context raises significant concerns, among other things, about the integration and working conditions for women in the seasonal work sectors in which men are overrepresented. This kind of portrait also raises questions related to MSD prevention interventions developed in a seasonal work context and the integration of a sex/gender sensitive approach.

3.2   Interventions and Recommendations in a Seasonal Work Context for Preventing MSDs

This section presents the findings of the analysis of the recommendations and interventions implemented in a seasonal work context that looked to prevent MSDs and that considered sex/gender in the included studies. We first analyzed the studies to see if sex/gender considerations and seasonal context were brought up or taken into consideration (e.g., seasonal context and particularities for women and men mentioned somewhere in the article, strategies considering the seasonal context and sex/gender in the recommendations or the transformation projects, etc.) and whether it involved the implementation of one or more transformation projects or only resulted in recommendations (or both). Next, we conducted a more specific analysis looking at the transformation targets of the interventions or the recommendations identified.

Of the 16 studies retained for this review, 10 involved the implementation of an intervention with one or several transformation projects while the remaining six involved recommendations only. Only a few studies incorporated both a sex/gender analysis and the influence of the seasonal context in the intervention-research study design (n = 7). Many studies did not specify the sex/gender of participants or failed to report sex/gender findings. Across all the interventions analyzed, six categories of transformation targets were identified, including the most reported category of technical devices/physical environment. This was followed by behavioral modification. Among the most frequently reported categories, a few highlighted a consideration of sex/gender (n = 7), notably, when considering the inter-individual differences of the workers when designing an intervention to meet physiological needs (e.g., exercise training focused on physiological strength capabilities). However, these considerations were mainly linked to physical capacity and only a few studies also considered the different exposures of sex/gender with respect to the work activity or other gender dimensions in this kind of atypical working context (e.g., load and time-based organization of extraprofessional activities during the working season). Indeed, one of the challenges for researching solutions to prevent MSDs is the invisibility of constraints [27], particularly overlooked in the context of seasonal work in low-prestige industries (atypical hours, low salary) that are also mostly masculine.

Several studies have also highlighted the importance of considering the sex/gender of the researchers or intermediaries during social interactions with the workplace in a seasonal context (e.g. worker recruitment [12], demonstration of credibility [15], even more so in workplace environments with a machoistic culture as reported in the seasonal context [22]). In one example from an intervention framework, Hudson (2013) highlighted the difficulties related to the recruitment and participation of seasonal workers, who were mainly seasonal female agricultural workers working in rural regions with low literacy levels. He reports that "These factors may have generated a perceived power dynamic that limited both interest and completion of the intervention, given that the researchers that contacted these workers were male university researchers" [12, p.81].

The importance of considering sex/gender when designing the methods/tools of knowledge transfer was also mentioned [12]. Notably, one of the successful strategies of building a collaborative knowledge transfer network is the understanding of stakeholder interactions and the power-dependance relationships between stakeholders [28]. This was recognized as a challenge in a seasonal work context because of the skepticism surrounding MSDs among seasonal workers for whom pain is considered inevitable and inherent to the work [22]. Furthermore, a macho culture in which resilience to MSDs is valued and rewarded [22] also makes interactions difficult. These « cultural norms» and beliefs may influence the type of transformation projects recognized as acceptable by the workplace and thus contribute to the fragmented knowledge transfer networks apparent in various seasonal industries, including agriculture [12].

Finally, our results demonstrate that several studies incorporating a sex/gender analysis were also tailored to meet various culture-specific needs and worker literacy levels. Considerations of sex/gender for preventing MSDs in the seasonal work context seem to be situated in an intersectionality of various social relationships (social class, gender, age, race, migratory status, culture, etc.) necessitating the development of MSD prevention actions that are sensitive to gender and social inequalities.

4   Conclusion

This study reveals the scarcity of literature integrating a sex/gender analysis within the development and implantation of interventions aiming to prevent MSDs in the context of seasonal work. Understanding the influence of seasonality and the mechanisms of action sensitive to gender and social inequalities within this context is essential in order to truly address the problem of MSDs among seasonal workers and to promote equitable working conditions for all.

Acknowledgements. This work was partially funded by the Institut de recherche Robert-Sauvé en santé et en sécurité du travail (IRSST) (grant number 2015–0017). We would like to thank Jean-Jacques Rondeau, librarian at the Université du Québec à Montréal for his guidance throughout the process of developing the literature search strategies.

References

1. Schweder, P., Quinlan, M., Bohle, P., Lamm, F., Ang, A.H.B.: Injury rates and psychological wellbeing in temporary work: a study of seasonal workers in the New Zealand food processing industry. N. Z. J. Employ. Relat. **40**(2), 24–46 (2015)
2. Major, M.E., Wild, P., Clabault, H.: Travail saisonnier et santé au travail : bilan des connaissances et développement d'une méthode d'analyse pour le suivi longitudinal des troubles musculo-squelettiques (R-1102). IRSST, p. 139 (2020)
3. Arksey, H., O'Malley, L.: Scoping studies: towards a methodological framework. Int. J. Soc. Res. Method. **8**(1), 19–32 (2005)
4. Peters, M.D.J, Godfrey, C., McInerney, P., Munn, Z., Tricco, A.C., Khalil, H.: Chapter 11: scoping reviews. In: Aromataris, E., Munn, Z (eds.) JBI Manual for Evidence Synthesis (2020)
5. St-Vincent, M., Vézina, N., Bellemare, M., Denis, D., Ledoux, E., Imbeau, D.: L'intervention en ergonomie. Québec (2011)
6. Laberge, M., Blanchette-Luong, V., Blanchard, A., Sultan-Taïeb, H., Riel, J., Lederer, V., et al.: Impacts of considering sex and gender during intervention studies in occupational health: researchers' perspectives. Appl. Ergon. **82**, 102960 (2020)
7. Major, M.E., Vézina, N.: Pour une prévention durable des troubles musculosquelettiques chez les travailleuses saisonnières : prise en compte du travail réel. PISTES **18**(2), 25 (2016)
8. Major, M.E., Vézina, N.: Analysis of worker strategies: a comprehensive understanding for the prevention of work related musculoskeletal disorders. Int. J. Ind. Ergon. **48**, 149–57 (2015)
9. Major, M.E., Vézina, N.: The organization of working time: developing an understanding and action plan to promote workers' health in a seasonal work context. New Solut. **27**(3), 403–23 (2017)
10. Imbeau, D., Dubé, P-A., Dubeau, D., LeBel, L.: Les effets d'un entrainement physique présaison sur le travail et la sécurité des débroussailleurs. Étude de faisabilité d'une approche de mesure (Rapport n°R-664). IRSST p. 75 (2010)
11. Slot, T.R., Dumas, G.A.: Musculoskeletal symptoms in tree planters in Ontario. Can. Work **36**(1), 67–75 (2010)
12. Hudson, D.S.: Development and validation of a proactive ergonomics intervention targeting seasonal agricultural workers. Department of kinesiology and physical education. Lethbridge, Alberta, Canada: University of Lethbridge, p. 159 (2013)
13. Major, M.E.: Étude ergonomique du travail saisonnier et de ses impacts sur les stratégies et les troubles musculo-squelettiques de travailleuses d'usines de transformation du crabe. Sciences biologiques. Montréal, Québec, Canada: Université du Québec à Montréal; 2011. p. 290.
14. Chapman, L.J., Newenhouse, A.C., Pereira, K.M., Karsh, B.T., Meyer, R.M., Brunette, C.M., et al.: Evaluation of a four year intervention to reduce musculoskeletal hazards among berry growers. J. Safety Res. **39**(2), 215–24 (2008)
15. Faucett, J., Meyers, J., Miles, J., Janowitz, I., Fathallah, F.: Rest break interventions in stoop labor tasks. Appl. Ergon. **38**(2), 219–26 (2007)
16. Holmes, W., Lam, P.Y., Elkind, P., Pitts, K.: The effect of body mechanics education on the work performance of fruit warehouse workers. Work **31**(4), 461–71 (2008)
17. Lipscomb, H.J., Loomis, D., McDonald, M.A., Kucera, K., Marshall, S., Li, L.: Musculoskeletal symptoms among commercial fishers in North Carolina. Appl. Ergon. **35**(5), 417–26 (2004)
18. Earle-Richardson, G., Fulmer, S., Jenkins, P., Mason, C., Bresee, C., May, J.: Ergonomic analysis of New York apple harvest work using a posture-activities-tools-handling (PATH) work sampling approach. J. Agric. Saf. Health **10**(3), 163–76 (2004)

19. Earle-Richardson, G., Jenkins, P., Fulmer, S., Mason, C., Burdick, P., May, J.: An ergonomic intervention to reduce back strain among apple harvest workers in New York state. Appl. Ergon. **36**(3), 327–34 (2005)
20. Roquelaure, Y., Dano, C., Dusolier, G., Fanello, S., Penneau-Fontbonne, D.: Biomechanical strains on the hand-wrist system during grapevine pruning. Int. Arch. Occup. Environ. Health **75**(8), 591–5 (2002)
21. Lovelock, K., Cryer, C.: Effective occupational health interventions in agriculture - summary report no.5. Injury Prevention Research Unit, University of Otago, Dunedin, New Zealand, p. 31 (2009)
22. Tappin, D.C., Bentley, T.A., Vitalis, A.: The role of contextual factors for musculoskeletal disorders in the New Zealand meat processing industry. Ergonomics **51**(10), 1576–93 (2008)
23. Habib, R.R., Hojeij, S., Elzein, K.: Gender in occupational health research of farmworkers: a systematic review. Am. J. Ind. Med. **57**(12), 1344–67 (2014)
24. Grzywacz, J.G., Lipscomb, H.J., Casanova, V., Neis, B., Fraser, C., Monaghan, P., et al.: Organization of work in the agricultural, forestry, and fishing sector in the US southeast: implications for immigrant workers' occupational safety and health. Am. J. Ind. Med. **56**(8), 925–39 (2013)
25. Fontaine, D., Gruaz, D., Guye, O., Medina, P., Dreneau, M.: Volet 1 : étude qualitative auprès des saisonniers, des employeurs et des professionnels. Étude régionale sur les conditions de travail, les conditions de vie et la santé des travailleurs saisonnier: Observatoire régional de la santé Rhône-Alpes, p. 1–131 (2008)
26. Payette, M.: Chantier sur la saisonnalité - Document de consultation - Synthèse des travaux de recherche de la phase 1 et identification des enjeux, pp. 1–25 (2010)
27. Messing, K., Boutin, S.: Les conditions difficiles dans les emplois des femmes et les instances gouvernementales en santé et en sécurité du travail. Relat. industrielles/Industrial Relat. **52**(2), 333–63 (1997)
28. Giannakis, M.: Facilitating learning and knowledge transfer through supplier development. Supply Chain Manage. Int. J. **13**(1), 62–72 (2008)

The "Woke" Ergonomist: How Can We, How Should We Improve Gender Equality as Well as Health?

Karen Messing[✉] [iD] and Nicole Vézina [iD]

CINBIOSE Research Centre, Université du Québec à Montréal, Montreal, QC H3C 3P8, Canada
messing.karen@uqam.ca

Abstract. Many workplaces segregate jobs, tasks, and responsibilities by gender, with negative effects on workers' health. Ergonomists can play a visible or a more subtle role in transforming these situations. Our experiences lead us to ask how to approach gender issues in interventions, how to deal with resistance from employers and employees, and how ergonomists' interest in social justice can inform our practice.

Keywords: Gender · Ergonomics practice · Intervention · Ethics · Workplace segregation

1 Problem Statement

Workplace segregation can impose different risks on women and men and threaten equality as well as health. But employers, unions, and workers may not be comfortable with open discussion of gender issues. Ergonomists may choose to ignore these issues, confront them openly, or quietly take them into account. This paper discusses practical and ethical issues arising during interventions.

2 Context

2.1 Authors' Context

The authors, who are based at universities and not financially dependent on contracts, have over thirty years' experience in ergonomic intervention, in various contexts. Both were trained in activity analysis in France and employ this approach in our interventions [1].We both have participated in studies involving ergonomics and gender since the 1980s [2]. Both have recently participated in analysis of the inclusion of sex and gender in twelve intervention-research projects, among them several of our own projects [3].

KM was co-director of a 17-year research partnership on gender and occupational health, involving university researchers, primarily from ergonomics and legal sciences, and the women's committees and health and safety committees of Québec's three major trade unions. The partnership was supported by public grants for scientific research and facilitated by the university outreach service [4: preface, ch. 5]. KM has also piloted some ergonomic interventions at the request of women's community organizations, again with external scientific funding [5: ch. 8). She has occasionally supervised student internships in or otherwise participated in projects developed with private-sector enterprises.

NV built and directed the ergonomics intervention programs at the Université du Québec à Montréal. She has supervised students' ergonomic interventions in a wide variety of workplaces, for over 27 years. These internships were usually carried out in response to requests from those responsible for health and safety in private-sector companies. NV also developed an independent research program on prevention of work-related musculoskeletal disorders that has led her to collaborate with employers, unions, public health authorities, and other community participants.

2.2 General Context

In most countries, women and men work in quite different industries and professions, and they have different task assignments and risk exposures even within the same jobs [5: ch. 4; 6]. Occupational segregation can contribute to intensifying some exposures and it can render them less visible. For example, gender can serve as an excuse for exposing one group or the other to health risks, as when men's gender justifies exposing them to a risk of accidents or requiring them to deploy sudden, excessive force, or when women's gender justifies their exposure to highly repetitive tasks requiring care, tensed muscles, and precise movements. In general, women workers enjoy less operational leeway to adjust their tasks to their own capacity and to changing conditions [7–9].

Occupational health researchers have concentrated disproportionately on men's jobs, over all disciplines [10–12], and specifically in ergonomics [13]. One consequence of this neglect is that judicial recognition of women's occupational health problems has been slow. This neglect has been documented in Canada [14, 15], more recently in France [16] and in Sweden, where women are four times as likely as men to be denied compensation for musculoskeletal disorders [17]. In Québec, women are a clear majority of workers in those industrial sectors (including health care, education, and retail sales) that are currently excluded from most prevention measures in the occupational health and safety law, although 86% of women compensated for musculoskeletal disorders work in those sectors [18: Fig. 2]. Researchers have also noticed that women are less often included in testing safety and protective equipment [19–21]. At the Université du Québec à Montréal, the GESTE[1] research group was intended in part to assess the success of attempts to remedy women's omission from occupational health and safety interventions. The present communication reports on the approaches taken by two GESTE researchers (KM and NV), with their differences, similarities, advantages, disadvantages, and consequences.

3 Methods

Twelve intervention-research projects were analyzed by the GESTE group, almost all of which involved ergonomics to some degree. Researchers and research partners were

---

[1] Abbreviation of the French words for Gender, Equity, Health, Work, and Environment.

interviewed, and a thematic content analysis of the interview transcripts was carried out, using NVivo 10 and focusing on s/g integration in the interventions. The interviews with researchers have been fully analyzed and those with partners are in progress. The analysis is described in detail by Laberge et al. [3] and in other communications at this symposium. The present communication primarily concerns the four projects with which we were directly involved, as well as some of our more recent interventions.

4   Results

Sometimes our interventions succeeded in improving the work and health of women. An early study by NV involved workers in nine poultry processing plants who responded to a detailed questionnaire about their health problems and working environment. There was a profound division of the assembly line according to sex, and a number of health problems were identified at the very repetitive positions assigned to women. The research team found musculoskeletal disorders, viral warts, and severe dysmenorrhea associated with exposure to cold temperatures [22–24]. This study was critical to getting viral warts recognized as an occupational disease of poultry processors [25, 26].

Later, in other poultry-processing plant where positions were assigned by sex, NV and her colleagues found several problems among the women workers assigned to deboning and trimming turkey parts at high speed. The intervention resulted in the addition of a woman to help debone and automation of carcass cutting. The employer was also induced to recognize the difficulties involved in trimming, a position assigned to women and to injured workers because it had been classed erroneously as "light work."

Some of the problems on the poultry-processing lines arose from the fact that workers' knives were too dull, forcing them to exert extra effort and making fine movements more difficult. Six joint management-labour health and safety committees asked the research team to tackle the issue of dull knives. The ensuing study identified efficient knife-sharpening practices and inspired a training film on knife sharpening that has been used internationally [27, 28]. This research effort was helpful both to the workers' union and to the employer, because it improved production as well as the health of the workers. An effort was made to recruit women as trainers, to optimize the chance that women's needs would be met by the training program. Thus, women's occupational health was improved without opposition from the employer or from colleagues.

NV and her colleagues also did an ergonomic intervention on a crab-processing line where men were assigned to breaking open the crab shells and women to packaging the crab meat [29]. The women's ability to do their physically-taxing job safely was negatively affected by the work of the men who, when rushed, downloaded some of their work on the women. The ergonomists worked toward getting recognition of the difficulty of the women's work, without insisting on gender as such. Researchers met separately with each group and then together with representatives of each group to resolve the problem.

An employer-initiated student internship supervised by NV concerned a dishwashing operation where two men supplied dirty dishes to a dishwasher, but one woman took them out and distributed them. The woman was overwhelmed by the required work speed. The ergonomist succeeded in getting a second woman hired, halving the workload.

More generally, employers often ask ergonomists to intervene in jobs with heavy lifting, occupied mainly by men, but when the ergonomists observe the work, they find very dangerous conditions at the neighboring positions, held by women. The ergonomists' work then involves making these risks visible to colleagues and management [30].

Two other union-initiated requests concerned jobs occupied by men and very few women. Equipment, tools and training were ill-adapted to the women's characteristics and the women's accident rate was much higher than the men's. The ergonomists reported on the women's difficulties to the employers and the unions, but nothing was done and the women gradually left. However, the unions used these experiences to pressure the government to favour adaptation of jobs for women, resulting in improvements in other male-dominated jobs. The union also produced training material for health and safety committees [5:ch. 1].

Another union-initiated request arose when male health care workers accused their female colleagues of not doing their share of heavy lifting. The employers allowed an intervention to protect workers from musculoskeletal disorders but prohibited discussion of gender. The ergonomists observed that women were actually doing 50% more of the heavy lifting, possibly impelled by guilt and a desire to do their part. Men were sometimes asked to do dramatically dangerous tasks because of their sex, but these requests were very rare and could be refused. The local union did not accept the results, and no changes were made. However, the study produced changes in the organization of teamwork that improved work organization in a different department [5:ch. 2].

Sometimes, the ergonomists were not sure that the gender-sensitive union-university intervention had been helpful. For example, several interventions succeeded in revealing hitherto unrecognized requirements of women's work in "light" cleaning [4:ch. 2;12]. These interventions resulted in higher pay for the women, and eventually to desegregation of cleaning. However, desegregation without adaptation of job parameters to women's physiology eventually led to many women leaving the cleaning profession [5:ch. 3]. It has also happened that interventions initiated with gender-based concerns uncovered issues of discrimination on other grounds, such as immigrant status or skin colour. The research team was able to make recommendations for change in some cases, but public policy changes are slow in coming.

5   Discusssion

We have developed two different ways of integrating gender into ergonomic studies. One approach is for the ergonomist to have gender in mind while performing an otherwise standard intervention [1] and making sure that inputs from all research participants are treated with interest and respect. Another is to raise gender issues explicitly. Is an ergonomist's responsibility to raise gender issues explicitly if they bear on workplace health and productivity? How can those issues be addressed in the most effective ways? Should we have publicized the women's higher accident rate, with the risk of stigmatizing them? What about other groups suffering discrimination, such as linguistic, immigrant, ethnic or racialized minorities? What is the ergonomist's responsibility? What if anything should be done in the case where no participants, neither the women, the men, the union nor the employer are asking for equity? How can ergonomists provide convincing science-based arguments that can make employers see that equity is good for productivity and work climate as well as for employees' mental and physical health?

We conclude that our approaches must vary according to the different contexts in which they are applied. Collaboration with unions has enabled us to help make the sex and gender issues more visible. Advances for women (and male co-workers) have come from explicitly taking sex and gender into account as well as from being conscious of gender issues while conducting interventions where sex and gender are not explicit concerns. Being aware of sex and gender issues is a necessary tool for ergonomists, due to the deep gender-segregation of industries, professions, task assignments, work activity and occupational health risks,

We have not yet developed interventions that have successfully dealt with other sources of inequality, such as immigrant or minority status. Ergonomists need to develop context-appropriate methods and tools to collaborate with workplace partners in advancing equality.

Acknowledgements. This study was funded by the Canadian Institutes of Health Research /Institute of Gender and Health (# IGK 153464 / GESTE Team). Nicole Vézina and Karen Messing are members of the SAGE (Santé, Travail, Genre) research team, supported by the Fonds de recherche du Québec – Société et culture.

References

1. St-Vincent, M., Vézina N., Bellemare, M.: Ergonomic Intervention. Bookbaby, e-book (2014)
2. European Trade Union Institute (ETUI): Integrating Gender in Ergonomic Analysis. Trades Union Technical Bureau, European Economic Community, Brussels (1999)
3. Laberge, M,. Blanchette-Luong, V., Blanchard, A., Sultan-Taïeb, H., et al.: Impacts of considering sex and gender during intervention studies in occupational health, researchers' perspectives. Appl. Ergon. **82**, 102960 (2020)
4. Messing, K.: Pain and Prejudice: What Science Can Learn about Work from the People Who Do It. BTL Books, Toronto (2014)
5. Messing, K.: Bent Out of Shape: Shame, Solidarity and Women's Bodies at Work. BTL Books, Toronto (2021)
6. Messing, K., Stock, S., Côté, J., Tissot, F.: Is sitting worse than static standing? How a gender analysis can move us toward understanding determinants and effects of occupational standing and walking. J. Occup. Environ. Hyg. **12**(3), D11-7 (2015)
7. Cailloux Teiger, C.: « Les femmes aussi ont un cerveau ! » Le travail des femmes en ergonomi : réflexions sur quelques paradoxes. Travailler **15**(1), 71–130 (2006)
8. Coutarel, F., Caroly, S., Vézina, N., Daniellou, F.: Marge de manœuvre situationnelle et pouvoir d'agir, des concepts à l'intervention ergonomique. Le Travail Humain **78**(1), 9–29 (2015)
9. Norval, M., Zare, M., Brunet, R., et al.: Operational leeway in work situations: do ergonomic risk assessment tools consider operational leeway? Int. J. Occup. Saf. Ergon. **25**(3), 429–442 (2018)
10. Stellman, J.M.: Women's Work, Women's Health: Myths and Realities, Pantheon, New York (1978)
11. Hunt, V.: Work and the Health of Women. CRC Press, Boca Raton, Florida (1979)

12. Messing, K.: One-Eyed Science: Occupational Health and Working Women. Temple University Press, Philadelphia (1998)
13. Habib, R., Messing, K.: Gender, women's work and ergonomics. Ergonomics **55**(2), 129–132 (2012)
14. Lippel, K.: Workers' compensation and stress. Gender and access to compensation. Int. J. Law Psychiatry. **22**(1), 79–89 (1999)
15. Lippel, K.: Compensation for musculoskeletal disorders in Quebec: systemic discrimination against women workers? Int. J. Health Serv. **33**(2), 253–281 (2003)
16. Serre, D.: La reconnaissance des maladies professionnelles dans les tribunaux. Les effets inégalitaires de la codification juridique. In: Cavalin, C., Henry, E., Jouzel, J-N., Pélisse, J. (eds.) : Cent Ans De Sous-Reconnaissance Des Maladies Professionnelles, Presses des Mines, Paris, pp. 255–274 (2020)
17. Leijon, O., Balliu, N., Lundin, A., et al.: Effects of psychosocial work factors and psychological distress on self-assessed work ability: a 7-year follow-up in a general working population. Am. J. Ind. Med. **60**(1), 121–130 (2017)
18. Stock, S., Nicolakakis, N., et al.: Inégalités De Santé Au Travail Entre Les Salariés Visés Et Ceux Non Visés Par Les Mesures Préventives Prévues Par La Loi Sur La Santé Et La Sécurité Du Travail. Institut national de sante publique du Quebec. Québec (2020)
19. McMahon, E., Wadam, K., Dufresne, A.: Implementing fit testing for N95 filtering facepiece respirators: practical information from a large cohort of hospital workers. Am. J. Infect. Control. **36**(4), 298–300 (2008)
20. Linder, A., Svedberg, W.: Review of average sized male and female occupant models in European regulatory safety assessment tests and European laws, gaps and bridging suggestions. Accid. Anal. Prev. **127**, 156–162 (2019)
21. Janson D., Newman S.T., Dhokia V.: Safety footwear: a survey of end-users. Appl. Ergon. **92**, 103333 (2021)
22. Mergler, D., Vézina, N., Beauvais, A., Everell, J.: The Effects of Working Conditions on the Health of Slaughterhouse Workers. Canadian Center for Occupational Health and Safety, Hamilton, Ontario (1983)
23. Mergler, D., Vezina, N.: Dysmenorrhea and cold exposure. J. Reprod. Med. **30**(2), 106–11 (1985)
24. Mergler, D., Brabant, C., Vézina, N., Messing, K.: The weaker sex? men in women's working conditions report similar health symptoms. J. Occup. Med. **29**(5), 417–21 (1987)
25. Mergler, D., Vezina, N., Beauvais, A.: Warts among workers in poultry slaughterhouses. Scand. J. Work Environ. Health. **8**(Suppl 1), 180–4 (1982)
26. Vézina, N., Mergler, D: Les verrues: une maladie professionnelle. Archives des Maladies Professionnelles **44**(8), 551–558 (1983)
27. Vézina, N., Prévost, J., Lajoie, A., Beauchamp, Y.: Élaboration d'une formation à l'affilage des couteaux: Le travail d'un collectif, travailleurs et ergonomes, [Preparation of training in knife sharpening: A collective effort by workers and ergonomists] Perspectives Interdisciplinaires sur le Travail et la Santé (PISTES) 1, 1 (1999).
28. Antle, D.M., MacKinnon, S.N., Molgaard, J., Vézina, N., et al.: Understanding knowledge transfer in an ergonomics intervention at a poultry processing plant. Work **38**(4), 347–57 (2011)
29. Major, M.E., Vézina, N.: The organization of working time: developing an understanding and action plan to promote workers' health in a seasonal work context. New Solut. **27**(3), 403–423 (2017)
30. Vézina, N., Chatigny, C., Calvet, B.: L'intervention ergonomique : que fait-on des caractéristiques personnelles comme le sexe et le genre ? Perspectives Interdisciplinaires sur le Travail et la Santé (PISTES) **18**(2), (2016)

31. Messing, K., Chatigny, C., Courville, J.: "Light" and "heavy" work in the housekeeping service of a hospital. Appl. Ergon. **29**(6), 451–9 (1998)
32. Pottern, L.M., Zahm, S.H., Sieber, S.S., et al.: Occupational cancer among women: a conference overview. J. Occup. Med. **36**(8), 809–13 (1994)

Facilitators and Obstacles to Sex/Gender-Conscious Intervention-Research on Occupational Health: Researchers and Partners Perspectives

Véronique Poupart-Monette[1,2]([✉]) [ID], Marie Laberge[1,2,3] [ID],
Marie-Laurence Genier[4] [ID], Jessica Riel[3,4] [ID], Karen Messing[3] [ID],
and Valérie Lederer[3,4] [ID]

[1] University of Montreal, Montreal, QC H3C 3J7, Canada
`veronique.poupart-monette@umontreal.ca`
[2] Sainte-Justine UHC Research Center, Montreal, QC H1T 1C9, Canada
[3] CINBIOSE Research Group, UQAM, Montreal, QC H3C 3P8, Canada
[4] Université du Québec en Outaouais, Gatineau, QC, Canada

Abstract. When trying to take sex and gender into account in participatory research, the challenges of knowledge users and researchers can be quite different. This communication aims to present perspectives of both stakeholders and researchers involved in occupational health intervention research (IR) studies about the facilitators and obstacles to considering sex and gender throughout the whole study, from the early stages to the final dissemination. Interviews were conducted with co-researchers and partners involved in seven occupational health IR projects integrating sex or gender considerations to some degree. The interviews were transcribed, and a qualitative content analysis was made. The obstacles and facilitators to sex/gender conscious interventions perceived by the investigators and the partners were then compared to bring out similarities and differences. Among the commonalities, not addressing sex and gender issues head on, a personal interest for s/g questions, the complexity related to studying s/g, the sociopolitical context were themes discussed by both researchers and partners. Partners also found that a positive relationship with the research team and an initial interest of the community or workplace for the s/g aspect of the project made the process easier. However, the facilitators or obstacles may differ from one context to another and it is mandatory for researchers to consider the characteristics of the community in which the intervention takes place, and the sensitivity to s/g matters in order to minimize resistance.

Keywords: Intervention-research study · Sex/Gender-based analyses · Integrated knowledge transfer · Stakeholders' views

1 Problem Statement

According to the Canadian Institutes of Health Research (CIHR), Knowledge Translation (KT) is about raising knowledge users' awareness about research findings as well as

N. L. Black et al. (Eds.): IEA 2021, LNNS 220, pp. 477–481, 2021.
https://doi.org/10.1007/978-3-030-74605-6_60

facilitating their use. The term integrated knowledge translation (iKT) describes the participation of knowledge users (KU) throughout the whole study process. The principle behind this idea is to bridge the gap between research results and their application in practice by taking their needs into account. In the field of Occupational Health and Safety (OHS), scientists often use this kind of study partnership because it may improve knowledge mobilization in terms of workplace and system changes [1] which is often the pursued objective. In the present communication, this kind of design study frequently used by ergonomists is called "Intervention-research study" (IR). Another important concern of research in OHS is to consider sex and gender. Sex refers to biological attributes associated mainly to physical and physiological characteristics. Gender, on the other hand, refers to the socially constructed characteristics of girls, women, boys, and men [2]. However, these two concepts are strongly linked.

The labor market is still segregated and the OHS risks are different for men and women [3]. Gender-sensitive approaches in research and interventions address differences between men and women in terms of exposure and experience. This analytic lens allows fairer and more specific prevention interventions in workplaces [4]. However, integrating sex and gender is not simple and gender-sensitive research teams may face obstacles. In the context of IR, the collaboration with KU has its own challenges. For instance, this may create resistance from the stakeholders [5], putting them in front of their stereotypes or power balance in their organization. The concern for sex/gender-sensitive research is not always shared by the partners or the stakeholders in the workplace or the target community. In 2017, in response to an initiative from the Institute for Gender and Health (IGH) of the Canadian Institutes for Health Research (CIHR), the GESTE team was created to model an approach of integrating sex and gender into iKT initiatives in the field of occupational health. Close collaboration with KU being an important part of our research process, the GESTE team wanted to know the stakeholders' point of view about this issue and to compare it with that of the researchers.

2 Objective

This study aims to identify obstacles and facilitators to the integration of sex and gender in occupational health research-intervention that combine a collaborative design with a sustained concern for integrating sex and gender. The objective of this paper is to present the distinct and common points of view of researchers and partners involved in such research.

3 Methodology

This research is a multiple case study based on the retrospective analysis of seven IR projects in the occupational health field that took sex or gender (s/g) into account in some way. All IR projects took place between 1990 and 2016. A call for IR projects having integrated the s/g was made to all the researchers of the GESTE team. Twelve IR studies were selected among the 27 projects initially proposed by all GESTE team (25 co-investigators). For general methodology and selection criteria of the studies, see Laberge et al. (2020) [3]. Our research team first read the reports and articles provided by the researchers to familiarize with the IR projects. Then, the researchers of the GESTE team involved in these IRs were interviewed. At the end of each interview, the researchers identified the key partners involved and provided contact information for a few partners still active in their organization who might be interested in discussing their experience with the projects in question. These partners, involved in seven of the twelve projects, were then contacted to participate in an interview. They were representatives of organizations such as unions, government organizations and community organizations. The interviews with the partners focused on four main themes: the origins of the project and the partners' involvement, the partnership relationship, the integration of s/g and the impacts of the projects. In addition to these themes, the methods used, the facilitators and obstacles to s/g integration as well as the impacts of taking s/g into account were discussed with the researchers. A thematic analysis was carried out from the transcriptions using NVivo. The interviews with the researchers were first examined according to three main themes: the context in which the IRs were conducted, the methods used, and the impacts of the projects. The data used for this study were drawn from the « context» and « methods» themes. A second analysis within these main themes then made it possible to determine the favorable (facilitators), the unfavorable (obstacles) and the neural elements, and to classify them by sub-themes that emerged while reading the verbatim. The analysis of the partners' interviews, on the other hand, directly focused on the elements identified as favorable, unfavorable, and neutral to then be grouped into sub-themes. These sub-themes were finally compared with those that emerged from the analysis of the researchers' corpus. The themes extracted for this paper are the facilitators and obstacles to the integration of s/g in these IR that were common to both groups, and those that came out of the interviews with the partners.

4   Results

Of the seven IRs studied, five were initially requested by a union, one was initially requested by an employer and one was initiated by the researcher herself. All the IRs conducted an activity analysis, except one that analyzed documents. Finally, four IRs were conducted in a workplace and three, in a community of interest.

Among the commonalities in the researchers' and the partners' points of view, not addressing s/g head on was mentioned as a way of minimizing resistance. For example, putting forward the project's contribution in terms of OHS without emphasizing the s/g component was identified as a way to promote a better reception from the community in some cases.

Participants raised the point that s/g are complex issues to study. They are easy to forget about during an IR, both for researchers who are absorbed by the work demands and for partners who are not used to having them in mind. Sophisticated data collection and analyses is required to document s/g or they may otherwise go unnoticed. Furthermore, researchers and partners have seen how sensitive these questions can be to address: they can be taboo, their relevance is not well known, and they raise identity issues for the actors in play. On that matter, one of the partner participants said: *"We're not comfortable to touch that because it's your deepest identity that you're questioning. And that's hard."*

In many cases, prior awareness of gender related questions helped raise interest and partner commitment Researchers also valued their partners' awareness and experience with the s/g issues, but also thought about their own personal feminist values and sensitivity as researchers as facilitators.

The partners discourse differs from the researchers on certain points. They place more importance on the initial interest of the union or community in the project. For example, a project that stemmed from the union's concern for discrimination against women in a community where justice is a fundamental value. It has proven to mobilize the stakeholders in a significant way. Moreover, the positive relationship with the researcher was mentioned by all the partners as an important way to ease sensitive discussions on s/g. A partner participant said about a researcher's attitude during the project meetings: "*She came in with two tangerines and shared them with everybody who was there and there was only one piece left for her. That set the tone, I think.*" Some projects helped women gain recognition for the value of their work, and that contributed to foster support, especially in a female-only environment. In other cases, the perceived neutrality of the research process and the researchers' objective attitude towards s/g issues was a better strategy to create favorable grounds. One of the researchers seemed to present the community's s/g issues in a very unbiased matter according to her partners: "*She brought it in a neutral way, it was not positive nor negative, it was really a matter of making observations first, I think*".

Since all interventions are contextualized, socio-political factors, such as current societal trends in feminism, and organizational factors, like budget cuts, were also mentioned by both researchers and partners. Depending on their nature, these factors can be facilitators or obstacles and do need to be considered to modulate the intervention.

Translating research findings into the necessary changes remains a challenge. For the partners, while the research results often confirmed, for example, a perceived discrimination against women, it was sometimes difficult to implement means to reduce gender inequalities. A partner reports: "*When we presented these studies, it confirmed their impressions. [...] This ability to understand the work and to see that there were differences between men and women, we did not feel a lot of resistance. It's more in the way to change that; how do we change that now?*". Certain researchers also find tricky to make recommendations that will not reinforce gender stereotypes and to see how recommendations will be interpreted by the decision-makers. In addition, for many, the fact that the interventions are punctual makes it difficult to follow-up on the outcomes of the projects to ensure sustainable transformations.

5 Discussion

The results show how complex the consideration of sex and gender can be, particularly in the context of research-intervention, as researchers may encounter resistance from the actors involved. A strategic social construction is essential not only to facilitate the reception of the project by the community, but also for the collection of data related to s/g. The researcher's openness to understand the needs of the community and to consider the context in which his/her intervention takes place is a key element in establishing a partnership relationship that promotes recognition of the importance of a gender-sensitive approach. In this research, the fact that the partners potentially interested in discussing with us were identified by the researchers might have resulted in the partner participants having a rather positive view of the outcome of the projects and of the importance of s/g analysis. However, their perspective is still very important to understand the reality experienced on their part of the partnership, which is often influenced by socio-political issues that can be overlooked by researchers. We have also seen that, depending on the environment in which the intervention takes place, the perception of the s/g aspect of the project can be different and that, for example, the promotion of women's work is a facilitator in one context and the neutrality of an objective approach is better in another. Other analysis exploring the link between the contextual elements surrounding IR projects and the researchers' thoughts on the methods used in the projects is currently being made by the GESTE team. The researchers' willingness to establish a positive relationship with stakeholders and to understand the environment is certainly essential to try to transform it.

References

1. Graham, I.D., Kothari, A., McCutcheon, C., et al.: Moving knowledge into action for more effective practice, programs and policy: protocol for a research program on integrated knowledge translation. Implement Sci. **13**(22), 1–15 (2018)
2. World Health Organization. https://www.who.int/health-topics/gender#tab=tab_1. Accessed 07 Feb 2021
3. Laberge, M., Blanchette-Luong, V., Blanchard, A., Messing, K., et al.: Impacts of considering sex and gender during intervention studies in occupational health: researchers' perspectives. Appl. Ergon. **82**, 102960 (2020)
4. Messing, K., Punnett, L., Bond, M., Alexanderson, K., Pyle, J., Zahm, S., Wegman, D., Stock, S.R., de Grosbois, S.: Be the fairest of them all: challenges and recommendations for the treatment of gender in occupational health research. Am. J. Ind. Med. **43**(6), 618–29 (2003)
5. Riel, J., Major, M.-E.: The challenges of mobilizing workers on gender issues: lessons from two studies on the occupational health of teachers in québec. New Solutions J. Environ. Occup. Health Policy **27**(3), 284–303 (2017)

Laying the Foundations to Build Ergonomic Indicators for Feminized Work in the Informal Sector

Sandra Liliana Ruiz-Amórtegui[1,3](✉) [iD], Sandra Liliana Joaqui-Galindo[1,3] [iD], and Martha Helena Saravia-Pinilla[2,3] [iD]

[1] Fundación Universitaria Escuela Colombiana de Rehabilitación, Bogotá, Colombia
[2] Pontificia Universidad Javeriana, Bogotá, Colombia
saravia@javeriana.edu.co
[3] Sociedad Colombiana de Ergonomía- SCE, Bogotá, Colombia

Abstract. Colombia has a population of 25 million women; almost half of these are economically active, and the majority are linked to the informal sector facing highly feminized jobs. This situation affects the development of their 'work activity' and dramatically decreases their quality of life. From the 'analysis of the work situation', the characteristics of the human being, the work environment and the social context in which the work activity takes place, this study aims to lay the foundations for building 'ergonomic indicators' that favour understanding and the transformation of feminized work systems. Using a mixed approach methodology, we seek to access a population of 80 women between 18 and 60 years old who are linked to the informal sector. The application of questionnaires with specific variables such as general context, family environment, socio-occupational aspects, work environment, individual conditions, among others, leads researchers to obtain the expected results. At the time of writing this paper, the project has partial results of the qualitative component. From there, the categories that will lead the construction of the indicators are defined, such as: occupations of opportunity, changes in operating modes, new work activities, space and proximity, new forms of employability, perceptions of the new way of working and more. As the project is currently under development and given the government policies associated with the pandemic, the development of the quantitative section has been delayed. It is expected that the results and general conclusions will be shared within the framework of the congress.

Keywords: Feminized work · Ergonomics · Gender · Systemic focus · Differential focus · Ergonomic indicators

1 Introduction

In Colombia there are 25 million women of which 10'567,000 are economically active, been approximately 8'945,000 employed and half of them are engaged on informal work [1]. Informal work is characterized by low scale activities, low productivity, high workforce and associated to "feminized works" performed in domestic habits or liveli-hoods/trades occupied principally by women [2], what produce a high schedule charge, work charge [3], mental charge, musculoskeletal disorders, less self-care and life qual-ity decrease [4]. On the other hand, ergonomics-using the systemic focus- analysed the different interactions produced in the micro and macro system scales to optimize it from the wellness indicators (health, security, satisfaction) as well of the technics indicators (quality, yields, innovation).

At the present global crisis caused by the pandemic, multiple interactions appeared and affect women inside and outside from work. Ergonomics, supported by the differen-tial approach-model-in which population groups differ from its own conditions-, seeks to understand works system and its effect on other human activity domains.

From the working situation analysis, the characteristics of the human being, the work means and the social context [5], in which the work activity is developed, it is proposed to structure a series of ergonomics indicators to favours the comprehension and transformation of the feminized work systems [6]. In this position, our contribution is related with the second proposal of the symposium: "Initiatives for the transfer of knowledge in ergonomics that have evaluated gender considerations".

The aim of the project is to set the bases to build ergonomic indicators, present on the feminized work from the systemic and differential focuses. Thus to understand the work activity, starting from the contextual, socio-labor, familiar and individual dimensions of a group of women linked with the informal work.

2   Methodology

2.1   Methodologic Foundation

Due the purposes of ergonomics and its holistic and systemic nature, the basis of this proposal has a mixed focus.

Quantitative Focus: Descriptive and transverse type design.

Qualitative Focus: Analysis perspective: Cases studies; Intrinsic reach when investigat-ing inside the real specific context.

Participants: 80 women between 18 and 60 years old, economically active and linked to the informal work sector.

Location: Women who reside and work in Apartadó (Urabá-Antioqueño), Chía (Cund-inamarca) and Bogotá D.C. – Colombia.

Sample: No probabilistic sampling. The Convenient Sampling Method and Snowball will be applied.

2.2 Recollection Technics

The collection of information processes and data have two moments: the first one of qualitative nature and the second one of quantitative character.

Qualitative Focus: Focal groups, semi-structured interviews, non-participant observation and risk cartography will be applied.

Quantitative Focus: Characterization format. Variables of the instrument: (1) General context (locality, housing, remuneration, time displacement, rural/urban population, public policies, vulnerability conditions). (2) Family environment (head of household, number of people with whom they live, relationship). (3) Socio-labor aspects (economic sector, training, hierarchy, time in workload), Work means (tools, equipment, utensils). (4) Individual conditions (age, symptoms, medical history, marital status, person with disability, level of education, ethnicity).

2.3 Analysis and Treatment of Data

Qualitative Information: In order to construct the proposed qualitative indicators and from the hermeneutic-dialectic perspective, all the information obtained from the understanding of the 'work activity' -carried out by the women linked to the study- is articulated analysed and synthesized.

Quantitative Information: Simple descriptive statistics that allow the numerical variables to be grouped and related for the construction of the ergonomics indicators of a quantitative nature.

Corpus Analysis: The corpus analysis is developed from the process of codification and categorization.

Codification Process: Through the Text separation processes, special registration and numbering units will be used.

Categorization Process: Through inferences, ascending conclusions are defined for the construction of ergonomic indicators with categories and subcategories.

3 Results

The close up with the target population, established at the first moment of the study, allows researchers identify the next categories:

1. *Opportunity occupations*: informality, entrepreneurship.
2. *Changes in operative modes*: adjustments in tasks, tools, cycles, rhythms, postures and bio-safety protocols.
3. *New work activities*: emerging jobs due to the pandemic, highly feminized jobs due to the 'care economy' and frequent exposure to risk.

4. *Space and proximity*: number of people in the interaction space, physical and environmental conditions, demarcations.
5. *New forms of employability*: salary adjustments, hiring conditions, equal pay, labour market opportunities.
6. *Perceptions of the new way of working*: links, feelings, interactions of the intra-family tissue, contact times, communication with a mask, domestic activities versus work activities.

4 Discussion

According to the literature consulted and when contrasting it with the first approximations to the context, it is evident the importance of recognizing the socioeconomic, political, historical, cultural, technological and productive aspects, among others, to address the new 'occupations of opportunity' and work activities.

It is confirmed that the basic categories of individual, family, general context and socio-labour environment conditions should be a point of reference to analyse the micro, macro and supra scales of the environment.

In this sense, facing the nascent works derived from the confinement situation, new links of interaction are established in the social tissue.

The transformation of work systems requires various forms of mental effort, physical workload and modes of execution that affect their quality of life and working conditions.

5 Conclusions

The project is currently under development and derived from the government policies due to the pandemic, the scope of the project has been restricted in terms of reaching the entire target population. Therefore, the project is positioned on the work-field phase for the recollection and systematization of the quantitative information. The qualitative data collect is now partially completed. It is expected to be socialized the in the setting of the congress. Thus, we are not able now to present the conclusions.

Glosary

Self-Care: It's a conduct that appears on specify life situations, when the individual guides itself to the regulation environment of the factors that affects their self-benefit, health and wellness.

Informal Sector: Group of production unities (non-constituted enterprises for head of household), included the "Self-Informal enterprises" and the "Informal workers enterprises".

Differential Focus: It's a progressive development of the principal of equality and no discrimination. Although all the people are equal to the law, this affects in a different way each one, according to their class condition, gender, ethnic group, age, physics or mental health and sexual orientation.

Systemic Focus: or system focus means that approaching method for the objects and phenomena cannot be isolated but it must be consider as whole. It´s not the sum of elements, but the set of interacting elements, in an integral way, that produce new qualities with different characteristics.

Feminized Work: Ideologically works associated to the women's work in the domestic sphere. Professions occupied mostly for women.

Work Charge: Set of physiological requirements that the employer develops throughout his working day, where the physical and mental work coexists on variable proportion, depending on the task.

Schedule Charge: Period of time where an assigned work or task required for the fulfilment of the working day are carried out.

References

1. Departamento Administrativo Nacional de Estadísticas (DANE). Encuesta Nacional de uso del tiempo - ENUT (2017). https://sitios.dane.gov.co/enut_dashboard/#!/. Accessed 09 Feb 2021
2. Gómez Bueno, C.: Mujeres y trabajo: principales ejes de análisis. Rev. de Sociología **63**(0), 123. (2001). https://papers.uab.cat/article/view/v63-64-gomez. Accessed 09 Feb 2021
3. Solís, M.: La construcción simbólica de un mercado de trabajo feminizado en la ciudad de Tánger: Una aproximación. Frontera Norte **22**(43). (2010). http://www.scielo.org.mx/scielo.php?script=sci_arttext&pid=S0187-73722010000100003. Accessed 08 Feb 2021
4. Zorrilla-Muñoz, V., Agulló-Tomás, M., García-Sedano, T.: Análisis socio-ergonómico en la agricultura. Evaluación del sector oleico desde una perspectiva de género y envejecimiento Dialnet. ITEA-Información Técnica Económica Agraria. **115**(1) 83–104. (2018). https://dialnet.unirioja.es/servlet/articulo?codigo=6903707. Accessed 05 Feb 2021
5. Gozalez, R., Hidalgo, G., Salazar, J., Preciado, M.: Calidad de Vida en el Trabajo. In: Ocupacional I de S. p. 59 (2009)
6. Masci, F., Rosecrance, J., Mixco, A., Cortinovis, I., Calcante, A., Mandic-Rajcevic, S., et al.: Personal and occupational factors contributing to biomechanical risk of the distal upper limb among dairy workers in the Lombardy region of Italy. Appl. Ergon. 83, 102796 (2020)

Upper and Lower Limb Work Injuries:
A Question of Sex or Gender?

Silvana Salerno[1]([✉]) and Claudia Giliberti[2]

[1] ENEA, National Agency for New Technologies, Energy and Sustainable Economic
Environment, SP Anguillarese SP 015, 00123 Rome, Italy
silvana.salerno@enea.it
[2] INAIL, National Institute for Insurance Against Accidents at Work, Via Roberto Ferruzzi
38-40, 00143 Rome, Italy

Abstract. Gender differences in non-vehicle work injuries compensated records
in Italy were studied for five years (2014–2018) using Inail (National Institute for
Insurance against Injuries at work) Data Records. Results showed 357.306 women
injuries and 908.139 men injuries with higher injury rate in both women 11‰ and
men 19.1‰ with upper and lower limb differently injured. *Upper limb* injuries
occurred more often among men *(women 34% vs 41% men, p < 0.05)* with
hand more injured. *Wrist* and *elbow* were significantly injured among women
(wrist OR: 2.09; IC95% 2.06–2.13 and elbow OR: 1.46; IC95% 1.42–1.50). A
higher women's injury rate was found in: *health care* activities (20‰, the highest
number of work accidents among women 83.029), *cleaning* (19‰), *transport*
(17‰) Women reported more *wrist fractures* in cleaning, *wrist dislocation* in
healthcare and more *wrist bruise* in post-service activities. *Lower limb* injuries
occurred more often among women (women 30% vs 26% men, p < 0.05) with
more *ankle (OR: 1.06; IC95% 1.05–1.08) and knee (OR: 1.10; IC95% 1.08–1.11)*,
particularly *ankle dislocation* among *cleaners* and *post-services* and bruise of the
knee in *healthcare* activities. The reasons of the high rate of wear and tear of *wrist,
elbow, ankle and knee* among women in analyzed work activities are discussed
taking s/g differences into account.

Keywords: Occupational injuries · Gender/sex · Upper/lower limb · Work
setting

1 Introduction

In Italy a work injury is a traumatic event resulted in a temporary or permanent work
inability for a minimum duration of three days.

All work injuries in Inail (National Institute for Insurance against Injuries at Work)
Data Records are classified into "*during work*" and "*commuting*" injuries [1]. The role of
any vehicle (car, motorcycles, bicycle, bus, etc.) is emphasized considering: "*vehicle and
non-vehicle during work accidents*" and "*vehicle and non-vehicle commuting accidents*".
Since last survey of Inail Disability Data Records, women have 53.054 occupational
disabilities (82% due to work accidents and 18% to occupational diseases) while men

© The Author(s), under exclusive license to Springer Nature Switzerland AG 2021
N. L. Black et al. (Eds.): IEA 2021, LNNS 220, pp. 487–494, 2021.
https://doi.org/10.1007/978-3-030-74605-6_62

432.063 disabilities (77% due to work accidents and 23% to occupational diseases). Work injury disabilities affect more women's musculoskeletal apparatus (women 62% *vs* 60% men) mainly upper and lower limbs [2]. A previous study on *non-vehicle commuting accidents* showed that women are more injured walking to work particularly at the ankle, foot and knee (Salerno and Giliberti, 2019) [3].

Women and men show sex (physical) and gender (social construction) (s/g) differences. Among others, physical differences are in upper and lower limb strength, body balance, body mass index that may rise further with age. In particular women over 50 years old lose more muscle mass into fat tissue, especially in lower limbs [4]. They also differ per work activities (horizontal and vertical segregation) and house activities (care activities). Interaction between s/g has to be taken into account when studying occupational injuries in order to orient prevention. No specific studies considering s/g difference in *work accidents* were available, although some papers, dealing with women falls, particularly in health care, and in older age, were found [5–7].

This study has the purpose to analyze *work accidents* exploring the "hows and whys" of s/g differences [8] in work injuries in different work activities and their impact on upper and lower limb lesions taking Inail records into account.

2   Methods

Data records on *non-vehicle work* accidents in Industry-Services (INAIL Data Base 2014–2018 update October 2019) were collected and analyzed per s/g taking part of the body (*upper limb*: hand, wrist, arm-forearm, elbow; *lower limb*: hallux, ankle, foot, knee, thigh), work activities, type of lesion (bruise, dislocation, wounds and fractures in 2017) and age interval into account. Injury rate per work accidents (work accidents/employed × 1000) and per work sector (work accidents in each work sector/employed in the work sector × 1000) was calculated. Work sectors with higher injury rate were selected and analyzed taking upper and lower limb impairments into account. Each upper and lower limb site was studied in order to better understand the prevalent lesion (%). Women and men employed were estimated from Italian National Institute of Statistics (ISTAT) [9] and applied to the work force given by INAIL where sex distribution was not available. Gender differences for each outcome (injury rate, main work sectors, lower and upper limb, type of lesions) were considered by using contingency tables 2 × 2 in which chi square value was calculated (significant level $p < 0.05$) and Odds Ratio was calculated per upper and lower limb sites and work activities.

3   Results

In the last five years women had 519.930 compensated injuries (injury rate 16‰) while men had 1.110.031 (injury rate 23.3‰). Higher injury rate was found in *during work accidents* (n. 375.653 women, 11.5‰ *vs* men n. 974.545, 20.5‰), particularly when *no vehicle* was involved (*non-vehicle during work* accidents n. 357.306 women 11‰ *vs* n. 908.139 men 19.1‰). Further analysis was then oriented towards these more numerous work accidents (from now "work accidents") (Table 1).

Gender differences in *upper and lower limb* injuries are shown in Table 2.

Table 1. Incidence rate of work-related compensated injuries in Industry-services in Italy per type of injury and gender (2014–2018 update October 2019)

	Women N.	Incidence rate ‰	Men N.	Incidence rate ‰
Workforce	32.534.391		47.565.143	
During work:	375.653	11.5	974.545	20.5
No vehicle	357.306	11.0	908.139	19.1
With vehicle	18.347	0.56	66.406	1.40
Commuting:	144.277	4.43	135.776	2.85
With vehicle	101.555	3.10	116.276	2.40
No vehicle	43.122	1.32	19.500	0.41
All	519.930	16.0	1.110.321	23.3

Table 2. Incidence rate of work-related compensated injuries in Industry-services in Italy per upper and lower limb sites and gender (2014–2018 update October 2019)

During work without vehicle compensated injuries						
2014–2018	Women 357.306		Men 908.139		OR	IC95%
	N	%	N	%		
Hand	77.534	64	277.002	75	0.59	0.59–0.60
Wrist	23.592	19.5	38.268	10.4	**2.09**	**2.06–2.13**
Elbow	8.686	7.2	18.591	5	**1.46**	**1.42–1.50**
Arm/forearm	11.329	9.4	35.565	9.6	0.97	0.95–0.99
Upper limb	121.141	100	369.426	100	0.75	0.74–0.75
Hallux	3.192	3.1	6.657	2.8	**1.07**	**1.02–1.11**
Foot	20.03	18.9	47.626	20.2	0.92	0.90–0.94
Ankle	45.451	42.9	97.797	41.6	**1.06**	**1.05–1.08**
Knee	33.589	31.7	70.018	29.7	**1.10**	**1.08–1.11**
Thigh	3.605	3.4	13.247	5.7	0.59	0.57–0.61
Lower limb	105.867	100	235.345	100	**1.20**	**1.19–1.21**
Other sites	117.887	100	280.207	100	–	–
All	344.895	96.5	884.978	100	–	–
Unidentified	12.411	3.5	23.161	2.6	–	–
Total	357.306	100	908.139	100	–	–

Upper limb injuries were more frequent among men (men 41% *vs* women 34%, p < 0.05) with *hand* more injured in both gender mainly among men (women 64% *vs* men 75%, p < 0.05) while *wrist* (women 19.5% *vs* men 10.4%, OR: 2.09; IC95% 2.06–2.13) and *elbow* (women 7.2% vs men 5%; OR: 1.46; IC95% 1.42–1.50) were more frequently injured among women if compared to men.

Lower limb injuries were more common among women (women 30% *vs* men 26%, OR: 1.20; IC95% 1.19–1.21) with more *ankle* (women 42.9% *vs* men 41.6%, OR: 1.06; IC95% 1.05–1.08) and *knee* (women 31.7% *vs* men 29.7, OR: 1.10; IC95% 1.08–1.11) injuries while *foot* among men (20.2% men *vs* 18.9% women, p < 0.05) (Table 2).

Work activities representing ninety-two per cent of women workforce were selected in order to determine injury rate (IR). A higher women's injury rate was found in: *health care activities* (20‰, the highest number of work accidents among women 83.029), *cleaning* (19‰), *transport* (17‰) and *food service and housing* (19.5‰). *Manufacturing and trade*, although having more employed women, showed lower injury rate (manufacturing 7‰, trade 8‰). Men, in the same work activities, showed the following injury rate: *health care* (27‰) *cleaning* (31‰), *transport* (28‰), *food and housing* (22‰), *manufacturing* (15‰), *trade* (17‰). In the *construction*, a typical male dominant activity, injury rate was also high (22.5‰) (table not shown).

Gender differences in upper and lower limb injury sites were analyzed in health care, cleaning and transport activities (Table 3 and Table 4) because of their higher injury rate among women.

Upper limb was more affected than lower limb, particularly among men (women 33.9% *vs* 40.7% men, p < 0.05). *Lower limb* was mainly affected among women (women 29.6% *vs* 26% men, p < 0.05). Women in health care reported higher risk for both upper and lower limbs as expected. In upper limb injuries, women always showed more *wrist injuries* in *health care* (women 26.3% vs men 17.1%; OR: 1.73; IC95% 1.62–1.84), *cleaning* (women 22.5% *vs* men 13.6%, OR 1.85; IC95% 1.73-1.97) and t*ransport* (women 21.3% *vs* men 16.2%; OR 1.39; IC95% 1.29–1.50). Women showed also more *elbow injuries* in *cleaning* (8.7% women *vs* men 6.9%; OR 1.30; IC95% 1.18–1.42) and *transport* (11% women *vs* 9.4% men; OR 1.19; IC95% 1.07–1.31). Men showed always more *hand injuries* than women particularly in cleaning activities (men 68.7% *vs* 59.6% women).

In *lower limb* women constantly showed more *ankle* injuries in *healthcare* (women 42% *vs* 36.4% men; OR 1.18; IC95% 1.12–1.24), *cleaning* (women 44.5% *vs* 42.8% men; OR 1.07; IC95% 1.01–1.13) and *transport* (women 46.1 *vs* 43.6 men; OR: 1.10; IC95% 1.05–1.16). *Knee* injuries were more frequent among women in *cleaning* (women 33.7% *vs* 32.4% men; OR 1.06; IC95% 1.00–1.12) and *transport* (women 32.6% *vs* 28.1% men; OR 1.24; IC95% 1.18–1.30). Men showed more often *knee* injuries in *healthcare* (men 38.6% *vs* 35.2% women, p < 0.05) and *ankle* injuries in *transport* (43.6%) and *cleaning* (42.8%) activities.

Type of lesions for upper and lower extremities in 2017 were also studied (table not shown). In *health care* women's *wrist* was more injured with *dislocation* (45%), *bruise* (41%) and *fractures* (21%) together with *hand-wounds* (19%). *Dislocation* of the ankle (78%) and *bruise* of the *knee* (55%) were the prevalent lesions in women's lower limb. Of

Table 3. Upper limb injury sites in health care, cleaning and transport per gender (2014–2018 update October 2019)

2014-2018	Women n. 357.306		Men n. 908.139			
Upper limb						
	N.	%	N.	%	OR	IC 95%
All work sectors	121.141	33.9	369.426	40.7	0.75	0.74–0.75
Healthcare						
Hand	11.924	54.7	5.047	64.0	0.68	0.64–0.72
Wrist	5.725	26.3	1.349	17.1	**1.73**	**1.62–1.84**
Elbow	1.757	8.1	606	7.7	1.05	0.96–1.16
Arm/forearm	2.373	10.9	873	11.2	0.98	0.90–1.06
Health care	21.779	100	7.875	100	10.1	9.80–10.34
Cleaning						
Hand	5.745	59.6	10.755	68.7	0.67	0.64–0.71
Wrist	2.166	22.5	2124	13.6	**1.85**	**1.73–1.97**
Elbow	842	8.7	1077	6.9	**1.30**	**1.18–1.42**
Arm/forearm	881	9.2	1701	10.8	0.83	0.76–0.90
Cleaning	9.634	100	15.657	100	1.95	1.90–2.00
Transport						
Hand	2.768	56.1	18.193	63.1	0.75	0.71–0.80
Wrist	1048	21.3	4.686	16.2	**1.39**	**1.29–1.50**
Elbow	542	11.0	2.723	9.4	**1.19**	**1.07–1.31**
Arm/forearm	573	11.6	3.251	11.3	1.04	0.94–1.14
Transport	4.931	100	28.853	100	0.50	0.49–0.52

all lower limb lesions 12% were *fractures* particularly of the *foot* (67% of all fractures). Men had more *hand-wounds* injuries (39.4%) and *dislocation* of the *knee* (61.3%).

In *cleaning* activities women's *wrist* was more injured with *bruise* (36%), *dislocation* (34%), and *fractures* (28%) and *bruise* of the elbow (53%). *Dislocation* of the *ankle* (71.5%) and *bruise of the knee* (57%) were the prevalent lesions in women's lower limb. Men had more *hand* injuries (66.3%) particularly *hand-wounds* (39.4%) and dislocation of the *ankle* (48%) and *knee* (41%).

In *transport* activities women's wrist was more injured with *bruise* (40%), *dislocation* (31%) and *fractures* (25%) and bruise of the *elbow* (54%). Men had more *hand-wounds* (33%), *hand-brui*se (33%) and *arm/forearm-dislocation* (20%). Women had mainly *ankle dislocation* (64%) and *bruise of the knee* (63%). Men had more *dislocation* of the *ankle* (60%) and of the *knee* (55%). *Fractures,* the most serious injury,

Table 4. Injury sites in lower limb sites in health care, cleaning and transport per gender (2014–2018 update October 2019)

2014–2018	Women n. 357.306		Men n. 908.139			
Lower limb						
	N.	%	N.	%	OR	IC 95%
All work sectors	105.867	29.6	235.345	25.9	1.20	1.19–1.21
Healthcare						
Hallux	860	3.7	419	5.3	0.67	0.60–0.76
Foot	4.104	17.6	1.171	15.0	**1.20**	**1.12–1.29**
Ankle	9.399	40.2	2.835	36.4	**1.18**	**1.12–1.24**
Knee	8.244	35.2	3007	38.6	0.87	0.82–0.91
Thigh	761	3.3	359	4.7	0.70	0.61–0.79
Health care	23.368	100	7791	100	8.27	8.05–8.50
Cleaning						
Hallux	183	1.9	308	2.2	0.88	0.73–1.05
Foot	1.612	17.1	2.551	18.3	0.92	0.86–0.99
Ankle	4.190	44.5	5.962	42.8	**1.07**	**1.01–1.13**
Knee	3.173	33.7	4.509	32.4	**1.06**	**1.00–1.12**
Thigh	268	2.8	603	4.3	0.65	0.56–0.75
Cleaning	9.426	100	13.933	100	1.55	1.51–1.60
Transport						
Hallux	144	1.7	984	2.6	0.66	0.55–0.79
Foot	1271	15.1	8.235	21.5	0.65	0.61–0.69
Ankle	3875	46.1	16.693	43.6	**1.10**	**1.05–1.16**
Knee	2745	32.6	10.743	28.1	**1.24**	**1.18–1.30**
Thigh	377	4.5	1.592	4.2	1.08	0.96–1.21
Transport	8.412	100	38.247	100	0.44	0.43–0.46

were more frequent in *upper limb* injuries with more *wrist fractures* among women and hand fractures among men particularly in cleaning activities. In lower limb *ankle* and *foot fractures* were more frequent among women with the exception of men in *transport* activities.

Age interval showed that *injured women* were older than men in cleaning and transport activities (women 45–54 vs 40–49 years old men). In health care activities women and men injured were in the same age interval (45–54 years old).

4 Discussion

Results showed higher injury rate in work accidents (non-vehicle) in both women and men with upper and lower limb differently injured.

Upper limb injuries occurred more often among men with *hand* more injured. *Wrist and elbow* were significantly injured among women. Women reported more *wrist fractures in cleaning, wrist dislocation in healthcare* and more *wrist bruise in post-activities. Bruise of the elbow* was the second significantly major upper limb injury among women working in the three analyzed work settings.

Lower limb injuries occurred more often among women if compared with men with more *ankle (dislocation)* particularly among *cleaners* and *post-services* and *knee (bruise)* in *health care. Dislocation* of the *ankle* was the major injured in all the three analyzed work setting among men. *Men* had more *dislocation* of the *knee* in *healthcare* and *bruise* of the *knee* in *post-activities.* Women in health care and cleaning reported more fractures of *ankle* while *foot fractures* were more reported in men during *post-service* activities.

Unfortunately no data on single dynamic of the upper and lower limb injuries are available in Inail data base and no studies addressing this specifically issue were found. Only an Italian Report based on European Statistic of Accidents at Work (Esaw) Codes [10] reported that the major women's activities during work accidents (non-vehicle) were walking, running, going up, going down, getting in or out, jumping, hopping, crawling, climbing, getting up, sitting down. Hypothesis is therefore that slips, trips and falls during work [11] could be the major cause of women injuries in the overall work actitivies causing different type of lesions in upper limb (wrist and elbow) and lower limb (ankle and knee). Moreover, women in the analyzed work sectors are exposed to repetitive tasks increasing the rate of wear and tear of the *wrist* and *elbow* that may lead to a higher incidence injury rate. This hypothesis of wrist and elbow overusing is confirmed by the higher prevalence among women of musculo-skeletal occupational diseases such as carpal tunnel syndrome and epicondylitis [12]. Carpal injuries and carpal tunnel syndrome can together explain the higher burden of *wrist pathologies* also due to women's lower strength of upper limb (40% less than men) [13]. Tasks and subtasks differ within the same work activities leading to a diverse gender exposure that can also produce overusing [14].

Lower limb in healthcare, cleaning and post-servicing women is also overused because women work in prolonged standing without possibility to rest or to change posture, have to move in many different workplaces often carrying loads. Slips, trips, and falls are frequent in these work settings, particularly post-servicing [15], healthcare [6, 16] and cleaning [17]. Finally repetitive tasks may easily produce less attentive behavior increasing the risk of having an injury while health caring, cleaning and post-servicing.

Reducing women repetitive tasks, enforcing upper and lower limb strength, using protective equipment such as wristband, together with a prevention plan on women's during work falls, could reduce injury rate. Applied ergonomics considering these results could design a new s/g approach [18] on preventing wrist, elbow, ankle and knee injuries among women in the specific analyzed work activities.

References

1. Inail Data base. https://bancadaticsa.inail.it/bancadaticsa/login.asp. Accessed 08 Feb 2021
2. Inail Disabilities data base. http://apponline.inail.it/DisabiliApp/Login.do. Accessed 08 Feb 2021
3. Salerno, S., Giliberti, C.: Non-vehicle commuting in Italy: need for ergonomic actions for women's lower limbs? Appl Ergon. **83**, 102982 (2020)
4. Anderson, L.J., Liu, H., Garcia, J.M.: Sex differences in muscle wasting. Adv. Exp. Med. Biol. **1043**, 153–197 (2017)
5. Scott, K.A., Fisher, G.G., Barón, A.E., Tompa, E., Stallones, L., DiGuiseppi, C.: Same-level fall injuries in US workplaces by age group, gender, and industry. Am. J. Ind. Med. **61**(2), 111–119 (2018)
6. Drebit, S., Shajari, S., Alamgir, H., Yu, S., Keen, D.: Occupational and environmental risk factors for falls among workers in the healthcare sector. Ergonomics **53**(4), 525–536 (2010)
7. Verma, S.K., Lombardi, D.A., Chang, W.R., Courtney, T.K., Brennan, M.J.: A matched case-control study of circumstances of occupational same-level falls and risk of wrist, ankle and hip fracture in women over 45 years of age. Ergonomics **51**(12), 1960–1972 (2008)
8. Laberge, M., Caroly, S., Riel, J., Messing, K.: Considering sex and gender in ergonomics: exploring the how and whys. Appl. Ergon. **85**, 103 (2020)
9. Dati occupati Istat. http://dati.istat.it/. Accessed 08 Feb 2021
10. Ires-Emilia Romagna su dati Inail. http://sicurinitinere.eu/il-progetto. Accessed 08 Feb 2021
11. Kemmlert, K., Lundholm, L.: Slips, trips and falls in different work groups–with reference to age and from a preventive perspective. Appl. Ergon. **32**(2), 149–153 (2001)
12. Kotejoshyer, R., Punnett, L., Dybel, G., Buchholz, B.: Claim costs, musculoskeletal health, and work exposure in physical therapists, occupational therapists, physical therapist assistants, and occupational therapist assistants: a comparison among long-term care jobs. Phys. Ther. **99**(2), 183–193 (2019)
13. Nuzzo, J.L., et al.: Measurement of upper and lower limb muscle strength and voluntary activation. J Appl Phys. **126**, 513–543 (2019)
14. Chen, H., Chang, CM., Liu,, Y.P., Chen, C.Y.: Ergonomic risk factors for the wrists of hairdressers Appl. Ergon. **41**(1), 98–105 (2010)
15. Bentley, T.A., Haslam, R.A.: Identification of risk factors and countermeasures for slip, trip and fall accidents during the delivery of mail. Appl. Ergon. **32**(2), 127–134 (2001)
16. Cherry, N., Parker, G., McNamee, R., Wall, S., Chen, Y., Robinson, J.: Falls and fractures in women at work. Occup Med (Lond), **55**(4), 292–297 (2005)
17. Alamgir, H., Yu, S.: Epidemiology of occupational injury among cleaners in the healthcare sector. Occup. Med. (Lond). **58**(6), 393–399 (2008)
18. Slopecki, M., Messing, K., Côté, J.N.: Is sex a proxy for mechanical variables during an upper limb repetitive movement task? An investigation of the effects of sex and of anthropometric load on muscle fatigue. 30;**11**(1), 60 (2020)

Dynamic Workstation Exposure: Does Sex Affect Response?

Mathieu Tremblay[1]([✉]) (iD), Nancy L. Black[2] (iD), and Jean-Philippe Morin[1] (iD)

[1] Université du Québec à Rimouski, Rimouski, QC, Canada
tremma11@uqar.ca
[2] Université de Moncton, Moncton, NB, Canada

Abstract. In the literature, little is known about the vagal response during exposure to a sit-stand workstation. This study measured the vagal response to exposure to a dynamic workstation that moved between sitting and standing heights for different regular durations and documented sex-related response. Fourteen workers (43.6 ± 4.0 years of age; 16.1 ± 4.1 years of experience) who work normally with computers (seven women, seven men of working age) were exposed to a dynamic workstation in their everyday office work environment. Heart rate variability (HRV) was used to measure the vagal activity with SD1, SD2 and MeanRR indicators, and questionnaires measured musculoskeletal health. Indicator of overall physiological response (HRV) to a dynamic workstation appears to be related to sex among a cohort of experienced office workers, where women showed a higher vagal response than men, and men had a decrease in body regions with musculoskeletal discomfort. More attention should provide to sex-specific responses to a dynamic workstation.

Keywords: Heart Rate Variability (HRV) · Dynamic workstation · Sex differences · Musculoskeletal discomfort · Physical activity

1 Introduction

Continuous sedentary work and physical inactivity increases physical health risks, including musculoskeletal discomfort, cardiovascular diseases (CVD) [1]. More importantly, workers who are exposed to high levels of occupational stress show an elevated risk of health impairments [2]. Over the years, many tools or indicators have been developed to identify and quantify health risks, including Heart Rate Variability (HRV). HRV is a tool to measure Autonomic Nervous System (ANS) modulation, and occupational stress and health impairments are recognized to modulate the activity of ANS [3]. The ANS is divided into two main branches, the sympathetic and the parasympathetic nervous systems. The vagus nerve is the main nerve of the parasympathetic nervous system and its activity is known as vagal tone or vagal response. Typically, HRV is lower when workers have high occupational demands (physical, psychosocial), but also when individuals have impaired health (e.g. chronic pain, CVD, diabetes, depression, anxiety) [4–8].

N. L. Black et al. (Eds.): IEA 2021, LNNS 220, pp. 495–500, 2021.
https://doi.org/10.1007/978-3-030-74605-6_63

In an effort to reduce the risk related to office work (including sedentary lifestyle and physical inactivity), regular workplace movement has been studied recently. Experts recommend regularly changing between sitting and standing posture [9]. However, little is documented about how this practice relates to ANS, and further investigation is needed. This study measured the ANS responses (more specifically, vagal response or vagal tone) to exposure to a workstation that moved between sitting and standing heights for different regular durations and documented sex-related response.

2   Methodology

Fourteen participants volunteered for this project (7 women, 44.9 ± 3.3 years of age, 14.3 ± 3.1 years of experience; 7 men, 42.4 ± 4.9 years of age, 17.9 ± 5.1 years of experience). All participants were university employees working full-time and regularly working on computer-intensive tasks. Participants' baseline HRV was recorded over 1 h in their regular sedentary work environment, pre- (baseline) and post-exposure to the dynamic workstation. During the data collection, the participants were asked to stay at their workstation to do their usual computer tasks to record similar tasks across the participants.

HRV was recorded using a Polar H10 thoracic belt, an IPhone 5 and a phone application (*Heart Rate Variability Logger*; version 4.6.2). The data were analyzed with *Kubios HRV Standard* (version 3.3.0) software. The HRV variables used were MeanRR, SD1 and SD2. These variables were known to be related to vagal activity [10].

- MeanRR: mean time between heart beats, being sensitive to both sympathetic and parasympathetic nervous system activity; it is strongly negatively associated to the heart rate) [10];
- SD1: standard deviation of points perpendicular to the line-of-equality, measuring the short-term HRV and being influenced by parasympathetic activity; it is strongly positively associated to the RMSSD [10];
- SD2: standard deviation of points along to the line-of-equality, measuring the long term HRV and being correlated to sympathetic and parasympathetic activity; it is strongly positively associated to the SDNN [10].

For this study, an "*elevated vagal response*" occurred when at least two of the three variables showed a positive difference between the post- and pre-conditions.

The dynamic workstation's settings included six different standing durations within a 30-min cycle, resulting in 0, 3, 6, 9, 12, and 15 min standing per period. Condition ordering was randomized, and each condition was experienced for at least two working days prior to the next condition. The total duration of exposure to the dynamic workstation conditions ranged from 40 to 96 working days. Concurrently to the HRV measures, participants were questioned about their regions with musculoskeletal discomfort (MSdi) in each of 10 body regions consistent with the Nordic questionnaire [11] for analysis of musculoskeletal symptoms. Additionally, participants were asked if they typically practice three or more bouts of moderate to vigorous physical activity per week, as well as if they were suffering from musculoskeletal pain or disorders (MSP) prior to the current study.

Considering that the statistical power was inferior to 0.8, the current study adopted a descriptive approach (proportion (%); mean ± standard error of means (M ± SE)). The statistics were computed with JASP version 0.13.1 (University of Amsterdam, Netherlands).

3   Results

Overall, 50% of this cohort presented an elevated vagal response to the dynamic workstation. A higher proportion of women presented an elevated vagal response than men (71.4% and 28.6%, respectively). Overall, it appears that women showed a greater vagal response after using the dynamic workstation than men compared to the baseline condition (mean differences ± SE: MeanRR 7.1 ± 6.0%; SD1 12.6 ± 15.6%; SD2 14.2 ± 14.3%;) (Fig. 1). Table 1 shows that exposure to the dynamic workstation decreased the musculoskeletal discomfort of body-region among men (difference of 2 pre vs. post) but did not change among the women participating (no difference pre vs. post). Among our participants, more men were more physically active than women (men 42.8% more) and reported higher MSP rates (men 14.3% more).

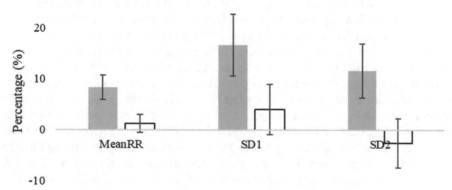

Fig. 1. Heart rate variability (HRV) values among participating women and men. HRV values were the variation between pre- (baseline) and post-exposure to the dynamic workstation. The values are presented in percentage (%) (i.e. (post HRV value – pre HRV value)/pre HRV value * 100)). The histograms are the mean and the error bars are standard error of means. Gray columns are women; white columns are men.

Table 1. Demographics and musculoskeletal health data

	N	Age (years)	Experience (years)	Physical activity	MSdi		MSP
					Pre	Post	
Women	7	44.9 ± 3.3	14.3 ± 3.1	42.9%	3.7	3.7	28.6%
Men	7	42.4 ± 4.9	17.9 ± 5.1	85.7%	4.4	2.4	42.9%

Notes. (N) number of participants; Experience refers to the number of years of intensive computer work experience; (Physical activity) proportion of individual that practice three or more bouts of moderate to vigorous physical activity per week before the study; (MSdi) number of regions with musculoskeletal discomfort; (Pre) before the exposition to the dynamic workstation; (post) post-exposure to the dynamic workstation; (MSP) percentage of participant group suffering from musculoskeletal pain or disorders before the study.

4   Discussion

The elevated vagal response is associated with an elevation in heart-rate variability, thus workers experienced an overall health condition improvement. In this sample, women were more likely to experience positive changes related to vagal response than men. Dynamic workstation exposure seems to enhance the women's occupational physical activity level. Increasing occupational physical activity is known to improve office workers' physical and psychosocial health [12]. Participating men were already prone to regular physical activities (i.e. during their leisure time), which may explain the observed sex-related vagal response change. It is possible that women's improvement was associated with an increasing level of occupational physical activity. Even though they did not show a physiological improvement, men experienced reduced regions with musculoskeletal discomfort after using the dynamic workstation. Therefore, women and men workers responded differently to the dynamic workstation by improving different domains of their respective health (i.e. general and musculoskeletal). Overall, it is difficult to compare the results of the current paper with the literature, considering that the specific question of sex differences has been poorly explored [13]. Partial explanation might be related to the proportion of women in the studies, considering that Mengistab [14] reported in a literature review that 18 of 23 sit-stand studies had predominantly women participants (ranging from 50 to 91%). Consequently, more attention should be paid to understand the workers' individuality.

5   Study Limitation

The authors acknowledge that the elevated vagal response associated with an elevation of HRV might be linked to an overall health condition improvement. The authors did not control for other covariables (e.g. weight, lifestyle habits, diet, leisure time, domestic physical activity), and further research is needed to better understand their influence on the workers' health. Initially, we planned to study more participants however, recruitment was challenging for this project. Details relating to challenges encountered during this study are presented in a paper published by Black et al. [15].

6 Conclusions

This study shows that vagal response as measured varied by sex in an age-matched population of 7 men and 7 women engaged in computer-intensive office-work prior to and after using a sit-stand dynamic workstation for several weeks. Confounding factors of differing physical activity levels and regions with musculoskeletal discomfort may contribute to this finding, but sex-related differences must not be ignored.

References

1. Koren, K., Pišot, R., Šimunič, B.: Active workstation allows office workers to work efficiently while sitting and exercising moderately. Appl. Ergon. **54**, 83–89 (2016). https://doi.org/10.1016/j.apergo.2015.11.013
2. Järvelin-Pasanen, S., Sinikallio, S., Tarvainen, M.P.: Heart rate variability and occupational stress—systematic review. Ind. Health **56**(6), 500–511 (2018). https://doi.org/10.2486/indhealth.2017-0190
3. Tonello, L., Rodrigues, F.B., Souza, J.W.S., Campbell, C.S.G., Leicht, A.S., Boullosa, D.A: The role of physical activity and heart rate variability for the control of work-related stress. Front. Physiol., **5**(67) (2014). https://doi.org/10.3389/fphys.2014.00067
4. Koenig, J., Loerbroks, A., Jarczok, M.N., Fischer, J.E., Thayer, J.F.: Chronic pain and heart rate variability in a cross-sectional occupational sample: evidence for impaired vagal control. Clin. J. Pain **32**(3), 218–25 (2016). https://doi.org/10.1097/AJP.0000000000000242
5. Wong, I.S., Ostry, A.S., Demers, P., Davies, H.W.: Job strain and shift work influences on biomarkers and subclinical heart disease indicators: a pilot study. J. Occup. Environ. Hyg. **9**, 467–477 (2012). https://doi.org/10.1080/15459624.2012.693831
6. Ramírez, E., Ortega, A.R., Reyes Del Paso, G.A.: Anxiety, attention, and decision making: The moderating role of heart rate variability. Int. J. Psychophysiol. **490**, 490–496 (2015). https://doi.org/10.1016/j.ijpsycho.2015.10.007
7. Kemp, A.H., Quintana, D.S.: The relationship between mental and physical health: insights from the study of heart rate variability. Int. J. Psychophysiol. **89**(3), 288–96 (2013). https://doi.org/10.1016/j.ijpsycho.2013.06.018
8. Hallman, D.M., Ekman, A.H., Lyskov, E.: Changes in physical activity and heart rate variability in chronic neck–shoulder pain: monitoring during work and leisure time. Int. Arch. Occup. Environ. Health **87**(7), 735–44 (2014). https://doi.org/10.1007/s00420-013-0917-2
9. Buckley, J.P., Hedge, A., Yates, T., Copeland, R.J., Loosemore, M., Hamer, M., Bradley, G., Dunstan, D.W.: The sedentary office: an expert statement on the growing case for change towards better health and productivity. Br. J. Sports Med. **49**(21), 1357–1362 (2015). https://doi.org/10.1136/bjsports-2015-094618
10. Shaffer, F., Ginsberg, J.P.: An overview of heart rate variability metrics and norms. Front. Public Health. **5**, 258 (2017). https://doi.org/10.3389/fpubh.2017.00258
11. Kuorinka, I., Jonsson, B., Kilbom, A., Vinterberg, H., Biering-Sørensen, F., Andersson, G., et al.: Standardised Nordic questionnaires for the analysis of musculoskeletal symptoms. Appl. Ergon. **18**(3), 233–237 (1987). https://doi.org/10.1016/0003-6870(87)90010-x
12. Lindberg, C.M., et al.: Effects of office workstation type on physical activity and stress. Occup. Environ. Med. **75**(10), 689–695 (2018). https://doi.org/10.1136/oemed-2018-105077
13. Chambers, A.J., Robertson, M.M., Baker, N.: The effect of sit-stand desks on office worker behavioral and health outcomes: a scoping review. Appl. Ergon. **7**, 37–53 (2019). https://doi.org/10.1016/j.apergo.2019.01.015

14. Mengistab, D.: Sedentariness, productivity, perception and long term health effects of sit-stand workstation at work: a literature review. Thesis. *New Jersey Institute of Tec*hnology. (2019). https://digitalcommons.njit.edu/theses/1657
15. Black, N.L., Tremblay, M., Mougnol, G., McGrath, M., Kengne, P.: Challenges of controlled measures in real Office environments: Impact of workstation stand-sit height variations. In: Proceedings of the 49th Annual Conference of the Association of Canadian Ergonomists and 6th Conference of CROSH, pp. 47–48 (2018). https://crosh.ca/wp-content/uploads/2018/10/FINAL-Conference-Proceedings-ACE-CROSH-2018_sm.pdf

Part V: Human Factors and Sustainable Development (Edited by Andrew Thatcher)

Eco-Drivers and Eco-Automation: A Case Study with Hybrid Electric Vehicle Drivers

Matthias G. Arend[1](✉) and Thomas Franke[2]

[1] Institute of Industrial Engineering and Ergonomics (IAW),
RWTH Aachen University, Aachen, Germany
m.arend@iaw.rwth-aachen.de

[2] Engineering Psychology and Cognitive Ergonomics, IMIS,
University of Lübeck, Lübeck, Germany
franke@imis.uni-luebeck.de

Abstract. Although the implications of increasingly automated road transport for driver behavior are often studied from the perspective of safety and comfort, automation is also expected to increase energy efficiency and thus contribute to environmental sustainability. However, drivers' interaction with automated systems that optimize the vehicle's energy efficiency by controlling the energy flows has not yet been well understood. Based on the perspective of user-energy interaction, the present research constitutes a first case study in this respect, focusing on hybrid electric vehicle (HEV) drivers. Results from an online questionnaire study with 121 HEV drivers indicated high user diversity in the interaction with the eco-automation, ranging from complete reliance to active disengagement of eco-automation. These interaction patterns were significantly related to differences in fuel efficiency, as well as the drivers perceived trust and knowledge of the eco-automation. The study provides evidence for the relevance of understanding drivers' interaction with eco-automation to ensure the sustainability of future road transport.

Keywords: Eco-driving · Automation · Hybrid electric vehicle

1 Introduction

For road vehicles, automation is overtaking more and more elements of the driving task [1]. Because a key goal of automation is to enhance the overall safety of road transport as well as driver comfort (e.g., [2]), most studies in the area of user-system interaction focus these aspects of driver behavior (e.g., take-over situations; [3]). Yet, beyond safety and comfort, another grand challenge for road transport is environmental sustainability and energy efficiency of vehicles in real-life usage [7]. Consequently, more sustainable vehicles are often equipped with automation designed to increase the energy efficiency of vehicle operation (e.g., [4, 5]). These eco-automation systems seek to manage the vehicles' energy flows in a more efficient way. Yet, driver behavior is a decisive factor for the ultimate effectiveness of eco-automation in real-life usage [6], since driver

© The Author(s), under exclusive license to Springer Nature Switzerland AG 2021
N. L. Black et al. (Eds.): IEA 2021, LNNS 220, pp. 503–511, 2021.
https://doi.org/10.1007/978-3-030-74605-6_64

inputs can integrate well with the eco-control algorithms or specify driving parameters for which eco-optimization is challenging for the eco-automation. Thus, understanding driver interaction with the eco-automation is important to facilitate energy-efficient human-automation collaboration.

Driver behaviors targeted towards increased energy efficiency are typically subsumed by the concept of eco-driving [7], including strategic (e.g., vehicle purchase), tactical (e.g., route selection) and operational (on-road) behaviors [8]. For eco-drivers who decide to purchase an energy-efficient vehicle such as a hybrid electric vehicle (HEV), optimal operational eco-driving can still be challenging due to the high temporal dynamics and complexity of energy flows [9]. Hence, HEVs are typically equipped with advanced eco-automation systems that dynamically manage the vehicle's energy flows based on the driver's discrete or continuous inputs. As such, the eco-automation constitutes the interface between driver inputs and vehicle actuators. The eco-automation readjusts the vehicle's energy flows to most efficiently provide the driving behavior required by the driver inputs (for present-day manual driving), while accounting for the current system and energy states. For example, when the driver increases the pressure on the throttle control (demanding an acceleration from the vehicle) in an HEV, the eco-automation seeks to optimally utilize the combustion engine and electric motor depending on the current energy status of the battery, to execute the acceleration with the ultimately lowest energy consumption possible.

At the same time, eco-drivers often seek to increase their on-the-road energy efficiency by applying (eco-)driving behaviors that they assume to be effective. To derive the effectiveness of certain behaviors, some HEV eco-drivers closely monitor the vehicle's energy flows and derive assumptions about the system [9], including the eco-automation. Yet, there have been indications that the real-world energy efficiency that HEV eco-drivers achieve depends on their conceptions of how the vehicle's energy flows are dynamically controlled, by the driver inputs and the eco-automation [10]. Consequently, from the perspective of Green Ergonomics [11, 12], it should be identified what constitutes and determines optimal driver-automation interaction in the context of eco-driving and how it can be supported through adequate system feedback design. Yet, while there is a plethora of technical research on eco-automation (e.g. [4, 5]), there is very few HF/E research to date examining actual driver interaction with eco-automation in everyday usage.

1.1 Present Research

The objective of the present research was to identify (a) eco-drivers' interaction with the eco-automation as measured by their usage of intervening driving modes, (b) the relationship of driving-mode usage to fuel efficiency, and (c) the role of eco-drivers' trust in and knowledge of the eco-automation for interacting with it. Therefore, research questions and hypotheses were specified as reported below.

In HEVs, different driving modes that relate to the eco-automation are available. The prototypical Toyota Prius models for which we examined user-automation interaction have three possible modes: (1) The *E-mode* switches the gasoline engine off and forces the eco-automation to propel the vehicle with electric energy as long as possible. Drivers can activate the E-mode by pressing the EV-button. (2) The *B-mode* is comparable to engine-braking in conventional vehicles and can be activated by setting the gearstick to 'B'. With an activated B-mode, the eco-automation cannot regenerate energy as efficiently as when deactivated, so it should only be used when additional deceleration is needed (e.g., to reduce usage of the mechanical brakes). (3) The *N-mode*, activated by setting the gearstick to 'N', enables the HEV to glide in neutral mode (i.e., without consuming energy, regenerative braking, and engine braking). Thus, the driver dictates the eco-automation to utilize kinetic energy for moving the vehicle instead of regenerating parts of it. In summary, drivers can directly intervene in the control of the energy flows by using a driving mode and at least partly uncouple the eco-automation. Hence, it should be determined how drivers interact with the eco-automation in terms of using the three driving modes (see Table 1, Q1).

Table 1. Research questions and hypotheses.

Research question (Q)		Hypothesis (H)	
Q1	How do drivers interact with the eco-automation?	H1	Drivers differ in their usage of the driving modes
Q2	How does the usage of each of the three driving modes relate to fuel efficiency?	H2a	Usage of the E-mode is related to fuel efficiency
		H2b	Usage of the B-mode is related to fuel efficiency
		H2c	Usage of the N-mode is related to fuel efficiency
Q3	How does trust in the eco-automation relate to drivers' interaction with it?	H3a	Trust is related to the usage of the E-mode
		H3b	Trust is related to the usage of the B-mode
		H3c	Trust is related to the usage of the N-mode
Q4	How does knowledge of the eco-automation relate to drivers' interaction with it?	H4a	Knowledge is related to the usage of the E-mode
		H4b	Knowledge is related to the usage of the B-mode
		H4c	Knowledge is related to the usage of the N-mode

Previous research indicates that the driver interaction with the energy dynamics related to the three driving modes impacted energy efficiency: Increased usage of the electric propulsion (e.g., by using the E-mode) was related to lower energy efficiency, and higher usage of neutral gliding (e.g., by using the N-mode) was related to higher energy efficiency [10]. Finally, in an interview study [9] drivers stated that the B-mode is often misunderstood as a stronger regenerative braking mode. Yet, the intensity of regenerative braking remains the same when the B-mode is activated, but more kinetic energy is converted into heat instead of electric energy due to added friction. Hence, usage of the driving modes should relate to fuel efficiency (see Table 1, Q2).

Furthermore, eco-drivers develop specific eco-driving strategies and system conceptualizations to increase their eco-driving success [13]. Hence, if drivers interact differently with the eco-automation, the question of what determines these differences arises. Trust in automation has been identified as a major factor for establishing an appropriate relationship between humans and automation [14], with humans generally more likely relying on automated systems they trust [14]. The question thus is how trust relates to drivers' interaction with the eco-automation (see Table 1, Q3).

Finally, for HEV eco-driving, individual differences in technical knowledge of the system have been identified as an important predictor of differences in eco-driving success [13]. Drivers who understand the system better also achieve higher energy efficiency [10, 13]. Hence, it is the question whether this finding also translates to drivers' knowledge of the eco-automation functioning (see Table 1, Q4).

2   Method

2.1   Participants

We wanted to study drivers who are generally motivated to eco-drive and can therefore be expected to regularly interact with the eco-automation. Therefore, HEV drivers were recruited via www.spritmonitor.de, a website on which they had constantly logged their fuel consumption. Thus, participants can be assumed to be eco-drivers because they had performed strategic (purchase of an HEV) as well as strategic (logging of refueling events) eco-driving behaviors (cf. [8]) prior to participation.

In total, $N = 121$ HEV drivers of the Toyota Prius (93% male, mean age $M = 48$ years; $SD = 11$) participated in an online questionnaire. The drivers most-used HEV were the Prius 3 (42%), Prius c (30%), and Prius 2 (28%). Drivers had a high mean driving experience with HEVs in general ($M = 62,392$ km; $SD = 52,324$).

2.2   Scales and Measures

Usage of the Driving Modes. Usage of each driving mode was assessed with one item, rated on a 6-point Likert scale from completely disagree (1) to completely agree (6). Each item was deduced from HEV drivers' statements in an interview study [9] and was formulated to assess drivers' usage of a driving mode with the intention to interrupt eco-automation control: "I use the EV-button to completely utilize the electric driving" (E-mode); "Downhill, I use the B-mode* to utilize the regenerative braking as much as possible. (*the B-mode can be chosen via the gearstick)" (B-mode); "I use the N-mode via the gearstick to completely utilize the neutral gliding" (N-mode).

Trust. Trust in the eco-automation was measured with a German translation [15] of the 12-item *Trust in Automated Systems Scale* [16]. The scale instruction was adapted to assess HEV drivers' trust in the eco-automation: "The energy flows in the HEV system (functional interaction between the gasoline engine, electric motor, regenerative braking) are controlled by an automated control system (specific algorithms). Hence, to a certain degree, the HEV system decides for itself how the energy for driving the wheels is supplied and how the battery is charged. How do you perceive this automated control system of the energy flows in your HEV?". Participants responded on a 7-point Likert scale from completely disagree (1) to completely agree (7).

Knowledge. To assess drivers' perceived knowledge of the eco-automation functioning, the technical system knowledge scale used in previous research [17] was adapted. The resulting five-item scale comprised several aspects of the eco-automation's energy flow management: (1) "I am familiar with the propulsion technology of hybrid cars (e.g., types and functionality of electric motors)"; (2) "I have an idea about how regenerative braking technically works"; (3) "I can explain the functioning of the planetary gearset in my HEV on a technical level"; (4) "I can explain on a technical level why the propulsion of my HEV uses respectively the gasoline engine, electric motor, or both"; (5) "I can explain why the gasoline engine sometimes does not switch off at the traffic lights on a technical level". The 6-point Likert scale was used again.

Fuel Efficiency. To first assess the validity of HEV drivers' fuel efficiency estimates, they were asked to estimate their average fuel consumption during the 6 months prior to the study. The correlation of these estimates with the actual fuel consumption recordings for the same period indicated that the HEV drivers were well-aware of their fuel consumption ($r = .86$, $N = 100$ drivers who provided their logged data).

To be able to account for systematic differences in the typical route profiles as well as weather conditions, we did not use drivers' recorded fuel consumption data but asked them to estimate their fuel consumption in two standardized scenarios, of which one was for an urban and one for a rural driving environment (for details on exact scenario and item texts see [10]). To further account for general differences in fuel consumption between Prius models, the fuel consumption estimates were standardized based on the mean and standard deviation from the distribution of logged fuel consumptions for each Prius model (i.e., extracted data from www.spritmonitor.de of >1200 vehicles). Finally, the resulting standardized values were inverted so that higher values corresponded to higher fuel efficiency.

3   Results

To model all hypothesized relationships in one path model and determine the most adequate measurement models for the latent constructs, structural equation modelling (SEM) was used to analyze the data. In the path model, fuel efficiency (outcome) was regressed on the usage of the E-, B-, and N-mode (predictors), which were again, as outcomes, regressed on the predictors trust and knowledge. To account for the non-normality of some items, parameter estimation was based on robust maximum likelihood estimators and scaled test statistics. The R-package 'lavaan' [19] was used.

The measurement model that best supported the aggregation of items (as indicators) to the scale [18] was examined for each construct. Therefore, parallel, tau-equivalent, and tau-congeneric models [18] were fitted and the one with the best fit was selected. For trust and fuel efficiency, an essentially tau-equivalent model, and for knowledge, a tau-congeneric model provided the best fit. All scales had acceptable to high reliabilities (.81 for fuel efficiency,.90 for knowledge,.93 for trust).

To assess Q1, the distribution of the single-item indicators was examined. In general, most drivers preferred to rely on the eco-automation over intervening by using the driving modes. 37.8% of the drivers reported to not use the E-mode (i.e., rating of "completely disagree") for driving only with electric energy; 49.6% of the drivers reported to use the B-mode to intensify the regenerative braking downhill; and 79.0% of the drivers reported to use the N-mode for letting the vehicle glide. To receive a global indicator of drivers' interaction with the eco-automation, the combined usage of the driving modes was assessed by dichotomizing the three single-item indicators based on their scale midpoint (3.5). Thus, drivers' usage of driving modes was aggregated, resulting in a binary variable with drivers who would rather (0) vs. rather not (1) rely on the eco-automation. Nearly half (50.8%) of the drivers reported relying on the co-automation by rather not using any driving mode, whereas the other drivers (49.2%) reported to rather use at least driving mode. Hence, there was substantial variance in driver's usage of the driving modes (H1 supported).

The relationships of using each driving mode (binary variable) to fuel efficiency (Q2) from the SEM path model indicated that usage of the E-mode was not significantly related to fuel efficiency (H2a rejected; see Table 2). Yet, usage of the B-mode was significantly related to lower energy efficiency and usage of the N-mode was significantly related to higher energy efficiency (H2b and H2c supported).

Table 2. Path coefficients of the full SEM. β = standardized path coefficient; z = test statistic; model RMSEA = 0.05, not significantly higher than 0.05 ($p = .473$), thus good fit.

Q	H	Outcome	Predictor	β	z	p	R^2
Q2	H2a	Fuel efficiency	E-mode	−0.01	−0.17	0.887	0.17
Q2	H2b		B-mode	−0.33	−2.84	0.005	
Q2	H2c		N-mode	0.23	2.47	0.014	
Q3	H3a	E-mode	Trust	−0.28	−2.42	0.015	0.06
Q4	H4a		Knowledge	0.07	0.7	0.486	
Q3	H3b	B-mode	Trust	−0.05	−0.44	0.66	0.11
Q4	H4b		Knowledge	−0.30	−2.21	0.027	
Q3	H3c	N-mode	Trust	−0.06	−0.61	0.539	0.03
Q4	H4c		Knowledge	0.21	1.88	0.059	

Furthermore, the standardized path coefficients for the relationships of trust with usage of the E-, B- and N-mode (Q3) indicated that higher trust was significantly related to lower usage of the E-mode (H3a supported; see Table 2). Yet, trust was not significantly related to the usage of the B- and N-mode (H3b and H3c rejected).

Finally, the standardized path coefficients for the relationships of knowledge with the usage of each driving mode (see Q4; Table 2) indicated that knowledge was not significantly related to usage of the E-mode (H4a rejected). However, higher knowledge was significantly related to lower usage of the B- and higher usage of the N-mode (H4b and H4c supported).

4 Discussion

The objective of the present research was to advance knowledge on the interaction between HEV eco-drivers and eco-automation in everyday usage. Thus, manual interventions of HEV drivers into the eco-automation's control of the vehicle's energy flows were studied. Half of the drivers reported using at least one driving mode to intervene in the eco-automation, whereas the other half refrained from interventions. Drivers differed regarding the type of driving mode used, with the E-mode being most frequently used, followed by the B-mode and N-mode. Hence, user-interaction with the eco-automation was diverse (Q1). Manual interventions by using the B-mode were negatively related to fuel efficiency, while usage of the N-mode was positively related to fuel efficiency (Q2). Finally, users' trust was related to reduced usage of the E-mode, leaving the management of electric energy resources to the eco-automation (Q3). Knowledge of the eco-automation was negatively related to drivers' usage of the B-mode, and positively related to usage of the N-mode (Q4).

4.1 Implications and Conclusion

Results from the present research indicate that, although eco-automation strongly supports energy-efficient driving, optimal human-system integration of the driver and eco-automation is necessary to fully realize the potential of more energy-efficient vehicles such as HEVs. Considering the results from Q1 and Q2, it becomes evident that many drivers reported interaction patterns with the eco-automation that can be deemed suboptimal from an energy-efficiency perspective: The N-mode was the least-used but most energy-saving driving mode, while the E- and B-mode, showing no and a negative relationship to fuel efficiency, were reported to having been used more frequently. Consequently, the question is how the integration of eco-drivers and eco-automation can be supported from the perspective of Green Ergonomics.

A first step towards achieving such human-automation integration can be derived from the results on drivers' trust in and knowledge of the eco-automation functioning: Higher trust in the eco-automation was related to usage of the E-mode, whereas higher knowledge of the eco-automation functioning related to lower usage of the B-mode and higher usage of the N-mode. Both factors thus seem to cover important aspects of the interaction and systems for supporting eco-driver's interaction with the eco-automation should facilitate the acquisition of relevant knowledge while maintaining appropriate levels of trust. As for specific system feedback design, an option is to provide drivers with feedback on the energy dynamics as controlled by the eco-automation (see [20] for considerations on how to design such energy displays).

In summary, the present research provided first evidence that eco-drivers showed diverse interaction patterns with the HEV eco-automation, which were related to differences in fuel efficiency, drivers' trust in and knowledge of the eco-automation. The results indicate that an optimal integration of driver and automation is necessary to utilize the full potential of more sustainable vehicles. The present study constituted a very first step in understanding the interaction of eco-drivers and eco-automation. Yet, with increasingly automated vehicles, the question of how drivers interact with the eco-automation systems also becomes increasingly important.

References

1. Walker, G.H., Stanton, N.A., Salmon, P.M.: Human Factors in Automotive Engineering and Technology. Aldershot, Ashgate, UK (2015)
2. Kauffmann, N., Winkler, F., Vollrath, M.: What makes an automated vehicle a good driver? In: Proceedings of the 2018 CHI Conference on Human Factors in Computing Systems (CHI 2018). Paper 168, pp. 1–9 (2018)
3. Mok, B., Johns, M., Miller, D., Ju, W.: Tunneled in: drivers with active secondary tasks need more time to transition from automation. In: Proceedings of the 2017 CHI Conference on Human Factors in Computing Systems, CHI 2017, pp. 2840–2844 (2017)
4. Song, Z., Hofmann, H., Li, J., Han, X., Ouyang, M.: Optimization for a hybrid energy storage system in electric vehicles using dynamic programing approach. Appl. Energy 139, 151–162 (2015)
5. Yu, H., Kuang, M., McGee, R.: Trip-oriented energy management control strategy for plug-in hybrid electric vehicles. IEEE Trans. Control Syst. Technol. 22, 1323–1336 (2014)
6. Zhang, Y., Chu, L., Fu, Z., Xu, N., Guo, C., Zhang, X., et al.: Optimal energy management strategy for parallel plug-in hybrid electric vehicle based on driving behavior analysis and real time traffic information prediction. Mechatronics 46, 177–192 (2017)
7. Barkenbus, J.N.: Eco-driving: an overlooked climate change initiative. Energy Policy 38, 762–769 (2010)
8. Sivak, M., Schoettle, B.: Eco-driving: Strategic, tactical, and operational decisions of the driver that influence vehicle fuel economy. Transp. Policy 22, 96–99 (2012)
9. Franke, T., Arend, M.G., McIlroy, R.C., Stanton, N.A.: Ecodriving in hybrid electric vehicles – exploring challenges for user-energy interaction. Appl. Ergon. 55, 33–45 (2016)
10. Arend, M.G., Franke, T.: The role of interaction patterns with hybrid electric vehicle eco-features for drivers' eco-driving performance. Hum. Factors 59(2), 314–327 (2018)
11. Thatcher, A.: Green ergonomics: definition and scope. Ergonomics 56, 389–398 (2013)
12. Hanson, M.A.: Green ergonomics: challenges and opportunities. Ergonomics 56, 399–408 (2013)
13. Arend, M.G., Franke, T., Stanton, N.A.: Know-how or know-why? The role of hybrid electric vehicle drivers' acquisition of eco-driving knowledge for eco-driving success. Appl. Ergon. 75, 221–229 (2019)
14. Hoff, K.A., Bashir, M.: Trust in automation: integrating empirical evidence on factors that influence trust. Hum. Factors 57, 407–434 (2014)
15. Beggiato, M., Krems, J.F.: The evolution of mental model, trust and acceptance of adaptive cruise control in relation to initial information. Transp. Res. Part Traffic Psychol. Behav. 18, 47–57 (2013)
16. Jian, J., Bisantz, A.M., Drury, C.G.: Foundations for an empirically determined scale of trust in automated systems. Int. J. Cogn. Ergon. 4, 53–71 (2000)
17. Franke, T., Rauh, N., Günther, M., Trantow, M., Krems, J.F.: Which factors can protect against range stress in everyday usage of battery electric vehicles? toward enhancing sustainability of electric mobility systems. Hum. Factors 58, 13–26 (2016)

18. Rosseel, Y.: Lavaan: an R package for structural equation modeling and more. J. Stat. Softw. **48**, 1–36 (2012)
19. Graham, J.M.: Congeneric and (essentially) Tau-equivalent estimates of score reliability: what they are and how to use them. Educ. Psychol. Measure. **66**(6), 930–944 (2006)
20. Franke, T., Görges, D., Arend, M.G.: The energy interface challenge. towards designing effective energy efficiency interfaces for electric vehicles. In: Proceedings of the 11th International Conference on Automotive User Interfaces and Interactive Vehicular Applications, pp. 35–48 (2019)

Scaling Micronarrative with Machine Learning to Model Human and Environmental Wellbeing in Macro, Meso and Micro Systems

Wendy Elford[1]([✉]) and Keil Eggers[2]

[1] Now to Next Pty Ltd., Canberra, ACT 2607, Australia
wendy@wendyelford.com
[2] George Mason University Jimmy and Rosalynn Carter School for Peace and Conflict Resolution, Fairfax, VA 22030, USA
keggers@masonlive.gmu.edu

Abstract. The UN Sustainable Development Goals (SDGs) reveal challenges in creating the social foundations that reduce poverty while protecting the environment, a concept recently popularized as 'Donut Economics'. Decision makers and program managers applying a vector theory of change for SDGs must track systems at the macro, meso and micro levels in real time. The emergence of new data may surface weak signals providing an early opportunity to adjust strategy and a timely reminder to continually monitor for impacts and unintended consequences. Fortunately, humans are born storytellers. A human sensor network using narrative provides data on intersecting social and environmental issues. Configured effectively, this narrative dataset can support pre-hypothesis testing and provide insight into the emergence of themes, scaffolding linkages between quantitative data and lived experience at multiple levels. The Our Tomorrows project in the state of Kansas, USA, captures self-interpreted micronarrative including demographics about families surviving or thriving using a process called naturalistic sensemaking. Stories were used in community workshops to design actionable projects to improve family wellbeing. This paper repurposes the original data set from Our Tomorrows to provide an early proof of concept for a multi-method analysis combining machine learning with naturalistic sensemaking. This approach shows how rapidly evolving data on environmental factors might be modeled in parallel with self-interpreted stories to show how interventions reduce poverty and improve the future for children and their families.

Keywords: Narrative · Text modeling · Naturalistic sensemaking · Sustainability integration · Vector change · Human sensor network

N. L. Black et al. (Eds.): IEA 2021, LNNS 220, pp. 512–520, 2021.
https://doi.org/10.1007/978-3-030-74605-6_65

1 Problem Statement

1.1 Human Wellbeing in a Planet Wide Environmental Sustainability Context

Multi-level, interacting systems present unique challenges for inquiry and intervention. Where both humans and technology are involved, systems seem to drift into levels of complexity based on individual expectations of human wellbeing that may not be environmentally sustainable. The United Nations Agenda for Sustainable Development [1] sets five areas, people, planet, prosperity, peace and partnership, and 17 goals, planetwide. The authors of this agenda acknowledge these goals are interdependent. This paper assumes that interventions and outcomes in each SDG must not just interoperate, they must seamlessly complement and coordinate across macro, meso and micro systems over time. Navigating these complex adaptive systems requires new analytical tools to improve situational awareness and decision-making [2, 3].

Integrated sustainability is central to Kate Raworth's Donut Economics [4]. Raworth presents the "imperative of eradicating poverty so that all people lead lives free of deprivation" with the "resources needed to provide a social foundation for leading lives of dignity, opportunity, and fulfilment". She uses the analogy of a donut with social foundation as the innermost ring, environmental thresholds as the outer ring, and a safe space for humans in between. Echoing Goldratt's 'Theory of Constraints' [5], Raworth urges us to strive to design for "… the space where both human well-being and planetary well-being are assured, and their interdependence is respected".

The interdependent systems within the donut present a granularity problem for researchers and practitioners that seek to enact systems change while maintaining dignity, opportunity and fulfillment for individual humans in the process. Managing the complex interactions between levels of a system is a long-term project that requires adequate mapping of the predisposition of the present to chart pathways to improve the world for future generations [6].

1.2 Human Wellbeing in a Local Sustainability Context

Our Tomorrows is a current project in the state of Kansas, USA, run by the University of Kansas Center for Public Partnerships and Research (CPPR). This project seeks to improve the early childhood system which comprises several elements of Raworth's 'safe space' for humans. Sponsors intend to improve the future for all citizens by ensuring families have what they need to thrive [7].

The funding for Our Tomorrows during the initial needs assessment came from a federal grant and was supported by state agency partners in the early childhood system [8]. The Early Childhood strategic plan has taken a complexity-informed approach, with strategies based in part on collecting micronarratives [9]. For example, Community Action Labs support small-scale interventions that respond to patterns in Our Tomorrows data and promote human wellbeing and sustainable systems.

A proposal was made through one of the advisors to Our Tomorrows to carry out a secondary analysis of the data and provide proof of concept of a way to increase the coherence and feasibility of qualitative data analytics for programs over the long-term. The advisors and CPPR team shared a joint aim to improve service to stakeholders, noting that the current qualitative analytics process to handle live queries, manage the program and write reports in real-time could falter under future resource constraints. This paper reports on the proof of concept project where a second analysis of existing data was completed that incorporated insights on environmental sustainability as a lens for publication.

Two software mediated approaches, SenseMaker® and Leximancer®, show promise for scaling narrative data through structured parallel analysis of associated quantitative data. Naturalistic sensemaking via distributed ethnography is one approach that allows large systems to be studied in context through self-interpreted narrative [9]. SenseMaker® is a software tool that supports the capture of self-interpreted micronarrative from citizen journalists and other stakeholders comprising a 'human sensor network' at scale. When analyzed at multiple levels of the system with other questions that provide structure and context, these micronarratives can reveal the nature and inclination for change within and between systems to multiple stakeholders near real-time [10]. Machine learning processes have the capacity to automatically produce models of text at scale. Leximancer® software carries out unsupervised machine learning of large volumes of text [11].

These approaches allow a larger system of narrative to be revealed to multiple stakeholders as dynamic models; the original data remaining unchanged and fully accessible at any level of granularity in the system. Micronarrative interpreted at source can scale cleanly because the 'first-order sensemaking' and 'theme finding' are done by the contributor and not by an external human coder. Machine learning takes that body of micronarratives, with or without themes or structuring variables, and returns a model of the text.

2   Objectives

The authors set up a pilot with CPPR using text modeling software to explore lexical patterns in Our Tomorrows SenseMaker® micronarratives collected during 2019. The pilot ought to achieve three objectives. First, the authors sought to complete an analysis of the existing data with text modeling software as a proof of concept to: a) learn about technical challenges; and b) to gain new insights. A second objective was to ask the CPPR sponsors: a) if they had gained any new insights; and b) to ask them to compare their now updated understanding of the data with the results from other analysis and activities, for example while running the community sensemaking workshops. A third objective was to carry out a simple test using text modeling to explore the Our Tomorrows data to identify factors related to the SDGs on the environment.

The authors will not present a full case study combining naturalistic sensemaking with machine learning in this paper. Interested practitioners and researchers are asked to read about these two approaches and supporting software tools [11, 12]. Further validation and case studies will follow as analysis of Our Tomorrows continues.

3 Methodology

The authors took an action learning approach to explore how the Our Tomorrows Sense-Maker® micronarrative dataset (n = 2450) collected from January to September 2019 could be analyzed further with machine learning software. Figure 1 shows the overall process of meta-analysis of the existing Our Tomorrows data in three phases aligned with three levels of the system; the macro (the state of Kansas), the meso (a subset of counties in Kansas) and micro (individual contributors). In all phases, the analyst used features of both software tools to zoom in and out, select and export data from different parts of the visualizations at macro, meso and micro levels. The statistical data associated with the original and processed micronarrative, available in both software packages, was not explicitly used in this proof of concept.

In phase 1, CPPR analysts identified three questions, one of which was the 'things got tough' triad question shown in Fig. 1 A1 and Fig. 2. Within these three questions there were eight clusters or groupings that CPPR analysts asked the authors to explore. This selection was based on the analysts' intuition of where additional insights might be found if they reviewed their initial analysis of SenseMaker® visualizations.

The three questions selected by CPPR plus another 12 multiple choice and demographics questions (a total of 15) were identified in the master data spreadsheet from Our Tomorrows. The authors edited this spreadsheet to retain only micronarratives written in English with permission to share publicly. Trial exports into Leximancer® established that these 15 questions of the total set of 32 variables could be used to produce a viable model of the total body of micronarrative. The decision to use a more structured approach with a larger count of variables when processing the text was made after the authors had first tested some initial strategies for text modeling using all of the Our Tomorrows micronarrative with smaller subsets of variables.

In phases 2 and 3, the processes of refining the identified clusters in SenseMaker® and creating text models of that narrative with Leximancer® were repeated at levels of finer granularity. More detail on the focus of analysis in the meso and micro systems appears in Fig. 2 and Fig. 3. The results of the analysis were presented to the CPPR team, and for the purposes of this paper, three team members involved in the analytics of Our Tomorrows 1.0 were interviewed for their insights about how the new analytics approach to analysing large qualitative data sets would benefit Our Tomorrows.

4 Results and Discussion

Sample outputs for this project from SenseMaker® for naturalistic sensemaking (Fig. 2) and Leximancer® A2 for text modeling (Fig. 3) show meta data at the macro level of Kansas. Visualizations in SenseMaker® (see Fig. 2) present interpreted micronarrative as single dots exactly as they were placed by each contributor at the time they answered each question. The top circle shows a pattern that might reveal a salient but weak signal of 'car' or 'house' within the micronarrative. The oval shows a cluster pattern where 'car' or 'house' content might appear within a larger cluster of micronarratives. Analysts at CPPR are familiar with outputs from SenseMaker®. Figure 3 shows a text model of the themes for all micronarrative in the Our Tomorrows project shared in a virtual

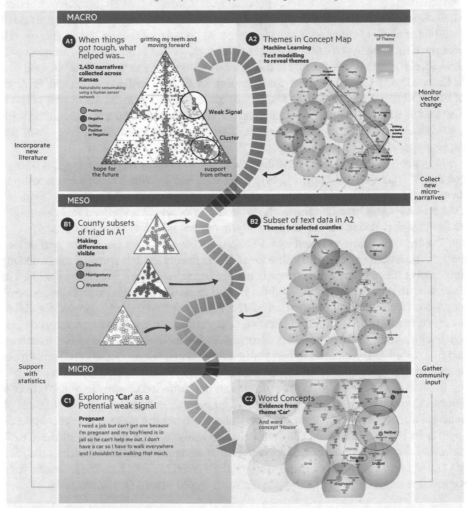

Fig. 1. Subsets of data are selected for further exploration and/or text modeling to allow comparisons at different levels of the systems. The vertical and horizontal arrows represent movement of the analyst's focus of exploration as they use the two software tools. A1 = triad from the full SenseMaker® project (See Fig. 2). A2 = text modeling for all micronarrative (see Fig. 3). B1, B2 = subsets A1 and A2 respectively. C1 = example of micronarrative with 'car' concept. C2 = close up of A2 showing 'car' theme and 'house' as a word concept with other adjacent concepts. Weak Signal is an early or isolated indicator of change.

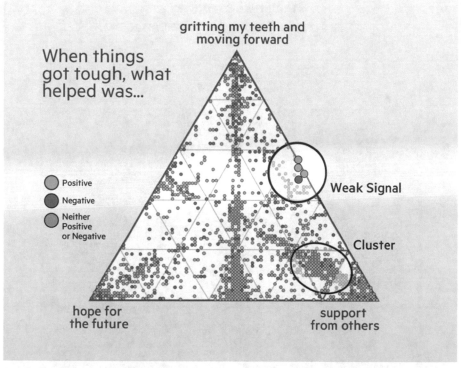

Fig. 2. Outputs for the "When things got tough" triad from SenseMaker®. Each dot locates a single micronarrative. Mousing over a dot reveals the source text, the coding and all demographics for that single unit of micronarrative. Capture tools allow export of micronarrative. A cluster is a grouping of micronarrative in one location of the question format. Positive and negative refers to sentiment.

presentation to the CPPR team. This presentation included support material on how to explore and interpret the text models as these were a new form of data visualization for this team.

The authors demonstrated that they had completed an analysis of the existing data with text modeling software as a proof of concept. The CPPR team confirmed that the authors' secondary analysis of their data was broadly consistent with the themes they found, for example, in comparing the different regions of Kansas. Text modeling was agreed to be a promising support to move towards real time analytics methods. It supported a multi-dimensional model of issues across Kansas. This was viewed as a useful artefact to consider in the next phases of the project.

One analyst (of two interviewed) confirmed that they believed the time-intensive hand coding of the data at scale wasn't sustainable. Both acknowledged that mining micronarratives for insights was necessary to answer stakeholders' questions quickly, but the re-coding often required was too time-intensive to effectively respond to these requests.

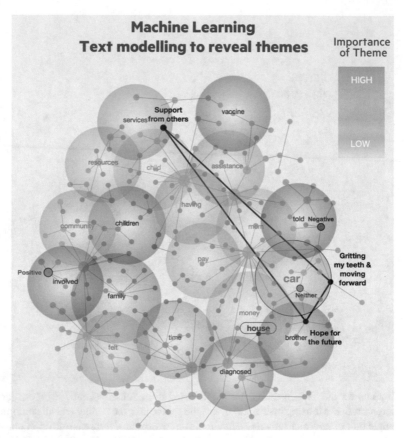

Fig. 3. A text model for all of the narrative in Our Tomorrows. The large, colored circles represent themes, and the small grey dots represent word concepts with grey lines showing relationships between concepts. The three black nodes represent the apices of the 'things got tough' triad. These black nodes are joined up by lines to show how the micronarrative from this specific question in Fig. 1 A1 and Fig. 2 relates to this text model. The theme 'car' and the concept 'house' are marked for further investigation.

Our Tomorrows has already noted the importance of contributors coding their stories at the time they share them. One interviewee noted the value of having a human sensor network where contributors code the stories themselves: "But in the sense of having (analysts) code these stories, I don't think it was very sustainable. I think that's why we stopped doing it and just allowed participants to code the stories themselves".

Finding weak signals in the data from Our Tomorrows was acknowledged to be a current and future challenge as the volume of data sets grows. In this pilot, the authors applied machine learning technology and text modelling to improve analysts' ability to locate themes which might be relevant to the environmental outcomes for Kansas in the future. Since associated lifestyle changes such as larger houses or multiple cars might be expected to have potential impacts on the environment, it could be useful to track these at a whole state level to promptly mitigate potential environmental issues.

The authors propose that the combination of these two approaches to qualitative data analytics has advantages in finding weak signals. For example, tracking the concepts 'car' and 'house' over time with text modeling has at least two benefits. It allows concepts relevant to, say, SDGs focusing on the environment, to be discovered, tested for salience and then followed over time. These concepts can then be integrated into wider models including quantitative data. A second and critical advantage to program managers and decision-makers is that any new initiatives such as programs to provide cars to raise people from poverty [13] have the potential to cause unintended consequences. Tracking weak signals in qualitative data with appropriately designed and scaled analytics can provide real benefits to ensuring the intended outcomes are achieved across time.

Interviews with two analysts from CPPR exploring the experience of recognising salience in micronarrative revealed that: "Concept salience tells a lot about where we should be placing our attention as people who are supposed to be helping people devise solutions to real time problems. I can do this within minutes with (text modeling) where it took me hours manually. I hear a lot about capacity, and this solves our capacity problem in many, many ways".

When asked about how a single concept relevant to the SDGs, such as 'car', might turn up as relevant, one analyst believed that transportation would come up frequently in peoples' experiences as a common obstacle for families.

"While it did appear every now and then, we found people will write about and prioritize their most urgent needs/crises when prompted. When transportation did appear in experiences of 'just surviving', it was often included in a long list of other challenges the individual and/or their family was facing," the analyst said. "I think if we went back now and looked at the data from our current collection effort, the role of personal transportation is more important and more likely to appear as a challenge because of the impact COVID has had on sharing spaces like public transportation". This insight is consistent with Klein's findings on the impact of life events on car ownership [14].

The current phase of Our Tomorrows commenced March 2020, just as COVID-19 hit the USA. This presents a unique chance to continue testing this analytics approach.

5 Conclusions

This paper presents a methodology to scale the analysis of qualitative data, specifically micronarrative. It supports multilevel analysis, especially where qualitative data must keep pace with quantitative data to establish how one level affects the other levels in complex adaptive systems. These parallel systems of qualitative data visualizations partnered with quantitative data from the supporting software and external sources will give better context for further research and decision making. It will effectively be like putting more wheels on a cart *and* improving the linkages in the steering mechanism.

Bliss [15] quotes Smart from Rutgers University as saying: "We don't want to try to balance our carbon emissions and budgets on the backs of the poor". This proof of concept provides early evidence that the unintended consequences harming the very humans we want to help can be tracked in a nuanced way to understand outcomes in multiple domains at multiple levels.

The combination of these two approaches—naturalistic sensemaking using human sensor networks and machine learning for text modeling—promises to help practitioners identify, model and respond to real life issues inside complex systems. Practitioners and designers can provide decision-makers with a more complete picture of context and help identify multiple pathways for change that integrate across the SDGs over time.

Three next steps seem useful: 1) to develop a validation model to test different types of narrative including formalised feedback from analysts; 2) to actively use quantitative data within both software tools and to actively integrate quantitative data from external sources; and 3) to explore options to model systems closer to real-time.

References

1. Transforming our world: The 2030 Agenda for sustainable development. United Nations. https://sustainabledevelopment.un.org/post2015/transformingourworld/publication. Accessed 16 Feb 2021
2. Kurtz, C.F., Snowden, D.J.: The new dynamics of strategy: sense-making in a complex and complicated world. IBM Syst. J. **42**(3), 462 (2003)
3. Elford, W.: Emerging Issues in Ergonomics: a Methodological Framework for Foresight and Sensemaking. University of Canberra (2011)
4. Raworth, K.: A safe and just space for humanity: Can we live within the doughnut? Oxfam Policy Pract. Climate Change Resilience **8**(1), 1–26 (2012)
5. Goldratt, E.M.: What Is This Thing Called Theory of Constraints and How Should It Be Implemented?. North River Press, Great Barrington, Massachusetts (1990)
6. Krznaric, R.: The Good Ancestor: How to Think Long Term in a Short-Term World. Random House, London (2020)
7. Our Tomorrows| University of Kansas Center for Public Partnerships & Research [Internet]. [cited 2021 Feb 9]. https://ourtomorrows.kucppr.org/. Accessed 16 Feb 2021
8. Observatory of Public Sector Innovation Our Tomorrows- A Community Sensemaking Approach. https://oecd-opsi.org/innovations/our-tomorrows-a-community-sensemaking-app roach/. Accessed 16 Feb 2021
9. University of Kansas Center for Public Partnerships and Research: Kansas early childhood systems building needs assessment. University of Kansas Center for Public Partnerships and Research, Lawrence, KA USA (2020)
10. Snowden, D.: Naturalizing Sensemaking. In: Informed by Knowledge: Expert Performance in Complex Situations, pp. 217–228. Psychology Press, New York, New York (2010)
11. Smith, A.E., Humphreys, M.S.: Evaluation of unsupervised semantic mapping of natural language with Leximancer concept mapping. Behav. Res. Meth. **38**(2), 262–279 (2006)
12. Van der Merwe, S.E., Biggs, R., Preiser, R., Cunningham, C., Snowden, D.J., O'Brien, K., Jenal, M., Vosloo, M., Blignaut, S., Goh, Z.: Making sense of complexity: using sensemaker as a research tool. Systems **7**(2), 25 (2019)
13. Klein, N.J.: Subsidizing car ownership for low-income individuals and households. J. Plan. Educ. Res. 0739456X20950428 (2020)
14. Klein, N.J., Smart, M.J.: Life events, poverty, and car ownership in the United States. J. Transp. Land Use **12**(1), 395–418 (2019)
15. Bliss, L.: As the planet warms, who should get to drive. https://www.bloomberg.com/news/art icles/2019–02-08/access-to-cars-could-help-the-poor-but-hurt-the-planet. Accessed 16 Feb 2021

Designing Sustainable Situations

Myriam Fréjus[✉]

EDF Recherche Et Développement, Palaiseau, France
myriam.frejus@edf.fr

Abstract. This paper aims to illustrate how the debate on sustainable development can be enriched through ergonomics. From our work relating to the reduction of households' energy consumption, we propose a shift in perspective from behavioral analysis to the study of situated human development over time. The analysis of everyday domestic situations makes it possible to identify both the contexts in which home occupants conduct activities and their experience of real-life situations, with a view to better understanding the mechanisms of energy consumption and reduction obstacles. Based on these criteria, it is possible to design "sustainable situations," whereby assistive solutions (tools, services) integrating extrinsic energy management objectives can assist actors in everyday situations. The proposed situation transformation entails, on the one hand, the development of adaptive, appropriable systems liable to contribute to in-home energy consumption regulation, and on the other, the development of reflective systems and resource supports to increase energy use awareness and commitments to energy saving. Energy use management is approached here as the result of structural changes across multiple systems (human, technological) emerging from their recurring interactions. By looking at these questions from the perspective of how to facilitate human activity, it is a matter of placing evolving human needs and situations and environmental resource management on an equal footing.

Keywords: Domestic activities · Appropriation · Experience · Development · Sustainable · Design · Energy

1 Ergonomics and Sustainable Development

The notion of sustainable development was first defined in 1987 as "development that meets the needs of the present without compromising the ability of future generations to meet their own needs" [3]. The definition of the term has since evolved beyond issues of natural resource conservation to include economic, ecological, and social dimensions, in order to "foster economic growth, advance social equity and ensure environmental protection" (Rio de Janeiro Earth Summit, 1992).

Research in sustainable ergonomics emerged more recently. Environmental and social inequality issues regarding pollution and resource misuse were addressed by [25] and [22]; in 2008, a dedicated sustainable ergonomics group was created at the International Ergonomics Association. Academic research has since addressed underlying issues across multiple fields, giving rise to studies in eco-ergonomics [4], green

© The Author(s), under exclusive license to Springer Nature Switzerland AG 2021
N. L. Black et al. (Eds.): IEA 2021, LNNS 220, pp. 521–529, 2021.
https://doi.org/10.1007/978-3-030-74605-6_66

ergonomics [33], HFE (Human Factors Ergonomics) and Sustainability [39, 40], and ergoecology [16].

We believe that ergonomics can provide specific insights to questions of sustainable development, on the one hand, by analyzing situations from the human perspective, with regards to sociotechnical environments, capacities for action, and human development; and on the other, by envisioning the transformation of situations with the aim of advancing human well-being (in accordance with the IEA definition) and protecting the environment. This implies promoting strategies of empowerment and resource system development over the adjustment of human behaviors [28]. We draw on our research on energy consumption management to present both the benefits of analyzing energy use mechanisms and the necessity for establishing design criteria for future sustainable situations.

1.1 Applying Ergonomics to Energy Management: Understanding the Mechanisms of Energy Consumption

The concept of "demand-side management" (DSM) emerged from the 2002 World Summit on Sustainable Development in Johannesburg. The goal of DSM was to at once maintain, and even increase, productivity using less energy, and to encourage "streamlined" energy uses. Central to this argument was the need to focus on consumer behavior.

Focusing On Domestic Situations Rather Than Energy Consumption "Behaviors." Prevailing studies frequently approach energy consumption from the angle of human behavior, and hence see the energy consumer as a rational actor whose actions can be influenced [1, 2, 38]. However, as [32] points out "*these approaches predominately follow the logic of resource management, rather than domestic life*" (Strengers, 2008, p. 9). Electricity consumption is indeed the result and not the purpose of day-to-day activities [31], in that all actions are inherently pluri-semantic and cannot emerge from a single goal [36]. Similarly, reducing energy consumption cannot only derive from supposed individual or collective concerns over energy and environmental issues. It is our belief that energy saving solutions can therefore be achieved through situated human-environment interaction analysis.

Consistent with ergonomics, we suggest that energy saving practices can only be effected (by interested individuals, energy control systems, or assistive household systems) when "invisibly" integrated into daily household activities, though appropriated tools and/or knowledge (namely, of links between the activities and associated energy consumption) may potentially assist occupants [8, 12]. This is why we examine both energy consumption mechanisms and energy reduction obstacles through the prism of everyday domestic situation analysis, with a specific focus on the everyday activity contexts and the lived and situated experiences of the actors. As such, activity-based ergonomics can provide invaluable insights to issues of environmental sustainability.

Understanding Energy Consumption Contexts. We are therefore interested in understanding the contexts in which inhabitants' concerns emerge by focusing on the meaning of individual actions and on the collective articulation of these meanings as construed by the inhabitants [12, 17]. This approach allows us to shed light on the relationships between actions and concerns, and to furthermore define such notions in energy use as forgetfulness and usefulness.

In terms of methodology, real-life recordings of domestic activities were made using mini-cameras with a 120° view angle and equipped with microphones [27]. In addition to these recordings, individual and collective self-confrontation interviews based on "Course-of-Action" principles [35] were conducted to identify meaningful factors from the actor's point of view.

This method of observation and domestic activity analysis allows us to identify a set of energy management actions carried out on an ad hoc basis in domestic activities [23]. Actions reflect such general concerns as reducing energy bills, protecting the environment, and achieving energy self-sufficiency. However, the analysis confirms that the activities are guided by concerns other than the efficient use and management of electrical appliances (putting children to bed, doing laundry, etc.). The considerations are multiple and arise intermittently over time, although from the actor's point of view they are consistent in terms of time. Indeed, the uses or non-uses of electrical devices are part of a collective process that is not easily described from an external point of view (such as not using a device to avoid disturbing other residents) [17]. Furthermore, events related to device or resident uses may prompt the redirection of an initial course of action, which can result in a device remaining in operation "while waiting" for the activity to be resumed (leaving the TV on while putting children to bed). Therefore, leaving a light or the TV on in an unoccupied room cannot be systematically characterized as an oversight from the actor's point of view. It signifies rather the intention to resume a previous activity, since domestic household activities are interrelated. It can also be indicative of the poor design of control systems, when switches are placed in an inconvenient location, for example. In this case, leaving on devices "when we aren't using them" derives from their "contextually rigid" nature and raises questions of (re)design.

Activity analysis also makes it possible to consider energy management on various timescales. For instance, the prior intention of lowering electricity bills is present when making the purchase of energy-efficient electrical appliances. Moreover, energy management practices are marked by the actor's personal story and background and arise from individual and, more importantly, collective constructions established over time: they are co-curated, negotiated, and evaluated according to the organization (spatial, technical, and temporal), norms, and conditions of individual households. Therefore, such energy saving practices are acceptable provided they do not interfere with ongoing domestic activities and concerns, that energy management decisions are determined by the inhabitants, and that the household's initial level of comfort is not too drastically decreased (according to the household norms).

The analysis of energy use contexts confirms our hypothesis that the appropriation of advantageous sales offers, services, and tools are crucial to the management of household energy use. The possibility of taking domestic energy management initiatives should thus be considered as a design criterion [8], some key aspects of which are described in the following section.

2   Designing Sustainable Situations

Rather than trying to lower energy use by influencing people and altering energy behaviors, sustainable situation design seeks to modify occupant-environment coupling dynamics [24], with a view to lowering energy consumption (energy efficiency). Our research is focused on providing assistive solutions (tools, services) for everyday situations while integrating extrinsic energy management objectives. By "sustainable situation" [8, 9, 10], we mean situations where the appropriation of new resources by the inhabitant (either owing to activity facilitating capabilities and/or activity enhancement, such as the addition of energy management properties) directly contributes to reduced energy use (either intentionally or system-induced). We differentiate "sustainable" from "efficient" situations, as efficiency applies to energy resources alone, and not to other resources potentially used by the actor. "Sustainable" reflects the time-based and changing nature of the occupant-environment coupling. In other words, the coupling itself is meant to last, whereas the individual elements that comprise it evolve independently of each other. The design objective is therefore more about aiming for a process (a coupling) that contributes to the actor's well-being, beyond issues of efficient household practices (a change of structure as defined by the enactive approach) and energy saving concerns, than it is about achieving a state of stability.

With regards to design directions, two main avenues for transforming domestic situations have been identified:

- the integration in the home of context-aware adaptive, appropriable systems capable of regulating energy consumption;
- the development of reflective systems and resource supports to raise energy awareness and reduction commitments.

The following section describes the research conducted in these two areas.

2.1   Designing Context-Aware Systems to Make Daily Life Easier and to Save Energy

We studied the potential of context-aware computing for providing in-home assistance to residents and lowering energy use, without necessarily requiring energy management guided interactions. [20] call this "context-aware power management." According to [6], *"a system is context-aware if it uses context to provide relevant information and/or services to the user, where relevancy depends on the user's task"* (p. 6). These systems, when relevant information about the actor's current situation is provided, can carry out control actions (turning off lights or devices, regulating heating) without any explicit interaction with "users," whose activities in progress may therefore be prioritized over the interaction. In an earlier case study by [7] and [15], a room-specific occupancy/vacancy system was designed and developed to identify situations where relevant actions for incidental device control (switching off, switching on, modulation), or direct control via the presence of interactive systems, could be of use to inhabitants.

More generally, interaction design approaches like these raise questions of system relevance, both in terms of context sensitivity and of technical capabilities for "transparent" inhabitant interactions, i.e., that are appropriated and comprised of the right level of automation and direct interaction [29]. Hence the importance of defining the contexts early on, based on ergonomics activities analysis. [17] and [18] drew on domestic context assessments to establish a set of design and interaction principles for a pervasive power management system, from which operational implementation parameters were deduced. Objectives of energy efficiency, as well as comfort and security, were integrated into these principles, while responding to the inhabitant's interaction needs.

We completed this approach by looking at the actors' actual evolution, along with the mechanisms behind their emerging energy concerns and reduction commitments.

2.2 Designing Reflective Systems and Resources for Energy Commitment

The goal of developing interactive systems (for monitoring use of energy, providing advice, and carrying out diagnostics) is to make energy consumption and the impact of domestic activities visible to the users. Energy data visibility in this case can be an effective trigger for self-reflection. Information here is not seen as an external reality that would be enough on its own, however, to effect activity changes. Rather it is viewed as a means for disrupting actors (in the sense of 'in-formation,' or 'forming from within,' as developed by [37] that could lead to structural reorganizations and to the constituting of a knowledge and experience base capable of modifying the actor's commitments. We approach these questions from the angle of how to develop activities, rather than restrict them. Three main areas of inquiry emerge from this avenue of research.

Designing Useful and Usable Energy Consumption Information Systems. An earlier ergonomic evaluation of existing systems [12] showed a demand for energy-consumption information systems ("consumption feedback" or "eco-feedback"), and especially real-time energy use. However, the various systems tested were all deemed inadequate in terms of usability, and none fully satisfied the users' needs or their requirements of simplicity. Moreover, the systems' inability to provide new information led to a drop in user involvement [19, 30]. We therefore insist on the need to adapt to the user's evolution (skills and knowledge acquired, various uses, new concerns) and needs (to take action, to modify activities…), to ensure a long-term energy saving commitment [13]. These changes need to be integrated early on in the design of information systems and complementary resources. To encourage the commitment to and/or undertaking of energy management practices, it is therefore necessary to study how information systems are appropriated in relation to the disruptions they generate and the need for complementary supports.

Monitoring System Appropriation Seen Through the Lens of Domestic Activities and Their Impact on Energy Use. To analyze the real-life experience of users, we set up an observatory dedicated to the study of how eco-feedback technologies are appropriated over time and to the new practices that emerge from their appropriation. Indeed, the nature of the project entailed making changes both to the duration of our case studies and to the methodology we employed [13, 14].

The findings of the study illustrate the relevance of studying system appropriation within the context of real-life user experience (energy problems to resolve, types of existing management actions, etc.). By taking a longitudinal approach, we were able to describe the various appropriation phases, from the initial discovery of how a household functions in terms of changing energy uses to the gradual increase of user proficiency and user awareness regarding the impact of their actions [11]. However, appropriation is not systematic, and the evolution of behaviors is subject to conditions, such as family contingencies, financial concerns, digital proficiency, prior energy knowledge, available time, and even emotional response to utilization [26].

Providing the Necessary Resources for the Development of Sustainable Situations. Users will abandon monitoring supports if the features do not allow them to respond to changing concerns, or if other systems cannot take over to assist them when necessary (other energy monitoring or control systems, for example). More generally, however, securing their commitment requires a complementary sociotechnical offer to meet needs for personalized support, interaction capabilities, and technical and financial assistance [14]. The service must in fact be approached as part of a much broader support system for fostering commitment through multiple resources, both digital and human, of which domestic energy management is just one aspect. It is therefore possible to lower energy consumption through actor development but on the condition that real-life experience be taken into account, with the aim of providing home occupants with appropriable relevant additional resources for decision-making, learning and action.

Therefore, thinking about energy use through the lens of sustainable situation design means (re)thinking the myriad components of which situations are comprised, including individual (knowledge, feelings, etc.), interindividual and collective, along with specific situations, backgrounds, and environments.

3   Conclusion: What Ergonomics Can Contribute to Sustainable Development

From the authors' perspective as French-speaking ergonomists concerned with situated activity, energy use management is approached here as the result of structural changes across multiple systems (human, technological) emerging from their recurring interactions. By intervening (through design) on technical systems and human-system interactions, it is possible to create new situations that are both energy efficient and that provide resources to users. It is not a question of taking an approach that is exclusively pro-nature [33], or merely sustainable, in the sense of "bearable." By looking at these questions from the perspective of how to facilitate human activities, it is therefore a matter of placing evolving human needs and situations and environmental resource management on an equal footing. Transformation we believe involves conditions that are both structural (modification of structure) and time-based (process). A sustainable situation can therefore not be equated with a state of stability. In keeping with the work of [34], we contend that sustainability cannot be bound by time or space. By focusing on actors in real-life situations, we are able to relate an intrinsic, situated point of view to the extrinsic perspective of the actor's environmental footprint (quantitatively estimated). As [5] point out, sustainability is context- and situation-sensitive, in terms of both outside criteria regarding sustainability (of designers, lawmakers, etc.) and real-life domestic experience. Thus, we consider the notion as both a criterion for transformation (how to achieve a sustainable situation) and an actual process (the situation taking place in an ever-shifting social, temporal and physical space). This raises the question of how sustainability (as an empirically studied process) can be dissociated from its technological embodiment as expressed by durability (as a design criterion, what appropriability is to appropriation, [21, 35]).

As such, addressing issues of "sustainable development" in ergonomics requires empirical research programs based on lengthier studies and the development of a new set of design criteria [14].

To meet the defined goals of sustainable development – ensuring environmental protection, advancing social equity, and fostering economic growth – we need to consider ongoing human development in response to the emerging human needs and ever-changing situations that result from the human-environment coupling [28, 35].

Acknowledgements. This work was conducted within the EDF Research and Development program and was made possible thanks to the many invaluable contributions of the authors of the cited works, to whom we would like to extend our sincere thanks and appreciation.

References

1. Arroyo, E., Bonanni, L., Selker, T.: Waterbot: exploring feedback and persuasive techniques at the sink. In: Proceedings of the SIGCHI Conference on Human Factors in Computing Systems, ACM DL, pp. 631–639 (2005)
2. Barr, S., Gilg, A., Ford, N.: The household energy gap: examining the divide between habitual- and purchase-related conservation behaviours. Energy Policy **33**, 1425–1444 (2005)
3. Brundtland, G.H.: The World Commission on Environment and Development. New York, Oxford University Press, Our Common Future. Oxford (1987)
4. Brown, C.: Eco-ergonomics. In: Proceedings of the New Zealand Ergonomics Society Conference. Waiheke Island (2007)
5. Dekker, S.W.A., Hancock, P.A., Wilkin, P.: Ergonomics and sustainability: towards an embrace of complexity and emergence. Ergonomics **56**(3), 357–364 (2013)
6. Dey, A., Abowd, G.: Towards a better understanding of context and context-awareness. Technical Report GIT-GVU-99–22, Georgia Institute of Technology, Atlanta, USA (1999)
7. Dominici, M., Fréjus, M., Guibourdenche, J., Pietropaoli, B., Weis, F.: Towards a system architecture for recognizing domestic activity by leveraging a naturalistic human activity model. In: Proceedings of the International Conference on Automated Planning and Scheduling. Freiburg, Germany (2011)
8. Fréjus, M.: Les questions de société comme nouveau territoire pour l'ergonomie : apports aux problématiques environnementales et à la conception de services associés. In : Proceedings of the 42d SELF congress. Toulouse: Octarès Editions (2007)
9. Fréjus, M.: La maîtrise de l'énergie vue comme la conception d'une situation durable (appropriée et efficace): apports de l'analyse ergonomique des activités domestiques. In: Les pratiques sociales et usages de l'énergie, Garabuau-Moussaoui, I., Pierre, M. (eds.). Lavoisier Tec&Doc. (2016)

10. Fréjus, M.: Expansion and renewal of the issues dealt with by ergonomics in the field of sustainable development: A 12-years review of researches on household activities and energy consumption management. Psychologie Française, 64(2) (2019)
11. Frejus, M., Cahour, B.: Reflection processes in energy regulation situations assisted with reflective tools. In: MobileHCI 2015: 17th International Conference on Human-Computer Interaction with Mobile Devices and Services Adjunct Proceedings. Copenhagen (2015)
12. Fréjus, M., Guibourdenche, J.: Analysing domestic activity to reduce household energy consumption. Work **41**, 539–548 (2012)
13. Fréjus, M., Martini, D.: Taking into Account User Appropriation and Development to Design Energy Consumption Feedback. In: CHI 2015 Extended Abstracts, 18–23 April, Seoul, Republic of Korea (2015)
14. Fréjus, M., Martini, D.: Why energy consumption feedback is not (only) a display issue. HCI International 2016, Toronto, 17–22 July (2016)
15. Fréjus, M., Dominici, M., Weis, F., Poizat, G., Guibourdenche, J., Pietropaoli, B.: Changing interactions to reduce energy consumption: specification of a context-aware system centered on the home occupants' concerns. In: Stephanidis, C. (ed.), HCI International 2013. Berlin: Springer (2013)
16. Garcia-Acosta, G., Saravia, M.H., Riba, C.: Ergoecology: evolution and challenges. Work **41**(Suppl. 1), 2133–2140 (2012)
17. Guibourdenche, J.: Préoccupations et agencements dans les contextes d'activité domestique. Contribution à la conception de situations informatiques diffuses, appropriables et énergétiquement efficaces (PhD thesis). University of Lyon, France (2013)
18. Guibourdenche, J., Vacherand-Revel, J., Fréjus, M., Haradji, Y.: Analysis of domestic activity contexts for the design of ubiquitous energy-efficient systems. Activités **12**(1), 46–69 (2015)
19. Hargreaves, T., Nye, M., Burgess, J.: Keeping energy visible: exploring how householders interact with feedback from smart energy monitors in the longer term. Energy Policy **52**, 126–134 (2013)
20. Harris, C., Cahill, V.: Exploiting user behaviour for context-aware power management. In: International Conference on Wireless and Mobile Computing, Networking and Communications, pp. 122–130. IEEE Computer Society Press, Los Alamitos (2005)
21. Haué, J.-B.: Étude de l'activité du quotidien de gestion d'énergie dans une finalité de conception. Journées Act'ing 2003, Quiberon, France (2003)
22. Helander, M.G.: Forty years of IEA: some reflections on the evolution of ergonomics. Ergonomics **40**(10), 952–961 (1997)
23. Lahoual, D., Fréjus, M.: Sustainability at Home: Monitoring Needs and Energy Management Actions of Solar Power Producers (2013). INTERACT 2013 Conference, Cape Town, South Africa, 2–6 September (2013)
24. Maturana, H.R., Varela, F.J.: The tree of Knowledge: a new look at the biological roots of human understanding. Shambhala/New Science Library, Boston (1987)
25. Moray, N.: Ergonomics and the global problems of the twenty-first century. Ergonomics **38**(8), 1691–1707 (1995)
26. Plancoulaine, A., Cahour, B., Fréjus, M., Licoppe, C.: Analyzing eco-feedback appropriation in a smart-home context. In: European Conference in Cognitive Ergonomics, Notthingam (2016)
27. Poizat, G., Fréjus, M., Haradji, Y.: Analysis of collective activity in domestic settings for the design of Ubiquitous Technologies. In: Proceeding of the European Conference on Cognitive Ergonomics. Otaniemi, Finland (2009)
28. Rabardel, P., Pastré, P.: Modèles du sujet pour la conception. Dialectique, activités, développement. Toulouse: Octarès (2005)

29. Salembier, P., Dugdale, J., Fréjus, M., Haradji, Y.: A descriptive model of contextual activities for the design of domestic situations. In: Proceeding of the European Conference on Cognitive Ergonomics. Otaniemi, Finland (2009)
30. Snow, S., Buys, L., Roe, P., Brereton, M.: Curiosity to cupboard: self-reported disengagement with energy use feedback over time. 25th OzCHI 2013 (2013)
31. Stern, P.C.: What psychology knows about energy conservation. Am. Psychol. **47**(10), 1224–1232 (1992)
32. Strengers, T.: Smart metering demand management programs: challenging the comfort and cleanliness habitus of households. In: Proceedings of the 20th OZ'CHI, Australia (2008)
33. Thatcher, A.: Green ergonomics: definition and scope. Ergonomics **56**, 389–398 (2013)
34. Thatcher, A., Yeow, H.P.: A sustainable system of systems approach: a new HFE paradigm. Ergonomics **59**, 167–178 (2016)
35. Theureau, J.: Course-of-action analysis and course-of-action-centered design. In: Cognitive Task Design, E. Hollnagel, ed, Erlbaum, London, pp. 55–81 (2003)
36. Tolmie, P., Pycock, J., Diggins, T., Maclean, A., Karsenty, A.: Unremarkable computing, Proceedings of CHI 2002, pp. 399–406. ACM Press, Minneapolis (2002)
37. Varela, F.J.: Principles of Biological Autonomy. Elsevier/North-Holland, New York (1979)
38. Wood, G., Newborough, M.: Energy-use information transfer for Intelligent Homes. Energy Build. **39**, 495–503 (2007)
39. Zink, K.J.: Designing sustainable work systems: the need for a systems approach. iFirst Appl. Ergon. **45** (1), 126–132 (2013)
40. Zink, K.J., Fischer, K.: Do we need sustainability as a new approach in human factors and ergonomics? Ergonomics **56**(3), 348–356 (2013)

Weaving the Net: Integrating Ergonomics and Sustainability in a Web-Based Co-creation Platform

Lia Buarque de Macedo Guimarães(✉) 📧

CNPq/ Universidade Federal do Rio Grande do Sul, Porto Alegre, Brazil
lia.buarque@pq.cnpq.br

Abstract. This article presents a platform for gathering information, producing and disseminating knowledge (co-production) on how ergonomics and sustainability interact, and for promoting experience exchange and collaboration among people from academy, company, government and society, interested in the topics and in contributing to solutions (co-design) for sociotechnical/environmental problems. The platform uses social media for public co-production and has a restricted forum space (with a virtual conference room and drawing tools) for co-design by registered participants. The platform is under continuous improvement and is being tested by the ABERGO Macroergonomics Technical Committee.

Keywords: Ergonomics · Macroergonomics · Sustainability · Co-creation platform · Knowledge production · Project development · Co-design

1 Introduction

Since its beginning with the Norwegian Iron and Metal Workers Union in the 1970s, [1], participatory ergonomics (PE) is the most widely used methodology in macroergonomic analysis and organizational design interventions and unique to the field of ergonomics [2]. PE implies that employees are valuable resources for problem solving and for the design, development, and implementation of technology to enhance organizational effectiveness, improve product quality, and the overall quality of work life [3]. Its application tends to result in greater feelings of solution "ownership" among those involved and affected, in increased job satisfaction and commitment to the changes being implemented [4]. Successful implementation of PE requires the empowerment of people to make decisions and to implement and evaluate them [5].

In the design field, user involvement in a project might have different denominations depending on project focus but the two best known are user centered design (UCD) and participatory design (PD). UCD focuses on usability and design is developed for potential users, who are informers and subjects of study [6]. Users are passively involved in the design process to "do" and "say" something in interviews only when designers and developers, who lead the process, analyze data and make design decisions, need their input. Observation reveals what people "do" and how they use products or services, and listening to what they say only return what designers want to hear. The user is not really a part of the design team [7]. In PD (as in PE) design is developed with users who "do" and "say" something, but also contribute with discussions and suggestions, taking part in the design process as collaborative partners [8].

Some authors (e.g. [6, 8]) consider that PD methods in which users are "expert actors" interviewed and observed by designers have limitations, since observing what exists cannot tell much about what could be; it cannot tell what human creativity and technological innovation could create [6]. The goals should expand from simply designing products for users, and move into focusing on people's purposes, i.e., future experiences of people, communities and cultures, which are now connected and informed [8]. It is necessary to use new "make" tools focusing on what people make, what they create while expressing their thoughts, feelings and dreams while jointly exploring and articulating their latent needs, exploring and "making" relevant solutions i.e., simultaneously useful, usable and desirable [7] Therefore, designer's role in PD should shift from "designer as a translator" to "designer as a facilitator" and a mediator in the design process where the end users (experts of their experiences) design together [7] i.e. they are co-designers during the entire process, exploring open questions in a critical and innovative way [6, 8]. People want to express themselves and to participate proactively and directly in the design process, and they realized that via networking they have an enormous amount of collective influence [7].

Advances in software technology and digital platforms have made it possible to virtually produce/disseminate knowledge (Wikipedia, Yahoo), sell products (Amazon, eBay, Alibaba), provide services (Uber, AirBnB) and engage people via hubs (Sustainability Science Hub, Desis Network, LeNS Labs), media sharing (Youtube, Spotify, Vimeo) and social platforms. The early 2000s boom of social platforms such as Friendster (in 2002), LinkedIn and MySpace (in 2003), Youtube (in 2005), Reddit (in 2005), Facebook (in 2006), Twitter (in 2006), Instagram (in 2010), Snapchat (in 2011) and TikTok (in 2016) became a means of communication for many people, allowing for the participation and interaction of users, who create, read, watch share, comment, like and rate content. Users and communities can more easily be involved in virtual collaborative, co-creative approaches to innovation, knowledge production and design.

Open source co-innovation platforms, exemplified by the Linux operating system, MySpace, Youtube and Wikipedia services enable creation by the users for the users. These are community-based, collaborative, non-competitive open space services for sharing and joint production, "where the value of openness is enhanced with every user as they directly contribute ideas and content to improve the variety and quality of the product" [9]. For [10], the motivation for collaboration on open innovation might be intrinsic (commitment, trust, desire to be involved in something that makes sense, that is important and interesting) or extrinsic (external compensation or rewards), and depends on the phases of the innovation process. The foresight (ideation) phase in the front end is more social, and more related to intrinsic motivations, creativity (generation of new ideas or concepts and new associations between existing ideas or concepts) is mostly driven by a combination of intrinsic and extrinsic motivations, while design is more concrete, using more extrinsic motivations.

Quirky.com is a user-driven open innovation platform, encouraging open design discussion among the crowd to produce a solution, allowing for collaborative participation and reward. Unlike typical crowdsourcing platforms, where only one person is rewarded for a chosen idea, the platform's algorithm weighs people's influences in any idea, and they are rewarded for their percentage of influence besides having their names stamped on the product's packaging. In most crowdsourcing innovation platforms, contributors, who are unknown to each other, do not typically collaborate on solutions, as they compete for a prize amount provided by companies for the best solutions to a problem. Therefore, companies have significant control over the creative process [9] while gathering feedback and suggestions of ideas for new products and services. Examples are IdeaConnection.com, Innocentive.com and eYeka.com and the platforms owed by companies such as Dell (Ideastorm), GE (Ecoimagination), Lego LegoIdeas) Nike, Nokia (InventWithNokia.nokia.com) and Starbucks.

OpenIdeo.com is a crowdsourcing platform for creating solutions for social issues. Sponsors set the project brief (for example, "a future where food is never wasted") and people worldwide come together to build on each other's ideas guided by experts. Innonatives.com uses crowdsourcing, crowd voting and crowdfunding to create radical innovation and design for sustainability (environment, sociocultural, economic).

Some platforms promote a combination of competition and cooperation among companies such as the coopetition platform for sustainable supply chains [11]. The aim of other non-competitive platforms is the collaborative production of knowledge (co-production). The platforms co-created by researchers of the Wageningen Centre of Sustainability Governance [12] enable the monitoring of environmental conditions, nature conservation, the tracing of sustainable products and services, peer-to-peer exchange of renewable energy, transparency and traceability in global value chains.

When the focus of co-creation is to gather people to conceptually develop and create things, the usually adopted term is co-design a "collective creativity as it is applied across the whole span of a design process" [8]. "The three premises of co-design are: democratization of society and democratization of knowledge, a source of new knowledge that can be turned into a meaningful and useful solution, and a practice that creates more meaningful and relevant futures for people that are engaged in the process, contributing to their social, economic and environmental sustainability and resilience" [13]. In this sense, the emphasis is on the initial phase, or ideation, in the front end of the design process, which is 'fuzzy' since it is often not known whether the answer to the question will be a product, a service, a process, an interface, a building [8]. U_CODE is a European Commission co-design platform for enabling the creative participation of citizens in urban planning through communication and collaboration between very large numbers of citizen and professional experts to ensure "higher public acceptance and understanding of complex urban planning projects, which otherwise are often subject to controversial debate" [14].

This article presents a co-creation platform for co-production and dissemination of knowledge on ergonomics and sustainability, and for co-design of sociotechnical/environmentally sustainable solutions for Brazil's most important challenges. The objectives were threefold: 1) to raise awareness of the importance of sustainability issues and how ergonomics can contribute to sustainable work systems, products and services; 2) to gather people with different backgrounds, expertise and from different areas of activity, representative of the quadruple helix, in collaborative knowledge production; 3) to involve them in discussions on how ergonomics and sustainability work together in order to explore open critical questions and opportunities for co-design and implementation of sustainable sociotechnical/environmental solutions.

2 Why an Ergonomics/sustainability Co-creation Platform

The reasons for building the platform were threefold: concentration of Brazilian research on diagnosis of microergonomic problems of specific companies with few proposals of solutions; little understanding of how ergonomics may contribute to solutions for socioetechnical/environmental problems; lack of interdisciplinary studies and collaboration among researchers.

A study [15] on the Brazilian ergonomics research showed that of the 1471 thesis and dissertations from 2007 to 2017, most of them (38.9%) end up in a diagnosis, while only 7.6% present a full ergonomics study, with proposals and validation of solutions either for improving physical products (53.6%) or processes (18.7%). The same research did not find any study stressing either social or environmental goals, although sustainability should be a concern for ergonomists (e.g. [16, 17]. These results were presented at Brazilian Ergonomics, Design and Engineering meetings aiming at highlighting the need for bridging the gap between sustainability and ergonomics, the importance of considering ergonomics as systemic and design driven, and that to reach sustainable systems, a joined effort of research groups working in an interdisciplinary way is necessary [18]. However, it had no echo maybe due to lack of interest, willingness, time and financial resources to promote the engagement.

The 20-year experience of the PPGEP/UFRGS Ergonomics Lab showed that it is easier for the interdisciplinary team (composed of architects, designers, engineers and healthcare professionals) to use a PE tool (MD) [19] for macroergonomic work analysis (MA) [20] in a company setting than using a macroergonomic method (SD) [21] for designing innovative solutions for basic needs of Brazilian society. A three-year participatory project aimed at addressing sociotechnical/environmental issues proved to be difficult to engage the participants with different backgrounds (architecture, chemistry, design, engineering, health) and level of expertise, maybe because the problems were "fuzzy" (i.e., not so straightforward as it use to be in the companies) demanding more creative effort in the front end (ideation phase) of the design process. With the closing of the Lab at the end of 2013, and considering that nowadays people can easily be involved in collaborative projects through the internet, its sociotechnical/environmental goals were transposed to a virtual space, an online platform named "ecoinnovate4sustain.com", presented in the following sections.

3 Method

Using the Wix cloud-based development platform, the ecoiinovate4sustain.com was designed by a designer/ergonomist and two engineers (electrical and industrial) to be an online space open to anyone interested in how ergonomics and sustainability interact, enabling knowledge and experience exchange, sociotechnical/environmental project development and network building by virtually engaging people from the quadruple helix (academy, companies, government, society) anywhere, anytime.

Prior to designing the platform, a literature review on ergonomics/macroergonomics and sustainability was carried out in order to build a reference text for the platform. Using the Internet, a search for cases on ergonomics/sustainability (mainly the ones dealing with residuals) was performed in broadcasted news, general TV programs, video interviews, talks etc. All links were copied and public/free information was recorded for later use on the platform.

The first version of the platform had three pages: 1) (who are we?) introducing the platform, its goals (co-production of content/knowledge and co-design of solutions) and the people responsible for the platform; 2) (how it works?) explaining the functioning of the platform, how to register and access the debate forum; 3) a page with the reference text on ergonomics and sustainability with links for the selected cases.

This version was pre-tested in October 2019, during the Sustainability Hackathon, a 50-h event hosted by SEEDS/PUCPR, where undergraduate students had to propose innovative sustainable/macroergonomic solutions using residuals [22]. The platform was used to gather and share information among participants, teachers and the organization team, and for keeping track of participants' progress as they have to deliver the results of each step of the project development process through the platform.

Based on data from spontaneous interviews with participants and direct observation of the hackathon dynamics, the platform was improved and introduced at the ABERGO Congress, on November 2020, to be used as an interaction/collaboration network, information/experience sharing and co-production/co-design tool by the participants of the ABERGO Macroergonomics Technical Committee (AMTC).

4 Results

The hackathon participants used the platform for in-group interaction/socialization, communication and information sharing, for exploring the cases for inspiration, and did not report having difficulties in using the platform. However, it was expected that they use it for more intense interaction with teachers and mentors that attended the hackathon, and even with other non-participant students, with different backgrounds, that could contribute to the project. Possible reasons for this behavior are the lack of familiarity with co-design, and also the fear of exposing their projects, since they were in a competition. Another finding is that participants did not use the reference text on ergonomics, sustainability and their interaction, in the third page, accessing directly the links to the cases. Possible reasons are they did not like reading long text (unlike the reference text, the cases have a very short text and many pictures and videos) or they did not want to spend time reading as they were under time pressure. Therefore, the platform should be tested in a non-competitive environment.

These results led to the following improvements of the platform: the third page was splited into two, one describing the development of ergonomics/macroergonomics and its importance for sustainability, and the other on the evolution of sustainability and how ergonomics can contribute to it; each page has links to each other and videos, pictures, graphics and links for academic papers. A fifth page hosts a bibliographic repository, a smart table which was added to a public Google spreadsheet, allowing for searching by title, author, year, and type of publication. Anyone can contribute to this repository by inserting new references on a Google form linked to the spreadsheet.

Social media (Facebook, Instagram, Twitter, Youtube) was introduced as the means for communication/interaction with the public, and is linked to the Forum space. Anyone can collaborate to knowledge production/dissemination, but only registered members (membership registration is needed for keeping track of the participant's profile and enable statistics) can access the Forum, which is formed from two parts:

1) the Contribution part, which combines contribution from both social media and Forum. Via social media (open access), anyone can participate on posts, chats, questionnaires, polls, share and publish documents, presentations, photographs, videos, and reference texts and cases to improve the platform and therefore become co-producers of content. Registered members may access the Forum (restricted access) and participate in the design process contributing their own briefings and design ideas and/or commenting on others, therefore becoming co-designers. When a registered member presents an idea briefing, it is discussed among the group (co-briefing) in order to prepare for the next project's stages of ideation, creativity, design and implementation, in a collaborative way (co-design). Co-briefing and co-design are done through private contact via social media and Forum space, or the virtual conference room, using its tools (chat, voice, video, screen sharing) and the drawing 'whiteboard' which has an annotate tool that allows participants to draw their ideas and build on others, simultaneously, therefore they form a blend of co-design innovation.

2) the Organization part, where all relevant contributions from both social media and Forum interaction are organized to allow for tracking the evolution of co-production and co-design. Organized co-production data allows for finding the most popular topics, the participants' profile, type and level of engagement as well as selecting important contents to enrich the platform. Results of co-production are made available to all via social media. Zoom meetings can be recorded and each step of the annotated presentations and whiteboard drawings can be saved as PNG or PDF. Results of the co-design process enter the Forum gallery so that registered participants can see and comment on the progress of the projects, anywhere, anytime.

Twelve people with different backgrounds (administrators, architects, designers, engineers, physiotherapists) have registered for the AMTC, and eight participated in the first meeting (December 2020), when AMCT goals and the functioning of the ecoiinovate4sustain.com platform were discussed. Twelve people participated in the second meeting (January 2021), when a proposed method for co-design was discussed. Five participants presented (through storytelling) various projects, opportunities, and ideas for: inclusion of older people and people with disabilities in society, improving children's safety and health, improving work in recycling cooperatives, and designing innovative business, service or industrial models for personnel qualification and job creation in small towns with no employment opportunity. They will be co-briefed in the next meetings for further analysis, prioritization, identification and engagement of stakeholders, and preparation for co-design.

5 Conclusion

This article presented a co-creation platform aiming at gathering people interested in discussing how ergonomics meets sustainability (and vice versa), to produce and disseminate knowledge, and to foresee opportunities, challenges and design solutions for sociotechnical/environmental problems. It hosts two integrated networks, the Ergonomics and the Sustainability one, each of them with relevant information about their research evolution, practical cases, and possible projects. The platform is under continuous improvement, depending on the contribution of people from the quadruple helix, who therefore become co-producers. Registered participants can contribute to project development, being co-designers of solutions for improving society's well being. The ABERGO Macroergonomics Technical Committee is using and testing the platform. Up to twelve ergonomists participated in the two meetings held so far, motivated by the innovative character of the project and the opportunity to contribute to the production/dissemination of knowledge, and to design solutions to critical national challenges. It is a start and it is expected that more people, from around the world, will join the platform when its English version be available in the near future.

It is worth noting that attention was paid to the sustainability of the platform: videos and documents were uploaded to a space in the cloud in order to make the platform lighter, therefore lowering energy consumption. Ryman Eco was the font used in all texts because it uses less ink than the standard ones reducing the impact of printing.

Acknowledgements. This research was supported by the Brazilian Conselho Nacional de Desenvolvimento Científico e Tecnológico – CNPq (grants 310536/2015-4 and 307716/2019-8).

References

1. Nygaard, K., Bergo, O.T.: The trade unions - new users of research. Pers. Rev. **4**(2), 5–10 (1975)
2. Brown, O., Jr.: Macroergonomic methods: participation. In: Hendrick, H.W., Kleiner, B. (eds.) Macroergonomics: Theory, Methods, and Applications, pp. 25–44. CRC Press, Boca Raton FL (2002)
3. Brown, O. Jr.: On the relationship between participatory ergonomics, performance and productivity in organisational systems. In: Marras, W., Karwowski, W., Smith, J., Pacholski, L. (eds.) Proceedings of the International Ergonomics Association, World Conference on Ergonomics of the Material Handling and Information Processing at Work, pp. 495–498. Taylor & Francis, London (1993)
4. Brown, O., Jr.: Participatory ergonomics. In: Stanton, N., Hedge, A., Brookhuis, K., Salas, E., Hendrick, H. (eds.) Handbook of Human Factors and Ergonomics Methods, vol. 81, pp. 1–7. CRC Press, Boca Raton FL (2005)
5. Imada, A.S.: The rationale and tools of participatory ergonomics. In: Noro, K., Imada, A.S. (eds.) Participatory Ergonomics, pp. 30–49. Taylor & Francis, London (1991)
6. Tosi, F.: Co-design and Innovation: tools, methods and opportunities for the generation of innovation through user involvement. In: Tosi, F. (ed.) Design for Ergonomics, vol. 8, pp. 143–159. Springer, Springer Series in Design and Innovation (2020)
7. Sanders, E.B.N.: From user-centered to participatory design approaches. In: Frascara, J. (ed.) Design and the Social Sciences, pp. 1–7. Taylor & Francis Books Limited (2002)

8. Sanders, E.B.N., Stappers, P.J.: Co-creation and the new landscapes of design. CoDesign **4**(1), 5–18 (2008)

9. Edwards, M., Logue, D., Schweitzer, J.: Towards an understanding of open innovation in services: beyond the firm and towards relational co-creation. In: Agarwal, R., Selen, W., Roos, G., Green, R. (eds.) The Handbook of Service Innovation, Chapter: 4, pp. 75–90. Springer, London (2015)

10. Battistella, C., Nonino, F.: Open innovation web-based platforms: The impact of different forms of motivation on collaboration. Innov. Manage. Policy Pract. **14**(4), 557–575 (2012).

11. Chen, Y.S.: An interactive platform for sustainable supply chains. Int. J. Interact. Commun. Syst. Technol. **8**(2), 56–73 (2018)

12. Wageningen Centre of Sustainability Governance (WCSG) Homepage. https://www.wur.nl/en/project/Incubator-project-Co-production-and-digital-platforms-for-sustainability-govern ance.htm. Accessed 15 Jan 2021

13. Zamenopoulos, T., Alexiou, K.: Co-Design as Collaborative Research. In: Facer, K, Dunleavy, K. (eds.) Connected Communities Foundation Series. Bristol: University of Bristol/ AHRC Connected Communities Programme (2018)

14. European Commission (EC): Urban Collective Design Environment: A new tool for enabling expert planners to co-create and communicate with citizens in urban design. https://cordis.europa.eu/article/id/413196-collaborative-urban-design-unites-architects-and-communities-in-creating-better-cities. Accessed 23 Jan 2021

15. Guimarães, L.B.M., Ribeiro, J.L., Bittencourt, R.S., Iida, I.: Investigation of the Brazilian academic production in Ergonomics, from 1987 to 2017. Production 29 e20190004 (2019)

16. Haslam, R., Waterson, P.: Ergonomics and sustainability. Ergonomics **56**(3), 343–347 (2013)

17. Lange-Morales, A., Thatcher, A., García-Acosta, G.: Towards a sustainable world through human factors and ergonomics: it is all about values. Ergonomics **57**(11), 1603–1615 (2014)

18. Guimarães, L.B.M.: An overview and some reflections on the ergonomics research in Brasil. Diálogo com a Economia Criativa 3(7), 50–65 (2018)

19. Guimarães, L.B.M., Fogliatto, F.S.: Macroergonomic design: a new methodology for ergonomic product design. In: Proceedings of the XIVth Triennial Congress of the International Ergonomics Association, vol. 2, pp. 328–328, IEA, San Diego (2000)

20. Guimarães, L.B.M.: Macroergonomic work analysis (MA). In: Guimarães, L.B. de M. (org.) Macroergonomics: concepts FEENG, Porto Alegre (2010)

21. Guimarães, L.B.M.: Sociotechnical design for a sustainable world. Theor. Issues Ergon. Sci. **13**(2), 240–269 (2012)

22. Guimarães, L.B.M., Bitencourt, R.S., Chrusciak, C.B., Derenevich, M.G., Poncini, C.R., Okumura, M.L.M., Canciglieri Jr., O.: Sustainability Hackathon: integrating academia and companies for finding solutions for socioenvironmental problems. In: Leal Filho, W., Tortato, U., Frankenberger, F. (eds.) Integrating Social Responsibility and Sustainable Development, World Sustainability Series. Springer International Publishing (2021)

Emerging Ergonomic Associations: Achievements, Obstacles, and Lessons Learned

Bouhafs Mebarki[1](✉) ⓘ, Rosemary R. Seva[2] ⓘ, Mohammed Mokdad[3] ⓘ, Serpil Aytac[4] ⓘ, and Ng Yee Guan[5] ⓘ

[1] Laboratory of Ergonomics, University of Oran 2, Oran, Algeria
mebarki.bouhafs@univ-oran2.dz
[2] Gokongwei College of Engineering, De La Salle University, Manila, Philippines
rosemary.seva@dlsu.edu.ph
[3] College of Arts, University of Bahrain, Zallaq, Bahrain
mmokdad@uob.edu.bh
[4] Labour Economics and Industrial Relations Department, Faculty of Economics and Administrative Sciences, Uludag University, Bursa, Turkey
saytac@uludag.edu.tr
[5] Department of Environmental and Occupational Health Faculty of Medicine and Health Sciences, Universiti Putra, Putra, Malaysia
shah86zam@gmail.com

Abstract. Self-evaluation and self-critics is a rare exercise, among the members or executive committees of academic and professional associations. Human factors and ergonomics associations throughout their seven decades of existence have rarely been evaluated. The aim of the present research is to highlight what objectives were achieved, what are the obstacles to attain the outlined objectives of the HF/E associations of the study sample, and what lessons can be learned throughout the existence of each society?

To answer these questions, five responsible/representatives of four (4) HF/E associations participated in the discussion panel. Their answers to the three questions on: achievements, obstacles and lessons learned were stratified into categories of (1) achievements: seven goals have been achieved, (2) eight obstacles are facing HF/E societies to achieve their missions, and (3) twelve lessons are learned during life time of HF/E society from its inception to today.

These results are discussed taking into account the context of each HF/E society, while having a critical eye when adopting experiences of other HF/E societies. Some of these are of great value, others cannot be applied locally. A particular emphasize steamed from the discussion among members of the panel is the implementation of workable strategies for short, medium and long terms to promote ergonomics at all levels.

Keywords: Emerging ergonomic associations · Achievements · Obstacles · Learned lessons

1 Introduction

Ergonomics societies are the guards of the temple of human factors and ergonomics discipline and profession. From its inception more than seventy years ago, these associations have not been subject to evaluation, except for rare history narrating cases [1, 2]. Evaluation actions are necessary operations for sustainability and efficacy of any scientific and professional organizations, to see to what extent the goals for which they were established have been achieved, to have a feedback to strengthen the positive practices, to correct errors that occur along the way, and benefit from experience of the well-established societies in the field of HFE, or that of the international ergonomics association (IEA) [3].

The 21st triennial Congress of the IEA seems to be the appropriate opportunity to raise these questions and discuss its different facets among HF/E specialists in a panel of ergonomists representing a sample of HF/E societies, and wishing to get feedback from interested colleagues in the congress, in the perspective of creating networks at regional or global levels, to exchange best practices, to organize common activities like, joint conferences, workshops, training courses, and so forth.

The aim of the present research is to shade light on three aspects of a sample of HF/E societies, namely: their achievements, the challenges facing them, and the lessons learned during the course of their existence.

Participating associations will be evaluated in terms of what they have been able to accomplish, the obstacles that may prevent achievement, and the lessons learned from work during the past years.

Accordingly, the following questions are asked:

1. What are the achievements of the ergonomic associations recently formed (the past twenty years) in developing countries?
2. What are the obstacles to carrying out their normal activity?
3. What are the lessons learned from these years on the job?

2 Methodology

Data related to the research methodology were collected from the participants in this panel (heads of some ergonomic associations or their representatives). The data included the method used in the research, research samples, and data collection tools. Each of the participants presented his/her report, in which he/she highlighted the elements of the aforementioned methodology. After that, these elements were reviewed in all reports, from which the methodology used in the current panel was derived.

2.1 Sample

Twelve (12) ergonomics societies' representatives have been contacted to participate in discussing points of achievements, obstacles and lessons learned during their course of existence as national ergonomics bodies which are concerned with the promotion of HF/E in their local or regional areas. Only five (5) persons representing four (4) ergonomics societies were willing to participate and have finished the different stages of the study, and ended up by constituting a discussion panel to debate the above mentioned three issues (See Appendix A). The rest eight (8) ergonomics societies' representatives, either they were not willing to participate in the panel or in the 21st IEA congress due to COVID-19 pandemic, or they just did not answer at all.

2.2 Data Collection Tool

A questionnaire investigating the three research variables of the study (achievements, challenges and lessons learned) was elaborated from the answers assigned to each variable. The process ended up with a twenty seven (27) statements' questionnaire, covering the three variables of this study as follows:

– Seven (7) statements describing the achievements of HF/E societies.
– Eight (8) statements describing the obstacles facing HF/E societies to achieve their missions, objectives and strategic plans and honor their commitments according to their creation status.
– Twelve (12) statements describing the lessons learned during life time of HF/E society from its inception to today.

3 Results

Analysis of the answers of each statement of the questionnaire showed that:

3.1 What Are the Achievements of the Ergonomic Associations Recently Formed (the Past Twenty Years) in Developing Countries?

The members of HF/E societies of the sample agreed on the following achievements of their societies:

1. They organized a number of promotional activities, such as, seminars, webinars, training courses, workshops, conferences, etc.
2. They Built or are in the process of building relationships with stakeholders at national level.
3. They Built or are in the process of building relationships with stakeholders at international level.
4. They are engaged in actions of dissemination of HF/E knowledge & practice among large public (outreach).
5. Their activities are attracting new membership & outreach among specialists
6. Since their formation, they have setup a number HF/E training courses.
7. Since their formation and even before, members of these societies have initiated or participated in a number of HF/E research project, and published a number of scientific research papers.

3.2   What Are the Obstacles to Carrying Out Their Normal Activity?

As for the obstacles facing HF/E societies to achieve their missions, objectives and strategic plans and honor their commitments according to their creation status:

1. Despite the acute need for ergonomists, there are no sufficient ergonomics training programs in universities.
2. A small number of well trained and recognized teaching staff exists in universities and training institutions.
3. The HF/E identity is being absorbed into dominant host disciplines, like engineering, occupational health and safety, or psychology [4].
4. HFE is not known to stakeholders (decision makers, government services, companies, etc.).
5. HFE societies suffer from some environment hurdles, like the level of technological mastery, cultural aspects of development, etc.)
6. HFE societies suffer from the weak commitment of the executive board committees & members of the society.
7. HFE societies suffer from financial aspects which hinder the activities of the society
8. Some societies are over dependent on well-established ergonomic models and practices which are not adapted to local realities.

3.3   What Are the Lessons Learned from These Years on the Job?

The lessons learned during life time of HF/E society from its inception to today:

1. The use of real life problems & cases in teaching ergonomics has a very good impact on the training quality.
2. The application of ergonomics principles in design courses enhanced the understanding of students.
3. To improve curricula, the feedback from alumni seems to be important, provided that their records are kept and updated.
4. The use of software to teach tools of ergonomics research & intervention has improved training and intervention.
5. The use & creation of videos & simulation material on ergonomics for/by students has improved training quality.
6. Use of videos & simulation material on ergonomics to disseminate ergonomics principals & benefits among stakeholders (decision makers, companies, trade unions, workers), seems to have a high impact.
7. The ratio of practical over theoretical aspects of ergonomics has improved training quality.
8. HFE society has to overcome the resistance to ergonomic changes through participative ergonomics intervention.
9. Missions, objectives and strategic plan of ergonomics society are aligned with the national interest and agenda in promoting HFE.
10. Clear distribution/delegation of tasks & missions among executive members of the society is the best way to its efficacy.

11. The executive members of the society are proactively to respond to issues and take lead in areas related to HFE.
12. Practical ergonomics problem are research topics in collaboration with companies at local/national level.

4 Discussion

According to responses of the members of this panel to the questions ergonomics societies have and are still accomplishing a number of goals in the process of ergonomics promotion in their respective countries. Their achievements are promising in the fields of ergonomics training, research and field intervention. Although, their formation dates are quit recent (around two decades), their achievements are encouraging. One of the many noticed achievements was the increasing acknowledgement of the ergonomics society presence through conferences. Establishment of Networks, like the South East Asian Network of Ergonomics Societies, in the case HFEM and HFESP, or at individual levels during different conferences which is a milestone in developing cooperation and thinking for different ways to strengthen relations among individual and collective initiatives.

The consensus among representatives of the HF/E societies of the present research on the different statements of the questionnaire ranged from 60% to 100%. This can be due to the maturity stage of each society, to the degree of technical and economic development and its related environmental factors [5–7].

Although there are some obstacles, as mentioned above, in the way of developing ergonomics, the ergonomic achievements in the fields of teaching, scientific research and practice in economic institutions give rise to hope. However, to develop ergonomics even more, it is necessary to benefit from the lessons mentioned above. We believe that well-known universities have been taking these lessons into consideration. These results are similar to those of Olabode, et al. [6] and Jaafar, et al. [5].

The members of the panel emphasized: (1) the need to strengthen the achievements realized, (2) To overcome the obstacles by implementing workable strategies for short, medium and long term. Some of the hurdles can be overcome throughout a time span, like the training of a sufficient number of qualified ergonomists, dissemination of HF/E principles and practices among stakeholders and the larger public alike, (3) Besides the lessons learned from the short experience of the new emerging HF/E societies, lessons and experiences of the well-established HF/E societies in developed nations are of great value, to cite examples of such societies, the CIEHF [1], and the HFES [2].

5 Conclusions

The organizers of the discussion panel on achievements, obstacles and lessons learned of the new generation of HF/E societies, were keen to gather more representatives of such societies in order to have a larger diversity of experiences, but for the above mentioned reasons this could not be possible. This fact does not hinder in any way the objectives of the present research work.

The authors of this paper are eager to share their experiences with the participants in the 21st triennial Congress of the IEA, in scope of developing their initiative on the periodic evaluation of HF/E societies, during IEA triennial congresses.

Although, the evaluation of the scientific and professional associations is not an easy exercise, as it deals with the efforts of the executive, steering committees and responsibles of the associations, and brings to light their missteps and failures (the forbidden zone), which stems from the human nature itself, besides, the self-evaluation and self-critics are seldom objective. We think that these hurdles can be overcome by the appropriate research methods and tools, and the will to evaluate and change to the better.

Appendix A

See Table 1.

Table 1. Sample members.

No	Member	Position
01	Prof. Mebarki Bouhafs	Algerian Ergonomic Association
02	Prof. Rosemary Seva	Ergonomics Society of Philippines
03	Prof. Mohamed Mokdad	Algerian Ergonomic Association
04	Prof. Serpil Aytac	Turkish Ergonomic Association
05	Dr. Ng, Y. G	Malaysian Ergonomic Association

References

1. Waterson, P., Sell, R.: Recurrent themes and developments in the history of the Ergonomics Society. Ergonomics **49**(8), 743–799 (2006)
2. The human factors and ergonomics society (HFES): Stories from the first 50 years. In: Stuster. J. (ed.). The Human Factors and Ergonomics Society. Santa Monica, CA, USA (2006)
3. Dul, J., Bruder, R., Buckle, P., Carayon, P., Falzon, P., Marras, W.S., Wilson, J.R., van der Doelen, B.: A strategy for human factors/ergonomics: developing the discipline and profession. Ergonomics **55**(4), 377–399 (2012)
4. Oakman, J., Hignett, S., Davis, M., Read, G., Aslanides, M., Mebarki, B., Legg, S.: Tertiary education in ergonomics and human factors: quo vadis? Ergonomics **63**(3), 243–252 (2020)
5. Jaafar, R., Libasin, Z., Razali, W.N.: Knowledge of ergonomics among technical staff in university technology of marapenang Malaysia. J. Eng. Technol. (JET) **10**(2), 220–226 (2019)
6. Olabode, S.O., Adesanya, A.R., Bakare, A.A.: Ergonomics awareness and employee performance: an exploratory study. Econ. Environ. Stud. **17**(44), 813–829 (2017)
7. Tan, L.W.H., Subramaniam, R.: Scientific academies and scientific societies have come of age. Int. J. Technol. Manage. **46**(1–2), 1–8 (2009)

Comparing Two Modalities of Urban Solid Waste Collection: Insights from Activity Analysis and Physiological Measurement

Talita M. Oliveira[1] , Andréa Regina Martins Fontes[1] , Esdras Paravizo[2](✉) ,
Renato Luvizoto Rodrigues de Souza[3] , Daniel Braatz[2] ,
and Márcia R. N. Guimarães[1]

[1] Department of Industrial Engineering, Federal University of São Carlos, Sorocaba, Brazil
afontes@ufscar.br
[2] Department of Industrial Engineering, Federal University of São Carlos, São Carlos, Brazil
[3] Department of Industrial Engineering, Federal University of Triângulo Mineiro,
Uberaba, Brazil

Abstract. The work of urban solid waste collectors requires handling household waste in an ever-changing environment characterized by a high variability level which is highly demanding. This paper compares two modalities of urban solid waste collection (manual and container-based), by applying the ergonomic work analysis and evaluating workers' lactate levels. The methodology employed can be classified as an exploratory and descriptive case study in a medium-sized city in the state of Sao Paulo, Brazil. Qualitative data collection, in this paper, includes semi-structured interviews with waste collectors and direct observation of their work routines and activities. Quantitative data collection measured workers' lactate levels before and after their workday. The analysis of the data comprised both qualitative and quantitative approaches, including coding interviews and statistical analysis. Results identified the core constraints (e.g. work rhythm, load handling, risk of accident and collective work) of the waste collection work and workers' perception of why those were critical determinants for their work. Comparing the work activity analysis for the manual and container-based collection modalities showed that both present physical overloads and that the workers can adapt their activities to both of these processes. The evaluation of workers' lactate levels indicates that the manual work is more strenuous than the container-based one, which is also corroborated by the insight from the ergonomics work analysis. Overall, the complementarity of the qualitative and quantitative approaches to understand and subsidize work transformation enables the consideration of mental, organizational, and physical dimensions of the activity and fosters communication and decision-making among managers and other indicator-oriented stakeholders.

Keywords: Municipal solid waste management · Ergonomics work analysis ·
Lactate levels · Activity-centered ergonomics

N. L. Black et al. (Eds.): IEA 2021, LNNS 220, pp. 544–551, 2021.
https://doi.org/10.1007/978-3-030-74605-6_69

1 Introduction

Urban solid waste management is currently one of the main challenges for cities, especially for those in developing countries. The collection activity is necessary to ensure correct waste treatment and destination, thus decreasing social and environmental impacts of its incorrect destination. Despite its importance, the collection activity still presents a series of physical and mental risks to workers, generally due to the materials variability, places where the collection is done and even the work equipment and processes.

In the Brazilian scenario this situation is also critical. Some authors presented a systematic review of published studies on the Brazilian context and identified twelve studies that addressed occupational risks related to working with solid waste. In these studies, biological, accident, chemical, ergonomic, physical and psychosocial risks were identified [1].

In the international literature, some authors discuss topics related to the collection activity and the impacts on the collectors. These studies corroborate the need to analyze and transform this activity, in order to improve safety and comfort during the execution of the waste collection task.

Regarding the analysis of physical risks, [2] analyzed waste collection in a residential region on the east coast of Malaysia. The study pointed out the prevalence of discomfort in the lumbar region in 54.5% of the workers interviewed in a sample of 44 individuals and showed that during the activity, 42.2% of the workers adopt high risk postures. The authors [3] found that the collection of solid waste can generate work-related musculoskeletal diseases (WMSD). The authors analyzed activities that involved the frequent handling of small containers (approximately 8 kg) and pointed out that this manipulation can mainly affect workers' back and lower limbs.

Regarding the analysis of cognitive risks, [4] point out that the waste collection activity, given the present variability, can be considered as complex work. The authors raised a series of variabilities, among them, the weight of the waste bags, the types of waste, the disposal of waste on the streets, the types of trucks and the weather, to demonstrate that the waste collection worker needs to continuously take decisions in scenarios of instability, unpredictability and uncertainty.

Regarding the organizational risks' analysis, in a study on outsourcing waste collection in a Brazilian city, [5] evidenced the consequent change in the work organization. This modification also appears as a factor that can contribute to the development of occupational diseases, as well as potentiate those that already exist. The authors indicate that, in the outsourced context, changes minimize the possibilities of managing the work itself, reducing the possibility of creating an affective bond with the community where the collection section is carried out (as the sections are modified according to the work organization), in addition to the decrease in the development of working links between the collection groups (the groups are defined and modified according to the work organization).

In this context and with an Activity-Centered Ergonomics approach [6], this paper was carried out from a case study in an urban solid waste collection enterprise located in a medium-sized city in the interior of the state of Sao Paulo, Brazil (about 680.000 inhabitants). The goal is to identify the variabilities and constraints involved in the work routine of urban solid waste collectors working in two collection modalities: manual and container-based. The city of the case study selected has both of these two modalities of collection: manual, in which workers collect garbage bags and place them into the truck; and container-based, in which workers position large waste containers in an automated device to unload them into the truck.

2 Methods

This study is an applied research and can be classified as an exploratory and descriptive case study. A mixed-methods approach was employed in the study, which was carried out in a medium-sized (approx. 680 thousand inhabitants) city in the interior of the state of Sao Paulo in Brazil. The city generates around 634 tons of solid waste daily, and the waste collecting company studied employs 473 people, out of which 192 workers are collectors, where 50 participated in this research for data collection.

The demand to analyze the collector's work was requested by the management group of the studied company. The initial demand assumed that the risks related to the work originated from the speed with which the workers completed the task, considering that this "attitude" made work even more tiring.

The adopted method was the Ergonomic Work Analysis (EWA), which made possible the global analysis of the work with the participation of the workers for a better understanding of the activity performed and, thus, to reconstruct the demand. The new demand had a systemic approach to the problem, considering physical (effort spent by the collector to perform the task), cognitive (action strategy necessary to deal with variability) and organizational aspects of the work situation (discrepancy between prescribed and real work).

Qualitative data was collected via semi-structured interviews with workers and collection routes observation, following the activity-centered ergonomics approach. In total, 50 workers were interviewed (covering all sectors of work), focusing on their perception of their own work. Furthermore, observation of all 8 collection teams in their collection routes was conducted, totaling 53 h of routes' observation.

Additionally, quantitative measurements of workers' lactate levels before and after their work shift were made both for container-based work ($n = 24$) and manual collection ($n = 12$). The data collected was divided in terms of the collection modality (container-based or manual) and period of collection (before or after the work shift). Normality tests were carried out to determine whether the data followed a normal distribution. Subsequent independent statistical sample tests were carried out to verify two core hypotheses: H1 - There is no significant difference of lactate levels before the work shift between the collection modalities and H2 - There is no significant difference of lactate levels after the work shift between the collection modalities. The main goal of this analysis was to understand if the different collection modalities imply in a different physiological response in workers.

3 Results

As previously presented, the article is based on the collection of qualitative data (interviews with workers, observation of collection routes and EWA fundamentals) and quantitative data (measurement of workers' lactate levels before and after their work shift).

In Fig. 1, two images related to the collection modalities are presented: on the left the manual collection and on the right the collection in container.

Fig. 1. Manual collection modality (left) and container-based modality (right).

3.1 Qualitative Analysis of Activity in Manual Collection

Manual collection can be divided into three main operations: team division and foot collection; stacking; and throwing the trash on the hopper.

- Division of the team and collection on the foot: the workers remain on the stirrup (step at the back of the truck) and they form into 2 groups where each one starts a race towards a different sidewalk. The teams are made up of three collectors, one of whom is responsible for doing the "heaping". When they do not heap up the garbage, then they "collect on the foot" where this third collector goes to the middle of the street helping the others. The pace of the "collection on the foot" is intense and the speed is high. During the execution of the task, the collectors accommodate the garbage in their hands holding 1 to 6 bags containing the waste. The plastic bags have different material and size (loads of up to 23 kg were found);
- Stacking: starts when one of the collectors at the front of the route, collects the garbage on both sides of the entire street and stacks them at a strategic point to optimize the collection. Then the accumulated pile is picked up and thrown into the hopper in one go. Collectors take turns based on the arrangement made beforehand by the team. The movements performed at this stage are similar to those in the "collecting on the foot" stage, although, the collector who builds up the heap walks a greater distance than the others;
- Throwing the garbage on the hopper: after picking up the garbage from the doorstep, the collector runs towards the truck to throw it on the hopper. He positions himself approximately one meter away from the hopper of the truck. In some occasions, due to the tacit knowledge of the collectors, the movement axis can be changed, rotating the trunk to throw the garbage on the hopper. The handle varies according to the material and the weight to be handled. There is an intense application of force to transport and throw trash to the hopper. The frequency of movement is high and lasts an average of four hours.

In workers' perception, the manual collection mode was reported by all collectors as being more difficult than collection using containers. There is little variation between the three operations: for 38% of the interviewees, the "foot collection" operation is the one that requires the greatest effort to be performed; however, not being too different from the "heap" operation, indicated by 36% of the interviewees; and 26% of the interviewees indicated that the "throwing the trash on the hopper" operation as the most difficult.

For the manual collection modality, it was observed that variations related to the limitations and state of conservation of the roads, lifting and handling of loads and high work pace hinder the execution of the task. In addition, each type of container and size requires a different way of working, which interferes with the operating mode, action strategy and pace during the execution of the activity.

3.2 Qualitative Analysis of Activity in Container Collection

Container collection can be divided into four main operations: opening the lifting arm; moving and positioning the container on the lift; handling the press; and returning the container to its place.

- Opening the lifting arm: the driver sees a container and reduces the truck's speed for the collector to jump off the stirrup. The most experienced collectors have the dexterity to get off the truck with the vehicle in motion. One of the collectors opens the lift (arm attached to the rear of the truck). The worker performs this process throughout the workday and repeats the movement at an average of 200 times. The responsibility for opening the lift arm rests on the collector who operates the press, and the lift arm is not allowed to remain open while the collectors are on the stirrup or with a moving truck;
- Moving and positioning the container in the lift: the route can present several variability and complications that can change the way the collector moves the container. The container can be moved by one or two collectors. They lift the lid and release the wheel locks. There is a considerable application of force to move the container considering that, at its maximum capacity, it weighs 450 kilos. The volume of garbage, the condition of the container and the floor interfere with this movements. As soon as they approach the rear of the truck, two collectors engage the container hitches on the lift hook and move away;
- Handling the press: with the container attached to the couplings, the collector responsible for handling the levers activates the command that raises the container. As soon as the tilting system finishes throwing the garbage on the hopper, the collector activates the lever that lowers the empty container;
- Returning the container to its place: the collectors are positioned at the rear of the truck, holding the hitches and moving the container to the curb. After returning the container back, they lock one of the wheels with one foot, close the lid and run back to the truck. Before leaving for another collection point, the collector in the press closes the lift arm to leave the stirrup free. Formally, the driver receives a signal from the collectors to continue the journey by a bell system, but in order to speed up the team, it communicates through whistles or by hitting the truck body. The driver has a view of the collectors through a reverse and rear-view camera.

In the workers' perception, the container collection method is less stressful than manual collection, although there is a great variation between the degrees of difficulty among different operations. For 78% of respondents, the operation of "moving and positioning the container on the lift" is the one that requires the greatest effort to be performed, while 12% of respondents think that the operation of "returning the container to its place" is hard and 6% find "opening the lifting arm" a hard work and 4% believe "handling the press" is difficult.

For the container collection modality, it was observed that the variability of misuse of the container by the population (placing more waste than the container can hold, placing the bags outside the containers, or even positioning the container on the sidewalk), lack of good preservation of the containers, as well as the state of conservation of the roads, make it difficult to move and handle containers during the journey.

3.3 Lactate Level Analysis

The lactate measurement was applied in both types of collection, being checked before and after the workday. As previously mentioned, the two core hypotheses of the statistical analysis are: H1 where "there is no significant difference of lactate levels before the work shift between the two collection modalities" and H2 where "there is no significant difference of lactate levels after the work shift between the collection modalities".

The results from the normality tests indicated that the data did not follow a normal distribution across all different groups. Thus, the non-parametric independent samples Wilcoxon Sign Rank test was conducted to test the hypotheses.

The first hypothesis (H1) was retained ($p = 0.7101$), indicating that there was no significant difference of the lactate levels of workers from the different collection modalities before the work shift. This makes it possible to further support the perception that possible differences in lactate level after work come directly from the differences in the work itself, namely the collection modality.

The second hypothesis was (H2) rejected ($p = 0.0095$), indicating that there are significant differences of lactate levels after work shifts, between the collection modalities. This result provides evidence that the workers' lactate levels for the manual modality are usually higher than those of workers' in the container-based modality.

Overall, the quantitative analysis of lactate levels provides direct, biological evidence that supports the findings from the observations, interviews and qualitative analysis that the manual modality of waste collection is more physically demanding than the container-based collection.

4 Discussion

Qualitative data analysis approaches through codification of the interviews enabled the identification of the main issues reported by workers (e.g. work rhythm, waste load handling, risk of accident, interaction among collectors – Table 1). A comparative analysis of the work activity for the manual and container-based collection modalities showed that both modalities present physical overloads (either on the handling of garbage bags

Table 1. Variability in manual and container collections

Difficulties	Manual collection	Container collection
Work rhythm	The pace of work is more intense in manual collection, the collection in the foot the rhythm is more intense than in the heap	The driver has a central role in the acceleration and speed of the task
Load handling [2, 3]	More flexible, since the collector can control the amount of load it moves (self-regulation). Difficulties when the bags break	Less direct contact with the garbage, but possible overload due to amount of waste in the container. Pavement conservation is a key factor, as it makes it difficult to move the container around especially when it's full
Risk of accident [1, 4]	Floor irregularities are critical, requiring constant attention to avoid tripping and falling during the run; greater exposure to dog attacks and traffic-related accidents; constant contact with garbage, increasing the possibility of cuts and contamination	In the container collection mode, the risk of falling on the ground is more associated with lack of synchronicity between the collector's accommodation in the stirrup and the truck's movement; less contact with garbage when compared to manual collection, reducing the risk of cutting and contamination
Collective work	Manual collection allows less dependence on the partners that make up the team, making the collector free to make decisions during the journey	In container collection mode, the activity becomes more susceptible to the division of tasks and requires negotiation with partners to select the strategy and effort distribution

of different shapes and weights, on the transportation of the containers towards the truck or in the routes traveled by workers).

Despite the perception of the difficulties for each modality, the choice of the collection method and possible improvements do not depend on the collector, but on the organizational determination negotiated between the company and the contracting municipality [5].

5   Conclusion

Both qualitative (from interviews and work observation) and quantitative results (from the lactate levels measurement) indicate that workers tend to adapt to their physically demanding activities. The qualitative analysis sheds some light on the complexity of their work and the explanations on how they adapt. The quantitative analysis, despite directly measuring an aspect of the physiological response to the work, is not able to provide a complete understanding of the complexity of the collection work. It does, however, support and further validate the findings uncovered in the qualitative analysis, especially in the activity-centered ergonomics approach. This validation can be fundamental for the process of consolidating the analysis, especially in corporate settings that usually rely on objective data and indicators.

The comparison of the work analysis for manual and container collection modalities showed that both have physical overloads and that workers can adapt their activities to both processes. The assessment of workers' lactate levels indicates that manual labor is more strenuous than that in containers, which is also supported by the insight of ergonomic work analysis. In general, the complementarity of qualitative and quantitative approaches to understand and support the transformation of work allows the consideration of the mental, organizational and physical dimensions of the activity and promotes communication and decision-making between managers and other stakeholders guided by indicators.

This study highlights that qualitative and quantitative analyzes can be used together to provide a better understanding of the complexity of the work and allow those responsible for management and coordination to act more effectively in improving working conditions.

Further studies may include data from other companies and municipalities, in addition to other types of collections. The application of other analysis protocols and techniques that include biological and biomechanical data can also enrich this type of comparative study and better understand the difference in collection modalities.

References

1. Paiva, M.H.P., Albuquerque, M.C.C., Latham, E.E., Bezerra, C.F., Sousa, A.S., Liege Araujo, L.C.S., Reis, M.R., Luz, R.F.: Occupational hazards of brazilian solid waste workers: a systematic literature review. Revista Brasileira de Medicina do Trabalho 15(4), 364–371 (2017)
2. Zakaria, J., Sukadarin, E.H., Omar, F.A.C., Salleh, N.F.M.: Musculoskeletal disorder among municipal solid waste collectors. Asia Pac. Environ. Occup. Health J. 3(1), 28–32 (2017)
3. Battini, D., Botti, L., Mora, C., Sgarbossa, F.: Ergonomics and human factors in waste collection: analysis and suggestions for the door-to-door method. IFAC-PapersOnLine 51(11), 838–43 (2018)
4. Vasconcelos, R.C., Lima, F.P.A., Camarotto, J.A., Abreu, A.C.M.S., Coutinho Filho, A.O.: Aspectos de Complexidade do Trabalho de Coletores de Lixo Domiciliar: A Gestão da Variabilidade do Trabalho na Rua. Gestão & Produção. 15(2), 407–419 (2008)
5. Santos, M.C.O., Lima, F.P.A., Murta, E.P., Motta, G.M.V.: Desregulamentação do Trabalho e Desregulação da Atividade: O Caso da Terceirização da Limpeza Urbana e o Trabalho dos Garis. Production 19(1), 202–213 (2019)
6. Guérin, F., Laville, A., Daniellou, F., Duraffourg, J., Kerguelen, A.: Compreender o trabalho para transformá-lo: a prática da ergonomia. Edgard Blücher, Fundação Vanzolini, São Paulo (2004)

Buyer Networking in Supplier HSEQ Development – A Macroergonomics Analysis in a CSR Framework

Arto Reiman[1]([⊠]) [iD], Henri Jounila[1] [iD], and Osmo Kauppila[1,2] [iD]

[1] Industrial Engineering and Management, University of Oulu, Oulu, Finland
arto.reiman@oulu.fi
[2] Quality Technology and Logistics, Luleå University of Technology, Luleå, Sweden

Abstract. Process industries focus on their core processes whilst certain activities are bought as outsourced services from a variety of suppliers. Corporate social responsibility highlights the need to manage and develop suppliers' HSEQ capabilities. This study focuses on large Finnish industrial companies' HSEQ cluster, and its' actions for supplier development. This study includes interviews for large Finnish industrial companies and a database analysis on a sample of supplier audit reports. A macroergonomics analysis is conducted to show how the observations made in the audits, i.e. identified development topics or deviations, are of internal origin and mainly identify issues related to suppliers' management processes and health and safety performance. In addition, suppliers' own stakeholder management practices and processes were questioned in some cases. This study shows that this current HSEQ assessment practice by the cluster somewhat strongly identifies issues related to CSR. Yet, some development topics and future research aspects are identified that could help in tying the assessment procedure better with CSR.

Keywords: Corporate social responsibility · HSEQ · Integrated management systems · Macroergonomics · Supplier development

1 Introduction

The trend in process industry has been to focus on core processes and purchase other services as outsourced support services from various suppliers. Often these support services include high-risk activities, such as industrial construction and maintenance. As a result of this outsourcing, industrial plants can be considered as multiemployer worksites (or shared workplaces) where employees representing different employers work together. Yet, the overall management of, and responsibility for this complexity lies under one principal actor (later buyer). In practice, industrial buyer-supplier development actions and work at such workplaces is often managed from an Integrated Management System (IMS) perspective [1] that ties together quality, environment, health and safety management perspectives. Often in an industrial context this entity is discussed under integrated Health, Safety, Environment and Quality (HSEQ) management framework (or another similar acronym, e.g. SHEQ, EHSQ, see [2]).

Based on the macroergonomics foundations [e.g. 3–5], such multiemployer worksites can be discussed as complex work system entities, where organizational, technological and personnel subsystems interact together. The organizational subsystem includes three interacting characteristics: complexity, formalization and centralization [4]. Complexity relates to segmentation of the organization [4] whereas formalization relates to the degree of standardization and centralization of the decision-making processes and the extent to which authority is concentrated within a few individuals. Personnel subsystem constitutes of those doing the work and technological subsystem relates to the means how the work is actually accomplished [4]. Design and management of such a complex work system and the stakeholders included is challenged by various forces set by the external environment [5].

Suppliers' HSEQ performance affects, directly or indirectly, the total performance of the buyer. Thus, supplier development is of interest for both the supplier and the buyer [6]. Local laws provide grounding for suppliers' and buyers' actions. However, research and practice has shown that merely focusing on fulfilling the laws is often considered inadequate and buyers and suppliers also have their own processes and procedures to raise the bar for their HSEQ performance below these minimum requirements. Corporate social Responsibility (CSR) is one framework that has been used for supplier development in this context [7] and for instance, Zink and Fischer [8] have highlighted the need for empirical CSR oriented macroergonomics studies focusing on whole value creation chains in industrial contexts.

Nordic countries are generally considered as forerunners in CSR. Despite this companies in the Nordic countries should not be considered a homogenous group as the level of CSR varies greatly between companies [9]. In this study, we focus on a Finnish HSEQ cluster and their approach on supplier's HSEQ performance assessment and development [10, 11] thus providing insight into Finnish industrial buyer-supplier context from the CSR perspective. The supplier assessment procedure, with supplier audits and the criteria utilized include various aspects that can be discussed under the topic of CSR from the supplier management perspective. Our objective is to deepen understanding about the nature of the assessment procedure and the development topics and deviations identified in the audit sessions by discussing them in a CSR framework. Within this approach, we aim to increase understanding on how well this established HSEQ assessment procedure corresponds to CSR.

2   Methodology

This study focuses on a Finnish HSEQ cluster, its' supplier assessment procedure and assessment database. HSEQ cluster is a network of twelve large industrial buyers. The cluster has actively developed procedures and processes for assessing and developing their industrial suppliers' HSEQ performance. Current assessment procedure is a product of a long fifteen-year collaboration process. During that time, a common procedure for assessing industrial suppliers' HSEQ performance and capabilities with altogether 41 criteria has been developed in collaboration within the cluster. The criteria include the following nine sub categories where these 41 criteria are divided; 1) Leadership, 2) Policy and strategy, 3) Personnel, 4) Partnerships and resources, 5) Processes, 6)

Customer results, 7) Personnel results, 8) Social results, and 9) Key performance results [12]. Every criterion is assessed on a four-step scale. Through the audit process, the auditees are provided with a numerical score on their HSEQ performance in total, and HS, E and Q performance separately. Numerical score is comparable with other audited companies' HSEQ audit results. In addition, a written audit report showing possible development topics and deviations is provided.

The assessment procedure includes self-audits by the supplier, followed by third-party audits where the buyers included in the cluster can participate at their will. The process is led by a lead auditor representing an external certification body. As a result of this cluster network the buyers have saved their own resources whilst HSEQ performance has been improved from the supplier perspective. There is also evidence on improved economic performance by the suppliers [10–12].

2.1 Study Process

The objective of this study was approached through buyer interviews and an analysis on the HSEQ audit database. The interviews were conducted at seven buyer companies in 2017. These companies were considered having the longest experience concerning HSEQ cluster networking. The interviewees were individuals responsible for HSEQ cluster actions at the company. In five companies the interviews were performed as group interviews with two interviewees participating, whilst in two companies the interviews were conducted as individual interviews. The interviews were arranged at companies' premises. Interviews were semi-structured in nature and they were recorded and transcribed. In this study, we focused on this interview material from the CSR perspective. Interview material has been analyzed earlier by Jounila et al. [10] who have analyzed the data as a whole from the HSEQ management perspective.

In the latter part of this study, a database analysis was conducted to the HSEQ audit database. The database covers over 340 supplier audit reports. In this study, we randomly selected a sample of 20 audit reports for further analysis. The audit reports contained in total 236 development topics and deviations (later observations). In the analysis phase, we applied a CSR framework by Baumgartner and Ebner [13] and re-categorized these 236 observations accordingly in eight CSR categories based on their origin. The eight categories in this CSR framework by Baumgartner and Ebner [13] include *Corporate governance, Motivation and incentives, Health and safety* and *Human capital development* as internal categories, and *Ethical behaviour and human rights, No controversial activities, No corruption and cartel* and *Corporate citizenship* as external categories.

3 Results

Buyer interviews focused on the benefits of the audit process, audit data utilization possibilities, experiences on supplier performance development, development topics for the audit process and the total coverage of the audits. In this study, we focus on buyers' views on the audit process from a CSR perspective. As a whole, the interviewees emphasized how HSEQ performance in practice can be comprehensively assessed through the criteria discussed and verified in the audit session. In general, the interviewees emphasized that the audit criteria coverage is in many ways adequate also from the CSR perspective. Interviewees highlighted that the audits were mainly conducted to Finnish suppliers. Accordingly, they considered that suppliers in Finland in principle have a high level of CSR in their actions. An interviewee quotation [translated from Finnish by the 1st author] from one interview concretizes this view in practice:

"...on the other hand, there is this thing that these [audited] *companies are from Finland. Surely, we have in our internal audits seen different violations* [concerning SR], *but certainly not on that level, that in Africa, East Asia and Southern America. There such ethical questions are somewhat different, and I don't think that we would need to focus on such ethical issues in Finland".*

Interviewees mentioned that the time might not be right to consider such issues in Finland. However, they pointed out that in the future buyers most likely will put more demands on CSR and especially on environmental efficiency. Partly, they considered that environmental responsibility might be an area that could be considered more in-depth in the audits and for instance raw material sourcing might be an area to consider more profoundly also when assessing suppliers and their sourcing processes.

As a whole, the interviewees were highly satisfied in HSEQ cluster networking and on the HSEQ audit process itself. The audit process was deemed comprehensive considering all major aspects that should be notified when assessing suppliers. However, we wanted to take a closer look on issues that have been identified in the audits to provide an external view on the coverage of the audits from the CSR perspective. Thus, we focused on the latter part of our analysis on the development topics and deviations that have been issued for the audited suppliers. For that purpose, we extracted a random sample of 20 audit reports from the audit database and categorized the observations on eight categories based on their internal or external origin. The analysis results (Table 1) show the division of the observations on eight categories.

Two thirds of the observations were of internal origin and roughly one third of the observations included in the analysis related to *Corporate governance* and on issues like the transparency of top management actions and unclearly defined processes and policies. One fifth of the observations related to *Health and safety* and on challenges related to its' arrangement, tools, and processes and on inadequate personnel health and safety training. Similarly, one fifth of the observations were categorized under *"No controversial actions"* category. Non-transparent partner selection processes and unclear customer relations management processes can be mentioned as typical examples of the observations in that category. One tenth of the observations related to the category *"Corporate citizenship"* with unclear communication with local communities and different environmental issues as typical examples of such observations. None of the observations in our sample related to *"No corruption and cartel"* category.

Table 1. Observations (n = 236) in eight CSR categories.

Categories	Examples*	Types of observations (most common)
Internal: Corporate governance	Transparency in actions, following rules of corporate governance, defining board responsibilities…	• Non-transparent management decision making • Non-transparent operative indicators • Insufficient process and task descriptions • Unclear operating policies • Insufficient long-term planning • Missing or unclear certificates
Internal: Motivation and incentives	Awareness of motivation factors, development incentives, reward systems…	• Missing or inadequate processes for suggestions • Unclear reward systems • Deficiencies in working hours monitoring and control • Challenges related to employee well-being
Internal: Health and safety	Health and safety at work, accident prevention, risk management programs…	• Insufficient accident & incident analyses • Unproper practices to orientation to work • Inadequate safety training • Unclear safety management processes • Unclear safety responsibilities
Internal: Human capital development	Education, training, job enrichment, job enlargement…	• Inadequate or missing personnel registers • Inadequate or missing knowledge and skill registers • Inadequate training
External: Ethical behaviour and human rights	Ethical behaviour, culture of respect, fair rules, equality…	• Inadequately defined ethical values and procedures
External: No controversial activities	Fair operating practices and investment policies…	• Challenges related to customer relations • Unclear supplier selection processes • Inadequately defined supplier responsibilities • Unclear stakeholder management processes
External: No corruption and cartel	Fair behaviour within practices, no rule-breaking…	• None

(*continued*)

Table 1. (*continued*)

Categories	Examples*	Types of observations (most common)
External: Corporate citizenship	Showing good corporate citizenship, showing interest on local communities…	• Inadequate environmental practices and processes • Inadequate actions and contacts to local communities and other stakeholders • Inadequate waste sorting practices

*As expressed by Baumgartner and Ebner [13].

4 Discussion and Conclusions

This study focused on supplier development processes and actions by a Finnish cluster comprised of large industrial buyer companies. The companies involved in the cluster include process industry companies and energy production. The companies are among the largest in Finland at their business sectors; thus, the cluster can be considered to represent adequately Finnish heavy industries in general. In this study, we focused on CSR issues related to supplier audits by the cluster. In general, we see that this study illustrated in practice the general development on CSR discussion in Finland during the past few years. Our empirical interview material from 2017 concluded that CSR was at that time mainly considered a by-product of the supplier audits whilst buyers' focus was merely on practical HSEQ performance issues. However, during the last years we, as long-lasting research partners of the cluster, have witnessed how the general discussion inside the cluster has shifted towards larger entities, like the ones of sustainability and CSR. This observed shift in the attitudes, along with current large-scale initiatives such as the European Union's Green Deal act which promotes CSR [14] and a growing trend to develop and deepen CSR reporting [15], made us ponder how well does this supplier audit process contribute to CSR in practice? Thus, we conducted an analysis on the audit database. In that analysis phase, we took a random sample of 20 audit reports and analyzed the development topics and deviations issued at the audits, i.e. observations, in a CSR framework, applied from Baumgartner and Ebner [13].

Our analysis shows how two thirds of the observations related to suppliers' internal processes and practices and a majority of those related to corporate governance and health and safety. From a macroergonomics perspective, we see here signs of unmatured organizational and technical subsystems. From the organizational subsystem perspective, we see centralization a challenge. In practice, centralization relates to suppliers' concentrated management decision making processes and practices, that seem not to be transparent at all levels. In addition, our analysis shows some signs of challenges related to stakeholder management from the supplier perspective as there were several observations that showed how suppliers' own supply chain processes were unmatured and not always transparent. In addition, there were some cases, where suppliers' own environmental practices and processes and interaction practices with the local communities were questioned.

Issues related to health and safety also stand out in our empirical material. This is not surprising considering the challenging nature of work that the suppliers perform at industrial sites. Being an important element of organizational subsystem that is also a challenge from the perspectives of personnel and technological subsystems. Our material showed challenges related to suppliers' personnel development systems and processes, practices on orientation to work and personnel training systems and their documentation.

Our macroergonomics analysis approach provided us with some evidence on IMS in industrial supply chain context. Contributing to the future research call by Nunhes et al. [16], we argue that the HSEQ supplier assessment approach studied provides means for systematic supplier management with standardized measures. Further, we argue that the assessment process provides knowledge that can be utilized broadly at strategic, tactic and operational levels. To support that, the assessment scores and reports can be utilized for inter- and intraorganizational learning steering thus towards continuous improvement actions.

As a future topic for research, we propose to study more in-depth the connections of and incentives for CSR and sustainability and health and safety in supplier development. For instance, Nawaz et al. [17] have in their recent review highlighted the close connections between safety and sustainability and concluded how the former offers in a sense an operational command on the latter one. This is a perspective that should be studied more in-depth in our HSEQ cluster environment. As another topic for future research, and for practical development actions inside the cluster, we propose a study that focuses on external CSR issues; like identifying challenges related to possible unfair operating practices. Our sample of 20 audit reports did not reveal any development topics or deviations related to unfair operation practices. However, considering our rather small sample size, we propose to study that more in-depth from a larger sample. In addition, we propose that to be discussed when the audit process and its's audit criteria are being developed.

4.1 Limitations

Our study was based on a fairly narrow sample. We highlight the need for more in-depth studies on the subject based on larger empirical data. The HSEQ assessment database introduced in this study is growing and will provide possibilities for such studies in the future. It should be noted that the audit process might contain potential biases as the audits are performed by humans. Supposedly it is possible that for instance the lead auditor might prefer some issues that he/she is more familiar with, thus making it possible for some other important topics to be left for a smaller discussion. However, a study by Jounila et al. [12] provides some indication on the objectivity of the audit process when different lead auditors' observations from a video material from one audit session were compared.

In addition, we highlight that the interviews we analyzed did not strictly focus on CSR as they were designed to cover the audit process more in general. It is possible that more specific CSR questions would have provided more in-depth information on CSR aspects from the buyer perspective.

References

1. Wilkinson, G., Dale, B.G.: Integrated management systems: an examination of the concept and theory. TQM Mag. **11**(2), 95–104 (1999)
2. Kauppila, O., Härkönen, J., Väyrynen, S.: Integrated HSEQ management systems: development and trends. Int. J. Qual. Res. **9**(2), 231–242 (2015)
3. Murphy, L.A., Robertson, M.M., Carayon, P.: The next generation of macroergonomics: integrating safety climate. Accid. Anal. Prev. **68**, 16–24 (2014)
4. Kleiner, B.M.: Macroergonomics: work system analysis and design. Hum. Fact. **50**(3), 461–467 (2008)
5. Carayon, P., Hankock, P., Leveson, N., Noy, I., Sznelwar, L., van Hootegem, G.: Advancing a sociotechnical systems approach to workplace safety – developing the conceptual framework. Ergonomics **58**(4), 548–564 (2015)
6. Chen, L., Ellis, S., Holsapple, C.: Supplier development: a knowledge management perspective. Knowl. Process Manage. **22**(4), 250–269 (2015)
7. Montero, M.J., Araque, R.A., Rey, J.M.: Occupational health and safety in the framework of corporate social responsibility. Saf. Sci. **47**(10), 1440–1445 (2009)
8. Zink, K.J., Fischer, K.: Do we need sustainability as a new approach in human factors and ergonomics? Ergonomics **56**(3), 348–356 (2013)
9. Kinderman, D.: The tenuous link between CSR performance and support for regulation: business associations and Nordic regulatory preferences regarding the corporate transparency law 2014/95/EU. Bus. Polit. **22**(3), 413–448 (2020)
10. Jounila, H., Reiman, A., Laine, J., Kauppila, O.: HSEQ at shared industrial workplaces – experiences from collaboration on supplier audits. Int. J. Qual. Res. **14**(1), 65–78 (2020)
11. Kauppila, O., Jounila, H., Reiman, A.: Networking for supplier development; evidence from a Finnish industrial cluster. Int. J. Occup. Environ. Saf. **4**(2), 22–36 (2020)
12. Jounila, H., Cajander, N., Reiman, A., Latva-Ranta, J., Väyrynen, S.: HSEQ assessment audit tool – consistency analysis of expert audits. In: Bernatik, A., Kocurkova, L., Jørgensen, K. (eds.). Prevention of Accidents at Work: Proceedings of the 9th International Conference on the Prevention of Accidents at Work (WOS 2017), pp. 115–119. Taylor & Francis Group, CRC Press/Balkema (2017)
13. Baumgartner, R.J., Ebner, D.: Corporate sustainability strategies: sustainability profiles and maturity levels. Sustain. Dev. **18**(2), 76–89 (2010)
14. Noti, K., Mucciarelli, C.A., Angelici, C., dalla Pozza, V.: Corporate social responsibility (CSR) and its implementation into EU Company law. Policy Department for Citizens' Rights and Constitutional Affairs, The European Union (2020)
15. Tsalis, T.A., Malamateniou, K.E., Koulouriotis, D., Nikolaou, I.E.: New challenges for corporate sustainability reporting: united Nations' 2030 Agenda for sustainable development and the sustainable development goals. Corp. Soc. Responsib. Environ. Manage. **27**(4), 1617–1629 (2020)
16. Nunhes, T.V., Bernardo, M., Oliveira, O.J.: Guiding principles of integrated management systems: towards unifying a starting point for researchers and practitioners. J. Clean. Prod. **210**, 977–993 (2019)
17. Nawaz, W., Linke, P., Koç, M.: Safety and sustainability nexus: a review and appraisal. J. Clean. Prod. **216**, 74–87 (2019)

Identifying Sustainability Attributes
of Products/Services with Ergoecology

Martha Helena Saravia-Pinilla$^{(\boxtimes)}$ and Lucas Rafael Ivorra-Peñafort ⓘ

Pontificia Universidad Javeriana, Carrera 7 #40 – 62 (Edificio 16), Bogotá, Colombia
saravia@javeriana.edu.co

Abstract. There are multiple tools in the market to define the scope of sustainable products in terms of their attributes [1], and sustainable corporate guidelines [2]. However, considering the principles of Hannover [3], the so-called "Social" aspects from the traditional TBL [4] are not incorporated into decision-making enough. Besides, some tools do not offer the possibility to adapt the decision-making process to the contexts or make decisions with more technical arguments. In the scenario of sustainable design teaching, the scope of products could be better supported in technical aspects when responding to ambiguous requirements such as "developing a sustainable product". In this situation, the framework of Green Ergonomics [5] and the Ergoecology [6] with its "eco-concepts" well developed, can help to ground product design in specific sustainability attributes.

Keywords: Ergoecology · Eco-productivity · Sustainable products · Corporate sustainability

1 Introduction

The critical-comparative review of specialised literature focused on eco-design and sustainable design tools and was conducted to identify those attributes and variables from sustainability that define a product/service as 'sustainable'. The researchers proposed a tool to assess and synthesise said attributes and variables; it also favours decision-making processes within organisations committed to sustainability.

Secondly, some eco-design perspectives are still limited to traditional approaches, such as "environmental" aspects referring to matter and energy, with a highly technical vision, reducing sociocultural aspects' relevance.

In the same way, today, a large part of the sustainability aspects when doing academic assessments of product/service design projects is still not clear or standardised. It is widespread to find sustainability as an ethereal and ambiguous design requirement, making it difficult for students and teachers to understand how to approach design decisions related to these attributes.

Finally, from the perspective of human and social aspects with an eco-spherical approach, favouring the inclusion of attributes for sustainability in the strategy of organisations -e.g., in the design and development of sustainable products and services-

© The Author(s), under exclusive license to Springer Nature Switzerland AG 2021
N. L. Black et al. (Eds.): IEA 2021, LNNS 220, pp. 560–565, 2021.
https://doi.org/10.1007/978-3-030-74605-6_71

must include variables associated with all the "stakeholders" so that decision-making encompasses the well-being and performance aspects of all of them.

The preceding's impact will be more evident when applying the proposed tool in further stages of this research.

2 Methodology

Due to the COVID-19 pandemic, the researchers had to adapt to the proposed activities, to be able to collect data to build the tool. In this sense, the researchers used the following methods from a wide variety of stakeholders related to the design of new sustainable products and services:

1. A literature review [7] to identify the status of the tools and decision-making processes.
2. Surveys to contrast literature, collect more in-depth data from individual stakeholders and complement how decisionmakers identify and assess sustainability attributes when designing new products and services.

2.1 Literature Review

It was a narrative/traditional literature review [8], both in English and Spanish. In this case, the researchers collected data from Pontificia Universidad Javeriana's databases and complementary sources (e.g., government documents, sustainability reports, degree projects, and other secondary sources) The literature review was developed with the "snowball" technique, with keywords and operators, looking for a wide range of cases and decision models.

2.2 Applied Surveys

The researchers sent online questionnaires via email to different stakeholders: students, lecturers, practitioners and the local environmental government. They collected data about different categories: demographic characteristics; basic knowledge about sustainability; criteria included in the definition of sustainability attributes in new products and services; and, decision-making processes.

2.3 Data Analysis

The team carried out a thematic analysis [9], listing key concepts [10] and then organising them in second or third level codes to group them. They used matrices in MS Excel, where key concepts were organised into criteria and decision processes categories. Similarly, the researchers documented critical questions used by different authors to identify key sustainability attributes of products and services. Subsequently, they supplemented this process with processed data from surveys to define the main criteria in the definition of sustainability attributes and their selection and prioritisation.

2.4 Ethics

The researchers followed the activities established in the approved research protocol, in line with the values and procedures of the Pontificia Universidad Javeriana, regarding the ethical component of the project (e.g., informing participants about the project, ensuring their voluntary participation and protecting their identity).

3 Results

The following were the key outcomes to this stage of the research: 1) A literature review report, and 2) a decision-making tool. In terms of the sustainable attributes of products, the researchers organised the criteria in five different general categories: 1) Humanity; 2) Next Life; 3) Context; 4) Inputs and outputs; and 5) Others. Concerning specific criteria, these are some examples of them: "It meets needs with simplicity", "The materials are reusable", "It can be upgraded", "It supports respect for human rights", among others. The tool also offers the possibility to assess the criteria regarding different life cycle stages of products and adjust their significance according to the project and the stakeholders' requirements.

For example, Fig. 1 shows a section of the tool with the twenty-six specific criteria initially defined; also, the tool offers the possibility to assess each criterion's relative significance (Column "%", showing a value 3.85% in this Figure). The tool also includes twelve different questions to evaluate each criterion (the last two columns on the right show some examples), each question with its value for its relative significance (8.33% in this Figure). With these data, from left to right, the tool offers the relative weight of each specific criteria after considering the relative significance of each criterion (Column "Val", on the left) and before considering the relative significance of each criterion (Columns ("Val" on the right). Besides, the tool shows the rank of each criterion based on the calculations explained above.

Regarding the decision-making processes, the tool offers twelve questions to assess every criterion and life-cycle stage, proposing the possibility to evaluate using a rubric with four levels of assessment: "0", if the criteria/stage do not apply; "1", if the criterion is not met; "2", if there is uncertainty about the compliance with the criterion; and "3" if the criterion is met. This section of the tool invites the stakeholders to hold dialogues to reach consensus about assessing the criteria.

After populating the tool with data, it offers the possibility to identify the most relevant life-cycle stages and criteria graphically, using the Pareto charts. The tool also allows filtering the criteria and stages based on the project team's compliance targets by adjusting the compliance percentage. Figure 2 shows an example of the graphics that summarises the data, setting the compliance target to 50%; in all the graphics, the darker columns show the criteria/stages which comply with the compliance target: the left chart, shows the specific criteria; the top-right chart shows the stages, and the bottom-right chart shows the general criteria.

Rank	Val	%	Restricciones	Val	¿Hay motivaciones suyas a nivel personal?	¿Hay motivaciones de su organización?
		100.00%	100.00%		8.33%	8.33%
13	0.0641	3.85%	Apoya el respeto a derechos humanos	1.6667	1	2
9	0.0673	3.85%	Difunde conocimiento sobre sostenibilidad	1.7500	2	2
9	0.0673	3.85%	Ayuda a modificar comportamientos	1.7500	3	2
12	0.0641	3.85%	Favorece la equidad	1.6667	3	3
20	0.0577	3.85%	Satisface necesidades con sencillez	1.5000	3	3
1	0.0801	3.85%	Las materias primas son locales	2.0833	3	3
3	0.0769	3.85%	La producción es local	2.0000	2	3
3	0.0769	3.85%	Incluye conocimiento local	2.0000	2	2
21	0.0577	3.85%	Apoya la restauración de ecosistemas	1.5000	2	2
15	0.0609	3.85%	Reducción de componentes	1.5833	0	1
24	0.0513	3.85%	Reducción de tipos de materiales	1.3333	0	1
9	0.0673	3.85%	Reducción de procesos	1.7500	0	2
21	0.0577	3.85%	Reducción de ruido	1.5000	0	1
5	0.0705	3.85%	Reducción de consumo de agua	1.8333	2	2
15	0.0609	3.85%	Reducción de consumo de energía	1.5833	2	1

Fig. 1. This section shows the specific criteria, relative values and ranks of each criterion, and an example of two columns of the assessment questions, using the assessment level (0–3).

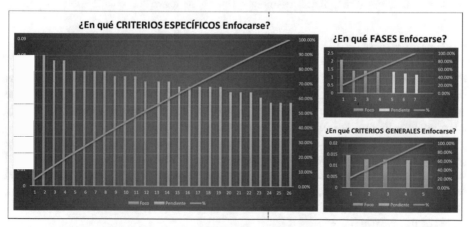

Fig. 2. An example of the assessment's graphic summary: the left's chart is about specific criteria; the top-right chart is about life cycle phases; the bottom-right chart is about general criteria. The darker columns show the criteria/phases, which were the top 50% most important criteria/phases in this example.

4 Discussion

Due to the complexity of projects and the resources constraints [11], decisionmakers need to find a balance between the sustainability attributes they want to include in new products and services, and the availability of resources. This balance needs to assess different criteria that comprise different aspects of the environmental, social and financial domains. Hence, it is virtually impossible to find/design a product/service which complies with all the potential sustainability attributes; for this reason, decisionmakers (e.g., designers, students) need to identify the most relevant in each new project.

Secondly, designers need to have more explicit criteria when making decisions, improve the rationale of the sustainable attributes of products/services, and avoid potential risks in their projects (e.g., communicating sustainability attributes as greenwashing). In this context, designers also need tools that allow them to make decisions in participatory design processes, considering the stakeholders' capabilities; they also need tools that help the stakeholders reach consensus with transparent information when making decisions. Besides, a new tool that helps designers must be flexible to adapt to the context's changing conditions and every new project (which, by definition, is always different); thus, the tool requires to allow decisionmakers to modify it according to every new project's requirements.

For example, in some projects, the stakeholders could reach a consensus to focus on some attributes. However, in another city, the same stakeholders could focus on other attributes (depending on different conditions: e.g., local environmental problems, local legal frameworks). This possibility of the tool aligns to current standards to prioritise the relevant sustainability issues, such as Materiality Analysis from the Global Reporting Initiative. It also helps the pedagogical processes, where students and lecturers reach a consensus that could help the assessment activities be more successful and transparent.

5   Conclusions

Defining sustainability attributes requires setting boundaries to the analysis, as it happens in the product/service life-cycle assessment. In complex systems, these boundaries are active, as their structure and dynamics; it means that decisionmakers must continuously adapt their decisions and adjust products/services' attributes.

Secondly, different drivers affect the selection of attributes and the decision-making process. There are aspects which affect the decisions at an organisational (e.g., financial status and strategic goals), context (e.g., environmental pressures) and worldwide level (e.g., global market trends). At the educational level, there are also different drivers: e.g., changes in the learning outcomes and adapting pedagogical strategies to the specific needs of the students).

In this sense, the tool offers the possibility to define the attributes with more specific criteria while serving in participatory design processes with different stakeholders, looking for more transparent decision-making and assessment processes of products and services which explicitly includes sustainability attributes.

References

1. Muriel, L.: Guía para diseñadores y desarrolladores de producto sobre métodos y tendencias con énfasis en factores ambientales. Universidad Nacional de Colombia, Bogotá, Colombia (2013)
2. Thatcher, A., Zink, K., Fischer, K. (eds.): Human Factors for Sustainability. CRC Press, Boca Raton (2020)
3. Heinz Kerry, T., Braungart, M., McDonough, W., William McDonough Architects. The Hannover principles: Design for sustainability. 10th anniversary ed., rev. and updated. W. McDonough Architects, New York (2003)

4. Elkington, J.: Enter the triple bottom line. In: Henriques, A., Richardson, J. (eds.) The Triple Bottom Line: Does It All Add up?, pp. 1–16. Earthscan, London (2004)
5. Thatcher, A., Garcia-Acosta, G., Lange-Morales, K.: Design principles for green ergonomics. In: Contemporary Ergonomics and Human Factors, pp. 319–326 (2013)
6. García-Acosta, G., Pinilla, M.H.S., Larrahondo, P.A.R., Morale, K.L.: Ergoecology: fundamentals of a new multidisciplinary field. Theoretical Issues in Ergonomics Science (2012)
7. Buchert, T., Neugebauer, S., Schenker, S., Lindow, K., Stark, R.: Multi-criteria decision making as a tool for sustainable product development – benefits and obstacles. Procedia CIRP **26**, 70–75 (2015)
8. Efron, S.E., Ravid, R.: Writing the Literature Review: A Practical Guide. Guilford Publications, New York (2018)
9. Ezzy, D. (ed.): Qualitative Analysis. Routledge, Florence (2003). (Adapted from Kellehear, 1993)
10. Ritchie, J., Spencer, L.: Qualitative data analysis for applied policy research. In: Burgess, R.G., Bryman, A. (eds.) Analysing Qualitative Data. Chapter 9, pp. 173–194. Routledge, London (1994)
11. PMI - Project Management Institute. A Guide to the Project Management Body of Knowledge (PMBOK Guide). (6th edn.): Project Management Institute, Inc., Newtown Square, Pennsylvania (2017)

A Comprehensive Overview on 'Eco-concepts' Use from Ergoecology Vision

Martha Helena Saravia-Pinilla[1]([⊠]) [iD], Gabriel García-Acosta[2] [iD],
and Carolina Daza-Beltrán[1] [iD]

[1] Pontificia Universidad Javeriana, Bogotá, Colombia
saravia@javeriana.edu.co
[2] Universidad Nacional de Colombia, Bogotá, Colombia

Abstract. A systematic theoretical-critical review was conducted to establish conceptual similarities and differences around the postulates of eco-productivity, eco-efficiency, and eco-effectiveness, to contribute to the epistemology of Ergoecology. This document shows the scope of the first review phase, which includes articles from 1989 to 2014, on which refinement criteria were used until 18 articles were obtained. Using the conglomerates analysis of the Nvivo-11 software, three groups of authors were obtained, from which it was possible to deduce the differences in approach in a critical reading under the vision of Ergoecology. It was established that there is not enough debate or consensus on eco-productivity; eco-efficiency is the concept most worked on by researchers and eco-effectiveness has been less developed by the scientific community. Emphasis is placed on the general vision of eco-concepts that pursue the understanding of sustainability and its impacts on how to achieve it. It is important to highlight the conceptual differences of the approaches offered by the authors that define each of the eco-concepts, since in some cases they have been misinterpreted without noticing the implications that this may have on the application of the corresponding strategies. It is expected that upon completion of the two review phases, the results will provide clues towards the unification of eco-concepts, allowing the development of effective strategies for sustainability that avoid the prolongation of the rebound effect.

Keywords: Product development · Eco-productivity · Eco-efficiency · Eco-effectiveness · Sustainability

1 Introduction

In ergonomics, some of the global concepts that are proposed as postulates are efficiency, productivity, and effectiveness, integrated with those of health, wellbeing, and quality of life of human beings. In the case of Ergoecology, these postulates are extended to eco-productivity, eco-efficiency, eco-effectiveness, socio-efficiency, and socio-effectiveness, integrated to sustainability, wellbeing, and quality of life as the diversity of living beings. It is necessary to relate, integrate and redefine these eco-concepts from the perspective of Ergoecology, to reinforce the epistemological basis of this recent multidiscipline. In this work, we will tackle eco-productivity, eco-efficiency and eco-effectiveness.

© The Author(s), under exclusive license to Springer Nature Switzerland AG 2021
N. L. Black et al. (Eds.): IEA 2021, LNNS 220, pp. 566–572, 2021.
https://doi.org/10.1007/978-3-030-74605-6_72

Even though the project has been structured in two phases, this paper describes what we have found into the scope of the first review phase, which includes 18 articles written from 1989 to 2014. The aim of this first phase was to establish conceptual similarities and differences around the postulates of eco-productivity, eco-efficiency, and eco-effectiveness carrying out a critical reading under the vision of Ergoecology. To make it possible, the Nvivo-11 software was used. By applying the conglomerates analysis tool, three groups of authors were obtained and from these three 'Conglomerates', the critical review was made as described in the following paragraphs.

As it can be seen at the results, it is expected that upon completion of the two review phases, the project provides clues towards the unification of eco-concepts, allowing the development of effective strategies for sustainability that avoid the prolongation of the so called 'Jevons paradox', also known as 'rebound effect'.

2 Methodology

A systematic theoretical-critical review was conducted. It was investigated how eco-productivity, eco-efficiency, and eco-effectiveness have been raised and interpreted in the scientific literature, to analyze similarities and differences. The project has been driven in two phases. The first one covered papers written between 1989–2014 and the second one—that is currently under development—between 2015–2021.

2.1 Search Equations

Search equations were constructed by crossing three framework concepts: (1) design and product development, (2) environmental and sustainability, and (3) ergonomics; resulting in 48 search equations. The databases consulted were: Scopus, IEEE, Compendex, Science direct, and Proquest. As a result of performing the first search, almost 1900 documents were obtained.

2.2 Selection of Papers

Refinement criteria were applied such as robustness, publication date, author name verification, as well as the expression 'product design' and relevance to product/service design and development, significantly reducing the database. Repeated documents were eliminated and access to each complete document was verified. The documents were filtered and the access to the full text was verified obtaining 696 documents as Saravia-Pinilla, Daza-Beltrán, & García-Acosta, described in 2016 [1]. Using the qualitative analysis software Nvivo-11, from the total number of papers, those that included at least two of the three 'eco-concepts' were selected, obtaining 18 full papers for deeper review.

2.3 Reading and Reviewing Papers

Using Nvivo-11 branching nodes were created with each of the three concepts. A collection was structured with the articles selected to make a reading focused on the three eco-concepts. Customized and coded text search was applied (Nvivo-11). Finally, memos and annotations were created for each of the resources.

2.4   Conglomerates Generation

Pearson correlation by 'words similarity' was applied using the NVivo Software to group the papers by maximum homogeneity between its arguments and the biggest differences between the created conglomerates. The tool allowed deep analysis about the closeness to each other helping to establish patterns of use of the eco-concepts. Three groups of conglomerates resulted from the analysis (Fig. 1).

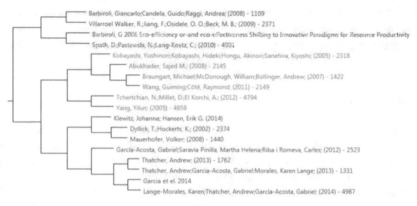

Fig. 1.   Three conglomerates obtained using Nvivo-11 Pearson coefficient by 'words similarity'.

3   Results

Considering the whole search, no more than four articles per year were found for the period from 1989 to 1996, and these were not accessible. Between 1997 and 1999, the number of proceedings and journals per year only reached 10. Between 2000 and 2013, yearly increased from 14 to 53. Found 2012 as an atypical year, with 72 documents, almost twice as many as in 2006.

An analytical-critical reading of the selected 18 papers by cluster was carried out, which allowed the construction of a matrix for each cluster. The matrix made it possible to compare not just the targets, definitions and terms of understanding, but also the contradictions and differences between the three concepts.

The following paragraphs present the main characteristics in terms of the eco-concepts interpretation and use by the authors assigned into each of the three conglomerates. Also, to illustrate, a representation of the frequency words is placed for each conglomerate (word cloud) showing the use of terms into the speech.

Regarding the clusters, it was found that Conglomerate-1 has a technical orientation and pursues eco-efficiency. Conglomerate-2 seeks eco-effectiveness as the ultimate goal the. And, Conglomerate-3 proposes two new concepts, 'systemic eco-efficiency' as the system's effective dynamics and it is assumed as eco-effectiveness synonymous; and 'eco-productivity' that looks forward to eliminating the negative impacts of production.

3.1   Conglomerate 1

Authors cluster formed by Pearson correlation coefficient: Braungart, McDonough, and Bollinger [2]; Wang and Côté [3]; Abukhader [4]; Kobayashi, Kobayashi, Hongu, and Sanehira [5]; Tchertchian and Millet [6] and, Yang [7] (Fig. 2).

Fig. 2. Word cloud obtained using Nvivo-11 for Conglomerate 1.

It focuses on the efficient use of resources associated with technologies, production and products. This cluster presents eco-efficiency as the main strategy to achieve sustainability from the Sustainable Development conception. Is the most traditionally used concept but not necessarily the most pertinent to achieve sustainability.

3.2   Conglomerate 2

Authors cluster formed by Pearson correlation coefficient: García-Acosta, Saravia-Pinilla, Romero and Lange-Morales [8]; Lange-Morales, Thatcher and García-Acosta [9]; Thatcher [10]; Thatcher, Garcia-Acosta and Lange-Morales [11]; García-Acosta, Saravia-Pinilla and Riba [12]; Dyllick and Hockerts [13]; Mauerhofer [14]; Klewitz and Hansen [15] (Fig. 3).

Fig. 3. Word cloud obtained using Nvivo-11 for Conglomerate 2.

They concentrate on the development of products with an environmental focus. The authors assume corporate management as the way to achieve sustainability, which ultimate goal is to achieve eco-effectiveness. They seek to avoid negative impacts on the environment.

3.3   Conglomerate 3

Authors cluster formed by Pearson correlation coefficient: Spath, Pastewski, and Lang-Koetz [16]; Barbiroli [17]; Barbiroli, Candela and Raggi [18]; Villaroel-Walker, Jiang, Osidele and Beck [19] (Fig. 4).

Fig. 4. Word cloud obtained using Nvivo-11 for Conglomerate 3.

It highlights the search for a balance between the human-social and the environmental-natural. Terms such as HFE appear, but their purpose is to achieve sustainability. They have a greater focus on eco-effectiveness but agree on the need of transition processes.

4   Discussion

Most of the documents reviewed have a clear definition of eco-efficiency, with no major differences between them. On the other hand, the concept of eco-effectiveness is seen by some authors as complementary, by others as opposed to eco-efficiency, and by a few as a utopian goal that could only be achieved through a long term transition. The concept of eco-productivity has not been considered by most authors and its development and definition is concentrated in Conglomerate 3. The authors of Conglomerate 2 mention it, but confuse it with the concept of resource productivity, following the line of eco-efficiency.

Conglomerate 1: It's technical oriented. They focussed to achieve eco-efficiency by material and energetic resources optimization into different states of the product life cycle (PLC). The social-human dimension is not considered.

Conglomerate 2: There is a strong environmental emphasis for product development, while corporate management is the key to achieve sustainability. The ultimate goal is to obtain eco-effectiveness.

Conglomerate 3: "Systemic eco-efficiency" is understood as the system's effective dynamics and it is assumed as eco-effectiveness synonymous. The authors insist to include eco-productivity as the system capability to transform resources into product/service without generating negative impacts.

5   Conclusions

The lack of consensus about eco-concepts among the authors reviewed in the first phase of the project is evident.

Some of these authors do not understand the conceptual differences between eco-efficiency and eco-effectiveness, nor do they understand how much the strategies proposed in each of them differ; for example the application of 'Rs-concepts' vs. applying the 'cradle to cradle' approach.

At one extreme, many authors continue seeking to increase productivity through the 'optimization of resources', based on the eco-efficiency approach. This approach i.e. doing more with less has caused the 'rebound effect' or Jevons paradox. At the other extreme, the authors who proposed the concept of 'eco-productivity' focus their efforts on eliminating negative impacts during the process of transforming resources into products or services.

It is necessary to finish the second phase of the project so this review can show the latest trends in the interpretation of eco-concepts. The results are expected to provide clues towards their unification, allowing the development of effective strategies for sustainability that avoid the prolongation of the rebound effect.

References

1. Saravia-Pinilla, M.H., Daza-Beltrán, C., García-Acosta, G.: A comprehensive approach to environmental and human factors into product/service design and development. A review from an ergoecological perspective. Appl. Ergon. **57**, 62–71 (2016)
2. Braungart, M., McDonough, W., Bollinger, A.: Cradle-to-cradle design: creating healthy emissions – a strategy for eco-effective product and system design. J. Clean. Prod. **15**(13–14), 1337–1348 (2007)
3. Wang, G., Côté, R.: Integrating eco-efficiency and eco-effectiveness into the design of sustainable industrial systems in China. Int. J. Sustain. Dev. World. Ecol. **18**(1), 65–77 (2011)
4. Abukhader, S.M.: Eco-efficiency in the era of electronic commerce - should 'Eco-Effectiveness' approach be adopted? J. Clean. Prod. **16**(7), 801–808 (2008)
5. Kobayashi, Y., Kobayashi, H., Hongu, A., Sanehira, K. A practical method for quantifying eco-efficiency using eco-design support tools (2005)
6. Tchertchian, N., Millet, D., El Korchi, A.: Design for remanufacturing: what performances can be expected? Int. J. Environ. Technol. Manage. **15**(1), 28–49 (2012)
7. Yang, Y.: Managing sustainable product design by integrating corporate product development practice with ISO14001 Environmental Management Systems. (3194990 Ph.D.), Arizona State University, Ann Arbo., ABI/INFORM Global; ProQuest Dissertations & Theses A&I database (2005). https://search.proquest.com/docview/305026696?accountid= 13250. Accessed 06 Feb 2021
8. García-Acosta, G., Saravia, M.H., Romero, P.A., Lange, K.: Ergoecology: fundamentals of a new multidisciplinary field. Theoret. Issues Ergon. Sci. **15**(2), 111–133 (2014)
9. Lange-Morales, K., Thatcher, A., García-Acosta, G.: Towards a sustainable world through human factors and ergonomics: it is all about values. Ergonomics **57**(11), 1603–1615 (2014)
10. Thatcher, A.: Green ergonomics: definition and scope. Ergonomics **56**(3), 389–398 (2013)
11. Thatcher, A., Garcia-Acosta, G., Lange Morales, K.: Design principles for green ergonomics. In: International Conference on Contemporary Ergonomics and Human Factors 2013, Cambridge, United kingdom (2013)

12. Garcia-Acosta, G., Saravia, M.H., Riba, C.: Ergoecology: evolution and challenges. Work **41**(Suppl 1), 2133–2140 (2012)
13. Dyllick, T., Hockerts, K.: Beyond the business case for corporate sustainability. Bus. Strategy Environ. **11**(2), 130–141 (2002)
14. Mauerhofer, V.: 3-D Sustainability: An approach for priority setting in situation of conflicting interests towards a Sustainable Development. Ecol. Econ. **64**(3), 496–506 (2008)
15. Klewitz, J., Hansen, E.G.: Sustainability-oriented innovation of SMEs: a systematic review. J. Clean. Prod. **65**, 57–75 (2014)
16. Spath, D., Pastewski, N., Lang-Koetz, C.: Managing new technologies for resource efficient innovations: results from current studies. In: Technology Management for Global Economic Growth (PICMET), Proceedings of PICMET 2010, 18–22 July 2010 (2010)
17. Barbiroli, G.: Eco-efficiency or/and eco-effectiveness? Shifting to innovative paradigms for resource productivity. Int. J. Sustain. Dev. World Ecol. **13**(5), 391–395 (2006)
18. Barbiroli, G., Candela, G., Raggi, A.: Implementing a new model to measure and assess eco-effectiveness as an indicator of sustainability. Int. J. Sustain. Dev. World Ecol. **15**(3), 222–230 (2008)
19. Villarroel Walker, R., Jiang, F., Osidele, O.O., Beck, M.B.: Eco-effectiveness, eco-efficiency, and the metabolism of a city: a multi-sectoral analysis (2009)

Supporting Interaction with CO_2 as a Resource with Individual Carbon Footprint Trackers as Everyday Assistants

Tim Schrills[✉], Laura Rosenbusch, Mourad Zoubir, Jacob Stahl, and Thomas Franke

Institute for Multimedia and Interactive Systems, University of Lübeck, Lübeck, Germany
schrills@imis.uni-luebeck.de

Abstract. A massive reduction in CO_2 emissions is needed to reach the Paris climate goals on many societal levels - including individual consumer decisions. In contrast to resources as time or money, it is challenging to monitor one's own impact on CO_2 emissions. Designing digital assistants to provide users with information about their CO_2 footprint could improve CO_2 literacy (i.e., mental models), enabling individual behavioural change. We reviewed how characteristics of human bounded rationality (c.f. behavioural economics), such as temporal discounting, hamper effective interaction with CO_2 as a resource. We examined user requirements for a carbon footprint tracker in an online study with 249 participants. Our study suggests CO_2 tracking apps should encompass three types of functions: presentation of concrete CO_2 emissions at a product or action level, direct comparisons between decision alternatives, and the proposal of better alternatives.

Keywords: Sustainable HCI · Eco-feedback · Carbon footprint tracking · Behavioural economics

1 Introduction

With many decisions and actions in diverse fields of everyday life, humans substantially contribute to greenhouse gas emissions (GHG, often aggregated to CO_2 equivalents [1], hereafter referred to as CO_2 for simplification). For instance, currently Germany emits 9.15 t CO_2 per capita per year [2]. However, based on the goals set in the Paris Climate Agreement and several further political agreements worldwide, greenhouse gas emissions have to be reduced massively in the coming years to effectively combat climate change and avoid severe consequences of global warming scenarios [3–5]. While this implies changes on many societal levels, it also points to a key need for significant reduction of CO_2 emissions via everyday individual decisions and actions (i.e., reducing the personal carbon footprint [6]).

Adapting behaviour to reduce the personal CO_2 footprint can be a challenging task for individuals, even if they are motivated to contribute to climate protection [7]. Knowledge on how different everyday decisions and actions affect CO_2 emissions and how to adapt behaviour accordingly on an everyday basis - which we refer to here as "climate literacy" - is difficult to gain in a precise and accurate manner. On the one hand, precise data on the relation between behaviour and CO_2 emissions are becoming increasingly available within the scientific community based on data and analyses from the field of life-cycle assessment [8]. On the other hand, digital end-user tools that facilitate every-day behaviour regulation for individual CO_2 footprint reduction are still in an early stage of development. That is, while extensive user research already exists in other fields of personal quantification and quantified self (e.g., [9, 10]). Theorising and empirical research on user-centred design challenges for software applications that support the tracking of individual CO_2 emissions and help individuals reduce their personal carbon footprint is lacking (for some promising first work, cf. [11]).

Consequently, the objective of the present research was to (1) apply action regulation in terms of a control loop to frame psychological challenges that digital tools for CO_2 tracking need to address and to (2) contribute first empirical insights into the needs and perspectives of potential early adopter users of CO_2 tracking apps. To this end, we present a focused summary and integration of key theoretical concepts from behavioural economics and human resource regulation and to explicate psychological challenges in CO_2 tracking and to derive first guidelines for digital tracking tools geared towards supporting individual CO_2 footprint regulation. In addition, we present results from an online questionnaire study with $N = 249$ young people who have at least a basic interest in their CO_2 footprint and can therefore be understood as potential early adopters of CO_2 tracking applications. Based on the results, the key design features for CO_2 trackers were derived.

2   Psychological Challenges for CO_2 Tracker Design

Many reasons for a lack of behaviour geared towards sustainability and climate protection have been discussed in the literature (cf. e.g. [12]). While a lack of motivation or trust in climate change information from science can play a central role (cf. The Dragons of Inaction, [13]), studies show that a considerable proportion of people are willing to make appropriate behavioural adjustments in favour of climate protection, even if this implies restrictions on other valuable resources such as time or money if e.g. social norms call for it [14].

CO_2 as a resource is not recognized within the sensory systems of a human and as such can - for all intents and purposes - be considered a rather abstract resource. To facilitate effective interaction with CO_2 within the environment of a tracking applica-tion it is therefore important to find a representation that lends CO_2 characteristics that enable a simpler resource regulation. This includes reframing CO_2 as 1) an exhaustible resource (cf. [15]), 2) with a short-term resource regulation cycle (cf. [16]), that 3) allows individual resource regulation. One method to accomplish this is in terms of a personal CO_2 budget. This directly creates an exhaustible individual resource with freely defin-able temporal resource-regulation dynamics (e.g., daily budget reducing psychological distances between action and consequences in terms of resource exhaustion).

Interestingly, this approach shares similarities with the definition of activity goals in personal fitness tracking applications [17]. This may allow for transfer of tracker design features like e.g. using ipsative norms (i.e., defining activity goals like steps per day based on previously assessed activity) to avoid frustration in the beginning of tracker usage [17]. However, tracking a ressource (like CO_2) may yield other, additional problems besides tracking a behavior.

2.1 A Control Loop Model of Individual CO_2 Regulation

In many everyday contexts resource regulation transactions are embedded in a cyclical process. Such aspects of behaviour can be modelled particularly well from a cybernetic perspective. An example of the basic architecture of a cybernetic human control loop is presented in the self-regulation theory of [18] (see Fig. 1). In this model, the input (actual state e.g., a first calculation of current CO_2 emissions) is compared with a goal (reference value e.g., a weekly CO_2 budget) and actions are chosen and adapted to reduce the discrepancy between input and goal by means of an output function. The effects of these actions in turn influence the environment. This effect on the environment in combination with further influencing factors from the environment (i.e., disturbances) again leads to a change in the input. Finally, the dynamics within the output function must be represented (e.g., by tracking the decisions made and supporting the comprehension of which effects can be achieved with different decision alternatives).

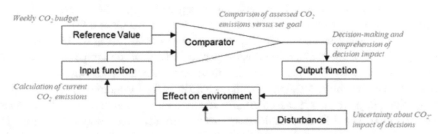

Fig. 1. Simplified self-regulation control loop by Carver and Scheier [18] applied to CO_2 emission regulation.

This model suggests that people need an accurate understanding of information regarding all components within the control loop for effective resource regulation - in other words, it is a critical component for climate literacy. Especially uncertainty about the input function (i.e., how much CO_2 their actions cause in each reference period) and the output function (i.e., which effect would different decision alternatives have) would make an effective regulation of behaviour difficult. Hence, a key need for empirical data collection is to better understand where uncertainties exist in the daily interaction with CO_2 and where potential users of CO_2 trackers perceive the need for support.

3 User Perspective on CO_2 Tracker Applications

The objective of the empirical study was to contribute first empirical insights into the perspective of potential early adopter users of CO_2 tracking apps with a specific focus on the uncertainties that they experience in the daily interaction with CO_2 and on the perceived specific needs for support. We focus on young people, who, in light of young activist movements like "Fridays for Future", we assume to have a high degree of involvement with the subject. These participants had to have at least a basic interest in their CO_2 footprint and therefore be seen as potential early adopters of CO_2 tracking applications. This was done as we believe that, given challenges like supporting user motivation and user understanding, we have to start user-centred development by focusing on target groups that may need less motivational support. To address this specific research objective, three research topics were formulated dealing with the following topics: 1) potential for CO_2 literacy improvement, 2) frequency of uncertainty regarding carbon footprint, 3) questions a carbon footprint tracking app needs to answer.

3.1 Method

Participants. We conducted an online survey via Google forms, which 249 people completed within a one-week-period in March 2020. The study was distributed via university email lists and social media. All participants had the chance to win one of two 20 € cash prizes of.

We included one filter question in the survey worded as: "I am interested in my CO_2 footprint." With a six-point Likert responses scale (from $1 =$ "Not true at all", $2 =$ "Mostly not true", $3 =$ "Rather not true", $4 =$ "Rather true", $5 =$ "Mostly true", $6 =$ "Absolutely true"). 12 participants disagreed to the filter question (i.e., had no specific interest in their CO_2 footprint) and were removed ($N = 237$).

The sample had a mean age of 23.5 years ($SD = 4.25$). 73.8% of the participants were female, 25.3% male, and 0.8% diverse gender. 94.1% of the sample were students, 5.1% professionals and 0.8% in other life situations. To control for possible sampling biases (i.e., risk that only participants with high affinity for technology react to a call for participation [19]) we also assessed affinity for technology interaction with the ATI-S short scale [20]. The ATI short scale describes affinity for technology interaction. The average ATI-score of the sample was 3.61 ($SD = 1.16$). Since the average of a comparable German population is 3.5 (cf. [20]) the sample was not seen as inducing any biases for the analysis.

Questionnaire. The online survey consisted of 19 qualitative and quantitative statements or questions and was originally conducted in German. All agreement items could be answered on a 6-point Likert scale (see above). For one question, aimed to determine frequencies of questions regarding CO_2, categories were predefined ("daily", "several times a week", "once a week", "once a month", "less than once a month", "never").

4 Thematic Analysis

The investigation of the context (Q2) as well as requirements regarding questions to be answered (Q3) was carried out by means of a reflected Thematic Analysis according to Brown and Clarke [21]. After familiarization with the data, the initial coding phase led to a list of codes that were relevant to the respective research question, hence, themes and sub-themes were defined. As only a relatively low level of abstraction of statements was targeted, this phase was less complex than for other topics in psychology (i.e., semantic rather than latent level analysis; [21]). In the final phase we again went through all transcripts and coded participants' statements based on the developed coding systems (i.e., thematic clusters and sub-clusters). Within this phase some final revisions and refinements of the coding system were performed. Clusters group similar statements of different participants (i.e., an overarching theme that is addressed by several participants). In the results section only clusters/sub-clusters with a prevalence of $n \geq 10$ (i.e., around 5% of the sample) are described.

5   Results

Question 1: How do potential early adopters perceive their own CO_2literacy? To determine participants' own perspective on individual literacy regarding CO_2 emissions (Q1) two items assessed key facets of this concept. Results regarding the first item (Q1.i1) revealed that participants' confidence in their own ability of estimating how their actions affect CO_2-emissions is relatively low ($M = 3.34$, $SD = 0.07$). Indeed 53% disagreed (i.e., after dichotomization of 6-point scale) with the given statement. Results regarding the second item (Q1.i2) revealed a similar pattern. On average, the perceived ability to accurately estimate the carbon footprint was rather low ($M = 2.79$, $SD = 0.07$). 73% at least rather disagreed with the statement. A scale combining both items showed a satisfactory internal consistency (Cronbach's $\alpha = .74$). The distribution of the resulting indicator of the subjectively perceived CO_2 literacy of the sample showed (see Fig. 2) there is considerable room for improvement in CO_2 literacy even in a sample of people who have already a considerable interest in their personal carbon footprint.

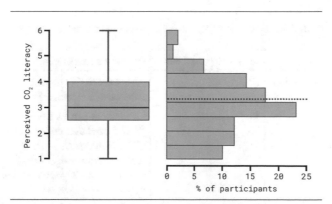

Fig. 2. Boxplot and histogram depicting the distributions of CO_2 literacy (dashed lines represent means).

Question 2: How often and when do such potential users perceive uncertainty about their carbon footprint? From $N = 249$ participants, 187 (i.e., 75%) answered that they wonder about the carbon footprint of products or services at least once a week. An overview of the various deducted thematic clusters and sub-clusters is presented in Table 1 (few answers did not fit to sub-clusters). A total of 3 themes and 4 sub-themes could be identified. In total, $n = 207$ (i.e., 87.3%) provided statements regarding the question of CO_2 tracker context. It is remarkable that shopping is mentioned much more often than mobility or housing. Tracking apps could increase attention to the latter two topics: it could be that conscious decisions are made less frequently in these categories than, for example, in shopping.

Table 1. Main thematic clusters ($n > 10$) for context of question regarding carbon footprint.

Cluster label	% of 207 participants	Examples (translated from German)
Shopping	**80**	(see subcategories below)
– Groceries	51	*"After I went shopping vegetables or fruits"*
– Clothes	9	*"Purchasing Equipment or clothes"*
Mobility	**47**	(see subcategories below)
– Travel	23	*"For vacation plans, e.g. flights"*
– Everyday mobility	17	*"While choosing means of transport e.g. car or bus"*
Housing	**6**	*"For Heating or energy supply at home"*

Question 3: Which questions would an app on your carbon footprint have to answer? In total, $n = 171$ (i.e. 72.2%) participants provided statements regarding which questions a CO_2 tracker should address A total of 5 thematic clusters were identified, with 2 sub-clusters for the theme "Alternatives" (see Table 2).

Table 2. Main thematic clusters ($N > 10$) for Questions for carbon footprint trackers.

Thematic clusters	% of 171 participants	Examples (translated from German)
Product/Action Emission	**67**	*"How much CO_2 does the consumption of a certain meal cause?"*
Alternatives - Suggestion - Comparison	**57** 36 21	(see subcategories below) *"I've heard that coffee causes a lot of CO_2. If that is true, are there (good!) alternatives for my coffee?"* *"How much CO_2 costs clothing (bought new vs. second-hand)?"*
Compensation	**31**	*"What are reputable ways to compensate for unavoidable travel?"*
Evaluation	**18**	*"When exactly do I produce "too much" CO_2?"*
Completeness	**8**	*"What are the CO_2 emissions of a product and in which processes is it divided (production phases, packaging, transport etc.)?"*

6 Discussion

The present research aimed to explicate key psychological challenges for the design of CO_2 trackers. We investigated which design recommendations could be garnered based on findings from the field of behavioural economics. This was further supported by gathering first empirical insights on the perspective of users who have at least a basic interest in their personal carbon footprint in an online study.

Based on the theoretical perspective of behavioural economics and control theoretical models, we concluded that by presenting CO_2 emissions as e.g. an individual budget, the shared task of reducing emissions can be dealt with on an individual level. In addition, when representing individual CO_2 emissions, it is important to ensure that the individual contribution to avoiding negative consequences is emphasised (i.e., to avoid loss of an individual CO_2 budget). Furthermore, comprehension of and assistance with behavioural control loops supports user's climate literacy.

We showed empirically that the perceived literacy in terms of the CO_2 footprint is low despite the high interest in the topic in the sample of participants (Q1). It was also found that many users very often have questions about their own CO_2 footprint. A large majority of users ask themselves questions about the CO_2 footprint at least once a week (Q2). This could be related to the fact that these questions arise in everyday situations. Especially the area of food shopping or individual daily mobility are contexts that are mentioned by the participants. The collection of questions users would address to a CO_2 tracking app revealed that the need for a decision support system is predominant (Q3). The support of decisions by proposing alternatives or comparing two similar products is particularly prominent.

Based on the collection of questions that would be asked of a CO_2 tracking app, it seems reasonable to distinguish between three types of functions which could best support climate literacy: 1) the presentation of CO_2 emissions at a concrete product or action level, 2) the direct comparison between two decision alternatives, and 3) the proposal of better alternatives. Considering the above-mentioned contexts, it is necessary to enable a comparison as a basis function that can be implemented very quickly and, if necessary, is exclusively based on a single CO_2 emission resource. For the implementation of the third function, it is important to take a closer look into the area of recommender systems and to check the suitability of corresponding systems (e.g., collaborative filtering or social navigation).

One further relevant topic from the field of user-centered design appears to be the examination of design possibilities to support the tangibility of CO_2 as a resource. Hence, the question is how a personal CO_2 budget should be best represented based on the theoretical consideration within the present paper. One next step with considerable HCI-potential is to examine what can be learned from this research for the design of optimal CO_2 budget metaphors and interface representations (e.g., temporal and quantitative representation of CO_2). A further empirical test of different design solutions with methods from behavioural economics appears promising here.

To further adapt an application to the needs of individual users, further research needs to address usage contexts and carbon footprint related questions to enable the formation of user groups. In this way, clusters could be developed that are differentiated in terms of their preferences (e.g.: "At what times should feedback be provided?" or "When should the budget be presented?"). Other elements that should be further considered in analyses are the issue of gamification [22] and the implementation of social comparisons. Here, however, tracking CO_2 as a shared resource could have different effects than other resources for which social comparisons have been used so far (for example, in the area of sport or engagement). The extent to which budgets can be shared across people (in e.g. families) and actions can be included in a common budget should also be evaluated in future studies.

Also, future studies should consider, which design features in an CO_2 tracking application could improve adherence, i.e. long-term tracker usage and implementation of user goals. Trackers are generally exposed to a high risk of being used for a short time and then abandoned [23]. This also endangers the effect of the tracker on a long-term change in behaviour. It should therefore be investigated which measures in the context of CO_2 tracking could contribute to increase the probability of long-term use.

7   Conclusion

Without a comprehensive and empirically grounded understanding of users' bounded rationality and behavioural control loops, the potential of CO_2 tracking applications to overcome current climate challenges cannot be exhausted. In a short literature summary and user study, we provide first work on developing tools to support climate literacy and the integration of climate-friendly behaviour into everyday life.

References

1. Gohar, L.K., Shine, K.P.: Equivalent CO2 and its use in understanding the climate effects of increased greenhouse gas concentrations. Weather **62**, 307–311 (2007). https://doi.org/10.1002/wea.103
2. Crippa, M., Oreggioni, G., Guizzardi, D., Muntean, M., Schaaf, E., Lo Vullo, E., Solazzo, E., Monforti-Ferrario, F., Olivier, J.G.J., Vignati, E., European Commission, Joint Research Centre: Fossil CO2 and GHG emissions of all world countries: 2019 report. Publications Office of the European Union, Luxembourg (2019)
3. United Nations Framework Convention on Climate Change ed: The Kyoto Protocol (1998)
4. United Nations Framework Convention on Climate Change ed: The Paris Agreement (2015)
5. United Nations Development Programme: Sustainable Development Goals. https://www.undp.org/content/undp/en/home/sustainable-development-goals.html. Accessed 24 Mar 2020
6. Torpman, O.: The case for emissions egalitarianism. Ethical Theory Moral Pract. **22**, 749–762 (2019). https://doi.org/10.1007/s10677-019-10016-8
7. Vermeir, I., Verbeke, W.: Sustainable food consumption: exploring the consumer "attitude – behavioral intention" gap. J Agric Environ Ethics **19**, 169–194 (2006). https://doi.org/10.1007/s10806-005-5485-3
8. Horne, R., Grant, T., Verghese, K.: Life Cycle Assessment: Principles, Practice, and Prospects. Csiro Publishing (2009)
9. Almalki, M., Gray, K., Sanchez, F.M.: The use of self-quantification systems for personal health information: big data management activities and prospects. Health Inf Sci Syst **3**, S1 (2015)
10. Etkin, J.: The hidden cost of personal quantification. J. Consum. Res. **42**, 967–984 (2016)

11. Guzman, L., Makonin, S., Clapp, A.: CarbonKit: designing a personal carbon tracking platform. In: Proceedings of the Fourth International Workshop on Social Sensing, pp. 24–29. Association for Computing Machinery, New York (2019). https://doi.org/10.1145/3313294. 3313385

12. Nielsen, K.S., Clayton, S., Stern, P.C., Dietz, T., Capstick, S., Whitmarsh, L.: How psychology can help limit climate change. Am Psychol (2020). https://doi.org/10.1037/amp0000624

13. Gifford, R.: The dragons of inaction: psychological barriers that limit climate change mitigation and adaptation. Am Psychol **66**, 290–302 (2011). https://doi.org/10.1037/a0023566

14. Nolan, J.M., Schultz, P.W., Cialdini, R.B., Goldstein, N.J., Griskevicius, V.: Normative social influence is underdetected. Pers Soc Psychol Bull **34**, 913–923 (2008). https://doi.org/10.1177/0146167208316691

15. Kahneman, D., Knetsch, J.L., Thaler, R.H.: Anomalies: the endowment effect, loss aversion, and status quo bias. J Econ Perspect **5**, 193–206 (1991). https://doi.org/10.1257/jep.5.1.193

16. Jacquet, J., Hagel, K., Hauert, C., Marotzke, J., Röhl, T., Milinski, M.: Intra- and intergenerational discounting in the climate game. Nat Clim Change **3**, 1025–1028 (2013). https://doi.org/10.1038/nclimate2024

17. Attig, C., Franke, T.: I track, therefore I walk – exploring the motivational costs of wearing activity trackers in actual users. Int J Hum-Comput Stud **127**, 211–224 (2019). https://doi.org/10.1016/j.ijhcs.2018.04.007

18. Carver, C.S., Scheier, M.F.: On the structure of behavioral self-regulation. In: Handbook of Self-Regulation, pp. 41–84. Elsevier (2000). https://doi.org/10.1016/B978-012109890-2/50032-9

19. Franke, T., Attig, C., Wessel, D.: A personal resource for technology interaction: development and validation of the affinity for technology interaction (ATI) scale. Int J Human-Comput Interact **35**, 456–467 (2019). https://doi.org/10.1080/10447318.2018.1456150

20. Wessel, D., Attig, C., Franke, T.: ATI-S - an ultra-short scale for assessing affinity for technology interaction in user studies. In: Proceedings of Mensch und Computer 2019 on – MuC 2019, pp. 147–154. ACM Press, Hamburg (2019). https://doi.org/10.1145/3340764.3340766

21. Braun, V., Clarke, V.: Using thematic analysis in psychology. Qual Res Psychol **3**, 77–101 (2006). https://doi.org/10.1191/1478088706qp063oa

22. Marques, B., Nixon, K.: The gamified grid: possibilities for utilising game-based motivational psychology to empower the Smart Social Grid. In: 2013 Africon, Pointe-Aux-Piments, Mauritius, pp. 1–5. IEEE (2013). https://doi.org/10.1109/AFRCON.2013.6757748

23. Attig, C., Franke, T.: Abandonment of personal quantification: a review and empirical study investigating reasons for wearable activity tracking attrition. Comput Hum Behav **102**, 223–237 (2020). https://doi.org/10.1016/j.chb.2019.08.025

The Ergonomics of Recycling Mattresses in Australia

Elizabeth M. Smith[(⊠)]

WorkSmith, Queanbeyan, Australia
service@worksmith.com.au

Abstract. The study analyses the ergonomics of manually recycling mattresses in an Australian context of a social enterprise. Mattress recycling in Australia is an environmentally conscious economy geared at diverting waste mattresses from landfill. Manual recycling of mattresses in the studied enterprise was a strategy for employing more people who had barriers to obtaining work. Analysis of a recycling task identified risk factors that required control. The analysis will guide decisions to enable healthier sustainable work for the person and the enterprise.

Keywords: Recycling · Mattress · Manual tasks · Ergonomics · Social enterprise

1 The Problem

Physical and psychological injuries from manual tasks in Australia impose high cost on the community (through compensation claims, lost productivity, social and individual impacts on health). Labourers lodged 10% of all serious body stressing claims [1].

Lack of application of reliable methods to inform how work is designed may expose vulnerable people to a higher risk of injury and threaten business viability. Continued employment and health and safety outcomes are highly reliant on how a manager acts as a decision maker to design work. Other factors include a manager's tolerance for risk and their ethics; and the workers' capabilities and work practices and a broader context of the enterprise's purpose in the community [2, 3].

2 Context

Mattress recycling occurs in broader social systems and sustainable use of resources (people and planet). Balancing risks for good work design is a challenge when an enterprise has a mission of creating employment opportunity. Risk is context sensitive and decisions are often based on the decision makers world view or experiences. The purpose of the studied enterprise is to provide access to sustainable employment - creating outcomes that help build a safe, productive community.

N. L. Black et al. (Eds.): IEA 2021, LNNS 220, pp. 582–587, 2021.
https://doi.org/10.1007/978-3-030-74605-6_74

Social enterprises may operate with thin financial margins and risk controls of high order may not be immediately viable. A higher order risk control is to mechanise the mattress recycling tasks which was not a viable option for the studied enterprise at this time. The analysis is part of 'discovery' phase [4] in an improvement program addressing an identified risk for injury in the enterprise, manual mattress recycling.

3 Actions

A Certified Professional Ergonomist analysed work of recyclers at two sites in one social enterprise.The analysis use a mix of methods selected to suit the type of task; and ease or cost to implement at two sites with least operational interruption. Further details of use of the tools and analysis is reported elsewhere [5].Table 1 outlines the methods and reasoning for selection.

Table 1. Methods applied in a case study of a mattress recycling enterprise.

Methods	Reasoning
Task observations, photographs & video recordings	Commonly used observational method to identify and measure steps, hazards and manual movements within a task or job role. Included to provide a whole view of the job roles and work activity (2 sites)
Regulatory WHS guidance: hazardous task risk factor assessment	Factor analysis to identify hazardous manual tasks as defined in legislation. Included for legal compliance documentation and verified the tasks with risk exposure
REBA Rapid Entire Body Assessment [6]	REBA is a quick reliable tool based on observational study. It provides for ranking of risks for task or job comparison. REBA analysis was based on the tasks analysis results. Helped to set priority for focus based on risk ranking of job activity by role at the sites (n = 3)
RULA Rapid Upper Limb Assessment [7]	A survey method for the investigation of work related upper limb disorders. Included as mattress cutting involves upper limb effort (n = 3)
Strain Index [8]	Observational rating scale for hand tasks (n = 1). Included based on observational analysis and RULA score indicating wrist and hand position may be a risk factor

(continued)

Table 1. (*continued*)

Methods	Reasoning
Assessment of repetitive tasks (ART) [9]	Observational analysis to identify common risk factors in repetitive work that contribute to the development of upper limb disorders (ULDs). Included to round out the risk factors and confirm focus areas for interventions and areas for job rotation options (n = 1)
Process analysis, flow analysis	Sequence of processes, tasks, inputs, outputs, stock, people and machines, movement and flow interactions (one site)
Focus Group	Small team facilitated discussion on the topic of discomfort and work tasks (participant n = 18, one site). Outputs: a map of discomfort at team level; verified areas for priority for interventions
Ergonomic systems model [10]	Factor analysis to understand systemic context. Included to understand broader context and system elements to support arguments for change with management

4   Outcomes

The task of manual mattress recycling is performed in a complex context within an operational production design. The recyclers perform a range of tasks (one with 25 recyclers in designated job for mattress disassembly, the other with 15 recyclers in rotated or combined jobs). They work a 7–8 hours day shift for 5–6 days per week (variance due to production demands). Paid an hourly rate, the recyclers agreed to meet a daily processing target of 45–50 disassembled mattresses per recycler.

Key steps in the mattress recycling task include:

1. In standing, pull or carry from stack to work station table.
2. Disassemble mattress into component materials (cloth, foam, latex, springs) by cutting with hand tool (retractable blade), pulling with hands or pliers.
3. As each layer is revealed, carry component materials to stacks.

The analysis with the assessment methods confirmed the manual activity of mattress disassembly has high exposure to injury (which aligns to the risk experience). Some sub steps in the task were defined as hazardous manual tasks according to Australian regulations (e.g. moving the mattress onto the workstation). The hand cutting risk factors were due to the arm and wrist position. The activity risks were due to duration (higher if a designated role compared to a combined role) and repetition; speed of work, and effort (subjective measures).

ART exposure score for work activity (n = 1) = 31 (high) for Left arm non dominant; 35 (high) for Right arm (dominant). RULA score = 7 (very high); and

REBA score = 11 (very high). Job strain index (forearm and hand) for cutting action = 13.5 (threshold 5). Cycle times range from 4–10 min depending on the size and nature of the mattress and skill of the operator.

Tactical interventions for risk control involved small changes to work methods and information about safer practices e.g. posters showing recommended hand position for cutting method (visual instructions being more accessible to people with language barriers); trials by the workers to use a hook tool rather than their hands for removing specific mattress materials such as coconut fibres; induction and education for work break stretches specific to relieve common areas of discomfort.

Higher order controls may relieve work demand on recyclers and support capability building objectives. Ideas under consideration include: some task steps may suit more mechanical handling systems or layout changes to reduce carry distances; or work design changes such as more flexible job rotations in teams; or competency programs e.g. the recyclers also doing plant operator rotations during shifts); as well as health strategies (primary or secondary interventions). Injury management (tertiary) support is in place for early intervention treatment support and return to work.

5   Discussion

The analysis used a variety of methods which were easy and suitable to apply in a operational workplace and engaged managers and workers. Inherent bias (in method selection) and influence of observation on workers' performing tasks may have affected results. The analysis helped to create a profile of the ergonomics for the work of mattress recyclers. Supervisors gained awareness of the methods and risks which supported a shift their attention to primary interventions. Managers and supervisors learnt methods to consult with the teams and test ideas. Workers observed management investing in safety improvement.

The analysis helped to understand the work and risks. The methods identified steps suitable for intervention to relieve the heavy work demands (e.g. changing the arm posture with different tools or cutting method). Objective validation of the hazardous nature of the task steps that created discomfort provided incentive for tactical interim controls to be adopted. The analysis will guide future risk control interventions to support the desired outcomes of healthier work.

The analysis may inform future policy decisions about mechanisation of whole or sub tasks e.g. based on return on investment for sustainable employment, production and injury exposure reduction. Resolving the tension between a policy favouring manual tasks in order to employ more people; tasks with injury risk exposure and viable access to higher order controls is a moral, legal and operational decision.

6 Conclusion

This study illustrates the importance of understanding work design for social sustainability (employment) and environmental sustainability (waste management). The study establishes an understanding of risk exposure factors in manual mattress recycling. The approach stimulated awareness of work design strategies with supervisors and managers (compared to assumptions about 'safe workers' following instructions or being better trained). The visibility of the assessment activity at the site provided interest and incentive for improving risk control in consultation with workers.

> The methods selected informed managers about the tasks and injury exposure factors and helped to prioritise effort. A single method did not adequately profile exposure to injury in a complex job and workplace. The mix of methods better identified the risk context and risk in sub tasks that could be improved if elimination of hazard itself is not viable.

> This mixed method approach to analyse work is useful where mechanisation or complete elimination of hazards are not reasonable options for a business; and when managers are open to creating a safer, more efficient design of the work in consultation with their workers. Targeted interventions were initiated on how tasks could be performed such as a change of technique and providing more tool options for workers (as interim risk controls). Higher order controls are being considered with management.

> Aligning strategic interventions to values and purpose of an enterprise is an important role for ergonomists. Social enterprises in the waste management sector operate in complex systems. Risks to productivity and health and safety are equally important to consider for commercially viable business models within circular economies. Improving work design supports systems for both productivity and health outcomes. Future analysis of interventions will inform how the enterprise can balance the benefits and risks of employing more people in the context of business operations that involve hazardous manual work.

References

1. Safe Work Australia. https://www.safeworkaustralia.gov.au/manual-handling. Accessed 28 Oct 2020
2. Fostervold, K.I., Koren, P.C., Nilsen, O.V.: Defining sustainable and 'decent' work for human factors and ergonomics. In: Thatcher, A., Yeow, P.H.P. (eds.) Chapter 3 in Ergonomics and Human Factors for a Sustainable Future (2018)
3. Parker, S., Van den Broeck, A., Holman, D.: Work design influences: a synthesis of multilevel factors that affect the design of jobs. Acad. Manag. Ann. **11**(1), 267–308 (2017)
4. Human factors & ergonomics society of australia good work design technical report, July 2020
5. Lizzy Smith Post. https://www.researchgate.net/post/Mattress_recycling-waste_manage ment_social_enterprise. Accessed 28 Feb 2021
6. Hignett, S., McAtamney, L.: Rapid entire body assessment (REBA). Appl. Ergon. **31**(2), 201–205 (2000)

7. McAtamney, L., Nigel Corlett, E.: RULA: a survey method for the investigation of work-related upper limb disorders. Appl. Ergon. **24**(2), 91–99 (1993)
8. Steven Moore, J., Garg, A.: The strain index: a proposed method to analyze jobs for risk of distal upper extremity disorders. Am. Ind. Hyg. Assoc. J. **56**(5), 443–458 (1995)
9. Assessment of repetitive tasks tool (ART) downloaded from the HSE (UK) Web page (2021)
10. Macdonald, W., Oakman, J.: Requirements for more effective prevention of work-related musculoskeletal disorders. BMC Musculoskelet. Disord. **16**, 293 (2015)

Ergonomics Role in Sustainable Development: A Review Article for Updates the Recent Knowledge

Mohammad Sadegh Sohrabi$^{(\boxtimes)}$ (iD)

Department of Industrial Design, School of Architecture and Urban Design,
Art University of Isfahan, Isfahan, Iran
ms.sohrabi@aui.ac.ir

Abstract. Having a greater role in the social and environmental sustainability has caused many challenges to addressing the paradigm of sustainable development in developing countries. The aim of this study is to update the uses and commons of the ergonomics with the sustainable development paradigm. In this review study, to find relevant literatures the "Ergonomics", "Human Factors", "Sustainable Development, and Sustainability" were searched as core keywords. The search was limited since 2000 to 2017. Finally, 13 articles were selected. The results indicated a dramatic increase in the number of articles in ergonomics and sustainable development field recently. These results indicate the role of micro-ergonomic interventions in sustainability that can take place in various economic, social or environmental domains. Reducing occupational accidents and illnesses and increasing the health of employees is related to aspects of social sustainability and leads to social sustainability in people's work life. Ergonomics attention to design/redesign of systems including production subsystem, communications, human resources and other support subsystems, such as health and well-being, and the system's life cycle consideration can be a move towards the sustainability.

Keywords: Ergonomics · Sustainable development · Macro-Ergonomics

1 Introduction

Sustainable development is one of the most important social transitions in the late twentieth and early 21st centuries which humans and organizations have to move towards this paradigm [1]. Sustainable development is stated in three basis of the environment, economic and social. It includes products and technologies that provide the needs of the present time without threatening future needs [2]. Sustainable development is recognized as a comprehensive approach which addresses development in the ways that don't endanger the environment [3]. These conditions are not only compatible with environmental policies, but also with economic and social ones [4]. According to the definition of the World Commission on Environment and Development (Brundtland Commission) in 1987, sustainable development is a development that provides current needs, without threatening future generations' ability [4]. This development improves the quality

© The Author(s), under exclusive license to Springer Nature Switzerland AG 2021
N. L. Black et al. (Eds.): IEA 2021, LNNS 220, pp. 588–602, 2021.
https://doi.org/10.1007/978-3-030-74605-6_75

of human's life and work [4, 5]. Previously, issues such as consumption and production, environment and resources, land use and agriculture, transportation, production and supply of energy, waste and recycling were main topics in sustainable development, but in addition to physical areas, sustainability of organizations and sustainable use of human resources are also concerns in the sustainable development [4]. Challenges for paying attention to the sustainable development paradigm in developing countries have more importance [6–9]. According to the statement of the "United Nations Sustainable Development Summit 2015" in New York 2015, sustainable development goals were identified in three areas including economic growth, social inclusion and environmental protection. Governments, non-government sectors, civil society, and other stakeholders committed to achieving these goals by 2030 to put an end to poverty and make a more sustainable world [10]. Recently, ergonomists' interest has grown in three pillars of sustainable development, and the number of articles in sustainable development areas has also grown [11]. In July 2008, the International Ergonomics Association launched the "Human Factors and Sustainable Development" technical committee for management and development of activities in this area [5]. This committee has 4 sub-committees entitled: 1) Theoretical viewpoint of human factors and sustainable development, 2) Sustainability and risk management, 3) Human factors and sustainable development in global value creation; 4) Ergonomics and design for sustainability. This committee with the slogan "We know where the world is moving, and if we know where the work will go, so we'll know what human factors will help," officially began their activities in 2006. Also the Journal of Ergonomics published a special issue with Ergonomics and sustainability topic, and pointed to Ergonomics role in industrial and environmental sustainable development [4]. In current century, attitude change in Ergonomics discipline towards the globalized Ergonomics and sustainable development is crucial for preservation of human and systems [8]. As a result, paying attention to socio-technical systems and human resources will help sustainable development benefits and will make a forward step to a sustainable future [4, 12].

In past review studies in the field of ergonomics and sustainable development, Martin et al. [13], Radjiyev et al. [11], Bolis et al. [14] and Thatcher [5] examined the theoretical relationship between the concepts of ergonomics and the field of sustainable development. Meyer et al. [15] has also identified ergonomics as a means of promoting sustainable development goals. One of the overviews of sustainable development by Olawumi and Chan has been devoted to the study of global trends and sustainability structures between 1991 and 2016 [16]. In that study, the map of sustainability studies in the world is drawn up and its interaction with the ergonomic knowledge or related sciences has not been addressed. Saravia-Pinilla et al. [17] also reviewed the relationship between ergonomics and product/service design from the perspective of sustainable environmental development. In these papers, the systematic review methodology is not precisely executed and has shortcomings in terms of method or time or did not all areas of the pillars of sustainable development are taken into account. Therefore, due to importance of sustainable development concept in societies as well as the growth of activities in Ergonomics knowledge, this study aims to update the Ergonomics literature with sustainable development concept through a systematic review.

2 Methodology

The research stages of this systematic review are implemented based on the official statement of PRISMA (Preferred Reporting Items for Systematic Reviews and Meta-Analyses) [18]. Papers are indexed in journals from the beginning of the 21st century to the end of 2017 were included. These papers have effectively compared common aspects of Ergonomics and foundations of sustainable development. These papers should also explain the implication of Ergonomics usage in sustainable development goals. Due to the lack of joint papers, a certain limitation to articles selection was not used. At the beginning of data gathering, search process was done in Scopus, PubMed and Web of Science, with main keywords such as "Ergonomics", "Human Factors", "Sustainable Development" and "Sustainability", in two ways of "OR" for increasing sensitivity and "AND" for specificity of the results among title, abstract and keywords. This protocol was in accordance with the method of reviewing the texts of Martin et al. [13]. (Appendix 1. Search strategies). First, 966 articles were obtained. After removing duplicate papers, 676 articles containing at least one of the main keywords in the full text were found. Then according to the method of selecting related texts, Radjiyev et al. [11], by reading carefully all abstracts, 103 articles were selected. Afterwards, by examining the full text of the selected articles in previous stage, 44 articles were selected in accordance to the inclusion and exclusion criteria of the protocol. Then, by measuring the qualitative criteria of articles, 31 articles were omitted and finally 13 articles were selected for information synthesis. This process is shown in Fig. 1.

Inclusion and Exclusion Criteria

Inclusion criteria contain English published articles between 2000 until the end of October 2017, which had surveyed Ergonomics and sustainable development. Exclusion criteria contain papers were presented at scientific conferences and seminars, letter to editors, review articles, reports and book sections, or articles that didn't have the qualitative criteria.

Evaluation of Articles Quality

Using the official checklist of STROBE's statement (Strengthening The Reporting of Observational Studies in Epidemiology) [19], the qualitative assessment for selecting papers was done by two evaluators separately. Differences between two evaluators were referred to the third person. It should be noted that this standard checklist has 22 items including title and abstract, introduction, method, results, discussion and other information and has acceptable credibility in systematic review research. To select the articles after the evaluation of the evaluators, if the article obtained at least 10 items from the checklist, it entered to the synthesis stage. The table of qualitative evaluation score of 44 papers is presented in the Appendix 2, qualitative evaluation.

Information Extraction:

After carefully studying and extracting the required information from the articles, the extracted results were first summarized in the extraction table and then analyzed manually.

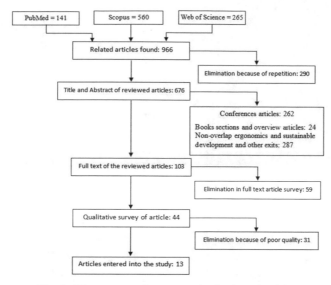

Fig. 1. The process of survey and selection of articles

3 Results

In Table 1 the highlights and sustainability consistent of 13 papers analyzed in this study are described.

Given the key pillars of sustainable development [32], which includes sustainable economic development, sustainable social development and sustainable environmental development, the findings are presented on the same basis.

a. *Economic Sustainability*

For sustained economic development, attention is focused on controlling income and expenditure flow, assets and financial liabilities, which public interventions and Ergonomics projects in this part, increase productivity and reduces work costs [32]. In economic sustainability, Ergonomics, with the look of socio-technical systems, analyzes and surveys support and communication systems and identifies the potential for improvement [33]. Another issue in business sustainability is waste and recycling that can occur in physical or human resource. In this case, the development of environment-friendly or waste reducer social-technical systems can guarantee the health and safety of employees and the efficiency of the business systems [4]. Ergonomics can also make a difference in the sustainable development of transportation systems. These changes can take place at the level of car factories, energy efficiency, transportation systems, vehicle life cycle, or socio-economic macroeconomic policies [29]. Sustainable production is a paradigm for production that has the least negative impact on the environment, energy conservation or natural resources and is safe and economical for employees and communities. Lee et al. introduced a model called MAS2 in their project, which is an integrated model for

Table 1. Specifications of articles published in the common area of ergonomics and sustainable development between 2000 and 2017, (sort by year).

Highlights	Sustainability pillar			Year	Author's
	Economic	Social	Environmental		
Move towards sustainability will result in many significant changes which present opportunities for E/HF professionals to improve work, systems, products and behaviors Design of products and systems that are "environmentally friendly" to facilitate their acceptability and use and how E/HF professionals can contribute to understanding and promoting behavioral change relating to environmental choices			*	2013	Hanson, M. A .[20]
The role of anthropometry in design process consisted of three iterations, with each iteration accounting for one of three sustainability concerns: reduction of raw material consumption, increase of usage lifetimes and consideration of ethical consequences of design decisions	*	*		2013	Nadadur, G. and M. B. Parkinson [21]
Web-based learning program that promote sustainable well-being at work were identified and described in the categories of the worker's individual capabilities and competencies, in the work organization and environment, and in the leadership The learning program can be considered a feasible and efficient in the light of promoting sustainable well-being at work/		*		2013	Randelin, M., T. Saaranen, P. Naumanen and V. Louhevaara [22]

(continued)

Table 1. (*continued*)

Highlights	Sustainability pillar			Year	Author's
	Economic	Social	Environmental		
Green ergonomics is defined as ergonomics interventions that have a pro-nature focus; specifically ergonomics that focuses on human affinity with the natural world The most important role for green ergonomics would be in facilitating larger, systemic behavior change in attempting to understand energy conservation behavior and other sustainable environmental behaviors The overlaps between ecological and ergonomics science are obvious and discuss about the challenge of ecological science to understand 'the intricate dependencies between humans and nature in society's endeavor to sustain long-term health and well-being			*	2013	Thatcher, A. [23]
Creating new and using well-known synergies between the domains of E/HF and sustainability could finally lead to mutual benefits: E/HF could offer its research results, methods and instruments as those are relevant for implementing sustainable development. This could also help to overcome the often rather 'green image' of sustainable development (reducing sustainability to an ecological approach), which does not take into account its character of an overall comprehensive concept		*		2013	Zink, K. J. and K. Fischer [24]

(continued)

Table 1. (*continued*)

Highlights	Sustainability pillar			Year	Author's
	Economic	Social	Environmental		
All the companies include care for the stakeholder "workers" in the information made available on their corporate websites in areas devoted to sustainability or social responsibility policies Ergonomics can be an important tool for sustainable policies since it's' contributions are related workers wellbeing, and to improvement in the production process, quality and productivity		*		2014	Bolis, I., C. M. Brunoro and L. I. Sznelwar [25]
Ergoecology proposes a multidiscipline for systematically studying the relationship between human activities and the natural environment, embracing complexity by extending the analysis of interactions (socio-technical systems with natural systems) Green ergonomics offers an approach to research and implement interventions with a pro–nature focus		*	*	2014	Lange-Morales, K., A. Thatcher and G. García-Acosta [26]
MAS² has been introduced for integrated modeling and simulation-based life cycle evaluation for sustainable manufacturing The MAS² system provides system architecture to communicate with heterogeneous engineering applications like human factors, to support sustainability assessment	*			2014	Lee, Ju Yeon. Kang, Hyoung Seok. Do Noh, Sang [27]
Green Ergo promotes simplicity in design, creativity, lower costs compared to store-bought items and a unified sense of pride in the workforce that everyone is protecting both people and planet	*		*	2014	Pilczuk, D. and K. Barefield [28]

(continued)

Table 1. (*continued*)

Highlights	Sustainability pillar			Year	Author's
	Economic	Social	Environmental		
There is an important role for Ergonomists/ Human Factors Engineers in contributing knowledge and wisdom, both in the design and operation of these sustaining systems and processes and ameliorating the undesirable effects of change on the recipients of changed processes	*	*	*	2015	Siemieniuch, C. E., M. A. Sinclair and M. J. Henshaw [29]
Occupational health and safety programs must not compromise work efficacy, efficiency and budgets Floor laying businesses place the stakes of sustainability in terms of their trade, where Occupational health and safety and competency issues are interrelated		*		2016	Lortie, M., S. Nadeau and S. Vezeau [30]
Green ergonomics approach can provide us with useful insights into sustainable relationships between humans and ecology in facilitating human well-being in consideration of the overall performance of the social-ecological system Policy interventions to change human behavior and achieve greater collaboration between various levels of government, academia, civil society, and businesses can help establish sustainable relationships between humans and ecology		*	*	2016	Poon, W. C., G. Herath, A. Sarker, T. Masuda and R. Kada [31]
3-pillar framework, applied at the activity levels, would help to excellent environmental performance without revealing the related potential negative impacts on human factors and costs Ergonomics professionals could contribute economic sub-sector specific metrics on worker and community health and safety, which can be incorporated into holistic activity level sustainability reporting Ergonomics could lift current sustainability reporting practices to the next level by promoting a balanced activity based sustainability reporting paradigm	*	*	*	2016	Samudhram, A., E. G. Siew, J. Sinnakkannu and P. H. Yeow [32]

assessing life cycle simulation for sustainable production. This model includes the fundamental principles of sustainable production, indicators of sustainable production (MSI),
evaluation method (e-MAS2) and information management (i-MAS2). The concept of
sustainable production in relation to the system of community and the earth ecosystem
is shown in Fig. 2. In the Sustainability Principles section, this model addresses 20
principles for sustainability, and then determines environmental, economic, and social
indicators in sustainable production, and an indicator for measuring the steady state
of the production system is determined. This model presents a method for evaluating
sustainability in production, which provides a quantitative assessment of the sustainability of production and work using statistical models. The proposed model is one of
the most complete models for measuring and determining sustainable production that
has the required extension of management and sustainability change in large and small
industries [27].

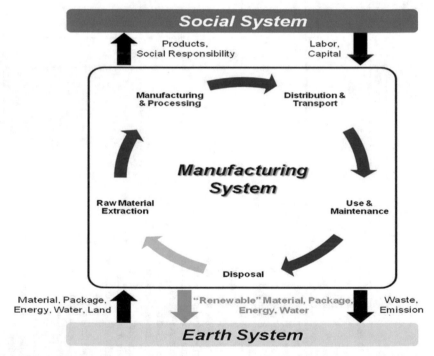

Fig. 2. Sustainable production in relation to the community system and ecosystem of the earth
[27]

b. *Social Stability*

The most important issues in social sustainability include education, employee development, social and gender equality, safety and health, and social communication [32]
From another viewpoint, musculoskeletal disorders, which are the main concern of

ergonomics around the world, will have a significant impact on sustainable development [22]. The goal of sustainable development is to preserve resources and utilize the existing resources. Maintaining and health of human resources will be in the direction of main goals of sustainable development [4]. Another topic in ergonomics and sustainable development is the use of anthropometric information in product design. In this view, Ergonomics knowledge in using human anthropometric changes procedures helps designers to increase the products life [21]. For example, the design of the seat for the work station in the process industry can be noted, which life-span and the use of chairs, are important elements in the sustainability of products and the creation of socio-economic sustainability [4].

c. Environmental Custainability

The main issues of sustainable environmental development are conservation and maintenance of energy resources, air and water, and renewable, waste and recycling of materials [32]. Ergo-Ecology is an interdisciplinary study of man and human-environment relations that examines the positive and negative effects of human-environmental relationships. This knowledge examines the flow of energy, materials and information in the Micro-Ergonomics and the socio-technical and natural systems from the Macro-Ergonomics perspective [26]. Ergo-Ecology provides a good basis for common ergonomic studies and environmental sustainability, and monitors the economic and social sustainability simultaneously [17, 26]. Green Ergonomics focuses on the common human-nature interaction level, and this approach addresses the maintaining and restoring ecosystems for human health [26]. This term, which was invented in Britain by Environment friendly efforts of Margaret Hanson, emphasizes on the use of clean energy, safety and health in the recycling, organic agriculture and sustainable buildings [23]. Green ergonomics addresses a two-way relationship between human and nature. In green ergonomics, two fundamental questions' answers are important; 1) how can Ergonomics designing and evaluating be used to preserve, maintain and restore the nature? 2) How can a service ecosystem be applied to the welfare and effectiveness of the human system? Green ergonomic goals include designing low resources systems and manufacturing, green jobs and design for behaviors change [20, 23]. After Ergonomic Green term, another term called Eco-Ergonomics is used, which deals with user interaction and recycling (recycling chemistry). Eco-Ergonomics is about equipment's recycling and factories, how to design and exploit them for system efficiency and human health [4].

Transportation is also a common area of ergonomics and sustainable development. Development sustainability thinking tries to create sustainability by decreasing energy waste, increasing productivity, and reducing greenhouse gas emissions. Ergonomics also accomplishes this with due regard to the effectiveness of the human-machine interface and the focus on the human sector in transportation systems. Ergonomics can achieve this goal with regard to the effectiveness of the human-machine interface and the focus on human resources in transportation systems [4]. According to previous models of ergonomics, Fig. 3, most of interventions have been conducted in the areas of productivity and effectiveness of social and economic fund [5]. But from Green Ergonomics perspective, attention to the efficiency and effectiveness of natural resources is also important and directs ergonomic interventions for eco-efficiency and effectiveness. In general, Green Ergonomics can be considered as a subscription of Ergonomics to sustainable environmental development [20, 23, 28]. In the early stages of sustainable development, attention has often been given to protecting natural resources, or development, taking into account environmental considerations, but in the third millennium and with the increasing need for sustainability, simultaneous attention to the three pillars of economic, social and natural capitals is a fundamental and obvious principle [5, 24, 32].

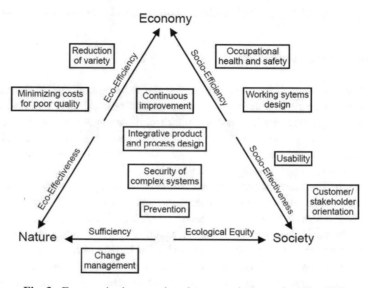

Fig. 3. Ergonomics interventions in companies' sustainability [34]

Micro-Ergonomics role interventions in sustainability can occur in various economic, social or environmental domains [35, 36]. For example, Ergonomic interventions in design for machinery maintenance and repair can change the life cycle of a machine, which will then improve the quality of work life of workers and, consequently, social sustainability [14, 37]. Ergonomic requirements in environmental design can make changes in its life cycle in line with the objectives of environmental and social sustainability [38]. Also, socio-technical designs as the micro-interventions in ergonomics can lead to evaluating and designing products and sustainable spaces by collaborative methods. These interventions, by physical resources (materials) and local human resources (users) can create changes in the socio-technical state of same place; the continuation of these changes can also help the cultural sustainability [39, 40]. Continuing efforts by ergonomists to improve working conditions can lead to social sustainability [41]. Incidents and diseases reduction in the workplace and increasing the health of employees are related to social sustainability aspects [3]. Ergonomic interventions aimed at increasing productivity and decreasing costs, including absenteeism and work-related injuries, can also contribute to the goals of commercial and economic sustainability of businesses. Service interventions selection, including supportive health workers subsystems, can provide the optimal social and economic sustainability. Micro-Ergonomic and Macro-Ergonomic attitude should be considered in sustainability interventions [36, 42].

4   Conclusion

Nowadays, a concept called organizational sustainability has expanded among governments and major organizations. This concept not only includes economic sustainability in an organization, but also sustainable social and environmental aspects [13]. The need for organizational sustainability is the continuation of business orientation for the satisfaction of all stakeholders inside and outside the organization [24]. In the meantime, general Ergonomic approaches to creating this satisfaction with respect to the technical, human and environmental subsystems can achieve sustainability goals. In these decades, Ergonomists have done interventions in areas of movement toward productivity, energy use, ease of use and extra costs. Also, attention to social and environmental issues has also grown by ergonomists. However, from sustainability viewpoint, these interventions can have little or no negative impact, regardless of the future focus on maintaining physical and human resources over long periods of time. Therefore, resource planning for making major changes should be done with sustainability goals [40, 43]. Imada states that values identification, system change and commit stakeholders are necessary to sustainable development in organizations [1]. Necessary approach to make these changes should be complex and comprehensive in order to evaluate all components of the systems involved [43]. One of the executive projects aimed at improving the system was presented by Engkvist et al. at the Swedish Recycling Center, which has been able to improve the implementation of sustainability goals through ergonomic interventions. These interventions have carried out in two areas: micro (environmental Ergonomics) and macro (improvement of management and recycling systems) [44]. Another project that has been implemented to improve the sustainable development of a wooden furniture industry in Iran has increased its environmental sustainability through systemic interventions such as multi-criteria decision making [45]. The study of Bolis et al. in Brazilian companies is also a proof of Ergonomic interventions impact aimed at increasing employees' welfare with regard to job issues on social sustainability. In this study, from a top-down perspective, sustainability strategies have come to the design of work and making small changes [46]. Another successful project in Ergonomics and sustainable development is the implementation of Ergonomic and sustainability interventions in the Australian mineral industry that considering the five capitals of nature, economic, financial, social, human, and manufacturing can be successful towards sustainable development in the mining industry [47]. Another comprehensive study with green ergonomics and environmental sustainability approach has been undertaken by Wai Ching Poon et al. in Malaysia, which was conducted in the river fishing industry. This study has been done with a look at the impact of human activities on river ecosystem and then human health, which shows the impact of pollution on water resources and fish. Finally, the researchers proposed macroeconomic interventions to change the behavior of humans at government levels, associations, and businesses, in order to control those effects [31]. The study of Ergonomic implementation as a strategy for sustainable development in the

British railways industry is also an indication of large-scale Ergonomic impact at senior policy and decision levels and its effect on achieving sustainable benefits in organizations [48]. A remarkable point in all introduced projects is the emphasis on learning organizations and decision-making models at all levels of the organization and the participation of all stakeholders [22, 24, 49]. Imada points out the achievement of sustainability through the management of Macro-Ergonomic changes and participation in his article. He knows the bottom-up changes strategy, legislation, and top-down policies as strategies for creating sustainability in organizations [1]. Macro-Ergonomics can bring together the concepts of management, Ergonomic technologies, change strategies, and participatory techniques to move towards reasonable use of the economy, community and environment [9, 33, 49]. The reason of Macro-Ergonomics approach application in sustainable development is that, firstly, Macro-Ergonomics examines the interface of human-organizational-technology that will lead to a systemic solution; Secondly, the relationship with management and organization stakeholders and investor can have a more comprehensive strategy for change management, which these two cause the Ergonomics encounter with the organization to integration in global sustainability [1, 43]. Basically, one of the Macro-Ergonomics challenges is job and occupation design, which inclusive attention to jobs and its impact on other social and environmental systems is important. Whit this approach, design as a main factor in creating a job life cycle or a production method that can affect other production and support subsystems simultaneously and acted on is the most important issue in macroergonomics and sustainability [50]. Human modeling methods such as simulation of work environment, simulation of health monitoring systems, injury prediction, robotics and augmented reality can help to establish sustainability goals in designing systems [51]. Ergonomics attention to the design/redesign of systems, including production subsystems, communications, human resources and other support subsystems, such as health and well-being, considering the life cycle of a system and its impact on internal and external organizational relationships, can create the movement towards sustainability and a long term sustainable development in all directions.

This research did not receive any specific grant from funding agencies in the public, commercial, or not-for-profit sectors.

Declarations of Interest.   None.

References

1. Imada, A.S.: Achieving sustainability through macroergonomic change management and participation. In: Corporate Sustainability as a Challenge for Comprehensive Management, pp. 129–138. Springer (2008)
2. Dorsey, J., Hedge, A., Miller, L.: Green ergonomics. Work (Read. Mass) **49**(3), 345 (2014)
3. Jilcha, K., Kitaw, D.: Industrial occupational safety and health innovation for sustainable development. Eng. Sci. Technol. Int. J. **20**(1), 372–380 (2017)
4. Haslam, R., Waterson, P.: Ergonomics and sustainability. Ergonomics **56**(3), 343–347 (2013)
5. Thatcher, A.: Early variability in the conceptualisation of "sustainable development and human factors." Work (Read. Mass) **41**(Suppl 1), 3892–3899 (2012)
6. O'Neill, D.: The promotion of ergonomics in industrially developing countries. Int. J. Ind. Ergon. **35**(2), 163–168 (2005)

7. Helali, F.: How could you use the ergonomics 'knowhow' transfer management to enhance human working for sustainable improvements in industrially developing countries? Work (Read. Mass) **41**(Suppl 1), 2730–2735 (2012)

8. Scott, P.A.: Ergonomics in Developing Regions: Needs and Applications. CRC Press, Boca Raton (2009)

9. Coelho, D.A., Ferrara, P.R., Couvinhas, A.F., Lima, T.M., Walter, J.K.: Macroergonomic aspects in the design of development programs in IDCs. Work (Read. Mass) **41**(Suppl 1), 2651–2655 (2012)

10. United Nations Sustainable Development Summit Statement New York (2015). https://www.un.org/sustainabledevelopment/summit/

11. Radjiyev, A., Qiu, H., Xiong, S., Nam, K.: Ergonomics and sustainable development in the past two decades (1992–2011): research trends and how ergonomics can contribute to sustainable development. Appl. Ergon. **46** Pt A, 67–75 (2015)

12. Thatcher, A., Yeow, P.H.: Human factors for a sustainable future. Appl. Ergon. **57**, 1–7 (2016)

13. Martin, K., Legg, S., Brown, C.: Designing for sustainability: ergonomics–carpe diem. Ergonomics **56**(3), 365–388 (2013)

14. Bolis, I., Brunoro, C.M., Sznelwar, L.I.: Mapping the relationships between work and sustainability and the opportunities for ergonomic action. Appl Ergon. **45**(4), 1225–1239 (2014)

15. Meyer, F., Eweje, G., Tappin, D.: Ergonomics as a tool to improve the sustainability of the workforce. Work (Read. Mass) **57**(3), 339–350 (2017)

16. Olawumi, T.O., Chan, D.W.M.: A scientometric review of global research on sustainability and sustainable development. J. Clean. Prod. **183**, 231–250 (2018)

17. Saravia-Pinilla, M.H., Daza-Beltran, C., Garcia-Acosta, G.: A comprehensive approach to environmental and human factors into product/service design and development. A review from an ergoecological perspective. Appl. Ergon. **57**, 62–71 (2016)

18. Moher, D., Liberati, A., Tetzlaff, J., Altman, D.G., The PRISMA Group: Preferred reporting items for systematic reviews and meta-analyses: the PRISMA statement. PLoS Med. **6**(7), e1000097 (2009)

19. Cevallos, M., Egger, M., Moher, D.: STROBE (STrengthening the Reporting of OBservational studies in Epidemiology). In: Guidelines for Reporting Health Research: A User's Manual, pp. 169–179 (2014)

20. Hanson, M.A.: Green ergonomics: challenges and opportunities. Ergonomics **56**(3), 399–408 (2013)

21. Nadadur, G., Parkinson, M.B.: The role of anthropometry in designing for sustainability. Ergonomics **56**(3), 422–439 (2013)

22. Randelin, M., Saaranen, T., Naumanen, P., Louhevaara, V.: Towards sustainable well-being in SMEs through the web-based learning program of ergonomics. Educ. Inf. Technol. **18**(1), 95–111 (2013)

23. Thatcher, A.: Green ergonomics: definition and scope. Ergonomics **56**(3), 389–398 (2013)

24. Zink, K.J., Fischer, K.: Do we need sustainability as a new approach in human factors and ergonomics? Ergonomics **56**(3), 348–356 (2013)

25. Bolis, I., Brunoro, C.M., Sznelwar, L.I.: Work in corporate sustainability policies: the contribution of ergonomics. Work (Read. Mass) **49**(3), 417–431 (2014)

26. Lange-Morales, K., Thatcher, A., García-Acosta, G.: Towards a sustainable world through human factors and ergonomics: it is all about values. Ergonomics **57**(11), 1603–1615 (2014)

27. Lee, J.Y., Kang, H.S., Do, N.S.: MAS 2: an integrated modeling and simulation-based life cycle evaluation approach for sustainable manufacturing. J. Clean. Prod. **66**, 146–163 (2014)

28. Pilczuk, D., Barefield, K.: Green ergonomics: combining sustainability and ergonomics. Work (Read. Mass) **49**(3), 357–361 (2014)

29. Siemieniuch, C.E., Sinclair, M.A., Henshaw, M.J.: Global drivers, sustainable manufacturing and systems ergonomics. Appl. Ergon. **51**, 104–119 (2015)
30. HSQE should be in your DNA. Maritime Holland, **60**(4), 56–59 (2011)
31. Poon, W.C., Herath, G., Sarker, A., Masuda, T., Kada, R.: River and fish pollution in Malaysia: a green ergonomics perspective. Appl. Ergon. **57**, 80–93 (2016)
32. Samudhram, A., Siew, E.G., Sinnakkannu, J., Yeow, P.H.: Towards a new paradigm: activity level balanced sustainability reporting. Appl. Ergon. **57**, 94–104 (2016)
33. Moore, D., Barnard, T.: With eloquence and humanity? Human factors/ergonomics in sustainable human development. Hum. Factors **54**(6), 940–951 (2012)
34. Zink, K.J., Steimle, U., Fischer, K.: Human factors, business excellence and corporate sustainability: differing perspectives, joint objectives. In: Corporate Sustainability as a Challenge for Comprehensive Management, pp. 3–18. Springer, Heidelberg (2008)
35. Pavlovic-Veselinovic, S.: Ergonomics as a missing part of sustainability. Work (Read. Mass) **49**(3), 395–399 (2014)
36. Genaidy, A.M., Sequeira, R., Rinder, M.M., A-Rehim, A.D.: Determinants of business sustainability: an ergonomics perspective. Ergonomics, **52**(3), 273–301 (2009)
37. Jasiulewicz-Kaczmarek, M. (ed.) The Role of Ergonomics in Implementation of the Social Aspect of Sustainability, Illustrated with the Example of Maintenance. Occupational Safety and Hygiene. - Proceedings of the International Symposium on Occupational Safety and Hygiene, SHO 2013 (2013)
38. Da Silva, A.M. (ed.) Ergonomics and Sustainable Design: A Case Study on Practicing and Teaching. In: 6th International Conference on Applied Human Factors and Ergonomics (2015)
39. De Macedo Guimarães, L.B.: Sociotechnical design for a sustainable world. Theor. Issues Ergon. Sci. **13**(2), 240–269 (2012)
40. Silveira, D.M., Brandão, E.L.: Ergonomics and education as a strategy for sustainable development in business. Work (Read. Mass) **41**(SUPPL.1), 3701–3708.
41. Fischer, K., Hobelsberger, C., Zink, K.: Social sustainability in global value creation: contributions of ergonomics interventions. Gesellschaft für Arbeitswissenschaft (Hrsg), Neue Arbeits-und Lebenswelten gestalten, Dortmund, GfA-Press, pp. 449–452 (2010)
42. Manuaba, A.: A total approach in ergonomics is a must to attain humane, competitive and sustainable work systems and products. J. Hum. Ergol. **36**(2), 23–30 (2007)
43. Thatcher, A., Yeow, P.H.: A sustainable system of systems approach: a new HFE paradigm. Ergonomics **59**(2), 167–178 (2016)
44. Engkvist, I.-L., Eklund, J., Krook, J., Björkman, M., Sundin, E.: Perspectives on recycling centres and future developments. Appl. Ergon. **57**, 17–27 (2016)
45. Azizi, M., Mohebbi, N., De Felice, F.: Evaluation of sustainable development of wooden furniture industry using multi criteria decision making method. Agric. Agric. Sci. Procedia **8**, 387–394 (2016)
46. Bolis, I., Brunoro, C.M., Sznelwar, L.I.: Work for sustainability: case studies of Brazilian companies. Appl. Ergon. **57**, 72–79 (2016)
47. Horberry, T., Burgess-Limerick, R., Fuller, R.: The contributions of human factors and ergonomics to a sustainable minerals industry. Ergonomics **56**(3), 556–564 (2013)
48. Ryan, B., Wilson, J.R.: Ergonomics in the development and implementation of organisational strategy for sustainability. Ergonomics **56**(3), 541–555 (2013)
49. Hasle, P., Jensen, P.L.: Ergonomics and sustainability–challenges from global supply chains. Work (Read. Mass) **41**(Suppl 1), 3906–3913 (2012)
50. Marano, A., Di Bucchianico, G., Rossi, E.: Strategies and arguments of ergonomic design for sustainability. Work (Read. Mass) **41**(Suppl 1), 3869–3873 (2012)
51. Kubek, V., Fischer, K., Zink, K.J.: Sustainable work systems: a challenge for macroergonomics? IIE Trans. Occup. Ergon. Hum. Factors **3**(1), 72–80 (2015)

Work Process and Restrictions Related to Activities Carried Out in a Waste Sorting Cooperative

Renato Luvizoto Rodrigues de Souza[1]($\boxtimes$) ⓘ, Andréa Regina Martins Fontes[2] ⓘ, João Alberto Camarotto[3] ⓘ, and Talita M. Oliveira[2] ⓘ

[1] Department of Industrial Engineering, Federal University of Triângulo Mineiro, Uberaba, Brazil
[2] Department of Industrial Engineering, Federal University of São Carlos, Sorocaba, Brazil
[3] Department of Industrial Engineering, Federal University of São Carlos, São Carlos, Brazil

Abstract. The informal structure of waste sorting workers' organizations in Brazil has two critical perspectives: the need to encourage solid waste management systems and difficult working conditions. The purpose of this paper is to present a case study that analyzed working conditions in a waste cooperative; highlighting variability associated with facilities, process, and materials faced worker risks and discomforts in their workplace. Data collection included systematic observations of the production process, interviews and use of the discomfort questionnaire. The results indicate that working in the process of sorting recyclable materials can cause several discomforts, in addition to offering risks to the worker. The discomforts are mainly associated with the movements necessary to separate the materials. Simultaneously, the risks come mainly from the types of materials that get to the conveyor belt, such as hospital material and sharp objects.

Keywords: Waste sorting · Cooperative · Work process · Ergonomics work analysis · Centered-activity ergonomics

1 Introduction

Solid waste management has been widely discussed with the aim of reducing the negative externalities caused by technological development and exploiting the potential of waste as a resource that can be transformed and reused. Some authors [1] discuss strategies for evaluating the municipal waste collection, while others [2] discuss how better waste separation at source could increase the quality of recyclable materials and increase their value in Bangladesh. Others still [3] show how greater waste separation at source can contribute to better municipal waste management in Bangkok.

The collection and sorting of solid waste in Brazil, as well as in low- and middle-income countries, is carried out predominantly by waste pickers, with no formal organization of the activity, considered as a poverty eradication strategy [4–7]. The challenge for the public management of solid waste in these countries refers to the need to develop

© The Author(s), under exclusive license to Springer Nature Switzerland AG 2021
N. L. Black et al. (Eds.): IEA 2021, LNNS 220, pp. 603–610, 2021.
https://doi.org/10.1007/978-3-030-74605-6_76

structures that enable its formalization using the formation of waste pickers cooperatives as a viable option [8, 9].

The activity of classifying recyclable materials is developed in degraded environments that present risks to the health of workers, including accidents and illnesses, and emotional vulnerabilities such as depression, stress and social stigma [10]. Workers face daily struggles engaging in activities that can harm their health and do not provide them with a better quality of life and higher pay [11–13].

This study aims to analyze the working conditions in a waste cooperative, highlighting variability associated with facilities, process, and materials faced worker risks and discomforts in their workplace. To reach the proposal, a case study by Activity-Centered Ergonomics approach was carried out in a waste sorting cooperative located in an inner-city in the state of São Paulo, Brazil.

In general, job analysis considers the prescribed task as a reference for assessing working conditions. This approach does not consider the risks, dangers and constraints of workers in their real work activities [14]. The ergonomic approach to the activity seeks to understand the activity of the workers, their real working conditions and the effective results sought, and the formal requirements of the task such as the conditions and expected results [15]. It is one of the focuses of this approach to identify the variabilities and constraints present in the work activities, as well as the operative strategies developed by the workers to achieve the expected results [16].

2 Methods and Techniques

A qualitative case study [17], faces a technically unique situation in which there are more variables of interest than data points. Data collection and analysis considered the prior development of theoretical propositions [18].

Data collection included the analysis of the production processes and the work carried out in the cooperative, focusing on the factors that affect the processes and pointing out possible determinants of the performance of the work task.

Fourteen interviews were conducted with workers, including spontaneous and simultaneous verbalizations, to determine the unobservable parameters of the process. Body discomfort data were also collected using the discomfort questionnaire [19].

Based on the evidence collected, a task description file was created, which allows an understanding of the factors that influence the operational techniques used by workers. However, due to the variability of situations found in the study, the data were systematized and organized to understand these techniques.

3 Results

The case study was carried out in a waste sorting cooperative located in an old municipal composting and recycling plant in an inner-city in the state of São Paulo-Brazil, where the collection of recyclables is carried out by the municipality. Recyclable materials are stored in a storage area until processing.

Cooperative operating hours are from 7:00 am to 4:30 pm with an interval of one hour (12:00 am to 1:00 pm) and a ten-minute coffee break (at 3:00 pm). About 150 tons of recyclable materials are sold per month, generating US$20,000 in revenue, on average. The monthly income per worker (all workers have the same monthly) is subject to fluctuations in the production of the cooperative; the workers receive, on average, US$150.00 per fortnight, totalling US$300.00 per month. Most workers called their salary "leftovers" because the amount paid is the difference between the profit generated and the operating expenses.

The cooperative has 40 members who perform the following tasks: 1 director, who also works on the conveyor belt; 3 members of the audit committee, who also work on the screening process; 20 persons responsible for sorting operations; 2 persons responsible for the removal of containers with classified material; 2 persons responsible for the cleaning tasks; 1 person responsible for the separation of metal; 1 claw operator; 2 persons responsible for the exchange of containers; 2 persons responsible for the removal of rejected materials; 4 people responsible for the compression of materials; and two persons responsible for administration services.

The main constraints observed during the analysis of this activity included the interviewees' verbalisations regarding their thoughts about different situations.

3.1 Variability Associated with Volume, Condition and Type of Material

The cooperative receives daily recyclable materials generated in a city with a population of 325 thousand inhabitants. One does not have the ability to process all the material that accumulates daily in the storage area awaiting classification. The presence of organic waste among recyclable materials results in contact with pests such as rats and cockroaches when materials are handled, imposing restrictions and risks of illness and accidents on workers.

The amount of recyclable materials in the conveyor belt directly influences sorting operations. If the conveyor is too full, workers should speed up sorting, which makes them vulnerable to accidents with sharp or penetrating materials, and they will not have enough time to open and check the packaging of each product. However, some interviewees claim that they prefer to work on a complete conveyor belt because they can have the fair perception of their workload.

> *"I prefer a complete conveyor belt because everyone has the same amount of work and they get the same, but it depends on the person carrying the conveyor (the person who has the control of the button) [...] I prefer when our director has control of the button, because it makes the difference, it increases the conveyor belt speed" (worker).*

> *"So we can increase production, I prefer it full to make the day pass faster" (worker).*

> *"You can see that today we are working with a complete transporter, because if we use a lot of trash, it will rot and we cannot use anything else" (worker).*

It is important to mention that the verbalization of the last interviewee indicated the need to always use overhead to meet the demand for materials to be classified and that even then, the materials should sometimes be sent to landfills before being classified.

In addition, the presence of organic materials among recyclable materials is associated with the inefficiency of selective collection or the poor separation of materials produced by the waste generators, according to the verbalizations of the respondents below:

"Some people (residents of the house) throw away the garbage all mixed thoroughly, and it shouldn't be thrown like that, for example, paper will go with paper, glass will go with glass, but they still don't know there is risk, not only to them, but also to the people who collect the garbage" (worker).

"I work this way, carefully. I open this box, take this piece of glass and wrap it in a newspaper to keep people from cutting themselves [...] if you can take the glass, you do, but if the milk box is too full and the glass is as glued, so it will take time and you will waste time, then leave it there and let it move down on the conveyor (the material is not separate)" (worker).

"But sometimes the problem is the time, right? Sometimes the organic garbage truck is late, so they (picking people) cannot separate (recyclable or not), so they end up picking up food too, but the majority (domestic residents) mix food and everything else" (worker).

This is a critical issue, since there is a conflict between two organizations, the company that performs selective collection and the cooperative. According to the respondents, conflicts between these two organizations are expected.

The following recyclable materials are separated in the cooperative: paper, cardboard, mixed paper (magazines, books, etc.), Tetra Pak®, PET, glass, copper, posters, food and beverage products, aluminum containers, metal cans (steel, iron, tin, eg.), hard plastic, soft plastic, buckets and basins. Many different types of these materials can be found on the classification conveyor belt, but, according to the verbalizations of the interviewees below, not all workers or classifiers have the necessary knowledge about all materials and their values:

"Sometimes I see a material and I don't know how to separate it, and sometimes I separate colored items and white items because I'm in a hurry, but, in general, each material has its own container. If you mix them too much, the buyer complains, you cannot make many mistakes" (worker).

"Every member of the cooperative should know about all the materials in the cooperative, but we don't and that's our problem." "You can see that many people still ask questions. If I take my stuff and throw it in your container, we are losing value because yours is cheaper than mine" (worker).

3.2   Risk of Accidents and Discomforts in the Workplace

All interviewees suffered accidents with sharp or penetrating materials and one respondent had his hand crushed on the mat. In sorting operations, workers need to spread the materials on the conveyor belt to improve separation, which causes accidents in hands and arms. The carrier has protection to prevent accidents, but parts of this protection are damaged, which makes the operation difficult.

Workers wear safety gloves provided by the cooperative, but complain that they are unreliable and therefore use other types of gloves that they find among recyclables or buy their gloves.

During screening operations, workers have to deal with hazardous materials that may contain a variety of pathogenic microorganisms and come into contact with poisonous animals. The statements of some respondents indicate a constant presence of risk factors:

"Today I'm scared to die in this trash every day. I'm going to end up cutting my finger. I think it's difficult because they (domestic people) mix everything" (worker).

"Because here you need to spread the waste on the carrier and have to be careful" (worker).

"There are a lot of diapers here, hospital waste that should not come here, and a lot of needles containing blood [...], and we have to be alert to avoid getting hurt here... because you know, here we have to work focused on what you are doing [...] You need to learn to be fast" (worker).

Out of the 14 interviewees, 10 (70%) reported having pains in the body, especially in the upper and lower limbs. Many have had back pain since they work standing up, ordering the waste. They believe that back pain is caused by the need to flex repeatedly to remove items from the conveyor belts.

In addition, workers often need to move forward or back because of the speed of the conveyor belt and the volume of materials:

"For example, if you work in the same place for a long period of time, many items move in front of you (items that were not separated) [...] Most people who work only locally pick up items that are there, but they do not pick up what is ahead of them, so we keep moving to avoid it" (worker).

4 Discussion

The discussion of the results is presented into two topics. The first refers to facilities, equipment and processes that can cause discomfort, while the second discusses the material variability and its impact on the work.

4.1 Facilities and Process

The cooperatives' facilities are from an old municipal composting and recycling plant with a layout designed according to the plants' old processing capacity, which was lower than that observed during the study. Also, the raw materials' storage area was not designed to fit the amount of organic and non-recyclable waste present among the recyclables.

In addition, it was not designed considering priority processing. Recyclable materials that were already stored in the plant must be processed before new arrivals. These factors prevent sorting operations and affect the quality of the classified material. The problems associated with facilities and processes for sorting recyclable materials are already addressed in the literature [13].

Therefore, the interviewees indicated the need to restructure the facility's layout for a storage that allows the entry of materials in the conveyor belt according to the first row of first-order priority.

Due to the discomfort observed in sorting operations and the inability to change the current facility structure, some suggestions and recommendations for improvement include adaptations at workstations based on the determinants of task performance, facilitating sorting and separation operations.

4.2 Materials' Classification

During the analysis of recyclable materials' classification activity, the variability associated with the volume, type and conditions of recyclable materials and the work constraints that this variability causes to work were observed. Also, this process and variability of the product are managed by classifiers, among which there is diversity in terms of age, place of work, competence and experience.

As regards the variability of types of recyclable materials, it is suggested to promote the education and training of workers in terms of various types of materials and their values. One of the interviewees highlighted the need to work in all sorting stations in order to gain experience and knowledge about all types of classified material in the cooperative.

Regarding the variability associated with material conditions, it is suggested that a manual of good practices for domestic residents be developed, containing instructions on the correct separation of household waste according to the type of material. This manual would also help to raise public awareness of the discomfort experienced during sorting of recyclable materials caused by poor separation of waste generators.

Also, about the variability of types of materials, all respondents have experienced or witnessed an accident during waste sorting operations. Sharp or penetrating materials caused the most common accidents. They also found medical waste, such as used needles, on the conveyor belt. Protective items such as gloves, masks, boots, goggles and clothing that protect the upper body during screening operations are recommended to reduce this type of risk.

It is also recommended to develop a good practice manual for industries that provide information on the proper disposal of materials containing chemical wastes and instructions on handling materials before selective disposal properly.

A better separation at the origin of the waste can improve the quality of the separated materials [2], above all, facilitate the sorting of materials in the cooperatives, possibly reducing the discomforts and risks associated with this activity.

5 Conclusion

This study aimed to show that the sorting of recyclable materials cannot be seen as an isolated activity of the cooperative. It is a social project in which the cooperative is inserted, which depends on the coordination of several actors, among them the population, the selective collection agents and the buyers of recycled materials. The interviewees' statements about the restrictions they face indicate the need to develop improvements since the organization of the chain related to the recycling of materials, such as the development of best practices in the separation of waste by generators.

In the current structure of the solid waste chain in Brazil, there is no system of costs or penalties, making it difficult to structure the entire process of managing this economic and social activity. Since the separation of the materials produced in the generators (homes, companies, industries, communities), the selective collection, the sorting and the commercialization.

It was found that waste separation operations are carried out in precarious environments and working conditions. The pungent odor and presence of pests that feed on decaying organic material present among the potentially recyclable ones creates a dangerous and degraded environment.

The analysis of the selective collection activity showed that workers process various information to make quick and effective decisions about the materials to be classified to reduce risks and obtain effective results. However, the inherent variability in recyclable materials makes it challenging to anticipate decision-making.

References

1. Ferreira, F., Avelino, C., Bentes, I., Matos, C., Teixeira, C.A.: Assessment strategies for municipal selective waste collection schemes. Waste Manage. 59, 3–13 (2017). https://doi.org/10.1016/j.wasman.2016.10.044. Accessed 21 Nov 2016 and 20 Mar 2020
2. Matter, A., Dietschi, M., Zurbrügg, C.: Improving the informal recycling sector through segregation of waste in the household - the case of Dhaka Bangladesh. Habitat Int. 38, 150–156 (2013). https://www.sciencedirect.com/science/article/pii/S0197397512000276. Accessed 16 June 2020
3. Sukholthaman, P., Sharp, A.: A system dynamics model to evaluate effects of source separation of municipal solid waste management: a case of Bangkok, Thailand. Waste Manage. 52, 50–61 (2016). https://doi.org/10.1016/j.wasman.2016.03.026. Accessed 15 Jan 2020
4. Medina, M.: Scavenger cooperatives in Asia and Latin America. Resour. Conserv. Recycl. 31(1), 51–69 (2000). https://doi.org/10.1016/S0921-3449(00)00071-9. Accessed 16 Feb 2020
5. Medina, M.: The informal recycling sector in developing countries: Organizing waste pickers to enhance their impact. Grid Lines (44) (2008). https://hdl.handle.net/10986/10586. Accessed 21 Nov 2016 and 16 Feb 2020
6. Asim, M., Batool, S.A., Chaudhry, M.N.: Scavengers and their role in the recycling of waste in Southwestern Lahore. Resour. Conserv. Recycl. 58, 152–162 (2012). https://doi.org/10.1016/j.resconrec.2011.10.013. Accessed 15 Mar 2020
7. Gutberlet, J.: Informal and cooperative recycling as a poverty eradication strategy. Geogr. Compass 6(1), 19–34 (2012). https://doi.org/10.1111/j.1749-8198.2011.00468.x. Accessed 20 May 2020
8. Aparcana, S.: Approaches to formalization of the informal waste sector into municipal solid waste management systems in low- and middle- income countries: Review of barriers and success factors. Waste Manage. 61, 593–607 (2017). https://doi.org/10.1016/j.wasman.2016.12.028. Accessed 21 Sept 2020
9. Tirado-Soto, M.M., Zamberlan, F.L.: Networks of recyclable material waste-picker's cooperatives: an alternative for the solid waste management in the city of Rio de Janeiro. Waste Manage. 33(4), 1004–1012 (2013). https://doi.org/10.1016/j.wasman.2012.09.025. Accessed 16 June 2020

10. Binion, E., Gutberlet, J.: The Effects of handling solid waste on the wellbeing of informal and organized recyclers: a review of the literature. Int. J. Occup. Environ. Health **18**(1), 43–52 (2012). https://doi.org/10.1179/1077352512Z.0000000001

11. Cockell, F.F., Carvalho, A.M., Camarotto, J.A., Bento, P.E.G.: A Triagem de Lixo Reciclável: Análise Ergonômica da Atividade. Revista Brasileira de Saúde Ocupacional **29**(110), 17–26 (2004)

12. Souza, R.L.R., Fontes, A.R.M., Salomão, S.: A triagem de materiais recicláveis e as variabilidades inerentes ao processo: Estudo de caso em uma cooperativa. Ciência Saúde Coletiva **19**(10), 4185–4195 (2014). https://doi.org/10.1590/1413-812320141910.09072014. Accessed 21 Nov 2020

13. de Souza, R.L.R., Camarotto, J.A., Fontes, A.R.M.: Ergonomics and technologies in waste sorting: usage and appropriation in a recyclable waste collectors cooperative. In: Bagnara, S., Tartaglia, R., Albolino, S., Alexander, T., Fujita Y. (eds.) Proceedings of the 20th Congress of the International Ergonomics Association (IEA 2018). IEA 2018. Advances in Intelligent Systems and Computing, vol. 825. Springer, Cham. (2019). https://doi.org/10.1007/978-3-319-96068-5_91

14. Lahoz, M., Camarotto, J.A.: Performance indicators of work activity. Work (Read. MA) **41**, 524–531 (2012)

15. Guérin, F., Laville, A., Daniellou, F., Duraffourg, J., Kerguelen, A.: Compreender o trabalho para transformá-lo: a prática da ergonomia. Edgard Blücher, Fundação Vanzolini, São Paulo (2004)

16. Béguin, P., Daniellou, F.: Metodologia da ação ergonômica: abordagens do trabalho real. In: Falzon, P. (ed.) Ergonomia, pp. 281–301. Edgar Blücher, São Paulo (2007)

17. Yin, R.K.: Estudo de caso: Planejamento e métodos, 4th edn. Bookman, Porto Alegre (2010)

18. Voss, C., Tsikriktsis, N., Frohlich, M.: Case research in operations management. Int. J. Oper. Prod. Manag. **22**(2), 195–219 (2002). https://doi.org/10.1108/01443570210414329. Accessed 15 Nov 2019

19. Corlett, E.N., Bishop, R.P.: A technique for assessing postural discomfort. Ergonomics **19**(2), 175–182 (1976)

Uncovering Sustainable System-of-Systems Elements in the Design of a Greywater Treatment System for Urban Informal Settlements

Andrew Thatcher[✉]

University of the Witwatersrand, Johannesburg 2050, South Africa
Andrew.Thatcher@wits.ac.za

Abstract. This study looks at urban informal settlements, a common feature of many cities in developing countries that arise when rapid urbanization is not supported by adequate social and physical infrastructure. This study looks at the application of the Sustainable System-of-Systems framework for human factors and ergonomics in an urban informal settlement. Using twelve months of photo-ethnographic and interview data, this paper shows how the four elements of this framework can be identified and how they might be applied to improve the design and implementation of a sustainable intervention to treat greywater effluent and improve the health of the environment.

Keywords: Participatory design · Green ergonomics · Sustainable system-of-systems · Informal settlements

1 Introduction

1.1 Informal Settlements Context

Urban informal settlements are a common feature of many cities in the Global South [1]. They arise when rapid urbanization is not supported by adequate social and physical infrastructure such as electricity, water, sewerage, schools, healthcare facilities, and recreational facilities. Under these circumstances urgent infrastructure, such as housing, precedes the construction of other important urban services. Some services such as water and electricity are relatively easy to retrofit in urban informal settlements because they require very little space and can be installed in a flexible manner. Other services, such as sewerage or greywater removal, are notoriously difficult to implement once an informal settlement has been established because they are less flexible and require a lot more space to implement. While not an ideal solution, some of these essential services are dealt with through temporary solutions. For example, sewerage is often viewed as an essential service due to its high health risks and is often dealt with through the provision of portable toilets or open-pit latrines.

The physical context for this study is an informal settlement, Setswetla, located along the Western bank of the Jukskei river in Johannesburg's oldest and poorest township,

N. L. Black et al. (Eds.): IEA 2021, LNNS 220, pp. 611–619, 2021.
https://doi.org/10.1007/978-3-030-74605-6_77

Alexandria [2]. The initial settlement of Setswetla started in the mid-1980s (during Apartheid) when Alexandria township, which also suffered major service delivery issues, could no longer support the continued influx of people coming from rural areas to seek employment in Johannesburg. Since then, Setswetla has seen continued growth and now has an estimated population of 30 000 people living in an area less than 1 km^2 in low-rise buildings. Many of the buildings are makeshift constructions consisting of "found" materials such as corrugated iron, recycled bricks, plastic sheeting, and cardboard. Local government has provided limited electricity and potable water (i.e. communal taps) and sewerage through the provision of portable toilets (with several households sharing a single portable toilet).

This study looks at the problem of greywater treatment and removal which is often neglected by local governments because it is perceived to have much lower health risks than sewerage (or "blackwater"). Greywater refers to wastewater from washing and other household chores. Due to the lack of formal sewerage services in Setswetla, greywater often ends up in the streets and the alleyways where people live, and then through the informal settlement into rivers and dams with almost no treatment of pathogens. Water quality testing of the greywater indicates that it is a significant health hazard (*eColi* counts of 5000 to 10000 cfu have been recorded – safe counts should be closer to 100–200 cfu). The investigations reported in this paper form part of a multidisciplinary research project, called URBWAT, whose aim is to design greywater treatment and removal solutions for urban informal settlements. From this perspective, the URBWAT project is an ideal HFE opportunity, where users are expected to interact with a novel technology.

1.2   Sustainable System-of-Systems (SSoS) Framework

The SSoS framework is green ergonomics [3] as it draws from an understanding of the connections between human factors and ergonomics (HFE) and ecological systems. The SSoS framework for HFE has been covered in-depth previously [4–8] and therefore only a summary is given here. The SSoS framework has four components.

The first component views systems as being part of a nested hierarchy with smaller, less complex systems being nested within larger, more complex systems [9]. The SSoS framework uses Wilson's [9] terms to describe the relationships between systems in the hierarchy. The system of interest is the "target" system. Systems with equivalent complexity and spatial influence are "sibling" systems. Systems of greater complexity and spatial reach than the target system are "parent" systems. Systems that are less complex and have a smaller spatial reach are "child" systems. There may be many levels of child, sibling, and parent systems representing the interrelationships with a target system.

The second component recognizes that facilitating the sustainability of the target system, many competing goals of the nested hierarchy of systems need to be balanced.

The third component notes that no system lasts forever and instead the sustainability of the hierarchy is dependent on systems reaching (but not going beyond) their 'natural lifespan'. The natural lifespan is determined by the relative placement of a system in the hierarchy. Larger, more complex systems have longer natural lifespans than smaller, less complex systems. Systems that last too long past their natural lifespan will become brittle and fail to adjust to external changes.

The fourth component incorporates the complex adaptive cycle [9], the cycle that every system follows: the exploitation of networked connections, the conservation/consolidation of those connections, the release/creative destruction of connections, and re-organisation/destructuring. Each system in the hierarchy has its own complex adaptive cycle with the rate of change determined by its natural lifespan (i.e. its relative position in the hierarchy of systems). However, larger, slower, more complex systems (with more interconnections) act as stabilizing influencers on faster, smaller, less complex systems. In contract, faster, smaller, less complex systems disrupt the slower, larger, more complex systems. These co-evolutionary interactions are what enable systems to be resilient and sustainable in unstable environments.

In implementing the SSoS framework, Thatcher and Yeow [6] emphasised the importance of methodological approaches embedded within complex systems analyses that use multi-voicedness to examine multiple design possibilities.

1.3 Problem Statement

While the SSoS framework is theoretically well-developed [4–8], the practical application is limited [10]. The URBWAT project therefore provides an ideal testing ground to empirically assess whether the SSoS framework has any practical value in understanding real-world HFE problems. The aim of this paper is to reflect on whether the four components of the SSoS framework are identifiable in the initial design stages of the research project and whether this identification can add value to the design process.

2 Methods

Following Thatcher and Yeow [6], the first step in the SSoS process is stakeholder identification. To determine the relevant stakeholders in the design, implementation, and use of any complex system design solution a stakeholder mapping exercise was first undertaken to identify relevant role players. Relevant stakeholders included the residents of Setswetla, the engineers and the designer team, the builders, the local community leadership forum, the local government officials responsible for water solutions, and finally the HFE specialist himself. The initial stakeholder map was not intended to be a final version, but was used as a template to determine the set of relevant actors to approach. In fact, during the course of data collection, it became necessary to separate out the users from the non-users of the design solution. Following methods used in complex systems modelling [11–13] the stakeholder map was used to identify relevant relationships between actors within the system.

The second step was to identify relevant systems and their relative placement within the hierarchy of systems. This process was far more difficult to determine. To identify relevant interacting systems involved careful observation of both pre- and post-intervention scenarios. The primary method of data collection for the second step was photo-ethnography [14]. Visits to Setswetla were made weekly for approximately twelve months (June 2019 to September 2020) carefully rotating the day of the week (including weekends) and the time of day. The first six months was before any intervention was implemented and the second six months was after two pilot systems were implemented. The photo-ethnography concentrated on water use; water collection, purposes of water use, and especially water disposal. The photo-ethnography enabled verification of each stakeholder identified in the first step (and the emergence of new stakeholders). The photo-ethnographic observations were augmented with iterative interviews with 40 community stakeholders. Community stakeholders included community leaders, residents who volunteered to take ownership of the system, residents who used the system, residents who didn't use the system, and the builders of the system. Each community stakeholders was interviewed at least twice (i.e. before and after the implementation of the system) and some stakeholders were interviewed several times. Combined, these data collection methods enabled the researcher to get an estimate of the relative geographical reach, complexity, and rate of change of each system.

The design of the treatment systems was done in a participatory, iterative, and co-design manner [15]. Six participatory design workshops were held in November 2019. The aims of the design workshops were to include the residents of Setswetla in the design process and to explore issues of the sustainability of the water treatment system that was implemented. The core principles of the workshops included: keeping costs as low as possible; using locally available materials; using locally available skills; causing minimal damage to the environment; incorporating residents' input in the design; and removing any implemented system that was not successful. In February 2020 two small, sub-surface, constructed wetlands [16] were installed by the engineering/design team working with builders from Setswetla, with all materials being sourced locally.

3 Results

3.1 Nested Hierarchy

The emergent nested hierarchy is presented in Fig. 1. Note that this is a simplified version of the actually nested hierarchy that the research team is using. Using the nested hierarchy as a tool it is possible to identify systems (not just individual stakeholders). This brings a different perspective to stakeholder maps or Actormaps [12]. Each system might be made up of different stakeholders and it is possible for a stakeholder to be a member of multiple systems. For example, two of the individuals were members of the Community Leadership Forum, users of the constructed wetland, and participants in some of the sibling systems and most of the child systems. The important observation from the nested hierarchy is that the unit of HFE analysis shifts from individuals to systems.

A related point is that systems consist of human actors, technology, and other non-human actors (such as infrastructure, services, and biological agents). The inclusion of non-human actors and agents are important elements required to facilitate sustainable systems [6]. In the full nested hierarchy other non-human actors include the river, housing infrastructure (such as electricity wiring, water pipes, ditches and culverts, plants, vermin, and stormwater protection).

However, constructing the nested hierarchy was not without problems. Spatial reach, complexity, and the natural lifespan of a system were difficult to unambiguously determine. Two systems might have similar spatial reach, but different levels of complexity (particularly interconnectedness with other systems) and natural lifespans. This raises the question of how to weight these different components to determine their relative placement in the nested hierarchy.

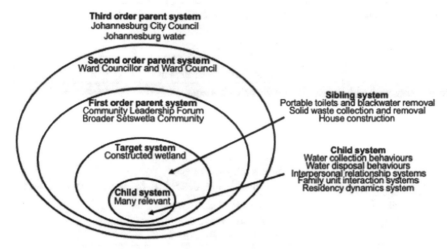

Fig. 1. Nested hierarchy with the constructed wetland as the target system.

3.2 Competing Goals

Previous theoretical work on the SSoS framework does not provide much guidance on determining goals [4–8]. There are several questions that arise from trying to address this second component. Whose goals should we be considering? Whose goals take precedence? Do the goals of the majority take precedence over the goals of the minority? Do the goals of influential actors take precedence over peripheral actors? What about the goals of "silent" actors such as plants or ecosystems? The original conceptualization of the SSoS framework only refers to the need for balance between the goals without specifying whose goals need to be balanced. The implication from this omission is that the goals of the designers appear to take precedence. During the interviews with community stakeholders it was apparent that while there was a great deal of commonality in the goals, there were also goals that were specific to particular stakeholders as shown in Table 1.

In Table 1 the goals of engineering and design team scarcely overlap with the goals of the other stakeholder groups. The other stakeholder groups each had fairly similar (but not entirely overlapping) goals aligned with issues of social security, food security, and health. It was only on the issue of health that there was any overlap between all four stakeholder groups. This would suggest that the intervention may meet with some resistance from the community during the implementation stage. Indeed, during the first few weeks of the installation of the constructed wetlands, cement had been poured onto one of the constructed wetlands and the tap closest to the most frequently used constructed wetland had been sabotaged.

Table 1. Goals of the different stakeholders (roughly in order of importance by stakeholder group).

Stakeholders	Goals
Community residents	Jobs and job security Affordable housing Food security Schools for their children Clean living environment
Community leadership forum	Affordable housing Safety and security (particularly women and children) Healthcare services Food security
Engineering/Design team	Low cost and easy to build Low ecological impact Improved health conditions (particularly for children)
Ward council	Safety and security for all Shack fire prevention and social security Health and wellbeing for all

3.3 Natural Lifespan of Systems

Identifying the natural end of a system's lifespan proved difficult to document because systems were always in a state of flux. In this regard it is difficult to definitively determine when a particular system has "ended" and novel system has emerged. Some systems, most notably the target system, nearly reached its "natural" lifespan during the course of this study because of a failure to make sufficient connections with other systems. Figure 2 shows how one constructed wetland looked when it was first installed and how it looked after four months.

3.4 Complex Adaptive Systems

The introduction of the target system into the existing matrix of systems provided a unique opportunity to see how the other systems in the nested hierarchy would react. In the nested hierarchy the positioning as a child, sibling, or parent system determines their potential to cause disruptions or to act as a stabilizing influence resisting change. As predicted, the child systems immediately reacted as disruptors to the target system and in turn, adaptations to these child systems arose as a consequence of this newly introduced system. Two of these adaptations are shown in Fig. 3.

Similarly, parent systems presented constraints on the target system that made community members resistant to using the constructed wetlands. For example, community behavioral habits (i.e. the larger social networks of washing behaviors, disposal behaviors, and community engagement) were not easily disrupted by the target system. In addition, new building infrastructure started encroaching on the space available for residents to continue with disposal at the constructed wetlands. There was therefore significant evidence to demonstrate that the parent systems acted to preserve existing network connections and resisted new connections being made with the target system.

Fig. 2. Constructed wetland just before final installation (left) and after four months (right).

Fig. 3. Adaptation to the water collection system where the constructed wetland was used as a "table" (left) and adaptation to the constructed wetland ecosystem with new plant species arising spontaneously (right).

4 Discussion

First it should be noted that all four components of the SSoS framework were easily identifiable in this study. It is important to emphasis that this observation in itself does not provide validation of the SSoS framework. Validation of the framework is possible only when it can be used to identify problems and solutions that are not identifiable from other methods and approaches.

Second, the issue of how to identify goals needs further articulation. Earlier work by Thatcher and Yeow [6] had not provided sufficient guidance on whose goals are relevant or what to do in the evident that the goals do not overlap. The results of this study indicated that the goals of the engineers/design team were markedly different from the goals of the other main stakeholder groups. These differences may have resulted in problems in the implementation of the constructed wetlands. It is also not immediately clear how this can be addressed. There is only a small area of overlap with respect to the issue of a healthy community. However, the other goals of the stakeholders place emphasis on issues such as job creation, adequate housing, and safety and security. Treating greywater does not match with these goals. A deeper understanding of the politics of co-production is required to resolve this mismatch [17].

Finally, the SSoS framework provided valuable insights to explain why the intervention was not working, as well as important input for the redesign of the system implementation. This is particularly important for iterative design interventions which have been recommended for addressing issues of sustainability [6]. The complex adaptive system understanding was particularly useful in identifying further design modifications that will be implemented in the second design iteration.

References

1. Lawhon, M., Nilsson, D., Silver, J., Ernstson, H., Lwasa, S.: Thinking through heterogeneous infrastructure configurations. Urban Stud. **55**(4), 720–732 (2018)
2. Bonner, P.L., Nieftagodien, N.: Alexandra: A history. Witwatersrand University Press, Johannesburg (2008)
3. Thatcher, A.: Green ergonomics: definition and scope. Ergonomics **56**(3), 389–398 (2013)
4. Thatcher, A., Yeow, P.H.P.: A sustainable system of systems approach: a new HFE paradigm. Ergonomics **59**(2), 167–178 (2016)
5. Thatcher, A., Yeow, P.H.P.: A sustainable system-of-systems approach: identifying the important boundaries for a target system in human factors and ergonomics. In: Thatcher, A., Yeow, P.H.P. (eds.) Ergonomics and Human Factors for a Sustainable Future: Current Research and Future Possibilities, pp. 22–45. Palgrave-Macmillan, Singapore (2018)
6. Thatcher, A., Yeow, P.H.P.: Factors to consider in the application of the sustainable system-of-systems model for human factors and ergonomics interventions. In: Thatcher, A., Zink, K.J., Fischer, K. (eds.) Human Factors for Sustainability: Theoretical Perspectives and Global Applications, pp. 217–236. CRC Press, Boca Raton (2020)
7. Thatcher, A.: Longevity in a sustainable human factors and ergonomics system-of-systems. In: 22nd Semana de Salud Occupacional in Medellin, Colombia (2016)
8. Thatcher, A.: The role of ergonomics in creating adaptive and resilient complex systems for sustainability. In: Proceedings of Ergonomics and Human Factors Conference 2017, pp. i–viii (2017)
9. Gunderson, L.H., Holling, C.S.: Panarchy: Understanding Transformations in Systems of Humans and Nature. Island Press, Washington DC (2002)
10. Thatcher, A., Nayak, R., Waterson, P.: Human factors and ergonomics systems-based tools for understanding and addressing global problems of the twenty-first century. Ergonomics **63**(3), 367–387 (2020)
11. Leveson, N.: A systems approach to risk management through leading safety indicators. Reliab. Eng. Syst. Saf. **136**, 17–34 (2004)
12. Svedung, I., Rasmussen, J.: Graphic representation of accident scenarios: mapping system structure and the causation of accidents. Saf. Sci. **40**(5), 397–417 (2002)
13. Vicente, K.J.: Cognitive Work Analysis: Toward Safe, Productive, and Healthy Computer-Based Work. Lawrence Erlbaum Associates, Mahwah (1999)
14. Harper, D.: Framing photographic ethnography: a case study. Ethnography **4**(2), 241–266 (2003)

15. Vink, P., Imada, A.S., Zink, K.J.: Defining stakeholder involvement in participatory design processes. Appl. Ergon. **39**(4), 519–526 (2008)
16. Sheridan, C., Hildebrand, D., Glasser, D.: Turning wine (waste) into water: toward technological advances in the use of constructed wetlands for winery effluent treatment. AIChE J. **60**(2), 420e431 (2014)
17. Turnhout, E., Metze, T., Wyborn, C., Klenk, N., Louder, E.: The politics of co-production: participation, power, and transformation. Curr. Opinion Environ. Sustain. **42**, 15–21 (2020)

Part VI: Slips, Trips and Falls (Edited by Richard Bowman)

How Might Slip Resistance Standards Become More Evidence Based?

Richard Bowman[✉]

Intertile Research, Brighton East 3187, Australia
slipbusters@gmail.com

Abstract. The purpose of slip resistance standards is to enable the specification of floors that will remain sufficiently during an economically reasonable life cycle, as well as to determine their relative safety and ensure their appropriate maintenance. It might be presumed that existing standards are evidence-based but where is the evidence to inform public good decision making? While many industries harness the power of historical data and use data analytics to make real time decisions, an appropriate database has yet to be established for any slip resistance test method variant. The data should ideally pertain to a currently used test, such as the wet pendulum test rather than a past variant that yielded somewhat different results. This paper considers many ways in which various organisations could help to establish evidence-based databases that would then enable data analytics to improve the specification of floor and ground surfaces, as well as their maintenance. Besides improved life cycle safety performance and reduced maintenance costs, there should also be fewer slip incidents and reduced health care costs.

Keywords: Slip resistance · Evidence based · Standards · Fall prevention · Public good · Data analytics

1 Responsible Slip Resistance Design

Whether we design for the whole population, or a special cohort, all design should be universal, and should thus focus on best satisfying the needs and expectations of all. However, if we have no evidence-based data relating to cohorts, we are restricted to designing for the masses. We might assume that some cohorts require more traction than others, but there is no evidence of a specific cohort that slips over more often than others thus representing the needs of the lowest common denominator. Indeed, if we consider any city, is there a data bank that reveals where people most frequently slipped, what the environmental conditions were, what the individuals were doing, their characteristics, footwear and any behavioural factors that might explain why the individuals failed to perceive any danger until it was too late? One may have to get down to some organizational level, say a council or shopping centre management, before one might obtain some fundamental data on incidents that were reported to management, which might exclude many where people chose not to become engaged with the

N. L. Black et al. (Eds.): IEA 2021, LNNS 220, pp. 623–630, 2021.
https://doi.org/10.1007/978-3-030-74605-6_78

bureaucracy, the questions asked might not probe deeply, and investigations may be more focused on ensuring relevant maintenance procedures had been followed rather than on obtaining a bespoke slip resistance test report. There may no records of incidents that occur on tenant properties within the organizational boundaries.

Where someone commissions a slip resistance test report at an incident location, it is quite possible that the operative may not be informed of the incident, and quite probable that the floor may be in a different condition. AS 4663:2013 [1] is helpful in this regard as it requires an identification of the test area, the nature and purpose of the test, the extent and type of cleaning performed, and any relevant observations such as maintenance cleaning procedures. Since the operative has a duty to determine the purpose of a test, a judge should be able to differentiate between routine audits and incident investigations. This distinction is also critical to better determining what levels of slip resistance are required in specific situations.

Personal injury lawyers typically advise potential clients who might experience a fall in a public space to:

1. Look to see what caused you to fall.
2. Use your phone to take a photo of what caused you to fall.
3. Get the names of all witnesses to the accident.
4. Report the fall to those responsible for the public space.
5. Do not sign any document (especially a Release) by those responsible for the space.
6. See a personal injury lawyer as soon as possible.

The lawyer should gather data related to probable cause and possible contributing factors, commissioning a slip resistance test if the incident may be due to a slippery floor. Some, or all, of this data might make its way to an insurance company. Similar data, possibly gathered by those responsible for the space or their insurance company, could materialise. If the person was working at the time of the incident, data might be gathered by the employer and their insurer, and perhaps by a governmental workplace authority that has a duty to ensure workplaces are safe. Such authorities might require the production of past test reports to confirm that the area has been maintained in a safe condition. If reports only exist where the floor was only tested in a clean, dry condition, they may be considered irrelevant if the floor was wet, dusty, or otherwise soiled at the time of the incident. Soiled conditions are foreseeable. If wet slippery surfaces pose a risk, the matter may focus on the adequacy of any periodic inspection system and if the operators were sufficiently vigilant and appropriately responsive.

While there are many possible scenarios, the establishment of relevant metrics for slip resistance control measures is ultimately dependent on access to slip incident data. Circa 2001, a National Occupational Health & Safety Commission Research Advisory Panel obtained approval to access some confidential data sources. We found the records contained insufficient detail that was worthy of further analysis. In 2005, the Australian Building Codes Board (ABCB) commissioned the Monash University Accident Research Centre (MUARC) to study the incidence of slips, trips and falls and their relationship to the design and construction of buildings. Unfortunately, the authors were unable to publish any data that quantified the level of slip resistance in circumstances where slips had occurred. The MUARC report [2] did not even start to consider what level of slip resistance might be required in specific situations. It failed to reflect there was no publicly available data that benchmarked the slip resistance in the Australian built environment. Where we lack data, do we know what is required to design successfully? Can we predict the probability of an outcome?

In Germany, the system for workplaces and for public wet barefoot areas is quite different. The Federal Institute for Safety at Work and Occupational Medicine and the German Statutory Accident Insurance are the respective competent authorities. They publish the minimum requirements for new floors, where compliance is essential to obtaining insurance. Given that these bodies are aware of any claims, they are well placed to amend any requirement if excessive incidents were to occur. Might a similar insurance-based system function be established and administered as effectively in other countries? Might the healthcare system or the aged care system collaborate to develop slip resistant design systems with inbuilt feedback loops to safeguard the needs of special populations?

2 An Inconvenient Reality

As newly installed floors are commissioned, the slip resistance will change due to factors such as wear, chemical attack (acid rain, cleaning products), and soiling, with potential fluctuations due to the frequency and intensity of cleaning operations. While the amount of change and the rate of change may vary considerably, most designers and property managers have little more to go on than an ex-factory classification, where this can cover a wide range of behaviour. Wear resistance, like slip resistance, is an engineering-system dependent property rather than a material-intrinsic surface property. Accelerated wear conditioning (AWC) protocols are routinely adopted in standard test procedures as an essential means of assessing durability or determining the long-term performance characteristics of building products. Each material will wear differently depending on the conditions to which it is exposed.

Specifiers and code writers want building owners to have floors that are safe at the end of an economically reasonable working life. Materials must have sustainable slip resistance (to avoid the unplanned premature use of costly remedial treatments). Good specifications identify appropriate maintenance practices, and adequate slip resistance throughout a life cycle. Overspecification can lead to cleaning issues. How does a lay person determine if initial excessive slip resistance provides a suitable safety factor?

Strautins [3] developed an accelerated wear conditioning (AWC) protocol that is considered to work well for ceramic tiles and natural and reconstituted stone tiles. Muñoz Lázaro [4] developed a similar AWC protocol and obtained good agreement between wet pendulum slip resistance results after pedestrian exposure and her AWC protocol for a wide range of 54 ceramic tiles [5]. Quite fortuitously, each of her AWC stages corresponded with about 10,000 pedestrian uses (in the relatively dry Castellon academic environment). However, the rate of slip resistance loss of these tiles may differ in other environments where there are different types and amounts of scratching dirt, different climatic exposures, different cleaning practices, etc. While Fig. 1 shows how much wet slip resistance was lost due to in situ wear, there was a similar rate of wear loss in each of the tiles when exposed to the Muñoz Lázaro AWC protocol.

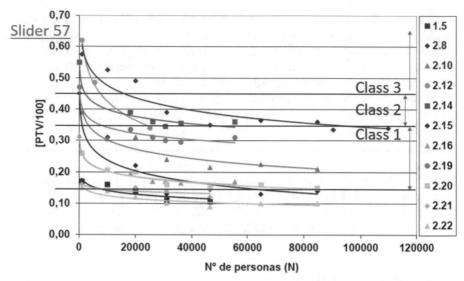

Fig. 1. Wet slip resistance loss for some smooth profiled ceramic tiles with a rough touch (after [4]). Classes 1, 2 and 3 are Spanish Building Code lifelong slip resistance requirements. However, tile 2.12 fell from well within class 3 to class 1 after only 25,000 pedestrian uses.

Although the Strautins protocol may not be suitable for conditioning resilient vinyl, timber, clay pavers and concrete, individual industries are ultimately responsible for establishing the life cycle slip resistance performance of their products. They should develop AWC protocols that are relevant to their product ranges, if they want them to be specified based on their life cycle slip resistance performance. While a few civic minded individuals have been seeking to develop an AWC protocol for resilient vinyl surfaces, progress has been slow without any external funding.

3 Australia, the Lucky Country

Australia is fortunate to use the wet pendulum as its slip resistance control procedure. Our NATA accredited (ILAC recognised) organisations participate in international proficiency studies [6]. This characterization process has increasingly led to improved metrological traceability, increasingly accurate results, and reduced bias. We question the worth of our codes and standards. We seek change that adds value. Compliance with criteria should provide purported benefits, without imposing unfair restrictions.

Designers have relied upon the wet pendulum recommendations made in HB 197 [7] and HB 198 [8] to provide an appropriate level of slip resistance. Bowman [7] based the initial recommendations on the German requirements for various areas. While brick industry literature suggested brick pavers might lose 10 to 15 BPN in service, the substantial amount of slip resistance loss in some other materials had yet to be appreciated. The existing system is inappropriately biased towards products with unsustainable ex-factory results, and against products with sustainable slip resistance.

HB 198 also includes the few mandatory requirements for stairways and ramps in new buildings that the ABCB introduced into the National Construction Code (NCC) in 2014. When or if these requirements apply to existing buildings, remains open to conjecture. Some believe these deemed-to-satisfy requirements to be ill considered and onerous, but there is still scope for alternative solutions. The legislation otherwise relies on an unquantified concept of slip resistance. It calls up AS 1428.1:2009 [9], to provide safe, equitable and dignified access for people with disabilities. This standard defines slip resistant as "A property of a surface having a frictional force-opposing movement of an object across a surface", which applies equally to wet ice and rough surfaces. Given this definition, is the requirement "A continuous accessible path of travel and any circulation spaces shall have a slip resistant surface" meaningful or nonsensical?

Since AS 1428.1:2009 is currently being reviewed, it is timely to wonder if a more appropriate definition of slip resistance has been proposed, or even some quantified requirements? If so, were such requirements based on evidence-based data? Have they been based on ex-factory criteria that may not provide ongoing safety? Does the committee have sufficient slip resistance expertise to ensure appropriate decisions? Unfortunately, too many standards committees operate as isolated silos. Guidance is sometimes solely fixated on ensuring that the floor surface should be able to provide sufficient traction, without adequately considering why so people may fail to observe hazardous conditions. It should consider what measures might assist the elderly who may be more likely to fall for reasons other than a lack of traction.

While it is easy to raise such issues, are they ever brought to the attention of parties who might ensure that appropriate action is taken? The ABCB has held many open public consultations on the draft Auditing and Compliance Publication Framework but has not sought opinions on slip resistance auditing and compliance issues.

Under Australian Consumer Law [10], suppliers are required to report any product-related death, or serious injury associated with a consumer product. Serious injury refers to an acute physical injury requiring medical or surgical treatment by, or under the supervision of, a qualified doctor or nurse. Although building products seem to be exempt from such a requirement, should they be? If the ABCB was to introduce a similar requirement, all participants in the supply chain (importers, manufacturers, distributors, retailers) and the supply chain for product related services (installers, cleaners, and service technicians, such as slip auditors) would be required to comply with the reporting requirement. This should enable the ABCB to develop a database benchmarking instances of possibly problematic slip resistance in the Australian built environment. However, such a database would still lack data on floors where products were being successfully used without incident. An ideal database would contain the full life cycle history of products in a wide range of settings.

Work Health and Safety Authorities have strategies to improve the prevention of occupational injuries and to provide leadership for the effective implementation and further development of their strategies, while also contributing to the development of a National Strategy. Since musculoskeletal disorders, (principally due to slips, trips and falls; and hitting, and being hit by, objects) have historically generated over 80% percent of compensated injuries, there is still a need for falls prevention initiatives on level surfaces even though all the many research efforts would appear to have ended. While much was learned, where is the data that relates available traction to incident occurrence in specific occupational settings?

The circumstances and occupational traction demands may be quite different in healthcare and aged care settings, where patients and the elderly may be at greater risk of falling due to loss of balance, and a range of impaired and diminished conditions. Falls prevention has many elements. While the provision and retention of sufficient slip resistance is important, any collection of incident data should be based on the fullest analysis possible of the widest range of possible contributing factors. Where there is less than a desired level of traction, this might be a contributing factor, just as it might be the primary causal factor. However, some scope should remain for the subsequent reanalysis of all data.

Periodic slip audits are a required component of some public liability insurance policies. Just as Governmental authorities and industry associations can choose whether to use a carrot or stick approach when seeking to compile important data, so can insurance companies (which also have a vested interest as large property owners). While insurance companies and other organisations have significant databases, past analyses revealed they lacked sufficient detail. Although many organisations could establish highly relevant databases, a collaborative exercise would be preferable, even if this were slightly complicated by the need for privacy protection.

Indeed, where countries share common means of measuring slip resistance, such as the pendulum in Australia, the United Kingdom, New Zealand, Singapore, and Spain, they should collaborate more. Significantly, these countries are also members of the Inter-jurisdictional Regulatory Collaboration Committee (IRCC) [11]. The IRCC promotes effective international collaboration concerned with 'best current practice' building regulatory systems, particularly those that are objective performance based. The IRCC members are sufficiently influential to aid local research and development of needed components of "best current practice" building regulatory systems, while seeking to minimise potential duplication nationally and internationally.

We live in an era of disruption where digital transformation can deliver more value for less cost, but only after the purpose has been defined, desired outcomes identified, and a clear direction determined. While conferences organized by the International Ergonomic Association Slip, Trip and Fall Technical Committee (IEA STF TC) have featured international discussions on specific topics, and further conferences will provide similar opportunities, more needs to be done between events. The IEA STF TC can establish agenda for various collaborative initiatives. There could be greater dialogue between national bodies such as the UK Slip Resistance Group (UKSRG), the Slip Resistance Group of Spain (SRGS) and similar entities.

In the meantime, what might be done to help establish objective performance-based requirements for AS 1428.1? The committee might convene a meeting to obtain external expert guidance, even if this only leads to an informative annex that provides interim partial solutions. Furthermore, they should consider the potential longer-term contributions of independent accredited slip assessors. An Australian Slip Resistance Group (ASRG) could give the regulators feedback on the perceived effectiveness of the AS 4586 [12] and AS 4663 [1] standards, and any related handbooks, as well as their application. The ASRG could use questionnaires to develop reports that might indicate which current slip resistance design measures are too lenient or too onerous. The ASRG might contribute to the design of a database to assist with data analytics.

Since slip assessors mainly produce data that belongs to their clients, would they be prepared to anonymize data for inclusion in a database, considering the associated costs of doing so? Might they be induced to do so?

4 Imperfect Fruits Can Be Highly Nutritious

While the highest prices are paid for visually perfect fruit, blemished fruit can still have great value. This metaphor relates to data obtained using slightly different test methods. Does a sample that has three specimens, each with eight pendulum readings, represent greater value than a sample of five specimens each with five pendulum readings. While the number of readings is similar, and it takes slightly longer to test five specimens, one might obtain useful data about consistency within a batch. One should examine the evidence (taste the fruit) to make meaningful comparisons, rather than being forced to make ad hoc decisions in standards meetings.

In Australia and Spain, wet slip resistance measurements are made after the rubber slider is prepared. In the UK, wet slip resistance measurements are only made after making 24 dry pendulum readings. Many would consider that such dry results are such limited value in clean dry situations, that the testing is rarely justified. Do the procedures yield significantly different results, and if so, does one method yield more relevant results than the other? Any difference may depend on the roughness of the specimens. However, having prepared the rubber on P400 paper and then on a 3-micron lapping film, is the time necessary to conduct a dry test justified if one only needs a wet test result? One could conduct several comparative tests over the widest range of products. However, is such effort justified if most ex-factory results are only transitory? Any studies might better be conducted on worn products where there is an increased likelihood of slips. Although the magnitude of the difference between wet and dry results may be a factor in product selection, it is a minor consideration when compared to the post AWC results.

The use of a 3-micron lapping film probably causes the test rubber surfaces to be far smoother than most soling materials, and thus causes results to be lower than might otherwise be obtained. The use of a 3-micron lapping film has certainly caused many surfaces to be assessed as being more likely to contribute to an incident than when the sliders were prepared using only P400 paper (in earlier standards). There is thus a significant disconnect between historical on-site test data and recent data, even though current results are assessed using the historical criteria. The consequences of changes to standard test procedures need to be well defined in informative guidance documents. Given the highly detailed nature of some issues, there is great scope for mistakes to be made if decision-makers are unaware of some of the fine detail. If AS 1428.1 is revised to include quantified slip resistance requirements, the committee should call upon the expert services of those who are aware of all the issues.

5 Closing Thoughts

Although much slip resistance guidance has been derived from a hypothetical basis, the folly of relying upon unsustainable ex-factory test data has become all too evident.

While acceptable AWC procedure have been developed for ceramic, natural stone and agglomerated stone tiles, other industries have still to develop appropriate protocols.

Just as standards test procedures cannot be delayed until they are perfected, neither can the implementation of new design methods be halted until every industry satisfies itself as to the probity of all proposed AWC protocols. However, all industries would benefit from improved databases and analytical systems that provide evidence of the life cycle performance of products in specific environments, including the influence of specified maintenance practices.

Most industries benefit from the real time application of data analytics to solving problems. The building industry, flooring manufacturers, building regulators, insurers, workplace regulators, health officials, and many other governmental and industrial organisations, locally and internationally, should collaborate to accumulate slip and fall data, and develop valuable analytics systems that yield universal benefits.

References

1. Standards Australia, AS 4663, Slip resistance measurement of existing pedestrian surfaces (2013)
2. Ozanne-Smith, J., Guy, J., Kelly, M., Clapperton, A.: The relationship between slips, trips and falls and the design and construction of buildings. Monash University Accident Research Centre - Report #281 (2008). https://www.monash.edu/muarc/archive/our-publications/reports/muarc281
3. Strautins, C.: Enhanced test method for assessing sustainable slip resistance. In: International Conference on Slips, Trips and Falls 2007: From Research to Practice (2007)
4. Muñoz Lázaro, A.: Problemática del resbalamiento en pavimentos cerámicos. Ph.D. thesis, Universitat Jaume I (UJI), Castellón (Spain) (2019)
5. Bowman, R.: A view of slip resistance and accelerated wear conditioning (AWC) post Muñoz (2020). https://www.researchgate.net/publication/341354262_A_view_of_slip_resistance_and_accelerated_wear_conditioning_AWC_post_Munoz
6. Strautins, C.: Pendulum calibration, metrological traceability and reference material. In: Slips, Trips and Falls. Conference Madrid 2020. Slip Resistance Group of Spain (2020)
7. Bowman, R.: Standards Australia Handbook 197. An introductory guide to the slip resistance of pedestrian surface materials (1999)
8. Standards Australia Handbook 198. Guide to the specification and testing of slip resistance of pedestrian surfaces (2014)
9. Standards Australia, AS 1428.1, Design for access and mobility – New building work (2009)
10. Australian Competition & Consumer Commission, (2021) Mandatory Reporting. https://www.productsafety.gov.au/product-safety-laws/legislation/mandatory-reporting
11. Inter-jurisdictional Regulatory Collaboration Committee (2020). https://www.ircc.info/
12. Standards Australia, AS 4586, Slip resistance classification of new pedestrian surface materials (2013)

Determining the Risk of Slipping
with Slip-Resistant Footwear

Davood Dadkhah[1,2(✉)], Danny Cen[1], and Tilak Dutta[1,2]

[1] Institute of Biomedical Engineering, University of Toronto, 164 College Street, Toronto
M5S3G9, Canada
davood.dadkhah@mail.utoronto.ca
[2] Kite Research Institute, Toronto Rehabilitation Institute, University Health Network,
550 University Avenue, Toronto M5G22, Canada

Abstract. The objective of this study was to investigate the relationship between the risk of slipping on a level wet ice surface and the scores provided from the Maximum Achievable Angle (MAA) footwear test. The numbers of slips experienced by nine participants each wearing three boots (MAA scores 0, 6, 11) were analyzed using logistic regression to determine how the risk of slipping (RoS) changed with the MAA score. Our findings showed that the risk of slipping was 0.03 (1 in 33 steps) for the best boot with an MAA score of 11, 0.25 (1 in 4) for the boot with an MAA score of 6, and 0.51 (1 in 2) for the boot with an MAA score of 0.

Keywords: Slips and falls · Slip prediction · Winter footwear · Risk of slipping

1   Introduction

Falls result in many injuries worldwide and are a major public health problem [1–3]. These injuries result in pain and suffering for individuals as well as large economic costs for the society [4]. For example, the cost of fall-related injuries in the United States is approximately 20 billion USD each year [5]. Icy walkways and stairs increase the risk of falls and result in higher rates of falls during the winter months [6, 7].

1.1   Importance of Footwear for Fall Prevention

Slip-resistant footwear plays an important role in the prevention of slips and falls by providing traction to prevent balance loss. A study in restaurant workers found that slip-resistant footwear was associated with a 54% reduction in the rate of slipping, demonstrating that slip-resistant footwear reduces falls [8, 9]. Another study among the personal support workers shows that wearing slip resistant footwear outdoors in winter conditions makes a huge difference in fall prevention [10]. In this study, the risk of falls among the intervention group (wearing the best performing slip resistant footwear) was 78% less than the control group (wearing their usual winter footwear).

© The Author(s), under exclusive license to Springer Nature Switzerland AG 2021
N. L. Black et al. (Eds.): IEA 2021, LNNS 220, pp. 631–637, 2021.
https://doi.org/10.1007/978-3-030-74605-6_79

1.2   Measuring Footwear Slip Resistance on Ice and Snow

There are a number of methods that have been used to evaluate footwear slip resistance on ice [11]. Our team has recently developed a new method called the MAA test, which measures the steepest incline that participants are able to walk up and down without experiencing a slip on ice-covered surfaces [12, 13]. These studies have found that most winter footwear performs poorly on ice and can lose grip on ice at slopes between 3 to 5 degrees (corresponding to MAA scores of 3 and 5, respectively) [14, 15]. These findings demonstrate why we see so many fall-related injuries every winter when we put them in the context of the results of a study published over 25 years ago describing the risk of slips based on the Available Coefficient of Friction (ACOF) [3, 16, 17]. It is important to note that this study did not include ACOF values in the range of those measured on icy surfaces. For instance, we can estimate the ACOF provided by a winter boot with reasonably good performance (scoring 9° on the MAA test) to an ACOF on ice of ~0.16 (evaluated by computing the tan(9°)).

Extrapolating the trend line in Pye's data suggests that practically every step should result in a slip for values of ACOF below ~0.24 (where the probability of slipping becomes 1). However, anyone who has walked on any icy surface will know that individuals do not slip with every step they take. In fact, our team's past research has also demonstrated that footwear with ACOF of 0.16 (MAA score of 9) and higher actually provides dramatically better slip resistance on ice compared to most commercially available footwear that scores between 3 and 5 in the MAA test which result in ACOF values of 0.05 to 0.09. Therefore, we have good reason to believe that the relationship between the probability of slipping and ACOF is quite different between ACOF values in the range of 0 to 0.2 (corresponding to icy conditions) than they are for ACOF values above 0.2. A better understanding of the relationship between MAA scores, ACOF, and the risk of slipping in icy conditions is needed for providing evidence-based recommendations for winter footwear for the public.

This study reports on the results of exploring the relationship between boot's MAA score and RoS. The goal of this work is to determine if there is a model that we can use to represent an equivalent value for MAA score in terms of RoS and vice versa. For this purpose, we used the data collected by researchers at KITE[1] in the WinterLab where carefully controlled icy winter conditions can be simulated.

2   Methodology

Ten healthy young adults (7 men, 3 women) participated in this study. Their average weight, age, and height were 74 ± 10 kg, 27 ± 6 years old, and 1.75 ± 0.05 m, respectively. Due to an observed gait abnormality, data from one male participant was excluded from the dataset (this participant's foot clearance was too low making it difficult to distinguish heel contact and toe-off events). Participants were asked to walk back and forth along a 4.5 m long on a zero inclined wet ice surface wearing three types of boots: Canadian Tire Woods Snow Peak Boots (MAA score: 0), Mark's WindRiver Canmore

---

[1] KITE is the research arm of the Toronto Rehabilitation Institute and is a world leader in complex rehabilitation science.

(MAA score: 6), and Mark's WindRiver Mallory (MAA score: 11). During the study, the ice floor is cooled via glycol tubes to 0.5 ± 1.0 °C and the ambient air temperature was maintained at 8.0 ± 2.0 °C. During each session, participant started by wearing the boot with lowest MAA score (0), then switched to the next lowest MAA score (6), and lastly wearing the highest MAA score (11). Participants walked in their self-selected pace and no gait control pattern took place during the study.

The total number of steps and slips were determined from data collected using a motion capture system (Raptor-E, utilizing Cortex 5.2.0.1518, Motion Analysis). This system traces 10 markers on each boot. During the classification stage, two raters independently identified slip events and in the case of disagreement, a third rater was used to make the final decision. Here, steps were categorized into three groups: normal step, toe slip, or heel slip. Each slip was further classified into a forward or backward slip [18]. Next, the number of steps and slips were recorded. These two numbers were used to calculate the RoS for each boot and participant. The collected data and MAA scores were used to fit a logistic regression model. The results of this model were compared to the previously fitted regression model based on ACOF and RoS.

3   Results

A total of 1732 steps were recorded, among them, 486 cases were slips. Table 1 summarizes the results of the data collection. To start with data analysis, a logistic regression model was fit to the collected data. Logistic regression modelling is a statistical modelling algorithm based on the logistic function. This function is mainly used to model a continuous binary dependent variable. We assigned 1 to each slip and 0 to each nonslip step for fitting the logistic regression model.

Results showed that the total RoS (among all participants) of boot number one (MAA score: 0), two (MAA score 6), and three (MAA score: 11) were 0.51, 0.25, and 0.03, respectively. Therefore, the probability of slipping decreased as a boot's MAA score increased.

Figure 1 shows the result of fitting a logistic regression model to the available data. The data points correspond to each of the three boots. In this figure, the red line shows the logistic regression model fitted to the collected data and the blue dots represent the original data, which are the total probability of slipping for each footwear.

The mean accuracy of the fitted model to the collected data was 73%. This accuracy has been calculated based on the probability of the slipping of the data collection footwear. According to the results, the logistic regression model fits the data, resulting in predicting the RoS based on the MAA score of the boots.

4   Discussion

Our results show a clear relationship between the MAA score and RoS. We can also determine the effective ACOF for each boot on our ice surface by computing the Tangent of the MAA score (since the MAA score represents the highest value for the ratio of the shear force and normal force present at the boot-ice interface without any slips occurring).

Table 1. Summary of the collected data.

Subject ID	Boot no.	Total steps	Number of slips	Probability of slipping
1	1	58	39	0.67
	3	40	0	0
2	1	63	25	0.40
	2	62	10	0.16
	3	61	0	0
4	1	78	36	0.46
	2	66	29	0.44
	3	58	6	0.10
5	1	53	5	0.09
	2	65	4	0.06
	3	62	0	0
6	1	84	36	0.43
	2	70	15	0.21
	3	64	3	0.05
7	1	79	65	0.82
	2	71	37	0.52
	3	55	7	0.13
8	1	74	31	0.42
	2	103	13	0.13
	3	60	1	0.02
9	1	75	47	0.63
	2	64	10	0.16
	3	66	0	0
10	1	78	44	0.56
	2	62	22	0.35
	3	61	1	0.02

Using these effective ACOF values with their associated RoS, we can extend the table produced by Pye [3] that shows the likelihood of slipping drops from 1 in 1,000,000 steps for an ACOF of 0.36 to 1 in 20 for ACOF of 0.24. We can now add ACOF values of 0.19 (corresponding to MAA score 11), 0.11 (MAA score 6) and 0 (MAA score 0) which fall below those provided by Pye [3]. According to our findings, the risk of slips for these is 1 in 33, 1 in 4, and 1 in 2, respectively.

If we add our findings to the data from Pye [16] to create Fig. 2, we can see that the relationship shown by our collected data is different from Pye [3]. There is an offset between the data provided by Pye and our dataset. There are a couple of logical reasons

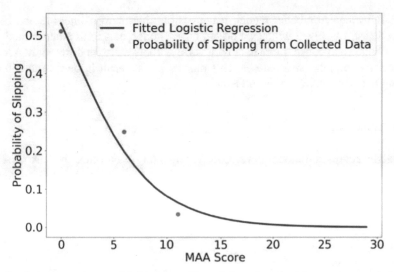

Fig. 1. Logistic regression model fitted to collected data plotted with respect to probability of slipping.

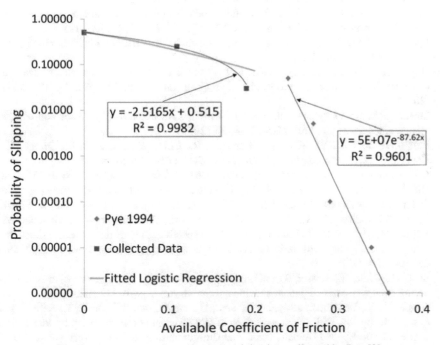

Fig. 2. Comparison of our dataset and the data collected by Pye [3].

that can explain this gap. First, no gait control parameters were set for our participants. This will result in conservative gait, which means equivalent RoS in lower ACOFs. Second, the amount of data that we have is limited. With more data in 0.2 to 0.3 region of ACOF, we can fit a better model. It is possible that there is linear region between the two datasets in Fig. 2 which we do not have enough data to fit a better model to it. We are planning to collect more data with various footwear with different MAA scores to collect a comprehensive dataset. This dataset could result in better modelling and mapping between MAA scores and RoS.

5   Conclusion

The logistic regression model developed in this study found that the risk of slipping drops as a boot's MAA score rises as expected. These findings can be used to extend our understanding of the relationship between ACOF and the risk of slipping in the range of ACOF values associated with wet ice surfaces (0 to 0.19) that have not been previously studied.

References

1. Chang, W.R., Leclercq, S., Lockhart, T.E., Haslam, R.: State of science: occupational slips, trips and falls on the same level. Ergonomics **59**(7), 861–883 (2016)
2. Li, J., Goerlandt, F., Li, K.W.: Slip and fall incidents at work: a visual analytics analysis of the research domain. Int. J. Environ. Res. Public Health **16**(24), 4972 (2019)
3. Pye, P.: A brief review of the historical contribution made by BRE to slip research. Slipping–Towards Safer Flooring (1994)
4. Huynh, N., Fernie, G., Dutta, T., Fekr, A.R.: A novel approach for slip resistance evaluation of winter footwear based on probability of slipping and cost analysis. Saf. Sci. **137**, 105133 (2021)
5. Stevens, J.A., Corso, P.S., Finkelstein, E.A., Miller, T.R.: The costs of fatal and non-fatal falls among older adults. Inj. Prev. **12**(5), 290–295 (2006)
6. Bell, J.L., Collins, J.W., Wolf, L., Gronqvist, R., Chiou, S., Chang, W.R., Sorock, G.S., Courtney, T.K., Lombardi, D.A., Evanoff, B.: Evaluation of a comprehensive slip, trip and fall prevention programme for hospital employees. Ergonomics **51**(12), 1906–1925 (2008)
7. Drebit, S., Shajari, S., Alamgir, H., Yu, S., Keen, D.: Occupational and environmental risk factors for falls among workers in the healthcare sector. Ergonomics **53**(4), 525–536 (2010)
8. Verma, S.K., Chang, W.R., Courtney, T.K., Lombardi, D.A., Huang, Y.H., Brennan, M.J., Mittleman, M.A., Ware, J.H., Perry, M.J.: A prospective study of floor surface, shoes, floor cleaning and slipping in us limited-service restaurant workers. Occup. Environ. Med. **68**(4), 279–285 (2011)
9. Staal, C., White, B., Brasser, B., LeForge, L., et al.: Reducing employee slips, trips, and falls during employee-assisted patient activities. Rehabil. Nurs. **29**(6), 211 (2004)
10. Bagheri, Z.S., Beltran, J., Holyoke, P., Sole, G., Hutchinson, K., Dutta, T.: Reducing the risk of falls by 78% with a new generation of slip resistant winter footwear. In: International Conference on Applied Human Factors and Ergonomics, pp. 279–285. Springer (2019)
11. Fekr, A.R., Li, Y., Gauvin, C., Wong, G., Cheng, W., Fernie, G., Dutta, T.: Evaluation of winter footwear: comparison of test methods to determine footwear slip resistance on ice surfaces. Int. J. Environ. Res. Public Health **18**(2), 405 (2021)
12. Hsu, J., Li, Y., Dutta, T., Fernie, G.: Assessing the performance of winter footwear using a new maximum achievable incline method. Appl. Ergon. **50**, 218–225 (2015)

13. Hsu, J., Shaw, R., Novak, A., Li, Y., Ormerod, M., Newton, R., Dutta, T., Fernie, G.: Slip resistance of winter footwear on snow and ice measured using maximum achievable incline. Ergonomics **59**(5), 717–728 (2016)
14. Bagheri, Z.S., Patel, N., Li, Y., Morrone, K., Fernie, G., Dutta, T.: Slip resistance and wearability of safety footwear used on icy surfaces for outdoor municipal workers. Work **62**(1), 37–47 (2019)
15. Bagheri, Z.S., Patel, N., Li, Y., Rizzi, K., Lui, K.Y.G., Holyoke, P., Fernie, G., Dutta, T.: Selecting slip resistant winter footwear for personal support workers. Work **64**(1), 135–151 (2019)
16. Pye, P., Harrison, H.: BRE building elements: Floors and flooring–performance, diagnosis, maintenance, repair and the avoidance of defects. BRE report **460** (2003)
17. Chang, W.R., Matz, S., Chang, C.C.: The available coefficient of friction associated with different slip probabilities for level straight walking. Saf. Sci. **58**, 49–52 (2013)
18. Cen, D.: Development of a slip analysis algorithm: automating the maximal achievable angle footwear slip resistance test. Master thesis (2018)

Alternative Measures for Determining the Risk of Tripping

Ghazaleh Delfi$^{(\boxtimes)}$, Abdulrahman Al Bochi, and Tilak Dutta

KITE Research Institute, Toronto Rehabilitation Institute, Toronto, Canada
Ghazaleh.delfi@mail.utoronto.ca

Abstract. Falls are a major public health issue and many are caused by tripping. An important indicator of the risk of tripping is the minimum foot clearance. Current practices assess the mean and standard deviation of minimum foot clearance values to measure the tripping risk with lower mean and/or higher minimum foot clearance variability being associated with higher risk of tripping. However, this method of representing the foot trajectory by a single point and using the most basic linear statistics to analyze the data may be an oversimplification. In this paper, we search the current literature for alternative approaches of interpreting foot trajectory data to more accurately assess the risk of tripping. We discuss methods outlined by five different papers, each introducing a novel analysis of foot clearance data. We also propose an improved general model to estimate an individual's probability of tripping by pooling the methods from the five papers.

Keywords: Falls · Tripping · Foot clearance · Foot trajectory

1 Introduction

Falls are a major public health issue. Each year, over 3 million people suffer from fall-related injuries. The annual economic burden of falls is estimated to be $6 billion in Canada [1]. Many of these falls are the result of tripping [2]. A large body of literature is dedicated to assessing the risk of tripping in different populations by investigating healthy/pathological gait parameters within the gait cycle. The gait cycle is comprised of two phases: the stance and swing phases. The distance between the foot and the ground during the swing phase is known as the foot clearance [3]. Commonly, the foot clearance will reach a local minima during the swing phase; this local minima is known as the Minimum Foot Clearance (MFC). The MFC value is often used as an indicator for the risk of tripping and is commonly described by investigating the mean and standard deviation of the MFC value.

However, using MFC mean and standard deviation to determine the risk of falls has a number of limitations. First, MFC may not occur in all gait cycles. Second, this approach assumes MFC values have a normal distribution, which usually is not the case. Studies have shown that the MFC distribution has a systematic positive skew [4]. Finally, potentially useful information may be lost when a three-dimensional foot trajectory is reduced to a single point. In this paper, we discuss some alternative methods for analyzing foot trajectories and foot clearance to estimate the risk of tripping.

N. L. Black et al. (Eds.): IEA 2021, LNNS 220, pp. 638–643, 2021.
https://doi.org/10.1007/978-3-030-74605-6_80

2 Methods

This study was a result of a scoping review currently under preparation. The scoping review was done in accordance with the Preferred Reporting Items for Systematic Reviews and Meta-Analyses (PRISMA) guidelines, to report on existing technologies for measuring MFC and gait abnormalities that affect MFC. Four databases (Medline, Embase, Compendex and Web of Science) were searched. Abstract and full-text screening was conducted by two independent reviewers. The papers discussed here were excluded from the main scoping review because they did not directly apply to the inclusion criteria. However, given the importance of these remaining papers to the field, we have summarized them in order to understand methods other than the use of MFC for analyzing foot trajectory data.

3 Results and Discussion

Our scoping review identified a total of 2976 papers and 61 of those met our inclusion criteria. This paper reports on five of the excluded papers which look at analyzing MFC and/or tripping risk in novel ways. Table 1 includes a summary of the five papers discussed in this article.

Table 1. Papers' summary

Paper	Title	Journal
Best et al. [7]	A method for calculating the probability of tripping while walking	Journal of biomechanics
Khandoker et al. [6]	A comparative study on approximate entropy measure and poincaré plot indexes of minimum foot clearance variability in the elderly during walking	Journal of neuroengineering and rehabilitation
Byju et al. [8]	Alternative measures of toe trajectory more accurately predict the probability of tripping than minimum toe clearance	Journal of biomechanics
Schulz et al. [9]	A new measure of trip risk integrating minimum foot clearance and dynamic stability across the swing phase of gait	Journal of biomechanics
Benson et al. [5]	A principal components analysis approach to quantifying foot clearance and foot clearance variability	Journal of biomechanics

All five papers recommend improvements on the current methods of analyzing gait for the purposes of assessing the risk of tripping. Two papers [5, 6] discuss improvements on current analysis of gait data by using non-linear metrics and generalizing to gait with no observable MFC. The other three papers [7–9] discuss new measures for calculating the probability of tripping.

3.1 Alternative Analysis of MFC

MFC height is commonly used to determine the risk of tripping. The mean and variability of an individual's (or a population's) MFC values are used to determine the risk of tripping. The lower the mean and the higher the variability, the higher the risk of a fall. Khandoker et al. [6] have noted that only analyzing the linear statistics of the MFC data will not capture its complexity and may lead to the loss of useful information. They proposed using non-linear statistics such as Poincare plots [10] and approximate entropy [11] for analysis. Using these measures, they distinguished walking patterns of balance-impaired subjects from normal gait. They stated that such measures can be used for early detection of gait pattern changes as well as clinical gait diagnostic markers. Their results showed that gait pathology due to balance impairments was reflected in indexes extracted from Poincare plots. They also identified Approximate Entropy as a measure of irregularity in gait and a reflection of stability in subject's foot motion control during walking.

Certain populations such as older adults, those with a history of stroke and people with bound feet do not always exhibit a local minimum in their gait trajectory. This makes it difficult to assess the risks of tripping for these individuals. Benson et al. [5] proposed using a non-discrete metric based on the foot trajectory that can provide an alternative to assess and rank these individuals, based on minimum foot clearance and variability. They proposed performing a Principal Component Analysis (PCA) on the trajectory signal [12]. Their proposed metric can be used on all trajectories, including those that do not exhibit a local MFC minima. PCA can provide "non-random behavioral components of toe height". They found that individuals can be *ranked* based on their foot clearance and foot clearance variability using the Principal Component score. However, to our knowledge, the relationship between this score and the risk of tripping has not yet been determined.

3.2 Novel Approaches to Calculating the Risk of Tripping

If a trip is defined as *foot-obstacle contact during the swing phase*, then to measure the risk of tripping on an obstacle of height x, the probability of a subject's MFC dropping below x should be calculated. Assuming that $f(y)$ denotes the probability density function of the random variable y, which represents MFC values, the probability of tripping can be calculated as below:

$$PT = \int_{-\infty}^{x} f(y)dy \tag{1}$$

The common practice is to assume that $f(y)$ is normal. We define the probability density function of MFC by its mean and variability. Assuming that μ denotes the distribution mean and σ denotes the variability, we can rewrite Eq. (1) as follows:

$$PT = \int_{-\infty}^{x} \frac{1}{\sqrt{2\pi}\sigma} e^{-\frac{1}{2}\left(\frac{y-\mu}{\sigma}\right)^2} dy \tag{2}$$

Best et al. [7] argue that MFC values do not follow a normal distribution. Rather, they have positive skewness and kurtosis values. Therefore, in order to have a better estimate of the risk of trips, skewness and kurtosis modelling should be performed when calculating the probability of tripping on an obstacle. This includes replacing the normal distribution in Eq. (2) with an exponential power distribution and replacing y with a skew-transformed value corresponding to MFC $= x$ cm. For a detailed formula of their approach, please refer to Best et al. [7]. Their results indicated that skewness and kurtosis modeling show significant differences compared to the probability of tripping calculated from a normal distribution, especially for smaller obstacles.

Byju et al. [8] also included the entire trajectory in their analysis rather than a single point (MFC). They assumed that a trip occurs if toe clearance drops below the present obstacle heights *at any point during the swing phase*. Therefore, to calculate the probability of tripping, they broke down the foot trajectory into 1 mm increments in the anterior-posterior direction. At each increment, the number of potential trip events were calculated by comparing the toe height with the distribution of the present obstacles in the environment. If the toe height dropped below an obstacle height, a potential trip was counted. Finally, the number of potential trip events was divided by the number of comparisons. They claimed that a good estimator for their probability of tripping is a parameter they called the MD40, which is calculated as follows:

$$MD40 = \int_{start_{swing}}^{end_{swing}} Trajectory(a)\delta(40-v)da \tag{3}$$

Where $\delta(v)$ is defined as follows:

$$\delta(v) = \begin{cases} 1 \; if \; v > 0 \\ 0 \; otherwise \end{cases} \tag{4}$$

Where the anterior-posterior direction is denoted as a and the vertical direction as v, we can assume that the foot trajectory is a function $Trajectory : a \rightarrow v$.

As we can see in Eq. (3), the cut-off value for obstacles was chosen to be 40 mm. This was due to the fact that the obstacles present in the environment studied by [8] were below 40 mm.

Schulz [9], proposed taking into account the dynamic stability of the subject, which indicates the ability to recover from potential disruptions to the gait by an obstacle, as well as considering the entire trajectory instead of a single point (i.e. MFC). Their proposed measure is called the Trip Risk Integral (TRI) and is calculated as follows:

$$TRI = \int_{start_{swing}}^{end_{swing}} \frac{MoI}{MFC} dt \tag{5}$$

Where *MoI* or the Margin of Instability is calculated by measuring the dynamic stability of the subject by considering the base of support, the position and the velocity of the center of mass [9]. To assess the risk of trips, the MOI is divided by the foot clearance of the subject in each time step. Therefore, the lower the foot clearance and the higher the instability of the subject, the higher the chance of a trip occurring.

3.3 Overall Model

There are many proposed ways to calculate the risk of trips. However, all of these metrics follow the same general model shown below to calculate the *true* probability of tripping [7]:

$$TPT(y) = f\{PT(y), P_{MTC}(y), P_{VOB}(y)\} \tag{6}$$

In this general model, the true probability of tripping over an obstacle of height x is calculated by taking three factors into account: (1) the probability of an obstacle of height y occurring ($P_{MTC}(y)$), (2) the probability of a minimum foot clearance value lower than y occurring ($PT(y)$) and (3) the probability of the pedestrian noticing the obstacle while walking ($P_{VOB}(y)$).

Most models presented in the literature attempt to estimate the $PT(y)$. As discussed in the previous sections, $PT(y)$ can be calculated using linear or non-linear statistics of MFC or by taking into account the entire foot trajectory rather than a single point.

All models discussed in the previous sections are based on the assumption that the obstacle present in the walkway will remain unseen by the pedestrian and their gait will not be adjusted (eliminating the function $P_{VOB}(y)$). However, this may not be a realistic assumption. In fact, we hypothesize that smaller obstacles will have a higher probability of remaining unseen. Our team's future work will attempt to test this hypothesis as it may have important implications for the sizes of walkway obstacles that should be repaired. Currently, many jurisdictions will repair obstacles that are larger than a given cut-off. For example, the accessibility guidelines for the City of Toronto recommends repairing obstacles over 13 mm on the outdoor walkways [13]. The Americans with disabilities act [14] allows vertical changes in walkways to be a maximum of 6.4 mm.

The P_{MTC} is also largely neglected in the literature. To calculate the tripping hazards of a certain environment, data on the sizes of obstacles that are present in that environment must be collected. Recently developed technologies including structured light sensors may provide efficient methods for collecting this type of data.

Finally, based on the studies done by Khandoker et al. [6] and Schulz et al. [9], we propose an addition to the general model in Eq. (6) [7] to include the probability of an individual losing their balance [9] in the event that their foot makes contact with an obstacle in the environment (since individuals will be able to recover their balance in many cases). To account for this probability, we propose to add a function to include dynamic stability in the general model. Note that the probability of a loss of balance depends on an individual's velocity and base of support. Therefore, it will be a function of time rather than obstacle height. If we set $P_{LOB}(t)$ to denote the probability of loss of balance after making contact with an obstacle at time t, we can write the final model as follows:

$$TPT(y, t) = f\{PT(y), P_{MTC}(y), P_{VOB}(y), P_{LOB}(t)\} \tag{7}$$

4 Conclusion

Five papers discussing alternative ways to analyze gait data to assess risk of falls were reviewed and a new general model to calculate the true probability of tripping was proposed. Our proposed model defines the true probability of a trip event to be a function with four factors: (1) the probability of an obstacle of a given height occurring, (2) the probability of a minimum foot clearance value lower than a given height occurring, (3) the probability of a pedestrian noticing the obstacle while walking, and (4) the probability of loss of balance after making contact with an obstacle.

References

1. Parachute! Fall prevention (2014). https://www.parachutecanada.org/Injury-topics/Item/fall-prevention1
2. Blake, A.J., Morgan, K., Bendall, M.J., Dallosso, H., Ebrahim, S.B.J., Arie, T.A., Bassey, E.J.: Falls by elderly people at home: prevalence and associated factors. Age Ageing 17(6), 365–372 (1988)
3. Winter, D.A.: Biomechanics and motor control of human gait: normal, elderly and pathological (1991)
4. Begg, R., Best, R., Dell'Oro, L., Taylor, S.: Minimum foot clearance during walking: strategies for the minimisation of trip-related falls. Gait Posture 25(2), 191–198 (2007)
5. Benson, L.C., Cobb, S.C., Hyngstrom, A.S., Keenan, K.G., Luo, J., O'Connor, K.M.: A principal components analysis approach to quantifying foot clearance and foot clearance variability. J. Appl. Biomech. 35, 116–122 (2019)
6. Khandoker, A.H., Palaniswami, M., Begg, R.K.: A comparative study on approximate entropy measure and poincare plot indexes of minimum foot clearance variability in the elderly during walking. J. Neuro-eng. Rehabil. 5(1), 4 (2008)
7. Best, R., Begg, R.: A method for calculating the probability of tripping while walking. J. Biomech. 41(5), 1147–1151 (2008)
8. Byju, A.G., Nussbaum, M.A., Madigan, M.L.: Alternative measures of toe trajectory more accurately predict the probability of tripping than minimum toe clearance. J. Biomech. 49(16), 4016–4021 (2016)
9. Schulz, B.W.: A new measure of trip risk integrating minimum foot clearance and dynamic stability across the swing phase of gait. J. Biomech. 55, 107–112 (2017)
10. Begg, R.K., Palaniswami, M., Owen, B.: Support vector machines for automated gait classification. IEEE Trans. Biomed. Eng. 52(5), 828–838 (2005)
11. Pincus, S.M., Goldberger, A.L.: Physiological time-series analysis: what does regularity quantify? Am. J. Physiol. Heart Circ. Physiol. 266(4), H1643–H1656 (1994)
12. Daffertshofer, A., Lamoth, C.J., Meijer, O.G., Beek, P.J.: PCA in studying coordination and variability: a tutorial. Clin. Biomech. 19(4), 415–428 (2004)
13. Toronto, C.O.: Accessibility Design Guidelines (2004)
14. Americans with disabilities act (ADA) standards

Effect of Test Conditions on COF Measurements on Ice Surfaces Using SATRA STM603 Whole Shoe Tester

Chantal Gauvin[1(✉)] and Yue Li[2]

[1] IRSST – Institut de Recherche Robert-Sauvé en Santé et en Sécurité du Travail, Montréal, QC H3A 3C2, Canada
chantal.gauvin@irsst.qc.ca
[2] KITE – Toronto Rehabilitation Institute, University Health Network, Toronto, ON M5G 22, Canada

Abstract. The SATRA STM603 whole shoe tester combined with a refrigerated ice tray to create ice surfaces can be used to measure the coefficient of friction (COF) between footwear and ice. However, performing tests on ice surfaces can be challenging. The objective of this study was to understand better the effect of ice surfaces (frosted, dry), consecutive runs (1 to 10), and different laboratories (L1, L2) on the COF measurements.

The first series of tests was done with two boots on two ice conditions, frosted and smooth dry, in one laboratory. The second series was done with three boots on dry ice, in two laboratories, and the ice temperature was monitored using thermistors.

The results of the first series showed that the COFs on the frosted ice declined with the runs until reaching a plateau that converged with the COFs on dry ice. Higher variability was observed with the frosted ice compared to dry ice. The results of the second series showed a slight decrease of the COFs over consecutive runs on dry ice, and a significant difference between labs, associated with the ice temperature and the polish of ice by consecutive runs.

This study provided a better understanding of the use and limitations of the SATRA 603ICE ice tray for measuring footwear slip resistance on ice. The method should be further developed, especially the method of controlling the properties of the ice surface, to better simulate ice surfaces in the real-world and to improve the reproducibility of COF measurements.

Keywords: Slip resistance measurements · Ice surfaces · Footwear · SATRA STM603

1 Introduction

Wearing footwear that offers good slip resistance on ice surfaces could effectively reduce slips and falls on the ice [1], which are very common in countries facing winters [2–4]. The whole shoe tester SATRA STM603 is a commonly used device, recommended

© The Author(s), under exclusive license to Springer Nature Switzerland AG 2021
N. L. Black et al. (Eds.): IEA 2021, LNNS 220, pp. 644–651, 2021.
https://doi.org/10.1007/978-3-030-74605-6_81

in ASTM F2913 [5] and ISO 13287 [6] standards, to measure the coefficient of friction (COF) between the footwear outsoles and surfaces. This device can be combined with a refrigerated ice tray (SATRA STM 603ICE) to create ice surfaces. The proprietary SATRA test method (SATRA TM144:2011, 2011 [7]) provides guidelines to test footwear on ice. However, performing tests on ice surfaces can be challenging [8]. It is difficult to maintain specific ice conditions at room temperature for the duration of the tests and reproduce the results in different laboratories. The ice surface temperature fluctuates as a function of the ice refrigeration cycle of the ice tray, and this fluctuation can show different patterns between ice machines [8]. In addition, the effect of several testing parameters on COF results is not well known since little information has been published about this method on ice.

The objective of this study was to understand better the effect of ice surfaces (frosted, smooth dry), consecutive runs (1 to 10), and different laboratories (L1, L2) on the COF measurements using a SATRA STM603 whole shoe tester in conjunction with an STM 603ICE Ice tray.

2 Methods

Two series of experiments were performed on winter boots. Tests were carried out using the SATRA STM603 whole shoe tester combined with an STM 603ICE ice tray (both from SATRA Technology Centre, Kettering, UK) according to ASTM F2913 to measure the COFs of footwear on ice surfaces (Fig. 1). As per this method, a vertical force of 500 N was applied to the test footwear against the ice test surface, which was then moved horizontally relative to the footwear at 0.3 m/s. The SATRA STM603 calculated the COF value as a function of time by computing the ratio: horizontal force/vertical force. A series of 5 to 10 consecutive runs is usually performed, and the final COF is the average of the last 5 consecutive runs. All the tests were done in heel slipping mode (Fig. 1).

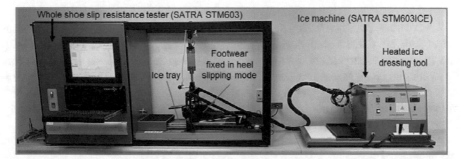

Fig. 1. The SATRA STM603 whole shoe slip resistance tester and the STM 603ICE ice machine were used to evaluate the COF between footwear and ice surfaces. The ice tray was placed under the footwear, which was fixed on the machine in heel slipping mode, by applying a 7° angle between the footwear sole and the test surface.

2.1 Effect of Ice Conditions

The first series of experiments were done in a laboratory (L1) with two winter boots (B1 and B2), on two ice conditions, frosted and smooth dry, and repeated 3 times by the same operator. The tests were conducted at ambient temperatures of 21°C and relative humidity of 52–56%. The boots were conditioned in the laboratory environment for testing.

In accordance with the SATRA TM144:2011 method, the ice was prepared by filling the ice tray with distilled water, setting the ice machine to −2 °C to obtain an ice surface temperature around −7 °C[1], and allowing the water to cool for around 2 h for the ice to be formed. The frosted ice was obtained by letting the frost form naturally on the ice until the depth of the frost was between 1 and 2 mm as recommended in SATRA TM144:2011. The ice was resurfaced before the tests by pressing the electrically heated ice dressing tool (Fig. 1) over the surface of the ice and waiting long enough for the frost to form again (30–45 min). The dry ice surface was obtained by setting the ice machine to −2 °C as well, but the frost was wiped off with a wet cloth a few minutes before the tests, as fully described in [8].

For this experiment, four COFs were calculated for each boot and each repetition, giving four types of ice condition:

1. $COF_{Frost\_1st\ run}$: COF obtained at the first run out of 10 consecutive runs on frosted ice. According to SATRA TM144:2011, this COF represents the slip resistance of footwear on frosted ice.
2. $COF_{Frost\_4th\ run}$: COF obtained at the fourth run out of 10 consecutive runs on frosted ice. According to SATRA TM144:2011, this COF represents the slip resistance of footwear on smooth ice.
3. COF_{Frost_Mean}: mean COF of the last 5 consecutive runs on frosted ice. According to ASTM F2913, this COF represents the slip resistance on a test surface, here the smooth ice.
4. COF_{Dry_Mean}: mean COF of the last 5 consecutive runs on smooth dry ice, according to [8].

ANOVA and post-hoc Tukey statistical analyses were performed using NCSS statistical software (NCSS Statistical Software, version 11, NCSS, LLC. Utah, USA [9]) with the independent variables footwear (B1, B2) and ice conditions (Frost_1st run, Frost_4th run, Frost_Mean, Dry_Mean), as well as the two-way interactions. The analyses had a significance level of 0.05, and the assumptions underlying the use of the models (homogeneity and normality of the residuals) were verified by examining the model's standardized residuals. The results are reported as mean ± standard deviation (SD).

2.2 Effect of Consecutive Runs, Session and Laboratory

The second series of experiments was done with three winter boots (B1, B2, B3), in the condition of dry ice (such as in the first series), in two laboratories (L1 and L2). For

---

[1] For laboratory L1, the ice machine calibration report indicated a difference of −5 °C between the set point and the temperature of the empty ice tray measured with an infrared reader. Thus, SATRA Technology Centre suggested using a set point of −2 °C to produce ice at −7 °C.

each test, a series of 10 consecutive runs was performed. The same operator in each lab repeated the tests four times (sessions), giving a total of 240 COFs. The tests were conducted at ambient temperatures of 22.0–23.0 °C with a relative humidity of 19–21% for L1, and of 23.8–24.5 °C with a relative humidity of 22–32% for L2. The boots were conditioned in the laboratory environment for testing. The exact same left boot for each type of footwear was used in both labs for testing. For this series, the temperature of the ice was monitored using thermistors (model SC50F103VN, Amphenol Thermometrics, Inc., St. Marys, PA, USA, for L1; Mon-a-therm™ temperature probe, Nellcor Puritan Bennett Inc., Pleasanton, CA, USA, for L2) connected to a data logger (USB-6002, National Instruments, TX, USA, for L1; Smartreader 8+, ACR Systems, Canada, for L2) and a computer to provide real-time temperature data in both labs.

At the temperature set point of −2 °C for dry ice, the display of the STM603ICE showed the temperature fluctuated between 0 °C and −2 °C, which corresponds to a fluctuation of the actual temperature of the ice between −3 °C and −7 °C. Because the fluctuation showed different patterns between the two labs, the COFs were measured within a specifically restricted temperature range in each lab in order to be as close as possible to the actual ice temperature of −7 °C and to have enough time to carry out the 10 test runs. For L1, tests were performed when the ice was warming up from the displayed temperature of −2 °C to −1 °C. For L2, tests were performed when the ice was cooling down from the displayed temperature of −1 °C to −2 °C.

ANOVA and post-hoc Tukey statistical analyses were performed using NCSS statistical software [9] with the independent variables footwear (B1, B2, B3), labs (L1, L2), test runs (10 levels), and sessions (4 levels), as well as the two-way interactions. The analyses had a significance level of 0.05, and the assumptions underlying the use of the models were verified by checking the model's standardized residuals. The results are reported as mean ± SD.

3   Results

3.1   Effect of Ice Conditions

The ANOVA for the first series of experiments showed that the footwear and the ice conditions both have a significant effect on COF measurements ($p < 0.0001$), but not the interaction between these two factors (Table 1).

The test results showed that:

(i)   On the frosted ice, the COFs declined with the runs (Fig. 2a) until almost reaching a plateau that converged with the COF on dry ice (Fig. 2b).

(ii)   The $COF_{Frost\_1st\,run}$ (0.24 ± 0.05 for B1, 0.38 ± 0.07 for B2) were significantly higher than COF_{Dry_Mean} (0.09 ± 0.01 for B1, 0.19 ± 0.01 for B2) (Fig. 2c).

(iii) The $COF_{Frost\_4th\,run}$, COF_{Frost_Mean} and COF_{Dry_Mean} were not significantly different from each other (0.11 ± 0.03, 0.09 ± 0.03 and 0.09 ± 0.01 respectively for B1; 0.24 ± 0.03, 0.20 ± 0.04 and 0.19 ± 0.01 respectively for B2).

(iv)   There was less variation between repetitions on the dry ice (SD = 0.01) than on the frosted ice (0.03 < SD < 0.07) (Fig. 2c).

Table 1. Test results in heel mode for two boots at lab L1 on four types of ice conditions (significant with $p \leq 0.05$).

Factor	F	p-value
Footwear	72.3	<0.0001*
Ice conditions	29.7	<0.0001*
Footwear*Ice	0.4	0.75

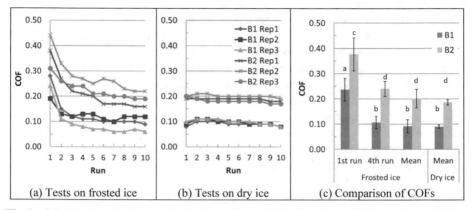

(a) Tests on frosted ice   (b) Tests on dry ice   (c) Comparison of COFs

Fig. 2. COF obtained in heel mode for boots B1 and B2 at lab L1 on (a) frosted ice condition and (b) wiped dry ice condition (10 test runs, 3 repetitions for each condition). (c) Comparison of COF evaluated for four types of ice condition (1st run, 4th run, and Mean of last 5 runs for frosted ice, and Mean of last 5 runs for dry ice), in which the histograms and error bars represent the mean ± SD over the three repetitions. Means that share the same letter are not significantly different, and on the contrary, means that do not share the same letter are significantly different.

3.2   Effect of Consecutive Runs, Session and Laboratory

The ANOVA for the second series of experiments showed that all factors have a significant effect on COF measurements ($p < 0.05$), as well as all two-way interactions between factors, except for interaction Test run*Session (Table 2).

The results of tests also showed that:

(i)   A slight decrease of the COFs was observed over consecutive runs, less pronounced in lab L1 (~0.02) compared to lab L2 (~0.04) (Fig. 3a). This decrease is observed for all boots (Fig. 3b and Fig. 3c).

(ii)   Overall COFs of the boots (Fig. 4a) were significantly different from each other. However, these results depend on the lab: for L1: B1 < B3 < B2, but for L2: B1 < B3 ≈ B2.

(iii)   The lab L1 obtained systematically higher COFs than the lab L2, 0.04 higher on average.

Table 2. Test results in heel mode for three boots at lab L1 and L2 on dry ice condition (significant with $p \leq 0.05$).

Factor	F	p-value
Footwear	2468.2	<0.0001*
Lab	2055.5	<0.0001*
Test run	48.0	<0.0001*
Session	39.7	<0.0001*
Footwear*Lab	82.5	<0.0001*
Footwear*Test run	2.0	0.013*
Footwear*Session	35.7	<0.0001*
Lab*Test run	5.8	<0.0001*
Lab*Session	13.5	<0.0001*
Test run*Session	1.3	0.203

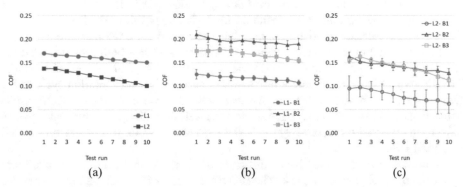

Fig. 3. Mean COF over the 10 test runs obtained for all boots and all sessions on dry ice condition, in heel slipping mode: (a) mean COF for each lab (L1 and L2), (b) mean COF and SD for each boot (B1, B2, B3) in lab L1, (c) mean COF and SD for each boot (B1, B2, B3) in lab L2.

4   Discussion

4.1   Effect of Ice Conditions

The $COF_{Fost\_1st\,run}$ varied a lot with the depth of the frost, which was difficult to control and measure. Over time, after a few consecutive runs on the frosted ice surface, the outsole made the ice smoother until reaching the COF_{Dry_Mean} obtained on the dry ice, which showed less variation and was easier to control. This trend was the same for the two boots tested, as shown by the non-significant interaction Footwear*Ice. Tests on frosted ice did not represent a common slippery surface situation since the boot sole has scraped the frost from the ice.

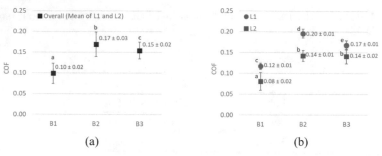

Fig. 4. Mean COF obtained for all test runs and sessions on dry ice condition, in heel slipping mode, for each boot (B1, B2, B3): (a) overall mean COF and SD for both labs, and (b) mean COF and SD for each lab (L1 and L2). Means that share the same letter are not significantly different, and on the contrary, means that do not share the same letter are significantly different.

4.2   Effect of Consecutive Runs, Session and Laboratory

Tests on dry ice revealed a drop in COF values over the consecutive runs, no matter the lab, even if the tests were performed during the increase in ice temperature for L1 and during the decrease in ice temperature for L12. The polish of the ice made by the footwear sole over consecutive runs may have an impact on COF measurements and on the practicability to get stable values. Despite the fact that both labs followed the same protocol, the lab-to-lab difference was one of the substantial sources of variation. The differences in ice temperature fluctuations caused by the refrigeration cycle of the two ice trays may have an impact on the systematic difference of ~0.04 in COF results between labs. Other factors may have an effect as well since disagreements between labs have been observed for tests using the SATRA STM603 whole shoe tester on dry and wet quarry tiles [10].

A limitation of this study is the difficulty of obtaining the actual ice temperature under the boot sole during the test. The SATRA STM603ICE machine does not give a precise value of ice temperature. In addition, it has been shown that these ice machines may have different refrigeration cycles from one another [8]. The use of thermistors can be a solution, but it has constraints. In fact, it is not easy to place a thermistor directly on the test zone, whereas this positioning would be ideal since the temperature of the ice is not homogeneous over the entire surface [8]. The two laboratories have developed their own way of doing things, but it would be better to harmonize the positioning and sampling in both laboratories and possibly to automate the taking of the ice temperature and synchronize it with the COF measurement. Ultimately, a better system to create ice surfaces should be developed to ensure the reproducibility of the ice surfaces.

5   Conclusion

This study provided a better understanding of the effect of ice surfaces, consecutive runs, and laboratories on the COF measurements, as well as the use and limitations of the SATRA 603ICE ice trays to obtain stable and replicable ice surfaces. On frosted ice, the boot sole has scraped the frost from the ice until reaching the dry ice condition after consecutive runs. Higher variability was encountered with the frosted ice compared to dry ice. A slight decrease of the COFs was observed with consecutive runs on dry ice, as well as a significant difference between labs. The ice temperature and the polish of ice by consecutive runs may have an impact on these outcomes. The method should be further developed to make COF measurements more reproducible and meaningful by refining the methods of creating realistic ice surfaces, for example, by better control of the properties of the ice surface and measurement of the actual temperature of the ice in the test zone during the footwear slip resistance testing on ice. The ice surfaces that are created in the lab should also be similar to the slippery ice surfaces that people regularly encountered in the real-world.

References

1. Bagheri, Z.S., Beltran, J.D., Holyoke, P., Dutta, T.: Reducing fall risk for home care workers with slip resistant winter footwear. Appl. Ergon. **90**, 103230 (2021)
2. Gronqvist, R., Hirvonen, M.: Slipperiness of footwear and mechanisms of walking friction on icy surfaces. Int. J. Ind. Ergon. **16**, 191–200 (1995)
3. Gao, C., Holmér, I., Abeysekera, J.: Slips and falls in a cold climate: underfoot surface, footwear design and worker preferences for preventive measures. Appl. Ergon. **39**, 385–391 (2008)
4. Tanner, L.M., Moffatt, S., Milne, E.M.G., Mills, S.D.H., White, M.: Socioeconomic and behavioural risk factors for adverse winter health and social outcomes in economically developed countries: a systematic review of quantitative observational studies. J. Epidemiol Community Health **67**, 1061–1067 (2013)
5. ASTM F2913-19: Standard Test Method for Measuring the Coefficient of Friction for Evaluation of Slip Performance of Footwear and Test Surfaces/Flooring Using a Whole Shoe Tester. ASTM International, West Conshohocken (2019)
6. ISO 13287:2019: Personal Protective Equipment – Footwear – Test Method for Slip Resistance. European Committee for Standardization, Brussels (2019)
7. SATRA TM144:2011: Friction (slip resistance) of footwear and floorings. SATRA Technology Centre (2011)
8. Roshan Fekr, A., Li, Y., Gauvin, C., Wong, G., Cheng, W., Fernie, G., Dutta, T.: Evaluation of winter footwear: comparison of test methods to determine footwear slip resistance on ice surfaces. Int. J. Environ. Res. Public Health **18**, 405 (2021)
9. Hintze, J.: NCSS and PASS. Number Cruncher Statistical Systems, Kaysville, Utah (2004). www.ncss.com
10. ASTM Research Report RR:F13-1005: Evaluation of Precision and Bias of ASTM F2913. ASTM International, West Conshohocken (2019)

Minimum Toe Clearance Estimation Using a Novel Wearable System

Shilpa Jacob[1,2(✉)], Geoff Fernie[1,3], and Atena Roshan Fekr[1,2]

[1] The Kite Research Institute, Toronto Rehabilitation Institute, University Health Network,
University of Toronto, Toronto, ON M5G A2A, Canada
shilpa.jacob@mail.utoronto.ca
[2] Institute of Biomedical Engineering, University of Toronto, Toronto, ON M5S 3G9, Canada
[3] The Creaghan Family Chair in Prevention and Healthcare Technologies,
Department of Surgery, University of Toronto, Toronto, ON M5S 3G9, Canada

Abstract. Slips, trips and falls are among the major causes of injury in Canada. The main reason for trip-related falls is inadequate Minimum Toe Clearance (MTC) in the mid-swing phase of the gait cycle when the foot is at its maximum forward speed. Motion capture systems are the current gold standard for measuring MTC, however they are expensive and have a restricted operating area. The main purpose of this study is to design and validate a novel wearable system that can estimate the MTC using sensor fusion. The system measures the toe clearance, acceleration and orientation of the foot by using a single Time of Flight (ToF) sensor and an Inertial Measurement Unit (IMU). An algorithm was introduced to detect the steps and the MTC events with about 95% accuracy. Our data analysis showed an average correlation coefficient of about 0.8 when comparing the ToF signals with motion capture. In addition, the proposed system can measure the MTC with a Mean Absolute Error (MAE) of 5.2 ± 3.4 mm. The proposed wearable system has the potential to perform real-time MTC estimation and can contribute to future work focused on minimizing tripping risks.

Keywords: Tripping · Minimum foot clearance · Wearable · Time-of-flight sensor · Inertial measurement units

1 Introduction

Slips, trips and falls are among the major causes of injury in Canada [1]. As reported by Parachute, seniors' falls were the primary contributors to injury costs in Canada totaling $8.7 billion in 2010 [2]. Falls not only have physical consequences, but can also negatively affect the mental state of individuals by causing a fear of falling, loss of independence, immobilization and depression [3]. Recent analysis revealed that 53% of seniors' falls are due to tripping [4]. Trip-related falls are predominantly caused by an unsuccessful foot-ground clearance during walking [5]. Minimum Toe Clearance (MTC) is defined as the distance between the toe and ground during the mid-swing phase of the gait cycle when the foot is at its maximum speed [6]. A low MTC, which is often apparent in individuals with shuffling gait or limited lower limb movement, can be a predictor of tripping risk [6]. Studies have found that by increasing the MTC, the risk of tripping can be minimized [6]. Therefore, to reduce the likelihood of trip-related falls, it is essential to have a system that can accurately measure the MTC in real time.

Motion capture (mocap) is considered the gold standard for estimating foot clearance as it can provide highly accurate measurements [7]. However, mocap data is often noisy and incomplete due to calibration error, poor sensor resolution, wrong marker placement and interference caused by body parts or clothing [8]. In addition, this is an expensive system which operates only in a restricted area [7]. Wearable systems have been introduced as an inexpensive, portable and lightweight alternative in gait analysis [9]. These systems provide flexibility to conduct research in both indoor and outdoor environments while minimize interference with an individual's natural gait during everyday activities [10]. Inertial Measurement Units (IMUs) are widely-used to measure different gait parameters such as the foot clearance [10]. Previous studies have investigated both different numbers and locations of the IMUs on the body (toe, heel and instep) to estimate the foot clearance [10]. For example, a recent study conducted by Fan *et al.* achieved the best accuracy for measuring MTC using a two-IMU configuration located at the toe and heel [10]. However, relying exclusively on IMU data to determine the foot displacement during walking provides challenges in data analysis [9]. For example, intermediate calculations need to be performed to convert the IMU data into displacement values which introduces a significant amount of noise and drift over time [11]. Due to the limited accuracy and indirect nature of measuring distance with IMU-based systems, other types of sensors have been investigated [12]. Distance sensors, such as infrared (IR) or ultrasonic sensors, have been used as another option to measure foot clearance [10, 13]. These sensors provide a direct method to measure the foot-ground distance without having to perform intermediate calculations that can cause cumulative drift errors [10, 14].

In this paper, a novel wearable system is introduced which uses a single IMU and a Time-of-Flight (ToF) sensor to estimate the MTC in real-time. The first part of this paper involves extracting the steps and time of the MTC from the ToF signal using data fusion. The second part of this study focuses on validating the MTC achieved from the proposed system versus the mocap as the ground truth. This proposed system has the potential to be integrated with assistive devices in healthcare settings in the future to minimize the risk of tripping and ultimately fall-related injuries.

2 Materials and Methods

2.1 System Design

The wearable system comprises one ToF sensor (SensorDots, Victoria, Australia) and one IMU (Bosch Sensortec, Reutlingen, Germany) mounted on a running shoe. As shown in Fig. 1, the ToF sensor is located near the fifth metatarsal on the outer part of the foot and the IMU is located near the heel of the foot. Reflective markers are placed on the shoe at approximately the same locations as the ToF and IMU sensor in order to minimize the error and perform an accurate comparison with the wearable system.

The ToF sensor outputs distance measurements ranging from 30 mm to 1200 mm with a 25° field of view. The IMU has 9 degrees of freedom and is used to determine the acceleration and orientation of the foot at different phases of the gait cycle. The

Fig. 1. Design components of the proposed wearable system

ToF sensor and IMU are securely attached to the shoes using custom-made 3D-printed enclosures. All the sensors are controlled with the Metro M4 Express microcontroller (Adafruit Industries, New York, USA) and the sensor outputs are recorded and saved using an SD card data logger (Adafruit Industries, New York, USA). The data logger includes a real-time clock which is used to timestamp the sensor data. All data was captured with a sampling rate of 50 Hz. An amber light was used to indicate when both IMUs were fully calibrated. All wiring was installed in a box which was connected to the sensors on the shoe through a 2.5 m ribbon cable. This box was attached to the participant's waist using a waist strap. The ribbon cable that extended from the shoe to the waist was taped to the participant's leg using adhesives to prevent any interference or tripping hazards during the experiment.

2.2 Experiment Setup

The experiment took place in KITE - Toronto Rehabilitation Institute (TRI), Challenging Environment Assessment Laboratory (CEAL). The Cortex motion capture system (Motion Analysis, California, USA) used ten cameras to track the participant's foot movements and serve as the gold standard measurement. Ten healthy female adults aged 25.5 ± 4.1 (Mean $\pm$ SD) years, with a height of 160.8 ± 4.2 cm, and a body weight of 56 ± 5.9 kg were recruited to participate in the study. The study protocol was approved by the University Health Network Research Ethics Board (REB). Participants provided consent before participating in the study. Each participant was asked to walk from one end of the walkway to the other end at their preferred normal speed, pause for a moment, turn around, pause for another moment and then walk back to the starting point (one complete trial). A total of two walking trials were completed for each participant which resulted in a total of 100 steps with their left foot.

2.3 Data Analysis

An algorithm was proposed to first detect the steps and then find the MTC moment within each step. In a typical toe-ground clearance graph as shown in Fig. 2, the first maximum toe clearance (MX1), second maximum toe clearance (MX2) and MTC are identified as key gait parameters [10, 15]. In a normal gait cycle, the MTC would be defined as the lowest minima between MX1 and MX2 [10].

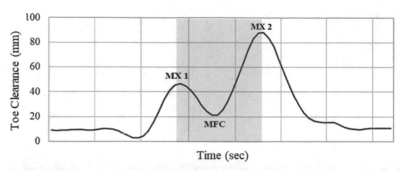

Fig. 2. The toe clearance of a normal gait cycle with the key gait parameters labeled. The grey shaded area represents the swing phase of the gait cycle.

In order to accurately estimate the MTC moments, a combination of ToF and IMU data was used. The raw data collected from the motion capture and wearable system were filtered using a low-pass filter with a passband frequency of 3 Hz and stopband frequency of 6 Hz. The motion capture data was downsampled to 50 Hz to match the sampling rate of the ToF data. Since the data was collected asynchronously by two systems, the motion capture and sensor signals were synchronized by computing the cross-correlations. The steps were extracted based on the orientation of the IMU on the heel of the shoe which was best represented as roll angles. The roll angles were calculated using Eq. (1) as follows:

$$Roll = tan^{-1}\left(\frac{a_y}{a_z}\right) \tag{1}$$

Where the a_y and a_z represent the acceleration in the y and z direction, respectively. Figure 3 shows a sample of three steps from a participant walking normally. The peaks and valleys in the roll angle were found to be located at the start and end of the swing phase of the gait cycle as indicated by the orange triangles. This information helped to define the region of interest where the MTC occurs in each step which is highlighted in gray. The region of interest starts at the MX1 of the ToF graph and ends at the time of the detected valley in the roll signal (V). This is done by comparing the current ToF value to the previous value from when the peak of the roll angle (P) occurs to determine if the trend is incremental or decremental. If the trend is incremental, then the algorithm will keep updating until it reaches the MX1 peak. The lowest ToF value in this region of interest is detected as the MTC value for that gait cycle. This process was repeated for the consecutive gait cycles.

3   Results and Discussion

The correlation coefficient was calculated to measure the strength of the relationship between the distance signals from the mocap and ToF sensor. In order to calculate the correlation coefficient, the signals were synchronized using cross-correlation. Figure 4 presents a sample plot of the mocap and ToF signals after being synchronized. The correlation values are summarized in Table 1. An average correlation coefficient of 0.79 ± 0.07 was obtained considering all 10 participants.

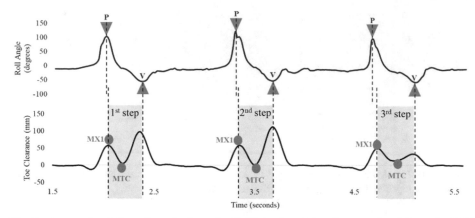

Fig. 3. A sample of the roll angle from the IMU (top) and the distance signal from the ToF (bottom) for a 3-step trial captured from one participant during normal walk.

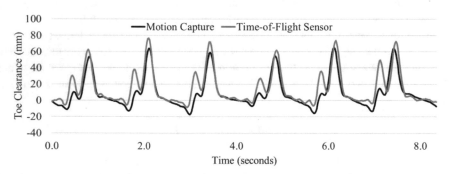

Fig. 4. A 6-step normal walking sample of the mocap and ToF signals after being synchronized through cross-correlation.

Table 1. The correlation coefficients between the motion capture and ToF distance signals

Sub#	Sub1	Sub2	Sub3	Sub4	Sub5	Sub6	Sub7	Sub8	Sub9	Sub10
r	0.83	0.88	0.85	0.84	0.80	0.77	0.74	0.81	0.61	0.81

The correlation coefficient (r) is used to determine if the two signals have a linear relationship meaning that similar trends exist in the data [16]. The MTC values calculated from the two systems were also compared. A total of 100 gait cycles were completed by ten participants over the two walking trials. The proposed step detection algorithm could identify 98 out of 100 steps properly. In addition, 95 MTC events were detected when compared with the mocap data. The proposed wearable system could measure the MTC with a Mean Absolute Error (MAE) of 5.2 ± 3.4 mm. A Bland-Altman (B&A) plot was created in Fig. 5 to graphically compare each MTC value from the mocap and wearable system. This graph indicates that in most cases the MTC from the wearable system was greater than the MTC from the mocap. The average bias between the two values was about 4.59 mm. This can also be seen in Fig. 4 where the peaks and valleys are sharper in the ToF signal compared to the mocap signal.

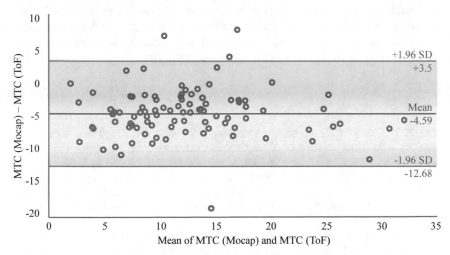

Fig. 5. A Bland-Altman plot for the MTC measurements from the motion capture and wearable system. The grey shaded area represents the limits of agreement around the mean.

3.1 Limitations and Future Work

The proposed wearable system was validated based on the mocap outputs. Due to the limited operating space of the mocap system, there were restrictions on the number of steps each participant could walk. A recommendation for future studies would be to conduct the experiment in a larger space and test the wearable system on different indoor and outdoor ground surfaces, different walking speeds and different inclines to determine if the accuracy of the system will be affected by these factors.

Another limitation was using only one ToF sensor to detect MTC events. Although the system was able to detect the MTC events with a reasonable accuracy, it was not able to measure other gait parameters such as Minimum Heel Clearance (MHC) which is another critical part of the gait cycle. Incorporating an additional ToF sensor at the heel can provide important information that can improve the foot clearance algorithm and possibly eliminate the need for the IMU. Removing the IMU from the system would result in less power, less equipment, simpler data analysis and easier operation. It is important to note that the distance measured from the ToF did not reflect the true toe-ground distance, but instead measured the perpendicular distance from the sensor to the ground. This could have introduced error to the measurements from the wearable system when comparing against the reference system as shown in the B&A plot in Fig. 5. In the future, the wearable system will be improved by compensating this angle.

4 Conclusion

In this paper, a new wearable system was proposed to measure the MTC events. The results from pilot data demonstrated the ability of the system to measure the MTC with an acceptable accuracy compared to previous work. The measurements can be further improved by compensating the foot angle and the observed bias as well as calibrating the sensors. In the future, the system will be validated in environments outside the laboratory to contribute to practical solutions to minimize tripping risk.

References

1. Do, M.T., Chang, V.C., Kuran, N., Thompson, W.: Fall-related injuries among Canadian seniors, 2005–2013: an analysis of the Canadian community health survey. Health Promot. Chronic Dis. Prev. Can. **35**, 99–108 (2015). https://doi.org/10.24095/hpcdp.35.7.01
2. Parachute: The Cost of Injury in Canada. Cost Inj Canada (2015)
3. Institute of Medicine (US) Division of Health Promotion and Disease Prevention, Berg, R.L., Cassells, J.S.: Falls in Older Persons: Risk Factors and Prevention. National Academies Press, Washington DC (1992)
4. Blake, A.J., Morgan, K., Bendall, M.J., Dallosso, H., Ebrahim, S.B.J., Arie, T.H.D., Fentem, P.H., Bassey, E.J.: Falls by elderly people at home: prevalence and associated factors. Age Ageing **17**, 365–372 (1988). https://doi.org/10.1093/ageing/17.6.365
5. Burpee, J.L., Lewek, M.D.: Biomechanical gait characteristics of naturally occurring unsuccessful foot clearance during swing in individuals with chronic stroke. Clin. Biomech. **30**, 1102–1107 (2015). https://doi.org/10.1016/j.clinbiomech.2015.08.018
6. Begg, R.K., Tirosh, O., Said, C.M., Sparrow, W.A., Steinberg, N., Levinger, P., Galea, M.P.: Gait training with real-time augmented toe-ground clearance information decreases tripping risk in older adults and a person with chronic stroke. Front. Hum. Neurosci. **8** (2014). https://doi.org/10.3389/fnhum.2014.00243
7. Benoussaad, M., Sijobert, B., Mombaur, K., Coste, C.A.: Robust foot clearance estimation based on the integration of foot-mounted IMU acceleration data. Sensors **16**, 1–13 (2015). https://doi.org/10.3390/s16010012
8. Mall, U., Lal, G.R., Chaudhuri, S., Chaudhuri, P.: A deep recurrent framework for cleaning motion capture data (2017)
9. Santhiranayagam, B.K., Lai, D.T.H., Sparrow, W.A., Begg, R.K.: A machine learning approach to estimate minimum toe clearance using inertial measurement units. J. Biomech. **48**, 4309–4316 (2015). https://doi.org/10.1016/j.jbiomech.2015.10.040
10. Fan, B., Li, Q., Liu, T.: Accurate foot clearance estimation during level and uneven ground walking using inertial sensors. Measur. Sci. Technol. **31** (2020). https://doi.org/10.1088/1361-6501/ab6917
11. Duong, P.D., Suh, Y.S.: Foot pose estimation using an inertial sensor unit and two distance sensors. Sensors **15**, 15888–15902 (2015). https://doi.org/10.3390/s150715888
12. Arami, A., Saint Raymond, N., Aminian, K.: An accurate wearable foot clearance estimation system: toward a real-time measurement system. IEEE Sens. J. **17**, 2542–2549 (2017). https://doi.org/10.1109/jsen.2017.2665624
13. Wahab, Y., Bakar, N.A., Mazalan, M.: Error correction for foot clearance in real-time measurement. J. Phys. Conf. Ser. **495** (2014). https://doi.org/10.1088/1742-6596/495/1/012046

14. Merat, P., Harvey, E.J., Mitsis, G.D.: A miniature multi-sensor shoe-mounted platform for accurate positioning. In: Proceedings of the 2018 IEEE International Conference on Systems, Man, and Cybernetics, SMC 2018, pp. 2772–2777 (2019). https://doi.org/10.1109/SMC.2018.00473
15. Mariani, B., Rochat, S., Büla, C.J., Aminian, K.: Heel and toe clearance estimation for gait analysis using wireless inertial sensors. IEEE Trans. Biomed. Eng. **59**, 3162–3168 (2012). https://doi.org/10.1109/TBME.2012.2216263
16. Giavarina, D.: Understanding bland altman analysis. Biochemia Medica **25**, 141–151 (2015). https://doi.org/10.11613/BM.2015.015

Can Tribometers and Testing Protocols Affect Slip Resistance Values and Opinions?

Timothy G. Joganich[(⊠)], Angela Levitan, and Tamara L. Cohen

ARCCA, Inc., Penns Park, PA 18943, USA
tjoganich@arcca.com

Abstract. Forensic investigations of slip and fall accidents often entail measuring the slip resistance of the subject floor with tribometers that are often different, which results in expectedly different slip resistance values. Differences in slip resistance measurements obtained on the same floor can be expected when measured with two different tribometers due to the nature of their operation and testing protocol. One such case involved slip resistance testing with two different tribometers using disparate protocols. The measured slip resistance values were substantially different from each other beyond what would be intuitively expected. Nevertheless, specious comparisons were made in this case between the slip resistance values that were measured with two different tribometers. A preliminary laboratory-based study was conducted to investigate the consistency of the differences in slip resistance measurements across floors, which underscores that the proper interpretation of the slip resistance values must be made within the framework of each tribometer.

Keywords: Slip resistance · Slip · Tribometers · Coefficient of friction

1 Introduction

Tribometers are often used during the adjudication process for assessing the adequacy of a floor surface to provide a reasonably safe walking surface and to assess the presence or absence of a causal relationship between a floor surface/contaminate and the incident. This process often involves the same floor surface being measured with two different tribometers, which is inherently confronted with challenges due to the different tribometers providing different slip resistance measurements on the same floor surface [1, 2].

Adjudicating the adequacy of a floor surface for providing a slip-resistant walking surface based on slip resistance measurements conducted with different tribometers is confronted with challenges. Powers et al. [2] references twelve studies that *"… have shown that different devices yield different COF measurements for the same surface."* The disparity of measurements between tribometers for the same floor surface renders the reliance on a single threshold value essentially untenable in an absolute sense. It is for this very reason that the walkway safety community, and specifically the ASTM

© The Author(s), under exclusive license to Springer Nature Switzerland AG 2021
N. L. Black et al. (Eds.): IEA 2021, LNNS 220, pp. 660–665, 2021.
https://doi.org/10.1007/978-3-030-74605-6_83

F13 Committee on Pedestrian/Walkway Safety and Footwear, moved toward a gait-based approach to assess the risk of a slip event based on the work of Powers et al. [3]. Efforts culminated in 2011 with the approval of ASTM F2508 Standard Practice for Validation and Calibration of Walkway Tribometers Using Reference Surfaces. Briefly, F2508 entails "validating and calibrating" individual tribometers with four reference tiles of different levels of slipperiness that represent the continuum from no slipping to slipping during human ambulation. The tribometer must be able to statistically rank order the tiles and differentiate between them. The slip resistance of the tile that presented no risk of a slip along the continuum is then determined to be the threshold value for that particular tribometer.

While the Brungraber Mark IIIB, in general, relies on a unique threshold value for each tribometer, determined in accordance with ASTM F2508, the BOT-3000E relies on a standard minimum dynamic coefficient of friction (DCOF) value of 0.42 as set forth in ANSI A137.1 American National Standard Specifications for Ceramic Tile. ANSI A137.1 Section 6.2.2.1.10 Coefficient of Friction states that *"Unless otherwise specified, tiles suitable for level interior spaces expected to be walked upon when wet shall have a wet DCOF of 0.42 or greater when tested using SLS solution as per the procedure outlined in Section 9.6.1."* The standard goes on to state *"The coefficient of friction (COF) measurement provided in this standard is an evaluation of a tile surface under known conditions using a standardized sensor material prepared according to a specific protocol. As such it can provide a useful comparison of the tile surfaces, but it does not predict the likelihood a person will or will not slip on a tile surface."* The BOT-3000E testing protocol entails validating the BOT-3000E using a provided reference surface prior to testing any tiles that are part of the forensic investigation per the protocol in ANSI A137.1 and ANSI A326.3 American National Standard Test Method for Measuring Dynamic Coefficient of Friction of Hard Surface Flooring Materials.

The foregoing challenges unfolded during a forensic investigation of a purported slip and fall event due to the presence of water within the stall of a public bathroom. Specifically, two different engineering firms conducted a forensic analysis using a Brungraber Mark IIIB and BOT-3000E. The flooring surface was a relatively heavily textured 12 × 12-in. glazed ceramic tile with 3/16-in. grout lines. The values measured with the BOT-3000E ranged from 58 to 78% less than those measured with the Mark IIIB.

The following study was undertaken in an attempt to understand the disparity of the above slip resistance measurements in light of the aforementioned challenges associated with measuring, and then interpreting, slip resistance values measured with two different tribometers on the same floor surface.

2 Methodology

Slip resistance testing was conducted on two different floor surfaces in a series of tests using the Mark IIIB and BOT-3000E tribometers. Testing was conducted in a laboratory type of setting with a temperature of 70.7 °F and a relative humidity of 47%. The floor surfaces were level within 0.2° across the four orthogonal directions. The first test measured the slip resistance of an epoxy floor using distilled water and sodium lauryl sulfate (SLS) as contaminates, which resulted in a 2×2 test matrix (device $\times$ contaminant). While standard protocol entailed using distilled water with the Mark IIIB and an SLS solution with the BOT-3000E, this testing matrix allowed the effects of the contaminant to be assessed. The second test measured the slip resistance of a lightly textured ceramic tile with the contaminate specified in the respective protocol of each tribometer. The slip resistance was measured at three separate locations on the floor surface and then collapsed into a single average. Testing using the BOT-3000E followed the ANSI A137.1/A326.3 standard. Testing using the Mark IIIB followed the manufacturer's instructions.

For reference purposes, the Mark IIIB (Fig. 1) is a mechanical device that operates by forcing a strut with an articulating test foot downwards by means of a spring at various angles onto a surface with water as a contaminate. The angle of the strut is increased until there are sufficient horizontal forces to cause the test foot to overcome the frictional forces causing it to slide forwards. The test foot is made from Neolite®. In contrast, the BOT-3000E (Fig. 2) is a motorized device that drags a sensor along the floor surface with SLS as a contaminate. Standard sensors for the BOT-3000E specified in the instruction manual are Neolite®, leather, and SBR rubber. Custom sensors are also available from the manufacture. An SBR sensor was used in this study per the ANSI protocol.

Fig. 1. Brungraber mark IIIB.

Fig. 2. BOT-3000E.

3   Results

3.1   Test 1

Table 1 provides the slip resistance measurements for both the BOT-3000E and the Mark IIIB on the epoxy floor using water and SLS as contaminates. The average (s.d.) slip resistance value when using the BOT-3000E was 0.55 (0.017) with distilled water, and 0.47 (0.030) with the SLS solution. The average (s.d.) slip resistance value when using the Mark IIIB was 0.59 (0.025) with distilled water, and 0.40 (0.006) with the SLS solution.

Table 1. Slip resistance measurements on the epoxy floor.

Tribometer	Contaminant	Slip resistance
BOT-3000E	Distilled water	0.54, 0.54, 0.57
	SLS	0.44, 0.50, 0.47
Mark IIIB	Distilled water	0.56, 0.59, 0.61
	SLS	0.40, 0.39, 0.40

3.2 Test 2

Table 2 provides the slip resistance measurements for both the BOT-3000E and the Mark IIIB on the ceramic tile using the respective protocols. The average (s.d.) slip resistance was 0.47 (0.017) when using the BOT-3000E with the SLS solution, and 0.56 (0.006) when using the Mark IIIB with distilled water.

Table 2. Slip resistance measurements following tribometer specific protocols.

Tribometer	Slip resistance
BOT-3000E	0.49
	0.46
	0.46
Mark IIIB	0.56
	0.56
	0.57

4 Discussion

Fundamentally, a measuring instrument will itself affect the results of the value being measured to some degree. It therefore comes as no surprise that the results of this study demonstrated that the slip resistance values of the same exact floor measured with the BOT-3000E and the Mark IIIB yielded different values. Furthermore, differences were expected since these two tribometers operate functionally in an entirely different manner with disparate testing protocols. The Mark IIIB tribometer is an articulating strut mechanical device, while the BOT-3000E is a motorized drag sled device. Standard protocol dictates distilled water and SLS solution for the Mark IIIB and BOT-3000E, respectively.

The differences between the two tribometers were relatively constant across the two floor samples. More specifically, the slip resistance values of the ceramic tile and epoxy floor when measured with the BOT-3000E were 16.6 and 19.9% less than those measured with the Mark IIIB, respectively, when using the contaminate as specified in their respective protocols. While these differences were present, both tribometers would characterize each of the floor surfaces as slip resistant by their respective standards and/or threshold values for delineating a slip resistant surface. The test results for the epoxy floor, which enabled for comparisons across devices and contaminates, showed that both the tribometer and contaminate accounted for the differences.

As would be expected, the SLS solution, which is a soap solution, resulted in a 14.5% and 32.4% decrease of slip resistance as compared to distilled water for the BOT-3000E and Mark IIIB, respectively. The slip resistance when measured with the BOT-3000E was 6.7% less than when measured with the Mark IIIB with distilled water as the contaminate but 15.6% greater with SLS solution as the contaminate. The underlying reason for this reversal in directionality is unclear.

5 Conclusion

The results of this study, while limited in scope, suggest that the differences in slip resistance when using the BOT-3000E and Mark IIIB can be expected to be relatively constant across floor surfaces on the order of 20% with the BOT-3000E providing the lower slip resistance value. The practitioner must ensure that they interpret the slip resistance values in accordance with the standards and/or threshold values established for the tribometer used, and avoid specious comparisons between slip resistance values measured with two different tribometers. Further studies should include other types of flooring surfaces such as stone, heavily textured ceramic, and polished marble in order to draw more robust conclusions.

References

1. Grieser, B.C., et al.: Slip resistance: field measurements using two modern slipmeters. Professional Safety, pp. 43–48 (2002)
2. Powers, C.M., et al.: Assessment of walkway tribometer readings in evaluating slip resistance: a gait-based approach. J. Forensic Sci. 52(2), 400–405 (2007)
3. Powers, C.M., et al.: Validation of walkway tribometers: establishing a reference standard. J. Forensic Sci. 55(2), 366–370 (2010)

The Misuse of Regulations, Standards and Acceptable Practice in Ambulation-Safety Analysis

Mark I. Marpet[✉]

(Emeritus) St. John's University, New York City, USA
mmarpet@comcast.net

Abstract. In United States jurisprudence, Reasonable Certainty is one of the criteria for the admissibility of expert opinion in litigation. One element of establishing Reasonable Certainty can be that the opinion comports with a code requirement, a voluntary-consensus standard, a handbook reference or, in their absence, with Acceptable Practice. From there, and importantly, that the claimed requirement, standard or practice is causally related to the accident under analysis. A key element in using a code, standard, or handbook reference in the Reasonably-Certain rubric is that all substantive elements, including temporality, must be met. The key elements in showing that something comports with Acceptable Practice are, in addition to the elements listed above, that the Acceptable Practice in fact exists beyond the imagination of the interested expert. Ignoring any of these elements, often deliberately, turns what should be dispositively significant elements of litigation into a meaningless check-box item. It has been my experience that many forensic practitioners simply ignore all this, citing for-one-reason-or-another irrelevant code and standards in their desire to give the work the appearance of a mantle of authority. That this is inappropriate is hopefully obvious.

Keywords: Ambulation safety · Reasonable certainty · Regulations · Standards

1 Introduction

1.1 Definitions

Reasonable Certainty is a term of legal art in the United States, in this paper relating to the admissibility of the opinion of an expert in a judicial proceeding. To have an opinion that is reasonably certain, it must be more probable than not. As one might imagine, that leaves significant wiggle room, especially when the opinion probability cannot be mathematically quantified[1] As a general rule, because expert opinion cannot be admissible without it being Reasonably Certain, a statement that an opinion is (or opinions are) Reasonably Certain is appended to each and every expert report.

Regulations are, in the context of this paper, statutes, or other elements that have the force of law behind them.

Standards are documents developed by various bodies to define an item or practice. One main purpose of a standard is to facilitate commerce. For example, rather than a contract specifying in detail the slip-resistance properties of a liquid floor polish, including the appropriate test protocols and acceptance-threshold criteria, the contract can simply specify that the polish must adhere to ASTM Standard D2047 Standard Test Method for Static Coefficient of Friction of Polish-Coated Flooring Surfaces as Measured by the James Machine, which lays out in detail these issues. Standards, at the risk of oversimplifying, come in various 'strengths.' The strongest is a standard developed through a Standards Development Organization, e.g., ASTM International or the International Standards Organization (ISO). Developed through such organizations, one can be reasonably assured that the many (often) divergent views of the stakeholders are taken into account. At the other end of the strength spectrum are company standards, which are essentially how-to instructions to use a specific product or class of products.

Reference and handbook entries often lack peer review, or at least, formal peer review. (Wikipedia entries often benefit from the public-review nature of the proceedings.)

Acceptable Practice characterizes the state of the industry (as opposed to the state of the art) at a certain point in time and place. It is important to actually define what constitutes Acceptable Practice: saying so doesn't make it so.

1.2 Temporal Relevance

There are generally two threshold dates in applying code: The building-erection date and the accident date. The building-erection date applies to the building's construction.

---

[1] Because the law and science have rather different worldviews, the relationship between the law and science is fraught. To cite an example: Many, many years ago, I was involved in an assessment of the *a priori* probability that a defendant would realize that his drinking would *probably* (as opposed to *possibly*) cause mishap, the probably-v.-possibly question being an important element in the seriousness of the charge against the defendant. There exists peer-reviewed, quantitative research that explicitly addressed the topic, so my analysis was made with mathematical rigor [1]. The court dismissed the work out of hand. It seems that the court—or at least, *this* court, was strongly against the very notion of quantification. I am not suggesting that all courts are against mathematical characterization of probability: one only has to think of DNA analysis. Rather, the courts are *extremely* conservative in their acceptance of such analysis. In 2009, the National Research Council published what is commonly known as the NAS report [2], which, in Peter Neufeld's words, "called on the scientific community to help the criminal justice system establish the resources and processes needed for forensics to move toward the promise of neutral truth teller. The progress that it set in motion cannot be understated—it is not an exaggeration to say that the report has freed innocent people and saved lives." [3]. That said, in 2021, sad to say, it is *still* a work in progress.

The accident date applies to maintenance issues, as building maintenance is and must be ongoing.[2]

2 Examples

2.1 Was There a Lack of Proper Illumination? Does the Alleged Violation of a Regulation *per se* Lead to an Unsafe Condition?

This litigation [4] involved an exterior staircase trip on a school staircase at night, where the allegation was that the plaintiff was unable to see the stairs because a light fixture was not working. The report concluded with this boilerplate, "that all of the writer's opinions have been offered within reasonable engineering certainty."

The expert, a Professional Engineer, without going into any detail[3], took illuminance measurements, finding that the light level was 0.5 foot-candles except in the shadows, where it was 0.2 foot-candles. The engineer writes that this violates Garfield's municipal ordinances, the International Property Maintenance Code, the New Jersey Uniform Construction Code, and the New Jersey Fire Code. Let's briefly look at each, keeping in mind that the issue is whether the stairs so lacked illumination that they were hazardous and causal in the accident under analysis:

Garfield's Municipal Code: This is cited to indicate that the City of Garfield has adopted the International Property Maintenance Code, published by the International Code Counsel.
The International Property Maintenance Code: cited to indicate that it applies to nonresidential structures, that property owners are responsible for the continued operation of safety-related equipment, and that non-residential buildings are required to have 1 foot-candle of illumination on exterior means of egress.
The New Jersey Uniform Construction Code: cited to indicate that municipalities are allowed to have stricter regulations.
The New Jersey Uniform Fire Code: cited for that same 1 foot-candle illumination requirement.

The first and third of these citations are on their face not germane to the question of whether there was a violation of code and, furthermore, whether that code violation was causal in the accident under analysis. In fact, the single relevant element of the three (!) pages of regulations cited was that there needed to be one foot-candle of illumination, measured at the floor of the exit path.

---

[2] There is a certain amount of interpretation here. If a building has undergone alteration or renovation, depending upon what was done, when it was done, and how much it cost, the alterations—or the whole building—may be required to conform to a later code edition. Also, if a Construction Code Official mandates that you need to upgrade some aspect of the building, or the building code explicitly requires updating *e.g.*, the installation of smoke detectors, you need to conform to such mandates. These issues are beyond the scope of this paper.

[3] I have stripped out pounds of dross in the interest of brevity. For the purpose of this paper, to keep things focused, let us assume that the engineer's measurements are correct.

Although the illuminance level that the engineer reportedly measured was below the code-mandated level, research and handbook data indicates the measured illumination level would not be low enough to cause an accident. To see this, we need to look at handbook data and peer-reviewed research as to how much illumination is actually required for safe egress from a building.

The Illumination Engineering Society of North America's *Lighting Handbook* [5] states (See Table 29–2) that, for safety, the minimum level of illuminance for a *Normal Activity Level* and *Slight Hazards Requiring Visual Detection* is ½ foot-candle.

Peer-reviewed research indicates that a much lower level of illumination is in fact safe. Oullette and Rea [6], using among other factors, crowd size, route familiarity, and the presence of stairs, concluded that a mean, i.e., average, illuminance of 0.04 foot-candles ($1/25^{th}$ the code-required minimum) on the stair was sufficient to ensure movement without collision with large objects. Boyce [7] found that exit speed decreased as illuminance levels went down, with a $1/3^{rd}$ reduction in speed for older pedestrians at a 0.09 foot-candles compared with 27 foot-candles 'normal' lighting. Jaschinski [8] found that research subjects did not collide with obstacles at a 0.02 foot-candle illuminance level ($1/50^{th}$ the code-required minimum).

In short, the research indicates that for normal egress, pedestrians need less than a tenth of the code-required minimum, bringing up the question, why is the code requirement so high *vis à vis* the research. There are at least two factors: (a) the code requirements long predate the research, and (b), emergent egress in fire or similar situations can have near panicked (or wholly panicked) pedestrians rushing the exits, a situation different in kind from what the researchers measured, and not-at-all not the situation confronting the plaintiff.

To Summarize the Engineer's Failings
Firstly, the engineer's methodology is, based upon the report supplied, not repeatable. The report was silent on the number and pattern of measurements, the instrumentation (including calibration information), the raw data, and any adjustments to that data. The *only* information supplied was that the illuminance was 0.5 footcandles except in the shadows, where it was 0.2 foot-candles. That's simply not enough information to evaluate the question of whether the testing was conducted within reasonable engineering certainty.

Secondly, the standards and regulations put forth in the report suffer from 'more-is-better' padding, taking three pages to get to the point that the codes call for a 1-foot-candle illumination level.

Thirdly, the engineer fails to show that failure to meet a code requirement was a causal element in the plaintiff's accident. This is arguably the most important failing, assuming that it the stairs did not in fact meet the one foot-candle building-code requirement. While the engineer never gets beyond the code issue, handbook and research data strongly refute the contention that one foot-candle is actually needed for safety in non-emergent situations.

2.2   Were the Church Steps Inherently Dangerous? Can We Hold Steps Built in the 1860s to a Regulation Promulgated in the 1960s?

The litigation involved the historic Holy Cross Roman Catholic church, located on the west side of 42nd Street in Manhattan, just across the street from the main Port Authority Bus Terminal [9]. The Plaintiff alleges that she had been exiting the church and tripped on the stairs leading to down to the street. An engineer retained by the plaintiff essentially opined that these stairs (a) were improperly maintained, (b) they lacked proper handrails and (c) the single step that plaintiff tripped upon was "inherently unsafe, dangerous and hazardous." To justify his opinions, the engineer cites the 1921,[4] 1938 and 1968 editions of the New York City Building Code, NFPA 101, the *Life Safety Code*, published by the National Fire Protection Association, and ASTM International's F1637 *Standard Practice for Safe Walking Surfaces*. Only the 1968, and in passing, the 2008, editions of the Building Code are cited as to the requirement that facilities be properly maintained. Secondly, the 1968 code is cited as to the requirement for handrails on stairs. The ASTM F1637 (2002 edition) standard and NFPA 101 (1994 edition) code were cited to make the points that single-riser steps are problematic (but not prohibited) and that enhancements to conspicuity are warranted.

The Church of the Holy Cross was, by its cornerstone, erected in the 1860s. As to the lack of maintenance, the engineer avers that the yellow paint on the noising of the step was somewhat worn.

The engineer's analysis fails in many ways. Firstly, as to construction, it is completely inappropriate to judge an 19th century building using 20th and 21st century building codes. The requirement for handrails that is (incorrectly[5]) cited was drafted 100 years after the church had been erected. The earliest requirement for handrails appeared in the 1916 edition of the New York City Building Code, about one-half century after the building came into being. (The installation of handrails is not a maintenance issue unless it is to repair or replace an existing handrail, not the case here.) As to the single-step issue, neither the Life-Safety Code or ASTM F1637, in spite of the good advice that they may confer, set a requirement that must be followed. And the advice that they give is not that single steps are prohibited, but rather, simply to make single steps more conspicuous. (In fact, the church did that by painting the step's nosing yellow. (The engineer asserts that the yellow paint, while clearly visible, was not as bright as it could have been.))

Ultimately, the matter was dismissed by summary judgment, *i.e.,* the court determined that the allegations against the church were without merit. These were not a set of ramshackle stairs jerry-built on the side of a barn; the 19th Century church stairs involved in this matter were built to the highest standards of their time, designed to last for centuries and designed to be impressive.

---

[4] There is no 1921 New York City Building Code; the edition before the 1938 code is the 1916 edition.

[5] In New York City, the stairs leading from the main entrance of a building to the street are not considered required exit stairs, and do not have to conform with the building code. (See *Gaston v. New York City Housing Authority*, 258 A.D. 2d 220 (1999).) Thus, the engineer's assertion that the step violated code is without merit.

What Are the Failings of the Engineer

Firstly, the engineer analyzing these steps ignored the issue of temporality, never relating these stairs to construction practices of the mid 1800s. The regulations he explicitly cites date from the mid 1960s. Thus, the analysis fails because 1860 construction and design practice cannot be judged by century-later requirements. To demand that is to demand that architects and builders be able to see far into the future. If engineers or architects could do that, it is clear that they would be far, far better off dropping engineering or architecture and investing in a futures market!

That existing construction is exempt from changes in the code is called grandfathering, and is explicitly permitted in the very 1968 code that the engineer cites, to wit, in section 27–111, "The lawful occupancy and use of any building, including the use of any service equipment therein, existing on the effective date of this code ... may be continued unless a retroactive change is specifically required by the provisions of this code."

Secondly, The other code citations, starting with §27–127, simply require a building to be safely maintained. To use this citation, one must first show that a defect actually existed. Here, the only maintenance 'failure,' according to the engineer, was that the paint on the edge of the step was faded. Clearly visible, but faded. And the citations to the Life Safety Code and ASTM F1637 standard are not requirements, they are recommendations. Moreover, neither of these required handrails. Rather, handrails were recommended as but one of a number of measures to increase the conspicuity of that single step. (Among the other recommendations was painting the landing edge.)

2.3 Was the Staircase Slippery? Does the Interpretation of a Code Provision Make Sense in the Context of Current Ergonomic Knowledge?

The requirement for floor friction set out in the New York City Building Code has no quantitative requirement, mandating only that the surface be "slip resistant." Given the need to adjust for differences in Required Friction for various activities, it is clear that this may well be as specific as the building code should (or could) get. To make sense of "slip resistant," one must fall back on basic ambulation ergonomics, *viz.,* the ergonomic criterion for not slipping is that the friction required for an ambulatory maneuver (the Required Friction, denoted by μ_R, where μ is the symbol for a coefficient of friction, a dimensionless parameter that essentially characterizes the relative force needed to institute or maintain slip. [11]) is available between the shoe bottom and the floor surface (the Available Friction, μ_A):

$$\mu_A > \mu_R,$$

Ergonomic research indicates that a mean Required Friction of just under 0.3 is required for stair descent [11]. In this matter [12], the involved engineer tested the ("COF") to be 0.34–0.40 using a "drag-sled" of unknown provenance.

The engineer involved writes that "several organizations" state "what they believe to be the threshold for safety when walking on a floor," citing "ADA (the American with Disabilities Act): flat surfaces" at $\mu \geq 0.6$ and OSHA (the Occupational Safety and Health Act), the US. Department of Commerce, and the NFPA (the National Fire Prevention

Association, Inc.) at $\mu \geq 0.5$. Notably, not one of these citations are a requirement, not one of these citations are for stair descent, and not one of these citations relate to the engineer's drag sled of unknown provenance.

The engineer calls the 0.5 threshold to be the "Working Definition," for safe floor traction. "Working Definition" is not a term of art in Walkway-Safety Tribometry, although a 0.5 threshold is accepted in certain circumstances, and it could well be this engineer's idiosyncratic Working Definition. It holds no sway in the context used here. Ironically, the 0.34–0.40 range of Available Friction found by the engineer was above what the slightly-under-0.3 mean friction required for stair descent. Thus, if the engineer's results had been meaningful (They are not.), he would have been able to make a convincing case against his client.

Ho Summarize the Failings of This Engineer

Firstly, the analytical work, if one could call it that, was engineering theater, unrepeatable test results compared with meaningless criteria, designed to sound like "Reasonable-ish Engineering Certainty." Problems abound: friction is both a material-dependent and a test-system-dependent property, and no apparatus was specified and no validation protocol, e.g., ASTM F-2508 *Standard Practice for Validation, Calibration, and Certification of Walkway Tribometers Using Reference Surfaces* [13] was utilized. Thus, the engineer's test results could not possibly be repeatable.

Secondly, the 0.5 (or 0.6) acceptance threshold that the engineer references is both non-mandatory and flawed. The ≥ 0.6 ADA threshold cited is for guidance only and has relevance only for those with mobility impairments. All the ≥ 0.5 COF thresholds are based upon the ASTM D2047 standard, which refers to testing liquid floor polish using a James tribometer.

Thirdly, and again, because the Required Friction varies with activity, it is meaningless to specify a single threshold without explicitly specifying the ambulatory activity. Here, there is a significant difference between the Required Friction for level-surface walking versus Required Friction for stair descent. The 0.5 threshold was originally set as an in-the-bottle acceptance threshold for liquid floor polish. It was set quite high because the end use of the polish was unknown, as was the footwear of the pedestrian. What it accomplished, and this was significant, was to greatly minimize the use of wax-based polishes on commercial floors, which reduced slip-induced fall accidents. The 0.5 threshold has little or nothing to do with whether or not a given fall was caused by a slippery floor. To determine that, one must examine the context of the fall.

References

1. Borkenstein, R.F., Crowther, R.F., Shumate, R.P., Ziel, W.B., Zylman, R.: The Role of the Drinking Driver in Traffic Accidents (The Grand Rapids Study). Blutalkohol, vol. II, no. Suppl. 1, pp. 1–131 (1974)
2. National Research Council of the National Academies: Strengthening Forensic Science in the United States: A Path Forward (2009). ISBN-13:978-0-309-13135-3
3. The Innocence Project: Ten Years Later: The Lasting Impact of the 2009 NAS Report. https://innocenceproject.org/lasting-impact-of-2009-nas-report/times. Accessed 22 Dec 2020

4. Zuest v. Garfield Board of Education, et al.: Docket Number BER–L–498–14, New Jersey (2014)
5. Rea, M.S. (ed.): The IESNA Lighting Handbook, Illuminating Engineering Society of North America, 9th edn., New York (2000). (Earlier editions of the handbook contained the same information cited in this paper)
6. Ouellette, M., Rea, M.: Illuminance requirements for emergency lighting. J. Illuminating Eng. Soc. **18**(1), 2742 (1989)
7. Boyce, P.: Human Factors in Lighting, 2nd edn. Taylor and Francis, New York (2003)
8. Jaschinski, W.: Conditions of emergency lighting. Ergonomics **25**(5), 363–372 (1982)
9. Baker v Roman Catholic Church of the Holy See (Index Number 113884/11, New York Supreme Court))
10. See, for example, 2008 New York City Building Code. https://www1.nyc.gov/assets/buildings/apps/pdf_viewer/viewer.html?file=2008CC_BC_Chapter_10_Means_of_Egress.pdf&section=conscode_2008. §1003.4, Accessed 23 Dec 2020
11. Redfern, M., et al.: Biomechanics of slips. Ergonomics **44**(13), 1138–1166 (2001)
12. Cunningham v. Long Island Rail Road. Index Number 700158/2015 (Queens Supreme Court)
13. ASTM F2508, Standard Practice for Validation, Calibration, and Certification of Walkway Tribometers Using Reference Surfaces, ASTM International, West Conshohocken, PA

Why, How, and How Effectively Do USA and Canadian Building Codes Address Two Leading Fall Sites in Homes?

Jake Pauls[1]([✉]) and Daniel Johnson[2]

[1] Jake Pauls Consulting Services, Silver Spring, MD, USA
bldguse@aol.com
[2] Daniel A. Johnson, Inc., Olympia, WA, USA
dajinc1@mac.com

Abstract. Despite abundant evidence, the most effective, ethics-driven, fall prevention and mitigation interventions have *not* been widely employed for new home settings in the USA and Canada in the last five decades. The Canadian and the two US model codes organizations came into existence independently and more or less in isolation with different histories, influential constituencies and procedures that developed in different places. Progress on fall prevention and mitigation efforts has been influenced by what can be thought of as an organizational personality or culture. With one exception, the National Fire Protection Association, NFPA, these organizations' codes and standards have generally been, at best, slow and, at worst, opposed to adopting fall prevention and mitigation requirements. Also, these organizations affect not just safety, but usability of homes and all other built environmental settings. For example, for stairways serving people in their homes, the most appropriate, minimum requirements should be based on public building requirements for stairways. Most generally, the three organizations operate in three very different political and cultural contexts that greatly influence their overall activity which is focused on differing emphasis on organization-funded and facilitated research, education, training, safety document production, and quality control generally.

Keywords: Home stairways · Home bathrooms · Building codes · Falls etiology · Injuries · Usability

1 Main Message of this Chapter

Despite abundant evidence, *from etiology (including macro-ergonomics and ergonomics generally), epidemiology, and economics*, the most effective, ethics-driven, fall prevention and mitigation interventions have *not* been widely employed for new home settings in the USA and Canada in the last five decades. There are multiple reasons for this state of affairs.

N. L. Black et al. (Eds.): IEA 2021, LNNS 220, pp. 674–681, 2021.
https://doi.org/10.1007/978-3-030-74605-6_85

1.1 Key Questions

Why? The two US and one Canadian model codes organizations came into existence independently and more or less in isolation with different histories, influential constituencies and procedures that developed in different places. Progress on fall prevention and mitigation efforts has been influenced by what can be thought of as an organizational personality or culture. With one exception, the National Fire Protection Association, NFPA, these organizations have generally been, at best, slow and, at worst, opposed to adopting fall prevention and mitigation requirements—*affecting the movement of individuals in homes*, based on public building requirements for stairways.

How? The three organizations operate in three very different political and cultural contexts that greatly influence their overall activity which is focused on differing emphasis on organization-funded and facilitated research, education, training, safety document production, and quality control generally.

How effectively? As perceived by whom? To which constituencies does something matter (like broad goals and objectives) and what is that something? Is it *evidence?* Does the organization actively participate in *evaluation* of *effectiveness* plus the development of—and *employing*—meaningful information on *epidemiology, etiology, economics* (e.g., of fall-related injury events), etc. Generally, it is useful to examine each organization in terms of its focus on these seven italicized "e" topics—along with an eighth, *ethics*. There are other "e" terms that could be utilized as well in organizational comparisons such as constituent (member, industry "partner" or code user) *energy, effort,* and *enthusiasm*. These three measures of engagement vary widely and are less prominent, especially currently, in the NFPA process and the Canadian one. On evaluation, NFPA leads the others, partly through its Research Foundation.

So What? The foregoing issues matter—including, especially, in the development of effective, respected and consistently practiced fall prevention and mitigation measures in building codes. Indeed, just like there are said to be three factors affecting the price of real estate, *"location, location, location,"* there are three factors affecting the extent to which code development bodies address fall safety in homes; they are *"personality, personality and personality."*

The lead author of this paper is in his sixth decade of witnessing this, as an active participant observer of organizational and individual activities. Notably, the ages of the three organizations—NFPA, the Canadian Commission on Building and Fire Codes (CCBFC), and the International Code Council (ICC)—are over a century for NFPA, about seven decades for the CCBFC (mostly operating as a very similar ACNBC and ACNFC during the 20th century) and about two decades for ICC. (The acronyms of two Canadian organizations noted here refer to the Associate Committee on the National Building Code and the Associate Committee of the National Fire Code which date back to the late 1940s.)

ICC is a mix of three earlier, *regional* code development organizations in the USA which had varying lives ranging, approximately, from five to seven decades, respectively for BOCA, SBCCI and ICBO. For completeness, these acronyms refer to Building Officials and Code Administrators, Southern Building Code Congress International and International Conference of Building Officials. Each of these three, so-called "Legacy Codes" developers had distinctive organizational personalities partly based on the geographical and cultural regions they operated in across the USA, i.e., the northeast, southeast and west. Their "personalities" or cultures are still readily observable—*and very relevant*. One of the informal expressions in code change deliberations, is to argue either explicitly or implicitly, "If it ain't broke, don't fix it." Surprisingly, this is still a mantra in code development processes, perhaps more so in the USA, even for as huge a problem as injurious falls are in built environmental settings, especially homes. Fall-related injuries exceed those from fire by orders of magnitude.

2   The Problem

Think of this as the opposite of "safety culture." Culture, generally, within a wide range of organizations and disciplines is a major aspect of the problem of impaired safety for new home stairways plus bathrooms and a key to achieving effective solutions. Responsibility for limited progress is shared widely over a spectrum of cultures dealing with national constitutional constraints severely limiting the powers of the national or federal government in matters of building control. Building industry culture (with tradition trumping technology) and constitutional traditions or laws have been factors over a long time scale including all six decades during which the lead author has been working on solutions to the problems, especially those involving home stairways, the more consequential of the two fall sites.

2.1   History

Stairway usability and safety have a long history, spanning millennia. Bathing and showering usability and safety have a much shorter history, on the order of a century; it tracks the growing incorporation of the related activities in increasingly lavish, space-consuming and technology-enhanced facilities and spaces in homes. While academic and technical books on stairways date back centuries (as documented in two volumes by Templer (1992), *The Bathroom,* an early book, by Kira (1976)), devoted to the ergonomics of bathrooms, dates back to only the 1970s.

This is about the same time the US Consumer Product Safety Commission, CPSC, began collecting hospital emergency department visit data which quickly revealed the stark epidemiological truth about stair and bathing/showering-related injuries. It is also the time that CPSC began funding some of the earliest comprehensive ergonomics research on both of these leading sources of injuries, especially in homes. The earliest publications on this work include a collection of etiological and epidemiological insights commissioned by the US National Bureau of Standards, NBS, now the National Institute of Standards and Technology, NIST (Alessi et al. 1978).

Part of the relatively recent impetus for greater attention to bathrooms came from the relatively new focus on usability of facilities by people with disabilities which, in the USA, was marked by the first edition of a national accessibility and usability standard, ANSI A117.1, in 1961 based on a meeting in 1959. Notably, in 1987, the Council of American Building Officials (CABO) took over the A117.1 secretarial role. In the 1990s, CABO morphed into the International Code Council (International Code Council 2017). ANSI A117.1 has provided some of the best criteria for not only usability of stairways, but for their safety as well (partly due to one of the two authors of this paper being appointed to the ANSI A117 Committee as its first *Individual Member* beginning with its 1992 edition).

These accessibility standards entail intervention mechanisms affecting both usability and safety *for all*, e.g., with attention to *universal design*. Moreover, falls are not just a problem for seniors and persons with disabilities although, clearly, injury consequences are more severe, life changing, and costly for older persons. Also, there are additional costs impacting families and society, for medical care plus public health.

3 Context

The lead author has worked on many aspects of stairways for five decades (with a shorter, several-year history with bathing/showering facilities). He has addressed them with research (in a national research agency, the National Research Council of Canada), 280 committee-years of model codes and safety standards activity in Canada and the USA, and forensics investigations plus analyses. (Note: as a measure of committee service, 280 committee-years represents, for example, 20 years of service—and active, voting participation—on 14 distinct committees of several organizations.)

Advocacy for building use and safety in mass media both before and during the Web era has been complemented by production of about 40 videos (with 30 freely streaming currently at www.bldguse.com/VideoPage.html).

One of these 40 videos was titled, "The Pathology of Everyday Things," focused on stairways and introducing ergonomists to the previously, largely ignored world of model building code development. The video was of an invited *Arnold Small Lecture* presented at the annual, 1996 conference of the Human Factors and Ergonomics Society, HFES (Pauls 1996). For his "punishment" in giving such a provocative, formal lecture, the author was appointed as Chair of several future, annual lectures in the series. This role was taken on with gusto, entailing the video production, and distribution, of all the lectures delivered under his chairmanship. Clearly, the blending of home stairways ("warts and all") and formal ergonomics was needed and undoubtedly valuable. There was a follow up revisiting the focus of the 1996 Arnold Small Lecture in a brief presentation and five-page paper in HFES 2013 proceedings (Pauls 2013). Here is the entire "Concluding Comment" from that 2013 paper.

"The Arnold M. Small Lecture in 1996 identified a pathology in everyday things, stairways, but it did not anticipate how important macro-ergonomics factors were to become—*especially for home stairways*, beginning about a year later in the US and nearly two decades later in Canada. Clearly, while improved understanding of micro-ergonomic factors—*notably geometry of steps and handrails*—is important, a broader social/organizational perspective is needed. A revisit now, applying human factors more comprehensively, is very timely."

Among its legacies was the collaboration of the two authors of this paper plus a few others, on stairways, including one presented to the then *Institute for Ergonomics and Human Factors* in the UK and one prepared for an organization of trial lawyers in the USA. The former dealt with societal (or macro-ergonomics) factors in stairway safety ranging from model code issues to the role of the public health field (Johnson and Pauls

2010). The latter exposed the flawed teaching of stairway safety inspection methods by the ICC (Johnson and Pauls 2012).

4   Actions

The 280 committee-years of experience have been documented with multi-format records. These records hold the full answers to the three questions posed in this presentation's title—"why, how, and how effectively." Revealed in the records are answers to other questions, e.g., who were the influential actors—individually and organizationally? The latter include the National Fire Protection Association (NFPA), the Canadian Commission on Building and Fire Codes (CCBFC), and the International Code Council (ICC). This listing is in decreasing order of achievement advancing improvements in stairway plus bathing/showering facilities' usability and safety in terms of published standards and model codes.

At this time (early 2021) there is some "jockeying" occurring that could affect the coverage and order of success with *application* of these organizations' codes and standards.

A clear leader, thus far, is not a model building code but, rather, the widely used *American National Standard for Accessible and Usable Buildings and Facilities* ("ANSI A117.1"), for which the first edition was published in 1961 and work has currently begun on its seventh edition—again with ICC as its Secretariat (International Code Council 2017). The latest, 2017, edition was developed by a committee of 48 organizations and 6 individual members. All editions of this standard have addressed usability and safety of stairways as well as bathing/showering facilities with state-of-the-art requirements. The latter are undergoing intensive, ICC Task Group examination relative to accessibility requirements as this abstract is submitted while a CCBFC Task Group is considering mainstreamed requirements focused on safety for all.

The CCBFC Task Group is proceeding less speedily than the ICC effort. However the Canadians are giving commendable, painfully detailed attention to all sides of the debate—including opposition from not only the home building industry, but also the North American plumbing products industry as well.

As this chapter is being submitted the Task Group has voted five to one—the housing industry representative being the "one"—to proceed with new requirements for grab bars in all bathing and showering facilities in new construction. Its final hurdles are with the CCBFC Standing Committee on Housing and Small Buildings and another governing committee, the Standing Committee on Use and Egress (which is also the committee responsible for accessibility requirements in the *National Building Code of Canada*). Results should be known when this paper is presented at the IEA Congress.

5   Outcomes

Clearly (relative to the "how" and "how well" questions) committee member-driven development of expertise-based and evidence-based usability and safety requirements worked best with the ANSI and NFPA standards and codes. Second-best (so far), but only for bathing and showering safety, were CCBFC staff-dominated procedures, but here this might have been due partly to the "personality" of the particular mix of Codes Canada staff in charge. They expertly processed the code-change proposals with fairness to all, while resisting unrelenting, homebuilder and plumbing industry pressures to delay, if not stop any improvements to the code.

ICC's process, on both the home stairway and bathing safety issues, is still an open question the ICC Board of Directors has refused to address with regard to a requested examination of committee member ethics in a January 6, 2021, meeting on grab bar requirements for safety of bathing and showering. The date is highly important for another, much more public ethical lapse in the US. Results will be known, on at least the grab bar issue, later in 2021.

Generally, on the reasons behind these outcomes is the "Why" question. Anyone involved with legal court proceedings, e.g., as a testifying expert—appreciates that "why" questions have the longest and most arguable answer(s) if great respect for evidence and truth generally is maintained.

6 Discussion

The "why" question entails the best use of evidence, e.g., *etiology (including ergonomics), epidemiology, and economics* examined in a process pursued with the highest regard for professional ethics by both the sponsoring organization and participating individuals. The personalities, especially the egos of both an organization and most-involved individuals, have the largest impact on success, for example, with addressing built environment-related fall prevention and mitigation.

Especially in the US, some of the most active participants in the ICC code development process have oversized egos. This is perhaps more evident when, as with ICC, there are limits for each person testifying, of two minutes, in code development hearings—for direct testimony—and only one minute for rebuttal. Rapid-fire, dramatic testimony, delivered without sufficient ethical care and evidence, distorts—*and retards*—the search for the best-founded consensus on an issue.

Code development hearings should be less like theater and more like a competently managed court proceedings where the evidence is not arbitrarily limited by a clock but rather is limited only by its relevance to establishing the truth on a carefully limited question or set of questions.

The truth here is that our human capabilities are as limited, plus more challenged—*not less*—in domestic settings when we use stairs and when we shower or bathe. There is no good rationale behind the double, lower standard for stair and bathing safety in homes—*relative to other buildings*—with their code requirements kept lower by the deliberate bias of as many homebuilder representatives, on committees, as ICC has written into its code development process. This means that home builder interests need only get two votes—beyond their own four votes, to defeat any proposals by others; it also means anyone else needs to win seven votes to prevail.

Also, as addressed in the prior (2018) IEA Congress, an open-minded approach is important to scope—*semantically*—of the problem, *missteps and falls*, not just "slips, trips and falls." This is especially relevant if we are to address effectively the full range of missteps and falls such as those occurring during use of stairways and bathing/showering facilities (plus "toileting" with its stand-to-sit and sit-to-stand transfers posing balance and strength issues). The vast majority—about 90 percent—of these incidents occur in home (domestic) settings. To give this some historical context, start your own professional review by reading one of the very early accounts of the problem seen in an ergonomics context as well as a recent discussion of the historic terminology issues pervading decades of work on falls (Pauls 1984, 2018).

7 Conclusion

Although the challenges we face could be monumental, careers building on the foregoing experience, working with built environment standards and codes in more than one country—addressing the age-old problem of falls—are worth pursuing. This holds especially for ergonomists who deal with a wide range of approaches including, for example, micro-ergonomics and macro-ergonomics—all pursued with the highest respect for evidence and all the other "e" terms covering other important concepts and approaches relevant to safety of built environments.

We look forward to further pursuits for the truth both *during* and *after* the COVID19 pandemic in which the rules and other conventions for where our daily activities occur have been completely upended since early 2020. How this is affecting everyone's propensity to fall, and how post-fall medical care plus epidemiology are affected, is discussed in the IEA presentation. The year 2021 is an exceptionally important one for all three of the model code development organizations addressed in this chapter, quite aside from the fact that it is also the first *full* year in which our world is being drastically altered by the pandemic.

For the Canadian code organization, the National Research Council of Canada, NRCC (along with its Canadian Commission on Building and Fire Codes), 2021 is especially important. As this chapter was being finalized (in February 2021), NRCC released a comprehensive evaluation of how its Codes Canada group was performing (NRCC 2021). It is an important document for those concerned with macro-ergonomics of building code development during this historic era, for example, to see the dearth of ergonomics addressed in the evaluation.

With this chapter's focus on homes, it is especially appropriate that most if not all participants in the IEA Congress will be participating from their homes which, if examined with new insights, hold many lessons that ergonomists will quickly appreciate. As home-based participants look around them, they will better understand the absurdity of compromised home design plus construction requirements that exist largely because this is the tradition. It is what poorly informed home builders selfishly demand—*and get, for example, in the ICC process but not in NFPA's process.* We need to demand better from not only the builders, but also from code authorities empowering them in model building code development, especially in the USA.

References

Alessi, D., Brill, M.: and associates: Home safety guidelines for architects and builders. NBS-GCR 78-156, National Bureau of Standards, Gaithersburg, MD (1978)

International Code Council: American National Standard on Accessible and Usable Buildings and Facilities ICC/ANSI A117.1 (2017)

Johnson, D.A., Pauls, J.: Systemic stair step geometry defects, increased injuries, and public health plus regulatory responses. In: Anderson M (ed) Contemporary Ergonomics and Human Factors 2010. CRC Press, pp. 453–461 (2010)

Johnson, D.A., Pauls, J.: Why should home stairs be less safe? Trial News **47**(8), 11–15 (2012). Washington State Association for Justice, Seattle

Kira, A.: The Bathroom (New and Expanded Edition). The Viking Press, New York (1976)

NRCC (2021) NRC'c Codes Canada Evaluation. National Research Council Canada, Office of Audit and Evaluation. Ottawa, 22 September 2020; released 23 February 2021. https://nrc.canada.ca/en/corporate/planning-reporting/evaluation-nrcs-codes-canada. Accessed 23 Feb 2021

Pauls. J.: Stair safety: review of research. In: Proceedings of the 1984 International Conference on Occupational Ergonomics, Toronto, pp. 171–180 (1984)

Pauls, J.: The pathology of everyday things: the role of building design standards in injury prevention and the role of ergonomics—and ergonomists—in the standards-development process. In: Proceedings of the Human Factors and Ergonomics Society 40th Annual Meeting, September, pp. 818–819 (1996)

Pauls. J.: The pathology of everyday things—stairs—revisited. In: Proceedings of the Human Factors and Ergonomics Society 57th Annual Meeting, San Diego (2013)

Pauls, J.: Identifying ambulation-related missteps and falls with ergonomically descriptive terminology, not as "slips, trips and falls". In: Proceedings of the 20th Congress of the International Ergonomics Association (IEA2018), Vol II, Springer, pp. 634–638 (2018)

Templer, J.: The Staircase: History and Theories; Studies of Hazards, Falls, and Safer Design. MIT Press, Cambridge (1992)

Effect of Combining Hydrophobic and Hydrophilic Treatments on Slip Resistance for Wet Flat Glass Flooring

Kei Shibata[1]([envelope]) [iD], Hirotaka Oguni[2], Hiromi Wada[3], Takeshi Yamaguchi[2,4], and Kazuo Hokkirigawa[2]

[1] Risk Management Reseach Group, National Institute of Occupational Safety and Health, Japan, 1-4-6 Umezono, Kiyose, Tokyo 204-0024, Japan
shibata-kei@s.jniosh.johas.go.jp
[2] Graduate School of Engineering, Tohoku University, 6-6-01 Aramaki Aza-Aoba, Aoba-ku, Sendai 980-8579, Japan
[3] LIXIL Corporation, Tokyo, Japan
[4] Graduate School of Biomedical Engineering, Tohoku University, Sendai, Japan

Abstract. To improve slip resistance of a flat flooring without any patterns, we proposed a combination of hydrophobic and hydrophilic treatments and investigated the effect of the combination on slip resistance between a flat glass plate and shoe sole under wet conditions. The concept of the combination is to make the hydrophilic area as a refuge for water films or droplets and increase the real dry contact between the hydrophobic area and shoe sole. The hydrophilic area was a circle shape and was allocated in a grid pattern on the hydrophobic sea while seven types of flat-glass-plate specimens were evaluated. Based on the friction test results, it was indicated that the combination of hydrophobic and hydrophilic treatments improves the slip resistance when the area of hydrophilic island was minute against the hydrophobic sea. From the observation of contact interface, the trend of the shear strength against the hydrophobic area ratio established the effect of the combination.

Keywords: Slip resistance · Glass flooring · Wettability · Treatment combination

1 Introduction

Slipping has well known to be one of the main causes of falling accidents, especially on wet surfaces. Shoe soles and flooring surfaces generally consist of various patterns, such as blocks and grooves, which can include a bit of roughness [1–3]. These patterns can drain liquid films or contaminants from the contact interface and increase an expected-dry contact between the shoe sole and flooring surface. However, the design range of these surface patterns is sometimes restricted because of both esthetic and cleaning issues. Those are conflicting issues against the safety of pedestrians. In response, surface treatments for flat flooring have been investigated in the present study to meet the conflicting requirements.

© The Author(s), under exclusive license to Springer Nature Switzerland AG 2021
N. L. Black et al. (Eds.): IEA 2021, LNNS 220, pp. 682–688, 2021.
https://doi.org/10.1007/978-3-030-74605-6_86

A hydrophobization treatment is an effective method for increasing the slip resistance for flat surfaces under wet conditions; this is because it helps the water films or droplets to easily move out from the contact interface [4]. However, the treatment has a potential risk to accumulate the water as a large droplet and lead to a slip. To increase the slip resistance of flat surfaces more, a combination of hydrophobic and hydrophilic treatments was proposed. The concept of the combination is to make the hydrophilic area as a refuge for water films or droplets and increase the real dry contact between the hydrophobic area and shoe sole. We investigated the effect of this combination on slip resistance for a flat glass plate under wet conditions.

2 Experimental Procedure

We developed seven types of flat-glass-plate specimens with hydrophobic/hydrophilic-area ratios as follows: i) 0:100 (wholly hydrophilic), ii) 21:79, iii) 50:50, iv) 65:35, v) 91:9, vi) 97:3, and vii) 100:0 (wholly hydrophobic) (See Table 1). The contact angle of water for the hydrophilic area was 100° while the angle for hydrophobic area was 8 degrees. The hydrophilic area was a circle shape and was allocated in a grid pattern (Figs. 1 and 2). To evaluate the slip resistance under wet sliding, a cart-type friction tester was used (Fig. 3), which was developed by the authors' research group [5, 6]. The static and dynamic coefficients of friction (SCOF and DCOF, respectively) between a rubber sole attached to a shoe and the glass specimens were measured. The natural rubber sole with the roughness of 14.3 μm had no block patterns while its contact angle of water was 123°. Tap water was spread on the specimen via a nebulizer. The normal load was 417 N while the number of replications under the same test condition was five.

Table 1. Specification of each glass sample for evaluation of slip resistance.

Sample	Distance between hydrophilic areas L, mm	Diameter of hydrophilic area φ, mm	Hydrophobic/hydrophilic-area ratio
i	—	—	0:100
ii	15	15	21:79
iii	15	12	50:50
iv	15	10	65:35
v	15	5	91:9
vi	15	3	97:3
vii	—	—	100:0

To observe the contact interface under wet sliding, a linear-sliding-friction tester was used (Fig. 4). The five hydrophobic/hydrophilic-area ratios for flat-glass-plate specimens

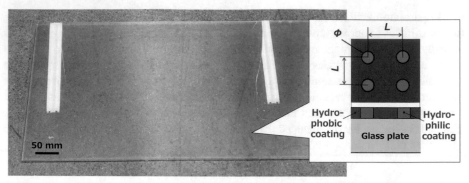

Fig. 1. A photo of a glass sample and schematic diagram of hydrophobic and hydrophilic coatings on the glass sample.

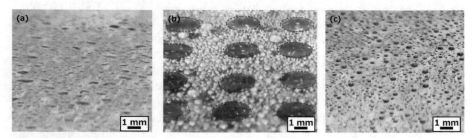

Fig. 2. Photos of water droplets on (a) sample i (wholly hydrophilic), (b) sample v, and (c) sample vii (wholly hydrophobic). It is noted that a large amount of water was spread to visualize droplets clearly.

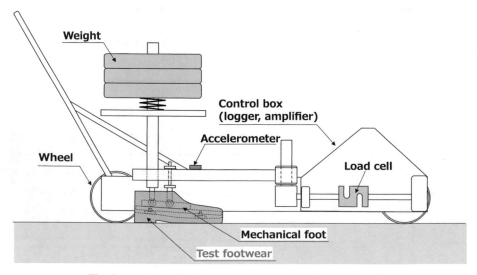

Fig. 3. A schematic diagram of the cart-type friction tester [2].

were: i) 0:100 (wholly hydrophilic), ii) 50:50, iii) 72:28, iv) 93:7, and v) 100:0 (wholly hydrophobic) (see Table 2). A cube-shaped natural rubber with the roughness of 17.7 μm was used for the block specimen. The size of the block was 28 mm × 40 mm with 5 mm height. The normal load was 26.8 N and the sliding velocity was 0.2 m/s. We used the total reflection method to observe the contact interface. A contact region appears brighter than the other regions because of the difference in reflective index of materials.

Table 2. Specification of each glass sample for the observation of contact interface.

Sample	Distance between hydrophilic areas L, mm	Diameter of hydrophilic area φ, mm	Hydrophobic/hydrophilic-area ratio
i	—	—	0:100
ii	10	8	50:50
iii	5	3	72:28
iv	10	3	93:7
v	—	—	100:0

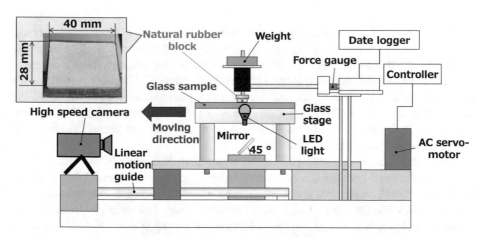

Fig. 4. A schematic diagram of the linear-sliding-friction tester.

3 Results and Discussion

Figure 5 shows the relationship between the mean coefficient of friction (COF) and the sliding velocity. The DCOFs decreased with an increase in the sliding velocity, irrespective of the glass specimens. From this, we could easily assume that water films or droplets probably existed between the contact interfaces. Surprisingly, for the wholly hydrophobic specimen, both the SCOF and DCOF changed from 0.93 to 0.17 with an increase in the sliding velocity. This corresponded with from quite high slip resistance to quite poor resistance.

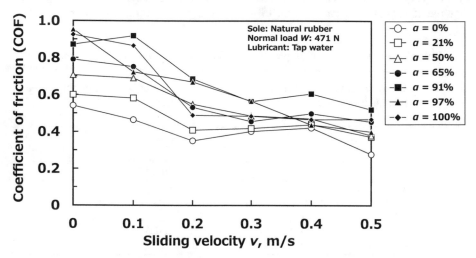

Fig. 5. Relationship between the COF and sliding velocity.

Figure 6 exhibits the relationship between the COF and the hydrophobic-area ratio (α). The SCOFs exhibited a peak with an increase in the hydrophobic-area ratio; the maximum SCOF was for the α of 97%, which means that the wholly hydrophobic specimen ($\alpha = 100\%$) did not return the maximum SCOF value. The DCOF also exhibited a peak with an increase in the hydrophobic-area ratios. Meanwhile, the maximum DCOF was seen for the 91% and 97% ratios. Therefore, it is briefly summarized that the combination of hydrophobic and hydrophilic treatments can improve the slip resistance of flat glass flooring under wet conditions.

From the contact area observation, no significant difference in the contact area ratio was observed between the specimens before applying a tangential force. Based on the measured contact area and friction force, the shear strength was calculated for the moments when the onset of slip and the steady sliding. The shear strengths showed a similar tendency at the maximum static friction and during sliding (Fig. 7). The shear strength exhibited a peak value at the 93% ratio. Furthermore, the shear strengths exhibited a proportional relationship to the hydrophobic region ratio, except for the wholly hydrophobic specimen (100%). Those indicated that for the wholly hydrophobic specimen, the water films or droplets hardly moved from the contact interface and then were accumulated. On the other hand, a few of the hydrophilic islands in the hydrophobic sea could act as a refuge for the water films or droplets.

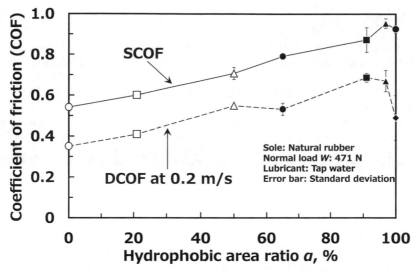

Fig. 6. Relationship between the SCOF and hydrophobic area ratio.

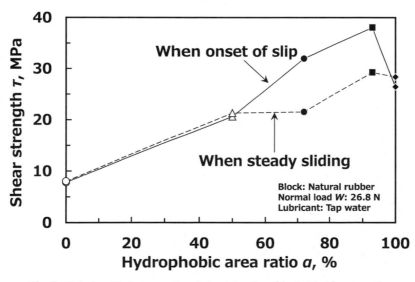

Fig. 7. Relationship between the shear strength and hydrophobic area ratio.

4   Conclusions

The SCOF exhibited a peak with an increase in the hydrophobic/hydrophilic-area ratios with the maximum value at the 97:3 ratio. For a 0.2 m/s sliding velocity, the DCOF also exhibited a peak with an increase in the hydrophobic/hydrophilic-area ratios with a maximum value seen at the 91:9 and 97:3 ratios. Thus, it is concluded that the combination of hydrophobic and hydrophilic treatments can improve slip resistance for flat glass flooring under wet conditions.

References

1. Yamaguchi, T., Umetsu, T., Ishizuka, Y., Kasuga, K., Ito, T., Ishizawa, S.: Development of new footwear sole surface pattern for prevention of slip-related falls. Saf. Sci. **50**(4), 986–994 (2012)
2. Yamaguchi, T., Hokkirigawa, K.: Development of a high slip-resistant footwear outsole using a hybrid rubber surface pattern. Ind. Health **52**(5), 414–423 (2014)
3. Shibata, K., Warita, I., Yamaguchi, T., Hinoshita, M., Sakauchi, K., Matsukawa, S., Hokkirigawa, K.: Effect of groove width and depth and urethane coating on slip resistance of vinyl flooring sheet in glycerol solution. Tribol. Int. **135**, 89–95 (2019)
4. Lin, S., Cai, H.: Preparation and properties of hydrophobic MMA floor coatings based on fluorine-containing methacrylic ester copolymers. J. Coatings Technol. Res. **10**(6), 841–847 (2001)
5. Shibata, K., Abe, S., Yamaguchi, T., Hokkirigawa, K.: Development of cart-type friction measurement system for evaluation for slip resistance of floor sheets. J. Jap. Soc. Des. Eng. **51**(10), 721–736 (2016)
6. Yamaguchi, T., Yamada, R., Warita, I., Shibata, K., Ohnishi, A., Sugama, A., Hinoshita, M., Sakauchi, K., Matsukawa, S., Hokkirigawa, K.: Relationship between slip angle in ramp test and coefficient of friction values at shoe-floor interface measured with cart-type friction measurement device. J. Biomech. Sci. Eng. **13**(1), 17–00389 (2018)

Estimation of Perceived Hand Force During Static Horizontal Pushing Tasks Using the Zero-Moment Point-Based Balance Control Model

Atsushi Sugama[1]([⊠]) [iD], Akiko Takahashi[1], and Akihiko Seo[2]

[1] Risk Management Research Group, National Institute of Occupational Safety and Health Japan, Tokyo, Japan
sugama@s.jniosh.johas.go.jp
[2] Faculty of Systems Design, Tokyo Metropolitan University, Tokyo, Japan

Abstract. Many fall accidents occur owing to loss of balance during tasks that involve external forces or reaction impacts. However, few studies have investigated the relationship between perceived hand force and postural balance. This paper proposes a method for estimating perceived hand force based on a model that uses the zero-moment point (ZMP), which is the ideal point of the center of pressure of the foot reaction force. Eleven men manually pushed a wall with maximum force for five seconds. The hand position was controlled using two experimental factors: the height of the pushing hand relative to the body height (35%, 60%, 85%, and 110%) and the distance between the hand and the foot (50%, 75%, and 100% of the upper limb length). The exerted hand forces, foot reaction forces, and whole-body posture were measured and used as input data to the analytical model. The perceived force was scored using the magnitude estimation technique after each trial and was modeled as an equation using the difference of ZMP position with or without hand forces. The ZMP-based model precisely estimated both the exerted force and the perceived force. These results imply that the somatosensory stimulus from soles is not only the key input for the control system for postural balance but also sensory information for force perception during manual pushing tasks.

Keywords: Force perception · Pushing task · Postural balance · Zero-moment point

1   Introduction

Falling from considerable heights is one of the leading causes of occupational fatalities and injuries. According to statistical reports on occupational accidents, slips, trips, and falls contribute to 26% of workplace injuries in the United States [1] and 40% of such injuries in Japan [2].

Many falls occur owing to workers losing their balance during tasks like pushing, pulling, lifting, or manipulation of tools [3]. The external forces and impacts created

N. L. Black et al. (Eds.): IEA 2021, LNNS 220, pp. 689–696, 2021.
https://doi.org/10.1007/978-3-030-74605-6_87

during these tasks act on the human body and destabilize balance. Therefore, maintaining postural balance under such external forces is an important constraint on the postural system and considerably influences the force capability of the musculoskeletal system [4, 5].

During these tasks, workers must predict the magnitude and direction of the reaction force accurately to maintain their postural balance. However, the characteristics of human perception are known to be nonlinear, and there can be differences between the actual force and the perceived force [6]. In psychophysical research, the characteristics of perceived force were originally examined by Stevens [7] and modeled as Stevens's power law. Recently, Kishishita et al. [8] investigated and estimated the force perceptual bias during unimanual steering. They demonstrated that the bias depends on changes in postures and the intensity of muscle activity changes. However, the characteristics of perceived force for tasks in upright stances have not been fully explained. The perceptual characteristics in upright stances may differ from those in sitting positions because of the difference of the limb position and the somatosensory stimulus caused by the reaction forces.

This study, therefore, aimed to investigate the relationship between the perceived hand force and the postural balance. We hypothesized that the force perception depends on the displacement of the center of pressure (CoP) because foot pressure is the major somatosensory input stimulus. To estimate the virtual position of the CoP using the presence or absence of hand forces, the zero-moment point (ZMP) was used.

2 ZMP-Based Balance Model

2.1 Modeling of Upright Posture Under Hand Reaction Forces

The ZMP is defined as the point, p, on the ground where the moments around the x- and y-axis are equal to zero ($T_x = 0$ and $T_y = 0$, respectively), generated by reaction forces and reaction torques [9]. When a position of ZMP, p_{ZMP} ($= [x_{ZMP}, y_{ZMP}, 0]$), exists within the domain of support surface S ($p_{ZMP} \in S$), the contact between the ground and the support leg is stable. If the foot reaction force balances all the active forces acting on the mechanism during the motion (a dynamically balanced gait), the CoP and the ZMP coincide [10].

Harada et al. [11] demonstrated the walking pattern of a humanoid robot during a pushing task using a ZMP-based balance model [12], which considers walking while touching an object. The received hand reaction forces affect the postural balance because the ZMP is shifted depending on the external forces applied.

Figure 1a presents the balance model for a humanoid robot during tasks under external hand reaction forces, as shown by Harada et al. [11]. f_{Hj} ($= [f_{Hjx} f_{Hjy} f_{Hjz}]^T$, where $j = 1, 2$) is the force applied on jth hands; forces f_Z ($= [f_{Zx} f_{Zy} f_{Zz}]^T$) and moments τ_Z ($= [\tau_{Zx} \tau_{Zy} \tau_{Zz}]^T$) are applied on the sole. $\sum_R$ is the reference frame, and $\sum_i$ is the fixed system of the coordinates on ith body segments. As the position vectors on $\sum_R$, p_i ($= [x_i y_i z_i]^T$), p_{Hj} ($= [x_{Hj} y_{Hj} z_{Hj}]^T$), and p_{Fj} ($= [x_{Fj} y_{Fj} z_{Fj}]^T$) indicate the origins of $\sum_i$, the points where the hand forces are applied, and the points inside the base of the support where the foot reaction forces are applied, respectively. p_G ($= [x_G y_G z_G]^T$) is the position vector of the center of mass, which is calculated as $p_G = \sum m_i p_i / \sum m_i$.

Further, $p_Z (= [x_Z\ y_Z\ z_Z]^T)$ is the position vector of the ZMP on the supporting surface. The inertia tensor and the angular velocity vector are denoted as I_i and ω_i, respectively. Here, when a person receives reaction forces on the hands, the forces and moments applied on the ZMP are, respectively,

$$f_z = M(\ddot{p}_G - g) - \sum_{j=1}^{2} f_{Hj} \tag{1}$$

$$\tau_z = \dot{L}_G + M(p_G - p_Z) \times (\ddot{p}_G - g) - \sum_{j=1}^{2} (p_{Hj} - p_Z) \times f_{Hj} \tag{2}$$

where $L_G (= [L_{Gx}\ L_{Gy}\ L_{Gz}]^T)$ is the angular momentum around the center of mass (CoM). For static and isometric manual tasks, $\ddot{p}_G$, $\dot{p}_i$ and ω_i are hypothesized to be zero. Equations (1) and (2) are solved for p_Z by assigning $\tau_{Zx} = \tau_{Zy} = 0$, which is the definition of the ZMP, and the x and y components of p_Z are derived, respectively, as.

$$x_z = \frac{Mx_G g - \sum_{j=1}^{2} \{x_{Hj} f_{Hjz} - (z_{Hj} - z_Z) f_{Hjx}\}}{Mg \sum_{j=1}^{2} f_{Hjz}} \tag{3}$$

$$y_z = \frac{My_G g - \sum_{j=1}^{2} \{y_{Hj} f_{Hjz} - (z_{Hj} - z_Z) f_{Hjy}\}}{Mg \sum_{j=1}^{2} f_{Hjz}} \tag{4}$$

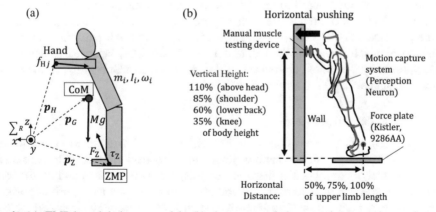

Fig. 1. (a) ZMP-based balance model. (b) Apparatus of the experiment and experimental variables.

2.2 Application to Static Horizontal Pushing Tasks

This study hypothesizes that a person perceives the displacement of the ZMP on the soles as the input stimulus for the pushing force perception. Therefore, we compare the ZMP coordinates for cases with or without the hand forces. First, the ZMP coordinates for cases without hand forces were calculated as $\tilde{p}_z \left(= [\tilde{x}_z\ \tilde{y}_z\ \tilde{z}_z]^T\right)$, assigning a value of zero to the f_{Hj} included in Eqs. (3) and (4). Here, when the vertical components of hand forces, f_{Hjz}, are zero, $\tilde{x}_Z$ and $\tilde{y}_Z$ are equal to that of CoM x_G and y_G. Then, Δx was defined as the difference in the ZMP coordinates between cases with and without hand forces, which are denoted as p_Z and $\tilde{p}_Z$, respectively. The x components are calculated as

$$\Delta x_z = \tilde{x}_z - x_z \frac{-x_G \sum_{j=1}^{2} f_{Hjz} + \sum_{j=1}^{2} \left\{ x_{Hj} f_{Hjz} - \left(z_{Hj} - z_Z \right) f_{Hjx} \right\}}{Mg \sum_{j=1}^{2} f_{Hjz}} \tag{5}$$

Next, the estimated hand forces are derived from Eq. (6) by solving Eq. (2) under the assumption that τ_{Zy} is zero because the static anterior-posterior balance is maintained. Here, to simplify the equation, the ratio of the vertical force to the horizontal force is considered to be zero because the tasks required only horizontal pushing.

$$f_H / Mg = (x_G - x_Z) / (z_H - z_Z) \tag{6}$$

3 Experimental Methods

3.1 Participants

Eleven right-handed men, between the age of 21–25 years, participated in the study. All participants were in good health, with no medical history of musculoskeletal injuries in the previous 12 months. The means and standard deviations for the age, height, and weight were 22.7 ± 1.2 years, 173.0 ± 3.6 cm, and 68.5 ± 4.7 kg, respectively. While standing upright, the upper limb length and the vertical height from the floor to eye level were 74.7 ± 1.5 cm and 162.2 ± 5.1 cm, respectively. The average foot length of the participants (ISO 7250-1, 2017) was 25.7 ± 0.8 cm. All participants wore the same model of safety shoes (MZ010J; Midori Anzen Co. Ltd., Japan). This experiment was approved by the ethics committee of Tokyo Metropolitan University, Hino Campus (approval number: 233).

3.2 Experimental Apparatus

Figure 1b illustrates the flow of their movements. The participants were required to push the wall horizontally with one hand while maintaining heel contact with force plates (9286B; Kistler Japan). For the first five seconds, the participants stood on the force plates while keeping their feet parallel and maintaining a stationary upright position. Thereafter, they adjusted their posture for manual force exertion, and pushed the wall with their right hand horizontally for five seconds with maximum effort. The width of the stance was established by each participant before the measurements and maintained in all trials.

The vertical height of the pushing hand on the wall and the horizontal distance between the wall and the participant's external malleolus were controlled as the experimental variables in this study. The vertical heights of the pushing hand were set at four levels: 110%, 85%, 60%, and 35% of the body height. The horizontal distances were set at three levels: 100%, 75%, and 50% of the upper limb length. The experimental conditions were completely randomized, and measurements were duplicated under each condition.

3.3 Measurement and Analysis

Body Posture. The entire body posture was captured through a motion capture system (Perception Neuron, Noitom Ltd., China) using software (Axis Neuron Ver. 3.8.42.8303, Noitom Ltd., China). The participants wore gloves and body straps equipped with 18 inertial measurement units (IMUs). The position and tilt angle of IMU were recorded at 120 fps and converted into the body posture angle as Biovision Hierarchy format files, including the hierarchy of the body skeleton and the rotational angles. The whole-body posture and CoM were calculated. The length and mass of each segment were determined as described by Chaffin et al. [13] and Ae et al. [14].

Foot Reaction Force. The force and moment components were sampled at 100 Hz using a single force-plate system with an analog-to-digital data converter (PH-703, DKH Co. Ltd, Japan) and analysis software (TRIAS2, DKH Co. Ltd, Japan). Subsequently, the coordinates of the CoP, p_P ($= [x_P \ y_P \ z_P]^T$), were calculated through standard transformations [15].

Subjective Sense for Force Perception. Each participant reported his subjective sense regarding the degree of force as a relative value against the reference stimulus. The task at the condition of 85% height $\times$ 75% distance was set as the reference stimulus, and the score under that condition Was assigned 100 points. After the measurement, the participants predicted the extent of force that had been exerted (Ex-post Rating). If they considered that the force exerted (or that was going to be exerted) was greater than that under the reference condition, they reported a score greater than 100, such as 110.

3.4 Statistical Analysis

The effects of the experimental factors on the measured indices were compared through analysis of variance (ANOVA) with a three-way factorial design (namely, the vertical heights, horizontal distances, and participants) and a post hoc Tukey's test. Sphericity was checked using the Mauchly sphericity test. The statistical significance level for all the tests was set to 5%. Data analyses were conducted out using BellCurve for Excel version 3.21 (Social Survey Research Information Co., Ltd., Japan).

4   Results

4.1 Effects of Experimental Factors

Figure 2 presents the results of the exerted forces and their ex-post perception. These values are presented relative to the reference stimulus, which is the task under 85% height $\times$ 75% distance. The exerted force ranged from 6.3 to 34.8 kgf, with a median of 14.8 kgf. The ANOVA revealed that, for the exerted force, the significant main effects of the vertical height, the horizontal distance, and the participant ($P < 0.001$ for all variables), and there was no interaction between variables. The multiple comparison test revealed that the exerted force increased under 60% height, decreased under 110% height, and decreased under 50% distance.

In terms of the perceived force, the main effects of the vertical height and the horizontal distance (P < 0.001 for both variables) were also significant. Among the vertical height conditions, the exerted force was maximum at 60% height, whereas the perceived force was maximum at 85% height. Hence, the trend of peak values for the vertical height differed for the exerted and perceived forces.

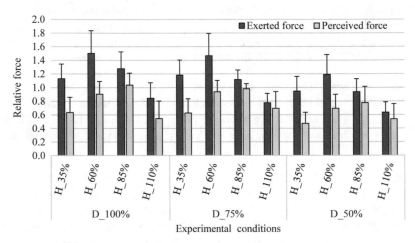

Fig. 2. Relative exerted forces against the reference stimulus and their ex-post perception under the vertical heights (H) and the horizontal distances (D).

4.2 Estimated Displacement of the ZMP During Horizontal Pushing

Figure 3 presents the estimated displacement of the ZMP, Δx, between the cases with and without hand forces. The Δx ranged from 8.5 cm to 30 cm depending on the experimental conditions. The ANOVA revealed the significant effects of the vertical height, horizontal distance, participant, and vertical height × horizontal distance (P < 0.001 for all variables). The vertical height had the most significant effect, and the displacement under 85% height was significantly larger, whereas that under 35% height was significantly smaller than those under other heights.

4.3 Relationship Between Estimated and Measured Forces

In this section, we evaluate the accuracy of the ZMP-based model against the data measured. First, as shown in Fig. 4a, the estimated hand force, described as the anterior-posterior coordinates of the CoM divided by the vertical height of the pushing hand, exhibited a high correlation with the real exerted force divided by the body mass ($r = 0.91$ for averaged data).

Next, Fig. 4b indicates that the estimated force perception, calculated as the ZMP displacement, had a linear trend with the ex-post score of force perception, and the correlation was 0.66. Because data for the condition of 110% height × 100% distance became outliers, they were excluded. When these data were excluded, the correlation was 0.96.

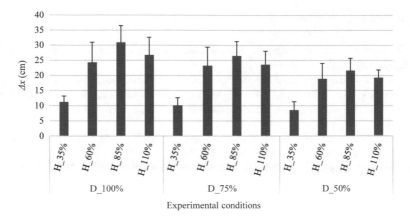

Fig. 3. Estimated displacements of the ZMP (Δx).

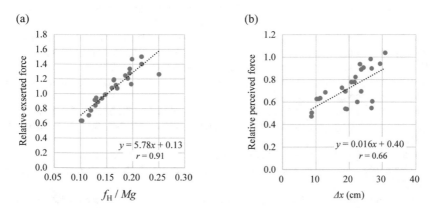

Fig. 4. (a) Relationship between the perception ratio and the height of the pushing hand. (b) Forces perceived versus the ZMP displacements.

5   Discussion

This paper proposed a postural balance model that uses the ZMP for the estimation of perceived force during manual horizontal pushing tasks. The estimation of perceived force was calculated as the displacement of the ZMP between cases with and without hand forces. The results revealed that both the perceived force and the exerted force had high linear relationships with the measured forces. These results imply that force perception during manual pushing tasks may depend on the somatosensory input and not on the hand or upper limbs, considering that the foot reaction force is the major somatosensory input for the control system for postural balance. The proposed model could contribute to the evaluation of the force perceptual bias for pushing tasks, as well as the assessment of risks owing to unexpected reaction forces, for ensuring proper working environments.

References

1. U.S. Bureau of Labor Statistics. Occupational Safety and Health Services. BLS Handb Methods, pp. 1–22 (2012)
2. Japan Industrial Safety & Health Association. General Guidebook on Industrial Safety (2018)
3. Fredericks, T.K., Abudayyeh, O., Choi, S.D., Wiersma, M., Charles, M.: Occupational injuries and fatalities in the roofing contracting industry. J. Constr. Eng. Manag. **131**(11), 1233–40 (2005)
4. Holbein, M.A., Redfern, M.S.: Functional stability limits while holding loads in various positions. Int. J. Ind. Ergon. **19**(5), 387–95 (1997)
5. Winter, D.A.: Sagittal plane balance and posture in human walking. IEEE Eng. Med. Biol. Mag. **6**(3), 8–11 (1987)
6. Stevens SS. Psychophysics: Introduction to Its Perceptual, Neural and Social Prospects. Stevens G, editor. John Wiley & Sons Inc; 1975.
7. Stevens, S.S., Galanter, E.: Ratio scales and category scales for a dozen perceptual continue. J. Exp. Psychol. **54**, 377–411 (1957)
8. Kishishita, Y., Tanaka, Y., Kurita, Y.: Force perceptual bias caused by muscle activity in unimanual steering. PLoS ONE **14**(10), e0223930 (2019)
9. Arakawa, T., Fukuda, T.: Natural motion generation of biped locomotion robot using hierarchical trajectory generation method consisting of GA, EP layers. In: Proceedings of International Conference on Robotics and Automation, pp. 211–216. IEEE (1997)
10. Vukobratović, M., Borovac, B.: Zero-moment point — thirty five years of its life. Int. J. Humanoid Robot. **01**(01), 157–73 (2004)
11. Harada, K., Kajita, S., Kanehiro, F., Fujiwara, K., Kaneko, K., Yokoi, K., et al.: Walking motion for pushing manipulation by a humanoid robot. J. Robot. Soc. Jpn. **22**(3), 392–9 (2004)
12. Harada, K., Kajita, S., Kanehiro, F., Fujiwara, K., Kaneko, K., Yokoi, K., et al.: ZMP analysis of a humanoid robot under coordination of arms and legs. J. Robot. Soc. Jpn. **22**(1), 28–36 (2004)
13. Chaffin, D.B., Andersson, G.B.J., Martin, B.J.: Occupational Biomechanics, 4th edn., pp. 37–51. Wiley, Hoboken (2006)
14. Ae, M., Tang, H., Yokoi, T.: Estimation of inertia properties of the body segments in Japanese athletes. Biomechanisms **11**, 23–33 (1992)
15. Winter, D.A.: Biomechanics and Motor Control of Human Movement, 4th edn. John Wiley & Sons, Inc., Hoboken (2009)

Do Stairs with Visual Cues Lead to Fewer Missteps?

Steve Thorpe[1](✉) and Mike Roys[2]

[1] Olver and Rawden, Consulting and Forensic Engineers, Green Lane, Balsall Common,
Coventry CV7 7EJ, UK
s.thorpe@olverandrawden.co.uk
[2] Rise and Going Consultancy, 26 Moor View, Watford W18 6JJ, UK
mike.roys@riseandgoing.co.uk

Abstract. This preliminary work considers alternatives to proprietary nosings, which could be equally effective at visually highlighting the edges of nosings. This paper considers two alternative designs: contrasting floor covering on alternate steps and localised LED lighting on alternate steps. The work illustrates how the two conditions compare visually against the baseline condition of a stair without nosing markings (typical in domestic settings) and a stair with contrasting proprietary nosings (typical of a public setting). It also explores the possibility of further experimental research which will consider the measurement of changes in gait which might result from the addition of visual nosing highlighting.

Keywords: Stair · Misstep · Visual cues

1 Introduction

Stairs are dangerous places, especially when you consider how little time the average person spends on stairs. Most people can traverse a domestic stair in 8 to 10 s, many are even quicker. Even with the current Covid-19 pandemic stay-at-home orders, and people working from home, it is likely that the stairs are travelled by users between 10 and 20 times a day. This equates to five to six minutes a day, which is about 0.6% of waking hours. In a typical year, the Health and Safety Executive estimate there are on average 1000 major accidents on workplace stairs in Great Britain. In addition, there are about 700 deaths on stairs and over 25,000 hospital admissions following accidents on stairs in dwellings in the UK every year. There is likely to be around a further 300,000 injuries from falls on dwelling stairs each year that are less serious, an injury rate of about 600 per 100,000. Death and injury rates are similar across the world.

We know from previous studies [1] that a significant amount of the risk associated with dwelling stairs is related to the small steep steps and the lack of graspable handrails. For stairs in buildings other than dwellings, the UK Slip Resistance Group guidance document [2] highlights in a similar way how step dimensions and step consistency along with graspable handrails are the main factors in reducing risk on stairs. Alongside these features the document highlights how step edge (nosing) visibility achieved through

© The Author(s), under exclusive license to Springer Nature Switzerland AG 2021
N. L. Black et al. (Eds.): IEA 2021, LNNS 220, pp. 697–704, 2021.
https://doi.org/10.1007/978-3-030-74605-6_88

the addition of contrasting proprietary nosings and good lighting can reduce the risk for unfamiliar users and people with impaired vision. It also emphasises the need for good maintenance and cleaning. In dwellings it is unusual for contrasting nosings to be used. In this setting lighting is typically two ceiling lights, one each in the top and bottom landing areas.

This leads to two interesting research questions. Is visual contrast information effective at reducing the risk of missteps on stairs? And if so, is the current proprietary nosing method the most effective option?

2 Background

In the late 1990s people with visual impairments were asked to consider steps with contrasting nosings, expressing what they were looking for in a stair to aid safe passage. This research formed the basis for introducing the requirement of colour contrasting nosings in the UK Building Regulations Approved Document M [3] and British Standard BS 8300: 2001 [4]. Further research undertaken at the University of Reading [5] on colour contrast influenced the specification of such nosings in later years. However, alternatives that could be equally effective at providing colour contrast were most likely not considered at this time.

One such alternative is the colour contrasting steps image used as the cover for Templer's book, The Staircase [6]. In this image the consecutive steps on a helical stair are clearly visible without any contrasting nosings. A second alternative was brought to our attention through lighting research conducted by Janssens et al. [7] in which one of the experimental conditions looked at lighting every other step in the experimental flight. Further research from this group has now been published [8]. Based on this evidence, alternative step highlights via lighting is included as a framework item in a RoSPA publication, Safer by Design, for new build homes [9].

We wanted to examine these alternatives further to determine whether a more in-depth experimental research project could illustrate the effectiveness of nosing highlighting through either proprietary nosings, visually contrasting step coverings, or localised LED lighting. We investigated these options using a short flight of steps, at a UK proprietary nosing manufacture's headquarters. We were able to visually assess a stair flight through direct observation, photographs, and video, both with and without traditional contrasting proprietary nosings. These conditions formed our baseline references for typical domestic and non-domestic stair coverings in the UK. The conditions were observed under three lighting conditions: indirect daylight, dusk and artificial lighting.

3 Experimental Options

The experimental conditions allow the observation of contrasting alternating steps, generated by either colour contrast or by the addition of localised lighting. Two sets of colour-contrasting flooring were selected, one carpet (a common covering on domestic stairs) and one resilient flooring (a common covering on many non-domestic stairs). It was expected that the lighting would reflect differently on these two surfaces. Similarly, with the lighting two different options were selected: LED spots with a cool white light were used to the side of the steps, and LED strip lights with a warmer white light were used at the back of the tread. It is noted that these options were chosen by availability; it is likely that there are more suitable products already on the market that would have been more effective at casting the appropriate amount of light on the stairs.

4   Results

4.1   Research Examples

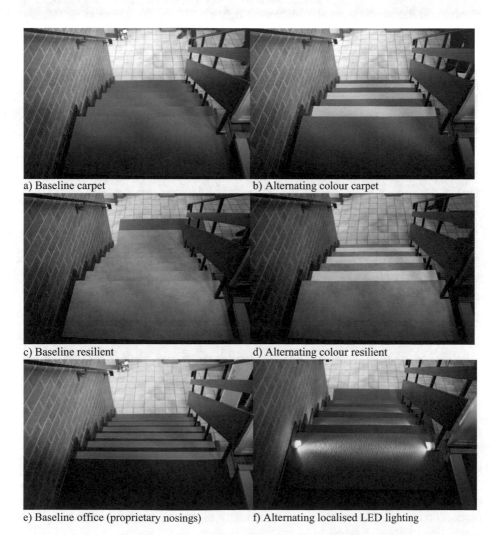

a) Baseline carpet

b) Alternating colour carpet

c) Baseline resilient

d) Alternating colour resilient

e) Baseline office (proprietary nosings)

f) Alternating localised LED lighting

Fig. 1. Examples of experimental conditions

4.2   Discussion

Each of the possible contrasting conditions were compared against their baseline options, see Fig. 1. In all cases, the application of two-colour step finishes or localised LED lighting provided contrast between a nosing and the step below. These alternatives seemed to be comparable to the contrasting proprietary nosings as described in the current guidance.

Although it was clear from observation, and from the sets of pictures, that the use of contrasting alternating steps was effective at highlighting the nosings, and that the localised LED lighting was also effective, we noticed that changing more than one condition, i.e. localised lighting and colour contrast on steps, only worked if the lighting emphasised the lighter steps (L). When the lighting was on the darker steps (D), the localised lighting decreased the effectiveness of the contrast, see Fig. 2.

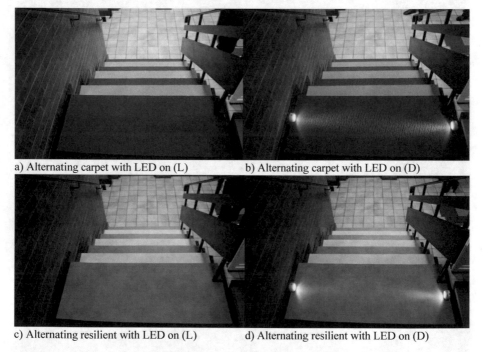

a) Alternating carpet with LED on (L)   b) Alternating carpet with LED on (D)

c) Alternating resilient with LED on (L)   d) Alternating resilient with LED on (D)

Fig. 2. Localised lighting on the lighter (L) and darker (D) steps

The appearance was made more complicated if the localised lighting was added to steps with proprietary nosings, or proprietary nosings were added to the alternating colour carpet, see Fig. 3. Clearly, if changes were applied inappropriately, the effect was to decrease nosing visibility rather than enhance it. Both these conditions led to the perception that there were fewer steps than reality, or that the edge of the tread (nosing) was midway through a step.

We were also aware that the magnitude, colour and location of the lighting had an effect on nosing visibility. It seemed that providing light across the nosing was most effective. This was true whether the light was generated by the LED spots being placed

a) Localised LEDs and nosings on carpet   b) Alternating carpet with nosings

Fig. 3. Confusing combinations with proprietary nosings

nearer the nosing at the side of the steps, or by angling the Strip LED lights to ensure the light fell over the whole tread including the nosing. The lighting used in the experiment did cause glare when viewed from the bottom of the flight and would, therefore, not be suitable for real world application. We have also noticed, in the trade press, stair lighting products that may be embedded into the underside of overhanging nosings. These can be designed to reduce glare in ascent while still providing illumination over the whole tread. Using such nosing light on alternating treads should therefore provide a similar result to our localised LED conditions. In some instances, these products only cast light onto the back half of the tread below, this also appeared to provide good contrast between the nosing and the tread below.

5 Some Practical Considerations

The location and effectiveness of the localised LED lighting may have more conse-quences than just providing light to the appropriate part of the steps. For example, it may be easier to retrofit side mounted lights to an existing stair than to try and add LED strip light to the nosings. The strip lighting may also be more prone to damage when installed on the nosing of a carpeted stair. A strip LED might be more appropriate on a stair in non-domestic settings where materials other than carpet are often used. In this scenario it might be possible to fix the strip light in a position less prone to damage and orientated to prevent glare. A lighting expert might help determine the best options available to ensure adequate lighting in the appropriate places, without adding glare to users in ascent.

6 Do These Alternatives Have a Place in Future Guidance?

Currently guidance in British Standards and Building Regulations is clear on the dimen-sions of colour contrast proprietary nosings that should be applied in public and assem-bly settings. There is no requirement for domestic stairs. Applying localised lighting to domestic steps is already becoming a trend, and good guidance on where to place this lighting would help support the market, while minimising the risks of poor solutions. A quick retrofit to an existing domestic stair shows how effective localised lighting could be. It also highlights how applying localised light on a narrower domestic stair can be more effective than the commercial stair used in the examples above, see Fig. 4. It was even effective on the winder steps near the bottom of the flight.

a) Localised LEDs on a domestic stair   b) Localised LEDs on a domestic stair

Fig. 4. Localised LEDs on alternate steps. a) from the landing b) from the first step down

The application of contrasting alternating treads to provide nosing contrast in non-domestic settings would require further evidence before it could be considered as a viable option. The application of localised lighting could be applied in some locations, but again how this might affect steps with existing proprietary nosings would need to be considered.

7   Next Steps for an Experimental Approach to Contrasting Nosings

Providing a subjective opinion of the effectiveness of methods to highlight nosings does not provide the level of evidence required to make substantive changes to standards and guidance. This is especially true when all the observers did not have visual impairments, for whom the contrasting nosings are intended. However, it is worth noting that the benefits of visible nosings may be apparent for all users.

We propose an experimental study using a stair laboratory with positional gait analysis and eye tracking software. Within these settings, alternative stair coverings and localised lighting settings could be established as experimental conditions in controlled ambient lighting conditions. It may be advantageous to try the options in both typical ambient lighting and dusk conditions.

At least two, but possibly three, groups of people (people with visual impairments, older users, and possibly younger people) would be asked to navigate at least four experimental stairs configurations multiple times. These four should include:

- stair with no highlighted nosings - all tread finishes the same.
- stair highlighted with proprietary nosings - all tread finishes the same.
- stair with different colours on alternate treads.

- stair with no highlighted nosings illuminated using LEDs on alternate treads - all tread finishes the same.

The experiment could be repeated over two step dimensions:

- conventional domestic stair (250 mm going, 200 mm rise).
- normal (public) stair (300 mm going, 180 mm rise).

Measurements of the foot position with reference to the nosings, especially in descent, would determine whether the addition of the contrast affects user's behaviour. The addition of eye tracking techniques would also allow observation of where users look when descending and ascending stairs. Trials should be randomised to reduce learning effects on the position of feet during the experiment. After each set of walks the users would also be asked to also provide an opinion of the stair: how comfortable it was to use, whether they could clearly see the edges of the steps and whether they felt safe using the stair. The experiment could be extended to include:

- stair with different colour nosings on alternate treads.
- stair with highlighted nosings illuminated using LEDs - all tread finishes the same.

These alternatives would highlight whether the complicated multiple level changes are detrimental to use.

Three research laboratories from different universities in the UK were approached at the observational stage and participated in the observations via a virtual meeting. With access to appropriate funding, it is expected that one of these universities would be able to conduct an experimental phase.

Acknowledgements. The authors would like to thank Diane Luther, Quantum Profile Systems Limited; and Nick Ferguson, Gradus; for providing the various stair coverings and their help with the practical work. We would also like to thank Tim Hayes, Quantum Profile Systems Limited; Neil Thompson, Gradus; Costis Maganaris, Liverpool John Moores University; John Buckley, Bradford University; and Neil Reeves and Steven Brown, Manchester Metropolitan University; for useful observations, discussion, and constructive comments on the work to date.

References

1. Roys, M.: FB 53: Refurbishing Stairs in Dwellings to Reduce the Risk of Falls and Injuries. BRE Press, Bracknell (2013)
2. UKSRG. Making Stairs Safer (2021). https://www.ukslipresistance.org.uk/publication/making-stairs-safer
3. DETR. Approved Document M: Access and Facilities for disabled people. The Stationary Office (1999)
4. British Standards Institute. BS 8300:2001 Design of buildings and their approaches to meet the needs of disabled people – Code of Practice BSI Publications (2001)
5. RGIE. Colour, contrast and perception. Design guidance for internal built environments. School of Construction Management, University of Reading (2004)

6. Templer, J.: The Staircase: Studies of Hazards, Falls, and Safer Design. MIT Press, Cambridge (1992)
7. Janssens, K., Vanrie, J., Quartier, K., Danschutter, S.: Light: towards an inclusive perspective. In: Di Bucchianico, G., Kercher, P. (eds.) Advances in Design for Inclusion. Advances in Intelligent Systems and Computing, vol. 500. Springer, Cham (2016). https://doi.org/10.1007/978-3-319-41962-6_14
8. Van de Perre, L., Danschutter, S., Janssens, K., Hanselaer, P., Dujardin, M., Smet, K., Ryckaert, W.: Safety perception of stairs with integrated lighting. Build. Environ. **166**, 106389 (2019). ISSN 0360-1323, https://doi.org/10.1016/j.buildenv.2019.106389
9. RoSPA. Safer by Design: A framework to reduce serious accidental injury in new-build homes (2019). https://www.rospa.com/home-safety/advice/safer-by-design

Part VII: Visual Ergonomics (Edited by Marino Menozzi)

Pragmatic Needs-Oriented Evaluation of Visibility, Impressions, Aesthetics and Eye Movement for Platform Display Design

Hirotaka Aoki[✉] [iD] and Naoto Koizumi

Tokyo Institute of Technology, Tokyo 152-8550, Japan
aoki.h.ad@m.titech.ac.jp

Abstract. In today's strict business environments, one key success factor for a platform display company seems to be making a product be different from those sold by other competing companies. The differentiator should be not only a functional one such as visibility, but also symbolic/experiential one such as impressions/aesthetics perceived. Considering this, effective/efficient evaluations of visibility, impressions and aesthetics that can be performed rapidly and easily are required. The objective of the present paper is to develop a pragmatic needs-oriented evaluation method to examine platform displays' visibility, impressions and aesthetics, which is scientifically rigorous yet also very simple and time-saving, and therefore acceptable for practitioners. By breaking down the needs of a company's need, multiple dimensions of evaluations were elicited. By performing a series of experiments, the multiple dimensional evaluations of visibility, impressions and aesthetics of a new product as well as its competing products were carried out. Results of each dimension as well as feasibility of the analysis procedure are discussed.

Keywords: Platform display · Visibility · Impression · Aesthetics

1 Introduction

In today's public display materials businesses context, the followings are of great importance: In order to strengthen business competitiveness, it is required that the materials provides both of high visibility and some additional value for customer such as positive impressions like clean, warm etc. This indicates that multiple evaluations for specific materials from not only visibility-related, but also some impression-related aspects are needed in the product development processes. The evaluation results, in addition, have to involve some new perspective to differentiate a company's sales promotions from competitors. In the present paper, we propose a new approach for multi-dimensional evaluation method where both of conventional methodology to evaluate visibility/impressions from subjective ratings and gaze behavior analysis are combined. Underlying idea of the proposed approach is to enable us to examine materials' quality in use needed in business environment from multiple dimensions (i.e., perceived visibility, aesthetics and gaze behavior).

© The Author(s), under exclusive license to Springer Nature Switzerland AG 2021
N. L. Black et al. (Eds.): IEA 2021, LNNS 220, pp. 707–714, 2021.
https://doi.org/10.1007/978-3-030-74605-6_89

2 Platform Displays and Business Context

One of Japan's manufacturing companies, with which we collaborated for the present study, started to release a new display where a novel material was implemented in the beginning of the present study. The material has a unique characteristic in its diffuse reflection of light. This characteristic was expected to contribute to effective and efficient reflection of outer illumination. By making platform displays by the material, it was expected that the displays would be brighter outer illumination type displays having good visibility but low operating cost (low electricity cost) compared to conventional materials. In addition to the visibility, the company needed to know unique/special benefits of the material which can be potential competing values for potential customers.

An example of platform displays made by the new material is shown in Fig. 1. This is an outer illumination type display. The size of the display is 450 mm × 1280 mm. The display shows the current station name as well as its preceding and succeeding stations. The current station name written in Kanji characters is shown in a large font in the center of the display with its Hiragana characters and Romanized versions. They are written by black characters on white background. The preceding and succeeding stations are shown in relatively a small font in the left and right of the display, respectively. These are white characters written on a green line.

Fig. 1. An example platform display showing current, preceding and succeeding stations.

3 Multi-dimensional Evaluation Scheme Developed

3.1 Needs Given by a Company

In the collaborating company, some effective visibility evaluation approach is strongly required. Its needs were given as follows: *Cost effective*, meaning that the evaluation can be performed rapidly. *Simple procedure*, meaning that the approach can be conducted easily with few knowledges relating to visibility such as cognitive psychology, human factors so forth. *Novel aspects*, meaning that some new visibility-related attribute rather than traditional ones should be unveiled by the approach.

3.2 Evaluation Scheme

By breaking down the above-mentioned needs, we developed an evaluation scheme composed of the following three dimensions: (1) Perceived visibility, (2) perceived visual aesthetics, and (3) gaze behavior.

First Dimension: Perceived Visibility. Subjectively perceived visibility of the platform display under real conditions can be characterized as the most fundamental dimension for evaluation. Subjectively perceived visibility is measured based on questionnaire items. We employed the following six questions to measure overall visibility and legibility (Table 1).

Table 1. Question items for first dimension (Perceived visibility).

Category	Statements	Response type
Overall visibility	1. How salient is the platform display? 2. How bright is the platform display? 3. How discomfortable is the glare? [1]	Five-point Likert scale (1: very obscure ~5: very salient) Five-point Likert scale (1: very dark ~5: very bright) Five-point Likert scale (1: just intolerable ~5: just not perceptible)
Legibility	1. How legible are the texts? [2] 2. How sharp are the texts? [2] 3. How fuzzy are the background?	Five-point Likert scale (1: very illegible ~5: very legible) Five-point Likert scale (1: very dim ~5: very sharp) Five-point Likert scale (1: very fuzzy ~5: very clear)

Second Dimension: Perceived Visual Aesthetics. The new material can be used not only for platform display but is strongly expected to be used for public displays like advertising boards. In advertising board design, it seems that visual impression given to consumers is important. Therefore, another evaluation dimension relating to impressions is employed. The question item used is shown in Table 2.

Table 2. Question item for second dimension (Perceived visual aesthetics).

Category	Statement	Response type
Overall aesthetics	How aesthetic is the display? [3]	Five-point Likert scale (1: very inaesthetic ~5: very aesthetic)

Third Dimension: Gaze Behavior. Gaze behavior is referred to as fixations sequences along with time-line during seeing. This can be seen as a novel one and is expected as an important and interesting dimension for visibility evaluation. From fixations sequences, two metrics representing the followings can be obtained as shown in Table 3. One is the time needed to find a platform display (abbreviated as *TF*). This metric can be obtained by measuring time spent before starting gazing at the platform display. TF seems to be directly connected with the degree in which how difficult it is to find a specific display. Another metric is the time needed to recognize information shown in a display (abbreviated as *TR*). This is measured by identifying time spent to finish reading stations' names after the display is detected. We can expect that former *TF* is connected with the degree in which how salient the specific display is, and the latter *TR* is strongly affected by the degree in which how readable/understandable information on a specific display is.

Table 3. Gaze metrics for third dimension (Gaze behavior).

Category	Eye movement-based metrics
Saliency	Time needed to find a platform display (*TF*) is measured Time duration from a point when a participant started to gaze at an initial fixated target until he/she directed his/her gaze to the display
Legibility	Time needed to read texts on a display (*TR*) is measured Time duration from a point when a participant started to gaze at the display until he/she directed his/her gaze back to the initial fixated target

4 Experiment

The objective of the experiment was to check feasibility of the multi-dimensional evaluation scheme developed. In the experiment, a new outer illuminated platform display made by new materials (abbreviated as D1) was compared with its competitive two displays (D2 and D3) by considering influences of eccentricity. D2 was also an outer illumination type display made by conventional material. D3 was an internally illuminated display which is illuminated by multiple LED lights. D3 was the brightest but requires both of much initial and running cost compared to D1 and D2. All displays' size was 450 mm × 1280 mm. Twenty-three healthy individuals (3 women and 20 men) participated as paid volunteers. They were university students with a median age of 21 years old (ranged from 18–24). They had normal or corrected-to-normal vision. All participants signed an informed consent form approved by the ethics committee of Tokyo Institute of Technology (A18087).

A schematic description of the experimental environment is shown in Fig. 2. Each display was set at a distance of 6.0 m from a participant, and the height of the display was 2.4 m. The eccentricity from a participant was set the following three conditions: 0°, 45° and 60°. This session used a 3 × 3 within-subjects design with eccentricity (3 levels of 0, 45 and 70°) and displays (3 levels of D1, D2 and D3) as factors. The participants were treated as repetitions. We used a head mount eye tracking system (TalkEye III, Takei Scientific Instruments) having a spatial accuracy of 0.1° and its sampling frequency was 60 Hz.

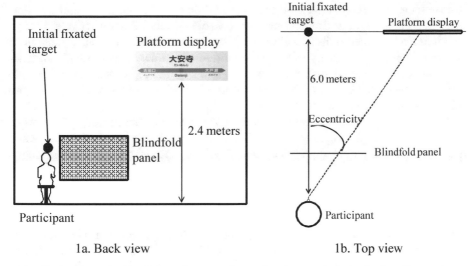

Fig. 2. A schematic description of an experimental environment: 1a back view, 1b top view.

The experimental task was to find a platform display shown in participants' peripheral visions (i.e., eccentricity) and read silently all the textual information as fast as possible. Upon arrival at our experimental site, each participant was briefed on the overall objective of the experiment, the tasks to be conducted, calibration processes of our eye tracker, and questionnaire. A participant was asked to be seated in a chair. Before starting, participant completed one practice circuit. This practice was performed to familiarize him/her with our experimental task. After carrying out calibration, experimental tasks composed of 11 trials were started. The trials included 9 experimental conditions (3 types of displays × 3 eccentricity levels) and 2 distracters where no display was exposed. In all conditions, a participant's view was obstructed by a blindfold. Immediately after the blindfold panel was removed, the participant started to view, from a seating position, the initial fixated target in front of them. During fixating at the target, he/she tried to find the platform display by using his/her peripheral vision. After finding the display, he/she looked at the all of textual information on the display as fast and accurate as possible and directed his/her gaze back to the target as fast as possible. In the end of each trial, the participant provided his/her responses to the questionnaire.

5   Result

5.1   First Dimension: Perceived Visibility

Table 4 shows the mean values for each condition and results of 2-way ANOVA (analysis of variance) of displays (D1, D2 and D3) and eccentricity (0, 45 and 60°). According to the ANOVA result on overall saliency scores, significant differences were found between display and eccentricity; no significant interaction effect was found from these two factors. As naturally predicted, D3 (an internally illuminated display) showed higher positive score (4.33) compared to other two outer illuminated displays (D1 and D2). Fortunately, D1 and D2 showed almost neutral scores of 3.07 and 3.22, respectively. Though negative effect of eccentricity was observed, the overall saliency maybe acceptable since the mean score at eccentricity 60-degree condition was almost neutral (3.13). In practical point of view, the interaction effect is of great importance because it may indicate a specific benefit that can be attributed to displays' materials. In "item 1," however, no interaction effect was observed.

We could identify significant main effects of display and eccentricity on scores of brightness. Subjective brightness evaluation of D3 was slightly positive (3.68), while those of D1 and D2 were slightly negative; 2.33 and 2.51, respectively. Interestingly, subjective brightness evaluation on eccentricity of 45-degree condition (2.91) seems a little improved than that in 0-degree condition. We could not identify any interaction effect here. From glare scores, there were no differences among displays. All displays showed highly positive scores (4.36, 4.28 and 4.13 for D1, D2 and D3, respectively), meaning that there were no glare-related problems. Although there was significant difference among eccentricity conditions, highly positive scores were obtained in all levels. Interaction effect seems to show that that D3's score on eccentricity condition of 45° is a little decreased compared to expected trend. In overall tendency, there were no severe problem caused by glare for all displays.

Table 4. Mean values and ANOVA results.

Item	Display				Eccentricity (degree)				Interaction
	D1	D2	D3	$F(2,176)$	0	45	60	$F(2,176)$	$F(4,176)$
Overall saliency	3.07	3.22	4.33	59.37^{**}	3.86	3.64	3.13	22.36^{**}	1.40
Brightness	2.33	2.51	3.68	102.62^{**}	2.88	2.91	2.72	5.28^{**}	1.25
Glare	4.36	4.28	4.13	2.12	4.04	4.17	4.55	9.13^{**}	6.98^{**}
Legibleness	3.42	3.49	3.84	11.67^{**}	4.48	3.71	2.57	107.86^{**}	2.64^{*}
Sharpness	3.88	3.93	4.49	22.52^{**}	4.62	4.19	3.49	52.73^{**}	3.18^{*}
Background fuzziness	3.67	3.91	4.35	21.13^{**}	3.96	3.97	4.00	5.28^{**}	1.25

**: $p < 0.01$, *: $p < 0.05$

In legibleness scores, significant main effects of display and eccentricity were found. Though D3 seemed to show relatively high legibleness (4.13), D1 and D2 showed higher than neutral scores (3.42 and 3.93). As for the effect of eccentricity on legibleness, only the condition of 60-degree eccentricity showed slightly negative score (2.57). Notably, we could find a significant interaction effect. Unexpectedly, D1's legibleness score became negative (1.85), while D2 and D3 seemed to keep approximately neutral scores (2.61 and 3.08, respectively) in 60-degree eccentricity condition.

Sharpness scores shared similar tendency with the legibleness scores. The D3 showed highly positive score (4.49), while D1 and D2 showed slightly positive scores (3.88 and

3.93). The eccentricity gave a negative effect on sharpness scores, but the scores could keep higher than neutral. There existed the following interaction effect: D1's score on eccentricity condition of 60° (2.80) is more decreased than expected trend.

As for back-ground fuzziness scores, main effects of display and eccentricity were found, though no interaction effect was identified. As predicted, D3 showed relatively higher scores compared to D1 and D2. Though significant differences were found among eccentricity conditions, their difference size seemed not so large. In total tendency, there were no problems in D1–D3 in terms of background fuzziness since all of scores were higher than neutral (ranged 3.67–4.35 and 3.96–4.00 for display and eccentricity conditions, respectively).

5.2 Second Dimension: Perceived Visual Aesthetics

2-way ANOVA revealed significant differences with the factors of display and eccentricity. D3 could obtain slightly positive score (3.78). D1 and D2 showed, on the other hand, almost neutral scores (3.07 and 3.09). The perceived overall aesthetics seemed to be significantly weakened on 60-degree eccentricity condition. We could identify an interesting tendency in the interaction effect. Though the interaction effects were not significant ($p = 0.067$), it seemed that material-attributed difference existed. D1 seemed to have a weakness at the eccentricity of 60° in terms of aesthetics.

5.3 Third Dimension: Gaze Behavior

As for *TF*, no difference was found among displays. A significant influence of eccentricity was found, but it was a tricky result. Unexpectedly, the mean *TF* at the eccentricity 0° was longer (1.11 s) than other angle conditions (0.84 s and 0.91 s). We could not identify significant interaction effect in *TF*. No difference could be found among displays and eccentricity conditions in *TR*. This seemed to indicate that time needed to read texts were identical for each display for each eccentricity condition.

6 Discussion

The results from the three dimensions clearly and quantitatively revealed the characteristics of the displays. For example, D1's overall saliency included in dimension 1 seemed to be acceptable considering the mean score of D1 and its comparison with D2. Furthermore, the experimental session and basic data processing could be carried out by persons who were not specialists/researchers. As a supporting evidence, additionally, we could obtain positive comments from people from the company. The comments are as follows: "We could easily understand the procedure and what outcome can be obtained clearly." "By just a few trials participation, we could easily understand how to conduct and collect data." Considering above-mentioned, we think that cost effectiveness and simple procedure of the approach proposed are satisfactory in terms of the company's needs.

Acknowledgments. This research was funded by FUJIFILM Imaging Systems Co.,Ltd. We would like to acknowledge Moriya Hagikubo, Kei-ichi Ikejima, Shuhei Uemura, Shinji Nagahara, FUJIFILM Imaging Systems Co., Ltd. and Kaitaro Hasegawa, Tokyo Institute of Technology, for their great supports for our study.

References

1. Kent, M.G., Forios, S., Altomonte, S.: Order effects when using Hopkinson's multiple criterion scale of discomfort due to glare. Build. Environ. **136**, 54–61 (2018)
2. Jankowski, J., Samp, K., Irzynska, I., Jozwowicz, M., Decker, S.: Integrating text with video and 3D graphics: the effects of text drawing styles on text readability. In: Proceedings of the SIGCHI Conference on Human Factors in Computing Systems, pp. 1321–1330 (2010)
3. Lavie, T., Tractinsky, N.: Assessing dimensions of perceived visual aesthetics of web sites. Int. J. Hum.-Comput. Stud. **60**(3), 269–298 (2004)

Preferences of People with Vision Impairment with Respect to Visibility of Elements in the Built Environment

Mei Ying Boon[1,2,3](✉) [iD] and Byoung Sun Chu[2,4] [iD]

[1] University of Canberra, Canberra, ACT 2617, Australia
MeiYing.Boon@canberra.edu.au
[2] University of New South Wales, Sydney, NSW 2052, Australia
[3] University of Sydney, Sydney, NSW 2006, Australia
[4] Daegu Catholic University, Gyeongsan, Korea

Abstract. The qualities of the built environment impact on the ability of people with vision impairment to move safely through the environment. It is important to revisit the evidence of the relationship between vision and the visibility of elements in the built environment to ensure accessibility standards and design guidelines are consistent with the latest evidence base. This paper reviews mixed method (qualitative and quantitative) research into visual and non-visual factors known to be implicated in injurious incidents in people with vision impairment. The evidence base for the visibility of simulated and real environmental elements such as stairs, doors, door handles, light switches, tactile ground surface indicators, traffic cones, road line markings and pedestrians will be reviewed. The evidence suggests that luminance contrasts of approximately $2.5\times$ current contrast standards, as current standards vary, would allow people with up to severe vision impairment to see objects of the dimensions of tactile ground surface indicators with ease. If people who are categorised as being blind by WHO are considered, about $3\times$ current contrast standards may be required. If lower contrasts are used, alternative provisions should be made to assist people with vision impairment to navigate the space safely.

Keywords: Visibility · Built environment · Contrast · Vision impairment · Low vision

Moderate to severe vision impairment affects 1 billion people globally [1]. While 949.7 million people may be helped with spectacle correction, there are 875 million people remaining who are significantly vision impaired due to disease or trauma. The moderate and severe categories of vision impairment (VI) are defined by the World Health Organization (WHO) according to visual acuity (VA), the ability to resolve fine detail. Individuals who have presenting Snellen VAs of 6/18 to better than 6/60, 6/60 to better than 6/120 and worse than 6/120 are categorised as having moderate VI, severe VI and blindness respectively. A person with normal vision can resolve details which subtend a visual angular subtense of 1 min of arc, hence the Snellen VAs of 6/18, 6/60 and 6/120 may be interpreted as requiring a person to be about 3x, 10x and 20x closer respectively than a person with normal vision (take the inverse of the VA fraction) in order to see the same detail as a person with normal vision.

Although the WHO categories of vision impairment reference VA, other qualities of vision may also be affected. Table 1 provides example data from people with VI that fall into different WHO categories. It is evident that individuals who have similar levels of VA may experience other vision deficits to a different extent (Table 1).

Table 1. Examples of patients with vision impairment ranging from mild, moderate and severe WHO categories of vision impairment, indicated by lightest to darkest grey shading respectively. Luminance contrast thresholds were recorded with either the MARS chart (own data) or the Colour Detective Test (UNSW Colour Vision Suite). Chromatic contrast thresholds were recorded using either the Cambridge Colour Trivector Test (AMD participants) or the Colour Detective Test.

Condition	n	Age (years)	Binocular VA (6/6 is normal)	Visual field loss	Luminance contrast threshold	Red-green contrast threshold	Blue-yellow contrast threshold
Optic Neuropathy [2]	1	29	6/8	Peripheral > central loss	Normal	2x worse than normal	2x worse than normal
Retinitis Pigmentosa [2]	8	33.9 (17–70)	6/23 (6/12–6/379)	Peripheral > central loss	Normal to 3x worse than normal	3–13x worse than normal	2.5–12x worse than normal
AMD (own data)	1	72	6/24	Central > peripheral loss	Normal	1.2x worse than normal	3x worse than normal
Corneal Dystrophy [2]	1	44	6/44	Central deficit	Normal	3.5x worse than normal	9x worse than normal
Cone-rod Dystrophy [2]	1	58	6/46	Central > peripheral loss	Normal	Normal	2x worse than normal
AMD (own data)	1	77	6/72	Central > peripheral loss	7x worse than normal	Could not see CCT stimulus	Could not see CCT stimulus
Stargardt Disease [2]	1	56	6/91	Not assessed	4x worse than normal	11x worse than normal	15x worse than normal

Why is altered perception of the built environment a problem? One reason is personal safety. Studies have shown that people with VI are more susceptible to injury. Incidents such as slips, trips, falls, collisions, traffic incidents result in soft-tissue injuries, fractures, head trauma, lacerations, twisting injuries, burns/scalds and sporting injuries [3, 4]. These injurious or near miss incidents occurred in a variety of environments, but significantly, most occurred within the built environment including at their own home or relative's home, on roads, footpaths, workplace, car park, shopping centre, hospital cafeteria, town hall and medical centre [3, 4]. Of concern, these patients had already consulted an eye care practitioner. Even for hospitalised patients, after adjusting for age, history of falls and use of walking aids, VI was found to significantly increase risk of falls. Falling is associated with injuries, fear of falling, loss of independence and death in one third of elderly (>65 year old) patients [5]. For these reasons, it is important to consider what can be done from the design standpoint to reduce risk of injury in people with VI.

Another reason that altered perception of the built environment is a problem is being unable to identify building elements, which can leave users feeling lost and wandering around trying to determine where to go, resulting in inefficiencies in orientation and mobility [6]. People with VI already experience high levels of fatigue due to the high cognitive load required to function with the impaired sense of vision; "paying attention to the environment and orientation in the surrounding environment" is fatiguing [7]. Facilitating ability to negotiate the environment by improving the visibility of building elements would improve the useability and enjoyment of spaces.

Accessibility standards have been designed to guide architects and builders to meet the needs of users of the built environment, however there are discrepancies between standards. To address this larger aim of improving accessibility and safety for people with VI as they navigate the built environment, the purpose of this paper is to revisit the evidence of the visibility of elements in the built environment for people with VI.

1 Which Visual Characteristics of the Built Environment Are of Relevance?

In improving the visibility of elements of the built environment, we seek to improve the ability of people with VI to identify and safely navigate elements of the built environment. Is improving visibility of elements of the built environment a useful approach? In a mixed methods prospective study of injurious incidents and near misses in older people (>60 years) with VI, participants who experienced an incident were asked to describe what visual and non-visual aspects they thought contributed to their near miss or incident [3]. The most frequently cited causative factors were contrast, depth perception, not seeing, central blur, dark/light adaptation problems and poor peripheral vision. Further, the same patients identified potential factors for prevention as using colour and pattern contrast, avoiding the use of transparent materials, improving balance, reducing clutter, modifying lighting (sunglasses and turning lights on), improving awareness of what is around them and learning to use peripheral vision. The quantitative analysis in the same group confirmed that poor contrast sensitivity and poor high contrast visual acuity were key visual predictors of incident occurrence in that group [3]. Good general fitness and health were also important to prevent incidents resulting in injury [3]. These results suggest that improving the contrast sensitivity of patients, such as by improving lighting or modification of the contrast of objects in the built environment, or increasing the size of objects observed, such as through the use of magnifying low vision aids, or coming closer to an object, are two key ways to improve visibility of elements in the built environment.

Is there any support for the notion that improving the contrast of objects has tangible benefits for orientation, mobility and personal safety? Home modifications have been found to prevent falls, with less clear evidence for other kinds of incidents, principally due to a lack of studies examining this issue [8, 9]. In Keall et al.'s study, aimed at preventing falls in older people but not specifically targeted at people with VI, two out of the eight interventions applied were aimed at improving visibility (improving lighting and using high contrast step edgings); the other interventions were designed to improving the levelness and slip-resistance of the walking surface or the provision of grab and handrails. Higher quality studies are required to evaluate interventions for other incidents apart from those on the falls causal pathway.

2 Contrast

This paper will focus on the quality of contrast. Accessibility standards such as AS 1428.1–2009 and AS 1428.4.1–2009 in Australia, BS 8300: 2009 in the United Kingdom [10–13], and 2010 ADA Standards for Accessible Design in the United States of America and the users of such standards, recognise the importance of contrast to support access and safety for individuals in public spaces. However, the evidence-base for contrast requirements that are stated in current standards is unclear and there are several equations currently in use to calculate contrast.

Contrast describes a difference in the quality of two or more things. To vision scientists, luminance contrast and chromatic contrast are commonly calculated as Weber or Michelson contrasts. Weber contrast is useful when there is an object against a background and is calculated as (Intensity of the object – Intensity of the background)/Intensity of the background. Michelson contrast is a useful measure for patterns where two elements alternate and is calculated as (Maximum intensity – Minimum intensity)/(Maximum intensity + Minimum intensity).

Accessibility standards provide minimum requirements for creating more accessible environments for people with disabilities, including people with VI. Within the accessibility and building code literature, contrast is calculated in different ways, which may impact on final outcomes in the selection of materials for building by architects, builders and designers [14]. For example, ISO21542 and ISO23599 calculate Weber contrast in the way described above multiplied by 100 to convert it into a percentage, however as light levels approach zero, intrinsic noise (a) within the visual system changes the perception of contrast by increasing the denominator value to (Intensity of the background + a) so alternatives have been suggested. In the accessibility literature, Michelson contrast has been defined the same as used by vision scientists, but multiplied by 100 to convert to a percentage (e.g. ISO21542). However, it has also been used with a different denominator, described as the average of the elements (Maximum intensity + Minimum intensity)/2 and multiplied by 100 to convert it into a percentage (AS/NZA 1428.4). Another modification of the Michelson equation is known as the Bowman-Sapolinski equation where contrast is defined as a percentage as ($125(Y2 – Y1)/(Y2 + Y1 + 25)$) where Y1 and Y2 are the luminance reflectances of the 2 surfaces. The variation is an attempt to account for the fact that at low average luminance, greater contrast is necessary to achieve equal visibility.

Regardless of which measure of contrast is used, it is possible to convert between the methods of calculating contrast, so the important question is what contrasts support visibility of building elements for people with VI, acknowledging that VI may range from mild to blindness. Studies have investigated this question using a variety of approaches.

Dain et al. reported an investigation into luminance contrast preferences using digital simulations of building elements of realistic visual angle that varied only in luminance contrast, not colour or shading [15]. The simulated representations were of door frames, door handles, light switches and stairs with nosings presented on a tablet computer. Participants with and without VI were asked to rate the visibility of each element on a four point scale, (1) not visible, (2) poorly visible, (3) easily visible and (4) extremely visible. Higher Michelson contrasts were associated with greater visibility ratings by participants. Further, participants with poorer high contrast VA required higher levels of contrast for each of the ratings. Two other trends were observed; elements that were larger or had fewer horizontal than vertical elements required lower contrast levels to be rated as "easily visible" than smaller objects or those that had a high proportion of horizontal elements. The latter is suggestive of a horizontal effect, which has been observed previously [16–18]. For people with normal contrast sensitivity (1.8) as measured on the MARS letter chart, the elements were rated as easily visible with Michelson contrasts ranging from 15–20%. For people with contrast sensitivity of at least 1.5 and 1.0 this changed to 15–31% and 22–48% respectively. For the people with the poorest contrast sensitivity, 33–69% contrast was required. Participants with moderate and severe VI required elements with 22% and 30% contrast to be rated easily visible. For the participants with the poorest vision, 69% was required. A limitation of the study is that it was a simulation and restricted to grey scale with uniform luminance, whereas building elements in the real world are more colourful and illuminated unevenly. However, the strength of the study is that it isolated the question to that of luminance contrast and shape.

Lukman et al. conducted a mixed methods study using real building elements commonly used by architects, builders and designers in a controlled laboratory environment (average of 230 lx room illumination) focusing on door frames [19] and tactile ground surface indicators (TGSIs) [14]. The latter are designed to provide both visual and haptic information as warning elements about hazardous changes in level, such as steps, ramps, for people with VI as they walk around. The luminances of the TGSIs and panels were measured and contrast calculated using the Bowman Sapolinski equation (Standards Australia, 2014) using light reflectance values. Luminance contrast ranged from 7 (stainless steel TSI on a timber background) to 90% (black TGSI on a white background). Building elements were rated using a rating scale from a distance of 1.5 m as (1) not visible at all, (2) poorly visible, (3) easily visible and (4) extremely easily visible. Visual detection and identification distance was assessed. Participants were required to walk towards the TGSI from a starting distance of 6 m and stop when they could first detect the TGSI and then identify it as a TGSI. The key findings were that people who had normal to severe levels of VI were all able to detect and identify all the TGSI/background combinations from approximately 5 to 6 m. However, people categorised as blind by the WHO needed to be closer, between 2 and 4 m, to achieve the same. The lower the contrast, the closer the required visual detection and identification distances. Lighting impacted on the relative visibility of the stainless steel TGSIs. Overall, people with mild to severe VI rated these real combinations from a distance of 1.5 m as easily visible when the elements had Bowman Sapolinski contrasts ranging from 35–66% for the TGSIs [14] and from 18–55% for door frames [19]. People who were categorised as blind by the WHO, rated elements from 77–90% for the TGSIs [14] and 62–100% for the door frames [19] as easily visible. The study showed overall that higher luminance contrasts benefit people categorised with blindness more than people with mild to severe VI as it allowed them to see the building element from longer distances away with greater ease.

3   Colour Considerations

Colour was found to have modified the order of visibility of the TGSI building elements from strictly following the order of luminance contrast in Lukman et al.'s study [14], however the impact of colour vision deficits on visibility of colourful elements could not be analysed due to the few participants who could see the Cambridge Colour Test stimulus, likely due to vision issues such as poor VA or poor visual fields impacting on their ability to do the test [19]. Lukman concluded from qualitative data that colour contrast aided people who had poor luminance contrast sensitivity to see building elements if they had sufficient luminance contrast sensitivity, agreeing with Legge et al., who stated that "readers rely on information conveyed by color contrast or luminance contrast, whichever yields the best performance" [20].

Additional clues as to the impact of colour on the preferences of people with VI with respect to elements within the built environment may be gained from a study which investigated ability to navigate in a virtual environment [2, 21]. In that study, most of the participants with VI could complete a different colour vision test, the Colour Detective Test [22]. The participants with VI navigated four virtual scenarios. They (1) slalomed between red and white horizontally striped traffic cones on a grey footpath, (2) walked down a grey footpath and avoided stationary pedestrians wearing yellow and black clothing, (3) followed a yellow line on a grey footpath and (4) walked down a grey footpath and avoided moving pedestrians wearing red and black clothing. Participants who had both poor luminance contrast sensitivity and chromatic contrast sensitivity had greater difficulty than people who had only poor luminance contrast sensitivity. The effect was colour-specific. Participants who had luminance contrast and blue-yellow vision deficits found task 3 difficult and participants who had luminance contrast and red-green colour vision deficiencies found pedestrian avoidance more difficult. Therefore, as red-green and blue-yellow contrast sensitivity deficits are a common characteristic of people with VI, colour contrast is a less reliable way of ensuring visibility than the use of high levels of luminance contrast in building elements for people with VI.

4   Conclusions

Collectively, the above findings support the use of luminance contrast requirements for accessibility standards. Lukman et al.'s (2020) findings provide the strongest evidence that real life building elements may be evaluated in terms of visibility using visibility rating scales and detection and identification distances and evaluated against equations used by accessibility standards to calculate contrast. Converting measures between the different contrast levels is possible however it requires knowledge of the original light reflectance values of the two elements, particularly when using the Bowman-Sapolinski equation for contrast. The results also suggest that there should be greater uniformity in the measures of contrast employed to provide greater certainty for designers when checking against the evidence. The evidence suggests that luminance contrasts of approximately 2.5x current contrast standards would allow people with up to severe VI to see objects of the dimensions of TGSIs with ease from 1.5 m. If people who are categorised as being blind by WHO are considered, about 3x current contrast standards may be required. If lower contrasts are used, alternative provisions should be made to assist people with VI to navigate and move around the space safely. If building elements are of insufficient contrast for a person with VI to see easily, moving to a closer distance can improve its visibility, but this is at the expense of time and energy needed to move around to search for the object, during which time the person would be at increased risk of injurious incidents. As VI is more prevalent in the elderly, this increased risk is borne by the most vulnerable in our population.

References

1. World Health Organisation. https://www.who.int/news-room/fact-sheets/detail/blindness-and-visual-impairment. Accessed 10 Nov 2020
2. Knopf, N.A., Boon, M.Y., Suaning, G.J., Zapf, M.P.H., Grigg, J.: Initial mobility behaviors of people with visual impairment in a virtual environment using a mixed methods design. In: 2017 IEEE Life Sciences Conference, Sydney, pp. 153–156 (2017)
3. Boon, M.Y., Chu, B.S., Lee, P.C., Chiang, T.J., Alshamli, N., Alghamdi, W., Lai, J., Yeung, W., Bridge, C.: Perceptions of older people regarding their vision and incident causation. Optom. Vis. Sci. **92**(10), 995–1002 (2015)
4. Wood, J.M., Lacherez, P., Black, A.A., Cole, M.H., Boon, M.Y., Kerr, G.K.: Risk of falls, injurious falls, and other injuries resulting from visual impairment among older adults with age-related macular degeneration. Ophthalmol. Vis. Sci. **52**(8), 5088–5092 (2011)
5. Ambrose, A.F., Paul, G., Hausdorff, J.M.: Risk factors for falls among older adults: a review of the literature. Maturitas **75**(1), 51–61 (2013)
6. Chang, K.J., Dillon, L.L., Deverell, L., Boon, M.Y., Keay, L.: Orientation and mobility outcome measures. Clin. Exp. Optom. **103**(4), 434–448 (2020)
7. Schakel, W., Bode, C., van der Aa, H.P.A., Hulshof, C.T.J., Bosmans, J.E., van Rens, G.H.M.B., van Nispen, R.M.A.: Exploring the patient perspective of fatigue in adults with visual impairment: a qualitative study. BMJ Open **7**(8), 1–8 (2017)
8. Sherrington, C., Fairhall, N., Wallbank, G., Tiedemann, A., Michaleff, Z.A., Howard, K., Clemson, L., Hopewell, S., Lamb, S.: Exercise for preventing falls in older people living in the community: an abridged Cochrane systematic review. Br. J. Sports Med. **54**(15), 885–891 (2020)
9. Keall, M.D., Pierse, N., Howden-Chapman, P., Cunningham, C., Cunningham, M., Guria, J., Baker, M.G.: Home modifications to reduce injuries from falls in the home injury prevention intervention (HIPI) study: a cluster-randomised controlled trial. Lancet **385**(9964), 231–238 (2015)
10. Standards Australia: AS 1428.4 Design for access and mobility part 4: tactile ground surface indicators for the orientation of people with vision impairment (2009)

11. Standards Australia: AS/NZS 1428.4.1 Design for access and mobility part 4.1: means to assist the orientation of people with vision impairment - tactile ground surface indicators (2009)
12. British Standards Institution.: BS8300 Design of buildings and their approaches to meet the needs of disabled people - code of practice (2009)
13. Bright, K., Cook, G.: The Colour, Light and Contrast Manual: Designing and Managing Inclusive Built Environments. Wiley, Hoboken (2010)
14. Lukman, A.L., Bridge, C., Dain, S.J., Boon, M.Y.: Luminance contrast of accessible tactile indicators for people with visual impairment. Ergon. Des. **28**(2), 4–15 (2020)
15. Dain, S.J., Manadhar, S., Boon, M.Y.: Luminance contrast preferences for the visual impaired in the built environment. In: American Academy of Optometry Annual Meeting, Orlando (2016)
16. Essock, E.A., DeFord, J.K., Hansen, B.C., Sinai, M.J.: Oblique stimuli are seen best (not worst!) in naturalistic broad-band stimuli: a horizontal effect. Vis. Res. **43**(12), 1329–1335 (2003)
17. Hansen, B.C., Essock, E.A.: A horizontal bias in human visual processing of orientation and its correspondence to the structural components of natural scenes. J Vis. **4**(12), 1044–1060 (2004)
18. Yap, T.P., Luu, C.D., Suttle, C.M., Chia, A., Boon, M.Y.: Electrophysiological and psychophysical studies of meridional anisotropies in children with and without astigmatism. Invest. Ophthalmol. Vis. Sci. **60**(5), 1906–1913 (2019)
19. Lukman, A.L.: Developing design criteria based on visual perception of people with visual impairment using contrast cues, Ph.D. thesis. The University of New South Wales, Sydney (2017)
20. Legge, G.E., Parish, D.H., Luebker, A., Wurm, L.E.: Psychophysics of reading. XI. Comparing color contrast and luminance contrast. J. Opt. Soc. Am. **7**(10), 2002–2010 (1990)
21. Knopf, N.A., Zapf, M.P., Suaning, G., Grigg, J., Bodduluri, L., Boon, M.Y.: Mobility performance in a virtual reality maze is related to luminance and chromatic sensitivity in people with vision impairment. In: CIE Australia Lighting Research Conference 2020. CIE Australia, Brisbane (2020)
22. Bodduluri, L., Boon, M.Y., Ryan, M., Dain, S.J.: Normative values for a tablet computer-based application to assess chromatic contrast sensitivity. Behav. Res. Methods **50**(2), 673–683 (2018)

Applied Visual Ergonomics - A Compelling Consideration for the New Normal

Nivedita Dabir[1]($\boxtimes$) and Prajakta Khanwalkar[2]

[1] Finevision Optometry and Contact Lens Clinic, Pune, Maharashtra, India
[2] MIT-WPU School of Design, Pune, Maharashtra, India

Abstract. Objective: To examine the relationship between practice of visual ergonomics in the work from home setup and its effect on eye health during COVID-19 pandemic. And to propose mitigation strategies via easy to implement visual ergonomic practices.

Methods: A standardized tool was used to gather information via an online survey conducted over a period of October-December 2020. Study population consisted of 231 professionals working from home (Mean age 37 years $\pm$ 6). The survey consisted of CVSS-17 questionnaire along with questions targeting ergonomics and human factors in the new work-from-home setups. The paper shows the association between impact of the new work environment and eye health using Pearson's correlation coefficient (r) for all the variables under ideal ergonomic practices.

Result: The study indicates that there is a marked increase in the hours spent in front of a screen for work ($r = 0.67$). The people who face eye strain reported that the letters on the screen became blurry after continuous screen use ($r = 0.56$). Screen size is negatively correlated to the ideal visual ergonomic position of eyes in relation to the screen ($r = -0.29$). Overall awareness about refresh rate is very low (21%).

Conclusion: The study has established a definite indication of onset of computer vision syndrome in the majority of the people who are now working from home on screens for extended hours. Further investigation is needed in understanding eye to screen relationship in the work from home situations.

Keywords: Computer vision syndrome · Visual ergonomics · Human factors · Digital eye strain

1 Introduction

In this pandemic situation, digital work has increased for each individual which was on the verge of happening as hybrid way of working has been taken up by a lot of work places. Eye strain is one of the important side effects of this new work culture. The use of computers for long periods of time is likely to lead to the development of a clinical syndrome called computer vision syndrome (CVS) [1] Computer vision syndrome or digital eye strain is a combination of eye and visual problems because of increased visual demands. Research has shown that, there is a prevalence of eyestrain among computer users that has been found to be between 31 and 57% [2, 3].

Multiple factors can give rise to unwanted glare in the field of view which can go un-noticed. It includes excessive artificial lighting, bright sunlight through windows or reflections from glossy surfaces. Glare can be of two types, discomfort glare (psychological) and disability glare (physiological). Discomfort glare originates when the differences in light conditions exist in the field of view which gives rise to light sensitivity. Glare is shown to lead to visual disability, and indirectly cause increased mental strain [4].

This paper is an attempt to establish the assumption that eye strain is one of the important side effects of this new work culture and it relates to other eye symptoms as well. It also proposes strategies for mitigation via appropriate implementation of visual ergonomics and human factors.

2 Methods and Methodology

A standardized tool was used to gather information via an online survey which was conducted over a period of October to December 2020. Study population consisted of 231 professionals working from home. The Mean Age of the subjects was 37 years ± 6 with age group range of 21 to 63 years. The survey consisted of CVSS-17 questionnaire [5] along with questions targeting Ergonomics and Human Factors. The questionnaire consisted of three sections, first section dealing with eye health, symptoms/observations which were experienced in four weeks prior to taking the survey, second section dealt with aspects of visual ergonomics and design during work, and third section dealt with computer activities and environment. Initial pilot study was done on 29 professionals and subsequent changes were made to the questionnaire as we found the need to probe into certain aspects deeper.

The data was compiled and analyzed using statistical tests. In this paper we attempt to show the association between impact of the new work environment and eye health using Pearson's correlation coefficient (r) for all the variables under ideal ergonomic practices.

Specific environmental variables like lumens, illumination level, ambient light, glare etc., were not collected in the study as in this global pandemic people are working from home setups which are very difficult to fine tune to the industry standards of 'good work space' norms.

3 Results

3.1 Change in Working Hours

The study indicates that there is a marked increase in the hours spent in front of a screen in the work from home scenarios as compared to the time spent in front of the screen during working hours in the office setups (r = 0.67) (Fig. 1).

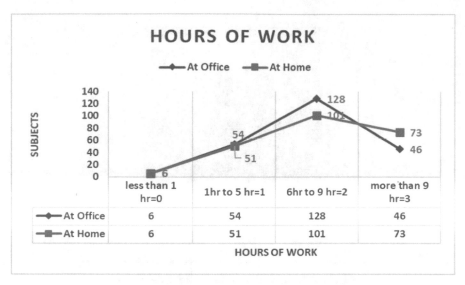

Fig. 1. Changes in working hours

3.2 Screen Time and Eye Health

Increase in the time of working from home is showing a correlation to tired eyes in the demographic we studied ($r = 0.22$). In the pandemic, mobile and tablet screen use has increased for work related activities; mobile or tab use has shown a correlation with squinting ($r = 0.30$) and we have also noticed that squinting to see and eye strain are correlated ($r = 0.45$).

The study shows that the people who have awareness about resolution of screens also have an awareness about refresh rate ($r = 0.49$) which is a significant environmental variable in visual ergonomics. Also, overall awareness about refresh rate is very low (21%) (Fig. 2).

Screen size is negatively correlated to the ideal visual ergonomic position of eyes in relation to the screen i.e., as screen size increases the top of the screen goes above the eye level ($r = -0.29$).

3.3 Eye Symptoms

The people who face eye strain reported that the letters on the screen became blurry after continuous use ($r = 0.56$) as per our study. Eye strain also correlates to increased light sensitivity ($r = 0.54$) and dry eyes ($r = 0.54$) People experiencing dry eyes are also bothered by lights after some time at the computer ($= 0.6$).

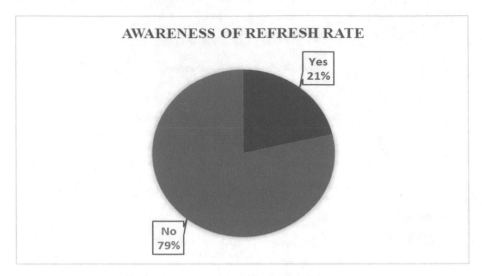

Fig. 2. Awareness about refresh rate of the screen.

4 Discussion

With high visual demands, combination of eye and visual problems occur indicating presence of CVS. During the global pandemic working population had to resort to work on computers from homes, with minimally optimal work conditions and longer working hours, this has definitely put them in a high-risk zone for developing a clinical syndrome called computer vision syndrome [1].

A significant number of people have reported eye strain which is an initial symptom for further problems like blurred vision or similar temporary visual difficulties [6, 7].

The refresh rate is the number of times per second that a raster-based display device displays a new image. Measured in Hertz (Hz), the refresh rate counts the number of times the display refreshes every second it is on. When the refresh rate is too slow it causes a flickering screen. Studies have proven that a higher refresh rate is associated with less flickering thus decreases ocular symptoms and is more user friendly. A minimal screen refresh rate of 75 Hz is needed, and much higher refresh rates (300 Hz or higher) may decrease ocular symptoms and increase user functionality [8–10].

In the work from home scenario during the pandemic, and also in the view of a hybrid work culture coming up, a poor working environment is rampant. It can be detrimental to the eye health and overall productivity of individuals [11]. Poor work conditions like a higher viewing angle, unclean computer screen, defective or poor-quality computer screens can lead to blurred images [12].

Some of the causes for a lack in ideal ergonomic work conditions at home offices are lack of awareness as users of the space are not professional to understand and implement the visual ergonomics principles of an ideal work space. As all offices are now on the verge of creating hybrid work culture the understanding of visual ergonomics is going to be essential and in fact compelling within the 'person to computer-screen' visual interaction. Table 1 mentions some of the remedies to improve the visual ergonomics in a work from home setup.

Table 1. Remedies to improve visual ergonomics in a work from home setup.

Sr. no.	Criteria	Suggestion
1.	Lighting	Screen lighting should be within 5× of average room lighting
2.	Screen reflections	Screen should be dust or smudge free. Use of anti-glare screen
3.	Glare from windows or overhead light	Glare from windows should be avoided by facing the workstation to the window
4.	Refresh rate	Computer screen constantly refreshes at a certain rate. By keeping refresh rate higher (>120 Hz) reduces the eye related symptoms and increases individual's functionality [8]
5.	Viewing angle	Screen should be 10–20° below the eye level [6]
6.	Viewing distance	As viewing distance between the eye & the computer is significant in causing eyestrain [13]. It is recommended that the viewing distance should be of 30–40 in [14]

4.1 Limitation and Future Work

There is not enough research done to understand the challenges faced in work from home environments pertaining to the eye to screen relationship under uncontrolled environmental variables. Due to the pandemic situation the physical parameters of work from home spaces were varied, thus it was not considered in the study. As work from home office setup cannot match the office setup in terms of Ergonomics, thus more research needs to be done to control the immediate eye to screen relationship.

5 Conclusion

The study has established a definite indication of onset of computer vision syndrome in the majority of the people who are now working from home on screens for extended hours. There is not much research done to understand the challenges faced in work from home environments pertaining to the eye to screen relationship. Further investigation is needed in these aspects and strategies need to be proposed for the way forward from the visual ergonomics and usability perspective to provide solutions for the problems noted. The most important strategy in managing of computer vision syndrome is to work towards its prevention. User friendly modifications in the visual ergonomic factors of the work-from-home-space, education about visual ergonomics in computer users and proper eye care are important strategies for the way forward in preventing computer vision syndrome in work from home scenarios.

References

1. Rosenfield, M.: Computer vision syndrome: a review of ocular causes and potential treatments. Ophthalmic Physiol. Optic. **31**(5), 502–515 (2011)
2. Bhanderi, D., Choudhary, S.K., Doshi, V.G.: A community-based study of asthenopia in computer operators. Ind. J. Ophthalmol. **56**(1), 51 (2008)
3. Mocci, F., Serra, A., Corrias, G.A.: Psychological factors and visual fatigue in working with video display terminals. Occup. Environ. Med. **58**(4), 267–271 (2001)
4. Garzia, R.P.: Vision and Reading, vol. 5. Mosby Incorporated, Maryland Heights (1996)
5. Gonz´alez-Perez, M., Susi, R., Antona, B., Barrio, A., Gonz´alez, E.: The computer-vision symptom scale (CVSS17): development and initial validation. Invest Ophthalmol. Vis. Sci. **55**, 4504–4511 (2014)
6. Anshel, J.: Visual Ergonomics Handbook. Taylor & Francis, New York (2005)
7. Sheedy, J.E., Parsons, S.D.: The video display terminal eye clinic: clinical report. Optom. Vision Sci. **67**, 622–626 (1990)
8. Blehm, C., Vishnu, S., Khattak, A., Mitra, S., Yee, R.W.: Computer vision syndrome: a review. Surv. Ophthalmol. **50**(3), 253–262 (2005)
9. Bonacker, J., Alshuth, E.: Accommodation, convergence, pupil diameter and eye blinks at a CRT display flickering near fusion limit. Ergonomics **39**(1), 152–164 (1996)
10. Kennedy, A., Murray, W.: The effects of flicker on eye movement control. Q. J. Exp. Psychol. Sect. A **43**(1), 79–99 (1991)
11. Richter, H., Sundin, S., Long, J.: Visually deficient working conditions and reduced work performance in office workers: is it mediated by visual discomfort? Int. J. Ind. Ergon **72**, 128–136 (2019)
12. Anshel, J.: Computer vision syndrome: causes and cures. Manag. Office Technol. **42**(7), 17–19 (1997)
13. Jaschinski, W.: The proximity-fixation-disparity curve and the preferred viewing distance at a visual display as an indicator of near vision fatigue. Optom. Vision Sci. **79**(3), 158–169 (2002)
14. Yan, Z., Liang, H., Chen, H., Fan, L.: Computer vision syndrome: a widely spreading but largely unknown epidemic among computer users. Comput. Human Behav. **24**(5), 2026–2042 (2008)

Visual Symptoms and Risk Assessment Using Visual Ergonomics Risk Assessment Method (VERAM)

Hillevi Hemphälä[1]($\boxtimes$), Marina Heiden[2], Per Lindberg[2], and Per Nylén[3]

[1] Division of Ergonomics and Aerosol Technology, Design Sciences, Lund University, 221 00 Lund, Sweden
`hillevi.hemphala@design.lth.se`

[2] Centre for Musculoskeletal Research, Department of Occupational Health Science and Psychology, University of Gävle, 801 76 Gävle, Sweden

[3] Swedish Work Environment Authority, 112 79 Stockholm, Sweden

Abstract. A visual environment impaired by e.g. glare can cause eyestrain, visual symptoms and musculoskeletal strain. A Visual Ergonomics Risk Assessment Method (VERAM) consisting of both a subjective questionnaire and an objective risk assessment, have been used at 217 workplaces, mainly computer work. VERAM can be used to examine and prevent deficiencies and increase wellbeing as well as detecting risks in the visual work environment and suggest measures that can be used to reduce the risks. The questionnaire showed that eyestrain, visual symptoms and musculoskeletal strain are common among Swedish workers. The overall risk assessments for glare and amount of illuminance on work surface are divided into three categories, green – no risk, yellow – risk, and red – high risk. Risk of glare and insufficient illuminance was present at 66% and 49% of the assessed workplaces, respectively. When the risk of glare and illuminance levels was rated as red, the frequency of the subjective strain was higher.

Keywords: Asthenopia · Eyestrain · Neck pain · Illuminance · Glare · Headache · Flicker · Temporal light modulation

1 Introduction

The visual environment has many times been shown to affect us in several ways. Visually demanding near work can cause eyestrain or asthenopia [1–3]. When straining your eyes to see clearly, you can experience eyestrain such as eye fatigue, gritty feeling and light sensitivity [4, 5]. Computer vision syndrome (CVS) or digital eyestrain is the combination of eye and vision problems associated with the use of computers [6] or digital devices. Eyestrain, asthenopia or CVS problems is shown to be present among 64–90% of computer workers [4, 5]. Asthenopia or eyestrain is also quite frequent among non-computer users; 54% of surgical personnel and 44% of mailmen reported eyestrain [7, 8], and 64% of cleanroom microscope workers reported eye fatigue [9].

© The Author(s), under exclusive license to Springer Nature Switzerland AG 2021
N. L. Black et al. (Eds.): IEA 2021, LNNS 220, pp. 729–735, 2021.
https://doi.org/10.1007/978-3-030-74605-6_92

If the visual environment is favourable, the visual system can function for many hours without eyestrain [10].

Boyce and Wilkins [11] states that visual discomfort can be caused by:

- Poor visibility – any visual task that has stimuli close to detection threshold contains information that is difficult to extract.
- Overstimulation – discomfort can result from overstimulation of the visual cortex by large-field, spatially or temporarily repetitive patterns. Prolonged work in such conditions can result in eyestrain, headaches and fatigue.
- Distraction – the human visual system has a large peripheral field that detects the presence of bright, mobbing or fluctuating objects that are then examined using the small, high-resolution fovea. If such objects in the peripheral field cannot be avoided, they become sources of distraction. Having to ignore objects that automatically attract attention can lead to visual discomfort.

The aspects of lighting that can cause visual discomfort and hence eyestrain are too little light, too much light, too much variation in illuminance between and across working surfaces, disability glare, discomfort glare, veiling reflections, shadows, and flicker [12]. Studies show that eyestrain can be caused by external factors in the visual environment such as glare or insufficient illuminance [13, 14]. The light distribution in the working environment should have both direct and indirect lighting to enhance the visual environment [14].

There is a connection between eyestrain and musculoskeletal strain [15]. When reporting eyestrain, the musculoskeletal strain can be 2–3 times as high [8, 16], and musculoskeletal strain can be reduced with good lighting and correct spectacles [17].

A good visual environment is crucial for visual performance [18]. Increased illuminance levels showed an increased working speed in an assembly line from 800 to 1200 lx [19].

Thus, the visual environment and its effect on our wellbeing and performance is well recorded an overall perspective is needed. The visual ergonomics risk assessment method (VERAM) presents this overall perspective with both subjective questionnaires and objective risk assessments together with measurements and has been shown to be valid and reliable [20, 21]. This paper describes the frequency of subjective strain such as eyestrain and musculoskeletal strain, as well as the objective risk assessment for glare and amount of illuminance on the work surface using VERAM.

2   Method

VERAM was used at 217 workplaces. It is an on-line method [20, 21] that consists of four parts. a subjective questionnaire for the workers ratings, objective measurements of illuminance and luminance together with evaluators assessment of the visual environment, a section with follow-up questions, and a final part for recommendations [20, 21]. This paper will focus on some of the results from the two first parts. The questionnaire for the worker consists mainly of frequency of perceived strain and preferences.

Forty-eight practitioners from the Occupational Health Services (OHS) in Sweden were recruited to perform the data collection. The majority of them were physiotherapists and/or ergonomists. Remaining practitioners were work environment engineers, occupational therapists and a low vision therapist. Each received a 7-day course with specific training in visual ergonomics and in VERAM. The OHS-practitioners are hereafter referred to as trained evaluators.

The trained evaluators performed the objective measurements with the type of instrument/light meter they had access to, typically a Hagner Screenmaster or a Hagner S1/S2/S3. In the objective risk assessment, the trained evaluators rated the risks in the visual environment using a checklist.

The trained evaluators recruited participants to the study mainly from their regular customers in the OHS sector. They were instructed to recruit participants with diverse characteristics to ensure high variability within the data, e.g. variability in work tasks, age, sex, and level of eye- and musculoskeletal symptoms. The participants are hereafter referred to as workers.

2.1 Subjective Strain and Visual Ability

Nine different symptoms of eyestrain were rated: smarting, itching, gritty feeling, eye pain, photophobia, redness, teariness, dryness and eye fatigue. The workers rated the frequency of experienced eyestrain during the last four weeks as $0 =$ never, $1 =$ occasionally, $2 =$ a few times per week and $3 =$ almost daily. The total frequency of eyestrain, all of the symptoms combined, was also calculated.

The workers also rated their visual ability on a scale from $0 =$ very bad to $4 =$ very good. The frequency of dim vision, diplopia and problems changing focus during the last four weeks were rated from $0 =$ never, $1 =$ occasionally, $2 =$ a few times per week and $3 =$ almost daily.

The frequency of musculoskeletal strain in the upper part of the body, (i e. neck, shoulders, upper back and arms, see Fig. 1), during the last four weeks, was rated on a scale of never (0) to almost daily (3).

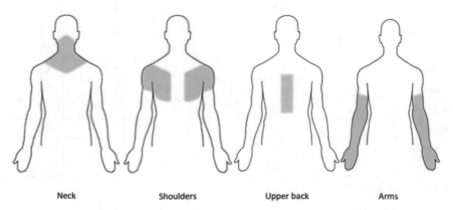

| Neck | Shoulders | Upper back | Arms |

Fig. 1. Instructions for locating the different areas for rating the musculoskeletal strain.

2.2 Risk Assessment

The illuminance levels were measured in lux at 3–10 places in each area of the workplace. Then the trained evaluator assessed if the illuminance requirements were fulfilled for the workplace (yes/no) with regard to the lighting recommendations for indoor workplaces [22]. The overall risk for illuminance levels was then rated as green/yellow/red.

The luminance was measured in cd/m^2 at 3–10 places in each area of the workplace and a luminance ratio was calculated. Similar to illuminance assessment, the overall risk of glare was then rated as green/yellow/red.

3 Results

Twenty of the workplaces did not have computer work as a main work task (9,2%). See [20, 21] for more information. The data from the lighting measurements, feed-back and recommendations will not be presented here.

3.1 Subjective Strain and Visual Function

Eyestrain (i. e., smarting, itching, gritty feeling, eye pain, photophobia, redness, teariness, dryness or eye fatigue) was present among 86% of the workers. The three most common symptoms the workers experienced during the last four weeks were eye fatigue (76%), dryness (47%) and photophobia (45%). See Table 1.

Table 1. The frequency of eyestrain during the last four weeks was rated as 0 = never, 1 = occasionally, 2 = a few times per week and 3 = almost daily.

Frequency of eyestrain n = 217					
	Min	Max	Average	Median	Percent*
Smarting	0	3	0.57	0	40.6
Itching	0	3	0.42	0	30.0
Gritty feeling	0	3	0.57	0	37.8
Eye pain	0	3	0.39	0	26.7
Photophobia	0	3	0.73	0	45.2
Redness	0	3	0.42	0	28.1
Teariness	0	3	0.49	0	30.9
Dryness	0	3	0.78	0	47.0
Eye fatigue	0	3	1.28	1	76.0
All eyestrain	0	27	5.65	4	85.7

* Percent with strain ≥ 1

On average, the workers rated their visual ability as 1.2 (median 1), and 9% of the workers rated their visual function as bad. None of the workers rated their vision as very

Table 2. The frequency of musculoskeletal strain during the last four weeks was rated as 0= never, 1= a few times, 2 = a few times a week and 3= almost daily.

Frequency of musculoskeletal strain n = 217				
	Neck	Shoulder*	Upper back*	Arms*
Min	0	0	0	0
Max	3	3	3	3
Average	1.3	1.1	0.7	0.7
Median	1	1	0	0
Percent (>0)	71.9	60.6	41.2	39.4
Percent (>2)	41.6	22.1	15.7	29.4

*n = 216 for Shoulder, Upper back and Arms

bad. The presence of dim vision among the workers was 60%, diplopia 15% and ability to focus/problems changing focus 62%.

The percentage of workers that reported any neck strain was 72%, shoulder strain 61%, strain from the upper back 41% and strain from the arms 39%. See Table 2.

3.2 Risk Assessments

The illuminance recommendations were not fulfilled at 27% of the assessed workplaces and the overall risk for illuminance levels was assessed to be yellow (risk) at 39% and red (high risk) at 10%. When the risk for illuminance was rated as red, the frequency of eyestrain and musculoskeletal strain was higher.

The luminance ratios were assessed to be yellow at 41% of the workplaces, and 19% of them were red. Assessment of the risk of glare showed that 40% of the workplaces were assessed to be yellow risk of glare, and 21% of the workplaces had red risk of glare from luminaires. The overall risk of glare was assessed to be yellow at 42% of the workplaces and red at 24%. When the risk of glare was rated as red, the frequency of eyestrain musculoskeletal strain was almost twice as high.

4 Discussion

VERAM showed that more than 86% of the workers reported eyestrain, with eye fatigue being the most frequent symptom. A feeling of dryness in the eyes was also common among the workers. Studies show that a lower blink frequency is common when performing computer work and focusing on a screen. The photophobia among 45% of the workers may also be connected to glare in the visual environment, as shown in other studies [23]. Taken together, these results are supported by other studies that show about 64–90% of computer work gave some sort of asthenopia or eyestrain [24].

Among the workers, 60% reported dim vision,62% had problems with focusing, and 15% reported diplopia. Only half of the workers that reported dim vision or diplopia rated their visual ability as bad even though they had problems. According to previous studies, glare can affect our ability to focus and therefore cause some of these symptoms. But there might also be some problems with accommodation and/or the ability to converge the eyes, maybe due to presbyopia.

Many of the studied workers reported musculoskeletal strain, especially from neck and shoulders. Other studies have clearly noticed a direct connection between eyestrain and musculoskeletal strain [8, 16]. Many individuals report neck and shoulder pain, which might contribute to lower performance levels and productivity. Studies show that good optical correction and a good visual environment can reduce such symptoms and increase productivity [8].

The risk of glare from luminaires was generally high and shows that the placement or configuration of luminaires is rarely taken into consideration when designing a workplace. The configuration or shape of a luminaire affects the light distribution and the risk for glare. LED panels is frequently installed at workplaces today and have no indirect lighting and often dark surroundings causing a glare situation.

The number of workplaces that did not fulfil the recommended illuminance levels was fairly high. There seems to be correlations between the low illuminance levels and lower performance as well as low illuminance levels and higher subjective strain.

The frequency of the subjective strain increased when the risk of illuminance levels and glare were risk assessed as red, as compared to green. This suggests that having a good visual environment is important. The gathered dataset will be used to analyse associations between subjective strain and objective assessments. It will be interesting to analyse the correlations between eyestrain and other symptoms such as musculoskeletal strain and headache.

5 Conclusion

The purpose of this article was to describe results from visual ergonomic risk assessments using VERAM. We found that many workers report a high frequency of eyestrain and musculoskeletal strain. Visual symptoms such as diplopia or dim vision are also quite frequent. Many of the studied workplaces had glare from luminaires or daylight, as well as insufficient illuminance levels or too high luminance ratio. The risks regarding glare needs to be addressed at workplaces to increase wellbeing. VERAM is a comprehensive, valid and reliable method for assessing risks of visual environments. A screening version of VERAM is under development, to be used as a first step in identifying areas that need more detailed assessment.

References

1. Anshel, J.R.: Visual ergonomics in the workplace. AAOHN J. **55**(10), 414–422 (2007)
2. Long, J., Helland, M.: A multidisciplinary approach to solving computer related vision problems. Ophthalmic Physiol. Opt. **32**(5), 429–435 (2012)
3. Bergqvist, U.O., Knave, B.: Eye discomfort and work with visual display terminals. Scand. J. Work Environ. Health. **20**(1), 27–33 (1994)
4. Knave, B.G., Wibom, R.I., Voss, M., Hedstrom, L.D., Bergqvist, U.O.V.: Work with video display terminals among office employees: 1. Subjective symptoms and discomfort. Scand. J. Work Environ. Hea. **11**(6), 457–466 (1985)

5. Gowrisankaran, S., Sheedy, J.E.: Computer vision syndrome: a review. Work **52**, 303–314 (2015)
6. Rosenfield, M.: Computer vision syndrome (aka digital eye strain). Optom. Pract. **17**(1), 1–10 (2016)
7. Hemphälä, H., Osterhaus, W., Larsson, P.A., Borell, J., Nylén, P.: Towards better lighting recommendations for open surgery. Lighting Res. Technol. **52**, 856–882 (2020)
8. Hemphälä, H., Eklund, J.: A visual ergonomics intervention in mail sorting facilities: effects on eyes, muscles and productivity. Appl. Ergonomics **43**(1), 217–229 (2012)
9. Lin, K.-H., Su, C.-C., Chen, Y.-Y., Chu, P.-C.: the effects of lighting problems on eye symptoms among cleanroom microscope workers. Int. J. Environ. Res. Public Health **16**(1), 101 (2019)
10. Boyce, P.R.: Review: the impact of light in buildings on human health. Indoor Built Environ. **19**(1), 8–20 (2010)
11. Boyce, P.R., Wilkins, A.: Visual discomfort indoors. Lighting Res. Technol. **50**(1), 98–114 (2018)
12. Boyce, P.: Human Factors in Lighting (2014). Taylor & Francis, Cornwall, ISBN 0-7484-0950-52003
13. Glimne, S., Seimyr, G.Ö., Ygge, J., Nylén, P., Brautaset, R.L.: Measuring glare induced visual fatigue by fixation disparity variation. Work **45**, 431–437 (2013)
14. Fostervold, K., Nersveen, J.: Proportions of direct and indirect indoor lighting — the effect on health, well-being and cognitive performance of office workers. Lighting Res. Technol. **40**(3), 175–200 (2008)
15. Kaldenberg, J., Richter, H.O., Zetterlund, C., Lundqvist, L.-O.: Eye-neck interactions triggered by visually deficient computer work. Work **39**(1), 67–78 (2011)
16. Helland, M., Horgen, G., Kvikstad, T.M., Garthus, T., Aarås, A.: Will musculoskeletal and visual stress change when Visual Display Unit (VDU) operators move from small offices to an ergonomically optimized office landscape? Appl. Ergonomics **42**(6), 839–845 (2011)
17. Hemphala, H., Nylen, P., Eklund, J.: Optimal correction in spectacles: Intervention effects on eyestrain and musculoskeletal discomfort among postal workers. Work-a J. Prev. Assess. Rehabil. **47**(3), 329–337 (2014)
18. Veitch, J.A., Newsham, G.R.: Lighting quality and energy-efficiency effects on task performance, mood, health, satisfaction, and comfort. J. Illum. Eng. Soc. **27**(1), 107–129 (1998)
19. Juslén, H.T., Wouters, M.C.H.M., Tenner, A.D.: Lighting level and productivity: a field study in the electronics industry. Ergonomics **50**(4), 615–624 (2007)
20. Zetterberg, C., Heiden, M., Lindberg, P., Nylén, P., Hemphälä, H.: Reliability of a new risk assessment method for visual ergonomics. Int. J. Ind. Ergonomics **72**, 71–79 (2019)
21. Heiden, M., Zetterberg, C., Lindberg, P., Nylén, P., Hemphälä, H.: Validity of a computer-based risk assessment method for visual ergonomics. Int. J. Ind. Ergonomics **72**, 180–187 (2019)
22. SS-EN. 12464–1 Light and Lighting - Lighting of Workplaces - Part 1 - Indoor Workplaces. Swedish Standard, SIS Förlag AB (2011)
23. Hashemi, H., Saatchi, M., Yekta, A., Ali, B., Ostadimoghaddam, H., Nabovati, P., et al.: High prevalence of asthenopia among a population of university students. J. Ophthalmic. Vis. Res. **14**(4), 474–482 (2019)
24. Anshel, J.R.: Visual Ergonomics Handbook. CRC Press, Boca Raton (2005)

Effects of the Use of a Widescreen Display on Information Retrieval

Kaoru Honda[⊠]

Yamagata University, Yamagata 990-8560, Japan
honda@human.kj.yamagata-u.ac.jp

Abstract. In recent years, PC screens have become wider and larger. The nature of our visual field is that visual acuity is at its highest when someone is looking at the center of something, making the central part look the clearest. This study used a widescreen display and a traditional display depicting a character to be retrieved at the center of the screen. Ten characters were displayed at 10 locations at the right or left edge of the screen. The study subjects were then asked to retrieve a particular character from among the 10 characters. Subsequently, this study analyzed the relationship between retrieval time and the display location of the character in the widescreen display and the traditional display. The effects of the use of the widescreen display on information retrieval were examined. Focused attention at the center of a screen can delay or even prevent the user's awareness of information displayed just above the center of the right edge, at the center of the right edge, and just below the center of the right edge. Information should be displayed on wide screens while considering these unique human visual characteristics.

Keywords: Widescreen display · Display location · Information retrieval · Visual field

1 Introduction

Recently, the number of widescreen displays for personal computers (PCs), the screens of which are larger and wider than those of conventional displays, has increased. In particular, the screen aspect ratio of displays for desktop computers has increased from 5:4 to 16:9 (the screen expands to the left and right), and the screen size has increased from approximately 17 in. to more than 24 in. [1]. The screen aspect ratio of 16:9 was adopted for high definition television. This ratio is suitable for movie viewing and does not presume visual display terminal work. When the screen size increases, the area in which information is displayed also increases. As a result, the amount of information to be displayed at the same time increases. However, because the amount of information that humans can process at one time is limited, there is apprehension that information displayed on widescreens may be noticed more slowly or overlooked (i.e., that the number of errors may increase). The visual information processing ability (visual field) of humans is such that an object at the center of the visual field can be clearly seen, but an object becomes more difficult to see as the distance between the object and the

© The Author(s), under exclusive license to Springer Nature Switzerland AG 2021
N. L. Black et al. (Eds.): IEA 2021, LNNS 220, pp. 736–741, 2021.
https://doi.org/10.1007/978-3-030-74605-6_93

center of the visual field increases [2]. Therefore, we must examine the effects of a large, widescreen display on the retrieval of information displayed at the periphery of the screen when the viewer focuses attention at the center of the screen.

This study used a widescreen display and a traditional display depicting a character (the Roman alphabet) to be retrieved at the center of the screen. Ten characters (the Roman alphabet) were displayed at 10 locations (one character at each location) at the right or left edge of the screen (five locations at the right edge and five locations at the left edge). The study subjects were then asked to retrieve a particular character from among the 10 characters. Subsequently, this study analyzed the relationship between retrieval time and the display location of the character in the widescreen display and the traditional display. Thus, the effects of the use of the widescreen display on information retrieval were examined.

2 Experiment

2.1 Subjects

The subjects were 10 university students aged 18–23 years. Before the experiment, each subject's eyesight and visual field were confirmed to be normal. The subjects were asked to get a full night's sleep by going to bed by 11:00 pm before the experiment to avoid sleepiness during the tasks.

2.2 Environment

Each subject was asked to sit on a chair in a comfortable position. The screen of the display was perpendicular (90°) to the desk, and the height of the display was adjusted so that the center of the screen was at eye level for each subject. Because the ideal working distance between the PC screen and a user is said to be 600 ± 150 mm (ISO 9241-5) [3], the distance between the screen and the subject's eye was set at 600 mm. Subjects were able to move their eyes as they searched for characters. The subjects were given the following instructions: "sit back in the chair with your back touching the backrest; do not to move your face closer to the display, and do not lean on the desk during the experiment."

2.3 Methods

The experiment used a 24-in. widescreen display (G2410; Dell Inc.). If different devices were used for the widescreen display and the traditional display, there would be differences in the character size, color, and brightness between the two devices. Therefore, the experiment used one display with a widescreen (531 mm × 299 mm) or a standard screen (374 mm × 299 mm), which was artificially produced. To examine the effects of the use of the widescreen display on information retrieval, the height of the display was unified to be 299 mm (see Fig. 1). The screen aspect ratio was 16:9 for the widescreen and 5:4 for the standard screen.

The experiment was explained to each subject, who then performed a preliminary training task for five minutes. After confirming that each subject understood the task, the

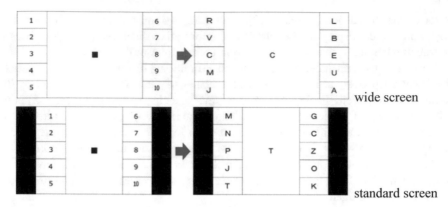

wide screen

standard screen

Fig. 1. An example of the experiment wide and standard screen. (display location No.)

experiment was launched. As shown in Fig. 1, a quadrangle was displayed at the center of the screen so that the mouse pointer and the fixation point could be placed at the center of the screen. When the left mouse button was used to click on this quadrangle, a character (alphabet A–Z) was displayed at the center of the screen, and 10 other characters were simultaneously displayed at 10 locations at the right or left edge of the screen. The subjects were asked to find and click the left mouse button on a character that was identical to the character displayed at the center of the screen (a retrieval task). The time between the display of a character at the center of the screen and the click of the left mouse button on a character identical to the character displayed at the center of the screen was recorded as the "retrieval time." When two seconds had passed without clicking the mouse button, the retrieval task was determined to be timed out. If you click the wrong character, the data is excluded. Both the presented characters and the display location were in a random order. The subjects were asked to perform retrieval tasks on each of the screens for 15 min (for a total time of 30 min). The subjects took a rest in the sitting position for 10 min between the tasks on the widescreen and those on the standard screen. After completing the retrieval tasks, the subjects were asked to fill out a subjective evaluation questionnaire. The background of the screen was white, and the characters in the retrieval tasks were black. The brightness of the white portion on the screen was 256 cd/m^2.

3   Results

3.1   Retrieval Time of a Character

Figure 2 shows the response time at each display location (10 locations at the right or left edge of the screen). Here, the average response time of the subjects is shown to shed light on overall tendencies. The retrieval time of a character was longer on the widescreen than on the standard screen, except at display location 5 (the lower-left corner). On the widescreen, the retrieval time was longest at display location 6 (the upper-right corner), followed by display locations 5 (the lower-left corner), 1 (the upper-left corner), and 10 (the lower-right corner), in that order. Moreover, the retrieval time was shortest at display location 8 (the center of the right edge), followed by display location 3 (the center of the left edge). A two-way analysis of variance using the factors of the type of the screen and the display location revealed that the differences between the screen type and the display location were statistically significant ($F(1,19) = 49.08$, $p < 0.01$); ($F(9,19) = 27.84$, $p < 0.01$).

To compare the retrieval time at each display location on the widescreen with that on the standard screen, the difference in the retrieval time at each display location between the widescreen and the standard screen was obtained. Figure 3 shows the obtained results. At display locations 7 (just above the center of the right edge), 8 (the center of the right edge), and 9 (just below the center of the right edge), the difference exceeded 100 ms. A negative value was observed only at display location 5 (the lower-left corner).

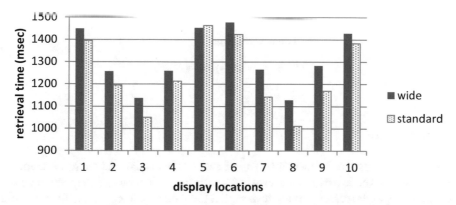

Fig. 2. The retrieval time of each display location.

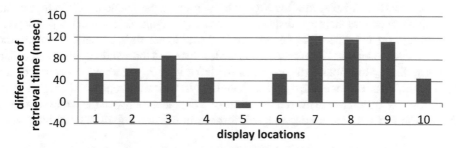

Fig. 3. The difference of retrieval time between widescreen and standard screen.

3.2 Subjective Evaluation

Figure 4 shows the results of the subjective evaluation. Here, the subjects were asked to identify "a display location at which the character was quickly found" and "a display location at which the character was slowly found." As shown in this figure, many subjects identified display locations 3 (the center of the left edge) and 8 (the center of the right edge) as areas at which the character was quickly found. Many subjects also identified display locations 1 (the upper-left corner), 5 (the lower-left corner), 6 (the upper-right corner), and 10 (the lower-right corner) as areas at which the character was slowly found. This tendency was observed both on the widescreen and the standard screen.

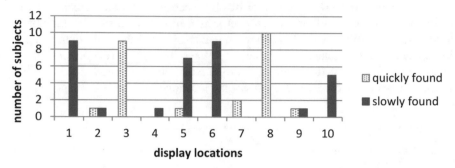

Fig. 4. A subjective evaluation.

4 Discussion

This experiment used a distance of 600 mm between the display and the subject, and the subjects were asked to perform retrieval tasks with Roman characters. A quadrangle was first displayed at the center of the screen so that the mouse pointer and the fixation point could be placed at the center of the screen. Between the widescreen and the standard screen, there was a difference in the moving distance of the mouse pointer required to click on a character displayed at the edge of the screen. In particular, the difference in the moving distance was largest at display locations 1 (the upper-left corner), 5 (the lower-left corner), 6 (the upper-right corner), and 10 (the lower-right corner). However, the difference in the retrieval time between the widescreen and the standard screen exceeded 80 ms at display locations 3 (the center of the left edge), 7 (just above the center of the right edge), 8 (the center of the right edge), and 9 (just below the center of the right edge). Therefore, the difference in the retrieval time of a character between the widescreen and the standard screen was not due to the difference in the moving distance of the mouse pointer.

Both on the widescreen and the standard screen, the retrieval time was longer at display locations 1 (the upper-left corner), 5 (the lower-left corner), 6 (the upper-right corner), and 10 (the lower-right corner) than at other display locations. A similar result was also observed in the subjective evaluation. Therefore, the subjects' line of sight was said to be difficult to move toward the four corners of the screen. The difference in the retrieval time of a character between the widescreen and the standard screen exceeded 100 ms at display locations 7 (just above the center of the right edge), 8 (the center of the right edge), and 9 (just below the center of the right edge). These three display locations were at the right edge of the screen. The human effective field of view lies in a range that can be used or that functions when a certain visual task is performed [4], usually 30° in the horizontal direction (15° to the right and left of center [5]). Using this assumption of 30°, the 600-mm distance between the subject and the screen gave an effective field of view of approximately 322 mm in the horizontal direction. However, the width of the widescreen display used in this experiment was 531 mm, which was considerably wider than that effective field of view. When monitoring a display or a dashboard, humans first look at the upper-left corner, then move the line of sight to the upper-right corner, the lower-left corner, and finally the lower-right corner [6]. When information is displayed on a screen, humans first look at the left side of the screen. In the case of a large and wide screen display, the right side of the screen is not included in the field of view. Therefore, in this experiment, the retrieval time of a character was longer on the widescreen than on the standard screen. When a large, widescreen display is used, information discovery is presumed to be delayed at these three display locations.

5 Conclusion

The human effective field of view is limited, and the operation of a PC is characterized by a small distance between the user and the screen. The use of a large, widescreen display is expected to result in increasing delays in the discovery of information displayed at the right side of the screen. Focused attention at the center of a screen can delay or even prevent the user's awareness of information displayed just above the center of the right edge, at the center of the right edge, and just below the center of the right edge. Information should be displayed on wide screens while considering these unique human visual characteristics. When the edge of a screen is used, measures to alert the user to that area must be taken.

Acknowledgements. I would like to express my appreciation to Dr. Tadasuke Monma. This work was supported by JSPS KAKENHI Grant Number 19K03051.

References

1. Information Terminals and Technologies Committee: Marketing research report about the information terminal. JEITA, IS-17–1, pp. 1–8, Tokyo (2017)
2. Alpern, M.: Movements of the Eyes. In: Davson, H. (ed.) The Eye, vol. 3, pp. 3–5. Academic Press, New York and London (1962)
3. ISO 9241–5: Ergonomic requirements for office work with visual display terminals (VDTs)? Part 5, Workstation layout and postural requirements. International Organization for Standardization (1998)
4. Mackworth, N.H.: Stimulus density limits the useful field of view. In: Monty, R.A., Senders, J. (eds.) Eye movements and psychological processes, pp. 307–321. Erlbaum, Hillsdale, NJ (1976)
5. Hatada, T.: Characteristics of human vision for VDT. Japanese J. Ergon. **22**(2), 45–52 (1986)
6. Fukuda, T., Watanabe, T.: Human Scape: Explore the world of vision. JUSE Press, pp. 171–207, Tokyo (1996)

Dynamic Signs: Appropriate Contrast and Speed for Older Adults and Low Vision

Nana Itoh[1]([⊠]) [iD], Ken Sagawa[1], Hiroshi Watanabe[1], and Reiko Sakata[2]

[1] National Institute of Advanced Industrial Science and Technology (AIST), Tokyo, Japan
nana-itoh@aist.go.jp
[2] Mitsubishi Electric Corporation, Tokyo, Japan

Abstract. The effects of contrast and speed of dynamic signs of visibility were experimentally examined. Thirty young adults, 30 older adults, and 20 persons with low vision participated in the experiment, wherein images of five different categories, namely lines, Japanese words, English words, simple figures, numbers, and pictograms were presented with varying speed and contrast. According to the results, an appropriate range of the speed and contrast of the dynamic signs was obtained considering older adults and persons with low vision. For persons with low vision, the results indicated an appropriate speed of 1.09 or less with a contrast of 0.89 or higher. In addition, it was found that the correct response rate of dynamic signs for young adults is high regardless of the visibility rating, whereas the correct response rate for persons with low vision is lower than that of young and older adults, even under conditions of "easy to see." The results of this study will be applied to the descriptions of accessibility that are a part of a series of dynamic sign standards under development.

Keywords: Dynamic signs · Visibility · Contrast · Speed · Accessible design · Older adults · Low vision

1 Introduction

Dynamic signs are a new technology for projecting additional information onto the building walls, floors, and streets. Recently, the number of cases in which dynamic signs are used is increasing because the contents can be easily changed according to the situation and users. Because these dynamic signs are typically used in public spaces, ensuring visibility is a critical consideration along with accessibility.

In terms of accessibility of visual information, some previous studies have discussed legibility for older adults and low vision (Sagawa and Itoh 2006). (Itoh et al. 2018), (Legge et al. 1997), (Arditi and Cho 2007). Numerous studies on static displays have been conducted. However, there is still no study on the visibility of a moving image of sign displays and their accessibility. One of the advantages of dynamic signs' visibility is that they can easily attract attention by moving or flashing. However, older adults and persons with low vision do not always see as well as younger adults with no impairments because of their reduced visual function.

To ensure the visibility of dynamic signs, as in the case of other static signs, it is important to have sufficient contrast against the background. In addition, speed is also important in terms of being able to follow the sign with one's eyes.

Therefore, in this study, the contrast and speed of the dynamic signs were randomly varied to investigate what range of each element is sufficient to ensure visibility for low vision and older adults.

In addition, contrast sensitivity depends on the fineness of the visual display, which is known as the special frequency. Therefore, the study investigated the effects of the contrast and speed on five types of relatively simple information (see Fig. 1) including single lines, numbers and symbols, English and Japanese words such as "EXIT," and pictographic signs such as toilets, assuming that the visibility of actual signs varies depending on the complexity of the information.

2 Method

Dynamic signs were projected onto the floor in front of participants and moved from right to left or vice versa with various contrasts and speeds. The visual distance between the participants sitting in a chair and images was approximately 1.1 m, visual angle of images approximately 18.9°, which is roughly equal to the size of a 50 cm square as seen by a person walking at a 1.5 m eye level.

Appropriate contrast and speed of dynamic signs for older adults and low-vision persons were investigated by conducting subjective evaluations of visibility. After the dynamic signs were projected, participants were asked to select the pattern of images to match the patters they saw and to perform the five-scale subjective evaluation of visibility for each image: very difficult to see, difficult to see, neither difficult nor easy (Intermediate level), easy to see, and very easy to see. After responding to the subjective evaluation on visibility, all participants selected what they saw from the list of images.

Figure 1 shows five different categories of images used in the experiment: lines, Japanese words, English words, simple figures, and numbers and pictograms were used. Each image category had several variations to prevent duplication. Three different Michelson contrasts (0.05, 0.28, and 0.87) and five different speeds: 0.27, 0.54, 1.09, 2.17, and 4.34 m/s (13.99, 27.58, 52.71, 89.21, and 126.24°/s) were employed for

Fig. 1. Visual information presented as dynamic signs used in the experiment. Three of each of the signs from each category except "Lines" are selected and randomly presented to participants. All signs in the "Lines" category were presented three times randomly to the participants.

those images. It was also confirmed that all used character sizes were larger than the size of "easy to read" when it was projected stationary with high contrast in to examine only the effects of various contrasts and speeds.

A total of 360 images with different contents, contrasts, and speeds were presented. Thirty young adults (22.5 ± 2.0), 30 older adults (69.5 ± 4.6), and 20 low-vision persons (56.9 ± 10.7) participated.

3   Results

3.1   Effects of Contrast and Speed

Figures 2, 3 and 4 show effects of the contrast and speed on visibility of numbers and figures, english words, and pictograms of dynamic signs. The vertical axis represents averages of subjective evaluation. The white bar shows the score higher than 4: easy to see. The gray bar shows the score between 3: neither difficult nor easy and 4: easy to see. The black bar shows the score lower than 3: neither difficult nor easy (intermediate level. it also includes 2: difficult to see, 1: very difficult to see, and 0: impossible to see. the numbers in the balloons show the average.

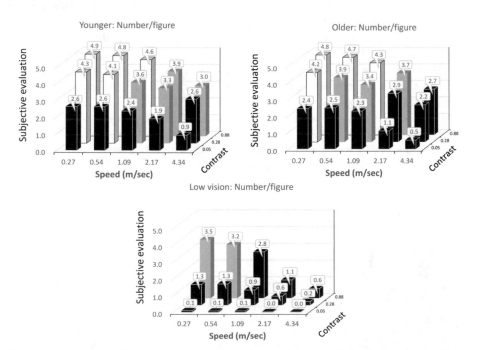

Fig. 2. Averages of subjective evaluation of numbers and figures of the dynamic sign. White, gray, and black bars indicate the difference in the average of the subjective evaluation of visibility. The white bar shows scores higher than 4: easy to see. The gray bar shows scores between 3: neither difficult nor easy and 4: easy to see. The black bar shows scores lower than 3: neither difficult nor easy (intermediate level). It also includes 2: difficult to see, 1: very difficult to see, and 0: impossible to see.

The horizontal axis represents speed of dynamic signs: 0.27, 0.54, 1.09, 2.17, and 4.34 m/s (13.99, 27.58, 52.71, 89.21, and 126.24°/s), whereas the depth axis represents the contrast of the dynamic signs (0.05, 0.28, and 0.87). The three graphs have the following points in common. When the contrast is high and the speed is low, the subjective evaluation scores of young, older, and low-vision participants are relatively good and the scores decrease when the contrast decreases or the speed increases. However, younger participants have more "5: very easy to see" or "4: easy to see" scores and fewer scores of "2: hard to see" or "1: very hard to see." In contrast, older participants have fewer scores of "5: very easy to see" or "4: easy to see" and more scores of "2: hard to see" and "1: very hard to see." In the case of the participants with low vision, the highest score was lower than "4: easy to see," and a large number of participants responded with scores "1: very hard to see" or "0: impossible to see." Furthermore, when the contrast is low, the scores for the low-vision participants were less than 1, even at low speeds. This indicates that persons with low vision have considerable difficulties in seeing signs at low contrast regardless of speed.

In addition, low-vision persons exhibit a steep decline in some areas when compared to young and older adults. For example, for speed, this decline is between 1.09 m/s and 2.17 m/s, and for contrast, between 0.29 and 0.05. These differences could be considered as one of the indicators in the presentation of dynamic signs that take into account persons with low vision.

Furthermore, for any image, the range where the average value of visibility is at least 3 or more is considered desirable.

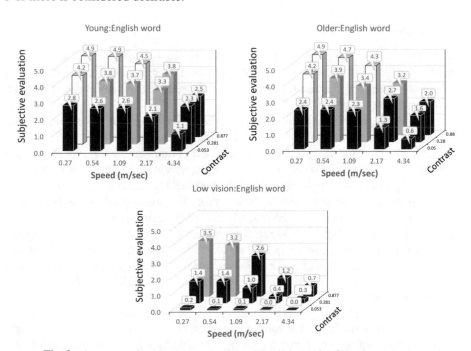

Fig. 3. Averages of subjective evaluation of English words of the dynamic sign.

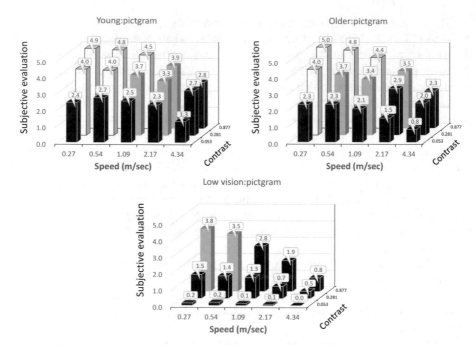

Fig. 4. Averages of subjective evaluation of pictograms of the dynamic sign.

3.2 Effects of Image Types

Upper Fig. 5 shows a comparison of the visibility of young, older, and low-vision participants when they see high contrast (0.88) images of numbers or figures, words, and pictograms. Lower Fig. 5 lower the correct rates of dynamic signs when choosing from a list of presented images.

Young participants have differences in visibility in images at the highest speed: 4.34 m/s, while older participants exhibited the same tendency at speeds of 2.17 m/s and above. In both cases, the ratings decrease in the order of numbers and figures, pictograph signs, and English letters. However, in the case of low-vision participants, the visibility of pictograms was relatively higher compared to other images when the speed is 2.17 m/s.

The correct rate does not decrease considerably for young participants even when the visibility rating decreases. In the case of older participants, the correct rate slightly decreases at the highest speed: 4.34 m/s. Low-vision participant, however, have a high correct rate only when the speed is 1.09 m/s or lower, but the correct rate decreases rapidly when the speed is higher. This also indicates that individuals with low vision encounter difficulties in seeing signs accurately if the speed is higher than 2.17 m/s, even with high contrast.

In addition, in the case of young and older participants, it was found that the complexity of the images also affected the correct rate when the speed was high (e.g., 2.17 m/s for older participants and 4.34 m/s for young participants.). Furthermore, older adults answered relatively correctly single-digit numbers or simple figures compared with pictograms and English words. However, low-vision participants tend to achieve a better correct rate score for pictograms than for numbers or figures and English words.

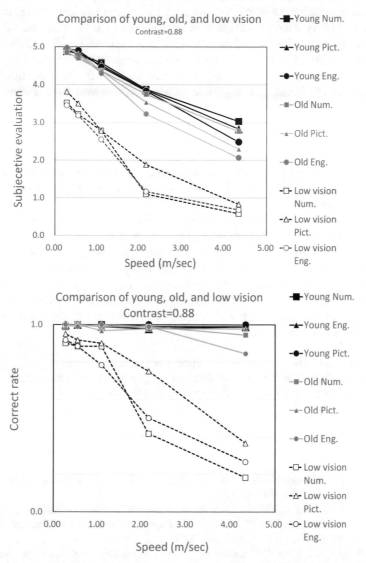

Fig. 5. (Upper) Comparison of subjective evaluations of young participants, older participants, and low-vision participants as the function of speed. (Lower) Comparison of the correct rate of young participants, older participants, and low-vision participants as the function of speed. Data for high contrast images: numbers or figures, English words, and pictograms.

4 Discussion and Conclusion

The experiment revealed the good visibility range of contrast and speed of dynamic signs for young participants, older participants, and participants with low vision. The present findings indicate that individuals with low vision can also see dynamic signs relatively accurately if the contrast of the image is high (0.88) and its speed is low (less than 1.09 m/s). It was also found that in the case of low-vision participants, the visibility score of pictograms was better compared with other images when the speed was 2.17 m/s. It is assumed that they may not be able to see the details of the images; thus, they may judge based on rough outlines. If people with low vision have such a view, it is also possible that some pictogram signs are easier to distinguish by their external shape than numbers and symbols of the same size or English letters that do not considerably in size or length. However, in this experiment, the answers of the correct rate were measured by selecting from those presented on paper to the participants; therefore, all comparisons were relative. This study did not determine whether the individuals with low vision could recognize individual pictograms accurately. Further investigation on the visibility of individuals with low vision is required.

As for correct rates of low-vision participants, they are always lower than those of the young and older participants, even when the evaluation is "easy to see." Therefore, for persons with low vision, it would be preferable to have other ways of considerations, such as to be informed in advance, provide simultaneously additional sensory information, or remove as many unnecessary restrictions as possible, and provide a time to read or space where people can approach the sign to reduce the chance of missing or misreading it. The results of this experiment will be applied to the international standardization of accessibility of dynamic signs.

Acknowledgement. These results were obtained through implementation of the project "International Standardization Relating to Dynamic Signing (Japanese Standards Association)" as part of a 2019 initiative by the Ministry of Economy, Trade and Industry.

References

Sagawa, K., Itoh, N.: Legible font size of a Japanese single character for older People. In: Proceedings of IEA, CD-ROM (2006)

Itoh, N., Lin, Q., Shimizu, T., Uchida, J., Ohyama, J., Sagawa, K.: Effects of luminance of projected letters on legibility. In: CIE 2017 Midterm Meetings and Conference on Smarter Lighting for Better Life. https://doi.org/10.25039/x44 (2018)

Legge, G.E., Ahn, S.J., Klitz, T.S., Luebker, A.: The visual span in normal and low vision. Vision Res. **37**(14), 1999–2010 (1997). https://doi.org/10.1016/S0042-6989(97)00017-5

Arditi, A., Cho, J.: Letter case and text legibility in normal and low vision. Vis. Res. **47**(19), 2499–505 (2007). https://doi.org/10.1016/j.visres.2007.06.010

Visual Ergonomics in a Virtual World: Examples of Lighting Assessments Conducted in Cyberspace

Jennifer Long[1,2](✉)

[1] Jennifer Long Visual Ergonomics, Katoomba, NSW 2780, Australia
jlong@visualergonomics.com.au

[2] School of Optometry and Vision Science, UNSW, Sydney, NSW 2052, Australia

Abstract. Although the COVID-19 pandemic has placed restrictions on travel and access to workplaces within Australia, people are still working, often from home, and may experience visual ergonomics issues associated with their work. This paper presents two case examples of visual ergonomics assessments conducted virtually: one for a large office where there were reports of reflected glare on computer displays, and another for a self-employed worker who experienced headaches associated with the lighting in her home office. In both cases it was not possible to conduct an onsite assessment due to COVID-19 travel restrictions. The cases demonstrate that virtual visual ergonomics assessments can be successful (1) if a triage is conducted prior to the assessment to confirm that the strategy is suitable, and (2) if there is good collaboration between the ergonomist and the worker during the assessment. A virtual assessment may also confer considerable financial savings to the workplace. In the case examples presented in this paper it was possible to observe the nature of the presenting problem and provide advice to mitigate the issue. It is not possible to report compliance with lighting standards without measuring the lighting in-situ.

Keywords: Visual ergonomics · Lighting · Virtual assessment · Telehealth · Glare · Migraines

1 Introduction

Telehealth refers to health services provided virtually, rather than in-person. The service can be categorized as synchronous whereby the assessor and the person being assessed have a conversation in real-time (for example, direct communication by telephone or by teleconference), or asynchronous whereby information or images (for example, photographs, videos, written questionnaires) are captured onsite and then sent to an assessor for analysis. Telehealth offers many advantages, including the ability for people in remote or regional areas to access healthcare services [1, 2] and cost savings for service delivery [2, 3].

Telehealth can be used for the delivery of ergonomics assessments. For example, Baker and Jacobs report the results of a study with 30 participants in which computer workstations were remotely assessed using photographs [4], and Liebregts and co-authors describe how 23 workers at computer workstations were assessed by taking photographs from different viewing angles and then analysing the images using the Rapid Office Strain Assessment (ROSA) tool [5]. Both papers reported that the online assessments tended to over-identify ergonomics problems, that is, detect issues that might be considered less severe when assessed in-person.

Visual ergonomics assessments can be conducted with tools such as the Visual Ergonomics Risk Assessment Method (VERAM). This is a two-part process in which the worker rates their workplace for eyestrain, visual symptoms, lighting conditions and musculoskeletal discomfort, and then a trained evaluator makes objective onsite measurements of the work area, for example, measurements of illuminance and luminance [6]. There are also published lighting questionnaires that ask workers to rate the quality of the lighting in their workspace [7]. However, there are no published reports describing virtual visual ergonomics assessments, most likely because of the limitations in their scope, for example, it can be difficult to assess the nuances of the visual environment when viewed online, and it is not possible to measure lighting parameters such as illuminance or luminance using photographs taken by a worker onsite.

On the 11th March 2020 the World Health Organization declared COVID-19 a global pandemic [8]. In Australia this resulted in a ban on overseas travel, intermittent border closures between Australian states and recommendations from the government to reduce unnecessary travel. Many workers started to work from home and communicate with colleagues and clients virtually via teleconference platforms such as Zoom and Microsoft Teams. Some businesses required their employees to physically attend their workplace, but placed restrictions on visitors attending the workplace. This was particularly an issue for critical infrastructure industries where a COVID-19 outbreak within the workplace could have dire consequences for service delivery. These responses to the COVID-19 pandemic create a challenge for conducting onsite assessments when visual ergonomics problems are reported in a workplace.

This paper provides two case examples of visual ergonomics assessments conducted virtually over a teleconference platform:

- A large office-based workplace where reflections were reported on computer displays.
- A microbusiness where the business owner was experiencing headaches from the lighting in her home office.

It was not possible to conduct a site assessment for either case due to COVID-19 travel restrictions. The cases have been deidentified to preserve anonymity.

2 Overview of the Assessments

Both visual ergonomics assessments described in this paper were client initiated: the client had identified an issue in their workplace, conducted a risk assessment, and determined that they required visual ergonomics advice to resolve the issue. A triage was conducted prior to the assessment by the ergonomist over the telephone and by email to determine whether a virtual assessment was a suitable course of action.

A formal risk assessment tool, such as VERAM, was not used in these cases because the client had already identified the nature of the problem in their workplace. Instead, the assessment structure was fluid: it was driven by the client's needs and by observations made by the ergonomist during the assessment.

Methods used during the assessment included (1) a conversation with the client to better understand the problem (2) observation of the workplace via a digital medium (3) instructing the client to make small interventions to test the effect of the intervention on the problem, for example, "switch off the light", and (4) a discussion with the client about possible remedies for the problem.

3 Example 1: Reflected Glare on Computer Displays in a Large Office

3.1 Problem

Office workers reported reflected glare on computer displays, and had attempted to minimize the reflections by switching off the ceiling luminaires. The workplace manager requested advice how to best mitigate the problem.

3.2 Virtual Assessment

The ergonomist conducted a virtual assessment using the Microsoft Teams teleconference platform. The onsite manager provided a virtual tour of the workplace using a camera on a tablet device. Trial actions to evaluate the reflected light were achieved by the ergonomist giving instructions to the onsite manager (for example, "turn the camera to the left/right", "switch the lights on/off"), observing these actions virtually, and making screen shots of the teleconference for more detailed analysis and for documentation in a report.

3.3 Outcomes

The ergonomist worked with the workplace manager to develop a solution strategy. The purpose was to provide information about alternative lighting and computer displays so that the manager could investigate the most appropriate solution for the business.

The range of solutions suggested to the business were determined by making observations during the assessment, assessing screen shots taken during the assessment, reading supporting documentation supplied by the workplace about the computer displays and the lighting, and taking into account interventions that the workplace had already tried.

4 Example 2: Headaches from Lighting in a Home-Based Office

4.1 Problem

A self-employed worker experienced an increased frequency of migraine headaches that she attributed to the lighting in her home office. Her normal occupation included meeting clients face to face and running workshops and courses in dedicated training facilities. With COVID-19 restrictions preventing travel and group interactions, the worker now exclusively conducted her work via teleconference, with up to 10 hours per day working online.

The worker had recently had an eye examination and her spectacle prescription was up-to-date. She had also engaged another professional for advice about her workstation furniture and set-up. Light was a known trigger for her migraines, so the worker requested assistance with setting up the lighting in her office for online meetings so that it was comfortable and did not exacerbate her headaches.

4.2 Virtual Assessment

A virtual assessment was conducted using the Zoom teleconference platform. The worker communicated via two different digital devices during the assessment: her desktop computer for general discussion with the ergonomist, and a mobile phone to show features of the office or to demonstrate a side-view of her posture.

The virtual assessment included interviewing the worker to better understand the nature of her headaches, giving instructions to the worker, for example, "Hold the phone-camera up to the ceiling so I can identify what type of lamp is in the light fitting", and observing her posture while she was sitting at her workstation.

4.3 Outcomes

The ergonomist developed a strategy in conjunction with the worker so that the worker could investigate the most appropriate solution for her business. This included recommendations for general lighting, workstation lighting and soft furnishings, and advice for the use of her computer monitor.

The range of solutions were determined by asking the worker what interventions she had already tried, drawing on experience gained from in-person assessments pre-COVID-19 for workers who had experienced similar problems in their workplace, and investigating products online that could improve the worker's visual comfort.

5 Discussion

5.1 Virtual Assessments Can Be Successful

This paper reports two successful virtual visual ergonomics assessments. The impetus for conducting the assessments using virtual media was COVID-19 travel restrictions.

The virtual assessments were successful for two reasons. Firstly, a triage was conducted prior to the assessment to ensure that the virtual assessment was a suitable course of action. Secondly, there was good collaboration between the ergonomist and the onsite manager/business owner. This echoes an observation made by Ritchie and co-authors that telehealth *"relies on the client taking a very active role in the process"* [9]. Part of the active role in these virtual assessments included the client setting up the technology in their workplace to enable photographs and video (these were "the eyes" of the ergonomist). It also required additional planning compared to an onsite assessment, for example, providing the client advance instructions about what would be required during the assessment. Similar observations have been documented by Ritchie and co-authors [9].

5.2 Quantifying Lighting Parameters

Under normal circumstances it would be preferable to undertake a lighting assessment onsite to observe the lighting, see how it illuminates the space, and to quantify lighting parameters such as illuminance and luminance. For some organisations, a report that quantifies the lighting and describes compliance with lighting standards is integral to justifying changes to workplace infrastructure. This was circumvented in case example #1 by including photographs of reflected light on the computer monitors to support the recommendations given in the report.

The worker in case study #2 had access to an illuminance meter and potentially could have placed the meter in locations according to instructions, for example, "Place the lux meter on the desk". However, this would not have added information relevant to the problem-at-hand: the more appropriate light-measurement tool would have been a luminance meter to measure the luminance (apparent brightness) of light sources, the ceiling and the walls.

There are many potential sources of error when measuring light [10], for example, casting a shadow over the photocell of an illuminance meter while making a measurement. It is also advisable that light meters are calibrated [7], otherwise the measurements may not be accurate. Therefore, it may not be valid to use the results of lighting measurements made by a worker, especially if the measurements need to be used to demonstrate compliance with lighting standards.

5.3 Financial Advantages

A virtual visual ergonomics assessment might not be indicated for all presenting problems. However, when it is suitable, there can be significant financial advantages [2, 3].

If the assessments described in this paper were conducted onsite, the ergonomist would have travelled to each site by a combination of rail, road and air. The relative cost savings for conducting each of the virtual assessments was calculated using Eq. 1.

$$[\text{Invoice cost(virtual assessment)}/\text{Invoice cost(onsite assessment)}]\% \tag{1}$$

Cost savings were achieved because there was no billable component for travel time to attend onsite nor for disbursements such as airfares and transfers. Table 1 shows that there was a 50% cost saving for the large office organization and an 83% cost saving for the microbusiness. This is a considerable price difference and could be an enabler for smaller size businesses to access visual ergonomics services.

Table 1. Financial savings achieved by conducting a virtual ergonomics assessment

	#1: Large office, reflected glare on computer monitors	#2: Microbusiness, headaches from lighting
Relative cost of the virtual assessment compared to an onsite assessment	50%	17%

No additional costs were incurred by the ergonomist or the clients for these virtual assessments because both parties were able to use teleconference equipment (for example, digital devices, web-camera, microphone) and services (for example, internet access, teleconference platforms) already owned or used within their respective businesses.

5.4 Overcoming Challenges

Participants in a virtual assessment require some technical literacy [9]. This issue was highlighted in case example #2 when the internet dropped-out multiple times during the assessment (at both the client's side and the ergonomist's side). Technical literacy [1, 2], availability of technology [2] and internet reliability [1] have been cited as barriers to telehealth. Good humour and patience is required for both parties, as well as a contingency plan for such events, for example, being able to dial into the assessment with an alternative mobile device, and having a power cord to charge the mobile phone because teleconference applications can quickly drain the phone battery.

Parallax errors are a possible source of error when conducting ergonomics assessments, for example, taking a photograph from an angle that does not accurately depict a worker's posture [5]. This potential problem was overcome by observations in real-time, whereby the worker in case study #2 was instructed to adjust the location of her mobile phone so her posture could be more easily observed.

Virtual interaction is not embraced by all people, with criticisms that face-to-face interaction is essential for building rapport. Ritchie and co-authors suggest that one option for building rapport between a worker and the assessor is to send a photograph and biography of the assessor in advance [9]. The worksite manager and the worker who participated in these virtual visual ergonomics assessments were comfortable with telecommunication platforms. Nevertheless, they had access to the ergonomist's website and were able to read her credentials before the assessment, they had several telephone conversations as well as email correspondence with the ergonomist prior to the assessment, and "chat time" was included at the start of the assessment for both parties to get to know each other.

6   Conclusion

This paper described two case examples of virtual visual ergonomics assessments. Two factors that contributed to the success of the assessments were (1) a triage was conducted prior to the assessment to confirm that the strategy was suitable, and (2) there was good collaboration between the ergonomist and the manager / worker. During the assessments it was possible to observe the nature of the presenting problem and provide advice to mitigate the issue. It was not possible to report compliance with lighting standards because the lighting was not measured in-situ.

A virtual assessment may also confer considerable financial savings to the workplace.

References

1. Abbott-Gaffney, C., Jacobs, K.: Telehealth in school-based practice: perceived viability to bridge global OT practitioner shortages prior to COVID-19 global health emergency. Work **67**, 20–35 (2020)

2. Green, N., Tappin, D., Bentley, T.: The impact of telehealth video-conferencing services on work systems in New Zealand: perceptions of expert stakeholders. In: Bagnara, S. (ed.) Proceedings of the 20th Congress of the International Ergonomics Association (IEA 2018), pp. 192–197. Springer (2019)
3. van Dyk, L.: A review of telehealth service implementation frameworks. Int. J. Environ. Res. Public Health **11**, 1279–1298 (2014)
4. Baker, N., Jacobs, K.: The feasibility and accuracy of using a remote method to assess computer workstations. Hum. Factors **56**(4), 784–788 (2014)
5. Liebregts, J., Sonne, M., Potvin, J.: Photograph-based ergonomic evaluations using the Rapid Office Strain Assessment (ROSA). Appl. Ergon. **52**, 317–324 (2016)
6. Heiden, M., et al.: Validity of a computer-based risk assessment method for visual ergonomics. Int. J. Ind. Ergon. **72**, 180–187 (2019)
7. International Commission on Illumination: CIE 213:2014 technical report: guide to protocols for describing lighting. International Commission on Illumination, Vienna (2014)
8. World Health Organization: WHO characterizes COVID-19 as a pandemic (2020). https://www.who.int/emergencies/diseases/novel-coronavirus-2019/events-as-they-happen. Accessed 31 Jan 2021
9. Ritchie, C., Miller, L., Antle, D.: A case study detailing key considerations for implementing a telehealth approach to office ergonomics. Work **57**, 469–473 (2017)
10. Standards Australia and Standards New Zealand, Australian/New Zealand Standards AS/NZS1680.1: 2006 interior and workplace lighting part 1: general principles and recommendations. Standards Australia (2006)

Error Rate as Mediators of the Relationships Among 2D/3D TV Environment, Eye Gaze Accuracy, and Symptoms

Yogi Tri Prasetyo[1](✉) and Retno Widyaningrum[2]

[1] School of Industrial Engineering and Engineering Management, Mapúa University, Manila, Philippines
ytprasetyo@mapua.edu.ph
[2] Department of Industrial Engineering, Institut Teknologi Sepuluh Nopember, Surabaya, Indonesia

Abstract. 3D TV is a new platform to enjoy the stereoscopic environment in the home and eye tracking technology has been extensively utilized to evaluate the 3D TV. This study was mainly intended to explore an additional eye movement parameter that can predict the eye gaze accuracy and symptoms while perceiving the image in the 3D TV. A total of 12 graduate students were asked to perform tapping task in the 2D and 3D TV using within-subject design under 6 different levels of index of difficulty (ID). Structural equation modeling (SEM) was applied to analyze the causal relationship between 2D/3D environment, a new eye movement parameter, eye gaze accuracy, and symptoms. The result showed that error rate was found as a significant mediator of the relationships. In addition, the SEM approach was also found as a new significant and reliable approach in the visual ergonomics particularly for bridging the objective and subjective measures. Finally, the new eye movement parameter can be an important key for predicting eye gaze accuracy in the stereoscopic display.

Keywords: Visual ergonomics · Eye movement parameter · Eye tracking · Structural equation modeling · Error rate

1 Introduction

3D TV is a new platform to enjoy the stereoscopic environment in the home-based setting [1–4]. In visual ergonomics, it is also a hot topic and has been widely investigated by many ergonomics researchers. They aim to maximize the perceived quality while also minimizing the side effects such as vergence-accommodation conflict [5].

Recently, eye tracker has been widely utilized as a powerful device to evaluate the eye tracker. It can collect many eye movement parameters which can be an important key in evaluating the performance in a stereoscopic environment. Visual ergonomics academicians, electrical engineers, and even virtual reality developers are consistently utilized eye tracker as a reliable tool to evaluate the performance in the stereoscopic

© The Author(s), under exclusive license to Springer Nature Switzerland AG 2021
N. L. Black et al. (Eds.): IEA 2021, LNNS 220, pp. 756–761, 2021.
https://doi.org/10.1007/978-3-030-74605-6_96

display. Eye tracker can collect several indicators which widely known as eye movement parameters [6].

One of the most important eye movement parameters is eye gaze accuracy. It is defined as the distance between the eye fixation position and actual target position [6, 7]. Academicians are continuously engaged in adding new eye movement parameters in order to get a better predictive model. Aside from eye gaze accuracy, symptoms are also an important consideration in the stereoscopic display. Eye tiredness, headache, eye clearness, and eye tiredness are some of the very important measures. Vergence-accommodation conflict is one of the widely known symptoms in the stereoscopic display when the user start experiencing the mismatch between the focusing distance required for the eyes to focus on the object and the distance of a virtual 3D object [5].

Although there were many previous studies related to 3D TV [1–4, 8, 9], there is still a few studies related to the predictive model of eye movement parameters in this stereoscopic environment. Our previous studies already proved that several eye movement parameters such as number of fixation and pupil size were found as significant predictors for eye gaze accuracy and symptoms respectively [6, 7]. New eye movement parameter would be required to explore the causal relationships between the eye movement parameter, eye gaze accuracy, and symptoms.

This study was mainly intended to explore a new eye movement parameter for predicting eye gaze accuracy and symptoms. Error rate was tested through structural equation modeling as a mediator between the stereoscopic environment, eye gaze accuracy, and symptoms (Fig. 1). This new eye movement parameter can be an important key for predicting eye gaze accuracy in the stereoscopic display.

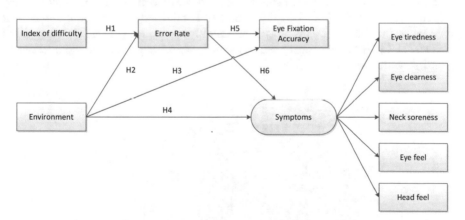

Fig. 1. The hypotheses construct in the current study.

2 Methodology

2.1 Participants

12 graduate students from National Taiwan University of Science and Technology were recruited in this study (mean: 25.08 years; sd: 3.09 years). Since this study was voluntary, all participants were not paid. This study was conducted in accordance to the National Taiwan University Research Ethics Committee. Thus, they were asked to fill a consent form and required to pass the Pelli Robson Contrast Sensitivity Test, Ishihara Color Vision Test, and the stereoscopic test in the excellent stereoscopic environment which covered by black curtains.

2.2 Apparatus and Stimuli

Tobii X2-60 eye tracker was utilized in this study. The sampling rate was 60 Hz and the accuracy was 0.4° visual angle. In addition, a Logitech webcam C-920 was also utilized to record the eye fixation point and eye gaze. When the participant was performing in 2D TV, the target was set on the screen while for 3D TV, the target was set 20 cm in front of the screen.

2.3 Procedures

All participants were required to utilize Sony 3D glasses and keep their head on a chin rest. This procedure was selected in order to get good eye fixation data. In addition, they were required to pass Tobii X2-60 calibration test. For the performance, multidirectional Fitts' Law test was utilized. This procedure is highly recommended since it is supported by ISO 9241-11. All participants were required to tap 12 target as fast and as accurate as possible with a mouse.

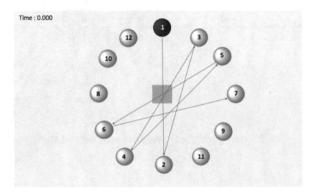

Fig. 2. Multidirectional fitts' law task based on ISO 9241-11 [6, 10–12].

2.4   Independent and Dependent Variables

The independent variables in this study were index of difficulty (ID) and TV environment. ID was set into 6 different levels (Table 1) while for environment, all participants were required to perform in 2D and 3D TV. Since there were 2 different environment and 6 ID, all participants were required to perform multidirectional Fitts' law tapping test in 12 different conditions.

Table 1. ID and task precision level [6].

Distance (unity unit)	Width (unity unit)	ID (bits)	Task Precision Level
40	3.3	3.7	Low
40	2.3	4.2	Medium
40	0.6	6.1	High
20	3.3	2.8	Low
20	2.3	3.3	Low
20	0.6	5.1	Medium

The dependent variables in this study were error rate, eye gaze accuracy, and symptoms. For symptoms, we measured eye tiredness, eye clearness, neck soreness, eye feel, and head feel by utilizing 5-points Likert scale. Following our previous study [10], the eye movement data were extracted by our proposed algorithm.

2.5   Structural Equation Modelling

AMOS 25 was utilized to perform structural equation modeling (SEM). Prior to that, 2D and 3D TV were dummy codded as 1 and 2 respectively in SPSS 25. Since there were 12 participants who performed in 12 different conditions, a total of 144 data were analyzed in this study. SEM standard model fit tests such as incremental fit indices, goodness of model fit, adjusted goodness of model fit, and even root mean square error of approximation were utilized.

3   Results and Discussion

Figure 3 illustrates the final of this study. Based on this figure, our SEM showed that the environment had significant direct effects on error rate (β: 0.161; p: 0.026), symptoms (β: 0.692; p: 0.001), and eye gaze accuracy (β: −0.263; p: 0.001). In addition, ID was found to have significant direct effects on error rate (β: 0.438; p: 0.001). Surprisingly, error rate was found to have a significant negative effect on eye gaze accuracy and a positive effect on symptoms. This new eye movement parameter can be utilized by future visual ergonomics study particularly for predicting eye gaze accuracy and symptoms in the stereoscopic display.

Table 2 illustrates the model fit of the study. Based on this table, all values were passed the suggested cut-off indicating that the model was very fit.

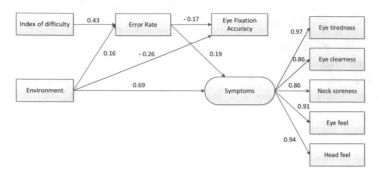

Fig. 3. The final model.

Table 2. Model fit.

Goodness of fit measures of the SEM	Parameter estimates	Suggested cut-off
p-value for Chi-square (χ^2)	0.138	>0.05
Chi-square statistic (χ^2)	29.228	
Degree of freedom (df)	22	
Normed chi-square (χ^2/df)	1.329	<2
Incremental fit indices		
Normed Fit Index (NFI)	0.969	>0.95
Tucker Lewis Index (TLI)	0.987	>0.95
Comparative Fit Index (CFI)	0.992	>0.96
Goodness-of-fit index		
Goodness of Fit Index (GFI)	0.958	>0.95
Adjusted Goodness of Fit Index (AGFI)	0.914	>0.90
Badness-of-fit index		
Root Mean Square Error of Approximation (RMSEA)	0.048	<0.07

4   Conclusions

3D TV is a new platform to enjoy the stereoscopic environment in the home and eye tracking technology has been extensively utilized to evaluate the 3D TV. This study was mainly intended to explore an additional eye movement parameter that can predict the eye gaze accuracy and symptoms while perceiving the image in the 3D TV. A total of 12 graduate students were asked to perform tapping task in the 2D and 3D TV using within-subject design under 6 different levels of index of difficulty (ID). Structural equation modeling (SEM) was applied to analyze the causal relationship between 2D/3D environment, a new eye movement parameter, eye gaze accuracy, and symptoms. The result showed that error rate was found as a significant mediator of the relationships. In addition, the SEM approach was also found as a new significant and reliable approach in the visual ergonomics particularly for bridging the objective and subjective measures. Finally, the new eye movement parameter can be an important key for predicting eye gaze accuracy in the stereoscopic display.

Acknowledgements. This study was funded by the Ministry of Science and Technology of Taiwan (MOST 103-2221-E-011-100-MY3).

References

1. Read, J.C.: Viewer experience with stereoscopic 3D television in the home. Displays **35**, 252–260 (2014)
2. Jang, J., Yi, M.Y.: Determining and validating smart TV UX factors: a multiple-study approach. Int. J. Hum. Comput. Stud. **130**, 58–72 (2019)
3. Read, J.C., Bohr, I.: User experience while viewing stereoscopic 3D television. Ergonomics **57**, 1140–1153 (2014)
4. Lubeck, A.J., Bos, J.E., Stins, J.F.: Equally moved and not really sick from viewing 2D and 3D motion stimuli on a TV screen. Displays **41**, 9–15 (2016)
5. Vienne, C., Sorin, L., Blondé, L., Huynh-Thu, Q., Mamassian, P.: Effect of the accommodation-vergence conflict on vergence eye movements. Vis Res. **100**, 124–133 (2014)
6. Lin, C.J., Prasetyo, Y.T., Widyaningrum, R.: Eye movement measures for predicting eye gaze accuracy and symptoms in 2D and 3D displays. Displays **60**, 1–8 (2019)
7. Prasetyo, Y.T., Widyaningrum, R., Lin, C.J.: Eye gaze accuracy in the projection-based stereoscopic display as a function of number of fixation, eye movement time, and parallax. In: 2019 IEEE International Conference on Industrial Engineering and Engineering Management (IEEM) (2019)
8. Lambooij, M., Ijsselsteijn, W., Heynderickx, I.: Visual discomfort of 3D TV: assessment methods and modeling. Displays **32**, 209–218 (2011)
9. Obrist, M., Wurhofer, D., Meneweger, T., Grill, T., Tscheligi, M.: Viewing experience of 3DTV: an exploration of the feeling of sickness and presence in a shopping mall. Entertain. Comput. **4**, 71–81 (2013)
10. Lin, C.J., Widyaningrum, R.: Eye pointing in stereoscopic displays. J. Eye Mov. Res. **9**(5), 4 (2016)
11. Lin, C.J., Widyaningrum, R.: The effect of parallax on eye fixation parameter in projection-based stereoscopic displays. Appl. Ergon. **69**, 10–16 (2018)
12. Lin, C.J., Prasetyo, Y.T., Widyaningrum, R.: Eye movement parameters for performance evaluation in projection-based stereoscopic display. J. Eye Mov. Res. **11**(6), 3 (2018)

Dynamic Signs: Field Test to Install Signs Around the Stairs

Reiko Sakata[1]([⊠]), Naoki Furuhata[1], Atsushi Shimada[1], Kenta Mishina[1], Hiroshi Watanabe[2], Nana Itoh[2], Hiroyasu Ujike[2], and Ken Sagawa[2]

[1] Mitsubishi Electric Corporation, Kanagawa 247-8501, Japan
Sakata.Reiko@ab.MitsubishiElectric.co.jp
[2] National Institute of Advanced Industrial Science and Technology, Tsukuba 305-8566, Japan

Abstract. This paper discusses the safety requirements to install dynamic signs around the stairs in the facility, in order to safely install and design dynamic signs in consideration of human cognitive characteristics. This paper discusses safety requirements when installing dynamic signs. The discussion is based on the results of observing behavior and measuring lines of sight of facility users in field tests where signs are installed around the stairs inside an event facility. The results reported in this paper shows that the dynamic signs provided on the floor at the bottom of the stairs exhibited a guiding effect on the facility users as they went down the stairs. Also, when the behavior of facility users going up and down stairs was observed, no congestion or contact accidents were caused due to people reading the content of the dynamic signs on the floor, or being preoccupied by the signs. However, facility users moved while watching the sign by central vision for a short time of approximately 2 s or less, and it was found that there is a possibility of misrecognition if the sign presentation position is not within the visual field during movement.

Keywords: Dynamic signs · Safety · Field test · Behavioral observation · Gaze point · Eye mark recorder

1 Problem Statement

Animated signs and signs presented in accordance with the movement of people or things are expected to be effective for improving facility convenience and the safety/security of movement. Signs of this type are called "dynamic signs," and proposals for international standardization have been made [1]. Dynamic signs are easier to understand than conventional static signs, and there is potential for presenting information to suit characteristics of the environment, but the technology is still immature, and there is a possibility that signs will be designed and used without considering the cognitive characteristics of human beings. Therefore, it will be important, when designing signs, to examine optimal designs based on consideration of visibility from a human factors perspective.

In a past report by the authors [2], field tests were conducted where dynamic signs were installed in a station facility, and it was confirmed that animation is effective for making signs more conspicuous. In addition, guidelines for gaze time by station facility users toward signs was obtained, and as a design requirement for dynamic signs, designs were considered which avoid the risk that facility users will overlook signs. Specifically, in a station facility, even the gaze times for the most referenced sign ware only about 1 s, so it is necessary to consider reducing the time when the sign is not displayed due to blinking or movement.

Also, Narumi et al. [3] have confirmed, by conducting field tests in an art museum, the guiding effectiveness of a feature for detecting people and presenting signs. However, the results of behavioral observation surveys and gaze point measurements have not been reported for facility users going up and down stairs when signs are installed around the stairs.

2 Objective

This paper discusses safety requirements when installing dynamic signs. The discussion is based on the results of observing behavior and measuring lines of sight of facility users in field tests where signs are installed around the stairs inside an event facility. Specifically, it is confirmed whether the dynamic sign installed around the stairs exhibited a guiding effect on the facility users without congestion or contact accidents. In addition, calculate the gaze time for each sign and consider the conditions under which the sign is referenced.

3 Methodology

3.1 Event Facility Where Field Tests Were Conducted

The event facility where tests were conducted was the Musashino Forest Sport Plaza [4, 5]. Tests were carried out in the corridors between the facility entrance and the event venue entrances. At this event facility, the facility entrance is on the top floor, and the event venue entrances are located on the intermediate floor and the bottom floor, and thus there is a need for visitors to enter the facility, and then go downstairs to the event venue entrances. However, typical experience when using the facility has shown it is hard for facility users to understand that the floor they need to go to is downstairs, and they sometimes get confused when entering. Therefore guidance to the event venue was provided by displaying dynamic signs on the floor, and affixing paper signs (static signs) to the walls. Multiple conditions were established, such as not presenting the dynamic signs on the floor, and varying the complexity of the presented information, and comparison was done between the conditions. Papers signs were always presented in every condition.

At the facility where the tests were conducted, no restrictions were imposed that might limit the behavior of ordinary users, aside from installing dynamic signs. Therefore, this was an environment where it was impossible to control the volume of human traffic (i.e., the flow and density of people) in the surrounding area during the test using test subjects, and this volume changed depending on the time slot and specific timing. Thus this was an environment with low reproducibility.

3.2 Signs Presented in the Facility

For dynamic signs on the floors and paper signs on the walls, Table 1 summarizes the informational content and installation position for each floor where signs are installed.

Table 1. Informational content and installation position of presented signs

Floor where installed	Informational content	Installation position	
		Dynamic signs	Posted paper signs
Top floor (facility entrance)	Event venue entrances are downstairs	Floor on near side of stairs*2 Dynamic signs	Handrails of stairs Posted paper signs
Intermediate floor (venue entrance)	Event venue entrances branch into intermediate floor and bottom floor	Floor at bottom of stairs*1*2 Dynamic signs	Handrails of stairs connecting to 1F Posted paper signs
Bottom floor (venue entrance)	Indicates event venue entrance	Floor at bottom of stairs*2 Dynamic signs	Column at bottom of stairs Posted paper signs

*1: The intention of the facility operator was to have visitors use the event venue entrance on the bottom floor with priority. In time slots where the venue on the bottom floor was not full and facility users could freely select a venue entrance, the dynamic signs on the intermediate floor presented guidance to the venue on the bottom floor larger than guidance to the venue on the intermediate floor.

*2: The displayed icon was animated. Sliding animation was provided for the arrow icon ($\rightarrow$) to indicate direction, and flashing animation was provided for the caution icon ($\triangle$+!).

Three types of dynamic sign conditions were used, as shown in Table 2. It was decided to set the dynamic sign presentation time to match the start and end time of the event held at the facility, and use an interval from 30 min before the start of the event to 30 min after its end for 1 condition, and management was done with a schedule so that conditions were switched 4–5 times during one day [6]. Dynamic signs were presented by projecting onto the existing floor of the facility using a projector. Brightness of each projected sign was affected by light from the outside and the floor materials, and varied depending on the time slot and floor where installed, but setting was done to ensure a brightness-contrast ratio ((projected surface brightness – non-projected surface brightness) ÷ non-projected surface brightness) of at least 10%.

Table 2. Dynamic sign conditions

Condition	Complexity of information	Content at top floor	Content at intermediate floor	Content at bottom floor
No. 1	Presented text information is given in Japanese only. Only guidance information is presented.	· Text: "Game venue" · Graphic: Animated arrow icon	· Text: "Arena" and "Stands" · Graphic: Animated arrow icon *No difference between condition No. 1 and 2	· Text: "Arena" · Graphic: Animated arrow icon
No. 2	Text information, switches between Japanese, English, and Korean, and a caution is provided in addition to guidance information.	· Text: "Game venue" and "Please use the stairs at left." Both are displayed by switching between Japanese, English, and Korean. · Graphic: Animated arrow and caution icon		· Text: "Arena" and "Proceed to the rear when going home." Both are displayed by switching between Japanese, English, and Korean. · Graphic: Animated arrow and caution icon
No. 3	No presentation of dynamic signs			

3.3 Behavioral Observation Survey of Facility Users Moving Between Floors

To confirm the response of ordinary users to dynamic signs, and the effectiveness of those signs, the behavior of ordinary users was observed at each floor. Also, at the branch point on the intermediate floor, the number of people who moved to each branch within a specified time were, respectively, counted, and a calculation was done of the percentage of the total number who moved according to the intention of the sign, relative to the total number of people who passed through.

3.4 Signs Referenced by Test Subjects and Survey of Gaze Time Towards Signs

Ordinary people who promised beforehand to participate in the tests (i.e., test subjects) were asked to carry out tasks of moving within the facility. The gaze points of the test subjects were measured using an eye mark recorder worn during the tasks, and gaze time towards each sign was calculated. Furthermore, after the task was finished, the subjects were given a multiple-choice survey about "signs referenced during the task."

The test subjects were 20 able-bodied people, able to walk on their own and with opportunities to go out, who were using the test venue facility for the first time (18 Japanese-speaking men and women aged 20–60, and 2 English-speaking men and women in their 20 s capable of reading and understanding Japanese). Two test subjects participated in one session, and a total of 10 sessions were carried out. Gaze point error in the specifications for the eye mark recorder was within 1° of visual angle (0.5° each way, up and down) near the center coordinate of the recorded eye mark. Also, the time spent by test subjects looking at a sign in the surrounding visual field was not included in the indicator of gaze time calculated in this case, and this was acquired as a reference value for the time needed by the test subject to understand the meaning of the sign. This experiment was carried out with the approval of the ethic examination of Research Institute of Human Engineering for Quality Life.

4 Results

4.1 Behavioral Observation Survey of Facility Users Moving Between Floors

At the branch point on the intermediate floor, the number of people who moved to the venue entrance on the bottom floor and the intermediate floor, within a specified time selected at random, were counted, and the percentage of the total number of people who passed through was calculated. As a result, it was found that the number of people who moved to the venue entrance on the bottom floor accounted for 74.7% of the total in the time slot where the dynamic signs were presented, and 49.6% of the total in the time slot where they were not presented (Fig. 1).

The intent of the information presented at the branch was for visitors to use the venue entrance at the bottom floor with priority. Therefore, this result shows that the dynamic signs provided on the floor at the bottom of the stairs on the intermediate floor exhibited a guiding effect on the facility users as they went down the stairs. Ito et al. [7] also reported that the gaze point fell to the floor regardless of age when using stairs, confirming this result.

Also, when the behavior of facility users going up and down stairs was observed, no congestion or contact accidents were caused due to people reading the content of the dynamic signs on the floor, or being preoccupied by the signs. In this field test, the brightness-contrast ratio at the display surface of dynamic signs on the floor was low at about 10%, and there is a possibility that the signs did not strongly attract attention, and thus it is difficult, based only on the results here, to state positively that dynamic signs on the floor around stairs have a low probability of causing congestion or contact accidents.

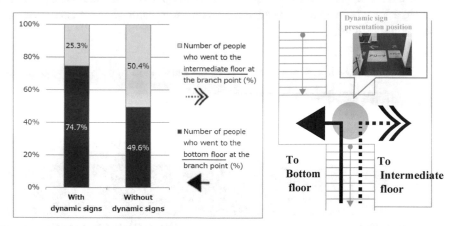

Fig. 1. Number of people moving to the venue on the bottom and intermediate floor depending on the presence of signs (percentages). The diagram at right is a top view of the branch point. The numbers of people who moved to the left or right at the branch were counted as the numbers of people who went to the intermediate floor or bottom floor, and then the percentage of the total people passing through was calculated.

4.2 Signs Referenced by Test Subjects and Survey of Gaze Time Towards Signs

There was no significant difference between conditions No. 1–2 for any of the dynamic signs, in terms of signs referenced by test subjects, or gaze time determined with an eye mark recorder. Therefore, results for each dynamic sign condition No. 1–2 were totaled, and the results for each sign are shown in Table 3. The signs with a high rate of being referenced were the dynamic signs on the intermediate floor (referenced by 85.7% of test subjects), posted paper signs on the top floor (85.0%), and dynamic signs on the bottom floor (78.5%). The number of signs reference by one test subject was about 3 to 5.

The signs with long gaze times were the posted paper signs on the intermediate floor (approx. 2.38 s), and the posted paper signs on the top floor (approx. 2.04 s). Regardless of the rate of being referenced, posted paper signs on columns had the longest gaze time. Also, gaze time was approx. 1.75 s for the dynamic signs on the floor of the intermediate floor which had the highest rate of being referenced, and the time was somewhat long because facility users continued to gaze at the signs while going down the stairs.

In interviews after the task, there were a number of test subjects who mistakenly perceived the content of posted paper signs. For this reason, when using the facility they moved while watching the sign by central vision for a short time of approximately 2 s or less, and it was found that there is a possibility of misrecognition if the sign presentation position is not within the visual field during movement. Also, based on comments from test subjects on their reasons for referencing signs, it was found that in order to determine the movement direction in a short time, there is a tendency to not read information thought to be irrelevant to oneself. In conditions No. 1 and No. 2, where there was a difference in the complexity of information given on dynamic signs, there was no significant difference in the degree signs were referenced or the gaze time, and that supports this trend.

Table 3. Referenced signs and gaze times of test subjects

	Top floor posted paper signs	Top floor dynamic signs	Interme-diate floor posted paper signs	Intermedi-ate floor dynamic signs	Bottom floor posted paper signs	Bottom floor dynamic signs
Percentage referencing (%)	85.0%	28.6%	25.0%	85.7%	5.0%	78.5%
Average gaze time (sec.)	Approx. 2.04 sec.	Approx. 0.16 sec.	Approx. 2.38 sec.	Approx. 1.75 sec.	Approx. 0.88 sec.	Approx. 0.72 sec.

5 Conclusions

Dynamic signs on the floor at the bottom of stairs exhibited a guiding effect on facility users going down the stairs. This is because the sign display position was appropriate with respect to the visual field during movement in the facility, and because the presented content was appropriate as auxiliary information for determining the direction of movement.

On the other hand, there is poor awareness of signs that do not come into the visual field during movement in the facility, and gaze time towards signs is also short, and thus misrecognition of content may occur depending on the sign installation position.

In this field test, the brightness-contrast ratio at the display surface of dynamic signs on the floor was low at about 10%, and there is a possibility that the signs did not strongly attract attention, and thus it is difficult, based only on the results here, to state positively that dynamic signs on the floor around stairs have a low probability of causing congestion or contact accidents. However, if factors such as the shortness of gaze time indicated above are taken into account, then even if signs are presented around stairs, it is conjectured that perhaps it will be more difficult for unsafe actions to occur such as suddenly stopping to gaze at a sign.

Acknowledgements. These results were obtained through implementation as the project "International Standardization Relating to Dynamic Signing (Japanese Standards Association)" as part of a 2019 initiative by the Ministry of Economy, Trade and Industry, etc.

Also, the authors would like to express their gratitude to everyone who cooperated with this test from the Japan Wheelchair Basketball Federation and the Musashino Forest Sport Plaza.

References

1. Watanabe, U., Itoh, S., Sakata, I., Furuhata, A.: Standardization of ergonomics requirements for 'dynamics sign' in ISO. In: Proceedings of International Display Workshop, VHF7-1 (2019)
2. Sakata, F., Aikawa, W., Ujike, I.: Sagawa, K.: "Dynamic signs" for the comfortable and safe society, optical Society of Japan. Jpn. J. Opt. **49**(7), pp 283–288 (2020). (in Japanese)
3. Narumi, H., Asama, T.: Modeling of guidance service by moving presentation. In: JSME Annual Conference on Robotics and Mechatronics (Robomec 2006), The Japan Society of Mechanical Engineers, 2P1-E12 (1) - (3) (2006). (in Japanese)
4. Musashino Forest Sport Plaza : https://www.musamori-plaza.com/english/. Accessed 01 Feb 2021
5. Mitsubishi Electric: Conducted a demonstration experiment for international standardization of "Dynamic Sign". https://www.mitsubishielectric.co.jp/news/2019/0826.html. Accessed 01 Feb 2021
6. Ogiya, S., Furuhata: A practical use of animation lighting equipment for hospital facilities. Japan Medical Welfare Information Association, Hospital Equipment, vol. 62, no. 3, pp. 38–41 (2020). (in Japanese)
7. Ito, F.: A study for age effects in reliance on lower visual information of environment while walking: the sequential change of eye movements. Jpn. Ergon. Soc. Ergon. **40**(5), 239–247 (2004). (in Japanese)

The Influence of Guiding Information Propagated from the Elbow on Foot Proprioception Among Severely Visually Impaired People

Tadashi Uno[1]([✉]) and Tetsuya Kita[2]

[1] National Institute of Technology, Tokuyama College, Yamaguchi 745-8585, Japan
t-uno@tokuyama.ac.jp

[2] National Institute of Technology, Oshima College, Yamaguchi 742-2193, Japan

Abstract. This study aimed to understand the influence of information propagated through the guide's elbow on foot proprioception among severely visually impaired people. Twelve male adults with pigmentary retinal degeneration were recruited for this study. Participants acquired information about steps (height of steps: 4, 10, and 20 cm) through two methods: being helped by a guide (grasping the guide's elbow as they climbed the steps; Condition A) or looking downward (viewing the obstacle at 30 cm from their toes; Condition B). Subsequently, participants performed two tasks. In task 1, participants reproduced the height of the obstacles by lifting their foot during static standing (10 times per leg). Task 2: After acquiring information about steps in both conditions, participants climbed the steps from a free position in which they could complete the movement with one step. For task 1, condition B, showed a higher toe rise and higher coefficient of variance in toe rise than condition A. Regarding Task 2, the highest points of the leading feet while stepping up were significantly higher under condition B. These results suggest that differences in information acquisition strategies affect the foot trajectory when climbing steps. Of the two methods used in this study, information acquisition through guide helpers may provide better feedback for individuals with low vision when climbing steps.

Keywords: Foot proprioception · Pigmentary retinal degeneration · Guide helper

1 Introduction

Visual impairment has a profound impact on daily life [1–3]. In recent years, it has been reported that people with low vision fall while navigating steps. Several reasons contribute to this mobility issue, including a lack of information on the surrounding environment and the barriers in it [4]. In addition, Haymes pointed out that contact with obstacles occurs due to visual field impairment and reduced contrast sensitivity [5]. These challenges are long-lasting in progressive eye diseases such as retinitis pigmentosa. Therefore, it is necessary to provide continuous mobility support to patients with low vision.

© The Author(s), under exclusive license to Springer Nature Switzerland AG 2021
N. L. Black et al. (Eds.): IEA 2021, LNNS 220, pp. 770–774, 2021.
https://doi.org/10.1007/978-3-030-74605-6_98

Two types of actions can help to avoid steps, "straddling" and "going around". Both actions require coordination of motor control. Consequently, visually impaired people employ low vision aids and sighted guides for orientation and mobility, to address the lack of visual information as well as to optimize the use of their remaining visual power [6]. In general, when using a guide, the visually impaired person grasps the guide's elbow or shoulder and moves according to the guidance information propagated through the grasped part. Among the mobility movements used by guides who help people with impaired vision, climbing steps is an essential skill to prevent falls and requires an adequate level of skill.

Previous studies have reported the importance of a multisensory approach in orientation, including auditory, tactile, and kinesthetic senses [7, 8]. Therefore, this study aimed to understand the influence of information propagated through the guide's elbow on foot proprioception among visually impaired people. Based on a series of research results, our team aims to develop safety guidelines for unskilled individuals to guide people with low vision.

2 Methods

Twelve male adults (44.8 ± 6.8 years) with pigmentary retinal degeneration (vision: 0.02–0.04, field of view: 10° and loss rate: 95%) were recruited for the study. Table 1 summarizes the disability information on individuals with retinitis pigmentosa. The participants had narrow peripheral vision and night blindness due to retinitis pigmentosa. The experimental room was adjusted beforehand using a dim light, a blackout curtain, and a digital illuminance meter (Shinwa) so that the illuminance around the participant converged within the range of 550 lx. Ethics Committee of the National Institute of Technology, Tokuyama College approved this study.

Participants acquired information about the steps (height of steps: 4, 10, and 20 cm) through two methods: being helped by a guide (the participant grasped the guide's elbow as they climbed the steps, Condition A) or looking downward (viewing the obstacle at 30 cm from their toes, Condition B). Subsequently, the participants performed two different tasks. In task 1, after being informed about the height of the steps, participants reproduced them by lifting their foot during static standing (10 times per leg). In task 2, after acquiring information about the step height in both conditions, participants climbed the steps from a free position in which they could complete the movement with one step. The steps were placed on a beige floor. In task 2, the assistants were placed diagonally behind the participants to avoid the risk of falling. In both tasks 1 and 2, the lower limb movement for each condition was recorded using high-speed cameras. The shooting range was defined as a space of 1.0 m (X axis) × 2.5 m (Y axis) × 2.0 m (Z axis). A calibration pole (2 m high, 5 calibration points) was set vertically in the space, and calibration was performed by photo-graphing a total of 90 control points. To measure movement, 12 spherical reflective markers were attached to the lower extremities of the participants. One-way analysis of variance between the conditions was used to analyze the differences in gait parameters (such as the height of toe elevation and the step length) and characteristics of the foot trajectory (such as the highest points of the leading and trailing feet while climbing the steps). Post-hoc pairwise Bonferroni-corrected comparison was used to examine mean differences in each condition.

Table 1. Characteristics of Participants with Disabilities

Partially sighted participants with pigmentary retinal degeneration

ID	Age (year)	Vision (Right eye)	Vision (Left eye)	Duration of cane use (years)
1	53	0.02	0.04	15
2	55	0.08	0.06	20
3	49	0.04	0.01	18
4	43	0.1	0.02	20
5	33	0.3	0.2	10
6	39	0.1	0.2	5
7	48	0.02	0.08	10
8	48	0.08	0.1	5
9	42	0.06	0.02	10
10	38	0.01	0.1	10
11	51	0.05	0.04	29
12	39	0.2	0.1	12

3 Results

For task 1, condition B showed greater toe elevation and a higher coefficient of variance for toe elevation ($p < 0.05$) than those in condition A at 10 and 20 cm. In Fig. 1, the crossing point, the highest point on the steps, and the highest point are illustrated as foot trajectories. For convenience, the ground contact point was added to the figures. Regarding Task 2, the highest points of the leading feet while stepping up were significantly higher ($p < 0.05$) under condition B. There were no significant differences in the crossing distance between the conditions for both step heights.

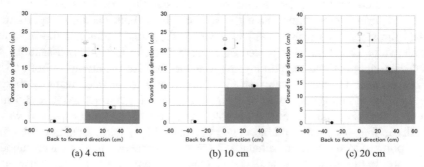

(a) 4 cm (b) 10 cm (c) 20 cm

Fig. 1. Trajectory of the leading limb at (a) 4, (b) 10, and (c) 20 cm step height, *$p < 0.05$, (Black round marker: Condition A, Square marker: Condition B)

4 Discussion

For task 1, condition B, showed greater elevation of the toe and higher coefficient of variance for toe elevation than condition A at 10 and 20 cm. Sensory inputs for postural control in humans are mainly visual, vestibular, and somatosensory. In this study, due to severe visual impairment, participants had difficulty in acquiring information for posture control from vision. Consequently, this suggests that participants with retinal degeneration had difficulty in controlling their posture when raising their legs.

On the other hand, using a walking guide is an effective way to solve mobility issues. Previous studies have shown that the acquisition of tactile sensory input may improve the accuracy of perceived information [9]. For task 2, the highest points of the leading feet while stepping up were significantly higher under condition B. As mentioned above, since the participant had severe visual field impairment, postural control associated with foot elevation became difficult in condition B, which was limited to the visual field, and variations in toe elevation height were observed. To avoid the risk of falling due to unstable foot-raising motions, each step motion was performed with greater emphasis on ensuring safety rather than on the efficiency of the motion. In contrast, under condition A, tactile information provided by the guide compensated for the lack of visual information and, thus, the integration of information was achieved. Therefore, it is inferred that variations in toe elevation when climbing steps were suppressed, leading to more stable motion.

Inadequate visual information is one of the main reasons why people with low vision are indecisive and uncertain when completing body movements. The results of our study suggest that differences in information acquisition strategies affect the foot trajectory when climbing steps. Of the two methods used in this study, information acquisition through guide helpers may provide better feedback for individuals with low vision when climbing steps. In the future, we will analyze the age of onset of visual impairment and the experience of gait rehabilitation.

Acknowledgement. This work is supported by JSPS KAKENHI Grant Numbers 19K20001.

References

1. Murray, C.J.L., Lopez, A.D.: The Global Burden of Disease. Harvard University Press, Cambridge (1996)
2. Brown, M.M., Brown, G.C., Sharma, S.: Evidence-Based to Value-Based Medicine. American Medical Association, Chicago (2005)
3. Brown, M.M., Brown, G.C., Sharma, S., Landy, J.: Health care economic analyses and value-based medicine. Surv. Ophthalmol. **48**(2), 204–223 (2003)
4. Uno, T.: Characteristics of lower limb position perception in response to environmental information in individuals with low vision. Adv. Intell. Syst. Comput. Intell. Hum. Syst. Integ. **2021**(1322), 591–596 (2021)
5. Haymes, S., Guest, D., Heyes, A.J.A.: Mobility of people with retinitis pigmentosa as a function of vision and psychological variables. Optom. Vis. Sci. **73**(10), 621–637 (1996)

6. Uno, T., Loh, P.Y., Muraki, S.: The influence of information acquisition strategies on foot proprioception and obstacle avoidance pattern in people with low vision. Adv. Intell. Syst. Comput. **819**, 786–790 (2019)
7. Forner-Cordero, A., Garcia, V.D., Rodrigues, S.T., Duysens, J.: Obstacle crossing differences between blind and blindfolded subjects after haptic exploration. J. Motor Behav. **48**(5), 468–478 (2016)
8. Patla, A.E., Davies, T.C., Niechwiej, E.: Obstacle avoidance during locomotion using haptic information in normally sighted humans. Exp. Brain Res. **155**, 173–185 (2004)
9. Ernst, M.O., Bülthoff, H.H.: Merging the senses into a robust percept. Trends Cogn. Sci. **8**(4), 162–169 (2004)

Data Visualization for Interdisciplinary Medical Research (Pilot Study)

Aleksandr Volosiuk[1,2](✉) ⓘ, Iaroslav B. Skiba[3] ⓘ, Alexey Polushin[3] ⓘ,
Daria Plotnikova[2] ⓘ, Daria Filippova[2] ⓘ, and Artem Smolin[2] ⓘ

[1] St. Petersburg Electrotechnical University, Saint Petersburg, Russia
[2] ITMO University, Saint Petersburg, Russia
[3] R.M. Gorbacheva Research Institute of Paediatric Oncology, Haematology and
Transplantation, First Pavlov State Medical University of St. Petersburg, Saint Petersburg, Russia

Abstract. Visualization is one of the key aspects of presenting the results of
scientific research. The authors propose an experiment design to analyze the perception of medical data visualizations in solving analytical problems. Perception
analysis involves processing a combination of data: eyetracking data, tasks solving
performance (time spent, answer accuracy, etc.), think-aloud data, and subjective
preferences survey. As the research material, the authors used an anonymized
database on 60 patients with Multiple Sclerosis treated by Hematopoietic Stem-Cell Transplantation (HSCT). The database contained about 150 parameters. The
study confirmed eligibility of the proposed approach.

Keywords: Medical data visualization · Usability testing · Eyetracking ·
Multiple sclerosis · Hematopoietic stem-cell transplantation

1 Introduction

1.1 Medical Data Visualization Studies

Visualization is one of the key aspects of presenting the results of scientific research.
Advanced visualization issues are extremely relevant for various fields of medicine,
especially those related to the processing of large data sets [1–3]. Along with clinical
and experimental medicine, visualization is also investigated in relation to the doctor's
educational process [4, 5].

Attention in a number of articles, published in the world's leading medical journals,
focused on choosing of a specific imaging method for research with a specific design
[6, 7]. At the same time, only in some studies the perception of various visualization
methods assessed by the users itself - medical specialists [8]. For this reason, eyetracking
technique as a quantitative analysis method could be useful to evaluate the perception
process of different types of medical data's graphic visualization.

Previously, quantitative monitoring of gaze patterns was used to objectively evaluate
Autism Spectrum Disorders treatments [9], as well as in a number of other diseases,

© The Author(s), under exclusive license to Springer Nature Switzerland AG 2021
N. L. Black et al. (Eds.): IEA 2021, LNNS 220, pp. 775–782, 2021.
https://doi.org/10.1007/978-3-030-74605-6_99

including Alzheimer's disease, schizophrenia [10]. In addition, this technique was also used to assess the skills of doctors of various qualifications [11].

In the present study, we are aiming at analyzing "doctors – medical data visualization" interactions to design tools for medical data visualization.

1.2   Research Material Multiple Sclerosis

As a test data, we used an anonymized database on 60 patients with Multiple Sclerosis (MS) treated by Hematopoietic Stem-Cell Transplantation (HSCT). The database consisted of almost 150 parameters including the following groups:

- Characteristics of patients and therapy before HSCT,
- Hospitalization and transplantation parameters,
- Haematological parameters during HSCT,
- Outcomes and functional tests results.

Multiple sclerosis (MS) continues to be a challenging and disabling condition [12]. Several disease-modifying therapies have become available making MS a treatable disease nowadays, but still, a large proportion of patients suffer from the poorly controlled progression of this disease [13]. Recently, immunoablation with autologous hematopoietic stem cell transplantation (AHSCT) has been offered as a treatment option to retard this inflammatory disease [14]. During two decades this treatment option became from an «expert opinion» based approach to strongly defined procedure with a standardized protocol [15]. Also changes the expectation of neurologists about the question: who should be treated with AHSCT and when? [16].

The main purpose of the information visualization is to support the analytical tasks [17]. For the current study, we designed a general analytical task, which was to compare the two groups of patients: those who underwent HSTC procedure wthin two separate periods: in 2000–2012 (wave 1), and in 2018–2020 (wave 2). The first period conducts the cases when the neurologist had no clear criteria of inclusion and exclusion for AHSCT and the procedure performed in-kind "life-saving therapy". In contrast, the second period includes the cases of AHSCT, when this treatment was performed based on the protocol of the European Blood and Marrow transplantation society and was supported by the Nation Ministry of Health care [18].

To compare the two waves of patients the authors selected 8 parameters according to the criterion of relevance. Thus, we limited the data needed to be visualized to 9 parameters, which were:

- Date of HSCT,
- Age at HSTC,
- MS Type,
- Time from diagnosis to HSCT (years),
- Time from frist symptoms to diagnosis (years),
- Duration of hospitalization for HSCT (bed-days),
- Number of Disease-Modifying Therapies (DMTs) for MS taken,
- Expanded Disability Status Scale (EDSS) value at the time of HSCT,
- Number of CD34+ cells injected during HSCT.

1.3   Visualizations

The information seeking mantra proposed by B. Shneiderman defines the three steps of the data exploration analysis: "Overview first, zoom and filter, then details-on-demand" [19]. In our previous study [20] we studied human interactions with 3 different visualizations of the same data, generated by Heating, Ventilation, & Air Conditioning system, in solving analytical tasks, and received significant confirmation of eligibility of the used approach.

Based on the same approach, and in accordance with findings from our previous studies [21, 22], we designed 3 visualizations of the same data differing in the degree of details presented. Thus, we received visualizations of the following types, presented in Figs. 1, 2, and 3: radar chart, box-and-whiskers, dot plots organized in table.

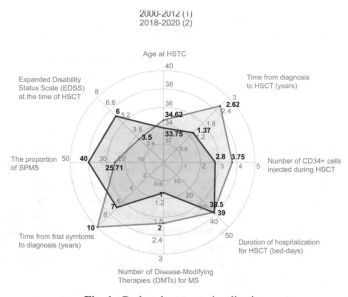

Fig. 1. Radar chart type visualization.

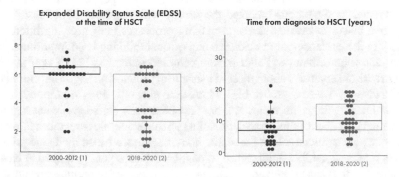

Fig. 2. A part of the box-and-whiskers type visualization.

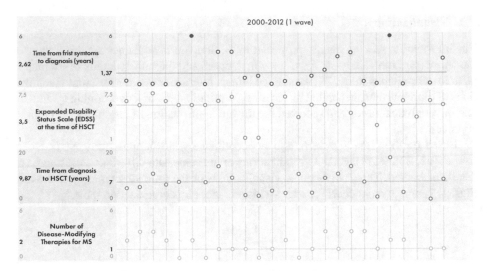

Fig. 3. A part of the dot plots organized in table visualization.

2 Methods

To study the interactions with visualizations the authors selected the usability-testing approach. The usability testing involves objective observation of how a user interacts with a studied object. We took medical workers and residents as users of medical data visualizations. To model the solution process of the previously designed general analytical we divided it into 7 tasks with increasing complexity: starting with comparing specific parameter median values of two waves of patients, and up to formulating conclusions and detecting relationships between factors. Thus, we observed how medical workers and residents solved the given analytical tasks of comparing characteristics of two waves of patients underwent HSTC procedure, finding possible interaction of factors, and drawing medical conclusions.

We conducted the usability testing in a usability laboratory with the correspondent room separated from the moderator's room by a one-way mirror. Before the usability testing procedure we surveyed the subjects, asking their age, sex, professional experience, hobbies, and we complimented the survey with cognitive biases test. The role of cognitive biases in medical decision-making processes is of growing interest right now [23]. In the evidence-based medicine era, critical thinking is an important skill for a doctor, and it contributes to better patient-centered outcomes [24]. Cognitive biases can distort the observations about disease causation, prognosis, diagnosis, and management of a disease. These cognitive biases influence how questions are framed, how risk factors and health status are measured, how decisions are made, and what actions are implemented [25]. The optimal translation of data from scientific researches into clinical practice can play a crucial role in the realization of evidence-based medicine principles. Thus, we may suggest that predisposed to cognitive biases person may also have specific features in the data visualization perception. We decided to include several specific questions in the survey to assess the possible features.

After the initial survey, we explained subjects the general information about the testing, underlying the idea that we evaluate only the visualizations and not the ability of the subjects to solve medical tasks. The instructions were followed by the calibration of an eyetracking system. After the calibration was complete, we presented to the subjects all three visualizations and the list with the analytical tasks. Subjects were asked to think aloud, including reading the tasks aloud. During the test, we communicated with the subjects, answering questions when needed.

Within the experiment, we controlled the following parameters:

- Order and duration of the visualizations used,
- Response speed and completeness of the solution,
- Gaze data (fixation duration, order and direction of saccades, saccades frequency and length).

After the testing, we interviewed the subjects about their subjective preferences for visualizations, as well as about what could help them to solve the tasks faster and more accurately.

3 Results and Discussion

Due to the COVID-19 pandemic, we were able to test only 5 subjects for the current pilot study, 3 of the subjects were medical workers of different age, sex and background, 1 of the other 2 subjects was data visualization specialist, and another was a psychologist.

The results showed very high diversity in how subjects approached the given tasks: subjects preferred different types of visualizations and showed various gaze patterns when working with visualizations (see Fig. 4), answers and findings given by the subjects were unique and sometimes mutually contradictory.

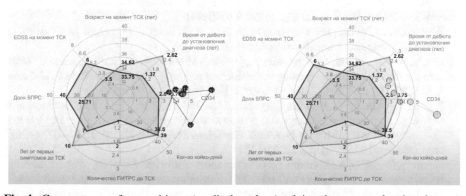

Fig. 4. Gaze patterns of two subjects (medical workers) solving the same task using the same visualization type.

Most of the subjects proposed the bar chart type visualization as a possible tool to solve some of the given tasks faster and more accurately.

It is obvious that to make conclusions on the different factors influence on the interaction patterns we need more subjects, but in general, the pilot study results confirmed the eligibility of the proposed experiment design. However, processing and analysis of the data proved to be extremely time-consuming process, which invoked the automation task. In this way, we are working on automating the data processing for the both surveys; fixing the duration and order of introductory presentation of visualizations; dividing the testing into parts with fixed duration, where a part would correspond to an analytical task.

At the same time the anti-coronavirus restrictions are being gradually decreased in Saint-Petersburg and we hope to conduct the testing on about 50 subjects – medical workers and residents by the time of presenting the paper at the IEA2021 Congress (please, refer to our presentation for more results and conclusions).

4   Conclusions

Studying gaze patterns of medical workers solving analytical tasks using data visualizations may provide important findings in medical data perception features. The pilot study results confirm the eligibility and the promise of the proposed and tested usability-testing design. The full study based on the given approach should lead to the discovery and classification of patterns in medical data perception that can be taken as a basis for improvement of the medical data visualization guidelines and for designing advanced visualization tools to be used by medical workers and researchers.

References

1. Vizcaíno, J.A., Barsnes, H., Hermjakob, H.: Proteomics data visualisation. Proteomics **15**(8), 1339–1340 (2015). https://doi.org/10.1002/pmic.201570063
2. Afonso, C., et al.: Data mining and visualisation: general discussion. Faraday Discuss. **218**, 354–371 (2019). https://doi.org/10.1039/C9FD90044F
3. Wieloch, W.: Chromosome visualisation in filamentous fungi. J. Microbiol. Methods **67**(1), 1–8 (2006). https://doi.org/10.1016/j.mimet.2006.05.022
4. Fanshawe, T.R., Power, M., Graziadio, S., Ordóñez-Mena, J.M., Simpson, J., Allen, J.: Interactive visualisation for interpreting diagnostic test accuracy study results. BMJ Evid.-Based Med. **23**(1), 13–16 (2018). https://doi.org/10.1136/ebmed-2017-110862
5. Kausar, T., Chandio, S., Quddus, I., Qureshi, G.S., Baloch, Z.H., Pario, A.: Effectiveness of teaching with visualisation table in comparison to traditional lecture in Anatomy Department, Jinnah Sindh Medical University. J. Coll. Physicians Surg. Pak. **30**(10), 1074–1077 (2020). https://doi.org/10.29271/jcpsp.2020.10.1074
6. Kiran, A., Crespillo, A.P., Rahimi, K.: Graphics and statistics for cardiology: data visualisation for meta-analysis. Heart **103**(1), 19–23 (2017). https://doi.org/10.1136/heartjnl-2016-309685
7. Bax, L., Ikeda, N., Fukui, N., Yaju, Y., Tsuruta, H., Moons, K.G.M.: More than numbers: the power of graphs in meta-analysis. Am. J. Epidemiol. **169**(2), 249–255 (2009). https://doi.org/10.1093/aje/kwn340
8. Terrin, N., Schmid, C.H., Lau, J.: In an empirical evaluation of the funnel plot, researchers could not visually identify publication bias. J. Clin. Epidemiol. **58**(9), 894–901 (2005). https://doi.org/10.1016/j.jclinepi.2005.01.006

9. Strobl, M.A.R., Lipsmeier, F., Demenescu, L.R., Gossens, C., Lindemann, M., De Vos, M.: Look me in the eye: evaluating the accuracy of smartphone-based eye tracking for potential application in autism spectrum disorder research. Biomed. Eng. Online **18**(1) (2019). https://doi.org/10.1186/s12938-019-0670-1

10. Oh, J., Chun, J.W., Lee, J.S., Kim, J.J.: Relationship between abstract thinking and eye gaze pattern in patients with schizophrenia. Behav. Brain Funct. **10**(1) (2014). https://doi.org/10.1186/1744-9081-10-13

11. Chen, H.E., et al.: Looks can be deceiving: gaze pattern differences between novices and experts during placement of central lines. Am. J. Surg. **217**(2), 362–367 (2019). https://doi.org/10.1016/j.amjsurg.2018.11.007

12. Thompson, A.J., Baranzini, S.E., Geurts, J., Hemmer, B., Ciccarelli, O.: Multiple sclerosis. The Lancet **391**(10130), 1622–1636 (2018). ISSN 0140-6736. https://doi.org/10.1016/S0140-6736(18)30481-1

13. Vargas, D.L., Tyor, W.R.: Update on disease-modifying therapies for multiple sclerosis. J. Invest. Med. **65**(5), 883–891 (2017). https://doi.org/10.1136/jim-2016-000339

14. Massey, J.C., Sutton, I.J., Ma, D.D.F., Moore, J.J.: Regenerating immunotolerance in multiple sclerosis with autologous hematopoietic stem cell transplant. Front. Immunol. **9** (2018). https://doi.org/10.3389/fimmu.2018.00410

15. Gavriilaki, M., Sakellari, I., Gavriilaki, E., Kimiskidis, V.K., Anagnostopoulos, A.: Autologous hematopoietic cell transplantation in multiple sclerosis: changing paradigms in the era of novel agents. Stem Cells Int. **2019** (2019). https://doi.org/10.1155/2019/5840286

16. Atkins, H.L., Freedman, M.S.: Five questions answered: a review of autologous hematopoietic stem cell transplantation for the treatment of multiple sclerosis. Neurotherapeutics **14**(4), 888–893 (2017). https://doi.org/10.1007/s13311-017-0564-5

17. Tufte, E.: Tech@State: Data Visualization – Keynote by Dr. Edward Tufte (2013). https://www.youtube.com/watch?v=g9Y4SxgfGCg. Accessed 02 Feb 2021

18. Sharrack, B., Saccardi, R., Alexander, T., Badoglio, M., Burman, J., Farge, D., Greco, R., Jessop, H., Majid, K., Kirgizov, K., Labopin, M., Mancardi, G., Martin, R., Moore, J., Muraro, P.A., Rovira, M., Sormani, M.P., Snowden, J.A.: Autologous haematopoietic stem cell transplantation and other cellular therapy in multiple sclerosis and immune-mediated neurological diseases: updated guidelines and recommendations from the EBMT Autoimmune Diseases Working Party (ADWP) and the Joint Accreditation Committee of EBMT and ISCT (JACIE). Bone Marrow Transplant. **55**, 283–306 (2020). https://doi.org/10.1038/s41409-019-0684-0

19. Shneiderman, B.: Dynamic queries for visual information seeking. IEEE Softw. **11**, 70–77 (1994). https://doi.org/10.1109/52.329404

20. Novikova, E., Belimova, P., Dzhumagulova, A., Bestuzhev, M., Bezbakh, Y., Volosiuk, A., Balkanskii, A., Lavrov, A.: Usability assessment of the visualization-driven approaches to the HVAC data exploration. In: CEUR Workshop Proceedings (2020). https://doi.org/10.51130/graphicon-2020-2-3-17

21. Svistelnikov, Y.A., Volosiuk, A.A., Voronina, O.V.: Shape and color coding: recall efficiency. In: Proceedings of the 2020 IEEE Conference of Russian Young Researchers in Electrical and Electronic Engineering, EIConRus 2020, №. 9039450, pp. 1441–1445 (2020). https://doi.org/10.1109/EIConRus49466.2020.9039450

22. Kartel, A., Novikova, E., Volosiuk, A.: Analysis of visualization techniques for malware detection. In: Proceedings of the 2020 IEEE Conference of Russian Young Researchers in Electrical and Electronic Engineering, EIConRus 2020, №. 9038910, pp. 337–340 (2020). https://doi.org/10.1109/EIConRus49466.2020.9038910

23. Blumenthal-Barby, J.S., Krieger, H.: Cognitive biases and heuristics in medical decision making: a critical review using a systematic search strategy. Med. Decis. Making **35**(4), 539–557 (2015)

782   A. Volosiuk et al.

24. Molony, D.A.: Cognitive bias and the creation and translation of evidence into clinical practice. Adv. Chronic Kidney Dis. **23**(6), 346–350 (2016)
25. Van der Wel, M.C., Sonke, G.S., Keijzers, G.: Kritische dokters en cognitieve bias, Nederlands Tijdschrift voor Geneeskunde, vol. 162. №. 51–52 (2018)

Dynamic Signs: Multiple Attributes Determining Visibility

Hiroshi Watanabe[1]([✉]), Nana Itoh[1], Hiroyasu Ujike[1], Ken Sagawa[1], Reiko Sakata[2], and Naoki Furuhata[2]

[1] National Institute of Advanced Industrial Science and Technology, Tsukuba 305-8566, Japan
h.watanabe@aist.go.jp
[2] Mitsubishi Electric Corporation, Kanagawa 247-8501, Japan

Abstract. Dynamic signs are an information presentation technology that changes the visual attributes of information displayed in public spaces in order to improve its visibility. With the development of new projector and display technologies, dynamic signs are already being put into practical use. However, it has not yet been established what kinds of signs should and should not be used. To ensure the continued development of dynamic signage as a new form of infrastructure, it is necessary to avoid unintended negative effects resulting from lack of systematic use. It is therefore important to accumulate ergonomic data that can be used toward the establishment of requirements for safe and easy-to-read dynamic signs. This study aims to elucidate visual requirements for signs that provide human traffic-flow guidance, which is one application of dynamic signage. The primary information provided by human traffic-flow guidance signs are the direction and distance to a destination. Herein, we consider the signage placement conditions and attributes required to convey this information, including interactions with aging effects. In this paper, we introduce the results from ergonomic experiments using immersive virtual reality that can be used as quantitative criteria for the visual design of dynamic signs.

Keywords: Dynamic signs · Visibility · Conspicuity · Discrimination · Virtual reality

1 Introduction

Dynamic signs are a technology for presenting information by using images that change in position, luminance, color, contents, and so on. Potential uses include presenting caution notifications to increase safety on roads, at factories, in outdoor spaces, and in public buildings as well as reliable guidance or notifications to increase convenience. With the development of new projector and display technologies, dynamic signs are already being put into practical use (Sakata et al. 2019; Watanabe et al. 2019). However, it has not yet been established what kinds of dynamic signs should and should not be used. To ensure the continued development of dynamic signage as a new infrastructure, it is necessary to avoid unintended negative effects resulting from lack of systematic

© The Author(s), under exclusive license to Springer Nature Switzerland AG 2021
N. L. Black et al. (Eds.): IEA 2021, LNNS 220, pp. 783–790, 2021.
https://doi.org/10.1007/978-3-030-74605-6_100

use. It is therefore important to accumulate ergonomic data that can be used toward the establishment of requirements for safe and easy-to-read dynamic signs.

This study aims to elucidate visual requirements for signs that provide human traffic-flow guidance, which is one application of dynamic signage. The primary information provided by human traffic-flow guidance signs are the direction and distance to a destination. We consider the signage placement conditions and attributes required to convey this information, including interactions with aging effects. The signage attributes considered are animation type (slide and blink), frequency, and presentation time.

2 Methods

2.1 Participants

To clarify the effect of age and cognitive function on sign reading, we performed experiments involving 60 male and female participants who were either in their twenties (mean 21.65, SD 0.37) or over the age of 60 (mean 70.56, SD 0.92). Participants were assigned to one of two animation conditions (slide or blink; see below), maintaining nearly equal male-to-female and young-to-old ratios for each group. All participants had normal vision, hearing, and walking ability, and all received compensation for their participation. On the day of the experiment, we verified that the participants were fit to participate by asking them to complete a questionnaire concerning their physical condition on the day, and by measuring their monocular and binocular vision using a Landolt ring test from 5 m and a Stereo Fly Test (Stereo Optical Co., Inc., Chicago, IL). We also administered the Mini-Mental State Examination (MMSE) in order to evaluate cognitive function.

No test participants had prior knowledge of the test contents. The experimental protocol was approved by the Ergonomics Committee of the National Institute of Advanced Industrial Science and Technology (AIST). All participants provided written informed consent before participating in the experiment.

2.2 Apparatus

Computer generated imagery was projected from 4,000-lm projectors (NP-M402XJD; NEC, Tokyo, Japan) onto four square screens measuring 3 m² placed to the left and right of the viewer as well as to the front and on the floor, using the CAVE immersive virtual reality device produced by the University of Illinois. Test participants viewed these projections through glasses polarized using the circular light polarization method (Fig. 1, left). We used the Vicon system (Vicon Motion Systems Ltd., Oxford, UK) to perform contactless measurements of each participant's head position at a sampling rate of 120 Hz and transmitted the position data to the CAVE system via an Ethernet connection. We used this information to correct rendering distortions according to participant head positions.

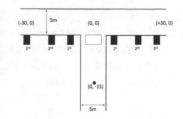

Fig. 1. Example VR representation for experiment participants (left) and layout of the underground passageway used in the experiment (right)

2.3 Stimulus

We performed the experiment in a virtual reality environment simulating an underground shopping center with a T-junction (Fig. 1, right). The passageway splits into left and right branches at the T-junction, with three destinations (1st, 2nd, and 3rd doors) along each branch. The passageway width was 5 m, and there was a series of shops over a 30-m range on both sides of the junction. All participants started at a point 15 m from the junction at coordinates $(x, y) = (0.0, -15.0)$. The sign display position was always just before the T-junction branch, such that the coordinates of the sign center were $(0.0, -4.25)$. The sign was approximately 2 m wide and 1.15 m tall.

The three destinations were depicted as circle, triangle, and star symbols, and the sign center had dimensions of 0.36×0.36 m (Fig. 2). In each test, participants were asked to read the position and direction of the star from the dynamic sign. A flashing or sliding arrow was added to the left or right of each symbol, with the distance from the junction implied by either the position of the arrows or the distance that the arrows slid. The distance between each arrow was 0.18 m.

The experimental parameters were "animation type," "alignment," and "presentation time."

The animation type was sliding or blinking. For the sliding type, arrows indicating the three destinations all moved 0.18 m per second, but the average positions of the arrows varied, with the distance between average positions and marks (0.49, 0.67, and 0.85 m) implying the positions of the destinations. In the blinking type, the arrow blinked at a frequency of 1 Hz at the final position under the sliding conditions.

The alignment parameter included four combinations of direction and distance information (Fig. 2), as follows:

Directions in sequence and positions in sequence (DI–PI): In this alignment, the direction arrows for all symbols were on either the right or the left. The travel distance indicators (shown by the arrow positions) are all in order (either "1st–2nd–3rd" or "3rd–2nd–1st"; Fig. 2a).

Directions in sequence and positions in disorder (DI–PD): In this alignment, the direction arrows for all symbols were on either the right or the left. However, travel distance indicators were not in a fixed order (Fig. 2b).

Directions in disorder and positions in sequence (DD–PI): In this alignment, some direction arrows were on the right and others were on the left. However, travel distance indicators were all in order (either "1st–2nd–3rd" or "3rd–2nd–1st"; Fig. 2c).

Directions in disorder and positions in disorder (DD–PD): In this alignment, some direction arrows were on the right and others were on the left. However, the travel distance indicators were not in a fixed order (Fig. 2d). Multiple signs were created to fulfill each of these conditions, with the circle, triangle, and star symbol positions randomized in each case and assigned for each subject.

The presentation time parameter was 2, 4, or 6 s for each sign. Frequencies were 1 Hz for each animation (slide and blink) and the numbers of repetitions were 2, 4, or 6 times per observation.

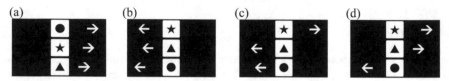

Fig. 2. Examples of four alignment combinations

2.4 Procedures

During the experiment, participants wore a VICON headset while standing in the center of the floor. The starting point in each trial was the base of the T-shaped passageway with coordinates $(x, y) = (0.0, -15.0)$, and participants automatically moved forward from that point at a speed of 4 km/h. The display position of the sign was always just in front of the T-junction branching, and presentation times for sliding and blinking were randomly selected as 2, 4, or 6 s, corresponding to the sign presentation starting when the participant is approximately 2.2, 4.4, or 6.6 m from the sign center.

Participants were asked to ascertain the target destination positions as quickly as possible while the sign was displayed and to verbally report the direction and distance. The experimenter used left and right buttons on a wireless device to record what they reported.

Each participant viewed 48 trials under all display conditions, as follows: for each of the four alignment conditions (DI–PI, DI–PD, DD–PI, and DD–PD), four types of signs were created with the circle, triangle, and star symbols in random positions, and each of these signs was viewed at three different presentation times for a total of $4 \times 4 \times 3 = 48$ trials.

2.5 Analysis

Four sign types were created to meet each set of alignment conditions, and the reading task results for each of these signs yielded five accuracy rates, namely 0%, 25%, 50%, 75%, and 100%. We measured these accuracy rates for each of the three presentation times and took the results as a measure of each participant's sign reading performance. We also calculated the average time required from sign display until participant report, taking this value as a measure of decision-making performance. We then conducted four-way ANOVA for accuracy rates and response time, taking animation method and age as between-subject factors and presentation time and alignment as within-subject factors.

2.6 Accuracy Rate

Main effect: All factors had a significant main effect on accuracy rates (dynamic display method $F(1,116) = 4.53, < .05$; age group $F(1,116) = 44.88, < .01$; presentation time $F(2,232) = 10.68, < .01$; alignment $F(3,348) = 11.64, < .01$). Tables 1 and 2 show average accuracy rates for each of these main effects. We also conducted multiple comparisons for display time and alignment combinations (Ryan's method, here and below). The results indicated that the correct ratio was significantly low when the duration was 2 s (0.93), as compared with 4 s (0.95, $t = 4.22$; significance threshold 5% here and below) and 6 s (0.96, $t = 3.74$). When the alignment type was DI–PI, the correct ratio was significantly high (0.98) as compared with DI–PD (0.93, $t = 4.34$), DD–PI (0.94, $t = 3.93$), and DD–PD (0.92, $t = 5.56$).

Interactions: We found significant interactions between age and duration ($F(2,232) = 6.42, < .01$), animation type and alignment ($F(3,348) = 10.96, < .01$), and age and alignment ($F(3,348) = 6.03, < .01$). Examining simple main effects, we obtained three results: (1) Duration had a significant effect on the accuracy rates of participants 60 years old or over ($F(2,232) = 16.16, < .01$). Accuracy rates decreased at 2 s durations more than at 4 s and 6 s (88%, 92%, and 93%, respectively). (2) Regardless of animation type (slide or blink), alignment had a significant effect on accuracy rates (slide: $F(3,348) = 13.34, < .01$, blink: $F(3,348) = 9.26, < .01$). In DD–PI, however, the accuracy rates for sliding were higher than those for blinking (99% and 90%, respectively). (3) Alignment had an effect on accuracy rates in the older group ($F(3,348) = 17.04, < .01$), but not those in the younger group ($F(3,348) = 0.63, < .01$). The older group showed significantly lower accuracy rates for DI–PD ($t = 5.37$), DD–PI ($t = 5.18$), and DD–PD ($t = 7.57$) as compared to DI–PI.

2.7 Response Time

Main Effect: We again found a significant main effect for age group ($F(1,116) = 89.64, < .01$; presentation time: $F(2,232) = 3.32, < .05$; alignment: $F(3,348) = 32.03, < .01$). Tables 3 and 4 show average response times for each of these main effects.

In relation to duration and alignment effects, multiple comparisons indicated that average response times for the 2-s presentation were significantly shorter than those for the 6-s presentation (2.04 and 2.08 s, respectively; $t = 2.51, p < .05$). We also found significant differences between all pairs other DD–PI and DD–PD (between DI–PI and DI–PD: $t = 3.66$; between DI–PI and DD–PI: $t = 8.17$; between DI–PI and DD–PD: $t = 8.35$; between DI–PD and DD–PI: $t = 4.51$; between DI–PD and DD–PD: $t = 4.68$; 5% significance thresholds in each case).

Interactions: We found significant interactions between age and duration (F(2,232) = 3.52, p < .05), so we investigated the simple main effects. The results indicated that duration had a significant effect on average response times of the older participants (F(2,232) = 6.83, p < .01). This suggests that shorter presentation times (2 s) result in shorter response times, but the difference is only about 50 ms.

Table 1. Mean and SE of accuracy ratios for older participants (here and below, upper rows show mean values and lower rows shows SE for slide and blink).

Age	Over 60											
Alignment	DI-PI			DI-PD			DD-PI			DD-PD		
Duration	2s	4s	6s	2s	4s	6s	2s	4s	6s	2s	4s	6s
Slide	0.98	0.98	1.00	0.88	0.94	0.92	0.98	0.98	0.98	0.79	0.85	0.88
	0.01	0.01	0.00	0.03	0.02	0.04	0.01	0.01	0.01	0.05	0.04	0.04
Blink	0.94	0.96	0.98	0.84	0.91	0.88	0.78	0.82	0.84	0.87	0.89	0.97
	0.02	0.02	0.01	0.04	0.03	0.03	0.05	0.05	0.03	0.03	0.03	0.02

Table 2. Mean and SE of accuracy ratio for younger participants

Age	Twenties											
Alignment	DI-PI			DI-PD			DD-PI			DD-PD		
Duration	2s	4s	6s	2s	4s	6s	2s	4s	6s	2s	4s	6s
Slide	0.99	1.00	1.00	1.00	0.97	0.98	0.98	1.00	0.99	0.96	0.98	0.98
	0.01	0.00	0.00	0.00	0.02	0.01	0.01	0.00	0.01	0.02	0.01	0.01
Blink	0.99	0.99	0.98	0.98	0.99	0.96	0.98	0.99	0.98	0.94	1.00	0.98
	0.01	0.01	0.01	0.01	0.01	0.02	0.01	0.01	0.02	0.02	0.00	0.01

Table 3. Mean and SE of response time for older participants

Age	Over 60											
Alignment	DI-PI			DI-PD			DD-PI			DD-PD		
Duration	2s	4s	6s	2s	4s	6s	2s	4s	6s	2s	4s	6s
Slide	2.30	2.26	2.43	2.49	2.44	2.49	2.49	2.65	2.59	2.47	2.62	2.56
	0.10	0.11	0.13	0.15	0.12	0.13	0.10	0.15	0.14	0.11	0.16	0.14
Blink	2.32	2.43	2.42	2.31	2.36	2.49	2.49	2.54	2.51	2.48	2.52	2.52
	0.12	0.10	0.11	0.10	0.09	0.12	0.10	0.12	0.11	0.10	0.09	0.11

Table 4. Mean and SE of response times for younger participants

Age	Twenties											
Alignment	DI-PI			DI-PD			DD-PI			DD-PD		
Duration	2s	4s	6s	2s	4s	6s	2s	4s	6s	2s	4s	6s
Slide	1.53	1.53	1.52	1.62	1.56	1.61	1.67	1.67	1.68	1.67	1.70	1.71
	0.06	0.05	0.05	0.06	0.06	0.07	0.05	0.07	0.07	0.06	0.07	0.06
Blink	1.65	1.60	1.58	1.65	1.71	1.69	1.69	1.75	1.71	1.77	1.71	1.75
	0.05	0.05	0.05	0.05	0.07	0.06	0.05	0.06	0.05	0.05	0.05	0.05

3 Discussion

The following summarizes the results of the experiment: (1) Regarding sign alignment, recognition rates decreased and response times increased when there was no consistency in the order of directions and distance. This trend was particularly apparent in the elderly. (2) Presenting signs for more than 4 s had little impact on accuracy rates, regardless of age group. (3) For the younger cohort, none of the presentation conditions considered dramatically lowered recognition rates or increased response times.

Recently, there has been increased research on the ability to read signs that lead to route-finding behavior in real-life situations, particularly emergency evacuations, under realistic environments in VR space (Jeon et al. 2019; Kewee et al. 2019, Vilar et al. 2014). One study employing ergonomic experiments with aging effects as a factor was a sign-reading experiment in evacuation situations by Kwee et al. (2019) in which experiment was conducted on directional sign-reading presented in a pathway using the same age structure as in our experiment (age 20–29 and 60–79 years). In their experiment, both an everyday scene and a fire evacuation scene were set up. Four types of digital escape route signs were selected to be read: a conventional static sign indicating an emergency exit, a sign with time information on when the change was made, a sign with a frame that flashed at 1 Hz, and a sign with an X in a direction that should not be taken. The participants' responses were evaluated according to the reaction time required to decide the direction of travel. Of the four signs, the study showed that signs other than that with an X were particularly effective in reducing decision-making time. However, their study found no effect of age on decision-making time, but there did seem to be an effect on sign preference; flashing signs were ranked highest in preference regardless of age.

The conditions of our experiment, which found significant differences in correct response rate and reaction time between older and younger participants, and those of Kwee et al. (2019) are very different. The main target of their experiment was to compare the influence of environmental affordances and signage on route choice, that is, whether people follow the instructions of a single sign. The fact that people of all ages received route selection instructions equally from the signs is important, and suggests that the current sign design, or a sign design modified with additional information, is an appropriate guidance method during evacuations. In contrast, our experiment was a complex task involving redundancy given that participants had to choose one of several destination signs and read its directions and distance. Accordingly, we believe this clearly shows the difference in selective attention function due to the effect of aging. Watanabe et al. (2019) reported an effect of sliding animation frequency (1, 2, or 3 Hz) on visibility in an experiment using the same device and procedure as the present study and suggested similar results to the present study for correct response rate and reaction time. In other words, although they found no main effect of frequency itself on the correct response rate, there was an interaction effect with age, suggesting that there are frequencies that are preferable for the elderly. The order of arrangement also had a strong effect on sign reading in the elderly, as in the present study. An effect of aging on increase in reaction time was also shown in the same way.

Additionally, the experimental conditions of this study involved passive movement scenarios, but if we consider interactions with signs in the spaces in which we actually conduct our lives, we might need to interpret sign meanings while actively moving. To avoid collisions resulting from scattered attention, we need further information relating to optimal sign placement and design that reduces the time required for interpretation. It is of course important to also consider aging effects in this case as well.

4 Conclusion

We presented the results of ergonomic experiments using immersive VR that can be used as quantitative criteria for the visual design of dynamic signs. The main information provided by signs for human traffic-flow guidance are the direction and distance to a destination. The study of sign placement conditions and attributes necessary to convey this information, including their interactions with aging, showed a strong effect of aging on visibility, consistent with the results of previous studies.

Acknowledgement. These results were obtained through a project conducted under the "International Standardization for Dynamic Signing (Japanese Standards Association)" initiative, part of the Ministry of Economy, Trade and Industry's "Activities for the acquisition/promotion of international standards for energy saving" for fiscal 2018. We thank Shingo Terada of Research & Telephone Technical Consultant, Yukie Tomidokoro, Kazue Goto, and Hiroko Ojima of the Human Informatics Research Institute at the National Institute of Advanced Industrial Science and Technology for their assistance in collecting and analyzing the data.

References

Watanabe, H., Ito, N., Ujike, H., Sagawa, K., Sakata, R., Imaishi, A., Furuhata, N., Aikawa, M.: Standardization of ergonomics requirements for 'Dynamics Sign' in ISO. In: Proceedings of the International Display Workshops 2019, vol. 26, pp. 1181–1184. Sapporo (2019)

Sakata, R., Imaishi, A., Furuhata, N., Aikawa, M., Watanabe, H, Ito, N., Ujike, H., Sagawa, K.: Standardization of "dynamic sign" for comfort and safe society: Volume VII: Ergonomics in design, design for all, activity theories for work analysis and design, affective design. In: Proceedings of the 20th Congress of the International Ergonomics Association (IEA 2018), pp. 147–151. Springer, Florence (2019)

Jeon, G.Y., Na, W.J., Hong, W.H., Lee, J.K.: Influence of design and installation of emergency exit signs on evacuation speed. J. Asian Archit. Build. Eng. **18**(2), 104–111 (2019)

Kwee-Meier, S.T., Mertens, A., Schlick, C.M.: Age-related differences in decision-making for digital escape route signage under strenuous emergency conditions of tilted passenger ships. Appl. Ergonomics **59**(A), 264–273 (2017)

Vilar, E., Rebelo, F., Noriega, P., Duarte, E., Mayhorn, C.B.: Effects of competing environmental variables and signage on route-choices in simulated everyday and emergency wayfinding situations. Ergonomics **57**(4), 511–524 (2014)

Correction to: Flat Cushion vs Shaped Cushion: Comparison in Terms of Pressure Distribution and Postural Perceived Discomfort

Iolanda Fiorillo, Yu Song, Maxim Smulders, Peter Vink,
and Alessandro Naddeo

Correction to:
Chapter "Flat Cushion vs Shaped Cushion: Comparison in Terms of Pressure Distribution and Postural Perceived Discomfort" in: N. L. Black et al. (Eds.): *Proceedings of the 21st Congress of the International Ergonomics Association (IEA 2021)*, LNNS 220, https://doi.org/10.1007/978-3-030-74605-6_31

The reference number [24] was misspelled and should be revised were incorrect in the original version of this chapter.

The correct version is given below:

Fiorillo, I., Song, Y., Vink, P. & Naddeo, A. 2021, Designing a shaped seat-pan cushion to improve postural (dis)comfort reducing pressure distribution and increasing contact area at the interface. In: Proceedings of the Design Society, pp. 1113. doi:10.1017/pds.2021.111

The original chapter has been corrected.

The updated original version of this chapter can be found at
https://doi.org/10.1007/978-3-030-74605-6_31

Author Index

Printed in the United States
by Baker & Taylor Publisher Services